CHILD RIGHTS & REMEDIES

Child Rights & Remedies

by

Robert C. Fellmeth

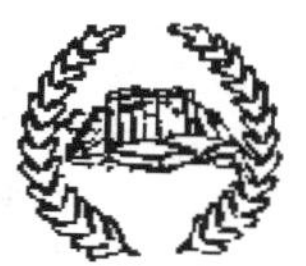

Clarity Press, Inc.

ISBN: 0-932863-47-7
978-0-932863-47-8

In-house editor: Diana G. Collier

Fellmeth, Robert C.
Child rights & remedies / by Robert C. Fellmeth.
— 2nd ed.
p. cm.
Child rights and remedies
Includes index.
ISBN-13: 978-0-932863-47-8
ISBN-10: 0-932863-47-7

1. Children—Legal status, laws, etc.—United States. 2. Minors—United States. 3. Children's rights—United States. 4. Children—Services for—United States. I. Title. II. Title: Child rights and remedies.

KF479.Z9F45 2006 346.7301'35
QBI06-200074

Clarity Press, Inc.
Ste. 469, 3277 Roswell Rd. NE
Atlanta, GA. 30305
http://www.claritypress.com

Table of Contents

Table of Cases

Acknowledgments

I am indebted to my colleagues in the child advocacy movement—the members of the National Association of Counsel for Children, Voices for America's Children, First Star, the Children's Defense Fund, the Child Welfare League, the ABA Center on Children and the Law, Foundation of America—Youth in Action, the Maternal and Child Health Access Project, Campaign for Tobacco-Free Kids, Children Now, the American Academy of Pediatrics, Children's Hospitals, teachers, social workers, child care providers, and the many other advocates who attempt to advance the interests of children. Those advocates include many attorneys from the heroic efforts of the Castano lawyers to protect children from tobacco, to the juvenile courts and legal aid attorneys who work one on one to help children day after day. They are joined by important foundations, including the David and Lucile Packard Foundation, the Robert Wood Johnson Foundation, The California Wellness Foundation, the ConAgra Foundation, the Rosenberg Foundation, the Sierra Health Foundation,the Leon Strauss Foundation, the Maximilian E. & Marion O. Hoffman Foundation, the Weingart Foundation, the Mattel Foundation, the Annie E. Casey Foundation, and the large number of anonymous givers who care about children and contribute for their effective representation.

I am grateful for the review and comments on early drafts of this work by Deborah Stein of the National Association of Child Advocates and by Nancy Fellmeth of Families for Early Autism Treatment. I am also grateful for the help and assistance from Public Citizen and other public interest advocates throughout the nation from Ralph Nader to Scott Harshbarger,Joshua Rosenkranz, and Charles Lewis—whose assistance in the first chapter of this work has been invaluable. In addition, Deans Daniel B. Rodriguez and Kevin Cole, the faculty of the University of San Diego (USD) School of Law, USD Presidents Alice Hayes and Mary Lyons, and USD Provosts Frank Lazarus and Julie Sullivan have been important supporters of our work over the years.

I am grateful for the editorial and research assistance of Elisa Weichel, Administrative Director of the Children's Advocacy Institute (CAI). Also, this book would have been impossible without the intellectual contribution and dedicated support of Julie D'Angelo Fellmeth, Administrative Director of CAI's parent organization, the Center for Public Interest Law (CPIL). Further, I am indebted to all of the other current and prior staff of CAI and CPIL, including Lupe Alonzo-Diaz, Steve Barrow, June Brashares, Collette Cavalier, Lillian Clark, Terry Coble, Leanne Cotham, Margaret Dalton, Cindy Dana, Kathryn Dresslar, Gene Erbin, Cheryl Forbes, Barry Fraser, Beth Givens, John Hardesty, Inez Hope, Jim Jacobson, Louise Jones, Sharon Kalemkiarian, Lynn Kersey, Joy Kolender, Christine Harbs Mailloux, Kathleen Murphy Mallinger, Marissa Martinez, Mark McWilliams, Claudia Terrazas Mellon, Betty Mulroy Mohr, Debra Back Marley, Rusty Nichols, Carl Oshiro, Kim Parks, Kathleen Quinn, Stephanie Reighley, Randy Reiter, Christina Riehl, Diana Roberts, Alecia Sanchez, Kathy Self, Kate Turnbull, Jim Wheaton, and Ellen Widess. And I thank Christine Basic, Hanna Gibson, Jessica Heldman, Catherine Learned, Molly Selway, and Melissa Stewart for their proofing, comments, and cite checks.

I am thankful for the enduring support of some of our leading child advocates in their service on CAI's Council for Children. These leaders in pediatrics, education, social work, business, and law serve without compensation and spend many hours helping to guide the Children's Advocacy Institute. They currently include Robert Black, M.D., John Goldenring, M.D., M.P.H., Louise Horvitz, M.S.W., Psy.D., the Hon. Leon Kaplan, James McKenna, Tom Papageorge, Gary Redenbacher, Gary Richwald, M.D., M.P.H., Blair Sadler, Gloria Perez Samson, Alan Shumacher, M.D., F.A.A.P., and Owen Smith, as well as *emeritus* members Paul A. Peterson and Birt Harvey, M.D. Past members of and/or special consultants to the Council have included Frank Alessio, Nancy Daly, Martin Fern, Robert Frandzel, Theodore Hurwitz, Ralph Jonas, Quynh Kieu, Harvey Levine, Mary O'Connor, the Hon. Robert Presley, and W. Willard Wirtz.

Finally, the spiritual underpinning for this book and for our child advocacy comes from our longstanding mentors, Sol and Helen Price.

Dedication

To Michael Q. and Aaron X.,
and to the memories of Robert B.,
Jane Z., Jimmy D., Jody B., and Aaron P.

Preface

Scholarship on children and the law reflects a movement from a view of children as property, to children as a protected underclass, to children as rights-based citizens. The first English book on children and the law, *Law, Both Ancient and Modern Relating to Infants*, published in 1697, described children as paternal chattel.[1] Subsequent scholarship from Elizabethan England to 20th Century America reflected changes in the status of children as they gradually came to be viewed as worthy of society's protection. This publication, *Child Rights & Remedies,* represents the next step in our evolving understanding of the place of children in society.

The evolutionary component of this work is found in its treatment of rights-based versus welfare-based thinking, and how that distinction dictates law and public policy. While it may be agreed that society as a whole probably cares about children, it can be more important to ask *how* we care about them. Whether we provide for children out of a benevolent sense of care-taking (a welfare-based approach) or because we believe children are *entitled* to certain treatment (a rights-based approach), these motives serve as ideological principles that guide our law and policy.

In the context of the legal representation of children, where we are situated on that ideological continuum determines in large part which type of legal representation we provide. If we take a welfare-based view, we are inclined to protect children by providing advocate-directed representation where the representative determines the best interests of a child (as is currently the norm in child abuse and neglect proceedings) and then advocates for it. If we take a rights-based approach, we are inclined toward client-directed representation where the child client is given an independent voice (as is the case in juvenile justice / delinquency proceedings).

It can be argued that as we review the history of juvenile law, we see progress toward better outcomes for children through the movement from welfare-based systems toward rights-based systems. At one time, the only protection children could receive from parental abuse was to see their parents prosecuted in criminal court. Children were not entitled to care or services; as one 19th century court wrote, "[t]he state, through its criminal laws, will give the minor child protection from parental violence and wrongdoing*, and this is all the child can be heard to demand*."[2] At the turn of the 20th century, however, with the advent of juvenile courts, society began to provide special care for children as part of the "child saving" movement. Ultimately, that child saving welfare-based movement was struck down (for delinquent children) by a Supreme Court which, having reviewed the history of the care-taking experiment, created a rights-based juvenile court in which youth would be *entitled* to the protections of due process of law.[3] The Court wrote, "[j]uvenile court history has again demonstrated that unbridled discretion, however benevolently motivated, is frequently a poor substitute for principle and procedure."[4]

But just how evolved was the new juvenile court? Did a rights-based due process court produce better outcomes for children? In many instances yes, but at the same time it can be argued that in actuality it tipped the balance too far away from beneficence and toward autonomy; resulting in a juvenile court that is essentially an adult criminal court which fails to treat children as children, and by so doing, actually infringes upon their rights.

So should we follow this evolutionary trend in the abuse and neglect court or other areas of law affecting children? Do we truly serve children by empowering them or does empowerment ultimately lead to the diminution of children's protected status? That is the question that serves as context for this book and gives us an analytical structure for responding.

It is also a theme that enables Professor Fellmeth to unite so many areas of law and policy affecting children. Children have historically been treated by legal scholars as either delinquent or dependent, but the all-important picture of the whole child — as determined not only by personal and familial circumstances, but also by the gamut of social policies through which governments seek to regulate or affect the socio-economic environment — has eluded them. By including not only delinquency and dependency, but also health care, education and property rights, poverty, mental health, civil liberties and reproductive law, *Child Rights & Remedies* provides a uniquely holistic analysis of children's law and policy.

With this comprehensive systemic analysis, Professor Fellmeth has made an important contribution to the growth of the field of children and the law.

Marvin Ventrell
Executive Director
National Association of Counsel for Children

ENDNOTES

[1] Juvenile Court historian Sanford J. Fox believed this to be the first English book on law relating to children.

[2] *Hewlett v. George*, 68 Miss. 703, 711, 9 So. 885, 887 (1891) (emphasis added).

[3] *In re Gault*, 387 U.S. 1 (1967).

[4] *Id.*, at 18.

Introduction

This text is intended for use in law school, political science, social science, and social work/public health graduate courses. The book focuses on the leading court cases interpreting and defining American law pertaining to children. It is supplemented with important data, brief commentaries, and questions to stimulate discussion.

The subject matter is deliberately broad, covering the political/legal context of rights and remedies available to children, and twelve substantive areas. Three themes tie together all of the issues and discussion of this work. First is a pervasive dichotomy underlying child-related public policies. On the one hand, children are all persons entitled to the rights and privileges of any citizen. Indeed, our affection for them gives them special status. In a sense, the status of adults is believed by many to be a floor above which children are properly elevated. On the other hand, however, children are immature. They are not merely "little adults" and cannot be relied upon to always judge their own self-interest. Rather, they require protection and guidance. This dualism underlies much public policy affecting children and has often worked to their disadvantage, as the materials to follow indicate. Sometimes children are not granted the minimum floor of rights reserved for adults. Their inferior status does not always relate to their immaturity or to their protection.

Second, children represent the politically weakest grouping of persons. Adults have organized across a wide spectrum of characteristics, from disabled status to sexual preference. To offend any grouping is to risk quick approbation. This status is reflected in many ways; for example, the media coverage of school shootings failed to report the marked diminution of youth crime and the fact that violence against children occurs hundreds of times more often than the reverse. Would similar reporting have occurred based on shootings by an Hispanic, a Lutheran, a gay man, or a senior citizen? A more critical reflection of this lack of status can be found in our attitude toward adult reproductive rights (which are expansively defended) as opposed to a posited right of a child simply to be intended by two adults. The statistical correlation between this rather simple stated "right" and child welfare is remarkable. But it brooks virtually no weight against the prerogatives of adult groupings. This political power deficit is exacerbated by their lack of organization, lobbying presence, ability to vote, lack of campaign finance resources, and limited access to court redress. How would the rights and remedies of children differ were they to have the organization and resources of energy corporations, trade associations, or senior citizens?

The final feature binding all of the chapters of this work is a cliche. But like many cliches, it covers a seminal truth. Children are our future, what we shall leave behind. One of the marks of civilization is the recognition of the sacrifices of our parents and of their parents—for us, and the ethical imperative to pass that legacy onto our own legatees. These sentiments cut across many cultures, from the People of Israel ("I have drunk from wells I did not dig, and warmed by fires I did not build") to the Native American ("I did not inherit this earth from my parents, I have borrowed it from my grandchildren").

CHAPTER ONE

The Underlying Context: Access to Political/Legal Remedies

INTRODUCTION: REPRESENTATION OF THE LONG-TERM PUBLIC INTEREST

Rights and remedies inevitably depend upon the political system that enacts laws, and then interprets and enforces them. Elected and appointed public officials decide federal, state, and local budgets, and prohibit or reward private acts affecting children. Using the power to invest public funds (including the provision of public education), the police power to tax (or to except from taxation), and the power to criminally or civilly prohibit, government exerts momentous and organized influence. Given the complexity of modern society, the public officials who make decisions necessarily depend upon outside advocacy to bring matters to their attention, to frame issues and present alternatives, and to provide information for decision making. Even the legislature, designedly the most proactive of the three branches, largely responds to advocacy before it. Who provides that advocacy? Is the result likely to reflect the ethical aspirations of the citizenry?

Child advocates argue that if decisions were made on their merits by those applying the underlying ethical mandate of the body politic, children would fare well. However, such a crucible for decisions may be distorted where public institutions are dominated by advocacy from those organized around a short-term profit/stake in public policy. To the extent the three branches are driven in vector fashion by advocacy before them, decisions may sacrifice unorganized, long-range interests not included within the cacophony before them. Children suffer particularly from such exclusion.

An examination of the rights and remedies available to children properly begins with an examination of the underlying process creating those rights and remedies. Their creation and amendment depend upon the political process within the three branches, federal, state and local. To what extent can children—or those who advocate on their behalf—participate in the process and achieve an appropriate impact on resulting policy?

Child advocates have undertaken two approaches to current advocacy imbalance. The first is to alter the rules to give non-profit/-stake interests (such as children) greater access to decision making. One theory holds that reforms to lessen the influence of organized short-term interests necessarily enhance the prospects of those currently excluded, as the tinkling of a glass at a dinner may quiet the crowd so a soft voice can be heard. Political reformers argue that children and other diffuse interests will achieve a seat at the table only if decisions are driven more "on the merits" and less based on organization and wealth alone. Accordingly, lessening dependence on private campaign contributors, on those able to provide employment to public officials, or on the information provided by organized interests may stimulate decisions that are responsive to accepted public values which otherwise lack sufficient consideration.

Such reform efforts vary from public financing of campaigns, providing incentives for more balanced advocacy before legislatures, increasing the independence of agencies, enhancing access to courts, and exposing governmental decisions to public examination. Such measures are intended to counterbalance the advantage of organization and money by raising considerations important to those interests—children's first among them—which otherwise are less heard.

The second approach is to work within whatever system is extant to maximize the influence of children by using available resources—however disadvantageous the structural setting. Hence, child advocates have increased political involvement (*e.g.,* formulating "report cards" on legislator votes, organizing to pose questions to candidates, etc.). Other child advocates devote resources to lobbying to the limited extent now feasible, and attempt to enlist powerful lobbyists with a tangential interest in policy benefiting children. Some child advocates use class action and mandamus tools in the courts. Others propose rules before federal and state agencies.

This Chapter explores the major political/structural impediments to child-sensitive public policies within the three branches, paying attention to the allegedly distorted "rules of the game" impeding balanced decision making, and identifying some of the successful tactics employed by child advocates to overcome existing barriers.

A. CHILDREN AND CAMPAIGN CONTRIBUTIONS

All three branches of government are necessarily affected by political elections. All legislators and major executive branch officials are elected. Judges are often appointed and confirmed by elected officials, but must run for subsequent election in most states. Campaigns have become increasingly expensive and most candidates depend upon private contributions to provide that funding. Such contributions often come from those with a vested profit stake in the decisions of the contested office. The extent to which such contributions influence later official acts varies, but few dispute that it provides an advantage, particularly in terms of access to elected officials. Such access can be a critical determinant of the decisions made. Understandably, large contributors tend to have a financial interest in those decisions. Large contributions are made or organized by corporations, unions, or trade associations across a spectrum of economic actors. However, three features often predominate: the defense of existing capital investment or occupational prerogatives, an advantage to those organized around their financial stake, and a focus on immediate economic consequences as opposed to longer range consequences. In contrast, children, who may benefit from new and different investment (capital) decisions, are inherently unorganized and incapable of direct political organization, and have an interest in longer term future impacts.

Children lack the policy leverage and access that often attends financial campaign support. On occasion, those who provide services to children may be organized and may contribute. But such organized support is insubstantial in comparison to vested profit/stake interests which dominate campaign giving. Such "surrogate" giving on behalf of the interests of children is hampered by three factors: (1) many who serve children are relatively unorganized and are paid close to minimum wage (*e.g.*, child care providers); (2) political giving by charitable interests (*e.g.*, foundations, churches, charities) organized around the interests of children is legally barred; and (3) such providers may not always place the interests of children above their own economic stake when the two conflict.

Current campaign regulation generally takes two forms: amount limitations per election on contributions to candidates (including an outright prohibition on corporate contributions for federal elections), and widespread required public identification of contributors. However, stated regulatory goals have been partially thwarted by two common problems: the increased use of political action committees (PACs) by organized interests, which frequently arrange for "independent expenditures" for and against candidates, and an even broader minimally monitored allowance for "soft money" contributions to national and state political parties, which was allowed with virtually no limitation until 2003. Such contributions may partially avoid financial limitations (and the effective attributable disclosures normally required) for contributors. By 2000, more than one-half of Congressional contributions by the major givers was channeled through political parties, totaling $457 million.[1] In addition, during the 1999–2000 cycle, a record $610 million in soft money contributions flowed to state and local candidates through similar state party contributions.[2]

The leading case casting a long shadow over all post-1976 regulatory efforts is *Buckley v. Valeo*, 424 U.S. 1 (1976), where the Supreme Court distinguished between campaign contributions (which may be regulated in amount) and campaign expenditures. The Court reasoned that unlike contribution limits, spending limits do not have the same "compelling state interest" in corruption diminution. Limiting campaign spending, including the amount a candidate could spend from her own assets, became problematical. Accordingly, campaign finance reformers developed a "quid pro quo" strategy: give the candidates something in return for a promise to limit spending. Different arrangements have allowed a public declaration that a candidate has "abided by a limitation" (sometimes to be placed on the ballot itself), or have allowed public financing (usually public funds to match small private contributions on a 1–to–1 or higher ratio), or have allowed a larger contribution limitation to candidates who agree to an expenditure ceiling.

The most prominent example of such a strategy is the Presidential election, financed through Form 1040 IRS tax check-off monies to political parties receiving more than 5% of the vote in the previous election, and whose candidates agree to abide by specified spending limitations. In addition, the cities of New York and Los Angeles, and the states of Maine, Massachusetts, and Arizona have implemented regimes which involve spending limitations and public matching funds for small individual contributions. However, the overwhelming influence of interests remains substantially intact, buttressed by the soft money and independent expenditure evasions which developed post-*Buckley*. One respected commentator summarizes the post-*Buckley* world:

The Post-*Buckley* World

In the generation since *Buckley*, the political landscape has undergone a seismic shift. A House seat is now six times as expensive as it was then, or more than triple after adjusting for inflation. In 1994, the average incumbent in a competitive House election spent $945,00 and the average incumbent in a competitive Senate election spent approximately $4.6 million. The 1996 federal elections cost over $2 billion, double the previous record.

These sky-high campaign costs have fixed an effective admission charge for candidates. And candidates who spend the most usually win. In 1996, 89 percent of all House winners outspent their opponents. In 1994, no House challenger spending under $100,000 won, and of those spending between $100,000 and $250,000 only 7 percent won. Only the wealthy, or candidates who can pick their pockets, have any real chance of being elected. In 1992, twelve Senate candidates each spent over $1 million of their own money on their campaigns. For the House, ten candidates spent more than $500,000 of their personal wealth. The result, predictably, is a plutocracy—a Congress, for example, in which thirty House members are worth more than $2 million and one out of four senators is a millionaire.

Candidates of more modest means must raise their money bit by bit. Even so, they are financed largely by the rich. Fewer than 1 percent of Americans contribute $200 or more to congressional candidates. Only 8 percent of voters make any political contribution of any size, in any election, federal, state, or local. The residents of one zip code on Manhattan's Upper East Side contributed more money to Congress in 1994 than did all the residents of each of twenty-one states. In contrast, the richest 10 percent of the population (those with family incomes over $75,000) contribute almost *half* of all campaign dollars.

All this money is certainly not buying competitive elections. In 1996, the House reelection rate was 95 percent—a lower turnover rate than the Politburo in Soviet days. No doubt, part of the problem is that legislative districts are gerrymandered to protect incumbents. But another part of the problem is that money follows the incumbent, regardless of political philosophy. Wealthy corporate PACs funnel huge sums to incumbents, Democrats and Republicans alike, in order to gain access and influence. In 1996, seventeen House incumbents ran unopposed, and another 111 were financially unopposed, facing challengers with less than $25,000 in campaign resources. They all won. A whopping 182 incumbents ran in financially uncompetitive races, where the incumbent had more than twice the challenger's campaign resources; 178, or 98 percent, won....

As campaign spending has increased, so has voter cynicism and disillusionment with politicians and with government, to the point where voter distrust is at an all-time high. One symptom of voter disillusionment is our shockingly low voter turnout, even as Congress has removed barriers to registration and even as the registration rolls have ballooned. The 49 percent voter turnout for the 1996 presidential election set a seventy-year low. Likewise, in the 1994 elections that transformed Congress, only approximately 39 percent of the electorate voted. Our turnout stands today at the lowest level of any democracy in the world. Why do we behave like spectators in our own democracy? Because we feel like spectators—spectators in an auction where the election goes to the highest bidder. And very few can afford to bid.

Source: Joshua Rosenkranz, Buckley Stops Here (Century Foundation Press, 1998) at 15-17 (cites omitted).

The Supreme Court decision in *Nixon v. Shrink Missouri Government PAC*, 528 U.S. 377 (2000), upheld a contribution limit of $1,075 imposed by Missouri on statewide races, noting that money is not directly equivalent to speech, and recognizing the legitimate public interest not only to prevent bribery, but "extending to the broader threat from politicians too compliant with the wishes of large contributors." Heartened by the judgment that money is not necessarily speech, reform efforts have been initiated in Vermont, Missouri, Oregon, Michigan, Idaho, Arizona, and Maine. Creative solutions have been advanced, including the following:

(1) "Clean Money Campaign Reform" where candidates qualify for public campaign funds through signatures or a minimum number of $5 contributions from registered voters in their jurisdiction, with private contributions limited to $100 per person.

(2) "Matching funds" allowing candidates to receive anywhere from a 1–to–1 match to 4–to–1 in public funds for every $250 in private contributions from a registered voter in the jurisdiction.

(3) Refundable tax credits for contributions to candidates who have agreed to spending limits.

(4) A system called "patriot dollars" where citizens are each given $200 in vouchers to commit to candidates for public office.

(5) Subsidized or free required time from the media for campaign messages by candidates, debates, and other means to lessen the increasing costs of candidate communications;

(6) A local charter provision enacted by citizen initiative in three California cities (San Francisco, Santa Monica, and Pasadena) which provides that where a local official has conferred a "public benefit" beyond a specified level to a corporation or person, that beneficiary may not give anything of value to the official for five years after the decision is made, or two years after leaving office, whichever is longer. Campaign contributions (as well as gifts and employment) may not be received by such an official during that period from such a beneficiary.

Public financing has been enacted for the presidential campaign, and recently for all statewide elected officials in Maine and Arizona. Both states report marked diminution of special interest influence. New Mexico and North Carolina have approved public financing for some public offices, and New Jersey has adopted a pilot program for two legislative districts. Many states provide tax incentives to individuals who contribute to a political party or a qualifying candidate, including Minnesota, Arkansas, Ohio, Oregon and Virginia.[3] Each such system varies in qualification for public finance help, residency requirements for matching public funds, sources of funding, spending limits (often imposed as a condition of public assistance), contribution limits, and waiver or extension of limits where high spending occurs by opponents or by independent expenditure committees. Beyond such state systems, the cities of Los Angeles and New York have implemented a partial system of public finance for some city positions. Notwithstanding these experiments, the vast majority of city, state, and all Congressional elections limit influence primarily through a regime of (a) campaign contribution amount limitations and (b) disclosure of contributors. As discussed above, the former is evaded through alleged "independent expenditures" and the latter by contributions received at or just after the election—inhibiting disclosure to voters. The more substantial proposals listed above have not been widely implemented.

Note on 2002 Bipartisan Campaign Reform Act

On March 27, 2002, the President signed the "Bipartisan Campaign

Reform Act of 2002,"[4] addressing the rapid "soft money" growth in campaign finance through the 1990s. As noted above, that soft money consisted of large contributions from corporations, unions, and wealthy individuals to the respective political parties. The monies were then channeled into the Presidential and Congressional campaigns, facilitating disproportionate influence by a small group of givers. Those givers also were able to effectively avoid disclosure of their identities as financiers of particular candidates as required by law due to the middleman role of the party. However, critics charged that party leaders knew well who the big givers were and would facilitate their influence on those public officials their funds helped to elect. In addition, the nation's political action committees began to use "independent expenditure" campaigns to influence elections—alleged public mailing and media advertising for and against candidates for office run by special interests independent of the candidates' political campaigns. These campaigns avoided the contribution limitations and contributor identification provisions of law applicable to the candidates.

The new law imposes some limitations on soft money contributions to political parties, prohibiting unions and corporations (already limited in federal candidate campaign giving) from making contributions for candidates through party giving. In addition, corporations and unions cannot fund ads for or against candidates for federal office within sixty days of a general election or thirty days of a primary election from their general treasury. Although addressing some important abuses, five factors limit its ability to redress campaign finance imbalance working to the disadvantage of children: (1) Independent expenditures immediately prior to an election remain lawful where funded by a political action committee. The law simply prohibits funding from the membership treasury where contributions presumably are not given voluntarily for that particular political purpose. Such PAC funding may still be substantial. (2) Corporations and unions may be able to tap their general treasuries for campaign spending outside the thirty and sixty-day prohibitory period, including substantial spending for ads attacking public officials with whom they disagree and who shortly face election. (3) The law may not apply fully to Internal Revenue Code § 527 organizations.[5] (4) The law does not apply at all to state and local office. Moreover, it does not prevent unlimited corporate or union soft money giving to state political parties, who can then funnel it into expenditure campaigns to assist state candidates allied with their federal counterparts. Most states do not have the federal limitation on corporate or union campaign funding, and the decried abuses leading to this legislation all remain largely unaddressed at the state level. (5) The law raises the limit on so-called "hard money" contributions (made by individuals to candidates directly) from $1,000 per person per election to $2,000, to be adjusted in the future by inflation.[6] Hence, a married couple can together give $8,000 to a candidate, $4,000 to the primary campaign and $4,000 to the general. These limits are subject to increase where a candidate spends substantial personal funds for his or her own election; such spending above two times the law's specified threshold will raise the $8,000 limit for the couple in the example above to $24,000. At a very high level of personal spending by a candidate on his or her own campaign, the individual limits are waived entirely for the opponents in that election.

In *McConnell v. Federal Election Commission*, 540 U.S. 93 (2003), the Court upheld most of the Bipartisan Campaign Reform Act of 2002. The Court applied a "heightened scrutiny" test (less than "strict scrutiny" but more rigorous than "rational relation") to limitations on contributions. As discussed above, the Court distinguished between "expenditures" where one is spending one's own money on one's speech (and subject to strict scrutiny) and "contributions" that involve giving money to another to finance his/her electoral speech. The test enunciated by the Court for contribution control is whether there is a "sufficiently important interest" at stake and whether the restriction is "closely drawn" to avoid unnecessary abridgement of First Amendment interests. Applying this test, the Court upheld the new statute's restrictions on soft money contributions via political parties, political advertising rate ceilings at the "lowest unit charge" for that class of advertising normally charged, and record keeping requirements imposed on broadcasters.

One aspect of the new statute suffered reversal—its prohibition on contributions by minor children. The government's justification that the restriction was necessary to prevent circumvention of limits based on family size was rejected as too attenuated given the lack of evidence presented of such abuse and the existing and still applicable general prohibition on giving or on receiving contributions "in the name of another person."

The soft money restriction on the pre-2003 common use of contributions to state and local parties—who then give to federal candidates free from otherwise applicable limitations on amount limitations, allowing avoidance of source disclosure—was upheld by a 5–4 margin, with Justice O'Connor providing the swing vote. The statute as upheld does not address the five tactics discussed above.

Since *McConnell*, political spending by the so-called Section 527 groups has increased dramatically—undermining the limitation and disclosure purposes of campaign regulation. Indeed, unlimited spending that is not controlled by or coordinated by a candidate (or his/her party under the expanded terms of the new statute) cannot be easily circumscribed given the Court's view of the first amendment speech and association rights connection.

To the extent hard money becomes the critical means of finance, it shifts influence somewhat from corporations and unions to professional associations of teachers, attorneys, physicians, and others able to organize substantial individual contributions. Moreover, it strongly favors the elderly—who dominate individual campaign giving—with the median age of givers over $1,000 above sixty-five years of age.

Child advocates argue that achieving decisions based on the merits, such as giving proper weight to the interests of children (and other diffuse, long-term interests) requires more substantial reduction of reliance on private giving, probably via some system of public financing as suggested by the six options listed above.

Questions for Discussion

1. Is a financial stake in public policy a surrogate measure of legitimate "intensity of interest?" At what point does influence based on a relatively short-term economic interest improperly compromise broader, long-range interests, such as the environment and children?

2. Does the assured disclosure of campaign contributors counterbalance the alleged disproportionate influence of profit/stake interests? Will the banning of soft money significantly lessen reliance on those organized around a proprietary profit/stake?

3. As noted above, those making large individual campaign contribu-

tions are disproportionately seniors. Does such dependence influence public policies in the direction of senior citizen benefits as opposed to investment in children (*e.g.*, private pension subsidies, property tax relief, Medicare, prescription drug coverage, social security)?

4. Some groups that provide services to children may be organized enough to provide campaign assistance, votes, and even independent expenditures on their behalf. Do the interests of such groups always correspond to the long-range interests of children in their respective economic territories?

5. Even if public financing of campaigns removed substantial private dependence and enhanced competitive elections, would the interests of children secure adequate attention? Do lobbying resources which frame public policy debates, employment of public officials, and other sources of influence based on proprietary stake remain as impediments to public policies in their long-range interests?

B. CHILDREN, LEGISLATURES, AND LOBBYING

In addition to a lack of campaign contribution assets, children lack substantial lobbying presence in Washington, D.C., and especially in state capitols. Lobbying maximizes the impact of campaign contributions or independent expenditures by providing advocacy tied to givers. Children are not represented in terms of direct campaign givers, and are minimally represented through surrogate givers. Similarly, they are under-represented in the lobbying of public officials in the executive and legislative branches.

The most prevalent lobbying presence on behalf of children comes from horizontally organized interests who provide services for them, such as social workers, child care providers, and teachers. However, except in limited degree for teachers, such lobbying is not often supported by campaign finance assets. In addition, such advocacy by child service providers may serve the interests of members as a priority. Political scientists have noted that political advocacy (PAC lobbying) for a group tends to focus on the defense or expansion of the client's "territory". Less attention may be given to prevention, competition, or alternatives that lessen resources or authority for those representing children's interests. For example, a child care providers' association may oppose increased inspections or remedies for safety violations by its licensed members. Or a teachers' association may focus more on member employee benefits than on class size reduction, or it may advocate that funding for schools be taken from high priority preschool preparation or special education where not taught by its membership.[7]

However, differences between child service providers and the interests of children may be less significant given the domination of lobbying advocacy by commercial and organized interests. The imbalance mirrors the power of high campaign contributing industries nationally (*e.g.*, oil and gas, manufacturing, telecommunications, powerful unions, the elderly). These interests are joined at the state level by effectively organized state groups, such as the alcohol and insurance industries, organized physicians, trial lawyers, and others much affected by state law. While not consciously hostile to the interests of children, the preoccupation of these groups with their own immediate self-interests often influences public policy adversely to those not so represented.

1. Legislative Passivity

State legislatures and the Congress became more professional during the 20th century. Such advancement implies an independent, proactive entity able to exercise its own prerogatives on behalf of its constituents and their values. However, the size and sophistication of private lobbies have also grown, while substantial legislative resources focus on constituent services. The drafting of bills, amendments, supporting documentation, and public advocacy is dominated by the private side. In many states, legislators serve on a part-time basis while maintaining relatively full-time employment elsewhere, are in session only several months a year, and have minimal staff to help with policy decisions. The term limits movement has further increased the power of private lobbies in states where short terms are imposed. Campaign money becomes more important as new offices must be won, more power is delegated to private lobbies, and higher legislative staff turnover means more former legislative staff are hired by profit interests to influence their previous legislative committees.

Washington, D.C. is home to approximately 20,000 registered lobbyists as well as thousands of unregistered attorneys and other advocates. The percentage of full-time, professional lobbyists representing the interests of children—and only children—is estimated to be approximately one-tenth of one percent of that number. The states are similarly balanced. For example, California has 1,050 full-time registered lobbyists (five times the number of legislative staffers). Two of those lobbyists represent the interests of children exclusively. The formal nomenclature of the state assigns the term "sponsor" not to the legislator carrying a bill, but to the private group proposing and supporting it.

2. Structural Problems

As noted above, child advocates argue that children benefit where public decisions are made "on the merits." Such decisions are more likely to be made in the long-range public interest where other considerations do not unduly interfere with such a *bona fide* attempt. One such variable is the domination of information and advocacy by those with a vested economic stake in the policy to be decided, buttressed by campaign finance influence. Another variable may be direct economic benefit to the decision maker arranged by similar interests, including direct conflicts of interest (*e.g.*, where legislators continue law practice or other occupations that allow for financial gain from those affected by decisions made), honoraria, or job interchange (where lobbyists, legislators, and legislative staff interchange hiring and make implied or explicit job offers while public officials are still in office). These avenues of influence potentially distort decisions away from the merits.

Everything I'm Telling You is Entirely Legal

by Charles Lewis
The Center for Public Integrity

In 1991, the Center issued a report called "Saving for a Rainy Day." We found that 112 former members of Congress had pocketed $10 million in leftover campaign funds. Some of them bought themselves Cadillacs or Lincoln Continentals.

Others used the money to pay their legal bills after being prosecuted for various ethical transgressions. But my personal favorite is that one fellow [Gene Taylor] actually opened up a museum about himself [in Sarcoxie, Mo.]

* * *

In 1994, 17 researchers, writers and editors at the Center put out an investigative report ("Well-Healed") about the lobbying for and against the Clinton health care plan, in which we tracked the Washington activities of 660 interest groups trying to influence the legislative process. We found that 80 former U.S. officials had tripled, quadrupled, quintupled their salaries by going to work for health care-related interests. Health care companies had contributed $30 million to congressional campaigns in the two years leading up to the Clinton health care legislation. They took members of Congress on 181 all-expenses-paid trips to nice locales such as Honolulu, the Caribbean and, well, Tampa, to "educate" them about health care, of course.

Forty members of Congress sitting on the five key committees with jurisdiction over health care reform legislation owned stock in various companies that would be affected by any new laws–some members actually were buying and selling pharmaceutical and other health care-related stocks during the mark-up sessions. One interest group, the people that brought America the "Harry and Louise" commercials, the Health Insurance Association of America, made a deal with then-House Ways and Means Committee Chairman Dan Rostenkowski. HIAA would pull the highly effective TV ads critical of the proposed reform legislation from the airwaves if the committee would make substantive policy concessions to the insurance industry. It was a done deal. The only reason it fell apart is that Rostenkowski was indicted on unrelated federal charges.

Remember, everything that I am telling you is entirely legal.

"So You Want to Buy a President?"

In 1996, we wrote the first book ever to identify the special interests behind the presidential candidates, released weeks before the election season began in Iowa....

What did we find? Well, take former GOP presidential candidate Bob Dole. Since he was a senator from Kansas, we assumed that he had strong agribusiness support, and we fully expected that his top career patron would be Archer Daniels Midland. But actually, that company was Dole's fourth-leading career patron. ADM gave Dole more than $200,000 during his career, took him on 35 trips on the corporate jet, and at the same time, Dole was helping ADM get billions of dollars in ethanol and other federal agricultural subsidies. And yes, the chairman of ADM, Dwayne Andreas, sold an oceanfront condominium right here in Florida to the Doles for $100,000 under the market price, and the first payment on the mortgage wasn't required for seven or eight months after the sale. The Senate Ethics Committee never had a problem with any of this. Don't get me started.

Bob Dole's Gallo connection

Dole's No. 1 career patron was the Ernest and Julio Gallo wine family, of Modesto, Calif. This really surprised us, because there are no grapes in Kansas. Gallo had given him nearly $400,000 and with Dole's help, gotten a special inheritance tax passed, saving the company millions of dollars. The legislation was known inside the Senate as the "Gallo amendment."

Now, ladies and gentlemen, most Americans never meet their member of Congress. Ninety-six percent of the American people never give a dime to any politician or party at the federal level. Only one-tenth of 1 percent of the American people actually make a campaign contribution of $1,000. And, of course, no one has a U.S. Senate amendment named after him.

* * *

"The Buying of the Congress"

Some politicians and their patrons would have you believe that all of this money and fund raising does not affect public policies that are enacted. Well, in 1998, 36 researchers, writers and editors at the Center for Public Integrity produced a book, *The Buying of the Congress.* It showed in stunning example after example that, on important health, safety, environmental and financial issues that affect every American's daily life, Congress frequently sides with powerful special interests, to our detriment. This book, unfortunately, was released in Washington the same day that Kenneth Starr released his report about Monica Lewinsky. I hate when that happens.

But we looked at the cost of groceries and how certain items cost more because of various deals with donors in Congress. Cable TV rates are higher because of legislation pushed by the cable industry....

Or take tobacco, a product that kills 400,000 Americans each year. Today, in the new millennium, we still have federal policies to help grow tobacco, insure it, export it, and protect it against foreign imports. In a 10-year period, the cigarette manufacturers have blown smoke and more than $30 million in contributions to members of Congress and the two major political parties. And who can forget the $50 billion tax credit given to tobacco companies in the middle of the night in 1997, and hastily repealed when the American people found out about it?

All of this is entirely legal. But, as all of you know too well, the problems of legal corruption are not just in Washington.

Pay attention to state capitols

For example, Americans need to pay more attention to what's happening in their state capitols. Last year, state governments enacted 25,000 bills and collected $470 billion in taxes....

We called and wrote to every state legislator in the U.S., asking about his or her personal financial interests. One state lawmaker was so angry that we were asking these basic, public interest questions that he actually had his mother call us: "Why are you calling my son?" And then he had the state Senate majority leader call us, and he asked, "Why are you harassing one of my members?" We were just asking simple, clarifying-type questions about his disclosure form.

Roughly 10 people at the Center for Public Integrity worked on this project for more than two years. What did we find? That literally hundreds of state lawmakers are engaged in unabashed self-dealing, all legal, of course, because they write the laws. That more than one in five state legislators today sits on a legislative committee that regulates his or her professional or business interest. At least 18 percent of state lawmakers have financial ties to businesses or organizations that lobby state government. Nearly one in four state legislators receives income from a government agency other than the state legislature.

* * *

One fellow in Illinois is a registered lobbyist for insurance companies fighting for tort reform at the same time he sits in the state legislature.

One-fourth of all Oregon lawmakers have a spouse on the public payroll, and last year—gosh, what a coincidence—legislative assistants were voted a 60 percent pay raise.

They had a tough time trying to outlaw the scandal-ridden sheriff system in Connecticut–eight lawmakers have family ties to local sheriffs.

One Maine state lawmaker is president and CEO of a multimillion-dollar health care claims processing corporation that gets $10 million in state contracts. The contracts have increased during his tenure in the legislature.

The Delaware legislature actually loosened ethics laws so that eight lawmakers could vote on a utility deregulation bill. All of these members had stock in the company being deregulated; all of them voted with the company.

On and on and on. It's bad, folks, and maybe it is about time somebody noticed.

Source: Remarks at the 22nd anual conference of the Council on Governmental Ethics Laws in Tampa, Fla., Dec. 5, 2000. See www.public-i.org/report.aspx?aid=440.

Questions for Discussion

1. Courts have *ex parte* contact restrictions to prohibit one party in a proceeding from privately communicating with a judge. The concept is to allow open examination of a matter where all parties hear what others say, with the right to cross-examine and rebut. Should some of these elements be introduced into the legislative branch, at least as to bills currently before a committee? Would such a change elevate the importance of open hearings and lessen the disproportionate influence of special interests meeting privately with legislators?

2. Should Congress and state legislators be restricted from working for industries with business before their bodies for at least one or two years after they leave office? Should the moratorium be longer? Should they be limited in the direct lobbying of their former colleagues?

3. Currently, we allow profit/stake interests to deduct lobbying expenses as a "normal business expense". We also exempt industry and trade groups of competitors organized to influence government from antitrust laws. Such groups have formed political action committees, institutes, and joint lobbying enterprises under first amendment dispensation and as an exception to federal and state antitrust laws (the "*Noerr-Pennington*" doctrine). Accordingly, many such associations assess themselves sums for lobbying and those costs are passed on to consumers as a *de facto* industry-wide assessment. At the same time, we prohibit or limit charities with a lesser profit/stake in public policy from lobbying legislatures or agencies. What are the arguments for and against the reversal of those two social policies: tax profit/stake lobbying expenses, but permit charities or others without a profit/stake in public policy to participate free from tax status penalty or other sanction? What would be the long-range effect of such a change on the influence of children and other future interests before legislatures and agencies?

C. CHILD ADVOCACY AND THE COURTS

1. Children and Standing to Litigate

Contrary to common belief, children theoretically have standing to sue and to be sued in court—that is, their property, liberty, and interests may be adjudicated. However, for the same reason immaturity limits the enforcement of a contract against children signators, their ability to gain access to courts is limited. Children are grouped with incompetent adults in their presumed incapacity to understand legal procedures. Accordingly, they require adult assistance to initiate or defend lawsuits. Historically, a plaintiff child sued through a "*prochein ami*" or "next friend," while a child defendant was guided by the "*guardian ad litem*"—the term now most commonly used for all child court representation. Most states model child rules of representation after Federal Rule of Civil Procedure 17(c). Typically, parents perform this function, although a court may appoint another representative for a child—usually where parents have a conflict of interest. The usual rule is that where a court appoints such a person, compensatory fees may be awarded as well.[8]

A court-appointed *guardian ad litem* may or may not be an attorney. Courts have discretion to make or not to make such appointments. Usually, a court must be shown that "prejudice" to a child will result from the failure to make such an appointment. Precedents vest with the court the responsibility of monitoring a case to assure the welfare of child litigants, with the charge of representing the "child's best interests."

Much controversy has surrounded the role of such a *guardian ad litem* (who may decline to represent a child's expressed preferences) *vis-a-vis* a traditional attorney (who has a fiduciary duty to the client first and foremost and is more obligated to represent the expressed desires of the client). The typical conundrum is framed as follows: Where the *guardian ad litem* is an attorney, but believes that the child's preferences are irrational or not in his best interests, what is the proper course of action?

But larger questions are raised by the *guardian ad litem* mechanism for child representation. As discussed in Chapters 8 and 10, children who are accused of crimes and face punishment by the state are entitled to an attorney. But otherwise, representation of children is limited. Most states require representation of an allegedly abused or neglected child by a *guardian ad litem*, but do not require that person to be an attorney. This is in contrast to the universal practice of appointing counsel for all parents whose parental rights are adjudicated. Some jurisdictions devolve child representation onto volunteers. Others designate the attorney for the state agency removing the child to serve as the *guardian ad litem*. However, this practice is problematic given the federally-established obligation of the local agencies represented by the same office to provide "reasonable services" for parents to facilitate reunification and to protect children who may be returned (see Chapter 8). Such agencies often have budgetary constraints, and the same legal office representing them as counsel may be placed in an irreconcilable conflict between the interests of their agency client (*e.g.*, to avoid imposition of expense) and their child client who needs services for health and safety protection.

Courts are generally authorized to appoint *guardians ad litem* to represent children where a child is an "indispensable party" or has a substantial interest in the outcome of a suit (*e.g.*, insurance policy beneficiary, inheritee, survivorship claimant). Where such a guardian is not an attorney, he or she has intrinsic authority to manage the lawsuit, including the retention of counsel. However, few jurisdictions appoint compensated counsel for children outside of juvenile court. For example, although critical to a child's future, family court disputes involving custody, probate court disputes involving inheritance, and other proceedings do not in the normal course result in a *guardian ad litem* appointment.[9]

Children suffer substantial practical barriers to court access beyond eligibility for court-appointed *guardians ad litem*. Those impediments include: (1) the catch-22 problem of gaining access to a court to enable the appointment of such a representative; (2) the anti-solicitation standards applicable to the bar which inhibit attorney-initiated contact; (3) the lack of sophistication or contacts to arrange representation for themselves; (4) the confidentiality of juvenile court proceedings—particularly in dependency court where children are victims and visibility may serve their interests in court and outside of it; (5) the lack of financial resources available to children to compensate counsel; and (6) the limitation of legal authority to speak for a child outside of parental consent or even, perhaps, to bring a matter to court to allow the court to make an appointment.

Cases involving children reach the courts in one of three ways: First, a parent or guardian may bring an action on behalf of children (usually arranging for counsel). Second, children may be brought before the court by other persons (as in juvenile, family, or probate court, or when a child is sued). Third, children may benefit from an *en masse* suit which may include or assist them. The third category of lawsuit in turn depends upon access to the courts for class actions, petitions for writs of mandate, civil rights injunctive actions, or other remedies which operate to change underlying policies (as discussed below). The class or categorical court access opportunity is particularly important for children given the inherent weaknesses in the first two avenues of judicial redress.

In general, the doctrine of *stare decisis* applies to court holdings, allowing a single case to have a mass impact on similar disputes or issues. However, the courts are passive. They entertain only such actions as are brought before them by litigants with the standing, ability and resources to litigate. Such individual cases need to be brought in order to reach appellate resolution and inclusion into the body of American law. Where a given group has limited access, relatively few such decisions will be rendered to adjudicate their interests and hence to produce a *stare decisis* benefit.

Mass remedy court options that include children as intended beneficiaries may allow effective court decisions defining their rights and providing remedies where these rights are abridged.

2. Right to Sue *En Masse*

a. Legal Aid Actions

"None of the funds appropriated...to the Legal Services Corporation may be used to provide financial assistance to any person or entity...that initiates or participates in a class action suit."[10] This 1996 federal restriction was copied by Texas and other states. The attorneys it affects constitute the primary source of legal representation for impoverished citizens.

The Legal Services Corporation restriction was revised slightly after 1996 to allow class actions, but only where approved by the administration (the Corporation's appointed officials nationally). The 1996 statute also included three additional measures which in effect restrict access to the courts on behalf of impoverished children. First, the Congress provided that "None of the funds appropriated...to the Legal Services Corporation may be used to provide financial assistance to any person or entity...unless such person or entity agrees...not [to] accept employment resulting from in-person unsolicited advice...[to] take legal action."[11] The Legal Services Corporation then expanded this anti-personal outreach provision to prohibit counsel from communicating about available legal rights by telephone or through the mail (45 CFR Section 1638.2). These restrictions go beyond the "solicitation" limitation applicable to attorneys, and may be unconstitutional.[12]

Second, the 1996 statute provided that "None of the funds appropriated...may be used to provide financial assistance to any person or entity...that claims...or collects and retains, attorneys' fees pursuant to federal or state law permitting or requiring ...such fees."[13] In other words, successful counsel may not collect fees from a defendant even where state or federal law otherwise allows or requires it. Children are generally unable to pay legal costs or to contribute to their legal representation. The possibility of recompense from the other party (which requires the beneficiary to prevail) may allow substantially more such actions to be brought. The possibility that such actions will provide their own costs and fees makes them feasible beyond the limited appropriations provided to the Legal Services Corporation.

A third provision was enacted applicable to any court challenge of federal welfare statutes. The Congress was particularly concerned with eliminating judicial challenges to the welfare reform provisions of the Personal Responsibility and Work Opportunity Reconciliation Act of 1996. That statute changed the Aid for Families with Dependent Children (AFDC) entitlement safety net for children to a capped, conditional, and time-limited Temporary Assistance to Needy Families (TANF) system which began in 1997 and remains in effect. Approximately 70% of TANF beneficiaries are children. Together with the food stamp program, TANF provides the basic safety net for the majority of children living in families below the federal poverty line (see discussion in Chapter 3). As to this statutory scheme, an individual client may seek specific relief, but no challenge may be brought to the law, including a constitutional challenge. This provision raises the same objections as do the class action and broad outreach bans. Its constitutionality was tested in *Velazquez*, below. The issues framed for court review pertained to access, the First Amendment, and the separation of powers doctrine. Can one branch prohibit another from checking it? Or is the Legal Services Corporation a discretionary benefit which may be provided or not—and accordingly may be, conditioned on the surrender of judicial review?

Legal Services Corporation v. Carmen Velazquez
531 U.S. 533 (2001)

OPINION: **JUSTICE KENNEDY** delivered the opinion of the Court.

In 1974, Congress enacted the Legal Services Corporation Act, 88 Stat. 378, 42 U.S.C. § 2996 et seq. The Act establishes the Legal Services Corporation (LSC) as a District of Columbia nonprofit corporation. LSC's mission is to distribute funds appropriated by Congress to eligible local grantee organizations "for the purpose of providing financial support for legal assistance in noncriminal proceedings or matters to persons financially unable to afford legal assistance." § 2996b(a).

LSC grantees consist of hundreds of local organizations governed, in the typical case, by local boards of directors. In many instances the grantees are funded by a combination of LSC funds and other public or private sources. The grantee organizations hire and supervise lawyers to provide free legal assistance to indigent clients. Each year LSC appropriates funds to grantees or recipients that hire and supervise lawyers for various professional activities, including representation of indigent clients seeking welfare benefits.

This suit requires us to decide whether one of the conditions imposed by Congress on the use of LSC funds violates the First Amendment rights of LSC grantees and their clients. For purposes of our decision, the restriction, to be quoted in further detail, prohibits legal representation funded by recipients of LSC moneys if the representation involves an effort to amend or otherwise challenge existing welfare law. As interpreted by the LSC and by the Government, the restriction prevents an attorney from arguing to a court that a state statute conflicts with a federal statute or that either a state or federal statute by its terms or in its application is violative of the United States Constitution.

...We agree that the restriction violates the First Amendment, and we affirm the judgment of the Court of Appeals.

I

* * *

The restrictions at issue were part of a compromise set of restrictions enacted in the Omnibus Consolidated Rescissions and Appropriations Act of 1996 (1996 Act), § 504, 110 Stat. 1321-53, and continued in each subsequent annual appropriations Act. The relevant portion of § 504(a)(16) prohibits funding of any organization

> "that initiates legal representation or participates in any other way, in litigation, lobbying, or rulemaking, involving an effort to reform a Federal or State welfare system, except that this paragraph shall not be construed to preclude a recipient from representing an individual eligible client who is seeking specific relief from a welfare agency if such relief does not involve an effort to amend or otherwise challenge existing law in effect on the date of the initiation of the representation."

The prohibitions apply to all of the activities of an LSC grantee, including those paid for by non-LSC funds. §§ 504(d)(1) and (2). We are concerned with the statutory provision which excludes LSC representation in cases which "involve an effort to amend or otherwise challenge existing law in effect on the date of the initiation of the representation."

In 1997, LSC adopted final regulations clarifying § 504(a)(16). 45 CFR pt. 1639 (1999). LSC interpreted the statutory provision to allow indigent clients to challenge welfare agency determinations of benefit ineligibility under interpretations of existing law. For example, an LSC grantee could represent a welfare claimant who argued that an agency made an erroneous factual determination or that an agency misread or misapplied a term contained in an existing welfare statute. According to LSC, a grantee in that position could argue as well that an agency policy violated existing law. § 1639.4. Under LSC's interpretation, however, grantees could not accept representations designed to change welfare laws, much less argue against the constitutionality or statutory validity of those laws....Even in cases where constitutional or statutory challenges became apparent after representation was well under way, LSC advised that its attorneys must withdraw. Ibid.

* * *

....[T]he LSC program was designed to facilitate private speech, not to promote a governmental message. Congress funded LSC grantees to provide attorneys to represent the interests of indigent clients. In the specific context of § 504(a)(16) suits for benefits, an LSC-funded attorney speaks on the behalf of the client in a claim against the government for welfare benefits. The lawyer is not the government's speaker. The attorney defending the decision to deny benefits will deliver the government's message in the litigation. The LSC lawyer, however, speaks on the behalf of his or her private, indigent client. Cf. *Polk County v.*

Dodson, 454 U.S. 312, 321-322... (1981) (holding that a public defender does not act "under color of state law" because he "works under canons of professional responsibility that mandate his exercise of independent judgment on behalf of the client" and because there is an "assumption that counsel will be free of state control").

The Government has designed this program to use the legal profession and the established Judiciary of the States and the Federal Government to accomplish its end of assisting welfare claimants in determination or receipt of their benefits. The advice from the attorney to the client and the advocacy by the attorney to the courts cannot be classified as governmental speech even under a generous understanding of the concept. In this vital respect this suit is distinguishable from *Rust.*

The private nature of the speech involved here, and the extent of LSC's regulation of private expression, are indicated further by the circumstance that the Government seeks to use an existing medium of expression and to control it, in a class of cases, in ways which distort its usual functioning.

* * *

By providing subsidies to LSC, the Government seeks to facilitate suits for benefits by using the State and Federal courts and the independent bar on which those courts depend for the proper performance of their duties and responsibilities. Restricting LSC attorneys in advising their clients and in presenting arguments and analyses to the courts distorts the legal system by altering the traditional role of the attorneys in much the same way broadcast systems or student publication networks were changed in the limited forum cases we have cited. Just as government in those cases could not elect to use a broadcasting network or a college publication structure in a regime which prohibits speech necessary to the proper functioning of those systems, see *Arkansas Ed. Television Comm'n, supra,* and *Rosenberger, supra,* it may not design a subsidy to effect this serious and fundamental restriction on advocacy of attorneys and the functioning of the judiciary.

LSC has advised us, furthermore, that upon determining a question of statutory validity is present in any anticipated or pending case or controversy, the LSC-funded attorney must cease the representation at once. This is true whether the validity issue becomes apparent during initial attorney-client consultations or in the midst of litigation proceedings. A disturbing example of the restriction was discussed during oral argument before the Court. It is well understood that when there are two reasonable constructions for a statute, yet one raises a constitutional question, the Court should prefer the interpretation which avoids the constitutional issue. *Gomez v. United States*, 490 U.S. 858, 864...(1989); *Ashwander v. TVA,* 297 U.S. 288, 346-348...(1936) (Brandeis, J., concurring). Yet, as the LSC advised the Court, if, during litigation, a judge were to ask an LSC attorney whether there was a constitutional concern, the LSC attorney simply could not answer. Tr. of Oral Arg. 8-9.

Interpretation of the law and the Constitution is the primary mission of the judiciary when it acts within the sphere of its authority to resolve a case or controversy. *Marbury v. Madison,* 5 U.S. 137... (1803) ("It is emphatically the province and the duty of the judicial department to say what the law is"). An informed, independent judiciary presumes an informed, independent bar. Under § 504(a)(16), however, cases would be presented by LSC attorneys who could not advise the courts of serious questions of statutory validity. The disability is inconsistent with the proposition that attorneys should present all the reasonable and well-grounded arguments necessary for proper resolution of the case. By seeking to prohibit the analysis of certain legal issues and to truncate presentation to the courts, the enactment under review prohibits speech and expression upon which courts must depend for the proper exercise of the judicial power. Congress cannot wrest the law from the Constitution which is its source. "Those then who controvert the principle that the constitution is to be considered, in court, as a paramount law, are reduced to the necessity of maintaining that courts must close their eyes on the constitution, and see only the law." Id. at 178.

The restriction imposed by the statute here threatens severe impairment of the judicial function. Section 504(a)(16) sifts out cases presenting constitutional challenges in order to insulate the Government's laws from judicial inquiry. If the restriction on speech and legal advice were to stand, the result would be two tiers of cases. In cases where LSC counsel were attorneys of record, there would be lingering doubt whether the truncated representation had resulted in complete analysis of the case, full advice to the client, and proper presentation to the court. The courts and the public would come to question the adequacy and fairness of professional representations when the attorney, either consciously to comply with this statute or unconsciously to continue the representation despite the statute, avoided all reference to questions of statutory validity and constitutional authority. A scheme so inconsistent with accepted separation-of-powers principles is an insufficient basis to sustain or uphold the restriction on speech.

* * *

The restriction on speech is even more problematic because in cases where the attorney withdraws from a representation, the client is unlikely to find other counsel. The explicit premise for providing LSC attorneys is the necessity to make available representation "to persons financially unable to afford legal assistance." *42 U.S.C. § 2996*(a)(3). There often will be no alternative source for the client to receive vital information respecting constitutional and statutory rights bearing upon claimed benefits. Thus, with respect to the litigation services Congress has funded, there is no alternative channel for expression of the advocacy Congress seeks to restrict.

Congress was not required to fund an LSC attorney to represent indigent clients; and when it did so, it was not required to fund the whole range of legal representations or relationships. The LSC and the United States, however, in effect ask us to permit Congress to define the scope of the litigation it funds to exclude certain vital theories and ideas. The attempted restriction is designed to insulate the Government's interpretation of the Constitution from judicial challenge. The Constitution does not permit the Government to confine litigants and their attorneys in this manner. We must be vigilant when Congress imposes rules and conditions which in effect insulate its own laws from legitimate judicial challenge. Where private speech is involved, even Congress' antecedent funding decision cannot be aimed at the suppression of ideas thought inimical to the Government's own interest....

The judgment of the Court of Appeals is Affirmed.

DISSENT: **JUSTICE SCALIA**, with whom **THE CHIEF JUSTICE**, **JUSTICE O'CONNOR**, and **JUSTICE THOMAS** join, dissenting.

Section 504(a)(16) of the Omnibus Consolidated Rescissions and Appropriations Act of 1996 (Appropriations Act) defines the scope of a federal spending program. It does not directly regulate speech, and it neither establishes a public forum nor discriminates on the basis of viewpoint. The Court agrees with all this, yet applies a novel and unsupportable interpretation of our public-forum precedents to declare § 504(a)(16) facially unconstitutional. This holding not only has no foundation in our jurisprudence; it is flatly contradicted by a recent decision that is on all fours with the present case. Having found the limitation upon the spending program unconstitutional, the Court then declines to consider the question of severability, allowing a judgment to stand that lets the program go forward under a version of the statute Congress never enacted. I respectfully dissent from both aspects of the judgment.

* * *

I

The LSC Act is a federal subsidy program, not a federal regulatory program, and "there is a basic difference between [the two]." *Maher v. Roe,* 432 U.S. 464, 475...(1977). Regulations directly restrict speech; subsidies do not. Subsidies, it is true, may indirectly abridge speech, but only if the funding scheme is "manipulated" to have a "coercive effect" on those who do not hold the subsidized position....

In *Rust v. Sullivan, supra,* the Court applied these principles to a statutory scheme that is in all relevant respects indistinguishable from § 504(a)(16). The statute in Rust authorized grants for the provision of family planning services, but provided that "none of the funds...shall be used in programs where abortion is a method of family planning." Id. at 178. Valid regulations implementing the statute required funding recipients to refer pregnant clients "for appropriate prenatal...services by furnishing a list of available providers that promote the welfare of mother and unborn child," but forbade them to refer a pregnant woman specifically to an abortion provider, even upon request. Id. at 180. We rejected a First Amendment free-speech challenge to the funding scheme, explaining that "the Government can, without violating the Constitution, selectively fund a program to encourage certain activities it believes to be in the public interest, without at the same time funding an alternative program which seeks to deal with the problem another way." Id. at 193. This was not, we said, the type of "discrimination on the basis of viewpoint" that triggers strict scrutiny, ibid., because the "decision not to subsidize the exercise of a fundamental right does not infringe the right," ibid. (quoting *Regan v. Taxation With Representation of Wash., supra*, at 549).

The same is true here....

* * *

The Court's "nondistortion" principle is also wrong on the facts, since there is no basis for believing that § 504(a)(16), by causing "cases [to] be presented by LSC attorneys who cannot advise the courts of serious questions of statutory validity," ante, at 11, will distort the operation of the courts. It may well be that the bar of § 504(a)(16) will cause LSC-funded attorneys to decline or to withdraw from cases that involve statutory validity. But that means at most that fewer statutory challenges to welfare laws will be presented to the courts because of the unavailability of free legal services for that purpose. So what? The same result would ensue from excluding LSC-funded lawyers from welfare litigation entirely....

Nor will the judicial opinions produced by LSC cases systematically distort the interpretation of welfare laws. Judicial decisions do not stand as binding "precedent" for points that were not raised, not argued, and hence not analyzed....

Finally, the Court is troubled "because in cases where the attorney withdraws from a representation, the client is unlikely to find other counsel."....That is surely irrelevant, since it leaves the welfare recipient in no worse condition than he would have been in had the LSC program never been enacted. Respondents properly concede that even if welfare claimants cannot obtain a lawyer anywhere else, the Government is not required to provide one.

Questions for Discussion

1. What if the political consequence of *Velazquez* was Congressional termination of the Legal Services Corporation? Could the Court prevent such an outcome?

2. Some Legal Aid offices formed separate voluntary entities to file class actions where warranted; would the dissenters allow the Congress to foreclose that alternative option?

3. Legal Aid attorneys argued that if they are prohibited from a mass remedy, or from constitutional challenge to a welfare provision, children are effectively deprived of the societal check provided by the courts for other persons, implying equal protection breach. What is the status of children for 14th Amendment equal protection purposes? Would a "due process" argument be stronger?

4. Does the *Velazquez* holding also eliminate the three other related restrictions to representation of impoverished children discussed above?

b. Current Barriers to Class Actions for Children

Federal Rule of Civil Procedure 23 provides the basis for class actions in federal court, and is roughly replicated in most states. The rule is divided into three kinds of class actions as specified by Rule 23(b)(1), (b)(2), and (b)(3), respectively. All three forms of class action require a class representative who is a part of the class and who is an "adequate class representative". There must be questions of fact and law common to all members of the class to allow the outcome to apply to all those within it. There must be an adequate number of class members ("numerosity") to make a consolidated suit naming each member impractical. The class must be "certified" by the court as qualifying, and limited discovery may be allowed on issues such as adequate commonality, adequacy of representation, and other requirements. Once certified, the representative must give court-approved notice of the class to those included within it to allow members to "opt out" of the case in order to pursue their remedies separately if they wish to do so. Any final settlement or judgment will only occur after additional notice and public proceedings. These basic requirements are necessary to give the final judgment binding effect on all members of the class. Absent these elements, the action would potentially foreclose the due process rights of absent class members by persons with different claims, not adequately representing their interests, or by failing to provide notice of the case or its possible outcome.

The third of these three specified types—the Rule 23(b)(3) class action—has suffered from "add-on" requirements which have limited its application. This third type of class action authorizes damage actions at law on behalf of a class of persons. That common judicial remedy not only requires common questions of fact and law, but that such questions "predominate." Such actions must be "manageable," and must be "superior" to alternative remedies capable of redressing the stated grievance. Finally, in most cases, notice must be to individuals rather than by publication or other indirect means and must be financed by the plaintiff.

These add-on requirements do not apply as stringently to the common fund and injunctive (*e.g.*, civil rights) actions respectively authorized by Rule 23(b)(1) and (b)(2).[14] Nevertheless, any class certification will require an adequate class representative who is a part of the class and whose claims are typical of the class claims. As such, many of the six impediments to individual access to the courts by children discussed above can also inhibit the bringing of actions on behalf of children. However, where a parent or *guardian ad litem* may exist willing to vindicate the rights of a child, or where an organization has standing to bring suit, the class action mechanism may allow the direct application of a judgment outcome to a large number of children similarly affected.

The bringing of a single action to vindicate the rights of a group of children across state lines is possible where multi-district assignment allows it. In addition, some authority exists for a state to include within its class action case members who reside in other states if the cause of action arose within its borders and the statutes of other states where class members reside are consistent with the state law invoked in the host state, subject to some new limitations by the Class Action Fairness Act of 2005, discussed below.[15]

Marisol A. v. Giuliani
126 F.3d 372 (2d Cir. 1997)

OPINION: **PER CURIAM, FEINBERG, WALKER, LEVAL**, Circuit Judges

...The defendants claim that certification of the plaintiff class was improper because the plaintiffs failed to demonstrate that the certified class adhered to the strictures of Fed. R. Civ. P. 23. Because we find that the district court, in certifying the class at this point in the litigation, has not abused its discretion, we affirm the decision of the district court.

BACKGROUND

Familiarity with the painful allegations of the named plaintiffs, eleven children who claim they were deprived of the services of the New York City child welfare system to their extreme detriment, is presumed....Briefly, in December 1995, the named plaintiffs brought this action by and through their adult next friends seeking declaratory and injunctive relief against the defendants to redress injuries caused by the alleged systemic failures of the City's child welfare system....The complaint charged that the manner in which the defendants operate that system violates a diverse array of federal and state laws, namely, the First, Ninth and Fourteenth Amendments to the United States Constitution; the Adoption Assistance and Child Welfare Act of 1980, 42 U.S.C. §§ 620-628, 670-679a; the Child Abuse Prevention and Treatment Act, 42 U.S.C. §§ 5101-5106a; the Early and Periodic Screening, Diagnosis and Treatment program of the Medicaid Act, 42 U.S.C. §§ 1396a, 1396d(a) & (r); the Multiethnic Placement Act of 1994, 42 U.S.C. § 622(b)(9); the Americans with Disabilities Act, 42 U.S.C. §§ 12101 et seq.; the Rehabilitation Act of 1973, 29 U.S.C. §§ 794, 794a; Article XVII of the New York State Constitution; the New York State Social Services Law Articles 2, 3, 6 & 7,; the New York State Family Court Act, Articles 6 & 10; and various state regulations, 18 N.Y.C.R.R. §§ 400-484.

Pursuant to Rule 23(b)(2) of the Federal Rules of Civil Procedure, the plaintiffs asked the district court to certify a class of similarly situated children who are the legal responsibility of the child welfare system. The defendants, maintaining that the requirements of Rule 23 were not met, opposed class certification. In an order dated July 3, 1996, the district court certified a plaintiff class consisting of

> All children who are or will be in the custody of the New York City Administration for Children's Services ("ACS"), and those children who, while not in the custody of ACS, are or will be at risk of neglect or abuse and whose status is or should be known to ACS.

DISCUSSION

* * *

The defendants argue that, except at the grossest level of generality, there are no questions of law or fact common to the class and that no named plaintiff may convincingly assert that his or her claim is typical of the class. See *K.L. ex rel. Dixon v. Valdez,* 167 F.R.D. 688, 691 (D.N.M. 1996) (refusing to certify similar class bringing variety of legal claims where "no named Plaintiff and no putative class member has allegedly suffered violations of all or even most of the statutory and constitutional rights listed."). The defendants point out that each named plaintiff challenges a different aspect of the child welfare system. These include allegations of inadequate training and supervision of foster parents, the failure to properly investigate reports of suspected neglect and abuse, unconscionable delay in removing children from abusive homes, and the inability to secure appropriate placements for adoption, see *Marisol A.*, 929 F. Supp. at 669-72. The claimed deficiencies implicate different statutory, constitutional and regulatory schemes. Further, the defendants note that no single plaintiff (named or otherwise) is affected by each and every legal violation alleged in the complaint, and that no single specific legal claim identified by the plaintiffs affects every member of the class. Thus, in light of the broad range of injuries which the named plaintiffs allegedly have suffered, defendants argue that the commonality and typicality requirements have not been satisfied.

* * *

We find that the district court did not abuse its discretion by certifying this class at this time, notwithstanding our view, expressed in Section III, infra, that the creation of subclasses will be necessary. Three considerations compel this conclusion. First, "Rule 23 is given liberal rather than restrictive construction, and courts are to adopt a standard of flexibility ...." *Sharif ex rel. Salahuddin v. New York State Educ. Dep't.*, 127 F.R.D. 84, 87 (S.D.N.Y. 1989). The rule's inherent flexibility, and the district court's ability to manage the litigation as it develops, counsel against decertification.

Second, although the district court's generalized characterization of the claims raised by the plaintiffs stretches the notions of commonality and typicality, we simply cannot say that these claims are so unrelated that their aggregation necessarily violates Rule 23. The plaintiffs allege that their injuries derive from a unitary course of conduct by a single system, and the district court agreed. At this stage of the litigation, we see no basis for finding that the district court abused its discretion in this regard.

Finally, we note that the only other circuit court which has considered this very question has held that it was an abuse of discretion not to certify a class nearly identical to the one considered here. See *Baby Neal*, 43 F.3d at 64-65; cf. *Jeanine B. ex rel. Blondis v. Thompson*, 877 F. Supp. 1268, 1287 (E.D. Wisc. 1995) (certifying two subclasses, one of children in foster care and one of children not in foster care about whom the county had received reports of neglect or abuse, where plaintiffs "challenged the operating practices of the...foster-care system, and generally alleged that the...program is systematically depriving children of their legal rights."). Although we believe that the district court is near the boundary of the class action device, we are not prepared to say that it has crossed into forbidden territory.

D. Rule 23(b)(2)

Class certification is appropriate where the defendant has acted or refused to act on grounds generally applicable to the class, thereby making injunctive or declaratory relief appropriate. Fed. R. Civ. P. 23(b)(2). Defendants argue that because the plaintiffs have alleged differing harms requiring individual remedies, no injunction will be appropriate for the entire class. Defendants further claim that due to the unique circumstances of each plaintiff's experience with the child welfare system, the defendants have not acted on grounds generally applicable to the class.

We disagree. Insofar as the deficiencies of the child welfare system stem from central and systemic failures, the district court did not abuse its discretion in certifying a 23(b)(2) class at this stage of the litigation. See *Comer v. Cisneros,* 37 F.3d at 796 (Rule 23(b)(2) satisfied "because the plaintiffs seek injunctive relief and they predicate the lawsuit on the defendants' acts and omissions with respect to" the class); *Jeanine B.*, 877 F. Supp. at 1288 ("civil rights cases seeking broad declaratory or injunctive relief for a large and amorphous class...fall squarely into the category" of 23(b)(2) actions); Advisory Committee Note to Subdivision (b)(2) ("Illustrative are various actions...where a party is charged with discriminating unlawfully against a class, usually one whose members are incapable of specific enumeration.").

* * *

As presently certified, the class certified by the district court implicitly consists of two large subclasses. The first is comprised of "children who are or will be in the custody of the New York City Administration for Children's Services ("ACS");" the second is comprised of "those children who, while not in the custody of ACS, are or will be at risk of neglect or abuse and whose status is or should be known to ACS." *Marisol A.*, 95 Civ 10533 at 3 (A628). But in reality, each of these subclasses consists of smaller groups of children, each of which has separate and discrete legal claims pursuant to particular federal and state constitutional, statutory, and regulatory obligations of the defendants. Each claim, in turn, is based on one or more specific alleged deficiencies of the child welfare system.

Well in advance of trial, the district court must engage in a rigorous analysis of the plaintiffs' legal claims and factual circumstances in order to ensure that appropriate subclasses are identified, that each subclass is tied to one or more suitable representatives, and that each subclass satisfies Rule 23(b)(2)....

* * *

Castano v. American Tobacco Co.

84 F.3d 734 (5th Cir. 1996)

OPINION: **JERRY E. SMITH**, Circuit Judge:

In what may be the largest class action ever attempted in federal court, the district court in this case embarked "on a road certainly less traveled, if ever taken at all,"...and entered a class certification order. The court defined the class as:

> (a) All nicotine-dependent persons in the United States...who have purchased and smoked cigarettes manufactured by the defendants;
> (b) the estates, representatives, and administrators of these nicotine-dependent cigarette smokers; and

(c) the spouses, children, relatives and "significant others" of these nicotine-dependent cigarette smokers as their heirs or survivors.

Id. at 560-61. The plaintiffs limit the claims to years since 1943.[1]

This matter comes before us on interlocutory appeal, under *28 U.S.C. § 1292*(b), of the class certification order. Concluding that the district court abused its discretion in certifying the class, we reverse.

I.

A. The Class Complaint

The plaintiffs...filed this class complaint against the defendant tobacco companies...and the Tobacco Institute, Inc., seeking compensation solely for the injury of nicotine addiction. The gravamen of their complaint is the novel and wholly untested theory that the defendants fraudulently failed to inform consumers that nicotine is addictive and manipulated the level of nicotine in cigarettes to sustain their addictive nature. The class complaint alleges nine causes of action: fraud and deceit, negligent misrepresentation, intentional infliction of emotional distress, negligence and negligent infliction of emotional distress, violation of state consumer protection statutes, breach of express warranty, breach of implied warranty, strict product liability, and redhibition pursuant to the Louisiana Civil Code.

The plaintiffs seek compensatory[4] and punitive damages[5] and attorneys' fees.[6] In addition, the plaintiffs seek equitable relief for fraud and deceit, negligent misrepresentation, violation of consumer protection statutes, and breach of express and implied warranty. The equitable remedies include a declaration that defendants are financially responsible for notifying all class members of nicotine's addictive nature, a declaration that the defendants manipulated nicotine levels with the intent to sustain the addiction of plaintiffs and the class members, an order that the defendants disgorge any profits made from the sale of ciga-

---

[1] The court defined "nicotine-dependent" as: (a) All cigarette smokers who have been diagnosed by a medical practitioner as nicotine-dependent; and/or (b) All regular cigarette smokers who were or have been advised by a medical practitioner that smoking has had or will have adverse health consequences who thereafter do not or have not quit smoking. *Id. at 561.* The definition is based upon the criteria for "dependence" set forth in AMERICAN PSYCHIATRIC ASSOCIATION, DIAGNOSTIC AND STATISTICAL MANUAL OF MENTAL DISORDERS (4th ed.).

[4] The plaintiffs seek compensatory damages for fraud and deceit, negligent misrepresentation, intentional infliction of emotional distress, breach of express and implied warranty, strict products liability, and redhibition.

[5] The plaintiffs seek punitive damages for fraud and deceit, intentional infliction of emotional distress, negligence, and negligent infliction of emotional distress.

[6] The plaintiffs seek attorneys' fees for violations of consumer protection statutes and redhibition.

[7] The district court did not adopt the plaintiffs' trial plan, but its order certifying the class incorporates many elements of it.

[9] Rule 23(a) states: One or more members of a class may sue or be sued as representative parties on behalf of all only if (1) the class is so numerous that joinder of all members is impracticable, (2) there are questions of law or fact common to the class, (3) the claims or defenses of the representative parties are typical of the claims or defenses of the class, and (4) the representative parties will fairly and adequately protect the interests of the class.

[10] Rule 23(b)(3) states, in pertinent part, that a class action may be maintained if the court finds that the questions of law or fact common to the members of the class predominate over any questions affecting only individual members, and that a class action is superior to other available methods for the fair and efficient adjudication of the controversy.

rettes, restitution for sums paid for cigarettes, and the establishment of a medical monitoring fund.

The plaintiffs initially defined the class as "all nicotine dependent persons in the United States," including current, former and deceased smokers since 1943. Plaintiffs conceded that addiction would have to be proven by each class member; the defendants argued that proving class membership will require individual mini-trials to determine whether addiction actually exists.

In response to the district court's inquiry, the plaintiffs proposed a four-phase trial plan.[7] In phase 1, a jury would determine common issues of "core liability." Phase 1 issues would include...(1) issues of law and fact relating to defendants' course of conduct, fraud, and negligence liability (including duty, standard of care, misrepresentation and concealment, knowledge, intent); (2) issues of law and fact relating to defendants' alleged conspiracy and concert of action; (3) issues of fact relating to the addictive nature/dependency creating characteristics and properties of nicotine; (4) issues of fact relating to nicotine cigarettes as defective products; (5) issues of fact relating to whether defendants' wrongful conduct was intentional, reckless or negligent; (6) identifying which defendants specifically targeted their advertising and promotional efforts to particular groups (*e.g.*, youths, minorities, etc.); (7) availability of a presumption of reliance; (8) whether defendants' misrepresentations/suppression of fact and/or of addictive properties of nicotine preclude availability of a "personal choice" defense; (9) defendants' liability for actual damages, and the categories of such damages; (10) defendants' liability for emotional distress damages; and (11) defendants' liability for punitive damages.

* * *

B. The Class Certification Order

Following extensive briefing, the district court granted, in part, plaintiffs' motion for class certification, concluding that the prerequisites of FED. R. CIV. P. 23(a) had been met.[9] The court rejected certification, under FED. R. CIV. P. 23(b)(2), of the plaintiffs' claim for equitable relief, including the claim for medical monitoring. 160 F.R.D. at 552. Appellees have not cross-appealed that portion of the order.

The court did grant the plaintiffs' motion to certify the class under FED. R. CIV. P. 23(b)(3),[10] organizing the class action issues into four categories: (1) core liability; (2) injury-in-fact, proximate cause, reliance and affirmative defenses; (3) compensatory damages; and (4) punitive damages. *Id* . at 553-58. It then analyzed each category to determine whether it met the predominance and superiority requirements of rule 23(b)(3). Using its power to sever issues for certification under FED. R. CIV. P. 23(c)(4), the court certified the class on core liability and punitive damages, and certified the class conditionally pursuant to FED. R. CIV. P. 23(c)(1).

1. Core Liability Issues

The court defined core liability issues as "common factual issues [of] whether defendants knew cigarette smoking was addictive, failed to inform cigarette smokers of such, and took actions to addict cigarette smokers. Common legal issues include fraud, negligence, breach of warranty (express or implied), strict liability, and violation of consumer protection statutes." 160 F.R.D. at 553.

The court found that the predominance requirement of rule 23(b)(3) was satisfied for the core liability issues....

* * *

II.

* * *

The district court erred in its analysis in two distinct ways. First, it failed to consider how variations in state law affect predominance and superiority. Second, its predominance inquiry did not include consideration of how a trial on the merits would be conducted.

Each of these defects mandates reversal. Moreover, at this time, while the tort is immature, the class complaint must be dismissed, as class certification cannot be found to be a superior method of adjudication....

* * *

A. Variations in State Law

* * *

In a multi-state class action, variations in state law may swamp any common issues and defeat predominance....

* * *

The able opinion in *School Asbestos* demonstrates what is required from a district court when variations in state law exist. There, the court affirmed class certification, despite variations in state law, because:

> To meet the problem of diversity in applicable state law, class plaintiffs have undertaken an extensive analysis of the variances in products liability among the jurisdictions. That review separates the law into four categories. Even assuming additional permutations and combinations, plaintiffs have made a creditable showing, which apparently satisfied the district court, that class certification does not present insuperable obstacles. Although we have some doubt on this score, the effort may nonetheless prove successful.

A thorough review of the record demonstrates that, in this case, the district court did not properly consider how variations in state law affect predominance. The court acknowledged as much in its order granting class certification, for, in declining to make a choice of law determination, it noted that "the parties have only briefly addressed the conflict of laws issue in this matter." 160 F.R.D. at 554. Similarly, the court stated that "there has been no showing that the consumer protection statutes differ so much as to make individual issues predominate." Id....

The Castano class suffers from many of the difficulties that the Georgine court found dispositive. The class members were exposed to nicotine through different products, for different amounts of time, and over different time periods. Each class member's knowledge about the effects of smoking differs, and each plaintiff began smoking for different reasons. Each of these factual differences impacts the application of legal rules such as causation, reliance, comparative fault, and other affirmative defenses.

Variations in state law magnify the differences. In a fraud claim, some states require justifiable reliance on a misrepresentation, while others require reasonable reliance. States impose varying standards to determine when there is a duty to disclose facts. Products liability law also differs among states. Some states do not recognize strict liability. Differences in affirmative defenses also exist. Assumption of risk is a complete defense to a products claim in some states. In others, it is a part of comparative fault analysis. others follow a "greater fault bar, and still others use an "equal fault bar."

Despite these overwhelming individual issues, common issues might predominate. We are, however, left to speculate. The point of detailing the alleged differences is to demonstrate the inquiry the district court failed to make.

The court also failed to perform its duty to determine whether the class action would be manageable in light of state law variations. The court's only discussion of manageability is a citation to Jenkins and the claim that "while manageability of the liability issues in this case may well prove to be difficult, the Court finds that any such difficulties pale in comparison to the specter of thousands, if not millions, of similar trials of liability proceeding in thousands of courtrooms around the nation." Id. at 555-56.

...In summary, whether the specter of millions of cases outweighs any manageability problems in this class is uncertain when the scope of any manageability problems is unknown. Absent considered judgment on the manageability of the class, a comparison to millions of individual trials is meaningless.

B. Predominance

* * *

In addition to the reasons given above, regarding the district court's procedural errors, this class must be decertified because it independently fails the superiority requirement of rule 23(b)(3). In the context of mass tort class actions, certification dramatically affects the stakes for defendants. Class certification magnifies and strengthens the number of unmeritorious claims. *Agent Orange,* 818 F.2d at 165-66. Aggregation of claims also makes it more likely that a defendant will be found liable and results in significantly higher damage awards.

In addition to skewing trial outcomes, class certification creates insurmountable pressure on defendants to settle, whereas individual trials would not. See Peter H. Schuck, Mass Torts: An Institutional Evolutionist Perspective, 80 Cornell L. Rev. 941, 958 (1995). The risk of facing an all-or-nothing verdict presents too high a risk, even when the probability of an adverse judgment is low. *Rhone-Poulenc,* 51 F.3d at 1298. These settlements have been referred to as judicial blackmail.

It is no surprise then, that historically, certification of mass tort litigation classes has been disfavored....The traditional concern over the rights of defendants in mass tort class actions is magnified in the instant case. Our specific concern is that a mass tort cannot be properly certified without a prior track record of trials from which the district court can draw the information necessary to make the predominance and superiority requirements required by rule 23. This is because certification of an immature tort results in a higher than normal risk that the class action may not be superior to individual adjudication.

* * *

The plaintiffs' claim also overstates the defendants' ability to outspend plaintiffs. Assuming arguendo that the defendants pool resources and outspend plaintiffs in individual trials, there is no reason why plaintiffs still cannot prevail. The class is represented by a consortium of well-financed plaintiffs' lawyers who, over time, can develop the expertise and specialized knowledge sufficient to beat the tobacco companies at their own game. See Francis E. McGovern, An Analysis of Mass Torts for Judges, 73 Tex. L. Rev. 1821, 1834-35 (1995) (suggesting that plaintiffs can overcome tobacco defendants' perceived advantage when a sufficient number of plaintiffs have filed claims and shared discovery).

> Courts can also overcome the defendant's alleged advantages through coordination or consolidation of cases for discovery and other pretrial matters....
>
> Severe manageability problems and the lack of a judicial crisis are not the only reasons why superiority is lacking. The most compelling rationale for finding superiority in a class action—the existence of a negative value suit—is missing in this case....
>
> As he stated in the record, plaintiffs' counsel in this case has promised to inundate the courts with individual claims if class certification is denied. Independently of the reliability of this self-serving promise, there is reason to believe that individual suits are feasible....
>
> * * *
>
> ...For the forgoing reasons, we REVERSE and REMAND with instructions that the district court dismiss the class complaint.

The relevance of *Castano* to child health includes the successful addiction of tobacco smokers at a median age of under 16 years, with most youthful smokers allegedly induced by industry promotion and peer pressure to begin smoking at between twelve and fifteen years of age. Note that, notwithstanding the certification denial, the plaintiff in *Castano* did not dismiss her action as an individual. That maintenance allowed a court order to remain in effect barring any destruction of documents by the industry. The early timing of that order and its continuation was propitious given subsequent events in the litigation.

Questions for Discussion

1. The *Castano* court's first reason for certification denial is the district court's failure to examine differences between states. Although states may have different rules regarding fraud and affirmative defenses, are there wide variations between the states relevant to misleading advertising (where the common test is simply "tendency to mislead"—with reliance, intent and other variations between states absent)? Is deliberate manipulation of addiction treated markedly different between states? Are they more varied than state statutes dealing with asbestos contamination? Why did the court not simply remand the matter to the district court to examine state statute variations?

2. Would the case have fared differently if confined to youth addiction, targeting and sales? Are these child-related policies markedly different among the several states?

3. Would this case have been certified if brought within a single state as a class action? Note that following *Castano*, plaintiff attorneys associated with that group filed class actions in 22 states. Except for California (relying on a private attorney general theory discussed below) and Louisiana, class action status failed for lack of adequate commonality or related objections where the certification issue was decided.

4. The *Castano* court acknowledges that a class action may be "superior" if a plethora of individual actions result from class denial and inefficiently swamp the courts in repetitive adjudication of similar issues of fact and law. It argues that such a proliferation of law suits is unlikely. But which way should such

a finding cut? If individualized remedies for a wrong are unlikely and court enforcement of the law is only viable on a class action basis, does not that condition argue for certification rather than against it? How does such a basis for class denial (if we deny class status, individual vindication of rights is unlikely) impact children's rights as victims with a relative lack of individualized access to the courts?

5. The *Castano* court also argues that defendants do not overwhelm plaintiffs in legal resources and that counsel for the latter can pursue trials against the tobacco industry via individual trials. Is this a realistic option? Note that fourteen states have punitive damage provisions which might apply to the allegations of plaintiff *Castano*. Those circumstances may provide inducement for such individual actions. During 2001, one jury made an award of $3 billion on behalf of a single individual, see *Boeken v. Philip Morris*, Los Angeles County Superior Court Case No. BC226593, later reduced on appeal to $100 million. In a 2001 Florida case, an unusual class action punitive damage award of $144.8 billion was handed down, see *Engle v. R.J. Reynolds Tobacco Co., et al.*, No. 94-08273 CA-22 (Fla. Cir. Ct., 11th Dist., Dade County).[16] Would it be "superior" and "more manageable" to distribute such a punitive penalty not to one or several plaintiffs who come to judgment first, or to those in a single state, but to the broader group of persons damaged by the practice (*e.g.*, through de-addiction services and child anti-smoking expenditures)?

6. One of the major allegations of *Castano* was the manipulation of nicotine by tobacco firms to create and enhance addiction, and to target children. Would the case be strengthened if it confined its scope to such marketing *and* pursued its claims in equity under 23(b)(2) as did the *Marisol* class, (seeking only an injunction and restitution—disgorgement of profits from sales to minors, or the payment for de-addiction services for persons addicted as children)? In fact, are not the differences in abuses, impact, and defenses substantially more significant among the *Marisol* class than would be the case in targeting children for nicotine addiction? Why did the *Castano* decision not remand to certify the injunctive aspects of the proposed class under Rule 23(b)(2)?

7. Many of the successful child class action cases have been brought in state court, avoiding some federal precedents applying Federal Rule of Civil Procedure 23 impediments to certification. However, some securities and consumer law class actions filed in pro-plaintiff state court jurisdictions won certification for national classes, conferring powerful leverage for settlements in venues disadvantageous to defendants. Citing these abuses, corporate interests won passage of the Class Action Fairness Act of 2005, which radically alters federal class action jurisdiction. Historically, state class actions were removed to federal court only where there was absolute diversity (parties from different states) and class members suffered a loss in excess of $75,000 each. The new law gives any defendant the right to remove class actions to federal court unless virtually all parties are from the same state and the total amount in dispute is over $5 million. If more than one-third of the class is from one state and the defendant operates primarily in that state, remand to state court may be possible. As noted above, after the decertification decision of the Fifth Circuit above, the *Castano* case was refiled in 22 states. Would such state court alternatives be possible under the 2005 Act? Could an action be brought in one state on behalf of only its children and/or waiving money claims over $5 million? State tort actions have traditionally been considered the bedrock territory of state com-

mon law. On the one hand, is a shift to required federal jurisdiction consistent with the stated federalist values of the Congressional proponents of this reform? On the other hand, what are the implications of state resolution of child-related grievances that extend across state lines, in a single state court unilaterally selected by a plaintiff attorney?

3. Alternatives to Class Actions

a. Public *Parens Patriae* Suit

One alternative to the class representative elements of the private class action is a similar action brought by a state attorney general, district attorney, or other authorized public counsel in *parens patriae* for citizens within their respective jurisdiction, including children. Such status may overcome the need to find a parent willing to have his or her child serve as class representative and then meet the various requirements of such class representatives, including the "adequacy of representation" and related requirements noted above.

b. Use of "Private Attorney General" Status

A few states allow their citizens to serve as a "private attorney general" and bring actions on behalf of the general public, including children. Such actions are brought in equity, but may yield disgorgement of ill-gotten gains and restitution. Most important, in some states they may be brought by any person, whether a part of the group aggrieved or not. That status allows public interest groups, or any litigant, to represent the interests of children without obtaining a child plaintiff. Such actions cannot be defeated based on lack of commonality since a right to sue for all who are injured or for the "general public" is explicitly authorized. And many of the defenses discussed above which undermine traditional class actions, such as inadequate commonality among the class for certification are also not available (*e.g.*, assumption of risk, reliance, and intent elements are irrelevant to an unfair competition action based on misleading advertising). Such actions focus on marketplace practices, and often seek the disgorgement of "unjust enrichment," which is assigned to a "fund" and which may allow attorney's fees to prevailing counsel for plaintiffs on a "private attorney-general fee award" basis, or alternatively on a "common fund" fee sharing theory (see discussion below).

California's Unfair Competition Act (Cal. Bus. & Prof. Code § 17200 *et seq.*) is a prime example of such a state statute. Its federal counterpart is Section 5 of the Federal Trade Commission Act, which is enforced exclusively by the Federal Trade Commission. But state unfair competition acts commonly provide for private enforcement. They allow equitable relief against private parties (business competitors) on behalf of children. Litigation is not confined to suit against government agencies to compel enforcement of standards, but can be brought directly against offending commercial operations.

Committee on Children's Television, Inc. v. General Foods Corporation
35 Cal. 3d 197 (1983)

OPINION: **Broussard, J.**—

Plaintiffs appeal from a judgment of dismissal following a trial court order sustaining demurrers without leave to amend to their fourth amended complaint. The complaint essentially charges defendants—General Foods Corporation, Safeway Stores, and two advertising agencies—with fraudulent, misleading and deceptive advertising in the marketing of sugared breakfast cereals. The trial court found its allegations insufficient because they fail to state with specificity the advertisements containing the alleged misrepresentations. We review the allegations of the complaint and conclude that the trial court erred in sustaining demurrers without leave to amend to plaintiffs' causes of action charging fraud and violation of laws against unfair competition and deceptive advertising.

I. Summary of the Pleadings and Procedure.

Plaintiffs filed their original complaint on June 30, 1977, as a class action on behalf of "California residents who have been misled or deceived, or are threatened with the likelihood of being deceived or misled," by defendants in connection with the marketing of sugared cereals....The named plaintiffs included five organizations..., individual adults, and individual children.

The principal defendant is General Foods Corporation, the manufacturer of five "sugared cereals"—Alpha Bits, Honeycomb, Fruity Pebbles, Sugar Crisp, and Cocoa Pebbles—which contain from 38 to 50 percent sugar by weight....

When the court sustained a demurrer to the third amended complaint, it ruled that no cause of action could be stated on behalf of the organizational plaintiffs. The individual plaintiffs remaining then filed their fourth amended complaint; the validity of this complaint is the principal issue on appeal.

... The first cause of action is based on Business and Professions Code sections 17200–17208, the unfair competition law. Paragraph 34 alleges that defendants "engaged in a sophisticated advertising and marketing program which is designed to capitalize on the unique susceptibilities of children and preschoolers in order to induce them to consume products which, although promoted and labeled as "cereals," are in fact more accurately described as sugar products, or candies." The complaint thereafter refers to sugared cereals as "candy breakfasts."

Paragraph 35 lists some 19 representations allegedly made in television commercials aimed at children. Most of these representations are not explicit but, according to plaintiffs, implicit in the advertising. They include, for example, the implied representation that "children...who regularly eat candy breakfasts are bigger, stronger, more energetic, happier, more invulnerable, and braver...," that eating such products is a "fun thing...to do," that the products possess or impart "magical powers," etc. Some representations, however, are more specific: that the sugared cereals are "grain products," are "healthful and nutritious," contain adequate amounts of elements essential to diet, and "are the most important part of a well balanced breakfast."[3]

---

[3] Paragraph 35 of the complaint reads as follows:

"35. The advertising scheme routinely and repeatedly employs and utilizes, in commercials aimed at children, each of the following representations which are conveyed both visually and verbally:

"(a) Children and young children who regularly eat candy breakfasts are bigger, stronger, more energetic, happier, more invulnerable, and braver than they would have been if they did not eat candy breakfasts.

"(b) Eating candy breakfasts is a "fun' thing for children to do, and is invariably equated with entertainment and adventure.

"(c) The sweet taste of a product ensures or correlates with nutritional merit.

"(d) Eating candy breakfasts will make children happy.

"(e) Bright colors in foods ensure or correlate with nutritional merit.

"(f) Candy breakfasts are grain products.

"(g) Candy breakfasts are more healthful and nutritious for a child than most other kinds and types of cereals.

Plaintiffs allege that commercials containing these representations are broadcast daily. Although the commercials changed every 60 days, "they retain consistent themes and each convey...the representations as set forth." Defendants, but not plaintiffs, know the exact times, dates, and places of broadcasts. Plaintiffs further allege that the same representations appear in other media, and on the cereal packages themselves.

Paragraph 42 asserts that defendants concealed material facts, such as the sugar content of their products, that "[there] is no honey in Honeycomb, no fruit in Fruity Pebbles," that sugared cereals contribute to tooth decay and can have more serious medical consequences, and that they cost more per serving than breakfast foods of greater nutritional value.[4] Such concealment, plaintiffs

---

[Cont'd from p. 55]

"(h) Adding small amounts of vitamins and minerals to a product automatically makes it "nutritious.'

"(i) Candy breakfasts inherently possess and/or impart to those ingesting them magical powers, such as the capacity to cause apes and fantastic creatures to appear or disappear.

"(j) Candy breakfasts contain adequate amounts of the essential elements of a growing child's diet, including protein.

"(k) The "premiums' (small toys packaged in with the candy breakfast as an inducement to the child) are very valuable and are offered free as a prize in each box of candy breakfast.

"(l) Candy breakfasts are the most important part of a "well-balanced breakfast' and are at least as nutritious as milk, toast and juice.

"(m) Candy breakfasts calm a child's fears and dispel a child's anxiety....

"(n) Candy breakfasts have visual characteristics which they do not in fact possess, such as vivid colors and the capacity to glitter or to enlarge from their actual size to a larger size.

"In addition to the foregoing representations specified in Paragraph 35 (a) through (n), in each of the commercials for each of the products specified below the advertising scheme repeatedly, uniformly and consistently utilizes and relies upon the following representations with respect to particular products:

"(o) Cocoa Pebbles are good for a child to eat whenever he or she is hungry, and it is a sound nutritional practice to eat chocolatey tasting foods, such as Cocoa Pebbles, for breakfast.

"(p) Honeycomb (i) contains honey and (ii) consists of pieces which are each at least two (2) inches in diameter and (iii) will make a child big and strong.

"(q) Alpha-Bits (i) will enable a child to conquer his or her enemies, (ii) can be used by a child easily to spell words in his or her spoon, (iii) are an effective cure for the child's anxieties, and (iv) have magical powers and can impart magical powers to a child....

"(r) Fruity Pebbles (i) contain fruit and (ii) emit auras, rainbows or mesmerizing colors.

"(s) Super Sugar Crisp (i) should be eaten as a snack food without danger to dental health, (ii) should be eaten as a nutritious snack whenever a child is hungry, (iii) makes a child smart and (iv) is coated with golden sugar and such sugar is very valuable."

[4] Paragraph 42 of the fourth amended complaint reads as follows:

"42. In the advertising scheme planned and participated in by each and every Defendant, none of the following facts are ever disclosed:

"(a) The percentage of sugar and chemicals together in the products advertised ranges from 38% to 50% of the total weight of the product;

"(b) There is no honey in Honeycomb, no fruit in Fruity Pebbles, and the premiums packed into the boxes of Alpha Bits and Super Sugar Crisp cost no more than a few pennies at most;

"(c) Eating candy breakfasts may contribute to tooth decay in children and adults;

"(d) Eating candy breakfasts as a snack will cause tooth decay;

"(e) Children should brush their teeth soon after eating sugary foods;

"(f) For many children, excessive sugar consumption will have serious and detrimental health consequences, including obesity, heart disease, and other adverse health consequences;

"(g) For children with already existing health problems, especially diabetes, consuming candy breakfasts may have serious and detrimental health consequences;

"(h) There is a serious controversy over the adverse effects of sugar on the health of children;

allege, when joined with the affirmative misrepresentations listed in paragraph 35, render the advertisements misleading and deceptive.

The complaint asserts at length the special susceptibility of children to defendants' "advertising scheme," and explains how defendants take advantage of this vulnerability. It further asserts that, as defendants know, the desires and beliefs of children influence and often determine the decision of adults to buy certain breakfast foods. Finally, claiming that defendants will continue deceptive practices unless enjoined, the first cause of action seeks injunctive relief, plus restitution of monies paid by plaintiff class for "candy breakfasts."

* * *

The third through sixth causes of action set out various aspects of the tort of fraud. The third cause of action charges deliberate fraud in violation of Civil Code section 1710, subdivision 1. Incorporating the allegations of the first cause of action, it adds allegations of plaintiffs' reasonable reliance upon defendants' representations, especially in light of defendants' claim to superior knowledge about the nutritional value of foods. The fourth cause of action adds allegations of negligent misrepresentation (Civ. Code, § 1710, subd. 2); the fifth cause of action adds fraudulent concealment (Civ. Code, § 1710, subd. 3). The sixth cause of action is based on common law fraud. Each of these causes of action asserts proximate causation, and claims compensatory damages of $10 million; those counts asserting intentional misrepresentation include a prayer for punitive damages.[5]

The prayer for relief is extensive, and includes some novel requests. In addition to seeking damages, restitution, and injunctive relief, plaintiffs seek warning labels in stores and on packages, creation of funds for research on the health effects of sugar consumption by young children, public interest representatives on defendants' boards of directors, and public access to defendants' research on the health effects of their products....

Defendants demurred to the fourth amended complaint for failure to state a cause of action and for uncertainty....The trial court sustained the demurrers without leave to amend. The trial judge explained the basis for his ruling: "[In] order to state a cause of action for fraud or for breach of warranty, there must be alleged with specificity the basis for the cause and that is, if there are advertisements which contain fraudulent matters, those advertisements must be set out. [para.] In paragraph 35, which is the heart of the allegations concerning the conveying of the representations, we have just a series of very general allegations to which there is no reference of an advertisement actually made....[para.] Paragraph 38 which makes the allegations concerning media dissemination set

---

[Cont'd from p. 56]

"(i) Candy breakfasts are not the most important part of a balanced breakfast;

"(j) If eaten at all, candy breakfasts should not be consumed in large quantities and whenever a child is hungry;

"(k) Candy breakfasts cost more per serving than non-pre-sweetened breakfast cereals or hot cereals and more than other foods of better nutritional value than candy breakfasts;

"(l) A child's welfare is best served by accepting nutritional advice from his or her parents when such advice conflicts with advice given in television commercials;

"(m) The happy, adventure-filled fantasy portrayal of eating candy breakfasts is unrealistic and cannot be duplicated by any child."

[5] Finally, plaintiffs asserted, but subsequently abandoned, a seventh cause of action claiming breach of express warranty. Defendants' general demurrer did not discuss the seventh cause of action for breach of warranty, and although the trial court entered judgment for defendants, it does not appear to have sustained a demurrer without leave to amend to this cause of action. On appeal, however, plaintiffs did not mention this cause of action, which led defendants to claim plaintiffs had abandoned any claim for breach of warranty. At oral argument plaintiffs acknowledged their failure to pursue this cause of action.

out no television stations, no other media, except for the fact that these ads were run on television stations every day in Southern California for a four-year period. [para.] This gives the defendant practically no kind of information concerning that which the defendant must answer, and it doesn't give the court a sufficient factual basis for its administration of the case."

* * *

II. Causes of Action Based on Consumer Protection Statutes.

Plaintiffs' first cause of action in the fourth amended complaint seeks injunctive relief and restitution under Business and Professions Code section 17200 and subsequent sections (the unfair competition law). The operative language appears in section 17203: "Any person performing or proposing to perform an act of unfair competition within this state may be enjoined in any court of competent jurisdiction. The court may make such orders or judgments...as may be necessary to prevent the use or employment by any person of any practice which constitutes unfair competition...or as may be necessary to restore to any person in interest any money or property, real or personal, which may have been acquired by means of such unfair competition.'

The term "unfair competition" receives a broad definition. A recent Court of Appeal decision summarized its breadth. "Historically, the tort of unfair business competition required a *competitive* injury. However, the language of section 17200..."demonstrates a clear design to protect consumers as well as competitors by its final clause, permitting inter alia, any member of the public to sue on his own behalf or on behalf of the public generally." (*Barquis v. Merchants Collection Assn.* (1972) 7 Cal.3d 94...) Thus, section 17200 is not confined to anticompetitive business practice but is equally directed toward "the right of the *public* to protection from fraud and deceit." (*Ibid.*) Furthermore, the section 17200 proscription of "unfair competition" is not restricted to deceptive or fraudulent conduct but extends to any *unlawful* business practice...The Legislature apparently intended to permit courts to enjoin ongoing wrongful business conduct in whatever context such activity might occur....

* * *

The fourth amended complaint in the present case describes the alleged deceptive scheme in considerable detail. Paragraph 35 alleges some 19 misrepresentations—some general, others relatively specific. Paragraph 42 lists material facts which are not disclosed. Finally, plaintiffs allege that each misrepresentation appears (and every listed material fact is concealed) in every advertisement for the specified product during the period in question.[13] There is thus no doubt as to what advertisements are at issue, nor as to what deceptive practices are called into question.[14] We believe these allegations are sufficient to notify the defendants of the claim made against them, and to frame the issues for litigation.[15]

---

[13] We are skeptical of plaintiffs' claim that every advertisement includes every misrepresentation. But to require plaintiffs in their complaint to review every advertisement to determine, for example, whether the April 1977 advertisements for Fruity Pebbles implied that they would dispel a child's anxiety, would greatly increase the complexity of the pleading without adding any significant increase in clarity.

[14] Plaintiffs' complaint may be uncertain, however, as to what media, other than television and cereal boxes, were employed to advertise the sugared cereals.

[15] We have not reviewed the allegations of paragraphs 35 and 42 to determine whether every alleged misrepresentation and nondisclosure is actionable. Some of the representations may constitute nonactionable expressions of opinion; likewise some nondisclosures may involve matters which defendants had no duty to disclose.

Defendants' objection, as we see it, is not really one of lack of specificity or notice. Basically defendants believe that the allegations of paragraph 35 are not a fair paraphrase of the actual language of the advertisements, and that if plaintiffs could be compelled to state the exact language, it would be clear, for example, that defendants are not really representing that Cocoa Puffs will make children braver or that Alpha Bits impart magical powers.

* * *

Important policy considerations also argue against requiring plaintiffs to set out the specific language of each advertisement. Plaintiffs allege that defendants carried out a large scale program of deceptive advertising in which the specific advertisements change constantly, but all follow a pattern of making, in one form or another, certain misleading and deceptive representations. If such is the case, to require plaintiffs to plead the specifics of each advertisement would render a suit challenging the overall program impractical. The complaint would have to include thousands of pages setting out specifics which are largely within defendants' knowledge. The cost and difficulty of compiling, organizing, and setting down the information would seriously deter the filing of any such complaint. The effect of such a pleading requirement, moreover, would not be limited to discouraging private suits; it would also seriously hamper suits by public officials seeking to enjoin schemes of unfair competition and deceptive advertising.

We conclude that the allegations of plaintiffs' fourth amended complaint are sufficient to overcome a general demurrer and to state causes of action for injunctive relief and restitution under both the unfair competition law and the false advertising law....

We also hold that the organizational plaintiffs have standing to sue under both the unfair competition law and the false advertising law. With respect to the former, section 17204 provides expressly that an action may be prosecuted "upon the complaint of any board, officers, person, corporation or association, or by any person acting for the interests of itself, its members or the general public." Construing this language, the court in *Hernandez v. Atlantic Finance Co.* (1980) 105 Cal.App.3d 65...stated that "we read the statute as expressly authorizing the institution of action by any person on behalf of the general public. The Legislature has provided that suit may be brought by any person acting in his own behalf *or* on behalf of the general public."....Substantially identical language appears in section 17535 of the false advertising law.

We do not, however, decide whether a plaintiff other than a business competitor can recover damages on a cause of action based on the unfair competition or false advertising law....Resolution of this issue is not essential to provide plaintiffs with an adequate remedy in the present case. As explained in part III of this opinion, the nonorganizational plaintiffs can recover damages under their causes of action for fraud, while the organizational plaintiffs have suffered no legally cognizable damages under any cause of action.

III. Causes of Action Based on Fraud.

* * *

Defendants also object that the complaint does not indicate that any particular child relied upon or even saw any particular television advertisement. They point out that although the complaint does assert that each of the adult plaintiffs purchased General Foods' products at a Safeway Store, it does not state which advertisements they, or their children, saw and relied upon.

A specific statement of the advertisements seen and relied upon by the individual plaintiffs would serve to demonstrate both that they possess a valid cause of action in their individual capacity and that they are proper representatives for the class plaintiffs. The realistic setting of the case, however, may make such specific pleading impossible. A long-term advertising campaign may seek to persuade by cumulative impact, not by a particular representation on a particular date. Children in particular are unlikely to recall the specific advertisements which led them to desire a product, but even adults buying a product in a store will not often remember the date and exact message of the advertisements which induced them to make that purchase. Plaintiffs should be able to base their cause of action upon an allegation that they acted in response to an advertising campaign even if they cannot recall the specific advertisements.

Defendants further claim that the complaint is deficient because it describes one group, children, who receive the misrepresentations and a different group, parents, who purchase the product. (This objection applies only to the television commercials, since the parents saw the advertisements on the cereal boxes and in printed media.) Defendants' argument is inconsistent with the strategy of their own advertising. They are aware that the parents purchase the cereals, but they are also aware that parents do not exercise a totally independent judgment, but are influenced by the desires of their children. If such were not the case, defendants would not spend millions to advertise cereals on children's programs watched by very few adult purchasers.

Restatement Second of Torts section 533, states that "[the] maker of a fraudulent misrepresentation is subject to liability...to another who acts in justifiable reliance upon it if the misrepresentation, although not made directly to the other, is made to a third person and the maker intends or has reason to expect that its terms will be repeated or its substance communicated to the other, and that it will influence his conduct."...

We turn finally to the question of damages. In an action for fraud, damage is an essential element of the cause of action...; the successful plaintiff recovers damages as a matter of right.

The present complaint describes three distinct groups of plaintiffs: the organizational plaintiffs, the parents who purchased the cereals, and the children who consumed them. With respect to the organizational plaintiffs, however, the allegations are inadequate to state a cause of action. Plaintiffs assert that some organizations such as the California Society of Dentistry for Children have spent funds to counter the influence of defendants' advertising; other organizations such as the American G.I. Forum of California have many members who have sustained injury. Neither theory justifies a damage claim by the organization itself. Any organizational expenditures were voluntary in character and not the result of any legally cognizable injury to the organization. If some of the members have suffered injury, they can seek redress in an individual or class action. Thus the trial court did not err in sustaining a demurrer without leave to amend as to the fraud causes of action on behalf of the organizations.

When we consider the damages claimed by the parents and children, we encounter a different problem. The allegations of the complaint are clearly sufficient to state a cause of action for restitution of the money spent to purchase the sugared cereals. The complaint also seeks additional damages, claiming that plaintiffs and members of their class encountered medical or dental injury from consuming sugared cereals and incurred expenses to treat those injuries. It does not, however, assert that any of the named children sustained any specific injury or that any of the named parents spent money to treat such injury. As a result, the allegations appear sufficient to assert injury to a subclass of parents and children (the class being all parents who purchased and children who consumed, even if no injury was incurred), but does not clearly place any of the individually named plaintiffs within their subclass. In view of the requirement for specific pleading in fraud actions, we believe the trial court could view the complaint as uncertain in its failure to make clear whether the individual child plaintiffs have incurred any specific health injury from the consumption of the sugared cereals, and whether their parents have spent any specific sums to treat those injuries.[20]

* * *

IV. Cause of Action for Breach of Fiduciary Duty.

The seventh cause of action of the second amended complaint asserted that General Foods owed, and breached, a fiduciary obligation to the child plaintiffs. The trial court sustained a demurrer without leave to amend, with the result that this cause of action did not appear in subsequent versions of the complaint.

Plaintiffs' assertion of fiduciary duty in a consumer context is unique. Plaintiffs argue that imposition of fiduciary obligations is appropriate whenever one party with a stronger bargaining position or greater knowledge has the ability to reach out and exploit the weaker party.[21] Such duties are particularly appropriate here, say plaintiffs, because General Foods purports to give expert advice on diet and nutrition, and directs that advice to children, exploiting their trusting and uncritical acceptance.

But the efforts of commercial sellers—even those with superior bargaining power—to profit from the trust of consumers is not enough to create a fiduciary duty. If it were, the law of fiduciary relations would largely displace both the tort of fraud and much of the Commercial Code. Something more is needed.

* * *

V. Conclusion.

Although the parties argue primarily the sufficiency and specificity of the pleadings, the underlying controversy is of much greater dimension. Defendants engaged in a nationwide, long-term advertising campaign designed to persuade children to influence their parents to buy sugared cereals. Adapted to its audience, the campaign sought to persuade less by direct representation than by imagery and example. While maintaining a constant theme, the particular advertisements changed frequently. Plaintiffs now contend that these advertisements were deceptive and misleading, and while we do not know the actual truth of those charges, we must assume them true for the purpose of this appeal. Yet, if we apply strict requirements of specificity in pleading as defendants argue, the result would be to eliminate the private lawsuit as a practical remedy to redress such past deception or prevent further deception. By directing their advertisements to children, and changing them frequently, defendants would have obtained practical immunity from statutory and common law remedies designed to protect consumers from misleading advertising.

* * *

The judgment is reversed, and the cause remanded for further proceedings consistent with this opinion.

Mosk, J., **Richardson, J.**, **Kaus, J.**, **Reynoso, J.**, and **Grodin, J.**, concurred.

---

[20] The damage allegations are also uncertain in their broad use of the term "plaintiffs" without distinguishing between the different damage suffered by the parents, the children, and the organizational plaintiffs.

[21] We do not agree that ability to exploit a disparity of bargaining power is a useful test of fiduciary duty. An agent owes a fiduciary duty to his principal, for example, even if the principal has the greater bargaining strength.

Questions for Discussion

1. The 2004 enactment in California of Proposition 64 altered the private Attorney General statute relied upon in *Children's Television.* The new law requires full class action qualification under state law. Would this case be certifiable as a class action? The court notes that "[i]t can be argued that administrative investigation and rule making would be a better method of regulating advertising of this scope and character." At the federal level, the Federal Trade Commission allegedly provides such a venue for advertising accuracy. Would a court then conclude that the class action mechanism is not a "superior" method of resolution? And would commonality of facts or issues among class members be an issue in a certification motion? On the other hand, the Unfair Competition Law in California (as in most states) lies in equity to regulate honest advertising. Unlike a mass tort or damage action, it authorizes injunctive relief—invoking more liberal allowance of class certification—without requiring that commonality "predominate" or that it be a "superior" method of resolution. Would that liberality allow *Children's Television* to proceed as a class action?

2. In addition to requiring full class certification, Proposition 64 also specifies that the class representative must suffer "financial harm" to bring the action. Do the allegedly misleading health statements in *Children's Television* cause "financial harm?" Can it be argued that parents are misled and unfairly lose monies in cereal purchases and such a parent may bring an action under this kind of statutory restriction? Does such a restriction preclude unfair competition actions where future harm or generalized child health is the only harm—rather than immediate financial injury (*e.g.*, marketing addictive cigarettes to children)?

3. What should be the final resolution of *Children's Television* if plaintiffs litigated it to final order? Should the specific alleged deceptions simply be prohibited? Should the court provide guidance by setting forth what information must be provided to avoid a deception judgment? How should such an order be worded? Should restitution be included in the remedy ("disgorgement of unjust enrichment")? How should such restitution be calculated? If these monies were collected, how could they be realistically distributed to victims (cereal purchasers)? Can and should the court order *cy pres* ("second best") relief in lieu of such repayment in order to fund child nutrition education? Healthy school lunches? Dental care for needy children?

c. Use of Mandamus

Most states allow a special kind of pleading, often called a "petition for ordinary mandamus." It lies in equity (court trial without a jury) and is based on an alleged "abuse of discretion" by a public official. The abuse of discretion occurs where such an official (in any of the three branches) violates a ministerial duty to act, or not to act. An action which violates statutory intent, or a failure to act notwithstanding a statutory duty to do so, is such an abuse. In many states, trial and appellate courts may have coextensive original jurisdiction to hear such writs (allowing possible leapfrogging to appellate or Supreme Court levels). Such an approach may result in an order directing the agency to act as prayed. Even if only one petitioner is named, it is not realistic that an agency will apply different policies to litigants. Accordingly, the petition acts as a class action. However, few of the impediments to class actions discussed above apply. There is no delay to certify a class or to explore class or counsel adequacy. The petition is generally entitled to calendar preference. Such an approach may afford child advocates more useful access to court redress where the grievance is with a public official.

Questions for Discussion

1. The petition for writ of mandate only applies to abuses of discretion by government officials. Can it be used where children are victimized by private parties to force government officials to act? See *DeShaney v. Winnebago County Dep't of Social Services*, 489 U.S. 189 (1989), discussed in Chapter 12.

4. Fees and Incentives to Sue

Attorney fee recovery by successful plaintiffs facilitates access to courts for children. Such contingent recompense allows attorneys to proceed on behalf of clients lacking resources.

a. Private Attorney General Fees

Some states have allowed what are termed "private attorney general" fees where an attorney prevails in a public interest action. In the leading case of *Serrano v. Priest*, 32 Cal. 3d 621 (1982), attorneys brought an action on behalf of California's children to alter the system of school finance (see Chapter 4). The Court held that where an attorney represents an interest substantially beyond the pecuniary stake of his named client, and successfully vindicates a right of such general application, attorneys' fees may be awarded at market rates. In addition, the court enunciated criteria for the enhancement of that market level figure by a "multiplier" based on the difficulty of the case and other enumerated factors. Many states have codified private attorney general fee recompense arrangements similar to the *Serrano* holding (see, *e.g.*, Cal. Civ. Proc. Code § 1021.5).

The U.S. Supreme Court has formulated a very different rule for generic private attorney general recovery, requiring plaintiffs to rely on specific attorney fee recovery provisions in federal statutes.

Alyeska Pipeline Service Co. v. Wilderness Society, et al.
421 U.S. 240 (1975)

OPINION BY: **WHITE**

This litigation was initiated by respondents Wilderness Society, Environmental Defense Fund, Inc., and Friends of the Earth in an attempt to prevent the issuance of permits by the Secretary of the Interior which were required for the construction of the trans-Alaska oil pipeline. The Court of Appeals awarded attorneys' fees to respondents against petitioner Alyeska Pipeline Service Co. based upon the court's equitable powers and the theory that respondents were entitled to fees because they were performing the services of a "private attorney general." Certiorari was granted, 419 U.S. 823 (1974), to determine whether this award of attorneys' fees was appropriate. We reverse.

* * *

With the merits of the litigation effectively terminated by this legislation, the Court of Appeals turned to the questions involved in respondents' request for an award of attorneys' fees.[13] 161 U.S. App. D.C. 446, 495 F. 2d 1026 (1974) (en banc). Since there was no applicable statutory authorization for such an award, the court proceeded to consider whether the requested fee award fell within any of the exceptions to the general "American rule" that the prevailing party may not recover attorneys' fees as costs or otherwise. The exception for an award against a party who had acted in bad faith was inapposite, since the position taken by the federal and state parties and Alyeska "was manifestly reasonable and assumed in good faith...." Id., at 449, 495 F. 2d, at 1029. Application of the "common benefit" exception which spreads the cost of litigation to those persons benefiting from it would "stretch it totally outside its basic rationale...." Ibid.[14] The Court of Appeals nevertheless held that respondents had acted to vindicate "important statutory rights of all citizens...," id., at 452, 495 F. 2d, at 1032; had ensured that the governmental system functioned properly; and were entitled to attorneys' fees lest the great cost of litigation of this kind, particularly against well-financed defendants such as Alyeska, deter private parties desiring to see the laws protecting the environment properly enforced. Title 28 U.S.C. § 2412....was thought to bar taxing any attorneys' fees against the United States, and it was also deemed inappropriate to burden the State of Alaska with any part of the award....But Alyeska, the Court of Appeals held, could fairly be required to pay one-half of the full award to which respondents were entitled for having performed the functions of a private attorney general. Observing that "[t]he fee should represent the reasonable value of the services rendered, taking into account all the surrounding circumstances, including, but not limited to, the time and labor required on the case, the benefit to the public, the skill demanded by the novelty or complexity of the issues, and the incentive factor," 161 U.S. App. D.C., at 456, 495 F. 2d, at 1036, the Court of Appeals remanded the case to the District Court for assessment of the dollar amount of the award.[17]

In the United States, the prevailing litigant is ordinarily not entitled to collect a reasonable attorneys' fee from the loser. We are asked to fashion a far-reaching exception to this "American Rule"; but having considered its origin and development, we are convinced that it would be inappropriate for the Judiciary, without legislative guidance, to reallocate the burdens of litigation in the manner and to the extent urged by respondents and approved by the Court of Appeals.

At common law, costs were not allowed; but for centuries in England there has been statutory authorization to award costs, including attorneys' fees. Although the matter is in the discretion of the court, counsel fees are regularly allowed to the prevailing party.

---

[13] Respondents' bill of costs includes a total of 4,455 hours of attorneys' time spent on the litigation. App. 209-219.

[14] "[T]his litigation may well have provided substantial benefits to particular individuals and, indeed, to every citizen's interest in the proper functioning of our system of government. But imposing attorneys' fees on Alyeska will not operate to spread the costs of litigation proportionately among these beneficiaries...." 161 U.S. App. D.C., at 449, 495 F. 2d, at 1029.

[17] The Court of Appeals also directed that "[t]he fee award need not be limited... to the amount actually paid or owed by [respondents]. It may well be that counsel serve organizations like [respondents] for compensation below that obtainable in the market because they believe the organizations further a public interest. Litigation of this sort should not have to rely on the charity of counsel any more than it should rely on the charity of parties volunteering to serve as private attorneys general. The attorneys who worked on this case should be reimbursed the reasonable value of their services, despite the absence of any obligation on the part of [respondents] to pay attorneys' fees." Id., at 457, 495 F. 2d, at 1037.

[35] "In any action commenced pursuant to this subchapter, the court, in its discretion, may allow the prevailing party, other than the United States, a reasonable attorney's fee as part of the costs, and the United States shall be liable for costs the same as a private person."

* * *

Congress has not repudiated the judicially fashioned exceptions to the general rule against allowing substantial attorneys' fees; but neither has it retracted, repealed, or modified the limitations on taxable fees contained in the 1853 statute and its successors. Nor has it extended any roving authority to the Judiciary to allow counsel fees as costs or otherwise whenever the courts might deem them warranted. What Congress has done, however, while fully recognizing and accepting the general rule, is to make specific and explicit provisions for the allowance of attorneys' fees under selected statutes granting or protecting various federal rights....These statutory allowances are now available in a variety of circumstances, but they also differ considerably among themselves. Under the antitrust laws, for instance, allowance of attorneys' fees to a plaintiff awarded treble damages is mandatory....Under Title II of the Civil Rights Act of 1964, 42 U.S.C. § 2000a-3 (b),[35] the prevailing party is entitled to attorneys' fees, at the discretion of the court, but we have held that Congress intended that the award should be made to the successful plaintiff absent exceptional circumstances. *Newman v. Piggie Park Enterprises, Inc.,* 390 U.S. 400, 402 (1968). See also *Northcross v. Board of Education of the Memphis City Schools,* 412 U.S. 427 (1973). Under this scheme of things, it is apparent that the circumstances under which attorneys' fees are to be awarded and the range of discretion of the courts in making those awards are matters for Congress to determine....

It is true that under some, if not most, of the statutes providing for the allowance of reasonable fees, Congress has opted to rely heavily on private enforcement to implement public policy and to allow counsel fees so as to encourage private litigation. Fee shifting in connection with treble-damages awards under the antitrust laws is a prime example; cf. *Hawaii v. Standard Oil Co.,* 405 U.S. 251, 265-266 (1972); and we have noted that Title II of the Civil Rights Act of 1964 was intended "not simply to penalize litigants who deliberately advance arguments they know to be untenable but, more broadly, to encourage individuals injured by racial discrimination to seek judicial relief under Title II." *Newman, supra,* at 402 (footnote omitted). But congressional utilization of the private-attorney-general concept can in no sense be construed as a grant of authority to the Judiciary to jettison the traditional rule against nonstatutory allowances to the prevailing party and to award attorneys' fees whenever the courts deem the public policy furthered by a particular statute important enough to warrant the award.

Congress itself presumably has the power and judgment to pick and choose among its statutes and to allow attorneys' fees under some, but not others. But it would be difficult, indeed, for the courts, without legislative guidance, to consider some statutes important and others unimportant and to allow attorneys' fees only in connection with the former. If the statutory limitation of right-of-way widths involved in this case is a matter of the gravest importance, it would appear that a wide range of statutes would arguably satisfy the criterion of public importance and justify an award of attorneys' fees to the private litigant. And, if any statutory policy is deemed so important that its enforcement must be encouraged by awards of attorneys' fees, how could a court deny attorneys' fees to private litigants in actions under 42 U.S.C. § 1983 seeking to vindicate constitutional rights? Moreover, should courts, if they were to embark on the course urged by respondents, opt for awards to the prevailing party, whether plaintiff or defendant, or only to the prevailing plaintiff?[37] Should awards be dis-

[37] Congress in its specific statutory authorizations of fee shifting has in some instances provided that either party could be given such an award depending upon the outcome of the litigation and the court's discretion, see, e.g., 35 U.S.C. § 285 (patent infringement) Civil Rights Act of 1964, 42 U.S.C. §§ 2000a-3 (b), 2000e-5 (k), while in others it has specified that only one of the litigants can be awarded fees. See, e.g., the antitrust laws, 15 U.S.C. § 15; Fair Labor Standards Act, 29 U.S.C. § 216 (b).

cretionary or mandatory?...Would there be a presumption operating for or against them in the ordinary case?...

* * *

The decision below must therefore be reversed.

MR. JUSTICE DOUGLAS and **MR. JUSTICE POWELL** took no part in the consideration or decision of this case.

* * *

MR. JUSTICE MARSHALL, dissenting.

In reversing the award of attorneys' fees to the respondent environmentalist groups, the Court today disavows the well-established power of federal equity courts to award attorneys' fees when the interests of justice so require. While under the traditional American Rule the courts ordinarily refrain from allowing attorneys' fees, we have recognized several judicial exceptions to that rule for classes of cases in which equity seemed to favor fee shifting. See *Sprague v. Ticonic National Bank,* 307 U.S. 161 (1939); *Mills v. Electric Auto-Lite Co.*, 396 U.S. 375, 391-392 (1970); *Hall v. Cole,* 412 U.S. 1, 5, 9 (1973). By imposing an absolute bar on the use of the "private attorney general" rationale as a basis for awarding attorneys' fees, the Court today takes an extremely narrow view of the independent power of the courts in this area—a view that flies squarely in the face of our prior cases.

The Court relies primarily on the docketing-fees-and court-costs statute, 28 U.S.C. § 1923, in concluding that the American Rule is grounded in statute and that the courts may not award counsel fees unless they determine that Congress so intended. The various exceptions to the rule against fee shifting that this Court has created in the past are explained as constructions of the fee statute. Ante, at 257. In addition, the Court notes that Congress has provided for attorneys' fees in a number of statutes, but made no such provision in others. It concludes from this selective treatment that where award of attorneys' fees is not expressly authorized, the courts should deny them as a matter of course. Finally, the Court suggests that the policy questions bearing on whether to grant attorneys' fees in a particular case are not ones that the Judiciary is well equipped to handle, and that fee shifting under the private-attorney-general rationale would quickly degenerate into an arbitrary and lawless process. Because the Court concludes that granting attorneys' fees to private attorneys general is beyond the equitable power of the federal courts, it does not reach the question whether an award would be proper against Alyeska in this case under the private-attorney-general rationale.

On my view of the case, both questions must be answered. I see no basis in precedent or policy for holding that the courts cannot award attorneys' fees where the interests of justice require recovery, simply because the claim does not fit comfortably within one of the previously sanctioned judicial exceptions to the American Rule. The Court has not in the past regarded the award of attorneys' fees as a matter reserved for the Legislature, and it has certainly not read the docketing-fees statute as a general bar to judicial fee shifting. The Court's concern with the difficulty of applying meaningful standards in awarding attorneys' fees to successful "public benefit" litigants is a legitimate one, but in my view it overstates the novelty of the "private attorney general" theory. The guidelines developed in closely analogous statutory and nonstatutory attorneys' fee cases could readily be applied in cases such as the one at bar. I therefore disagree with the Court's flat rejection of the private-attorney-general rationale for fee shifting. Morover, in my view the equities in this case support an award of attorneys' fees against Alyeska.

Accordingly, I must respectfully dissent.

* * *

...The cases plainly establish an independent basis for equity courts to grant attorneys' fees under several rather generous rubrics. The Court acknowledges as much when it says that we have independent authority to award fees in cases of bad faith or as a means of taxing costs to special beneficiaries. But I am at a loss to understand how it can also say that this independent judicial power succumbs to Procrustean statutory restrictions—indeed, to statutory silence—as soon as the far from bright line between common benefit and public benefit is crossed. I can only conclude that the Court is willing to tolerate the "equitable" exceptions to its analysis, not because they can be squared with it, but because they are by now too well established to be casually dispensed with.

B

* * *

Starting with the early common-fund cases, the Court has consistently read the fee-bill statute of 1853 narrowly when that Act has been interposed as a restriction on the Court's equitable powers to award attorneys' fees. In *Trustees v. Greenough*, 105 U.S. 527 (1881), the Court held that the statute imposed no bar to an award of attorneys' fees from the fund collected as a result of the plaintiff's efforts, since: "[The fee bill statute addressed] only those fees and costs which are strictly chargeable as between party and party, and [did not] regulate the fees of counsel and other expenses and charges as between solicitor and client.... And the act contains nothing which can be fairly construed to deprive the Court of Chancery of its long-established control over the costs and charges of the litigation, to be exercised as equity and justice may require...." Id., at 535-536...

* * *

In sum, the Court's primary contention—that Congress enjoys hegemony over fee shifting because of the docketing-fee statute and the occasional express provisions for attorneys' fees—will not withstand even the most casual reading of the precedents. The Court's recognition of the several judge-made exceptions to the American rule demonstrates the inadequacy of its analysis. Whatever the Court's view of the wisdom of fee shifting in "public benefit" cases in general, I think that it is a serious misstep for it to abdicate equitable authority in this area in the name of statutory construction.

I

The statutory analysis aside, the Court points to the difficulties in formulating a "private attorney general" exception that will not swallow the American Rule. I do not find the problem as vexing as the majority does. In fact, the guidelines to the proper application of the private-attorney-general rationale have been suggested in several of our recent cases, both under statutory attorneys' fee provisions and under the common-benefit exception...

* * *

...[I]t is possible to discern with some confidence the factors that should guide an equity court in determining whether an award of attorneys' fees is appropriate.[7] The reasonable cost of the plaintiff's representation should be placed upon the defendant if (1) the important right being protected is one actually or necessarily shared by the general public or some class thereof; (2) the plaintiff's pecuniary interest in the outcome, if any, would not normally justify incurring the cost of counsel; and (3) shifting that cost to the defendant would effectively place it on a class that benefits from the litigation.

---

[7] These teachings have not been lost on the lower courts in which the elements of the private-attorney-general rationale have been more fully explored. See, e.g., *Souza v. Travisono*, 512 F. 2d 1137 (CA1 1975); *Hoitt v. Vitek*, 495 F. 2d 219 (CA1 1974); *Knight v. Auciello*, 453 F. 2d 852 (CA1 1972); *Cornist v. Richland Parish School Board*, 495 F. 2d 189 (CA5 1974); *Fairley v. Patterson*, 493 F. 2d 598 (CA5 1974); *Cooper v. Allen*, 467 F. 2d 836 (CA5 1972); *Lee v. Southern Home Sites Corp.*, 444 F. 2d 143 (CA5 1971); *Taylor v. Perini*, 503 F. 2d 899 (CA6 1974); *Morales v. Haines*, 486 F. 2d 880 (CA7 1973); *Donahue v. Staunton*, 471 F. 2d 475 (CA7 1972), cert. denied, 410 U.S. 955 (1973); *Fowler v. Schwarzwalder*, 498 F. 2d 143 (CA8 1974); *Brandenburger v. Thompson*, 494 F. 2d 885 (CA9 1974); *La Raza Unida v. Volpe*, 57 F.R.D. 94 (ND Cal. 1972); *Wyatt v. Stickney*, 344 F. Supp. 387 (MD Ala. 1972); *NAACP v. Allen*, 340 F. Supp. 703 (MD Ala. 1972).

b. The Common Fund Doctrine

The private attorney general basis for fees is considered a "fee shifting" approach because it takes fees from the losing party separate and apart from damages or restitutionary funds obtained for alleged victims. In contrast, a separate basis for fees has evolved out of the "common fund" doctrine. This concept takes funds not from the defendant, but from the proceeds due the victims represented by counsel. As such, it is considered a "fee sharing" approach, as named litigants do not bear the full cost of providing a fund benefiting a large group—rather, the entire group receiving an advantage share in paying attorney compensation, *i.e.*, it comes from the fund recovered.

Although rejecting fee shifting without a specific statute, the federal courts allow such common fund fee sharing. Moreover, in many cases where financial recovery is substantial, plaintiff attorneys favor a common fund recovery because it may allow for a percentage of the large fund comparable to market contingent fee arrangements in an amount above compensation for hours times a multiplier—particularly given a tradition of multipliers in the 1.2 to 3.6 range.

Lealao v. Beneficial California, Inc.
82 Cal. App. 4th 19 (2000)

KLINE, P. J.

Appellants Richard U. Lealao and his wife Sese Lealao, who commenced this successful consumer class action, claim that the attorney fees awarded class counsel were unreasonably low. The questions before us are whether, under the circumstances of this case, the trial court had discretion to award a fee based solely on a percentage of the class benefit or, in the alternative, to measure an award calculated under the lodestar methodology by a percentage-of-the-benefit yardstick and to adjust the lodestar upward or downward on that basis. Our answers are no to the first question and yes to the second.

* * *

DISCUSSION

* * *

II.

The parties' dispute centers on the validity and continuing jurisprudential viability of the distinction between "fee shifting" and "fee spreading."

In so-called fee shifting cases, in which the responsibility to pay attorney fees is statutorily or otherwise transferred from the prevailing plaintiff or class to the defendant, the primary method for establishing the amount of "reasonable" attorney fees is the lodestar method. The lodestar (or touchstone) is produced by multiplying the number of hours reasonably expended by counsel by a reasonable hourly rate. Once the court has fixed the lodestar, it may increase or decrease that amount by applying a positive or negative "multiplier" to take into account a variety of other factors, including the quality of the representation, the novelty and complexity of the issues, the results obtained, and the contingent risk presented....

Fee spreading occurs when a settlement or adjudication results in the establishment of a separate or so-called common fund for the benefit of the class. Because the fee awarded class counsel comes from this fund, it is said that the expense is borne by the beneficiaries. Percentage fees have traditionally been allowed in such common fund cases, although, as will be seen, the lodestar methodology may also be utilized in this context.

Respondent maintains that, because the settlement in this case did not result in the establishment of a traditional common fund, the percentage-of-the-benefit approach cannot be utilized, even in connection with the lodestar formulation. Appellant, conceding a conventional common fund does not exist, answers with federal cases suggesting that the distinction between "fee shifting" and "fee spreading" is an illusory jurisprudential construct, and that unless the fee award is in some fashion considered as a percentage of the monetary benefit received by the class the law will create counterproductive economic incentives and disincentives that should no longer be tolerated.

* * *

Despite its primacy, the lodestar method is not necessarily utilized in common fund cases. The common fund or "fund-in-court" doctrine, first articulated by the United States Supreme Court in *Trustees v. Greenough* (1881) 105 U.S. 527..., is a venerable exception to the general American rule disfavoring attorney fees in the absence of statutory or contractual authorization. (Code Civ. Proc., § 1021.5) The exception "is grounded in 'the historic power of equity to permit the trustee of a fund or property, or a party preserving or recovering a fund for the benefit of others in addition to himself, to recover his costs, including his attorneys' fees, from the fund of property itself or directly from the other parties enjoying the benefit.'" (*Serrano III, supra,* 20 Cal. 3d at p. 35, quoting *Alyeska Pipeline Co. v. Wilderness Society* (1975) 421 U.S. 240, 257).

Because the common fund doctrine "rest[s] squarely on the principle of avoiding unjust enrichment" ...attorney fees awarded under this doctrine are not assessed directly against the losing party (fee shifting), but come out of the fund established by the litigation, so that the beneficiaries of the litigation, not the defendant, bear this cost (fee spreading). Under federal law, the amount of fees awarded in a common fund case may be determined under either the lodestar method or the percentage-of-the-benefit approach, although, about a decade ago, as the Ninth Circuit then noted, there commenced a "ground swell of support for mandating the percentage-of-the-fund approach in common fund cases."...

III.

Class counsel's argument rests heavily on federal cases. During the nearly quarter of a century since Serrano III, many federal courts, heavily burdened with the class and derivative actions that give rise to the need to adjudicate fee issues, became disillusioned with the lodestar method. This shift is perhaps most dramatically exemplified by the Third Circuit, whose 1973 opinion in *Lindy I, supra,* 487 F.2d 161, which was relied upon in *Serrano III* (20 Cal. 3d at p. 49, fn. 23), pioneered adoption of the lodestar methodology. (See also *Lindy Bros. Builders, Inc. v. Am. Radiator, etc.* (3d Cir. 1976) 540 F.2d 102 (Lindy II).) The so-called "Lindy lodestar' technique quickly gained wide acceptance among the federal circuits, sometimes in modified fashion...,and was eventually approved by the United States Supreme Court. (*Hensley v. Eckerhart* (1983) 461 U.S. 424, 433)....[40]

However, in 1985, concerned about increasing criticism of the lodestar method, the Third Circuit reexamined the concept it is credited with inventing in *Lindy I...,* and concluded it was seriously deficient and subject to abuse when applied in cases resulting in the creation of a fund. A task force commissioned by the Third Circuit concluded that the lodestar approach (1) "increases the workload of an already overtaxed judicial system," (2) is "insufficiently objective and produce[s] results that are far from homogenous," (3) "creates a sense of mathematical precision that is unwarranted in terms of the realities of the practice of law," (4) "is subject to manipulation by judges who prefer to calibrate fees in terms of percentages of the settlement fund or the amounts recovered by the plaintiffs or of an overall dollar amount," (5) "encourages lawyers to expend excessive hours, and...engage in duplicative and unjustified work," (6) "creates a disincentive for the early settlement of cases," (7) deprives trial courts of "flexibility to reward or deter lawyers so that desirable objectives, such as early settlement, will be fostered," (8) "works to the particular disadvantage of the public interest bar," and (9) results in "confusion and lack of predictability."...[41] Due to these perceived deficiencies, the Report of the Third Circuit Task Force concluded that the lodestar technique is a "cumbersome, enervating, and often surrealistic process of preparing and evaluating fee petitions that now plagues the Bench and Bar"...,and recommended a return to the percentage of the recovery fee formula in cases involving a settlement fund.

...This now widely shared view has stimulated greater judicial willingness to evaluate a fee award as a percentage of the recovery....It is for present purposes significant, as class counsel are at great pains to emphasize, that the federal trend in favor of the percentage-of-the-benefit approach has been extended to cases in which (1) the "fund" that results from an adjudication or settlement is not deposited in a separate account; (2) the value of the "fund" depends on the number of valid claims presented or is imprecise for other rea-

---

[40] Adoption of the lodestar methodology in the early 1970's was stimulated by the view that awards based on a reasonable percentage of the fund, historically the preferred method of fee setting in common fund cases, was yielding fee awards that were excessive and unrelated to the work actually performed by counsel....

[41] The task force concluded that fund cases should be treated differently from the conventional statutory fee case, involving the declaration or enforcement of rights or relatively modest sums of money. It felt the lodestar method necessary in statutory fee cases "because it is reasonably objective, neutral, and does not require making monetary assessments of intangible rights that are not easily equated with dollars and cents." (Report of the Third Circuit Task Force, supra, 108 F.R.D. at p. 255.) The task force felt "these protections were not...needed in the traditional fund case or in those statutory fee cases likely to produce a sizeable fund from which counsel fees could be paid." (Ibid.)

sons; and (3) attorney fees are not deducted from monies made available to the class, but are paid by the defendant directly. All that has been required in many such cases is that the benefits received by the class, or the range thereof, can be monetized without undue speculation.

* * *

IV.

The cases just described reflect the growing willingness of federal courts to disregard the strict theoretical distinction between fee shifting and fee spreading in cases in which fees are not authorized by statute, no separate fund is established, and fees are paid directly by the defendant—provided, of course, that the monetary value of the class recovery is reasonably ascertainable.

* * *

...What constitutes a reasonable fee in a representative action has been shown to be a far more complex question than the judiciary once thought it to be. There are no easy answers. The lodestar methodology originated as an alternative to percentage recoveries, which often resulted in exorbitant fee awards clearly unjustified by the contributions of counsel, which in turn undermined public confidence in the bench and bar....Considering the fee only as a percentage of the benefit would simply resurrect that problem. Refusing ever to take that consideration into account, however, would, as we have indicated, create equally pernicious problems. The federal judicial experience teaches that the "reasonableness" of a fee in a representative action will often require some consideration of the amount to be awarded as a percentage of the class recovery. How much weight that factor should receive may well be, as an experienced trial judge has said, "the most difficult question in present-day jurisprudence concerning attorney's fees.' (Grady, Reasonable Fees: A Suggested *Value-Based Analysis for Judges, supra,...*) However difficult this question, it cannot be avoided; and the ability of California courts to intelligently address it would not be enhanced by diminishing the tools with which they have to work.

VI.

The order denying the motion for new trial as to fees is reversed and the matter remanded to the trial court for reconsideration of the reasonable fee to which class counsel is entitled.

Haerle, J., and Lambden, J., concurred.

Attorneys' fees are available to a child advocate in federal court under the following circumstances: (1) a diversity case in federal court where state causes of action are pled and that state allows such fees; (2) the specific statute litigated authorizes or mandates fees; and (3) a common fund is created to allow "fee sharing."

Statutory attorneys' fees are common in many areas of public interest practice: environmental law, sunshine statutes (such as public records act statutes), taxpayer waste (*qui tam*) actions, antitrust, and civil rights cases. But note that most statutes giving rights or benefits to children lack such clauses, at both state and federal levels. In some cases, a child rights case may invoke civil rights concepts. But unlike groups delineated by race, religion, or gender, children are not a suspect class entitled to strict or heightened scrutiny (see Chapters 3 to 13).

Questions for Discussion

1. As Justice Kline describes, federal policy permits liberal allowance of fees as a percentage of a recovery fund (often millions of dollars). Is it current federal policy to make such awards where monetary benefits are conferred to a fund beyond the named plaintiffs, but to categorically deny fees where a momentous non-economic benefit is conferred to a large societal group? What is the policy rationale to stimulate representation of an economic interest, but exclude interests not translatable into immediate financial recovery?

2. One common form of *en masse* suit on behalf of children is a filing to compel state authorities to comply with minimum federal standards. Such cases have been brought on behalf of foster care children and others. The outcome of such a case may require redistribution of millions of dollars for the benefit of ignored children, but no direct fund is created for private collection. Few such statutes directly allow for attorney fees to prevailing plaintiffs. Is there a basis for an attorney fee claim in such cases under civil rights law (42 U.S.C. § 1983)? Where courts grant immunity or deny standing to preclude such civil rights statute invocation, what alternative is available for attorney recompense and effective court access (see discussion below)?

3. How important are these questions where the Legal Services Corporation (LSC), including a substantial portion of the nation's attorneys able to sue without compensation, is precluded by federal law from bringing class actions? Where the LSC is precluded by federal law from collecting fees if it prevails in an action? (See discussion above.)

5. Constitutional Remedies: Limitations and a Proposed New Amendment

The U.S. Constitution provides the primary court-enforced standard entitled to supersession within federalist constraints. State constitutions provide theoretical cover where federal constitutional standards may be precluded by notions of state sovereignty. However, two major factors impede application of constitutional protection for the benefit of children. First, as noted above, children are not considered a "suspect" classification—thus, discrimination against them invokes neither the "strict scrutiny" test nor a "heightened scrutiny" test. In general, the state need only show a "rational relation" between a legitimate state interest and the practice that the complaint addresses.

The second impediment is the focus of constitutional rights on "state action." They occur in the context of limiting the state *vis-à-vis* an individual subject to police power intrusion or abuse. The assumption is that the state is the only power capable of organized abuse, and by limiting it we preserve the individual liberty it may threaten. However, abuse may emanate from private power as well—as the residents of a one-company town, victims of a trust or cartel, or members of a corrupt union may attest. Children are among the weakest of private groupings. Indeed, one primary role of the state has been the protection of the weak from private power abuse, whether from labor conditions, institutional exploitation, or parental neglect. To the extent that constitutional standards are applied, they are asymmetrical. They limit the state—which may be the only check on private power disadvantage available to children. Hence, for example, constitutional police power limitations to protect individuals from state intrusion where there is suspected child abuse has consequences beyond the simple state vs.

individual (adult) paradigm. From the child's perspective, a proper analysis must be tripartite and include the state, the strong private entity, and the weak private entity.

Over the past two decades, many have undertaken to add the "Equal Rights Amendment" to more specifically secure the rights of women. Some child advocates argue that the rationale for constitutional protection for children is *a fortiori* to any competing interest. They argue, as noted above, that children lack protected constitutional status, are politically and financially weak, and warrant protection written into the governmental structure. One advocate has proposed a constitutional amendment directed at protecting children's rights.[17] In amended form, it would read:

> We, the citizens of the United States, declare that our highest societal priority is the long term welfare of children and of the earth which shall be their home. We declare our interest in the welfare of children of all nations, recognizing that the suffering of any child diminishes all of us. Our commitment to our own children, to whom we have special responsibility, includes the following rights, which are here constitutionally secured against infringement by the state, and is an affirmative obligation of the state to preserve wherever abridged:
>
> All children residing within the United States shall enjoy the right to live in a home which is safe and secure, to adequate nutrition and health care, to protection from abuse, injury and environmental harm, and to meaningful educational opportunity.
>
> All children under the age of 16 years shall enjoy the right to publicly provided counsel in any legal proceeding that substantially affects their interests.
>
> In all governmental actions, the best interests of children shall be a primary consideration.
>
> These rights may be secured and protected by all means afforded for the vindication of constitutionally based civil rights under existing law. [18]

6. Statutorily Implied Remedies

Chapters 2 through 13 discuss the specific, substantive statutes conferring rights and benefits to children and forming the basis for court redress. And most cases litigated involve the invocation of statutory remedies.

a. Statutorily Implied Remedies

Franklin v. Gwinnett County Public Schools
503 U.S. 60 (1992)

JUSTICE WHITE delivered the opinion of the Court.

This case presents the question whether the implied right of action under Title IX of the Education Amendments of 1972, 20 U.S.C. § 1681–1688 (Title IX),[1] which this Court recognized in *Cannon v. University of Chicago*, 441 U.S. 677 (1979), supports a claim for monetary damages.

I

Petitioner Christine Franklin was a student at North Gwinnett High School in Gwinnett County, Georgia, between September 1985 and August 1989. Respondent Gwinnett County School District operates the high school and receives federal funds. According to the complaint filed on December 29, 1988 in the United States District Court for the Northern District of Georgia, Franklin was subjected to continual sexual harassment beginning in the autumn of her tenth grade year (1986) from Andrew Hill, a sports coach and teacher employed by the district. Among other allegations, Franklin avers that Hill engaged her in sexually-oriented conversations in which he asked about her sexual experiences with her boyfriend and whether she would consider having sexual intercourse with an older man,...that Hill forcibly kissed her on the mouth in the school parking lot,...that he telephoned her at her home and asked if she would meet him socially,...and that, on three occasions in her junior year, Hill interrupted a class, requested that the teacher excuse Franklin, and took her to a private office where he subjected her to coercive intercourse....The complaint further alleges that though they became aware of and investigated Hill's sexual harassment of Franklin and other female students, teachers and administrators took no action to halt it and discouraged Franklin from pressing charges against Hill....On April 14, 1988, Hill resigned on the condition that all matters pending against him be dropped....The school thereupon closed its investigation....

In this action,[3] the District Court dismissed the complaint on the ground that Title IX does not authorize an award of damages. The Court of Appeals affirmed.

* * *

I

In *Cannon v. University of Chicago*, 441 U.S. 677 (1979), the Court held that Title IX is enforceable through an implied right of action. We have no occasion here to reconsider that decision. Rather, in this case we must decide what remedies are available in a suit brought pursuant to this implied right. As we have often stated, the question of what remedies are available under a statute that provides a private right of action is "analytically distinct" from the issue of whether such a right exists in the first place....Thus, although we examine the text and

---

[1] This statute provides in pertinent part that "No person in the United States shall, on the basis of sex, be excluded from participation in, be denied the benefits of, or be subjected to discrimination under any education program or activity receiving Federal financial assistance." 20 U.S.C. § 1681(a).

[3] Prior to bringing this lawsuit, Franklin filed a complaint with the Office of Civil Rights of the United States Department of Education (OCR) in August 1988. After investigating these charges for several months, OCR concluded that the school district had violated Franklin's rights by subjecting her to physical and verbal sexual harassment and by interfering with her right to complain about conduct proscribed by Title IX. OCR determined, however, that because of the resignations of Hill and respondent William Prescott and the implementation of a school grievance procedure, the district had come into compliance with Title IX. It then terminated its investigation. First Amended Complaint, Exh. A, pp. 7–9.

history of a statute to determine whether Congress intended to create a right of action,...we presume the availability of all appropriate remedies unless Congress has expressly indicated otherwise....This principle has deep roots in our jurisprudence.

A

"Where legal rights have been invaded, and a federal statute provides for a general right to sue for such invasion, federal courts may use any available remedy to make good the wrong done." *Bell v. Hood*, 327 U.S. 678 (1946). The Court explained this longstanding rule as jurisdictional, and upheld the exercise of the federal courts' power to award appropriate relief so long as a cause of action existed under the Constitution or laws of the United States....

The *Bell* Court's reliance on this rule was hardly revolutionary. From the earliest years of the Republic, the Court has recognized the power of the judiciary to award appropriate remedies to redress injuries actionable in federal court, although it did not always distinguish clearly between a right to bring suit and a remedy available under such a right. In *Marbury v. Madison*, 1 Cranch 137, 163 (1803), for example, Chief Justice Marshall observed that our government "has been emphatically termed a government of laws, and not of men. It will certainly cease to deserve this high appellation, if the laws furnish no remedy for the violation of a vested legal right." This principle originated in the English common law, and Blackstone described "it is a general and indisputable rule, that where there is a legal right, there is also a legal remedy, by suit or action at law, whenever that right is invaded." 3 W. Blackstone, Commentaries 23 (1783). See also *Ashby v. White*, 1 Salk. 19, 21, 87 Eng. Rep. 808, 816 (Q.B. 1702) ("If a statute gives a right, the common law will give a remedy to maintain that right...").

* * *

The general rule, therefore, is that absent clear direction to the contrary by Congress, the federal courts have the power to award any appropriate relief in a cognizable cause of action brought pursuant to a federal statute.

* * *

IV

Respondents and the United States nevertheless suggest three reasons why we should not apply the traditional presumption in favor of appropriate relief in this case.

A

First, respondents argue that an award of damages violates separation of powers principles because it unduly expands the federal courts' power into a sphere properly reserved to the Executive and Legislative Branches....In making this argument, respondents misconceive the difference between a cause of action and a remedy. Unlike the finding of a cause of action, which authorizes a court to hear a case or controversy, the discretion to award appropriate relief involves no such increase in judicial power....Federal courts cannot reach out to award remedies when the Constitution or laws of the United States do not support a cause of action. Indeed, properly understood, respondents' position invites us to abdicate our historic judicial authority to award appropriate relief in cases brought in our court system. It is well to recall that such authority historically has been thought necessary to provide an important safeguard against abuses of legislative and executive power,...as well as to insure an independent judiciary....Moreover, selective abdication of the sort advocated here would harm separation of powers principles in another way, by giving judges the power to render inutile causes of action authorized by Congress through a decision that no remedy is available.

B

Next, consistent with the Court of Appeals's reasoning, respondents and the United States contend that the normal presumption in favor of all appropriate remedies should not apply because Title IX was enacted pursuant to Congress's Spending Clause power. In *Pennhurst State School and Hospital v. Halderman*, 451 U.S. 1, 28–29 (1981), the Court observed that remedies were limited under such Spending Clause statutes when the alleged violation *was unintentional*. Respondents and the United States maintain that this presumption should apply equally to *intentional violations*. We disagree. The point of not permitting monetary damages for an unintentional violation is that the receiving entity of federal funds lacks notice that it will be liable for a monetary award....This notice problem does not arise in a case such as this, in which intentional discrimination is alleged. Unquestionably, Title IX placed on the Gwinnett County Schools the duty not to discriminate on the basis of sex, and "when a supervisor sexually harasses a subordinate because of the subordinate's sex, that supervisor discriminate[s] 'on the basis of sex.'....We believe the same rule should apply when a teacher sexually harasses and abuses a student. Congress surely did not intend for federal monies to be expended to support the intentional actions it sought by statute to proscribe....

* * *

V

In sum, we conclude that a damages remedy is available for an action brought to enforce Title IX. The judgment of the Court of Appeals, therefore, is reversed and the case is remanded for further proceedings consistent with this opinion.

So ordered.

Questions for Discussion

1. In *Franklin*, the Court found an "implied" right of action for enforcement of the statute, including damages—although no remedy is explicitly provided in the statute. In 2005, the Ninth Circuit held in *Sanchez v. Johnson*, 416 F.3d 1051 (9th Cir., 2005) that an attempt to enforce Medicaid standards lacked private remedy recourse without clear Congressional statement of intent to include it. Substantively, the case involved the federal statutory mandate that federally-financed medical services not discriminate against any particular patient group. Pediatric specialists in many states, including California, Oklahoma, and Pennsylvania suffer Medicaid rates at less than one-half the levels paid under Medicare for identical services for the elderly. Providers serving impoverished children are allegedly in short supply for orthopod, neurosurgery, and other specialties. Suits in the latter two states contend that the statute is

violated, with long delays and service unavailability a common result. If the *Sanchez* case stands and no private remedy is available, by what means are the statute's terms enforced?

2. How does the *Sanchez* conclusion that the lack of explicit Congressional remedy invokes a default rule of "no private remedy" comport with the *Franklin* holding of an implied private remedy—not only to compel prospective injunctive compliance, but to obtain private damages?

b. Violation of Federal Standards as a Civil Rights Violation

In addition to possible generic remedy available where federal statutes are violated, it also may be possible to invoke coverage of broad federal civil rights statutes, potentially applying their remedies on behalf of children. Although some cases have succeeded in that invocation, *Suter v. Artist M.* sets forth a major limiting line.

Suter v. Artist M.
503 U.S. 347 (1992)

THE CHIEF JUSTICE delivered the opinion of the Court.

This case raises the question whether private individuals have the right to enforce by suit a provision of the Adoption Assistance and Child Welfare Act of 1980 (Adoption Act or Act), 42 U.S.C. §§ 620–628, 670–679a, either under the Act itself or through an action under 42 U.S.C. § 1983.[1] The Court of Appeals for the Seventh Circuit held that 42 U.S.C. § 671(a)(15) contained an implied right of action, and that respondents could enforce this section of the Act through an action brought under § 1983 as well. We hold that the Act does not create an unenforceable right on behalf of the respondents.

The Adoption Act establishes a federal reimbursement program for certain expenses incurred by the States in administering foster care and adoption services. The Act provides that States will be reimbursed for a percentage of foster care and adoption assistance payments when the State satisfies the requirements of the Act. 42 U.S.C. §§ 672–674, 675(4)(A)....

* * *

Petitioners in this action are Sue Suter and Gary T. Morgan, the Director and the Guardianship Administrator, respectively, of the Illinois Department of Children and Family Services (DCFS). DCFS is the state agency responsible for, among other things, investigating charges of child abuse and neglect and providing services to abused and neglected children and their families. DCFS is authorized under Illinois law,...to gain temporary custody of an abused or neglected child after a hearing and order by the Juvenile Court. Alternatively, the court may order that a child remain in his home under a protective supervisory order entered against his parents....

---

[1] Section 1983 provides, in relevant part: "Every person who, under color of any statute, ordinance, regulation, custom, or usage, of any State or Territory or the District of Columbia, subjects or causes to be subjected, any citizen of the United States or other person within the jurisdiction thereof to the deprivation of any rights, privileges, or immunities, secured by the Constitution and laws, shall be liable to the party injured in an action at law, suit in equity, or other proper proceeding for redress."

Respondents filed this class-action suit seeking declaratory and injunctive relief under the Adoption Act....They alleged that petitioners, in contravention of 42 U.S.C. § 671(a)(15) failed to make reasonable efforts to prevent removal of children from their homes and to facilitate reunification of families where removal had occurred....This failure occurred, as alleged by respondents, because DCFS failed promptly to assign caseworkers to children placed in DCFS custody and promptly to reassign cases when caseworkers were on leave from DCFS....The District Court, without objection from petitioners, certified two separate classes seeking relief, including all children who are or will be wards of DCFS and are placed in foster care or remain in their homes under a judicial protective order....The District Court denied a motion to dismiss filed by petitioners, holding, as relevant here, that the Adoption Act contained an implied cause of action and that suit could also be brought to enforce the Act under 42 U.S.C. § 1983....[the generic federal civil rights statute]

The District Court then entered an injunction requiring petitioners to assign a caseworker to each child placed in DCFS custody within three working days of the time the case is first heard in Juvenile Court, and to reassign a caseworker within three working days of the date any caseworker relinquishes responsibility for a particular case....

We granted certiorari, and now reverse....

In *Maine v. Thiboutot*, 448 U.S. 1...(1980), we first established that § 1983 is available as a remedy for violations of federal statutes as well as for constitutional violations. We have subsequently recognized that § 1983 is not available to enforce a violation of a federal statute "where Congress has foreclosed such enforcement of the statute in the enactment itself and where the statute did not create enforceable rights, privileges, or immunities within the meaning of § 1983." *Wright v. Roanoke Redevelopment and Housing Authority*, 479 U.S. 418, 423...(1987).

* * *

In both *Wright* and *Wilder* the word "reasonable" occupied a prominent place in the critical language of the statute or regulation, and the word "reasonable" is similarly involved here. But this, obviously, is not the end of the matter. The opinions in both *Wright* and *Wilder* took pains to analyze the statutory provisions in detail, in light of the entire legislative enactment, to determine whether the language in question created "enforceable rights, privileges, or immunities within the meaning of § 1983."....And in *Wilder*, we caution that "section 1983 speaks in terms of 'rights, privileges, or immunities,' not violations of federal law."....

Did Congress, in enacting the Adoption Act, unambiguously confer upon the child beneficiaries of the Act a right to enforce the requirement that the State make "reasonable efforts" to prevent a child from being removed from his home, and once removed to reunify the child with his family? We turn now to that inquiry.

As quoted above, 42 U.S.C. § 671(a)(15) requires that to obtain federal reimbursement, a State have a plan which "provides that, in each case, reasonable efforts will be made...to prevent or eliminate the need for removal of the child from his home, and...to make it possible for the child to return to his home...."...In the present case, however, the term "reasonable efforts" to maintain an abused or neglected child in his home, or return the child to his home from foster care, appears in quite a different context. No further statutory guidance is found as to how "reasonable efforts" are to be measured. This directive is not the only one which Congress has given to the States, and it is a directive whose meaning will obviously vary with the circumstances of each individual case. How the State was to comply with this directive, and with the other provisions of the Act, was, within broad limits, left up to the State....

The regulations promulgated by the Secretary to enforce the Adoption Act do not evidence a view that § 671(a) places any requirement for state receipt of federal funds other than the requirement that the State submit a plan to be approved by the Secretary....The regulations provide that to meet the requirements of § 671(a)(15) the case plan for each child must "include a description of the services offered and the services provided to prevent removal of the child from the home and to reunify the family."....Another regulation, entitled "requirements and submittal," provides that a state plan must specify "which preplacement preventive and reunification services are available to children and families in need." 1357.15(e)(1).[14] What is significant is that the regulations are not specific, and do not provide notice to the States that failure to do anything other than submit a plan with the requisite features, to be approved by the Secretary, is a further condition on the receipt of funds from the Federal Government. Respondents contend that "neither [petitioners] nor amici supporting them present any legislative history to refute the evidence that Congress intended 42 U.S.C. § 671(a)(15) to be enforceable."....To the extent such history may be relevant, our examination of it leads us to conclude that Congress was concerned that the required reasonable efforts be made by the States, but also indicated that the Act left a great deal of discretion to them....

Careful examination of the language relied upon by respondents, in the context of the entire Act, leads us to conclude that the "reasonable efforts" language does not unambiguously confer an enforceable right upon the Act's beneficiaries. The term "reasonable efforts" in this context is at least as plausibly read to impose only a rather generalized duty on the State, to be enforced not by private individuals, but by the Secretary in the manner previously discussed.

* * *

Reversed.

Justice Blackmun, with whom **Justice Stevens** joins, dissenting.

The Adoption Assistance and Child Welfare Act of 1980 (Adoption Act) conditions federal funding for state child welfare, foster care, and adoption programs upon, inter alia, the State's express commitment to make, "in each case, reasonable efforts" to prevent the need for removing children from their homes and "reasonable efforts," where removal has occurred, to reunify the family....The Court holds today that the plaintiff children in this case may not enforce the State's commitment in federal court either under 42 U.S.C. § 1983 or under the Act itself.

In my view, the Court's conclusion is plainly inconsistent with this Court's decision just two Terms ago in *Wilder v. Virginia Hospital Assn.*, 496 U.S. 498,...(1990), in which we found enforceable under § 1983 a functionally identical provision of the Medicaid Act requiring "reasonable" reimbursements to health care providers. More troubling still, the Court reaches its conclusion without even

---

[14] The regulation, 45 CFR § 1357.15(e)(2) (1990), goes on to provide a list of which services may be included in the State's proposal:

"Twenty-four hour emergency caretaker, and homemaker services; day care; crisis counseling; individual and family counseling; emergency shelters; procedures and arrangements for access to available emergency financial assistance; arrangements for the provision of temporary child care to provide respite to the family for a brief period, as part of a plan for preventing children's removal from home; other services which the agency identifies as necessary and appropriate such as home-based family services, self-help groups, services to unmarried parents, provision of, or arrangements for, mental health, drug and alcohol abuse counseling, vocational counseling or vocational rehabilitation; and post adoption services."

stating, much less applying, the principles our precedents have used to determine whether a statute has created a right enforceable under § 1983. I cannot acquiesce in this unexplained disregard for established law. Accordingly, I dissent.

I

A

Section 1983 provides a cause of action for the "deprivation of any rights, privileges, or immunities, secured by the Constitution and laws" of the United States. We recognized in *Maine v. Thiboutot*, 448 U.S. 1,...(1980), that § 1983 provides a cause of action for violations of federal statutes, not just the Constitution. Since Thiboutot, we have recognized two general exceptions to this rule. First, no cause of action will lie where the statute in question does not "create enforceable rights, privileges, or immunities within the meaning of § 1983." *Wilder*, 496 U.S. at 508...Second, § 1983 is unavailable where "Congress has foreclosed enforcement of the statute in the enactment itself."....

In determining the scope of the first exception—whether a federal statute creates an "enforceable right"—the Court has developed and repeatedly applied a three-part test. We have asked (1) whether the statutory provision at issue "was intended to benefit the putative plaintiff."....If so, then the provision creates an enforceable right unless (2) the provision "reflects merely a congressional preference for a certain kind of conduct rather than a binding obligation on the governmental unit,"...or unless (3) the plaintiff's interest is so "vague and amorphous" as to be "beyond the competence of the judiciary to enforce."....The Court today has little difficulty concluding that the plaintiff children in this case have no enforceable rights, because it does not mention—much less apply—this firmly established analytic framework.

* * *

C

These principles, as we applied them in Wilder, require the conclusion that the Adoption Act's "reasonable efforts' clause[1] establishes a right enforceable under § 1983. Each of the three elements of our three-part test is satisfied. First, and most obvious, the plaintiff children in this case are clearly the intended beneficiaries of the requirement that the State make "reasonable efforts" to prevent unnecessary removal and to reunify temporarily removed children with their families.

Second, the "reasonable efforts" clause imposes a binding obligation on the State because it is "cast in mandatory rather than precatory terms," providing that a participating State "*shall* have a plan approved by the Secretary which...*shall be in effect* in all political subdivisions of the State, and, if administered by them, *mandatory* upon them." Further, the statute requires the plan to "provide that, in each case, reasonable efforts *will be made*." Moreover, as in *Wilder*, the statutory text expressly conditions federal funding on state compliance with the plan requirement and requires the Secretary to reduce payments to a State, if "in the administration of [the State's] plan there is a substantial failure to

---

[1] "In order for a State to be eligible for payments under this part, it shall have a plan approved by the Secretary which—...(3) provides that the plan shall be in effect in all political subdivisions of the State, and, if administered by them, mandatory upon them; [and]...(15)...provides that, in each case, reasonable efforts will be made (A) prior to the placement of a child in foster care, to prevent or eliminate the need for removal of the child from his home, and (B) to make it possible for the child to return to his home." 42 U.S.C. § 671(a).

comply with the provisions of the plan." 42 U.S.C. § 671(b). Under our holding in *Wilder*, these provisions of the Adoption Act impose a binding obligation on the State. Indeed, neither the petitioner state officials nor amicus United States dispute this point....

* * *

Petitioners also argue that the right to "reasonable efforts" is "vague and amorphous" because of substantial disagreement in the child-welfare community concerning appropriate strategies. Furthermore, they contend, because the choice of a particular strategy in a particular case necessarily will depend upon the facts of that case, a court-enforced right to reasonable efforts either will homogenize very different situations or else will fragment into a plurality of "rights" that vary from State to State. For both of these reasons, petitioners contend, Congress left the question of what efforts are "reasonable" to state juvenile courts, the recognized experts in such matters.

Here again, comparison with *Wilder* is instructive. The Court noted the lack of consensus concerning which of various possible methods of calculating reimbursable costs would best promote efficient operation of health care facilities....The Court further noted that Congress chose a standard that leaves the States considerable autonomy in selecting the methods they will use to determine which reimbursement rates are "reasonable and adequate." *Id.*, at 506–508, 515. The result, of course, is that the "content" of the federal right to reasonable and adequate rates—the method of calculating reimbursement and the chosen rate—varies from State to State. And although federal judges are hardly expert either in selecting methods of Medicaid cost reimbursement or in determining whether particular rates are "reasonable and adequate," neither the majority nor the dissent found that the right to reasonable and adequate reimbursement was so vague and amorphous as to be "beyond the competence of the judiciary to enforce."....

* * *

Even assuming that it is accurate to call the statute and regulations involved in that case "detailed,"[4] the Court has misread *Wilder*. The Court there referred to the relative specificity of the statute and regulations not to demonstrate that the health-care providers enjoyed a substantive right to reasonable and adequate rates—we had already concluded that the State was under a binding obligation to adopt such rates,...but only to reinforce our conclusion that the providers' interest was not so "vague and amorphous" as to be "beyond the competence of judicial enforcement."....Under our three-part test, the Court would not have inquired whether that interest was "vague and amorphous" unless it had *already* concluded that the State was required to do more than simply file a paper plan that lists the appropriate factors.

Second, the Court emphasizes: "Other sections of the [Adoption] Act provide enforcement mechanisms for the reasonable efforts clause of § 671(a)(15)."....Such "mechanisms" include the Secretary's power to cut off or reduce funds for noncompliance with the State plan, and the requirement of a state judicial finding that "reasonable efforts" have been made before federal funds may

---

[4] Petitioners suggest a sharp contrast between the implementing regulations considered in *Wilder* and the implementing regulation for the Adoption Act "reasonable efforts" provision: The former, they say, require the State to consider certain factors, but the latter merely provides "a laundry list of services the States may provide." Brief for Petitioners 34 (citing 45 CFR § 1357.15(e) (1991)). Further, petitioners emphasize HHS's remark during rulemaking that States must retain flexibility in administering the Adoption Act's "reasonable efforts" requirement....

be used to reimburse foster care payments for a child involuntarily removed.

The Court has apparently forgotten that ever since *Rosado v. Wyman*, 397 U.S. 397...(1970), the power of the Secretary to enforce congressional spending conditions by cutting off funds has not prevented the federal courts from enforcing those same conditions....Indeed, we reasoned in Wilder that a similar "cutoff" provision *supports* the conclusion that the Medicaid Act creates an enforceable right, because it puts the State "on notice" that it may not simply adopt the reimbursement rates of its choosing....As for the Court's contention that § 671(a)(15) should be enforced through individual removal determinations in state juvenile court, the availability of a state judicial forum can hardly deprive a § 1983 plaintiff of a federal forum. *Monroe v. Pape*, 365 U.S. 167,...(1961). The Court's reliance on enforcement mechanisms other than § 1983, therefore, does not support its conclusion that the "reasonable efforts" clause of the Adoption Act creates no enforceable right.

The Court, without acknowledgement, has departed from our precedents in yet another way. In our prior cases, the existence of other enforcement mechanisms has been relevant not to the question whether the statute at issue creates an enforceable right, but to whether the second exception to § 1983 enforcement applies—whether, that is, "Congress has foreclosed enforcement of the statute in the enactment itself." *Wilder*, 496 U.S. at 508...In determining whether this second exception to § 1983 enforcement applies, we have required the defendant not merely to point to the existence of alternative means of enforcement, but to demonstrate "by express provision or other specific evidence from the statute itself that Congress intended to foreclose [§ 1983] enforcement." 496 U.S. at 520–521. We have said repeatedly that we will not "lightly" conclude that Congress has so intended....In only two instances, where we concluded that "the statute itself provides a comprehensive remedial scheme which leaves no room for additional private remedies under § 1983," have we held that Congress has intended to foreclose § 1983 enforcement....

The Court does not find these demanding criteria satisfied here....Instead, it simply circumvents them altogether: The Court holds that even if the funding cutoff provision in the Adoption Act is not an "express provision" that "provides a comprehensive remedial scheme" leaving "no room for additional private remedies under § 1983,"...that provision nevertheless precludes § 1983 enforcement. In so holding, the Court has inverted the established presumption that a private remedy is available under § 1983 unless "Congress has affirmatively withdrawn the remedy."....

III

In sum, the Court has failed, without explanation, to apply the framework our precedents have consistently deemed applicable; it has sought to support its conclusion by resurrecting arguments decisively rejected less than two years ago in *Wilder*, and it has contravened 22 years of precedent by suggesting that the existence of other "enforcement mechanisms" precludes § 1983 enforcement. At least for this case, it has changed the rules of the game without offering even minimal justification, and it has failed even to acknowledge that it is doing anything more extraordinary than "interpreting" the Adoption Act "by its own terms."....Readers of the Court's opinion will not be misled by this hollow assurance. And, after all, we are dealing here with children....I dissent.

Neither of these factors marks a significant difference between Wilder and the present case. The difference between *requiring* States to *consider* certain factors, as in *Wilder*, and *permitting* States to *provide* certain listed services, as in the present case, is hardly dramatic. As for the second asserted difference, *Wilder* itself emphasized that States must retain substantial discretion in calculating "reasonable and adequate" reimbursement rates.

Questions for Discussion

1. The *Suter* Court implies that the general nature of the "reasonable efforts" requirement is critical to its holding that there is no implied private enforcement remedy. Can this defect be cured by enumerating specific standards in federal law, and invoking the many precedents finding implied private enforcement remedies where such specificity exists? If the statute deliberately delegates such specificity to a federal agency (DHHS), and such specificity is produced by its rules, would that suffice?

2. Would it suffice if the Congress intended such specificity to exist, but delegated the precise line drawing to a state? Does broad discretion to a state to fashion substantive policy preclude enforcement of the standard selected?

c. Note on Enforcement of Federal Standards Through Funding Cut-Off

Many of the rights and benefits of children derive from publicly funded programs. Their federal enabling statutes often reflect liberal legislative intent to provide benefits, and are fleshed out in federal agency rulemaking. This body of federal law forms a minimum standard for state and local compliance. How are such standards to be enforced? Commonly, suit is brought by public interest counsel against state or local officials for failure to meet those standards, often by denying assistance to children in violation of federal law. The facial remedy sought is necessarily the termination of federal assistance to the state. Such redress involves a certain game of "chicken," since the plaintiffs do not want the remedy sought. They rather rely on the desire of the state to retain federal funding (or to avoid the embarrassment of losing federal funds to other states). As discussed above, these cases may raise attorney fee uncertainty and are the target of 1996 Congressional limitations on court challenge by federally funded attorneys representing the impoverished.

7. Federal Spending Standards Applicable to State Recipients and Possible "Sovereign Immunity" Bar

Child advocates commonly utilize 42 U.S.C. §1983 civil rights actions to compel state compliance with federal standards. Such actions are brought on three bases: (1) a state action is unconstitutional; (2) a federal statute entitled to supremacy is violated; or (3) a federal precondition for federal funding is breached. In each of these cases states have invoked the 11th Amendment to the Constitution, raising "state sovereign immunity" doctrine to avoid federal court jurisdiction. The concept is that "the Constitution does not provide for federal jurisdiction over suits against non-consenting states." However, the leading case of *Ex Parte Young*, 209 U.S. 123 (1908), and its progeny have held that where state officials act in violation of the constitution, or where federal statutes are entitled to supremacy,[19] state actors enjoy no such immunity. The 14th Amendment to the Constitution, adopted after the 11th Amendment, refines the former. To the extent state and local officials act in violation of the federal constitution or effective federal law, they are shorn of the protective cloak of the state. Such a basis for suit has been broadly interpreted to allow for prospective injunctive relief where state officials violate effective federal mandates, including those requirements preconditioning the receipt of federal funds. See *Joseph A. v. Ingram*, 275 F.3d 1253 (10th Cir., 2002).

In addition to the 14th Amendment/*Ex Parte Young* basis for such suit in federal court, a state (or its officials) may also be sued where it has "consented" to such federal jurisdiction. Arguably, such consent is implied where the federal jurisdiction provides funds on the condition that the state expend those funds as stipulated, and the state accepts the funding on those terms.

In *Will v. Michigan Department of State Police*, 491 U.S. 58 (N.D. Ill. 2002), the Court held that municipalities and local government units which are not part of the "state" are not covered by 11th Amendment immunity, citing the leading case of *Monell v. New York City Dept. of Social Services*, 436 U.S. 658 (1978). However, cities administer few child related programs; most are administered by the state, or by counties considered to be "political subdivisions" of the state. *Will* otherwise affirmed the immunity of the state, and of state officials sued in their official capacity, from damage actions in federal court. It distinguished actions for prospective injunctive relief, holding that they are not "actions against the state" within the meaning of the 11th Amendment. In *Hafer v. Melo*, 502 U.S. 21 (1991), the Court narrowed *Will*, holding that state officials sued in their individual capacities are "persons" for purposes of 42 U.S.C. § 1983, and are subject to suit, reasoning that their violation of federal law strips them of the protective cloak of state immunity. Then in *Patterson v. McLean Credit Union*, 491 U.S. 164 (1989), the Court limited the reach of the related 42 U.S.C. § 1981 (guaranteeing the "same right" to all persons "to make and enforce contracts").

In *Jett v. Dallas Independent School District*, 491 U.S. 701 (1989), the Court went further and held that § 1981 creates no remedy against a "state actor," effectively foreclosing remedy for § 1981 civil rights actions to state civil rights or related statutes, or to allegations of constitutional breach. Congress responded to the 1989 *Jett* decision by amending 42 USC § 1981(c) to state: "The rights protected by this section are protected against impairment by nongovernmental discrimination *and impairment under color of State law*" (emphasis added). However, despite this apparent Congressional repudiation, *Jett* has been cited in a substantial number of federal court opinions as controlling while a small minority of decisions have held that it is effectively reversed by this amendment. In *Joseph A. v. Ingram*, 275 F.3d 1253 (10th Cir. 2001), the court upheld a case brought by a class of New Mexico foster children who had suffered excessive movement between placements and other violations of applicable federal law. The court held that where the remedy sought was "prospective" injunctive relief, immunity would not lie to protect state officials under the Younger (or other) doctrine. The *Joseph A.* litigation consumed twenty years of proceedings and consent decree oversight. However, in repeated cases federal appellate courts have contradicted such a holding to preclude access to federal judicial remedy for violations of federal standards—particularly for children.

Two years after *Joseph A.*, the Eleventh Circuit decided *31 Foster Children v. Jeb Bush*, 329 F.3d 1255 (10th Cir., 2003), a class action brought by Florida foster children to require compliance with the law. The court narrowly construed standing, denying it to children who had left the foster care system, and then barred even prospective relief for those currently suffering violations. The court held that as Congress did not clearly manifest an unambiguous intent for those provisions of the Adoption Assistance and Child Welfare Act of 1980 to provide a basis for private enforcement, there were no individual rights to be pursued under 42 U.S.C.S. § 1983. The court went on to hold that continuing state dependency proceedings involving each of the plaintiffs "were ongoing state proceedings for the purposes of *Middlesex* abstention analysis" and that the requested declaratory judgment and injunction "would interfere with the state proceedings in numerous ways." Since several forms of relief existed at the state level, including the state courts' protective order and contempt powers, the court held that such a theoretical state remedy (in an action against state officials) effectively bars federal remedy under the *Younger* doctrine. Similarly, in *Olivia Y. v. Barbour*, 351 F.Supp.2d 543 (2004), the court manifested new and creative judicial obstacles to federal standards enforcement for children. There, plaintiffs sought to represent two classes, consisting of children who were in the Mississippi Division of Family and Children's Services (DFCS) custody, and children who were not in DFCS custody—but had been or were at risk of being abused or neglected. Granting defendants' motion in part, the court held, *inter alia*, that (1) there was no protectable liberty interest in that state's protective measures for foster children because they did not guarantee a specific substantive outcome; (2) the equal protection claim failed because plaintiffs failed to allege that defendants' action toward them was based on an illegitimate *animus* directed against them individually or as an identifiable class; (3) the substantive due process claim on behalf of the protective services class was subject to dismissal because the U.S. Court of Appeals for the Fifth Circuit had declined to adopt the "state-created danger" theory of liability; (4) plaintiffs' allegations did not support a conclusion of deliberate indifference; and (5) none of the provisions of the Adoption Assistance and Child Welfare Act of 1980 created an individual federal right enforceable under 42 U.S.C.S. § 1983.

The problems confronting child access to the courts for statutory compliance are illustrated in *Laurie Q. v. Contra Costa County*, 304 F.Supp.2d 1185 (2004), where the plaintiff class of disabled foster children filed under 42 U.S.C.S. § 1983. The class alleged that the county applied federal benefits to purposes unrelated to the children and violated state and federal mandates for that spending. The county claimed state sovereign immunity from damages and also argued that ongoing judicial oversight of the county's foster care activities required abstention which precluded injunctive relief, and that injunctive relief was moot as to children who were now adopted. The court found mootness as to adopted children and upheld immunity as to the remainder because state courts had jurisdiction over the children until their adoptions and held ultimate review authority over the case plans providing for the children's care. Hence, abstention was warranted since any injunctive relief concerning case plan management would constitute unwarranted federal intervention in state judicial proceedings.

While state immunity doctrine would appear to leave intact at least a 42 U.S.C. § 1983 claim against state officials for prospective relief for violation of constitutional substantive due process rights by those foster children in state custody, the creative invocation of collateral immunity concepts increasingly inhibits access to federal court for aggrieved children. As indicated above, these doctrines include standing impediments (*e.g.*, foster children are now over 18 years of age—not normally a basis for rejection where the issue is "likely to reoccur").

Indeed, the seminal case of *Roe v. Wade* (discussed in Chapter 2) was decided years after the pregnancy giving rise to the case. Other judicially extended obstacles include deference to the state where it may offer a theoretical remedy, or the recitation, as in *Laurie Q.*, of the theoretical jurisdiction of juvenile courts (a jurisdiction that does not include practically the issue here contested—appropriation of funds powers). Since juvenile courts in every state exercise purported jurisdiction over foster children, such an immunity concept may effectively bar access to federal court for foster children victimized by federal constitutional or statutory violations.

8. Federal Statutory Minimum Standards to Protect Children and Possible Contraction of Federal Supremacy and Jurisdiction

The expansion of state immunity barring federal jurisdiction over federal spending standards may not apply to direct federal statutes entitled to supremacy. Accordingly, child advocates here commonly use 42 U.S.C. § 1983 and other tools to compel compliance with such directly stated national minimum terms. However, in *U.S. v. Lopez*, 514 U.S. 549 (1995), the Supreme Court invalidated the Gun-Free School Zones Act of 1990, raising a possible new obstacle to enforcement of direct federal statutory minimums. The challenged statute made it a federal crime to carry a concealed handgun and bullets onto or within 1,000 feet of a school property. The Court held 5–4 that because the regulation was not of "commerce" (an "economic activity") it did not "affect interstate commerce" sufficiently to confer federal jurisdiction under Article I, § 8 of the Constitution (see also discussion of *Lopez* in Chapter 4).[20]

The context of the decision is significant—occurring after five decades of expansive interpretation of "affecting interstate commerce" federal jurisdiction. For example, racial discrimination in local restaurants has been held to confer federal jurisdiction.[21] The presence of automobiles from other states in the parking lot of a motel justifies federal jurisdiction to prohibit accommodations discrimination.[22] In *McLain v. Real Estate Board*, 444 U.S. 232 (1980), the Court found an effect on interstate commerce in real estate sales—perhaps the ultimate local and untransportable commodity—because sales may involve title insurance and some title insurance firms conduct business across state lines.

Lopez may be overcome by the inclusion of "Congressional findings" in federal legislation explicating the impact on commerce of a measure (lacking with the Gun-Free School Zones Act). Such findings may persuade the Court that a given statute has a commercial impact sufficient to confer federal jurisdiction and possible supremacy.[23] However, the *Lopez* holding is a concern for child advocates because statutory protections for children are more often of a "social" nature than of a "commerce regulating" character. Hence, minimum federal standards may here involve public health and medical care, child abuse and foster care standards, special needs children, nutrition, education opportunity *et al.* Query, under the *Lopez* rationale, can the Congress mandate immunizations to protect children? Is that sufficiently "commercial?" To the extent *Lopez* is not surmountable, it could relegate federal health and social minimums to the states and inhibit a direct national health, safety, or other mandated floor for children.

D. CHILD ADVOCACY AND THE EXECUTIVE BRANCH

Within the Executive Branch, agencies carry out the intent of legislative enactments and budget decisions. However, the work of agencies is not purely ministerial. The trend has been to enact broad enabling statutes and to allow executive branch rulemaking to flesh out specific standards.

1. Note on Executive Branch Advocacy

Two sets of statutes facilitate procedural advocacy for children before executive branch agencies. The first are administrative procedure acts (APAs) at the federal and state level. These statutes govern how agencies adopt rules and generally require a public process, including notice, opportunity for public comment, public hearings, and public vote (where the agency is governed by a multi-member board or commission). In addition, the federal and most state APAs not only assure a public process and opportunity for public comment, but also allow proposals for new rules or amendments under liberal standing criteria. See, for example, 5 U.S.C. section 500 *et seq.*, which requires federal agencies to give an interested person the right to petition for the issuance, amendment, or repeal of a rule.

The other set of relevant laws are generally termed "sunshine statutes" and require multi-member boards and commissions to conduct business in open meetings, with advance agenda notice of items to be acted upon. In addition, the federal Freedom of Information Act (5 U.S.C. § 552) and most state public records acts give citizens access to all documents held by agencies unless specifically exempt. These statutes do not impose standing requirements on those requesting documents. Further, they place the burden of non-disclosure on the agency. Both types of sunshine statutes (open meetings and public records) generally provide for attorney's fees for plaintiffs successfully vindicating their terms.

The formal requirements of broad public visibility and disclosure provide an opportunity for child advocates. Those with a vested profit/stake in the business of public agencies are generally well represented and aware of prospective agency action. Accordingly, wider exposure provides some counterbalance to otherwise unchecked influence from profit/stake advocates alone. However, the size of the public bureaucracy and its esoteric proceedings, combined with insubstantial resources and presence from child advocates in that forum marginalize their influence.

The imbalance of advocacy before agencies is exacerbated by continuing conflicts of interest similar to those discussed above and applicable to legislators. Such conflicts undermine "decisions on the merits" and can further bias public decisions in the direction of short term economic advantage for those with a stake in agency decisions. The primary current checks on such conflicts are federal (and common state) requirements applicable to high agency officials to (1) disclose holdings in industries regulated, (2) recuse themselves from participating in decisions where they have a material financial interest, and (3) to a limited extent, refrain for a period of time from accepting employment as a lobbyist before their previous agency. However, common problems undermining such conflict checks include:

(1) Many regulatory agencies (particularly at the state level) are literally governed by persons currently in the trade or profession their agency regulates;[24]

(2) Job interchange between executive agencies and private industry is common, even prevalent, at both the state and federal levels;

(3) Those with a vested profit/stake in agency policies engage in extensive socialization with agency officials, including banquets, conferences, trips, entertainment, and awards;

(4) *Ex parte* contact (private communications between agency officials and private industry) is common and is generally not prohibited outside of adjudications and some rate proceedings;

(5) External information and advocacy on pending issues is dominated by profit/stake interests, and many agencies (particularly at the state and local levels) lack independent professional staffs capable of advancing internal agendas on behalf of diffuse and long term interests.

Two mechanisms have demonstrated success in providing some counterbalance on behalf of broader constituencies. First is the reform of creating an internal advocate with some structural independence.[25] Second is the award of intervenor compensation on behalf of public interest organizations who represent broad and otherwise unrepresented interests and who prevail or contribute to the outcome of an agency proceeding. These two checks on profit/stake interest domination of agency proceedings have most often been invoked on behalf of consumer interests, but could be extended to or could collaterally benefit those advocating for children.

2. Standard Setting and Children

Most regulatory agencies operate through the issuance of "rules" to guide private action or the government's own allocation of services. Rules often set standards to protect the health and safety of the citizenry. To what extent do such standards take into account the physiological characteristics of children? The medical profession has recognized the importance of such developmental differences in its creation of the separate branch of pediatrics, with separate hospitals, practitioners, and procedures substantially attending to their special needs. Similarly, research has documented extraordinary dangers applicable to children which may not be as manifest when applied to adults, ranging from the impact of alcohol and drugs *in utero* to relatively minute lead contaminant damage to developing brains. (See Chapter 5 for detailed discussion of the differences between children and adults for regulatory purposes and the current state of the law in acknowledging them.)

E. CHILD ADVOCACY AND PUBLIC BUDGETS

Child service providers are sometimes organized to advocate for public spending on behalf of the children they serve. That advocacy is more effective for some accounts than for others. For example, education spending is promoted by organized teacher groups, and covers a subject matter of concern across the electorate. However, in areas such as child welfare (child abuse/neglect and foster children), special education, or child care the practitioners are less organized. The children they serve may lack media visibility and come disproportionately from impoverished families. In general, budget advocacy for children implicates the priority distortions from the under-representation of diffuse, long run interests discussed above. To the extent that structural political reforms are implemented (*e.g.*, public financing of campaigns, reductions in conflicts of interest, less reliance on information/lobbying from profit/stake interests), the consideration of children is enhanced.

Currently, the budget process varies widely between the federal jurisdiction and the states, and among the states. At the federal level, public spending is first "authorized" by legislation. Then monies are "appropriated" in a separate budgetary process. Where revenue does not match total sums appropriated, the Congress engages in deficit spending, borrowing from buyers of treasury instruments or adding to the money supply. Such a deficit may benefit children if its proceeds are invested effectively in their future; but where expended for current adults, it constitutes a taking for the present from revenues to be generated by today's children, who must repay or pay interest on these amounts.

Almost all federal spending for children is in the form of either (1) capped grants to states, or (2) entitlement spending that is open-ended—expended based on numbers who qualify for that spending. Both forms of spending often require a state or local contribution.

Unlike the federal jurisdiction, states are unable to engage in substantial deficit spending. Budgets must balance. Hence, an unexpected revenue downturn imposes special problems and hard choices, particularly where new taxation is politically foreclosed. States often devolve services for children to counties and school districts similar to federal spending devolution to the states. Local governments actually administer most programs affecting children, receiving funds based on population, need, or other criteria. Although local budgets must balance, they often lack broad revenue generating authority (taxation power).

1. Issues and Problems

a. Proper Adjusters

Official governmental budgets often compare amounts proposed to prior years' budgets in terms of raw numbers ("current dollars"). Child advocates argue that all figures should be adjusted by the proper measure of inflation, and by population. Only "adjusted" dollars are relevant when looking at trends over time. More money may be printed and the population of taxpayers (as well as those requiring services) changes year to year. Hence, the common claim that "spending for education is at or above previous levels" may often be misleading. It is not uncommon for official press releases to claim 2–3% increases each year, while in actuality constant dollar/child spending reductions have been effectuated.

b. Block Grants and Supplantation

Federal to state devolution through block grants rather than entitlement spending for qualified children raises the danger of state "supplantation"—referring to the dynamic of accepting new funds intended to supplement an existing purpose, then removing a similar amount from monies already addressing that function. For example, the federal jurisdiction may give the states $10 million for a given purpose only to find that states subtract a similar amount from current spending in the subject area, effectively diverting the intended sum to another purpose. The same process may occur within a state where counties and school districts undermine an intended *additive* effect of state directed funds by reducing their own current spending for the same project or purpose. Supplantation occurs commonly unless there is strong "anti-supplantation" language, usually in the form of "maintenance of effort" (MOE) requirements on the jurisdiction receiving the intended augmenting funds.

c. State "Suspense File" Referrals

State legislation that requires measurable public funding is normally referred to appropriations committees after passing out of one or more substantive committees in each legislative house. A typical initiative or reform intended to benefit children will be introduced by legislative authors, often with press release announcement. Such measures will be voted out of the one or more policy committees where they are initially referred, pass out of appropriations, and then may pass the floor of the house where introduced. Such legislation may then go to the second house, pass out of one or more policy committees and then be referred to the appropriations committee of the second house. During this travail, some measures enjoy strong public support and pass through public votes with few and sometimes no negative votes. However, as they reach the first or the second appropriations committee, they will commonly be referred to what is termed a "suspense file." In many states, unless a measure is affirmatively brought out of "suspense" by the decision of the appropriations committee chair (usually in consultation with the Governor or the Department of Finance), it is effectively defeated. Accordingly, where a legislative body whose appropriations committee is holding a measure in suspense is controlled by the same political party holding the Governorship, these bills are commonly killed. The spending they would authorize is defeated entirely through inaction and without public vote.[26]

d. Intra-State Realignment

Many states have replicated the federal Personal Responsibility Act's (PRA) format within their boundaries. Called "devolution" or "realignment," state requirements or mandates to provide minimum services are removed, and counties are assigned what were previously state responsibilities. Again, as with the PRA at the federal level, the state may create or designate a special fund to finance locally administered state programs. The assigned fund may be capped or have a source unrelated to the services allocated to it. In addition, the money from the state for such child related accounts may be "supplanted" locally, as discussed above with state supplantation of federal money intended for children.

Supplantation may often be stimulated by other financial pressure on states or counties. The local entity administering a program may lack control over the revenue source assigned, and lack realistic alternative funding. For example, in California, mental health spending for children comes from a pre-set fund fed by motor vehicle registration fees, which may not relate to mental health spending needs.

Child advocates argue that the result of such devolution is the severance of policy from appropriately related funding sources, resulting in cuts which occur in fragmented fashion, and increasing variations between states and locales as time passes—implicating equality of opportunity goals.

e. Entitlement Status

Federal "entitlement status" means that children meeting statutory qualification for a service are entitled to it. Appropriations vary with need. Within states, such a status may be delineated with slightly different terminology, *e.g.,* "state mandate" or "mandated service." In either case, financing is provided so long as the standards and requirements of the funder are met. Such mandatory language gives child advocates the legal tool to compel performance—the teeth of court-ordered enforcement. The public record on spending for children includes many examples of spending shortfall and service cut-offs, and some examples of litigation to compel compliance with promises made. Historical examples include the failure of Medicaid state accounts to meet EPSDT requirements benefiting children, the failure to provide required "reunification" services to protect children in foster care, and the denial of JOBS child care subsidies to TANF mothers.

f. Tax Expenditures

The tax side of public budgets is a form of spending. Federal and state tax codes include numerous tax deductions and credits allowing taxpayers to forego or reduce tax burdens. That dispensation is regarded by economists as a form of spending, often termed a "tax expenditure." Unlike straight spending, however, such benefits are often not examined. They are not reappropriated annually, but rather continue indefinitely unless affirmatively terminated. In addition, some states require a supermajority legislative vote to raise taxes, and the ending of such a tax benefit is technically an increase requiring such a vote. Hence, tax expenditures are understandable targets for lobbyists. Each year additional tax expenditures are enacted to add to those currently in place. They tend to subtract future revenue from the federal and state general funds, which are the sources of most child related funding. Some tax expenditures may themselves benefit children, but except for the Earned Income Tax Credit assisting impoverished working families, few are "refundable credits." In other words, they only serve to offset tax liability and hence provide no benefit for those who meet their conditions, but who earn too little to have a sufficient tax liability to offset.

g. Disinvestment in Children and Obligation Deferral

Note on Child Budget Disinvestment 2003–2013
By Robert C. Fellmeth

Federal spending and taxation policy raises six questions relevant to children: (a) What are the federal deficit projections? (b) How have the federal tax cuts after 2000 affected resources for future child investment? (c) What are the long run federal spending commitments for non-child purposes vs. the health coverage and education investment promises made post 2000? (d) What proposed federal budget rule changes are relevant to children? (e) How does the "design" of federal income taxation (who pays what amount, who receives credits/deductions) affect children, particularly impoverished children? (f) What are the implications for children of the projected Social Security and Medicare obligation accrual—financed from payroll tax deductions and employer contributions?

A. A Different Kind of Federal Deficit

During the Clinton Administration, the federal budget projected a surplus of $5.6 trillion over fiscal years 2002 to 2011. That surplus allowed for possible child investment in medical coverage and education. The Congressional Budget Office then revised the estimate to a reduced $1.6 trillion surplus in January 2002.[1] The tax cuts and defense/security spending decisions of

2001 and 2003 have now substituted a long-term debt for the surplus. The Congressional Budget Office predicted last year that annual budget shortfalls would total a cumulative $4.2 trillion over the next decade—unless tax cuts are sunsetted. More recently, the estimate has been raised to over $7 trillion.

Defenders of the current deficit contend that the level is not as alarming as a percentage of Gross Domestic Product (GDP). However, three factors demark this developing long-term deficit: (1) the new estimate is at a high level, even factoring in the larger size of the future economy, and it substitutes a burden on future generations to replace a surplus available for investment in them—a turnaround of a remarkable $12 trillion, or $35,000 per American; (2) the largest share of the deficit is held by the People's Republic of China—giving it power over U.S. interest rates upon which millions of Americans depend for home ownership under variable rate mortgages[2]; and (3) the historical deficit budgets cited as comforting precedent generally bought enhanced infrastructure that benefit the future generations burdened by the debt financing it (water projects, park purchases, higher education investment), but the current deficit purchases tax reductions and consumables for the wealthy and the elderly (*e.g.*, tax breaks for private pensions, prescription drug benefits). Previous deficits have invested in future generations with proper assessment of the beneficiaries, while the current deficit largely finances benefits for a single generation of the elderly, with the obligations financing them largely imposed on the young and the future.

B. Federal Income Tax Cuts in 2001, 2003 and Child Investment Capacity

In 1997, the Congress granted tax relief to wealthy, middle class, and elderly taxpayers in a heavy "back-end benefit" pattern—with the tax expenditures growing as time passes. The 1997 reductions were then supplemented by larger cuts in 2001, followed by yet additional reductions in 2003. These reductions require increased interest payments on the debt, which brings their average cost to approximately $3 trillion through 2013. In the following 2014–24 ten-year period, the cost will rise to $4.5 trillion in general fund reduction.

As currently enacted, the tax cuts will reduce non-defense spending by 2011 to the lowest percentage of GDP since the data was collected in 1962. Overall federal revenue as a percentage of GDP is now at its lowest level since 1950. Spending on discretionary programs, where most child-related spending occurs, reached a modern-era record low of 3% of GDP in 2000; dropping even lower to 2.6% in 2004. Revenue capacity injury from the 1997, 2001 and 2003 cuts continue to accrue, and will likely further depress the child investment percentage.

C. Federal Budget Trends and Proposals

1. Discretionary Spending Non-Child Commitments

Separate from the payroll-tax-financed Social Security and Medicare systems discussed below, federal discretionary spending is dominated by five programs: defense spending, Medicaid, public pensions, veterans, and interest on the debt. The last three amounts are substantially locked-in by prior commitments. Defense spending and Medicaid account for most federal public spending.

a. Defense Spending

Despite the end of the cold war, U.S. defense spending has reinflated. Some of that increase may be traced to Homeland Security and the terrorist attacks of 9/11. But the vast majority of such spending is not directly related to such threats. The 2003 defense budget reached $390 billion. The next nearest defense budget in the world was Russia—at $60 billion. This count does not include the Homeland Security spending accelerating after fiscal 2002, and it does not include the non-defense budget sum expended on Iraq—most of $87.5 billion for 2003 and $79.5 billion for fiscal 2004. The fiscal 2005 defense budget has reached $450 billion—a level substantially above the total military spending of the rest of the world combined. Defense and related spending is projected to be $600 billion by fiscal 2007. Given some contraction in the defense budgets of other nations, the U.S.—with 4.6% of the world's population and no superpower enemies—is likely to account for over 60% of the world's cumulative military-related spending by 2007.

b. Medicaid

The next largest discretionary account financed from general fund sources is Medicaid. Although children below the poverty line are covered by this federal program, two factors affect its utility for children. First, the Congress is threatening to cut $11 billion in funding for the program for 2006 and thereafter. Second, most of the account's expenditure focuses upon the elderly; child medical coverage costs roughly one-fifth the level of older adults. And those older adults may be able to shift to Medicare or other coverage more easily than can impoverished children. Both Medicare and Medicaid costs are dominated by end-of-life expenses. That application is to a population that has universal preventive and on-going coverage, in contrast to the six million children in America who lack coverage and must rely on emergency room treatment.

California's spending is illustrative of cost allocation nationally. The state currently spends $13 billion per annum on Medi-Cal (the state's Medicaid program), with the federal jurisdiction adding $19 billion more. The total of $32 billion approaches the state's entire public investment in K–12 education. A study by the Public Policy Institute found that five percent of California's Medicaid recipients consume over sixty percent of its cost. One summary of the report notes that "even if the healthiest 75% of the state's recipients were to cut their Medicaid expenses in half, the reduction in cost would amount to 3% of current spending."[3] The vast majority of the "intensive 25%" of users are the elderly.

c. Other Major Discretionary Spending

Beyond these traditional and expanding accounts, and the Iraq war, the Congress is considering more than $200 billion in federal funds—beyond insurance coverage—to rebuild the Gulf states following hurricanes Katrina and Rita. Other large accounts include agricultural subsidies, and space exploration plans (including an expensive planned human revisit to the Moon). Much of the spending on these discretionary programs may have merit, but in balancing priorities, they have advantages borne of media coverage, ideological commitment, and strong political/campaign finance support. In stark contrast to the defense establishment, the elderly, and big agriculture, children do not vote, lack lobbying influence, and do not contribute to the campaign finance needs of public officials.

2. Caps (Mandated Reductions) on Child-Related Spending

Federal budget policy was substantially altered in 1996. Major accounts affecting children were changed from entitlement status (where services were provided based on need and poverty qualification) to a "capped grant" system. These grant amounts have generally been static levels that do not increase with inflation and population—allowing annual reductions of 3%–5% to be cumulatively imposed without Congressional review or action. For major accounts, such a policy accrues a reduction of 34% from 1996 to 2006 in per capita real spending impact.

The largest such block grant program is the Personal Responsibility Act of 1996 (federal welfare reform). States have not been required to cut safety net levels because rolls have declined more than the 34% reduction in population/inflation adjusted federal assistance. However, many of those who left welfare rolls have not, in fact, obtained and maintained employment. Few have achieved self-sufficiency, and many—now deprived of basic safety net support—are subsisting below 50% of the poverty line. Of comparable concern, should an economic downturn reinflate these rolls, the accumulated reductions from 1996 will jeopardize safety net assurance unless independently financed by the state. Further reauthorization of block grant amounts, without adjustment for population/inflation, will continue that constriction year to year.

The President's 2005 and now 2006 budget proposals would expand the "block grant" approach to Medicaid, foster care, housing vouchers, and other child-related accounts. Some have suggested its application to child support enforcement, school meals, Food Stamps, substance abuse prevention and treatment, special education, and Head Start. These programs are not as amenable to caseload reduction from economic upturn that softened the TANF block grant constriction. And welfare reform devoted substantial monies to job training, job search, and child care to facilitate employment and somewhat lower demand for assistance. But in many areas proposed for movement from entitlement to block grant format, related budget proposals do not provide for prevention or caseload reduction. In many cases, existing prevention spending is recommended for cuts. Examples include Centers for Disease Control (CDC) child-related health accounts, juvenile justice, child protection reduction, and the termination of 48 education programs.

No proposal has been presented to cap the number of prisoners who may be incarcerated, or the number of children who may be admitted to public school, but the defined expenditure approach in protecting injured or molested children—where need may increase— necessarily implies funding denial. Similarly, the block grant approach to Medicaid takes the notion of entitlement to basic medical coverage and rations it unrelated to need. Importantly, the current system of health care confines those lacking coverage to emergency room treatment *post hoc*, with limited preventive health care. Because organized health plans may bargain for rates at the marginal cost of providing treatment, hospitals and providers commonly charge uncovered individuals two to four times the bargained prices for procedures—in an attempt to recover the significant hospital overhead costs from less organized purchasers. Standard tests, relatively routine surgery, or an extended stay as a hospital in-patient at such extraordinary prices can exhaust the life savings of many working poor families lacking coverage. Such consequences may regrettably induce parents to postpone or forego medical treatment for their children.

Beyond the expansion of the block grant format, the Bush Administration proposes to retract current block grant commitment where that methodology is currently in place. Assistance may be limited by either caps, or by changing qualification criteria. For example, the Personal Responsibility Act reauthorization proposed in 2004, and reproposed in 2005 will require all TANF parents to work a minimum of 34 to 40 hours. While such full-time employment is preferable, for many parents it is not realistic because of employer needs, physical constraints, or child care limitations. But the Administration's proposal ignores the realities facing parents who are new entrants to the workforce, and punishes their families with benefit reductions and loss of all safety net support for their children after sixty months of benefits.

3. Federal Spending Promises to Children: Health Coverage and Education

Two accounts reflect additional investment intent in children, borne by the anticipated surpluses available during the Clinton Administration. Both the State Child Health Insurance Program (SCHIP) and the No Child Left Behind Act were publicly advanced by the new Bush Administration as emblematic of the nation's commitment to children. These new programs promised medical coverage to virtually all American children, and major educational investment, accountability, and enhanced performance. Together, they purportedly balanced the older adult solicitude of deficit obligations, future payroll tax burdens, and conversion from entitlements to block grants for many child-related accounts, as well as renewed spending on defense and the war on terror.

a. State Child Health Insurance Program (SCHIP)

The State Child Health Insurance Program (SCHIP) promised to extend medical coverage to children in families living above the poverty line and below a set ceiling. The program provides a federal match at a generous 2–1 ratio, for state investment in the basic health coverage for children in families from the poverty line up to 250% of the line—and up to 300% of the line in some states and for some groups of children. This demographic definition matches the current gap in coverage because the vast majority of high-earning adults receive employee benefits that medically cover their children.

Although states were awarded potentially billions annually in federal grant funds to expand child health care at a 2–1 match, a substantial portion of these funds were not expended. Much of this money has been effectively returned to the federal government, undermined by state-based impediments to coverage notwithstanding available federal monies adequate to insure almost every American child. The SCHIP program has brought increased medical coverage for children, but over five million of those eligible for medical coverage remain uninsured. Their current treatment often depends upon emergency room visits. Moreover, clinics, hospitals and providers commonly charge such uncovered families two to four times the price paid by public coverage or organized private insurers. Recent surveys have revealed that a major source of working family bankruptcy comes from medical costs for uncovered care—which triggers often aggressive collection tactics. Parents of children who are uncovered face a Hobson's choice: risk the health of their child and avoid treatment, or risk the thousands of dollars even a short hospital stay will incur—an expense that may jeopardize college and pension savings accrued over many years.

The failure of intended coverage for all of those between 100% to 250% of the poverty line is joined with a decline in coverage for those below the poverty line eligible for traditional Medicaid—substantially driven by the reduction in TANF rolls to families who remain below the poverty line and whose children are Medicaid eligible, but who lack the social worker to arrange enrollment. The enrollment obstacle to receiving treatment is imposed notwithstanding the fact that over 96% of children in most states are covered privately or are eligible for Medicaid or SCHIP. To prevent less than 4% income unqualified children from medical coverage—states set up obstacles that effectively bar 12%–18%.[4]

Beyond the issue of coverage efficacy are contemporaneous Congressional cuts to the underlying Medicaid account and also to the medical infrastructure supporting uninsured children. Nationally, net reductions here total $36.9 billion over ten years—more than the amount SCHIP will expend. Moreover, the President now has proposed the reversion of much of the authorized and not-yet-spent monies from SCHIP back to the federal treasury, inhibiting further child coverage.

b. No Child Left Behind Act of 2001

Education investment in children was a centerpiece of President Bush's first presidential campaign. The Administration borrowed heavily from the catch-phase of the Children's Defense Fund, and won enactment of the "No Child Left Behind Act." The new law emphasized statewide student testing, revenue penalties, student transfer allowance from low-performing schools, and other measures for enhanced accountability. At the same time, the enactment promised substantial new resources for the reward side of the equation—including the promise of enhanced teacher supply, quality, and rewards. However, the appropriated amounts made available to the states under its aegis did not correspond to expectations or to promises made. New monies were not sufficient to lower classroom size measurably, or to increase teacher supply or quality, or to provide bonuses or rewards on a meaningful scale. The Congress allocated $5.97 billion to the Act in fiscal 2003, $6.69 billion in 2004, and $6.73 billion in fiscal 2005. The amount appropriated as of 2006 is more than $9 billion under the amount authorized for annual investment.

4. Federal Spending Trends and Projections in Child Related Accounts

Continuing and current reports on Congressional budgetary decisions are available from the *Children and Youth Funding Report*.[5] In general, child-related accounts have suffered from the whipsaw of an underlying structural deficit and continuing revenue shortfall. Other accounts discussed below suffer from static funding without adjustment for inflation or population. For example, the apparent increase in Head Start funding from $6.77 in 2004 to $6.88 billion in 2006 actually represents a decline in the account. The number of children able to participate in Head Start, in relation to the population of four-year-olds eligible, will decline from 5%–8% over the two-year period.

Budget reconciliation bills face the Congress during 2006–10. Amounts scheduled for mandatory reduction range from $34.7 billion to $53 billion to 2010. Additional cuts may be compelled by the extraordinary burden of hurricane relief for the Gulf states, continued spending for Iraq occupation, and future expenses from an anticipated 15,000 to 25,000 newly-wounded veterans from Middle East hostilities. These cuts may largely come from Medicaid, the Child Care and Development Block Grant, Foster Care, Adoption Assistance, Promoting Safe and Stable Families, and the Social Services Block Grant.

D. Federal Budget Procedure Changes

The Bush Administration proposes systemic changes beyond the ongoing shift toward capped block grants for child related programs. The first such change would set a statutory cap on the total sum that may be appropriated for all "discretionary" programs. Much child-related spending is in this category—particularly given the growth of the "block grant" format. The scope of this over-all cap would include education, child care, many medical accounts, and any program not given "entitlement" status. The grouping of programs subject to this overall limit would include defense spending—a category supported by influential lobbies and patriotic appeal. The programs within this umbrella would then have to compete in a "zero sum" game fashion for available resources. Rather than reductions through population and cost of living increases year to year, child investment would depend on its priority over other programs and could lead to substantial raw number reductions. By 2010, conservatively projected defense and homeland security increases would require a $65 billion cut in other programs, disproportionately affecting children. That amounts to a 16% raw spending cut from 2005 levels.

The second proposed change is a "Pay as You Go" design principle advanced by the Bush Administration. This concept requires any spending increase in a particular area to be matched by a reduction in another area. While that philosophy protects future taxpayers from additional deficits, the Administration refuses to apply it to tax reductions. Hence, tax deductions and credits for various purposes need not receive countervailing revenue increase. The asymmetrical approach, when combined with continued support for additional tax reductions, may produce deficit growth on the tax side of greater consequence than likely through spending increases—as recent tax decreases indicate. As discussed above, the fact that defense and security spending is within the "discretionary spending" category of much child related spending would likely lead to cuts for the latter. A military emergency would not be financed through additional revenue, but from cuts to discretionary programs without budgetary consideration of consequences.

E. Federal Income Tax Design

Beyond the amount of public resources available for child investment is the issue of tax design. What portion of the "tax expenditures" (tax exceptions, deductions, credits) benefit children as opposed to other populations? What income groupings benefit the most directly from new tax forbearance? How do the children in the working poor to middle class families fare? The distribution of the new tax forbearance largely excludes impoverished children as beneficiaries. In terms of wealth distribution, the one percent at the income top receive about 40% of the tax benefits, the bottom 80% receive 29%, and the bottom 20% a negligible amount. An estimated 12.2 million low- and moderate-income families with children (accounting for 33.5% of the nation's children) received no tax reduction.[6]

The distribution of benefits to exclude working poor parents and families occurs in the context of record income disparities between the top and the bottom. Nationally, income disparities are at their widest point since World War II. From 1977–95, the after tax income of the bottom fifth of the population fell 14% in constant dollars. The after-tax income of the top fifth of households rose 27%, while the after-tax income of the top 1% increased by 87%. These widening after-tax disparities form the context for the tax changes enacted by the Congress in 2001.

Some of the elements of the 2001 federal tax plan have benefits for children and families, chiefly the doubling of the dependent tax credit from $500 to $1,000, but as with other administrations' tax proposals, it is a non-refundable credit. It does not benefit those who pay payroll and property taxes but earn below the personal income tax line. Moreover, such dependent credits start to phase out as income rises above $110,000, but the 2001 tax system raises that ceiling to $200,000—assuring full benefit to the latter level. Hence, for a substantial share of families above $100,000, the credit will mean a new (previously unavailable) tax reduction of $1,000 per child. While adding tax forbearance to this new group of wealthy citizens, the strange design of the credit restricts benefits beyond usual tax credit application. Families with four children and $34,000 of income paying $4,000 in taxes can claim only $2,350—a family earning $20,500 can claim only $1,000.

While the plan reduced marginal tax rates generally, they are not reduced for working families with children earning from $13,000 to $20,000. For each additional dollar these families earn, they lose up to 21 cents in Earned Income Tax Credit phase-out, 15.3 cents in payroll taxes, and 24–36 cents in lost Food Stamp benefits and child care credits.

The 2003 round of tax cuts was represented to cost an additional $350 billion in foregone revenue. The actual cost is between $800 billion and $1 trillion. The lower, figure advanced during Congressional debate, was obtained by disingenuously imposing a "sunset" date on seven of the eight tax reductions in 2004, 2005, or 2008, respectively. But the Congress did not terminate any of the cuts in 2004 or 2005 and the Bush Administration—notwithstanding extraordinary expenses from Iraq and two devastating hurricanes—proposes to reject their sunset. Adding increased interest payments to the cost, the sum grows to an estimated $1.9 trillion. And combined with the 2001 changes and interest due on it, the sum will total $3 trillion over ten years, averaging about $300 billion per annum, with that total increasing after 2013, as discussed above.

The 2003 changes benefit children—and in particular, impoverished and lower middle class children—even less than did the 2001 cuts. The reformulation did expand to a minor degree the lowest tax bracket, and reduced slightly two income joint return rates (the so-called marriage penalty revision). But its most costly three changes: (1) capped dividend income and capital gains profits; (2) reduced top-income bracket rates; and (3) allowed immediate deduction of 50% of new investment in equipment and facilities. Tax filers with incomes above $1 million will average $93,500 in reductions, those in the middle fifth of income will average $217 in benefit, and those in the bottom fifth will gain, on average, $1. Beyond a lack of federal revenue, the changes reverberate at the state level to reduce public revenue there. In order to compensate for those reductions, the Congress conferred a one-time grant of $20 billion for state fiscal relief; a small portion of lost monies, and one terminating after 2004–05.

Nationally, the IRS released data in 2003 concerning the taxation of the wealthiest 400 American taxpayers from 1992–2000. In 1992, that group averaged $46.8 million in income and paid 26.4% in taxes; in 2000, the group averaged $174 million in income and paid 22.3% in taxes. These figures comprise part of the context for the tax reductions decisions of 2001 and 2003. If these cuts had been in effect in 2000, the $38.8 million they paid would have been $26.8 million. The tax rate of the extremely wealthy currently averages well below 15%—a record low and substantially below rates (including payroll taxes) paid by working poor families at the bottom 40% of average family income.

F. Payroll Tax Future Obligations: Social Security/Medicare

Two government programs are of special concern to children separate and apart from general fund spending. Both Social Security and Medicare are funded by payroll taxes—a set percentage deduction from payroll checks, plus required employer contributions. These payroll taxes are capped as income approaches six figures, and the working poor pay a much larger percentage of their income than do the wealthy. Such taxation for a family of two parents and two children earning $25,000 currently amounts to $3,825.

The Social Security system is a "defined benefit" plan, not a "defined contribution" plan. In other words, the amount to be paid is politically determined separate and apart from contributions. Retired adults over the next twenty years will receive many times their contribution—and those benefits will be subsidized by today's children. The actuarial liability to make those payments amounted to $10.1 trillion at the beginning of 2002. Interest on this accruing amount would properly place the actual current year federal deficit not at $534 billion, but at $930 billion.

These calculations do not include the Medicare entitlement obligation, perhaps the most troubling liability facing children. The Medicare accrued liability is estimated to reach $20 trillion by the time today's children have to pay the bill—one likely "off the top" from paychecks with required employer contribution as well. The number of taxpayers supporting seniors has declined from over four per senior to 2.3 as projected by 2020. The Social Security and Medicare payroll obligations imposed upon our children will amount to a debt on each of them of over $300,000 to be paid to current adults in their old age. If one were to impose the projected annual sum required after 2013 in today's dollars, a tax increase seven times the size of the Bush Administration's income tax cuts would be required to pay its annual bill.

These Medicare estimates do not include the recent addition of prescription drug benefits for seniors. This cost is estimated by the Congressional Budget Office at $851 billion between 2005 and 2015. This one new addition of $85 billion per year contrasts with the total new education promise of $15 billion and actual appropriations of $6 billion and the reversion of SCHIP money back to the treasury with 6 million children remaining medically uncovered.

The older adult beneficiaries are increasingly organized politically, vote at a high percentage, and have made their health and security essential campaign issues. Politicians otherwise favoring limited government and inveighing against state "welfare" vie to assure voters of their devotion to both Social Security and Medicare, and tout pension subsidies, as well as the tax cuts normally a part of their appeal to the public. The political power of the "Boomer" generation is buttressed by a dynamic well known by political operatives: The median age of those with sufficient disposable income to fund charities, public interest groups, and political campaigns, is well over 65, with the median age of large givers over 70 years of age.

The increasing private pension tax subsidies and reductions, safety net assurance, new sums for medical care, and other commitments to older adults are based on the obligation of society to its elders. Children as a group have traditionally enjoyed a commitment in balance—one protectively provided by many generations of adults investing in those who follow them. Older adults, with less than one-half of the poverty rate of children, and with medical coverage 6 million of them lack, alter that historical American intergenerational commitment.

---

1. Kaiser Family Foundation, *The President's Fiscal Year 2003 Budget: An Overview of Health Programs* (March 8, 2002) Chart 3 at 8, citing CBO estimates of January 2002.

2. Note that the People's Republic of China is the largest purchaser of U.S. debt. Conservative economists point to the danger of dependence on the world's largest totalitarian nation for U.S. deficit financing. Unlike private buyers within capitalist nations, the PRC can coordinate all of its purchasing policy as a single borrower. They argue that with a share of over 30% of all government deficit bonds, it is in a position more advantageous than the Arab oil nations upon whom the U.S. is dependent for oil supply. This position is significant because of the possible impact on interest rates in the U.S. At the same time, record numbers of Americans have purchased their homes in an inflated real estate market, or have borrowed close to its market value at variable interest rates. A relatively small increase in such rates by historical standards will create massive foreclosures and home ownership loss, particularly by working middle class and poor families with children.

3. See *Medi-Cal Growth 'Unsustainable', Study Says Revenue Can't Meet Costs as 5% of Clients Require 60% of the Spending* Capital Bureau, SACRAMENTO BEE, June 15, 2005 (commenting on the June 14, 2005 Report of the Public Policy Institute of California).

4. One factor explaining the continuing lack of medical coverage for so many children—notwithstanding Congressional intent and a generous match—is the continuing reliance on enrollment. States require laborious, affirmative acceptance of children one at a time, replete with paperwork and premiums, before coverage is granted. Those premiums are not co-pays to discourage overuse, but required advance monthly or quarterly payments—asked of parents who are often making barely enough to cover rent, utilities, food and clothing costs—and whose children are not ill when the money must be paid.

5. See www.cdpublications.com.

6. Center on Budget and Policy Priorities, *Overview Assessment of President Bush's Tax Proposal* (Washington, D.C.; February 15, 2001) at 1–2 (see www.cbpp.org).

2. Advocacy Strategies for Public Investment in Children

Child advocates have employed diverse and creative tactics to stimulate public investment in children, including:

* **A Minimum Floor.** A minimum percentage of general fund spending, or a special fund may be allocated for children. San Francisco's Children's Amendment (Proposition J) and California's Proposition 98 are examples of such alternatives. Sponsors of floors warn that such a floor may well become an effective ceiling. Further, any newly directed spending faces the risk of supplantation, as discussed above.

* **Special District or Other Special Fund Financing.** Florida allows for the formation by local vote of special districts to fund children's services.

* **Use of 501(c)(3) Status.** Most jurisdictions employ public counsel to represent abused children in court. Sacramento and other counties contract out that representation to an independent 501(c)(3) entity. That structure allows tax benefits to flow to private contributors, and removes conflicts of interest common where counsel employed by a county to represent a child also represents county agencies.

* **Bonds/Debt Instruments**. Bond financing is a substantial source of public capital investment—even to build prisons and other facilities which generate no return. Could one create a social service system, which demonstrably saves money through prevention? Why shouldn't such ventures be funded through general revenue bond sales, with the return on public savings designated for repayment?

* **Crime Victim Restitution Funds**. Almost every state has a crime victim restitution fund fed by court assessed fines *et al.* and the federal jurisdiction adds funds to each state's fund, declaring child victims to be of high priority for recompense, see 42 USC 10601 *et seq.* Such funds finance medical treatment and assistance for injured and traumatized youngsters. Many states impede child access, *e.g.*, by requiring traditional police reports when much child abuse is investigated civilly by child protective services. Expanding eligibility beyond police reports opens funding for children.

* **Leveraging Maximum Federal Dollars.** Most federal funding for children comes with a state match requirement. Federal funds tend not to supply the outreach monies needed to maximize participation. State investment in full participation leverages maximum use of available federal funds. For example, summer school, school breakfasts, and child care nutrition programs for impoverished

children are underutilized. Typically, state spending in these areas is less than 10% of the federal program dollars at issue. Often, additional state outreach dollars can yield a better than 5 to 1 ratio in additional federal dollars.

* **New Grants.** There are new grant opportunities emerging from the federal administration and from the private sector. From the latter: a new fund from Hewlett, a strong continuing commitment from the Annie Casey Foundation, a major effort from Carnegie, a Center for the Future of Children from Packard, a new Ford Foundation initiative, and others. Advocacy funding is growing as a foundation priority given the leveraged impact it has demonstrated.

* **Required Bulk Purchasing.** In the 1980s, national pharmaceutical companies successfully sponsored legislation within states to prohibit state bulk purchase of vaccines at a discount. Some states have won reversal of that policy and such bulk purchasing of products directed at impoverished children (such as vaccines and WIC nutritional supplements) saves substantial public monies, allowing more extensive coverage without appropriations increase.

* **Use of Existing Bureaucracy and Legal Regimes.** Even where paternity is known and child support orders are entered, child support collection is paltry. Over 25% of America's children are eligible for child support from an absent parent. Although collections have been increasing, they remain relatively trivial, with children of unwed parents receiving less than $45 per month each in support, on average. Over one-half of these children live below the poverty line. One possible improvement puts existing bureaucracies to work collecting support. For example, some states have given their state tax collection agencies the authority to collect support payments delinquent over 90 days. The advantages include: use of an existing bureaucracy already engaged in money collection, agency tie-in to the IRS sources of information for collection, and legal status as a "tax lien" which is not dischargeable.

* **Tax Expenditures**. As discussed above, tax expenditures have focused on organized interests, the elderly, and middle class adults. One major exception is the federal earned income tax credit (EITC) which provides substantial income to working poor parents earning near the poverty line. As a refundable tax credit, it is paid to an eligible family regardless of income or tax liability. The federal EITC can currently add up to $2,353 to the income of a working family with one child and up to $3,888 for families with two or more children. Only a few states have enacted state supplemental credits (*e.g.*, calculated at 10% to 30% of the federal credit). Such additions create substantial benefits for impoverished children, helping working families at the margin. Aside from allowances for dependents, the other major source of federal assistance is child care credits, but—as noted above—these have generally not been refundable and tend to benefit middle class families rather than children living in families near the poverty line.

* **Interest Deferral and Forgiveness**. Many states provide limited scholarships for students admitted to higher education institutions. The federal government and many states also provide loan assistance, including low interest loans, and interest deferral until after graduation. Expansion of these programs can leverage opportunity for youth.

* **Tuition Reductions**. In addition to providing additional funds for children, another alternative is to reduce costs which serve as a barrier to their advancement. Low tuition for community colleges and state university systems provides such a child-related public benefit.

* **Regulatory Cross Subsidies and Incentives**. Public investment in children can take the form of little discussed regulatory subsidies. Such subsidies

are often not a part of the continuing budget process, are not always subject to wide public debate, and continue automatically unless affirmatively ended. Such subsidies often involve rate or insurance systems which socialize costs for the benefit of those especially in need. Expansion of health insurance for children, or lower utility rates for the first increment of power usage by families with children are examples.

* **Industry fees.** Legislatures may address a social harm by allowing the financial assessment of an industry responsible for it. For example, in 1991 the California legislature enacted AB 2038 (Connelly) the Childhood Lead Poisoning Prevention Act, which assesses the paint and oil industries based on their contribution to environmental lead to pay for monitoring of children and mitigation. Although many of the firms in the assessed industries are reconstituted or different from those contributing to lead contamination, the court has upheld the fee's constitutionality.[27]

* ***Cy Pres* Funds.** Class action or private attorney general cases may allow for the creation of a residuary fund after all identifiable claimants are paid damages or restitution or where payment to victims directly may be impractical. *Cy pres* ("second best") relief allows courts to direct such sums disgorged from wrongdoers to the general benefit of the aggrieved group, or to a charity serving them. Organizations serving children can be eligible for such funds.

* **Punitive Damage Awards.** The primary purpose of punitive damages is to sanction a wrongdoer and to deter similar future conduct. But the incentive for a plaintiff or his counsel to add such a claim may not require its entire award to them. The named plaintiff may be one of many injured by the defendant. A statute allowing allocation of a portion of punitive damage awards to the broader group harmed, and/or to children's programs on a *cy pres* basis could spread their benefits to a larger population.

* **Special Products.** In 1992, the Children's Advocacy Institute sponsored legislation to create the California Kids' Plates Program, which added four new symbols to customized vehicle license plates (a child's handprint, a star, a heart, and a plus sign). Revenues from the sales of these special license plates, now reaching millions of dollars annually, are directed to a special fund for child care facility inspections, poison control centers, safety, child abuse prevention, and related purposes.

F. ADVOCACY FOR CHILDREN AND THE MEDIA

1. Story Selection: Setting the Public Agenda

Notwithstanding the disappointment of many child advocates with the evolution of news toward entertainment, it remains the major tool available to them given general public sympathy for children. Those public sentiments are of marginal use in direct public policy negotiations because of the skill of special interest public relations experts in framing their arguments around other commonly revered points of agreement. However, to the extent the media pays attention to issues and reports on the actions of public officials, underlying public priorities can affect public decisions. Media attention requires that the subject matter for attention relate somehow to the needs of children, that the "media agenda" as reflected in subject matter (story selection) includes their issues.

THE MEDIA AND THE COVERAGE OF CHILDREN*

By Robert C. Fellmeth

Kathie Lee Gifford faces the camera dramatically, her hair is uncharacteristically dishevelled; she looks a mess. She speaks in tremulous tones, about her outrage over accusations that the clothes sold under her name come from exploited children. Her appearance was preceded and followed by substantial attention to the issue of child labor. The trigger for the increased attention could have been the GATT treaty, but that was not a trigger. Nor was the trigger the gradual increase in child labor over the last decade—as international firms gravitate to the lowest common denominator for market advantage. Rather, it was a celebrity caught in a bind, boy bites dog—the "petty irony."

What the media chooses to cover may determine public policies. Our values are largely shaped by what we are thinking about. It is the subject matter of our thought—how much time and attention we devote to a problem that determines our priorities. They are especially important for the diffuse and future interests not well represented in Washington or state capitols. Although representing ethical sensibilities (to provide a better life for those who follow us)—these interests may depend on the bright light of repeated media attention.

The bias of story selection by journalists is not a matter of "liberal" or "conservative." It is a cultural phenomenon operating by predictable profession-specific rules. Journalists can be defensive about these biases, and often deny they exist. They not only exist, but can be catalogued.

The factors counting strongly toward "news" coverage include: (1) events involving a celebrity; (2) naughty sex or nudity (often at an adolescent-sniggering level); (3) violence; (4) a "contest," or an event involving a record; (5) something "cute" (*e.g.*, animals); (6) a story involving strong sentiment (*e.g.*, an individual rescue or sacrifice); (7) anything with an unexpected "twist," the petty irony noted above (*e.g.*, the EPA Director driving gas guzzling car); and (8) a story recently or contemporaneously covered elsewhere, or where there is a photograph or video tape available.

Increasingly, TV news has added coverage of the fictional characters of their respective network's entertainment offerings and characters—as actual news events.

Does what is put "on our table" by news editors define what is important for us to know among the thousands of events which occurred on a given day? Were scientific discoveries surveyed? Substantial acts of charity? A momentous institutional achievement by a foundation, or government agency or corporation? Most important, the abandonment of impoverished children by some mothers, many fathers?

One problem is that the media is not good at covering anything gradual, even if massive. There is no "handle." To cover it implies that the journalist *has* a bias, has made a *substantive* judgment that something warrants attention; believe it or not, such a judgment apart from the eight factors listed above, is commonly considered unprofessional.

We have to find a way to pay attention to a gradual process affecting the people we care the most about, to declare some subjects "stories" on some rational basis. And I do not mean the occasional feature or oblique try for the Pulitzer—I mean coverage, the kind of coverage that was given to Hugh Grant's tryst with a hooker (4 of the 7 factors: celebrity, sex, the petty irony of a leading man paying for sex, and coverage elsewhere). The kind of coverage given to Tom Cruise and Jennifer Lopez.

---

*Revised and excerpted from Robert C. Fellmeth, "Budget Advocacy for Children," *Children's Law, Policy and Practice*, National Association of Counsel for Children (1995) Chapter 14, at 323–34.

2. Child Advocacy Media Strategies

A child advocate engaged in media relations must be aware of the need for a recognized "handle" for story coverage or opinion piece entry. In general, such a handle must correspond to one or more of the factors listed above. For example, a story must be spun around an "event" which is a "record" or involves "conflict or a contest." A personal profile with pathos must be found. Such management is not dishonest, nor are all of the biases of the media irrational. The media depend upon market interest and whatever is featured must be *interesting* or somehow noteworthy.

One child advocate known for her media skill is Margaret Brodkin of Coleman Advocates for Children in San Francisco. During a recent December she had a parade of school children dragging their little red wagons to city hall to present their "wish list" to the Mayor. Santa Claus accompanied them, along with television cameras from the local news. When they arrived at the Mayor's office, apparently unexpected, Santa was seen trying to arrange for a short visit with the Mayor. "I'm sorry," said his secretary in the high ceilinged anteroom, "he is very busy and can't see you." Without missing a beat, Brodkin's Santa turned full face to the camera and intoned, "gee that's too bad, because, you see, this is Santa's busy time also." Coverage was pervasive and children's needs were on the table for discussion.

Questions for Discussion

1. Many child advocates argue that current juvenile dependency court confidentiality disadvantages child abuse victims. They point out that where an offense is committed by an adult against another adult, the entire process is public, but when a child is the victim most states invoke strong presumptive confidentiality. Allegedly, that secrecy impedes public coverage of the conditions leading to abuse and neglect, and to the plight of children in the foster care system. Other child advocates argue that confidentiality is important to protect the privacy of children. Is it possible to have a presumptively open system where counsel for the child (or perhaps other parties) can petition for a protective order in cases where the best interests of the child warrant confidentiality? What would be the political implications of more extensive coverage of these children?

2. Some political scientists are critical of legislative enactments (or other public policy decisions) driven by a single dramatic incident (statutes may be enacted based on (and even named after) a highly publicized child victim). The political scientists argue that such drama may skew outcomes to address what may be an unusual wrong, while creating injustices in more prevalent circumstances. On the other hand, the human consequences of public policies are important, and without the public attention they bring, child advocates argue that it is difficult to gain attention to counterbalance financially dominant special interest advocacy. How can these two concerns be reconciled?

3. Public officials who advocate new revenue for child investment—even when an economic downturn chokes off general fund spending for children in need—are ostentatiously labeled "tax and spenders." Does the media bear any responsibility for the common anathema to a tax increase to benefit children? Does a new tax expenditure for commercial interests depleting the general fund warrant equivalent public attention? Does it receive it? Do the consequences of not spending for children in need properly yield media discussion?[28]

ENDNOTES

[1] The Center for Responsive Politics data indicates that in 1992, the ten major campaign contribution sectors to Congressional campaigns gave 23% of their funds through the soft money vehicle, climbing to 54% by 2000 (see www.opensecrets.org; see also *Killing Us Softly: Soft Money's Phenomenal Growth and Its Harm to the Public,* Public Citizen's Congress Watch (Washington, D.C.; January 2001).

[2] *State Secrets: A Joint Investigation of Soft Money in the States,* National Institute on Money in State Politics (July 30, 2001). Only five states impose any limitation on national party contributions to state and local political parties. Thirty-six states do not prohibit corporate contributions to state and local parties, thirteen of which have no amount limitation. Twenty-two states have no limitation on PAC contributions to state parties, eighteen have no limitation on labor union contributions, and twenty have no limitation on individual contributions. Where limitations are applicable they generally range from $5,000 to $20,000 per election. *Survey of Campaign Finance Laws,* Common Cause (Washington, D.C.; 2001) Appendix A at 38-42.

[3] For a chart of state-level public financing arrangements and a listing of the funding sources drawn upon, see Center for Governmental Studies, CGS Publishes Comprehensive Overview of State Public Financing Laws," November 17, 2005 at www.cgs.org.

[4] 2001 H.R. 2356 (Shays, Meehan).

[5] For a discussion of the § 527 evasion of soft money reform, see Public Citizen, *Deja Vu Soft Money: Outlawed Contributions Likely to Flow to Shadowy 527 Groups that Skirt Flawed Disclosure Law* (Washington, D.C.; April 2002).

[6] The statute prohibits contributions from persons under 18 years of age to avoid multiplication of the limits for families with children. Would the same basic purpose be accomplished through a tighter maximum limit for children, *e.g.*, $100 for children 14 to 18 years of age and $20 for children from 5 to 14 years of age? Some child advocates argue that such limits would correspond more to possible contributions from child earnings without unduly expanding the maximum $2,000 limit for adults through the artifice of counting children. Would such a compromise provide opportunity to some children for the civics lesson benefit of contributing to candidates they support? Is a categorical ban constitutional, given this or other less restrictive alternatives?

[7] See *California Teachers Association v. Hayes*, 5 Cal. App. 4th 1513 (1992).

[8] See *Friends for All Children, Inc. v. Lockheed Aircraft*, 533 F. Supp. 895 (D. D.C. 1982).

[9] See *contra* the states of New Hampshire and Wisconsin, which require appointment of a *guardian ad litem* for a child in all disputed custody cases. Montana and several other states require a court to consider such an appointment and state for the record why one is not made.

[10] Omnibus Consolidated Rescissions and Appropriations Act of 1996, Pub. L. No. 104-134, § 504(a)(7).

[11] *Id.* at § 504(a)(18).

[12] In the 1950s, the state of Virginia attempted to prohibit the NAACP from encouraging African-American parents to file suits against segregated school systems. Its ban, which includes attorneys and non-attorneys (as does the Legal Services prohibition above), was overturned by the Supreme Court as an infringement on free speech. See *NAACP v. Button*, 371 U.S. 415 (1963).

[13] Omnibus Consolidated Rescissions and Appropriations Act of 1996, *supra* note 10, at § 504(a)(13).

[14] The (b)(1) class includes cases where the defendant is obliged to treat class members alike, or where members claim money from a fund insufficient to satisfy all claimants. The 23(b)(2) provision focuses on cases where broad, injunctive or declaratory relief is sought. Note that under some circumstances such injunctive relief may include restitution.

[15] See *Phillips Petroleum Co. v. Shutts*, 472 U.S. 797 (1985); see also *Norwest Mortgage, Inc. v. Superior Court of San Diego County*, 72 Cal. App. 4th 214 (1999). See also *In Re Asbestos Sch. Litig.,* 104 F.R.D. 422, 434 (E.D. Pa. 1984) (discussing the similarity of negligence and strict liability in U.S. jurisdictions) *aff'd in part and reversed in part sub nom*; *School Dist. of Lancaster v. Lake Asbestos, Ltd.* (*In re Sch. Asbestos Litig.*), 789 F.2d 996, 1010 (3d Cir. 1986), *cert. denied*, 479 U.S. 852 (1986).

[16] Defendants filed an appeal of this decision in November 2001. However, in order to avoid posting $145 billion in escrow until all appeals are complete, the defendants agreed to pay the plaintiff class almost $710 million—which the plaintiff class will keep regardless of the outcome. See Terri Somers, *Tobacco Appeals Record Payout* SUN-SENTINEL (Nov. 27, 2001) at 1B. *Query*: if one or more cases exhaust all or most of the tobacco companies' resources, is the resulting distribution adequately wide? The disproportionate remedy problem is even more pronounced in cases brought by individuals.

[17] For discussion of the need for such an amendment, with several additional provisions, see Hon. Charles D. Gill, *Essay on the Status of the American Child, 2000 AD: Chattel or Constitutionally Protected Child-Citizen?*, Children's Law Manual Series 1998, National Association of Counsel for Children, at 337.

[18] For a more extensive list of potential constitutional rights, see the excerpts of the United Nations' Convention on the Rights of the Child reproduced in the Postscript following Chapter 13.

[19] Although *Ex Parte Young* concerned allegedly unconstitutional state actions, the doctrine has been extended to violations of federal statute; see *e.g., Idaho v. Coeur d'Alene Tribe*, 521 U.S. 261, 281 (1997).

[20] The dissent in *Lopez* advanced two arguments: (1) gun sales, possession, and use by youth have significant effects on interstate commerce (including a lengthy appendix listing studies, reports and

references of those impacts); and (2) the distinction that federal jurisdiction should depend on a direct "commercial character" is not a useful basis for federal supremacy line-drawing. *Query*, how does the Court find gun regulation insufficiently in "commerce" (a matter of local health and safety precluding federal activity), and then invalidate state law allowing limited, local marijuana use for medicinal purposes? See *Gonzales v. Angel McClary Raich*, 125 S.Ct. 2195 (2005).

[21] See note 19.

[22] *Heart of Atlanta Motel v. U.S.*, 379 U.S. 241 (1964).

[23] Note that the criminal format of the statute was noted by and may have also influenced the majority, although if the "commercial" or "non-commercial" characterization is determinative—as the majority opinion implies, it is unclear how the criminal or civil format of the statute would be influential.

[24] For example, state bars exercising public police powers over attorneys commonly are governed by boards of practicing lawyers selected by a vote of their peers. Similarly, state medical boards include primarily practicing physicians, etc.

[25] Another option could be an independent advocacy office within state government empowered to intervene and represent children before different child-related agencies.

[26] See *e.g.*, Robert Fellmeth, *California's Legislative Graveyard for Children*, Sacramento Bee (Oct. 8, 2000).

[27] See *Sinclair Paint Co. v. State Board of Equalization*, 15 Cal. 4th 866 (1997).

[28] A revealing example of media value judgment comes from the coverage of a revenue increase proposed by California Governor Gray Davis in 2002. Facing a $23.5 billion state deficit—the largest such shortfall in the nation's history—the Governor included in his revised budget proposed on May 15, 2002 a tobacco tax and vehicle fee increase. The additional revenues amounted to less than 10% of the calculated deficit. Child advocates protested the new budget (see http://www.cbp.org). Some argued that the state and local tax burden (and general fund per child spending) was substantially below the percentage of personal income committed for children by the previous, less wealthy generation. Advocates argued that program spending cuts proposed on the same date concentrated on health, child care, safety net, and other child related accounts. They further argued that the cuts were planned during a state economic downturn and when federal safety net time deadlines were looming for impoverished families. The revised state budget presented a number of topics for possible media emphasis: (a) the cigarette/motor vehicle fee increase, (b) new tax expenditures for organized interests, (c) overall revenues/personal income reductions from previous levels, (d) substantial cuts to children in need, and (e) the consequences of such disinvestment. Is it a value-neutral decision to give the revenue increase more emphasis than the other four topics above? As much emphasis as the other four? Some media did include discussion of spending cuts, but front page headlines typically read something to the effect of "Governor Proposes Tax Increase" (see *e.g.*, *Davis Budget Seeks Tax Hikes*, San Diego Union Tribune (May 15, 2002) at 1; see also *Davis Seeks Tax Hikes to Bridge Gap*, Los Angeles Times (May 15, 2002) at 1; see also *Governor Backtracks on Budget. He Proposes Raising Taxes and Cutting Programs*, San Francisco Chronicle (May 15, 2002) at 1).

CHAPTER TWO

Reproductive Rights, Reproductive Responsibilities

A. POVERTY AND CHILDBEARING DECISIONS

Reproductive rights relate to deeply held views of morality, religion, and human purpose. How we decide to have children profoundly determines the world we create. Child advocates argue that currently children occur substantially as the happenstance byproduct of adult sexual pleasure. Surveys indicate that a majority of American babies born were not intended by either biological parent; fewer are the result of a commitment by two parents who intend and prepare for a new human being. Births to unwed mothers have risen to a 30% rate overall, and make up close to two-thirds of African-American births. The increase in unwed births (and single parenthood in general) is not confined to the poor, but has occurred across all income groups.

Because of continuing high rates of divorce and unwed births, over one-third of children in America will live with only one of their biological parents for most of their childhood—usually a mother. As discussed below, the financial assistance paid by absent parents subject to child support collection and received by the families caring for America's 19 million eligible children amounts to $45 per month per child.

1. Single-Parent Families, Unwed Births

a. Incidence, Relation to Poverty

Children living in two-parent families consistently have median household incomes three to five times the amount in female-headed single-parent households. The disparity holds for all ethnic groups.[1] The median income of a

All Races	MEDIAN INCOME	
	Married Parents	Female Single Parent
1 child, under 6	$40,938	$11,243
1 child, 6-17	$48,869	$18,050
2 or more children, all under 6	$40,952	$6,948
2 or more children, some under 6, some 6-17	$40,815	$9,742
2 or more children, all 6-17	$47,429	$16,330
No children	$39,766	$27,495

Table 2-A. U.S. Income of Families with Children: Married vs. Single Parents

married couple with children exceeds that of childless couples (partly reflecting couples waiting to have children a number of years after marriage and as incomes begin to rise).[2] The data indicate poverty for a large proportion of children in single parent households, and extreme poverty (generally defined as below one-half of the poverty line) for most of those single parent households with more than one young child.

In 2004, the poverty rate and the number in poverty for related children under 6 living in families were 19.9% and 4.7 million; of related children under 6 living in families with female householders with no husband present, 52.6% were in poverty, about five times the rate of their counterparts in married couple families (10.1%).[3] Table 2-B presents data on the poverty status of people in families with related children under 18 years of age.

	Married Couple with Children	Single Female with Children
All Races	8.9%	41.8%
White	5.2%	31.5%
African American	12.6%	49.1%
Hispanic	20.7%	51.8%

Table 2-B. Percent of Families with Related Children Under 18 in Poverty, 2004

National data from 2004 finds 49.6 million children living with two parents; 17 million live with only their mother; and 3.4 million live only with their father.[4] The 2004 median income of households with married couples present was $58,109, compared to $44,923 for households headed by a male, no wife present, and $29,826 for households headed by a female, no husband present.[5]

b. Exacerbating Factors: Multiple, Young Children, Unwed Births

Looking within the single parent population allows us to see which factors most correlate with extreme child poverty. In female-headed single parent households, 43.6% of the women have never been married, compared to 35.3% who are divorced, 17% who are separated, and 4.1% who are widowed.[6] For those women who have never married, the poverty rate is 54.5%, compared to 23.9% for those divorced, 18.5% for those separated, and 3.1% for those widowed.[7]

The breakdown by age of child indicates that youngest children—in greatest need of adequate nutrition for developing brains—fare the worst. The median income of unwed single mothers with children under 6 years of age sinks to $11,687.[8] And, as noted above, the number goes down further where there are two or more younger children in such families—to a median of just over $9,000 per year, to be divided between those additional children. A U.S. Census Bureau Population Report, covering data through 1998, concluded: "children under 6 remained particularly vulnerable....[R]elated children under age 6 living in families with a female householder, no husband present, had a poverty rate (54.8%) that was more than five times the rate for their counterparts in married-couple families (10.1%)."[9]

The close correlation between unwed births and child poverty holds true for all ethnic groups. The poverty rate of white children of single mothers is 40%, and for children under 6 the percentage grows to 50.4%. Among African-American children of unwed mothers, 55% live under the poverty line, and 60% of those under 6 years of age are below the line. Among Hispanic children living with single mothers, 60% live below the poverty line, and 67% of those under six years of age live in impoverished conditions.[10]

National income trends since 1969 show that income in constant dollars is up 10% for single mothers with children, down 8% for single fathers with children, and up a remarkable 25% for married couples with children—much of it driven by the increased work participation of married women.[11]

c. Trends in Single Parent Incidence

Despite the strong correlation between child poverty and single parenthood, the number of parents choosing single parenthood has grown substantially throughout the nation. The percentage of first births to unmarried women was static at 8% to 10% of all births from the 1930s through the 1960s. However, as Table 2-C indicates, the percentage of mothers giving birth to their first child without marriage almost doubled to 18% by the early 1970s, and over the subsequent twenty years, has more than doubled again, to 42% in 2003. These percentages count premarital births; another relatively constant 10% to 12% of births come from sexual acts conceiving children that occur prior to marriage.[12] As of the mid-1990s, for perhaps the first time in the nation's history, the majority of mothers giving birth to their first children conceived that child prior to marriage.[13]

Period	All Women
1970-74	18.0%
1980-84	29.6%
1990-94	40.5%
2003	42.0%

Table 2-C. U.S. Premarital First Birth Rates[14]

Parents choosing to have children without a second parent, divorcing, or parenting alone for other reasons more than doubled from 1974 to 1994. While one in seven families with children were headed by a single parent in 1970, by 1998 that number had increased to 28.8%; 40.4% of these were never married and 21.4% had been married but the spouse was absent from the home without a divorce. Only 34% derive from traditional divorces with court ordered child support and visitation rights defining parental involvement.[15]

Marriage, traditionally representing a formalized commitment to family, now has markedly lower incidence: in 1970, 71.7% of all adults (over 18) were married; in 1996 the percentage had declined to 60.3%—with the decrease attributable to roughly equal increases in divorce and in decisions not to marry at all.[16] However, the decision not to marry has not substantially influenced the decision to have children—with the incidence of childbirth outside of marriage growing markedly. In 1970, 40.3% of all households consisted of a married couple with children; by 1996 that percentage dropped to 25%.[17] The Bureau of the Census projections for the coming decade estimate an increase of single parent households with children from 24% to 28%—from 8 million such families to 9 million, including the addition of 800,000 more single mother families (from 6.4 to 7.2 million). Two parent families are projected to decline yet further, from 24.8 million in 1998 to 23.1 million by 2010.[18]

By 1996, unwed births accounted for as many single parent families as did divorce.[19] The 1998 to 2000 data show a remarkable growth in unwed-birth caused single parent families, then accounting for one million more children in single parent homes than were caused by divorce.

d. Unwed Teen Parents

The most comprehensive study of teen pregnancy nationally to date was released in November 1998, covering the 1990–95 period.[20] The national teen pregnancy rate was 83.6 per thousand, down 13% between 1990 and 1995. The decrease in pregnancies is attributed to somewhat less sexual activity and increased use of contraceptives.[21] However, pregnancy rates do not correspond to birth rates because of abortions (30% to 40% of teen pregnancies) or involuntary "fetal loss" (12% of teen pregnancies). The study found that the pregnancy reduction resulted in a substantial 21% abortion rate decline, but only a 9% teen birth rate decline.[22] Moreover, most of this decline occurred among married teens; the unwed teen birthrate nationally declined by only 1% during the five-year period.[23]

The study found almost one in ten teenage females becoming pregnant each of the study years. It found 51% of the women 15–19 years of age had sexual experience, and that 40% were "sexually active," defined as having had sexual intercourse within the prior 90 days.[24] The pregnancy rate within this sexually active group amounts to more than one in five becoming pregnant in 1995, with two-thirds of them choosing to give birth.[25] The study also noted that 78% of teen births are unintended; acknowledged some increases in contraceptive use, with rate of use at first intercourse increasing from 65% to 76% between 1988 and 1995; and found that 18% are not "current contraceptive users."[26] The data supports the conclusion that the minority not using contraception, or those using it improperly or inconsistently, account for an extraordinary fertility rate notwithstanding lack of pregnancy intent.

Trends to 2006 indicate continued high levels of sexual activity among high school students, notwithstanding a leveling from the early 1990s. In 1997, about one-half of high school students nationally had experience with sexual intercourse and about one-third was "sexually active."[27] Moreover, 90% of those in the "sexually experienced" category had sexual intercourse within the last year, and among those who were sexually active, 56% of males and 38% of women had experienced sex with two or more different partners. All of the high school survey figures discussed above are amplified by the inclusion in the sampled population of 12th grade students—down to 9th graders. The contraceptive use increase of 1982–95 among high schoolers nationally has lessened since 1995, particularly for those teens who are "sexually active."[28] Two other recent related trends also cause concern: an increase in sex by those under the age of 15, and a marked increase in Hispanic sexual activity.[29]

e. The Most Critical Factor: Unwed Births to Adult Women

The finding that unwed teen births are down somewhat must be placed in the context of the much higher teen pregnancy rates in the 1960s and 1970s. These and other data make clear that while teen pregnancies remain a serious problem, child poverty is driven substantially beyond the purview of that issue—by births to unwed mothers in general.[30] High unmarried incidence applies to all income and age groups.[31] The age breakdown is illustrative:

Age	Total Number of Unwed Births	White	Black	Hispanic
Under 15 years	6,469	1,353	2,633	2,224
15–19 years	337,201	132,482	93,918	97,925
20–24 years	549,353	224,941	155,153	146,729
25–29 years	287,205	101,454	80,087	91,644
30–34 years	147,555	52,167	39,926	46,995
35–39 years	69,071	26,352	18,400	20,158
40 years and over	19,141	8,242	4,714	4,945

Table 2-D. Groupings of Unwed Mothers[32]

Counts of families on welfare consistently find fewer than 2% headed by a mother under 18 years of age, and fewer than 5% under 20 years of age.[33] A somewhat larger percentage receiving support may have had their first child as a teen, thus placing themselves in economic jeopardy for later TANF need, particularly where they have additional children. National TANF surveys breaking down age of mother at first birth find substantially more African American and Hispanic women having their first babies at an earlier maternal age, with 40% of African American women and 33.7% of Hispanic women under 20 years of age when giving birth to their first child.[34] But women in all groups are giving birth in substantial numbers to their first children, as well as subsequent children, without husbands or other paternal commitment across the spectrum of their childbearing years.

The Centers for Disease Control and Prevention study "Nonmarital Childbearing in the United States, 1940–99" concluded: "Because of steep increases in birth rates for unmarried women aged 20 years and over and in the number of these women...the proportion of all nonmarital births that are to teenagers has dropped considerably."[35]

B. REPRODUCTIVE RESPONSIBILITY

1. Media and Culture

Cultural influences on personal decisions are momentous, and are substantially driven by the media, the entertainment industry, and commercial discourse—the sources of much public discussion in the modern era. A recent survey found the following self-identified information sources about sex for children 10–12 years of age: Mothers 38%, TV-Movies-Entertainment 38%, Schools and Teachers 38%, Fathers 34%, Friends 31%. For children 13–15 years of age, the five most acknowledged information sources change to: Friends 64%, TV-Movies-Entertainment 61%, Schools and Teachers 44%, Internet 40%, Mothers 38%.[36] The increased reliance on TV-Movies-Entertainment as adolescence begins is significant, particularly given its influence on the other leading source (friends).

A recent Children Now study of the incidence and content of sexual messages during television's "family hour" compared three-week periods of 8:00 p.m.–9:00 p.m. major network programming in 1976, 1986, and 1996, finding sexual content in 43% of the shows in 1976, rising to 65% in 1986, and 75% in 1996. Most important, the study found little mention of the consequences of sex:

pregnancy, a new human being with rights, at least 18 years of costs and support, and a lifetime of obligation.[37] Consistent with Children Now's findings, child advocates argue that the underlying problem with television, the entertainment industry, the Internet, and commercial advertising as they have evolved culturally is not that sex is discussed, but that its domination of story lines cumulatively imbalances developing priorities, and that its omissions are irresponsibly misleading.

Child advocates contend that the culture emphasizes the importance of allure to females and denigrates the traditional paternal male role—the steady provider, the reliable anchor. Forty-three percent of the fathers of the children of teen mothers are 20–24 years of age.[38] Two-thirds of pregnant and parenting teens were sexually abused by men (55% molested, 42% attempted rape, 44% raped).[39] Advocates argue that the problem indicated by these numbers is reflected in the comic book "macho-bravado" values promoted by action adventure entertainment and manifested in youth gang behavior. It is also the failure to emphasize as a legitimate image those male traits that are valuable to children, starting with a commitment to marriage and fatherhood. Or indeed, notwithstanding expressed respect for family values, to valorize women as mothers or grandmothers.

The impact of the cultural dissonance between how we are entertained and informed and how we should live—particularly *vis-à-vis* our reproductive decisions—is not confined to the adolescent population. The unwed birth rates to older women and paternal abandonment at all ages suggest a similar effect on the older audience. Those making incremental decisions as to what will be the news, entertainment, and advertising subject matter do not consider the cumulative effect of thousands of individual but similar decisions to focus on sexual allure. Child advocates argue that those decisions affect what adults and children think about—a matter arguably of greater import than the transmitted message itself.

2. The Reproductive Rights Debate

Competing political ideologies interact in a manner disadvantageous to the long range interests of children, as follows: (1) Most groups regard a direct state role in adult reproductive decisions as dangerous "social engineering." (2) However, liberals support state intervention to provide birth control and abortion options—including the public subsidy for the poor of both, but they oppose state measures to discourage unwed births—with the limited exception of teen pregnancies, which are politically correct to condemn. (3) Neo-conservatives favor policies that would: require women giving birth and eligible for welfare to work (at least within two years), limit lifetime cash safety net assistance to 60 months, and deny further assistance to a second child born to a woman receiving assistance. While these measures are intended to serve as an incentive for responsible adult procreation (children born to those able to afford their cost), they may gratuitously injure children. (4) Sexual conservatives oppose the abortion option, favoring required maternal birth of conceived children and supporting sexual abstinence as birth control. (5) Some judicial conservatives focus on the political process leading to reproductive policies, opposing judicial line-drawing due to the unelected status of judges and because the courts provide a poor forum for broad policy debate.

The contention between these points of view has informed constitutional argument in repeated cases. As sexual conservatives and neo-conservatives have sporadically obtained criminal prohibitions against birth control and abortion, those who disagree (liberals, libertarians) have argued that sexual matters are an area of privacy intended by the framers to be free from state intrusion, while judicial conservatives argue that the matters are constitutionally irrelevant and should be properly determined by electoral and legislative vote.

The context of reproductive rights and public policy now includes the rescission of child statutory "entitlement" to assured safety net support, and reductions or cut-off. What are the implications of child sustenance diminution? Would it be a more effective deterrent to pregnancies without financial means if the work requirement were not delayed two or more years and the cut-off not imposed after five years, but immediately? How would this affect the innocent children who would be penalized by such a regime? How would the various political groupings respond to an immediate means test (if you lack the means to provide for a child, he or she will be taken at birth for adoption)? Is there merit to the conclusion that the current delayed means test is the worst possible alternative for children, i.e. that the delay removes substantial deterrent impact on adult procreation decisions, while the cut off two to five years after birth will have permanent detrimental effects on impoverished children, who are then unlikely to be adopted elsewhere?

More generally, do future children have a stake in the reproductive rights of adults? What is that stake, and is it considered in the leading adjudications considering fundamental rights? What is the policy underpinning of constitutional holdings relating to adult procreative decisions? Are they based on a neutral "zone of privacy" concept? On the merits of the particular state intervention at issue? What part do the interests (and constitutional rights) of children play in the equations produced?

Griswold v. Connecticut
381 U.S. 479 (1965)

MR. JUSTICE DOUGLAS delivered the opinion of the Court.

Appellant Griswold is Executive Director of the Planned Parenthood League of Connecticut. Appellant Buxton is a licensed physician and a professor at the Yale Medical School who served as Medical Director for the League at its Center in New Haven—a center open and operating from November 1 to November 10, 1961, when appellants were arrested.

They gave information, instruction, and medical advice to *married persons* as to the means of preventing conception. They examined the wife and prescribed the best contraceptive device or material for her use. Fees were usually charged, although some couples were serviced free.

The statutes whose constitutionality is involved in this appeal are §§ 53-32 and 54-196 of the General Statutes of Connecticut.... The former provides:

> "Any person who uses any drug, medicinal article or instrument for the purpose of preventing conception shall be fined not less than fifty dollars or imprisoned not less than sixty days nor more than one year or be both fined and imprisoned."

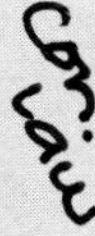

Section 54-196 provides:

> "Any person who assists, abets, counsels, causes, hires or com-

mands another to commit any offense may be prosecuted and punished as if he were the principal offender."

The appellants were found guilty as accessories and fined $100 each, against the claim that the accessory statute as so applied violated the Fourteenth Amendment.

* * *

Coming to the merits, we are met with a wide range of questions that implicate the Due Process Clause of the Fourteenth Amendment. Overtones of some arguments suggest that *Lochner v. New York*, 198 U.S. 45, should be our guide. But we decline that invitation as we did in *West Coast Hotel Co. v. Parrish*, 300 U.S. 379;...We do not sit as a super-legislature to determine the wisdom, need, and propriety of laws that touch economic problems, business affairs, or social conditions. This law, however, operates directly on an intimate relation of husband and wife and their physician's role in one aspect of that relation.

The association of people is not mentioned in the Constitution nor in the Bill of Rights. The right to educate a child in a school of the parents' choice—whether public or private or parochial—is also not mentioned. Nor is the right to study any particular subject or any foreign language. Yet the First Amendment has been construed to include certain of those rights.

By *Pierce v. Society of Sisters*, *supra*, the right to educate one's children as one chooses is made applicable to the States by the force of the First and Fourteenth Amendments. By *Meyer v. Nebraska*, *supra*, the same dignity is given the right to study the German language in a private school. In other words, the State may not, consistently with the spirit of the First Amendment, contract the spectrum of available knowledge. The right of freedom of speech and press includes not only the right to utter or to print, but the right to distribute, the right to receive, the right to read (*Martin v. Struthers*, 319 U.S. 141, 143) and freedom of inquiry, freedom of thought, and freedom to teach (see *Wieman v. Updegraff*, 344 U.S. 183, 195)—indeed the freedom of the entire university community....Without those peripheral rights the specific rights would be less secure....

* * *

The foregoing cases suggest that specific guarantees in the Bill of Rights have penumbras, formed by emanations from those guarantees that help give them life and substance....Various guarantees create zones of privacy. The right of association contained in the penumbra of the First Amendment is one, as we have seen. The Third Amendment in its prohibition against the quartering of soldiers "in any house" in time of peace without the consent of the owner is another facet of that privacy. The Fourth Amendment explicitly affirms the "right of the people to be secure in their persons, houses, papers, and effects, against unreasonable searches and seizures." The Fifth Amendment in its Self-Incrimination Clause enables the citizen to create a zone of privacy which government may not force him to surrender to his detriment. The Ninth Amendment provides: "The enumeration in the Constitution, of certain rights, shall not be construed to deny or disparage others retained by the people."

* * *

The present case, then, concerns a relationship lying within the zone of privacy created by several fundamental constitutional guarantees. And it concerns a law which, in forbidding the *use* of contraceptives rather than regulating their manufacture or sale, seeks to achieve its goals by means having a maximum destructive impact upon that relationship. Such a law cannot stand in light of the familiar principle, so often applied by this Court, that a "governmental purpose to control or prevent activities constitutionally subject to state regulation may not be achieved by means which sweep unnecessarily broadly and thereby invade the area of protected freedoms." *NAACP v. Alabama*, 377 U.S. 288, 307. Would we allow the police to search the sacred precincts of marital bedrooms for telltale signs of the use of contraceptives? The very idea is repulsive to the notions of privacy surrounding the marriage relationship.

We deal with a right of privacy older than the Bill of Rights—older than our political parties, older than our school system. Marriage is a coming together for better or for worse, hopefully enduring, and intimate to the degree of being sacred. It is an association that promotes a way of life, not causes; a harmony in living, not political faiths; a bilateral loyalty, not commercial or social projects. Yet it is an association for as noble a purpose as any involved in our prior decisions.

Reversed.

* * *

Mr. Justice Black, with whom **Mr. Justice Stewart** joins, dissenting.

I agree with my Brother Stewart's dissenting opinion. And like him I do not to any extent whatever base my view that this Connecticut law is constitutional on a belief that the law is wise or that its policy is a good one....

* * *

Had the doctor defendant here, or even the nondoctor defendant, been convicted for doing nothing more than expressing opinions to persons coming to the clinic that certain contraceptive devices, medicines or practices would do them good and would be desirable, or for telling people how devices could be used, I can think of no reasons at this time why their expressions of views would not be protected by the First and Fourteenth Amendments, which guarantee freedom of speech....But speech is one thing; conduct and physical activities are quite another....The two defendants here were active participants in an organization which gave physical examinations to women, advised them what kind of contraceptive devices or medicines would most likely be satisfactory for them, and then supplied the devices themselves, all for a graduated scale of fees, based on the family income. Thus these defendants admittedly engaged with others in a planned course of conduct to help people violate the Connecticut law. Merely because some speech was used in carrying on that conduct—just as in ordinary life some speech accompanies most kinds of conduct—we are not in my view justified in holding that the First Amendment forbids the State to punish their conduct....

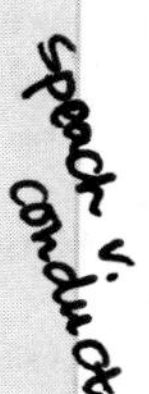

The Court talks about a constitutional "right of privacy" as though there is some constitutional provision or provisions forbidding any law ever to be passed which might abridge the "privacy" of individuals. But there is not. There are, of course, guarantees in certain specific constitutional provisions which are designed in part to protect privacy at certain times and places with respect to certain activities. Such, for example, is the Fourth Amendment's guarantee against "unreasonable searches and seizures." But I think it belittles that Amendment to talk about it as though it protects nothing but "privacy."...

One of the most effective ways of diluting or expanding a constitutional guarantee another word or words, more or less flexible and more or less restricted in meaning. This fact is well illustrated by the use of the term "right of privacy" as a comprehensive substitute for the Fourth Amendment's guarantee against "unreasonable searches and seizures." "Privacy" is a broad, abstract and ambiguous concept which can easily be shrunken in meaning but which can

> also, on the other hand, easily be interpreted as a constitutional ban against many things other than searches and seizures....
>
> * * *

The first ten amendments to the federal constitution do not address private action. They were drafted because of the framers' suspicion of centralized governmental power—"state action." Since the primary fear in 1787 was the possible coercive power of the newly formed federal authority, they explicitly focus on the limitation of federal powers *vis-a-vis* the citizenry. In order to impede the power of the sovereign states, protections must be considered to be within the due process and equal protection guarantees of the 14th Amendment—an amendment which explicitly applies to the states as well. Hence, until the 1960s, constitutional law was unclear as to whether one or all of the traditional constitutional guarantees of speech, search and seizure protection, *et al.* (the first eight amendments) would be considered a part of the 14th Amendment and hence limit state as well as federal acts.

This setting explains the references of Douglas to the inclusion or exclusion of various amendments and protections, including marital privacy interests of *Griswold*, within the 14th Amendment. Such inclusion was required for such a "penumbral" privacy right to apply to the state of Connecticut. Justice Goldberg's concurring opinion argued that the mention of eight enumerated freedoms did not imply an exhaustive list. They are framed in light of the specific grievances of 1787. The Ninth Amendment implies a recognition of such additional freedoms and Goldberg would include the freedom to make marital decisions within such an *a fortiori* zone.

Questions for Discussion

1. What are the implications of a declared reservoir of presumed basic rights within the constitution and applicable to the states *vis-à-vis* children? Clearly, a child is a person entitled to some constitutional protection; is that protection different given the helplessness of the child? Do those rights include only speech/privacy/belief rights? What about state action that deprives citizens of life or health? Can the state be affirmatively obligated to protect endangered children? To provide sustenance? Emergency medical care? What would trigger such affirmative obligations for the state under current constitutional doctrine?

2. Is it reasonable to cite the precise language of the founders as the outer limit of state intrusion or minority protection? Are the first eight amendments limited to their precise subject matter in protecting individuals from state intrusion, or do they imply that other, more egregious, intrusions are similarly prohibited?

3. Do many of our criminal prohibitions have an ethical base shared by religious leaders? If a religious doctrine is hostile to sexual liberties, does that preclude society from dealing with the same issue? Assuming that there is a legitimate social issue and impact apart from religious beliefs, and that persons are not compelled to engage affirmatively in the practice of religions other than their own, may not the "religion based" moral precepts of the majority be reflected in the criminal code? Do not many criminal prohibitions relate to the Ten Commandments? Does their enforcement thereby violate the religious rights of "non-believers" who violate their terms?

4. If the list of freedoms cited in the Constitution is to be expanded based on rights of "privacy," where is the bright line to demark the limits of majority rule? Is it based on the perceived wisdom of a particular state requirement? By its degree of coercion? By its intrusiveness? By its connection with religious values? By its infringement on the conflicting rights or legitimate needs of others, particularly vulnerable groups?

Roe v. Wade
410 U.S. 113 (1973)

Mr. Justice Blackmun delivered the opinion of the Court.

* * *

We forthwith acknowledge our awareness of the sensitive and emotional nature of the abortion controversy, of the vigorous opposing views, even among physicians, and of the deep and seemingly absolute convictions that the subject inspires. One's philosophy, one's experiences, one's exposure to the raw edges of human existence, one's religious training, one's attitudes toward life and family and their values, and the moral standards one establishes and seeks to observe, are all likely to influence and to color one's thinking and conclusions about abortion.

* * *

...[W]e have inquired into, and in this opinion place some emphasis upon, medical and medical-legal history and what that history reveals about man's attitudes toward the abortion procedure over the centuries. We bear in mind, too, Mr. Justice Holmes' admonition in his now-vindicated dissent in *Lochner v. New York*, 198 U.S. 45, 76 (1905):

> "[The Constitution] is made for people of fundamentally differing views, and the accident of our finding certain opinions natural and familiar or novel and even shocking ought not to conclude our judgment upon the question whether statutes embodying them conflict with the Constitution of the United States."

I

The Texas statutes that concern us here...make it a crime to "procure an abortion," as therein defined, or to attempt one, except with respect to "an abortion procured or attempted by medical advice for the purpose of saving the life of the mother." Similar statutes are in existence in a majority of the States....

Texas first enacted a criminal abortion statute in 1854....This was soon modified into language that has remained substantially unchanged to the present time....The final article in each of these compilations provided the same exception, as does the present Article 1196, for an abortion by "medical advice for the purpose of saving the life of the mother."

* * *

V

The principal thrust of appellant's attack on the Texas statutes is that they improperly invade a right, said to be possessed by the pregnant woman, to choose to terminate her pregnancy. Appellant would discover this right in the concept of personal "liberty" embodied in the Fourteenth Amendment's Due Process Clause; or in personal, marital, familial, and sexual privacy said to be protected by the Bill of Rights or its penumbras, see *Griswold v. Connecticut*, 381 U.S. 479 (1965)....

VI

It perhaps is not generally appreciated that the restrictive criminal abortion laws in effect in a majority of States today are of relatively recent vintage. Those laws, generally proscribing abortion or its attempt at any time during pregnancy except when necessary to preserve the pregnant woman's life, are not of ancient or even of common-law origin. Instead, they derive from statutory changes effected, for the most part, in the latter half of the 19th century.

* * *

...*The American law*. In this country, the law in effect in all but a few States until mid-19th century was the pre-existing English common law. Connecticut, the first State to enact abortion legislation, adopted in 1821 that part of Lord Ellenborough's Act that related to a woman "quick with child."...The death penalty was not imposed. Abortion before quickening was made a crime in that State only in 1860....In 1828, New York enacted legislation...that, in two respects, was to serve as a model for early anti-abortion statutes. First, while barring destruction of an unquickened fetus as well as a quick fetus, it made the former only a misdemeanor, but the latter second-degree manslaughter. Second, it incorporated a concept of therapeutic abortion by providing that an abortion was excused if it "shall have been necessary to preserve the life of such mother, or shall have been advised by two physicians to be necessary for such purpose." By 1840, when Texas had received the common law,...only eight American States had statutes dealing with abortion....It was not until after the War Between the States that legislation began generally to replace the common law. Most of these initial statutes dealt severely with abortion after quickening but were lenient with it before quickening. Most punished attempts equally with completed abortions. While many statutes included the exception for an abortion thought by one or more physicians to be necessary to save the mother's life, that provision soon disappeared and the typical law required that the procedure actually be necessary for that purpose.

Gradually, in the middle and late 19th century the quickening distinction disappeared from the statutory law of most States and the degree of the offense and the penalties were increased. By the end of the 1950's, a large majority of the jurisdictions banned abortion, however and whenever performed, unless done to save or preserve the life of the mother....

It is thus apparent that at common law, at the time of the adoption of our Constitution, and throughout the major portion of the 19th century, abortion was viewed with less disfavor than under most American statutes currently in effect. Phrasing it another way, a woman enjoyed a substantially broader right to terminate a pregnancy than she does in most States today. At least with respect to the early stage of pregnancy, and very possibly without such a limitation, the opportunity to make this choice was present in this country well into the 19th century. Even later, the law continued for some time to treat less punitively an abortion procured in early pregnancy.

* * *

VII

Three reasons have been advanced to explain historically the enactment of criminal abortion laws in the 19th century and to justify their continued existence.

It has been argued occasionally that these laws were the product of a Victorian social concern to discourage illicit sexual conduct. Texas, however, does not advance this justification in the present case, and it appears that no court or commentator has taken the argument seriously....The appellants and amici contend, moreover, that this is not a proper state purpose at all and suggest that, if it were, the Texas statutes are overbroad in protecting it since the law fails to distinguish between married and unwed mothers.

A second reason is concerned with abortion as a medical procedure. When most criminal abortion laws were first enacted, the procedure was a hazardous one for the woman....Thus, it has been argued that a State's real concern in enacting a criminal abortion law was to protect the pregnant woman, that is, to restrain her from submitting to a procedure that placed her life in serious jeopardy.

Modern medical techniques have altered this situation. Appellants and various amici refer to medical data indicating that abortion in early pregnancy, that is, prior to the end of the first trimester, although not without its risk, is now relatively safe. Mortality rates for women undergoing early abortions, where the procedure is legal, appear to be as low as or lower than the rates for normal childbirth....Consequently, any interest of the State in protecting the woman from an inherently hazardous procedure, except when it would be equally dangerous for her to forgo it, has largely disappeared. Of course, important state interests in the areas of health and medical standards do remain. The State has a legitimate interest in seeing to it that abortion, like any other medical procedure, is performed under circumstances that insure maximum safety for the patient. This interest obviously extends at least to the performing physician and his staff, to the facilities involved, to the availability of after-care, and to adequate provision for any complication or emergency that might arise. The prevalence of high mortality rates at illegal "abortion mills" strengthens, rather than weakens, the State's interest in regulating the conditions under which abortions are performed. Moreover, the risk to the woman increases as her pregnancy continues. Thus, the State retains a definite interest in protecting the woman's own health and safety when an abortion is proposed at a late stage of pregnancy.

The third reason is the State's interest—some phrase it in terms of duty—in protecting prenatal life. Some of the argument for this justification rests on the theory that a new human life is present from the moment of conception....The State's interest and general obligation to protect life then extends, it is argued, to prenatal life. Only when the life of the pregnant mother herself is at stake, balanced against the life she carries within her, should the interest of the embryo or fetus not prevail. Logically, of course, a legitimate state interest in this area need not stand or fall on acceptance of the belief that life begins at conception or at some other point prior to live birth. In assessing the State's interest, recognition may be given to the less rigid claim that as long as at least *potential* life is involved, the State may assert interests beyond the protection of the pregnant woman alone.

Parties challenging state abortion laws have sharply disputed in some courts the contention that a purpose of these laws, when enacted, was to protect prenatal life....Pointing to the absence of legislative history to support the contention, they claim that most state laws were designed solely to protect the woman. Because medical advances have lessened this concern, at least with respect to abortion in early pregnancy, they argue that with respect to such abortions the laws can no longer be justified by any state interest. There is some scholarly support for this view of original purpose....The few state courts called upon to interpret their laws in the late 19th and early 20th centuries did focus on the State's interest in protecting the woman's health rather than in preserving the embryo and fetus. Proponents of this view point out that in many States, including Texas, by statute or judicial interpretation, the pregnant woman herself could not be prosecuted for self-abortion or for cooperating in an abortion performed upon her by another. They claim that adoption of the "quickening" distinction through received common law and state statutes tacitly recognizes the greater health hazards inherent in late abortion and impliedly repudiates the theory that life begins at conception.

It is with these interests, and the weight to be attached to them, that this case is concerned.

VIII

The Constitution does not explicitly mention any right of privacy. In a line of decisions, however, going back perhaps as far as *Union Pacific R. Co. v. Botsford*, 141 U.S. 250, 251 (1891), the Court has recognized that a right of personal privacy, or a guarantee of certain areas or zones of privacy, does exist under the Constitution. In varying contexts, the Court or individual Justices have, indeed, found at least the roots of that right in the First Amendment,...in the Fourth and Fifth Amendments,...in the penumbras of the Bill of Rights,...or in the concept of liberty guaranteed by the first section of the Fourteenth Amendment.... These decisions make it clear that only personal rights that can be deemed "fundamental" or "implicit in the concept of ordered liberty,"...are included in this guarantee of personal privacy. They also make it clear that the right has some extension to activities relating to marriage...; procreation...; contraception...; family relationships...; and child rearing and education....

This right of privacy, whether it be founded in the Fourteenth Amendment's concept of personal liberty and restrictions upon state action, as we feel it is, or, as the District Court determined, in the Ninth Amendment's reservation of rights to the people, is broad enough to encompass a woman's decision whether or not to terminate her pregnancy. The detriment that the State would impose upon the pregnant woman by denying this choice altogether is apparent. Specific and direct harm medically diagnosable even in early pregnancy may be involved. Maternity, or additional offspring, may force upon the woman a distressful life and future. Psychological harm may be imminent. Mental and physical health may be taxed by child care. There is also the distress, for all concerned, associated with the unwanted child, and there is the problem of bringing a child into a family already unable, psychologically and otherwise, to care for it. In other cases, as in this one, the additional difficulties and continuing stigma of unwed motherhood may be involved. All these are factors the woman and her responsible physician necessarily will consider in consultation.

On the basis of elements such as these, appellant and some *amici* argue that the woman's right is absolute and that she is entitled to terminate her pregnancy at whatever time, in whatever way, and for whatever reason she alone chooses. With this we do not agree. Appellant's arguments that Texas either has no valid interest at all in regulating the abortion decision, or no interest strong enough to support any limitation upon the woman's sole determination, are unpersuasive. The Court's decisions recognizing a right of privacy also acknowledge that some state regulation in areas protected by that right is appropriate. As noted above, a State may properly assert important interests in safeguarding health, in maintaining medical standards, and in protecting potential life. At some point in pregnancy, these respective interests become sufficiently compelling to sustain regulation of the factors that govern the abortion decision. The privacy right involved, therefore, cannot be said to be absolute. In fact, it is not clear to us that the claim asserted by some amici that one has an unlimited right to do with one's body as one pleases bears a close relationship to the right of privacy previously articulated in the Court's decisions. The Court has refused to recognize an unlimited right of this kind in the past. *Jacobson v. Massachusetts*, 197 U.S. 11 (1905) (vaccination); *Buck v. Bell*, 274 U.S. 200 (1927) (sterilization).

We, therefore, conclude that the right of personal privacy includes the abortion decision, but that this right is not unqualified and must be considered against important state interests in regulation.

* * *

Where certain "fundamental rights" are involved, the Court has held that regulation limiting these rights may be justified only by a "compelling state interest,"...and that legislative enactments must be narrowly drawn to express only the legitimate state interests at stake....

* * *

The Constitution does not define "person" in so many words. Section 1 of the Fourteenth Amendment contains three references to "person." The first, in defining "citizens," speaks of "persons born or naturalized in the United States." The word also appears both in the Due Process Clause and in the Equal Protection Clause. "Person" is used in other places in the Constitution....But in nearly all these instances, the use of the word is such that it has application only postnatally. None indicates, with any assurance, that it has any possible pre-natal application.[54]

All this, together with our observation, *supra*, that throughout the major portion of the 19th century prevailing legal abortion practices were far freer than they are today, persuades us that the word "person," as used in the Fourteenth Amendment, does not include the unborn....This is in accord with the results reached in those few cases where the issue has been squarely presented....

* * *

B. The pregnant woman cannot be isolated in her privacy. She carries an embryo and, later, a fetus, if one accepts the medical definitions of the developing young in the human uterus....The situation therefore is inherently different from marital intimacy, or bedroom possession of obscene material, or marriage, or procreation, or education, with which *Eisenstadt* and *Griswold*, *Stanley*, *Loving*, *Skinner*, and *Pierce* and *Meyer* were respectively concerned. As we have intimated above, it is reasonable and appropriate for a State to decide that at some point in time another interest, that of health of the mother or that of potential human life, becomes significantly involved. The woman's privacy is no longer sole and any right of privacy she possesses must be measured accordingly.

Texas urges that, apart from the Fourteenth Amendment, life begins at conception and is present throughout pregnancy, and that, therefore, the State has a compelling interest in protecting that life from and after conception. We need

---

[54] When Texas urges that a fetus is entitled to Fourteenth Amendment protection as a person, it faces a dilemma. Neither in Texas nor in any other State are all abortions prohibited. Despite broad proscription, an exception always exists. The exception contained in Art. 1196, for an abortion procured or attempted by medical advice for the purpose of saving the life of the mother, is typical. But if the fetus is a person who is not to be deprived of life without due process of law, and if the mother's condition is the sole determinant, does not the Texas exception appear to be out of line with the Amendment's command?

There are other inconsistencies between Fourteenth Amendment status and the typical abortion statute. It has already been pointed out,...that in Texas the woman is not a principal or an accomplice with respect to an abortion upon her. If the fetus is a person, why is the woman not a principal or an accomplice? Further, the penalty for criminal abortion specified by Art. 1195 is significantly less than the maximum penalty for murder prescribed by Art. 1257 of the Texas Penal Code. If the fetus is a person, may the penalties be different?

not resolve the difficult question of when life begins. When those trained in the respective disciplines of medicine, philosophy, and theology are unable to arrive at any consensus, the judiciary, at this point in the development of man's knowledge, is not in a position to speculate as to the answer.

* * *

In areas other than criminal abortion, the law has been reluctant to endorse any theory that life, as we recognize it, begins before live birth or to accord legal rights to the unborn except in narrowly defined situations and except when the rights are contingent upon live birth. For example, the traditional rule of tort law denied recovery for prenatal injuries even though the child was born alive....That rule has been changed in almost every jurisdiction. In most States, recovery is said to be permitted only if the fetus was viable, or at least quick, when the injuries were sustained, though few courts have squarely so held....In a recent development, generally opposed by the commentators, some States permit the parents of a stillborn child to maintain an action for wrongful death because of prenatal injuries....Such an action, however, would appear to be one to vindicate the parents' interest and is thus consistent with the view that the fetus, at most, represents only the potentiality of life. Similarly, unborn children have been recognized as acquiring rights or interests by way of inheritance or other devolution of property, and have been represented by guardians *ad litem*....Perfection of the interests involved, again, has generally been contingent upon live birth. In short, the unborn have never been recognized in the law as persons in the whole sense.

X

In view of all this, we do not agree that, by adopting one theory of life, Texas may override the rights of the pregnant woman that are at stake. We repeat, however, that the State does have an important and legitimate interest in preserving and protecting the health of the pregnant woman, whether she be a resident of the State or a nonresident who seeks medical consultation and treatment there, and that it has still another important and legitimate interest in protecting the potentiality of human life. These interests are separate and distinct. Each grows in substantiality as the woman approaches term and, at a point during pregnancy, each becomes "compelling."

With respect to the State's important and legitimate interest in the health of the mother, the "compelling" point, in the light of present medical knowledge, is at approximately the end of the first trimester. This is so because of the now-established medical fact, referred to above at 149, that until the end of the first trimester mortality in abortion may be less than mortality in normal childbirth. It follows that, from and after this point, a State may regulate the abortion procedure to the extent that the regulation reasonably relates to the preservation and protection of maternal health. Examples of permissible state regulation in this area are requirements as to the qualifications of the person who is to perform the abortion; as to the licensure of that person; as to the facility in which the procedure is to be performed, that is, whether it must be a hospital or may be a clinic or some other place of less-than-hospital status; as to the licensing of the facility; and the like.

This means, on the other hand, that, for the period of pregnancy prior to this "compelling" point, the attending physician, in consultation with his patient, is free to determine, without regulation by the State, that, in his medical judgment, the patient's pregnancy should be terminated. If that decision is reached, the judgment may be effectuated by an abortion free of interference by the State.

With respect to the State's important and legitimate interest in potential life, the "compelling" point is at viability. This is so because the fetus then presumably has the capability of meaningful life outside the mother's womb. State regulation protective of fetal life after viability thus has both logical and biological justifications. If the State is interested in protecting fetal life after viability, it may go so far as to proscribe abortion during that period, except when it is necessary to preserve the life or health of the mother.

* * *

Mr. Justice Rehnquist, dissenting.

* * *

I

Even if there were a plaintiff in this case capable of litigating the issue which the Court decides, I would reach a conclusion opposite to that reached by the Court. I have difficulty in concluding, as the Court does, that the right of "privacy" is involved in this case. Texas, by the statute here challenged, bars the performance of a medical abortion by a licensed physician on a plaintiff such as Roe. A transaction resulting in an operation such as this is not "private" in the ordinary usage of that word. Nor is the "privacy" that the Court finds here even a distant relative of the freedom from searches and seizures protected by the Fourth Amendment to the Constitution, which the Court has referred to as embodying a right to privacy. ., 389 U.S. 347 (1967).

If the Court means by the term "privacy" no more than that the claim of a person to be free from unwanted state regulation of consensual transactions may be a form of "liberty" protected by the Fourteenth Amendment, there is no doubt that similar claims have been upheld in our earlier decisions on the basis of that liberty. I agree with the statement of Mr. Justice Stewart in his concurring opinion that the "liberty," against deprivation of which without due process the Fourteenth Amendment protects, embraces more than the rights found in the Bill of Rights. But that liberty is not guaranteed absolutely against deprivation, only against deprivation without due process of law. The test traditionally applied in the area of social and economic legislation is whether or not a law such as that challenged has a rational relation to a valid state objective.... The Due Process Clause of the Fourteenth Amendment undoubtedly does place a limit, albeit a broad one, on legislative power to enact laws such as this. If the Texas statute were to prohibit an abortion even where the mother's life is in jeopardy, I have little doubt that such a statute would lack a rational relation to a valid state objective under the test stated in *Williamson, supra*. But the Court's sweeping invalidation of any restrictions on abortion during the first trimester is impossible to justify under that standard, and the conscious weighing of competing factors that the Court's opinion apparently substitutes for the established test is far more appropriate to a legislative judgment than to a judicial one.

* * *

The fact that a majority of the States reflecting, after all, the majority sentiment in those States, have had restrictions on abortions for at least a century is a strong indication, it seems to me, that the asserted right to an abortion is not "so rooted in the traditions and conscience of our people as to be ranked as fundamental," *Snyder v. Massachusetts*, 291 U.S. 97, 105 (1934). Even today, when society's views on abortion are changing, the very existence of the debate is evidence that the "right" to an abortion is not so universally accepted as the appellant would have us believe.

To reach its result, the Court necessarily has had to find within the scope of the Fourteenth Amendment a right that was apparently completely unknown to the drafters of the Amendment. As early as 1821, the first state law dealing directly with abortion was enacted by the Connecticut Legislature....By the time of the adoption of the Fourteenth Amendment in 1868, there were at least 36 laws enacted by state or territorial legislatures limiting abortion....While many States have amended or updated their laws, 21 of the laws on the books in 1868 remain in effect today....Indeed, the Texas statute struck down today was, as the majority notes, first enacted in 1857 and "has remained substantially unchanged to the present time."....

There apparently was no question concerning the validity of this provision or of any of the other state statutes when the Fourteenth Amendment was adopted. The only conclusion possible from this history is that the drafters did not intend to have the Fourteenth Amendment withdraw from the States the power to legislate with respect to this matter.

III

Even if one were to agree that the case that the Court decides were here, and that the enunciation of the substantive constitutional law in the Court's opinion were proper, the actual disposition of the case by the Court is still difficult to justify. The Texas statute is struck down *in toto*, even though the Court apparently concedes that at later periods of pregnancy Texas might impose these selfsame statutory limitations on abortion. My understanding of past practice is that a statute found to be invalid as applied to a particular plaintiff, but not unconstitutional as a whole, is not simply "struck down" but is, instead, declared unconstitutional as applied to the fact situation before the Court....

For all of the foregoing reasons, I respectfully dissent.

Planned Parenthood of Southeastern Pennsylvania v. Casey
(1992) 505 U.S. 833

Justice O'Connor, **Justice Kennedy**, and **Justice Souter** announced the judgment of the Court and delivered the opinion of the Court with respect to Parts I, II, III, V-A, V-C, and VI, an opinion with respect to Part V-E, in which **Justice Stevens** joins, and an opinion with respect to Parts IV, V-B, and V-D.

I

Liberty finds no refuge in a jurisprudence of doubt. Yet 19 years after our holding that the Constitution protects a woman's right to terminate her pregnancy in its early stages, *Roe v. Wade*, 410 U.S. 113 (1973), that definition of liberty is still questioned. Joining the respondents as *amicus curiae*, the United States, as it has done in five other cases in the last decade, again asks us to overrule *Roe*....

At issue in these cases are five provisions of the Pennsylvania Abortion Control Act of 1982 as amended in 1988 and 1989....The Act requires that a woman seeking an abortion give her informed consent prior to the abortion procedure, and specifies that she be provided with certain information at least 24 hours before the abortion is performed....For a minor to obtain an abortion, the Act requires the informed consent of one of her parents, but provides for a judicial bypass option if the minor does not wish to or cannot obtain a parent's consent....Another provision of the Act requires that, unless certain exceptions apply, a married woman seeking an abortion must sign a statement indicating that she has notified her husband of her intended abortion....The Act exempts compliance with these three requirements in the event of a "medical emergency," which is defined in § 3203 of the Act....In addition to the above provisions regulating the performance of abortions, the Act imposes certain reporting requirements on facilities that provide abortion services....

* * *

After considering the fundamental constitutional questions resolved by *Roe*, principles of institutional integrity, and the rule of *stare decisis*, we are led to conclude this: the essential holding of *Roe v. Wade* should be retained and once again reaffirmed.

It must be stated at the outset and with clarity that *Roe*'s essential holding, the holding we reaffirm, has three parts. First is a recognition of the right of the woman to choose to have an abortion before viability and to obtain it without undue interference from the State. Before viability, the State's interests are not strong enough to support a prohibition of abortion or the imposition of a substantial obstacle to the woman's effective right to elect the procedure. Second is a confirmation of the State's power to restrict abortions after fetal viability, if the law contains exceptions for pregnancies which endanger a woman's life or health. And third is the principle that the State has legitimate interests from the outset of the pregnancy in protecting the health of the woman and the life of the fetus that may become a child. These principles do not contradict one another; and we adhere to each.

I

Constitutional protection of the woman's decision to terminate her pregnancy derives from the Due Process Clause of the Fourteenth Amendment. It declares that no State shall "deprive any person of life, liberty, or property, without due process of law." The controlling word in the case before us is "liberty." Although a literal reading of the Clause might suggest that it governs only the procedures by which a State may deprive persons of liberty, for at least 105 years, at least since *Mugler v. Kansas*, 123 U.S. 623, 660-661 (1887), the Clause has been understood to contain a substantive component as well, one "barring certain government actions regardless of the fairness of the procedures used to implement them." *Daniels v. Williams*, 474 U.S. 327, 331 (1986)....

The most familiar of the substantive liberties protected by the Fourteenth Amendment are those recognized by the Bill of Rights. We have held that the Due Process Clause of the Fourteenth Amendment incorporates most of the Bill of Rights against the States....It is tempting, as a means of curbing the discretion of federal judges, to suppose that liberty encompasses no more than those rights already guaranteed to the individual against federal interference by the express provisions of the first eight amendments to the Constitution...But of course this Court has never accepted that view.

* * *

Neither the Bill of Rights nor the specific practices of States at the time of the adoption of the Fourteenth Amendment marks the outer limits of the substantive sphere of liberty which the Fourteenth Amendment protects....

Our law affords constitutional protection to personal decisions relating to marriage, procreation, contraception, family relationships, child rearing, and education. *Carey v. Population Services International*, 431 U.S. at 685. Our cases recognize "the right of the individual, married or single, to be free from unwarranted governmental intrusion into matters so fundamentally affecting a person as the decision whether to bear or beget a child." *Eisenstadt v. Baird*, *supra*, at 453 (emphasis in original). Our precedents "have respected the private realm of family life which the state cannot enter." *Prince v. Massachusetts*, 321 U.S. 158, 166,...(1944). These matters, involving the most intimate and personal choices a person may make in a lifetime, choices central to personal dignity and autonomy, are central to the liberty protected by the Fourteenth Amendment. At the heart of liberty is the right to define one's own concept of existence, of meaning, of the universe, and of the mystery of human life. Beliefs about these matters could not define the attributes of personhood were they formed under compulsion of the State.

These considerations begin our analysis of the woman's interest in terminating her pregnancy but cannot end it, for this reason: though the abortion decision may originate within the zone of conscience and belief, it is more than a philosophic exercise. Abortion is a unique act. It is an act fraught with consequences for others: for the woman who must live with the implications of her decision; for the persons who perform and assist in the procedure; for the spouse, family, and society which must confront the knowledge that these procedures exist, procedures some deem nothing short of an act of violence against innocent human life; and, depending on one's beliefs, for the life or potential life that is aborted. Though abortion is conduct, it does not follow that the State is entitled to proscribe it in all instances. That is because the liberty of the woman is at stake in a sense unique to the human condition and so unique to the law. The mother who carries a child to full term is subject to anxieties, to physical constraints, to pain that only she must bear. That these sacrifices have from the beginning of the human race been endured by woman with a pride that ennobles her in the eyes of others and gives to the infant a bond of love cannot alone be grounds for the State to insist she make the sacrifice. Her suffering is too intimate and personal for the State to insist, without more, upon its own vision of the woman's role, however dominant that vision has been in the course of our history and our culture. The destiny of the woman must be shaped to a large extent on her own conception of her spiritual imperatives and her place in society.

It should be recognized, moreover, that in some critical respects the abortion decision is of the same character as the decision to use contraception, to which *Griswold v. Connecticut*, *Eisenstadt v. Baird*, and *Carey v. Population Services International*, afford constitutional protection. We have no doubt as to the correctness of those decisions. They support the reasoning in *Roe* relating to the woman's liberty because they involve personal decisions concerning not only the meaning of procreation but also human responsibility and respect for it. As with abortion, reasonable people will have differences of opinion about these matters. One view is based on such reverence for the wonder of creation that any pregnancy ought to be welcomed and carried to full term no matter how difficult it will be to provide for the child and ensure its well-being. Another is that the inability to provide for the nurture and care of the infant is a cruelty to the child and an anguish to the parent. These are intimate views with infinite variations, and their deep, personal character underlay our decisions in *Griswold*, *Eisenstadt*, and *Carey*. The same concerns are present when the woman confronts the reality that, perhaps despite her attempts to avoid it, she has become pregnant.

* * *

To eliminate the issue of reliance that easily, however, one would need to limit cognizable reliance to specific instances of sexual activity. But to do this would be simply to refuse to face the fact that for two decades of economic and social developments, people have organized intimate relationships and made choices that define their views of themselves and their places in society, in reliance on the availability of abortion in the event that contraception should fail. The ability of women to participate equally in the economic and social life of the

Nation has been facilitated by their ability to control their reproductive lives....The Constitution serves human values, and while the effect of reliance on *Roe* cannot be exactly measured, neither can the certain cost of overruling *Roe* for people who have ordered their thinking and living around that case be dismissed.

* * *

We have seen how time has overtaken some of *Roe*'s factual assumptions: advances in maternal health care allow for abortions safe to the mother later in pregnancy than was true in 1973..., and advances in neonatal care have advanced viability to a point somewhat earlier....But these facts go only to the scheme of time limits on the realization of competing interests, and the divergences from the factual premises of 1973 have no bearing on the validity of *Roe*'s central holding, that viability marks the earliest point at which the State's interest in fetal life is constitutionally adequate to justify a legislative ban on nontherapeutic abortions. The soundness or unsoundness of that constitutional judgment in no sense turns on whether viability occurs at approximately 28 weeks, as was usual at the time of *Roe*, at 23 to 24 weeks, as it sometimes does today, or at some moment even slightly earlier in pregnancy, as it may if fetal respiratory capacity can somehow be enhanced in the future. Whenever it may occur, the attainment of viability may continue to serve as the critical fact, just as it has done since *Roe* was decided; which is to say that no change in *Roe*'s factual underpinning has left its central holding obsolete, and none supports an argument for overruling it.

* * *

...But whatever the premises of opposition may be, only the most convincing justification under accepted standards of precedent could suffice to demonstrate that a later decision overruling the first was anything but a surrender to political pressure, and an unjustified repudiation of the principle on which the Court staked its authority in the first instance. So to overrule under fire in the absence of the most compelling reason to reexamine a watershed decision would subvert the Court's legitimacy beyond any serious question....

* * *

We conclude the line should be drawn at viability, so that before that time the woman has a right to choose to terminate her pregnancy....

* * *

The trimester framework no doubt was erected to ensure that the woman's right to choose not become so subordinate to the State's interest in promoting fetal life that her choice exists in theory but not in fact. We do not agree, however, that the trimester approach is necessary to accomplish this objective. A framework of this rigidity was unnecessary and in its later interpretation sometimes contradicted the State's permissible exercise of its powers.

Though the woman has a right to choose to terminate or continue her pregnancy before viability, it does not at all follow that the State is prohibited from taking steps to ensure that this choice is thoughtful and informed. Even in the earliest stages of pregnancy, the State may enact rules and regulations designed to encourage her to know that there are philosophic and social arguments of great weight that can be brought to bear in favor of continuing the pregnancy to full term and that there are procedures and institutions to allow adoption of unwanted children as well as a certain degree of state assistance if the mother chooses to raise the child herself. "'The Constitution does not forbid a State or city, pursuant to democratic processes, from expressing a preference for normal childbirth.'"...

* * *

These principles control our assessment of the Pennsylvania statute, and we now turn to the issue of the validity of its challenged provisions.

V

The Court of Appeals applied what it believed to be the undue burden standard and upheld each of the provisions except for the husband notification requirement. We agree generally with this conclusion,....

A

* * *

Because it is central to the operation of various other requirements, we begin with the statute's definition of medical emergency. Under the statute, a medical emergency is

> "that condition which, on the basis of the physician's good faith clinical judgment, so complicates the medical condition of a pregnant woman as to necessitate the immediate abortion of her pregnancy to avert her death or for which a delay will create serious risk of substantial and irreversible impairment of a major bodily function."...

* * *

...We...conclude that, as construed by the Court of Appeals, the medical emergency definition imposes no undue burden on a woman's abortion right.

B

We next consider the informed consent requirement....Except in a medical emergency, the statute requires that at least 24 hours before performing an abortion a physician inform the woman of the nature of the procedure, the health risks of the abortion and of childbirth, and the "probable gestational age of the unborn child." The physician or a qualified nonphysician must inform the woman of the availability of printed materials published by the State describing the fetus and providing information about medical assistance for childbirth, information about child support from the father, and a list of agencies which provide adoption and other services as alternatives to abortion. An abortion may not be performed unless the woman certifies in writing that she has been informed of the availability of these printed materials and has been provided them if she chooses to view them.

Our prior decisions establish that as with any medical procedure, the State may require a woman to give her written informed consent to an abortion....In this respect, the statute is unexceptional....

* * *

It cannot be questioned that psychological well-being is a facet of health. Nor can it be doubted that most women considering an abortion would deem the impact on the fetus relevant, if not dispositive, to the decision. In attempting to ensure that a woman apprehend the full consequences of her decision, the State furthers the legitimate purpose of reducing the risk that a woman may elect an abortion, only to discover later, with devastating psychological consequences, that her decision was not fully informed. If the information the State requires to be made available to the woman is truthful and not misleading, the requirement may be permissible.

* * *

C

Section 3209 of Pennsylvania's abortion law provides, except in cases of medical emergency, that no physician shall perform an abortion on a married woman without receiving a signed statement from the woman that she has notified her spouse that she is about to undergo an abortion. The woman has the option of providing an alternative signed statement certifying that her husband is not the man who impregnated her; that her husband could not be located; that the pregnancy is the result of spousal sexual assault which she has reported; or that the woman believes that notifying her husband will cause him or someone else to inflict bodily injury upon her. A physician who performs an abortion on a married woman without receiving the appropriate signed statement will have his or her license revoked, and is liable to the husband for damages.

* * *

This information and the District Court's findings reinforce what common sense would suggest. In well-functioning marriages, spouses discuss important intimate decisions such as whether to bear a child. But there are millions of women in this country who are the victims of regular physical and psychological abuse at the hands of their husbands. Should these women become pregnant, they may have very good reasons for not wishing to inform their husbands of their decision to obtain an abortion. Many may have justifiable fears of physical abuse, but may be no less fearful of the consequences of reporting prior abuse to the Commonwealth of Pennsylvania. Many may have a reasonable fear that notifying their husbands will provoke further instances of child abuse; these women are not exempt from § 3209's notification requirement. Many may fear devastating forms of psychological abuse from their husbands, including verbal harassment, threats of future violence, the destruction of possessions, physical confinement to the home, the withdrawal of financial support, or the disclosure of the abortion to family and friends. These methods of psychological abuse may act as even more of a deterrent to notification than the possibility of physical violence, but women who are the victims of the abuse are not exempt from § 3209's notification requirement. And many women who are pregnant as a result of sexual assaults by their husbands will be unable to avail themselves of the exception for spousal sexual assault, § 3209(b)(3), because the exception requires that the woman have notified law enforcement authorities within 90 days of the assault, and her husband will be notified of her report once an investigation begins. § 3128(c). If anything in this field is certain, it is that victims of spousal sexual assault are extremely reluctant to report the abuse to the government; hence, a great many spousal rape victims will not be exempt from the notification requirement imposed by § 3209.

The spousal notification requirement is thus likely to prevent a significant number of women from obtaining an abortion. It does not merely make abortions a little more difficult or expensive to obtain; for many women, it will impose a substantial obstacle. We must not blind ourselves to the fact that the significant number of women who fear for their safety and the safety of their children are likely to be deterred from procuring an abortion as surely as if the Commonwealth had outlawed abortion in all cases.

* * *

...Respondents speak of the one percent of women seeking abortions who are married and would choose not to notify their husbands of their plans. By selecting as the controlling class women who wish to obtain abortions, rather than all women or all pregnant women, respondents in effect concede that § 3209 must be judged by reference to those for whom it is an actual rather than irrelevant restriction.

* * *

...If this case concerned a State's ability to require the mother to notify the father before taking some action with respect to a living child raised by both, therefore, it would be reasonable to conclude as a general matter that the father's interest in the welfare of the child and the mother's interest are equal.

Before birth, however, the issue takes on a very different cast. It is an inescapable biological fact that state regulation with respect to the child a woman is carrying will have a far greater impact on the mother's liberty than on the father's. The effect of state regulation on a woman's protected liberty is doubly deserving of scrutiny in such a case, as the State has touched not only upon the private sphere of the family but upon the very bodily integrity of the pregnant woman....

* * *

D

We next consider the parental consent provision. Except in a medical emergency, an unemancipated young woman under 18 may not obtain an abortion unless she and one of her parents (or guardian) provides informed consent as defined above. If neither a parent nor a guardian provides consent, a court may authorize the performance of an abortion upon a determination that the young woman is mature and capable of giving informed consent and has in fact given her informed consent, or that an abortion would be in her best interests.

We have been over most of this ground before. Our cases establish, and we reaffirm today, that a State may require a minor seeking an abortion to obtain the consent of a parent or guardian, provided that there is an adequate judicial bypass procedure....Under these precedents, in our view, the one-parent consent requirement and judicial bypass procedure are constitutional.

* * *

Justice Blackmun, concurring in part, concurring in the judgment in part, and dissenting in part.

* * *

C

Application of the strict scrutiny standard results in the invalidation of all the challenged provisions. Indeed, as this Court has invalidated virtually identical provisions in prior cases, *stare decisis* requires that we again strike them down.

* * *

The 24-hour waiting period following the provision of the foregoing information is also clearly unconstitutional. The District Court found that the mandatory 24-hour delay could lead to delays in excess of 24 hours, thus increasing health risks, and that it would require two visits to the abortion provider, thereby increasing travel time, exposure to further harassment, and financial cost. Finally, the District Court found that the requirement would pose especially significant burdens on women living in rural areas and those women that have difficulty explaining their whereabouts....In *Akron* this Court invalidated a similarly arbitrary or inflexible waiting period because, as here, it furthered no legitimate state interest.[8]

* * *

III

* * *

The Chief Justice's criticism of *Roe* follows from his stunted conception of individual liberty. While recognizing that the Due Process Clause protects more than simple physical liberty, he then goes on to construe this Court's personal-liberty cases as establishing only a laundry list of particular rights, rather than a principled account of how these particular rights are grounded in a more general right of privacy....This constricted view is reinforced by The Chief Justice's exclusive reliance on tradition as a source of fundamental rights....

Even more shocking than The Chief Justice's cramped notion of individual liberty is his complete omission of any discussion of the effects that compelled childbirth and motherhood have on women's lives. The only expression of concern with women's health is purely instrumental—for The Chief Justice, only women's psychological health is a concern, and only to the extent that he assumes that every woman who decides to have an abortion does so without serious consideration of the moral implications of their decision....In short, The Chief Justice's view of the State's compelling interest in maternal health has less to do with health than it does with compelling women to be maternal.

* * *

IV

In one sense, the Court's approach is worlds apart from that of The Chief Justice and Justice Scalia. And yet, in another sense, the distance between the two approaches is short—the distance is but a single vote.

I am 83 years old. I cannot remain on this Court forever, and when I do step down, the confirmation process for my successor well may focus on the issue before us today. That, I regret, may be exactly where the choice between the two worlds will be made.

Chief Justice Rehnquist, with whom **Justice White**, **Justice Scalia**, and **Justice Thomas** join, concurring in the judgment in part and dissenting in part.

The joint opinion, following its newly-minted variation on stare decisis,

[8] The Court's decision in *Hodgson v. Minnesota*, 497 U.S. 417 (1990), validating a 48-hour waiting period for minors seeking an abortion to permit parental involvement does not alter this conclusion. Here the 24-hour delay is imposed on an adult woman....Moreover, the statute in *Hodgson* did not require any delay once the minor obtained the affirmative consent of either a parent or the court.

retains the outer shell of *Roe v. Wade*, 410 U.S. 113,...(1973), but beats a wholesale retreat from the substance of that case. We believe that *Roe* was wrongly decided,..

* * *

In *Roe v. Wade*, the Court recognized a "guarantee of personal privacy" which "is broad enough to encompass a woman's decision whether or not to terminate her pregnancy." 410 U.S., at 152–153. We are now of the view that, in terming this right fundamental, the Court in *Roe* read the earlier opinions upon which it based its decision much too broadly. Unlike marriage, procreation and contraception, abortion "involves the purposeful termination of potential life." *Harris v. McRae*, 448 U.S. 297, 325,...(1980). The abortion decision must therefore "be recognized as sui generis, different in kind from the others that the Court has protected under the rubric of personal or family privacy and autonomy."...One cannot ignore the fact that a woman is not isolated in her pregnancy, and that the decision to abort necessarily involves the destruction of a fetus....

* * *

Justice Scalia, with whom **The Chief Justice**, **Justice White**, and **Justice Thomas** join, concurring in the judgment in part and dissenting in part.

* * *

...The States may, if they wish, permit abortion-on-demand, but the Constitution does not require them to do so. The permissibility of abortion, and the limitations upon it, are to be resolved like most important questions in our democracy: by citizens trying to persuade one another and then voting....

* * *

The emptiness of the "reasoned judgment" that produced *Roe* is displayed in plain view by the fact that, after more than 19 years of effort by some of the brightest (and most determined) legal minds in the country, after more than 10 cases upholding abortion rights in this Court, and after dozens upon dozens of amicus briefs submitted in this and other cases, the best the Court can do to explain how it is that the word "liberty" must be thought to include the right to destroy human fetuses is to rattle off a collection of adjectives that simply decorate a value judgment and conceal a political choice. The right to abort, we are told, inheres in "liberty" because it is among "a person's most basic decisions,"...; it involves a "most intimate and personal choice,"....it is "central to personal dignity and autonomy,"...; it "originates within the zone of conscience and belief,"...; it is "too intimate and personal" for state interference,...; it reflects "intimate views" of a "deep, personal character,"...; it involves "intimate relationships," and notions of "personal autonomy and bodily integrity,"...; and it concerns a particularly "'important decision,'"....[2] But it is obvious to anyone applying "reasoned judgment" that the same adjectives can be applied to many forms of conduct that this Court (including one of the Justices in today's majority,...) has held are not entitled to

---

[2] Justice Blackmun's parade of adjectives is similarly empty: Abortion is among "the most intimate and personal choices,"...; it is a matter "central to personal dignity and autonomy,"...; and it involves "personal decisions that profoundly affect bodily integrity, identity, and destiny,"...Justice Stevens is not much less conclusory: The decision to choose abortion is a matter of "the highest privacy and the most personal nature,"...; it involves a "difficult choice having serious and personal consequences of major importance to [a woman's] future,"...; the authority to make this "traumatic and yet empowering decision" is "an element of basic human dignity,"...; and it is "nothing less than a matter of conscience,"...

constitutional protection—because, like abortion, they are forms of conduct that have long been criminalized in American society. Those adjectives might be applied, for example, to homosexual sodomy, polygamy, adult incest, and suicide, all of which are equally "intimate" and "deeply personal" decisions involving "personal autonomy and bodily integrity," and all of which can constitutionally be proscribed because it is our unquestionable constitutional tradition that they are proscribable. It is not reasoned judgment that supports the Court's decision; only personal predilection...."Liberty finds no refuge in a jurisprudence of doubt."...

One might have feared to encounter this august and sonorous phrase in an opinion defending the real *Roe v. Wade*, rather than the revised version fabricated today by the authors of the joint opinion. The shortcomings of *Roe* did not include lack of clarity: Virtually all regulation of abortion before the third trimester was invalid. But to come across this phrase in the joint opinion—which calls upon federal district judges to apply an "undue burden" standard as doubtful in application as it is unprincipled in origin—is really more than one should have to bear.

* * *

The joint opinion explains that a state regulation imposes an "undue burden" if it "has the purpose or effect of placing a substantial obstacle in the path of a woman seeking an abortion of a nonviable fetus."...An obstacle is "substantial," we are told, if it is "calculated, [not] to inform the woman's free choice, [but to] hinder it."[4]...This latter statement cannot possibly mean what it says. Any regulation of abortion that is intended to advance what the joint opinion concedes is the State's "substantial" interest in protecting unborn life will be "calculated [to] hinder" a decision to have an abortion. It thus seems more accurate to say that the joint opinion would uphold abortion regulations only if they do not unduly hinder the woman's decision. That, of course, brings us right back to square one....

* * *

The Imperial Judiciary lives. It is instructive to compare this Nietzschean vision of us unelected, life-tenured judges—leading a Volk who will be "tested by following," and whose very "belief in themselves" is mystically bound up in their "understanding" of a Court that "speaks before all others for their constitutional ideals"—with the somewhat more modest role envisioned for these lawyers by the Founders.

> "The judiciary...has...no direction either of the strength or of the wealth of the society, and can take no active resolution whatever. It may truly be said to have neither FORCE nor WILL but merely judgment...." The Federalist No. 78, 393–394...

* * *

...The only principle the Court "adheres" to, it seems to me, is the principle that the Court must be seen as standing by *Roe*. That is not a principle of law

---

[4] The joint opinion further asserts that a law imposing an undue burden on abortion decisions is not a "permissible" means of serving "legitimate" state interests....This description of the undue burden standard in terms more commonly associated with the rational-basis test will come as a surprise even to those who have followed closely our wanderings in this forsaken wilderness....

(which is what I thought the Court was talking about), but a principle of Realpolitik—and a wrong one at that.

I cannot agree with, indeed I am appalled by, the Court's suggestion that the decision whether to stand by an erroneous constitutional decision must be strongly influenced—against overruling, no less—by the substantial and continuing public opposition the decision has generated. The Court's judgment that any other course would "subvert the Court's legitimacy" must be another consequence of reading the error-filled history book that described the deeply divided country brought together by *Roe.* In my history-book, the Court was covered with dishonor and deprived of legitimacy by *Dred Scott v. Sandford*, 60 U.S. 393,...(1857), an erroneous (and widely opposed) opinion that it did not abandon,....

But whether it would "subvert the Court's legitimacy" or not, the notion that we would decide a case differently from the way we otherwise would have in order to show that we can stand firm against public disapproval is frightening. It is a bad enough idea, even in the head of someone like me, who believes that the text of the Constitution, and our traditions, say what they say and there is no fiddling with them. But when it is in the mind of a Court that believes the Constitution has an evolving meaning,...that the Ninth Amendment's reference to "other" rights is not a disclaimer, but a charter for action, *ibid.*; and that the function of this Court is to "speak before all others for [the people's] constitutional ideals" unrestrained by meaningful text or tradition—then the notion that the Court must adhere to a decision for as long as the decision faces "great opposition" and the Court is "under fire" acquires a character of almost czarist arrogance. We are offended by these marchers who descend upon us, every year on the anniversary of *Roe*, to protest our saying that the Constitution requires what our society has never thought the Constitution requires. These people who refuse to be "tested by following" must be taught a lesson. We have no Cossacks, but at least we can stubbornly refuse to abandon an erroneous opinion that we might otherwise change—to show how little they intimidate us.

* * *

We should get out of this area, where we have no right to be, and where we do neither ourselves nor the country any good by remaining.

Questions for Discussion

1. Justice O'Connor recognizes in her opinion that a husband has a "deep and proper concern and interest...in his wife's pregnancy." Why is that interest more easily overcome than the interest of the parents of a pregnant minor? The parents of the minor may have an enhanced stake should a child be born to their dependent child, but doesn't a husband have a similar stake? Does the likely genetic contribution and possible affective interest of the husband constitutionally allow a permissible role (to be informed)? Is it relevant that a woman may end her marital status on a no-fault basis (divorce) while the state will likely return a runaway child to his or her parents?

2. Defenders of the parental consent requirement for an abortion by a minor point out that there is a medical emergency exception, that a single parent may consent and is obligated to make a decision considering the child's "best interests." The law also allows the child to appear in the court of common pleas where she resides and petition the court to allow an abortion without notice (or where consent was denied). The court shall grant the petition where the woman is "mature and capable of giving informed consent," and if the court cannot make

such a finding, where "in the best interests of the woman" in his or her judgment. Would a roughly parallel set of provisions for wives reasonably afraid of spousal abuse make required spousal consent constitutional?

3. According to the record, states (such as Massachusetts) with judicial redress for abortions by minors in lieu of parental consent approve those requests at close to a 100% rate; does the apparently gratuitous nature of such a hoop make it an "undue barrier"?

4. Justice Blackmun would allow none of the provisions of the Pennsylvania law to stand. Does it make sense to prohibit a 24-hour waiting period on a decision as momentous—and irreversible—as is an abortion, while upholding required two-day rescission rights on all door-to-door sales, or on all loans secured by real property under the federal Truth-in-Lending law? Numerous statutes and rules require physician or hospital disclosures to patients. What would make such a legislatively determined informational or "cooling off" requirement unconstitutional here?

5. If a description of the fate of the aborted fetus (as Pennsylvania requires) is accurate, on what basis should its recitation be barred as an intrusion? Can the mere disclosure of truthful information interfere with and hence violate a constitutional right to decide a personal matter? Is our free will so sensitive that mere mention of adverse consequences threatens its exercise? On the other hand, what if the "truthful information" is on the other side of the issue—consisting of a detailed presentation on the implications of parenting—particularly single parenting—for future income levels and personal freedom, and on non-surgical options for terminating a pregnancy? Should the state take a side in its selection of which truths to disclose? Does it matter if the issue is steeped in religious belief?

6. Rehnquist would reverse *Roe* entirely, finding no liberty interest in a woman's decision as to a fetus within her prior to viability. Should protection depend upon the redcoats being unBritish enough to issue edicts about colonial sexual practices? Should we be tied to the happenstance customs of 1787, or rather to the values and zones of privacy impliedly addressed?

7. Another rationale of Chief Justice Rehnquist's opinion is the distinction that abortion involves the "purposeful termination of potential life." But does not birth control in any form involve the purposeful termination of potential life? The dissent states that the constitution should "get out of this area," referring to all of the birth control privacy decisions of the Court. Would it make sense to allow a state to make the use of condoms by a married couple a criminal offense but declare that an officer investigating a murder cannot intrude into the property of a citizen without a warrant? Should we defend the "reasonable expectation of privacy" protected by the 4th Amendment against such a compelling interest (homicide prevention), but allow the state to imprison those who do not have sex with their spouses as prescribed by the state? Is that the reasonable privacy line intended by the founding fathers?

8. Justice Scalia's dissent argues that the plurality opinion creates the notion of "undue burden" out of whole cloth, attacking it as objectionably vague—allowing excessive judicial discretion. How does this lack of specificity comport with constitutional jurisprudence extensively defining concepts such as "free

speech," "reasonable expectation of privacy," "equal protection of the laws," *et al.* How does it comport with the extensive body of judicially created law interpreting the "combination in restraint of trade" prohibition in antitrust law? Do not courts draw such lines inevitably and as a matter of course?

9. How different is "undue burden" as a standard from traditional "strict scrutiny" involving a fundamental liberty (requiring a "compelling state interest" and a least restrictive alternative approach)? Is it close to the "heightened scrutiny" approach the Court has taken as a middle ground, short of the more permissive "rational relation" test? On the other hand, if the concepts are similar to either strict or heightened scrutiny, is O'Connor's invocation of different nomenclature gratuitous and confusing?

10. If Justice Scalia would simply confine constitutional limitation on the states to the precise words of the first eight amendments, what does the term "liberty" mean in the 14th Amendment? Is a general term to be ignored because it is difficult to interpret? If drawing such lines should be done with care and only at the extremes, does that excuse not drawing them at all? Justice Scalia partly quotes Lord Acton's famous dictum that "power corrupts, absolute power corrupts absolutely" to apply to the judiciary. But if the judiciary removes itself as the check on majoritarian legislative imposition (often with criminal sanctions) related to sacrosanct aspects of individual conscience, who is left to check such abuses of power against a minority?

11. Justice Scalia would extend fundamental liberty interests to those "traditionally protected by society." How would such criteria have been applied in the *Dred Scott* case? In *Brown v. Board of Education*? Does the Constitution only apply to halt changes in *status quo* tradition?

Note on Fetus Hazard Incidence. A 1992 National Institute of Drug Abuse study surveyed admitted use of alcohol/drugs/tobacco during pregnancy. The survey of four million women who gave birth found that 5.5% used illicit drugs while they were pregnant.[40] The self-reporting of alcohol or cigarette use involves somewhat less stigma and 18.8% of pregnant women admitted to exposing their fetuses to alcohol, and 20.4% to cigarette smoking.[41]

The Centers for Disease Control found that the rate of American babies born with health problems caused by diagnosed Fetal Alcohol Syndrome (FAS) rose almost six fold from 1979 through 1993.[42] Babies born with FAS suffer central nervous system dysfunction, including delayed motor development, mild to profound mental retardation, and learning disabilities.[43] FAS also causes problems that affect speech, language, swallowing, and hearing development.[44]

Another statistical indicator of potential abuse/neglect has been low birthweights. Although not indicative of direct abuse *in utero,* they statistically correlate closely with later child neglect risk. Delicate health and enhanced family stress are associated with neglect and/or abuse problems. The rate differs greatly for African American babies; 12.6 of every 100 African American births are underweight, compared to 5.4 of every 100 white births.[45]

Whitner v. State of South Carolina
328 S.C. 1 (1997)

Opinion by **TOAL**, Justice.

This case concerns the scope of the child abuse and endangerment statute in the South Carolina Children's Code (the Code)....[1] We hold the word "child" as used in that statute includes viable fetuses.

FACTS

On April 20, 1992, Cornelia Whitner (Whitner) pled guilty to criminal child neglect, S.C.Code Ann. § 20-7-50 (1985), for causing her baby to be born with cocaine metabolites in its system by reason of Whitner's ingestion of crack cocaine during the third trimester of her pregnancy. The circuit court judge sentenced Whitner to eight years in prison. Whitner did not appeal her conviction.

Thereafter, Whitner filed a petition for Post Conviction Relief (PCR), pleading the circuit court's lack of subject matter jurisdiction to accept her guilty plea as well as ineffective assistance of counsel. Her claim of ineffective assistance of counsel was based upon her lawyer's failure to advise her the statute under which she was being prosecuted might not apply to prenatal drug use. The petition was granted on both grounds. The State appeals.

LAW/ANALYSIS

A. Subject Matter Jurisdiction

* * *

S.C.Code Ann. § 20-7-50 (1985) provides: Any person having the legal custody of any child or helpless person, who shall, without lawful excuse, refuse or neglect to provide, as defined in § 20-7-490, the proper care and attention for such child or helpless person, so that the life, health or comfort of such child or helpless person is endangered or is likely to be endangered, shall be guilty of a misdemeanor and shall be punished within the discretion of the circuit court...

The State contends this section encompasses maternal acts endangering or likely to endanger the life, comfort, or health of a viable fetus.

Under the Children's Code, "child" means a "person under the age of eighteen." S.C.Code Ann. § 20-7-30(1) (1985). The question for this Court, therefore, is whether a viable fetus is a "person" for purposes of the Children's Code.

In interpreting a statute, this Court's primary function is to ascertain the intent of the legislature....South Carolina law has long recognized that viable fetuses are persons holding certain legal rights and privileges. In 1960, this Court decided *Hall v. Murphy*, 236 S.C. 257, 113 S.E.2d 790 (1960). That case concerned the application of South Carolina's wrongful death statute to an infant who died four hours after her birth as a result of injuries sustained prenatally during viability. The Appellants argued that a viable fetus was not a person within the purview of the wrongful death statute, because, inter alia, a fetus is thought to have no separate being apart from the mother.

We found such a reason for exclusion from recovery "unsound, illogical and unjust," and concluded there was "no medical or other basis" for the "assumed identity" of mother and viable unborn child. Id. at 262. In light of that conclusion, this Court unanimously held: "We have no difficulty in concluding that a fetus having reached that period of prenatal maturity where it is capable of

---

[1] Section 20-7-50 was amended in 1993 to make violation of the section a felony and to make the maximum term of imprisonment conform to the new crime classification system....

independent life apart from its mother is a person." Id. at 263....

Four years later, in *Fowler v. Woodward*...we interpreted *Hall* as supporting a finding that a viable fetus injured while still in the womb need not be born alive for another to maintain an action for the wrongful death of the fetus.

Since a viable child is a person before separation from the body of its mother and since prenatal injuries tortiously inflicted on such a child are actionable, it is apparent that the complaint alleges such an 'act, neglect or default' by the defendant, to the injury of the child....

* * *

Once the concept of the unborn, viable child as a person is accepted, we have no difficulty in holding that a cause of action for tortious injury to such a child arises immediately upon the infliction of the injury....

More recently, we held the word "person" as used in a criminal statute includes viable fetuses. *State v. Horne*...concerned South Carolina's murder statute,... The defendant in that case stabbed his wife, who was nine months' pregnant, in the neck, arms, and abdomen. Although doctors performed an emergency caesarean section to deliver the child, the child died while still in the womb. The defendant was convicted of voluntary manslaughter and appealed his conviction on the ground South Carolina did not recognize the crime of feticide.

This Court disagreed. In a unanimous decision, we held it would be "grossly inconsistent ... to construe a viable fetus as a 'person' for the purposes of imposing civil liability while refusing to give it a similar classification in the criminal context."...Accordingly, the Court recognized the crime of feticide with respect to viable fetuses.

Similarly, we do not see any rational basis for finding a viable fetus is not a "person" in the present context. Indeed, it would be absurd to recognize the viable fetus as a person for purposes of homicide laws and wrongful death statutes but not for purposes of statutes proscribing child abuse. Our holding in *Hall* that a viable fetus is a person rested primarily on the plain meaning of the word "person" in light of existing medical knowledge concerning fetal development. We do not believe that the plain and ordinary meaning of the word "person" has changed in any way that would now deny viable fetuses status as persons.

The policies enunciated in the Children's Code also support our plain meaning reading of "person."...[It] expressly states: "It shall be the policy of this State to concentrate on the prevention of children's problems as the most important strategy which can be planned and implemented on behalf of children and their families." (emphasis added). The abuse or neglect of a child at any time during childhood can exact a profound toll on the child herself as well as on society as a whole. However, the consequences of abuse or neglect which takes place after birth often pale in comparison to those resulting from abuse suffered by the viable fetus before birth. This policy of prevention supports a reading of the word "person" to include viable fetuses. Furthermore, the scope of the Children's Code is quite broad. It applies "to all children who have need of services."...

* * *

Whitner also argues an interpretation of the statute that includes viable fetuses would lead to absurd results obviously not intended by the legislature. Specifically, she claims if we interpret "child" to include viable fetuses, every action by a pregnant woman that endangers or is likely to endanger a fetus, whether otherwise legal or illegal, would constitute unlawful neglect under the statute. For example, a woman might be prosecuted under section 20-7-50 for smoking or drinking during pregnancy. Whitner asserts these "absurd" results could not have been intended by the legislature and, therefore, the statute should not be construed to include viable fetuses.

We disagree for a number of reasons. First, the same arguments against the statute can be made whether or not the child has been born. After the birth of a child, a parent can be prosecuted under section 20-7-50 for an action that is likely to endanger the child without regard to whether the action is illegal in itself. For example, a parent who drinks excessively could, under certain circumstances, be guilty of child neglect or endangerment even though the underlying act—consuming alcoholic beverages—is itself legal. Obviously, the legislature did not think it "absurd" to allow prosecution of parents for such otherwise legal acts when the acts actually or potentially endanger the "life, health or comfort" of the parents' born children. We see no reason such a result should be rendered absurd by the mere fact the child at issue is a viable fetus.

Moreover, we need not address this potential parade of horribles advanced by Whitner. In this case, which is the only case we are called upon to decide here, certain facts are clear. Whitner admits to having ingested crack cocaine during the third trimester of her pregnancy, which caused her child to be born with cocaine in its system. Although the precise effects of maternal crack use during pregnancy are somewhat unclear, it is well documented and within the realm of public knowledge that such use can cause serious harm to the viable unborn child....There can be no question here Whitner endangered the life, health, and comfort of her child. We need not decide any cases other than the one before us.

We are well aware of the many decisions from other states' courts throughout the country holding maternal conduct before the birth of the child does not give rise to criminal prosecution under state child abuse/endangerment or drug distribution statutes. [citations omitted] Many of these cases were prosecuted under statutes forbidding delivery or distribution of illicit substances and depended on statutory construction of the terms "delivery" and "distribution." Obviously, such cases are inapplicable to the present situation. The cases concerning child endangerment statutes or construing the terms "child" and "person" are also distinguishable, because the states in which these cases were decided have entirely different bodies of case law from South Carolina.[citations omitted]. In *Reyes v. Superior Court*, the California Court of Appeals noted California law did not recognize a fetus as a "human being" within the purview of the state murder and manslaughter statutes, and that it was thus improper to find the fetus was a "child" for purposes of the felonious child endangerment statute. *Reyes*, 75 Cal.App.3d at 217.

Massachusetts, however, has a body of case law substantially similar to South Carolina's, yet a Massachusetts trial court has held that a mother pregnant with a viable fetus is not criminally liable for transmission of cocaine to the fetus. See *Commonwealth v. Pellegrini* [superior court decision, no citation]. Specifically, Massachusetts law allows wrongful death actions on behalf of viable fetuses injured in utero who are not subsequently born alive....Similarly, Massachusetts law permits homicide prosecutions of third parties who kill viable fetuses. See Commonwealth v. Cass,...(ruling a viable fetus is a person for purposes of vehicular homicide statute);...(viable fetus is a person for purposes of common law crime of murder)....In *Pellegrini*, the Massachusetts Superior Court found that state's distribution statute does not apply to the distribution of an illegal substance to a viable fetus. The statute at issue forbade distribution of cocaine to persons under the age of eighteen. Rather than construing the word "distribution," however, the superior court found that a viable fetus is not a "person under the age of eighteen" within the meaning of the statute. In so finding, the court had to distinguish *Lawrence* and *Cass, supra*, both of which held viable fetuses are "persons" for purposes of criminal laws in Massachusetts.

The Massachusetts trial court found *Lawrence* and *Cass* "accord legal rights to the unborn only where the mother's or parents' interest in the potentiality of life, not the state's interest, are sought to be vindicated."[citation omitted] In other words, a viable fetus should only be accorded the rights of a person for the sake of its mother or both its parents. Under this rationale, the viable fetus lacks rights of its own that deserve vindication....

...*First, Hall, Fowler,* and *Horne* were decided primarily on the basis of the meaning of "person" as understood in the light of existing medical knowledge, rather than based on any policy of protecting the relationship between mother and child. As a homicide case, *Horne* also rested on the State's—not the mother's—interest in vindicating the life of the viable fetus. Moreover, the United States Supreme Court has repeatedly held that the states have a compelling interest in the life of a viable fetus. See *Roe v. Wade*...; see also *Planned Parenthood v. Casey*..., Webster v. Reproductive Health Servs....If, as Whitner suggests we should, we read Horne only as a vindication of the mother's interest in the life of her unborn child, there would be no basis for prosecuting a mother who kills her viable fetus by stabbing it, by shooting it, or by other such means, yet a third party could be prosecuted for the very same acts. We decline to read *Horne* in a way that insulates the mother from all culpability for harm to her viable child. Because the rationale underlying our body of law—protection of the viable fetus—is radically different from that underlying the law of Massachusetts, we decline to follow the decision of the Massachusetts Superior Court in *Pellegrini.*

* * *

...[W]e do not believe the statute is ambiguous and, therefore, the rule of lenity does not apply. Furthermore, our interpretation of the statute is based primarily on the plain meaning of the word "person" as contained in the statute. We need not go beyond that language. However, because our prior decisions in *Murphy, Fowler,* and *Horne* support our reading of the statute, we have discussed the rationale underlying those holdings. We conclude that both statutory language and case law compel the conclusion we reach. We see no ambiguity.

* * *

C. Constitutional Issues

1. Fair Notice/Vagueness

Whitner argues that section 20-7-50 does not give her fair notice that her behavior is proscribed.[6] We disagree.

The statute forbids any person having legal custody of a child from refusing or neglecting to provide proper care and attention to the child so that the life, health, or comfort of the child is endangered or is likely to be endangered. As we have found above, the plain meaning of "child" as used in this statute includes a viable fetus. Furthermore, it is common knowledge that use of cocaine during pregnancy can harm the viable unborn child....

2. Right to Privacy

Whitner argues that prosecuting her for using crack cocaine after her fetus attains viability unconstitutionally burdens her right of privacy, or, more specifically, her right to carry her pregnancy to term. We disagree.

Whitner argues that section 20-7-50 burdens her right of privacy, a

---

[6] In a related argument, Whitner suggests section 20-7-50 is void for vagueness. This argument lacks merit. As we noted in our interpretation of section 20-7-50, *supra,* the same argument could be made about the statute as applied to a child who has already been born.

right long recognized by the United States Supreme Court. See, *e.g., Eisenstadt v. Baird* [citations omitted], as standing for the proposition that the Constitution protects women from measures penalizing them for choosing to carry their pregnancies to term.

In *LaFleur*,...the United States Supreme Court...found that "[b]y acting to penalize the pregnant teacher for deciding to bear a child, overly restrictive maternity leave regulations can constitute a heavy burden on the exercise of these protected freedoms." The Court then scrutinized...the policies to determine whether "the interests advanced in support of" the policy could "justify the particular procedures [the School Boards] ha[d] adopted." [ed. note: using the rational relationship test; citation omitted] Although it found that the purported justification for the policy—continuity of instruction—was a "significant and legitimate educational goal," the Court concluded that the "absolute requirement[ ] of termination at the end of the fourth or fifth month of pregnancy" was not a rational means for achieving continuity of instruction and that such a requirement "may serve to hinder attainment of the very continuity objectives that they are purportedly designed to promote." Finding no rational relationship between the purpose of the maternity leave policy and the means crafted to achieve that end, the Court concluded the policy violated the Due Process Clause of the Fourteenth Amendment.

Whitner argues that the alleged violation here is far more egregious than that in *LaFleur*. She first suggests that imprisonment is a far greater burden on her exercise of her freedom to carry the fetus to term than was the unpaid maternity leave in *LaFleur*. Although she is, of course, correct that imprisonment is more severe than unpaid maternity leave, Whitner misapprehends the fundamentally different nature of her own interests and those of the government in this case as compared to those at issue in *LaFleur*.

First, the State's interest in protecting the life and health of the viable fetus is not merely legitimate. It is compelling. The United States Supreme Court in *Casey* recognized that the State possesses a profound interest in the potential life of the fetus, not only after the fetus is viable, but throughout the expectant mother's pregnancy....

Even more importantly, however, we do not think any fundamental right of Whitner's—or any right at all, for that matter—is implicated under the present scenario. It strains belief for Whitner to argue that using crack cocaine during pregnancy is encompassed within the constitutionally recognized right of privacy. Use of crack cocaine is illegal, period. No one here argues that laws criminalizing the use of crack cocaine are themselves unconstitutional. If the State wishes to impose additional criminal penalties on pregnant women who engage in this already illegal conduct because of the effect the conduct has on the viable fetus, it may do so. We do not see how the fact of pregnancy elevates the use of crack cocaine to the lofty status of a fundamental right.

Moreover, as a practical matter, we do not see how our interpretation of section 20-7-50 imposes a burden on Whitner's right to carry her child to term. In *LaFleur*, the Supreme Court found that the mandatory maternity leave policies burdened women's rights to carry their pregnancies to term because the policies prevented pregnant teachers from exercising a freedom they would have enjoyed but for their pregnancies. In contrast, during her pregnancy after the fetus attained viability, Whitner enjoyed the same freedom to use cocaine that she enjoyed earlier in and predating her pregnancy—none whatsoever. Simply put, South Carolina's child abuse and endangerment statute as applied to this case does not restrict Whitner's freedom in any way that it was not already restricted. The State's imposition of an additional penalty when a pregnant woman with a viable fetus engages in the already proscribed behavior does not burden a woman's right to carry her pregnancy to term; rather, the additional penalty simply recognizes that a third party (the viable fetus or newborn child) is harmed by the behavior.

* * *

For the foregoing reasons, the decision of the PCR Court is REVERSED.

WALLER and **BURNETT**, JJ., concur.

FINNEY, C.J., and **MOORE**, J., dissenting in separate opinions.

FINNEY, Chief Justice:

I respectfully dissent, and would affirm the grant of post-conviction relief to respondent Whitner.

The issue before the Court is whether a fetus is a "child" within the meaning of S.C.Code Ann. § 20-7-50 (1985), a statute which makes it a misdemeanor...for a "person having legal custody of any child or helpless person" to unlawfully neglect that child or helpless person. Since this is a penal statute, it is strictly construed against the State and in favor of respondent....

The term child for purposes of § 20-7-50 is defined as a "person under the age of eighteen" unless a different meaning is required by the circumstances. S.C.Code Ann. § 20-7-30(1) (1985). We have already held that this same definition found in another part of the Children's Code means a child in being and not a fetus. *Doe v. Clark* [citation omitted] It would be incongruous at best to hold the definition of "child" in the civil context of Doe is more restrictive than it is in the criminal context we consider today.

More importantly, it is apparent from a reading of the entire statute that the word child in § 20-7-50 means a child in being and not a fetus. [citation omitted] A plain reading of the entire child neglect statute demonstrates the intent to criminalize only acts directed at children, and not those which may harm fetuses. First, § 20-7-50 does not impose criminal liability on every person who neglects a child, but only on a person having legal custody of that child. The statutory requirement of legal custody is evidence of intent to extend the statute's reach only to children, because the concept of legal custody is simply inapplicable to a fetus. [citation omitted] Second, ...the vast majority of acts which constitute statutory harm under § 20-7-490 are acts which can only be directed against a child, and not towards a fetus.[2]...

At most, the majority only suggests that the term "child" as used in § 20-7-50 is ambiguous. This suggestion of ambiguity is created not by reference to our decisions under the Children's Code or by reference to the statutory language and applicable rules of statutory construction, but by reliance on decisions in two different fields of the law, civil wrongful death and common law feticide. Here, we deal with the Children's Code, and the meaning of language used in a criminal statute under that Code. We have already indicated that a child within the meaning of § 20-7-90(A) (1985), which criminalizes non-support, must be one already born. State v. Montgomery [citations omitted] Even if these wrongful death, common law, and Children's Code decisions are sufficient to render the term child in § 20-7-50 ambiguous, it is axiomatic that the ambiguity must be resolved in respondent's favor. [citation omitted]

I would affirm.

---

[2] Examples include condoning delinquency, using excessive corporal punishment, committing sexual offenses against the child, and depriving her of adequate food, clothing, shelter or education.

MOORE, Justice:

I concur with the dissent in this case but write separately to express my concerns with today's decision.

In my view, the repeated failure of the legislature to pass proposed bills addressing the problem of drug use during pregnancy is evidence the child abuse and neglect statute is not intended to apply in this instance. This Court should not invade what is clearly the sole province of the legislative branch. At the very least, the legislature's failed attempts to enact a statute regulating a pregnant woman's conduct indicate the complexity of this issue. While the majority opinion is perhaps an argument for what the law should be, it is for the General Assembly, and not this Court, to make that determination by means of a clearly drawn statute. With today's decision, the majority not only ignores legislative intent but embarks on a course of judicial activism rejected by every other court to address the issue.

* * *

In construing this statute to include conduct not contemplated by the legislature, the majority has rendered the statute vague and set for itself the task of determining what conduct is unlawful. Is a pregnant woman's failure to obtain prenatal care unlawful? Failure to quit smoking or drinking? Although the majority dismisses this issue as not before it, the impact of today's decision is to render a pregnant woman potentially criminally liable for myriad acts which the legislature has not seen fit to criminalize. To ignore this "down-the-road" consequence in a case of this import is unrealistic. The majority insists that parents may already be held liable for drinking after a child is born. This is untrue, however, without some further act on the part of the parent. A parent who drinks and then hits her child or fails to come home may be guilty of criminal neglect. The mere fact of drinking, however, does not constitute neglect of a child in being.

The majority attempts to support an overinclusive construction of the child abuse and neglect statute by citing other legal protections extended equally to a viable fetus and a child in being. The only law, however, that specifically regulates the conduct of a mother toward her unborn child is our abortion statute under which a viable fetus is in fact treated differently from a child in being....

The majority argues for equal treatment of viable fetuses and children, yet its construction of the statute results in even greater inequities. If the statute applies only when a fetus is "viable," a pregnant woman can use cocaine for the first twenty-four weeks...of her pregnancy, the most dangerous period for the fetus, and be immune from prosecution under the statute so long as she quits drug use before the fetus becomes viable. Further, a pregnant woman now faces up to ten years in prison for ingesting drugs during pregnancy but can have an illegal abortion and receive only a two-year sentence for killing her viable fetus....

Because I disagree with the conclusion § 20-7-50 includes a viable fetus, I would affirm the grant of post-conviction relief.

Questions for Discussion

1. Does the federal constitutional right of a biological mother to abort a child imply a lesser included right to injure him or her? Does it include a right to injure a child *in utero* to whom the mother intends to give birth?

2. South Carolina's neglect statute only covers "viable fetuses" (presumably well into the second trimester). Where a mother intends to give birth, can

South Carolina protect a fetus during its first four months from illegal drug use which will demonstrably produce a severely handicapped baby?

3. Does this "child neglect" case turn on the illegal nature of the contaminant threatening the child? How is child neglect vitiated because the chemical is legal to ingest, but has the same devastating effect on the child as an illegal drug?

4. Can the legislature protect a child from threatened severe Fetal Alcohol Syndrome injury *in utero*? Can the state regulate other actions hazardous to a child *in utero*, such as ingestion of foods hazardous to a fetus, frequenting rooms with heavy second hand tobacco smoke, extreme weight gain jeopardizing the health of the fetus? Does it matter that recent research discounts the long-term harm to children from moderate cocaine use during pregnancy? If evidence of harm is stronger as to tobacco or alcohol use, can "child neglect" be a constitutional basis for criminal penalties where cocaine is found at birth?

5. What is the assumption in *Whitner* about the status of the unborn child? Is the fetus considered a "person" capable of constitutional protection? If not a competing constitutional right *vis-à-vis* the mother, is its health nevertheless a "compelling state interest" warranting possible limitation on her constitutional rights? Because such a status may invoke "strict scrutiny" the state may be required to choose the least restrictive alternative to advancing that state interest. What measures would pass constitutional muster under both Blackmun's and O'Connor's acknowledged right of the state to protect the health of a fetus who will be born?

6. As the opinion indicates, a third party who intentionally injures a child *in utero* may be criminally prosecuted, or may be civilly liable where negligently injuring a baby in gestation. Usually, the parents are the recovering plaintiffs. Can the state constitutionally recover against a negligent mother who injures her child *in utero* and imposes substantial costs of care on the public?

7. Note that in *Ferguson v. City of Charleston*, 532 U.S. 67 (2001), the Supreme Court invalidated the South Carolina hospital practice of testing pregnant women suspected of drug use. Where samples tested positive during the first 27 weeks of pregnancy, the woman was charged with possession of an unlawful drug. Where testing positive after 27 weeks of pregnancy, she would be charged with possession and "distribution to a person under the age of 18." Where testing positive during delivery she could be charged with unlawful neglect of a child. The Court held that where hospital employees take samples with the intent to obtain evidence for a criminal prosecution, they must obtain a knowing waiver (and patients must be informed of their constitutional right to refuse such a sample). Would *Ferguson* be decided differently if there is "probable cause" that such a mother is using drugs? Is a search warrant required? Would the bar the Court imposes here apply if the remedy were civil rather than criminal? What kind of remedy might protect a fetus which is viable or where birth is intended? Does the viable fetus have any constitutional rights whatever? If not, to what extent is his or her protection a "compelling state interest" and what are the alternatives available to the state to constitutionally protect that interest?

Reproductive Responsibility and Child Poverty in America

Robert C. Fellmeth

Originally Printed in the American Bar Association's *Human Rights Magazine* (Winter 2005)

Johnny S. was eleven years old and his homeless mother had his five-year-old sister to worry about. So she left him on a street corner in Ocean Beach, a neighborhood in San Diego. Johnny looked for his mom for four days before he was picked up by social workers. He scrounged for odd jobs and conned a restaurant manager into letting him wash dishes for three hours a night, earning just over $135. When the social workers found him, he had every penny in his pockets. He had confined himself to just one meal at the restaurant because "Mom needs [the money]." Johnny is a bright-eyed boy with above average intelligence. However, he has a slight stoop due to a correctable bone malformation, and his teeth have painful cavities. He has not been to school for two years. He presents a microcosm of child poverty in America: a child with strong potential and admirable character but with health problems, an educational deficit, and likely relegation to group home foster care or to the streets. Regrettably, Johnny is not unique. He lives in our wealthiest state and, until gathered up, was sleeping under bushes by the beach, in the shadows of $5 million homes.

For two decades, child poverty has been fluctuating between 10-20% of the population, with an overall upward trend. It declined somewhat during the late 1990s, and welfare rolls fell substantially. But those hopeful signs obscure three *caveats*: (1) the increase appears to have resumed since 2000, and in the context of a now-limited and reduced welfare reform safety net; (2) "severe poverty," that is, income less than half of the federal poverty line, has increased (but is not precisely measured); and (3) large numbers of children are living below or near the poverty line. This last grouping now represents 37% of all American children, 42% of its infants and toddlers, 58% of its African American children, and 62% of its Latino children. National Center for Children in Poverty, Columbia University, *Low Income Children in the United States–2004*, at www.nccp.org.

Child advocates are concerned about both ends of this spectrum: the severe poverty, portending permanent damage, and the imminent creation of a large Third World underclass of intractable poverty. The latter concern is reflected in overall increasing income disparities, with the upper 1% of Americans now earning as much as the bottom 38% combined. And the concern is underlined by barriers to upward mobility driven not only by childhood poverty but by preclusive real estate and rent inflation; growing energy, gasoline, and healthcare costs; and small increases in the higher education capacity—including community college and technical training—that most will need for employment in the international economic labor niche of the United States. This effective contraction is joined by many years of tuition increases well above inflation. Impediments to mobility for the young include unprecedented economic solicitude for older adults and a record federal deficit for the future taxpayers who are now our children. Add to this deficit more ominous Social Security and Medicare obligations. Harvard Law School's Howell Jackson projects an obligation of more than $30 trillion, $300,000 for each child over the next generation. Unless policies radically change, it will double and perhaps quadruple the regressive and already substantial payroll deductions for the youth who secure employment. Child advocates increasingly decry our unique cross-generational taking. Instead of the long-standing American tradition of older adults investing in the young, which particularly represents an opportunity for the impoverished, we are burdening our children with unprecedented debts and future costs.

A Closer Look

Contrary to public perception, the parents of impoverished children are not consuming beer while watching soap operas, engaging in what some call "welfare as a way of life." Data reveal that 56% of these low-income families have at least one full-time working parent, 28% work part time, and only 16% are unemployed, many of whom would be willing to work if employment were available. *Id.* However, the single most striking variable underlying child poverty is single parenthood, caused by divorce and unwed births. The latter have risen over the last thirty years from below 10% of all births to over 30%. Contrary to the common view, these births are not to teenagers; the vast majority are to adult women. Paternal support for these children is minimal, with average payments amounting to less than $35 per month per child, and almost half of that going not to families but to repay state and federal governments for welfare payments. See Children's Advocacy Institute, *California Children's Budget 2004-05*, Ch. 2, at www.caichildlaw.org. Most of these children live below the poverty line. Perhaps the most remarkable number from the U.S. Census reports is the difference between the median income of a female single head of household with two or more young children (about $11,000 in annual income) and the median for those children in a family of a married couple (well over $50,000). *Id.*

The conundrum for children like Johnny is the need for two incomes to support high rents and other rising costs of living. His mother is caught between the rock of child care obligations for her children—which she either provides or finds $5,000 per year per child to finance—and the hard place of a single wage earner unlikely to net much more than her child care costs for two or more children. Current federal policy makes the hard place harder because she is limited to sixty months of Temporary Aid to Needy Families and, even if working part time, is given no credit for those months of income where she works less than thirty-two hours. Remarkably, the Bush administration currently proposes a forty-hour minimum work week for such parents, with each month of full-time shortfall generating possible sanction, including the sixty-month lifetime cutoff.

Child poverty involves both private decisions and public disinvestment. Hence, the causes mentioned by commentators tend to turn on their respective political leanings. Conservatives cite reproductive irresponsibility, sexual license, lack of paternal commitment, as well as deficits and unfair burdens imposed on the young by the old, limiting their future aspirations. Liberals cite reduction of the safety net, a minimum wage that is not adjusted to inflation and has declined to below the poverty level for parents of two or more children, and education disinvestment that jeopardizes future employability for an impoverished class. Is it possible that both are correct?

According to many child advocates, the problem facing children is the truce silently in force between these traditional political antagonists. Each appears to have surrendered its agenda favorable to impoverished children in return for the surrender of the other's. Hence, popular culture now purveys with impunity the notion that single parenthood is simply a different and somehow charming choice, with those dozens of sit-com and other adult models (from Rachel on *Friends* to Roz on *Frasier*) suffering no financial repercussions, child care dilemmas, or worries. Indeed, our fantasy parents in the media often do not seem to work for a living; the rent is magically paid. No male appears to pay child support, nor does any child appear to need it. Rather, our media flood us with sexual stimulation and commendation without apparent negative childbirth consequences, replete with Cialis and Viagra ads for hours of male "hardening" while hypocritically eschewing condom ads. Child advocates contend that liberal adults have surrendered (or been overborne) in the direction of momentous public disinvestment in children, especially impoverished children, with safety net support and education opportunity suffering the largest cuts. And child advocates complain that both adult political groupings (although purportedly deeply divided) have conspired to violate through deficits and huge obligations to the elderly the one pact always drawn in favor of children: that adults do not take from their children, but give to them.

A Search for Answers

If these complaints have merit, what is the answer? One prescription is to reverse the trade-off between private license and child disinvestment into the opposite proposition, one demanded from the body politic. The Honorable Charles D. Gill has advanced the public commitment aspect in a proposed constitutional amendment. NACC CHILDREN'S LAW MANUAL, *Essay on the Status of the American Child—2000 AD: Chattel or Constitutionally Protected Child-Citizen?* at 337 (1998). The U.S. Constitution is oriented to inhibit the coercive power of the state vis-à-vis private, individual liberties. However, the constitutions of most developed nations also interpose some affirmative obligations on the state, obligations that need not impede checks on state coercion. Similarly, the UN Convention on the Rights of the Child, signed and ratified by every nation except the United States and Somalia, posits some minimal affirmative obligations to our children. Such a compact may properly specify only those obligations that are clearly commended as a common floor: that our children will not be homeless, will receive adequate care and nutrition to develop healthy brains, will have minimal health coverage and educational opportunity so they may provide for themselves and their children in turn. What is the opposition to such a constitutional amendment, spelled out with sufficient specificity to be enforceable? Is it that we, unlike our less affluent contemporaries in Europe, cannot afford it?

We reserve for our Constitution measures that may be politically unpopular but are a consensus "rule of the game" underlying our society. Although denied "suspect class" status in equal protection cases, what group is more politically impotent than impoverished children? And what commitment do we have more basic than this one?

Would support for such a formalized pledge benefit from a cultural sea change that private decisions to have children warrant the preparation and respect that the miracle of childbirth implies? That the decision includes the simple and minimal obligation of parents simply to intend a child, and of a father to provide for his children? Assume such a commitment were an acknowledged part of our culture and became as politically incorrect to transgress as would an insult to a gay person or someone dependent on a wheelchair. What would be the prospects for such a constitutional commitment, and to child investment in general, in such an altered environment?

One need not have a long conversation with Johnny to appreciate the merits of both a constitutional amendment and a cultural commitment to children.

ENDNOTES

[1] U.S. Department of Commerce, Bureau of the Census; *Money Income of Households, Families, and Persons in the United States: 1992* (Current Population Reports, Consumer Income, Series P60-184) (Washington, D.C.; 1993) Table 18 at 68–76; see also http://www.census.gov.

[2] This is partly a reflection of length of time working, because younger couples who have not yet had children are closer statistically to initial entry into the workforce. It also suggests enhanced resources for children where there is such a delay.

[3] U.S. Census Bureau, *Income, Poverty and Health Insurance in the United States* (Washington, D.C.; August 2005) at 11 (see www.census.gov).

[4] U.S. Census Bureau, *America's Families and Living Arrangements: 2004* (Washington, D.C.; 2004) at Table C2 (see www.census.gov).

[5] U.S. Census Bureau, *Income, Poverty and Health Insurance in the United States* (Washington, D.C.; August 2005) at Table 1 (see www.census.gov).

[6] U.S. Census Bureau, *America's Families and Living Arrangements: 2004* (Washington, D.C.; 2004) at Table FG6 (see www.census.gov).

[7] *Id.*

[8] Terry Lugaila, *Marital Status and Living Arrangements: March 1998 (Update)*, Current Population Report P20-514, Bureau of the Census, Department of Commerce (Washington, D.C.; Dec. 1998) Table 6 at 36.

[9] *Id.*

[7] *Id.*

[8] U.S. Department of Commerce, Bureau of the Census; *Consumer Income 1998* (Current Population Reports, Consumer Income, Series P60-206) (Washington, D.C.; 2000) at viii, Table A; see also http://www.census.gov.

[10] *Poverty in the United States 1998* (Current Population Reports, Consumer Income, Series P60-207) (Washington, D.C.; 9-99) at Table 2; see also http://www.census.gov.

[11] See John McNeil, *Changes in Median Household Income: 1969 to 1996* (Current Population Report Special Study P23-196) Bureau of the Census, U.S. Department of Commerce (Washington, D.C.; July 1998) at 2-4. This study used data from the Survey of Current Business of August 1997.

[12] U.S. Department of Commerce, Bureau of the Census, *Trends in Premarital Childbearing 1930 to 1994* (Current Population Reports P23-197, Washington, D.C.; Oct. 1999) Table 1, column 4, at 2.

[13] 47.2% of births were "post maritally conceived first births" counted in 1990–94; *id.* at Table 1, column 5, at 2.

[14] National Center for Health Statistics, National Vital Statistics Report, *Births, Final Data for 2003* (Vol. 54, No. 2; Sept. 2005) at 8.

[15] Terry Lugaila, *Marital Status and Living Arrangements: March 1998 (Update)*, Current Population Report P20-514, Bureau of the Census, Department of Commerce (Washington, D.C.; Dec. 1998) at 36, Table 6. The percentages do not total 100% because of approximately 4% of single parent households with children deriving from the death of a spouse. Where this occurs, median income for widows with children is $23,192, and for male widowers it is $43,575.

47 (No. SS-3).

[28] Although contraceptive use at first sex has increased sharply from 1982 to 1995 (from 48% to 76%), much of it has come from increased condom use. Declining pill use and less reliable condom use by those more sexually experienced has led to a decline in contraceptive use among that large group, with "contraception use with most recent sex" declining from 77% in 1988 to 69% in 1995. Elizabeth Terry, MPP and Jennifer Manlove, PhD, *Trends in Sexual Activity and Contraceptive Use Among Teens*, Child Trends Research Brief (Washington, D.C.; March 2000) at Figures 7 and 8.

[29] Hispanic female sexual experience rates grew from 49% in 1988 to 55% in 1995; see *Trends in Sexual Activity, supra* note 28, at 2.

[30] One study reached similar conclusions, finding teen pregnancy to be a relatively minor contributor to TANF caseload, but that overall (older) single parenthood was the most correlative single factor for TANF, and correlates even more highly with the "highly dependent" or longer-term population within the TANF recipient group. See Thomas MaCurdy, Margaret O'Brien-Strain, Public Policy Institute of California, *Who Will Be Affected by Welfare Reform in California?* (San Francisco, CA; Feb. 1997) at 96–100.

[31] The increase in single-parent births is society-wide. It is occurring among middle class and wealthy populations at the same or higher rates than among the poor; it occurs regardless of welfare level changes over time, and independent of welfare level disparities between states. Unwed birth increases are also international in scope, with some European rates surpassing American levels.

[32] National Center for Health Statistics, National Vital Statistics Report, *Births, Final Data for 2003* (Vol. 54, No. 2; Sept. 2005) at Table 17.

[33] For example, 96.6% of TANF parents in California are over 19 years of age, and one quarter of these are married. See California Department of Social Services, *TANF Characteristics Survey 1998* (Sacramento, CA; 1999) Tables 18 and 19 at 34.

[34] National Vital Statistics Reports, *Births and Deaths: Preliminary Data for 1997,* Vol. 47, No. 4 (Oct. 1998); percentages calculated from data presented in Table 2 at 11.

[35] Stephanie Ventura and Christine Bachrach, *Nonmarital Childbearing in the United States, 1940–99*, Centers for Disease Control and Prevention, National Vital Statistics Report, Vol. 48, No. 16 (Oct. 2000) at 7.

[36] Children Now survey of 880 parents and 348 children (from 10 to 15 years of age), conducted by Princeton Survey Research Associates. See Report of Results in Christine Russell, *The Talk with Kids Should Occur Early, Often*, Washington Post (Apr. 6, 1999) at Z10.

[37] Children Now and the Kaiser Family Foundation, *Sex, Kids and the Family Hour: A Three-Part Study of Sexual Content on Television* (San Francisco, CA; 1996).

[38] See California State Board of Education Policy Publication "*Adolescent Pregnancy and Parenting*" at http://www.cde.ca.gov/cyfsbranch/lsp/teen/teenpolicy.htm. The average age of an impregnating male is over three years older than the female.

[39] *Id.*

[40] Robert Mathias, National Institute on Drug Abuse, *NIDA Survey Provides First National Data on Drug Use During Pregnancy,* NIDA NOTES (Bethesda, MD; Jan./Feb. 1995).

[41] *Id.*

[42] See *Use of Alcohol Linked to Rise in Fetal Illness*, N.Y. TIMES (Apr. 7, 1995) at A27.

[43] American Speech-Language-Hearing Association, *Fetal Alcohol Syndrome* (1996).

[44] *Id.*

[45] Children's Defense Fund, *The State of America's Children, Yearbook 1996* (Washington, D.C.; 1996) at 90.

CHAPTER THREE

Child Poverty and Safety Net Sustenance

A. CHILD POVERTY

Child poverty correlates with critical health measures: low birthweights, undernutrition, lower cognitive development and IQ, and low height for age. It also correlates with child neglect and delinquency incidence. Perhaps most profoundly, it has a close relationship to long-term educational achievement and economic opportunity.

As of January 2006, the federal poverty line for the benchmark family of three is an annual income of $16,090.[1] The National Center for Children in Poverty at Columbia University estimates the number and rate of U.S. children living below the federal line at twelve million (4.2 million under the age of six). The number of impoverished children has increased by 1.6 million since 1979. Despite improvements since 1993, the child poverty rate as of 2006 is estimated at 18%, slightly above its 1979 level of 17%.

1. Child Poverty Demographic Breakdown

The child poverty rate is highest for African American (33 percent) and Latino (30 percent) children. By international standards, it is also high for white children at 9%. The young-child poverty rate follows a similar pattern: 37% for African American children under age six, 31% for Latino young children, and 10% for white young children.

Of greatest concern are the 7% of America's children who live in extreme poverty (8% of U.S. children under age six). Such extreme poverty is defined as families with incomes below 50% of the poverty line. Research indicates that extreme poverty during the first five years of life has especially deleterious effects on children's future life chances compared to less extreme poverty experienced later in childhood. Finally, 39% of American children live in or near poverty (41 percent of U.S. children under age six), in families with incomes below 200 percent of the poverty line.[2]

In February 2001, a Syracuse University study concluded that California and New York had the highest child poverty rates among the developed nations of the world. All of Europe, including Russia, achieved lower child poverty rates, *e.g.*, Germany's rate is 8.7%, Sweden's is 2.5%.[3]

2. Nutrition and Hunger

The brain is vulnerable to damage from undernutrition far short of gross physical symptoms, particularly for children under six years of age. Even where noticeable emaciation may occur from severe malnutrition, the preschool children who are most vulnerable are not commonly seen by the "mandated reporters" relied upon to detect child abuse and neglect (*e.g.*, school nurses, teachers, school counselors).

For pregnant women and young children, such undernutrition correlates statistically with low birthweight babies, retarded physical growth, higher infant mortality, brain underdevelopment, cognitive disability, language dysfunction, and other long-run costs (see below for a discussion of consequences). It also correlates with measurable cognitive and concentration shortfall, in turn reflected in school performance.[4]

Nine national or multi-state studies of hunger released since 1997 indicate unexpected levels of undernutrition for large numbers of U.S. children, particularly among impoverished families losing food stamps, and immigrant children. The largest studies include the following:

• In September 1997, the U.S. Department of Agriculture released its Food Security Measurement Study from April 1995, finding nationally 11.9 million households with 34.7 million persons threatened by hunger.[5] In early 2000 the Department analyzed data from September 1996, April 1997, and August 1998 to rank the states according to "food insecurity" of its residents. Food insecurity is defined narrowly as: "limited or uncertain access to enough safe, nutritious food for an active and healthy life. These households have reduced quality...and may have irregular food intake. There may be a need for recourse to emergency food sources or other extraordinary coping behaviors to meet their basic food needs." The Department concluded: "Although most U.S. households are food secure, during the period 1996–1998 some 10 million households (9.7%) were food insecure...The incidence is significantly above the national average in eleven states—Arizona, Arkansas, California, Florida, Louisiana, Mississippi, New Mexico, Oklahoma, Oregon, Texas, and Washington."[6] These states have a child hunger incidence almost 20% above the national average, and affecting approximately one million children.

• A study released in 1997 measured a well-known result of nutrition shortfall: stunting (low height for age). According to the U.S. Public Health Service, the Surgeon General's 1990 goal of eliminating growth retardation of infants and children caused by inadequate diets was not met because significant numbers of low-income children continued to suffer retarded growth. In 1992, almost twice as many low-income children as would be expected were short for their age.[7]

• A national study published in 1998 found that 13.4% of children and 29% of poor children lived in households experiencing food insecurity without hunger being evident from their physical appearance.[8]

• A survey of 30 cities across the nation revealed that from 1997 to 1998, requests for emergency food assistance by families with children increased by an average of 14%. Of greater concern, a 1999 update found that during 1999 emergency food assistance increased (further) by 18%.[9] On average, 21% of the requests for emergency food assistance are estimated to have gone unmet during 1998–2000. Fifty-eight percent of the people requesting emergency food assistance in 1999 were members of families—children and their parents. Contrary to common perception, 67% of the adults asking for food in 1999 were employed at least part time. That percentage had increased substantially from previous numbers, further indicating that while welfare reform may be inducing employment, it is not protecting children or moving families out of harsh poverty.[10] Notwithstanding increasing need, the 1999 results report that 73% of city emergency food assistance facilities have had to decrease the number of bags of food provided and/or the number of times people can receive food.[11]

• A 1998 survey of randomly-selected immigrant families in Los Angeles (403 families surveyed in November 1997 and 376 in March 1998) found "severe hunger" in 40% of the households where at least one member had lost food stamps. By March of 1998, the number had risen to 50%. The study calculated that families losing stamps were 30% more likely to suffer extreme hunger. A January 1998 survey of 241 San Francisco households included random samples of those with children and those without, and yielded similar results.[12] There, 33% of children living in immigrant households with food stamp cuts were experiencing moderate to severe hunger.

• A 1999 study surveyed 44,461 households in 13 states in 1997. The survey found that among low income families (below 200% of the poverty line) 58.9% "worried about or had difficulty affording food for their children."[13]

• In January 2000, the Center on Hunger and Poverty at Tufts University released its national review of the impact of welfare reform to date on the impoverished, concluding that despite a strong economy, welfare reform dynamics have increased damaging undernutrition, particularly among impoverished children and immigrant families. The report's findings include the following: (1) workers with earnings below the poverty line report little job security; (2) about 15% of Americans with children were food insecure in 1995 through 1998, including 12.4 million children; (3) nearly one in three single parent households is food insecure, and one in ten is hungry; (4) families leaving welfare struggle to provide food for their children; (5) emergency food programs are reporting increasing demand of 14% to 38%; (6) children leaving the food stamp program number three times as many as those rising above the poverty line; (7) the percentage of poor children whose families received food stamps dropped from 94% in 1994 to 75% in 1998; and (8) immigrants are in particular difficulty, with over 500,000 immigrants ineligible for federal food stamps and leery of any participation in the program (even where states make assistance available).[14]

Table 3-A displays results from a dietary intake study of impoverished children by the Tufts School of Nutrition Science and Policy. Compared to the non-poor, children living in families with income below 130% of the poverty line had significantly greater incidence of deficits for ten of the sixteen nutrients measured, including food energy and critical vitamins and minerals.[15] The deficit in calories helps explain the observation that hungry children have less energy to interact socially, explore their environment actively, and attend to tasks at school. Other deficits, particularly the substantial lack of zinc, iron, and vitamin E, have developmental implications.

Lack of child nutrition is associated with the depth of poverty. The original federal poverty level (FPL) assumed that adequate nutrition requires one-third of a family's income.[16] However, food costs have risen faster than the general inflation rate used to annually adjust the federal poverty line,[17] and other costs—especially housing costs—increasingly require a higher percentage of income.

Nutrient	Poor*	Non-Poor	Rel. Risk**	Deficiency Effect
Food Energy (calorie intake)	15.80%	6.00%	26	attention, concentration, learning deficits, cognitive disorders
Folate	13.20%	6.30%	21	anemia, forgetfulnes, immune response, depression, mental functions
Iron	40.80%	25.20%	1.6	anemia, fatigue, distractibility, cognitive development
Magnesium	11.70%	2.30%	5.1	weakness, growth failure; teeth, protein building
Thiamin	3.50%	0.00%	n/a	nervous and cardiovascular systems, energy reproduction, cell reproduction
Vitamin A	11.1%	1.90%	5.8	vision, bones, teeth, reproduction; infectious chronic diseases
Vitamin B6	16.90%	6.40%	26	weakness, irritability, red blood cells
Vitamin C	18.20%	6.20%	29	bone strength, wound healing, infection resistance
Vitamin E	33.20%	18.80%	1.8	muscle coordination, nervous system
Zinc	51.20%	34.80%	1.5	immune response, blood clotting, mental lethargy, growth, night blindness

Nutrients with non-significant differences: calcium, niacin, phosphorus, protein, riboflavin vitamin B12 (for all, prevalence for poor>non-poor).
*Poor: below 130% of federal poverty threshold. **Relative Risk Ratio of Poor to Non-Poor Prevalences.

Source: J. Cook & K. Marth, "Differences in Nutrient Adequacy Among Poor and Non-Poor Children," Tufts Univ. 1995.

Table 3-A. Percent of Children Aged 1-5 With Nutrient Intakes Less Than 70% of RDA by Income Level and Nutrient

B. CHILD POVERTY-RELATED PUBLIC POLICIES

Child poverty in the United States has been driven by a mix of factors: unemployment, wage depression below self-sufficiency for families, increased births to unwed mothers and more single-parent households, continued low rate of child support collection, tax policies, and substantial cuts in the safety net for impoverished children.

Other factors commonly cited include high unemployment among the young and the poor; high real estate prices requiring two incomes to maintain a household with children; decline in blue collar compensation and job opportunities; disinvestment in trade schools, community colleges, and university opportunities combined with fee increases and loan reductions; a minimum wage below the poverty line for full time work for a family of three (after its 1996 increase); lack of medical coverage; substantial decline in public safety net assistance for children; and the isolation of the poor into neighborhoods where connections for upper mobility are lacking. International migration has also been a factor in some states, although less so than the negative impact of wage, education, regressive tax, and safety net policies.[18]

The overall economic condition of children contrasts with that of the elderly. Social investment in Medicare and social security has decreased the poverty rate for senior citizens to 7%, less than one-half the rate applicable to children. The combination of social security, Medicare, and Medicaid services to the elderly consume almost 35% of the federal budget. Those currently employed have seen contributions increase steadily to the point of almost 20% in employee/employer gross wage deductions for social security plus medical (public and private) insurance—consumed primarily by the elderly.

In contrast, the major safety net program for children (Temporary Assistance to Needy Families) (TANF) consumes 1.5% of the federal budget—with two-thirds of that amount, or 1%, attributed to child beneficiaries. However, unlike senior citizen support, this account was removed as an entitlement in 1996 and capped at lower levels (see discussion below).

In addition to high poverty rates, children lack the assured medical coverage of Medicare; almost one-fifth lack private or public medical coverage (see Chapter 5). The current elderly were given the benefits of the GI Bill of Rights, which allowed many of them to obtain higher education and to advance beyond their parents. Current students face highly escalating tuition costs—even at public colleges and universities, and now bear unprecedented levels of debt upon graduation. Many of the loan programs for students are currently suffering reductions, precluding advanced education for some who would have advanced in prior years.

Those who do graduate with higher debts and seek to purchase a home face unprecedented housing costs. Senior citizens are likely to have purchased their homes at a fraction of current market value. Under property tax systems such as California's, older citizens are locked into those low market values—and pay only a fraction of the property taxes of a young person purchasing his or her first house. The major tax reform backed by both political parties since 1996 is to forgive capital gains entirely on home sales.

1. Minimum Wage and Employment

In October 1997, the federal minimum wage increased to $5.15 per hour. Some states specify slightly higher minimum wage levels.[19] However, the minimum wage has declined substantially over the past three decades in constant dollars. If the 1968 level were maintained in constant dollars, the minimum wage would have been $8.37 per hour by 2000.[20] From well above the poverty line, the minimum wage has moved to a current level of 73% of the poverty line for a family of three. Actual take-home pay for minimum wage workers is 8–12% below these levels, given social security and other "payroll tax" deductions.[21]

Advocates for the poor and children have argued for a minimum wage which allows a parent who works full time to reach the poverty level. A minimum of $7.25 per hour would yield gross income close to the poverty line for the benchmark family of a parent and two children. Objections to such increases center on job losses at the low-wage end, possibly focusing on youth unemployment. However, these fears were somewhat undermined in California, where the minimum wage increased markedly from $4.25 to $5.75 from September 1996 to April 1998 while a record 701,000 new jobs were created in the state during the same period, and unemployment fell from 7% to 4.9%. More recent studies confirm that the 1996 to 2000 federal minimum wage increases did not stimulate unemployment to the extent feared.[22]

Of those benefiting from minimum wage increases, 19% are under 20, and 36% are adult parents supporting children. National studies find that single mothers benefit disproportionately from minimum wage increases, making up 5.7% of the total workforce, but 10% of those who would benefit directly. In particular, African American and Hispanic workers would benefit, with 18% and 14% respectively affected by minimum wage hikes. The majority of the 1996–97 raise (58%) went to working, prime age adults in the bottom 40% of income distribution.[23] Experts calculate that in addition to those earning under the minimum wage, those at or near that level also enjoy a boost in earnings (termed "spillover effect").[24]

2. Tax Policies

The tax statutes and rules allow tax forbearance, termed "tax expenditures" (see Chapter 1). While the activity stimulated by a tax deduction or credit may ameliorate child poverty, these tax benefits may also reduce general fund revenues upon which impoverished children may rely for assistance. More generally, taxes affect income distribution. Taxation policies, including inheritance or estate transfers from the wealthy to their heirs, and tax rates imposed on various income levels, can either stimulate or impede equality of opportunity and upward mobility.

Tax subsidies are commonly arranged in three ways. The refundable tax credit allows a payment in the specified subsidy amount where the behavior to be subsidized occurs. This type benefits the poor as well as the wealthy. A nonrefundable tax credit does not benefit those who do not pay taxes, but it does benefit equally all taxpayers who owe taxes at or above the level of the credit. Hence, a state tax credit of $300 can be subtracted from taxes owed of $300 or more. If poverty reduces a parent's tax liability to $150, he or she will be able to benefit from only one-half of the subsidy. And those below the poverty line who pay no personal income taxes will receive no benefit whatsoever.

The third type of tax expenditure, a deduction from taxable income, is the most disadvantageous to the poor. It does not benefit the poor, and rewards in direct proportion to the tax bracket of the taxpayer. Hence, a taxpayer subtracting a $1,000 tax deduction from taxable income who is in the 35% bracket receives a $350 benefit while a taxpayer in the 5% bracket receives a $50 benefit.

a. Earned Income Tax Credit (EITC)—Refundable

The largest current tax benefit directed to impoverished children is the refundable federal Earned Income Tax Credit (EITC), which can provide up to $4,400 per year for a working family with two or more children. For a parent with one child, the credit essentially adds about 30% to income to a break point of $7,000; for a parent with two or more children it adds about 40% up to a break point of $10,000. After these levels are respectively reached, the subsidy declines steadily as earned income increases. This assistance allows many working poor parents to reach at least marginally above the poverty line.

b. Child and Dependent Care Tax Credit—Not Refundable

The federal Child and Dependent Care Tax Credit allows up to $720 in child care costs for one child, and up to $1,440 in total (more than one child). However, it is only available as a credit against taxes owing, thus depriving the families of most impoverished children from any benefit[25] (see discussion in Chapter 7).

c. 1997 Federal Tax Changes

In 1997, Congress enacted a major new tax package which creates a non-refundable child tax credit of up to $500 per child. Its other major provision lowered capital gains taxes to 18% on profits from assets held more than five years—a rate lower than at any time in the post-World War II era. The new law reduced the corporate alternative minimum tax by $20 billion through 2007, reduced estate taxes (increasing the exempt amount to $1 million by 2006), raised the income limits so more taxpayers can add on private Individual Retirement Accounts [IRA] apart from co-existing employer pension plans, allowed a new type of IRA where contributions are not deductible, but earnings on deposits are tax-free, provided a tax credit for up to $1,500 (non-refundable) of tuition and expenses for the first two years of higher education, allowed deduction of interest paid on student loans for five years after interest payments start, and created an education "IRA"-type account, allowing up to $500 per family per year to be deposited tax-free into an account for education purposes.

The major measure applicable to impoverished children was a limited "empowerment zone" subsidy to promote economic growth in low-income communities by an increase in tax benefits for employers who hire former TANF recipients. But these provisions are limited and declining in amount, already reduced to $400 million per annum. By 2007, their total value will be a symbolic $20 million per annum.

Budget experts note that these changes deepen a regressive taxation trend. Those earning the top one percent of income will receive 32% of the benefit from the changes made; the top 20% of taxpayers will receive 78% of the benefits.[26] Moreover, the cost of the package is "backloaded". The legislation will cost a total of $95 billion from 1997 through 2002, but cost a total of $180 billion from 2003 through 2007. By 2007, the annual cost will be $39 billion. From 2008 through 2017, the annual cost will average $50 billion.

Two of the federal tax benefits seemingly benefit children. First is the $500 child tax credit. But, unlike the Earned Income Tax Credit, it is not a "refundable" tax credit. As noted above, those parents who earn too little to pay taxes receive nothing. Those in the upper middle class with three children will receive $1,500 in reduced taxation. Nationally, 31% of all children—including those below the poverty line and those in working poor families near it—will not qualify for any of the credit. Second is the tuition credit. However, the incentive is also "non-refundable" and thereby excludes 30% of the nation's children from its education investment.[27]

d. 2001 and 2003 Federal Tax Changes

During 2001, Congress enacted major new legislation effectively setting societal priorities for the next decade for the disposition of anticipated budget surpluses. As discussed in Chapter 1, while these changes include a number of benefits for children, they exclude the impoverished. The changes raised the child tax credit from $500 to $1,000. However, as noted above, it remains a non-refundable credit and will provide no benefit to those now below the poverty line and most in need of assistance. Nor will the working poor be able to take full advantage of the benefit until their earnings are well above the poverty line. On the other hand, the top 20% of families in income receive 46% of its benefit.[28]

Nationally, 31.5% of all families (24.1 million children, including all of the nation's impoverished children) will not receive any tax benefit whatever from the new tax package. The majority of minority children in the nation will receive nothing (55% of African-American children, 56% of Hispanic children).[29] The taxes of working poor parents will be unaffected by the reductions, including federal payroll taxes amounting to $3,825 for a two-parent family of four with an income of $25,000 in 2001 (when including both employee and employer shares which must be paid).

The change includes the phased abolition of federal taxation on estates—where the first $1 million was already exempt. A study of African American families found that inheritance opportunities for that group were a small fraction of the inheritance expected by the children of white Americans,[30] with the average white child standing to inherit $65,000 and the average black child $8,000. Impoverished children generally do not live with parents able to take proportionate advantage of pension plan subsidies. The focus on pension benefits continues the trend of subsidy increase for older Americans.

The momentous, long-term tax expenditure deprives the government of resources to invest in children and the future, which will be difficult to regenerate politically. According to one source, the $1.35 trillion eleven-year tax reduction final plan actually amounts to $2.3 trillion when the 11th year totals are properly included and increased interest payments are counted.[31] In the following 2012–21 ten-year period, the cost will rise to $4.3 trillion, excluding substantially increased interest payments.[32] Adding the 2003 tax breaks to this total raises the ten-year price from 2003 to 2012 to over $3 trillion, as discussed in Chapter 1.

3. Safety Net Assurance

a. History

Historically, the nation has had two major programs to address the basic shelter, clothing and food needs of its poorest children: Aid to Families with Dependent Children (AFDC) and food stamps. Seventy percent of the recipients of funds expended on these two programs are children.[33]

Unlike the case in much of Europe, the U.S. Constitution does not cover economic rights, including an assured safety net for children. However, since the 1960s federal statutes established both AFDC and food stamps as entitlements for children whose parents' income falls below a level likely to allow minimal housing and adequate nutrition. The states have been required roughly to match the AFDC contribution from the federal jurisdiction, but were allowed to individually set the total benefit levels. During the 1980s many states began to reduce AFDC benefits—often by failing to adjust for inflation over an extended period—with total safety net provision (AFDC plus food stamps) commonly declining to below 75% of the poverty line. This trend was limited by the federal entitlement status of AFDC. States could be granted "waivers" to experiment with terms separate and apart from federal minimums (in order to test theses for possible improvement or to reflect local conditions). However, after 1989 states were required to maintain their respective benefit levels per person at least at their chosen 1989 level unless granted a federal waiver. That limit was based on the raw numbers, allowing an effective 2% to 3% per annum further real spending reduction as inflation occurred thereafter. However, the 1989 floor provided some restraint on cuts below those levels during the early 1990s (see *Beno v. Shalala*, below).

During the middle 1990s, the opponents of AFDC contended that it stimulated "welfare as a way of life", *e.g.*, unwed births funded by the state without paternal involvement. Critics contended that the program discouraged work and suffered widespread abuse, including teen pregnancies, movement of claimants between states seeking higher benefits (and immigrants from other nations), and sequential children for higher grants. Although some of these criticisms may have some merit, the overall demographics of recipients reveals the typical parental recipient to be a mother, over thirty years old, white, with two children, averaging under $50 per month per child in support from the father. She works part time and would work more if child care and employment were available. Fewer than 5% are unwed teens, fewer than 2% have been in the state less than one year—none are undocumented immigrants. Studies indicate that the major causes of caseload include: unemployment, divorce, paternal abandonment, and declining wage levels. The available evidence suggests that changes in benefit levels (beyond extremes) do not influence caseloads substantially.[34]

b. Personal Responsibility and Work Opportunity Reconciliation Act of 1996 (PRA)

As the Congress changed composition in 1996, it enacted the Personal Responsibility and Work Opportunity Reconciliation Act of 1996 (PRA). The new statute removed AFDC as an entitlement, replacing it with "Temporary Assistance to Needy Families (TANF)", and capped it and other safety net programs under several "block grants."

For a family with dependent children to receive benefits under TANF (as with prior AFDC), most states impose asset limits, *e.g.*, no more than $2,000 and an auto allowance (a market value of no more than $4,500[35]). Recipients must be U.S. citizens or qualified legal aliens. If eligible, a family may receive monthly cash grants based on family size and income. If a family has earned income, the grant is reduced by the amount of earnings; but to encourage employment, recipients may disregard certain expenses, including actual child care expenses up to a set level.[36] In addition, states have JOBS training programs through which TANF parents may receive education, training, and child care assistance to achieve independent employment (see below).

The block grant could not be increased for at least five years (in fact, extended to ten years), accomplishing assured reductions of 3%–5% each year from inflation and population gain—assuming static need for the account. The state must meet Maintenance of Effort (MOE) requirement to obtain TANF funding. However, the state contribution is no longer a match of federal monies—which were themselves once based on the safety net needs of children. Instead, both are capped.

The five states most successful at reducing unwed births receive a bonus from the federal jurisdiction. A bonus is also possible for "high performance" (to be determined by the Secretary of the Department of Health and Human Services), based on the movement of TANF recipients into work.

The state must assess the skills, work experience, and employability of each adult recipient. Under the Act, a specific percentage of families must participate in work activities. If it fails to comply, a state may lose up to 5% of its block grant. In addition, families face a five-year lifetime limit on use of block grant funds. The state may exempt up to 20% of families from the five-year limit, and from work requirements for "hardship" (*e.g.*, disabled or abused recipients).

Under the Act, teen parents may not receive TANF unless they attend school and live with their parents or in another approved adult setting. The state may deny benefits for additional children born while the parent is receiving TANF. The state may deny cash assistance to non-citizens legally residing in the state. The statute also provided that a state may limit benefits for persons from another state to the grant level of the former state (a provision struck by the U.S. Supreme Court in late 1999, see discussion below).

The Act imposed work requirements on TANF families. For a two-parent family to count as "working", the adults must work at least a combined 35 hours per week. A single parent must work at least 30 hours per week in 2000 and beyond. A parent is "working" if employed or participating in on-the-job training, vocational education, job search, or community service. The state may exempt families with children under the age of one from TANF's work requirements.

The new statute requires a 25% reduction in TANF benefits (and allows states to cut more) where a parent "fails to cooperate" in identifying and finding the non-custodial biological parent, usually an absent father. It is not clear what constitutes a "failure to cooperate". The law also includes a confusing requirement that the state's plan provide for work "once the parent...has received assistance under the program for 24 months [whether or not consecutive], whichever is earlier."[37] The "ready to engage" clause indicates that where a TANF parent is able to work and is offered employment, it must be accepted. The second clause requires work after 24 months of total assistance (after January 1, 1998) as an outside limit. However, this requirement is not imposed on individuals, but on states. That is, states must have a mechanism in place to assure employment of all recipients after no more than 24 months of assistance after January 1, 1998. The mechanism to enforce state compliance with its plan requiring work within 24 months is unclear—few large states have fully complied as of 2006.

(i) PRA Consequences

The initial study of New York's TANF population reflected a national trend of substantial roll reductions after 1996. However, only about one-third of those dropped from TANF rolls from July 1996 to March 1997 achieved wages beyond $100 in total over three months after departure; most were driven by sanctions or new qualification or paperwork requirements into deep poverty without any employment whatever—and with dire implications for involved children.[38] Studies during 1997 and 1998 have partly confirmed these findings. Summarizing from 11 state studies, experts concluded that approximately 50% to 60% of those who leave welfare find jobs, only slightly higher than the percentage leaving welfare for jobs prior to 1996. Most of the jobs obtained pay between $5.50 and $7 per hour, not enough to lift families out of poverty, and far short of self-sufficiency. Child care and transportation remain major barriers to economic improvement for families.[39]

The Urban Institute's study released in August 1999 found that about two-thirds of those exiting welfare had found jobs, and generally achieved more income than TANF grants in their respective states. However, the average wage for those so employed was $6.61 per hour, still below the poverty line for a family of three.[40] Another study used census data to compare income trends among single mother households from 1993–95 compared to 1995–97. It found income rising during 1993–95 due to economic expansion and the Earned Income Tax Credit, but it found incomes falling from 1995–97 as welfare reform implementation began. The cause of the downturn is the diminution in means tested benefits (income decline from TANF assistance loss exceeded gains from new employment). Welfare is being replaced by working poverty.[41]

Studies published after 2000 indicate young children may benefit in terms of academic achievement and other indices where parents work *and* family income increases, although the lessening of parental attention has some negative impacts on adolescents. The positive results appear to correlate with quality child care and education/training investment in parents.[42] An economic downturn without concomitant employment assistance (less likely with lower tax revenues) will subject many recently employed parents to lay-off and reliance on safety net provision to the extent eligible.

The safety net retraction nationally has been momentous. In 1995, 57% of impoverished children received safety net cash assistance; by 1998 the percentage of poor children receiving TANF assistance had fallen dramatically to 40%. Similarly, food stamp participation fell from 88% to 70% of children living below the poverty line.[43] The prime directive of welfare reform—moving parents out of poverty while holding children harmless—has not succeeded as promised. Notwithstanding a major economic boom, a relatively small number of children have risen above the poverty line. A recent national study attributes the expansion of the Earned Income Tax Credit in 1993–96 for the substantial mitigation of what would otherwise have been a further deepening of poverty. Nevertheless, the study found that while the number of poor children decreased modestly between 1995 and 1997, children living in poverty were, on average, somewhat poorer in 1997 than in 1995.[44] As discussed above, the trend after 1997 has been toward a yet higher average "deficit below the poverty line," now reaching down to $7,000 below the line for single parent impoverished families.[45]

(ii) PRA Future Implications

As indicated, the PRA reverses federal policy from a required floor to a required ceiling. The ceiling terms raise two dominant concerns:

(1) The law imposes a lifetime five-year (sixty-month) limit on all such assistance. Any month where any assistance amount is received counts against the maximum. Hence, if a parent works half time for five years and receives a small TANF amount, then loses her job, her family is cut off entirely. Except for a few states (*e.g.*, Illinois), credit is not provided for part-time work. About one-half of TANF parents traditionally work ten hours per week or more. The impact of the five year cut-off will become apparent for large numbers of children after 2005.

(2) The statute requires that "adequate child care be provided," but supply is unavailable to many impoverished parents, and most who obtain jobs suffer the cut-off of all such child care help at the one- or two-year mark of post-TANF employment.

These concerns are supported by a major study by the University of California and Yale University, released in February 2000. The study focuses on three major states. Compared to control groups, the study found: (1) young children are moving into low-quality child care as their mothers move from welfare to work; (2) child care centers are in short supply in the neighborhoods where needed and almost half are compelled to leave children with family or friends; (3) the early development of young children is limited by uneven parenting practices and high rates of maternal depression; and (4) although a sizable percentage are moving into jobs, wages are low and income remains below the poverty line, with average hourly wages of $6.36 and a median monthly income of $700 before deductions. About one-third of the mothers surveyed admitted that they had difficulty buying enough food for their children "often or sometimes."[46]

More recent TANF parents entering employment (post-1998) are achieving somewhat higher wages (up to $14,660) or close to the poverty line for the benchmark family of three.[47] However, payroll taxes push most back below the poverty line in take-home pay. Many do not receive medical coverage through their employer, and are denied Medicaid coverage due to their income. Their children may be eligible for the new State Child Health Insurance Program, but coverage requires co-payments plus premium payments difficult for many to afford (see Chapter 5).

c. Food Stamps

Under the Food Stamp Act of 1964, low-income households are provided with coupons (or electronic credit) redeemable for food at retail food stores. The federal government pays for 100% of the coupons. The program is administered on the federal level by the U.S. Department of Agriculture (USDA) and in most states through departments of social services, usually at the county level. Most states pay about 60% of the limited "administrative costs" of the program, but the stamps themselves are federally funded.

Food stamps are generally considered the nation's broadest and most basic safety net program, because there are no eligibility restrictions other than income, assets, and citizenship. The program includes TANF recipients by operation of law, but is more expansive. Hence, some parents leaving TANF for employment, or who are disqualified from TANF, may qualify for food stamp assistance for their children. Food stamps are available to any household with a gross income below 130% of the federal poverty line, a net income below the poverty line, and less than $2,000 in disposable assets (higher for the disabled and those over 65). Benefits have never been claimable by undocumented immigrants.

Categorical food stamps are well targeted to people below 130% of the federal poverty threshold; over half the benefits go to families with incomes less than half of the poverty level.[48] Families with children receive over 80% of food stamp benefits.[49] Of the families receiving food stamps, 46.6% of the children in these families are under six years of age—during active brain development—and 71% are under eleven years of age. Studies indicate that the Food Stamp Program has historically increased the nutritional intake of impoverished children by 20-40%.[50]

Studies in the middle 1990s estimated that 60% of persons legitimately needing and qualifying for food stamps receive them.[51] The percentage now is closer to 50%. Many thousands of persons who could qualify for food assistance—most of them children—remain unserved. A hunger study in the Central Valley of California, ironically the most productive agricultural area of the nation, indicated that while 98% of the poor know about food stamps, about half of those eligible don't know that they qualify, are embarrassed to seek assistance, or are intimidated by the paperwork required.[52]

(i) Food Stamp Benefit Levels

The basis for food stamps benefits, USDA's Thrifty Food Plan, has been judged to be inadequate to meet nutritional needs, and to significantly underestimate the actual costs of purchasing the necessary component foods. Consistent with the Tufts University study cited above, USDA studies indicate that among low-income families whose total spending for food equaled the value of food stamps, only 12% obtained the minimum recommended daily allowances (RDAs) of basic nutrients.[53] For those spending between 1.5 and two times that amount for food, 66% obtained the RDAs, compared to 92% of those spending three times the food stamps levels for food.[54]

As noted above, food stamp benefits are based on income, and so increase at least somewhat as TANF benefits decline. However, these increases only amount to $3 for every $10 in TANF reduction. Using illustrative California data, adjusted food stamp value peaked at about $76.01 in 1997–98, partly reflecting average increases historically keyed to TANF decreases from 1989. In the 1997–98 year, both TANF and food stamps were cut simultaneously for the first time. The PRA both cut off groups of children from food stamp eligibility, and reduced benefits for those still eligible (see discussion below). From 1996 to the present, as the parents of over five million children have pulled off of welfare rolls, almost three million have lost not only TANF, but also Medicaid coverage and food stamps. Among those still receiving help, the adjusted per capita assistance received has fallen from $76.01/month per person in 1997 to $72.78 in 2000.

One study from the Tufts University Center on Hunger and Poverty examined the total reductions in the food stamp program implemented by the PRA from 1997 to 2003. The study noted that the reductions approved are "the equivalent of removing 24 billion pounds of food from low-income households—enough to fill a line of Army convoy trucks stretching to the moon and back, and then more than four times around the earth."[55]

USDA estimated that for January 2000, a nutritionally adequate diet under a "low-cost plan" costs an average of $139.50 per month for a woman adult from 20 to 50 years of age, and $159.50 for a man of the same age. The cost for a child varies from $83.60 per month up to two years of age, increasing to $159.50 for a child 15 to 19 years of age.[56] Using the profile of the average food stamp family above as a guide, the benchmark family of a mother and two children 7 to 8 years of age would require $402.50 per month for the low cost plan.[57] The average food stamp benefits paid are less than one half these levels. Hence, if rent and utilities consume the cash from TANF assistance and/or earnings, the food stamp allotment will not meet nutritional needs, even where all food is prepared at home on a low cost basis.

(ii) Personal Responsibility Act (PRA) Food Stamp Changes

As discussed above, one result of the PRA has been the premature disenrollment of those leaving TANF from food stamp help for their children. Large numbers of the working poor are eligible for some (albeit reduced) nutritional help. For example, a typical parent with two children leaving TANF and working 34 hours a week at $6.50 per hour remains eligible for $150 per month or $1,800 per year in food stamp help to assure proper nutrition for her children. However, TANF caseworkers do not consistently inform such parents of available help. Other parents long off welfare share a similar ignorance.[58] Almost one-half of the nation's children below the poverty line receive no food stamp help. Because some benefits can be paid over the poverty line, over sixty percent of the children eligible for some food stamp aid do not receive it.

Traditionally, food stamp recipients have been required to "register for work." The PRA allows states to require recipients with children over the age of one to work in order to receive benefits. However, the amounts appropriated will not fund training for an appreciable percentage of out-of-work recipients. Some states disqualify persons from food stamps who refuse to work or voluntarily quit "without cause"—a disqualification the PRA allows. The PRA provision authorizing work requirements for able-bodied adults without children within 90 days would affect children indirectly by adding substantially to the pool of persons competing for a limited number of jobs, thereby driving down wages, and potentially burdening counties to provide yet more workfare.

The PRA also gives states the option to disqualify individuals from food stamps aid who are delinquent in court-ordered child support, and to disqualify parents who do not cooperate with the child support program. Finally, where TANF aid is cut down, normally there is a partial increase in food stamps, as discussed above. However, this partial food stamp increase is prohibited if the TANF reduction is due to a failure to comply with a requirement, including reductions "until paternity is established," or failure to meet the 32-hour and other work requirements. The full measure of any TANF reduction must be absorbed without mitigation from food stamps.

The PRA mandated food stamp cut-offs for many legal immigrants. One impetus for this ban was the perception that persons were moving to the United States to abusively take advantage of public benefits. However, data from California, where almost half of the nation's immigrants settle, indicate that less than 2% of its TANF recipients had less than twelve months tenure in the state (from another nation or another state) when first applying for aid.

Of special concern is the group of legal immigrants arriving post-1996, whose children are barred from most safety net protection. Although citizenship makes these families eligible, there is a five-year mandatory waiting period applicable to immigrants during which federal food stamp assistance is categorically barred for adults and children.[59] California and several other states have established state-only funded food stamps for children excluded from federal coverage.[60]

4. Other Federal Safety Net Related Programs

a. Special Child Meal Programs

In addition to food stamps, the federal government funds specialized food subsidy programs for impoverished children, including the National School Lunch Program, School Breakfast Program, Child and Adult Care Food Program, Special Milk Program, Summer Food Service, and Commodities Aid program. More than 26 million children (66% of children aged 6–10) participate in the National School Lunch Program daily.

Current federal law requires that the National School Lunch Program be available free to every child with income up to 130% of the poverty line, and that it provide children with at least one-third of their daily nutritional requirements. Studies indicate that the noon meal is important to children's health.[61] In addition, smaller programs provide summer food service to children, school breakfasts, and a child care food program. Children from families below 130% of the poverty line are subsidized with a free meal; children from families below 185% of the poverty line receive a reduced-price meal. The programs are administered nationally by USDA, and by state departments of education. The lunch program started in 1946, after the Army found high levels of nutritional problems in its recruit pool. Beginning in the 1960s, the scope was expanded to include—for a limited number of children—breakfasts, summer lunches, and child care meals.

These federal meal programs remain as entitlements; all meal providers who have applied and are qualified may be reimbursed for meals provided to eligible children. In addition to the federal funding, which underwrites over 90% of the meal benefits, some states provide a supplement targeted for meals for the neediest children. Where applicable, this state money adds about 5 to 15 cents per meal for local providers serving free meals to the lowest-income children.

b. WIC Nutrition

The Special Supplemental Food Program for Women, Infants, and Children (WIC) provides vouchers for nutritious foods, assessment, counseling, and health care referrals for low-income pregnant, breastfeeding, and post-partum women, their infants, and children under the age of five, based on income level below 185% of FPL and an assessment of being at nutritional risk.

WIC is widely regarded as one of the most successful federal benefit programs in terms of benefits conferred and costs saved. A USDA study concluded that for every WIC dollar spent on prenatal care, between $1.92 and $4.21 is saved in later Medicaid expenses during the first few months after birth.[62] A U.S. General Accounting Office study concluded that the $296 million spent by the federal government during 1990 on WIC prenatal assistance will save more than $1 billion in health-related costs over an eighteen-year period. Savings to states are estimated at 31% of that total.[63] The WIC program has been evaluated as successful in preventing poor birth outcomes (such as infant mortality and low birthweight), and facilitating earlier use of prenatal care and healthier pregnancies, births, and infants.[64]

WIC is a categorical program, funded from an annual federal appropriation. States' shares are allocated based on a distributional formula. WIC's national enrollment as of January 2001 was 1,242,092. In general, 17.4% of participants are pregnant or breast feeding women, 6.2% postpartum non-breast feeding women, 22.9% infants, and 53.5% young children (1–5 years of age). The ethnic composition is 69% Hispanic; 14% White; 9% African-American; 7% Asian; and 2% other.[65] Enrollment has leveled from 1998. The group with the lowest percentage participation among the eligible are children from 1 to 4 years of age. This is the population most excluded from the federally subsidized meals program, which is still centered on school year attendees.

5. Employment Development for Parents

a. JOBS History

The federal Family Support Act of 1988 established a Jobs Opportunities and Basic Skills (JOBS) program: States are required to set up an employment, training, and education program for TANF recipients. At least 11% of a state's TANF families not exempt from work were required to be enrolled by 1992–93. About two-thirds of state JOBS spending had been traditionally from the federal jurisdiction. The PRA merges the federal funding of this account into the broad TANF block grant, to be frozen for at least five years.

b. Job Training Partnership Act/1998 Federal Workforce Investment Act[66]

Separate and apart from Welfare-to-Work funding, the federal Department of Labor also provides funds to states through another vehicle, the "Federal

Workforce Investment Act". Congress enacted the Workforce Investment Act of 1998 to replace the longstanding Job Training Partnership Act (JTPA). The new law focuses not on a new substantive program, but on compelling states to rationalize and organize existing efforts. The program includes the Summer Youth program providing summer employment. However, federal allocations have declined substantially since 1992–93 levels of $204 million, down to $146 million in 1996–97, and below $100 million for the years after 2001. Youth unemployment nationally has fallen somewhat with the post-1996 economic recovery, but remains more than three times the adult unemployment rate.

6. Higher Education Necessity

Many young parents earn somewhat above the current minimum wage. However, the income trend for those working at low-skill levels has been downward. Nationally, average hourly wages of females from 15 to 24 years of age who have not completed high school or who have only a high school diploma dropped 16% between 1979 and 1993 in constant dollars. In 1979, 18.5% of all households headed by females from 15 to 24 years of age lived below the poverty line; by 1993, the proportion climbed to 38.1% for all races, and to 63% for young African American women. In comparison, over the same 1979–93 period, the top 5% of all income earners increased their income 35% in constant dollars, from $89,000 to $121,000.[67]

A more recent study of California wages found that from 1979 to 1998 those earning in the bottom 20% suffered an income decline of 19% in constant dollars, and only the upper 30% in income achieved real economic gain over this twenty-year span.[68] Among California men who lack a high school diploma, real wages declined a remarkable 34% from 1979 to 1998. Women lacking a high school diploma fell 21% in average constant dollar wages over the same period. Only those who had "some" college gained in real income from earnings over the last twenty years, with income gains directly proportional to educational attainment. Men with advanced degrees enjoyed a 27% earnings rise and women a 39% increase in constant dollars over the 1979–98 period surveyed.[69]

As discussed in Chapter 4, investment in higher education—from community colleges to universities—is critical to child poverty amelioration over the next two decades. The international economic niche of the United States is in technology and advanced services, not in assembly line or agricultural employment. The nation has an extensive program of college loan assistance, but strong countervailing trends include rising tuition, higher living costs, and a general failure to invest in higher education capacity. The number of "slots" or seats available in higher education has increased in raw numbers nationally, but has decreased in relation to youth population[70]—the important measure.

7. The Barrier to Self-Sufficiency at the Poverty Line

For those who are able to obtain work, the EITC and higher minimum wage promise to move large numbers of parents and families to the area of $1,000–$1,400 per month in take-home income. But the various subsidies for impoverished parents—some designed to protect children—here interact to create a difficult barrier to increasing income from the poverty line to a "liveable wage" of above $2,000 per month to allow modest shelter, adequate nutrition, and child care without public subsidy.

As the income of a single mother of two passes $1,000 per month, she sequentially: (a) loses TANF assistance; (b) suffers withholding on income, as federal tax liability starts at this low income level; (c) loses food stamps; (d) progressively loses the EITC; (e) loses eligibility for subsidized school lunches; (f) loses priority for subsidized child care; (g) may lose some support obligation from the absent spouse; and (h) either loses Medicaid coverage or gains monthly premium obligations if she qualifies for the new State Child Health Insurance program (see Chapter 5). The rate of fall-off of this assistance places many parents in a quandary—additional earnings may not appreciably increase (or even reduce) net benefits to support their children.

Meanwhile, two economic trends post-2000 exacerbate child poverty. Rental vacancy rates are low and are unlikely to increase markedly; accordingly, rent increases are likely to outpace inflation over the long term. In addition, two basic commodities are projected for substantial long term price increases: energy (electricity and natural gas) and gasoline for automobiles.

C. INTERPRETING ELIGIBILITY

1. AFDC (TANF) Assistance Standards

Townsend v. Swank
404 U.S. 282 (1971)

MR. JUSTICE BRENNAN delivered the opinion of the Court.

Appellants, two college students and their mothers, brought this class action in the District Court for the Northern District of Illinois alleging that...the Illinois Public Aid Code...and the implementing Illinois Public Aid Regulation 150 violate the Equal Protection Clause of the Fourteenth Amendment, and, because inconsistent with...the Social Security Act, 42 U.S.C. § 606 (a)(2)(B), also violate the Supremacy Clause of the Constitution.[1] Under the Illinois statute and regulation needy dependent children 18 through 20 years of age who attend high school or vocational training school are eligible for benefits under the federally assisted Aid to Families With Dependent Children (AFDC) program, 42 U.S.C. § 601 *et seq.*, but such children who attend a college or university are not eligible.[2] Section 406 (a)(2) of the Social Security Act, on the other hand, defines "dependent child" to

---

[1] Section 4-1.1 of the Illinois Public Aid Code, Ill. Rev. Stat., c. 23, § 4-1.1 (1967), provides:

"Child Age Eligibility. The child or children must be under age 18, or age 18 or over but under age 21 if in regular attendance in high school or in a vocational or technical training school. 'Regular Attendance,' as used in this Section, means attendance full time during the regular terms of such schools, or attendance part time during such regular terms as may be authorized by rule of the Illinois Department for the purpose of permitting the child to engage in employment which supplements his classroom instruction or which otherwise enhances his development toward a self-supporting status."

Illinois Department of Public Aid Regulation 150 provides:

"Age Requirements:

"A.D.C. Dependent children under 18 years of age, unless 18 through 20 years of age and in regular attendance in high school or vocational or technical training school. (This does not include 18 through 20 year old children in college.)"

[2] Appellant Loverta Alexander lives with her son Jerome in Chicago. Jerome reached his 18th birthday in August 1968 and enrolled in junior college about a month later. In early October a Cook County welfare officer notified Mrs. Alexander that the AFDC benefits received by her

include a child "...(B) under the age of twenty-one and (as determined by the State in accordance with standards prescribed by the Secretary) a student regularly attending a school, college, or university, or regularly attending a course of vocational or technical training designed to fit him for gainful employment."....

I

Section 402 (a)(10) of the Social Security Act provides that state participatory plans submitted under the AFDC program for the approval of the Secretary of the Department of Health, Education, and Welfare (HEW) must provide "that aid to families with dependent children shall be furnished with reasonable promptness to *all eligible* individuals." (Emphasis supplied.) In *King v. Smith*, 392 U.S. 309 (1968), we considered whether a State participating in an AFDC program may, consistently with the Supremacy Clause, adopt eligibility standards that exclude from benefits needy dependent children eligible for benefits under applicable federal statutory standards. There was before us in that case a regulation of the Alabama Department of Pensions and Security that treated a man who cohabited with the mother of needy dependent children in or outside the home as a nonabsent "parent" within the federal statute. Since aid can be granted under § 406 (a) of the Federal Act only if a "parent" of the needy child is continually absent from the home, Alabama's regulation resulted in the ineligibility of the children for benefits. We held that the Alabama regulation defined "parent" in a manner inconsistent with § 406 (a) of the Social Security Act and therefore that in "denying AFDC assistance to [children] on the basis of this invalid regulation, Alabama has breached its federally imposed obligation to furnish 'aid to families with dependent children...with reasonable promptness to all eligible individuals....'" 392 U.S., at 333.

Thus, *King v. Smith* establishes that, at least in the absence of congressional authorization for the exclusion clearly evidenced from the Social Security Act or its legislative history, a state eligibility standard that excludes persons eligible for assistance under federal AFDC standards violates the Social Security Act and is therefore invalid under the Supremacy Clause....

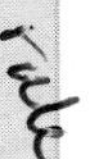

I

It is next argued that in the case of 18–20-year-old needy dependent children, Congress authorized the States to vary eligibility requirements from federal standards. In other words, it is contended that Congress authorized the States to discriminate between these needy dependent children solely upon the basis of the type of school attended. Our examination of the legislative history has

---

since 1963 would be terminated as of November 1, 1968. Though Mrs. Alexander was able to obtain general assistance benefits from the State, the termination of AFDC payments resulted in a loss of $23.52 per month in the family's income. The only reason given by the State for the termination was that Jerome had reached his 18th birthday and was not attending high school or vocational school.

Appellant Georgia Townsend is the sole support of Omega Minor, her only child. Mrs. Townsend, who is disabled, received AFDC benefits for herself and her daughter from 1953 through 1960. Thereafter she received an AFDC grant for Omega, and benefits for herself under the Aid to the Disabled provisions of the Social Security Act, 42 U.S.C. § 1351 *et seq.* In September 1966, Omega enrolled in junior college. Two months later a Cook County welfare officer notified Mrs. Townsend that Omega's monthly AFDC payment would be canceled as of January 1967. While Mrs. Townsend's disability payments were increased to meet her own needs, the loss of AFDC benefits resulted in a reduction of $47.94 per month in family income. Again the only reason given was the failure to comply with the Illinois statute and regulation.

* * *

uncovered no evidence that Congress granted the asserted authority. On the contrary, we are persuaded that the history supports the conclusion that Congress meant to continue financial assistance for AFDC programs for the age group only in States that conformed their eligibility requirements to the federal eligibility standards.

* * *

...Notwithstanding the view of the majority of the District Court, 314 F.Supp., at 1088–1089, we think there is a serious question whether the Illinois classification can withstand the strictures of the Equal Protection Clause. The majority justified the classification as designed to attain the twin goals of aiding needy children to become employable and self-sufficient, and of insuring fiscal integrity of the State's welfare program. We doubt the rationality of the classification as a means of furthering the goal of aiding needy children to become employable and self-sufficient... we are not told what basis in practical experience supports the proposition that children with a vocational training are more readily employable than children with a college education. And a State's interest in preserving the fiscal integrity of its welfare program by economically allocating limited AFDC resources may not be protected by the device of adopting eligibility requirements restricting the class of children made eligible by federal standards. That interest may be protected by the State's "undisputed power to set the level of benefits...." *King v. Smith*, 392 U.S., at 334. See *Dandridge v. Williams*, 397 U.S. 471 (1970).[8]

Reversed.

Mr. Chief Justice Burger, concurring in the result.

I concur in the result reached by the Court, but add this brief comment. In dealing with these cases—and the other AFDC cases on the Court's docket—it seems appropriate to keep clearly in mind that Title IV of the Social Security Act governs the dispensation of federal funds and that it does no more than that. True, Congress has used the "power of the purse" to force the States to adhere to its wishes to a certain extent; but adherence to the provisions of Title IV is in no way mandatory upon the States under the Supremacy Clause. The appropriate inquiry in any case should be, simply, whether the State has indeed adhered to the provisions and is accordingly entitled to utilize federal funds in support of its program....I agree that the answer to that inquiry here must be in the negative; I therefore concur in the result reached by the Court.

---

[8] The concurring opinion below acknowledged that the reasonable basis for the classification would not be apparent if incentives to learn white- and blue-collar trades and the supply and demand for professional and labor positions were the same. The opinion concluded, however, that the classification could be reasonable in the context of a labor market in which "the skills of manual laborers are in short supply," because in such a market, "as a means of utilizing limited state funds in an effort to channel persons into those employment positions for which the society has great need, the statutory discrimination between college students and post-high school vocational trainees is not purely arbitrary or invidious, but rather, a rational approach designed to correct a perceived problem." 314 F.Supp., at 1091. Apart from the fact that nothing appears about the nature of the market, a classification that channels one class of people, poor people, into a particular class of low-paying, low-status jobs would plainly raise substantial questions under the Equal Protection Clause.

Questions for Discussion

1. Under current federal law, states are permitted to vary aid based on the "type of institution" attended, among other locally determined factors. If the

equal protection issue (which would apply notwithstanding federal statutes on spending) were to reach the Supreme Court, how would it be decided? Is there a suspect classification here, or a fundamental liberty interest to trigger strict scrutiny? The Court explicitly "doubts the rationality" of the limitation and implies that it might be unconstitutional even under a "rational relation" test. Would the current Supreme Court agree?

2. In terms of a "rational relation" policy argument, are college-educated youth likely to earn more money and hence need less federal assistance? On the other hand, how many will be academically qualified but compelled to sacrifice college to contribute to family income if TANF help is subtracted from their impoverished family? Can we rely on generic college aid, such as loan interest deferral, to facilitate entry? What is the return on investment for the public where a youth attends college who would otherwise be foreclosed? Are these questions well suited to court findings?

3. Note that this case assumes an age of majority of 21. Given the current 18-year-old age of majority, will the family qualify for TANF support for children in school (in any form) after that age?

4. This decision does not merely rest on compliance with a federal statute to receive federal monies. It purports to rest directly on Supremacy Clause supersession (generating a concurring note in disagreement from the Chief Justice). If the state sought to exclude college attendees from state-only assistance would this holding apply? Would the current Supreme Court apply the Supremacy Clause here (beyond a federal funding precondition) to require state compliance?

Bowen v. Gilliard

483 U.S. 587 (1987)

Justice Stevens delivered the opinion of the Court.

As part of its major effort to reduce the federal deficit through the Deficit Reduction Act of 1984, 98 Stat. 494, Congress amended the statute authorizing Federal Aid to Families with Dependent Children (AFDC)...to require that a family's eligibility for benefits must take into account, with certain specified exceptions, the income of all parents, brothers, and sisters living in the same home....The principal question presented in this litigation is whether that requirement violates the Fifth Amendment to the United States Constitution when it is applied to require a family wishing to receive AFDC benefits to include within its unit a child for whom child support payments are being made by a noncustodial parent.

I

This litigation began in 1970. At that time the federal statute did not require that all parents and siblings be included in an AFDC filing unit. Thus, for example, if a teenage child had significant income of her own, perhaps from wages or perhaps in support payments from an absent parent, the other members of her family could exclude her from the filing unit in order to avoid disqualifying the entire family from benefits or reducing its level of benefits.

Beaty Mae Gilliard, one of the named class members in the 1970 suit,...began receiving public assistance from North Carolina under AFDC in 1962. In February 1970, after her seventh child was born, the State automatically included him in the filing unit, thereby increasing the family's monthly allotment from $217 to $227 to reflect the difference between the benefit for a family of seven and the benefit for a family of eight. Gilliard was, however, also receiving $43.33 each month in child support from the baby's father. When a formal parental support order was entered in April 1970, the State credited the support payments against her account and reduced her monthly benefit to $184. Gilliard sued, contending that she had a statutory right to exclude her seventh child from the unit and thus to continue to receive the $217 benefit for a family of seven and also to retain the $43.33 paid by her youngest child's father. A three-judge District Court agreed with her reading of the statute and entered an order requiring the State to reinstate her benefits at the $217 level and to reimburse her for the improper credits of $43 per month....

Congress amended the AFDC program in 1975 to require, as a condition of eligibility, that applicants for assistance must assign to the State any right to receive child support payments for any member of the family included in the filing unit....In response, North Carolina amended its laws to provide that the acceptance of public assistance on behalf of a dependent child would constitute an assignment of any right to support for that child....These amendments, however, did not harm recipients like Gilliard because they did not affect the right to define the family unit covered by an application and thereby to exclude children with independent income, such as a child for whom support payments were being made.

In 1983, the Secretary of Health and Human Services proposed certain amendments to the Social Security Act to "assure that limited Federal and State resources are spent as effectively as possible."....One of the Secretary's proposals was "to establish uniform rules on the family members who must file together for AFDC, and the situations in which income must be counted. In general, the parents, sisters, and brothers living together with a dependent child must all be included; the option of excluding a sibling with income, for example, would no longer be available."....The Secretary stressed that the improvements would result in an AFDC allocation program that "much more realistically reflects the actual home situation."....

* * *

Because the 1984 amendment forced families to include in the filing unit children for whom support payments were being received, the practical effect was that many families' total income was reduced.[6] The burden of the change was mitigated somewhat by a separate amendment providing that the first $50 of child support collected by the State must be remitted to the family and not counted as income for the purpose of determining its benefit level.[7] ....Thus, the net effect of the 1984 amendments for a family comparable to Gilliard's would include three changes: (1) the addition of the child receiving support would enlarge the filing unit and entitle the family to a somewhat larger benefit; (2) child support would be treated as family income and would be assigned to the State, thereby reducing the AFDC benefits by that amount; and (3) the reduction would be offset by $50 if that

---

[6] For example, under the July 1985 levels of payment in North Carolina, a family of four with no other income would have received $269. A child's support income of $100 would therefore reduce the family's AFDC payment to $169 if that child was included in the filing unit. The family would have a net income of $269. But if the family were permitted to exclude the child from the unit and only claim the somewhat smaller benefit of $246 for a family of three, it could have collected that amount plus the excepted child's $100 and have a net income of $346. See App. 85.

[7] Therefore, under our example, n. 6, *supra*, the net income with the child included in the unit would have been $319.

amount was collected from an absent parent. In sum, if the assigned support exceeded $50 plus the difference in the benefit level caused by adding the child or children receiving support, the family would suffer; if less than $50 and the difference in the benefit level was collected as support, it would not.

* * *

III

* * *

Appellees argue (and the District Court ruled),...that finding that Congress acted rationally is not enough to sustain this legislation. Rather, they claim that some form of "heightened scrutiny" is appropriate because the amendment interferes with a family's fundamental right to live in the type of family unit it chooses.[16] We conclude that the District Court erred in subjecting the DEFRA amendment to any form of heightened scrutiny. That some families may decide to modify their living arrangements in order to avoid the effect of the amendment, does not transform the amendment into an act whose design and direct effect are to "intrud[e] on choices concerning family living arrangements." *Moore v. East Cleveland*, 431 U.S. 494, 499 (1977).[17] As was the case with the marriage-related provision upheld in *Califano v. Jobst*, 434 U.S. 47 (1977), "Congress adopted this rule in the course of constructing a complex social welfare system that necessarily deals with the intimacies of family life. This is not a case in which government seeks to foist orthodoxy on the unwilling."....

* * *

IV

Aside from holding that the amendment violated the Due Process Clause of the Fifth Amendment and its equal protection component, the District Court invalidated the DEFRA amendments as a taking of private property without just compensation. The court based this holding on the premise that a child for whom support payments are made has a right to have the support money used exclusively in his or her "best interest." Yet, the court reasoned, the requirements (1) that a custodial parent who applies for AFDC must include a child's support money in computing family income, and (2) that the support must be assigned to the State, effectively converts the support funds that were once to be used exclusively for the child's best interests into an AFDC check which, under federal law, must be used for the benefit of all the children. § 405, 42 U.S.C. § 605. Therefore, the District Court held that the State was "taking" that child's right to exclusive use of the support money....

...Congress is not, by virtue of having instituted a social welfare program, bound to continue it at all, much less at the same benefit level. Thus,

---

[16] For example, the District Court had before it an affidavit from one mother who stated that she had sent a child to live with the child's father in order to avoid the requirement of including that child, and the support received from the child's father, in the AFDC unit. 633 F.Supp., at 1537–1538.

[17] If the DEFRA amendment's indirect effects on family living arrangements were enough to subject the statute to heightened scrutiny, then the entire AFDC program might also be suspect since it generally provides benefits only to needy families without two resident parents. Surely this creates incentive for some needy parents to live separately. The answer, of course, is that these types of incentives are the unintended consequences of many social welfare programs, and do not call the legitimacy of the programs into question.

notwithstanding the technical legal arguments that have been advanced, it is imperative to recognize that the amendments at issue merely incorporate a definitional element into an entitlement program. It would be quite strange indeed if, by virtue of an offer to *provide* benefits to needy families through the entirely voluntary AFDC program, Congress or the States were deemed to have *taken* some of those very family members' property.

The basic requirement that the AFDC filing unit must include all family members living in the home, and therefore that support payments made on behalf of a member of the family must be considered in determining that family's level of benefits, does not even arguably take anyone's property. The family members other than the child for whom the support is being paid certainly have no takings claim, since it is clear that they have no protected property rights to continued benefits at the same level....Nor does the simple inclusion of the support income in the benefit calculation have any legal effect on the child's right to have it used for his or her benefit. To the extent that a child has the right to have the support payments used in his or her "best interest," he or she fully retains that right. Of course, the effect of counting the support payments as part of the filing unit's income often reduces the family's resources, and hence increases the chances that sharing of the support money will be appropriate....But given the unquestioned premise that the Government has a right to reduce AFDC benefits generally, that result does not constitute a taking of private property without just compensation.

The only possible legal basis for appellees' takings claim, therefore, is the requirement that an applicant for AFDC benefits must assign the support payments to the State, which then will remit the amount collected to the custodial parent to be used for the benefit of the entire family. This legal transformation in the status of the funds, the argument goes, modifies the child's interest in the use of the money so dramatically that it constitutes a taking of the child's property. As a practical matter, this argument places form over substance, and labels over reality. Although it is true that money which was earmarked for a specific child's or children's "best interest" becomes a part of a larger fund available for all of the children, the difference between these concepts is, as we have discussed, more theoretical than practical.[20]

* * *

✎ The law does not require any custodial parent to apply for AFDC benefits. Surely it is reasonable to presume that a parent who does make such an application does so because she or he is convinced that the family as a whole—as well as each child committed to her or his custody—will be better off with the benefits than without. In making such a decision, the parent is not taking a child's property without just compensation; nor is the State doing so when it responds to that decision by supplementing the collections of support money with additional AFDC benefits.

* * *

---

[20] In analyzing the effect of the assignment it is again instructive to ask what would happen to the support payments if there were no AFDC program at all. In that case, it would appear that custodial parents would have to use a much greater portion of the support payments to sustain the family unit, since it could hardly be deemed in the child's best interest for his custodial parent and siblings to have no funds whatsoever. The overall practical effect of the AFDC program (even after the 1984 amendment), therefore, is to enhance the probability that a child whose custodial parent is receiving support payments in the child's behalf will obtain direct economic benefit from those funds, in addition to the benefits that result from preserving the family unit. A reduction in that enhancement is no more a taking than any other reduction in a Social Security program.

Justice Brennan, with whom **Justice Marshall** joins, dissenting.

* * *

The very pervasiveness of modern government,...creates an unparalleled opportunity for intrusion on personal life. In a society in which most persons receive some form of government benefit, government has considerable leverage in shaping individual behavior. In most cases, we acknowledge that government may wield its power even when its actions likely influence choices involving personal behavior. On certain occasions, however, government intrusion into private life is so direct and substantial that we must deem it intolerable if we are to be true to our belief that there is a boundary between the public citizen and the private person.

This is such a case. The Government has told a child who lives with a mother receiving public assistance that it cannot both live with its mother and be supported by its father. The child must either leave the care and custody of the mother, or forgo the support of the father and become a Government client. The child is put to this choice not because it seeks Government benefits for itself, but because of a fact over which it has no control: the need of *other* household members for public assistance. A child who lives with one parent has, under the best of circumstances, a difficult time sustaining a relationship with both its parents. A crucial bond between a child and its parent outside the home, usually the father, is the father's commitment to care for the material needs of the child, and the expectation of the child that it may look to its father for such care. The Government has thus decreed that a condition of welfare eligibility for a mother is that her child surrender a vital connection with either the father or the mother.

The Court holds that the Government need only show a rational basis for such action. This standard of review has regularly been used in evaluating the claims of applicants for Government benefits, since "a noncontractual claim to receive funds from the public treasury enjoys no constitutionally protected status." *Weinberger v. Salfi*, 422 U.S. 749, 772 (1975). Plaintiff child support recipients in this case, however, are children who wish *not* to receive public assistance, but to continue to be supported by their noncustodial parent. Their claim is *not* that the Government has unfairly denied them benefits, but that it has intruded deeply into their relationship with their parents. More than a mere rational basis is required to withstand this challenge, and, as the following analysis shows, the Government can offer no adequate justification for doing such damage to the parent-child relationship.

I

A

The family is an institution "deeply rooted in this Nation's history and tradition." *Moore v. East Cleveland*, 431 U.S. 494, 503 (1977). Our society's special solicitude for the family reflects awareness that "it is through the family that we inculcate and pass down many of our most cherished values, moral and cultural." *Id.*, at 503–504 (footnote omitted).[2] As a result, we have long recognized that "freedom of personal choice in matters of family life is a fundamental liberty interest protected by the Fourteenth Amendment."....Therefore, "when the

---

[2] See also *Smith v. Organization of Foster Families for Equality and Reform*, 431 U.S. 816, 844 (1977) (importance of the family "stems from the emotional attachments that derive from the intimacy of daily association, and from the role it plays in 'promot[ing] a way of life' through the instruction of children, as well as from the fact of blood relationship") (citation omitted).

government intrudes on choices concerning family living arrangements, this Court must examine carefully the importance of the governmental interests advanced and the extent to which they are served by the challenged regulation."....

A fundamental element of family life is the relationship between parent and child....

...When parents make a commitment to meet those responsibilities, the child has a right to rely on the unique contribution of each parent to material and emotional support. The child therefore has a fundamental interest in the continuation of parental care and support, and a right to be free of governmental action that would jeopardize it. As the next section discusses, a child in modern society faces perhaps more difficulty than ever before in sustaining a relationship with both parents.

B

It is increasingly the case that a child in contemporary America lives in a household in which only one parent is present. The percentage of households headed by one parent has doubled since 1970, from 13% to 26%....[5] Researchers predict that "close to half of all children living in the United States today will reach age 18 without having lived continuously with both biological parents." Furstenberg, Nord, Peterson, & Zill, The Life Course of Children of Divorce: Marital Disruption and Parental Contact, 48 Am. Sociological Rev. 656, 667 (1983).

Almost 90% of single-parent households are headed by women,[6] and a considerable percentage of them face great financial difficulty. One prominent reason is that divorce "produces a precipitous decline in women's household incomes."....In 1977, one-half of *all* related children under age 18 in female-headed households were below the poverty level....Not surprisingly, many such households must rely on public assistance.[8]

Increasing numbers of children in this country thus reside only with their mother, in a household whose financial condition is precarious. These children have a fundamental interest in sustaining a relationship with their mother, since she is their primary source of daily emotional support. They also have a fundamental interest, of course, in sustaining a relationship with their father, whose absence from the household does not diminish the protection that must be afforded this parent-child relationship. The need for connection with the father is underscored by considerable scholarly research, which indicates that "the optimal situation for the child is to have both an involved mother and an involved father." H. Biller, Paternal Deprivation 10 (1974).[9] Research indicates that maintenance of a relationship with both parents is particularly important for children whose parents have divorced: "By his or her presence or absence, the visiting parent remains central to the psychic functioning of the children."....

In short, "training, nurture, and loving protection...are at the heart of the parental relationship protected by the Constitution,"...and a child's relationship with a father outside the home can be an important source of these benefits.

C

---

[5] Almost 60% of all black families with children are headed by one parent, compared with only 36% in 1970. While only 1 in 10 white families were headed by a single parent in 1970, the figure is now 1 in 5. Current Population Reports, at 5.

[6] Families headed by women accounted for 25% of the households added from 1980 to 1984, compared to 18% of the households added from 1970 to 1980....

[8] In May 1982, of all AFDC families, only 9.4% had a father present in the home.

[9] "Paternal deprivation, including patterns of inadequate fathering as well as father absence, is a highly significant factor in the development of serious psychological and social problems." H. Biller, Paternal Deprivation 1 (1974)....

The Government's insistence that a child living with an AFDC mother relinquish its child support deeply intrudes on the father-child relationship, for child support is a crucial means of sustaining the bond between a child and its father outside the home. A father's support represents a way in which the father can make an important contribution to raising the child, and the benefits to the child are both financial and emotional.

* * *

...[T]he Government in these cases has...told children who live with mothers who need AFDC that they cannot both live with their mothers and receive child support from their fathers. Rather than terminate either relationship itself, the Government requires the *child* to choose between them. It has declared that, for an indigent mother with a child receiving child support, a condition of *her* AFDC eligibility is that *her child* relinquish its fundamental constitutional interest in maintaining a vital bond with either her or the child's father.

On the one hand, if the child stays with its mother, the father is told that henceforth the Government, not he, will support the child. Unless he is wealthy enough to support the entire household, all but $50 of any support payment that the father makes will be used to reimburse the Government for making a welfare payment for use by the whole family. This conversion of the father's support payment into Government reimbursement means that the father is rendered powerless in most cases to respond to the special financial needs of his child.

It is important to illustrate why this is the case. Let us suppose that a couple with one child obtains a divorce, that the mother has a child by a previous marriage, and that the mother has custody of the two children. The mother has no source of income, but the father from whom she obtained her recent divorce provides $150 a month to support his child. If the mother desires to keep both her children, the $150 in child support must be assigned to the State. In return, the three-person household receives, let us say, $400 a month in AFDC. Of the $150 in child support assigned to the State, $50 is returned for use of the child for whom it was paid, and $100 is kept by the State as reimbursement for its welfare payment.

If the father wanted to increase the amount of child support, say to $200, because of the child's special needs, *none of the extra money would go to the child.* The family would still receive $400 in AFDC, and the child would still receive $50 of the support payment. The only difference would be that the State would now get to keep $150 as reimbursement for the welfare payment. By continuing to live with the mother, the child has lost not only the financial benefit of the father's support, but a father-child relationship founded on the father's commitment to care for the material needs of his child. If the child has a conscientious father who has shouldered his paternal duty, that father will be enlisted to help defray the cost of providing for *other* children whose fathers are not so responsible. A child thus must pay a high price for continuing to live with its mother.

This price is not merely speculative. The affidavits in these cases establish it....

* * *

B

The nature of the interest asserted in these cases, as well as the direct disruption produced by the Government, distinguishes this litigation from typical challenges to the operation of Government benefit programs.

* * *

Finally, the disruption directly produced by the household filing requirement distinguishes these cases from cases in which we have upheld Government benefit provisions from a challenge that they interfered with family life. In *Lyng, supra,* for instance, we upheld the food stamp program's presumption that parents, children, and siblings who live together constitute a single "household," so that such persons could not individually apply for benefits as separate households. We noted that the definition "does not order or prevent any group of persons from dining together. Indeed, in the overwhelming majority of cases it probably has no effect at all." *Id.*, at 638. In *Califano v. Jobst*, 434 U.S. 47 (1977), we upheld a provision whereby a recipient of dependent Social Security benefits lost those benefits upon marriage to anyone other than another beneficiary, even though we acknowledged that the provision "may have an impact on a secondary beneficiary's desire to marry, and may make some suitors less welcome than others." *Id.*, at 58. These cases reflect recognition that the extensive activities of Government in modern society inevitably have the potential for creating incentives and disincentives for certain behavior. By itself, plausible speculation about the effect of Government programs generally cannot provide the basis for a constitutional challenge.

In these cases, however, the impact of Government action is not speculative, but direct and substantial. If a child support recipient lives with a mother who needs public assistance, AFDC will be provided *only* if the child either leaves the household or gives up its right to support from its father. Determining whether other eligibility requirements for Government assistance will influence family choices may call for subtle inquiry into the nuances of human motivation. Here, however, the burden on family life is inescapable, because it is *directly required* by the Government as a condition of obtaining benefits. "'Governmental imposition of such a choice puts the same kind of burden upon [the child's rights] as would a fine imposed against'" the child for living with its mother or being supported by its father....

* * *

IV

In The Republic and in The Laws, Plato offered a vision of a unified society, where the needs of children are met not by parents but by the government, and where no intermediate forms of association stand between the individual and the state....The vision is a brilliant one, but it is not our own:

* * *

"Happy families," wrote Tolstoy, "are all alike; every unhappy family is unhappy in its own way." L. Tolstoy, Anna Karenina 1...Contemporary life offers countless ways in which family life can be fractured and families made unhappy. The children who increasingly live in these families are entitled to the chance to sustain a special relationship with both their fathers and their mothers, regardless of how difficult that may be. Parents are entitled to provide both daily emotional solace and to meet their child's material needs; the fact that in some families a different parent may take on each role does not diminish the child's right to the care of both parents. The Government could not prohibit parents from performing these duties, and what it cannot do by direct fiat it should not be able to do by economic force. The Government has decreed that the only way a child can live with its mother and be supported by its father is if the mother is wealthy enough not to require public assistance. A child cannot be held responsible for the indigency of its mother, and should not be forced to choose between parents because of something so clearly out of its control. No society can assure its children that there will be no unhappy families. It can tell them, however, that their Government will not be allowed to contribute to the pain.

I dissent.

* * *

Questions for Discussion

1. AFDC (TANF) assistance increases with the number of children, with the increment declining per child added. *Bowen* asks: If the seventh child costs the state an additional $10 but his absent father pays $43, does the family keep the $33 the state is not spending on that child? If the state takes all $43, is the father's right to contribute to his child abridged? If he had nothing to do with the other six children, and he wants to contribute to his own child beyond the state's contribution for him, on what basis can the state take his money for his child?

2. If the mother refuses the AFDC (TANF) for the seventh child, knowing child support will be paid in a larger amount, can North Carolina say "you can't exclude a child from our assistance"? What if the father takes voluntary custody of his child, necessarily making the mother's family one child less for assistance? If the only way the father can give more to his son is to take custody of him, how does that impact the right of the child to live with his siblings? The right of the mother to have custody of children without state impediment?

3. Can the state argue that the seventh child benefits from the overall support of the family and accordingly all income generated by the family—however tied to a member—is owed back to the state for state assistance up to the total amount given by the state?

4. Can the state argue that the children within the family with outside child support will receive disproportionate income, which interferes with the mother's right to manage the family equitably? Or does the father have the right to give his child an advantage over his child's siblings who are biologically unrelated to him?

5. Assume a state gives "child only" benefits of $341 for a single child living with her grandmother (*e.g.*, kin foster care) as a "one person assistance unit" (AU). Assume the grandmother then accepts two nieces into her care from different parents, constituting a separate "child only" AU of two children at $561 per month for a $901 total. Can California refuse to acknowledge these separate units, but consider all three children as a single AU eligible for only $694 in total support? See the affirmative answer in interpreting federal law and rules implementing AFDC in *Anderson v. Edwards*, 514 U.S. 143 (1995). If another person receives the two nieces, total payment received for the care of the three children will be $901. How is this California rule likely to affect custody decisions? Much has been written about the "marriage penalty" of federal income taxation—which has historically imposed lower taxes to two unmarried people filing separately than for a joint return as a married couple. The political upheaval has led to

adjustment in federal tax rates. Does the welfare payment design effect on child custody decisions warrant similar attention?

6. The Court rejects impoverished children or the poor as a suspect class or even for heightened scrutiny, noting that it is not powerless but that "the opposite is true"? What is the evidence that impoverished children are politically powerful?

Saenz v. Roe
526 U.S. 489 (1999)

JUSTICE STEVENS delivered the opinion of the Court.

In 1992, California enacted a statute limiting the maximum welfare benefits available to newly arrived residents. The scheme limits the amount payable to a family that has resided in the State for less than 12 months to the amount payable by the State of the family's prior residence. The questions presented by this case are whether the 1992 statute was constitutional when it was enacted and, if not, whether an amendment to the Social Security Act enacted by Congress in 1996 affects that determination.

I

California is not only one of the largest, most populated, and most beautiful States in the Nation; it is also one of the most generous. Like all other States, California has participated in several welfare programs authorized by the Social Security Act and partially funded by the Federal Government. Its programs, however, provide a higher level of benefits and serve more needy citizens than those of most other States. In one year the most expensive of those programs, Aid to Families with Dependent Children (AFDC), which was replaced in 1996 with Temporary Assistance to Needy Families (TANF), provided benefits for an average of 2,645,814 persons per month at an annual cost to the State of $2.9 billion. In California the cash benefit for a family of two—a mother and one child—is $456 a month, but in the neighboring State of Arizona, for example, it is only $275.

In 1992, in order to make a relatively modest reduction in its vast welfare budget, the California Legislature enacted § 11450.03 of the state Welfare and Institutions Code. That section sought to change the California AFDC program by limiting new residents, for the first year they live in California, to the benefits they would have received in the State of their prior residence....Because in 1992 a state program either had to conform to federal specifications or receive a waiver from the Secretary of Health and Human Services in order to qualify for federal reimbursement, § 11450.03 required approval by the Secretary to take effect. In October 1992, the Secretary issued a waiver purporting to grant such approval.

* * *

PRWORA replaced the AFDC program with TANF. The new statute expressly authorizes any State that receives a block grant under TANF to "apply to a family the rules (including benefit amounts) of the [TANF] program...of another State if the family has moved to the State from the other State and has resided in the State for less than 12 months." 42 U.S.C. § 604(c) (1994 ed., Supp. II)....The California Department of Social Services therefore issued an "All County Letter" announcing that the enforcement of § 11450.03 would commence on April 1, 1997.

The All County Letter clarifies certain aspects of the statute. Even if members of an eligible family had lived in California all of their lives, but left the State "on January 29th, intending to reside in another state, and returned on April

15th," their benefits are determined by the law of their State of residence from January 29 to April 15, assuming that that level was lower than California's....Moreover, the lower level of benefits applies regardless of whether the family was on welfare in the State of prior residence and regardless of the family's motive for moving to California. The instructions also explain that the residency requirement is inapplicable to families that recently arrived from another country.

I

* * *

The State relied squarely on the undisputed fact that the statute would save some $10.9 million in annual welfare costs—an amount that is surely significant even though only a relatively small part of its annual expenditures of approximately $2.9 billion for the entire program. It contended that this cost saving was an appropriate exercise of budgetary authority as long as the residency requirement did not penalize the right to travel. The State reasoned that the payment of the same benefits that would have been received in the State of prior residency eliminated any potentially punitive aspects of the measure. Judge Levi concluded, however, that the relevant comparison was not between new residents of California and the residents of their former States, but rather between the new residents and longer term residents of California. He therefore again enjoined the implementation of the statute.

* * *

III

The word "travel" is not found in the text of the Constitution. Yet the "constitutional right to travel from one State to another" is firmly embedded in our jurisprudence....

...We [have] squarely held that it was "constitutionally impermissible" for a State to enact durational residency requirements for the purpose of inhibiting the migration by needy persons into the State....We further held that a classification that had the effect of imposing a penalty on the exercise of the right to travel violated the Equal Protection Clause "unless shown to be necessary to promote a compelling governmental interest,"..., and that no such showing had been made.

In this case California argues that § 11450.03 was not enacted for the impermissible purpose of inhibiting migration by needy persons and that, unlike the legislation reviewed in *Shapiro*, it does not penalize the right to travel because new arrivals are not ineligible for benefits during their first year of residence. California submits that, instead of being subjected to the strictest scrutiny, the statute should be upheld if it is supported by a rational basis and that the State's legitimate interest in saving over $10 million a year satisfies that test. Although the United States did not elect to participate in the proceedings in the District Court or the Court of Appeals, it has participated as amicus curiae in this Court. It has advanced the novel argument that the enactment of PRWORA allows the States to adopt a "specialized choice-of-law-type provision" that "should be subject to an intermediate level of constitutional review," merely requiring that durational residency requirements be "substantially related to an important governmental objective."...The debate about the appropriate standard of review, together with the potential relevance of the federal statute, persuades us that it will be useful to focus on the source of the constitutional right on which respondents rely.

IV

The "right to travel" discussed in our cases embraces at least three different components. It protects the right of a citizen of one State to enter and to leave another State, the right to be treated as a welcome visitor rather than an unfriendly alien when temporarily present in the second State, and, for those travelers who elect to become permanent residents, the right to be treated like other citizens of that State.

It was the right to go from one place to another, including the right to cross state borders while en route, that was vindicated in *Edwards v. California*, 314 U.S. 160...(1941), which invalidated a state law that impeded the free interstate passage of the indigent....

The second component of the right to travel is...expressly protected by the text of the Constitution. The first sentence of Article IV, § 2, provides:

> "The Citizens of each State shall be entitled to all Privileges and Immunities of Citizens in the several States."

Thus, by virtue of a person's state citizenship, a citizen of one State who travels in other States, intending to return home at the end of his journey, is entitled to enjoy the "Privileges and Immunities of Citizens in the several States" that he visits....This provision removes "from the citizens of each State the disabilities of alienage in the other States."...Those protections are not "absolute," but the Clause "does bar discrimination against citizens of other States where there is no substantial reason for the discrimination beyond the mere fact that they are citizens of other States." 334 U.S. at 396. There may be a substantial reason for requiring the nonresident to pay more than the resident...to enroll in the state university, see *Vlandis v. Kline*, 412 U.S. 441...(1973), but our cases have not identified any acceptable reason for qualifying the protection afforded by the Clause for "the 'citizen of State A who ventures into State B' to settle there and establish a home."...

What is at issue in this case, then, is this third aspect of the right to travel—the right of the newly arrived citizen to the same privileges and immunities enjoyed by other citizens of the same State. That right is protected not only by the new arrival's status as a state citizen, but also by her status as a citizen of the United States.[15]...That additional source of protection is plainly identified in the opening words of the Fourteenth Amendment:

> "All persons born or naturalized in the United States, and subject to the jurisdiction thereof, are citizens of the United States and of the State wherein they reside. No State shall make or enforce any law which shall abridge the privileges or immunities of citizens of the United States;...."[16]

---

[15] The Framers of the Fourteenth Amendment modeled this Clause upon the "Privileges and Immunities" Clause found in Article IV. Cong. Globe, 39th Cong., 1st Sess., 1033-1034 (1866) (statement of Rep. Bingham). In *Dred Scott v. Sandford*, 60 U.S. 393, 19 HOW 393, 15 L. Ed. 691 (1857), this Court had limited the protection of Article IV to rights under state law and concluded that free blacks could not claim citizenship. The Fourteenth Amendment overruled this decision. The Amendment's Privileges and Immunities Clause and Citizenship Clause guaranteed the rights of newly freed black citizens by ensuring that they could claim the state citizenship of any State in which they resided and by precluding that State from abridging their rights of national citizenship.

[16] U.S. Const., Amdt. 14, § 1. The remainder of the section provides: "nor shall any State deprive any person of life, liberty, or property, without due process of law; nor deny to any person within its jurisdiction the equal protection of the laws."

Despite fundamentally differing views concerning the coverage of the Privileges or Immunities Clause of the Fourteenth Amendment, most notably expressed in the majority and dissenting opinions in the *Slaughter-House Cases*, 83 U.S. 36, 16 Wall. 36, 21 L. Ed. 394 (1873), it has always been common ground that this Clause protects the third component of the right to travel....

* * *

V

Because this case involves discrimination against citizens who have completed their interstate travel, the State's argument that its welfare scheme affects the right to travel only "incidentally" is beside the point. Were we concerned solely with actual deterrence to migration, we might be persuaded that a partial withholding of benefits constitutes a lesser incursion on the right to travel than an outright denial of all benefits....But since the right to travel embraces the citizen's right to be treated equally in her new State of residence, the discriminatory classification is itself a penalty.

It is undisputed that respondents and the members of the class that they represent are citizens of California and that their need for welfare benefits is unrelated to the length of time that they have resided in California. We thus have no occasion to consider what weight might be given to a citizen's length of residence if the bona fides of her claim to state citizenship were questioned. Moreover, because whatever benefits they receive will be consumed while they remain in California, there is no danger that recognition of their claim will encourage citizens of other States to establish residency for just long enough to acquire some readily portable benefit, such as a divorce or a college education, that will be enjoyed after they return to their original domicile....

...To justify § 11450.03, California must...explain not only why it is sound fiscal policy to discriminate against those who have been citizens for less than a year, but also why it is permissible to apply such a variety of rules within that class.

These classifications may not be justified by a purpose to deter welfare applicants from migrating to California for three reasons. First, although it is reasonable to assume that some persons may be motivated to move for the purpose of obtaining higher benefits, the empirical evidence reviewed by the District Judge, which takes into account the high cost of living in California, indicates that the number of such persons is quite small—surely not large enough to justify a burden on those who had no such motive....Second, California has represented to the Court that the legislation was not enacted for any such reason.[19] Third, even if it were, as we squarely held in *Shapiro v. Thompson*, 394 U.S. 618...(1969), such a purpose would be unequivocally impermissible.

Disavowing any desire to fence out the indigent, California has instead advanced an entirely fiscal justification for its multitiered scheme. The enforcement of § 11450.03 will save the State approximately $10.9 million a year. The question is not whether such saving is a legitimate purpose but whether the State may accomplish that end by the discriminatory means it has chosen. An evenhanded, across-the-board reduction of about 72 cents per month for every beneficiary would produce the same result. But our negative answer to the question does not rest on the weakness of the State's purported fiscal justification. It rests on the fact that the Citizenship Clause of the Fourteenth Amendment expressly equates citizenship with residence: "That Clause does not provide for, and does not allow for, degrees of citizenship based on length of residence." *Zobel*, 457 U.S. at 69. It is equally clear that the Clause does

[19] The District Court and the Court of Appeals concluded, however, that the "apparent purpose of § 11450.03 was to deter migration of poor people to California." *Roe v. Anderson*, 134 F.3d 1400, 1404 (CA9 1998).

not tolerate a hierarchy of 45 subclasses of similarly situated citizens based on the location of their prior residence....Thus § 11450.03 is doubly vulnerable: Neither the duration of respondents' California residence, nor the identity of their prior States of residence, has any relevance to their need for benefits. Nor do those factors bear any relationship to the State's interest in making an equitable allocation of the funds to be distributed among its needy citizens. As in *Shapiro*, we reject any contributory rationale for the denial of benefits to new residents:

> "But we need not rest on the particular facts of these cases. Appellants' reasoning would logically permit the State to bar new residents from schools, parks, and libraries or deprive them of police and fire protection. Indeed it would permit the State to apportion all benefits and services according to the past tax contributions of its citizens."

394 U.S. at 632-633.

* * *

VI

The question that remains is whether congressional approval of durational residency requirements in the 1996 amendment to the Social Security Act somehow resuscitates the constitutionality of § 11450.03. That question is readily answered, for we have consistently held that Congress may not authorize the States to violate the Fourteenth Amendment....Moreover, the protection afforded to the citizen by the Citizenship Clause of that Amendment is a limitation on the powers of the National Government as well as the States.

* * *

The Solicitor General does not unequivocally defend the constitutionality of § 11450.03. But he has argued that two features of PRWORA may provide a sufficient justification for state durational requirements to warrant further inquiry before finally passing on the section's validity, or perhaps that it is only invalid insofar as it applies to new arrivals who were not on welfare before they arrived in California....

He first points out that because the TANF program gives the States broader discretion than did AFDC, there will be significant differences among the States which may provide new incentives for welfare recipients to change their residences. He does not, however, persuade us that the disparities under the new program will necessarily be any greater than the differences under AFDC, which included such examples as the disparity between California's monthly benefit of $673 for a family of four with Mississippi's benefit of $144 for a comparable family. Moreover, we are not convinced that a policy of eliminating incentives to move to California provides a more permissible justification for classifying California citizens than a policy of imposing special burdens on new arrivals to deter them from moving into the State. Nor is the discriminatory impact of § 11450.03 abated by repeatedly characterizing it as "a sort of specialized choice-of-law rule."...California law alone discriminates among its own citizens on the basis of their prior residence.

The Solicitor General also suggests that we should recognize the congressional concern addressed in the legislative history of PRWORA that the "States might engage in a 'race to the bottom' in setting the benefit levels in their TANF programs."[24] Again, it is difficult to see why that concern should be any greater under TANF than under AFDC. The evidence reviewed by the District Court indicates that the savings resulting from the discriminatory policy, if spread equitably throughout the entire program, would have only a minuscule impact on benefit levels. Indeed, as one of the legislators apparently interpreted this concern, it would logically prompt the States to reduce benefit levels sufficiently "to encourage emigration of benefit recipients."...But speculation about such an unlikely eventuality provides no basis for upholding § 11450.03.

Finally, the Solicitor General suggests that the State's discrimination might be acceptable if California had limited the disfavored subcategories of new citizens to those who had received aid in their prior State of residence at any time within the year before their arrival in California. The suggestion is ironic for at least three reasons: It would impose the most severe burdens on the neediest members of the disfavored classes; it would significantly reduce the savings that the State would obtain, thus making the State's claimed justification even less tenable; and, it would confine the effect of the statute to what the Solicitor General correctly characterizes as "the invidious purpose of discouraging poor people generally from settling in the State."...

* * *

Citizens of the United States, whether rich or poor, have the right to choose to be citizens "of the State wherein they reside." U.S. Const., Amdt. 14, § 1. The States, however, do not have any right to select their citizens.[27] The Fourteenth Amendment, like the Constitution itself, was, as Justice Cardozo put it, "framed upon the theory that the peoples of the several states must sink or swim together, and that in the long run prosperity and salvation are in union and not division." *Baldwin v. G. A. F. Seelig, Inc.*, 294 U.S. 511...(1935).

The judgment of the Court of Appeals is affirmed.

It is so ordered.

CHIEF JUSTICE REHNQUIST, with whom **JUSTICE THOMAS** joins, dissenting.

The Court today breathes new life into the previously dormant Privileges or Immunities Clause of the Fourteenth Amendment....It uses this Clause to strike down what I believe is a reasonable measure falling under the head of a "good-faith residency requirement." Because I do not think any provision of the Constitution—and surely not a provision relied upon for only the second time since its enactment 130 years ago—requires this result, I dissent.

I

* * *

...I cannot see how the right to become a citizen of another State is a necessary "component" of the right to travel, or why the Court tries to marry these separate and distinct rights. A person is no longer "traveling" in any sense of the

---

[24] Id., at 8. See H. R. Rep. No. 104-651, p. 1337 (1996) ("States that want to pay higher benefits should not be deterred from doing so by the fear that they will attract large numbers of recipients from bordering States");

[27] As Justice Jackson observed, "it is a privilege of citizenship of the United States, protected from state abridgment, to enter any State of the Union, either for temporary sojourn or for the establishment of permanent residence therein and for gaining resultant citizenship thereof. If national citizenship means less than this, it means nothing." *Edwards v. California*, 314 U.S. 160, 183, 86 L. Ed. 119, 62 S. Ct. 164 (1941) (concurring opinion).

word when he finishes his journey to a State which he plans to make his home. Indeed, under the Court's logic, the protections of the Privileges or Immunities Clause recognized in this case come into play only when an individual stops traveling with the intent to remain and become a citizen of a new State....

No doubt the Court has, in the past 30 years, essentially conflated the right to travel with the right to equal state citizenship in striking down durational residence requirements similar to the one challenged here....

Instead, the Court in these cases held that restricting the provision of welfare benefits, votes, or certain medical benefits to new citizens for a limited time impermissibly "penalized" them under the Equal Protection Clause of the Fourteenth Amendment for having exercised their right to travel....The Court thus settled for deciding what restrictions amounted to "deprivations of very important benefits and rights" that operated to indirectly "penalize" the right to travel. See *Attorney General of N.Y. v. Soto-Lopez*, 476 U.S. 898...(1986) (plurality opinion). In other cases, the Court recognized that laws dividing new and old residents had little to do with the right to travel and merely triggered an inquiry into whether the resulting classification rationally furthered a legitimate government purpose. See *Zobel v. Williams*, 457 U.S. 55...(1982); *Hooper v. Bernalillo County Assessor*, 472 U.S. 612...(1985)....While *Zobel* and *Hooper* reached the wrong result in my view, they at least put the Court on the proper track in identifying exactly what interests it was protecting; namely, the right of individuals not to be subject to unjustifiable classifications as opposed to infringements on the right to travel.

The Court today tries to clear much of the underbrush created by these prior right-to-travel cases, abandoning its effort to define what residence requirements deprive individuals of "important rights and benefits" or "penalize" the right to travel....Under its new analytical framework, a State, outside certain ill-defined circumstances, cannot classify its citizens by the length of their residence in the State without offending the Privileges or Immunities Clause of the Fourteenth Amendment. The Court thus departs from Shapiro and its progeny, and, while paying lipservice to the right to travel, the Court does little to explain how the right to travel is involved at all. Instead, as the Court's analysis clearly demonstrates..., this case is only about respondents' right to immediately enjoy all the privileges of being a California citizen in relation to that State's ability to test the good-faith assertion of this right. The Court has thus come full circle by effectively disavowing the analysis of Shapiro, segregating the right to travel and the rights secured by Article IV from the right to become a citizen under the Privileges or Immunities Clause, and then testing the residence requirement here against this latter right. For all its misplaced efforts to fold the right to become a citizen into the right to travel, the Court has essentially returned to its original understanding of the right to travel.

I

In unearthing from its tomb the right to become a state citizen and to be treated equally in the new State of residence, however, the Court ignores a State's need to assure that only persons who establish a bona fide residence receive the benefits provided to current residents of the State....

...[T]he Court has consistently recognized that while new citizens must have the same opportunity to enjoy the privileges of being a citizen of a State, the States retain the ability to use bona fide residence requirements to ferret out those who intend to take the privileges and run....

While the physical presence element of a bona fide residence is easy to police, the subjective intent element is not. It is simply unworkable and futile to require States to inquire into each new resident's subjective intent to remain. Hence, States employ objective criteria such as durational residence requirements to test a new resident's resolve to remain before these new citizens can enjoy certain in-state benefits. Recognizing the practical appeal of such criteria, this Court has repeatedly sanctioned the State's use of durational residence requirements before new residents receive in-state tuition rates at state universities....The Court has done the same in upholding a 1-year residence requirement for eligibility to obtain a divorce in state courts..., and in upholding political party registration restrictions that amounted to a durational residency requirement for voting in primary elections....

If States can require individuals to reside in-state for a year before exercising the right to educational benefits, the right to terminate a marriage, or the right to vote in primary elections that all other state citizens enjoy, then States may surely do the same for welfare benefits. Indeed, there is no material difference between a 1-year residence requirement applied to the level of welfare benefits given out by a State, and the same requirement applied to the level of tuition subsidies at a state university. The welfare payment here and in-state tuition rates are cash subsidies provided to a limited class of people, and California's standard of living and higher education system make both subsidies quite attractive. Durational residence requirements were upheld when used to regulate the provision of higher education subsidies, and the same deference should be given in the case of welfare payments....

* * *

In one respect, the State has a greater need to require a durational residence for welfare benefits than for college eligibility. The impact of a large number of new residents who immediately seek welfare payments will have a far greater impact on a State's operating budget than the impact of new residents seeking to attend a state university. In the case of the welfare recipients, a modest durational residence requirement to allow for the completion of an annual legislative budget cycle gives the State time to decide how to finance the increased obligations.

The Court tries to distinguish education and divorce benefits by contending that the welfare payment here will be consumed in California, while a college education or a divorce produces benefits that are "portable" and can be enjoyed after individuals return to their original domicile....But this "you can't take it with you" distinction is more apparent than real, and offers little guidance to lower courts who must apply this rationale in the future. Welfare payments are a form of insurance, giving impoverished individuals and their families the means to meet the demands of daily life while they receive the necessary training, education, and time to look for a job. The cash itself will no doubt be spent in California, but the benefits from receiving this income and having the opportunity to become employed or employable will stick with the welfare recipient if they stay in California or go back to their true domicile....

I therefore believe that the durational residence requirement challenged here is a permissible exercise of the State's power to "assure that services provided for its residents are enjoyed only by residents."...

Finally, Congress' express approval in 42 U.S.C. § 604(c) of durational residence requirements for welfare recipients like the one established by California only goes to show the reasonableness of a law like § 11450.03. The National Legislature, where people from Mississippi as well as California are represented, has recognized the need to protect state resources in a time of experimentation and welfare reform. As States like California revamp their total welfare packages,...they should have the authority and flexibility to ensure that their new programs are not exploited. Congress has decided that it makes good welfare policy to give the States this power. California has reasonably exercised it through an objective, narrowly tailored residence requirement. I see nothing in the Constitution that should prevent the enforcement of that requirement.

* * *

Questions for Discussion

1. If California provides $645 a month in AFDC (TANF) safety-net assistance for a mother and two children based on a legislative intent to assure rent, utilities and basic necessities for child protection, how is that intent effectuated for newly arrived children whose benefit is cut to $145 per month based on the rent extant in another state? Assuming parental responsibility, does not such a policy necessarily implicate a right to travel from such a state to California? Note that the "portability" discussion of *Saenz* suggests that California may restrict its benefits to only those children who are currently living in California and subject to its higher rents.

2. The dissent argues that the California policy is simply a variation of a commonly approved state "residency" requirement to assure state presence and prevent fraud. Is this posited *bona fide* residency intent actually the purpose or effect of the policy? How is that state interest consistent with California's stated primary motivation to save $10 million in public funds?

3. Would it be permissible for California to set its tuition for out-of-state students based on the average tuition charged by each student's previous state of residence?

4. Is it important that the total number of TANF applicants in California who have been in the state less than one year before applying for assistance amounts to less than 2% of those enrolled? If such is the case, where is the empirical basis that the reduction policy is needed to discourage welfare movement between states seeking lucrative California benefits? Does that fact undermine the dissent's argument that the restriction is akin to a residency requirement for divorce, *i.e.*, intended to prevent fraud? Is the argument that such a condition prevents evasion of the divorce requirements of the real state of residency applicable at all to welfare benefits received only while a family is in California?

5. Assume that the purpose of the AFDC (TANF) program is to provide basic sustenance for the safety net protection of children, primarily money for rent to avoid homelessness. Is it consistent with such Congressional intent for one state to set benefit levels at median rent levels, while another state sets them at one-third its median rent? If a child in one state receives enough to pay for his family's rent, while a child in another state is rendered homeless, is the latter child receiving the "equal protection" of federal law?

6. Assume that a state does not use the "state of origin" level approach of California, but simply lowers its benefits so that its impoverished families are compelled to leave. The Court holds that California cannot influence families in Mississippi to stay put by refusing to allow them better benefits if they enter its domain. Is there a "freedom of travel" difference between impeding travel by sanctioning new entrants, and compelling travel by sanctioning your own impoverished population to force their departure?

7. Do the low benefits of a state such as Mississippi set at a small fraction of local median rent impede entry into that state from a California family receiving full median rent assistance? The Court might argue that equal protection principles are not violated where Mississippi treats all of its own residents

similarly and that the difference is based on permissibly varying state policies. But does such a wide disparity between states implicate interstate "freedom of travel," regardless of benefit level consistency within a state?

8. What would be the equal protection implications of a holding that children had a "fundamental liberty interest" in shelter and food for minimal health and safety? What would be the equal protection implications for *Saenz* of a holding that as with race, religion and gender, children as a group have suffered historical discrimination and lack political power sufficiently to constitute a protected class, thus invoking "strict scrutiny"?

2. Foster Care Assistance Standards

Miller v. Youakim

440 U.S. 125 (1979)

MR. JUSTICE MARSHALL delivered the opinion of the Court.

At issue in this appeal is whether Illinois may exclude from its Aid to Families with Dependent Children-Foster Care program children who reside with relatives.

The Aid to Families with Dependent Children-Foster Care program (AFDC-FC) authorizes federal financial subsidies for the care and support of children removed from their homes and made wards of the State pursuant to a judicial determination that the children's homes were not conducive to their welfare....42 U.S.C. §§ 608 (a)(1), (2).... To qualify for Foster Care assistance, these children must be placed in a "foster family home or child-care institution."...The basic AFDC program, already in existence when the Foster Care program was enacted in 1961, provides aid to eligible children who live with a parent or with a relative specified in § 406 (a) of the Act....In administering these programs, Illinois distinguishes between related and unrelated foster parents. Children placed in unrelated foster homes may participate in the AFDC-FC program. But those who are placed in the homes of relatives listed in § 406 (a), and who are entitled to basic AFDC benefits, cannot receive AFDC-FC assistance because the State defines the term "foster family home" as a facility for children unrelated to the operator....Foster children living with relatives may participate only in Illinois' basic AFDC program, which provides lower monthly payments than the Foster Care program.[5] The specific question presented here is whether Illinois has correctly interpreted the federal standards for AFDC-FC eligibility set forth in § 408 (a) of the Act to exclude children who, because of placement with related rather than unrelated foster parents, qualify for assistance under the basic AFDC program.

I

Appellees are four foster children, their older sister (Linda Youakim), and her husband (Marcel Youakim). In 1969, Illinois removed the children from their mother's home and made them wards of the State following a judicial determination of neglect. The Department of Children and Family Services (Department), which became responsible for the children,...placed them in unrelated foster care facilities until 1972. During this period, they each received full AFDC-FC benefits of

---

[5] Illinois, like most other States, has consistently authorized substantially greater AFDC-FC payments than basic AFDC benefits....

$ 105 a month. In 1972, the Department decided to place two of the children with the Youakims, who were under no legal obligation to accept or support them....The Department investigated the Youakim home and approved it as meeting the licensing standards established for unrelated foster family homes, as required by state law.[8] Despite this approval, the State refused to make Foster Care payments on behalf of the children because they were related to Linda Youakim.

The exclusion of foster children living with related caretakers from Illinois' AFDC-FC program reflects the State's view that the home of a relative covered under basic AFDC is not a "foster family home" within the meaning of § 408 (a)(3), the federal AFDC-FC eligibility provision at issue here. Interpreting that provision, Illinois defines a "foster family home" as

> "a facility for child care in residences of families who receive no more than 8 children *unrelated to them*...for the purpose of providing family care and training for the children on a full-time basis....".…

Homes that do not meet the definition may not be licensed,...and under state law, only licensed facilities are entitled to Foster Care payments....

Although Illinois refused to make Foster Care payments, it did provide each child basic AFDC benefits of approximately $63 a month, substantially less than the applicable $105 AFDC-FC rate.[12] The Youakims, however, believed that these payments were insufficient to provide proper support, and declined to accept the other two children. These children remain in unrelated foster care facilities and continue to receive AFDC-FC benefits.

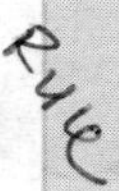

In 1973, the Youakims and the four foster children brought a class action under 42 U.S.C. § 1983 for themselves and persons similarly situated, challenging Illinois' distinction between related and unrelated foster parents as violative of the Equal Protection Clause of the Fourteenth Amendment....

* * *

I

A participating State may not deny assistance to persons who meet eligibility standards defined in the Social Security Act unless Congress clearly has indicated that the standards are permissive....Congress has specified that programs, like AFDC-FC, which employ the term "dependent child" to define eligibility must be available for "all eligible individuals."...Section 408 (e) reinforces this general rule by requiring States to provide Foster Care benefits to "any" child who satisfies the federal eligibility criteria of § 408 (a). Thus, if foster care in related homes is encompassed within § 408, Illinois may not deny AFDC-FC benefits when it places an eligible child in the care of a relative.

---

[8] Ch. 23, §§ 4-1.2 and 2217...; Illinois Department of Children and Family Services, Child Welfare Manual 2.8.2 (1976).... The DCFS Welfare Manual recently has been revised to conform to the decisions below.

The Agency documented its approval in two "Relative Home Placement Agreements" which were identical, both in form and in obligations imposed, to those used for unrelated foster care placements, except that the term "foster" was sometimes crossed out, two references were made to the familial relationship among appellees, and the usual promise of AFDC-FC benefits was deleted. See 431 F.Supp. 40, 43–44, and nn. 4, 5 (ND Ill. 1976); App. 20–23.

[12] As an exception to this benefit differential, the State has authorized special supplemental payments, upon an adequate showing of need by related foster parents, to bring basic AFDC related foster care assistance up to $105 per month. Brief for Appellants 5; 374 F.Supp. 1204, 1206 (ND Ill. 1974). Since September 1, 1974, the Youakims have received these need-based payments for their foster children. This Court previously held that receipt of the supplemental benefits does not render the case moot. *Youakim v. Miller*, 425 U.S. 231, 236 n. 2 (1976) (*per curiam*).

In arguing that related foster care does not fall within § 408's definition of "foster family home," appellants submit that Congress enacted the Foster Care program solely for the benefit of children not otherwise eligible for categorical assistance. We disagree. The purpose of the AFDC-FC program was not simply to duplicate the AFDC program for a different class of beneficiaries. As the language and legislative history of § 408 demonstrate, the Foster Care program was designed to meet the particular needs of all eligible neglected children, whether they are placed with related or unrelated foster parents.

A

* * *

Had Congress intended to exclude related foster parents from the definition of "foster family home," it presumably would have done so explicitly, just as it restricted the definition of "child-care institution."[15] Instead, the statute plainly states that a foster family home is the home of any individual licensed or approved by the State as meeting its licensing requirements, and we are unpersuaded that the provisions on which appellants rely implicitly limit that expansive definition.

* * *

III

* * *

...Accordingly, we hold that the AFDC-FC program encompasses foster children who, pursuant to a judicial determination of neglect, have been placed in related homes that meet a State's licensing requirements for foster homes.

The judgment below is

Affirmed.

* * *

---

[15] In contrast to the broad definition of "foster family home," the term "child-care institution" is explicitly qualified to exempt private institutions operated for profit and public institutions....

Unlike generic TANF, the AFDC-foster care program was not altered by the PRA and remains an entitlement, involving a higher benefit than straight AFDC (or TANF presently) provided in Illinois. States vary in their compensation for TANF versus "kin-care" versus regular licensed foster care. Usually TANF compensation is the lowest and licensed foster care the highest, particularly where multiple children are involved (unlike TANF parents, foster care rates are generally fully multiplied by number of children under care). From 40% to 50% of foster care children are cared for by relatives. Some kin are given "formal" foster care status, achieving what amounts to licensed status at full foster care rates. But most such providers are simply relatives helping out, and states vary in their compensation from traditional TANF benefits to full foster care-level compensation. Where receiving TANF benefits, they may receive a family grant if their income is low enough to qualify, or alternatively may qualify for a lower "child only" coverage amount. If they choose the family grant, however, they will be subject to the PRA restrictions listed above, including the work requirement and the 60 month absolute time limit.

The PRA creates a potential incentive shift in state funding by removing TANF as an entitlement and capping it as a block grant. Since foster care funds remain a federally matched entitlement without a lid, states can move children into foster care compensation (through "kin care" foster status), and use the TANF block grant money thus saved and already "in-hand" for other purposes.

Questions for Discussion

1. Can the state argue that a child's relative has a duty of care and that state compensation is inappropriate? Is such a duty to support enforceable? Could a statute theoretically impose such an obligation (similar to the obligation of parental support)? Assuming it could impose such a duty constitutionally, can it do so through a policy of non-payment for care by relatives where it imposes upon them no statutory duty of care? Does the state opportunity to save money by assigning foster children to relatives at no or lower compensation provide an economic incentive to do so apart from the merits (*e.g.*, where relatives are highly marginal or risky placements)?

2. Can the state pay higher foster care compensation to "licensed providers"? If so, can it enforce foster care by relatives on an unlicensed, and hence uncompensated basis? What if the relatives could qualify for licensure?

3. Does a higher grant for foster care than for TANF-in home care provide an incentive for parents to abandon children to relatives who will receive more for them than will they? Note that TANF is to be cut off after sixty months, and may be reduced by up to one-half (the "parent's share" cut sanction). Will that drive large numbers of children into foster care with relatives after 2002 (where either foster care or TANF compensation may be more available), when the sixty months will begin to expire for the parents of many children? How else will these children be supported absent other alternatives?

D. STATE WAIVERS AND BENEFIT LEVELS

Beno v. Shalala
30 F.3d 1057 (9th Cir. 1994)

GOODWIN, Circuit Judge:

Plaintiffs, California residents who receive Aid to Families with Dependant Children ("AFDC"), appeal the denial of their request for a preliminary injunction enjoining California's public benefits experiment. Plaintiffs object to a statewide benefits cut enacted as part of an experimental work-incentive project and challenge the Secretary of Health and Human Services' ("Secretary of HHS")...waiver of certain federal laws related to the project. They argue that the Secretary's waiver violates the Administrative Procedures Act, ("APA"), 5 U.S.C. § 701 *et seq.* and § 211 of the HHS Appropriations Act, 42 U.S.C. § 3515b, which prohibits HHS from spending federal money on experimental projects which pose a danger to human research subjects without their informed consent. In addition, they contend that California's project violates the Americans with Disabilities Act ("ADA"), 42 U.S.C. §§ 12131–12213, by failing to make reasonable accommodations for AFDC recipients with disabilities. We reverse.

I. CALIFORNIA'S PROGRAM

The benefits cut at issue in this appeal is part of a five-year Assistance Payments Demonstration Project ("APDP") enacted at Cal. Welf. & Inst. Code § 11450.01 *et seq.* APDP includes both a "residency requirement" and a "work-incentive" program. The former, which has been preliminarily enjoined on constitutional grounds, aims to discourage poor families from moving to California by limiting recent entrants' AFDC benefits to the amount received in their state of former residence. See *Green v. Anderson*, 811 F. Supp. 516 (E.D. Cal. 1993), aff'd 26 F.3d 95 (9th Cir. 1994). The latter, which is the subject of this appeal, aims to encourage AFDC recipients to find work by decreasing benefits and allowing recipients to keep more of their earned income.[2]

The work-incentive benefits cut affects all California AFDC families (approximately 826,000 families and 2.4 million persons,...) without regard to family composition or disabilities,[3] except for a "control group" of 5,000 families randomly selected from four counties. The control group receives AFDC benefits at their former levels and is subject to the old income-disregard rules. In order to assess the impact of the work-incentive program, the state plans to compare data about these control group families with data on 10,000 families randomly selected from the same four counties. The state does not plan to study most of the other approximately 800,000 families affected by the cut.

II. THE FEDERAL WAIVERS

The benefits program at issue, AFDC, is a cooperative federalism program created by the Social Security Act of 1935, 42 U.S.C. §§ 601–687. Participating states and the federal government jointly finance the program and state governments administer it under plans approved by the Secretary of Health and Human Services. *Id.* While states are not required to participate, participating states must comply with a variety of federal requirements....

California concedes that APDP violates several of these requirements, including the "Maintenance of Effort" requirement of 42 U.S.C. § 1396a(c)(1).[4] This section provides that:

> the Secretary shall not approve any State plan for medical assistance if—(1) the state has in effect [AFDC] payment levels that are less than the payment levels in effect under such plan on May 1, 1988.

---

[2] Specifically, the Project reduces the 1992 Maximum Aid Payments ("MAP") (*i.e.* the benefits) provided to needy families, but retains the 1992 Minimum Basic Standard of Adequate Care ("MBSAC") (with cost of living adjustments in 1992–96). Cal. Welf. & Inst. Code § 11452. Families are permitted to "fill the gap" between the MAP and the MBSAC by working and keeping their earnings as long as their total income does not exceed the MBSAC.

[3] Thus, the "work-incentive" benefits cut will affect not only AFDC families headed by "able-bodied" adults, but also families headed by adults who cannot work because of their disabilities and "child-only" AFDC families which contain no adult recipient.

[4] APDP also conflicts with (1) federal rules prohibiting states from basing AFDC benefits on the length of state residency; (2) federal income-disregard rules, including the "100 hour rule" which prohibits AFDC recipients from working more than 100 hours a month, 45 C.F.R. §§ 233.100(a)(1)(i), 233.100(c)(1)(iii) and the "thirty dollars and one-third earnings disregard" which restrict AFDC recipients' ability to retain earned income without losing benefits, 45 C.F.R. §§ 233.20(a)(11)(i)(D), 233.20(a)(11)(ii)(B); and (3) rules requiring states to provide uniform benefit payments statewide.

42 U.S.C. § 1396a(c)(1). California's experiment reduces AFDC benefits to below their May 1988 levels. Thus, absent a waiver, the state could not implement the experiment without jeopardizing federal funding of its $14 billion Medicaid program. The California statutes enacting APDP, therefore, refer explicitly to obtaining HHS approval, and do not become effective until thirty days after state officials receive such approval....

* * *

(2) The Plain Language of § 1315

Moreover, § 1315(a) plainly requires the Secretary to review state proposals. On its face, the statute allows waivers only (1) for experimental, demonstration or pilot projects, which (2) in the judgment of the Secretary are likely to assist in promoting the objectives of the Social Security Act and only (3) for the extent and period she finds necessary. Thus, while the Secretary has considerable discretion to decide which projects meet these criteria, she must, at a minimum, examine each of these issues.

* * *

As this statute, its legislative history, and courts have made clear, the AFDC program's main objective is to support needy children....Thus, in determining that a state project is "likely to further the goals of the Act," the Secretary must obviously consider the impact of the state's project on the children and families the AFDC program was enacted to protect....

* * *

D. The Administrative Record

Plaintiffs have indisputably shown that California's experiment has serious problems, both as an experiment and as an attempt at welfare reform. The actors in this case—including the Secretary, the district court, and impressively credentialed *amici*[39]—agree that both the statewide scope of the benefits cut as well as the decision to cut benefits to individuals who cannot work appear wholly unjustified by any legitimate experimental goal. State officials have advanced no such experimental goal, and we are unable to explain how it would advance social science to cut benefits to recipients who are not even included in the study. Amici accurately observe that such a design is "methodologically indefensible" in that it exposes a large number of subjects to potential harm, yet studies only a few....

Moreover, the idea of imposing a work-incentive benefits cut on individuals whose disabilities preclude work can only be called absurd. As the district court found, "the Demonstration Project was intended to create work-incentives for recipients able to work; the effect of the project on those disabled recipients who are unable to work appears unintended and serves no stated goal of the project."...."The State could exclude from the benefit cut those of the disabled who are unable to work" and "it would be humane to do so." *Id.* at 35....

---

[39] *Amici* include 19 biomedical and social scientists, physicians and other health care professionals, philosophers, and lawyers who served on the National Commission for the Protection of Human Subjects of Biomedical and Behavioral Research or its staff or on the President's Commission for the Study of Ethical Problems in Medicine and Biomedical and Behavioral Research or its staff.

Nearly everyone also agrees that California's experiment will put "child-only" AFDC families, AFDC families headed by adults who are too disabled to work, and families whose heads are unable to find work—or cannot work due to child-care, transportation, and other difficulties—at increased risk of homelessness, inadequate nutrition, and a variety of emotional and physical problems....The program offers no work-training, child-care, or any other assistance designed to enable recipients to find and keep jobs. Moreover, given the minimum level of benefits already paid to AFDC families, it is difficult to imagine that the benefits cut would radically change the existing incentives to work. As plaintiffs point out, California could have accomplished its goal of increasing recipients' incentive to work without cutting AFDC benefits at all, by simply allowing recipients to keep more of their earned income.

Given these various problems, plaintiffs' expert contends that California's experiment is "utterly unconscionable,"...and *amici* argue that it "flagrantly disregards the basic norms of research."....

* * *

In the present case, the record contains a rather stunning lack of evidence that the Secretary gave plaintiffs' objections any...consideration. Except for the Secretary's conclusory letter to plaintiffs' counsel and possibly her decision to limit California's authority to cut benefits, the record contains no evidence that the Secretary ever considered the danger California's benefits cut would pose to recipients, the state's decision to impose a statewide benefits cut, the need for cutting benefits as a work-incentive, the merits of imposing a work-incentive cut on individuals whose disabilities preclude work, or the feasibility of excluding individuals who receive federal disability benefits or have already been adjudged unable to work in the context of other government programs such as California's Greater Avenue for Independence ("GAIN") program. Neither the Secretary nor California ever responded to the substance of plaintiffs' objections, and the Secretary did not revise the Terms and Conditions at all in response to plaintiffs' comments.

* * *

Here, the record contains no evidence that the Secretary considered the materials plaintiffs submitted. While the state and HHS exchanged detailed drafts of the Terms and Conditions, these drafts did not address any of plaintiffs' objections. Even if these drafts show, as the district court found, that a "good deal of thought went into approval of the research design," ...they do not show that HHS gave any such thought to plaintiffs' objections or proposed alternatives. If anything, the timing of the waiver approval—HHS's final changes to the draft Terms were made on the very day it received plaintiffs' objections—suggests the opposite....

* * *

...The Secretary's waiver of 42 U.S.C. § 1396a(c)(1) is VACATED...and the case is REMANDED to the district court with instructions to remand to the Secretary for additional consideration of plaintiffs' objections....

REVERSED AND REMANDED.

O'SCANNLAIN, Circuit Judge, dissenting:

I respectfully dissent. For the reasons expressed in Judge Levi's well-crafted memorandum of decision and order (unpublished), I would affirm. Given the extremely deferential standard under which we review the Secretary's decisions under 42 U.S.C. § 1315, I believe that the agency record provides more than sufficient support for the Secretary's waiver.

* * *

...[T]he instant proceeding is very similar to *Aguayo v. Richardson*, 473 F.2d 1090 (2d Cir. 1973), the only other appellate case to review the Secretary's waiver of federal requirements under Section 1315 and approval of an experimental welfare project. In *Aguayo*, as here, the Secretary approved New York's proposed welfare program without a statement of the grounds for its decision. *Id.* at 1103....

The majority attempts to distinguish *Aguayo* because the Aguayo agency record included not only the plaintiffs' objections to the welfare plan, but also a memorandum prepared by the state responding to these objections. This is both true and irrelevant. Although California did not similarly respond to the appellants' objections, the agency record does include extensive information on the proposed program. Besides California's application for the waiver, the Secretary had before her the appellants' "voluminous materials" about the claimed harms the program would cause....

* * *

Because the extremely deferential standard for reviewing the agency's process controls the decision in this case, I need not comment on other issues discussed in the court's opinion.

Questions for Discussion

1. Assuming one wants to engage in an experiment with a control group, why would one test 2.4 million children and use 5,000 as the control group rather than vice versa? Would the state's experiment qualify as acceptable under "human subjects" ethical scrutiny?

2. Are state experiments acceptable where there is already an existing body of data on the impact of benefit reductions on percentage of recipients working? AFDC benefits at the time of *Beno* were about $7,000 per year for the benchmark mother and two children; does that assistance remove her incentive to work for more income? Are a substantial number of parents going to work hard at $6,000 per year in assistance, but reject additional work if receiving $7,000?

3. Is it relevant that from 1989 to 1994, AFDC benefits in California were already cut in constant dollars (by over 15% by excluding any cost of living adjustment)? Hadn't the state been experimenting with benefit reductions for the prior five years (during which numbers of claimants increased markedly)?

4. Would the state have a stronger case for reductions to test unwed birth rates at different compensation levels? Or the degree to which child support is generated from absent parents to make up for public aid subtractions?

E. NOTE ON CHILD OPPORTUNITY, POVERTY, AND AMERICA'S TWO PROMISES

The longstanding American commitment to succeeding generations has included a notion of egalitarianism—the chance for children born in poverty to advance, and with two hallmark promises from the previous generation: meaningful employment and home ownership. Chapter 1 discusses the growth of regressive taxation and the deferral of obligation onto future generations that may affect these aspirations. In particular, regressive payroll taxes are relied upon to fund both Social Security and Medicare, together imposing a projected debt of over $30 trillion to be borne by the next generation. Other public policies and private cost trends supplement these trends to the disadvantage of upward fluidity and opportunity.

1. Inheritance Taxation

The Congress has voted to phase-out entirely federal inheritance/estate taxes by 2010 (after having already exempted the first $1.5 million in each estate from taxation in 2001). Half of all estate taxes are currently paid by the 2,400 largest estates, and the elimination of this tax confers a benefit on their heirs averaging $3.5 million each. The defenders of the abolition claim that family-owned businesses or farms are lost to family succession, but only 3% of taxed estates have such assets, and these paid less than one-half of one percent of existing estate taxes.

African-American children inherit less than one-fifth the average amount of white children. Child advocates argue that modest inheritance taxes allow a small sharing of unearned wealth by those born to privilege to other children—serving egalitarian principles of opportunity equity and meritocracy.

2. Necessity Cost Increases and Minimum Wage Decline

Energy costs have increased substantially above inflation; in California, for example, inflation was marked by the 2000 and 2001 energy deregulation market failures producing $40 billion in costs above the rates of other markets. These utility costs have been exacerbated nationally by gasoline prices that have risen to almost $3 per gallon. In this context, the Republican Congress in October 2005 rejected an attempt to increase the minimum wage along a party line vote—it remains at $5.15 per hour and has not been increased since 1997. The maintenance of the minimum wage accomplishes a 24% reduction in spending power over the last eight years based on the Consumer Price Index from 1997 through 2005. Because of increases well above the CPI in the practical necessities of energy, gasoline and rent, effective earning diminution has been higher for parents working at—or influenced by—the minimum wage floor.

3. Promise #1: Higher Education Opportunity

Parents have historically taken pride in seeing their children attend a university and enjoy wealth and life options unavailable to them or their forebearers. Higher education tuition has joined energy and rents in a twenty year rise at well beyond CPI increase levels. College graduates depend on federal and state low interest loans—now under budgetary pressure and now proposed at higher cost and less availability. Living cost increases for students have also increased and even if loans cover tuition, those costs may limit opportunity. These decisions contrast with the "GI Bill of Rights" spirit of the previous generation in allowing many thousands to attend college who would otherwise not be able to afford it. Those able to obtain tuition or additional loans now face unprecedented debt levels upon graduation. This cost inflation is joined by a more troubling failure to expand higher education capacity. That shortfall relates directly to the employability of the next generation given the evolving international job market—where American opportunity for youth depends upon advanced and technical education (see Chapter 4 below).

4. Promise #2: Home Ownership

Beyond educational opportunity for meaningful employment, American tradition has also provided a second intergenerational promise: the chance for a family with home ownership. The median price of homes has passed $300,000 and has now reached $500,000 in coastal states and for most of the California population. The prices are now at a level inhibiting home ownership. The barrier will be insurmountable for the vast majority of children not positioned to inherit real property should interest rates increase. In October 2005, the federal reserve announced the nation's highest monthly inflationary measure in more than a decade and home interest rates continued a gradual rise to average above 6% nationally. Such mortgage rate increase radically limits ownership opportunity for youth.

ENDNOTES

[1] Note that there are two separate federal measures of poverty. The "poverty thresholds" for various family sizes were the original format developed by Mollie Orshanksy of the Social Security Administration. These thresholds are used for statistical purposes, *e.g.*, estimating the number of children in poverty each year.

In contrast, the "poverty guidelines" are issued each year in the Federal Register by the U.S. Department of Health and Human Services (DHHS). They are a simplification of the more complex "thresholds" above for administrative purposes, including eligibility for income related programs. The guidelines below went into effect as of February 2005 and are popularly referred to as the "federal poverty line." For the 48 contiguous states, they are:

Size of family unit	Poverty guideline
1	$9,570
2	$12,830
3	$16,090
4	$19,350
5	$22,610
6	$25,870
7	$29,130
8	$32,390
additional members	$3,260

Source: Federal Register, Vol. 70, No. 33, February 18, 2005 at 8373–75; see also http://aspe.hhs.gov/poverty/05poverty.shtml.

[2] National Center for Children in Poverty at Columbia University, *Child Poverty Fact Sheet, June 2001*. Note that the conclusions are based on 1999 census data. See http://cpmcnet.columbia.edu/dept/nccp/ycpf.html.

[3] See Timothy Smeeding, *Child Well-Being, Child Poverty and Child Policy in Modern Nations*, Syracuse University, 2001, *passim*. Note that the study is based on 1995–97 data and does not use the federal poverty line criterion due to its inapplicability in other nations. It rather defines poverty as those living at under one-half of the net median income within the jurisdiction. Hence, it tends to measure relative income inequality.

[4] Linda Neuhauser, Doris Disbrow, and Sheldon Margen, University of California at Berkeley School of Public Health, *Hunger and Food Insecurity in California,* California Policy Seminar Brief (Berkeley, CA; April 1995) at 2.

[5] U.S. Department of Agriculture, *Food Security Measurement Study* (Washington, D.C.; Sept. 15, 1997) at ES 1-6 (available at http://www.usda.gov).

[6] U.S. Department of Agriculture, *Measuring Food Insecurity in the United States: Prevalence of Food Insecurity and Hunger by State, 1996–1998* (Washington, D.C.; 2000) News Release at 1 (http://www.usda.gov).

[7] Food Research and Action Center, *Health Consequences of Hunger* (http://www.frac.org).

[8] Federal Interagency Forum on Child and Family Statistics, *America's Children: Key National Indicators of Well-Being, 1998* (Washington, D.C.; 1998) at 15.

[9] See United States Conference of Mayors, *A Status Report on Hunger and Homelessness in America's Cities 1999, A 26 City Survey* (Dec. 1999) at 1 (http://www.usmayors.org).

[10] U.S. Conference of Mayors, *A Status Report on Hunger and Homelessness in American Cities, 1998* (Dec. 1999) at Summary (http://usmayors.org).

[11] *Status on Hunger, supra* note 9, at 1.

[12] California Food Policy Advocates, *Legal Immigrant Households in Two California Counties: The Impact of Food Stamp Cuts* (San Francisco, CA; May 26, 1998).

[13] Snapshots of America's Families, *National Survey of America's Families* (Jan. 1999) at 3 (California) (see http://newfederalism.urban.org).

[14] Sandra H. Venner, Ashley F. Sullivan, Dorie Seavey, Tufts University School of Nutrition Science and Policy, Center on Hunger and Poverty, *Paradox of Our Times: Hunger in a Strong Economy* (Medford, MA; Jan. 2000) at "Highlights of the Paradox" preceding p. 1.

[15] John T. Cook and Katie S. Martin, Tufts University School of Nutrition Science and Policy, Center on Hunger and Poverty, *Differences in Nutrient Adequacy Among Poor and Non-Poor Children* (Medford, MA; March 1995) at 7.

[16] *Hunger in California, supra* note 4, at 5.

[17] *Id.* at 6; see also Center on Budget and Policy Priorities, *Discussion of Selected Food Stamp Provisions in the Personal Responsibility Act* (Washington, D.C.; Apr. 7, 1995) at 1–2.

[18] See Mary C. Daly, Deborah Reed, and Heather N. Royer, *Population Mobility and Income Inequality in California*, Public Policy Institute of California, California Counts, Vol. 2, No. 4 (May 2001), at 1–2. The Institute places the impact of immigration as accounting for one-third of the income inequality growth in California, but adds: "However, other forces explain the bulk of the growth in inequality. The rising value of skills such as schooling and labor market experience has been one of the most important factors behind the growing inequality. Thus, the concern over the economic opportunities available to low- income families, particularly those headed by low-skilled workers, is well-founded" (at 2).

[19] For example, in March 1998, California's minimum wage was raised to $5.75 per hour. On October 24, 2000, the state's Industrial Welfare Commission increased the state minimum wage to $6.25 effective January 1, 2001, and to $6.75 per hour on January 1, 2002. Eight other states have a minimum wage set at between $6.25 and $6.75 per hour.

[20] See data and discussion in California Budget Project, *California's Recent Minimum Wage Increases: Real Wage Gains with No Loss of Jobs, Minimum Wage Remains Inadequate to Meet California's Cost of Living,* Budget Brief (June 2000) at 4 (see http://www.cbp.org).

[21] Federal legislation introduced in 2001 (H.R. 665, S. 272) would raise the minimum wage to $6.65 over two years, still well below the poverty line for the benchmark family of three.

[22] See research compiled by the Economic Policy Institute at http://www.epinet.org. See esp. the resources bibliography and the EPI post 1999 publications accessible at this site. See *e.g.*, Edith Rasell, Jared Bernstein and Heather Boushey, *Step up, Not Out: The Case for Raising the Federal Minimum Wage for Workers in Every State,* EPI (Feb. 2001); Jared Bernstein and John Schmitt, *The Impact of the Minimum Wage: Policy Lifts Wages, Maintains Floor for Low-Wage Market*; see also confirming conclusions in *California's Recent Minimum Wage, supra* note 20.

[23] See Economic Policy Institute, *Minimum Wage Facts at a Glance* (Washington D.C.; 2001) at http://www.epinet.org.

[24] Some cities (*e.g.*, Baltimore and San Francisco) have implemented "living wage" policies boosting hourly rates for City and other work to above $10 per hour and attempting to target a higher percentage of working poor.

[25] A study by Harvard University's Professor Bruce Fuller surveyed 1,800 child care centers in 36 states and concluded that families with annual incomes over $50,000 pay just 6% of their incomes for child care, while families earning under $15,000 devote 23% of their income for child care. One-third of the

annual $4 billion in credits goes to families with incomes above $50,000 per year. For a discussion, see Diego Ribadeneira, *Day Care Credits Said to Favor Well Off*, Boston Globe, Sept. 18, 1992, at 3.

[26] See, *e.g.*, Iris J. Lav, Center on Budget and Policy Priorities, *The Final Tax Bill: Assessing the Long-Term Costs and the Distribution of Tax Benefits* (Washington, D.C.; Aug. 1, 1997) at 1.

[27] Note the interesting argument of William Gale, The Brookings Institution, *Tax Reform is Dead, Long Live Tax Reform* (Washington, D.C.; 1997) (Policy Brief No. 12), which explores the thesis that deductible savings accounts for higher education will lead to higher tuition and reduced Pell Grants and other financing for poorer students, perhaps actually lowering opportunity for children most needing college assistance. Although such tax incentives may be a net gain for children in terms of dollars provided overall, they exclude the large impoverished population most in need of assistance. Making the incentive into a "refundable tax credit," as with the EITC, extends the education incentive evenly across society, including those most in need. While an argument can be made for focusing such a subsidy on those lacking other resources to obtain employment in the future, it is difficult to understand how their effective *exclusion* can be justified.

[28] Center on Budget and Policy Priorities, *Bush Tax Plan Offers No Benefits to One in Three Families* (Feb. 7, 2001) at 1(see http://www.cbpp.org).

[29] *Id.*

[30] See Tom Shapiro, Northeastern University, *Black Wealth, White Wealth* (1995).

[31] Joel Friedman, Richard Kogan, and Robert Greenstein, *Final Tax Bill Ultimately Costs as Much as Bush Plan*, Center for Budget and Policy Priorities (Washington, D.C.; May 29, 2001) at 1–3 (see http://www.cbpp.org).

[32] *Id.*

[33] Note that the percentage of child recipients varies from 69%–72% for the largest TANF category "family groups"; the percentage of child recipients for the smaller TANF unemployed category is 61–63%. See Children's Advocacy Institute, *California Children's Budget 2001–02* (San Diego, CA; June 2001) at Chapter 2.

[34] Reducing TANF (AFDC) levels would have little impact on impoverishment caused by divorce, or by male abandonment or rejection. Proponents of reduction argue that it would stimulate employment. There may be some relationship between benefit levels and incentive to work, but the analyses of poverty incidence and TANF caseloads do not correlate closely with benefit levels, either over time or between states with very different benefit systems. Rather, TANF claims correlate with unemployment levels and prevailing wages for the working poor. See *e.g.*, Tufts University School of Nutrition Science and Policy, Center on Hunger and Poverty, *Statement on Key Welfare Reform Issues, The Empirical Evidence*, (Medford, MA; 1995), referencing 73 studies and statistical sources.

[35] These are California's current requirements, which are not atypical. Note that certain assets are exempt from the limitation, including the family home, an automobile worth under $1,500, burial insurance, tools of trade needed for employment, household furniture, and "other items essential for day-to-day living" (such as dishes, flatware, toilet paper, etc.).

[36] For example, in California the level is $175 per month ($200 for children younger than two), and $90 of work-related expenses. In addition, the first $30 earned each month for up to one year is not counted, and an additional one-third of earnings is disregarded (termed the "30 and one-third rule" to encourage work). If received, the first $50 per month in child support is also not counted. The first $225 in earnings each month plus 50% of what is earned may be kept, with TANF assistance reduced as the counted 50% of earnings raises income.

[37] Pub. L. No. 104-193, § 103 of the Act, 42 U.S.C. § 602.

[38] See Raymond Hernandez, *Most Dropped from Welfare Don't Get Jobs*, N.Y. Times, Mar. 22, 1998, at 1 (survey by New York State Office of Temporary and Disability Assistance).

[39] Staff of NGA, NCSL, and APWA, *Tracking Recipients after They Leave Welfare*, July 1998, at 1 (see http://www.nga.org/welfare/statefollowup.htm).

[40] Urban Institute, *Families Who Left Welfare: Who Are They, and How Are They Doing?* (Washington D.C.; Aug. 1999) at 1–5; note that these findings were generally supported by the independent study of the General Accounting Office: "*Welfare Reform: Information on Former Recipients' Status*," released in April 1999.

[41] Wendell Primus, Lynette Rawlings, Kathy Larin, Kathryn Porter, *The Initial Impacts of Welfare Reform on the Incomes of Single-Mother Families*, Center on Budget and Policy Priorities (Aug. 22, 1999) at 1–3 (see http://www.cbpp.org).

[42] See Brooks, J. L., Hair, E. C. & Zaslow, M. J., *Welfare Reform's Impact on Adolescents: Early Warning Signs*, Child Trends Research Brief (Washington, D.C.; July 2001); see also Duncan, G. J. & Chase-Lansdale, P.L., *Welfare Reform and Children's Well-Being*, in R. Blank and R. Haskins (eds.), *The New World of Welfare* (Washington, D.C.; 2001) at 391–417; see also Hamilton, G., Freedman, S., Gennetian, L., Michalopoulos, C., Walter, J., Adams-Ciardullo, D., Gassman-Pines, A., McGroder, S., Zaslow, M., Ahluwalia, S., and Brooks, J., *How Effective Are Different Welfare-to-Work Approaches? Five-Year Adult and Child Impacts for Eleven Programs*, U.S. Department of Health and Human Services (Washington, D.C.; Dec. 2001); see also Morris, P. A., Huston, A.C., Duncan, G. J., Crosby, D. A., & Bos, J. M., *How Welfare and Work Policies Affect Children: A Synthesis of Research*, Manpower Demonstration Research Corporation (New York, NY; March 2001); see also Morris, P., Knox, V., and Gennetian, L. A.,

Welfare Policies Matter for Children and Youth: Lessons for TANF Reauthorization, MDRC Policy Brief (New York, NY; March 2002); see also Shields, M.K. (Ed.), *Children and Welfare Reform*, The Future of Children, Vol. 12, No. 1 (2002); see also Zaslow, M., Brooks, J. L., Moore, K. A., Morris, P., Tout, K., and Redd, Z., *Impact on Children in Experimental Studies of Welfare-to-Work Programs*, Child Trends (Washington, D.C.; 2001). Note that earnings increases for some parents benefit their children, and for young children the increased hours employed do not correlate with measurable indices of child well-being. However, supporters of welfare reform have largely relied on welfare caseload reductions as the criterion for success. Impacts on children are rarely discussed or closely examined, and have had little impact on reauthorization of the PRA—now proposing minimum work requirements of 38 to 40 hours per week and permission to pay "workfare" at levels below minimum wage, *et al.*

[43] *Initial Impacts of Welfare Reform on the Incomes of Single-Mother Families, supra* note 41, at 2.

[44] *Id.* at 6.

[45] U.S. Census Bureau, *Poverty in the United States—1999*, Current Population Reports P60-210 (Washington, D.C.; Sept. 2000) Table D at xv.

[46] Bruce Fuller, Sharon Lynn Kagan, *Remember the Children: Mothers Balance Work and Child Care Under Welfare Reform, Growing Up in Poverty Project 2000, Wave 1 Findings: California, Connecticut, Florida* (U.C. Berkeley and Yale University; Feb. 2000) at 3–6.

[47] See Research Development Division, Department of Social Services, *Characteristics and Employment of Current and Former CalWORKs Recipients: What We Know From Statewide Administrative Data* (June 6, 2000) at 16–17.

[48] Center on Budget and Policy Priorities, *Should Federal Food Assistance Programs Be Converted to Block Grants?* (Washington, D.C.; Jan. 27, 1995) at 13.

[49] California Rural Legal Assistance Foundation, *Hunger in the Heartland: Community Childhood Hunger Identification Project in California's Central Valley* (San Francisco, CA; March 1991) at 28.

[50] Barbara Howell and Lynette Engelhardt, Bread for the World, *Elect to End Childhood Hunger*, "Childhood Hunger Facts,"(Silver Spring, MD; Feb. 1996) at 4 (citing USDA).

[51] California Food Policy Advocates, *California Food Stamp Facts* (San Francisco, CA; June 1994) estimates 60%; the Statewide Food Stamp Outreach Task Force estimated participation by about half of those eligible (see *Hunger in California, supra* note 4, at 17).

[52] *Hunger in the Heartland, supra* note 49, at 27–28.

[53] See *Hunger in California, supra* note 4, at 6.

[54] *Id.*

[55]J. Larry Brown, Tufts University School of Nutrition Science and Policy, Center on Hunger and Poverty, *What Does a $27 Billion Cut in Food Stamps Mean?* (Medford, MA; July 11, 1997).

[56]USDA, Center for Nutrition Policy and Promotion, *Official USDA Food Plans: Cost of Food at Home at Four Levels, U.S. Average, January 2000.* See http://www.usda.gov.

[57]*Id.* Note that the low cost of a 6- to 8-year-old is $121.80 per month, and that the numbers for individuals assume purchasing for a four person family, requiring a 5% add-on for a three person family (see footnote 2 on table). Note also that there is a super "thrifty plan" below the low-cost plan, which would cost $307.65.

[58] See Sharon Parrott and Stacy Dean, *Food Stamps Can Help Low Income Working Families Put Food on the Table*, Center on Budget and Policy Priorities (March 31, 1999) at 1.

[59] Marriage to a citizen can shorten the waiting period to three years. Note also that veterans and those serving in the active duty military are exempt from the legal immigrant PRA bar to public assistance. Children who are born in the United States may be eligible for food stamp and TANF assistance because they are U.S. citizens at birth. However, many legal immigrants have withdrawn from TANF (and food stamp) assistance because of fears that accepting such help, even where needed for their children, will cause them to be designated a likely "public charge" and preclude their citizenship in their new country. According to the federal Immigration and Naturalization Service, the definition of public charge focuses on cash assistance (*e.g.*, TANF) and is supposed to measure future dependency on public funds, not prior use based on need not likely to recur.

[60]See AB 1576 (Bustamante) (Chapter 287, Statutes of 1997), which—effective August 18, 1997—added section 18930 *et seq.* to the Cal. Welfare & Institutions Code.

[61]See Laurie True, *Hunger in the Balance: The Impact of the Proposed AFDC Cuts on Childhood Hunger in California* (San Francisco, CA; March 1992) at 14.

[62]See Center on Budget and Policy Priorities and Center for the Study of the States, *The States and the Poor: How Budget Decisions Affected Low-Income People in 1992* (Washington, D.C.; 1993) at 67.

[63] *Id.*

[64]See *Hunger in California, supra* note 4, at 18. For a discussion (and critique) of positive WIC research findings, see Douglas Besharov and Peter Germanis, *Is WIC as Good as They Say?* The Public Interest (Jan. 1, 1999). Note that although the authors state a strong case for more extensive and properly blind tested measurement of WIC, the evidence is substantial that it has important health benefits for the children in circumstances of extreme poverty. Direct familiarity with the program and its workings—what it provides to women and infants that they are otherwise not reliably receiving indicates a substantial beneficial effect in light of double blind tested literature correlating the effect of nutrients on

child development.

[65] California Department of Health Services, *Women, Infants and Children* (March 2000) at 1 (see http://www.dhs.ca.gov).

[66] Federal Workforce Investment Act of 1998 (Pub. L. No 105-220).

[67] Richard May, Center on Budget and Policy Priorities, *1993 Poverty and Income Trends* (Washington, D.C.; March 1993) at 19–20, 61.

[68] Jean Ross, Jesse Rothstein, *Will Work Pay? Job Creation in the New California Economy,* California Budget Project (Sacramento, CA; April 2000) at 5 and Table 3 at 15.

[69] *Id.*

[70] See, *e.g.*, the California data indicating a failure to match population increase over the past decade, at Children's Advocacy Institute, *California Children's Budget 2001–02* (San Diego, CA; June 2001) at Chapter 7 (http://www.caichildlaw.org).

CHAPTER FOUR

Education Rights and Investment

A. EDUCATION AND EQUALITY OF OPPORTUNITY

The educational level of children correlates with their future economic success. Figure 4-A indicates the existing strong and positive relationship between education and earnings in the United States. In 1998, a male high school drop-out earned a median salary of $16,818 annually; a female earned $8,861. A male high school graduate earned a median of $25,453 per year; females earned $13,407. A male with a bachelor's degree earned a median annual salary of $41,949; a female earned $26,401. As the figure indicates, employment and domestic wage levels directly relate to educational attainment.

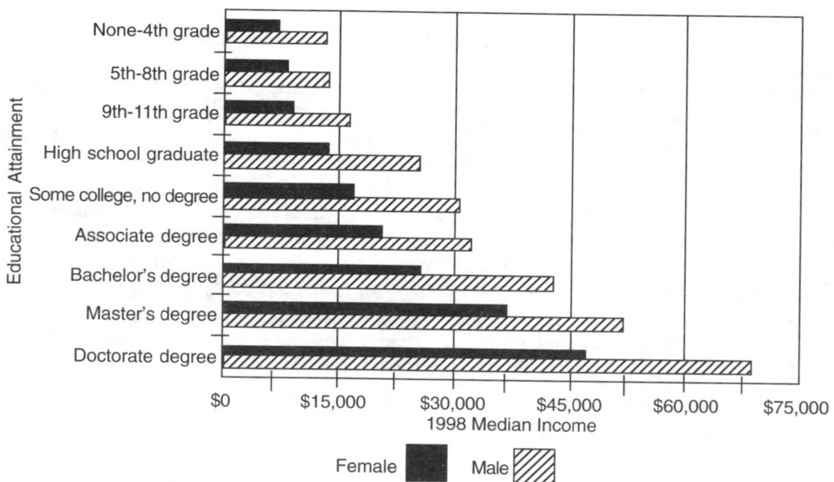

Source: Department of Commerce, Bureau of the Census, *Educational Attainment in the United States: March 1998 (Update)* Table 8. Restricted to persons 25 years and over.

Figure 4-A. Median Income by Higher Education

That correlation is likely to be further enhanced by the evolving international labor marketplace, where the American niche is likely to be technical services. Future projections anticipate continued international competition for low skill jobs, particularly factory and other non-service manual labor. In 1984, 24% of U.S. jobs were characterized as "high skill" and 40% as "low skill." Trends as projected past 2002 reverse that balance to 41% high skill and 27% low skill.[1]

Brown v. Board of Education of Topeka
347 U.S. 483 (1954)

Mr. Chief Justice Warren delivered the opinion of the Court.

* * *

Today, education is perhaps the most important function of state and local governments. Compulsory school attendance laws and the great expenditures for education both demonstrate our recognition of the importance of education to our democratic society. It is required in the performance of our most basic public responsibilities, even service in the armed forces. It is the very foundation of good citizenship. Today it is a principal instrument in awakening the child to cultural values, in preparing him for later professional training, and in helping him to adjust normally to his environment. In these days, it is doubtful that any child may reasonably be expected to succeed in life if he is denied the opportunity of an education. Such an opportunity, where the state has undertaken to provide it, is a right which must be made available to all on equal terms.

We come then to the question presented: Does segregation of children in public schools solely on the basis of race, even though the physical facilities and other "tangible" factors may be equal, deprive the children of the minority group of equal educational opportunities? We believe that it does.

In *Sweatt v. Painter*,...in finding that a segregated law school for Negroes could not provide them equal educational opportunities, this Court relied in large part on "those qualities which are incapable of objective measurement but which make for greatness in a law school." In *McLaurin v. Oklahoma State Regents*,...the Court, in requiring that a Negro admitted to a white graduate school be treated like all other students, again resorted to intangible considerations: "...his ability to study, to engage in discussions and exchange views with other students, and, in general, to learn his profession." Such considerations apply with added force to children in grade and high schools. To separate them from others of similar age and qualifications solely because of their race generates a feeling of inferiority as to their status in the community that may affect their hearts and minds in a way unlikely ever to be undone. The effect of this separation on their educational opportunities was well stated by a finding in the Kansas case by a court which nevertheless felt compelled to rule against the Negro plaintiffs:

> "Segregation of white and colored children in public schools has a detrimental effect upon the colored children. The impact is greater when it has the sanction of the law; for the policy of separating the races is usually interpreted as denoting the inferiority of the negro group. A sense of inferiority affects the motivation of a child to learn. Segregation with the sanction of law, therefore, has a tendency to [retard] the educational and mental development of negro children and to deprive them of some of the benefits they would receive in a racial[ly] integrated school system."[10]

---

[10] A similar finding was made in the Delaware case: "I conclude from the testimony that in our Delaware society, State-imposed segregation in education itself results in the Negro children, as a class, receiving educational opportunities which are substantially inferior to those available to white children otherwise similarly situated." 87 A. 2d 862, 865.

Whatever may have been the extent of psychological knowledge at the time of *Plessy v. Ferguson*, this finding is amply supported by modern authority.[11] Any language in *Plessy v. Ferguson* contrary to this finding is rejected.

We conclude that in the field of public education the doctrine of "separate but equal" has no place. Separate educational facilities are inherently unequal. Therefore, we hold that the plaintiffs and others similarly situated for whom the actions have been brought are, by reason of the segregation complained of, deprived of the equal protection of the laws guaranteed by the Fourteenth Amendment. This disposition makes unnecessary any discussion whether such segregation also violates the Due Process Clause of the Fourteenth Amendment....

Because these are class actions, because of the wide applicability of this decision, and because of the great variety of local conditions, the formulation of decrees in these cases presents problems of considerable complexity. On reargument, the consideration of appropriate relief was necessarily subordinated to the primary question—the constitutionality of segregation in public education. We have now announced that such segregation is a denial of the equal protection of the laws. In order that we may have the full assistance of the parties in formulating decrees, the cases will be restored to the docket, and the parties are requested to present further argument on Questions 4 and 5 previously propounded by the Court for the reargument this Term.[13] The Attorney General of the United States is again invited to participate. The Attorneys General of the states requiring or permitting segregation in public education will also be permitted to appear as *amici curiae* upon request to do so by September 15, 1954, and submission of briefs by October 1, 1954....

It is so ordered.

---

[11] K.B. Clark, Effect of Prejudice and Discrimination on Personality Development (Midcentury White House Conference on Children and Youth, 1950); Witmer and Kotinsky, Personality in the Making (1952), c. VI; Deutscher and Chein, The Psychological Effects of Enforced Segregation: A Survey of Social Science Opinion, 26 J. Psychol. 259 (1948); Chein, What are the Psychological Effects of Segregation Under Conditions of Equal Facilities?, 3 Int. J. Opinion and Attitude Res. 229 (1949); Brameld, Educational Costs, in Discrimination and National Welfare (MacIver, ed., 1949), 44–48; Frazier, The Negro in the United States (1949), 674–681. And see generally Myrdal, An American Dilemma (1944).

[13] "4. Assuming it is decided that segregation in public schools violates the Fourteenth Amendment

"*(a)* would a decree necessarily follow providing that, within the limits set by normal geographic school districting, Negro children should forthwith be admitted to schools of their choice, or

"*(b)* may this Court, in the exercise of its equity powers, permit an effective gradual adjustment to be brought about from existing segregated systems to a system not based on color distinctions?

"5. On the assumption on which questions 4 *(a)* and *(b)* are based, and assuming further that this Court will exercise its equity powers to the end described in question *4 (b)*,

"*(a)* should this Court formulate detailed decrees in these cases;

"*(b)* if so, what specific issues should the decrees reach;

"*(c)* should this Court appoint a special master to hear evidence with a view to recommending specific terms for such decrees;

"*(d)* should this Court remand to the courts of first instance with directions to frame decrees in these cases, and if so what general directions should the decrees of this Court include and what procedures should the courts of first instance follow in arriving at the specific terms of more detailed decrees?"

Questions for Discussion

1. Was it important that *Brown* was a unanimous decision of the Court? Why?

2. Is the judgment that separation is itself *prima facie* discriminatory an insult to minorities? Does it imply that minority children cannot achieve academic excellence except with the help of white children and their teachers? Does it portend the absorption of a viable African-American culture into a homogenous whole? If a black community were predominantly Muslim and did not want its children to be subject to outside influence, how would that situation differ from *Wisconsin v. Yoder* (Chapter 13 below), allowing the Amish to *segregate* as a constitutional right?

3. Have we conferred similar constitutional education integration rights to Native American children? Should we?

4. If opportunity involves social connections and if the dominant race tends to obtain the most skilled teachers and extensive facilities, is integration then necessary for a more level playing field? What remedies did the federal courts then impose to accomplish integration? Was their detailed oversight of public education, including busing orders, calculation of percentage of minority students, *et al.* an appropriate court function? If relegated to legislative decision, is it likely that a legislature dominated by the majority race would represent the interests of another group to raise the floor, at the partial expense of its own group?

5. Would housing integration be more effective at equalizing opportunity since it could act to integrate schools, as well as other institutions?

Lau v. Nichols
414 U.S. 563 (1974)

Mr. Justice Douglas delivered the opinion of the Court.

The San Francisco, California, school system was integrated in 1971 as a result of a federal court decree, 339 F.Supp. 1315....The District Court found that there are 2,856 students of Chinese ancestry in the school system who do not speak English. Of those who have that language deficiency, about 1,000 are given supplemental courses in the English language.[1] About 1,800, however, do not receive that instruction.

This class suit brought by non-English-speaking Chinese students against officials responsible for the operation of the San Francisco Unified School District seeks relief against the unequal educational opportunities, which are alleged to violate, *inter alia*, the Fourteenth Amendment. No specific remedy is urged upon us. Teaching English to the students of Chinese ancestry who do not speak the language is one choice. Giving instructions to this group in Chinese is another. There may be others. Petitioners ask only that the Board of Education be directed to apply its expertise to the problem and rectify the situation.

---

[1] A report adopted by the Human Rights Commission of San Francisco and submitted to the Court by respondents after oral argument shows that, as of April 1973, there were 3,457 Chinese students in the school system who spoke little or no English. The document further showed 2,136 students enrolled in Chinese special instruction classes, but at least 429 of the enrollees were not Chinese but were included for ethnic balance. Thus, as of April 1973, no more than 1,707 of the 3,457 Chinese students needing special English instruction were receiving it.

* * *

The Court of Appeals reasoned that "every student brings to the starting line of his educational career different advantages and disadvantages caused in part by social, economic and cultural background, created and continued completely apart from any contribution by the school system," 483 F.2d, at 797. Yet in our view the case may not be so easily decided. This is a public school system of California and § 71 of the California Education Code states that "English shall be the basic language of instruction in all schools." That section permits a school district to determine "when and under what circumstances instruction may be given bilingually." That section also states as "the policy of the state" to insure "the mastery of English by all pupils in the schools." And bilingual instruction is authorized "to the extent that it does not interfere with the systematic, sequential, and regular instruction of all pupils in the English language."

Moreover, § 8573 of the Education Code provides that no pupil shall receive a diploma of graduation from grade 12 who has not met the standards of proficiency in "English," as well as other prescribed subjects. Moreover, by § 12101 of the Education Code...children between the ages of six and 16 years are (with exceptions not material here) "subject to compulsory full-time education."

Under these state-imposed standards there is no equality of treatment merely by providing students with the same facilities, textbooks, teachers, and curriculum; for students who do not understand English are effectively foreclosed from any meaningful education.

Basic English skills are at the very core of what these public schools teach. Imposition of a requirement that, before a child can effectively participate in the educational program, he must already have acquired those basic skills is to make a mockery of public education. We know that those who do not understand English are certain to find their classroom experiences wholly incomprehensible and in no way meaningful.

We do not reach the Equal Protection Clause argument which has been advanced but rely solely on § 601 of the Civil Rights Act of 1964, 42 U.S.C. § 2000d, to reverse the Court of Appeals.

That section bans discrimination based "on the ground of race, color, or national origin," in "any program or activity receiving Federal financial assistance." The school district involved in this litigation receives large amounts of federal financial assistance. The Department of Health, Education, and Welfare (HEW),...in 1968 issued one guideline that "school systems are responsible for assuring that students of a particular race, color, or national origin are not denied the opportunity to obtain the education generally obtained by other students in the system."....In 1970 HEW made the guidelines more specific, requiring school districts that were federally funded "to rectify the language deficiency in order to open" the instruction to students who had "linguistic deficiencies,"...

* * *

Discrimination is barred...even though no purposeful design is present: a recipient "may not...utilize criteria or methods of administration which have the effect of subjecting individuals to discrimination" or have "the effect of defeating or substantially impairing accomplishment of the objectives of the program as respect individuals of a particular race, color, or national origin."....

It seems obvious that the Chinese-speaking minority receive fewer benefits than the English-speaking majority from respondents' school system which denies them a meaningful opportunity to participate in the educational program—all earmarks of the discrimination banned by the regulations....

Reversed and remanded.

* * *

Bilingual students and others with English language difficulties are referred to as Limited English Proficiency (LEP) students. They currently make up 13% of all students nationwide,[2] but some major states have an extraordinary proportion, *e.g.*, California's percentage is at 24.6%.[3]

Questions for Discussion

1. Is the state policy "to bring English mastery to all" constitutionally compelled?

2. The Court does not address the equal protection issue, but notes that education is compulsory and that the Chinese will be deprived of meaningful education if they cannot understand the lessons. Does Section 601 of the Civil Rights Act or the Constitution require the state to bring each child to the same level of English proficiency? To some minimum level? Is equal protection provided where an equivalent effort is made as to each that is sufficient for some to achieve it? If some students start with languages particularly disparate from English (*e.g.*, an Asian language) is additional effort required on their behalf?

3. Some states have recently enacted statutes reducing bilingual education, and requiring that English be learned on an "immersion" basis (*e.g.*, by limiting bilingual opportunity to a single year or less). Does that limitation discriminate against children with a primary language so difficult that they cannot learn sufficient English within one year and are unable to learn other subjects? Are these students deprived of educational opportunity in violation of the 14th Amendment or Section 601 of the Civil Rights Act? If such difficulties are particularly marked for Asian children, does their race afford them strict scrutiny protection, since race is a "suspect" classification?

Serrano v. Priest
5 Cal. 3d 584 (1971)

OPINION: SULLIVAN, J.—

We are called upon to determine whether the California public school financing system, with its substantial dependence on local property taxes and resultant wide disparities in school revenue, violates the equal protection clause of the Fourteenth Amendment. We have determined that this funding scheme invidiously discriminates against the poor because it makes the quality of a child's education a function of the wealth of his parents and neighbors. Recognizing as we must that the right to an education in our public schools is a fundamental interest which cannot be conditioned on wealth, we can discern no compelling state purpose necessitating the present method of financing. We have concluded, therefore, that such a system cannot withstand constitutional challenge and must fall before the equal protection clause.

Plaintiffs, who are Los Angeles County public school children and their parents, brought this class action for declaratory and injunctive relief against certain state and county officials charged with administering the financing of the California public school system. Plaintiff children claim to represent a class consisting of all public school pupils in California, "except children in that school district, the identity of which is presently unknown, which school district affords the greatest educational opportunity of all school districts within California." Plaintiff parents purport to represent a class of all parents who have children in the school system and who pay real property taxes in the county of their residence.

* * *

The complaint sets forth three causes of action. The first cause alleges in substance as follows: Plaintiff children attend public elementary and secondary schools located in specified school districts in Los Angeles County. This public school system is maintained throughout California by a financing plan or scheme which relies heavily on local property taxes and causes substantial disparities among individual school districts in the amount of revenue available per pupil for the districts' educational programs. Consequently, districts with smaller tax bases are not able to spend as much money per child for education as districts with larger assessed valuations.

* * *

I

We begin our task by examining the California public school financing system which is the focal point of the complaint's allegations. At the threshold we find a fundamental statistic—over 90 percent of our public school funds derive from two basic sources: (a) local district taxes on real property and (b) aid from the State School Fund.[2]

By far the major source of school revenue is the local real property tax. Pursuant to article IX, section 6 of the California Constitution, the Legislature has authorized the governing body of each county, and city and county, to levy taxes on the real property within a school district at a rate necessary to meet the district's annual education budget. (Ed. Code, § 20701 *et seq.*)....The amount of revenue which a district can raise in this manner thus depends largely on its tax base—*i.e.*, the assessed valuation of real property within its borders. Tax bases vary widely throughout the state; in 1969–1970, for example, the assessed valuation per unit of average daily attendance of elementary school children[3] ranged from a low of $103 to a peak of $952,156—a ratio of nearly 1 to 10,000....

The other factor determining local school revenue is the rate of taxation within the district. Although the Legislature has placed ceilings on permissible district tax rates (§ 20751 *et seq.*), these statutory maxima may be surpassed in a "tax override" election if a majority of the district's voters approve a higher rate. (§ 20803 *et seq.*) Nearly all districts have voted to override the statutory limits. Thus the locally raised funds which constitute the largest portion of school revenue are primarily a function of the value of the realty within a particular school district, coupled with the willingness of the district's residents to tax themselves for education.

Most of the remaining school revenue comes from the State School Fund pursuant to the "foundation program," through which the state undertakes to supplement local taxes in order to provide a "minimum amount of guaranteed

---

[2] California educational revenues for the fiscal year 1968–1969 came from the following sources: local property taxes, 55.7 percent; state aid, 35.5 percent; federal funds, 6.1 percent; miscellaneous sources, 2.7 percent.

[3] Most school aid determinations are based not on total enrollment, but on "average daily attendance" (ADA), a figure computed by adding together the number of students actually present on each school day and dividing that total by the number of days school was taught. (§§ 11252, 11301, 11401.) In practice, ADA approximates 98 percent of total enrollment....When we refer herein to figures on a "per pupil" or "per child" basis, we mean per unit of ADA.

support to all districts...." (§ 17300.) With certain minor exceptions,[6] the foundation program ensures that each school district will receive annually, from state or local funds, $355 for each elementary school pupil (§§ 17656, 17660) and $488 for each high school student. (§ 17665.)

The state contribution is supplied in two principal forms. "Basic state aid" consists of a flat grant to each district of $125 per pupil per year, regardless of the relative wealth of the district...."Equalization aid" is distributed in inverse proportion to the wealth of the district.

To compute the amount of equalization aid to which a district is entitled, the State Superintendent of Public Instruction first determines how much local property tax revenue would be generated if the district were to levy a hypothetical tax at a rate of $1 on each $100 of assessed valuation in elementary school districts and $.80 per $100 in high school districts.[7]....To that figure, he adds the $125 per pupil basic aid grant. If the sum of those two amounts is less than the foundation program minimum for that district, the state contributes the difference....Thus, equalization funds guarantee to the poorer districts a basic minimum revenue, while wealthier districts are ineligible for such assistance.

An additional state program of "supplemental aid" is available to subsidize particularly poor school districts which are willing to make an extra local tax effort. An elementary district with an assessed valuation of $12,500 or less per pupil may obtain up to $125 more for each child if it sets its local tax rate above a certain statutory level. A high school district whose assessed valuation does not exceed $24,500 per pupil is eligible for a supplement of up to $72 per child if its local tax is sufficiently high....

Although equalization aid and supplemental aid temper the disparities which result from the vast variations in real property assessed valuation, wide differentials remain in the revenue available to individual districts and, consequently, in the level of educational expenditures. For example, in Los Angeles County, where plaintiff children attend school, the Baldwin Park Unified School District expended only $577.49 to educate each of its pupils in 1968–1969; during the same year the Pasadena Unified School District spent $840.19 on every student; and the Beverly Hills Unified School District paid out $1,231.72 per child....The source of these disparities is unmistakable: in Baldwin Park the assessed valuation per child totaled only $3,706; in Pasadena, assessed valuation was $13,706; while in Beverly Hills, the corresponding figure was $50,885—a ratio of 1 to 4 to 13....Thus, the state grants are inadequate to offset the inequalities inherent in a financing system based on widely varying local tax bases.

Furthermore, basic aid, which constitutes about half of the state educational funds...actually widens the gap between rich and poor districts....Such aid is distributed on a uniform per pupil basis to all districts, irrespective of a district's wealth. Beverly Hills, as well as Baldwin Park, receives $125 from the state for each of its students.

* * *

III

---

[6] Districts which maintain "unnecessary small schools" receive $10 per pupil less in foundation funds....

Certain types of school districts are eligible for "bonus" foundation funds. Elementary districts receive an additional $30 for each student in grades 1 through 3; this sum is intended to reduce class size in those grades....Unified school districts get an extra $20 per child in foundation support....

[7] This is simply a "computational" tax rate used to measure the relative wealth of the district for equalization purposes. It bears no relation to the tax rate actually set by the district in levying local real property taxes.

...[W]e take up the chief contention underlying plaintiffs' complaint, namely that the California public school financing scheme violates the equal protection clause of the Fourteenth Amendment to the United States Constitution....

* * *

A
Wealth as a Suspect Classification

In recent years, the United States Supreme Court has demonstrated a marked antipathy toward legislative classifications which discriminate on the basis of certain "suspect" personal characteristics. One factor which has repeatedly come under the close scrutiny of the high court is wealth. "Lines drawn on the basis of wealth or property, like those of race [citation], are traditionally disfavored."....Invalidating the Virginia poll tax in *Harper*, the court stated: "To introduce wealth or payment of a fee as a measure of a voter's qualifications is to introduce a capricious or irrelevant factor."...."[A] careful examination on our part is especially warranted where lines are drawn on the basis of wealth...[a] factor which would independently render a classification highly suspect and thereby demand a more exacting judicial scrutiny...."

* * *

...[W]e reject defendants' underlying thesis that classification by wealth is constitutional so long as the wealth is that of the district, not the individual. We think that discrimination on the basis of district wealth is equally invalid. The commercial and industrial property which augments a district's tax base is distributed unevenly throughout the state. To allot more educational dollars to the children of one district than to those of another merely because of the fortuitous presence of such property is to make the quality of a child's education dependent upon the location of private commercial and industrial establishments.[16] Surely, this is to rely on the most irrelevant of factors as the basis for educational financing.

Defendants, assuming for the sake of argument that the financing system does classify by wealth, nevertheless claim that no constitutional infirmity is involved because the complaint contains no allegation of purposeful or intentional discrimination....Thus, defendants contend, any unequal treatment is only de facto, not de jure. Since the United States Supreme Court has not held de facto school segregation on the basis of race to be unconstitutional, so the argument goes, de facto classifications on the basis of wealth are presumptively valid.

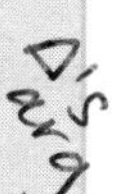

[16] Defendants contend that different levels of educational expenditure do not affect the quality of education. However, plaintiffs' complaint specifically alleges the contrary, and for purposes of testing the sufficiency of a complaint against a general demurrer, we must take its allegations to be true.

Although we recognize that there is considerable controversy among educators over the relative impact of educational spending and environmental influences on school achievement...we note that the several courts which have considered contentions similar to defendants' have uniformly rejected them.

In *McInnis v. Shapiro* (N.D.Ill. 1968) 293 F.Supp. 327, affd. mem. *sub nom. McInnis v. Ogilvie* (1969) 394 U.S. 322...heavily relied on by defendants, a three-judge federal court stated: "Presumably, students receiving a $1,000 education are better educated that [sic] those acquiring a $600 schooling."....

Spending differentials of up to $130 within a district were characterized as "spectacular" in *Hobson v. Hansen*, *supra*, 269 F.Supp. 401. Responding to defendants' claim that the varying expenditures did not reflect actual educational benefits, the court replied: "To a great extent...defendants' own evidence verifies that the comparative per pupil figures do refer to actual educational advantages in the highcost schools, especially with respect to the caliber of the teaching staff."....

We think that the whole structure of this argument must fall for want of a solid foundation in law and logic....[N]one of the wealth classifications previously invalidated by the United States Supreme Court or this court has been the product of purposeful discrimination. Instead, these prior decisions have involved "unintentional" classifications whose impact simply fell more heavily on the poor.

* * *

We turn now to defendants' related contention that the instant case involves at most de facto discrimination. We disagree. Indeed, we find the case unusual in the extent to which governmental action *is* the cause of the wealth classifications. The school funding scheme is mandated in every detail by the California Constitution and statutes. Although private residential and commercial patterns may be partly responsible for the distribution of assessed valuation throughout the state, such patterns are shaped and hardened by zoning ordinances and other governmental land-use controls which promote economic exclusivity....

Finally, even assuming arguendo that defendants are correct in their contention that the instant discrimination based on wealth is merely de facto, and not de jure,...such discrimination cannot be justified by analogy to de facto *racial* segregation. Although the United States Supreme Court has not yet ruled on the constitutionality of de facto racial segregation, this court eight years ago held such segregation invalid, and declared that school boards should take affirmative steps to alleviate racial imbalance, however created. (*Jackson v. Pasadena City School Dist.* (1963) 59 Cal.2d 876, 881)....

B

Education as a Fundamental Interest

* * *

Until the present time wealth classifications have been invalidated only in conjunction with a limited number of fundamental interests—rights of defendants in criminal cases...and voting rights....Plaintiffs' contention—that education is a fundamental interest which may not be conditioned on wealth—is not supported by any direct authority.[22]

---

[22] In *Shapiro v. Thompson* (1969) 394 U.S. 618..., in which the Supreme Court invalidated state minimum residence requirements for welfare benefits, the high court indicated, in dictum, that certain wealth discrimination in the area of education would be unconstitutional: "We recognize that a State has a valid interest in preserving the fiscal integrity of its programs. It may legitimately attempt to limit its expenditures, whether for public assistance, public education, or any other program. But a State may not accomplish such a purpose by invidious distinctions between classes of its citizens. It could not, for example, reduce expenditures for education by barring indigent children from its schools."....Although the high court referred to actual exclusion from school, rather than discrimination in expenditures for education, we think the constitutional principle is the same. (See fn. 24, and accompanying text.)

A federal Court of Appeals has also held that education is arguably a fundamental interest. In *Hargrave v. McKinney* (5th Cir. 1969) 413 F.2d 320, the Fifth Circuit ruled that a three-judge district court must be convened to consider the constitutionality of a Florida statue which limited the local property tax rate which a county could levy in raising school revenue. Plaintiffs contended that the statute violated the equal protection clause because it allowed counties with a high per-pupil assessed valuation to raise much more local revenue than counties with smaller tax bases. The court stated: "The equal protection argument advanced by plaintiffs is the crux of the case. Noting that lines drawn on wealth are suspect [fn. omitted] and that we are here dealing with interests which may well be deemed fundamental, [fn. omitted] we cannot say that there is no reasonably arguable theory of equal protection which would support a decision in favor of the plaintiffs. [Citations.]" (*Id.* at p. 324.)

We, therefore, begin by examining the indispensable role which education plays in the modern industrial state. This role, we believe, has two significant aspects: first, education is a major determinant of an individual's chances for economic and social success in our competitive society; second, education is a unique influence on a child's development as a citizen and his participation in political and community life. "[The] pivotal position of education to success in American society and its essential role in opening up to the individual the central experiences of our culture lend it an importance that is undeniable."....Thus, education is the lifeline of both the individual and society.

The fundamental importance of education has been recognized in other contexts by the United States Supreme Court and by this court. These decisions—while not *legally* controlling on the exact issue before us—are persuasive in their accurate factual description of the significance of learning....

The classic expression of this position came in *Brown v. Board of Education* (1954) 347 U.S. 483..., which invalidated de jure segregation by race in public schools....

* * *

When children living in remote areas brought an action to compel local school authorities to furnish them bus transportation to class, we stated: "We indulge in no hyperbole to assert that society has a compelling interest in affording children an opportunity to attend school. This was evidenced more than three centuries ago, when Massachusetts provided the first public school system in 1647. [Citation.] And today an education has become the *sine qua non* of useful existence....In light of the public interest in conserving the resource of young minds, we must unsympathetically examine any action of a public body which has the effect of depriving children of the opportunity to obtain an education." (Fn. omitted.)....

And long before these last mentioned cases, in *Piper v. Big Pine School Dist., supra*, 193 Cal. 664, where an Indian girl sought to attend state public schools, we declared: "[The] common schools are doorways opening into chambers of science, art, and the learned professions, as well as into fields of industrial and commercial activities. Opportunities for securing employment are often more or less dependent upon the rating which a youth, as a pupil of our public institutions, has received in his school work. These are rights and privileges that cannot be denied." (*Id.* at p. 673;...) Although *Manjares* and *Piper* involved actual exclusion from the public schools, surely the right to an education today means more than access to a classroom.[24]....

On remand, a three-judge court held the statute unconstitutional because there was no rational basis for the discriminatory effect which it had in poor counties. Having invalidated the statute under the traditional equal protection test, the court declined to consider plaintiffs' contention that education was a fundamental interest, requiring application of the "strict scrutiny" equal protection standard. (*Hargrave v. Kirk, supra*, 313 F.Supp. 944.) On appeal, the Supreme Court vacated the district court's decision on other grounds, but indicated that on remand the lower court should thoroughly explore the equal protection issue. (*Askew v. Hargrave* (1971) 401 U.S. 476...)

[24] Cf. *Reynolds v. Sims* (1964) 377 U.S. 533, 562–563..., where the Supreme Court asserted that the right to vote is impaired not only when a qualified individual is barred from voting, but also when the impact of his ballot is diminished by unequal electoral apportionment: "It could hardly be gainsaid that a constitutional claim had been asserted by an allegation that certain otherwise qualified voters had been entirely prohibited from voting for members of their state legislature. And, if a State should provide that the votes of citizens in one part of the State should be given two times, or five times, or ten times the weight of votes of citizens in another part of the State, it could hardly be contended that the right to vote of those residing in the disfavored areas had not been effectively diluted....Of course, the effect of state

* * *

We are convinced that the distinctive and priceless function of education in our society warrants, indeed compels, our treating it as a "fundamental interest."...

First, education is essential in maintaining what several commentators have termed "free enterprise democracy"—that is, preserving an individual's opportunity to compete successfully in the economic marketplace, despite a disadvantaged background. Accordingly, the public schools of this state are the bright hope for entry of the poor and oppressed into the mainstream of American society....

Second, education is universally relevant. "Not every person finds it necessary to call upon the fire department or even the police in an entire lifetime. Relatively few are on welfare. Every person, however, benefits from education...."....

Third, public education continues over a lengthy period of life—between 10 and 13 years. Few other government services have such sustained, intensive contact with the recipient.

Fourth, education is unmatched in the extent to which it molds the personality of the youth of society....

Finally, education is so important that the state has made it compulsory—not only in the requirement of attendance but also by assignment to a particular district and school....

C
The Financing System Is Not Necessary to Accomplish a Compelling State Interest

* * *

[E]ven assuming arguendo that local administrative control may be a compelling state interest, the present financial system cannot be considered necessary to further this interest. No matter how the state decides to finance its system of public education, it can still leave this decision-making power in the hands of local districts.

The other asserted policy interest is that of allowing a local district to choose how much it wishes to spend on the education of its children. Defendants argue: "[If] one district raises a lesser amount per pupil than another district, this is a matter of choice and preference of the individual district, and reflects the individual desire for lower taxes rather than an expanded educational program, or may reflect a greater interest within that district in such other services that are supported by local property taxes as, for example, police and fire protection or hospital services."

We need not decide whether such decentralized financial decision-making is a compelling state interest, since under the present financing system, such fiscal freewill is a cruel illusion for the poor school districts. We cannot agree that Baldwin Park residents care less about education than those in Beverly Hills solely because Baldwin Park spends less than $600 per child while Beverly Hills spends over $1,200....

* * *

---

legislative districting schemes which give the same number of representatives to unequal numbers of constituents is identical....One must be ever aware that the Constitution forbids 'sophisticated as well as simpleminded modes of discrimination.' [Citation.]" (Fn. omitted.)

Defendants' second argument boils down to this: if the equal protection clause commands that the relative wealth of school districts may not determine the quality of public education, it must be deemed to direct the same command to all governmental entities in respect to all tax-supported public services;...and such a principle would spell the destruction of local government. We unhesitatingly reject this argument. We cannot share defendants' unreasoned apprehensions of such dire consequences from our holding today. Although we intimate no views on other governmental services,[31] we are satisfied that, as we have explained, its uniqueness among public activities clearly demonstrates that *education* must respond to the command of the equal protection clause.

* * *

By our holding today we further the cherished idea of American education that in a democratic society free public schools shall make available to all children equally the abundant gifts of learning. This was the credo of Horace Mann, which has been the heritage and the inspiration of this country. "I believe," he wrote, "in the existence of a great, immortal immutable principle of natural law, or natural ethics,—a principle antecedent to all human institutions, and incapable of being abrogated by any ordinance of man...which proves the *absolute right* to an education of every human being that comes into the world, and which, of course, proves the correlative duty of every government to see that the means of that education are provided for all...."

* * *

[31] We note, however, that the Court of Appeals for the Fifth Circuit has recently held that the equal protection clause forbids a town to discriminate racially in the provision of municipal services. In *Hawkins v. Town of Shaw, Mississippi, supra*, 437 F.2d 1286, the court held that the town of Shaw, Mississippi had an affirmative duty to equalize such services as street paving and lighting, sanitary sewers, surface water drainage, water mains and fire hydrants. The decision applied the "strict scrutiny" equal protection standard and reversed the decision of the district court which, relying on the traditional test, had found no constitutional infirmity.

Although racial discrimination was the basis of the decision, the court intimated that wealth discrimination in the provision of city services might also be invalid: "Appellants also alleged the discriminatory provision of municipal services based on wealth. This claim was dropped on appeal. It is interesting to note, however, that the Supreme Court has stated that wealth as well as race renders a classification highly suspect and thus demanding of a more exacting judicial scrutiny. [Citation.]" (*Id.* at p. 1287, fn. 1.)

Questions for Discussion

1. The court writes that wealth is a "suspect classification" where a "basic right" is at issue. Does that apply to free speech or to media access? Precedents have applied this concept to the right to vote, and to an attorney in a criminal matter; is education a different kind of application?

2. The court recognizes that "local democracy" is a "compelling state interest" warranting some variations based on wealth. Under what circumstances can that justify spending more on children? Can it be based on factors unrelated to need? Simply on the enhanced property values available to a school and its students? If everyone is assured a minimum floor of educational resources, can some parents/communities add to their floor? Does it matter if students from

poorer neighborhoods are barred entry? What is the difference between such favoritism and the disparity created when the wealthy send their children to well-financed private schools?

Note on the Aftermath of *Serrano*

In *San Antonio Independent School District v. Rodriguez*, 411 U.S. 1 (1973), the U.S. Supreme Court was presented with a Texas system of school finance similar to California's. Wide disparities in funding meant that students in poor areas would receive a fraction of the public investment committed to children in wealthier neighborhoods. As with California, locally financed schools meant that wealthy parents paid a lower property tax rate on their higher valued homes and were able to provide substantially more per student in K–12 spending. Nevertheless, the Court held that poor children were not a "suspect classification." The Court wrote that no one is "absolutely barred" from education, and concluded that "the class (impoverished children) is not saddled with such disabilities, or subjected to such a history of purposeful unequal treatment, or relegated to such a position of political powerlessness as to command extraordinary protection from the majoritarian political process." Hence, the Court found that strict scrutiny did not apply, and further held that the rational relation test was met because of the state's interest in "local participation and control." Accordingly, the means of funding chosen "is not invidiously discriminatory." The Court added that school taxation was a complex concept and that reforms in such areas "are matters reserved for the legislative processes of the various states."

Questions for Discussion

1. Can we rely on majority decision of legislatures where a minority of impoverished children are disadvantaged *vis-à-vis* a majority? If a majority wishes to relegate such a group to an inferior public education system, who but the Court will draw a line for its protection? Is it a purpose of constitutional protections to limit the exploitation of the weak by the majority?

2. Is the cited fact that the poor are not "absolutely barred" from education an appropriate criterion for constitutional acceptability? Are impoverished children not "saddled with disabilities?"

3. Is education spending based explicitly on neighborhood wealth a form of "unequal treatment" as to the unwealthy? Is such inequality permissible so long as it is not "purposeful," as the Court suggests in *Rodriguez*? The state is purposefully basing school funding on the wealth of real property, knowing that substantial unequal funding will result. The Court might argue that the state's purpose is not unequal treatment, but "local control." But local control to do what? One could draw local lines to include the wealthy and poor together in a district, and have local control and little unequal treatment within the state. Where the state draws lines with substantial wealth disparity, knowing it will produce unequal education spending, is not unequal funding one (if not the central) purpose?

4. Are questions of school finance impossibly complex? Has *Serrano* been impossible to implement in California? Is a command that financing not be based on the wealth of parents or neighborhoods, or commanding basic equality based on children served that difficult of a concept? Has the Court used the

complexity concern to eschew complex judgments in patent cases? In civil rights busing cases? In antitrust cases?

5. Could the University of Texas spend less on the education of an admittee (or demand a higher tuition payment) because he grew up in a poor Texas town? Could it spend more on the education of a Texas student from a wealthy family for that reason? Could it discount his tuition? What is the difference between such a policy and the financing disparities found constitutional in *Rodriguez*?

6. Is "local control" a factor with sufficient weight to vary education resources and opportunity based on wealth? Could the University of Texas, in the example above, argue that those citizens from the poorer areas do not contribute as much to the state budget financing the University and therefore their children should not receive the same educational value as those whose parents contribute more? What if the University operates a major on-line educational program for students who remain in their home towns, and charges less or offers more courses for students from wealthy towns? If such a University policy would be struck, would not twelve years of financial discrimination in basic, required public education—based on the wealth of parents, or on the locale of residence—be *a fortiori* objectionable?

7. Would it be constitutionally permissible for a state to issue a contract to build a road, but pay workers less who come from poorer communities? To pay workers less for construction through poorer neighborhoods? On the other hand, if a poor town builds a road, must it pay wages at the same level as a wealthier community would offer? Must a wealthier town deny itself an extensive fancy local library because a poor town cannot afford one? Must it cross subsidize libraries throughout the state if it wishes to build one for its own residents?

8. Do the answers to the questions above suggest that the decision in *Serrano/Rodriguez* turns on one's vision of whose children these are? Are they the children of a town, with understandable variations based on local preferences, traditions, and wealth variations, or are they all properly children of California and Texas, respectively, entitled to equal educational opportunity before the sovereign state? Would such a judgment change if the local entity receiving deference is not a "town," but a school district? Does it matter that states commonly have from 200 to 1,200 such districts, with separate boundaries from other jurisdictions and usually performing only the function of school finance and control under the mandatory guidelines of the state?

9. The difference between *Serrano* and *Rodriguez* also necessarily turns on the weight given to K–12 education as a right/opportunity. Child advocates cite three features commending its elevated status: (a) its provision by the state or its subdivisions, (b) its compulsory nature, and (c) its direct relationship to higher education opportunity, future income, and livelihood. Can a strong argument be made for equal provision of many public services, *e.g.*, water, sewage, parks, trash collection? Many of these services are financed by special districts similar in structure to school districts and allowed relative financial autonomy. Those in the district pay fees and finance what is provided to those who pay for it. Is education different, or does the equality principle of *Serrano* (where the state or its

agencies provide a basic service) properly apply beyond education? What factors should dictate line drawing for equal protection application?

As noted above, the federal jurisdiction refused to follow *Serrano*. However, California subsequently reaffirmed its holding, stating that it rested on California's constitution (on "independent state grounds") regardless of federal constitutional status.[4] Following *Serrano*, thirty-four states have heard similar challenges, and fourteen of them have similarly found their systems to be unconstitutional,[5] while twenty have affirmed alleged funding disparities.[6] Some child advocates have accomplished funding reforms without litigation.[7]

Millions of American children remain in schools where equality of opportunity is denied in the most basic sense: the state allows unequal K–12 education spending, based on the wealth of parents. The discrimination is not in favor of impoverished children, to give them a boost to the starting line, but against them. Currently, the richest school districts spend 56% more per student than do the poorest.[8]

Plyler v. Doe
457 U.S. 202 (1982)

Justice Brennan delivered the opinion of the Court.

The question presented by these cases is whether, consistent with the Equal Protection Clause of the Fourteenth Amendment, Texas may deny to undocumented school-age children the free public education that it provides to children who are citizens of the United States or legally admitted aliens.

I

Since the late 19th century, the United States has restricted immigration into this country. Unsanctioned entry into the United States is a crime, 8 U.S.C. § 1325, and those who have entered unlawfully are subject to deportation...But despite the existence of these legal restrictions, a substantial number of persons have succeeded in unlawfully entering the United States, and now live within various States, including the State of Texas.

In May 1975, the Texas Legislature revised its education laws to withhold from local school districts any state funds for the education of children who were not "legally admitted" into the United States. The 1975 revision also authorized local school districts to deny enrollment in their public schools to children not "legally admitted" to the country....These cases involve constitutional challenges to those provisions.

* * *

...[T]he District Court made extensive findings of fact. The court found that neither § 21.031 nor the School District policy implementing it had "either the purpose or effect of keeping illegal aliens out of the State of Texas." 458 F.Supp. 569, 575 (1978). Respecting defendants' further claim that § 21.031 was simply a financial measure designed to avoid a drain on the State's fisc, the court recognized that the increases in population resulting from the immigration of Mexican nationals into the United States had created problems for the public schools of the State, and that these problems were exacerbated by the special educational needs of immigrant Mexican children. The court noted, however, that the increase in school enrollment was primarily attributable to the admission of children who were legal residents....It also found that while the "exclusion of all undocumented children from the public schools in Texas would eventually result in economies at some level,"...funding from both the State and Federal Governments was based primarily on the number of children enrolled. In net effect then, barring undocumented children from the schools would save money, but it would "not necessarily" improve "the quality of education."....The court further observed that the impact of § 21.031 was borne primarily by a very small subclass of illegal aliens, "entire families who have migrated illegally and—for all practical purposes—permanently to the United States." *Id.*, at 578.[3] Finally, the court noted that under current laws and practices "the illegal alien of today may well be the legal alien of tomorrow,"[4] and that without an education, these undocumented children, "[already] disadvantaged as a result of poverty, lack of English-speaking ability, and undeniable racial prejudices,...will become permanently locked into the lowest socio-economic class." *Id.*, at 577.

* * *

I

The Fourteenth Amendment provides that "[no] State shall...deprive any person of life, liberty, or property, without due process of law; nor deny to *any person within its jurisdiction* the equal protection of the laws." (Emphasis added.) Appellants argue at the outset that undocumented aliens, because of their immigration status, are not "persons within the jurisdiction" of the State of Texas, and that they therefore have no right to the equal protection of Texas law. We reject this argument. Whatever his status under the immigration laws, an alien is surely a "person" in any ordinary sense of that term. Aliens, even aliens whose presence in this country is unlawful, have long been recognized as "persons" guaranteed due process of law by the Fifth and Fourteenth Amendments....[9]

* * *

Sheer incapability or lax enforcement of the laws barring entry into this country, coupled with the failure to establish an effective bar to the employment of undocumented aliens, has resulted in the creation of a substantial "shadow population" of illegal migrants—numbering in the millions—within our borders.[17] This

---

[3] The court contrasted this group with those illegal aliens who entered the country alone in order to earn money to send to their dependents in Mexico, and who in many instances remained in this country for only a short period of time. 458 F.Supp., at 578.

[4] Plaintiffs' expert, Dr. Gilbert Cardenas, testified that "fifty to sixty per cent...of current legal alien workers were formerly illegal aliens."....A defense witness, Rolan Heston, District Director of the Houston District of the Immigration and Naturalization Service, testified that "undocumented children can and do live in the United States for years, and adjust their status through marriage to a citizen or permanent resident."....The court also took notice of congressional proposals to "legalize" the status of many unlawful entrants. *Id.*, at 577–578....

[9] It would be incongruous to hold that the United States, to which the Constitution assigns a broad authority over both naturalization and foreign affairs, is barred from invidious discrimination with respect to unlawful aliens, while exempting the States from a similar limitation. See 426 U.S., at 84-86.

[17] The Attorney General recently estimated the number of illegal aliens within the United States at between 3 and 6 million. In presenting to both the Senate and House of Representatives several Presidential proposals for reform of the immigration laws—including one to "legalize" many of the illegal entrants currently residing in the United States by creating for them a special status under the immigration laws—the Attorney General noted that this subclass is largely composed of persons with a permanent attachment to the Nation, and that they are unlikely to be displaced from our territory:

situation raises the specter of a permanent caste of undocumented resident aliens, encouraged by some to remain here as a source of cheap labor, but nevertheless denied the benefits that our society makes available to citizens and lawful residents.[18] The existence of such an underclass presents most difficult problems for a Nation that prides itself on adherence to principles of equality under law.[19]

The children who are plaintiffs in these cases are special members of this underclass. Persuasive arguments support the view that a State may withhold its beneficence from those whose very presence within the United States is the product of their own unlawful conduct. These arguments do not apply with the same force to classifications imposing disabilities on the minor *children* of such illegal entrants. At the least, those who elect to enter our territory by stealth and in violation of our law should be prepared to bear the consequences, including, but not limited to, deportation. But the children of those illegal entrants are not comparably situated. Their "parents have the ability to conform their conduct to societal norms," and presumably the ability to remove themselves from the State's jurisdiction; but the children who are plaintiffs in these cases "can affect neither their parents' conduct nor their own status."....Even if the State found it expedient to control the conduct of adults by acting against their children, legislation directing the onus of a parent's misconduct against his children does not comport with fundamental conceptions of justice.

* * *

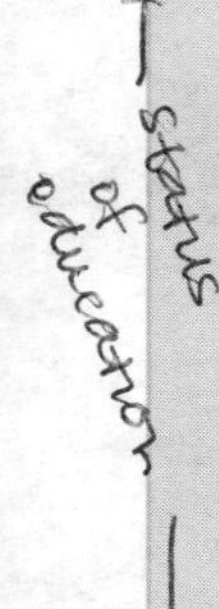

Public education is not a "right" granted to individuals by the Constitution....But neither is it merely some governmental "benefit" indistinguishable from other forms of social welfare legislation. Both the importance of education in maintaining our basic institutions, and the lasting impact of its deprivation on the life of the child, mark the distinction. The "American people have always regarded education and [the] acquisition of knowledge as matters of supreme importance."....We have recognized "the public schools as a most vital civic institution for the preservation of a democratic system of government,"....In addition, education provides the basic tools by which individuals might lead economically productive lives to the benefit of us all. In sum, education has a fundamental role in maintaining the fabric of our society. We cannot ignore the significant social costs borne by our Nation when select groups are denied the means to absorb the values and skills upon which our social order rests.

In addition to the pivotal role of education in sustaining our political and cultural heritage, denial of education to some isolated group of children poses an

---

"We have neither the resources, the capability, nor the motivation to uproot and deport millions of illegal aliens, many of whom have become, in effect, members of the community. By granting limited legal status to the productive and law-abiding members of this shadow population, we will recognize reality and devote our enforcement resources to deterring future illegal arrivals."....

[19] We reject the claim that "illegal aliens" are a "suspect class." No case in which we have attempted to define a suspect class,...Unlike most of the classifications that we have recognized as suspect, entry into this class, by virtue of entry into this country, is the product of voluntary action. Indeed, entry into the class is itself a crime. In addition, it could hardly be suggested that undocumented status is a "constitutional irrelevancy." With respect to the actions of the Federal Government, alienage classifications may be intimately related to the conduct of foreign policy, to the federal prerogative to control access to the United States, and to the plenary federal power to determine who has sufficiently manifested his allegiance to become a citizen of the Nation. No State may independently exercise a like power. But if the Federal Government has by uniform rule prescribed what it believes to be appropriate standards for the treatment of an alien subclass, the States may, of course, follow the federal direction....

affront to one of the goals of the Equal Protection Clause: the abolition of governmental barriers presenting unreasonable obstacles to advancement on the basis of individual merit. Paradoxically, by depriving the children of any disfavored group of an education, we foreclose the means by which that group might raise the level of esteem in which it is held by the majority. But more directly, "education prepares individuals to be self-reliant and self-sufficient participants in society."....Illiteracy is an enduring disability. The inability to read and write will handicap the individual deprived of a basic education each and every day of his life. The inestimable toll of that deprivation on the social, economic, intellectual, and psychological well-being of the individual, and the obstacle it poses to individual achievement, make it most difficult to reconcile the cost or the principle of a status-based denial of basic education with the framework of equality embodied in the Equal Protection Clause.[20] ...

* * *

...In determining the rationality of § 21.031, we may appropriately take into account its costs to the Nation and to the innocent children who are its victims. In light of these countervailing costs, the discrimination contained in § 21.031 can hardly be considered rational unless it furthers some substantial goal of the State.

need substantial state goal

* * *

To be sure, like all persons who have entered the United States unlawfully, these children are subject to deportation....But there is no assurance that a child subject to deportation will ever be deported. An illegal entrant might be granted federal permission to continue to reside in this country, or even to become a citizen....In light of the discretionary federal power to grant relief from deportation, a State cannot realistically determine that any particular undocumented child will in fact be deported until after deportation proceedings have been completed. It would of course be most difficult for the State to justify a denial of education to a child enjoying an inchoate federal permission to remain.

We are reluctant to impute to Congress the intention to withhold from these children, for so long as they are present in this country through no fault of their own, access to a basic education....

V

Appellants argue that the classification at issue furthers an interest in the "preservation of the state's limited resources for the education of its lawful residents."[21] ....Of course, a concern for the preservation of resources standing

---

[20] Because the State does not afford noncitizens the right to vote, and may bar noncitizens from participating in activities at the heart of its political community, appellants argue that denial of a basic education to these children is of less significance than the denial to some other group. Whatever the current status of these children, the courts below concluded that many will remain here permanently and that some indeterminate number will eventually become citizens. The fact that many will not is not decisive, even with respect to the importance of education to participation in core political institutions. "[The] benefits of education are not reserved to those whose productive utilization of them is a certainty...." 458 F.Supp., at 581, n. 14. In addition, although a noncitizen "may be barred from full involvement in the political arena, he may play a role—perhaps even a leadership role—in other areas of import to the community." *Nyquist v. Mauclet*, 432 U.S. 1, 12 (1977). Moreover, the significance of education to our society is not limited to its political and cultural fruits. The public schools are an important socializing institution, imparting those shared values through which social order and stability are maintained.

[21] Appellant School District sought at oral argument to characterize the alienage classi

alone can hardly justify the classification used in allocating those resources....The State must do more than justify its classification with a concise expression of an intention to discriminate....

First, appellants appear to suggest that the State may seek to protect itself from an influx of illegal immigrants. While a State might have an interest in mitigating the potentially harsh economic effects of sudden shifts in population,[23] § 21.031 hardly offers an effective method of dealing with an urgent demographic or economic problem. There is no evidence in the record suggesting that illegal entrants impose any significant burden on the State's economy. To the contrary, the available evidence suggests that illegal aliens underutilize public services, while contributing their labor to the local economy and tax money to the state fisc. 458 F.Supp., at 578; 501 F.Supp., at 570–571. The dominant incentive for illegal entry into the State of Texas is the availability of employment; few if any illegal immigrants come to this country, or presumably to the State of Texas, in order to avail themselves of a free education.[24] Thus, even making the doubtful assumption that the net impact of illegal aliens on the economy of the State is negative, we think it clear that "[charging] tuition to undocumented children constitutes a ludicrously ineffectual attempt to stem the tide of illegal immigration," at least when compared with the alternative of prohibiting the employment of illegal aliens....

* * *

VI

If the State is to deny a discrete group of innocent children the free public education that it offers to other children residing within its borders, that denial must be justified by a showing that it furthers some substantial state interest. No such showing was made here. Accordingly, the judgment of the Court of Appeals in each of these cases is

---

fication contained in § 21.031 as simply a test of residence. We are unable to uphold § 21.031 on that basis. Appellants conceded that if, for example, a Virginian or a legally admitted Mexican citizen entered Tyler with his school-age children, intending to remain only six months, those children would be viewed as residents entitled to attend Tyler schools....It is thus clear that Tyler's residence argument amounts to nothing more than the assertion that illegal entry, without more, prevents a person from becoming a resident for purposes of enrolling his children in the public schools. A State may not, however, accomplish what would otherwise be prohibited by the Equal Protection Clause, merely by defining a disfavored group as nonresident. And illegal entry into the country would not, under traditional criteria, bar a person from obtaining domicile within a State....Appellants have not shown that the families of undocumented children do not comply with the established standards by which the State historically tests residence. Apart from the alienage limitation, § 21.031(b) requires a school district to provide education only to resident children. The school districts of the State are as free to apply to undocumented children established criteria for determining residence as they are to apply those criteria to any other child who seeks admission.

[23] Although the State has no direct interest in controlling entry into this country, that interest being one reserved by the Constitution to the Federal Government, unchecked unlawful migration might impair the State's economy generally, or the State's ability to provide some important service. Despite the exclusive federal control of this Nation's borders, we cannot conclude that the States are without an power to deter the influx of persons entering the United States against federal law, and whose numbers might have a discernible impact on traditional state concerns....

[24] The courts below noted the ineffectiveness of the Texas provision as a means of controlling the influx of illegal entrants into the State...("The evidence demonstrates that undocumented persons do not immigrate in search for a free public education. Virtually all of the undocumented persons who come into this country seek employment opportunities and not educational benefits....There was overwhelming evidence...of the unimportance of public education as a stimulus for immigration")...

Affirmed.

Justice Marshall, concurring.

While I join the Court opinion,...I continue to believe that an individual's interest in education is fundamental, and that this view is amply supported "by the unique status accorded public education by our society, and by the close relationship between education and some of our most basic constitutional values."...

* * *

Chief Justice Burger, with whom **Justice White, Justice Rehnquist,** and **Justice O'Connor** join, dissenting.

Were it our business to set the Nation's social policy, I would agree without hesitation that it is senseless for an enlightened society to deprive any children—including illegal aliens—of an elementary education. I fully agree that it would be folly—and wrong—to tolerate creation of a segment of society made up of illiterate persons, many having a limited or no command of our language.[1] However, the Constitution does not constitute us as "Platonic Guardians" nor does it vest in this Court the authority to strike down laws because they do not meet our standards of desirable social policy, "wisdom," or "common sense." See *TVA v. Hill*, 437 U.S. 153, 194–195 (1978). We trespass on the assigned function of the political branches under our structure of limited and separated powers when we assume a policymaking role as the Court does today.

The Court makes no attempt to disguise that it is acting to make up for Congress' lack of "effective leadership" in dealing with the serious national problems caused by the influx of uncountable millions of illegal aliens across our borders.[2]....The failure of enforcement of the immigration laws over more than a decade and the inherent difficulty and expense of sealing our vast borders have combined to create a grave socioeconomic dilemma. It is a dilemma that has not yet even been fully assessed, let alone addressed. However, it is not the function of the Judiciary to provide "effective leadership" simply because the political branches of government fail to do so.

The Court's holding today manifests the justly criticized judicial tendency to attempt speedy and wholesale formulation of "remedies" for the failures—or simply the laggard pace—of the political processes of our system of government. The Court employs, and in my view abuses, the Fourteenth Amendment in an effort to become an omnipotent and omniscient problem solver. That the motives for doing so are noble and compassionate does not alter the fact that the Court distorts our constitutional function to make amends for the defaults of others.

* * *

---

[1] It does not follow, however, that a state should bear the costs of educating children whose illegal presence in this country results from the default of the political branches of the Federal Government. A state has no power to prevent unlawful immigration, and no power to deport illegal aliens; those powers are reserved exclusively to Congress and the Executive. If the Federal Government, properly chargeable with deporting illegal aliens, fails to do so, it should bear the burdens of their presence here. Surely if illegal alien children can be identified for purposes of this litigation, their parents can be identified for purposes of prompt deportation.

[2] The Department of Justice recently estimated the number of illegal aliens within the United States at between 3 and 6 million....

In the end, we are told little more than that the level of scrutiny employed to strike down the Texas law applies only when illegal alien children are deprived of a public education,...[3] If ever a court was guilty of an unabashedly result-oriented approach, this case is a prime example.

(1)

The Court first suggests that these illegal alien children, although not a suspect class, are entitled to special solicitude under the Equal Protection Clause because they lack "control" over or "responsibility" for their unlawful entry into this country....Similarly, the Court appears to take the position that § 21.031 is presumptively "irrational" because it has the effect of imposing "penalties" on "innocent" children....[4]...

* * *

(2)

The second strand of the Court's analysis rests on the premise that, although public education is not a constitutionally guaranteed right, "neither is it merely some governmental 'benefit' indistinguishable from other forms of social welfare legislation."....Whatever meaning or relevance this opaque observation might have in some other context,[8] it simply has no bearing on the issues at hand. Indeed, it is never made clear what the Court's opinion means on this score.

The importance of education is beyond dispute. Yet we have held repeatedly that the importance of a governmental service does not elevate it to the status of a "fundamental right" for purposes of equal protection analysis....Moreover, the Court points to no meaningful way to distinguish between education and other governmental benefits in this context. Is the Court suggesting that education is more "fundamental" than food, shelter, or medical care?

* * *

Without laboring what will undoubtedly seem obvious to many, it simply is not "irrational" for a state to conclude that it does not have the same responsibility to provide benefits for persons whose very presence in the state and this country is illegal as it does to provide for persons lawfully present. By definition, illegal aliens have no right whatever to be here, and the state may reasonably, and

---

[3] The Court implies, for example, that the Fourteenth Amendment would not require a state to provide welfare benefits to illegal aliens.

[4] Both the opinion of the Court and Justice Powell's concurrence imply that appellees are being "penalized" because their parents are illegal entrants....However, Texas has classified appellees on the basis of their own illegal status, not that of their parents. Children born in this country to illegal alien parents, including some of appellees' siblings, are not excluded from the Texas schools. Nor does Texas discriminate against appellees because of their Mexican origin or citizenship. Texas provides a free public education to countless thousands of Mexican immigrants who are lawfully in this country.

[8] In support of this conclusion, the Court's opinion strings together quotations drawn from cases addressing such diverse matters as the right of individuals under the Due Process Clause to learn a foreign language, *Meyer v. Nebraska*, 262 U.S. 390 (1923); the First Amendment prohibition against state-mandated religious exercises in the public schools, *Abington School District v. Schempp*, 374 U.S. 203 (1963); and state impingements upon the free exercise of religion, *Wisconsin v. Yoder*, 406 U.S. 205 (1972). However, not every isolated utterance of this Court retains force when wrested from the context in which it was made.

constitutionally, elect not to provide them with governmental services at the expense of those who are lawfully in the state.[11] ...

* * *

Denying a free education to illegal alien children is not a choice I would make were I a legislator. Apart from compassionate considerations, the long-range costs of excluding any children from the public schools may well outweigh the costs of educating them. But that is not the issue; the fact that there are sound *policy* arguments against the Texas Legislature's choice does not render that choice an unconstitutional one.

I

The Constitution does not provide a cure for every social ill, nor does it vest judges with a mandate to try to remedy every social problem.

* * *

The solution to this seemingly intractable problem is to defer to the political processes, unpalatable as that may be to some.

---

[11] The Court suggests that the State's classification is improper because "[a]n illegal entrant might be granted federal permission to continue to reside in this country, or even to become a citizen."....However, once an illegal alien is given federal permission to remain, he is no longer subject to exclusion from the tuition-free public schools under § 21.031. The Court acknowledges that the Tyler Independent School District provides a free public education to any alien who has obtained, *or is in the procession of obtaining*, documentation from the United States Immigration and Naturalization Service. Thus, Texas has not taken it upon itself to determine which aliens are or are not entitled to United States residence....

Questions for Discussion

1. In California, voters approved Proposition 187 barring undocumented immigrants from public school attendance. The initiative was struck by a federal district court judge and its appeal was dropped by the Gray Davis administration in 2000. However, if the state could demonstrate its purpose was not to "save money," but to discourage unlawful immigration by accommodating the children of parental violators, would it pass constitutional muster if reviewed today? If the state could show some inducement impact from free public education, would *Plyler* be decided differently?

2. Assume that the undocumented immigrants who are lawfully here (*e.g.*, "permanent residents under color of law" or PRUCOL residents) are excluded from the education ban. Would that make it constitutional?

3. Is it relevant that undocumented parents pay sales and other taxes, but their children would be deprived of public services they help finance?

4. The Court notes that undocumented immigrants are "persons" under the Constitution. Is it relevant that the sanction punishes children who have no control over the immigration status of their parents? If the immigration statutes

could be enforced directly with greater efficacy than using denial of schooling for their children as a disincentive, would that be relevant? If undocumented immigrant parents are working the fields, caring for the yards, and supervising the children of upper class Americans, what are the ethical implications of education denial for children in lieu of enforcing immigration at point of employment? If such school denial were to be examined under strict scrutiny, can the state satisfy the "least restrictive alternative" requirement if it were shown to be avoiding enforcement through employer sanctions and that such employment is the primary inducement for immigration?

5. Are undocumented immigrant children a suspect class entitled to strict scrutiny? The *Serrano* case labeled education a "fundamental right"—is that status confirmed in *Plyler*? Blackmun's concurring opinion argues that although education is not a fundamental right, its denial must be based on more than rational relation. Is this a "heightened scrutiny" standard? What is its basis?

6. Is the denial of education to the undocumented so steeped in federal immigration policy that the states' options are pre-empted? Can they be required to fund the schooling of persons unlawfully in the state (and nation) insofar as the federal jurisdiction has failed to stop them at the border?

B. NOTE ON CHILD LABOR

Child labor problems may involve issues of child neglect, abuse and exploitation due to the onerous nature of assigned work. However, beyond the working conditions themselves, the time demanded for substantial child employment may foreclose educational opportunity and limit a child's potential. Accordingly, the extent to which a child may work has been limited by law in the United States. The Fair Labor Standards Act of 1938 (FLSA, 29 U.S.C. § 201 *et seq.*) includes a ceiling on such employment, with states permitted to lower that ceiling further. *U.S. v. Darby*, 312 U.S. 100 (1941), upheld the constitutionality of this state interference with parental and contract rights of adults, *et al.* Many states have enacted stricter standards to protect children from work exploitation beyond applicable federal standards. In *Prince v. Massachusetts*, 321 U.S.158 (1944), the Supreme Court upheld the conviction of an aunt (given parental status in the decision) for violating state child labor law where she took her nine year old niece to help her sell Jehovah's Witness periodicals on the street. The prohibition was upheld against the invocation of constitutional religious and parental rights. On the other hand, *Wisconsin v. Yoder*, 406 U.S. 205 (1972), upheld a religion-based limitation on public education, allowing Amish children to leave public school at the age of 16, even though they were subject to long hours of work, and most of the affected children thus leave Amish communities without traditional schooling beyond the 8th grade (see discussion in Chapter 13).

The Federal FLSA prohibits "oppressive child labor," defined as the employment of a child under 16 years of age (except by a parent or guardian). Even a parent or guardian cannot employ a child in "manufacturing or mining," or in work listed by the Secretary of Labor as particularly "hazardous" (*e.g.*, explosives, meat packing, roofing, and excavation). As to the hazardous list, child labor is considered unlawfully oppressive to age 18. However, it is not "oppressive" to employ children down to the age of 14 outside of hazardous work, manufacturing or mining, if not interfering with education or jeopardizing child health and safety. In addition, work on farms is permitted for children down to the age of 12.

Remedy for violation of the FLSA rests with criminal and civil remedies available to the Secretary of Labor, primarily against employers. However, enforcement of these limited standards is rare. The Act provides for no private enforcement of its standards, and courts have refused to imply such a remedy, leaving enforcement to parallel state enactments.

State laws generally protect children from excessive work where they are under 18 years of age, and are not emancipated by court order or marriage, are not parents or have not graduated from high school. The states may and do add to the federal FLSA a list of jobs unacceptably hazardous for children, including dangerous machinery and sometimes construction.

Hours are commonly limited by the week and for school nights while children are in school. Most states also require work permits from a school (or other) official where children work during the school year. The federal statute includes no such requirement and so the terms vary among the states. The permit may require attestation that the child is satisfactorily attending school. It usually includes a description of the work, hours, and commonly requires a physician's attestation that the child is able to perform the assigned tasks without health risk. Finally, it requires a signature indicating parental or guardian consent.

The agricultural exemption affords unusual latitude for child labor (and education avoidance) beyond that granted to the Amish in *Yoder*. The agricultural exemption in federal and state statutes allows children to be used for labor with little limitation. While the exemption may have envisioned children helping with the harvest on a family farm, it also applies to the highly mechanized farm operations of the modern era. Child labor and educational foreclosure are particularly prevalent among the children of undocumented agricultural workers. Pay is often below poverty levels in such families, safety net support is barred (TANF and food stamps), and children are conscripted as workers to assist their families to survive. This work may involve dangerous machinery, pesticide exposure with enhanced child susceptibility to harm, and long hours. Although *Plyler v. Doe*, 457 U.S. 202 (1982), rejected the categorical exclusion of undocumented immigrants from public education (see discussion above), movement between fields may further preclude educational opportunity.

Exemptions also often apply to children working for their own parents or guardians, including employment in family owned businesses, such as restaurants. Moreover, some states define "work" and "labor" as restricted to remunerative work, and fail to limit child employment at all for so-called "volunteer" work that is not compensated.

The lack of private federal remedy places substantial burden on state enforcement of child labor violations. State worker compensation statutes commonly bar private tort causes of action separate and apart from the compensation statute extant—if the law includes child labor prohibitions and hence occupies that field. Where the statute is silent about such requirements, a private tort action against an employer may generally lie. However, most such statutes include or address unlawful child labor sufficiently to foreclose private tort remedies. Hence, enforcement against employers where there is injury (usually the context) is usually confined to the remedies enumerated in that law. Often, violation of a child related provision may trigger an enhanced award from 150% to 300% of the remedy for other violations, but that enhancement is from the low base allowed for worker's compensation. It does not include pain and suffering, nor lost future wages, nor punitive damages. It often covers only medical or funeral expenses, and perhaps lost wages while unable to work, often a non-existent sum for a child legally barred from that work in the first place.

Worker compensation statutes may bar remedies outside their confines against employers, but traditional tort actions remain viable against other actors where injury or death has occurred to children who are unlawfully employed. Where such causes of action are allowed they serve as an important deterrent to stimulate compliance. The standard defenses of contributory negligence, assumption of risk, or consent are unavailable.

State "Unfair Competition Acts" may be the most potent enforcement alternative. The hiring of underage labor may provide a business with a competitive advantage in violation of law and give rise to injunctive and restitutionary relief. Here, suit is not brought by the child or employees, but by a competitor, or by a public prosecutor in many states under unfair competition statutes.

C. PUBLIC SCHOOL SANCTIONS/EXPULSION

Goss v. Lopez
419 U.S. 565 (1975)

MR. JUSTICE WHITE delivered the opinion of the Court.

This appeal by various administrators of the Columbus, Ohio, Public School System (CPSS) challenges the judgment of a three-judge federal court, declaring that appellees—various high school students in the CPSS—were denied due process of law contrary to the command of the Fourteenth Amendment in that they were temporarily suspended from their high schools without a hearing either prior to suspension or within a reasonable time thereafter, and enjoining the administrators to remove all references to such suspensions from the students' records.

I

Ohio law, Rev. Code Ann. § 3313.64 (1972), provides for free education to all children between the ages of six and 21. Section 3313.66 of the Code empowers the principal of an Ohio public school to suspend a pupil for misconduct for up to 10 days or to expel him. In either case, he must notify the student's parents within 24 hours and state the reasons for his action. A pupil who is expelled, or his parents, may appeal the decision to the Board of Education and in connection therewith shall be permitted to be heard at the board meeting. The Board may reinstate the pupil following the hearing. No similar procedure is provided in § 3313.66 or any other provision of state law for a suspended student....

* * *

The proof below established that the suspensions arose out of a period of widespread student unrest in the CPSS during February and March 1971. Six of the named plaintiffs, Rudolph Sutton, Tyrone Washington, Susan Cooper, Deborah Fox, Clarence Byars, and Bruce Harris, were students at the Marion-Franklin High School and were each suspended for 10 days on account of disruptive or disobedient conduct committed in the presence of the school administrator who ordered the suspension. One of these, Tyrone Washington, was among a group of students demonstrating in the school auditorium while a class was being conducted there. He was ordered by the school principal to leave, refused to do so, and was suspended. Rudolph Sutton, in the presence of the principal, physically attacked a police officer who was attempting to remove Tyrone Washington from the auditorium. He was immediately suspended. The other four Marion-Franklin students were suspended for similar conduct. None was given a hearing to determine the operative facts underlying the suspension, but each, together with his or her parents, was offered the opportunity to attend a conference, subsequent to the effective date of the suspension, to discuss the student's future.

Two named plaintiffs, Dwight Lopez and Betty Crome, were students at the Central High School and McGuffey Junior High School, respectively. The former was suspended in connection with a disturbance in the lunchroom which involved some physical damage to school property. Lopez testified that at least 75 other students were suspended from his school on the same day. He also testified below that he was not a party to the destructive conduct but was instead an innocent bystander. Because no one from the school testified with regard to this incident, there is no evidence in the record indicating the official basis for concluding otherwise. Lopez never had a hearing.

Betty Crome was present at a demonstration at a high school other than the one she was attending. There she was arrested together with others, taken to the police station, and released without being formally charged. Before she went to school on the following day, she was notified that she had been suspended for a 10-day period. Because no one from the school testified with respect to this incident, the record does not disclose how the McGuffey Junior High School principal went about making the decision to suspend Crome, nor does it disclose on what information the decision was based. It is clear from the record that no hearing was ever held.

There was no testimony with respect to the suspension of the ninth named plaintiff, Carl Smith. The school files were also silent as to his suspension, although as to some, but not all, of the other named plaintiffs the files contained either direct references to their suspensions or copies of letters sent to their parents advising them of the suspension.

On the basis of this evidence, the three-judge court declared that plaintiffs were denied due process of law because they were "suspended without hearing prior to suspension or within a reasonable time thereafter,"...

* * *

I

* * *

...School authorities here suspended appellees from school for periods of up to 10 days based on charges of misconduct. If sustained and recorded, those charges could seriously damage the students' standing with their fellow pupils and their teachers as well as interfere with later opportunities for higher education and employment.[3] It is apparent that the claimed right of the State to determine unilaterally and without process whether that misconduct has occurred immediately collides with the requirements of the Constitution.

Appellants proceed to argue that even if there is a right to a public education protected by the Due Process Clause generally, the Clause comes into play only when the State subjects a student to a "severe detriment or grievous loss." The loss of 10 days, it is said, is neither severe nor grievous and the Due Process Clause is therefore of no relevance....

A short suspension is, of course, a far milder deprivation than expulsion. But, "education is perhaps the most important function of state and local governments," *Brown v. Board of Education,* 347 U.S. 483, 493 (1954), and the

---

[3] Appellees assert in their brief that four of 12 randomly selected Ohio colleges specifically inquire of the high school of every applicant for admission whether the applicant has ever been suspended. Appellees also contend that many employers request similar information.

total exclusion from the educational process for more than a trivial period, and certainly if the suspension is for 10 days, is a serious event in the life of the suspended child. Neither the property interest in educational benefits temporarily denied nor the liberty interest in reputation, which is also implicated, is so insubstantial that suspensions may constitutionally be imposed by any procedure the school chooses, no matter how arbitrary....

III

"Once it is determined that due process applies, the question remains what process is due." We turn to that question, fully realizing as our cases regularly do that the interpretation and application of the Due Process Clause are intensely practical matters and that "[the] very nature of due process negates any concept of inflexible procedures universally applicable to every imaginable situation." [citation omitted] We are also mindful of our own admonition:

> "Judicial interposition in the operation of the public school system of the Nation raises problems requiring care and restraint....By and large, public education in our Nation is committed to the control of state and local authorities."...

* * *

The difficulty is that our schools are vast and complex. Some modicum of discipline and order is essential if the educational function is to be performed. Events calling for discipline are frequent occurrences and sometimes require immediate, effective action. Suspension is considered not only to be a necessary tool to maintain order but a valuable educational device. The prospect of imposing elaborate hearing requirements in every suspension case is viewed with great concern, and many school authorities may well prefer the untrammeled power to act unilaterally, unhampered by rules about notice and hearing. But it would be a strange disciplinary system in an educational institution if no communication was sought by the disciplinarian with the student in an effort to inform him of his dereliction and to let him tell his side of the story in order to make sure that an injustice is not done....[9]

We do not believe that school authorities must be totally free from notice and hearing requirements if their schools are to operate with acceptable efficiency. Students facing temporary suspension have interests qualifying for protection of the Due Process Clause, and due process requires, in connection with a suspension of 10 days or less, that the student be given oral or written notice of the charges against him and, if he denies them, an explanation of the evidence the authorities have and an opportunity to present his side of the story. The Clause requires at least these rudimentary precautions against unfair or mistaken findings of misconduct and arbitrary exclusion from school....

---

[9] The facts involved in this case illustrate the point. Betty Crome was suspended for conduct which did not occur on school grounds, and for which mass arrests were made—hardly guaranteeing careful individualized factfinding by the police or by the school principal. She claims to have been involved in no misconduct. However, she was suspended for 10 days without ever being told what she was accused of doing or being given an opportunity to explain her presence among those arrested. Similarly, Dwight Lopez was suspended, along with many others, in connection with a disturbance in the lunchroom. Lopez says he was not one of those in the lunchroom who was involved. However, he was never told the basis for the principal's belief that he was involved, nor was he ever given an opportunity to explain his presence in the lunchroom. The school principals who suspended Crome and Lopez may have been correct on the merits, but it is inconsistent with the Due Process Clause to have made the decision that misconduct had occurred without at some meaningful time giving Crome or Lopez an opportunity to persuade the principals otherwise....

There need be no delay between the time "notice" is given and the time of the hearing. In the great majority of cases the disciplinarian may informally discuss the alleged misconduct with the student minutes after it has occurred. We hold only that, in being given an opportunity to explain his version of the facts at this discussion, the student first be told what he is accused of doing and what the basis of the accusation is....Since the hearing may occur almost immediately following the misconduct, it follows that as a general rule notice and hearing should precede removal of the student from school. We agree with the District Court, however, that there are recurring situations in which prior notice and hearing cannot be insisted upon. Students whose presence poses a continuing danger to persons or property or an ongoing threat of disrupting the academic process may be immediately removed from school. In such cases, the necessary notice and rudimentary hearing should follow as soon as practicable, as the District Court indicated.

In holding as we do, we do not believe that we have imposed procedures on school disciplinarians which are inappropriate in a classroom setting. Instead we have imposed requirements which are, if anything, less than a fair-minded school principal would impose upon himself in order to avoid unfair suspensions. Indeed, according to the testimony of the principal of Marion-Franklin High School, that school had an informal procedure, remarkably similar to that which we now require, applicable to suspensions generally but which was not followed in this case....

We stop short of construing the Due Process Clause to require, countrywide, that hearings in connection with short suspensions must afford the student the opportunity to secure counsel, to confront and cross-examine witnesses supporting the charge, or to call his own witnesses to verify his version of the incident. Brief disciplinary suspensions are almost countless. To impose in each such case even truncated trial-type procedures might well overwhelm administrative facilities in many places and, by diverting resources, cost more than it would save in educational effectiveness. Moreover, further formalizing the suspension process and escalating its formality and adversary nature may not only make it too costly as a regular disciplinary tool but also destroy its effectiveness as part of the teaching process.

* * *

We should also make it clear that we have addressed ourselves solely to the short suspension, not exceeding 10 days. Longer suspensions or expulsions for the remainder of the school term, or permanently, may require more formal procedures. Nor do we put aside the possibility that in unusual situations, although involving only a short suspension, something more than the rudimentary procedures will be required.

IV

The District Court found each of the suspensions involved here to have occurred without a hearing, either before or after the suspension, and that each suspension was therefore invalid and the statute unconstitutional insofar as it permits such suspensions without notice or hearing. Accordingly, the judgment is

Affirmed.

DISSENT: **MR. JUSTICE POWELL,** with whom **THE CHIEF JUSTICE, MR. JUSTICE BLACKMUN,** and **MR. JUSTICE REHNQUIST** join, dissenting.

The Court today invalidates an Ohio statute that permits student suspensions from school without a hearing "for not more than ten days."[1] The decision unnecessarily opens avenues for judicial intervention in the operation of our public schools that may affect adversely the quality of education. The Court holds for the first time that the federal courts, rather than educational officials and state legislatures, have the authority to determine the rules applicable to routine classroom discipline of children and teenagers in the public schools. It justifies this unprecedented intrusion into the process of elementary and secondary education by identifying a new constitutional right: the right of a student not to be suspended for as much as a single day without notice and a due process hearing either before or promptly following the suspension.[2]

...In my view, a student's interest in education is not infringed by a suspension within the limited period prescribed by Ohio law. Moreover, to the extent that there may be some arguable infringement, it is too speculative, transitory, and insubstantial to justify imposition of a constitutional rule.

* * *

The Ohio suspension statute allows no serious or significant infringement of education. It authorizes only a maximum suspension of eight school days, less than 5% of the normal 180-day school year. Absences of such limited duration will rarely affect a pupil's opportunity to learn or his scholastic performance. Indeed, the record in this case reflects no educational injury to appellees. Each completed the semester in which the suspension occurred and performed at least as well as he or she had in previous years....Despite the Court's unsupported speculation that a suspended student could be "seriously [damaged]" there is no factual showing of any such damage to appellees.

* * *

I

In prior decisions, this Court has explicitly recognized that school authorities must have broad discretionary authority in the daily operation of public schools. This includes wide latitude with respect to maintaining discipline and good order....

The Court today turns its back on these precedents. It can hardly seriously be claimed that a school principal's decision to suspend a pupil for a single day would "directly and sharply implicate basic constitutional values."...

Moreover, the Court ignores the experience of mankind, as well as the long history of our law, recognizing that there are differences which must be accommodated in determining the rights and duties of children as compared with those of adults. Examples of this distinction abound in our law: in contracts, in torts, in criminal law and procedure, in criminal sanctions and rehabilitation, and in the right to vote and to hold office. Until today, and except in the special context of the First Amendment issue in Tinker, the educational rights of children and teenagers in the elementary and secondary schools have not been analogized to the rights of adults or to those accorded college students. Even with respect to the

---

[1] The Ohio statute actually is a limitation on the time-honored practice of school authorities themselves determining the appropriate duration of suspensions. The statute allows the superintendent or principal of a public school to suspend a pupil "for not more than ten days..." (italics supplied); and requires notification to the parent or guardian in writing within 24 hours of any suspension.

[2] Section 3313.66 also provides authority for the expulsion of pupils, but requires a hearing thereon by the school board upon request of a parent or guardian. The rights of pupils expelled are not involved in this case, which concerns only the limited discretion of school authorities to suspend for not more than 10 days. Expulsion, usually resulting at least in loss of a school year or semester, is an incomparably more serious matter than the brief suspension, traditionally used as the principal sanction for enforcing routine discipline. The Ohio statute recognizes this distinction.

First Amendment, the rights of children have not been regarded as "co-extensive with those of adults." *Tinker, supra, at 515* (STEWART, J., concurring).

A

* * *

The facts set forth in the margin[10] leave little room for doubt as to the magnitude of the disciplinary problem in the public schools, or as to the extent of reliance upon the right to suspend. They also demonstrate that if hearings were required for a substantial percentage of short-term suspensions, school authorities would have time to do little else.

* * *

C

One of the more disturbing aspects of today's decision is its indiscriminate reliance upon the judiciary, and the adversary process, as the means of resolving many of the most routine problems arising in the classroom. In mandating due process procedures the Court misapprehends the reality of the normal teacher-pupil relationship. There is an ongoing relationship, one in which the teacher must occupy many roles—educator, adviser, friend, and, at times, parent-substitute....It is rarely adversary in nature except with respect to the chronically disruptive or insubordinate pupil whom the teacher must be free to discipline without frustrating formalities....

* * *

If, as seems apparent, the Court will now require due process procedures whenever such routine school decisions are challenged, the impact upon public education will be serious indeed. The discretion and judgment of federal courts across the land often will be substituted for that of the 50 state legislatures, the 14,000 school boards,...and the 2,000,000 teachers who heretofore have been responsible for the administration of the American public school system. If the Court perceives a rational and analytically sound distinction between the discretionary decision by school authorities to suspend a pupil for a brief period, and the types of discretionary school decisions described above, it would be prudent to articulate it in today's opinion. Otherwise, the federal courts should prepare themselves for a vast new role in society.

IV

...In recent years the Court, wisely in my view, has rejected the "wooden distinction between 'rights' and 'privileges,'" [citation omitted] and looked instead to the significance of the state-created or state-enforced right and to the substantiality of the alleged deprivation. Today's opinion appears to abandon this reasonable approach by holding in effect that government infringement of any interest to which a person is entitled, no matter what the interest or how inconsequential the infringement, requires constitutional protection. As it is difficult to think of any less consequential infringement than suspension of a junior high school student for a single day, it is equally difficult to perceive any principled limit to the new reach of rocedural due process....

---

[10] An amicus brief filed by the Children's Defense Fund states that at least 10% of the junior and senior high school students in the States sampled were suspended one or more times in the 1972–1973 school year...

Questions for Discussion

1. The majority in *Goss* argues that students subject to a sanction of less than ten days of school suspension must receive two elements of due process: notice and a chance to be heard. They are not entitled to a hearing, right to counsel, testimony under oath, right to cross-examine, transcript, neutral adjudicator, or other formal due process rights. Are these elements sufficient to assure consistency? Is more impractical?

2. The dissent would not require these elements, and rejects formal due process even for permanent expulsion. How is the dissent's view of expulsion due process consistent with the complete panoply of procedural due process rights (including notice, hearing before a neutral adjudicator, right to confront, testimony under oath, right to present evidence, transcript, right to appeal) offered adults where: (a) an employer wishes to garnish wages (see *Sniadach v. Family Finance Corp. of Bay View*, 395 U.S. 337 (1969)); (b) a state agency cuts off welfare payments (see *Goldberg v. Kelly*, 397 U.S. 254 (1970) and *Board of Regents v. Roth*, 408 U.S. 564 (1972)); (c) a state university denies tenure (see *Garnel v. Bunzel*, 68 Cal. App. 3d 999 (1977)); or (d) a state agency disciplines a trade licensee (contractor, pharmacist)? As to licensure discipline, the full panoply of due process also includes a burden on the state to prove its case by "clear and convincing evidence," and applies short of revocation and to cases where the sanction is a fine or short suspension. Yet other cases find due process procedures constitutionally compelled where official charges, "however informal,... threaten to stain [a] personal or professional future" (*Endler v. Schutzbank*, 68 Cal.2d 162 (1968)). What would be the dissenters' explanation for the differences between due process requirements imposed for adult takings or sanctions in (a) through (d) above and those required for the state to expel a student from school?

3. Assume, as the majority implies, that a suspension from school for alleged misconduct must be disclosed and may be given substantial weight by universities and employers. Is the loss to a student of admission to the college he or she has hoped to attend a significant consequence warranting some safeguards? Are the safeguards enumerated sufficient?

4. If there is a serious reputational impact, why doesn't the majority consider allowing the quick decision with only the two due process elements it imposes, but then allow a student a traditional due process hearing after the suspension has been served so an unjust, inaccurate, or arbitrary stain on reputation may be removed or adjusted? Assuming that only those students who were damaged and feel it was incorrect factually or unjust will request such a remedy, why not provide some hearing opportunity?

5. How would a demonstration of substantial future reputational harm (with real impact on college and job prospects) affect the dissent's judgment that a suspension is categorically different from an expulsion? What if expulsions do not result in the loss of a school year, but merely require a student to attend school elsewhere or at a county- administered facility (as is commonly the case)?

6. The dissent argues that "the interests here implicated—of the State through its schools and of the pupils—are essentially congruent." Are the interests of an accused child to be suspended and the principal suspending him

congruent? Are the interests of the police and the citizenry at large "essentially congruent?" Similarly, the dissent cites the large number of students subject to suspension. Would the dissenters agree that a rising or high crime rate justifies the abrogation of criminal justice system due process?

7. Should the dissent have considered the range of discipline available to a school short of suspension (a required assignment related to the offense, after-hours detention, loss of privileges)? If such measures are available, would that tend to place a suspension in a qualitatively different category warranting some due process as imposed by the majority, although perhaps substantially less than a formal hearing for expulsion?

D. U.S. EDUCATION POLICIES AND INVESTMENT

1. Kindergarten to Grade 12 Federal/State Investment

As of 2000, the United States had 118,464 K–12 schools with a total enrollment of 51.6 million. Standard public schools enroll 90% (46.5 million), with 580,000 of this number in "charter schools." Of the private school 5.1 million enrollment, 2.5 million were in Catholic schools.[9] The total $326 billion expended on public education came from the states (48.4%), local sources (school districts, counties) (42.3%), the federal jurisdiction (6.8%), and private sources such as foundations (2.6%).[10]

Total spending per public K–12 student increased marginally above inflation since 1990, but as of 2002 stood at a modest $7,670 per pupil per year in total investment,[11] 52% of which is expended on teachers.[12] The increase is offset by a reduction in the percentage directed at teaching and instruction, and by an increasing population of special needs and Limited English Proficiency (LEP) students (see Chapter 6).

The shortfall and remaining disparities between wealthy and impoverished districts (particularly in those states rejecting the *Serrano* equality of opportunity spending mandate) produce a list of problems cited by education experts and child advocates, including:

- 38% of the nation's 4th graders do not read at a basic level.
- 77% of 4th graders, 73% of 8th graders, and 78% of 12th graders scored below minimal writing proficiency levels of the National Association of Education Progress (NAEP).
- U.S. 4th graders score above most nations in both math and science, but fall behind substantially in both areas by the time they reach the 12th grade.
- More than 25% of newly-hired teachers begin teaching without state licensure as competent to teach.
- More than 25% of students in public schools are being taught English by teachers who did not even major in the subject.
- Only 38% of those teaching have an undergraduate or graduate degree in any academic field (*e.g.*, in biology to teach biology); 18% have a major in reading education, and 37% in general education.

- Those teaching in poor communities are less likely to have a major in the subject matter they teach—including those teaching core subjects.[13]

Experts agree that more than 2.2 million new, trained and qualified teachers will be necessary to replace those scheduled to retire and currently uncertified teachers, and to meet population increases and modest class size reduction goals.[14] Investment in teacher compensation and education to meet that need has not occurred and is not proposed in state budgets. Rather, and with rare exception, state officials view new taxation for such investment in children as politically untenable, and likely to raise the feared "tax and spend" label. In contrast, public opinion polls have reflected a strong public commitment to children and in particular to their education—including additional taxation for that investment if prudently expended. Elected officials have reconciled this dichotomy by campaigning vigorously as "pro-education", with candidates and newly elected officials throughout the nation commonly adopting the informal title "the Education Governor", or the "Education President". However, those claims have not always produced actual new significant investment in education for public K–12 or for higher education (see discussion below).

2. Underlying Major Federal K–12 and Vocational Education Funding Programs

Most federal education programs provide grants to states or to local agencies. Four of the major continuing programs are listed below (they exclude the school nutrition and special education programs discussed briefly in Chapters 3 and 6, respectively):

Program	FY 2004	FY 2005	FY 2006 (as proposed by President Bush)
Title I Basic Grants	$6,934	$6,934	$6,934
Title I Concentration	$1,365	$1,365	$1,365
Targeted Grants	$1,969	$2,219	$2,822
Education Finance Incentive Grants	$1,969	$2,219	$2,219
Reading First Teacher Quality	$1,041	$1,041	$1,041
State Grants	$2,930	$2,916	$2,916
21st Century Learning Centers	$999	$999	$999
TRIO	$836	$836	$369
Source: CD Publications, *Children & Youth Funding Report* (Nov. 11, 2005) at 3. $ in millions.			

Table 4-A. Funding for Selected Education Programs

3. Federal Title I Funding

Outside of nutrition and special education, the largest single federal contribution for K–12 education has been basic education Title I funds to help the 20% economically poorest children in school. The program, started in 1965 as part of President Johnson's "War on Poverty," has increased over the years to provide tutoring and more than 132,000 classroom positions (about half paraprofessionals—mostly school aides and teacher's assistants).

The results of Title I spending are in dispute, with the overall gap in reading and math scores between the impoverished and average student populations virtually unchanged over the past two decades, notwithstanding increases in the account from its original $1 billion to its current level. However, adjusting the original amount in 1965 for population and inflation indicates very little actual spending power increase. Further, the growth of LEP populations, and increasing poverty over the past decade may have led to a substantially larger gap without this continuing investment. Finally, the initial impact of the program from 1965 to 1980 correlated with a marked improvement in test scores of impoverished children, with about one-third of the pre-1965 gap made up during the early years of the war on poverty. Final judgment about the program's efficacy is limited by a lack of control group comparison.

Whatever the historical or theoretical advantages of the Title I program, educators generally contend that its stimulation of substantial numbers of relatively unqualified "aides" and "clerks" is less beneficial than hiring fewer persons who are more highly trained and proficient in the teaching task. Others argue that the program's tactic of "pulling children out" of class for individual tutoring can backfire if the rest of the class is getting more advanced material by a trained educator. Many such tutors have uncertain teaching ability, and only 13% have college degrees. As of 1994, Title I hired aides must have at least a high school diploma.

4. Major Federal Programs

From 1998 through 2005, education has been a major stated priority of two presidential administrations. Programs beyond or within the major accounts of Table 4-A indicate the range (and fragmentation) of federal support. Discrete programs includes:

- A smaller class size initiative to stimulate the hiring of over 100,000 new teachers.

- Summer jobs for youth in school funds summer employment for impoverished youth. The Summer Youth program is now rolled into a larger Youth Training Account.

- Education Technology to stimulate computer access by students, educational software, and technology training of teachers.

- Eisenhower Professional Development Grants provide support to states for training to upgrade the skills of teachers and principals.

- Child Literacy funds work-study students from 1,000 colleges to tutor children in reading, and similarly organizes Ameri-Corps members and senior volunteers to provide after-school reading programs (tutor costs), teacher training in reading instruction, and helps parents teach children how to read. The goal: every child able to read well by completion of third grade.

- Bilingual Education grants to local schools and agencies support LEP student learning.

- Immigrant Education assistance is paid to schools with large numbers of new immigrant students.

- Safe and Drug Free Schools grants are currently part of a larger school and community antidrug program.

- High Hopes College Preparation Program provides state grants to partner with colleges, community organizations, and schools to prepare impoverished children for college and to encourage their application, intended to reach one million students nationally.

- Charter School Funding provides charter school start-up funding for 3,000 or more nationwide.

- Teacher Preparation and Recruitment enhances the supply of qualified new teachers for impoverished areas through recruitment and training.

- A Safe Schools Initiative provides safety related grants.

- A federal tax credit may pay interest on $22 billion in bond authority to build and repair school facilities, at a federal cost of $10 billion in lost federal revenue over ten years.

- The non-refundable Tax Credit Alternative and Higher Education Savings Account allows family members, charitable groups, or private donors to contribute up to $2,000 per year to a special "savings account" for each student of K–12 age. Interest and money contributed and withdrawn is tax free to the extent used for education related expenses, including tutoring, computers, and private school tuition. The account would cost the government $1.6 billion over ten years and would be phased out for those earning more than $95,000 per year. The system's non-refundable nature excludes impoverished children most in need.

- 21st Century Learning Centers for after school services and child care (see Chapter 7).

- Head Start for preschool education of 4-year-olds (see Chapter 7).

- Other school-related accounts include school nutrition, special education, and school-based delinquency intervention programs, discussed in other chapters.

A package of new reforms is now in place consistent with the testing and accountability agenda of the Bush Administration. Its major elements include: annual state tests in reading and math for children in grades 3 through 8; extra aid for low performing schools (which could be required to replace some staff); and $1 billion per annum provided for five years to improve reading, with the goal of making sure every child can read by third grade. Other new federal policies include the funding of partnerships with universities to improve science and math instruction; required school "report cards" to compare academic progress statewide; required English proficiency after three years of U.S. school attendance; and peer mediation programs for students. Federal policy encourages "charter" schools or transfer options for children in low performing schools. Increasing support has developed for both accountability and competitive choice—including the evolution of "voucher" systems to finance K–12 education, even where applied to parochial schools (see Chapter 13 discussion). Public spending to implement the post-2000 reforms has been minimal. Additional education investment has focused on the No Child Left Behind Act, authorized at $15 billion but funded at $6 billion as of 2005–06 (see budget discussion in Chapter 1).

E. U.S. HIGHER EDUCATION INVESTMENT

Perhaps the most important federal higher education assistance provides loan interest deferral and opportunity for youth. Current policies include:

- The low interest rate on student loans (at 7.46%).

- Gear Up Grants. $120 million appropriated for competitive grants to colleges that partner with schools to tell impoverished families about available financial aid and to provide long term mentoring and other assistance to help their children enter college.

- High Quality Distance Education. This program includes the Learn Anytime Anywhere Partnership (LAAP) initiative, and expands student aid to distant learners. Again, competitive grants are given to "partnerships" between schools and other entities to explore innovation in learning through the Internet, software, or other device. The emphasis is on higher education for those otherwise unable to receive it (full-time workers, those in rural areas, disabled students).

However, as discussed in Chapter 4, federal assistance and state educational grant and loan programs have been increasingly offset by tuition and living expense increases running at two to three times inflation levels. Most importantly, although higher education "slots" or capacity has increased since 1990, it has actually contracted in relation to population in major states.[15] Hence, a lower percentage of 18-year-olds have been and are being given higher education opportunity (vocational school to university graduate studies). This constriction occurs at the very time a much larger proportion of youth requires such additional education to secure employment given the nation's economic niche in technical services within the evolving international economy, as discussed at the beginning of this Chapter.

The failure to expand higher education capacity and to invest in tuition assistance even commensurate with population gain is of special concern during the period from 2000 to 2008, where the children of the "baby boomer" generation will increase child population markedly. The number of high school graduates will continue to rise during this period to produce in 2008 the largest high school graduating class in U.S. history: 3.2 million students. These youth will encounter opportunities as provided by current investment. The projected shortfall in that investment will be disproportionately felt by students on the Pacific Coast, Southwest and Southeast, and in states that already have low college participation rates, high percentages of children in poverty, and projected revenue deficiencies.[16]

The federal government has not significantly assisted the needed capacity expansion, either in the regions with projected severe shortfalls or nationally. Child advocates argue that this relative disinvestment in our children contrasts with the massive "GI Bill of Rights" and other federal and state higher education opportunity provided for today's adults by their parents and grandparents.

ENDNOTES

[1] Children Now, *Report Card '95* (Oakland, CA; 1995) chart at 9. See also M. Gittell, J. Fross, and J. Holdaway, Howard Samuels State Management and Policy Center, *Building Human Capital: The Impact of Post-Secondary Education on AFDC Recipients in Five States* (New York, NY; Sept. 1993).

[2] Policy Analysis for California Education (PACE), University of California at Berkeley School of Education, *Conditions of Education in California 1994–95* (Berkeley, CA; 1995), at 96–97.

[3] California Department of Education, *Statewide Profile* (Sacramento, CA; 2000) at 3, using 1997–98 data.

[4] See *Serrano v. Priest*, 18 Cal. 3d 728 (1976), *cert. denied*, 432 U.S. 907 (1977) (adhering to decision in *Serrano I* on state equal protection grounds).

[5] The following challenges to public education funding systems were successful: *Opinion of the Justices No. 338*, 624 So. 2d 107 (Ala. 1993); *Roosevelt Elementary Sch. Dist. No. 66 v. Bishop*, 179 Ariz. 233 (1994); *Dupree v. Alma Sch. Dist. No. 30*, 279 Ark. 340 (1983); *Horton v. Meskill*, 172 Conn. 615 (1977); *Rose v. Council for Better Educ., Inc.*, 790 S.W.2d 186 (Ky. 1989); *McDuffy v. Secretary of the Executive Office*, 415 Mass. 545 (1993); *Helena Elementary Sch. Dist. No. 1 v. State*, 236 Mont. 44 (1989); *Abbott v. Burke*, 119 N.J. 287 (1990); *Robinson v. Cahill*, 62 N.J. 473 (1973); *Bismarck Pub. Sch. Dist. No. 1 v. State*, 511 N.W.2d 247 (N.D. 1994); *Tennessee Small Sch. Sys. v. McWherter*, 851 S.W.2d 139 (Tenn. 1993); *Edgewood Indep. Sch. Dist. No. 1 v. Kirby*, 777 S.W.2d 391 (Tex. 1989); *Seattle Sch. Dist. No. 1 v. State*, 90 Wn.2d 476 (1978); *Pauley v. Kelly*, 162 W.Va. 672 (1979); *Washakie County Sch. Dist. No. 1 v. Herschler*, 606 P.2d 310 (Wy. 1990).

[6] The following challenges to public education funding systems were unsuccessful: *Hargrave v. McKinney*, 413 F.2d 320 (5th Cir. 1969), *vacated sub nom. Askew v. Hargrave,* 401 U.S. 576 (1971) (challenging Florida's system); *Lujan v. Colorado State Bd. of Educ.*, 649 P.2d 1005 (Colo. 1982); *McDaniel v. Thomas*, 248 Ga. 632 (1981); *Idaho Sch. for Equal Educ. Opportunity v. Evans*, 123 Idaho 573 (1993) (remanding for consideration whether funding given was sufficient to allow compliance with the constitutionally sufficient standards); *Thompson v. Engelking,* 96 Idaho 793 (1975); *People ex rel. Jones v. Adams*, 40 Ill. App. 3d 189 (1976); *Knowles v. State Bd. of Educ.*, 219 Kan. 271 (1976); *Hornbeck v. Somerset County Bd. of Educ.*, 295 Md. 597 (1983) ; *East Jackson Pub. Sch. v. State*, 133 Mich. App. 132 (1984); *Skeen v. State*, 505 N.W.2d 299 (Minn. 1993); *Gould v. Orr*, 244 Neb. 163 (1993); *Board of Educ., Levittown Union Free Sch. Dist. v. Nyquist*, 57 N.Y.2d 27 (1982), *appeal dismissed* 459 U.S. 1138 (1983); *Reform Educ. Fin. Inequities Today v. Cuomo*, 606 N.Y.S.2d 44 (1993); *Britt v. North Carolina State Bd. of Educ.*, 86 N.C. App. 282 (1987); *Board of Educ. v. Walter*, 58 Ohio St. 2d 368 (1979); *Fair Sch. Fin. Council v. State*, 1987 Ok. 114 (1987); *Coalition for Equitable Sch. Funding, Inc. v. State*, 311 Ore. 300 (1991); *Olsen v. State ex rel. Johnson,* 276 Ore. 9 (1976); *Danson v. Casey*, 484 Pa. 415 (1979); *Richland County v. Campbell*, 294 S.C. 346 (1988); *Scott v. Commonwealth*, 247 Va. 379 (1994); *Kukor v. Grover*, 148 Wis.2d. 469 (1989).

[7] See, *e.g.*, William S. Koski, *Note, Equity in Public Education: School-Finance Reform in Michigan*, 26 U. Mich. J.L. Ref. 195 (1992).

[8] Children's Defense Fund, *Key Facts About Education* (Washington, D.C.; 2002) at 1.

[9] Center for Education Reform, *Elementary and Secondary Education Statistics at a Glance* (Washington D.C.; 2000), quoting U.S. Department of Education Statistics 2000 and other data.

[10] *Id.*

[11] National Center for Education Statistics, *Projections of Education Statistics to 2011* (2001) at Table 34. In constant 1999 dollars per pupil spending has increased from $6,640 in 1990 to a projected $7,443 in 2002.

[12] *Elementary and Secondary Education Statistics, supra* note 9, at 4.

[13] *Key Facts About Education, supra* note 8 at 1.

[14] *Id.*

[15] See *e.g.,* California, a state with a longstanding tradition of investment for low-cost higher education, has reduced population adjusted slots for vocational to university higher education from 1.543 million in 1990–91 to 1.518 million in 2001–02. See Children's Advocacy Institute, *California Children's Budget 2001-02* (San Diego, Ca; June 2001) Table 7-G at 7-12.

[16] National Center for Public Policy and Higher Education, *Coping with Recession: Public Policy, Economic Downturns and Higher Education* (Feb. 2002) at 10 (see http://www.highereducation.org). States facing the greatest enrollment pressure with coextensive budget shortfalls and high child poverty rates include: Nevada, Arizona, Florida, Georgia, California, New Jersey, North Carolina, Washington, Maryland, Colorado, Connecticut, Oregon, Tennessee, Virginia, Texas, Idaho, and New York. *Id.* at Table 3.

CHAPTER FIVE

Health, Medical Care, and Safety

A. CHILD RIGHT TO TREATMENT

Public policy obligating parents to medically care for their children is reflected in the common civil requirement to provide "necessaries." Failure to so provide is a basis for juvenile dependency court termination of parental rights. In addition, criminal liability for involuntary manslaughter may lie where death is the result of gross negligence. Some states have a "poverty exemption" to civil neglect charges where parents are not financially able to provide medical care or other necessities for their children.[1] However, the most extensive source of asserted parental exemption rests with the *bona fide* religious beliefs of parents in faith healing. The courts have ruled consistently that first amendment religious or other parental constitutional rights do not cover allowing harm to befall a child. In one early leading case, the U.S. Supreme Court upheld mandatory vaccination laws against a parental religious challenge.[2] In perhaps the leading state case, Mississippi held in 1979 that "innocent children, too young to decide for themselves" should not be denied the protection against crippling or death that immunization provides because of a religious belief adhered to by a parent.[3]

However, over the past thirty years partial, often confusing religious exemption statutes have been enacted in all fifty states. They tend not to cover diagnosis and vaccination, but rather medical treatment for existing and known illness. In possibly applicable *dictum*, the U.S. Supreme Court held in *Prince v. Massachusetts* that a Jehovah's Witness could not compel her daughter to sell literature on the streets in violation of child labor laws,[4] writing: "The right to practice religion freely does not include liberty to expose the community or child to communicable disease or the latter to ill health or death....Parents may be free to become martyrs themselves. But it does not follow that they are free, in identical circumstances, to make martyrs of their children before they have reached the age of full and legal discretion when they can make that choice for themselves."[5]

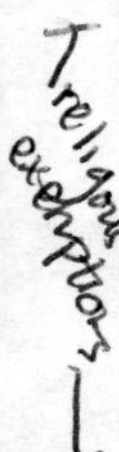

However, notwithstanding this *Prince* reference, since the 1970s most states have enacted some religious exemption to civil dependency or neglect charges,[6] and/or a religious defense to a criminal charge involving the care of their children.[7] These exemptions permit parents to pray and otherwise use faith healing to address a child's illness. Most are not intended to exempt from civil or criminal liability a failure to medically treat a child where his or her life is in danger; however their ambiguous wording has created some effective barrier to criminal prosecution—even in relatively egregious failures to treat.[8]

One source has counted 172 deaths of U.S. children from 1975 to 1995 related to parental religious refusals to medically treat. Only 43 criminal prosecutions followed those deaths, with seven more prosecutions initiated after 1995.

Of those fifty cases, 38 resulted in convictions, three are pending, and nine were dismissed or yielded acquittals. Of the 38 convictions, six were overturned on appeal. All of the dismissals and some of the reversals were based on a broad interpretation of a statutory religious exemption, or on its mitigation of a necessary intent or notice requirement.[9]

Some child advocates contend that the religious exemption itself is a constitutional affront to the equal protection and due process rights of children.[10] They contend that adults' failure to provide assistance where a duty lay should not be excused on religious grounds, and that the religion defense rests on the premise that the child is the property of the parent. The problem is complicated by the inclusion within parental rights of the prerogative to raise a child in the parent's religion, including to compel practice of that religion. It is clear that where a child's life is threatened, the state may supervene the religion-based decision of a parent not to treat a child and compel that treatment. What is less certain is the termination of parental rights or criminal sanctions for such failures where they do not occur *in extremis*. Some child advocates argue that a broad spectrum of sanctions is necessary to protect children.[11]

In Re Phillip B.
92 Cal. App. 3d 796 (1979)

OPINION: **Caldecott, P.J.**—

A petition was filed by the juvenile probation department in the juvenile court, alleging that Phillip B., a minor, came within the provision of Welfare and Institutions Code section 300, subdivision (b),...because he was not provided with the "necessities of life."

The petition requested that Phillip be declared a dependent child of the court for the special purpose of ensuring that he receive cardiac surgery for a congenital heart defect. Phillip's parents had refused to consent to the surgery. The juvenile court dismissed the petition. The appeal is from the order.

Phillip is a 12-year-old boy suffering from Down's Syndrome.[2] At birth, his parents decided he should live in a residential care facility. Phillip suffers from a congenital heart defect—a ventricular septal defect[3] that results in elevated pulmonary blood pressure. Due to the defect, Phillip's heart must work three times harder than normal to supply blood to his body. When he overexerts, unoxygenated blood travels the wrong way through the septal hole reaching his circulation, rather than the lungs.

If the congenital heart defect is not corrected, damage to the lungs will increase to the point where his lungs will be unable to carry and oxygenate any blood. As a result, death follows. During the deterioration of the lungs, Phillip will suffer from a progressive loss of energy and vitality until he is forced to lead a bed-to-chair existence.

Phillip's heart condition has been known since 1973. At that time Dr. Gathman, a pediatric cardiologist, examined Phillip and recommended cardiac catheterization to further define the anatomy and dynamics of Phillip's condition. Phillip's parents refused.

In 1977, Dr. Gathman again recommended catheterization and this time Phillip's parents consented. The catheterization revealed the extensive nature of

---

[2] "Down's syndrome or mongolism is a chromosomal disorder producing mental retardation caused by the presence of 47 rather than 46 chromosomes in a patient's cells, and marked by a distinctively shaped head, neck, trunk, and abdomen."....

[3] In other words, a hole between his right and left ventricles.

Phillip's septal defect, thus it was Dr. Gathman's recommendation that surgery be performed.

Dr. Gathman referred Phillip to a second pediatric cardiologist, Dr. William French of Stanford Medical Center. Dr. French estimates the surgical mortality rate to be 5 to 10 percent, and notes that Down's Syndrome children face a higher than average risk of postoperative complications. Dr. French found that Phillip's pulmonary vessels have already undergone some change from high pulmonary artery pressure. Without the operation, Phillip will begin to function less physically until he will be severely incapacitated. Dr. French agrees with Dr. Gathman that Phillip will enjoy a significant expansion of his life span if his defect is surgically corrected. Without the surgery, Phillip may live at the outside 20 more years. Dr. French's opinion on the advisability of surgery was not asked.

I

It is fundamental that parental autonomy is constitutionally protected....

Inherent in the preference for parental autonomy is a commitment to diverse lifestyles, including the right of parents to raise their children as they think best. Legal judgments regarding the value of child rearing patterns should be kept to a minimum so long as the child is afforded the best available opportunity to fulfill his potential in society.

Parental autonomy, however, is not absolute. The state is the guardian of society's basic values. Under the doctrine of *parens patriae*, the state has a right, indeed, a duty, to protect children. (See *e.g., Prince v. Massachusetts, supra*, 321 U.S. 158 at p. 166....) State officials may interfere in family matters to safeguard the child's health, educational development and emotional well-being.

One of the most basic values protected by the state is the sanctity of human life. (U.S. Const., 14th Amend., § 1.) Where parents fail to provide their children with adequate medical care, the state is justified to intervene. However, since the state should usually defer to the wishes of the parents, it has a serious burden of justification before abridging parental autonomy by substituting its judgment for that of the parents.

Several relevant factors must be taken into consideration before a state insists upon medical treatment rejected by the parents. The state should examine the seriousness of the harm the child is suffering or the substantial likelihood that he will suffer serious harm; the evaluation for the treatment by the medical profession; the risks involved in medically treating the child; and the expressed preferences of the child. Of course, the underlying consideration is the child's welfare and whether his best interests will be served by the medical treatment.

Section 300, subdivision (b), permits a court to adjudge a child under the age of 18 years a dependent of the court if the child is not provided with the "necessities of life."

* * *

Turning to the facts of this case, one expert witness testified that Phillip's case was more risky than the average for two reasons. One, he has pulmonary vascular changes and statistically this would make the operation more risky in that he would be subject to more complications than if he did not have these changes. Two, children with Down's Syndrome have more problems in the postoperative period. This witness put the mortality rate at 5 to 10 percent, and the morbidity would be somewhat higher. When asked if he knew of a case in which this type of operation had been performed on a Down's Syndrome child, the witness replied that he did, but could not remember a case involving a child who had the degree of pulmonary vascular change that Phillip had. Another expert witness testified that one of the risks of surgery to correct a ventricular septal defect was damage to the nerve that controls the heartbeat as the nerve is in the same area as the defect. When this occurs a pacemaker would be required.

The trial judge, in announcing his decision, cited the inconclusiveness of the evidence to support the petition.

On reading the record we can see the trial court's attempt to balance the possible benefits to be gained from the operation against the risks involved. The court had before it a child suffering not only from a ventricular septal defect but also from Down's Syndrome, with its higher than average morbidity, and the presence of pulmonary vascular changes. In light of these facts, we cannot say as a matter of law that there was no substantial evidence to support the decision of the trial court.

I

In denying the petition the trial court ruled that there was no clear and convincing evidence to sustain the petition. The state contends the proper standard of proof is by a preponderance of the evidence and not by the clear and convincing test. The state asserts that only when a permanent severance of the parent-child relationship is ordered by the court must the clear and convincing standard of proof be applied. Since the petition did not seek permanent severance but only authorization for corrective heart surgery, the state contends the lower standard of proof should have been applied.

* * *

The order dismissing the petition is affirmed.

Questions for Discussion

1. This case involves the invocation of a parent's fundamental right to make a decision about his or her child's health. Would it matter if the decision were based on a *bona fide* religious belief that the proposed treatment was against a Divine directive?

2. Is this fundamental right to parent mentioned in the Constitution? How do the literalist Justices (such as Scalia) find it to be implied?

3. If the child is a "person" under the Constitution, does "the right to life, liberty, and the pursuit of happiness" mentioned in the Declaration of Independence apply to him or her? Are the words of the Declaration of Independence relevant to constitutional doctrine?

4. Can the parents argue that as the procreators, parents and caretakers of Phillip, they best determine what his happiness involves, and what risks it should entail, even including the risk of death? Don't parents make decisions about their children which commonly involve some measure of risk? Does it matter that these parents may have a conflict of interest with regard to care obligations? Does it matter that they have placed Phillip in substantial state care and the state bears the expense of caring for him? Should the economics matter?

B. PUBLIC COVERAGE AND SUBSIDY

1. Demographics of Child Health Coverage

The United States has established goals for child health, referred to as "Year 2010 Objectives." Table 5-A below lists some of these longstanding targets.

Health Issue	1998 Baseline	Year 2010 Objective
Increase early and adequate prenatal care	74% of live births	90% of live births
Reduce low birth weight	7.6% of live births	5.0% of live births
Reduce very low birth weight	1.4% of live births	0.9% of live births
Reduce all infant deaths (within 1 year)	7.2 per 1,000 live births	4.5 per 1,000 live births
Reduce child deaths, ages 1– 4	34.6 per 100,000	18.6 per 100,000
Reduce child deaths, ages 5–9	17.7 per 100,000	12.3 per 100,000
Reduce adolescent deaths, ages 10–14	22.1 per 100,000	16.8 per 100,000
Reduce adolescent deaths, ages 15–19	70.6 per 100,000	39.8 per 100,000
Increase use of child restraints in vehicles	92% of motor vehicle occupants aged 4 and under	100% of motor vehicle occupants aged 4 and under
Reduce measles breakouts	74 cases	0 cases
Increase number of children aged 19 to 35 months who received all recommended vaccines	73%	80%

Source: U.S. Department of Health and Human Services, Office of Disease Prevention and Health Promotion, *Healthy People 2010* (www.healthypeople.gov)

Table 5-A. Selected Year 2010 Objectives for Child Health

As the millennium ended, most states met the Year 2000 goals only in infant mortality. In addition, health experts remain concerned about continuing environmental health hazards, particularly lead[12] and pesticides—which can permanently harm developing brains.[13]

Health care tends to be more extensively available to wealthier children, than to the disadvantaged who are more often in need of it. The problem is exacerbated by health care inflation which ran roughly double that of the rest of the economy from 1990 to 2006.[14]

2. Child Health Coverage Correlations

Uninsured children lack a regular medical professional to monitor their development—and are three times more likely than covered children to lack a regular source of care.[15] They are less likely to have regular health examinations for early detection of problems. Timely treatment of children for infectious and chronic diseases such as strep throat, asthma, and ear infections is important to prevent the development of more serious medical conditions.[16] Fewer immunizations, well baby checks, and genetic/chronic disease screening are related consequences. Lower rates of adolescent sexual health care, failed responses to fluid loss and diarrhea, and expensive or debilitating outcomes occur more frequently where coverage is lacking. Overall, uninsured children receive only 70% of the outpatient visits of their insured peers, and 71% of the care received for serious injuries. Of particular concern, uninsured children under six are almost three times more likely to use no health services than are their covered counterparts.[17]

One survey from the late 1990s found that 34% of the parents of insured children reported difficulties in obtaining medical services for their kids, while 56% of those parents whose children lacked insurance coverage reported problems.[18] The medical areas with the most limited access for the uninsured include dental care, health care after hours, basic health care, preventive care, and mental health services.

Evidence of coverage benefits include both private and public insurance. From 1986 to 1995, the average Medicaid income eligibility set by states rose from 55% to 169% of the poverty level—substantially increasing care for impoverished pregnant women; as care increased, U.S. infant mortality dropped 21%—from 10.8 per 1,000 live births in 1988 to 8.5 in 1992 to 7.0 in 2002.[19]

Uninsured children are more likely to be perceived by their parents as being in poor or fair health, and are more likely to be hospitalized for potentially preventable conditions, to be discharged from the hospital early after birth, and to have an increased risk of adverse outcomes after birth.[20] A study of 2,126 children participating in a New York state program to cover children above the poverty line (on terms similar to the subsequently enacted federal program) was released in February 2000. The study concluded: the statewide health insurance program for low-income children was associated with improved access, utilization and quality of care.[21]

3. Child Health Public Insurance Costs

Medicaid has long been the primary federal program covering the health of impoverished children (as well as adults). The program generally requires a 50% state match and covers all children living below the poverty line. Further, some children (such as the very young) are often covered at higher income levels; in some states coverage for younger children reaches 200% of the poverty line.

Nationally, children make up about 49% of Medicaid recipients,[22] but use only about 15.1% of the dollars spent.[23] Adults and children in low-income families make up three-fourths of Medicaid beneficiaries, but account for only 25% of Medicaid spending. The elderly and disabled account for 65% of expenditures due to their intensive use of acute and long term care services.[24] Medicaid payments for maternity and infant care through the first year of life are estimated at less than 7% of total Medicaid expenditures.[25] As Table 5-B indicates, children cost relatively little to cover; the vast majority of public subsidy is expended on the elderly—much of it during the final weeks or months of life.

Children cost about one-third as much to publicly cover medically as do adults, and one-seventh as much as senior citizens cost. The numbers of Table 5-B have gone up somewhat since 2003 for all groups, but with the relative ratios substantially retained.

In terms of broader medical investment, spending for the health care of adults (and the elderly in particular) is substantially beyond these ratios. Almost all of the Medicare budget is devoted to the medical and care needs of the elderly, as is part of the Veteran's Administration budget and portions of other budgets. The overall ratio of public medical subsidy per person for the elderly versus children is in excess of ten to one overall.

Beneficiary	Average Medicaid Payment per Person Served
Children	$1,746
Disabled	$12,279
Elderly	$12,828

Table 5-B. Average Medicaid Payments per Person Served, 2003[26]

4. Extent of Child Medical Coverage

Unlike Medicaid coverage relied upon by impoverished children, the children of middle class and wealthy parents tend to be covered by private employer coverage. Working poor families whose parents earn above the federal poverty line (and work for employers who do not provide dependency coverage) account for most of the nation's uncovered children. At least one of the parents of 89% of these uncovered children works, and 58% of them work full time.[27] A substantial number of uncovered children (52%) have parents who work for small businesses of fewer than 25 employees that do not provide coverage.[28]

The 2000 estimate of medical coverage status for children by the American Academy of Pediatrics[29] is as follows: privately financed coverage: 64%; Medicaid: 21%; uninsured: 15%.

5. State Child Health Insurance Program (SCHIP) Coverage

In order to address the child coverage shortfall, Congress enacted the "State Children's Health Insurance Program" (SCHIP) as part of the Balanced Budget Act of 1997. The federal assistance, at a rate of $2 for every $1 in state money, may cover children up to 200% of the poverty line, and up to 250% for some children. However, several problems have impeded the program from covering enough children to lower the uninsured portion below 15% of the child population. First, those families leaving TANF coverage for employment remain qualified for Medicaid or for SCHIP coverage. However, large numbers are losing that coverage as social worker contact is lost. Hence, in some states almost as many children lose medical coverage for which they are qualified as are signed into SCHIP coverage. Second, bureaucratic barriers have impeded more extensive coverage. Paperwork requirements and advance monthly premiums are required in most states. Those premiums are in addition to co-payments, and may amount to over $300 per family per year, which is a significant amount for a family earning just above the poverty line.

6. Other Public Child Health Programs

Beyond generic Medicaid or SCHIP coverage, many federal and state health programs have been created to address specific health care needs (*e.g.*, prenatal care and immunizations). Each reflects public policy judgments that those eligible should have access to at least a specified set of services. The result is the current "system" of from 9 to 16 incrementally added programs, each with its own administration, eligibility, funding criteria, benefits, set of providers, payment sources and mechanisms, reporting requirements, and constituency. Each is subject to ongoing contention for political support and available public dollars.

Most of these programs provide direct clinical and/or educational services to a defined group. In addition, states operate a variety of programs to fulfill the public health functions of quality assurance, policy development, and assessment. Health programs are funded by federal, state, and county money. Their mix has been changing in recent years, but one common state strategy is to shift costs to the federal or to the county level.

One such specialized program operates within Medicaid: Early Preventive Screening, Diagnosis, and Treatment services (EPSDT) to eligible children. Most states also have special programs outside Medicaid to cover children with severe and chronic disabilities or diseases. Almost all states have a program called Child Health and Disability Prevention (CHDP), which provides health screens for low-income children not eligible for Medicaid. Funding for Maternal and Child Health Programs (MCH) is allocated to states to promote health care for mothers and children and provide it to those with inadequate access.[30] State Genetic Disease Testing Programs conduct screening, diagnosis, education, and prevention programs for genetic diseases. The Childhood Immunization Program assists state and local programs to immunize children against vaccine-preventable diseases. The Preventive Health and Health Services Block Grant supports a variety of state programs in health prevention. Migrant and Community Health Centers grants are administered directly by the federal Health Resources and Services Administration (HRSA) to the health centers.

The array of categorical programs presents a complex landscape of public programs to families trying to meet their needs. A child eligible for services one year may be ineligible the next, based on age, income status, length of residence, school enrollment, health needs, or changing program requirements. A parent may have different children in different programs and may herself be in yet another—if indeed all are covered. The annual budget struggles over funding levels and policy goals may cause program slots to open or close and program staff to disappear or suffer high turnover.

Some child advocates point out that the proportion of children uncovered and not eligible for public coverage is small. A California study concluded that if coverage were raised to 250% of the poverty line only 3.3% of those privately uncovered would be ineligible for public coverage. An additional 2.4% are undocumented children and are ineligible for that reason, bringing the total ineligible proportion to 5.7%. Accordingly, the numbers warrant deeming all children covered, with the *post hoc* billing of parents making over 250% of the poverty line on a sliding scale where significant expenses are incurred for their children. Such a change would result in both efficient universal child public health measures and considerable savings in paperwork, qualification, delay, and inconvenience. A further argument in favor: This is not a cash benefit amenable to abuse, and the current fragmented system of barriers is more expensive than the amount necessary to cover the small percentage of ineligible children. Thus far, no state has enacted such a paradigm shift.

7. Shift to Managed Care

Concern about services under capitated managed care plans for adults also applies to children. Such arrangements pay a per/person annual rate up front for health care coverage, creating an incentive to deny services in order to save costs and enhance profit. Typically driven by cost-saving intentions, managed care capitation rates are generally based on 95%-97% of fee-for-service costs under the pre-existing system. Children are not themselves articulate advocates for their own preventive health, which raises enhanced concern about managed care growth. Nevertheless, such coverage will apply to the majority of Medicaid children early in the 21st century. The abuses of concern to advocates and the subject of initial litigation include barriers to disenrollment where a plan is incorrect or inconvenient for covered children, misleading marketing practices, obstacles to specialized care, and avoidance of children with special needs. As with insurance coverage, there is a natural incentive to "skim the cream," or to enroll only those who will demand or require little cost producing services.

C. CHILD PUBLIC MEDICAL COVERAGE INTERPRETATION AND STANDARDS

Stanton v. Bond
504 F.2d 1246 (7th Cir.1974)

OPINION: **SPRECHER**, Circuit Judge.

We are asked to determine whether failure of a state to comply with the requirements of the early and periodic screening, diagnosis and treatment (for persons under 21 years of age) provisions of the Social Security Act justifies injunctive relief.

Plaintiffs, representing the class of persons under age 21 who are eligible for medical benefits under Title XIX of the Social Security Act, brought this action under 42 U.S.C. § 1983, against various Indiana state officials, challenging their failure to implement a mandatory federal health program for needy children.

On March 22, 1974, the district court partially granted plaintiffs' motion for summary judgment and enjoined the state officials from continuing to administer the state program in violation of the statute and regulations, and ordered that a complying program be instituted by July 1, 1974. The defendants have appealed.

I

In 1965 Congress added Title XIX to the Social Security Act, which created a comprehensive program of medical assistance for the needy (popularly called Medicaid).[2] The medical assistance program is administered by the states...with the federal government participating through financial grants to the states....States are not required to operate medical assistance plans, but if they elect to do so they must comply with the requirements of Title XIX....

Title XIX requires...that each state plan provide five basic services: inpatient hospital services, outpatient hospital services, laboratory and x-ray services, skilled nursing home services and physicians' services....Originally nine

[2] 42 U.S.C. §§ 1396–1396g.

other medical services were optional with the states,[7] and additional optional categories of care have been added by Congress from time to time.

In 1967 Congress amended one of the five mandatory requirements to, in effect, require each participating state to furnish a sixth basic service....

> Effective July 1, 1969, such early and periodic screening and diagnosis of individuals who are eligible under the plan and are under the age of 21 to ascertain their physical or mental defects, and such health care, treatment, and other measures to correct or ameliorate defects and chronic conditions discovered thereby, as may be provided in regulations of the Secretary.

The addition of "early and periodic screening and diagnosis" and "treatment" (EPSDT) of persons under the age of 21 was the result of a growing need for child health care among the needy....

* * *

Most childhood handicaps can be prevented or cured or corrected if detected early enough. One-third of the chronically handicapped conditions of children in the United States could be corrected or prevented by preschool care, and continuing care to age eighteen would correct or prevent 60 percent.[14]

* * *

The regulations seek "to assure that individuals under 21 years of age who are eligible for medical assistance may receive the services of such facilities..."...and "assuring that such individuals are informed of such services...."...States are required to enter into "agreements to assure maximum utilization of existing screening, diagnostic, and treatment services provided by other public and voluntary agencies...."...State plans are to assure that the necessary services "will be available to all eligible individuals under 21 years of age...."...

* * *

I

The mandatory obligation upon each participating state to aggressively notify, seek out and screen persons under 21 in order to detect health problems and to pursue those problems with the needed treatment is made unambiguously clear by the 1967 act and by the interpretative regulations and guidelines.

Indiana is a participating state....

* * *

In defendants' reply brief, they summarize the nature of Indiana's compliance with EPSDT:

---

[7] The nine original optional services were (1) medical or remedial care furnished by state licensed practitioners; (2) home health care services; (3) private duty nursing services; (4) clinic services; (5) dental services; (6) physical therapy; (7) prescribed drugs, dentures, prosthetic devices and eyeglasses; (8) other diagnostic, screening, preventive and rehabilitative services; and (9) tubercular and mental institution services for the aged. *Id.* §§ 1396d(a)(6)—(14).

[14] White House Conference on Children, Report to the President, 184 (1970). Routine throat screening of children age 5—15 with respiratory illness or unexplained fever could prevent 75 percent of rheumatic fever cases....Early detection and treatment of lead poisoning, which leads to mental retardation, seizure disorder, kidney diseases and other handicaps, can reduce blood lead to safe levels before permanent handicaps occur....

> Any of the eligible children in this state can secure all of the requested services merely by requesting them from their local health provider....[Recipients] need merely take their children to the health providers of their choice and obtain for their children the required services.

On March 22, 1974, the district court in its memorandum opinion granting in part plaintiffs' motion for summary judgment, found:

> A careful reading of the original and supplemental materials filed in this case indicates, in a clear and convincing fashion, that little, if any, headway has been made by the State as far as the implementation of the EPSDT program is concerned. From the information supplied by the Lake County Welfare Department as well as that supplied by the state, it appears to a certainty that the welfare procedures are nearly the same as they were last year. No special training is required for the caseworkers and there have been only minimal attempts to communicate this program to either the caseworkers or to the ultimate recipients. A few letters and directives, clothed in bureaucratic prose, have been issued to the local units of the Department of Public Welfare of Indiana. In fact, there is no evidence of a comprehensive EPSDT program, nor even any semblance of any screening program however minimal.

The court enjoined defendants "from continuing to administer EPSDT in violation of 42 U.S.C., Section 1396d (a)(4)(B) and the regulations established thereunder" and ordered defendants to have a program meeting the minimum standards of, and in substantial compliance with, the regulations and guidelines, "in effect in every county in Indiana by July 1, 1974."

There is no genuine issue as to any material fact and the plaintiffs were entitled to judgment as a matter of law.

Indiana's somewhat casual approach to EPSDT hardly conforms to the aggressive search for early detection of child health problems envisaged by Congress. It is difficult enough to activate the average affluent adult to seek medical assistance until he is virtually laid low. It is utterly beyond belief to expect that children of needy parents will volunteer themselves or that their parents will voluntarily deliver them to the providers of health services for early medical screening and diagnosis. By the time an Indiana child is brought for treatment it may too often be on a stretcher. This is hardly the goal of "early and periodic screening and diagnosis." EPSDT programs must be brought to the recipients; the recipients will not ordinarily go to the programs until it is too late to accomplish the congressional purpose.

* * *

JUDGMENT IS AFFIRMED.

Questions for Discussion

1. Indiana announced that EPSDT was "available"—what more should it have done? Is the court engaged in micro-management? If the court does not intervene, what other remedies are available?

2. Can Indiana be forced to engage in outreach if the underlying program is not federally funded? What if its failure incurs additional federal Medicaid dollars because of the state's failure to screen and prevent?

Oklahoma Chapter of the American Academy of Pediatrics v. Fogarty
366 F. Supp. 2d 1050 (ND. Okla., 2005)

Claire V. Eagan, District Judge

FINDINGS OF FACT AND CONCLUSIONS OF LAW

Introduction

Plaintiff Oklahoma Chapter of the American Academy of Pediatrics is a non-profit professional organization of pediatricians and pediatric specialists....The individual named plaintiffs are thirteen children and their parents; they also serve as representatives of the class certified by the Court. Defendants are officials of the State of Oklahoma and Oklahoma Health Care Authority ("OHCA"), the designated agency responsible for implementing and administering Oklahoma's program to provide eligible children with the health and medical services at issue in thiscase.

Plaintiffs filed this action in March 2001, alleging essentially that defendants' policies and procedures denied or deprived eligible children of the health and medical care to which those children are entitled by federal law. Plaintiffs seek injunctive relief to ensure that eligible children receive that care. After the Court ruled on motions to dismiss, plaintiffs filed an amended complaint in May 2002. The Court defined and certified the plaintiff class of children on May 30, 2003. The Court then held a non jury trial for 19 days in April and May 2004.

• • •

Findings of Fact: ...

17. The United States is one of twenty-five countries with established market economies—so-called developed nations. Of all nations, the United States, at $5,440 per capita, spends more on health care per person than any other country. The rest of the market-economy nations spend about $ 2,400 per capita for health care. The United States, however, is near the bottom of the market economies in the health of its population, as measured by life expectancy, infant mortality, age-adjusted death rates, and other health standards.

18. Among the fifty states, Oklahoma ranks third highest in per capita cost of health insurance premiums. Despite these health insurance premiums, Oklahoma is the only state whose health status has worsened since 1990, as measured by life expectancy and age-adjusted death rates. In other words, poor health is a problem in Oklahoma for both Medicaid and non-Medicaid recipients. The health status of Oklahoma's poor children, in particular, has declined since 1990....

• • •

25. From 1995 through December 31, 2003, provider reimbursement under Oklahoma's Medicaid's fee-for-service schedule never exceeded 72% of Medicare.

• • •

27. Under commercial plans, Oklahoma physicians are reimbursed at rates of 130% to 180% of Medicare.

28. While most of the medical services provided by Primary Care Physicians are included in a monthly capitated rate...the medical services provided by non-

pediatrician specialists and sub-specialists are paid for on a fee-for-service basis...and are paid approximately 72% of Medicare for most of their services....

• • •

45. According to a 2003 survey conducted by the AAP, only 34% of Oklahoma's pediatricians participate fully in the Medicaid program by accepting all new Medicaid patients. At the same time, 69% of Oklahoma's pediatricians accept all new privately-insured patients....

• • •

49. The lack of pediatricians denies children needed diagnostic and treatment services. A pediatric cardiologist testified that he sees an "extraordinary number" of Medicaid children who find themselves in the hospital when their undiagnosed congenital heart disease becomes malignant....

• • •

53. Children living in rural Oklahoma counties often do not have access to pediatricians for primary care....

• • •

56. ...PCPs are experiencing difficulty in locating speciality providers for their SoonerCare Choice patients....The proportion of Medicaid specialty providers that are willing to accept their patients has steadily dropped since the inception of the program....

[Findings 57 to 91 concern insufficient supply of pediatric orthopods, ENT specialists, neurologists, psychiatrists, urologists, electrophysiologists (specialists who treat children with congenital heart deformities), nephrology, pediatric ER, cardiology, pediatric surgery.
Findings 135 to 199 concern failures to provide require Early Periodic Screening, Diagnosis and Treatment (EPSDT) required under federal Medicaid law.]

• • •

Conclusions of Law...

• • •

6. ...The "equal access" provision, 42 U.S.C. § 1396a(a)(30)(A), has been a part of the Medicaid Act since 1989. As codified, it requires that a State plan...assure that payments are consistent with efficiency, economy, and quality of care and are sufficient to enlist enough providers so that care and services are available under the plan at least to the extent that such care and services are available to the general population in the geographic area;....

• • •

9. The Court finds that those authorities holding that providers do not have enforceable rights under 1396a(a)(30)(A)....Accordingly, the Court concludes that [the Oklahoma Chapter of the American Academy of Pediatrics...does not have enforceable rights under § 1396a(a)(30)(A), and should be dismissed from this lawsuit....However, the Court concludes that the individual class members continue to have standing to enforce § 1396a(a)(30) as Medicaid recipients....

• • •

19. The second "major factor" which the Clark court considered in assessing compliance with the equal access mandate was the level of reimbursement....In deciding that California's dental rates were inadequate, the *Clark* court considered the fact that the rates there fell well short of the defendant's stated goal of "90% of the average allowance of private insurers." [In the instant case], the effect of defendants' rate-setting and implementation speaks for itself.

• • •

21. While there is no established percentage for sufficient Medicaid reimbursement rates under federal law, rates which consistently fall well below what is allowed under Medicare, let alone under private insurance, have been shown to be inadequate to attract enough providers so that health care services are available to Medicaid recipients to the same extent as those services are available to the general population....

• • •

39. As discussed above, the United States Supreme Court subsequently held that, in order for a statute to be individually enforceable under § 1983, the statutory language at issue must unambiguously confer a right. *Gonzaga University v. Doe*, 536 U.S. 273 (2002). After *Gonzaga*, at least four courts have found that the EPSDT provisions of the Medicaid Act are enforceable by private right of action under 42 U.S.C. § 1983....The Court concludes that the EPSDT provisions of the Medicaid Act unambiguously confer rights upon the class members in this case.

• • •

Sanchez v. Johnson

416 F.3d 1051 (9th Cir. 2005)

O'Scannlain, Circuit Judge

We must decide whether developmentally disabled recipients of Medicaid funds and their service providers have a private right of action against state officials to compel the enforcement of a federal law governing state disbursement of such funds....

I.

In May, 2000, seven named plaintiffs representing a class of developmentally disabled individuals, and six organizations that advocate for, or provide community-based services to, the developmentally disabled, brought this action against California officials who manage and administer various state programs for the developmentally disabled.

• • •

Sanchez and the Providers claim that, because California pays wages to community-based service providers...at a lower rate than it pays employees in state institutions, the State is in violation of the provision of the Medicaid Act that requires that:

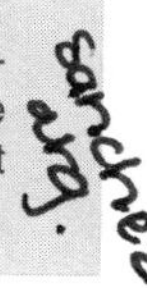

> A State plan for medical assistance—[must] provide such methods and procedures relating to the utilization of, and the payment for, care and services available under the plan...as may be necessary to...assure that payments are consistent with efficiency, economy, and quality of care and are sufficient to enlist enough providers so that care and services are available under the plan at least to the extent that such care and services are available to the general population in the geographic area[.]
>
> 42 U.S.C. § 1396a(a)(30)(A).

• • •

In *Maine v. Thiboutot*, 448 U.S. 1 (1980), the Supreme Court held for the first time that § 1983 permits suits against state officials to enforce statutes enacted pursuant to Congress's spending power. The scope of these new remedies available under § 1983 was clarified in *Pennhurst State School and Hospital v. Halderman*, 451 U.S. 1 (1981), in which the Court explained that *Thiboutot* did not alter the fact that "the typical remedy for state noncompliance with federally imposed conditions is not a private cause of action for noncompliance but rather action by the Federal Government to terminate funds to the State."...*Pennhurst* established that the remedy announced in *Thiboutot* was to be applied sparingly and only to statutes in which Congress "speaks with a clear voice," and "unambiguously" creates a "right secured by the laws of the United States." ...

• • •

In *Blessing v. Freestone*, 520 U.S. 329 (1997),the Court finally provided an analytical framework for courts to use when evaluating whether or not a statute creates a right enforceable under § 1983. *Blessing* requires a court to consider three factors: (1) "Congress must have intended that the provision in question benefit the plaintiff," (2) "the plaintiff must demonstrate that the right assertedly protected by the statute is not so 'vague and amorphous' that its enforcement would strain judicial competence," and (3) "the statute must unambiguously impose a binding obligation on the States. In other words, the provision giving rise to the asserted right must be couched in mandatory rather than precatory terms." *Id.* Somewhat confusingly, the first *Blessing* factor addressed whether or not the plaintiff receives an intended "benefit" from the statute, whereas the second factor referred not to a "benefit" but to a "right." In *Gonzaga*, the Court resolved this inconsistency.

• • •

...The Court repeatedly stressed that it is Congress's use of explicit, individually focused, rights-creating language that reveals congressional intent to create an individually enforceable right in a spending statute. *See Gonzaga*, 536 U.S. 273 (2002) at 283-84[2]

• • •

...[W]hen there is evidence that a State has in place a comprehensive deinstitutionalization scheme, which, in light of existing budgetary constraints and the competing demands of other services that the State provides, including the maintenance of institutional care facilities is "effectively working," *Olmstead* 527 U.S. at 605, the courts will not tinker with that scheme. *Olmstead* does not require the immediate, state-wide deinstutionalization of all eligible developmentally disabled persons, nor that a State's plan be always and in all cases successful..... The record supports the district court's finding that California has a successful record of personalized evaluations leading to a reasonable rate of deinstutionalization and, moreover, that California has undertaken to continue and to increase its efforts to place current residents of Developmental Centers into the community when such placement is feasible. Sanchez's and the Providers' requested relief would require us to disrupt this working plan and to restrict impermissibly the leeway that California is permitted in its operation of developmentally disabled services under *Olmstead.*

• • •

Congress did not unambiguously create an individually enforceable right in § 30(A) that would be remediable under § 1983 either by recipients or providers of Medicaid services. Furthermore, Sanchez's and the Providers' requested relief under Title II of the ADA and § 504 of the Rehabilitation Act would require the "fundamental alteration" of a comprehensive, working plan for deinstitutionalization in contravention of *Olmstead.*

Affirmed.

---

[1]*Gonzaga* involved an alleged violation of the Family Educational Rights and Privacy Act of 1974 ("FERPA"), 20 U.S.C. § 1232g, which prohibits "the federal funding of educational institutions that have a policy or practice of releasing education records to unauthorized persons." 536 U.S. at 276. Gonzaga University disclosed a student's alleged sexual misconduct to the state agency responsible for teacher certification, whereupon the student sued to enforce the privacy provisions of FERPA. The Court held that "such an action [was] foreclosed because the relevant provisions of FERPA create no personal rights to enforce under 42 U.S.C. § 1983." *Id.*

D. CHILD SAFETY

1. Causes of Child Deaths and Injuries

The leading non-disease causes of death of children have remained consistent since the late 1980s: for very young children to age 4, drownings, auto accidents, homicides and accidental suffocations are the four leading causes. For children 5 to 15, auto accidents, homicides (especially those involving firearms), and accidental drownings head the list. For children 16–20, causes shift markedly to homicide (especially those involving firearms and knives) as the leading cause, followed by traffic accidents and suicides.

By gender, unintentional injuries (primarily motor vehicle accidents) are the leading cause of death for all girls after age one. Among boys over one year of age, unintentional injury is the leading cause of death through age 14, and homicide is the number one cause among boys aged 15–19. Improvements in infectious disease control and unintentional injury prevention may be offset by increases in violence, especially homicides, suicides, and injuries by firearms.[31]

2. Auto Safety

All states require that infants in a moving vehicle be in a child restraint car seat. However, coverage does not extend to all types of vehicles, with commercial and even school vehicles commonly exempt. Moreover, although federal law requires that state laws include obligatory adult seat belt use,[32] it does not specify proper safety standards for post-infant small children. In particular, children from 3 to 8 years of age are often too large for standard infant child seat restraints, but are still too small to use adult seat belts safely. Their use for these children places severe pressure in an accident on soft stomach tissue, often causing permanent spinal damage or head/neck trauma where the chest strap does not fit as designed. Children under 60 pounds of weight may only be safe in those restraints if adult belts are used in combination with "booster" seats so the belts restrain the body in the correct anatomical locations. Most states do not distinguish between child restraints and adult seat belt use consistent with the small child physiology. Moreover, child advocates contend that even where portable booster seats are required, they present some dangers in an accident due to their instability. Rather, advocates argue that the optimum solution is to build such booster seats into the seat back to "fold down" for use where needed. Citing the relatively low cost of such a design and the large number of children it would protect, groups such as Public Citizen have argued for a federal standard from the National Highway Traffic Safety Administration requiring their future inclusion. Thus far, no such standard has been adopted.

Some states have independently required proper booster seats for children up to 60 pounds;[33] however, most states do not cover the distinct needs of such children. More basic omissions in state auto safety regimes for children include: (1) seat belt use enforcement only on a "secondary basis" (cannot be the basis for a traffic stop, but may be issued only where the stop was for another purpose); (2) lack of belt use coverage (for adults or children) for backseat riders—where children are commonly carried; (3) an exemption for seat belt use in trucks; and (4) an absence of protection for children riding in the cargo areas of vehicles—including pick-up trucks (although some states prohibit untethered dog transportation in pick-up beds).

3. Motor Vehicle Operations

Almost all American children begin to drive just after reaching the age of 16. The auto accident incidence among youth is extraordinary, and is reflected in disparate insurance rates that will often amount to five times or more the rates extant for adults over 25 years of age.

Most states prohibit youth motor vehicle driving until the age of 15 or 16 years, with higher ages required for commercial vehicles. States increasingly regulate the details of license qualification, including the imposition of a graduated license, with an initial "learner's permit" allowing driving only where being tutored by a parent, driving instructor, or other qualified adult. This is followed by a restricted or probationary license including additional training and testing, before a standard license is issued, usually at 17 or 18 years of age.

Some states require parental (or other qualified adult) sponsorship and assumption of joint liability for youth licensure. A parent may avoid liability by reporting a possibly dangerous youth to the state department of motor vehicles for license revocation. In addition, states are increasingly using the revocation of the license privilege as a sanction to deter undesirable youth behavior, including truancy, school drop-outs, or the commission of specified crimes (including tobacco purchase, graffiti offenses or other violations unrelated to driving). Most states will suspend the license of a person under 21 for possessing or using drugs or alcohol even if not connected to vehicle operation.

4. Firearm Safety

The Gun-Free Schools Act of 1990 made it a federal crime to carry a concealed handgun or ammunition on or within 1,000 feet of a school. In *U.S. v. Lopez*, 514 U.S. 549 (1995), the Supreme Court struck the statute as insufficiently "commercial" in character to confer federal interstate commerce jurisdiction. Such a prohibition must rest exclusively with the states (see discussion of *Lopez* in Chapter 1).

Congress has enacted two major statutes since 1994 that strike a more "commercial" format. The Violent Crime Control and Law Enforcement Act of 1994 prohibits sale or transfer to a person reasonably known or believed to be under the age of 18 as a federal offense.[34] States are permitted to detain juveniles arrested or convicted of possessing handguns in "secure" juvenile facilities. The amended Gun-Free Schools Act of 1994 requires that local schools receiving federal funds have a "zero tolerance" firearm policy requiring a minimum one year expulsion for any student bringing a firearm to school.[35] These approaches purport to regulate commerce or use federal funding conditions to avoid *Lopez* problems.

In addition, almost all states have policies consistent with these federal statutes, including prohibitions on possession of firearms on school grounds. Many states also include liability where negligent storage allows juveniles to obtain weapons. California, for example, imposes liability for "criminal storage of the first degree" where an individual stores a loaded firearm at a location he or she reasonably knows is accessible to a child and such a weapon is discharged with death or serious injury resulting. "Criminal storage of the second degree" applies to such keeping where the result is any injury or the firearm is discharged at all or is carried to a public place.[36] Defenses to the crime include the illegal entry of the child to obtain the weapon, that it is in a locked container reasonably believed to be secure, or that it had a trigger lock.

Child advocates generally support restrictions on hand gun sales to minors, firearm registration, and most important, required trigger locks.

5. Alcohol Use

Alcohol consumption by youth occurs at a higher incidence than illegal drug use and correlates closely with violence related delinquency (and firearm fatalities) where victims are most often other youth (see discussion in Chapter 10). Alcohol is also ubiquitous where fatal automobile accidents occur, especially those involving youth. When the 21st Amendment to the Constitution was repealed, ending prohibition of alcohol sales, most states set 21 years of age as the minimum age to lawfully imbibe. However, the lowering of the voting age to 18 years of age and other youth advocacy efforts of the 1960s and 1970s led to the lowering of the drinking age in almost half of the states. In reaction to this reduction, Congress enacted the National Minimum Drinking Age Act in 1984,[37] withholding federal highway funds from states allowing alcohol purchase or possession by persons under 21 years of age. This spending power standard was upheld in

South Dakota v. Dole, 483 U.S. 203 (1987), and all fifty states have now raised the minimum age to 21.

Some states allow prescription of alcohol by physicians and religious use of alcohol by clergy. Some states go further and exempt parental provision of alcohol to their own children—which may trigger enhanced parental tort liability should an intoxicated child thus injure a third party. Further, where this parental exemption is used to permit excessive youth intoxication, the parent may suffer criminal or civil liability for parental neglect, for "contributing to the delinquency of a minor," reckless endangerment or other state law violations.

Federal law now reflects a national theoretical "zero tolerance" policy for underage drinking. As of 1995, federal highway funds are jeopardized to states failing to enact statutes setting the prohibited blood alcohol concentration for "driving under the influence" (DUI) by those under 21 years of age at or below .02% per liter of blood.[38] That level represents the effect of approximately one can of beer, glass of wine, or shot of hard liquor on a person of average body weight, and is one-third to one-fifth the typical level establishing DUI for adults.

6. Accident Injury Prevention

Most states have a program directed at injury prevention. In some states, it is called an Emergency Preparedness and Injury Control Program (EPIC), or a similar title. These agencies conduct epidemiological investigations and control programs for prevention of unintentional and intentional injuries. They generally include programs, education, an advisory task force and a state injury control plan.

These injury prevention programs are structured differently from state to state. However, they are eligible for MCH Title V block grant funds (see discussion above) and are sometimes administered as part of a state MCH office. Unintentional injuries remain the leading cause of death for all youth from ages 1 to 12. Given the costs of such injuries, spending for prevention from federal or state sources is low, even in major states.[39]

Federal standards have been imposed historically to address some lethal dangers. For example, Federal Trade Commission standards altered flammable fabric use in child night clothing and blankets after some horrendous deaths of children by fire in the 1960s.[40] The widespread use of smoke alarms in homes since the 1980s has also saved increasing numbers of children from fire death or injury. Child proof medicine bottles, some household product safety lids, and the crib and other standards of the Consumer Product Safety Commission have evolved over the past two decades to contribute to child safety.

However, the incidence of serious injury and deaths to children remains high. Beyond automobile accidents, firearms, and alcohol as discussed above, death or unintentional injury to children particularly arise from eight preventable causes: drownings (most notably in home swimming pools), bicycle accidents, playground injuries (from unsafe equipment or surfaces), electrocution, parental shaking, being left unattended in cars, and strangulation or suffocation from such things as window blind cords or thin dry cleaner bags. Except for the last instance, most public sector prevention initiatives have come primarily from the state or local levels.

A Phoenix ordinance, enacted into law in California, has reduced child swimming pool drownings by requiring a fence with lockable gate, or a secure cover, or a buzzer on the back doors leading to the pool.[41] States increasingly require children who ride bicycles to wear helmets given the devastating impact of head injuries on pavement.[42] One state has adopted statewide public playground safety standards.[43] Many states have created a system of "poison control centers" including a hotline to call for immediate antidote information. Devices to block infant access to wall sockets and to provide additional circuit breakers have become common. Some states have initiated education campaigns on the theme "never, never shake a baby" to stress the danger, given the weak necks and vulnerable heads of infants. And an increasing number of states are addressing the problem of babies left unattended in cars without consideration of the often startling and sometimes fatal temperature effect of sunlight on a closed vehicle.[44] However, these measures, notwithstanding some evidence of preventive impact, provide protection in only a minority of states covering a fraction of the nation's children.

E. ENVIRONMENTAL HEALTH

One 1997 report identifies five common environmental dangers disproportionately endangering children: lead, air pollution, pesticides, environmental tobacco smoke, and drinking water contamination.[45] As to each of these sources, children are not merely "little adults," but suffer more harm from levels of exposure which adults can tolerate. Child health advocates contend that federal and state regulatory officials have set standards based on danger to adults without adequately factoring in impacts on children, who are more vulnerable.

Environmental Policy: Increasing Focus on Children's Health

The George Washington University Medical Center
4:1 HEALTH POLICY: CHILD HEALTH (Winter 1997)

For decades, the federal government has registered, regulated and sometimes restricted potential environmental pollutants, from industrial chemicals to lawn fertilizers. Yet, until very recently, the potential adverse effects of these substances on the health of children had rarely been addressed. This is largely the result of environmental policy that has generally emphasized protection of the environment over the health of the public.

Recently, however, environmental policy took a new turn with the enactment of the Food Quality Protection Act of 1996 and the Safe Drinking Water Act of 1996. Both of these new laws pay special attention to the health considerations of children and other vulnerable populations in defining food and water quality standards.

A trend toward growing concern for pediatric environmental health is further evidenced by proponents who tout the benefits to children's health of other environmental measures. Among these are proposed Environmental Protection Agency (EPA) regulations to lower ozone levels and particulate matter emissions, as well as legislation introduced to reform the Superfund and possible legislation to reauthorize the Clean Water Act.

Still, critics contend that the methodologies employed to assess the risks of various materials, even if increasingly sensitive to the dangers to children, remain inadequate and lead to unjustifiable consequences for children.

Children Are Not "Little Adults"

Children are more susceptible than adults to environmental pollutants due to physiological differences and developmental factors. At each stage of development, a child faces exposure to external hazards that may be harmful to her health.

The fetus, for example, is exposed to the same harmful substances to which the mother herself is exposed. An example is exposure to polychlorinated biphenyls (PCBs), which were produced in the U.S. between 1929 and 1977 to serve as insulating liquids in electrical transformers and capacitators.

Although no longer produced, PCBs released into the environment long ago are still present, as they take several decades to decompose. Measurable amounts of PCBs have been detected in soil, water, fish, milk and human tissues. Several studies show that pregnant women who chronically ingested PCBs through their food gave birth to babies with low birth weights, small head circumferences, and signs of developmental delay that persist over time.

Likewise, newborns can be exposed to harmful substances in milk, whether it be breast milk or cow's milk used in infant formula, polluted indoor air, and contaminated tap water. Infants are often placed on floors, carpets and lawns where they are more vulnerable to exposure to chemicals associated with these surfaces. And because of their greater proximity to the source, infants are more likely to inhale toxic fumes from such sources.

Toddlers engage in sucking and mouthing behaviors which increase their chances of ingesting environmental pollutants. A clear relationship has been established between these behaviors and increased blood lead levels, for example. A common source of lead is paint dust and chips in older homes which children eat directly or lick from their hands.

The most important adverse health effect of a high concentration of lead in children is cognitive deficiencies. One study shows that the higher the level of lead concentration in blood, the lower the IQ of the child.

Preschool and school-aged children consume more fluids and food, have higher rates of breathing and blood flow, and are in contact with the outside environment more often than adults. These factors expose children to an increased quantity of environmental pollutants and put them at greater risk of toxicity than any other age group.

Accumulation of pesticides from food, particularly fruits and vegetables, and the outside environment, such as treated lawns, is particularly high during childhood.

* * *

Risk Assessment vs. the "Precautionary Principle"

...One major point of contention revolves around"risk assessment," the methodology used to evaluate the dangers of any given chemical substance. Risk assessment is a technique used to determine whether the risks associated with the use of a pollutant are outweighed by the environmental, social and economic benefits associated with its use. If the net benefit is positive, a pollutant is deemed safe and therefore allowed for general use. Safety is defined as "a reasonable certainty of no harm" or "negligible risk,"often determined to be a probability of less than "a one in a million lifetime risk of cancer."

This approach, therefore, promotes the greater good at the expense of the few people who may be harmed. Under EPA policy and new federal law, determination of safety must now take into account whether a permissible pollutant is safe, not just for adults, but for infants and children as well..... [however, such risk assessment] is flawed for two main reasons.

First, it is based on assumptions of acceptable levels of harm set by regulators and imposed on unconsenting people. Second, it is based on data that are very limited, particularly when it comes to children.

Rather, these critics argue, a stricter methodology known as the "precautionary principle" or the "zero risk standard" should be used. This approach justifies the prohibition of the use of a pollutant if it can not be proven to be totally safe. In other words, as long as some individuals run the risk of being harmed from the use of a specific pollutant, that pollutant should be banned altogether.

...In 1988, Congress requested the National Academy of Sciences (NAS) to examine the issue of pesticide residues in food and children's health. The examination resulted in a 1993 report, Pesticides in the Diets of Infants and Children, which pointed to the need for a comprehensive strengthening of pesticide qualifications. Specifically, the report called for more stringent pesticide regulations to protect children's inherent vulnerabilities to toxic substances. It recommended that all testing for pesticide registration include children's dietary patterns.

The report also suggested improving the monitoring and tracking of pesticide residue found in children's food and establishing a full assessment of its distinctive risks to children's cognitive and physical development....

F. JUDICIAL REVIEW OF CHILD HEALTH AND SAFETY REGULATION

Aqua Slide 'N' Dive Corp. v. Consumer Product Safety Commission

569 F.2d 831 (5th Cir. 1978)

OPINION: **RONEY**, Circuit Judge:

In this proceeding for review authorized by the Consumer Product Safety Act, 15 U.S.C.A. §§ 2051 *et seq.*, Aqua Slide 'N' Dive Corporation, an interested manufacturer, challenges the legality of a "Safety Standard for Swimming Pool Slides" adopted by the Consumer Product Safety Commission.

The primary issue is whether substantial evidence supports the Commission's finding, required by statute, that this standard is "reasonably necessary to eliminate or reduce an unreasonable risk of injury." § 2058(c)(2)(A). The Commission demonstrated that adults who slide into the water headfirst encounter a one in 10 million risk of spinal injury and paralysis. The Commission, however, has only an untested theory to support its conclusion that the warnings required by the standard to be affixed to slides will actually reduce such injuries, and has failed to produce adequate evidence to show the chain required by the standard to be fixed to the slide ladder will avert drownings which might result from the installation of slides in deep water, and has further failed to consider adequately the effect of these standards on slide purchasers. Accordingly, we grant the petition for review and set aside challenged sections of the standard relating to warning signs, a ladder chain, and installation instructions.

I. Introduction

Congress created the Consumer Product Safety Commission, an independent regulatory agency, in 1972. Among the purposes of the Commission are protection of the public "against unreasonable risks of injury associated with consumer products" and assistance to consumers "in evaluating the comparative safety" of such products....

* * *

The Act took effect in late 1972. In mid-1973 both a trade association known as the National Swimming Pool Institute and the plaintiff in this action, Aqua Slide, petitioned the Commission under § 2059 seeking promulgation of a safety

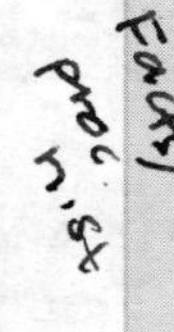

standard for swimming pool slides. Aqua Slide's admitted motive was to prevent a product ban or forced repurchase threatened by the Bureau of Product Safety, a predecessor of the Commission,...

The Commission granted the petition and sought offers to develop the requested standard....The Institute appointed a committee and hired an engineering consultant, Weiner Associates, Inc., to assist it. Members of the committee included two pool builders, an orthopedic surgeon specializing in sports injuries, the president of Aqua Slide...[and others].

The Commission modified the Institute's proposal in several respects. It rewrote the warning signs, and included a specific mention of the danger of paralysis....The Commission decided it did not have jurisdiction to regulate slide installation, and so it substituted required instructions which recommended appropriate installation depths....The ladder chain provision, however, remained mandatory....The Commission published its proposed rule on September 15, 1975. An oral proceeding took place in Washington, D.C., on October 10. Aqua Slide did not participate, and during the course of the comment period, which closed on October 15, submitted only a brief written criticism of the rule....

Aqua Slide brought a timely petition for review to this Court. The Court denied Aqua Slide's motion to stay enforcement and the standard became effective on July 17, 1976.

II. Standard of Review

* * *

[T]he Court will defer to Commission fact-finding expertise, but it can do so only when the record shows the Commission has made an actual judgment concerning the significance of the evidence....Also, the extent to which data and views in the record have been exposed to public comment will affect their reliability. Technical studies which have survived scrutiny of the scientific community and the public provide sounder footing for an inexpert judiciary to base its decision on than do facts which first see the light of day in a court proceeding....

* * *

III. "Reasonable Necessity"

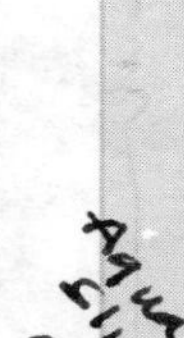

The Act requires a finding that the standard is "reasonably necessary to eliminate or reduce an unreasonable risk of injury."....Aqua Slide argues that substantial evidence does not support the Commission's conclusion,...that this standard is "reasonably necessary," in two particulars: (i) the warning signs have not been tested, may not work, and may be so explicit as to deter slide use unnecessarily, (ii) the ladder chain has not been shown effective.

* * *

The Act does not define the term "reasonably necessary," and apparently Congress intended the Commission and the courts to work out a definition on a case-by-case basis....The legislative history, and the holdings of other cases decided under similar statutes, do discuss the meaning of "unreasonable risk," and indicate that term is interrelated with the "reasonably necessary" requirement. The necessity for the standard depends upon the nature of the risk, and the reasonableness of the risk is a function of the burden a standard would impose on a user of the product.

* * *

The Senate Report provides an example of the kind of analysis Congress had in mind. It said a sharp knife might pose a reasonable risk of injury, because dulling the blade to make it safe would also make it useless. A sharp knife in a child's silverware set, however, might be unreasonable....In the *Forester* case, the D.C. Circuit found the Commission failed to show the risk of protrusions on a bicycle frame was unreasonable because it had not considered the extent to which a regulation which banned the protrusions would impair the bicycle's utility....In *Clever Idea Company v. Consumer Product Safety Commission*, 385 F. Supp. 688, 694 (E.D.N.Y.1974), another Federal Hazardous Substances Act case, the Commission failed to prove a risk of injury from plastic toy mouthpieces was unreasonable. There the risk was never shown to exist. No injuries had been reported, and the Commission's simulated "bite test" was not shown reliable. The Commission does not have to conduct an elaborate cost-benefit analysis....It does, however, have to shoulder the burden of examining the relevant factors and producing substantial evidence to support its conclusion that they weigh in favor of the standard.

In this case, the severity of the risk is so terrible that virtually any standard which actually promised to reduce it would seem to be "reasonably necessary." Both the Commission and the Institute concentrated their fact-gathering efforts on an attempt to identify the precise nature of the risk. After surveying slide accidents,...and considering the result of scientific studies of slide dynamics,...the Commission identified a risk of "quadriplegia and paraplegia resulting from users (primarily adults using the swimming pool slide for the first time) sliding down the slide in a head first position and striking the bottom of the pool."....The risk is greater than an inexperienced "belly-slider" would anticipate, because improper headfirst entry can cause an uncontrollable "snap rotation of the body" that "allows the arms to clear the bottom prior to head impact."....Also, a curved slide can disorient persons who are using it for the first time....Without question, paraplegia is a horrible injury....

The risk of paraplegia from swimming pool slides, however, is extremely remote. More than 350,000 slides are in use, yet the Commission could find no more than 11 instances of paraplegia over a six-year period. According to Institute figures, the risk, for slide users, is about one in 10 million, less than the risk an average person has of being killed by lightning. App. 583. The standard faces an initial difficulty because it is not easy to predict where paraplegia will next occur, and to burden all slide manufacturers, users, and owners with requirements that will only benefit a very few, is questionable. Remote risks have been found "unreasonable," but the context was one in which the safety standard promised to eliminate the danger entirely...see *Bunny Bear v. Peterson*, 473 F.2d 1002 (1st Cir. 1973) (risk of crib mattress fires, Flammable Fabrics Act, 15 U.S.C.A. § 1193)....

A. *Warning signs*

Given the infrequency of the risk, it was incumbent upon the Institute and the Commission to produce evidence that the standard actually promised to reduce the risk. Instead, both the Institute and the Commission gave the matter short shrift. To begin with, the standard only applies to new slides. It does not affect slides now in use, despite an Institute finding that "there are many more slides in use than produced per year by a factor of ten to one."....It is odd that the Commission chose this limited method of addressing the risk rather than deciding to use its power to conduct a public education campaign, which could reach far more slide users....A Red Cross representative told the Institute that its safety courses could inform 3,000,000 people a year of the risk of slide injury....

Furthermore, the record contains only the most ambiguous of indications that the warning signs would actually be heeded by slide users. The Commission did not test the signs....The only testing was done at the last minute by one Institute committee member, who conducted experiments for two days. The letter describing the tests, although it concluded that the signs "would seem capable of effecting significant risk reduction," also indicated that the test subjects "claimed they understood the belly slide message, but this seemed questionable," the message was "long," few readers "did more than glance" at it, and "it should be cautioned that the signs will not be a strong countermeasure to unsafe acts, but of limited effectiveness."....

...While it is no doubt rational to assume the warning signs would be heeded, mere rationality is not enough. The statute requires substantial evidence to support the Commission's ultimate conclusion that the signs are a reasonably necessary means of reducing an unreasonable risk....Unarticulated reliance on Commission "experience" may satisfy an "arbitrary, capricious" standard of review,...but it does not add one jot to the record evidence....

In short, the Commission provided little evidence that the warning signs would benefit consumers. The risk is remote. The evidence that the signs would reduce the risk rests more on inference than it does on proof. In weighing the "reasonable necessity" for the signs, the crucial question then, is whether the benefit has a reasonable relationship to the disadvantages the sign requirement imposes.

In this case, the prime disadvantage to which Aqua Slide points is the warning's effect on the availability of the slides. Because the Commission did not test the signs, it provided little evidence of whether the signs were so explicit and shocking in their portrayal of the risk of paralysis as to constitute an unwarranted deterrent to the marketing of slides, and, hence, their availability to users. The record provides only scant assurance that purchasers would not be so alarmed by the warning signs that they would unnecessarily abstain. The signs do not indicate paralysis is a one in 10 million risk....

Certainly, on this record, the economic finding is crucial. The only way to tell whether the relationship between the advantages and disadvantages of the signs is reasonable is to know exactly what those disadvantages are. Yet the Commission's study of the standard's economic impact lacks the indicia of reliability. At the same time, the proof that signs will significantly reduce the risk is weak. We consequently hold that the Commission has failed to provide substantial evidence to demonstrate the reasonable necessity of the warning signs. We set aside the warning sign requirement and the mandatory intended use instructions which repeat the warning,....

B. *Ladder Chain*

The one aspect of the standard which does promise to reduce the risk of paraplegia is the placement of large slides in deep water....The Commission concluded it did not have jurisdiction over slide placement, so it included placement "recommendations" in the standard, and made them a part of the required intended use instructions....Deep water placement, however, presented the Commission with an increased risk of child drownings.

* * *

The Commission took two steps to reduce the risk of drowning associated with deep water slides. It redrew the warning sign to include a drowning figure, and it required all such slides to have a ladder chain. That warning sign, however, was never tested for effectiveness. The only tests performed on the ladder chain were done by Institute consultant Robert Weiner, who tried one out on his neighbors' children at a pool in his own back yard....The scant five pages of Institute committee discussion, which provides the only support for the chain cited by the Government, does not provide persuasive evidence that the chain would prevent children from using the slides....Weiner thought the chain would serve as a warning device, but he apparently did not think it would prevent a child from climbing the ladder....One Institute committee member, who had observed chains in use, said the chains would "create some difficulty."....The Commission concluded the chain's presence "should, on balance, create a safer product."....

This is not the stuff of which substantial evidence is made....

...Because the Commission failed to produce substantial evidence to show the ladder chain and warning sign would work, its balance collapses and all of 16 C.F.R. § 1207.6 must be set aside.

* * *

WISDOM, Judge, concurring.

... As I read the record, there was substantial evidence to support a conclusion that warning signs would reduce the risk, although the majority says that the Commission was operating on an "untested theory." This theory was that some people will read and be affected by warning signs. When the group for whom the message is intended is first-time adult and teenage sliders, such a theory needs little, if any, empirical support to meet the substantial evidence standard. In this case the theory was supported, not only by the Commission, but by the National Swimming Pool Institute. The petitioner does not disagree. It has not pressed the question of the effectiveness of the signs; it questions only the relationship between the effectiveness and its economic cost. The changes the Commission made in the Institute's signs could only have strengthened them, as far as effectiveness is concerned.

Furthermore, there was a study made of the effectiveness of the Institute's signs. The majority properly notes that the researcher concluded that signs provided only a qualified benefit, but he did decide that they would be beneficial. His research dealt with children, rather than with the adults and teenagers at whom the Commission aimed its signs. That should make even stronger his conclusion that "they seem a desirable behavior modification device, but no panacea."....

The majority responds by pointing to evidence in the record that shows the signs will not solve the problem. Yet that evidence does not prove that signs will not work; it shows only that their effectiveness is limited....

* * *

Questions for Discussion

1. Assume that the Commission's *Aqua-Slide* order were upheld and thereafter violated. Can the Commission effectively void its own standards through non-enforcement? Note that the Consumer Product Safety Act (15 U.S.C. §§ 2051–2084) includes a right of private action for damages (15 U.S.C. § 1702) where rules are violated. Such a federal cause of action is concurrent with existing state tort or product liability damage actions. Is such enforcement viable through class actions given the commonality and other requirements now imposed for federal class certification? (See discussion in Chapter 1.) Is there adequate incentive for counsel to file such an action on an individual case basis where attorney's fees must be taken from a fund which may require a large group of victims (class format)?

2. Assume that the Commission had rejected the proposed *Aqua-Slide* order as to both a warning and a ladder sign. If a private tort action were filed in state court based partly on the failure to have such warnings, with an offer of proof that such warnings would have prevented an injury, what impact would the Commission's rejection have on the case? Could the defense use the Commission's rejection to bar liability for that notice failure?[46]

Anheuser-Busch, Inc. v. Mayor and City Council of Baltimore City
101 F.3d 325 (4th Cir. 1996)

NIEMEYER, Circuit Judge:

I

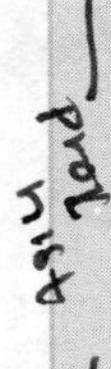

In Anheuser-Busch I, we upheld against a constitutional challenge a city ordinance prohibiting the placement of stationary, outdoor advertising that advertises alcoholic beverages in certain areas of *Baltimore City*....The ordinance was designed to promote the welfare and temperance of minors exposed to advertisements for alcoholic beverages by banning such advertisements in particular areas where children are expected to walk to school or play in their neighborhood....Applying the four-prong test for evaluating commercial speech announced in *Central Hudson Gas & Elec. Corp. v. Public Serv. Comm'n*, 447 U.S. 557...(1980), we concluded, in respect to the disputed prongs, that the ban of outdoor advertising of alcoholic beverages in limited areas directly and materially advances Baltimore's interest in promoting the welfare and temperance of minors....

* * *

If the target is simply higher prices generally to discourage consumption, the regulation imposes too great, and unnecessary, a prohibition on speech in order to achieve it...."The objective of lowering consumption of alcohol by banning price advertising could be accomplished by establishing minimum prices and/or by increasing sales taxes on alcoholic beverages."Id. at 1521-22 (O'Connor, J., concurring in the judgment) (quoting 44 *Liquormart, Inc. v. Rhode Island,* 39 F.3d 5, 7 (1st Cir. 1994)....

III

While Rhode Island's blanket ban on price advertising failed Central Hudson scrutiny, Baltimore's attempt to zone outdoor alcoholic beverage advertising into appropriate areas survived our "close look" at the legislature's means of accomplishing its objective in Anheuser-Busch I. Baltimore's ordinance expressly targets persons who cannot be legal users of alcoholic beverages, not legal users as in Rhode Island. More significantly, Baltimore does not ban outdoor advertising of alcoholic beverages outright but merely restricts the time, place, and manner of such advertisements. And Baltimore's ordinance does not foreclose the plethora of newspaper, magazine, radio, television, direct mail, Internet, and other media available to Anheuser-Busch and its competitors.

* * *

...Baltimore's interest is to protect children who are not yet independently able to assess the value of the message presented. This decision thus conforms to the Supreme Court's repeated recognition that children deserve special solicitude in the First Amendment balance because they lack the ability to assess and analyze fully the information presented through commercial media. In the context of cable television, the Supreme Court recently upheld restrictions on programming imposed by the Cable Television Consumer Protection and Competition Act as a means of protecting children from indecent programming....The underlying reason for the special solicitude of children was articulated long ago: "A democratic society rests, for its continuance, upon the healthy, well-rounded growth of young people into full maturity as citizens." *Prince v. Massachusetts,* 321 U.S. 158, 168...(1944).

DISSENT: **BUTZNER**, Senior Circuit Judge, dissenting:

I dissent because I believe we should vacate the district courts' judgments and remand these cases for evidentiary hearings. I address in this dissent both the cases pertaining to advertising of alcoholic beverages and the case pertaining to the advertising of cigarettes.

* * *

...Even assuming, as common sense might suggest, that Baltimore's restrictions will reduce underage drinking to some degree, without any findings of fact we cannot determine whether the effect will be significant....

Baltimore must also show that its speech regulation is narrowly tailored. Anheuser-Busch argued that the city could implement other measures that would reduce underage drinking as effectively as the advertising restrictions without regulating speech. The company specifically suggested education programs and increased law enforcement efforts....The company's argument should be evaluated on the strength of the facts that support and negate it. The parties should be given the opportunity to present and contest those facts.

The same reasoning applies to Baltimore's restriction on cigarette advertising. Whether that restriction advances the asserted governmental interest and whether it is unnecessarily extensive raise factual questions that only an evidentiary hearing can answer. For example, Baltimore's transit buses, which carry children as well as adults, are exempted from the ordinance that restricts advertising of cigarettes. The ordinance permits such advertising at a ball park where minors watch games. What effect these and similar facts have on the validity of the city ordinance should be weighed by a court.

Lorillard Tobacco Co. v. Reilly

533 U.S. 525 (2001)

JUSTICE O'CONNOR delivered the opinion of the Court.

In January 1999, the Attorney General of Massachusetts promulgated comprehensive regulations governing the advertising and sale of cigarettes, smokeless tobacco, and cigars....Petitioners, a group of cigarette, smokeless tobacco, and cigar manufacturers and retailers, filed suit in Federal District Court claiming that the regulations violate federal law and the United States Constitution. In large measure, the District Court determined that the regulations are valid and enforceable....The first question presented for our review is whether certain cigarette advertising regulations are pre-empted by the Federal Cigarette Labeling and Advertising Act (FCLAA), 79 Stat. 282, as amended, 15 U.S.C. § 1331 et seq. The second question presented is whether certain regulations governing the advertising and sale of tobacco products violate the First Amendment.

I

In November 1998, Massachusetts, along with over 40 other States, reached a landmark agreement with major manufacturers in the cigarette industry. The signatory States settled their claims against these companies in exchange for monetary payments and permanent injunctive relief.... At the press conference covering Massachusetts' decision to sign the agreement, then-Attorney General Scott Harshbarger announced that as one of his last acts in office, he would create consumer protection regulations to restrict advertising and sales practices for tobacco products. He explained that the regulations were necessary in order to "close holes" in the settlement agreement and "to stop Big Tobacco from recruiting new customers among the children of Massachusetts."

In January 1999, pursuant to his authority to prevent unfair or deceptive practices in trade, Mass. Gen. Laws, ch. 93A, § 2 (1997), the Massachusetts Attorney General (Attorney General) promulgated regulations governing the sale and advertisement of cigarettes, smokeless tobacco, and cigars. The purpose of the cigarette and smokeless tobacco regulations is "to eliminate deception and unfairness in the way cigarettes and smokeless tobacco products are marketed, sold and distributed in Massachusetts in order to address the incidence of cigarette smoking and smokeless tobacco use by children under legal age....[and] in order to prevent access to such products by underage consumers."...

The cigarette and smokeless tobacco regulations being challenged before this Court provide:

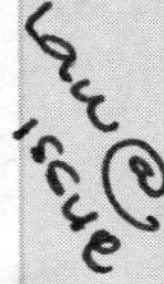

> "(2) Retail Outlet Sales Practices. Except as otherwise provided in [§ 21.04(4)], it shall be an unfair or deceptive act or practice for any person who sells or distributes cigarettes or smokeless tobacco products through a retail outlet located within Massachusetts to engage in any of the following retail outlet sales practices:
>
> .....
>
> "(c) Using self-service displays of cigarettes or smokeless tobacco products;
>
> "(d) Failing to place cigarettes and smokeless tobacco products out of the reach of all consumers, and in a location accessible only to outlet personnel." §§ 21.04(2)(c)-(d).
>
> "(5) Advertising Restrictions. Except as provided in [§ 21.04(6)], it shall be an unfair or deceptive act or practice for any manufacturer, distributor or retailer to engage in any of the following practices:
>
> "(a) Outdoor advertising, including advertising in enclosed stadiums and advertising from within a retail establishment that is directed toward or visible from the outside of the establishment, in any location that is within a 1,000 foot radius of any public playground, playground area in a public park, elementary school or secondary school;
>
> "(b) Point-of-sale advertising of cigarettes or smokeless tobacco products any portion of which is placed lower than five feet from the floor of any retail establishment which is located within a one thousand foot radius of any public playground, playground area in a public park, elementary school or secondary school, and which is not an adult-only retail establishment." §§ 21.04(5)(a)-(b).

* * *

I

Before reaching the First Amendment issues, we must decide to what extent federal law pre-empts the Attorney General's regulations. The cigarette petitioners contend that the FCLAA, *15 U.S.C. § 1331* et seq., pre-empts the Attorney General's cigarette advertising regulations.

A

Article VI of the United States Constitution commands that the laws of the United States "shall be the supreme Law of the Land;...any Thing in the Constitution or Laws of any State to the Contrary notwithstanding." Art. VI, cl. 2....In the FCLAA, Congress has crafted a comprehensive federal scheme governing the advertising and promotion of cigarettes. The FCLAA's pre-emption provision provides:

"(a) Additional statements

"No statement relating to smoking and health, other than the statement required by section 1333 of this title, shall be required on any cigarette package.

"(b) State regulations

"No requirement or prohibition based on smoking and health shall be imposed under State law with respect to the advertising or promotion of any cigarettes the packages of which are labeled in conformity with the provisions of this chapter." 15 U.S.C. § 1334.

The FCLAA's pre-emption provision does not cover smokeless tobacco or cigars.

In this case, our task is to identify the domain expressly pre-empted,...we "work on the assumption that the historic police powers of the States are not to be superseded by the Federal Act unless that [is] the clear and manifest purpose of Congress."...Our analysis begins with the language of the statute....In the pre-emption provision, Congress unequivocally precludes the requirement of any additional statements on cigarette packages beyond those provided in § 1333...). Congress further precludes States or localities from imposing any requirement or prohibition based on smoking and health with respect to the advertising and promotion of cigarettes. § 1334(b). Without question, the second clause is more expansive than the first; it employs far more sweeping language to describe the state action that is pre-empted....

* * *

B

...Although they support the Court of Appeals' result, the Attorney General and United States as amicus curiae do not fully endorse that court's textual analysis of the pre-emption provision. Instead, they assert that the cigarette advertising regulations are not pre-empted because they are not "based on smoking and health." The Attorney General and the United States also contend that the regulations are not pre-empted because they do not prescribe the content of cigarette advertising and they fall squarely within the State's traditional powers to control the location of advertising and to protect the welfare of children.

* * *

JUSTICE STEVENS finds it ironic that we conclude that "federal law precludes States and localities from protecting children from dangerous products within 1,000 feet of a school," in light of our prior conclusion that the "Federal Government lacks the constitutional authority to impose a similarly-motivated ban" in *United States v. Lopez*, 514 U.S. 549 (1995)....Our holding is not as broad as the dissent states; we hold only that the FCLAA pre-empts state regulations targeting cigarette advertising. States remain free to enact generally applicable zoning regulations, and to regulate conduct with respect to cigarette use and sales....The reference to *Lopez* is also inapposite. In *Lopez*, we held that Congress exceeded the limits of its Commerce Clause power in the Gun-Free School Zones Act of 1990, which made it a federal crime to possess a firearm in a school zone....This case, by contrast, concerns the Supremacy Clause and the doctrine of pre-emption as applied in a case where Congress expressly precluded certain state regulations of cigarette advertising. Massachusetts did not raise a constitutional challenge to the FCLAA, and we are not confronted with whether Congress exceeded its constitutionally delegated authority in enacting the FCLAA.

In sum, we fail to see how the FCLAA and its pre-emption provision permit a distinction between the specific concern about minors and cigarette advertising and the more general concern about smoking and health in cigarette advertising, especially in light of the fact that Congress crafted a legislative solution for those very concerns. We also conclude that a distinction between state regulation of the location as opposed to the content of cigarette advertising has no foundation in the text of the pre-emption provision. Congress pre-empted state cigarette advertising regulations like the Attorney General's because they would upset federal legislative choices to require specific warnings and to impose the ban on cigarette advertising in electronic media in order to address concerns about smoking and health. Accordingly, we hold that the Attorney General's outdoor and point-of-sale advertising regulations targeting cigarettes are pre-empted by the FCLAA.

* * *

III

By its terms, the FCLAA's pre-emption provision only applies to cigarettes. Accordingly, we must evaluate the smokeless tobacco and cigar petitioners' First Amendment challenges to the State's outdoor and point-of-sale advertising regulations. The cigarette petitioners did not raise a pre-emption challenge to the sales practices regulations. Thus, we must analyze the cigarette as well as the smokeless tobacco and cigar petitioners' claim that certain sales practices regulations for tobacco products violate the First Amendment.

A

For over 25 years, the Court has recognized that commercial speech does not fall outside the purview of the First Amendment....

Petitioners urge us to reject the *Central Hudson* analysis and apply strict scrutiny. But...we see "no need to break new ground. *Central Hudson*, as applied in our more recent commercial speech cases, provides an adequate basis for decision." 527 U.S. at 184.

Only the last two steps of *Central Hudson's* four-part analysis are at issue here. The Attorney General has assumed for purposes of summary judgment that petitioners' speech is entitled to First Amendment protection....With respect to the second step, none of the petitioners contests the importance of the State's interest in preventing the use of tobacco products by minors....

The third step of *Central Hudson* concerns the relationship between the harm that underlies the State's interest and the means identified by the State to advance that interest. It requires that

> "the speech restriction directly and materially advance the asserted governmental interest. 'This burden is not satisfied by mere speculation or conjecture; rather, a governmental body seeking to sustain a restriction on commercial speech must demonstrate that the harms it recites are real and that its restriction will in fact alleviate them to a material degree.'"

We do not, however, require that "empirical data come...accompanied by a surfeit of background information....We have permitted litigants to justify speech restrictions by reference to studies and anecdotes pertaining to different locales altogether, or even, in a case applying strict scrutiny, to justify restrictions based solely on history, consensus, and 'simple common sense.'"...

B

* * *

1

The smokeless tobacco and cigar petitioners contend that the Attorney General's regulations do not satisfy *Central Hudson's* third step.... In previous cases, we have acknowledged the theory that product advertising stimulates demand for products, while suppressed advertising may have the opposite effect....The Attorney General cites numerous studies to support this theory in the case of tobacco products.

* * *

Our review of the record reveals that the Attorney General has provided ample documentation of the problem with underage use of smokeless tobacco and cigars. In addition, we disagree with petitioners' claim that there is no evidence that preventing targeted campaigns and limiting youth exposure to advertising will decrease underage use of smokeless tobacco and cigars. On this record and in the posture of summary judgment, we are unable to conclude that the Attorney General's decision to regulate advertising of smokeless tobacco and cigars in an effort to combat the use of tobacco products by minors was based on mere "speculation [and] conjecture." *Edenfield v. Fane*, 507 U.S. at 770.

2

Whatever the strength of the Attorney General's evidence to justify the outdoor advertising regulations, however, we conclude that the regulations do not satisfy the fourth step of the *Central Hudson* analysis. The final step of the *Central Hudson* analysis, the "critical inquiry in this case," requires a reasonable fit between the means and ends of the regulatory scheme. 447 U.S. at 569. The Attorney General's regulations do not meet this standard. The broad sweep of the regulations indicates that the Attorney General did not "carefully calculate the costs and benefits associated with the burden on speech imposed" by the regulations....

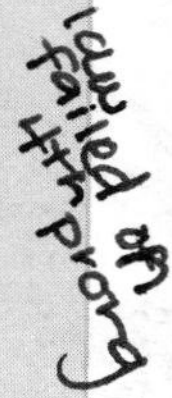

The outdoor advertising regulations prohibit any smokeless tobacco or cigar advertising within 1,000 feet of schools or playgrounds. In the District Court, petitioners maintained that this prohibition would prevent advertising in 87% to 91% of Boston, Worchester, and Springfield, Massachusetts. 84 F. Supp. 2d at

191. The 87% to 91% figure appears to include not only the effect of the regulations, but also the limitations imposed by other generally applicable zoning restrictions.... The Attorney General disputed petitioners' figures but "conceded that the reach of the regulations is substantial."...Thus, the Court of Appeals concluded that the regulations prohibit advertising in a substantial portion of the major metropolitan areas of Massachusetts....

The substantial geographical reach of the Attorney General's outdoor advertising regulations is compounded by other factors. "Outdoor" advertising includes not only advertising located outside an establishment, but also advertising inside a store if that advertising is visible from outside the store....

* * *

The State's interest in preventing underage tobacco use is substantial, and even compelling, but it is no less true that the sale and use of tobacco products by adults is a legal activity. We must consider that tobacco retailers and manufacturers have an interest in conveying truthful information about their products to adults, and adults have a corresponding interest in receiving truthful information about tobacco products. In a case involving indecent speech on the Internet we explained that "the governmental interest in protecting children from harmful materials . . . does not justify an unnecessarily broad suppression of speech addressed to adults." *Reno v. American Civil Liberties Union*, 521 U.S. 844, 875 ...(1997) (citations omitted).

* * *

C

Massachusetts has also restricted indoor, point-of-sale advertising for smokeless tobacco and cigars. Advertising cannot be "placed lower than five feet from the floor of any retail establishment which is located within a one thousand foot radius of" any school or playground....

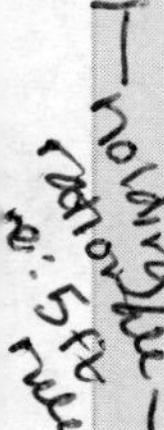

We conclude that the point-of-sale advertising regulations fail both the third and fourth steps of the *Central Hudson* analysis. A regulation cannot be sustained if it "'provides only ineffective or remote support for the government's purpose,'"...or if there is "little chance" that the restriction will advance the State's goal,...As outlined above, the State's goal is to prevent minors from using tobacco products and to curb demand for that activity by limiting youth exposure to advertising. The 5 foot rule does not seem to advance that goal. Not all children are less than 5 feet tall, and those who are certainly have the ability to look up and take in their surroundings....

Massachusetts may wish to target tobacco advertisements and displays that entice children, much like floor-level candy displays in a convenience store, but the blanket height restriction does not constitute a reasonable fit with that goal....

D

The Attorney General also promulgated a number of regulations that restrict sales practices by cigarette, smokeless tobacco, and cigar manufacturers and retailers. Among other restrictions, the regulations bar the use of self-service displays and require that tobacco products be placed out of the reach of all consumers in a location accessible only to salespersons....[These] sales practices provisions regulate conduct that may have a communicative component, but Massachusetts seeks to regulate the placement of tobacco products for reasons unrelated to the communication of ideas.. We conclude that the State has demonstrated a substantial interest in preventing access to tobacco products by minors and has adopted an appropriately narrow means of advancing that interest....

Unattended displays of tobacco products present an opportunity for access without the proper age verification required by law. Thus, the State prohibits self-service and other displays that would allow an individual to obtain tobacco products without direct contact with a salesperson. It is clear that the regulations leave open ample channels of communication. The regulations do not significantly impede adult access to tobacco products.

* * *

JUSTICE STEVENS, with whom **JUSTICE GINSBURG** and **JUSTICE BREYER** join, and with whom **JUSTICE SOUTER** joins as to Part I, concurring in part, concurring in the judgment in part, and dissenting in part.

This suit presents two separate sets of issues. The first—involving preemption—is straightforward. The second — involving the First Amendment—is more complex. Because I strongly disagree with the Court's conclusion that the Federal Cigarette Labeling and Advertising Act of 1965 (FCLAA or Act), 15 U.S.C. § 1331 et seq. as amended, precludes States and localities from regulating the location of cigarette advertising, I dissent from Parts II-A and II-B of the Court's opinion. On the First Amendment questions, I agree with the Court both that the outdoor advertising restrictions imposed by Massachusetts serve legitimate and important state interests and that the record does not indicate that the measures were properly tailored to serve those interests. Because the present record does not enable us to adjudicate the merits of those claims on summary judgment, I would vacate the decision upholding those restrictions and remand for trial on the constitutionality of the outdoor advertising regulations. Finally, because I do not believe that either the point-of-sale advertising restrictions or the sales practice restrictions implicate significant First Amendment concerns, I would uphold them in their entirety.

* * *

...To this day, the stated federal policies in this area are (1) to inform the public of the dangers of cigarette smoking and (2) to protect the cigarette companies from the burdens of confusing and contradictory state regulations of their labels and advertisements....The retention of this provision unchanged is strong evidence that Congress' only intention in expanding the preemption clause was to capture forms of content regulation that had fallen through the cracks of the prior provision—for example, state laws prohibiting cigarette manufacturers from making particular claims in their advertising or requiring them to utilize specified layouts or include particular graphics in their marketing.[17]

* * *

I am firmly convinced that, when Congress amended the preemption

[17] Because of the nature of magazine publishing and distribution, it is conceivable that a State or locality might cause the kind of regulatory confusion the statute was drafted to prevent by adopting a law prohibiting the advertising of cigarettes in any publication distributed within its boundaries. There is at least a modicum of support for the suggestion that Congress may have intended the preemption of such restrictions. See *id.* at 515, n. 11 (noting that California was considering such a ban at the time Congress was considering the 1969 Act). However, the concerns posed by the diverse regulation of national publications are not present with regard to the local regulation of the location of signs and billboards....

provision in 1969, it did not intend to expand the application of the provision beyond content regulations.[6] I, therefore, find the conclusion inescapable that the zoning regulation at issue in this suit is not a "requirement or prohibition...with respect to...advertising" within the meaning of the 1969 Act....Even if I were not so convinced, however, I would still dissent from the Court's conclusion with regard to preemption, because the provision is, at the very least, ambiguous. The historical record simply does not reflect that it was Congress'" 'clear and manifest purpose,'"...to preempt attempts by States to utilize their traditional zoning authority to protect the health and welfare of minors. Absent such a manifest purpose, Massachusetts and its sister States retain their traditional police powers.[8]

I

...[N]oble ends do not save a speech-restricting statute whose means are poorly tailored. Such statutes may be invalid for two different reasons. First, the means chosen may be insufficiently related to the ends they purportedly serve. See, e.g., *Rubin v. Coors Brewing Co.*, 514 U.S. 476...(1995) (striking a statute prohibiting beer labels from displaying alcohol content because the provision did not significantly forward the government's interest in the health, safety, and welfare of its citizens). Alternatively, the statute may be so broadly drawn that, while effectively achieving its ends, it unduly restricts communications that are unrelated to its policy aims. See, e.g., *United States v. Playboy Entertainment Group, Inc.*, 529 U.S. 803, 812...(2000) (striking a statute intended to protect children from indecent television broadcasts, in part because it constituted "a significant restriction of communication between speakers and willing adult listeners"). The second difficulty is most frequently encountered when government adopts measures for the protection of children that impose substantial restrictions on the ability of adults to communicate with one another....

To my mind, the 1,000-foot rule does not present a tailoring problem of the first type. For reasons cogently explained in our prior opinions and in the

---

[6] Petitioners suggest in passing that Massachusetts' regulation amounts to a "near-total ban," Brief for Petitioners Lorillard Tobacco Co. et al. 22, and thus is a de facto regulation of the content of cigarette ads. But we need not consider today the circumstances in which location restrictions approximating a total ban might constitute regulation of content and thus be preempted by the Act, because petitioners have failed to introduce sufficient evidence to create a genuine issue as to that claim. Petitioners introduced maps purporting to show that cigarette advertising is barred in 90.6% of Boston proper, 87.8% of Worcester, and 88.8% of Springfield. See App. 165-167. But the maps do not distinguish between the area restricted due to the regulation at issue here and the area restricted due to pre-existing regulations, such as general zoning requirements applicable to all outdoor advertising. Nor do the maps show the percentage (with respect to either area or population) of the State that is off limits to cigarette advertising; they cover only three cities containing approximately 14% of the State's population..... And even on the interpretation of this data most favorable to petitioners, the Massachusetts regulation still permits indoor and outdoor cigarette advertising in at least 10% of the geographical area of the State. In short, the regulation here is not the equivalent of a total ban on cigarette advertising.

[8] The Court's holding that federal law precludes States and localities from protecting children from dangerous products within 1,000 feet of a school is particularly ironic given the Court's conclusion six years ago that the Federal Government lacks the constitutional authority to impose a similarly-motivated ban. See *United States v. Lopez,* 514 U.S. 549 (1995). Despite the absence of any identified federal interest in creating "an invisible federal zone extending 1,000 feet beyond the (often irregular) boundaries of the school property," as the majority construes it today, the "statute now before us forecloses the States from experimenting and exercising their own judgment in an area to which States lay claim by right of history and expertise," *id.* at 583 (KENNEDY, J., concurring). I wonder why a Court sensitive to federalism concerns would adopt such a strange construction of statutory language whose quite different purpose Congress took pains to explain.

opinion of the Court, we may fairly assume that advertising stimulates consumption and, therefore, that regulations limiting advertising will facilitate efforts to stem consumption. Furthermore, if the government's intention is to limit consumption by a particular segment of the community—in this case, minors—it is appropriate, indeed necessary, to tailor advertising restrictions to the areas where that segment of the community congregates—in this case, the area surrounding schools and playgrounds.

However, I share the majority's concern as to whether the 1,000-foot rule unduly restricts the ability of cigarette manufacturers to convey lawful information to adult consumers. This, of course, is a question of line-drawing. While a ban on all communications about a given subject would be the most effective way to prevent children from exposure to such material, the state cannot by fiat reduce the level of discourse to that which is "fit for children."...On the other hand, efforts to protect children from exposure to harmful material will undoubtedly have some spillover effect on the free speech rights of adults....

Finding the appropriate balance is no easy matter. Though many factors plausibly enter the equation when calculating whether a child-directed location restriction goes too far in regulating adult speech, one crucial question is whether the regulatory scheme leaves available sufficient "alternative avenues of communication." Because I do not think the record contains sufficient information to enable us to answer that question, I would vacate the award of summary judgment upholding the 1,000-foot rule and remand for trial on that issue.

* * *

The Sales Practice and Indoor Advertising Restrictions

Second, I would...uphold the regulation limiting tobacco advertising in certain retail establishments to the space five feet or more above the floor.[11] When viewed in isolation, this provision appears to target speech. Further, to the extent that it does target speech it may well run into constitutional problems, as the connection between the ends the statute purports to serve and the means it has chosen are dubious. Nonetheless, I am ultimately persuaded that the provision is unobjectionable because it is little more than an adjunct to the other sales practice restrictions. As the Commonwealth of Massachusetts can properly legislate the placement of products and the nature of displays in its convenience stores, I would not draw a distinction between such restrictions and height restrictions on related product advertising. I would accord the Commonwealth some latitude in imposing restrictions that can have only the slightest impact on the ability of adults to purchase a poisonous product and may save some children from taking the first step on the road to addiction.

---

[11] This ban only applies to stores located within 1,000-feet of a school or playground and contains an exception for adult-only establishments.

Note on Tobacco Case Aftermath

The median age for initial tobacco addiction is under 16 years of age. Although most of its debilitating and lethal health consequences occur in adulthood, public health officials contend that youth-targeted advertising and nicotine manipulation for early addiction make it a child health problem. In early 1994, a combine of plaintiff lawyers organized nationally to challenge tobacco marketing practices, and successfully certified a federal class action in Louisiana, alleging addiction manipulation (see the *Castano* case and discussion in Chapter 1).

These *Castano* attorneys obtained an immediate order prohibiting destruction of documents, and obtained a critical early settlement from defendant Liggett. Their work from 1994 to 1999 developed insiders willing to testify, created a depository of over one million documents, developed expert witnesses, and deposed witnesses. After the national class was decertified, they filed similar class action suits in over twenty states, often including "targeting youth" allegations. Various state attorneys general, spurred by Mississippi, joined or filed parallel state lawsuits.

A negotiated settlement with the remaining tobacco defendants required Congressional approval and was narrowly rejected in 1998, but that same year the industry nevertheless settled with 40 state attorney generals to create a "Master Settlement Agreement" (MSA), including $196 billion to be paid to states over twenty years for tobacco related prevention and amelioration (although some states facing budget shortfalls have allocated these sums for their general funds). It also requires tobacco funding of charities to reduce teen smoking, prohibits targeting of youth or cartoon use in ads, bans all outdoor advertising (except at the site of a sponsored event), limits retail ad signs outside of retail stores to 14 square feet, bans transit ads, bans brand name apparel (caps, t-shirts, backpacks), limits tobacco companies to only one brand name sponsorship per year, prohibits brand name sponsorship of events with a significant youth audience, or sponsorship of team sports, allows corporate sponsorship of athletic, musical, and other events as long as the brand name is not used, stops free samples unless underage safeguards are in place, prohibits gifts based on tobacco purchases without proof of age, disbands the Council for Tobacco Research (CTR), the Tobacco Institute (TI), and the Council for Indoor Air Research (CIAR), and purports to prohibit tobacco industry political opposition to state or local laws intended to deter youth tobacco use. (For a complete listing, see http://www.wa.gov/ago/tobaccosettlement/summary.html.) The restrictions do not apply to the foreign sales and promotion activities of American tobacco firms, which continue to promote their products to youth overseas.

Questions for Discussion

1. Two of the three child safety regulatory cases above shift the burden to the state to show the efficacy of its health and safety protections for children. In the two advertising cases, this shift occurs because of the stated commercial free speech rights of advertisers. The Court acknowledges that the first amendment provides no protection to misleading commercial messages. Can it be argued that messages on behalf of alcohol and tobacco are inherently misleading as applied to children?

2. Neither the Court's opinion nor the dissent in *Lorillard* acknowledge that the Master Settlement Agreement (MSA) entered into by the tobacco industry and state attorneys general (including Massachusetts) prohibits virtually all outdoor sign advertising, not merely advertising near schools and playgrounds (see Note above). How should that fact affect the "commercial free speech" impact and "tailoring" discussion of the majority and dissent?

3. The First Amendment analysis of *Lorillard* and *Anheuser-Busch* implies a presumptive right to advertise without regulatory impediment. Such impediments may be created by the state, but they must not merely be rationally

related to a compelling state interest, they must demonstrably and materially advance such an interest; further, the state must consider other alternatives. Is the Court the ideal forum to decide the efficacy of regulatory measures to protect children? Should the burden on such regulation be "show me it works and you can do it," or should it be "if it might work do it, but stop it if it turns out to have no substantial impact"?

4. In *Lorillard*, Justice O'Connor rejects a Massachusetts restriction on tobacco advertising located below the five-foot level in retail stores because "not all children are less than five feet tall and those who are certainly have the ability to look up...." What evidence underlies her implied conclusion that locating this advertising above five feet does not advance a governmental interest by reducing to some degree child exposure? Is she equipped to make her own findings about child exposure to messages closer to their height level than above it? Is a state assumption that children are generally shorter and that the advertising of an addictive substance that produces illness and death should be made less noticeable to children reasonable? Is tobacco advertising that does not disclose its addictive and dangerous qualities misleading? Can the state prohibit all tobacco advertising that does not ostentatiously so warn?

5. Some states have a different mix of constitutional guarantees than the federal Constitution includes. For example, California has a "right to safety" enumerated as a primary citizen right (Cal. Const. Art. I, Sec. 1). If this right (or a hypothetical child's right to safety) is coextensive with First Amendment rights, would the analyses of the courts above differ?

Association of American Physicians and Surgeons, Inc. v. U.S. Food and Drug Administration

226 F. Supp. 2d 204 (D.C. District, 2002)

Henry H. Kennedy Jr., United States District Judge:

The Federal Food Drug and Cosmetic Act ("FDCA"), 21 U.S.C. § 321 *et seq.*, provides a systematic scheme for the approval of new drugs and new drug formulations intended to be marketed for use in interstate commerce. Under the FDCA, a new drug product cannot be marketed unless the FDA approves the product and determines that it is safe and effective for its intended use. *See* 21 U.S.C. § 355(a). When the FDA approves a drug, it approves the drug only for the particular use for which it was tested, but after the drug is approved for a particular use, the FDCA does not regulate how the drug may be prescribed. Thus, a drug that has been tested and approved for adult use only can be prescribed by a physician for her pediatric patients.

Because of the expense and difficulty in finding substantial pediatric populations to undergo tests, along with the ethical complications associated with testing new drugs on children, many drugs are tested for safety and effectiveness in adults only. As a result, even though there are many diseases and ailments that are common to both children and adults, physicians with pediatric patients often find their treatment options limited. Some physicians, forced "to choose between prescribing drugs without well-founded dosing and safety information or utilizing other, potentially less effective, therapy" respond by prescribing adult-approved drugs to children, but in a smaller dose. *See* Regulations Requiring Manufacturers to Assess the Safety and Effectiveness of New Drugs and Biological Products in Pediatric Patients, 62 Fed. Reg. 43,900 (Aug. 15, 1997).

Prescribing adult-approved drugs to children is often referred to as going "off-label." An off-label use is the prescription of a drug by a doctor for a condition not indicated on the label or for a dosing regimen or patient population not specified on the label. Off-label use of pharmaceuticals appears to be "generally accepted" in the medical community. ... While it is a common practice for physicians to prescribe to children pharmaceuticals only approved for adult use, by doing so, they can expose children to various hazards. Children may be given an ineffective dose or an overdose, and they face an increased risk of side effects. ...This happens because correct pediatric dosing cannot necessarily be extrapolated from adult dosing information using an equivalence based either on weight...or body surface area....Potentially significant differences in pharmacokinetics may alter a drug's effect in pediatric patients. The effects of growth and maturation of various organs, maturation of the immune system, alterations in metabolism throughout infancy and childhood, changes in body proportions, and other developmental changes may result in significant differences in the doses needed by pediatric patients and adults....

In the face of insufficient information about a new medication, pediatricians do not merely prescribe inexact doses, however. Physicians sometimes prescribe for their young patients older, less effective, but well-tested medication—as opposed to newer, more effective, medication that has not been subjected to rigorous study on pediatric populations. This practice keeps children from benefitting from state-of-the-art medication....In response to these concerns, in 1994, the FDA issued a regulation requiring manufacturers of marketed drugs to survey existing data and determine whether the data was sufficient to support pediatric use information on the drug's labeling. If so, the FDA required manufacturers to submit a supplemental new drug application seeking the FDA's approval of the labeling change. If the drug had not been sufficiently tested on children, the rule required the manufacturer to include in the product's labeling a statement to read: "Safety and effectiveness in pediatric patients have not been established."

Also in an effort to encourage pediatric testing, in 1997, Congress passed the Food and Drug Administration Modernization Act ("FDAMA")....This Act established a five-year experimental program to encourage pediatric drug-testing . Under this Act, the FDA could request (but never require) manufacturers of new drugs to conduct studies on pediatric patients. Drug manufacturers that agreed to conduct these pediatric tests could receive six months of market exclusivity for their products.

Finding that the voluntary incentive provisions of FDAMA did not increase pediatric testing as much as the FDA had hoped, after proper notice-and-comment, the FDA issued the "Pediatric Rule" in 1998. This Rule's legitimacy is challenged here.

In application, the Pediatric Rule distinguishes new drugs from already-marketed drugs. Manufacturers of new drugs "may be required to submit an application containing data adequate to assess whether the drug is safe and effective in pediatric populations. The application may be required to contain adequate evidence to support dosage and administration in some or all pediatric subpopulations, including neonates, infants, children, and adolescents....."...This means, in effect, drug manufacturers may now be obligated to study their product on pediatric populations, even if the product is not explicitly marketed for children's use. In addition, the "applicant may also be required to develop a pediatric formulation for a drug product that represents a meaningful therapeutic benefit to such patients over existing therapies."

The FDA presumes that sponsors will study all new drugs in pediatric patients unless the applicant can show that waiver is appropriate. Waivers are granted if: (1) necessary studies are impossible or highly impractical because, e.g., the number of such patients is so small or geographically dispersed; or (2) there is evidence strongly suggesting that the product would be ineffective or unsafe in all pediatric age groups.

• • •

For already-marketed drugs, the Pediatric Rule still applies, but it has a more narrow sweep. For such drugs, the FDA may still require a manufacturer to submit an application containing adequate evidence to support dosage and administration in some or all pediatric subpopulations, and the FDA may also still require an applicant to develop a pediatric drug formulation. In this context, however, the burden is on the FDA show that such testing and analysis is required. The FDA satisfies this burden only if the absence of adequate labeling could pose significant risks to pediatric patients; and either (1) the drug is "used in a substantial number of pediatric patients for the labeled indications;" or (2) there is "reason to believe that the drug product would represent a meaningful therapeutic benefit over existing treatments for pediatric patients for one or more of the claimed indications." This Rule's application, for both new and existing drugs, is limited in three other respects as well. First, the Rule does not require a manufacturer to study its product for unapproved or unclaimed indications, even if the product is widely used in pediatric patients for those indications. This means that a drug marketed as a cure for one disease in adults does not need to be tested for its ability to cure an entirely different disease in children. Second, the Pediatric Rule allows drug manufacturers to defer pediatric testing until after the FDA has approved the product for adult use. Third, the Rule only requires testing of new "innovator" drugs. The Rule does not apply to generic copies of previously-approved drugs or for suitability petitions for a change in dosage strength.

• • •

Since the filing of this lawsuit, Congress has passed, and the President has signed into law, the "Best Pharmaceuticals for Children Act," Public Law No. 107-109, 115 Stat. 1408 (2002) ("BPCA"). This Act reauthorized and expanded the pediatric testing incentives set forth in FDAMA. The BPCA endorses the goal of increasing the number of drugs studied in pediatric populations but does not authorize FDA to require manufacturers to conduct pediatric testing. Instead, the Act establishes a legislative framework to encourage voluntary testing. Under the Act, a manufacturer receives an additional six months of market exclusivity on a new or marketed drug if: (1) FDA determines that pediatric testing of the drug "may produce health benefits in that population;" (2) FDA makes a written request to the manufacturer to conduct such testing; (3) the manufacturer agrees to test the drug within an appropriate time-frame; (4) the manufacturer conducts the tests and submits reports of these tests to the FDA; and (5) the FDA accepts the testing reports.

• • •

...We first turn to the FDCA, which the FDA claims serves as the basis for its authority. The FDA claims that its authority to promulgate the Pediatric Rule comes, generally, from 21 U.S.C. § 371(a). This Section provides: "The authority to promulgate regulations for the efficient enforcement of this chapter...is vested with the Secretary." As the Second Circuit has provided "'the validity of a regulation promulgated'" under § 371 "will be sustained so long as it is 'reasonably related to the purposes of the enabling legislation.'"

• • •

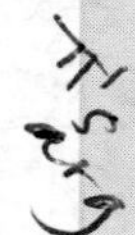

The FDA bases the Pediatric Rule, in part, on its authority under 21 U.S.C. §§ 352(a), 352(f), 355(d)(7), and 321(n), which pertain to labeling....Section 352(a) provides that drugs or devices are misbranded if they contain false or misleading labels, and Section 352(f) requires labels to contain adequate directions for use. Section 321(n) defines labeling as misleading if it "fails to reveal facts...material with respect to consequences which may result" from the use of the product as labeled or "from use of the article...under such conditions of use as are customary or usual."

Plaintiffs claim that § 352(n) and the other labeling provisions cannot support the Pediatric Rule because,...the FDA's ability to require manufacturers to include "adequate directions for use," simply permits the FDA to ensure that a product bears adequate directions for its *claimed* uses. In addition, plaintiffs contend that these provisions give the FDA limited power—power that truly extends to only "labeling and reporting" matters. According to plaintiffs, these provisions only authorize the FDA to require manufacturers to "(a) include in their labeling certain *known* material facts about products and (b) report to FDA on the use of the drugs in certain circumstances."...The question is a close one, however. Section 321(n) plainly provides that, in determining whether a label is misleading, the agency should look to whether the "labeling fails to reveal [material] facts...under such conditions of use as are *customary or usual*" (emphasis added). In adopting the Pediatric Rule, the FDA relied on extensive evidence demonstrating that at least some drugs are "commonly" or "usually" used by children, despite the absence of pediatric labeling. In addition, there is authority for the proposition that a label can be misleading based on what it fails to say, in addition to what is actually said. (Citations omitted).

Although § 201(n) and the other sections regarding labeling speak to some of the matters at issue here, FDA's power to promulgate the Pediatric Rule cannot rest solely on these provisions. Most problematic are those Pediatric Rule provisions that require manufacturers to (1) conduct studies of drugs for unclaimed uses or (2) devise formulations of the drug tailored to those uses. It is simply difficult to see how such power can be wholly derived from the FDA's power over drug labeling. Moreover, if Congress had intended for these sections to authorize the FDA to require manufacturers to test their drugs for unclaimed uses, Congress would likely have spoken more clearly, especially since "Congress can reasonably be expected to be quite precise in defining critical jurisdictional terms going to the very power of the agency to regulate." The FDCA's labeling provisions, therefore, do not provide a clear basis for the Pediatric Rule.

• • •

The FDA also relies upon 21 U.S.C. §§ 321(p), 331(a) and (d), and 355(a), (j), and (d). Section 321(p) defines "new drugs" as those not recognized to be safe and effective under conditions "prescribed, recommended, or suggested" in product labeling. Section 355(a) forbids new drugs' distribution. Section 352(j), provides that a drug shall be deemed misbranded if it is "dangerous to health when used in the dosage or manner, or with the frequency or duration prescribed, recommended, or suggested in the labeling thereof." § 352(j). Sections 331(a) and (d) proscribe misbranded drugs' sale or introduction into interstate commerce. Finally, § 355(d) provides that manufacturers seeking to market a new drug must demonstrate that the product is safe "for use under the conditions prescribed, recommended, or suggested in the proposed labeling thereof."

The applicability of the above provisions all turns on what is "*prescribed, recommended, or suggested*" in a product's labeling. Thus, the import of those three words must be scrutinized, and the analysis may apply to all....To begin,...the Act defines "labeling" to include "all labels and other written, printed, or graphic matter (1) upon any article or any of its containers or wrappers, or (2) accompanying such article." The FDA argues, in essence, that notwithstanding the plain meaning of the statutory language, these provisions give the agency the authority to regulate drugs for pediatric uses even when such uses are not explicitly claimed by a drug manufacturer in a product's labeling.

• • •

FDA counters by claiming that the Pediatric Rule does not so expand its reach. FDA argues that the Rule "simply requires, in some instances, data on a reasonable sample of patients likely to be given a drug or biological product."... FDA provides that, since there is uncontroverted evidence that many drugs officially indicated for adult use are *routinely* used by pediatric patients, "such pediatric use is 'suggested.'"...This is true, according to the FDA, even if pediatric use is specifically disclaimed on the product's labeling.

• • •

In *Weinberger*, the plaintiffs challenged an FDA regulation restricting the distribution of methadone. The FDA promulgated the regulation because the agency feared that methadone was being diverted from its intended use—that of a "safe, useful, and effective agent in the treatment of severe pain." *See Weinberger*, 377 F. Supp. at 825. The question for the court was whether, under the FDCA, the FDA had the authority to enact the regulation....The *Weinberger* court found that "the term 'safe' was intended to refer to a determination of the inherent safety or lack thereof of the drug under consideration [only] when used for its intended purposes." After this determination, the court went on to conclude "that FDA has overstepped the bounds of its authority in purporting to limit the distribution of methadone in the manner contemplated by its regulations."...This court concludes that use of a drug nowhere indicated by the label and, in fact, specifically disclaimed by the label is, quite simply, not "suggested" by that label. For that reason, the court finds that the FDA's expansive interpretation of the FDCA lacks firm support in law.

• • •

Lastly, given that the court is to examine the statute in context, the court must consider the effects of 21 U.S.C. § 355(c) and (d), if any. These sections provide that once the FDA has determined that the new drug is safe and effective "for use under the conditions prescribed, recommended, or suggested in the proposed labeling thereof," and once the manufacturer meets certain other requirements not at issue here, the FDA "*shall* issue an order approving the application." (emphasis added).. While approval appears nondiscretionary once certain congressionally-prescribed conditions are satisfied, under the Pediatric Rule, the FDA can withhold approval merely because a manufacturer has failed to test the drug on children. This tension between § 355(c) and (d) and the Pediatric Rule suggests at least some inconsistency between the Pediatric Rule and the broader context of the FDCA.

For the foregoing reasons, this court concludes that the Pediatric Rule does not have a sound statutory basis in the FDCA.

• • •

...[M]ilitating in the Pediatric Rule's favor is the fact that, when enacting the BPCA, Congress failed to expressly reject the Pediatric Rule, even though Congress was well aware of its existence. Generally, Congress' "failure to revise or repeal the agency's interpretation is persuasive evidence that the interpretation is the one intended by Congress." ....[In addition]some affirmative legislative history does support the Pediatric Rule,...the Senate Report accompanying the BPCA...provides:

> [The Pediatric Rule] requires the manufacturers of certain new and marketed drugs and biological products to provide adequate labeling for the use of the products in children. The rule is both broader and narrower than the pediatric exclusivity provision enacted by congress in 1997. When their scopes overlap, Congress provided that pediatric studies required under the rule could also satisfy the requirements for market exclusivity.

S. Rep. No. 107-79, at 4 (2001). This language demonstrates some desire for the Pediatric Rule to exist along-side Congress' scheme, and it is somewhat persuasive. However, given that the relevant legislative history is contradictory,...this statement shall not be accorded undue weight.

• • •

b. BPCA and the Pediatric Rule are Incompatible

Congress adopted an incentive scheme while the FDA adopted a command and control approach. The two schemes differ in almost every possible regard. First, as far as drug approval, the Pediatric Rule gives the FDA the authority to refuse to approve new drug applications if manufacturers refuse to conduct pediatric studies. The BPCA does not. Second, in terms of drug testing on pediatric populations, the Pediatric Rule provides that the FDA may "require" manufacturers to tests new drugs on pediatric populations. In contrast, the BPCA provides these tests may be merely "requested," and the BPCA establishes a public fund to pay for third parties to conduct pediatric tests if the FDA determines that such tests are necessary but the manufacturer elects not to conduct them....For already-marketed drugs, the BPCA, unlike the Pediatric Rule, allows manufacturers to decline to conduct pediatric testing without any risk that their products will be deemed misbranded and pulled off the market. As for labeling changes, the BPCA sets up an elaborate scheme to force labeling changes if, as a result of what was unearthed during pediatric testing, the FDA determines that such changes are necessary. In contrast, the Pediatric Rules gives the FDA the authority to simply declare a drug misbranded. In regard to pediatric formulations, the Pediatric Rule requires their development, but the BPCA provides that the FDA "shall send a nonbinding letter" recommending a change in formulation "if a pediatric study completed under public contract indicates that a formulation change is necessary and the Secretary agrees."...Finally, the very thrust of the BPCA—providing marketing incentives to encourage voluntary testing—is entirely anomalous with the very thrust of the Pediatric Rule—requiring such tests in the absence of a deferral or waiver.

Far from complementing Congress' voluntary incentive scheme, the Pediatric Rule usurps it by superimposing an often-incompatible regime.

Questions for Discussion

1. The court holds that the BCPA and the Pediatric rule are incompatible. Are they? What requirement cited by the court contradicts FDA authority to

include child testing where it finds treatment of children is likely or is occurring? As the court acknowledges, Congress was well aware of the pediatric rule when it enacted the BCPA. What indication is there of its intent to abrogate it?

2. The labels on new drugs are drafted by the pharmaceutical company holding the relevant patent. Must that label specifically instruct use on a particular patient group for that group's safety to be a part of required testing? Does it matter that children are over 20% of the population and that they often have different responses to drugs than do adults—particularly infants and young children (as the court acknowledges)? Does it matter if the illness addressed by the drug as stated occurs often in children? Are these factors relevant to the existing regulatory structure? To Congressional intent?

3. The court holds that the labeling authority of the FDA does not extend to pediatric testing because new drugs used on children do not have "customary or usual use" as noted in the statute. But does any new drug have such customary or usual use—whether prescribed to children or adults? Doesn't the phrase parsed by the court simply mean in such a prospective context the "usual" use as intended or as specified or as likely?

4. If a drug is developed that combats infections common with sickle-cell anemia victims (who are predominantly African-American) would the FDA lack the authority to require the drug testing to include persons of that racial background? Does it lack that authority unless the label specifies "to be used by African Americans" or "use to treat sickle cell anemia"?

5. Perhaps the major historical event informing Congressional intent in enacting FDA related statutes was the thalidomide scandal of the 1960s, where women in Europe took the drug, leading to tens of thousands of deformed babies for those who were pregnant. Can the FDA require testing for mutagenesis (birth defect properties) of drugs that might be prescribed for pregnant women under this decision's prescribed charter for the agency?

6. Is the methadone case partly relied upon by the court applicable to a decision denying authority to protect children from off-label uses that the agency finds occur?

7. The plaintiffs challenging the FDA's rule to protect children argued that even where use on children is explicitly disclaimed the rule might require testing on that population—delaying the introduction of needed drugs to adult patients for whom they are intended. Would an FDA rule that applies only to drugs that are not so disclaimed pass muster with this court? What of a rule that requires such testing where the drug's target or features would likely lead to substantial child use or which does lead to such use (off-label or not)? How does the Pediatric rule described by the court differ from such a regime?

ENDNOTES

[1] See *e.g.*, Iowa Code Ann. § 232.68(2)(d) (West 1998).
[2] *Jacobson v. Massachusetts*, 197 U.S. 11 (1905).
[3] *Brown v. Stone*, 378 So. 2d 218 (Miss 1979).
[4] *Prince v. Massachusetts*, 321 U.S. 158 (1944).
[5] *Id.*, at 165, 169.

[6] States include Alabama, Alaska, Arizona, Arkansas, California, Connecticut, Delaware, DC, Florida, Georgia, Idaho, Illinois, Kansas, Kentucky, Louisiana, Michigan, Minnesota, Mississippi, Montana, North Dakota, New Hampshire, New Jersey, Nevada, New Mexico, Oregon, Pennsylvania, Rhode Island, Vermont, Virginia, Washington, Wisconsin, Wyoming. For statutory citations, see Rita Swan, *On Statutes Depriving a Class of Children of Rights to Medical Care: Can this Discrimination be Litigated,* KIDS, COURTS AND COMMUNITY: PROVIDING CHILDREN ACCESS TO JUSTICE, NACC Children's Law Manual Series (1999) note 46 at 224.

[7] Alabama, Arkansas, California, Colorado, Delaware, Georgia, Idaho, Indiana, Iowa, Kansas, Louisiana, Minnesota, Missouri, New Jersey, Nevada, New Hampshire, New York, Ohio, Oklahoma, Oregon, South Carolina, Tennessee, Texas, Utah, and Wisconsin. For specific statutory citations within each state's codes, see *id.*, note 47 at 225.

[8] The problems attending the religious exemption are illustrated in *Lybarger v. People*, 807 P.2d 570 (Colo. 1991); see also *Walker v. Keldgord*, No. CIV S-93-0616 LKK JFM P (Cal. 1996); see discussion in Swan, *supra* note 6, at 229–31.

[9] See detailed discussion in Swan, *supra* note 6, at 227–230.

[10] Note that one circuit declined to dispositively decide the 14th Amendment equal protection issue raised by the plaintiffs in *Children's Healthcare Is a Legal Duty, Inc. v. Deters*, 92 F.3d 1412 (6th Cir. 1996). No other federal case has directly addressed the issue of the constitutional rights of affected children where medical care is denied and they are treated differently than are other persons in the state's response to that failure.

[11] See A. Massie, *The Religion Clauses and Parental Health Care* Health Policy Research, *The Consequences of Being Uninsured in California* (Policy Brief) (Los Angeles, CA: Feb. 1998) at 2.

[12] The Children's Defense Fund contends that 900,000 U.S. children under the age of five have dangerously elevated lead blood levels. See Children's Defense Fund, *General Health Facts* (April 24, 2002) , available at www.childrensdefense.org/hs_tp_genfacts.php; see also discussion of recent screening results indicating high levels of lead in substantial populations of children in Children's Advocacy Institute, *California Children's Budget 2001–02* (San Diego, CA; June 2001) at 4-54 to 4-58; see also discussion in Chapter 1 of different environmental standards properly applicable to children *vis-a-vis* adults.

[13] For example, California allows pesticides which are banned from certain agricultural use due to worker safety concerns to be used on the landscaping of school grounds.

[14] See Children's Advocacy Institute, *California Children's Budget 2000–01* (San Diego, CA; June 2000), Appendix A (Methodology) at Table A-A.

[15] Children Now, *Working Families and Their Uninsured Children* (Oakland, CA; 1997) at viii.

[16] Roberta Wyn, Rebecka Levan, E. Richard Brown, UCLA Center for Health Policy Research, *The Consequences of Being Uninsured in California* (Policy Brief) (Los Angeles, CA: February 1998) at 2.

[17] *Id.* at ix.

[18] The Field Institute for California Center for Health Improvement, *Parents Report Many Problems in Accessing Health Care Services for Their Children* (Sacramento, CA; Jan. 15, 1998). The survey covered October–November 1997.

[19] See Center for Health Statistics, *Data Summary: California's Infant Death Rate 2002* (Dec. 2002) at 1). See also March of Dimes, *Facts on Medicaid for Pregnant Women and Infants* (Washington, D.C.; 1995) at 1–2.

[20] Peter G. Szilagy, M.D., M.P.H., et al., *Evaluation of a State Health Insurance Program for Low-Income Children: Implications for State Child Health Insurance Program,* PEDIATRICS, Vol. 105, No. 2 (Feb. 2000), at 363–364.

[21] *Id.* at 363.

[22] Kaiser Commission on Medicaid and the Uninsured, overhead presentation by Barbara Lyons, Ph.D., Deputy Director, "Building on Medicaid and CHIP to Expand Coverage of the Low-Income Population," Families U.S.A. Annual Meeting (Jan. 27, 2001).

[23] Kaiser Commission on Medicaid and the Uninsured, *Medicaid Facts: The Medicaid Program at a Glance* (July 1999) at 1.

[24] *Id.*

[25] Maternal and Child Health Coalition, *Medicaid Protects Maternal and Child Health* (March 1995) at 2.

[26] Alliance for Health Reform, *Sourcebook for Journalists, 2004* (Washington, D.C.; 2004) at 33 (see www.allhealth.org).

[27] E. Richard Brown, Ninez Ponce, Thomas Rice, *The State of Health Insurance in California: Recent Trends, Future Prospects,* UCLA Center for Health Policy Research (March 2001) at 20 and Ex. 14 at 21.

[28] Nadereh Pourat, E. Richard Brown, Roberta Wyn, UCLA Center for Health Policy Research, *1.6 Million California Children Are Uninsured* (Los Angeles, CA; March 1997) at 2.

[29] American Academy of Pediatrics, *Children's Health Insurance in the United States, 2000 Projections* (Elk Grove Village, Il.; 2000) at 1–2.

[30] The majority of MCH funds come from the federal Social Security Act Title V Block Grant. Current law requires that a portion of this funding be spent to assure child and adolescent access to preventive and

primary care, another share for children with special needs (part for perinatal access), and places a 10% cap on administration. The incremental parts of a typical state MCH program vary somewhat in terminology, but generally include physician residency training, an MCH Epidemiology Unit for surveillance of health indicators, and various projects in which local health departments participate, such as Comprehensive Perinatal Services Program (CPSP), Adolescent Family Life Program (AFLP), High-Risk Infant Follow-Up (HRIF), Perinatal Regionalization (PERI) programs, in some states an African-American Infant Death Program, Perinatal Substance Abuse Project, the Sudden Infant Death Syndrome (SIDS) programs, and Childhood Injury Prevention Programs (MCH-CHIPP).

[31] G. K. Singh, S. M. Yu, *U.S. Childhood Mortality, 1950 through 1993: Trends and Socioeconomic Differentials*, 86:4 Am. J. Pub. Health 505-13 (Apr. 1996); C. W. Sells, R. W. Blum, *Morbidity and Mortality among U.S. Adolescents: An Overview of Data and Trends*, 86:4 Am. J. Pub. Health 513-19 (Apr. 1996); G. K. Singh, S. M. Yu, *Trends and Differentials in Adolescent and Young Adult Mortality in the United States, 1950 through 1993*, 86:4 Am. J. Pub. Health 560-65 (Apr. 1996).

[32] See 23 U.S.C. § 153

[33] See *e.g.*, California Statutes of 2000, Chapter 675, adding § 27360 *et seq.* to the Vehicle Code.

[34] 18 U.S.C. § 922 *et seq.*

[35] 20 U.S.C. § 8921 *et seq.*

[36] Cal. Pen. Code § 12035.

[37] 23 U.S.C. § 158.

[38] 23 U.S.C. § 161(a)(3).

[39] For example, the total appropriation in California for its EPIC account, of which 46% derived from federal sources, ranged from $3 to $4 million during the 1990s falling to $600,000 in total by 2001–02, see Children's Advocacy Institute, *California Children's Budget 2001–02* (San Diego, CA; June 2001) at 4-62.

[40] See Flammable Fabrics Act of 1953, as amended by Pub. L. No. 90-189, then administered by the FTC.

[41] See AB 3305 (Setencich and Speier) (Chapter 925, Statutes of 1996) adding § 115920 *et seq.* to the Cal. Health & Safety Code; the measure also includes disclosures of options for safety additions in escrow for all real property sold with a pool in place.

[42] See AB 2268 (Caldera) (Chapter 1000, Statutes of 1993), adding § 21212 to the Cal. Vehicle Code; the provision was based on a successful law in Victoria, Australia to require approved helmets (meeting the standards of the American National Standards Institute) for children riding bicycles. A first offense yields a warning, with a further offense yielding a $25 fine. The law has increased helmet use substantially among children.

[43] To date, California is the only state to adopt comprehensive public playground safety standards. The rules were mandated by statute enacted in 1990 (Chapter 1163, Statutes of 1990), which required the California Department of Health Services (DHS) to adopt the regulations by January 1, 1992. Following years of delay and in response to litigation brought by the Children's Advocacy Institute, DHS adopted the standards in December 1999; the promulgated rules are largely based on recommendations of the National Consumer Product Safety Commission.

[44] See, *e.g.*, Texas Penal Code § 22.10, prohibiting the leaving of a child younger than seven not attended by someone 14 years of age or over for more than five minutes; approximately twelve other states have varying prohibitions, usually with citation or misdemeanor sanctions. See also extensive data regarding incidence and state responses at http://www.kidsncars.org.

[45] Lawrie Mott, Natural Resources Defense Council, *Our Children at Risk: The Five Worst Environmental Threats to Their Health* (New York, NY; Nov. 1997).

[46] Note that the Act also allows private injunctive enforcement by "any interested person" after advance notice is given to the Commission and the Attorney General and where neither then files a preemptive case. Unlike the damage action under § 1702, reasonable attorneys' fees are provided for prevailing petitioners (15 U.S.C. § 1703).

CHAPTER SIX

Children with Special Needs

A. DEMOGRAPHIC BACKGROUND

Children with special needs vary widely by disability and circumstance. They include children injured prenatally, genetically disabled, or subject to post-birth injury or illness. Children with physical handicaps, and those with a mental illness, learning disability, or severe emotional problems also have special needs. On a national basis, about one in every eight children aged 6–14 has some type of disability; 6.8% of children in that age-range have difficulty doing regular schoolwork, 5.2% have a learning disability; 1.5% have a developmental disability (including mental retardation, autism, or cerebral palsy), and 3.7% have some other developmental condition for which they have received therapy or diagnostic services.[1] States provide services directly, and through federally-funded programs—administered through the Social Security Administration (SSA), the Department of Education, or the Department of Health and Human Services.

Although the Census Bureau places the Severe Emotional Disability (SED) rate at a conservative 4.8% of all school age children,[2] a broader definition of mental health disorder yields estimates in the 12–20% range. Related to mental stability, persons under the age of 26 accounted for 10.5% of all suicides in 2002.[3] In 2003, an estimated 124,409 visits to U.S. emergency departments were made after attempted suicides or other self-harm incidents among persons aged 10–24 years.[4] U.S. youth attempts at suicide and suicide deaths are high compared to other nations, and suicide now constitutes the third leading cause of death for those from 15 to 24 years of age.[5]

B. CAUSAL CORRELATIONS

1. Undernutrition

Longstanding research has established a strong connection between nutrition and optimum brain development. One leading source has concluded that even moderate but chronic undernutrition correlates with lower scores in cognitive function tests, and found "substantial relations between nutrition and mental development."[6] A decades long longitudinal study of diet and mental development from 1968 into the 1990s found that nutrition is highly correlated with cognitive competence, especially between ages 3 and 7, including language test performance results.[7]

Some harm is permanent—particularly where malnutrition occurs during the first five years of brain development. Recent research shows that even low levels of malnutrition for various nutrients harm children in a variety of ways; some—but not all—are irreversible. These developmental, growth, health, and educational effects are all preventable—and some can be wholly or partly reversed—if children are properly fed.[8]

2. Fetal Drug Injury and Fetal Alcohol Syndrome

Parental abuse and neglect is a cause of child disability across a range of injuries. Children are particularly vulnerable *in utero*, where permanent damage can come from alcohol ingestion or drug use. A 1993 study indicates that one of every nine babies born in California in 1992 was exposed to alcohol or drugs. The authors of this *New England Journal of Medicine* study concluded: "[W]e estimate that 11.35% of maternity patients at California hospitals in 1992 (approximately 67,000 women) had used a licit or illicit drug or alcohol within hours or days of delivery."[9] The study also found that an additional one in eleven mothers admitted that she continued to smoke during pregnancy.[10] The chemicals here of concern—alcohol, tobacco-borne substances, opiates, amphetamines, and cocaine—are not blocked by the placenta, and may infuse the small body-weight fetus at effective concentrations many times the level felt by the mother.

The results in California are lower than a 1992 national study which did not rely on use within several days or weeks before birth. The larger study relied on self-reporting—also likely to understate use of dangerous substances. The National Institute on Drug Abuse gathered self-reported information from a national sample of women who delivered babies. Of the four million women who gave birth, 5.5% used illicit drugs while they were pregnant, close to the California results.[11] However, the self-reporting of alcohol or cigarette use involves less stigma (and only recent use would be detected by the California survey). Alarmingly, 18.8% of pregnant women admit to exposing their fetuses to alcohol, and one recent self-report of smoking during pregnancy is 13.6%.[12]

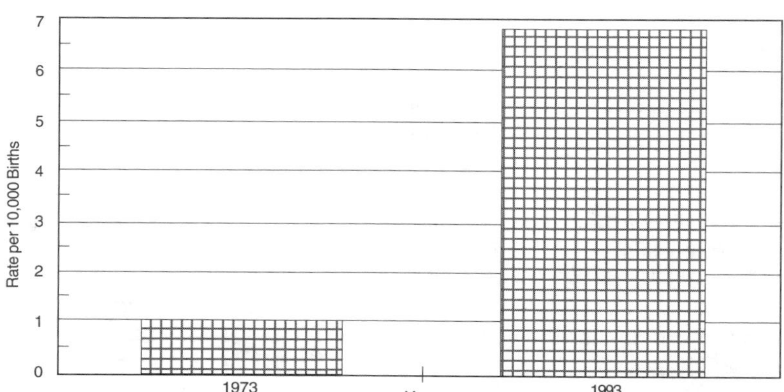

Figure 6-A U.S. Trend in Alcohol-Injured Infants per 10,000 Births

Figure 6-A, based on data from the Centers for Disease Control, presents an indicator of the trend in perinatal alcohol abuse harm. The CDC found that the rate of American babies born with health problems caused by diagnosed fetal alcohol syndrome (FAS) rose almost sixfold from 1979 through 1993. Babies born with FAS suffer central nervous system dysfunction, including delayed motor development, mild to profound mental retardation, and learning disabilities.[13] FAS also causes problems that affect speech, language, swallowing, and hearing development.[14] The Centers for Disease Control put more recent FAS rates somewhat above the 1993 levels, with some surveys indicating rates up to 15 per 10,000, double the 1993 rate. Prenatal harm—including neurodevelopment disorders—short of diagnosed FAS is estimated at three times the FAS rate.[15]

The effects of FAS are well-documented. In one large study in the state of Washington, FAS correlated with an average IQ of 79. Other problems revealed:[16]

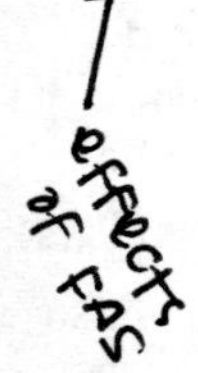

- Nearly all FAS children had reading and spelling levels below their IQs;
- Only 10% lived independently after emancipation (reaching adult years);
- 60% were suspended, expelled, or dropped out of school prior to high school graduation;
- 50% had been confined or were confined in mental hospitals, rehab facilities, or prisons;
- 30% had drug or alcohol problems; and
- Of those studied who had given birth to a child themselves, 57% no longer had the child in their custody, 40% drank during their own pregnancies, and 17% had children diagnosed with FAS, with another 13% suspected as FAS injured.

3. Lead Contamination/Environmental Injury

As discussed briefly in Chapter 5, several environmental contaminants are disproportionately dangerous to children, particularly lead. Although blood lead levels in children have decreased approximately 80% since the late 1970s, elevated levels remain more common among low-income children, urban children, and those living in older housing.[17] Substantial lead-based paint remains in fragile condition in older buildings. Lead remains environmentally common due to decades of leaded gasoline, and most ominously, there are signs of excessive lead in some drinking water supplies. The most recent large-scale study of lead exposure in California involved a state Department of Health Services (DHS) survey of drinking water, paint, and soil at elementary schools and child care centers from 1994 to 1998 and found that 37% of public elementary schools have deteriorating lead-containing paint significant enough to pose a hazard, 18% have lead levels in drinking water above the federal action level of 15 parts per billion (ppb), and 6% have soil lead levels above the federal action level of 400 ppb.[18] Nationally, the CDC surveys indicate some progress in lowering blood lead levels (BLL), with an overall prevalence of 0.7% during the most recent surveyed period of 1999–2002, a marked decrease from the 2.2% level of the 1991–94 survey. But the most vulnerable population of children ages 1–5 had the highest prevalence of damaging exposure—at a 1.6% rate, representing 310,000 American children.[19]

For young children, serious brain damage—including IQ diminution and ability to read and write—correlate in the research to low exposure levels (well short of visible lead poisoning symptoms). Most important, intake of lead poses a cumulative danger—each exposure adds to an overall tolerance threshold which must not be exceeded. The health evidence is summarized by one expert: "Recent studies of children with low but elevated blood-lead levels strongly link lead with decreased intelligence and impaired neurobehavioral development."[20] Another leading 1995 study concludes that "even low levels of lead in blood (10 ug/dL) can drop the IQ of young children measurably—and to below normal ranges."[21] The 10 ug/dL level is one-eighth the "lead poisoned" line of 80 ug/dL where diagnosis from observable symptoms most often occurs. The leading study concludes that the result of current "low level" exposure "could be a tripling of the number of youngsters who need specialized educational services."[22] Figure 6-B presents the research findings published in the *Journal of the American Medical Association* on February 7, 1996. The data indicate a high, statistically significant, and consistent correlation between bone lead levels and delinquent and dysfunctional behaviors in young boys.[23]

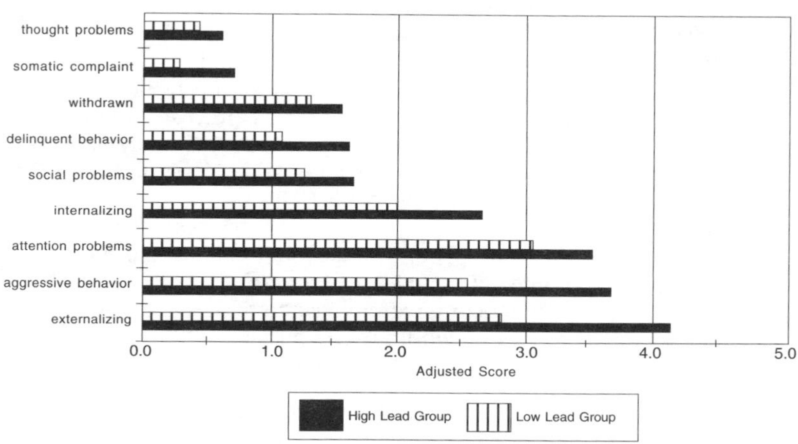

Figure 6-B. Bone Lead Concentration and Behavior Correlations

4. Causes Unknown: Autism and Related Disabilities

The precise cause remains unknown for a substantial number of child handicaps. Among the most troubling is autism and related disabilities.[24] Autism is a disorder with symptoms that become manifest at any point from birth to three years of age. Most autistic children are normal in appearance, but engage in abnormal and disturbing behaviors: staring into space for hours, uncontrollable tantrums, exhibiting no interest in people (including their parents), pursuit of strange, repetitive activities with no apparent purpose. They appear to be severely "inner directed," as if only vaguely aware of the reality outside of their minds. Most have extreme difficulty communicating or integrating socially and many may be unresponsive to common hazards, from poisons to fire to vehicular traffic—so as to pose a danger, particularly to themselves.

Prior to 1990, autism was considered a rare disorder affecting 1 in 10,000 individuals. Five years ago, researchers, including those at the National Institutes of Health (NIH), Centers for Disease Control and Prevention (CDC), and the Department of Education, estimated that as many as 1 in 500 individuals had autism or a related disorder. Some researchers contend that the number afflicted with autism or a related disorder may be closer to 3 in 500, which would translate to 1.8 million persons in the United States.[25]

The increase does not appear to be solely from improved diagnosis and identification. Rather, reports from the U.S. Department of Education and state agencies suggest a steady and alarming increase of above 10% per annum, and 3% above the increase of other reported disabilities.[26] If the increase continues, incidence would surpass mental retardation as the most common developmental disability in the nation before 2010. Identifying causes for this childhood disability carries special urgency.

Autism appears to be a biological brain disorder, and hypotheses about causes (or contributing factors) have sparked vigorous controversy within the medical community. It is clear that autistic children benefit from early diagnosis and early intervention—capable of ameliorating many symptoms and allowing some to be mainstreamed.[27] Regrettably, many children do not receive that attention. At current levels of incidence, estimates of the cost of autism range from $20 billion to $60 billion annually, projected to $120 billion by 2010.[28]

In 2003–04, ten collaborative programs of 129 researchers were studying 2,000 families with autism incidence. The most recent research indicates an overall national autism rate of 3.4 per 1,000 children, far higher than in the 1970s and 1980s. The recent 2001 NIH study of Brick Township, New Jersey, found a 6.7 per 1,000 rate, similar to some other small community findings.

The Children's Health Act of 2000 requires annual reports to Congress on the status of autism incidence and response. The federal government now has eight facilities under the Studies to Advance Autism Research and Treatment (STAART) Centers Program. The new research centers are funded at a total of $13 million per annum. The Act also creates an Interagency Autism Coordinating Committee to organize government efforts across relevant agencies. Total autism research has grown from $22 million in 1997 to $74 million as of 2003, mostly in the form of grants administered by the National Institutes of Health.[29]

The total budget expended as of 2004–05 from NIH and CDC and other agencies remains under $100 million annually. Although monitoring and research spending has grown, child advocates contend that it represents less than half the sum needed for prevention and cause related research, based on the severity and incidence of the problem. And the funds devoted to treatment—largely through the Individuals with Disabilities Education Act (IDEA)—are a small fraction of sums needed for amelioration. The individualized attention required for autism education makes treatment for these children extremely expensive and pressures educators into making hard choices to limit or avoid the treatment, or avoid obligations to other disabled children more easily addressed.

C. MAJOR PUBLIC PROGRAMS ADDRESSING DISABILITY

1. Programs Available

The programs designed to help children with special problems are scattered widely through governmental departments in most states. The pattern has been to provide special attention to children in various "categories" of need, primarily (1) developmental disabilities, (2) mental health problems, and (3) learning disabilities.

As Tables 6-A and 6-B indicate, programs for disabled children originate from a variety of different and substantially unconnected programs. In addition to those listed above, the Medicaid program discussed in Chapter 5 covers 35 million impoverished persons, providing medically related services to 830,000 children with disabilities. And as discussed in Chapter 7, approximately one million children are enrolled in federal Head Start pre-school,[30] of whom more than 100,000 are special needs children. Others may come to the

TABLE 6-A. MAJOR FEDERAL CHILD DISABILITY PROGRAMS SERVING SPECIAL NEEDS CHILDREN				
PROGRAM/LAW	**FEDERAL AGENCY**	**EST/NO. SERVED**	**PURPOSE**	**ADMIN**
Supplemental Security Income (SSI) Social Security Act, Title XVI 42 US Code § 1381 20 CFR § 300	Social Security Administration	Established 1972 Number served 65 million including 900,000 youths with disabilities (approximately 66% children with mental impairments) (fiscal 1994-96)	To assure a minimum level of income to persons with income and resources below specified levels	Administered through direct cash payments to recipients
Special Education—State Grants Program for Children with Disabilities Individuals with Disabilities Education Act (IDEA), Part B 20 U.S. Code § 1400 34 CFR § 300	U.S. Department of Education Office of Special Education Programs	Established 1975 7 million children	To ensure that all children with disabilities receive a free, appropriate public education (FAPE)	Administered by state and local education agencies
Early Intervention Program for Infants and Toddlers with Disabilities Education Act (IDEA), Part H 20 U.S. Code § 1471 34 CFR § 308	U.S. Department of Education, Office of Special Education Programs	Established 1986 250,000 children	To provide a statewide system of comprehensive, multi-disciplinary, coordinated services to infants and toddlers with disabilities and to their families	Administered by states: *Education Departments in 15 states *Health Departments in 21 states *Other agencies and co-leads in remaining states
Disabilities Prevention Public Health Service Act §§301, 317 42 U.S. Code § 6000 42 CFR §§ 52, 74	U.S. Department of Health and Human Services, Centers for Disease Control and Prevention, Disabilities Prevention Program	Established 1988 Prevention	Funds educational efforts and epidemiological projects to prevent primary and secondary disabilities	Administered by state-bsed offices of disabilities prevention
Comprehensive Mental Health Services for Children and Adolescents with Serious Emotional Disturbances and Their Families Public Health Service Act, Title V 42 U.S. Code § 250	U.S. Department of Health and Human Services, Center for Mental Health Services	Established 1992 200 to 400 children per million in a community (fiscal 1994-96)	The development of collaborative community-based mental health service delivery systems	Administered by state agencies

TABLE 6-A. MAJOR FEDERAL CHILD DISABILITY PROGRAMS SERVING SPECIAL NEEDS CHILDREN				
PROGRAM/LAW	**FEDERAL AGENCY**	**EST/NO. SERVED**	**PURPOSE**	**ADMIN**
Temporary Child Care for Handicapped Children and Crisis Nurseries Act of 1986 42 U.S. Code § 5117 45 CFR § 1355	U.S. Department of Health and Human Services, Children's Bureau	Established 1986 Number served Respite care 6,201 children with disabilities Crisis care 6,525 at-risk children (fiscal 1994-96)	To alleviate social and emotional stress on families of children with special needs, families and children at risk of abuse and/or neglect	Administered by state agencies
Supportive Housing National Affordable Housing Act 42 U.S. Code § 8013 24 CFR § 890	U.S. Department of Housing and Urban Development (HUD), Office of Multifamily Housing Development	Established 1990 Total new housing units: 2384 units for persons with Disabilities (fiscal 1995-96)	To expand supply of housing that enables persons with disabilities to live independently	Administered by HUD-approved nonprofit organizations
Protection and Advocacy for Persons with Developmental Disabilities Developmental Disabilities and Bill of Rights Act 42 U.S. Code § 6000 45 CFR § 1395	U.S. Department of Health and Human Services, Administration Developmental Disabilities	Established 1975 Number served 36,000 received individual advocacy (61% were 22 years of age) 114,000 received information or referral 109,000 received training	To protect the legal and human rights of individuals with developmental disabilities	Administered through state Protection and Advocacy system
Maternal and Child Health Services Social Security Act, Title V 42 U.S. Code § 701 45 CFR § 96	U.S. Department of Health and Human Services, Maternal and Child Health Bureau	Established 1986 128 million women and children 750,000 children with special health needs	To provide basic public health functions to improve the health of mothers and children	Administered by state Maternal and Child Health programs in cooperatioon with local public and private providers

TABLE 6-B. MAJOR FEDERAL PROGRAMS AFFECTING SPECIAL NEEDS CHILDREN

PROGRAM/LAW	FEDERAL AGENCY	EST/NO. SERVED	PURPOSE	ADMIN
Foster Care Social Security Act TItle IV-E, Section 470 42 U.S. Code § 511 45 CFR § 1355	U.S. Department of Health and Human Services, Children's Bureau	Established 1961 Average monthly number of children with disabilities served 35,000	To assist states with the costs of *foster care maintenance *administrative costs *training for staff foster parents, and private agency staff	Administration by state public child welfare agencies or departments of social services
Adoption Assistance Social Security Act, Title IV-E Section 470 42 U.S. Code §1501 20 CFR §625	U.S. Department of Health and Human Services, Children's Bureau	Established 1980 Average monthly number of children receiving support 100,000	To assist states in paying maintenance costs for adopted children with special needs (disabled or older youths) and prevent inappropriate stays in foster care	Administered by state public child welfare agencies or departments of social services
Summer Employment (Title II-B) Youth Training Program (Tittle II-C) Job Training Partnership Act 29 U.S. Code §1501 20 CFR §625	U.S. Department of Labor, Employment and Training Administration	Established 1988 Number served Total Title II-B 55,000 Youth with disabilities: 86,000 Total Title II-C.181,982 Youth with disabilities 30,000	To improve long term employability of disadvantaged youths, encourage school completion, and assist in transition from school to work	Administered through state award of federal funds by statutory formula
Vocational Rehabilitation The Rehabilitation Act of 1973, Title 1 as amended 29 U.S. Code §720 34 CFR §361	U.S. Department of Education, Rehabilitation Services Administration	Established 1921 Number served unknown	To prepare persons with disabilities to engage in competitive employment	Administered by state Vocational Rehabilitative offices
Supported Employment The Rehabilitation Act of 1973 Title VI-C	U.S. Department of Education, Rehabilitation Services Administration	Established 1986 Number served 26,000	Employment for disabled individuals who require support and supervision	Administered by state Vocational Rehabilitation offices

TABLE 6-B. MAJOR FEDERAL PROGRAMS AFFECTING SPECIAL NEEDS CHILDREN

PROGRAM/LAW	FEDERAL AGENCY	EST/NO. SERVED	PURPOSE	ADMIN
Projects with Industry The Rehabilitation Act 1973 29 US Code § 795 34 CFR § 379	U.S. Department of Education, Rehabilitation Services Administration	Established 1986 Number served 20,000 (72% with severe disabilities)	To stimulate private industry training/living of persons with disabilities	Administered through federal Rehabilitation Services Administration competitive discretionary grants to employer
Projects for Initiating Recreational Programs for Individuals with Disabilities The Rehabilitation Act of 1973 Title I 29 U.S. Code § 777 34 CFR § 38	U.S. Department of Education, Rehabilitation Services Administration	Established 1996 Number served 22,000	To aid in employment and mobility, independent socialization, and community integration	Administered by federal Rehabilitation Services Administration
Client Assistance Programs (CAPs) The Rehabilitation Act of 1973 Title I, Part B 29 U.S. Code § 732 34 CFR § 30	U.S. Department of Education, Rehabilitation Services Administration	Established 1984 Number served 54,000 adults and youths	To provide information and assist Vocational Rehabilitation clients in identifyinng and accessing services	Administered by state designated Client Assistance Program offices
Protection and Advocacy for Individual Rights (PAR) The Rehabilitation Act of 1978 29 U.S. Code § 794 34 CFR § 381	U.S. Department of Education, Rehabilitation Services Administration	Established 1994 Number served 50,000 adults and youths	To enable persons with disabilities to function and continue by protecting their legal rights	Administered by state Protection and Advocacy agencies

Sources: See Packard Foundation, *The Future of Children* (Vol. 6, No. 1) Spring 1996

[1] Participation Estimates 1/1/2000.

attention of the state because of criminal acts, an arrest, and "ward of the court" status. Children with special needs may generate SSI assistance, special education, special regular hospital services, outpatient counseling, drug testing, treatment at a "regional" mental health center, a boot camp, forced confinement in a mental health hospital or facility operated by the state, or other services.

2. The "System of Care" Approach

Among the more promising reforms in special needs services is a "bottom up" approach sometimes called "system of care," or "self-determination". Rather than a system of top-down directed services which rely on applications and decisions by agencies, this alternative allocates a sum to be expended by or on behalf of the child. A child's guardian or other representative "shops" between applicable programs. A market dynamic based on the judgment of those only concerned with results for affected children may result, with the possible elimination of those service providers failing to achieve results. One parallel model is the Monadnock Project in New Hampshire funded in 1992 by the Robert Wood Johnson Foundation. Consumers controlled the planning process, and "bought" their own services; each was given 85% of previous average levels, and the remaining 15% was placed in a "risk pool" for allocation where individual programs failed. Initial external reviews of the program are positive, indicating greater efficacy, enhanced consumer control, and lower cost. Similar projects under varying formats and nomenclature are underway in thirty other states.

D. TWO MAJOR FEDERAL BENEFIT PROGRAMS

Among the list of programs available to prevent and mitigate child disability, two programs cover the largest number of children and expend the most in public funding: SSI and the IDEA statute (see the first three cells of Table 6-A).

1. Federal Supplemental Security Income/State Supplementary Program (SSI/SSP)

The Supplementary Security Income (SSI) Program provides cash grants to aged, blind, or disabled persons, including children. The program is administered by the federal Social Security Administration. Some states supplement federal SSI payment with a State Supplementary Payment (SSP). Approximately 33% of SSI/SSP recipients receive help under the "aged" category, but children make up a share of the remaining 67% in the disabled and blind recipient categories.

Sullivan v. Zebley
493 U.S. 521 (1990)

JUSTICE BLACKMUN delivered the opinion of the Court.

This case concerns a facial challenge to the method used by the Secretary of Health and Human Services to determine whether a child is "disabled" and therefore eligible for benefits under the Supplemental Security Income Program, Title XVI of the Social Security Act...42 U.S.C. § 1381 *et seq*....

The program went into effect January 1, 1974. Currently, about 2 million claims for SSI benefits are adjudicated each year. Of these, about 100,000 are child-disability claims....

A person is eligible for SSI benefits if his income and financial resources are below a certain level, § 1382(a), and if he is "disabled." Disability is defined in § 1382c(a)(3) as follows:

> "(A) An individual shall be considered to be disabled for purposes of this subchapter if he is unable to engage in any substantial gainful activity by reason of any medically determinable physical or mental impairment which can be expected to result in death or which has lasted or can be expected to last for a continuous period of not less than twelve months (or, in the case of a child under the age of 18, if he suffers from any medically determinable physical or mental impairment of comparable severity).
>
> "(B) For purposes of subparagraph (A), an individual shall be determined to be under a disability only if his physical or mental impairment or impairments are of such severity that he is not only unable to do his previous work but cannot, considering his age, education, and work experience, engage in any other kind of substantial gainful work which exists in the national economy....
>
> "(C) For purposes of this paragraph, a physical or mental impairment is an impairment that results from anatomical, physiological, or psychological abnormalities which are demonstrable by medically acceptable clinical and laboratory diagnostic techniques."

This statutory definition of disability was taken from Title II of the Social Security Act, 70 Stat. 815, as amended, 42 U.S.C. § 423 *et seq.*...

Pursuant to his statutory authority to implement the SSI Program,...the Secretary has promulgated regulations creating a five-step test to determine whether an *adult* claimant is disabled....

The Secretary's test for determining whether a *child* claimant is disabled is an abbreviated version of the adult test. A child qualifies for benefits if he "is not doing any substantial gainful activity,"...if his impairment meets the duration requirement,...and if it matches or is medically equal to a listed impairment,...In evaluating a child's claim, both the general listings and a special listing of children's impairments,...are considered. If a child cannot qualify under these listings, he is denied benefits. There is no further inquiry corresponding to the fourth and fifth steps of the adult test.

I

Respondent Brian Zebley, a child who had been denied SSI benefits, brought a class action in the United States District Court for the Eastern District of Pennsylvania to challenge the child-disability regulations....His complaint alleges that the Secretary

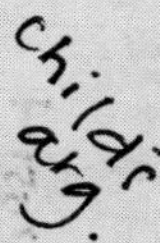

> "has promulgated regulations and issued instructions...whereby children have their entitlement to SSI disability benefits based solely on the grounds that they have a listed impairment or the medical equivalent of a listed impairment...in contravention of the Act's requirement that a child be considered disabled 'if he suffers from any medically determinable physical or mental impairment of comparable severity' to that which disables an adult under the program."

* * *

III

Since the Social Security Act expressly grants the Secretary rulemaking power,..."'our review is limited to determining whether the regulations promulgated exceeded the Secretary's statutory authority and whether they are arbitrary and capricious.'"....

The statute generally defines "disability" in terms of an individualized, functional inquiry into the effect of medical problems on a person's ability to work....

The statutory standard for child disability is explicitly linked to this functional, individualized standard for adult disability. A child is considered to be disabled "if he suffers from any...impairment of comparable severity" to one that would render an adult "unable to engage in any substantial gainful activity." 42 U.S.C. § 1382c(a)(3)(A)...The next paragraph of the statute elaborates on the adult disability standard, providing that an adult is considered unable to engage in substantial gainful activity, and is therefore disabled, if he is unable to do either his own past work or other work. § 1382c(a)(3)(B). In plain words, the two provisions together mean that a child is entitled to benefits if his impairment is as severe as one that would prevent an adult from working.

The question presented is whether the Secretary's method of determining child disability conforms to this statutory standard. Respondents argue, and the Third Circuit agreed, that it does not, because the regulatory requirement that a child claimant's impairment must match or be equivalent to a listed impairment denies benefits to those children whose impairments are severe and disabling even though the impairments are not listed and cannot meaningfully be compared with the listings....

IV

The listings set out at 20 CFR pt. 404, subpt. P, App. 1 (pt. A)..., are descriptions of various physical and mental illnesses and abnormalities, most of which are categorized by the body system they affect.[6] Each impairment is defined in terms of several specific medical signs, symptoms, or laboratory test results.[7] For a claimant to show that his impairment matches a listing, it must meet *all* of the specified medical criteria. An impairment that manifests only some of those criteria, no matter how severely, does not qualify.[8]....

---

[6] There are 125 impairments defined in the adult listings, and an additional 57 in the child listings. The body system categories in the adult listings are: musculoskeletal, special senses and speech, respiratory, cardiovascular, digestive, genito-urinary, hemic and lymphatic, skin, and endocrine. In addition, there are four groups of listings not categorized by body system: multiple body system impairments, neurological impairments, mental disorders, and malignant neoplastic diseases. The child-disability listings include, in addition to all these, a category for growth impairment.

[7] For example, under the "growth impairment" category of the child-disability listings, 20 CFR pt. 404, subpt. P, App. 1 (pt. B), § 100.00 *et seq.* (1989), there is a listing the medical criteria of which require the claimant to show both a "[f]all of greater than 25 percentiles in height which is sustained" and "[b]one age greater than two standard deviations...below the mean for chronological age." § 100.03. Another example is the listing for "mental retardation," which requires that a child claimant show "achievement of only those developmental milestones generally acquired by children no more than one-half the child's chronological age," or "IQ of 59 or less," or "IQ of 60–69, inclusive, and a physical or other mental impairment imposing additional and significant restriction of function or developmental progression." § 112.05.

[8] For example, in the growth impairment listing described in n. 7, *supra*, a child claimant whose "bone age" was slightly less than two standard deviations below normal would not qualify under the listing, even if his height was much more than 25 percentiles below normal.

For a claimant to qualify for benefits by showing that his unlisted impairment, or combination of impairments, is "equivalent" to a listed impairment, he must present medical findings equal in severity to *all* the criteria for the one most similar listed impairment.[10] 20 CFR § 416.926(a) (1989) (a claimant's impairment is "equivalent" to a listed impairment "if the medical findings are at least equal in severity" to the medical criteria for "the listed impairment most like [the claimant's] impairment");...when a person has a combination of impairments, "the medical findings of the combined impairments will be compared to the findings of the listed impairment most similar to the individual's most severe impairment").[11] A claimant cannot qualify for benefits under the "equivalence" step by showing that the overall functional impact of his unlisted impairment or combination of impairments is as severe as that of a listed impairment....

* * *

When the Secretary developed the child-disability listings, he set their medical criteria at the same level of severity as that of the adult listings....

Thus, the listings in several ways are more restrictive than the statutory standard. First, the listings obviously do not cover all illnesses and abnormalities that actually can be disabling. The Secretary himself has characterized the adult listing as merely containing "over 100 *examples* of medical conditions which ordinarily prevent" a person from working, and has recognized that "it is difficult to include in the listing all the sets of medical findings which describe impairments severe enough to prevent any gainful work."....Similarly, when the Secretary published the child-disability listings for comment in 1977, he described them as including only the "more common impairments" affecting children....[13]

* * *

For *adults*, these shortcomings of the listings are remedied at the final, vocational steps of the Secretary's test. A claimant who does not qualify for benefits under the listings, for any of the reasons described above, still has the opportunity to show that his impairment in fact prevents him from working....

For children, however, there is no similar opportunity. Children whose impairments are not quite severe enough to rise to the presumptively disabling level set by the listings; children with impairments that might not disable any and all children, but which actually disable *them*, due to symptomatic effects such as pain, nausea, side effects of medication, etc., or due to their particular age, educational background, and circumstances; and children with unlisted impairments or combinations of impairments[16] that are not equivalent to any one listing—

---

[10] For example, a child claimant with Down syndrome (which currently is not a listed impairment), a congenital disorder usually manifested by mental retardation, skeletal deformity, and cardiovascular and digestive problems, would have to fulfill the criteria for whichever single listing his condition most resembled....

[11] For example, if a child has both a growth impairment slightly less severe than required by listing § 100.03, and is mentally retarded but has an IQ just above the cut-off level set by § 112.04, he cannot qualify for benefits under the "equivalence" analysis—no matter how devastating the combined impact of mental retardation and impaired physical growth.

[13] There are, as yet, no specific listings for many well-known childhood impairments, including spina bifida, Down syndrome, muscular dystrophy, autism, AIDS, infant drug dependency, and fetal alcohol syndrome....The Secretary, however, has proposed new listings for "Down syndrome and other Hereditary, Congenital, and Acquired Disorders."....

[16] As the dissent points out,...42 U.S.C. § 1382c(a)(3)(F)...requires that "the combined impact of [multiple] impairments shall be considered throughout the disability determination process," and 20 CFR § 416.923...promises that "we will consider the combined effect of all your impairments." This assurance may be of value to adult claimants, but not to children, for whom the combined effect of multiple impairments is considered *only* within the confines of

all these categories of child claimants are simply denied benefits, even if their impairments are of "comparable severity" to ones that would actually (though not presumptively) render an adult disabled.

The child-disability regulations are simply inconsistent with the statutory standard of "comparable severity."[18] ...

V

* * *

The Secretary's claim that a functional analysis of child-disability claims is not feasible is unconvincing. The fact that a *vocational* analysis is inapplicable to children does not mean that a *functional* analysis cannot be applied to them....

VI

We conclude that the Secretary's regulations and rulings implementing the child-disability statute simply do not carry out the statutory requirement that SSI benefits shall be provided to children with "any...impairment of comparable severity" to an impairment that would make an adult "unable to engage in any substantial gainful activity."...

The judgment of the Court of Appeals, vacating in part the District Court's grant of summary judgment in the Secretary's favor as to the claims of the plaintiff class, is affirmed.

It is so ordered.

Justice White, with whom The Chief Justice joins, dissenting.

Only two Terms ago, when reviewing an aspect of the Secretary's methodology for evaluating disability applications under this Act, we emphasized that "Congress has 'conferred on the Secretary exceptionally broad authority'" in this context, and we stated that the Secretary's regulations were therefore en-

---

the equivalence determination, "whether the combination of your impairments is medically equal to *any listed impairment*."....As the Court of Appeals noted, *if* children are afforded the Benefits (1988).

A telling example of the effect of the listings-only approach is found in *Wilkinson ex rel. Wilkinson v. Bowen*, 847 F.2d 660 (CA11 1987) (child with rare liver disorder causing severe swelling, food allergies, and fever, and requiring constant care and confinement at home, does not qualify for benefits because his impairment does not meet or equal the criteria for any listing); see also *Zebley ex rel. Zebley v. Bowen*, 855 F.2d 67 (CA3 1988) (plaintiff Zebley denied benefits, despite evidence of congenital brain damage, mental retardation, development delay, eye problems, and musculoskeletal impairment, because his condition did not meet or equal any listing).

The disparity in the Secretary's treatment of child and adult claimants is thrown into sharp relief in cases where an unsuccessful child claimant, upon reaching age 18, is awarded benefits on the basis of the *same* impairment deemed insufficient to qualify him for child disability benefits....

[18] The dissent proposes that children who fail to qualify for benefits under the Secretary's current approach can simply "make their case before the Secretary, and take the case to court if their claims are rejected."....We fail to see why each child denied benefits because his impairment falls within the several categories of impairments that meet the statutory standard but do not qualify under the Secretary's listings-only approach should be compelled to raise a separate, as-applied challenge to the regulations, or why a facial challenge is not a proper response to the systemic disparity between the statutory standard and the Secretary's approach to child-disability claims.

titled to great deference....Because the majority has failed to abide by this principle, I respectfully dissent.

* * *

At the end of 42 U.S.C. § 1382c(a)(3)(A)..., with its definition of disability, is a parenthetical provision defining that term in the case of persons under 18: "or, in the case of a child under the age of 18, if he suffers from any medically determinable physical or mental impairment of comparable severity." There is no reference to nonmedical factors in this definition and no references to specific consequences that an impairment must or should produce. Furthermore, neither "comparable," "severity," nor the two words together are there or elsewhere defined in the Act, and their meaning is anything but clear. The severity of an impairment that disables an adult is measured by its effects on the ability to engage in gainful employment. But that yardstick is not useful with respect to children, whose inability to work is not due to mental or physical impairment, but to the stage of their development and the labor market. Given this task of comparing apples and oranges, it is understandable that the Secretary implemented the statute with respect to children in a somewhat different manner than he did for adults, and surely there is no direction in the statute to employ the same methodology for both groups.

* * *

...Surely it cannot be said that the regulations, insofar as they use the Part A and Part B listings, singly or in combination, to identify disability in children, are inconsistent with the statute and void on their face. And as I understand it, no one claims that they are. What is submitted is, first, that the listings do not identify all of the specific medical impairments that should be considered disabling, and second, that each child not deemed disabled under Parts A and B must be evaluated in terms of both his or her medical impairments and nonmedical factors, as are adults.

These alleged deficiencies are said to be sufficient to invalidate the regulations on their face. But surely these claims, if true, only would demonstrate that the regulations do not go far enough. Furthermore, the claims purport to be supported by descriptions of various unlisted impairments and anecdotal evidence, none of which, it seems to me, has been adjudged by a court to be sufficient to demonstrate that the Part B impairments, or their equivalents, fail to identify impairments that will have comparably severe effects on a child's development as the disabling impairments for an adult will have on an adult's ability to engage in substantial gainful employment. If there are medically determinable diseases or impairments that should be considered disabling because of comparable severity to those affecting adults, the children suffering from them should claim disability, make their case before the Secretary, and take the case to court if their claims are rejected....

* * *

I also note that the majority faults the regulations on the grounds that they do not adequately provide for considering multiple impairments together...[H]owever, the regulations expressly provide that impairments in combination may add up to qualify for benefits....The Court of Appeals recognized that the Secretary's regulations faithfully implement the statutory mandate "by providing generally that the combined effect of all of a claimant's impairments will be considered throughout the disability determination process." *Zebley v. Bowen*, 855 F.2d 67, 76 (CA3 1988). There is no cross-petition challenging this aspect of the judgment below, and the Court should therefore not expand the relief obtained in the Court of Appeals.

In sum, because I cannot conclude that the Secretary's method for evaluating child-disability claims is an impermissible construction of the Act, I dissent. The Social Security Administration processes over 100,000 child-disability claims a year. The agency has a finite amount of funds with which to work. By requiring the Secretary to conduct unspecified individualized determinations in cases where an applicant fails to satisfy the agency that he is otherwise disabled, the majority imposes costs on the agency that surely will detract from the pool of benefits available to the unfortunate children that Congress has sought to protect through the Supplemental Security Income Program.

Note on Developments After *Sullivan v. Zebley*: PRA Contraction

Six years after the *Zebley* decision, Congress enacted the Personal Responsibility and Work Opportunity Reconciliation Act (PRA), adversely affecting child eligibility for SSI/SSP. The new guidelines change the definition of disability. Under the old standards, children were eligible for SSI benefits if an impairment existed that prevented them from performing age-appropriate activities.[31] The new statute and implementing rules eliminate references to the "comparable severity standard," the "individual functional assessment," and "maladaptive behavior."[32]

The new rules adopted by the Social Security Administration include a set of "medical listings."[33] All children who qualified on the basis of comparable severity, the individual functional assessment, or maladaptive behavior must be reevaluated under the new PRA criteria.[34] SSI critics contended that some adults were "coaching" children to elicit a disabled diagnosis. However, the U.S. General Accounting Office independently investigated SSI child claimants to ascertain the prevalence of fabricated or coached child symptoms. In 1995, GAO released its report, concluding that the coaching and fabrication allegations regarding child claimants were not supported by the evidence.[35] Grant monies for children are not as susceptible to discretionary spending for non-medical purposes as they are for adults; their regimen is more likely to involve SSI-financed therapy, special diets, or rehabilitation after a third-party diagnosis.

As of May 30, 1998, 245,349 children had been reevaluated out of the country's 998,280 child recipients of SSI. Of that number, 147,933 (54%) were continued and 125,740 (46%) were terminated from SSI. In addition, 56.7% of the 61,402 adolescents turning age 18 were removed from SSI based on adult criteria even though many had been qualified previously under the strict "listings" criteria.[36] The two largest categories of SSI/SSP withdrawal appear to be those who qualified based on non-medical referrals: "maladaptive behavior," as noted above, and children with respiratory problems. The former often involves seriously mentally retarded, ADD, or ADHD children who were born drug-addicted. While disability is clear and serious, there is no organ dysfunction, illness, or traditionally treatable medical condition involved. The condition does not meet the "list" oriented to common adult illness and injury which dominates qualification.

The second group suffering withdrawal of assistance, those with respiratory problems, confronts the same adult list. Under its terms, children must often show respiratory failure in a Forced Expiratory Volume Test in a doctor's office. Unfortunately, the often serious asthma disability of children can be episodic and may not be reflected in an office test while no asthma attack is occurring. However, for children with the affliction, living with the suffocating feeling of not being able to breathe for many hours during an attack can be a serious and dangerous disability—requiring close monitoring and often expensive medicine.[37]

Adding to the concern over the withdrawal of SSI/SSP is the record of those cases reviewed by independent administrative law judges. Over the first two years of review, 63% of the terminations nationally have been reversed.[38] This extraordinary rate suggests a pattern of broad-brush denial, followed by reinstatement of those able to obtain independent review. In addition to the issue of terminations, the same new strict criteria are used to deny new child claimants since the effective date of the PRA (August 22, 1996); here, the rejection rate nationally has risen to 56%.

Washington State Department of Social and Health Services v. Guardianship Estate of Danny Keffeler
537 U.S. 371 (2003)

Justice Souter delivered the opinion of the Court:

At its own expense, the State of Washington provides foster care to certain children removed from their parents' custody, and it also receives and manages Social Security benefits for many of the children involved, as permitted under the Social Security Act and regulations. The question here is whether the State's use of Social Security benefits to reimburse itself for some of its initial expenditures violates a provision of the Social Security Act protecting benefits from "execution, levy, attachment, garnishment, or other legal process."...We hold that it does not.

...A child may get OASDI payments if, say, the minor is unmarried and was dependent on a wage earner entitled to OASDI benefits..., including children, whose income and assets fall below specified levels (the level for the latter currently being $ 2,000). Although the Social Security Administration generally pays OASDI and SSI benefits directly, it may distribute them "for [a beneficiary's] use and benefit" to another individual or entity as the beneficiary's "'representative payee.'"...In the exercise of its rulemaking authority,...the Administration has given priority to a child's parent, legal guardian, or relative when considering such an appointment. While the Act and regulations allow social service agencies and custodial institutions to serve in this capacity, such entities come last in order of preference....Whoever the appointee may be, the Commissioner of Social Security must be satisfied that the particular appointment is "in the interest of" the beneficiary. Detailed regulations govern a representative payee's use of benefits. Generally, a payee must expend funds "only for the use and benefit of the beneficiary," in a way the payee determines "to be in the [beneficiary's] best interests."...The regulations get more specific in providing that payments made for "current maintenance" are deemed to be "for the use and benefit of the beneficiary," defining "current maintenance" to include "costs incurred in obtaining food, shelter, clothing, medical care, and personal comfort items."...Although a representative payee "may not be required to use benefit payments to satisfy a debt of the beneficiary" that arose before the period the benefit payments are certified to cover, a payee may discharge such a debt "if the current and reasonably foreseeable needs of the beneficiary are met" and it is in the beneficiary's interest to do so. Finally, if there are any funds left over after a representative payee has used benefits for current maintenance and other authorized purposes, the payee is required to conserve or invest the funds and to hold them in trust for the beneficiary.

• • •

The State of Washington, through petitioner Department of Social and Health Services, makes foster care available to abandoned, abused, neglected, or orphaned children who have no guardians or other custodians able to care for them adequately.... Although the department provides foster care without strings attached to any child who needs it, the State's policy is "to attempt to recover the costs of foster care from the parents of [the] children,"...and to use "moneys and other funds" of the foster child to offset "the amount of public assistance otherwise payable,"....The department accordingly adopted a regulation providing that public benefits for a child, including benefits under SSI or OASDI, "shall be used on behalf of the child to help pay for the cost of the foster care received."...When the department receives Social Security benefits as representative payee for children in its care, it generally credits them to a special Foster Care Trust Fund Account kept by the state treasurer, which includes subsidiary accounts for each child beneficiary. When these accounts are debited, it is only rarely for a direct purchase by the State of a foster child's food, clothing, and shelter. The usual purchaser is a foster care provider, who is then paid back by the department according to a fixed compensation schedule. Every month, the department compares its payments to the provider of a child's care with the child's subsidiary account balance, on which the department then draws to reimburse itself. Since the State's outlay customarily exceeds a child's monthly Social Security benefits, the reimbursement to the State usually leaves the account empty until the next federal benefit check arrives.

• • •

As of September 1999, there were 10,578 foster children in the department's care, some 1,500 of them receiving OASDI or SSI benefits. The Commissioner had appointed the department to serve as representative payee for almost all of the latter children,...who are among respondents in this action brought on behalf of foster care children in the State of Washington who receive or have received OASDI or SSI benefits and for whom the department serves or has served as representative payee. In their 1995 class action filed in state court, they alleged, among other things, that the department's use of their Social Security benefits to reimburse itself for the costs of foster care violated,...commonly called the Act's "antiattachment" provision, provides that "the right of any person to any future payment under this subchapter shall not be transferable or assignable, at law or in equity, and none of the moneys paid or payable or rights existing under this subchapter shall be subject to execution, levy, attachment, garnishment, or other legal process, or to the operation of any bankruptcy or insolvency law."

• • •

For obvious reasons, respondents do not contend that the department's activities involve any execution, levy, attachment, or garnishment. These legal terms of art refer to formal procedures by which one person gains a degree of control over property otherwise subject to the control of another, and generally involve some form of judicial authorization....Thus, the case boils down to whether the department's manner of gaining control of the federal funds involves "other legal process," as the statute uses that term....On this restrictive understanding of "other legal process," it is apparent that the department's efforts to become respondents' representative payee and its use of respondents' benefits in that capacity involve nothing of the sort. Whereas the object of the processes specifically named is to discharge, or secure discharge of, some enforceable obligation, the State has no enforceable claim against its foster children. And although execution, levy, attachment, and garnishment typically involve the exercise of some sort of judicial or quasi-judicial authority to gain control over another's property, the department's reimbursement scheme operates on funds already in the department's possession and control, held on terms that allow the reimbursement.

• • •

The regulations previously quoted specify that payments made for a beneficiary's "current maintenance" are deemed to be "for the use and benefit of the beneficiary," and define "current maintenance" to include "costs incurred in obtaining food, shelter, clothing, medical care, and personal comfort items."...There is no question that the state funds to be reimbursed were spent for items of "current maintenance," and although the State typically makes the accounting reimbursement two months after spending its own funds, this practice is consistent with the regulation's definition of "current maintenance" as "costs incurred" for food and the like. That the State is dealing with the funds consistently with Social Security regulations is confirmed by the Commissioner's own interpretation of those regulations as allowing reimbursement by a representative payee for maintenance costs, at least for costs incurred after the first benefit payment is made to the payee.

• • •

Although it is true that the State could not directly compel the beneficiary or any other representative payee to pay Social Security benefits over to the State, that fact does not render the appointment of a self-reimbursing representative payee at odds with the Commissioner's mandate to find that a beneficiary's "interest...would be served" by the appointment....Respondents' premise that promoting the "best interests" of a beneficiary requires maximizing resources from left-over benefit income ignores the settled principle of administrative law that an open-ended and potentially vague term is highly susceptible to administrative interpretation subject to judicial deference....Under her statutory authority, the Commissioner has read the "interest" of the beneficiary in light of the basic objectives of the Act: to provide a "minimum level of income" to children who would not "have sufficient income and resources to maintain a standard of living at the established Federal minimum income level,"..., and to provide workers and their families the "income required for ordinary and necessary living expenses,"....The Commissioner, that is, has decided that a representative payee serves the beneficiary's interest by seeing that basic needs are met, not by maximizing a trust fund attributable to fortuitously overlapping state and federal grants.

• • •

...If respondents had their way, however, public offices like the department might well not be there to serve as payees even as the last resort, for there is reason to believe that if state agencies could not use Social Security benefits to reimburse the State in funding current costs of foster care, many States would be discouraged from accepting appointment as representative payees by the

> administrative costs of acting in that capacity...many eligible children would either obtain no Social Security benefits or need some very good luck to get them. With a smaller total pool of money for their potential use, the chances of having funds for genuine needs beyond immediate support would obviously shrink, to the children's loss. Respondents' position, in sum, would tend to produce worse representative payees in these cases, with less money to spend.
>
> • • •

Questions for Discussion

1. If a foster child gets a paper route or otherwise earns money for his college education, should his parents take those earnings from the child's account to recompense them for rent, utilities, and food expenses of the child? Under current law, the child is entitled to a cumulative total of $2,000 in assets from such sources, but under this Court's decision is effectively entitled to no monies from SSI funds due and payable to him. For these foster children, the state exercises "parental jurisdiction." Is the taking of monies earned by (or due to) a child by a parent to pay for the living expenses of the child at home reflective of a responsible parent? Is it a typical approach of parents in our culture?

2. As the opinion discusses, the Social Security Act provisions on SSI benefits to children require the appointment of someone to act as the fiduciary of the child. The Court argues that the state does act in the best interests of the child in taking away these payments because the Commissioner has determined that paying the state is in the child's interests. Repayment of foster care benefits both the state and federal jurisdictions who may receive recompense. Is the taking of money due a person to whom one is owed a fiduciary duty—for the benefit of the fiduciary's employer—the proper discharge of that duty? Does the agreement to that diversion by an agent of the other beneficiary (the federal jurisdiction) provide convincing support for fiduciary compliance? The Court then argues that if the state cannot take the child's money, it will be unable to pay for the fiduciary payee to act for the child. Are there no alternative payees to serve as financial fiduciaries for foster children? If the state functions as the child's parent, does it not have the independent duty to seek funds for the child and to preserve monies due that child for the child's future use?

3. The purpose of SSI disability and death benefits is as a supplement to the other income or wealth of the recipient—for reasons of qualification separate and apart from foster care status. Does the child in foster care "owe" the state the cost of his care? Ironically, if the state openly declared that such a "debt" existed and could be enforced by garnishment or other legal process, *Keffeler* would hold that it could not be taken from the child because such "debt"

payments are barred. Why does the direct taking of monies due a child warrant approval, while its classification as a debt subject to procedural due process would allow the child to keep the funds? Is this the intent of the Congress?

4. *Keffeler* lacked a dissent and was buttressed by a puzzling brief by the Children's Defense Fund advancing the arguments of the state that these monies are properly (and advantageously) taken from the child and paid to it as recompense for child foster care expenses. What does this advocacy and this unanimous decision indicate about the political and legal status of children in American law? (See discussion of child protection in Chapter 8; *see also Parham v. J.R.*, 442 U.S. 584 (1979) and *Deshaney v. Winnebago County,* 489 U.S. 189 (1989) discussed in chapters 10 and 12, respectively.)

2. Individuals with Disabilities Education Act (IDEA)

The Individuals with Disabilities Education Act (IDEA) guides the federal government's spending for special education. On June 4, 1997, the Congress enacted substantial amendments to the statute.[39] The changes added federal funds and, when that addition surpassed $4.9 billion, changed the distribution formula for additional money to schools. Instead of their respective numbers of "identified" disabled children, distribution is based on broader population and poverty characteristics. States are required to "maintain" effort by spending the same per child as was previously expended.

Part C of IDEA concerns special education programs for infants and toddlers up to three years of age, and Section 619 covers children from three to five years of age. The original IDEA statute included a minimum guidepost of $1,500 per annum per child in Section 619 (over $2,200 in current dollars), spending that would be approximately three times actual appropriations as of 2004–05. IDEA as amended in 1997 included the following basic elements:

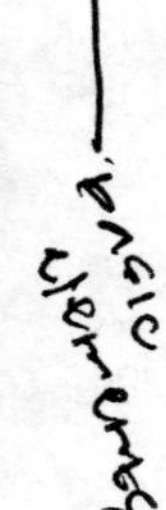

- Parents are to participate in all eligibility and placement decisions, and have access to records concerning their child;
- If the child is in regular school, a regular teacher must be on the Individual Education Plan (IEP) team formulating what services will be provided;
- School districts must "ensure" that parents participate in placement decisions;
- Disabled students must be allowed to participate in districtwide assessments, or the district must explain its reasons for excluding them;
- IEPs must outline how a disability affects a student's performance in the general education curriculum, include goals and short-term objectives (rather than the often common formulaic generalizations), and identify the support needed to participate in general education;
- Attorneys' fees for an IEP meeting are eliminated, unless court- or administratively-ordered;
- Attorneys' fees for mediation prior to the filing of a due process action are prohibited;

- Awarded fees will be reduced if the attorney fails to provide the district with information included in the notice provisions of IDEA; and
- Parents are required to notify school districts of their concerns in detail before filing a due process action in order to receive later attorney fees.

Child advocates contend that the final four changes constitute a considerable impediment to effective implementation. Only a small percentage of the parents of disabled children can afford legal representation. Critics contend that school districts commonly ignore special education requests until contacted by counsel for a child. A growing number of legal practitioners now specialize in securing special education benefits. They are paid under current arrangement only if they prevail, limiting attorney attraction to marginal cases. The 1997 federal changes preclude compensation in the early proceedings where the presence of counsel may often resolve matters short of litigation. And they reduce incentives to pursue cases, including meritorious cases, based on ancillary procedural failings of counsel or of parents.

Oberti v. Board of Education of the Borough of Clementon School District
995 F.2d 1204 (3rd Cir. 1993)

BECKER, Circuit Judge.

The Individuals with Disabilities Education Act (IDEA), 20 U.S.C. §§ 1400–1485 (formerly the "Education for All Handicapped Children Act"), provides that states receiving funding under the Act must ensure that children with disabilities are educated in regular classrooms with nondisabled children "to the maximum extent appropriate." 20 U.S.C. § 1412(5)(B). Plaintiff-appellee Rafael Oberti is an eight-year-old child with Down's syndrome who was removed from the regular classroom by defendant-appellant Clementon School District Board of Education (the "School District") and placed in a segregated special education class. In this appeal, we are asked by the School District to review the district court's decision in favor of Rafael and his co-plaintiff parents Carlos and Jeanne Oberti concerning Rafael's right under IDEA to be educated in a regular classroom with nondisabled classmates. This court has not previously had occasion to interpret or apply the "mainstreaming" requirement of IDEA.[1]

We construe IDEA's mainstreaming requirement to prohibit a school from placing a child with disabilities outside of a regular classroom if educating the child in the regular classroom, with supplementary aids and support services, can be achieved satisfactorily. In addition, if placement outside of a regular classroom is necessary for the child to receive educational benefit, the school may still be violating IDEA if it has not made sufficient efforts to include the child in school

[1] Integrating children with disabilities in regular classrooms is commonly known as "mainstreaming."....The Obertis point out that some educators and public school authorities have come to disfavor use of the term "mainstreaming" because it suggests, in their view, the shuttling of a child with disabilities in and out of a regular class without altering the classroom to accommodate the child. They prefer the term "inclusion" because of its greater emphasis on the use of supplementary aids and support services within the regular classroom to facilitate inclusion of children with disabilities....While "inclusion" may be a more precise term, we will nonetheless use the term "mainstreaming" because it is currently the common parlance. Moreover, as we discuss below, "mainstreaming" as required under IDEA does not mean simply the placement of a child with disabilities in a regular classroom or school program....

programs with nondisabled children whenever possible. We also hold that the school bears the burden of proving compliance with the mainstreaming requirement of IDEA, regardless of which party (the child and parents or the school) brought the claim under IDEA before the district court.

* * *

I. FACTUAL AND PROCEDURAL BACKGROUND

A. Rafael Oberti's educational history

Rafael is an eight-year-old child with Down's syndrome, a genetic defect that severely impairs his intellectual functioning and his ability to communicate. Now and throughout the period in question, Rafael and his parents have lived within the Clementon School District, in southern New Jersey. Prior to his entry into kindergarten, Rafael was evaluated in accordance with federal and state law by the School District's Child Study Team (the "Team"). See 20 U.S.C. § 1412(c);...[2] Based on its evaluation, the Team recommended to Rafael's parents that he be placed in a segregated special education class located in another school district for the 1989–90 school year. The Obertis visited a number of special classes recommended by the School District and found them all unacceptable. Thereafter the Obertis and the School District came to an agreement that Rafael would attend a "developmental" kindergarten class (for children not fully ready for kindergarten) at the Clementon Elementary School (Rafael's neighborhood school) in the mornings, and a special education class in another school district in the afternoons.

The Individualized Education Plan (IEP) developed by the School District for Rafael for the 1989–90 school year, see 20 U.S.C. §§ 1401(19), 1414(a)(5);...assigned all of Rafael's academic goals to the afternoon special education class. In contrast, the only goals for Rafael in the morning kindergarten class were to observe, model and socialize with nondisabled children.

While Rafael's progress reports for the developmental kindergarten class show that he made academic and social progress in that class during the year, Rafael experienced a number of serious behavioral problems there, including repeated toileting accidents, temper tantrums, crawling and hiding under furniture, and touching, hitting and spitting on other children. On several occasions Rafael struck at and hit the teacher and the teacher's aide.

These problems disrupted the class and frustrated the teacher, who consulted the school psychologist and other members of the Child Study Team to discuss possible approaches to managing Rafael's behavior problems. The teacher made some attempts to modify the curriculum for Rafael, but Rafael's IEP provided no plan for addressing Rafael's behavior problems. Neither did the IEP provide for special education consultation for the kindergarten teacher, or for communication between the kindergarten teacher and the special education teacher. In March of 1990, the School District finally obtained the assistance of an additional aide, which had been requested by the parents much earlier in the school year, but the presence of the extra aide in the kindergarten class did little to resolve the behavior problems. According to Rafael's progress reports for the afternoon special education class, and as the district court found, Rafael did not experience similar behavior problems in that class.

---

[2] The Child Study Team is "an interdisciplinary group of appropriately certified persons," which, pursuant to New Jersey regulations, includes a school psychologist, a learning disabilities teacher-consultant and a school social worker, all of whom are employees of the School District....The Team was responsible for evaluating Rafael to determine his eligibility for special education and related services under IDEA, and continues to be responsible for developing, monitoring and evaluating the effectiveness of his individualized education program.

At the end of the 1989–90 school year, the Child Study Team proposed to place Rafael for the following year in a segregated special education class for children classified as "educable mentally retarded." Since no such special education class existed within the Clementon School District, Rafael would have to travel to a different district. The Team's decision was based both on the behavioral problems Rafael experienced during the 1989–90 school year in the developmental kindergarten class and on the Team's belief that Rafael's disabilities precluded him from benefiting from education in a regular classroom at that time.

The Obertis objected to a segregated placement and requested that Rafael be placed in the regular kindergarten class in the Clementon Elementary School. The School District refused, and the Obertis sought relief by filing a request for a due process hearing.[3] The parties then agreed to mediate their dispute, pursuant to New Jersey regulations, as an alternative to a due process hearing. See N.J.A.C. 6:28-2.6. Through mediation, the Obertis and the School District came to an agreement that for the 1990–91 school year Rafael would attend a special education class for students labeled "multiply handicapped" in a public elementary school in the Winslow Township School District ("Winslow"), approximately 45 minutes by bus from Rafael's home. As part of the agreement, the School District promised to explore mainstreaming possibilities at the Winslow school and to consider a future placement for Rafael in a regular classroom in the Clementon Elementary School.[4]

The special education class in Winslow that Rafael attended during the 1990–91 school year was taught by an instructor and an instructional aide and included nine children. Although Rafael initially exhibited some of the same behavioral problems he had experienced in the Clementon kindergarten class, his behavior gradually improved: he became toilet trained and his disruptiveness abated. Rafael also made academic progress. However, by December of 1990, Rafael's parents found that the School District was making no plans to mainstream Rafael. The Obertis also learned that Rafael had no meaningful contact with nondisabled students at the Winslow school.[5]

B. The Due Process Hearing

In January of 1991, the Obertis brought another due process complaint, renewing their request under IDEA that Rafael be placed in a regular class in his neighborhood elementary school. A three-day due process hearing was held in February of 1991 before an Administrative Law Judge (ALJ) of the New Jersey Office of Administrative Law....On March 15, 1991, the ALJ affirmed the School District's decision that the segregated special education class in Winslow was the "least restrictive environment" for Rafael.[6] Based on the testimony of Rafael's kindergarten teacher and other witnesses for the School District who described Rafael's disruptive behavior in the developmental kindergarten class, the ALJ found that Rafael's behavior problems in that class were extensive and that he had

---

[3] When a dispute arises between the parents of a disabled child and the school over the adequacy of the IEP proposed for the child, either party has a right to resolve the matter through a state administrative proceeding known as an "impartial due process hearing." 20 U.S.C. § 1415(b)(2)....

[4] Although Rafael was placed in a school within the Winslow Township School District, the Clementon School District has remained responsible for Rafael's education under IDEA because Rafael resides within the Clementon School District.

[5] Rafael's class went to the lunchroom and assemblies with nondisabled children, but he and his classmates had no opportunity to socialize with the other children. Rafael did not participate in any classes, such as art, music, or physical education, with nondisabled children.

[6] Compliance with IDEA's mainstreaming requirement is sometimes referred to as placement in the "least restrictive environment."....

achieved no meaningful educational benefit in the class.[7] The ALJ concluded that Rafael was not ready for mainstreaming.[8]

In reaching this conclusion, the ALJ discounted the testimony of the Obertis' two expert witnesses. Dr. Gail McGregor, a professor of education at Temple University and an expert in the education of children with disabilities, testified that Rafael could be educated satisfactorily in a regular class at the Clementon Elementary School with supplementary aids and services, and that Rafael would learn important skills in a regular classroom that could not be learned in a segregated setting.[9] The ALJ disregarded Dr. McGregor's testimony because, unlike the School District's witnesses, she did not have daily experience with Rafael. Likewise, the ALJ discounted the testimony of the Obertis' other expert

---

[7] The School District presented eight witnesses before the ALJ. Melinda Reardon, the teacher of the developmental kindergarten class, testified to Rafael's behavioral problems that disrupted the class throughout the year, including repeated toileting accidents, touching and hitting other children, throwing objects, not following instructions, and running and hiding from the teacher and the aides. She also testified that throughout the year she had great difficulty communicating with Rafael, and that she had consulted with the school psychologist to come up with methods of controlling Rafael's behavior. Karen Lightman, the speech therapist at the Clementon Elementary School, testified that Rafael regularly disrupted her small-group speech therapy sessions during the 1989–90 school year. She testified that Rafael slapped her on one occasion, refused to follow instructions, threw paper, and touched other students. She stated that these behaviors disrupted the session and took away therapy time from the other students. William Sherman, the superintendent of Schools for the School District and acting principal of the Clementon Elementary School in May and June of 1990 testified that he was called to Rafael's kindergarten class several times by the teacher to help her address Rafael's disciplinary problems. Valeria Costino, an instructional aide for that class, corroborated the testimony of the teacher and the acting principal regarding Rafael's behavior problems.

Peggy McDevit, the Clementon Elementary School psychologist, a member of the Child Study Team, and a qualified expert in child placement and child psychology, testified that she had observed Rafael engaging in disruptive behavior in the kindergarten class and that, in her opinion, placement in a regular classroom would not be feasible for Rafael at that time because of his behavior problems. David Hinlicky, the principal of the Clementon Elementary School, described a visit he paid to a summer school class Rafael attended in 1991 in which he observed Rafael misbehaving and disrupting the class.

In contrast, Nancy Leetch, Rafael's speech therapist at Winslow, and Lisa Mansfield, the special education teacher at Winslow, both testified that Rafael had made significant academic and social progress in the Winslow special education class.

[8] Although the ALJ upheld the School District's decision to place Rafael in the segregated class in Winslow, he added: This is not to say that the time may not come when mainstreaming in Winslow Tp. and/or Clementon will not be called for. The present record discloses only that now is not such a time....

[9] Based on her observation of Rafael in the Winslow program, observation of the Clementon Elementary School, review of Rafael's education records, and her expertise in this area, Dr. McGregor testified that there were no aspects of Rafael's disability that would preclude him from being educated in a regular classroom with supplementary aids and services. She testified that many of the educational aids and techniques that were provided for Rafael at Winslow could be transferred to a regular classroom. She described various types of special support that could be provided to enable Rafael to learn in a regular classroom, including use of a behavior modification plan to address Rafael's specific behavior problems, working in small groups with tutoring by peers, and multisensory instructional techniques that are often used in special education classes.

As to the behavioral problems Rafael experienced in the kindergarten class in 1989–90, Dr. McGregor testified that those problems could be contained through use of adequate supplementary aids and services (such as those described above), which, she explained, had not been provided for Rafael in the kindergarten class.

Dr. McGregor also testified that it is extremely important for a child like Rafael to learn to work and communicate with nondisabled peers, and that this type of learning could only be provided by including him as much as possible in a regular classroom. Finally, Dr. McGregor testified that she did not observe any opportunities for Rafael to interact with nondisabled students in the Winslow program.

witness, Thomas Nolan, a teacher and special education specialist who had taught a child with Down's syndrome in a regular classroom, because he too had not had day-to-day experience with Rafael.[10] The ALJ thus concluded that the Winlsow placement was in compliance with IDEA.

C. The Proceedings Before the District Court

Seeking independent review of the ALJ's decision pursuant to 20 U.S.C. § 1415(e)(2), the Obertis filed this civil action in the United States District Court for the District of New Jersey. In addition to the IDEA claim, the Obertis pleaded a claim of unlawful discrimination under § 504 of the Rehabilitation Act of 1973, 29 U.S.C. § 729. Soon thereafter, the court denied both parties' motions for summary judgment, finding "genuine issues of material fact...about the feasibility of including Rafael in a regular classroom setting now."....

In May of 1992, the district court held a three-day bench trial, receiving new evidence from both parties to supplement the state agency record. See 20 U.S.C. § 1415(e)(2).[11] The Obertis presented the testimony of two additional experts who had not testified in the administrative proceedings: Dr. Lou Brown, a professor of special education at the University of Wisconsin, and Amy Goldman, an expert in communication with children with developmental disabilities.

Dr. Brown, who over the past twenty years has been a consultant to hundreds of school districts throughout the country regarding the education of severely disabled children, interviewed and evaluated Rafael on two occasions, and reviewed Rafael's educational records, as well as a set of videotapes showing Rafael at age seven working with his mother, being taught by a language professional, and participating in a Sunday school class with nondisabled children. Dr. Brown testified that he saw no reason why Rafael could not be educated at that time in a regular classroom with appropriate supplementary aids and services. He told the court that if such aids and services were provided, he had no reason to believe that Rafael would be disruptive at that time (more than two years after the experience in the Clementon kindergarten class). He also stated that integrating Rafael in a regular class at his local school would enable Rafael to develop social relationships with nondisabled students and to learn by imitating appropriate role models, important benefits which could not be realized in a segregated, special education setting.

Dr. Brown outlined a number of commonly applied strategies which could be used, in combination, by the School District to integrate Rafael in a regular classroom....

---

[10] In addition to the two experts, the Obertis presented the testimony of both of Rafael's parents, who testified that from their experience with and understanding of their son, they were convinced that Rafael would be successful in a regular classroom with adequate aids and services. Jeanne Oberti testified that she believed the segregated Winslow class had a negative emotional impact on Rafael, who would cry regularly before boarding the bus for the 45 minute trip to Winslow. She also testified that she and her husband understood that Rafael could not be expected to master the curriculum in a regular class in the same way as the nondisabled students, but that they did not believe Rafael should be excluded for that reason. Michelle Zbrozek, a neighbor of the Obertis and a parent of a nondisabled child in the Clementon kindergarten class, testified that her son played with Rafael and other neighborhood children and that she believed Rafael and the nondisabled children learned from each other by working and playing together....The ALJ considered this testimony but was nonetheless convinced by the School District's witnesses that Rafael's behavior problems in the kindergarten class during the 1989-90 school year precluded an integrated placement at that time.

[11] 20 U.S.C. § 1415(e)(2) provides in part: ...the court shall receive the records of the administrative proceedings, shall hear additional evidence at the request of a party, and, basing its decision on the preponderance of the evidence, shall grant such relief as the court determines is appropriate.

* * *

In August of 1992, after reviewing all of this new evidence along with the evidence that had been adduced at the administrative proceedings, the district court issued its decision, finding that the School District had failed to establish by a preponderance of the evidence that Rafael could not at that time be educated in a regular classroom with supplementary aids and services. The court therefore concluded that the School District had violated IDEA....

In particular, the court was persuaded by the Obertis' experts that many of the special education techniques used in the Winslow class could be implemented in a regular classroom....The court also found that the School District did not make reasonable efforts to include Rafael in a regular classroom with supplementary aids and services (*e.g.*, an itinerant teacher trained in aiding students with mental retardation, a behavior management program, modification of the regular curriculum to accommodate Rafael, and special education training and consultation for the regular teacher); that Rafael's behavior problems during the 1989–90 school year in the developmental kindergarten class were largely the result of the School District's failure to provide adequate supplementary aids and services; and that the record did not support the School District's contention that Rafael would present similar behavior problems at that time (more than two years after the kindergarten class) if included in a regular classroom setting with adequate aids and services....

* * *

II. THE MAINSTREAMING REQUIREMENT OF IDEA

The Education for All Handicapped Children Act (IDEA's predecessor statute) was enacted in 1975 in response to a Congressional finding that "more than half of the children with disabilities in the United States do not receive appropriate educational services." 20 U.S.C. § 1400(b)(3);...The Act provides federal funds to participating states for the education of children with disabilities....As a condition of receiving these funds, states must have "in effect a policy that assures all children with disabilities the right to a free appropriate public education."....

In *Board of Educ. v. Rowley*, 458 U.S. 176, 188–89 (1982), the Supreme Court held that a "free appropriate public education" under the Act "consists of educational instruction specially designed to meet the unique needs of the handicapped child, supported by such services as are necessary to permit the child 'to benefit' from the instruction." This court in turn interpreted Rowley to require the state to offer children with disabilities individualized education programs that provide more than a trivial or de minimis educational benefit. *Polk v. Central Susquehanna Intermediate Unit 16*, 853 F.2d 171, 180–85 (3d Cir. 1988), cert. denied, 488 U.S. 1030 (1989).[16]

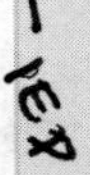

[16] The "centerpiece" of the Act is the "individualized education program" or IEP, see 20 U.S.C. §§ 1401(19), 1414(a)(5);..."The IEP consists of a detailed written statement arrived at by a multi-disciplinary team summarizing the child's abilities, outlining the goals for the child's education and specifying the services the child will receive." Polk, 853 F.2d at 173. The IEP must include, among other things, a statement of the child's current level of educational performance, annual goals for the child, specific educational services to be provided, and the extent to which the child will participate in regular educational programs....The Act imposes numerous procedural safeguards to ensure proper development of the IEP and to protect the rights of parents and guardians to challenge the IEP....The Obertis do not claim that the School District has failed to comply with any of these procedural requirements; rather, their claim concerns the Act's substantive requirements.

In addition to the free appropriate education requirement, IDEA provides that states must establish

> procedures to assure that, to the maximum extent appropriate, children with disabilities...are educated with children who are not disabled, and that special classes, separate schooling, or other removal of children with disabilities from the regular educational environment occurs only when the nature and severity of the disability is such that education in regular classes with the use of supplementary aids and services cannot be achieved satisfactorily....

20 U.S.C. § 1412(5)(B).[17] As numerous courts have recognized, this provision sets forth a "strong congressional preference" for integrating children with disabilities in regular classrooms....

* * *

...[C]ourts must be careful to avoid imposing their view of preferable educational methods upon the States."....We are mindful that the Act leaves questions of educational policy to state and local officials....On the other hand, as the Supreme Court recognized in *Rowley*, the Act specifically "requires participating States to educate handicapped children with nonhandicapped children whenever possible."....It is our duty to enforce that statutory requirement....

* * *

A third factor the court should consider in determining whether a child with disabilities can be educated satisfactorily in a regular classroom is the possible negative effect the child's inclusion may have on the education of the other children in the regular classroom. While inclusion of children with disabilities in regular classrooms may benefit the class as a whole,...a child with disabilities may be "so disruptive in a regular classroom that the education of other students is significantly impaired."....

In sum, in determining whether a child with disabilities can be educated satisfactorily in a regular class with supplemental aids and services (the first prong of the two-part mainstreaming test we adopt today), the court should consider several factors, including: (1) whether the school district has made reasonable efforts to accommodate the child in a regular classroom; (2) the educational benefits available to the child in a regular class, with appropriate supplementary aids and services, as compared to the benefits provided in a special education class; and (3) the possible negative effects of the inclusion of the child on the education of the other students in the class.[25]

---

[17] The federal and state regulations include a similar mandate that children with disabilities be educated in the "least restrictive environment."...:

(b) Each public agency shall insure:

(1) That to the maximum extent appropriate, handicapped children...are educated with children who are not handicapped, and

(2) That special classes, separate schooling or other removal of handicapped children from the regular educational environment occurs only when the nature or severity of the handicap is such that education in regular classes with the use of supplementary aids and services cannot be achieved satisfactorily.

[25] Additional factors may be relevant depending on the circumstances of the specific case. For example, other courts have considered cost as a relevant factor in determining compliance with the Act's mainstreaming requirement....Since the parties have not raised cost as an issue, we do not consider it here....

* * *

III. BURDEN OF PROOF UNDER IDEA's MAINSTREAMING REQUIREMENT

Before we apply the two-part analysis discussed above to the facts in this case, we must address the School District's argument that the district court improperly placed the burden of proof under the Act on it. In the School District's view, while it may have had the initial burden at the state administrative level of justifying its educational placement, once the agency decided in its favor, the burden should have shifted to the parents who challenged the agency decision in the district court. Courts must place the burden on the party seeking to reverse the agency decision, the School District argues, in order to effectuate IDEA's requirement that "due weight shall be given to [the state administrative] proceedings,"...We disagree.

IDEA instructs district courts and state trial courts reviewing the decisions of state educational agencies to "receive the records of the administrative proceedings,...hear additional evidence at the request of a party, and, basing its decision on the preponderance of the evidence,...grant such relief as the court determines is appropriate."....As construed by the Supreme Court in *Rowley*, § 1415(e)(2) requires courts to give "due weight" to the agency proceedings. Rowley, 458 U.S. at 206,...However, neither Rowley nor the Act itself specifically addresses which party bears the burden of proof at the district court level, an issue which we believe is quite different from the district court's obligation to afford due weight to the administrative proceedings.

* * *

B. Application of the Daniel R.R. test

* * *

Although the School District presented ample evidence of Rafael's disruptive behavior in the 1989–90 kindergarten class, the Obertis' evidence supports the district court's finding that Rafael would not have had such severe behavior problems had he been provided with adequate supplementary aids and services in that kindergarten class, and that Rafael (who at the time of the district court trial was two years older than when he attended the kindergarten class) would most likely not present such problems if he were included in a regular class at that time. We therefore conclude that the district court's findings on this issue are not clearly erroneous, and, accordingly, that consideration of the possible negative effects of Rafael's presence on the regular classroom environment does not support the School District's decision to exclude him from the regular classroom.

* * *

For all of these reasons, we agree with the district court's conclusion that the School District did not meet its burden of proving by a preponderance of the evidence that Rafael could not be educated satisfactorily in a regular classroom with supplementary aids and services. We will therefore affirm the district court's decision that the School District has violated the mainstreaming requirement of IDEA. Because we have come to this conclusion based on application of the first part of the *Daniel R.R.* two-part test, we need not apply the second part of the test (whether the child has been included in programs with nondisabled children whenever possible)....We note, however, that in the event that the Child Study Team were to determine in designing an IEP for Rafael in the future that education in a regular classroom with supplementary aids and services could not be achieved satisfactorily at that time and therefore would not be required under

IDEA, the Team would then have to satisfy the second part of the *Daniel R.R.* test, ensuring that Rafael is included in regular school programs with nondisabled students whenever possible.[30]

* * *

The order of the district court will be affirmed.

---

[30] We also note that, as the Obertis'counsel acknowledged at oral argument, inclusion in regular academic classes may become less appropriate for Rafael, given his cognitive disability, as he reaches the higher grades. Dr. Brown testified before the district court:

> ...as Rafael—children [with similar disabilities] all over this country, as they increase in chronological age, they spend more and more of their time learning to function in non-school settings; in respected, valued integrated settings like vocational environments. Rafael, as he gets older, will have to leave school and learn how to function in a real job as part of his school program.

Questions for Discussion

1. Can the district argue that economies of scale dictate the movement of children with like disabilities into a single program, *e.g.,* one nine-person special class with two instructors rather than nine separate tutors? Are the two teachers in such a system likely to be more qualified than would be the case with nine separate persons required?

2. If separate one-on-one treatment costs substantial monies, will it lessen services to other students? What obligation do we owe other students in terms of balanced resources? Do students who demonstrate genius potential warrant special investment? Are they likely to manifest a special return on such an investment? Is it necessary to make such choices, *i.e.*, why would funding necessarily come from the same pot? Can the benefit of investment in special needs children versus gifted children be compared to alternatives such as military weapons spending, agricultural subsidies, or major tax expenditures?

3. Is mainstreaming appropriate even if it "holds the other students back?" What benefits accrue to other children from contact with their special needs peers? How do you balance those benefits against possible educational distraction?

4. How does the *Oberti* child prove he is ready for mainstreaming if the evidence is confined to prior behavior? Are such children likely to be in a catch-22 once they are removed from the general student body?

5. What if the school district proposed to remove the student from the neighborhood school where he was being "mainstreamed" to another school at a greater distance because it included a program for his disability? Would the school district be able to take advantage of the economies of scale of the alternative school (so an individual tutor would not be required)? Would it be considered "mainstreaming" if the new school had a substantial population of nondisabled students who would be in contact with the IDEA student? See *Murray v. Montrose County School District RE-1J*, 51 F.3d 921 (10th Cir., 1995).

6. How important for this child was the additional evidence provided by two expert witnesses added at the trial court level? How important was the law's instruction that education be provided in regular classes "where possible?" How important was the preponderance of evidence test employed? Are many children in a position to mount such an empirically rich case?

Florence County School District Four v. Carter
510 U.S. 7 (1993)

JUSTICE O'CONNOR delivered the opinion of the Court.

The Individuals with Disabilities Education Act (IDEA),...20 U.S.C. § 1400 *et seq*..., requires States to provide disabled children with a "free appropriate public education,"...This case presents the question whether a court may order reimbursement for parents who unilaterally withdraw their child from a public school that provides an inappropriate education under IDEA and put the child in a private school that provides an education that is otherwise proper under IDEA, but does not meet all the requirements of § 1401(a)(18). We hold that the court may order such reimbursement, and therefore affirm the judgment of the Court of Appeals.

I

Respondent Shannon Carter was classified as learning disabled in 1985, while a ninth grade student in a school operated by petitioner Florence County School District Four. School officials met with Shannon's parents to formulate an individualized education program (IEP) for Shannon, as required under IDEA....The IEP provided that Shannon would stay in regular classes except for three periods of individualized instruction per week, and established specific goals in reading and mathematics of four months' progress for the entire school year. Shannon's parents were dissatisfied, and requested a hearing to challenge the appropriateness of the IEP....Both the local educational officer and the state educational agency hearing officer rejected Shannon's parents' claim and concluded that the IEP was adequate. In the meantime, Shannon's parents had placed her in Trident Academy, a private school specializing in educating children with disabilities. Shannon began at Trident in September 1985 and graduated in the spring of 1988.

Shannon's parents filed this suit in July 1986, claiming that the school district had breached its duty under IDEA to provide Shannon with a "free appropriate public education,"...and seeking reimbursement for tuition and other costs incurred at Trident. After a bench trial, the District Court ruled in the parents' favor....

* * *

I

In *School Comm. of Burlington v. Department of Ed. of Mass.*, 471 U.S. 359...(1985), we held that IDEA's grant of equitable authority empowers a court "to order school authorities to reimburse parents for their expenditures on private special education for a child if the court ultimately determines that such placement, rather than a proposed IEP, is proper under the Act." Congress intended that IDEA's promise of a "free appropriate public education" for disabled children would normally be met by an IEP's provision for education in the regular public schools or in private schools chosen jointly by school officials and parents. In cases where cooperation fails, however, "parents who disagree with the proposed IEP are faced with a choice: go along with the IEP to the detriment of their child if it turns out to be inappropriate or pay for what they consider to be the appropriate placement."....For parents willing and able to make the latter choice, "it would be an empty victory to have a court tell them several years later that they were right but that these expenditures could not in a proper case be reimbursed by the school officials."....Because such a result would be contrary to IDEA's guarantee of a "free appropriate public education," we held that "Congress meant to include retroactive reimbursement to parents as an available remedy in a proper case."....

As this case comes to us, two issues are settled: 1) the school district's proposed IEP was inappropriate under IDEA, and 2) although Trident did not meet the § 1401(a)(18) requirements, it provided an education otherwise proper under IDEA. This case presents the narrow question whether Shannon's parents are barred from reimbursement because the private school in which Shannon enrolled did not meet the § 1401(a)(18) definition of a "free appropriate public education."* We hold that they are not, because § 1401(a)(18)'s requirements cannot be read as applying to parental placements.

Section 1401(a)(18)(A) requires that the education be "provided at public expense, under public supervision and direction." Similarly, § 1401(a)(18)(D) requires schools to provide an IEP, which must be designed by "a representative of the local educational agency,"...and must be "established," "revised," and "reviewed" by the agency, § 1414(a)(5). These requirements do not make sense in the context of a parental placement. In this case, as in all *Burlington* reimbursement cases, the parents' rejection of the school district's proposed IEP is the very reason for the parents' decision to put their child in a private school. In such cases, where the private placement has necessarily been made over the school district's objection, the private school education will not be under "public supervision and direction." Accordingly, to read the § 1401(a)(18) requirements as applying to parental placements would effectively eliminate the right of unilateral withdrawal recognized in *Burlington*. Moreover, IDEA was intended to ensure that children with disabilities receive an education that is both appropriate and free....To read the provisions of § 1401(a)(18) to bar reimbursement in the circumstances of this case would defeat this statutory purpose.

Nor do we believe that reimbursement is necessarily barred by a private school's failure to meet state education standards. Trident's deficiencies, according to the school district, were that it employed at least two faculty members who were not state-certified and that it did not develop IEPs....

* * *

III

The school district also claims that allowing reimbursement for parents such as Shannon's puts an unreasonable burden on financially strapped local educational authorities. The school district argues that requiring parents to choose a state-approved private school if they want reimbursement is the only meaningful way to allow States to control costs; otherwise States will have to reimburse dissatisfied parents for any private school that provides an education that is

---

* Section 1401(a)(18) defines "free appropriate public education" as, "special education and related services that

(A) have been provided at public expense, under public supervision and direction, and without charge,

(B) meet the standards of the State educational agency,

(C) include an appropriate preschool, elementary, or secondary school education in the State involved, and

(D) are provided in conformity with the individualized education program...."

proper under the Act, no matter how expensive it may be.

There is no doubt that Congress has imposed a significant financial burden on States and school districts that participate in IDEA. Yet public educational authorities who want to avoid reimbursing parents for the private education of a disabled child can do one of two things: give the child a free appropriate public education in a public setting, or place the child in an appropriate private setting of the State's choice. This is IDEA's mandate, and school officials who conform to it need not worry about reimbursement claims.

* * *

Accordingly, we affirm the judgment of the Court of Appeals.

So ordered.

Questions for Discussion

1. The *Florence* child was given an IEP for ninth grade in 1985. The decision was handed down in 1993. Given this timing, how important is the parental option to provide required services immediately and obtain recompense? How does the *Florence* precedent work for the vast majority of parents who cannot afford to up-front finance a private alternative?

2. Can parents receive a "blank check" where the school district fails to provide a program fully complying with IDEA? Should parents be required to pursue IDEA specified remedies prior to the pursuit of a private alternative with *post hoc* public funding? Should administrative/court remedies include timelines for expeditious resolution? Should such timelines bind the courts in their review?

3. What discretion do parents have to choose their private alternative? Should a district failing to provide required services be strictly liable for alternative expenses? In *Florence,* the Trident school allegedly failed to meet some state standards. What if the child had not done well? Do we know that the child may have achieved better results in other settings? Do we know whether the child would have done as well under the District's plans?

Cedar Rapids Community School District v. Garret F.
526 U.S. 66 (1999)

MR. JUSTICE STEVENS delivered the opinion of the Court, Justices Thomas and Kennedy dissenting.

...The question presented in this case is whether the definition of "related services" in [the Individuals with Disabilities Education Act (IDEA)][1] requires a public school district in a participating State to provide a ventilator-dependent

---

[1] "The term 'related services' means transportation, and such developmental, corrective, and other supportive services (including speech pathology and audiology, psychological

terms of what a licensed physician does. However, isn't a licensed physician exclusively authorized to "practice medicine?" Here, a body of law prohibits others from "unauthorized practice of medicine". Does such a "scope of practice" definition apply to auto mechanics? Or to the other dissent example: food preparation?

2. The dissent proposes an alternative test: that medical services exempt from IDEA funding be broadly defined, but that it include those services provided to *non*-handicapped students which are medical in nature, such as those provided by school nurses. However, what is the "medical services" definition proposed by the dissent? Is it ascertainable? What if a school does not have a school nurse, or the only nurse is busy with non-handicapped children and the extensive services provided by the handicapped will require hiring additional nurses?

3. If you were drafting amendments to IDEA, would you want to consider allowing IDEA "medical service funding" where it affirmatively saved education funds otherwise required? For example, assume that a special needs student could eliminate a disability with a major operation and hence save all future special education costs. Assume that the operation (or other medical cure) costs less than the special education costs to be saved. Assume that the child's parents do not qualify for public medical subsidy and cannot afford the operation. Should those medical expenses then be included within the scope of IDEA?

Note on IDEA Improvement Act of 2004

The Congress amended the IDEA statute through the Individual with Disabilities Education Improvement Act of 2004. Some of the changes were supported by child advocates, including the following:

- New language instructs use of "research-based teaching methods" allowing empirical results as a guidepost.
- The amendments broaden the scope of intervention to "maximizing a child's potential" and meeting "developmental" goals beyond mere instruction, and including "related services" such as speech, occupational and physical therapy, counseling, and behavior intervention services. The IEP must include "functional goals" beyond academics where applicable.
- The mandate now includes preparing students for "further education" beyond public school.
- A foster child's foster parent is a "parent" for IDEA purposes, ending denials of services based on confusion over who had the authority to speak for these children—although still leaving uncertain in some jurisdictions who speaks for the child in the group home foster setting.
- Early intervention is authorized (eliminating the "wait first for the child to fail" problem), and that intervention may be authorized pre-school (from birth to three years of age).

Three aspects of the 2004 statutory changes were opposed by child advocates:

- School districts are given wide latitude to change child placements where students violate the applicable "code of student conduct."

• A new layer of administrative delay has been interposed after the request for hearing by the parent. Instead of a 45 day timeline for hearing on the IEP, a "resolution" session must be held within 15 days at the request of either party. More important, attorney's fees are not available for these sessions—discouraging legal representation of children and facilitating possible adhesive influence by school districts.

• Of related and greater concern, the amendments allow the school authorities to seek attorney's fees from the child's counsel or parents where the child does not prevail. Such fees are limited to circumstances where the school district can show that the request for hearing was frivolous, unreasonable or without foundation, or if the child's attorney is shown to have litigated beyond what was needed, or presented issues for an improper purpose. Child advocates argue that it is relatively easy for a prevailing school district (or any party) to argue that the rejected case presented by the child's attorney was "without foundation" or was litigated "beyond what was needed." After all, if the attorney's position is rejected, was its advocacy "founded" or "needed"? Child advocates note that under previous IDEA law, those attorneys representing parents without wealth undertook substantial work only with the prospect of fees if they prevailed. The added element of out-of-pocket loss to a state agency based on its substantial hourly fees to its counsel is not a common feature of American law where citizens challenge government and serves to markedly chill representation of children.

Schaffer v. Jerry Weast

___U.S.___(2005) (2005 U.S. LEXIS 8554)

Justice O'Connor delivered the opinion of the Court:

The Individuals with Disabilities Education Act (IDEA or Act), 84 Stat. 175, as amended,...is a Spending Clause statute that seeks to ensure that "all children with disabilities have available to them a free appropriate public education,"....Under IDEA, school districts must create an "individualized education program" (IEP) for each disabled child....If parents believe their child's IEP is inappropriate, they may request an "impartial due process hearing."...The Act is silent, however, as to which party bears the burden of persuasion at such a hearing. We hold that the burden lies, as it typically does, on the party seeking relief.

This case concerns the educational services that were due, under IDEA, to petitioner Brian Schaffer. Brian suffers from learning disabilities and speech-language impairments. From prekindergarten through seventh grade he attended a private school and struggled academically. In 1997, school officials informed Brian's mother that he needed a school that could better accommodate his needs. Brian's parents contacted respondent Montgomery County Public Schools System (MCPS) seeking a placement for him for the following school year.

MCPS evaluated Brian and convened an IEP team. The committee generated an initial IEP offering Brian a place in either of two MCPS middle schools. Brian's parents were not satisfied with the arrangement, believing that Brian needed smaller classes and more intensive services. The Schaffers thus enrolled Brian in another private school, and initiated a due process hearing challenging the IEP and seeking compensation for the cost of Brian's subsequent private education.

In Maryland, IEP hearings are conducted by administrative law judges (ALJs).... After a 3-day hearing, the ALJ deemed the evidence close, held that the parents bore the burden of persuasion, and ruled in favor of the school district. The parents brought a civil action challenging the result.

•••

The term "burden of proof" is one of the "slipperiest members of the family of legal terms."... Part of the confusion surrounding the term arises from the fact that historically, the concept encompassed two distinct burdens: the "burden of persuasion," *i.e.*, which party loses if the evidence is closely balanced, and the "burden of production," *i.e.*, which party bears the obligation to come forward with the evidence at different points in the proceeding....We note at the outset that this case concerns only the burden of persuasion.

•••

We therefore begin with the ordinary default rule that plaintiffs bear the risk of failing to prove their claims....

•••

Petitioners contend first that a close reading of IDEA's text compels a conclusion in their favor. They urge that we should interpret the statutory words "due process" in light of their constitutional meaning, and apply the balancing test established by *Mathews* v. *Eldridge,* 424 U.S. 319 (1976). Even assuming that the Act incorporates constitutional due process doctrine, *Eldridge* is no help to petitioners, because "outside the criminal law area, where special concerns attend, the locus of the burden of persuasion is normally not an issue of federal constitutional moment."

•••

Petitioners also urge that putting the burden of persuasion on school districts will further IDEA's purposes because it will help ensure that children receive a free appropriate public education. In truth, however, very few cases will be in evidentiary equipoise. Assigning the burden of persuasion to school districts might encourage schools to put more resources into preparing IEPs and presenting their evidence. But IDEA is silent about whether marginal dollars should be allocated to litigation and administrative expenditures or to educational services. Moreover, there is reason to believe that a great deal is already spent on the administration of the Act. Litigating a due process complaint is an expensive affair, costing schools approximately $ 8,000-to-$ 12,000 per hearing....Congress has also repeatedly amended the Act in order to reduce its administrative and litigation-related costs....

Petitioners in effect ask this Court to assume that every IEP is invalid until the school district demonstrates that it is not. The Act does not support this conclusion. IDEA relies heavily upon the expertise of school districts to meet its goals. It also includes a so-called "stay-put" provision, which requires a child to remain in his or her "then-current educational placement" during the pendency of an IDEA hearing....Congress could have required that a child be given the educational placement that a parent requested during a dispute, but it did no such thing. Congress appears to have presumed instead that, if the Act's procedural requirements are respected, parents will prevail when they have legitimate grievances....Petitioners' most plausible argument is that "the ordinary rule, based on considerations of fairness, does not place the burden upon a litigant of establishing facts peculiarly within the knowledge of his adversary."...But this "rule is far from being universal, and has many qualifications upon its application."...School districts have a "natural advantage" in information and expertise, but Congress addressed this when it obliged schools to safeguard the procedural rights of parents and to share information with them....As noted above, parents have the right to review all records that the school possesses in relation to their child....They also have the right to an "independent educational evaluation of their child." The regulations clarify this entitlement by providing that a "parent has the right to an independent educational evaluation at public expense if the parent disagrees with an evaluation obtained by the public agency."...IDEA thus ensures parents access to an expert who can evaluate all the materials that the school must make available, and who can give an independent opinion. They are not left to challenge the government without a realistic opportunity to access the necessary evidence, or without an expert with the firepower to match the opposition.

Additionally, in 2004, Congress added provisions requiring school districts to answer the subject matter of a complaint in writing, and to provide parents with the reasoning behind the disputed action, details about the other options considered and rejected by the IEP team, and a description of all evaluations, reports, and other factors that the school used in coming to its decision....

• • •

We hold no more than we must to resolve the case at hand: The burden of proof in an administrative hearing challenging an IEP is properly placed upon the party seeking relief. In this case, that party is Brian, as represented by his parents. But the rule applies with equal effect to school districts: If they seek to challenge an IEP, they will in turn bear the burden of persuasion before an ALJ.

Justice Ginsburg, dissenting:

...The IDEA is atypical in this respect: It casts an affirmative, beneficiary-specific obligation on providers of public education. School districts are charged with responsibility to offer to each disabled child an individualized education program (IEP) suitable to the child's special needs.... The proponent of the IEP, it seems to me, is properly called upon to demonstrate its adequacy.

Familiar with the full range of education facilities in the area, and informed by "their experiences with other, similarly-disabled children,"..."the school district is...in a far better position to demonstrate that it has fulfilled [its statutory] obligation than the disabled student's parents are in to show that the school district has failed to do so,"...."In practical terms, the school has an advantage when a dispute arises under the Act: the school has better access to relevant information, greater control over the potentially more persuasive witnesses (those who have been directly involved with the child's education), and greater overall educational expertise than the parents."...[The] parent's obligation "should be merely to place in issue the appropriateness of the IEP. The school board should then bear the burden of proving that the IEP was appropriate. In reaching that result, we have sought to implement the intent of the statutory and regulatory schemes."...

Understandably, school districts striving to balance their budgets, if "left to [their] own devices," will favor educational options that enable them to conserve resources....Saddled with a proof burden in administrative "due process" hearings, parents are likely to find a district-proposed IEP "resistant to challenge."...Placing the burden on the district to show that its plan measures up to the statutorily mandated "free appropriate public education,"...will strengthen school officials' resolve to choose a course genuinely tailored to the child's individual needs.[7]

The Court acknowledges that "assigning the burden of persuasion to school districts might encourage schools to put more resources into preparing IEPs."...Curiously, the Court next suggests that resources spent on developing IEPs rank as "administrative expenditures" not as expenditures for "educational services."...Costs entailed in the preparation of suitable IEPs, however, are the very expenditures necessary to ensure each child covered by IDEA access to a free appropriate education. These outlays surely relate to "educational services." Indeed, a carefully designed IEP may ward off disputes productive of large administrative or litigation expenses.

This case is illustrative. Not until the District Court ruled that the school district had the burden of persuasion did the school design an IEP that met Brian Schaffer's special educational needs....

Notably, nine States, as friends of the Court, have urged that placement of the burden of persuasion on the school district best comports with IDEA's aim....If allocating the burden to school districts would saddle school systems with inordinate costs, it is doubtful that these States would have filed in favor of petitioners....It bears emphasis that "the vast majority of parents whose children require the benefits and protections provided in the IDEA" lack "knowledge about the educational resources available to their [child]" and the "sophistication" to mount an effective case against a district-proposed IEP....In this setting, "the party with the 'bigger guns' also has better access to information, greater expertise, and an affirmative obligation to provide the contested services."...Policy considerations, convenience, and fairness, I think it plain, point in the same direction. Their collective weight warrants a rule requiring a school district, in "due process" hearings, to explain persuasively why its proposed IEP satisfies IDEA's standards. I would therefore reverse the judgment of the Fourth Circuit.

• • •

---

[7] The Court observes that decisions placing "the *entire* burden of persuasion on the opposing party at the *outset* of a proceeding...are extremely rare."...In cases of this order, however,the persuasion burden is indivisible. It must be borne *entirely* by one side or the other: Either the school district must establish the adequacy of the IEP it has proposed or the parents must demonstrate the plan's inadequacy.

Questions for Discussion

1. The majority opinion concludes that whoever challenges the IEP—whether parents or the local educational agency (LEA)—should bear the burden of persuasion, implying symmetry. How often does a school district challenge an IEP that is generally formulated by its own agents?

2. Justice O'Connor emphasizes the collaborative nature of the IDEA process and the costs of litigation. Do these factors commend a burden of persuasion on the child (or parents) or on the LEA? If litigation is expensive, is it not generally more expensive for parents than for the LEA? What should be the impact of the 2004 amendments discussed above (including the lack of pay-

ment for parents' counsel at pre-hearing proceedings, and possible assessment of LEA fees against parents) on the burden of persuasion? Does it signal Congressional intent to rely on LEA judgment? Or does it signal Congressional assumption that obstacles to child (parental) legal access further commend a burden of persuasion on the LEA when a challenge does reach hearing?

3. Is the fact emphasized by Ginsburg of an *amicus* filing by nine states in favor of an LEA burden of persuasion significant? Is it fair to conclude from such a filing that putting the burden of persuasion on the LEA will not involve inordinate costs?

4. The dissent disputes the majority view that IDEA proceedings involve administrative costs, characterizing the development of the IEP as determining the educational content of a child's program. But doesn't this case concern the legal proceedings challenging the IEP, properly characterized as a transaction or process cost separate from the actual delivery of services? How much does the LEA spend per hour on counsel to meet the burden of persuasion before an ALJ or in court versus amount per hour for a child's special education tutor?

ENDNOTES

[1] U.S. Department of Commerce, Economics and Statistics Administration, Bureau of the Census, *Disabilities Affect One-Fifth of All Americans; Proportion Could Increase in Coming Decades* (Dec. 1997) at 1 and 8.

[2] *Id.,* at Table 5; see also *Emotional Disturbance*, National Information Center for Children and Youth with Disabilities (Jan. 2001) at 1, noting that—nationally—463,172 children were provided services in public schools based on diagnosis of serious emotional disturbance in the 1998–99 school year (citing the U.S. Department of Education's 2000 annual report); see http://www.nichcy.org.

[3] Centers for Disease Control, National Center for Health Statistics, *Health, United States, 2004* (Hyattsville, MD; 2004) at Table 46.

[4] Centers for Disease Control, *Morbidity and Mortality Weekly Report*, Vol. 53, No. 22 (Washington, D.C., June 11, 2004).

[5] Centers for Disease Control, National Center for Injury Prevention and Control, *Suicide Fact Sheet* (Atlanta, GA; Oct. 13, 2005) (see www.cdc.gov/ncipc/factsheets/suifacts.htm).

[6] A. B. Wilson, *Longitudinal Analysis of Diet, Physical Growth, Verbal Development and School Performance*, in Balderston, *et al.* (eds.) MALNOURISHED CHILDREN OF THE RURAL POOR (Auburn House, Boston) at 40.

[7] See, *e.g.*, H. E. Freeman, R. E. Klein, J. W. Townsend, and A. Lechtig, *Nutritional and Cognitive Development Among Rural Guatemalan Children*, AM. J. PUB. HEALTH (1980) at 1277–85.

[8] Information about the effects of nutrition deficits on children's development are summarized in Tufts University School of Nutrition Science and Policy, Center on Hunger, Poverty and Nutrition Policy, *The Link Between Nutrition and Cognitive Development in Children* (Medford, MA; 1995). See also J. Larry Brown and Ernesto Pollitt, *Malnutrition, Poverty and Intellectual Development*, SCIENTIFIC AMERICAN (February 1996) at 38–43.

[9] William A. Vega, Ph.D., Bohdan Kolody, Ph.D., Jimmy Hwang, Ph.D., and Amanda Noble, Ph.D., *Prevalence and Magnitude of Perinatal Substance Exposures in California*, 329:12 NEW ENG. J. MED. 850, at 853 (Sept. 16, 1993).

[10] *Id.* at 852–54.

[11] Robert Mathias, National Institute on Drug Abuse, *NIDA Survey Provides First National Data on Drug Use During Pregnancy,* NIDA NOTES (January/February 1995).

[12] *Id.* Note that the American Lung Association reported the level nationally at 20.4% in 1990. The decline to 13.6% by 1996 is significant, but given the ability of nicotine and carbon monoxide to pass through the placenta, remains of great concern. It is unclear, given increases in smoking by young women through the 1980s and 1990s, whether the decrease from the 1990 level to 1996 reflects lower smoking incidence, or lower self-reporting from increased recognition of the hazards posed to their children and the self-guilt an admission implies. See *Smoking and Pregnancy*, Fact Sheet, American Lung Association (April 13, 2000) (available at http://www.lungusa.org/tobacco/ pregnancy_factsheet.html).

[13] American Speech-Language-Hearing Association, *Fetal Alcohol Syndrome* (1996).

[14] *Id.*

[15] Centers for Disease Control, *Fetal Alcohol Syndrome* (Atlanta, GA; Sept. 29, 2005) at 1–2 (see www.cdc.gov/ncbddd/fas/faqs.htm).

[16] *Fetal Alcohol Syndrome in Our Community*, Online Clinic, 1999 (available at http://www.online-clinic.com/community.html).

[17] Centers for Disease Control and Prevention, Morbidity and Mortality Weekly Report, *Blood Lead Levels in Young Children—United States and Selected States, 1996–1999* (Dec. 22, 2000) available at http://www.cdc.gov/mmwr/preview/mmwrhtml/mm4950a3.htm.

[18] California Department of Health Services, *Lead Hazards in California's Public Elementary Schools and Child Care Facilities* (Sacramento, CA; 1998).

[19] Centers for Disease Control, Morbidity and Mortality Weekly Report, *Blood Lead Levels—United States, 1999–2002*, 54(20);513-516 (Atlanta, GA; May 27, 2005) at 1 (see www.cdc.gov/mmwr/preview/mmwrhtml/mm5420a5.htm).

[20] See Lawrie Mott, Natural Resources Defense Council, *Our Children at Risk: The Five Worst Environmental Threats to Their Health* (New York, NY; 1997) at 12, citing P. Mushak, *et al., Prenatal and Postnatal Effects of Low-Level Lead Exposure: Integrated Summary of a Report to the U.S. Congress on Childhood Lead Poisoning,* 50 Env. Res. (1989) at 11–36; see also P. Baghurst, *et al., Exposure to Environmental Lead and Visual-Motor Integration at Age 7 Years: The Port Pirie Cohort Study*, 6:2 Epidemiology (March 1995) at 104–09.

[21] *Exposure to Environmental Lead, supra* note 20, at 4–09.

[22] See *Our Children at Risk, supra* note 20, at 13.

[23] Herbert L. Needleman, M.D.; Julie A. Riess, Ph.D.; Michael J. Tobin, Ph.D.; Gretchen E. Biesecker; Joel B. Greenhouse, Ph.D., *Bone Lead Levels and Delinquent Behavior*, 275:5 JAMA 363 (Feb. 7, 1996). The study focused on 11-year-old boys.

[24] Autistic spectrum disorders include autism, Aspergers Disorder, and PDD-NOS (Pervasive Developmental Disorder - Not Otherwise Specified).

[25] Testimony of Lee Grossman, Committee on Government Reform, U.S. House of Representatives, *Hearing on Autism* (April 18, 2002), citing 2001 CDC data.

[26] California Department of Developmental Services, *Changes in the Population of Persons with Autism and Pervasive Developmental Disorders in California's Developmental Services System: 1987 through 1998,* Report to the Legislature (March 1, 1999).

[27] The most effective single therapy thus far has been the "ABA" (Applied Behavior Analysis) method developed by Ivar Lovaas to teach autistic children. Its use involves intensive, mostly one-on-one therapy. Its success, together with diet alteration, vitamin and some drug therapy, has increased the percentage of children able to attend school with normal children and to live somewhat independently. Some treatment results suggest that up to 50% of children subject to intensive and early therapy of more than 40 hours per week of such therapy can be mainstreamed into public schools and become significantly contributing adults. Importantly, the more common commitment of ten or fewer hours per week of therapy does not yield a consistently measurable gain for these children. The cost of the required intensive treatment is substantial and is not assuredly available for autistic U.S. children, notwithstanding its high long-term benefit-cost ratio. For more information, see http://www.feat.org, http://www.autism.org, or http://www.autism-society.org.

[28] This estimate is based on a per-person cost of $40,000, based on the range of current incidence of from 500,000 to 1,500,000 individuals with autism. The 2010 estimate assumes continued growth at current rates. See Testimony of Lee Grossman, *supra* note 25. Mr. Grossman, President of the Autism Society of America, places the high estimate at $300 billion by 2010.

[29] Department of Health and Human Services, National Institute of Mental Health, *Report to Congress on Autism* (Dec. 2003) at 1–4. For current information about autism, see www.nimb.nih.gov or www.feat.org.

[30] See 42 USC § 9801, 45 CFR § 1301.

[31] See Legislative Analyst's Office, *Federal Welfare Reform (H.R. 3734): Fiscal Effect on California* (Sacramento, CA; Aug. 20, 1996) at 19.

[32] See Judge David L. Bazelon Center for Mental Health Law, *New Rules for Children's SSI Program* (Washington, D.C.; Feb. 11, 1997) at 2.

[33] *Id.*, at 1–2.

[34] *Id.*, at 5.

[35] See U.S. General Accounting Office, *Social Security: New Functional Assessments for Children Raise Eligibility Questions* (GAO/HEHS-95-66) (Washington, D.C.; March 1995) at 18; see also *Study: Kids on SSI Not Faking*, Sacramento Bee, May 8, 1995, at A-9 (separate study by National Academy of Social Insurance contradicts claims that parents are coaching children to gain eligibility for SSI).

[36] Prepared Statement of Robert E. Cooke, MD, Before the Senate Finance Committee/Social Security and Family Policy Subcommittee, July 7, 1998.

[37] For a detailed discussion of the elimination of children with serious asthmatic conditions, see Chris Palamountain, National Center for Youth Law, *Children with Asthma Prove Vulnerable to SSI Cuts*, XIX:1 Youth Law News (San Francisco, CA; January–February 1998) at 1–8.

[38] See David Lash, *Cease Fire*, L.A. Daily J. (Jan. 22, 1998) at 6.

[39] H.R. 5, Pub. L. No. 105-17, the IDEA Improvement Act of 1997.

CHAPTER SEVEN

Child Care

A. CHILD CARE DEMOGRAPHICS

1. Demand

Child care is divided into two markets: full-time child care for children under five years of age, and part-time (usually after school) care for older children. Full-time child care is in turn divided into two submarkets: full-day infant care and full-day toddler care.

a. U.S. Full Day Infant and Toddler Care

Children may enter organized child care as early as six weeks of age and remain in full day care until kindergarten, sometimes with the option of nursery or preschool for three or four year olds. The growth of preschool has been driven by the radical change in demographics partly discussed in Chapter 2, including the growth of unwed births and other single parent families, higher real estate (and rent) costs requiring more than one income in a two-parent household, and the concomitant growth in the employment of mothers. Currently, sixty-five percent of mothers with children under 6 are in the labor force.[1] Less than 25% of families with these preschool children conform to the historical model of one parent working and one parent at home.[2] Twelve million American preschoolers are in child care, another twelve million are income-eligible for child care assistance but do not receive it due to the block grant structure limiting allocation (see budget discussion in Chapter 1). The preschoolers with working mothers are now cared for by parents, relatives, or friends (57.5%), in-home (non-relative) care for the more affluent (3.3%), child care centers (22.1%), and licensed family child care providers (16.9%).[3] Census data place 45,000 preschoolers in "self-care," 432,000 cared for by a "sibling", and 565,000 with "no regular arrangement."[4]

The census data breakdown by income and race confirm the thesis of advocates that non-relative family child care remains either unaffordable or is unavailable for minority parents (*i.e.*, available slots are not located in urban low-income neighborhoods), that Head Start has yet to be embraced by or is unavailable to Hispanic parents, and that relatives of minority children bear a substantial child care burden.

b. U.S. Part-time Care for Children 5 to 14 Years of Age

Part-time child care for children in school is also driven by maternal employment. Of the 38.8 million U.S. children between 5 and 14 years of age, only

14.4 million have a parent at home who is neither working nor in school.[5] Public schools provide some 18,000 after-school care programs nationally.[6] However, 70% of U.S. public schools fail to offer any significant services.[7] Accordingly, experts cite census data to estimate that over 6 million children spend substantial time in "latchkey status"—home alone without adult supervision.[8]

The National Center for Education Statistics finds that 20% of children in kindergarten though eighth grade had regularly scheduled nonparental arrangements before school in 2001, and 50% had such arrangements after school. The most common after-school programs were center or school-based (19%), relative care (17%), and self-care (13%). Few of these elementary and middle school children were in the care of a nonrelative (6%) or in supervised extracurricular activities such as sports (7%). The children with regular weekly before school arrangements spent an average of one hour a day there, and those with after-school programs spent two hours a day. Important differences delineate the races, with African American children more likely to be cared for a relative or in "self-care."[9] Many of the relative providers are grandparents (52%), and a large percentage are siblings (21%)—14% of whom are brothers or sisters between the ages of 10 and 12.[10]

c. New Demand from Federal Welfare Reform Requiring Employment

In addition to the current child care demand created by households where both parents work outside the home, additional demand comes from unemployed parents who live below the poverty line and who would require child care in order to work. Federal welfare reform (the 1996 Personal Responsibility and Work Opportunity Reconciliation Act or "PRA") requires such employment by most parents receiving Temporary Assistance to Needy Families (TANF), formerly Aid to Families with Dependent Children (AFDC).

The PRA includes a two-year maximum period before just under 80% of those receiving TANF theoretically must be in a "work activity," and a 60-month lifetime limit on safety net assistance for their children. For the vast majority of parents receiving aid, work will require child care, which the PRA requires states to provide.[11] Literal compliance with the law will require an extraordinary bolus of child care capacity and subsidy if an economic downturn increases unemployment and reinflates TANF rolls.

2. Distribution of Supply

The distribution of supply versus demand is another concern. A study of licensed child care supply in Los Angeles County found the most affluent quarter of communities (by zip code) had more than twice the spaces available to the poorest quarter.[12] In poor areas of Los Angeles, where over one-third of the children live in TANF-receiving homes, there are 10 to 20 children under 6 years of age for every available licensed child care space.[13]

The shortage of licensed spaces is most severe in minority neighborhoods. In an examination of one such neighborhood—with a 59% Latino population—a *Los Angeles Times* investigation found "six slots in licensed day-care centers for every 100 children under 6 years of age"—about one-fifth the rate of spaces/child extant in Burbank or Pasadena, with a middle class population and a 22% Latino make-up.[14]

In October of 2000 the Human Services Alliance released a report on the current undersupply of child care slots in Los Angeles. The report surveyed 500 low income parents and put a human face on the numbers. Virtually all of those surveyed qualify for child care subsidies, but supply does not exist for their use. Of concern, 52% reported that a lack of child care caused them to lose a job, and 68% reported that it impeded them from attempting employment. One half of those surveyed did not have a provider outside the family of any type, although 87% of those without placement were actively seeking it. As the data for California indicates, parents stay home and eschew employment (now required for safety net assistance) or count on family or friends.[15]

3. Child Care Costs

For after-school care, the National Association of Education Statistics survey found that fees paid by parents averaged $5.60 per hour for relative-, center- or school-based care, and $7.90 per hour for non-relative outside care.[16] After-school child care costs from $3,500 to $4,500 per year at the common utilization of two hours a day and up to $6,000 if before school care is required at the rate of one hour per day. Full-day child care for a preschool toddler costs from $5,000 to $8,000 per year; infant care costs from $6,000 to $10,000.[17] A family with two young children and both parents working full-time at minimum wage would have to pay over two-thirds of their take-home pay in such costs—leaving less than $7,000 a year for rent, utilities, food, clothing, and other costs. One quarter of America's families with young children earn less than $25,000 per year, before payroll deductions and child care costs.

The problem becomes a Hobson's dilemma where there is only one parent. A single parent earning minimum wage with a single toddler would pay about 60% of her net pay for child care—leaving just over $5,000 to finance total shelter, food, clothing, and other costs for herself and her child.

B. MAJOR FEDERAL STATUTES

1. Generic Federal Child Care Programs

In 2003, an estimated 2.5 million children were served by all of the federal child care funding streams. These major sources of assistance are the Child Care Development Block Grant (CCDBG), the Temporary Assistance to Needy Families (TANF) block grant, and the Social Services Block Grant. Together, these programs would require service to 2.8 million by 2010 to keep even with general child population growth. However, the number served fell to 2.3 million in 2004, and under current budget plans will fall to 2 million by 2010—with some experts predicting a larger diminution.[18] Under the more conservative projection, child care will suffer a 29% population adjusted reduction over seven years to 2010.

These withdrawals of assistance are related to their means of delivery. The block-grant structure commonly sets a static ceiling on monies available to states for at least five years and commonly for longer periods. They do not usually adjust for inflation and population, accomplishing a gradual, constricting cut of 2%–5% per annum in per capita spending power (see discussion of budget policy in Chapter 1). Further complications affect the TANF block grant source. This grant includes child care grouped with obligations to pay for job search, training, and safety net assistance payments under the PRA. The portion of this grant used for child care reached a peak of $4 billion in 2000, and has declined to $3.5 billion to 2005, with the Congressional Budget Office projecting further raw number reductions. In addition, many states have expended prior surpluses created by TANF caseload decline from 1997 to 2002. Even a small increase in unemployment and TANF need after 2005 could produce extraordinary TANF shortfall. The pressure is likely to be felt disproportionately in child care assistance because the TANF block grant covers a package of welfare-to-work spending (assistance grants, training, job search, etc.). As those expenses increase, child care investment necessarily decreases under the zero-sum block-grant structure.

The largest alternative source of child care funding is the CCDBG noted above, set at $4.8 billion—without raw number increase from 2002. As with block grant static funding in general, this policy will accomplish more than a 20% cut by 2010 in population/inflation adjusted investment. Child advocates contrast the total child care investment nationally (including state supplemental spending) with spending for space exploration, agricultural subsidies, and defense spending. The total federal investment in child care and education is a small fraction of the national financial commitment for homeland security, the Iraq war, or hurricane Katrina (see budget discussion in Chapter 1).

2. Federal Head Start

The federal Head Start program is not a part of the state budget, but is one of the few child-related federal programs administered and funded directly by a federal agency. It has increased modestly since 1989–90, and now serves just over 40% of the eligible population, providing additional "catch-up" preparation for four-year-olds who live in families making under $16,090 per year.[19]

Head Start provides preschool preparation for impoverished children, focusing on three- and four-year-olds about to enroll in the public school system. About 13% of the enrollment consists of children with disabilities. Ninety percent of Head Start teachers have degrees in early childhood education or have obtained a credential or state certificate to teach preschool children. Large numbers of parents participate as volunteers in Head Start classes. Traditionally, Head Start has been a part-day, four-days-per-week program for four-year-olds. It has been expanding its scope gradually to provide full-day coverage to assist parents who need to work full-time, with about 50% of the programs now offering such care.

Another area of expansion is the inclusion of children under 4 years of age. An "Early Head Start" program was initiated by Congress with the reauthorization of the Head Start Act in 1994. However, this program for three-year-olds remains insubstantial in scope, with less than 3% of eligible children covered. The main Head Start program for four-year-olds, despite repeated political promises of universal coverage during its 40-year tenure, still serves less than one-half of the eligible population. Appropriations for Head Start have not increased since 2000 commensurate with inflation/population changes. Fiscal 2004 spending of $6.77 billion would have to increase to $7.3 billion by 2006 to match conservative measures of population growth (1.5%/annum) and inflation (2.5%/annum). Total Head Start funding was $6.84 billion in 2005 and $6.89 billion for 2006.[20] A similar, gradual constriction is predicted to at least 2010 given the Deficiency Act appropriations decisions and priorities of the Congress in 2005–06—obligating reductions for the subsequent five years.

3. Other Federal Programs: 21st Century Learning Center Grants

One substantial federal program approved and expanded after 1998 provides indirect resources to facilitate after-school activities to ease child care burdens to some extent: the 21st Century Learning Centers Program. This program was established by Congress to award grants to rural and inner-city public schools, or consortia of such schools, for projects that benefit the educational, health, and related needs of the community. It is administered by the U.S. Department of Education. Grants awarded under this program fund community learning centers. The program is designed to target funds to high-need low-achieving students where there are high rates of juvenile crime, school violence, and student drug abuse, but where resources for after-school centers are lacking.

By statute, a 21st Century Community Learning Center grant cannot exceed three years. Currently, the average grant size is approximately $500,000 and supports four Centers, at an average cost per Center of approximately $125,000. Annual costs per Center range from $35,000 to $200,000, depending on the array of proposed activities and the availability of additional resources. Funding has been static at $999 million from 2003 to at least 2007, effectuating a 3%–5% adjusted reduction each year.

4. Tax Subsidies

Public subsidies are also provided through federal and state tax credits for child care, based on income eligibility. A family whose income is less than $10,000 annually may claim 30% of their child care costs as a federal tax credit; a family whose income is over $28,000 annually may claim 20%. The maximum tax credit which may be claimed is $2,400 for one child and $4,800 for two or more children.[21] However, it is a nonrefundable credit—that is, it merely offsets tax liability. The working poor who pay little in income taxes receive limited benefit from it, as discussed in Chapter 3 above. Studies of the federal system indicate that the credit benefits relatively few poor families, and extends into the middle class more than do the direct subsidy programs.[22] Some states have similar credit or deduction allowances for child care, but most are modest in amount, are not refundable, and provide little assistance for the children of the working poor.

C. THE PROBLEM OF CHILD CARE PROVISION FOR THE WORKING POOR

Although the federal jurisdiction has increased child care funding as a part of welfare reform, the Congressional Budget Office has estimated that if states simply maintain current spending for the working poor so they can remain on the job and meet the minimum work requirements of TANF recipients, their spending will still be $8.4 billion short over its six-year period.[23] Moreover, two serious problems remain. First, as discussed above, quality child care is not available in the areas where the PRA creates new need. Accordingly, the work requirement is imposed without the assurance of "adequate child care" notwithstanding the theoretical appropriation of funds. As the data show, impoverished parents use relatives, neighbors and latchkey their children. Beyond the latchkeying of children from toddlers to teens, recent studies show lack of parental supervision over teen youth by now-working TANF parents. Most states do not interpret the "adequate child care" assurance to apply to children over 12 years of age—and little assistance is provided for them.

The second problem is the actual diminution of child care for the working poor. In many states, child care is divided into three stages: Stage 1 is six months of child care while a parent is in training for employment; Stage 2 covers those who have obtained work and are transitioning off aid; and Stage 3 consists of those who have been employed more than one year (more than two years in some states). Child care subsidy is provided in theory to meet the full need (assuming availability as noted above) for Stages 1 and 2. But Stage 3 child care is excluded from assured provision. TANF recipients, who receive assistance to leave welfare rolls and for one year post-employment, do not achieve a sudden pay raise of $4,000 to $10,000 in net pay at the one- or two-year mark to pay for child care. Under current practice, most are then cut off from assured child care help under the TANF block grant. They then depend on eligibility as part of the general working poor population from another child care funding source. However, only one in seven eligible children of the working poor receive child care assistance.[24]

Those who receive help from other accounts generally qualify based on income. Those who have been on the TANF rolls are subject to a difficult choice—because where welfare to work has succeeded, their income may be too high to qualify for subsidy, but is likely to be far short of the amount allowing them to pay the full cost of licensed care for even one young child and remain above the poverty line. Those who are forced back (or newly) onto welfare rolls because they are unwilling to latchkey their children and lack relatives or other alternatives to provide care now also face a lifetime limit of 60 months of safety net TANF assistance, as noted in Chapter 3.

The acknowledged goal of welfare reform is to lift families with children above the poverty line and to "self-sufficiency". Such self-sufficiency would require a monthly gross income of $1,900 to $2,900 for the benchmark family of a mother and two children when including average child care costs.[25] However, a single mother of two passing $1,000 per month in income sequentially loses TANF, begins to pick up federal (and some state) tax liability, loses food stamps, progressively loses the Earned Income Tax Credit (EITC), loses eligibility for subsidized school lunches, loses priority for subsidized child care (if available), and loses Medicaid (or picks up premium obligations for child coverage under federal SCHIP).

The major costs impeding self-sufficiency as subsidies drop off at the poverty line are housing and child care. Child care costs are the single largest expense for working parents with two or more young children. Private sector child care coverage for dependents is rare. Hence, shortfall in public child care subsidies creates a ceiling in net income for living expenses for many working poor families. Assistance with this single expense makes self-sufficiency a more realistic prospect—allowing the drop-off of TANF, Food Stamps, school lunch subsidy, and the EITC, and gradually increasing contribution in tax contribution.

D. SUBSIDY OPPORTUNITY: INTERPRETATION OF FEDERAL FAMILY SUPPORT ACT

Miller v. Carlson

768 F. Supp. 1331 (N.D. Cal. 1991)

STANLEY A. WEIGEL, UNITED STATES DISTRICT JUDGE

I. BACKGROUND

Plaintiffs are California recipients of Aid to Families with Dependent Children ("AFDC") who need child care in order to participate in educational or training activities likely to provide them opportunities to secure employment and remove themselves from the welfare rolls. Defendants include the California Department of Social Services ("DSS"), the United States Department of Health and Human Services ("HHS"), and the Directors of DSS, HHS, and the California Department of Finance.

At issue is a provision of the Family Support Act of 1988 which requires all states to guarantee child care to each recipient of AFDC who is participating satisfactorily in an education or training activity approved by the state. 42 U.S.C. § 602(g)(1)(A)(i)(II).

On March 3, 1991, plaintiffs filed a complaint for declaratory and injunctive relief, contending that defendants have violated their rights under the Family Support Act of 1988, 42 U.S.C. § 602(g)(1)(A)(i)(II)..., by limiting the guarantee of child care exclusively to AFDC recipients enrolled in the state sponsored employment and training program known as Greater Avenues to Independence ("GAIN"). Defendants maintain that such a policy is in compliance with the Act.

* * *

A. The Family Support Act of 1988

Congress enacted the Family Support Act of 1988...(codified in scattered sections of 42 U.S.C.), to "profoundly and fundamentally change the welfare system...[by creating] opportunities for recipients of Aid to Families with Dependent Children to further their education and job training and ultimately to remove themselves from the welfare rolls and gain self sufficiency through meaningful employment."....

The Act requires each state, as a condition of participation in the AFDC program, to create a "Job Opportunities and Basic Skills" ("JOBS") program in order to provide training, education, and work opportunities for AFDC recipients. 42 U.S.C. § 681 *et seq*...JOBS participants are entitled to support services necessary for participation, including costs of transportation and other work-related expenses....

A separate section of the Act requires the state to "guarantee" child care

> for each individual [AFDC recipient] participating in an education and training activity (*including* participation in a program that meets the requirements of [the JOBS provision]) if the State agency approves the activity and determines that the individual is satisfactorily participating in the activity.

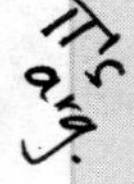

....Plaintiffs argue (1) that on its face, this child care guarantee includes, but is not limited to, JOBS participants; (2) that the structure of the Family Support Act confirms that the child care guarantee is not limited to JOBS participants; and (3) that the legislative history of this provision demonstrates that it extends beyond JOBS.

Yet HHS has promulgated a regulation which requires states to offer child care assistance to AFDC recipients *only* if they "participate in an approved education or training activity *under* JOBS."[2] 45 C.F.R. § 255.2(a)(2) (emphasis

---

[2] The regulation also provides that states may provide child care to AFDC recipients in non-JOBS areas (areas of the state which do not have a JOBS program). In California, there are no non-JOBS areas. California AFDC recipients who are unable to participate in GAIN [California's JOBS program] are denied child care.

added). In reliance on this regulation, California has denied child care to AFDC recipients who are participating satisfactorily in education or training programs but who, due to capped GAIN [the name of California's JOBS' progam] funds, have not been admitted into or have been terminated from GAIN. Both HHS and DSS defend their actions as consistent with the Family Support Act.

B. Plaintiffs' Predicament

Plaintiffs are recipients of AFDC who are currently participating or wish to participate in educational or training programs likely to lead to permanent employment. The named plaintiffs have chosen programs such as nursing, court reporting, and paralegal training. Their declarations indicate that lack of affordable child care is the primary obstacle to successful completion of their education and training.

Members of the class seeking preliminary injunctive relief were participating in training or education activities approved through the GAIN program until they were recently terminated from the program due to budget reductions. As a result, these plaintiffs lost their child care assistance....

In support of this motion, class members describe their inability to participate in training and educational activities without child care assistance....Their declarations indicate that they cannot afford to pay for child care without sacrificing basic necessities. The AFDC grant, which is their only source of income, is often insufficient even for essentials.[4] This money must be stretched to pay for housing, food, utilities, clothing, transportation, personal hygiene and miscellaneous necessities for the entire family. There is no money left to pay for child care....

* * *

As plaintiffs argue, the plain language of the Family Support Act provides that JOBS participants comprise one group of AFDC recipients entitled to child care. The use of the word "including" indicates Congress's intent to extend the child care guarantee *beyond* the JOBS program to *all* eligible AFDC recipients. Any other interpretation renders the word "including" meaningless. In construing a statute, courts are "obliged to give effect, if possible, to every word Congress used."....

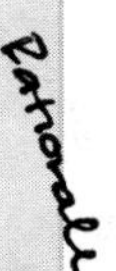

* * *

The child care provisions of the statute are not only broadly delineated, but also mandatory. The Family Support Act dictates that a state "must guarantee" child care for each eligible individual. 42 U.S.C. § 602(g)(1)(A)(i). Child care for *all* eligible individuals is therefore a requirement, not an option. Congress established only two criteria that an AFDC recipient must meet in order to qualify for child care: satisfactory participation in an educational or training activity, and approval of this activity by the state....

California has no authority to deny child care to plaintiffs to whom a federal statute guarantees such assistance....

---

[4] The AFDC grant for a parent and two children in California, for instance, is only $694 per month, or 74.8% of the federal poverty level....

2. *Structure of the Family Support Act*

The plain meaning derived from the language of the Family Support Act is further supported by an examination of the structure of the Act....

Title II of the Family Support Act, entitled "Job Opportunities and Basic Skills Program," contains the requirements for the JOBS program. Federal funding for JOBS is capped and each state's share determined by the state's percentage of the total national AFDC caseload....Funding for transportation and other work-related expenses, provided only to JOBS participants, is limited by this provision....

By contrast, the child care provisions are found in Title III of the Act, entitled "Supportive Services for Families" (not, significantly, "Supportive Services for JOBS Families"), and funding for child care is uncapped. 42 U.S.C. § 602(g)(3). States receive open-ended federal matching funds for child care provided to those who need it to accept employment or to remain employed, to JOBS participants, and to "each individual participating in an education and training activity...if the State agency approves the activity...." 42 U.S.C. § 602 (g)(1)(A). Funding for child care, unlike JOBS funding, is therefore limited only by the number of eligible individuals.

* * *

C. Dispute Over What Constitutes a State Approved Activity

* * *

...Defendants admit that the educational or training activities of plaintiffs seeking preliminary relief were previously approved by the state under California's GAIN program. Defendants also admit that plaintiffs were removed from the program due to program reductions *not* because their activity was no longer approved.[11] Plaintiffs were terminated because they were not in the target population prioritized to remain in GAIN....The State has approved plaintiffs' educational and training activities pursuant to the only criteria it has developed for that purpose in connection with GAIN....

* * *

In addition, defendants imply that by granting plaintiffs child care assistance, the court would directly diminish GAIN funds. They assert that plaintiffs seek to deprive "more deserving" or higher priority recipients of their right to GAIN services. As plaintiffs argue, this claim is based on an erroneous construction of the Family Support Act. Plaintiffs do not seek entry or reentry into GAIN at the expense of participants who are in higher priority groups. They seek only the child care assistance to which they are entitled under the Family Support Act. Funding for this child care assistance is uncapped and separate from JOBS funding. Moreover, fiscal constraints cannot justify the state's failure to comply with its legal obligations.

* * *

[11] See notices of termination attached to Declaration of Tom Burke. For each of the named plaintiffs who were terminated from GAIN, the Notices read in relevant part:

As of December 31, 1990: Payment for your GAIN Child Care Will Stop. Here's Why:....

( ) Your child is 13 years old, which is over the age we can pay for.

( ) Your child care provider is your child's parent, legal guardian, or a member of your assistance unit.

( ) You are not attending an approved GAIN activity.

(x) other: Your GAIN Program Services are discontinued.

Questions for Discussion

1. Why would the state want to preclude private training if it works to qualify AFDC (TANF) parents for employment?

2. Could the state partially accomplish elimination of non-JOBS training programs by requiring special and strict licensure of all such private programs? Would some state controls on this vocational education be warranted based on possible abuse (tuition charges for dubious training)? Does the state's provision of child care give it a special stake in the quality of training provided?

3. The system described in *Miller* remains generally in place, buttressed by a two-year time limit to seek JOBS training, and a five-year lifetime TANF aid limit, as discussed above. What happens to a trainee who is educated for jobs which are not available? Can such parents seek new or additional training and another round of child care provision?

4. What happens after Miller obtains employment and her Stage 2 child care runs out? What if she is laid off within the first year of her employment due to economic downturn and her junior status? Can she re-enter TANF and obtain new and different training until her five years of lifetime aid reservoir is exhausted? Will she receive child care during this period, and for at least the first year of her subsequent employment?

E. CHILD CARE QUALITY

1. Safety

Increasingly, parents entrust their children for most of the day to the care and facilities of strangers, either in a commercial center context, or in the home of a day care provider. Safety issues are of particular importance given the tendency of young children to test their environment, and the increase in allowable children per facility discussed above. In January 2000, the General Accounting Office released a national review of state child care safety and health regulation using 1999 data. The results indicated the inspections are not generally assured and that caseloads are high.[26] Meanwhile, only California has issued playground safety standards applicable to day care facilities.

2. Quality of Care

Both adequacy and quality of child care have become a subject of scholarship and commentary. Since 1995, more than twenty major reports, studies, and surveys have covered basic child care issues, particularly in light of welfare reform. Studies generally conclude that attention in the early developmental years is important and has lasting impact. They also find that the supply of subsidized child care is inadequate, and the quality is uneven and disappointing.[27]

A four-state study of quality in child care centers found that only 14% could be rated as high in quality.[28] The Packard Foundation's Center for the Future of Children concluded that "(1) the quality of services is mediocre, on average; (2) the cost of full-time care is high; (3) at the present time, the cost of increasing quality from mediocre to good is not great, about 10%; [and] (4) good child care is dependent on professionally approved staffing ratios, well educated staff, low staff turnover...."[29] One of the leading authorities in the field concludes that the state of child care "reflect[s] the low priority given to children's care and women's work in American society."[30]

Other recent studies have raised serious questions about the impact of low-quality child care on children, exacerbated by its substitution for parental time and attention. The reported problems with older children of TANF parents now forced to work (and hence forego substantial parental monitoring) are underlined by data showing low levels of parental or other adult supervision for children over the age of ten. These children are increasingly latchkeyed home alone, and are sometimes themselves relied upon to care for younger siblings. An increasing number lack direct paternal impact and male models. The popular culture tends to fill that vacuum with regrettable messages about laudable male qualities: being decisive, forceful, tough, threatening, violent. Although such *caveats* are discounted by many child care advocates, the implications of enhanced peer group influence, or reliance on popular cultural, are not a source of comfort.

The concerns of many were heightened by some preliminary findings released in April 2001 from the most substantial longitudinal study of child care consequences conducted to date. Financed by the National Institute of Child Health and Human Development (NICHHD), the study started in 1991 with 1,364 children from ten cities who underwent detailed surveys and a follow-up study—including observation of class room and social behavior. Three preliminary findings have emerged from the first seven years of observation: (1) 17% of kindergartners who had been in child care showed more assertive and aggressive behaviors; (2) family relationships correlate more closely with measures of aggression than does child care; and (3) higher quality child care correlates with academic success in early school years.

The first finding produced great controversy because of the political ramifications implicit in a message that child care was not beneficial to children. While the degree of aggression increase is not severe, it is statistically significant and not appropriately rejected based on notions of political correctness. Rather than view such findings as an assault on parental prerogative, it should trigger active further inquiry. What are the implications of the aggression measured? What is their relation to delinquency? What are the detailed characteristics of child care provided which correlate with such aggression, *e.g.*, age of child, extent of adult supervision, degree of cognitive stimulation?

A full-time parent is not an option for millions of children, and the findings of the NICHHD and other studies confirm the advantages of high quality child care where it is provided, with this study confirming: "The quality of child care over the first three years of life is consistently but modestly associated with children's cognitive and language development. the higher the quality of child care (more positive language stimulation and interaction between the child and provider), the greater the child's language abilities at 15, 24, and 36 months, the better the child's cognitive development at age two, and the more school readiness the child showed at age three." The study also acknowledged that other variables were more influential, including family income, maternal vocabulary, home environment, and maternal cognitive stimulation.[31]

Recent additional evidence has been presented during 1999–2005 concerning the deleterious consequences of latchkeying children and the advantages of high quality child care. In addition to four new studies,[32] the *Journal of the*

American Medical Association published a peer reviewed article on May 8, 2001 which involved a long-term (17 year) study of 1,539 low income children enrolled as 3- and 4-year-olds in Chicago Public Schools' Child-Parent Centers, with half-day care similar to Head Start, and some school-age services linked to elementary schools at ages 6 to 9. The results were more decisive than the NICHHD study discussed above, with those admitted in the program 33% less likely to be arrested, 41% less likely to be arrested for a violent crime, and 20% more likely to finish high school *vis-a-vis* control groups. The study concluded: "Participation in an established early childhood intervention for low-income children was associated with better educational and social outcomes up to age 20 years."[33]

Child care quality is compromised by three factors: (1) a general lack of any certification or other system to provide enhanced status to providers as a positive incentive to learn and improve;[34] (2) high staff turnover (now at 20% to 30% per annum), and (3) low pay. The last factor is of particular importance, and influences the first two. Some family day care workers do not earn minimum wage. Current compensation allows a full-time child care worker providing for a 6-year-old to receive $527 per month. These workers, in whose hands children are placed, may live below the poverty line themselves.[35] At the higher end for child care, the average salary of a preschool teacher in California is about $24,600 for twelve months of work. An elementary school teacher *starts* at $24,835 for a ten-month year with a realistic career track to earn $50,000.[36] In contrast, the average pay of child care workers nationally is $18,060 per year—one of the lowest levels of any occupation tracked by the Department of Labor.[37] Their conditions of employment also generally exclude medical benefits, retirement accounts, paid leave, or other common compensation. These levels of pay contrast markedly with the higher levels (comparable to teacher salaries and benefits) extant in Western Europe. Consistent with these salary levels, training and quality control in most states is confined to sexual predator list clearance, and rarely includes required training in child development or substantive teaching knowledge or experience.

On April 29, 2001, a University of California at Berkeley study focusing on California reported that salaries for child-care teachers have fallen over the last six years in relation to inflation. The study focuses on child care centers in Santa Cruz, Santa Clara, and San Mateo counties, but its results appear to be fairly generalized. In examining centers, the study overstates income because of the much smaller compensation (generally close to minimum wage) available for licensed family day care providers. But the study found that "just 24% of teaching staff employed in 1996 were still on the job in 2000, more than half of the centers reporting turnover last year had not replaced the staff they lost, when teachers leave a center about one-half leave child care provision entirely, and wages for teachers decreased 6% adjusted for inflation since 1994."[38] The study found "the presence of a greater proportion of highly trained teaching staff in 2000 is the strongest predictor of whether a center can sustain quality improvements over time. Wages are also a significant predictor."[39]

ENDNOTES

[1] Bureau of the Census, Current Population Survey, quoted in Children's Defense Fund, *Child Care Basics* (April 2005) at 1 (see www.childrensdefense.org).

[2] *Id.* at note 4 (data is from 2001).

[3] See detailed breakdown for unemployed mothers at Bureau of the Census, *Current Population Reports–2005* (Washington, D.C.; 2005) at 14–18 (www.census.gov).

[4] *Id.* Note the "no regular arrangement" census category does not imply a mix of care sources (a category denoted as "multiple arrangements" and including 3 million children), nor does it include care by a relative. It rather indicates no identifiable arrangement.

[5] Based on 1997 data, see Administration for Children and Families, Department of Health and Human Services' Child Care Bureau, *Out-of-School Time School-Age Care*.

[6] *Id.*

[7] *Id.*

[8] Note that 1997 data from the Bureau of Children and Families estimated 5 million such children. The six million estimate comes from Bureau of Census, *Current Population Reports, 1999* (Washington, D.C.) at Table 4 (see www.census.gov).

[9] See U.S. Department of Education, National Center for Education Statistics, *Before- and After-School Care, Programs, and Activities of Children in Kindergarten Through Eighth Grade: 2001* (Washington, D.C.; April 2004) at v.

[10] *Id.* at vii.

[11] See discussion in Chapter 3.

[12] Bruce Fuller and Casey Connerty, PACE Center, University of California, Berkeley; Fran Kipnix, California Child Care Resource & Referral Network; Yvonne Choong, University of Chicago, *An Unfair Head Start: California Families Face Gaps in Preschool and Child Care Availability* (1997).

[13] Little Hoover Commission, *Caring for Our Children: Our Most Precious Investment* (Sacramento, CA; Sept. 1998) at 41.

[14] Melissa Healy, *Latinos at Center of Chicken-Egg Debate Over Child-Care Funds*, L.A. Times, Sept. 29, 1998, "Community Section" at 1.

[15] Sam Mistrano, *Transforming Child Care from the Ground Up*, Human Services Alliance (Los Angeles, CA; Oct. 2000), passim.

[16] See U.S. Department of Education, National Center for Education Statistics, *Before- and After-School Care, Programs, and Activities of Children in Kindergarten Through Eighth Grade: 2001*(Washington, D.C.; April 2004) at vii.

[17] Karen Schulman, Issue Brief: *The High Cost of Child Care*(Children's Defense Fund, Washington D.C.; 2000). See also Children's Defense Fund, *Green Book (State of America's Children) 2005* at Chapter 3 (www.childrensdefense.org). See also Children's Advocacy Institute, *California Children's Budget 2004-05* (San Diego, CA; 2004) at Chapter 6 (www.caichildlaw.org) for discussion of the Regional Market Surveys of California tracking market charges for child care in urban and rural areas.

[18] These are administration estimates as of 2005. See Hannah Matthews and Danielle Ewen, Center for Law and Social Policy, *President's Budget Projects 300,000 Low-Income Children to Lose Child Care by 2010* (Washington, D.C.; Feb. 7, 2005) at 1 (www.clasp.org). The CLASP discussion uses raw numbers unadjusted for increases in child population (and child care demand). On the other hand, the CLASP estimate of reductions is not the 300,000 conceded by the Bush Administration, but 375,000 in raw numbers. See *id.*, note 1, an estimate derived by dividing average slot costs (adjusted by the inflation measure of the Congressional Budget Office) into total proposed spending amounts.

"Family" here refers to the benchmark of one parent and two children (see poverty line discussion in Chapter 3).

[19] Unlike most federal subsidy programs, Head Start is not channeled through a state agency but is dispensed through direct federal contracts with providers.

[20] To track federal spending for child care, education, and other accounts, see CD Publications, *Children & Youth Funding Report* (Silver Springs, MD), a subscription-based weekly compendium of data and reports on child-related funding (www.cdpublications.com).

[21] A separate federal "Wee Tot" Earned Income Tax Credit (EITC) Supplement allowed a credit of 5% of earned income up to $388 for a parent who stays home to care for a newborn and in so doing loses eligibility for straight earned income tax credit benefits. That credit was repealed in 1994.

[22] A study by Harvard University's Professor Bruce Fuller surveyed 1,800 child care centers in 36 states and concluded that families with annual incomes over $50,000 pay just 6% of their incomes for child care, while families earning under $15,000 devote 23% of their income for child care. The tax credits provide a tax expenditure of $4 billion annually. One-third of the credit goes to families with incomes above $50,000 per year. For a discussion, see Diego Ribadeneira, *Day Care Credits Said to Favor Well Off*, Boston Globe, Sept. 18, 1992, at 3.

[23] See Shelley Smith, Mary Fairchild, and Scott Groginsky, National Conference of State Legislatures, *Early Childhood Care and Education: An Investment that Works* (Washington, D.C.; Jan. 1997) at 68, citing an August 14, 1996, Congressional Budget Office memorandum.

[24] See Children's Defense Fund, *Child Care Basics* (Washington, D.C.; April 2005) at 1. Note that waiting lists are long in most states—with subsidy limited to those of lowest income.

[25] See, *e.g.*, Diane Pearce, Wider Opportunities for Women, *The Self Sufficiency Standard for California* (1996) at 5.

[26] General Accounting Office, *Child Care: State Efforts to Enforce Safety and Health Requirements,* GAO/HEHS-00-28 (Jan. 2000) at 19, 28, 37.

[27] See, *e.g.*, David Illig, California Research Bureau, *Birth to Kindergarten: The Importance of the*

Early Years (Sacramento, CA; Feb. 1998) (conducted at the request of Senator Dede Alpert); Jane Knitzer and Stephen Page, Columbia University National Center for Children in Poverty, *Map and Track: State Initiatives for Young Children and Families* (New York; NY; 1998); Anne Mitchell, Louise Stoney, and Harriet Dichter, *Financing Child Care in the United States*, Ewing Marion Kauffman Foundation and The Pew Charitable Trusts (1997); Sharon L. Kagan and Nancy E. Cohen, Yale University, The Bush Center in Child Development and Social Policy, *Not By Chance: Creating an Early Care and Education System for America's Children* (New Haven, CT; 1997); Mary L. Culkin, Scott Groginsky, and Steve Christian, National Conference of State Legislatures, *Building Blocks: A Legislator's Guide to Child Care Policy* (Washington, D.C.; 1997); Children's Defense Fund, *Study Reveals Working Families Are Locked Out of Child Care*, 19:4/5 CDF Reports 1 (Washington, D.C.; April/May 1998); U.S. General Accounting Office, *Welfare Reform: Implications of Increased Work Participation for Child Care* (GAO/HEHS-97-75) (Washington, D.C.; 1997); Mark H. Greenberg, Center for Law and Social Policy, *The Child Care Protection Under TANF* (Washington, D.C.; 1998); U.S. General Accounting Office, *Welfare Reform: States' Efforts to Expand Child Care Programs* (GAO/HEHS-98-21) (Washington, D.C.; 1998); Center for the Future of Children, The David and Lucile Packard Foundation, The Future of Children: Financing Child Care (Richard E. Behrman, M.D., ed.) (Los Angeles, CA; Summer/Fall 1996).

[28] Suzanne W. Helburn, ed., University of Colorado, Center for Research in Economic and Social Policy, *Cost, Quality, and Child Outcomes in Child Care Centers: Technical Report* (Denver, CO; 1995).

[29] Suzanne W. Helburn and Carollee Howes, Center for the Future of Children, The David and Lucile Packard Foundation, *Child Care Cost and Quality*, 6:2 The Future of Children: Financing Child Care (Richard E. Behrman, M.D., ed.) (Los Angeles, CA; Summer/Fall 1996) at 79–80.

[30] *Id.*, at 80.

[31] See Robin Peth-Pierce, *Early Child Care: About the NICHD Study of Early Child Care* (2001) at 10.

[32] *Child Care Outcomes When Center Classes Meet Recommended Standards for Quality*, American Journal of Public Health, 1999; National Center for Early Development and Learning, *The Children of the Cost, Quality, and Outcomes Study Go to School* (1999); Nancy Kerrebrock, Eugene Lewitt, *Children in Self-Care*, The Future of Children 9(2), Packard Foundation (1999), at 151–160; Jill Posner and Deborah Candell, *After-school Activities and the Development of Low-Income Urban Children: A Longitudinal Study*, Developmental Psychology 35(3): 868-879.

[33] Arthur J. Reynolds, PhD, Judy A. Temple, PhD, Dylan L. Robertson, Emily A. Mann MSSW, *Long-term Effects of an Early Childhood Intervention on Educational Achievement and Juvenile Arrest: A 15-Year Follow-up of Low-Income Children in Public Schools*, 285 Journal of the American Medical Association 2339–2346 (May 9, 2001), see http://www.jama.com.

[34] See the interesting study by William T. Gormley, Jr. and Jessica Lucas, *Money, Accreditation and Child Care Center Quality,* Foundation for Child Development, Working Paper Series (August 2000) passim (see http://www.ffcd.org). The study cites eighteen states providing certification to assure and demonstrate enhanced child care quality, and which also triggers enhanced compensation. Evidence is compelling that this incentive driven technique for enhancing quality works.

[35] For a discussion of labor commissioner protests by workers and rate levels extant, see Carla Rivera, *Day-Care Providers Say State Reimbursements Fail to Pay a Living Wage*, Los Angeles Times (May 19, 2000) at B-3.

[36] California Child Care Resource and Referral Network, *1999 California Child Care Portfolio* (San Francisco, CA; 1999) at 2–5.

[37] See U.S. Department of Labor, Bureau of Labor Statistics, *National Occupational Employment and Wage Estimates* (Washington, D.C.; Nov. 2004) at www.bls.gov.

[38] See Marcy Whitebrook, Laura Sakai, Emily Gerber, Carollee Howes, *Then & Now: Changes in Child Care Staffing, 1994–2000,* Institute of Industrial Relations (Berkeley, CA; April 2001) *passim.*

[39] *Id.*, summary at 4.

CHAPTER EIGHT

Child Protection from Abuse

The term "child welfare" services does not refer to cash safety net assistance programs (AFDC or TANF) but to the system addressing child abuse and neglect. As described in Chapter 10 below, the juvenile courts evolved under a *parens patriae* concept that did not clearly distinguish between juvenile law violators, and juvenile child abuse victims. Many of those subject to the "House of Refuge Movement" were impoverished children who had committed no criminal offense. Many were abandoned, orphaned, or neglected. Most suffered extreme poverty.

When the Illinois Act, widely replicated in the states, established a juvenile court it similarly grouped minor offenders and child abuse victims into a single system designedly to aid children in trouble. The Illinois Act defined "dependency and neglect" to include "(1) any child...destitute or homeless or abandoned, (2) [without] proper parental care or guardianship, (3) who habitually begs or receives alms, (4) who is found living in any house of ill fame or with any vicious or disreputable person, (5) whose home, by reason of neglect, cruelty, or depravity on the part of its parents, guardian or other person in whose care it may be, is an unfit place for such a child, (6) [who is] under the age of 8 years who is found peddling or selling any article or singing or playing any musical instrument upon the street or giving any public entertainment."[1]

Current notions of child abuse based on excessive corporal punishment, failure to treat for medical ailments, or even molestation were not ascendant in the early formation of juvenile courts. Parental authority over children was close to absolute and the system focused on children effectively abandoned or orphaned by parents. Over time, the delinquency system discussed in Chapter 10 evolved to incorporate some adult criminal justice procedures, particularly after the *Gault* decision. Meanwhile, the "dependency" jurisdiction of juvenile court separated into a system where children enjoyed broader state protection. That protection covered physical abuse, psychological abuse (where *in extremis*), sexual abuse, medical neglect, and general neglect. In addition, "status offenses" marked the entry of juvenile court jurisdiction for runaways, truants, curfew violators, "incorrigible" children, and those with intractable drug addiction problems. As discussed below, mandated reporting and investigations have increased caseloads markedly in most states. Much of the increase and many of the problems of children relate to poverty and parental drug and alcohol abuse, both at high incidence, as the data presented below reflect.

A. NATIONAL INCIDENCE OF ABUSE AND NEGLECT

National data gathered in 2003 on child abuse reports and disposition find:[2]

Reports, Victims, Perpetrators

- 2,958,000 child abuse reports were received, 32.1% screened out, and the remainder transferred for investigation or assessment.
- 56.8% of the reports were received from professionals (most of the remaining 43.2% were submitted by family, neighbors and nonprofessionals).
- Most states have established time standards for initiating the investigation of reports. The median response time to initiate a report investigation is 3 days.
- 26.4% of investigations were found to be "substantiated" (indicated maltreatment), 57.7% found the report unsubstantiated, and the remaining 15.9% were given another status.
- An estimated 826,000 children were believed to be abused nationwide and reported to authorities, with a 1999 rate of 11.8 per 1,000 children.
- 60.9% of all victims were alleged to have suffered neglect, 18.9% physical abuse, and 9.9% sexual abuse.
- The highest victimization rate is for the 0–3 age group (16.4 per 1,000) with rates declining with the age of the child.
- The victimization rate ranged from a low of 2.9 per 1,000 for Asian victims to a high of 26.4 African-American victims per 1,000.
- Over 60% of perpetrators are female, and the most common pattern is a child neglected by a female parent (40.8%)with no other perpetrators identified.

Fatalities

- 1,500 children died of abuse or neglect (2.0 per 100,000 child population), with 43.6% not yet one year of age.
- 17.7% of the fatalities were of children not in parental custody (relative, foster care, legal guardian, etc.).

Services

- 1.85 million children received preventive services, with the average time from the start of investigation to provision of service being 43 days.
- 691,540 child victims received post-investigative services, and an estimated 424,441 children who were the subjects of unsubstantiated reports also received services.
- 92,258 children were removed for their homes, and placed in foster care; another 41,642 children who were not themselves victims were placed in protective supervision during the investigation.
- About 80% of the victims subject to court action were appointed counsel or other representation.
- 22.8% of victims had received family preservation services within the previous five years, while 6.4% had been removed previously, and reunited with their families.
- Average annual caseload for a Child Protective Service investigation/assessment worker was 63.1 investigations.

State	Children in Foster Care
California	97,261
New York	37,067
Florida	30,677
Texas	22,191
Pennsylvania	21,768
Illinois	21,608
Michigan	21,376
Ohio	19,323
Other 42 States	251,791
Total	**523,062**
Number awaiting adoption	118,000[3]

Table 8-A. Children in Foster Care in the United States, Fiscal 2003–04[4]

B. CHILD ABUSE/NEGLECT CAUSAL CORRELATIONS

In September 1996, the U.S. Department of Health and Human Services released a national incidence study of child abuse and neglect which tested important correlations.[5]The Department's second study used data from 1986; its 1996 study was based on 1993 surveys of 5,600 professionals working in 842 agencies serving 42 counties. The study compared 1986 and 1993 results, using two standards: "harm"—meaning experienced abuse or neglect, and "endangerment"—meaning at risk of harm. The researchers arrived at the following conclusions:

- The total number of abused and neglected children in 1993 was 67% higher than in 1986; the number of children endangered roughly doubled. The total number of children seriously injured quadrupled in this seven-year span.
- Girls were sexually abused three times more often than boys.
- No investigation by local child protective service workers occurs concerning an estimated three-quarters of the children seriously injured by parents or caretakers.

The study found the following correlations between families and child abuse:

- Children of single parents had a 77% greater risk of physical abuse, an 87% greater risk of neglect, and an 80% greater risk of serious injury than children living with two parents.
- Children in the largest families were physically neglected at three times the rate of one-child families.
- Compared to children from families with annual incomes above $30,000, children from families with annual incomes below $15,000 were 22 times more likely to be harmed, 25 times more likely to be endangered, and 56 times more likely to be educationally neglected.

Most studies find that for between one-third and two-thirds of children involved with the child welfare system, parental substance abuse is a contributing factor; data from the 1996 National Household Survey on Drug Abuse reveal that an estimated 8.3 million children in the U.S.—11% of all children in the country—live in households in which at least one parent is either alcoholic or in need of substance abuse treatment.[6]

C. FEDERAL STATUTES, FUNDING, MAJOR POLICY ISSUES

1. Evolution to the Current System

a. The Formative Statutes

In 1980, the Congress began to rationalize the nation's treatment of abused and neglected children through a system of funding assistance and minimum standards. In 1980, Congress passed the Adoption Assistance and Child Welfare Act[7] directed at state and local child protection and foster care systems. In 1981, Title XX of the Social Security Act was amended to include the Social Services Block Grant to provide child protective service funding for states. Federal funding has required state compliance with minimum standards. In 1983, the Act was amended to include required "reasonable efforts" before removing children from homes and to reunify them with parents after removal.

The Child Abuse Victims' Rights Act was enacted in 1986, giving child victims of federal sexual exploitation laws a private right of action. In 1991, Congress enacted the Victims of Child Abuse Act of 1990 to upgrade the investigation and prosecution of child abuse laws. As part of the Omnibus Budget and Reconciliation Act of 1993, the Congress provided funding to study performance of the Adoption Assistance and Child Welfare Act of 1980, particularly focusing on dependency court practices.

b. Brief Outline of Traditional Procedure

Spurred by federal statutes which required some common elements between states to qualify for federal funds, states developed "child welfare" systems which required certain professionals (such as teachers or physicians) to report suspected child abuse or neglect, and established both hotline intake systems and emergency response protocols. For about two-thirds of the children where reports are deemed founded and response appropriate, the result is "family preservation" services in their homes. However, where the county contends that the child is in substantial danger, children are removed to a "receiving" facility or into temporary foster care.

Where children are removed, the child protective services agency at the county level files a petition with the juvenile court to take "jurisdiction" of the child. Within a short time frame (less than one week), a "detention hearing" is held before a juvenile court (dependency) judge to determine if the state has an adequate basis for its initial removal. At this point counsel is appointed for parents at public cost if necessary, and counsel or a "*guardian ad litem*" is usually appointed for the child. A critical "jurisdictional" hearing is generally held within the subsequent thirty days to consider the county petition for court jurisdiction over the child. If granted, the child then becomes a "dependent" of the court and parental authority is supplanted *pendente lite*. A "dispositional" hearing will be held with or close to the jurisdictional hearing to determine where the child shall be placed pending further proceedings. As discussed below, federal policy—adopted by all of the states—requires the state to engage in reasonable efforts to accomplish the reunification of children who have been removed from parental custody and control. These services often include parenting classes, psychological counseling, alcohol or drug rehabilitation, or other programs, depending on the basis for removal. Generally, twelve months are allowed for such services to provide an acceptably safe home for the children, with review hearings scheduled at six-month intervals. At the end of that period (or sooner under extraordinary conditions) a "termination" hearing may consider a county agency petition to terminate parental authority. The burden is on the state to prove that a parent whose parental rights are terminated is "unfit" as a parent, under a "clear and convincing" evidentiary showing, as the leading cases presented below hold. A "permanent placement" hearing is coextensively or subsequently held to determine the child's future care and custody.

During the pendency of the dependency court proceedings (and often after), children are placed into foster care under the jurisdiction of the juvenile court. That care is usually provided by one of three types of entities: family foster care providers, foster care agencies, and more institutional group homes. Group homes can vary between a home-like setting with five or six children, to a larger facility associated in the public mind with traditional "orphanages". Children may also be placed with relatives (so-called "kin-care") who may receive guardianship status from the courts in most states. Finally, children are eligible for adoption upon the termination of previously applicable parental rights. Such adoptions are most easily accomplished for younger, healthy white children, often through family foster care providers when they are so placed.

Children who are not adopted remain in foster care status, with the juvenile court supervising those assigned the parental role. At the age of 18, they are "emancipated" by age from the foster care system—at which point public assistance to foster care parents or agencies for their care generally stops.

c. Current Major Federal Funding

Federal funding for abused or neglected children is distributed through the following vehicles:

(1) Federal funding to states under Title IV-B of the Social Security Act,[8] usually allocated to county child protective services to cover administrative expenses, including staff training. It is a "closed-end appropriation," meaning Congress allocates a finite amount of money each year. In most states, these "child welfare accounts" fund county intake systems where social workers receive "hotline" calls of possible child abuse or neglect, most from "mandated reporters" (physicians, teachers, *et al.* obligated by law to report suspected abuse or neglect). Local ("child protective") social workers receive calls, investigate, perhaps visit placements, and in coordination with peace officers, may remove allegedly endangered children and place them in foster care, as discussed above. The cost of this initial placement, usually up to the first month, is borne by "child welfare" accounts in most state budgets.

(2) After the initial child welfare account expenditure, the federal government subsidizes the costs of foster care for children who are eligible for Temporary Aid for Needy Families (TANF) through the TANF–Foster Care (TANF-FC) program. In addition, it provides adoption aid for children with special needs who are eligible for TANF and Supplemental Security Income (SSI) under Title IV-E of the Social Security Act.[9] This money is an "open-ended entitlement" for eligible children administered by a state department of social services (SDSS) in most states.

The TANF-FC program provides payments for the out-of-home placement of children who: (1) have been relinquished for purposes of adoption, or whose parents have lost their parental rights by court order; (2) have been removed from the physical custody of their parents or guardians as a result of a voluntary placement agreement or judicial determination that the child is a dependent (finding of abuse or neglect) or a ward of the court (finding of delinquency); (3) are living in the home of a non-related legal guardian; or (4) have been placed in foster care under the federal Indian Child Welfare Act.[10]

Children eligible for TANF-FC payments are placed in foster family homes, licensed group homes, and, in some cases, more intensive treatment facilities. Federal TANF-FC pays 50% of the cost of child placement and related administrative costs. Spending from other state and federal accounts, including Child Welfare Services, Medicaid and mental health services, provides supplemental services for children in TANF-FC placement.

(3) Less substantial federal grant programs include (a) the Child Abuse/Neglect Prevention and Treatment Act[11] (CAPTA) through which states receive modest grants to fund child abuse prevention and treatment efforts and which funded the National Center on Child Abuse and Neglect (NCCAN) to serve as an information clearinghouse; (b) small training grants are available for universities training social workers under Section 426 of the Social Security Act; (c) the federal "Independent Living Program" through Title IV-E of the Social Security Act provides some children modest assistance as they reach 18 and are no longer eligible for foster care; (d) a small number of competitive grants are available under Title III of the Juvenile Justice Act to help homeless and runaway youth, and provide some emergency assistance to homeless youth under the Stewart B. McKinney Act.

The vast majority of spending relevant to child protection is routed through the five accounts of Table 8-B below.

	FY 2000	FY 2004	FY 2005	FY 2006
Foster Care (Title IV-E)	$4,537	$4,974	$4,895	$4,685
Social Services (Title XX)	$1,775	$1,700	$1,700	$1,700
Adoption Assistance (Title IV-E)	$1,020	$1,699	$1,770	$1,795
Family Preservation and Support	$295	$305	$305	$305
Child Welfare Services (Title VI-B)	$292	$289	$291	$291
TOTAL:	$7,919	$8,967	$8,967	$8,776
Adjusted Total*:	$9,699	$9,589	$8,967	$8,493

* Adjusted to population and inflation (CPI). FY 2005 = 1.00

Table 8-B. Major Federal Child Welfare Accounts ($ millions)

The adjusted total of Table 8-B puts prior spending in 2005 dollars by factoring in population and CPI changes. The overall trend is toward disinvestment. Projected trends to 2010 are for further decreases as the 2001 and 2003 tax cuts are extended (see budget discussion in Chapter 1).

d. Adoption Tax Expenditures

The Small Business Job Protection Act of 1996 included a new adoption tax credit to stimulate more adoptions and lessen the population of children in less secure foster care placement (see discussion below).[12] The law allows married couples filing a joint return to claim a credit for "adoption expenses" for an eligible child (a person under 18 years of age unable to care for himself or herself) through 2001. Since 2001, the credit has been limited to children "with special needs," defined as a citizen or resident of the United States for whom the state has determined assistance is needed to effectuate an adoption—that is, someone the state cannot place. The credit is limited to necessary adoption fees, court costs, legal fees, and similar costs. The maximum credit claimable is $5,000 per child, and it is not refundable; it may only be used to offset tax liability, and is accordingly of no value to those who lack tax liability. A similar credit is available to an employer who pays such costs for an employee seeking to adopt.

2. Post-1996 Federal Legislation

a. The Federal Adoption and Safe Families Act of 1997

During 1997, Congress passed a conference committee bill (H.R. 327) which supplanted prior House and Senate initiatives to stimulate adoptions and further protect children.[13] The new statute was driven by highly publicized cases of children "reunified" with parents who subsequently murdered those children, as well as the following alleged conditions: evidence of harm given the long 18-month period then allowed to parents to win reunification, use of procedures to extend beyond that period, and "permanency plans" which maintained children in unstable foster care settings, often with little subsequent court review.

The 1997 statute reauthorized the pre-existing Family Preservation and Support Services Act and imposed new requirements on the "state plan" necessary for federal funding. Changes included the "safety of children" as the paramount concern in state administration, and the following specific adjustments to prior law:

- "Reasonable efforts" to reunify are guided by "the child's health and safety" as the paramount concern, and 12 months instead of 18 months is allowed in the normal course to make the disposition decision, with even shorter time spans allowed under some circumstances.

- "Reasonable efforts" may not be required where there is abandonment, chronic abuse, torture, sexual abuse, the parent has seriously injured a child or sibling, or parental rights to a sibling have been terminated. The first two elements on this list are both new and potentially applicable to large numbers of children in the juvenile court dependency system.

- Where the court has determined that no reasonable efforts are required, a permanency hearing is to be held within 30 days.

- Permanency planning and reasonable efforts to reunify with parents can proceed *concurrently*, to enable preparation for a permanent alternative (such as adoption) if reunification is denied.

- The "disposition hearing" is replaced by a "permanency hearing." The previous terminology appeared to sanction a continued "holding pattern" status for affected children. Permanency options include return to the parent(s), termination of parental rights and placement for adoption, referral for legal guardianship, or placement in another planned living arrangement.

- A petition for termination of parental rights must be filed for foster children who have been in state custody for 15 out of the most recent 22 months, and for all children for whom reasonable efforts to reunify are not required. However, exceptions are allowed where children are placed with a relative of a parent, where services have not been completed to allow safe return of a child (and that is the permanency plan), or where there is a compelling reason why it would not be in the best interests of the child to so terminate parental rights.

- Foster parents, pre-adoptive parents, or relatives providing care have a right to notice and opportunity to be heard in any review or hearing about a child, but do not have "party" status.

- States may receive an "adoption incentive payment" of $4,000 times the number of increased foster child adoptions (above a base period average from 1995 through1997); the money must be used for child welfare services. An amount of up to $20 million each year is authorized (not appropriated) for this purpose.

- To receive incentive payments, a state must provide health insurance coverage to any child with special needs who is subject to an adoption assistance agreement.

b. Federal Foster Care Independence Act of 1999[14]

In 1999, Congress enacted the Federal Foster Care Independence Act, a statute focusing on youths from 18 to 21 years old who age out of the foster care program but are often not given the kind of support youths receive from their families, and are often left without resources, prospects, or income for basic expenses once on their own. Federal funding for "independent living" programs doubled with the legislation, from $70 million to $140 million and requires only a 20% state match. The funds can be used to help youths transition to independence by financing: education, training in daily living skills, substance abuse and pregnancy prevention, and health services. Those in foster care as of their 16th birthday can use these funds even if adopted before their 18th birthday. States can use up to 30% of the funds for supervised room and board for youths of 18 to 21 years of age.

The law increases the amount of assets allowable for children in foster care to retain foster care assistance (from $1,000 to $10,000). Hence, a youth may save up to $10,000 for further education without reduction of benefits for his/her care. The law also allows states to provide Medicaid to those emancipated from foster care, and increases funding for adoption assistance payments to states.

c. Federal Child Abuse Prevention and Enforcement Act of 2000

On February 1, 2000, the House of Representatives passed H.R. 764, the Child Abuse Prevention and Enforcement Act of 2000. The law (1) allows state grants under the Crime Identification Technology Act of 1998 to be used to deliver timely and complete criminal history information to child welfare agencies (*e.g.*, to guide foster care placements); (2) allows state law enforcement ("Byrne") grants to enforce child abuse laws and to prevent child abuse, including cooperation between law enforcement and the media to apprehend serious criminal abusers of children; and (3) provides additional money (doubling from $10 million to $20 million) for child abuse victims under the Victims of Crime Act of 1984.

3. Current Policy Issues

Notwithstanding the evolution of state child protection, six problem areas concern child advocates, as follows:

a. Prevention/Early Intervention/Education Failure

A disproportionate share of abused children come from births where one or both parents did not intend to create a child, often from an unwed mother, with minimal biological father involvement. Unwed birth rates remain near historical highs and while child support collection from absent fathers has increased, it remains at low levels (below $50/month received per eligible child in single parent households).

As discussed above, the second highly correlated variable is alcohol/drug abuse. A review of over 18,000 child abuse court orders in Los Angeles County Juvenile Dependency Court in 1989 indicated that substance abuse was a significant factor in at least 90% of the cases.[15] A similar study in Washington D.C. found that parental substance abuse was an important contributing factor in 80% of the cases.[16] Although the development of drug courts and other preventive measures has increased, as the budget figures outlined above indicate, this and related prevention measures remain a relatively low funding priority.

In addition to underlying prevention, there is a growing movement in support of "early preventive intervention". "Family preservation" is one alternative response to a report of abuse or neglect. A child is not removed from the home and the juvenile court does not formally assume jurisdiction over him or her. Rather, a parent signs an agreement to receive services (*e.g.*, drug rehabilitation, anger management, living skills) and such services are provided while the child remains at home. An earlier intervention model originated in Hawaii during the late 1980s (sometimes termed the "Hawaii model"). Rather than wait for an abuse report, new mothers who fit a profile for high-risk abuse are visited in their homes by social workers shortly after they give birth. These "house call" social and public health workers proactively check on the status of the new child and provide on-site individual instruction and advice. This model has enjoyed increasing political support and it has been implemented in many counties in varying forms over the last decade.

However, "home visitation" to large numbers of new mothers without prior abuse reports is expensive. Nevertheless, the early intervention model shows substantial promise compared to the "report response" standard approach, since such reports may not occur, particularly for young pre-school children who do not come into contact often with mandated reporters.

The almost universal support for such intervention contrasts with opposition to an approach facially even more cost effective in preventing abuse/neglect: mandatory parenting education. Child advocates supporting such education argue that most children will become parents, and all are likely to perform some parenting functions. These advocates argue that this momentous task with profound social consequences is amenable to useful instruction. Young parents currently lack basic information about the care of an infant, dangers, and optimum child rearing practices. Parenting education advocates ask: Why should this critical information not be taught in classes where future parents are gathered in groups of 20 to 30—an apparently more efficient means of delivery than the one-on-one limited in-home format?

Some information relevant to child rearing may be included in home economics classes largely attended by girls. However, parenting advocates argue that a single class, and one confined to a single gender, is not as effective as modular lessons repeated at different age levels to all students. Those lessons need not sacrifice substantial time from important education in English, math, science, and other important subjects. They would include important information ranging from the difficulties and financial costs of parenthood to basic facts about infant care: nursing, food, physiology, development, health needs, etc. An educated parent would know not only that an infant must never be shaken, but would understand why—the weak neck and brain trauma from whiplash. Students would be taught about common hazards, from leaving children unattended in cars in hot weather to swimming pool dangers to the special vulnerability of young brains to lead contamination, *et al.* Future parents would learn why children cry, what they should eat, and when to seek medical attention. Social services departments would provide current material based on errors and abuses evident from their investigations.

Most high school curricula will include substantial coverage of a wide range of subjects from how to fill out a tax form to Hannibal's conquests to the trigonometric use of the cosign and tangent. But few include basic parenting information—notwithstanding three million reports of abuse/neglect annually, and the many child developmental benefits that follow from informed and skilled parenting. Parenting education opponents have thus far contended successfully that such information is properly confined to family, non-profit and religious instruction.[17]

b. Foster Care Drift and Adoption Failure

Removal from a home, even a dangerous and harmful one, can be a devastating disruption for a child. That disruption is exacerbated by the normal course of proceedings of dependency court and the foster care system. Only a minority of children achieve quick and certain stability, usually when a relative previously known to them is an acceptable alternative or they are reunited expeditiously with parents. About 20%–25% of the children entering foster care are reunited with their parents, and about 20% of these children will subsequently re-enter the system. Another 25% of the children will be adopted and achieve a stable family by that means. A majority of children (roughly 55%) who become foster children will remain so until they emancipate into adulthood. Of this group, for most of their foster years 8.6% will be placed in group homes, 7.8% in "other" placements, including juvenile incarceration, 39% in family foster care settings, and 44.4% with kin. This last category has grown significantly with relatives of children increasingly qualified for foster care compensation to facilitate the care of those children.[18]

Child advocates use the term "foster care drift" to refer to the repeated placement changes affecting many children in foster care. Children often are moved from an initial receiving facility to temporary foster care, to family foster care, then to one or more other families, and often to multiple group home placements. Psychologists term one consequence of such drift "detachment syndrome" as children lack the reliable, certain anchor that a parent can provide.

One study of California found that children placed in foster care with relatives have less movement between caregivers,[19] but much of the total foster care population measured had been in three or more separate placements within six years.[20] A study by California's Office of Legislative Analyst confirms these levels of instability, finding that overall, one-third of current foster care children have been subject to three or more separate placements (with different families or institutions).[21]

Exacerbating foster care drift is the deliberate pacing of judicial proceedings. Although the Federal Adoption and Safe Families Act of 1997 discussed above has moved the normal course eighteen-month period for reunification to twelve months, it is in practice often well beyond one year. During this period, children are often in a temporary waiting status. Reunification does not occur in the majority of cases, and in less than 30% of the cases where parental rights are terminated is an adoption with permanent new parents the outcome. In some states, a large percentage of children in foster care are designated as "unadoptable" and are designated for permanent foster care status until emancipating out of the system at 18 years of age.

Adoptions are impeded by the confidentiality of the dependency system which advocates argue allows more effective exposure of canine adoption needs than human. They are also limited by the practice of many jurisdictions to refuse Adoption Assistance payments to adoptive parents who the state believes may be able to afford their costs.

One impediment to adoption is racial "preference", often reflected within departments of social services. Such bias is not at all confined to whites, but often is reflected in the attitudes of social workers of minority ethnicity, who are offended by the adoption of a child by white parents. The placement of a child with an adoptive parent of his or her own ethnic group has advantages—including those which flow from appearance similarity between parent and child. But over 70% of foster care children are minorities and insistence on matching them with minority parents precludes adoption for many of these children. Paradoxically, departments of social services have little objection to foster care placement of children in homes of different races, placements that can well last until emancipation.

The Congress has enacted two successive statutes to address racially based adoptive rejection: the Multiethnic Placement Act of 1994, and the Interethnic Adoption Provisions of 1996, which further amended the law to prioritize interracial adoptions over foster care drift. In 1998, the General Accounting Office issued a report on the statute, indicating substantial failure to comply.[22]

- **c. Family Foster Care Supply and Quality**

One of the impediments to foster care stability is low compensation paid to foster family care providers. Commonly at $500 to $700 per month per child, the amount available in most states does not meet the out-of-pocket costs of children, particularly for families seeking just two or three children for possible adoption. These family foster care providers make up almost 80% of the adoptive parents of children who are adopted. In contrast, group homes are generally paid between $3,000 and $5,000 per month per child. The result has been a failure in the supply and quality of family foster care providers, who often lack the political representation in state capitols of the more organized and commercial group home providers (see discussion of lobbying and influence in Chapter 1). Child advocates within the states have argued, generally without success, for increased compensation for family foster care to stimulate supply, maintenance of compensation into adoption, and certification of advanced care skills (especially for special needs children) warranting augmented payment.

d. Independent, Quality Representation

Children in foster care are relatively inarticulate and depend upon external representation. The juvenile courts, as with the judiciary in general, are inherently passive. The affirmative supervision duties of the dependency court, however, are extraordinary given its direct parental function for the foster care children under its charge. Many courts have attempted to develop more affirmative contact with the children under their jurisdiction through a widespread national program of Court Appointed Special Advocates (CASA). These volunteers, often retired persons, monitor foster children in placements and independently report to the court on their status. Although an important contribution, child advocates concede that the CASA program is not a substitute for professional, competent representation of children before the court. An attorney is required to present evidence to the court—consistent with the legal basis for the court's decisions. An attorney is capable of filing a writ or otherwise contesting an action by the county or a parent.

Despite the cases presented below indirectly guaranteeing parents an attorney for legal representation, involved children have not been so universally advantaged. Although federal law requires an appointment of a "guardian ad litem" by the dependency court, interpretations of who such a person may be vary widely. Some contend that the CASA volunteer can fulfill such a role. Others argue that county counsel (or the attorney for the agency) may perform such a role. Still others contend that the social worker assigned to the case may qualify. The consensus view of child advocates is that a child pulled from a home is about to undertake a serious legal proceeding of far reaching consequences. Accordingly, the child needs legal representation meeting minimal standards (as to qualification and performance),[23] as well as sufficiently low caseloads to adequately represent child clients.

e. Safety Net Cut-Off Endangerment

The Personal Responsibility and Work Opportunity Reconciliation Act of 1996 (PRA) does not directly alter child protection programs. The traditional requirements of the federal Adoption Assistance and Child Welfare Act remain in force. Eligibility, entitlement status, and funding for TANF-FC, Adoptions Assistance, and Medicaid for foster care and adopted children were substantially maintained. A child's eligibility for federal foster care and adoption assistance is based on the eligibility of the child's family for AFDC according to the rules in effect on June 1, 1995, rather than on the family's eligibility for the new TANF welfare block grant post 1996.

Overall, the PRA cut federal contribution for state safety-net (TANF) provision substantially. Funds for the Social Services Block Grant, which is used in part for child protection services, were reduced 15% in fiscal year 1997, and have been maintained at static levels since 2000. Inflation and child population gain will produce per capita real spending cuts 20%–25% lower to 2005, with a similar real spending reduction projected to 2010. Similar reductions have been implemented in food stamp benefits, the other major child safety-net federal program. The end result has been a decline in safety net support for those fully eligible from close to the poverty line in the 1970s, to 70% of the line in major states, and below half the poverty line in others.[24]

Some of the evidence of welfare reform outcome is favorable to impoverished children. Employment has increased. Child poverty and unwed births appear to have leveled. However, the primary visible sign of success—substantial diminution in welfare rolls—is misleading. Studies indicate that at least one-third of those not receiving TANF have not found employment. Of those who have, few earn incomes above the poverty line. Moreover, as discussed in Chapter 7, child care financial assistance—necessary for continued work for these parents[25] is assured in most states for only one to two years after initial employment. The children of immigrants who arrived in the United States after 1996 are likely to be in particularly dire straits due to their ineligibility for most safety net assistance, including food stamps, SSI, TANF, and non-emergency Medicaid. Some states have limited state-only assistance for some children, but the evidence indicates that although the percentage of children living in poverty has declined slightly, a larger number are living in extreme poverty, defined as under one-half of the federal poverty line.

Punitive provisions of the federal statute which threaten children include lifetime cut-off of the "parent's share" (which could be up to one-half of the grant) from TANF and food stamps to any person convicted of a drug offense. Children with parents attempting rehabilitation (or successfully accomplishing it) suffer safety net reductions to minimal levels (generally below one-half of the poverty line). Mothers are also required to assist in the identification of biological fathers for child support collection purposes. Child advocates argued unsuccessfully that alleged "parent share" reductions primarily impacted children. More ominous is the prospective cut-off of all assistance to any parent after sixty months of benefits. The limitation applies even for parents who have worked continuously on a part time basis during this period and received only small public payments. It has started to affect millions of children as of 2005, with uncertain consequences.

A state is allowed to use up to 30% of its TANF funds to carry out programs under the Social Services Block Grant and the Child Care and Development Block Grant, provided that not more than one-third of the transferred amount may be used for Title XX child welfare programs.[26] Hence, up to 10% of federal TANF funds may be used for child abuse/neglect spending—an important provision if TANF cut-downs produce substantial foster care demand increases as children are surrendered or taken from families unable to provide basic sustenance. However, reliance on the child welfare system as the final safeguard for children is problematical. Parental rights are normally not terminated based on poverty alone, but require *post hoc* proof of child endangerment. Further, even severe harm is not likely to be reported for children aged 0–5, who are less visible to teachers and other mandated child abuse reporters—at the same time, these children are at an age where nutritional deficiency can portend permanent damage.

Finally, reliance on child protective services is uneconomic given its substantially higher cost over denied TANF. The policy rationale of removing an otherwise competent and loving parent from a child (and vice versa) when the cost to do so is greater than public assistance in place is questionable. One explanation may be an unstated theory akin to "don't feed the pigeons"—if you deny help to impoverished adults, they will not have children they cannot afford. Child advocates argue that children are not pigeons, and that adult influence is best not accomplished through child deprivation. They contend that the political and media strength of children is so minimal that a direct discussion of adult reproductive responsibility, incentives, birth control, parenting education, or other subjects addressing decisions to have children is *verboten*, but cutting children to below one-half of the federal poverty line, with attendant nutritional shortfall and brain development implications, is not.

f. Emancipation Abandonment

Foster children reaching 18 years of age are commonly sent into the world without the family platform that supports most children during their early years of adulthood. Surveys of emancipated foster youth two to four years after emancipation find that fewer than half had completed high school or were employed, 30% did not have access to health care, 60% of the women had already given birth (the vast majority unmarried), and less than 20% were self supporting. Males made up a highly disproportionate share of incarcerated populations, at least five times the incidence of the general population.[27]

4. The Special Problem of Child Sexual Abuse

a. Protection Difficulties

Sexual abuse of children presents special enforcement and prosecutorial problems. Such abuse usually involves a betrayal of trust by persons on whom a child relies. It does not occur in public. It may not leave unambiguous physical evidence. It involves an area of human function steeped in understandable privacy. It is often not reported, or not immediately disclosed by a victim, due to what is termed the "Child Sexual Abuse Accommodation Syndrome," and which can be stimulated by threats from a perpetrator and/or by the underlying dependent position of the child, as well as the possibly embarrassing nature of the events. The syndrome also frequently produces common "retractions" of sexual abuse disclosures, even in cases where abuse is well documented from other evidence. Expert testimony as to the "syndrome" is normally not permitted to buttress the credibility of a child witness, unless the defense opens the door by challenging the failure of the child to report clearly and expeditiously, or raising statements of retraction.

Where children themselves report offenses, they are sometimes not believed. Tragically, they are often not believed by the other adult protectors of the child with a relationship to the offender. The most common such scenario is a mother's defense of a husband or boyfriend implicated in such an offense, even where the evidence may be substantial. That posture makes detection more difficult and subjects the child to the possible additional trauma of removal from the home due to that parent's "failure to protect" the child. The end result may be the loss of contact with the only parent a child victim has known and trusted.

Children suffer from the format and timing of societal response to alleged sexual offenses against them. First, the state may not only pursue a civil case to remove a child, but also a criminal prosecution against the suspected offender. The criminal case usually precedes the final civil determination but requires the high "proof beyond a reasonable doubt" burden of proof. An acquittal or plea to a lesser charge may have an impact on the civil dependency court proceedings. The criminal nature of such a prosecution also invokes due process rights of the accused, including the appointment of counsel, discovery rights, and cross examination. Although often assigned an attorney for the dependency court proceeding, children as victims or witnesses are not assured appointment of counsel on that basis or for those purposes.

The confluence of a criminal and civil case together thus raises problems for affected children. One such problem is the sequential interviews of a child by a relative, physician, police officer, Child Protective Service social worker, DA investigator, assigned attorney, attorney investigator, therapist, and others. These interviews may cause a child to relive a molestation or other offense repeatedly. In addition, they produce interview summaries that necessarily vary given the different styles of reporting, and are subject to discovery. Such early questioning may include interviewers insensitive to the misleading consequences of excessive suggestion, thus weakening a meritorious case. To address this problem, some jurisdictions have instituted a "single interview" multi-disciplinary videotape technique. It provides for a single interview as early as possible by a trained professional in a child-friendly room on video tape and observed by a multi-disciplinary group behind one way mirrors. The child must talk about the events once, with others able to suggest to the interviewer questions they need answered, and with a video tape recording the nature of the questions and the answers, including precise tone and body language. This format has enhanced the reliability and credibility of child victims. Studies also indicate its success in reducing the number of sequential interviews.[28]

Other problems for child victims attending the child sexual abuse civil/ criminal trials are discussed in Chapter 9 below, and include (1) the difficulty in testifying against a powerful adult in his or her close physical proximity, particularly if prior threats have been made to the child and the allowance of one-way or two-way testimony by videotape;[29] (2) the attempted discovery of psychological counseling records (even those occurring post-arrest) by defense counsel and involving the conflict between psycho-therapist-patient confidentiality, and the due process rights of a criminal defendant to discovery; and (3) the challenged credibility of child witnesses based on an alleged "False Memory Syndrome," or possible manipulation by biased adults.

b. Civil Commitment of Offenders

Adult pedophiles exhibit high rates of recidivism. The rights of child sexual molestation victims may be affected by the ability of the state to civilly commit such persons, or to track their presence and activities post-release. Some states have enacted statutes to accomplish such treatment/child protection on a civil basis. The Kansas Sexually Violent Predator Act provides for such commitment where a court finds that a "mental abnormality" makes a respondent "likely to engage" in future violent sexual predation. The statute covers those convicted of violent sexual offenses and awaiting release, those found so mentally defective they are incompetent to stand trial and those found not guilty by reason of a mental defect or disease. The Act was upheld in *Kansas v. Hendricks*, 521 U.S. 346 (1997).[30]

c. Mentally Disordered Sex Offender (MDSO) Tracking

Many states require persons convicted of certain sexual offenses to "register" as "Mentally Disordered Sex Offenders" after their release, and even after their period of parole has expired. Such registration allows further monitoring of the location of such persons for public protection. The states providing for such registration increased substantially in number, and public notice of the location of such persons was added, following the brutal rape and murder of seven-year-old Megan Kanka in 1994 by a neighbor who, unknown to the Kankas, had two prior child sex-related convictions. Within two years most states had enacted "Megan's Law" statutes requiring registration with local police departments by persons previously convicted of criminal child-sexual offenses, and "community notification" of their presence and respective names and addresses—to theoretically allow parental safeguards. During 1994, Congress enacted the Jacob Wetterling Crimes

Against Children and Sexually Violent Offender Registration Act[31] that financially sanctioned states (reduction in federal law enforcement assistance funding) where they failed to create a sex offender registration program. The Act was amended in 1996 to require an additional "notification" element for full federal funding, and most states now include both elements in their statutes, with some posting the information on the Internet. These statutes have been upheld even as to the registration and disclosure of persons engaging in sex offenses while under the age of 18 and purportedly subject to the confidentiality/rehabilitation policies of juvenile court.

Child advocates are sympathetic to the statute's intent, but it is unlikely that effective child protection can be achieved through the happenstance of actual parental knowledge of the identity and location of such persons, particularly in urban areas.

d. Child Pornography

Child pornography may involve child actors forced into unlawful sexual acts for the gratification of certain adults, and for the profit of its producers. Its proliferation may stimulate child molestation incidence. While some argue that child pornography may serve as an alternative outlet for pedophiles, reducing child victimization, others contend it has the opposite impact—feeding the interest and libido of those predisposed to its attraction. In *New York v. Ferber*, 458 U.S. 747 (1982), the Court upheld the criminal conviction of a bookstore owner who sold films to an undercover officer of young boys masturbating. The holding rejected the proffered First Amendment defense, finding that apart from the issue of expression and viewing, depictions of the sexual activity of children was itself a form of child abuse as to those performing.[32] After *Ferber,* and reflecting its holding, the Congress expanded its 1977 Act in 1984 to criminalize the transportation across state lines of material depicting sexual activity by children even if not obscene and with or without profit motive. In 1986 the Congress expanded the child sexual activity prohibition to include not merely transport or receipt across state lines, but production and advertising even if intra-state. It also created a civil remedy allowing private enforcement where personal injury occurs.[33]

The Supreme Court upheld the criminalization of private possession and viewing of non-obscene child pornography in the home and without any commercial intent—reflecting a generous reach as a "compelling state interest" of the *Ferber* protection for underage performers (*Osborne v.* Ohio, 495 U.S. 103 (1990)). The court implicitly recognized the market incentive such possession provides for child performer sexual exploitation. In addition, many states enacted photo processor reporting statutes, requiring the reporting of child sexual activities on film given to processors for developing, and providing civil immunity for such reports where filed in good faith.

The *Ferber* analysis and its related federal legislation leave open the possibility of First Amendment protection for "artificial" child pornography (*e.g.*, explicit sexual acts by persons who appear to be minors but who are in fact 18 years of age or older, or computer-generated images of even younger children). This technological advance has combined with the rapid growth of pornography sites on the Internet, a situs allowing intrusive entry of easily accessible or unsolicited pornography into homes with uncertain parental ability to block or oversee.

In 1996, Congress enacted the Child Pornography Prevention Act[34] to extend the reach of prohibition beyond the use of underage performers condemned in *Ferber* and focusing upon the prurient effect on viewers. It prohibits "any visual depiction" (computer-generated or actors over 18 years of age who appear younger) where the appearance is created of a minor engaging in "sexually explicit conduct."[35]

However, on April 16, 2002, the Supreme Court decided *Ashcroft v. Free Speech Coalition*, 535 U.S. 234 (2002), a 7–2 decision invalidating the Child Pornography Act of 1996 as overly broad and violative of the First Amendment. The fact that the prohibition reached sexual acts by persons who were not children and extended beyond the definition of "obscenity" allegedly prohibited by separate statute[36] was determinative. The *Ferber* Court had upheld the 1984 prohibition as addressing images where the "creation of the speech is itself the crime of child abuse." The 1996 Act's prohibition is based on the content of the communication. The images may be (and increasingly are) altered photos of persons over 18 or are entirely computer generated.[37] The Court noted that the 1996 Act's prohibition would apply to a picture in a psychology manual, or in a movie depicting the horrors of child sexual abuse; it could apply to a modern movie adaptation of Shakespeare's Romeo and Juliet, involving love between young teens, and might reach award winning movies such as Traffic and American Beauty.[38] The Court noted that one section of the law prohibits advertising or promotion that vaguely "conveys the impression" that the product includes children engaging in sex. And the Court also found objectionable the alleged broad liability imposed by the law to "knowing" reproduction, distribution, sale, reception, or possession of such materials, which compounds its vagueness.

The Court's holding did not grant dispensation for child pornography, reiterating support of the separate federal obscenity statute which requires that the "work taken as a whole, appeals to the prurient interest, is patently offensive in light of community standards, and lacks serious literary, artistic, political, or scientific value."[39]

Questions for Discussion

1. The Court acknowledges the compelling state interest in preventing child sexual abuse. It finds the Government's evidence of connection between the prohibited depictions and child abuse incidence to be weak. Would the 1996 Act withstand scrutiny if the Government produced an evidentiary record indicating a strong correlation between the depiction of children engaged in sex and child molestation incidence?

2. If the law were to be rewritten to prohibit only the depiction of children appearing to be under the age of twelve engaged in sex acts, would the Court approve of that narrower category? If not, would it approve of a rebuttable presumption that depiction of children engaged in sex acts was obscene, allowing a defendant to then demonstrate that the three elements of "obscenity" listed above did not apply? Would it approve such a presumption shift where the objectionable depiction appeared to be children under the age of twelve? Under the age of six? Where the sex depicted also included violence?

3. Would the Court approve a similar statute but more narrowly prohibiting the viewing of child sexual depictions by children? A ban on depiction to persons without prior consent?

D. REPORTING CHILD ABUSE

People v. Stritzinger

34 Cal. 3d 505 (1983)

OPINION: **MOSK**, J.—Defendant appeals from a judgment convicting him of multiple counts of child molestation. He contends that certain evidentiary rulings at his trial violated his psychotherapist-patient privilege and his right to confrontation. As will appear, we conclude that both points are well taken and compel reversal of the judgment.

During a 15-month period ending May 1981 defendant allegedly engaged in various acts of fondling, mutual masturbation, and oral copulation with his stepdaughter Sarah.[1] When Sarah's mother—defendant's wife—learned of these activities she arranged for her daughter and her husband each to see Dr. Walker, a licensed clinical psychologist. During Sarah's counseling session on July 28, 1981, she revealed that she had engaged in sexual activity with her stepfather. Dr. Walker reported the conversation to the child welfare agency that same afternoon.[2] The agency in turn relayed the information to the sheriff's office.

The next day Deputy Buttell of the sheriff's office telephoned Dr. Walker to investigate the child abuse report. Dr. Walker told Buttell that he had seen Sarah the day before, and related the substance of her discussion of sexual relations with her stepfather. He also informed Buttell that he was scheduled to meet with defendant himself later that afternoon, July 29, and with Sarah's older sister two days later, July 31. The deputy asked the doctor to call back after his session with Sarah's sister because he was concerned that she might also be the victim of child abuse. However, he hesitated on the issue of defendant's communications, acknowledging there might be a "confidentiality" problem. This telephone conversation was tape recorded.

Defendant saw Dr. Walker as scheduled, and during his conversation with the psychotherapist discussed his sexual relations with Sarah. Deputy Buttell telephoned the doctor again the next day, July 30, to inquire further about the reported child abuse. When Dr. Walker expressed reservations about disclosing defendant's confidential communications, Buttell read him Penal Code section 11171, subdivision (b), part of the Child Abuse Reporting Act, which he described as providing an applicable exception to the psychotherapist-patient privilege. The doctor then recounted the substance of defendant's session of July 29. This telephone conversation was also tape recorded, and a written report summarizing the conversation was prepared.

At the opening of trial defendant moved that Dr. Walker's testimony be excluded on the basis of the psychotherapist-patient privilege. (Evid. Code, § 1014.) The court held that Penal Code section 11171, subdivision (b), provides an applicable exception to the privilege and ruled the testimony admissible.

* * *

---

[1] Sarah turned 14 on July 13, 1980.

[2] Defendant concedes Evidence Code section 1027 provides an exception to the psychotherapist-patient privilege that allowed Dr. Walker to disclose Sarah's confidential communications. The section provides that "There is no [psychotherapist-patient] privilege under this article if all of the following circumstances exist:

"(a) The patient is a child under the age of 16.

"(b) The psychotherapist has reasonable cause to believe that the patient has been the victim of a crime and that disclosure of the communication is in the best interest of the child."

Defendant was convicted of one count of lewd and lascivious conduct with a minor, a felony, in violation of Penal Code section 288a, subdivision (b)(2); one count of misdemeanor child molestation, a necessarily included lesser offense under this section, based on an act of oral copulation; and seven counts of misdemeanor child molestation in violation of Penal Code section 647a. The verdict on one of the latter counts was set aside on defendant's motion to dismiss. Defendant was sentenced to three year's probation with ninety days in the county jail.

I

The Psychotherapist-Patient Privilege and the Child Abuse Reporting Act.

Defendant first contends that Dr. Walker's testimony regarding the consultation of July 29 was erroneously admitted at trial in violation of the psychotherapist-patient privilege, a relationship subsumed in the right to privacy and defined by statutory provision. On the facts of this case, we agree that the doctor's testimony should have been excluded.

Evidence Code section 1014 provides in part that "the patient, whether or not a party, has a privilege to refuse to disclose, and to prevent another from disclosing, a confidential communication between patient and psychotherapist...." We acknowledged in *In re Lifschutz* (1970) 2 Cal.3d 415, 421..., "the growing importance of the psychiatric profession in our modern, ultracomplex society." Thus for reasons of policy the psychotherapist-patient privilege has been broadly construed in favor of the patient....Confidential communications between psychotherapist and patient are protected in order to encourage those who may pose a threat to themselves or to others, because of some mental or emotional disturbance, to seek professional assistance....

The psychotherapist-patient privilege has been recognized as an aspect of the patient's constitutional right to privacy. (Cal. Const., art. I, § 1; *In re Lifschutz*, *supra*, 2 Cal.3d at pp. 431–432, citing *Griswold v. Connecticut* (1965) 381 U.S. 479, 484....

* * *

To determine whether the psychotherapist-patient privilege embraced by the right to privacy has impermissibly been violated, we begin by considering the state's competing interest. Here that interest is the detection and prevention of child abuse, and is expressed in the recently enacted Child Abuse Reporting Act. (Pen. Code, § 11165 et seq.) Section 11166, subdivision (a), of the act provides in part that "any child care custodian, medical practitioner, nonmedical practitioner, or employee of a child protective agency who has knowledge of or observes a child in his or her professional capacity or within the scope of his or her employment whom he or she knows or reasonably suspects has been the victim of child abuse shall report the known or suspected instance of child abuse to a child protective agency immediately or as soon as practically possible by telephone and shall prepare and send a written report thereof within 36 hours of receiving the information concerning the incident." Section 11165 of the act provides the following: subdivision (g) defines "child abuse" to include "the sexual assault of a child..."; subdivision (i) defines "medical practitioner" to include licensed psychiatrists and psychologists...

Together these provisions impose on psychotherapists the affirmative duty to report to a child protective agency all known and suspected instances of child abuse. Lest there be any doubt that the Legislature intended the child abuse reporting obligation to take precedence over the physician-patient or psychotherapist-patient privilege, section 11171, subdivision (b), explicitly provides an exception to these very privileges: "Neither the physician-patient privilege nor the psychotherapist-patient privilege applies to information reported pursuant to this article in any court proceeding or administrative hearing."...

Defendant neither challenges the constitutionality of the child-abuse reporting exception to the psychotherapist-patient privilege, nor argues that the state's interest in protecting children is less than compelling. Rather, he contends that on the particular facts of his case the exception provided in Penal Code section 11171, subdivision (b), was unnecessarily and therefore erroneously applied to his confidential communications with Dr. Walker. We agree.

* * *

Dr. Walker was under no statutory obligation to make a second report concerning the same activity. Had he learned from defendant of possible further child abuse—whether additional incidents involving Sarah, or other incidents with another child—he would, of course, have been required to report these new suspicions. Or, if Dr. Walker had first learned of the fondling incidents from defendant himself, he would have been bound to report that information as provided in the act. However, on the facts of this case, we conclude that Dr. Walker satisfied his statutory reporting obligation when he divulged Sarah's revelations; he was not required to reiterate his suspicion following consultation with defendant.

* * *

Richardson, J.—I respectfully dissent.

The majority finds prejudicial error was committed in admitting (1) Dr. Walker's testimony regarding defendant's admissions to him that he had sexually abused his stepdaughter Sarah, and (2) Sarah's own preliminary hearing testimony confirming that such abuse had occurred. In my view, *both* Dr. Walker's and Sarah's testimony were admissible and fully support defendant's conviction of child molestation.

1. *Dr. Walker's Testimony*

The majority concedes that Dr. Walker's initial report regarding his interview with Sarah was not rendered inadmissible by the psychotherapist-patient privilege....Yet the majority holds that Dr. Walker's supplemental report, discussing his interview with defendant himself, was protected by that privilege. With due respect, this holding is patently incorrect.

The Child Abuse Reporting Act (Pen. Code, § 11165 *et seq.*) unequivocally provides that the psychotherapist-patient privilege shall not apply "to information reported pursuant to" the act....Thus, if Dr. Walker's supplemental report was made "pursuant to" the act's provisions, the report was unprivileged and Dr. Walker was free to testify regarding its contents.

The act's provisions impose on psychotherapists such as Dr. Walker an affirmative duty to report to a child protective agency all known or suspected instances of child abuse, even though they may learn of such incidents through otherwise confidential communications with their patients....

The majority holds that, because Dr. Walker initially reported Sarah's own communications with him regarding defendant's misconduct, Dr. Walker's statutory obligations were somehow satisfied and permanently discharged and, accordingly, the psychotherapist-patient privilege was revived. It is claimed that the privilege thereafter protected any further disclosure regarding the same incidents of sexual abuse.

With deference, I suggest that the majority's interpretation of the Child Abuse Reporting Act is erroneous. Under section 11171, subdivision (b), the privilege is rendered inapplicable to *any* information "reported pursuant to" the act.

The provision is not limited merely to information *required* to be reported thereunder. Certainly Dr. Walker was *permitted* (if indeed, not required) to file a supplemental report which *corroborated* the victim's unsubstantiated charges by reporting admissions from the alleged offender himself. How can it reasonably be argued that such a critical follow-up report, confirming what otherwise might be deemed mere fantasy or fabrication by a young child, was not issued "pursuant to" the act? In my view, in order to carry out the act's salutary purposes, such confirmatory reports should be encouraged and the information contained therein made freely available for use in criminal proceedings. I have no doubt whatever that this was the legislative intent underlying section 11171, subdivision (b).

* * *

I would affirm the judgment.

Questions for Discussion

1. Should Dr. Walker be seeing both the defendant and his daughter, particularly after he knows of a conflict of interest? Would Dr. Walker be obligated to report the molestation if only the defendant were his patient and he confessed to molestation? If the information of molestation only concerned prior events that were not continuing and in Dr. Walker's professional opinion were not likely to reoccur?

2. The court notes that the patient holds the psychotherapist-patient privilege. What would happen if Sara were to tell Dr. Walker that her disclosures to him were privileged and she wanted him to assert that privilege? Should the court recognize such a decision by Sara given her age? What if Sara's mother were loyal to the defendant (or doubted her daughter's allegations) and informed Dr. Walker that, speaking as Sara's parent, the privilege should be asserted?

3. What if a client informs an attorney that not only has he committed a crime, but that he is now in the course of planning and carrying out additional crimes. The "continuing crime exception" limits even the attorney-client privilege. Is this molestation a continuing crime?

4. The California Constitution buttresses the privilege with an explicit "right to privacy", which would possibly apply to the defendant's statements to Dr. Walker during the course of treatment. But the same section (Cal. Const. Art. I, Sec. 1) also confers a "right to safety". Does such a right apply to Sara, who may be facing rape within her own home? Is it a factor which is reflected in the court's decision? Should it be?

5. Is it persuasive that the initial report by Dr. Walker satisfies the statute and the majority implies that further reports may be gratuitous? What if the matter is disregarded by child protective services due to a lack of corroboration? Is confirmation not relevant? Is a mandated reporter excused from reporting if another report has been made by another reporter?

6. What happens if the child receives psychotherapy—with the privilege applied so she is not betrayed by another adult—and the defendant seeks those

records to impeach her testimony? What if her disclosures were, in fact, exculpatory and would preclude his conviction—does he have a due process right to that information? Can these competing interests be reconciled through *in camera* review by a court to determine if exculpatory material is present and germane, and with confidentiality otherwise maintained?

E. RIGHT TO COUNSEL

1. Parents

Lassiter v. Department of Social Services
452 U.S. 18 (1981)

JUSTICE STEWART delivered the opinion of the Court.

I

In the late spring of 1975, after hearing evidence that the petitioner, Abby Gail Lassiter, had not provided her infant son William with proper medical care, the District Court of Durham County, N.C., adjudicated him a neglected child and transferred him to the custody of the Durham County Department of Social Services, the respondent here. A year later, Ms. Lassiter was charged with first-degree murder, was convicted of second-degree murder, and began a sentence of 25 to 40 years of imprisonment.[1] In 1978 the Department petitioned the court to terminate Ms. Lassiter's parental rights because, the Department alleged, she "has not had any contact with the child since December of 1975" and "has willfully left the child in foster care for more than two consecutive years without showing that substantial progress has been made in correcting the conditions which led to the removal of the child, or without showing a positive response to the diligent efforts of the Department of Social Services to strengthen her relationship to the child, or to make and follow through with constructive planning for the future of the child."

* * *

A

The pre-eminent generalization that emerges from this Court's precedents on an indigent's right to appointed counsel is that such a right has been recognized

---

[1] The North Carolina Court of Appeals, in reviewing the petitioner's conviction, indicated that the murder occurred during an altercation between Ms. Lassiter, her mother, and the deceased:

"Defendant's mother told [the deceased] to 'come on.' They began to struggle and deceased fell or was knocked to the floor. Defendant's mother was beating deceased with a broom. While deceased was still on the floor and being beaten with the broom, defendant entered the apartment. She went into the kitchen and got a butcher knife. She took the knife and began stabbing the deceased who was still prostrate. The body of deceased had seven stab wounds...." *State v. Lassiter*, No. 7614SC1054 (June 1, 1977).

After her conviction was affirmed on appeal, Ms. Lassiter sought to attack it collaterally. Among her arguments was that the assistance of her trial counsel had been ineffective because he had failed to "seek to elicit or introduce before the jury the statement made by [Ms. Lassiter's mother,] 'And I did it, I hope she dies.'" Ms. Lassiter's mother had, like Ms. Lassiter, been indicted on a first-degree murder charge; however, the trial court granted the elder Ms. Lassiter's motion for a nonsuit. The North Carolina General Court of Justice, Superior Court Division, denied Ms. Lassiter's motion for collateral relief....

to exist only where the litigant may lose his physical liberty if he loses the litigation....

* * *

B

The case of *Mathews v. Eldridge*, 424 U.S. 319, 335, propounds three elements to be evaluated in deciding what due process requires, viz., the private interests at stake, the government's interest, and the risk that the procedures used will lead to erroneous decisions. We must balance these elements against each other, and then set their net weight in the scales against the presumption that there is a right to appointed counsel only where the indigent, if he is unsuccessful, may lose his personal freedom.

This Court's decisions have by now made plain beyond the need for multiple citation that a parent's desire for and right to "the companionship, care, custody, and management of his or her children" is an important interest that "undeniably warrants deference and, absent a powerful countervailing interest, protection." *Stanley v. Illinois*, 405 U.S. 645, 651. Here the State has sought not simply to infringe upon that interest, but to end it. If the State prevails, it will have worked a unique kind of deprivation....A parent's interest in the accuracy and justice of the decision to terminate his or her parental status is, therefore, a commanding one.[3]

Since the State has an urgent interest in the welfare of the child, it shares the parent's interest in an accurate and just decision. For this reason, the State may share the indigent parent's interest in the availability of appointed counsel. If, as our adversary system presupposes, accurate and just results are most likely to be obtained through the equal contest of opposed interests, the State's interest in the child's welfare may perhaps best be served by a hearing in which both the parent and the State acting for the child are represented by counsel, without whom the contest of interests may become unwholesomely unequal. North Carolina itself acknowledges as much by providing that where a parent files a written answer to a termination petition, the State must supply a lawyer to represent the child....

The State's interests, however, clearly diverge from the parent's insofar as the State wishes the termination decision to be made as economically as possible and thus wants to avoid both the expense of appointed counsel and the cost of the lengthened proceedings his presence may cause. But though the State's pecuniary interest is legitimate, it is hardly significant enough to overcome private interests as important as those here, particularly in light of the concession in the respondent's brief that the "potential costs of appointed counsel in termination proceedings...is [*sic*] admittedly *de minimis* compared to the costs in all criminal actions."

Finally, consideration must be given to the risk that a parent will be erroneously deprived of his or her child because the parent is not represented by counsel....

* * *

Yet the ultimate issues with which a termination hearing deals are not always simple, however commonplace they may be. Expert medical and psychiatric testimony, which few parents are equipped to understand and fewer still to confute, is sometimes presented. The parents are likely to be people with little education, who have had uncommon difficulty in dealing with life, and who are, at

---

[3] Some parents will have an additional interest to protect. Petitions to terminate parental rights are not uncommonly based on alleged criminal activity. Parents so accused may need legal counsel to guide them in understanding the problems such petitions may create.

the hearing, thrust into a distressing and disorienting situation. That these factors may combine to overwhelm an uncounseled parent is evident from the findings some courts have made....Thus, courts have generally held that the State must appoint counsel for indigent parents at termination proceedings....

C

.

The dispositive question, which must now be addressed, is whether the three *Eldridge* factors, when weighed against the presumption that there is no right to appointed counsel in the absence of at least a potential deprivation of physical liberty, suffice to rebut that presumption and thus to lead to the conclusion that the Due Process Clause requires the appointment of counsel when a State seeks to terminate an indigent's parental status. To summarize the above discussion of the *Eldridge* factors: the parent's interest is an extremely important one (and may be supplemented by the dangers of criminal liability inherent in some termination proceedings); the State shares with the parent an interest in a correct decision, has a relatively weak pecuniary interest, and, in some but not all cases, has a possibly stronger interest in informal procedures; and the complexity of the proceeding and the incapacity of the uncounseled parent could be, but would not always be, great enough to make the risk of an erroneous deprivation of the parent's rights insupportably high.

* * *

III

.

Here, as in *Scarpelli*, "[it] is neither possible nor prudent to attempt to formulate a precise and detailed set of guidelines to be followed in determining when the providing of counsel is necessary to meet the applicable due process requirements," since here, as in that case, "[the] facts and circumstances...are susceptible of almost infinite variation...." 411 U.S., at 790. Nevertheless, because child-custody litigation must be concluded as rapidly as is consistent with fairness,[7] we decide today whether the trial judge denied Ms. Lassiter due process of law when he did not appoint counsel for her.

The respondent represents that the petition to terminate Ms. Lassiter's parental rights contained no allegations of neglect or abuse upon which criminal charges could be based, and hence Ms. Lassiter could not well have argued that she required counsel for that reason. The Department of Social Services was represented at the hearing by counsel, but no expert witnesses testified, and the case presented no specially troublesome points of law, either procedural or substantive. While hearsay evidence was no doubt admitted, and while Ms. Lassiter no doubt left incomplete her defense that the Department had not adequately assisted her in rekindling her interest in her son, the weight of the evidence that she had few sparks of such an interest was sufficiently great that the presence of counsel for Ms. Lassiter could not have made a determinative difference. True, a lawyer might have done more with the argument that William should live with Ms. Lassiter's mother—but that argument was quite explicitly made by both Lassiters, and the evidence that the elder Ms. Lassiter had said she could not handle another child, that the social worker's investigation had led to a similar conclusion, and that the grandmother had displayed scant interest in the child once he had been removed from her daughter's custody was, though controverted, sufficiently

---

[7] According to the respondent's brief, William Lassiter is now living "in a pre-adoptive home with foster parents committed to formal adoption to become his legal parents." He cannot be legally adopted, nor can his status otherwise be finally clarified, until this litigation ends.

substantial that the absence of counsel's guidance on this point did not render the proceedings fundamentally unfair.[8] Finally, a court deciding whether due process requires the appointment of counsel need not ignore a parent's plain demonstration that she is not interested in attending a hearing. Here, the trial court had previously found that Ms. Lassiter had expressly declined to appear at the 1975 child custody hearing, Ms. Lassiter had not even bothered to speak to her retained lawyer after being notified of the termination hearing, and the court specifically found that Ms. Lassiter's failure to make an effort to contest the termination proceeding was without cause. In view of all these circumstances, we hold that the trial court did not err in failing to appoint counsel for Ms. Lassiter.

* * *

For the reasons stated in this opinion, the judgment is affirmed.

* * *

Justice Blackmun, with whom **Justice Brennan** and **Justice Marshall** join, dissenting.

The Court today denies an indigent mother the representation of counsel in a judicial proceeding initiated by the State of North Carolina to terminate her parental rights with respect to her youngest child. The Court most appropriately recognizes that the mother's interest is a "commanding one,"...and it finds no countervailing state interest of even remotely comparable significance, ...Nonetheless, the Court avoids what seems to me the obvious conclusion that due process requires the presence of counsel for a parent threatened with judicial termination of parental rights, and, instead, revives an ad hoc approach thoroughly discredited nearly 20 years ago in *Gideon v. Wainwright*, 372 U.S. 335 (1963). Because I believe that the unique importance of a parent's interest in the care and custody of his or her child cannot constitutionally be extinguished through formal judicial proceedings without the benefit of counsel, I dissent.

---

[8] Ms. Lassiter's argument here that her mother should have been given custody of William is hardly consistent with her argument in the collateral attack on her murder conviction that she was innocent because her mother was guilty. See n. 1, *supra*.

Questions for Discussion

1. What of the child's right to an attorney? Is a state order terminating a parental relationship any less of a constitutional taking for the child than for the parent? Can we assume that the attorney for the county represents the child's interests? Can an attorney for the county appeal or otherwise seek, on behalf of a child, review of a decision by a county official who is also that attorney's client?

2. The dissent believes the parent's right to counsel should be absolute. It is then left with the task of distinguishing *Parham*, where counsel (and hearing) are denied children subject to civil commitment (see Chapter 10). The dissent contends that (a) dependency court proceedings are complex, (b) error is more likely, and (c) the parent is not trained in the law. However, isn't the *Parham* civil commitment process less complex because there is virtually no due process? Is there more or less risk of error where an independent judge takes testimony than

where medical professionals and parents make the final judgment (as in *Parham*)? Why would not the County "professionals" exercise the same neutrality in dependency court as the state psychiatrists who are relied on in *Parham*? Is the parent here less articulate than the child in *Parham*—who need not be apprised of the basis for his commitment?

3. The holding of *Lassiter* is that appointed counsel was not required for this parent. However, the case had the practical effect of mandating counsel for parents in virtually all proceedings where the right to parent is at risk. Why?

2. Children

Kenny A. v. Sonny Purdue (attny wrld)
356 F. Supp. 2d 1353 (2005)

Marvin H. Shoob, Senior Judge:

• • •

In both Fulton and DeKalb Counties, child advocate attorneys are responsible for representing allegedly deprived children in all of these proceedings. Fulton County employs four child advocate attorneys, while DeKalb County employs five....As of March 2004, there were 1,757 plaintiff foster children in custody in Fulton County and 914 in DeKalb County. This equates to a caseload of 439.2 child clients per attorney in Fulton County, and 182.8 child clients per attorney in DeKalb County. The American Bar Association, the United States Department of Health and Human Services, and the National Association of Counsel for Children (NACC) have each established standards of practice for lawyers who represent children in abuse and neglect cases. In light of the minimum requirements for effective advocacy set forth in these standards, the NACC recommends that no child advocate attorney should maintain a caseload of over 100 individual child clients at a time. facts

• • •

The Court concludes that plaintiff foster children have both a statutory and a constitutional right to counsel in all deprivation proceedings, including but not limited to TPR (termination of parental rights) proceedings. The Court further concludes that plaintiffs have presented sufficient evidence to create a genuine issue for trial as to whether they are threatened with irreparable harm because they are receiving, or face a substantial risk of receiving, ineffective assistance of counsel in such proceedings....[T]he Court rejects County Defendants' argument that only the legislature has the authority to correct this problem. If plaintiffs prove their case at trial, then this Court has not only the authority but the obligation to grant appropriate injunctive relief.

• • •

...[T]he Court concludes that in a deprivation proceeding there is an inherent conflict of interests between the child and his or her parent, guardian, or custodian, which requires appointment of separate counsel for the child pursuant to [state law]....There is no conflict, however, in requiring the appointment of both an attorney and a guardian ad litem for the child. Indeed, the two Code sections expressly require the appointment of both an attorney and a guardian ad litem in cases where the child is not represented by his or her parent, guardian, or custodian....

• • •

III. Constitutional Right to Counsel

Even if there were not a statutory right to counsel for children in deprivation cases and TPR proceedings, the Court concludes that such a right is guaranteed under the Due Process Clause of the Georgia Constitution, Art. I, § 1, P 1. It is well settled that children are afforded protection under the Due Process Clauses of both the United States and Georgia Constitutions and are entitled to constitutionally adequate procedural due process when their liberty or property rights are at stake. See, *e.g., Goss v. Lopez*, 419 U.S. 565 (1975) (lack of adequate procedures used by school in suspending students violated due process); *In re Gault*, 387 U.S. 1 (1967) (holding that minors have due process right to counsel in delinquency proceedings)....The question, therefore, is whether plaintiff foster children have liberty or property interests at stake in deprivation and TPR proceedings, and, if so, what process is due when those interests are threatened.

The Court finds that children have fundamental liberty interests at stake in deprivation and TPR proceedings. These include a child's interest in his or her own safety, health, and well-being, as well as an interest in maintaining the integrity of the family unit and in having a relationship with his or her biological parents. On the one hand, an erroneous decision that a child is not deprived or that parental rights should not be terminated can have a devastating effect on a child, leading to chronic abuse or even death. On the other hand, an erroneous decision that a child is deprived or that parental rights should be terminated can lead to the unnecessary destruction of the child's most important family relationships.

Furthermore, a child's liberty interests continue to be at stake even after the child is placed in state custody. At that point, a "special relationship" is created that gives rise to rights to reasonably safe living conditions and services necessary to ensure protection from physical, psychological, and emotional harm....Thus, a child's fundamental liberty interests are at stake not only in the initial deprivation hearing but also in the series of hearings and review proceedings that occur as part of a deprivation case once a child comes into state custody.

Given the liberty interests at stake, the question becomes what process is constitutionally required to safeguard those interests. To determine what process is due under the Due Process Clause of the Georgia Constitution, Georgia courts apply the three-part federal test enunciated in *Mathews v. Eldridge* 424 U.S. 319, 334-35 (1976):

> [O]ur prior decisions indicate that identification of the specific dictates of due process generally requires consideration of three distinct factors: First, the private interest that will be affected by the official action; second, the risk of an erroneous deprivation of such interest through the procedures used, and the probable value, if any, of additional or substitute procedural safeguards; and finally, the Government's interest, including the function involved and the fiscal and administrative burdens that the additional or substitute procedural requirement would entail.

...Applying the Mathews test to this case, the Court concludes that plaintiff foster children have a right to counsel in deprivation and TPR proceedings under the Due Process Clause of the Georgia Constitution.

...[T]he evidence shows that foster children in state custody are subject to placement in a wide array of different types of foster care placements, including institutional facilities where their physical liberty is greatly restricted. Indeed, plaintiffs have pointed to evidence that foster children are often forced to live in such institutional settings because suitable family foster homes are not available. The Court concludes that the private liberty interests at stake support a due process right to counsel in deprivation and TPR proceedings.

Second, the Court finds that there is a significant risk that erroneous decisions will be made during the course of deprivation and TPR proceedings. As an initial matter, the standards employed by juvenile courts in deprivation and TPR proceedings allow wide room for judicial discretion and thus for subjective determinations....Such "imprecise substantive standards that leave determinations unusually open to the subjective values of the judge" serve "to magnify the risk of erroneous factfinding."...In addition, plaintiffs have pointed to strong empirical evidence that DFCS makes erroneous decisions on a routine basis that affect the safety and welfare of foster children.

Contrary to County Defendants' argument, juvenile court judges, court appointed special advocates (CASAs), and citizen review panels do not adequately mitigate the risk of such errors. Judges, unlike child advocate attorneys, cannot conduct their own investigations and are entirely dependent on others to provide them information about the child's circumstances. Similarly, citizen review panels must rely on facts presented to them by state and county personnel, including local DFCS offices. As a result, their reviews are only as good as the information provided to them by DFCS and other state and local agencies. CASAs are also volunteers who do not provide legal representation to a child. Moreover, CASAs are appointed in only a small number of cases. The Court concludes that only the appointment of counsel can effectively mitigate the risk of significant errors in deprivation and TPR proceedings.

Finally, the Court must consider the government's interest, including the function involved and the fiscal and administrative burdens that a right to counsel would entail. In this case, the function involved is that of the state as *parens patriae*, which refers to "the state in its capacity as provider of protection to those unable to care for themselves."

• • •

Plaintiffs cite deposition testimony and documentary evidence showing that effective assistance of counsel by a child advocate attorney requires that he or she carry out certain minimum legal tasks as part of the representation. These tasks include meeting with the child prior to court hearings and when apprised of emergencies or significant events impacting the child; conducting investigations and discovery, including interviewing individuals involved with the child, such as caseworkers and foster parents, and reviewing all judicial, medical, social services, educational, and other records pertaining to the child; evaluating the child's need for particular services; monitoring the implementation of all court orders; participating in all hearings; and filing all relevant motions and appeals.

Plaintiffs also cite the NACC recommendation that, in order to perform these essential tasks, a child advocate attorney should represent no more than 100 individual clients at a time. The evidence shows that this recommendation is based on the assumption that a child advocate attorney will spend an average of 20 hours representing each child and will work 2000 hours in a year. The recommended caseload limit is meant to apply regardless of how many support

> staff an attorney might have and assumes that child advocate attorneys are not required to perform non-legal, administrative tasks. Based on his extensive experience in the child welfare area and his participation in the development of the NACC caseload limit, NACC Executive Director Marvin Ventrell testified that a child advocate attorney could not possibly provide effective representation if the attorney had a number of clients significantly above 100, and certainly not if the attorney had a caseload of 200 clients. The evidence shows that each of the four child advocate attorneys in Fulton County represent almost 450 clients, while the five child advocate attorneys in DeKalb County each represent approximately 200 clients.
>
> In addition, plaintiffs have presented testimonial and documentary evidence showing that Fulton and DeKalb Counties' child advocate attorneys are overwhelmed by their caseloads and cannot provide effective representation to their child clients....Plaintiffs also point to evidence from the named plaintiffs' own child advocate attorney files. This evidence shows that the child advocate attorneys often failed to meet with their clients, failed to monitor compliance with court orders, and failed to ensure that their clients' foster care placements were safe and appropriate. All of this evidence is more than sufficient to create a genuine issue for trial as to whether plaintiff foster children, including the named plaintiffs, are receiving, or face a substantial risk of receiving, ineffective assistance of counsel.
>
> • • •
>
> County Defendants argue that public policy considerations mandate that plaintiffs not be allowed to circumvent the Georgia legislature, which has sole authority to determine the appropriate amount of funding for child advocate attorneys. This argument is without merit. If this Court finds that plaintiff foster children's right to counsel is being violated, then it is the obligation of the Court to order an appropriate remedy even if such an order requires the state to appropriate additional funds to hire more child advocate attorneys. County Defendants cite no authority to the contrary.

Questions for Discussion

1. Is this published holding limited to Georgia on an independent state basis? Given the extensive discussion of federal constitutional standards (held to be here applicable as well), is this decision binding as a federal precedent? Is it being followed as to either its attorney representation or caseload limitation holding?

2. Should standards allow higher caseloads where attorneys for children are given investigators or social workers to assist them? Will a jurisdiction meet the suggested 100 case per attorney maximum by dismissing existing support staff in order to finance new attorney hiring?

3. What of the status of child's counsel if provided? Are children parties in dependency court proceedings? For example, if the county bringing the case and the attorneys for the defense agree to dismiss, or to drop certain charges, does counsel for the child have standing to object? See *Allen M. v. Superior Court of San Diego County*, 6 Cal.App.4th 1069 (1992). If a child is given counsel

at the trial level in juvenile court, does he or she have continuing rights to that representation on appeal? See *In re Josiah Z.*, 36 Cal.4th 664 (2005). What is the role of a child's attorney as to ancillary legal needs outside of dependency court? Can the child's attorney represent the child for SSI benefits? Qualification for education disability benefits (*e.g.*, under the federal IDEA statute)? Medical coverage? Tort injury?

F. TERMINATION OF PARENTAL RIGHTS: STANDARDS AND BURDEN

Santosky v. Kramer
455 U.S. 745 (1982)

JUSTICE BLACKMUN delivered the opinion of the Court.

Under New York law, the State may terminate, over parental objection, the rights of parents in their natural child upon a finding that the child is "permanently neglected." N.Y. Soc. Serv. Law §§ 384-b.4.(d), 384-b.7.(a)...The New York Family Court Act § 622...requires that only a "fair preponderance of the evidence" support that finding. Thus, in New York, the factual certainty required to extinguish the parent-child relationship is no greater than that necessary to award money damages in an ordinary civil action.

Today we hold that the Due Process Clause of the Fourteenth Amendment demands more than this. Before a State may sever completely and irrevocably the rights of parents in their natural child, due process requires that the State support its allegations by at least clear and convincing evidence.

I

A

New York authorizes its officials to remove a child temporarily from his or her home if the child appears "neglected," within the meaning of Art. 10 of the Family Court Act....Once removed, a child under the age of 18 customarily is placed "in the care of an authorized agency,"...usually a state institution or a foster home. At that point, "the state's first obligation is to help the family with services to...reunite it...."...But if convinced that "positive, nurturing parent-child relationships no longer exist,"...the State may initiate "permanent neglect" proceedings to free the child for adoption.

* * *

B

Petitioners John Santosky II and Annie Santosky are the natural parents of Tina and John III. In November 1973, after incidents reflecting parental neglect, respondent Kramer, Commissioner of the Ulster County Department of Social Services, initiated a neglect proceeding under Fam. Ct. Act § 1022 and removed Tina from her natural home. About 10 months later, he removed John III and placed him with foster parents. On the day John was taken, Annie Santosky gave birth to a third child, Jed. When Jed was only three days old, respondent transferred him to a foster home on the ground that immediate removal was necessary to avoid imminent danger to his life or health.

In October 1978, respondent petitioned the Ulster County Family Court to terminate petitioners' parental rights in the three children.[4] Petitioners challenged the constitutionality of the "fair preponderance of the evidence" standard specified in Fam. Ct. Act § 622. The Family Court Judge rejected this constitutional challenge,

App. 29–30, and weighed the evidence under the statutory standard. While acknowledging that the Santoskys had maintained contact with their children, the judge found those visits "at best superficial and devoid of any real emotional content." *Id.*, at 21. After deciding that the agency had made "'diligent efforts' to encourage and strengthen the parental relationship," *id.*, at 30, he concluded that the Santoskys were incapable, even with public assistance, of planning for the future of their children. *Id.*, at 33–37. The judge later held a dispositional hearing and ruled that the best interests of the three children required permanent termination of the Santoskys' custody.[5] *Id.*, at 39.

Petitioners appealed, again contesting the constitutionality of § 622's standard of proof....

* * *

I

* * *

...When the State moves to destroy weakened familial bonds, it must provide the parents with fundamentally fair procedures.[7]

In *Lassiter*, the Court and three dissenters agreed that the nature of the process due in parental rights termination proceedings turns on a balancing of the "three distinct factors" specified in *Mathews v. Eldridge*, 424 U.S. 319, 335 (1976): the private interests affected by the proceeding; the risk of error created by the State's chosen procedure; and the countervailing governmental interest supporting use of the challenged procedure....

* * *

Thus, while private parties may be interested intensely in a civil dispute over money damages, application of a "fair preponderance of the evidence" standard indicates both society's "minimal concern with the outcome," and a conclusion that the litigants should "share the risk of error in roughly equal fashion." 441 U.S., at 423....

* * *

---

[4] Respondent had made an earlier and unsuccessful termination effort in September 1976. After a factfinding hearing, the Family Court Judge dismissed respondent's petition for failure to prove an essential element of Fam. Ct. Act § 614.1.(d). See *In re Santosky*, 89 Misc. 2d 730, 393 N.Y.S. 2d 486 (1977). The New York Supreme Court, Appellate Division, affirmed, finding that "the record as a whole" revealed that petitioners had "substantially planned for the future of the children." *In re John W.*,...404 N.Y.S. 2d 717, 719 (1978).

[5] Since respondent Kramer took custody of Tina, John III, and Jed, the Santoskys have had two other children, James and Jeremy. The State has taken no action to remove these younger children. At oral argument, counsel for respondents replied affirmatively when asked whether he was asserting that petitioners were "unfit to handle the three older ones but not unfit to handle the two younger ones."....

[7] We therefore reject respondent Kramer's claim that a parental rights termination proceeding does not interfere with a fundamental liberty interest. See Brief for Respondent Kramer 11–18; Tr. of Oral Arg. 38. The fact that important liberty interests of the child and its foster parents may also be affected by a permanent neglect proceeding does not justify denying the *natural parents* constitutionally adequate procedures. Nor can the State refuse to provide natural parents adequate procedural safeguards on the ground that the family unit already has broken down; that is the very issue the permanent neglect proceeding is meant to decide.

This Court has mandated an intermediate standard of proof—"clear and convincing evidence"—when the individual interests at stake in a state proceeding are both "particularly important" and "more substantial than mere loss of money." *Addington v. Texas*, 441 U.S., at 424. Notwithstanding "the state's 'civil labels and good intentions,'"...the Court has deemed this level of certainty necessary to preserve fundamental fairness in a variety of government-initiated proceedings that threaten the individual involved with "a significant deprivation of liberty" or "stigma." 441 U.S., at 425, 426....

* * *

III

In parental rights termination proceedings, the private interest affected is commanding; the risk of error from using a preponderance standard is substantial; and the countervailing governmental interest favoring that standard is comparatively slight. Evaluation of the three *Eldridge* factors compels the conclusion that use of a "fair preponderance of the evidence" standard in such proceedings is inconsistent with due process.

A

* * *

The factfinding does not purport—and is not intended—to balance the child's interest in a normal family home against the parents' interest in raising the child. Nor does it purport to determine whether the natural parents or the foster parents would provide the better home. Rather, the factfinding hearing pits the State directly against the parents. The State alleges that the natural parents are at fault....The questions disputed and decided are what the State did—"made diligent efforts,"...—and what the natural parents did not do—"maintain contact with or plan for the future of the child."....The State marshals an array of public resources to prove its case and disprove the parents' case. Victory by the State not only makes termination of parental rights possible; it entails a judicial determination that the parents are unfit to raise their own children.[10]

At the factfinding, the State cannot presume that a child and his parents are adversaries. After the State has established parental unfitness at that initial proceeding, the court may assume at the *dispositional* stage that the interests of the child and the natural parents do diverge. See Fam. Ct. Act § 631 (judge shall make his order "solely on the basis of the best interests of the child," and thus has no obligation to consider the natural parents' rights in selecting dispositional alternatives). But until the State proves parental unfitness, the child and his parents share a vital interest in preventing erroneous termination of their natural relationship.[11] Thus, at the factfinding, the interests of the child and his natural parents coincide to favor use of error-reducing procedures.

* * *

[10] The Family Court Judge in the present case expressly refused to terminate petitioners' parental rights on a "non-statutory, no-fault basis."....Nor is it clear that the State constitutionally could terminate a parent's rights *without* showing parental unfitness. See *Quilloin v. Walcott*, 434 U.S. 246, 255 (1978) ("We have little doubt that the Due Process Clause would be offended '[if] a State were to attempt to force the breakup of a natural family, over the objections of the parents and their children, without some showing of unfitness and for the sole reason that to do so was thought to be in the children's best interest,'" quoting *Smith v. Organization of Foster Families*, 431 U.S. 816, 862–863 (1977)...

B

Under *Mathews v. Eldridge*, we next must consider both the risk of erroneous deprivation of private interests resulting from use of a "fair preponderance" standard and the likelihood that a higher evidentiary standard would reduce that risk. See 424 U.S., at 335. Since the factfinding phase of a permanent neglect proceeding is an adversary contest between the State and the natural parents, the relevant question is whether a preponderance standard fairly allocates the risk of an erroneous factfinding between these two parties.

In New York, the factfinding stage of a state-initiated permanent neglect proceeding bears many of the indicia of a criminal trial....

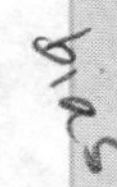

At such a proceeding, numerous factors combine to magnify the risk of erroneous factfinding. Permanent neglect proceedings employ imprecise substantive standards that leave determinations unusually open to the subjective values of the judge....Because parents subject to termination proceedings are often poor, uneducated, or members of minority groups,...such proceedings are often vulnerable to judgments based on cultural or class bias.

The State's ability to assemble its case almost inevitably dwarfs the parents' ability to mount a defense. No predetermined limits restrict the sums an agency may spend in prosecuting a given termination proceeding. The State's attorney usually will be expert on the issues contested and the procedures employed at the factfinding hearing, and enjoys full access to all public records concerning the family. The State may call on experts in family relations, psychology, and medicine to bolster its case. Furthermore, the primary witnesses at the hearing will be the agency's own professional caseworkers whom the State has empowered both to investigate the family situation and to testify against the parents. Indeed, because the child is already in agency custody, the State even has the power to shape the historical events that form the basis for termination.[13]

* * *

C

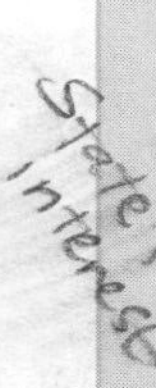

Two state interests are at stake in parental rights termination proceedings—a *parens patriae* interest in preserving and promoting the welfare of the child and a fiscal and administrative interest in reducing the cost and burden of such proceedings. A standard of proof more strict than preponderance of the evidence is consistent with both interests.

---

[11] For a child, the consequences of termination of his natural parents' rights may well be far-reaching. In Colorado, for example, it has been noted: "The child loses the right of support and maintenance, for which he may thereafter be dependent upon society; the right to inherit; and all other rights inherent in the legal parent-child relationship, not just for [a limited] period..., but forever."....

Some losses cannot be measured. In this case, for example, Jed Santosky was removed from his natural parents' custody when he was only three days old; the judge's finding of permanent neglect effectively foreclosed the possibility that Jed would ever know his natural parents.

[13] In this case, for example, the parents claim that the State sought court orders denying them the right to visit their children, which would have prevented them from maintaining the contact required by Fam. Ct. Act. § 614.1.(d)....The parents further claim that the State cited their rejection of social services they found offensive or superfluous as proof of the agency's "diligent efforts" and their own "failure to plan" for the children's future....

We need not accept these statements as true to recognize that the State's unusual ability to structure the evidence increases the risk of an erroneous factfinding. Of course, the disparity between the litigants' resources will be vastly greater in States where there is no statutory right to court-appointed counsel....

> "Since the State has an urgent interest in the welfare of the child, it shares the parent's interest in an accurate and just decision" at the factfinding proceeding. *Lassiter v. Department of Social Services*, 452 U.S., at 27. As *parens patriae*, the State's goal is to provide the child with a permanent home....Yet while there is still reason to believe that positive, nurturing parent-child relationships exist, the *parens patriae* interest favors preservation, not severance, of natural familial bonds.[17] ...."[The] State registers no gain towards its declared goals when it separates children from the custody of fit parents." *Stanley v. Illinois*, 405 U.S., at 652.

* * *

Like civil commitment hearings, termination proceedings often require the factfinder to evaluate medical and psychiatric testimony, and to decide issues difficult to prove to a level of absolute certainty, such as lack of parental motive, absence of affection between parent and child, and failure of parental foresight and progress....The substantive standards applied vary from State to State. Although Congress found a "beyond a reasonable doubt" standard proper in one type of parental rights termination case, another legislative body might well conclude that a reasonable-doubt standard would erect an unreasonable barrier to state efforts to free permanently neglected children for adoption.

A majority of the States have concluded that a "clear and convincing evidence" standard of proof strikes a fair balance between the rights of the natural parents and the State's legitimate concerns....We hold that such a standard adequately conveys to the factfinder the level of subjective certainty about his factual conclusions necessary to satisfy due process. We further hold that determination of the precise burden equal to or greater than that standard is a matter of state law properly left to state legislatures and state courts....

* * *

It is so ordered.

Justice Rehnquist, with whom **The Chief Justice, Justice White,** and **Justice O'Connor** join, dissenting.

I believe that few of us would care to live in a society where every aspect of life was regulated by a single source of law, whether that source be this Court or some other organ of our complex body politic. But today's decision certainly moves us in that direction. By parsing the New York scheme and holding one narrow provision unconstitutional, the majority invites further federal-court intrusion into every facet of state family law. If ever there were an area in which federal courts should heed the admonition of Justice Holmes that "a page of history is worth a volume of logic,"...it is in the area of domestic relations. This area has been left to the States from time immemorial, and not without good reason.

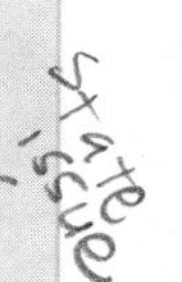

Equally as troubling is the majority's due process analysis. The Fourteenth Amendment guarantees that a State will treat individuals with "fundamental fairness" whenever its actions infringe their protected liberty or property interests. By adoption of the procedures relevant to this case, New York has created an exhaustive program to assist parents in regaining the custody of their children and to protect parents from the unfair deprivation of their parental rights. And yet the majority's

---

[17] Any *parens patriae* interest in terminating the natural parents' rights arises only at the dispositional phase, *after* the parents have been found unfit.

myopic scrutiny of the standard of proof blinds it to the very considerations and procedures which make the New York scheme "fundamentally fair."

* * *

I

As the majority opinion notes, petitioners are the parents of five children, three of whom were removed from petitioners' care on or before August 22, 1974. During the next four and one-half years, those three children were in the custody of the State and in the care of foster homes or institutions, and the State was diligently engaged in efforts to prepare petitioners for the children's return. Those efforts were unsuccessful, however, and on April 10, 1979, the New York Family Court for Ulster County terminated petitioners' parental rights as to the three children removed in 1974 or earlier. This termination was preceded by a judicial finding that petitioners had failed to plan for the return and future of their children, a statutory category of permanent neglect. Petitioners now contend, and the Court today holds, that they were denied due process of law, not because of a general inadequacy of procedural protections, but simply because the finding of permanent neglect was made on the basis of a preponderance of the evidence adduced at the termination hearing.

* * *

Parents subjected to temporary removal proceedings are provided extensive procedural protections. A summons and copy of the temporary removal petition must be served upon the parents within two days of issuance by the court... and the parents may, at their own request, delay the commencement of the factfinding hearing for three days after service of the summons. FCA § 1048.[6] The factfinding hearing may not commence without a determination by the court that the parents are present at the hearing and have been served with the petition....At the hearing itself, "only competent, material and relevant evidence may be admitted," with some enumerated exceptions for particularly probative evidence....In addition, indigent parents are provided with an attorney to represent them at both the factfinding and dispositional hearings, as well as at all other proceedings related to temporary removal of their child....

An order of temporary removal must be reviewed every 18 months by the Family Court....Such review is conducted by hearing before the same judge who ordered the temporary removal, and a notice of the hearing, including a statement of the dispositional alternatives, must be given to the parents at least 20 days before the hearing is held....As in the initial removal action, the parents must be parties to the proceedings, and are entitled to court-appointed counsel if indigent....

One or more years after a child has been removed temporarily from the parents' home, permanent termination proceedings may be commenced by the filing of a petition in the court which ordered the temporary removal. The petition must be filed by a state agency or by a foster parent authorized by the court, SSL § 384-b.3.(b), and must allege that the child has been permanently neglected by the parents....Notice of the petition and the dispositional proceedings must be served upon the parents at least 20 days before the commencement of the hearing,...must inform them of the potential consequences of the hearing,...and must inform them "of their right to the assistance of counsel, including [their] right...to have counsel

---

[6] The relatively short time between notice and commencement of hearing provided by § 1048 undoubtedly reflects the State's desire to protect the child. These proceedings are designed to permit prompt action by the court when the child is threatened with imminent and serious physical, mental, or emotional harm.

assigned by the court [if] they are financially unable to obtain counsel."....

As in the initial removal proceedings, two hearings are held in consideration of the permanent termination petition....At the factfinding hearing, the court must determine, by a fair preponderance of the evidence, whether the child has been permanently neglected...."Only competent, material and relevant evidence may be admitted in a factfinding hearing."....The court may find permanent neglect if the child is in the care of an authorized agency or foster home and the parents have "failed for a period of more than one year...substantially and continuously or repeatedly to maintain contact with or plan for the future of the child, although physically and financially able to do so."....In addition, because the State considers its "first obligation" to be the reuniting of the child with its natural parents,...the court must also find that the supervising state agency has, without success, made "*diligent* efforts to encourage and strengthen the parental relationship."....

Following the factfinding hearing, a separate, dispositional hearing is held to determine what course of action would be in "the best interests of the child."....A finding of permanent neglect at the factfinding hearing, although necessary to a termination of parental rights, does not control the court's order at the dispositional hearing. The court may dismiss the petition, suspend judgment on the petition and retain jurisdiction for a period of one year in order to provide further opportunity for a reuniting of the family, or terminate the parents' right to the custody and care of the child....The court must base its decision solely upon the record of "material and relevant evidence" introduced at the dispositional hearing,...and may not entertain any presumption that the best interests of the child "will be promoted by any particular disposition."....

As petitioners did in this case, parents may appeal any unfavorable decision to the Appellate Division of the New York Supreme Court. Thereafter, review may be sought in the New York Court of Appeals and, ultimately, in this Court if a federal question is properly presented.

As this description of New York's termination procedures demonstrates, the State seeks not only to protect the interests of parents in rearing their own children, but also to assist and encourage parents who have lost custody of their children to reassume their rightful role. Fully understood, the New York system is a comprehensive program to *aid* parents such as petitioners. Only as a last resort, when "diligent efforts" to reunite the family have failed, does New York authorize the termination of parental rights. The procedures for termination of those relationships which cannot be aided and which threaten permanent injury to the child, administered by a judge who has supervised the case from the first temporary removal through the final termination, cannot be viewed as fundamentally unfair. The facts of this case demonstrate the fairness of the system.

* * *

It is inconceivable to me that these procedures were "fundamentally unfair" to petitioners. Only by its obsessive focus on the standard of proof and its almost complete disregard of the facts of this case does the majority find otherwise.[11] ....

B

In addition to the basic fairness of the process afforded petitioners, the standard of proof chosen by New York clearly reflects a constitutionally permissible

---

[11] The majority finds, without any reference to the facts of this case, that "numerous factors [in New York termination proceedings] combine to magnify the risk of erroneous factfinding."....In short, the majority characterizes the State as a wealthy and powerful bully bent on taking children away from defenseless parents....Such characterization finds no support in the record....

balance of the interests at stake in this case. The standard of proof "represents an attempt to instruct the factfinder concerning the degree of confidence our society thinks he should have in the correctness of factual conclusions for a particular type of adjudication."....[12]

* * *

On the other side of the termination proceeding are the often countervailing interests of the child.[13] A stable, loving homelife is essential to a child's physical, emotional, and spiritual well-being. It requires no citation of authority to assert that children who are abused in their youth generally face extraordinary problems developing into responsible, productive citizens. The same can be said of children who, though not physically or emotionally abused, are passed from one foster home to another with no constancy of love, trust, or discipline. If the Family Court makes an incorrect factual determination resulting in a failure to terminate a parent-child relationship which rightfully should be ended, the child involved must return either to an abusive home[14] or to the often unstable world of foster care.[15] The reality of these risks is magnified by the fact that the only families faced with termination actions are those which have voluntarily surrendered custody of their child to the State, or, as in this case, those from which the child has been removed by judicial action because of threatened irreparable injury through abuse or neglect. Permanent neglect findings also occur

---

[12] It is worth noting that the significance of the standard of proof in New York parental termination proceedings differs from the significance of the standard in other forms of litigation. In the usual adjudicatory setting, the factfinder has had little or no prior exposure to the facts of the case. His only knowledge of those facts comes from the evidence adduced at trial, and he renders his findings solely upon the basis of that evidence. Thus, normally, the standard of proof is a crucial factor in the final outcome of the case, for it is the scale upon which the factfinder weighs his knowledge and makes his decision.

Although the standard serves the same function in New York parental termination proceedings, additional assurances of accuracy are present in its application. As was adduced at oral argument, the practice in New York is to assign one judge to supervise a case from the initial temporary removal of the child to the final termination of parental rights. Therefore, as discussed above, the factfinder is intimately familiar with the case before the termination proceedings ever begin. Indeed, as in this case, he often will have been closely involved in protracted efforts to rehabilitate the parents....

[13] The majority dismisses the child's interest in the accuracy of determinations made at the factfinding hearing because "[the] factfinding does not purport...to balance the child's interest in a normal family home against the parents' interest in raising the child," but instead "pits the State directly against the parents."....Only "[after] the State has established parental unfitness," the majority reasons, may the court "assume...that the interests of the child and the natural parents do diverge."....

This reasoning misses the mark. The child has an interest in the outcome of the factfinding hearing independent of that of the parent. To be sure, "the child and his parents share a vital interest in preventing *erroneous* termination of their natural relationship."....But the child's interest in a continuation of the family unit exists only to the extent that such a continuation would not be harmful to him. An error *in the factfinding hearing* that results in a failure to terminate a parent-child relationship which rightfully should be terminated may well detrimentally affect the child....

The preponderance-of-the-evidence standard, which allocates the risk of error more or less evenly, is employed when the social disutility of error *in either direction* is roughly equal—that is, when an incorrect finding of fault would produce consequences as undesirable as the consequences that would be produced by an incorrect finding of *no* fault. Only when the disutility of error in one direction discernibly outweighs the disutility of error in the other direction do we choose, by means of the standard of proof, to reduce the likelihood of the more onerous outcome....

New York's adoption of the preponderance-of-the-evidence standard reflects its conclusion

only in families where the child has been in foster care for at least one year.

* * *

III

For the reasons heretofore stated, I believe that the Court today errs in concluding that the New York standard of proof in parental-rights termination proceedings violates due process of law. The decision disregards New York's earnest efforts to *aid* parents in regaining the custody of their children and a host of procedural protections placed around parental rights and interests. The Court finds a constitutional violation only by a tunnel-vision application of due process principles that altogether loses sight of the unmistakable fairness of the New York procedure.

Even more worrisome, today's decision cavalierly rejects the considered judgment of the New York Legislature in an area traditionally entrusted to state care. The Court thereby begins, I fear, a trend of federal intervention in state family law matters which surely will stifle creative responses to vexing problems. Accordingly, I dissent.

---

that the undesirable consequence of an erroneous finding of parental unfitness—the unwarranted termination of the family relationship—is roughly equal to the undesirable consequence of an erroneous finding of parental fitness—the risk of permanent injury to the child either by return of the child to an abusive home or by the child's continued lack of a permanent home....Such a conclusion is well within the province of state legislatures. It cannot be said that the New York procedures are unconstitutional simply because a majority of the Members of this Court disagree with the New York Legislature's weighing of the interests of the parents and the child in an error-free factfinding hearing.

[14] The record in this case illustrates the problems that may arise when a child is returned to an abusive home. Eighteen months after Tina, petitioners' oldest child, was first removed from petitioner's home, she was returned to the home on a trial basis. Katherine Weiss, a supervisor in the Child Protective Unit of the Ulster County Child Welfare Department, later testified in Family Court that "[the] attempt to return Tina to her home just totally blew up."....When asked to explain what happened, Mrs. Weiss testified that "there were instances on the record in this court of Mr. Santosky's abuse of his wife, alleged abuse of the children and proven neglect of the children." *Ibid.* Tina again was removed from the home, this time along with John and Jed.

[15] The New York Legislature recognized the potential harm to children of extended, nonpermanent foster care. It found "that many children who have been placed in foster care experience unnecessarily protracted stays in such care without being adopted or returned to their parents or other custodians. Such unnecessary stays may deprive these children of positive, nurturing family relationships and have deleterious effects on their development into responsible, productive citizens."....Subsequent studies have proved this finding correct. One commentator recently wrote of "the lamentable conditions of many foster care placements" under the New York system even today. He noted: "Over fifty percent of the children in foster care have been in this 'temporary' status for more than two years; over thirty percent for more than five years. During this time, many children are placed in a sequence of ill-suited foster homes, denying them the consistent support and nurturing that they so desperately need." Besharov, State Intervention To Protect Children: New York's Definition of "Child Abuse" and "Child Neglect," 26 N.Y.L.S.L. Rev. 723, 770–771 (1981) (footnotes omitted). In this case, petitioners' three children have been in foster care for more than four years, one child since he was only three days old. Failure to terminate petitioners' parental rights will only mean a continuation of this unsatisfactory situation.

Questions for Discussion

1. The majority argues that the burden of "clear and convincing" is compelled by the extraordinary taking of a child. Can it be argued that the court's analysis treats the child as a valuable chattel which the state cannot take without an enhanced burden of proof beyond preponderance? That is, if the court were to represent the interests of a child who may be subject to unfit parents endangering his safety, and the contest is between the state on the one side and the parents on the other, would preponderance be the more likely test?

2. Is the clear and convincing burden required only for the final termination of parental rights? Should it apply at the detention and jurisdictional stages as well?

3. The majority writes that the "child and foster parent" are involved at the fact-finding stage but "the focus is not on them." What does that mean? The behavior of the parents may be a focus, but does that mean that the issue is simply state vs. parents? How is the child's interest in the proceeding and its outcome any less important than the outcome to the parent?

4. In terms of distribution of risk, what is the consequence of placing a child back with the Kramers if they are a danger to the child? Imagine a parent who may be raping a child every night; if the evidence is more than 50% that the rapes have occurred and will continue, what burden should we impose for loss of custody? For termination of parental rights? If we impose a lesser standard for loss of custody, will the outcome of the "clear and convincing for termination" outcome preclude adoption for the child (and a parental relationship elsewhere)?

5. Is the solemnity with which the court considers parental rights consistent with the way adults decide to reproduce (with a substantial percentage of pregnancies unintended and over 30% of current births to unwed mothers)?

6. The dissent argues that the confidence needed to warrant termination of parental rights may be provided by a variety of means, of which the burden of proof is one, and that states should be free to develop their own combination of notice, compensated counsel, hearing procedures, *et al.* How would the Supreme Court establish due process lines under such flexibility? Would a system which is less adversarial (more on the continental European model of active, neutral investigation by the court) warrant a preponderance type burden of proof?

G. FOSTER CARE REGULATION

Smith v. Organization of Foster Families For Equality & Reform
431 U.S. 816 (1977)

MR. JUSTICE BRENNAN delivered the opinion of the Court.

Appellees, individual foster parents...and an organization of foster parents, brought this civil rights class action pursuant to 42 U.S.C. § 1983 in the United States District Court for the Southern District of New York, on their own behalf and on behalf of children for whom they have provided homes for a year or more. They sought declaratory and injunctive relief against New York State and New York City officials,...alleging that the procedures governing the removal of foster children from foster homes provided in N.Y. Soc. Serv. Law...violated the Due Process and Equal Protection Clauses of the Fourteenth Amendment....The District Court appointed independent counsel for the foster children to forestall any possibility of conflict between their interests and the interests asserted by the foster parents....A group of natural mothers of children in foster care...were granted leave to intervene...on behalf of themselves and others similarly situated....

A divided three-judge District Court concluded that "the pre-removal procedures presently employed by the State are constitutionally defective," holding that "before a foster child can be peremptorily transferred from the foster home in which he has been living, be it to another foster home or to the natural parents who initially placed him in foster care, he is entitled to a hearing at which all concerned parties may present any relevant information to the administrative decisionmaker charged with determining the future placement of the child,"...We reverse.

* * *

Foster care has been defined as "[a] child welfare service which provides substitute family care for a planned period for a child when his own family cannot care for him for a temporary or extended period, and when adoption is neither desirable nor possible." Child Welfare League of America, Standards for Foster Family Care Service 5 (1959).[8] Thus, the distinctive features of foster care are, first, "that it is care in a *family*, it is noninstitutional substitute care," and, second, "that it is for a *planned* period—either temporary or extended. This is unlike adoptive placement, which implies a *permanent* substitution of one home for another."....

Under the New York scheme children may be placed in foster care either by voluntary placement or by court order. Most foster-care placements are voluntary.[9] They occur when physical or mental illness, economic problems, or other family crises make it impossible for natural parents, particularly single parents, to provide a stable home life for their children for some limited period.[10] Resort to such placements is almost compelled when it is not possible in such circumstance to place the child with a relative or friend, or to pay for the services of a homemaker or boarding school.

Voluntary placement requires the signing of a written agreement by the natural parent or guardian, transferring the care and custody of the child to an authorized child welfare agency.[11] ....Although by statute the terms of such agreements are open to negotiation,...it is contended that agencies require execution of standardized forms....The agreement may provide for return of the child to the natural parent at a specified date or upon occurrence of a particular event, and if it does not, the child must be returned by the agency, in the absence of a court order, within 20 days of notice from the parent....

---

[8] The term "foster care" is often used more generally to apply to any type of care that substitutes others for the natural parent in the parental role, including group homes, adoptive homes, and institutions, as well as foster family homes....Since this case is only concerned with children in foster family homes, the term will generally be used here in the more restricted sense defined in the text.

[9] The record indicates that as many as 80% of the children in foster care in New York City are voluntarily placed....

[10] Experienced commentators have suggested that typical parents in this situation might be "[a] divorced parent in a financial bind, an unwed adolescent mother still too immature to rear a child, or a welfare mother confronted with hospitalization and therefore temporarily

* * *

B

The provisions of the scheme specifically at issue in this litigation come into play when the agency having legal custody determines to remove the foster child from the foster home, either because it has determined that it would be in the child's best interests to transfer him to some other foster home, or to return the child to his natural parents in accordance with the statute or placement agreement. Most children are removed in order to be transferred to another foster home.[23] The procedures by which foster parents may challenge a removal made for that purpose differ somewhat from those where the removal is made to return the child to his natural parent.

Section 383(2)...provides that the "authorized agency placing out or boarding [a foster] child...may in its discretion remove such child from the home where placed or boarded." Administrative regulations implement this provision. The agency is required, except in emergencies, to notify the foster parents in writing 10 days in advance of any removal....The notice advises the foster parents that if they object to the child's removal they may request a "conference" with the Social Services Department....The department schedules requested conferences within 10 days of the receipt of the request. § 450.10(b). The foster parent may appear with counsel at the conference, where he will "be advised of the reasons [for the removal of the child] and be afforded an opportunity to submit reasons why the child should not be removed."....The official must render a decision in writing within five days after the close of the conference, and send notice of his decision to the foster parents and the agency....The proposed removal is stayed pending the outcome of the conference....

If the child is removed after the conference, the foster parent may appeal to the Department of Social Services for a "fair hearing," that is, a full adversary administrative hearing, under Soc. Serv. Law § 400,...the determination of which is subject to judicial review...; however, the removal is not automatically stayed pending the hearing and judicial review....

This statutory and regulatory scheme applies statewide.[28] In addition,

---

incapable of caring for her child."....A leading text on child-care services suggests that "[family] disruption, marginal economic circumstances, and poor health" are principal factors leading to placement of children in foster care....Other studies suggest, however, that neglect, abuse, abandonment and exploitation of children, which presumably account for most of the children who enter foster care by court order,...are also involved in many cases of voluntary placement....

[11] "Authorized agency" is defined in N.Y. Soc. Serv. Law § 371(10) (McKinney 1976) and "includes any local public welfare children's bureau, such as the defendants New York City Bureau of Child Welfare and Nassau County Children's Bureau, and any voluntary child-care agency under the supervision of the New York State Board of Social Welfare, such as the defendant Catholic Guardian Society of New York." 418 F.Supp., at 278 n. 5.

An *amicus curiae* brief states that in New York City, 85% of the children in foster care are placed with voluntary child-care agencies licensed by the State, while most children in foster care outside New York City are placed directly with the local Department of Social Services.

[23] The record shows that in 1973–1974 approximately 80% of the children removed from foster homes in New York State after living in the foster home for one year or more were transferred to another foster placement. Thirteen percent were returned to the biological parents, and 7% were adopted.

[28] There is some dispute whether the procedures set out in 18 N.Y.C.R.R. § 450.10 and Soc. Serv. Law § 400 apply in the case of a foster child being removed from his foster home to be returned to his natural parents. Application of these procedures to children who have beenplaced voluntarily, for example, arguably conflicts with the requirement of § 384-a (2)(a) that children in that situation be returned to the natural parent as provided in the placement

regulations promulgated by the New York City Human Resources Administration, Department of Social Services—Special Services for Children (SSC) provide even greater procedural safeguards there. Under SSC Procedure No. 5..., in place of or in addition to the conference provided by the state regulations, the foster parents may request a full trial-type hearing before the child is removed from their home. This procedure applies, however, only if the child is being transferred to another foster home, and not if the child is being returned to his natural parents....

One further preremoval procedural safeguard is available. Under Soc. Serv. Law § 392, the Family Court has jurisdiction to review, on petition of the foster parent or the agency, the status of any child who has been in foster care for 18 months or longer.[30] ...

* * *

Appellee foster parents as well as natural parents question the accuracy of the idealized picture portrayed by New York. They note that children often stay in "temporary" foster care for much longer than contemplated by the theory of the system....The District Court found as a fact that the median time spent in foster care in New York was over four years. 418 F.Supp., at 281. Indeed, many children apparently remain in this "limbo" indefinitely....The District Court also found that the longer a child remains in foster care, the more likely it is that he will never leave: "[T]he probability of a foster child being returned to his biological parents declined markedly after the first year in foster care." 418 F.Supp., at 279 n. 6....It is not surprising then that many children, particularly those that enter foster care at a very early age[38] and have little or no contact with their natural parents during extended stays in foster care,[39] often develop deep emotional ties with their foster parents.[40]

---

agreement or within 20 days of demand. Similarly, if the child has been ordered returned by a court, it is unclear what purpose could be served by an administrative conference or hearing on the correctness of the decision to remove the child from the foster home. Moreover, since the § 400 hearing takes place after removal of the child from the foster home, the hearing would have no purpose if the child has been returned to its parents, since the agency apparently has no authority to take the child back from its parents against their will without court intervention.

Nevertheless, nothing in either the statute or the regulations limits the availability of these procedures to transfers within the foster-care system. Each refers to the decision to *remove* a child from the foster family home, and thus on its face each would seem to cover removal for the purpose of returning the child to its parents. Furthermore, it is undisputed on this record that the actual administrative practice in New York is to provide the conference and hearing in all cases where they are requested, regardless of the destination of the child. In the absence of authoritative state-court interpretation to the contrary, we therefore assume that these procedures are available whenever a child is removed from a foster family home.

[30] The agency is required to initiate such a review when a child has remained in foster care for 18 months, § 392(2)(a), and if the child remains in foster care, the court "shall rehear the matter whenever it deems necessary or desirable, or upon petition by any party entitled to notice in proceedings under this section, but at least every twenty-four months." § 392(10).

[38] In New York City, 23.1% of foster children enter foster care when under one year of age, and 43% at age three or under...(18% of foster-care children in Rhode Island study were under one year of age when they entered foster care, and 43% were under the age of three).

[39] One study of parental contacts in New York City found that 57.4% of all foster children had had no contact with their natural parents for the previous six months....

[40] The development of such ties points up an intrinsic ambiguity of foster care that is central to this case. The warmer and more homelike environment of foster care is intended to be its main advantage over institutional child care, yet because in theory foster care is intended to be only temporary, foster parents are urged not be become too attached to the children in their care....Indeed, the New York courts have upheld removal from a foster home for the very reason that the foster parents had become too emotionally involved with the child.

Yet such ties do not seem to be regarded as obstacles to transfer of the child from one foster placement to another. The record in this case indicates that nearly 60% of the children in foster care in New York City have experienced more than one placement, and about 28% have experienced three or more....The intended stability of the foster-home management is further damaged by the rapid turnover among social work professionals who supervise the foster-care arrangements on behalf of the State....Moreover, even when it is clear that a foster child will not be returned to his natural parents, it is rare that he achieves a stable home life through final termination of parental ties and adoption into a new permanent family....

* * *

I

A

Our first inquiry is whether appellees have asserted interests within the Fourteenth Amendment's protection of "liberty" and "property." *Board of Regents v. Roth*, 408 U.S. 564, 571 (1972).

* * *

The appellees' basic contention is that when a child has lived in a foster home for a year or more, a psychological tie is created between the child and the foster parents which constitutes the foster family the true "psychological family" of the child....That family, they argue, has a "liberty interest" in its survival as a family protected by the Fourteenth Amendment....Upon this premise they conclude that the foster child cannot be removed without a prior hearing satisfying due process. Appointed counsel for the children,...however, disagrees, and has consistently argued that the foster parents have no such liberty interest independent of the interests of the foster children, and that the best interests of the children would not be served by procedural protections beyond those already provided by New York law. The intervening natural parents of children in foster care,...also oppose the foster parents, arguing that recognition of the procedural right claimed would undercut both the substantive family law of New York, which favors the return of children to their natural parents as expeditiously as possible,...and their constitutionally protected right of family privacy, by forcing them to submit to a hearing and defend their rights to their children before the children could be returned to them.

The District Court did not reach appellees' contention "that the foster home is entitled to the same constitutional deference as that long granted to the more traditional biological family." 418 F.Supp., at 281. Rather than "reach[ing] out

---

In re Jewish Child Care Assn. (Sanders), 5 N.Y. 2d 222 (1959). See also the case of the Lhotans, named appellees in this case,...

On the other hand, too warm a relation between foster parent and foster child is not the only possible problem in foster care. Qualified foster parents are hard to find,...and very little training is provided to equip them to handle the often complicated demands of their role,...; it is thus sometimes possible that foster homes may provide inadequate care. Indeed, situations in which foster children were mistreated or abused have been reported. Wald 645. And the social work services that are supposed to be delivered to both the natural and foster families are often limited, due to the heavy caseloads of the agencies....Given these problems, and given that the very fact of removal from even an inadequate natural family is often traumatic for the child,...it is not surprising that one commentator has found "rather persuasive, if still incomplete, evidence that throughout the United States, children in foster care are experiencing high rates of psychiatric disturbance."....

to decide such novel questions," the court based its holding that "the pre-removal procedures presently employed by the state are constitutionally defective,"...not on the recognized liberty interest in family privacy, but on an independent right of the foster child "to be heard before being 'condemned to suffer grievous loss,' *Joint Anti-Fascist Committee v. McGrath*, 341 U.S. 123, 168...(1951)..."

The court apparently reached this conclusion by weighing the "harmful consequences of a precipitous and perhaps improvident decision to remove a child from his foster family,"... and concluding that this disruption of the stable relationships needed by the child might constitute "grievous loss." But if this was the reasoning applied by the District Court, it must be rejected.[43] *Meachum v. Fano*, 427 U.S. 215, 224 (1976), is authority that such a finding does not, in and of itself, implicate the due process guarantee. What was said in *Board of Regents v. Roth*, *supra*, at 570–571, applies equally well here:

> "The District Court decided that procedural due process guarantees apply in this case by assessing and balancing the weights of the particular interests involved....[A] weighing process has long been a part of any determination of the *form* of hearing required in particular situations by procedural due process. But, to determine whether due process requirements apply in the first place, we must look not to the 'weight' but to the nature of the interest at stake....We must look to see if the interest is within the Fourteenth Amendment's protection of liberty and property."...

* * *

B

....There does exist a "private realm of family life which the state cannot enter," *Prince v. Massachusetts*, 321 U.S. 158, 166 (1944), that has been afforded both substantive...and procedural...protection. But is the relation of foster parent to foster child sufficiently akin to the concept of "family" recognized in our precedents to merit similar protection?...

* * *

...[T]here are also important distinctions between the foster family and the natural family. First, unlike the earlier cases recognizing a right to family privacy, the State here seeks to interfere, not with a relationship having its origins entirely apart from the power of the State, but rather with a foster family which has its source in state law and contractual arrangements....Here, however, whatever emotional ties may develop between foster parent and foster child have their origins in an arrangement in which the State has been a partner from the outset. While the Court has recognized that liberty interests may in some cases arise from positive-law sources,...in such a case, and particularly where, as here, the claimed interest derives from a knowingly assumed contractual relation with the State, it is appropriate to ascertain from state law the expectations and entitlements of the parties. In this case, the limited recognition accorded to the foster family by the New York statutes and the contracts executed by the foster parents argue against any but the most limited constitutional "liberty" in the foster family.

---

[43] The dissenting judge argued that the court's underlying premise was a holding "over the objection of the representative of the children...that the foster children have a 'liberty' interest in their relationship with the foster parents." 418 F.Supp., at 288. If this was in fact the reasoning of the District Court, we do not see how it differs from a holding that the foster family relationship is entitled to privacy protection analogous to the natural family—the issue the District Court purported not to reach.

* * *

Reversed.

Mr. Justice Stewart, with whom **The Chief Justice** and **Mr. Justice Rehnquist** join, concurring in the judgment.

The foster parent-foster child relationship involved in this litigation is, of course, wholly a creation of the State. New York law defines the circumstances under which a child may be placed in foster care, prescribes the obligations of the foster parents, and provides for the removal of the child from the foster home "in [the] discretion" of the agency with custody of the child....

* * *

In these circumstances, I cannot understand why the Court thinks itself obliged to decide these cases on the assumption that either foster parents or foster children in New York have some sort of "liberty" interest in the continuation of their relationship.[1] Rather than tiptoeing around this central issue, I would squarely hold that the interests asserted by the appellees are not of a kind that the Due Process Clause of the Fourteenth Amendment protects.

* * *

...[U]nder New York's foster-care laws, any case where the foster parents had assumed the emotional role of the child's natural parents would represent not a triumph of the system, to be constitutionally safeguarded from state intrusion, but a failure. The goal of foster care, at least in New York, is not to

---

[1] The Court's opinion seems to indicate that there is no reason to distinguish between the claims of the foster parents and the foster children, either because the parents have standing to assert the rights of the children or because the parents' interest is identical to that of the children....I cannot agree.

First, it is by no means obvious that foster parents and foster children have the same interest in a continuation of their relationship. When the child leaves the foster family, it is because the agency with custody of him has determined that his interests will be better served by a new home, either with his natural parents, adoptive parents, or a different foster family. Any assessment of the child's alleged deprivation must take into account not only what he has lost, but what he has received in return. Foster parents, on the other hand, do not automatically receive a new child with whom they will presumably have a more profitable relationship.

Second, unlike the situation in *Craig v. Boren*, 429 U.S. 190, 195–196, this is not a case where the failure to grant the parents their requested relief will inevitably tend to "[dilute] or adversely [affect]" the alleged constitutional rights of the children. Denying the parents a hearing simply has no effect whatever on the children's separate claim to a hearing, and does not impair their alleged constitutional rights. There is therefore no standing in the parents to assert the children's claims....

I would nevertheless consider both the parents' and the children's claims in these cases, but only because the suit was originally brought on behalf of both the parents and the children, all of whom were parties plaintiff. While it is true that their interests may conflict, there was no reason not to allow counsel for the parents to continue to represent the children to the extent that their interests may be compatible. The conflict was avoided by the District Court's appointment of independent counsel, who took a position opposite to that of the foster parents as to where the children's welfare lay. The appointment of independent counsel, however, should not have left the children without advocacy for the position, right or wrong, that they are entitled to due process hearings. That position should have been left to be asserted by the counsel who originally brought the suit for the children. My view, therefore, is that the parents and the children are properly before the Court and entitled to assert their own separate claims, but that neither group has standing to assert the claims of the other.

> provide a permanent substitute for the natural or adoptive home, but to prepare the child for his return to his real parents or placement in a permanent adoptive home by giving him temporary shelter in a family setting....
>
> * * *
>
> ...The family life upon which the State "intrudes" is simply a temporary status which the State itself has created. It is a "family life" defined and controlled by the law of New York, for which New York pays, and the goals of which New York is entitled to and does set for itself.
>
> For these reasons I concur in the judgment of the Court.

Questions for Discussion

1. Do the majority or concurring opinions analyze the issues from the child's point of view?

2. Under New York law, foster care parents may appeal to the local agency making the decision to remove a child from their care within the first eighteen months of their custody. What elements of traditional due process are missing from such a review?

3. The Court opines that there is no reason to assume bonding takes place before eighteen months. Is there any evidence to support this extraordinary finding? If one were to place a child or puppy or new car with the justices authoring that opinion, what would they say to summary retrieval after fifteen months? Six months? Three weeks? Does a young child bond with non-parents who may be performing the parental function before eighteen months transpires?

4. Over 70% of adoptions come from family foster care providers. Most of the children removed from their homes are not reunified but rather remain in foster care until emancipation (see discussion above). Do we want bonding to take place between foster parents and the children entrusted to them in such a setting? Or is the Court's footnote correct that such bonding violates public policy and can properly justify removal of children from foster parents? Or the concurring opinion's conclusion that such bonding constitutes a "failure" of foster care?

5. The Court's holding may apply not only to decisions to move a child from foster care back to a parent (reunification) but to the much more common case where the transfer is between foster care placements. What is the downside of a hearing on the issue of transfer as a check on possible local agency error (as well as gratuitous foster care drift)? If the foster care parent is the agent of the court in caring for the child, why would the court deny its own agent access to its offices to inform it of the status of children where the courts function as the *de jure* parents?

6. If the county agency decides to move a child from a foster parent who seeks adoption to a group home with delinquents who the foster parent believes would be detrimental for the child, what is the likelihood of court review or other check under the *OFFER* standard?

7. The concurring opinion notes that the issue is not the "weight of the loss" but its nature, and that its nature does not involve deprivation of life or property. How does that square with *Lassiter*, where the parental loss of a child is a sufficient taking of something to warrant publicly financed counsel if it could make a difference in the outcome?

8. Is it relevant that in New York City, where a local rule permits some neutral hearings prior to removing children from objecting foster care parents, the local agency was reversed in 45% of its reviewed decisions?

9. Is any Constitutional weight due to a child's reasonable perception that an adult has functioned as his or her parent? If a child is a "person" for purposes of Constitutional rights, how is the "right to parent" a fundamental liberty interest, but the child's counterpart relationship entirely devoid of Constitutional status? Since the *OFFER* case in 1977, state courts have increasingly entertained the status of "*de facto*" parents—delineating a person who may not have a parental claim from biology or marriage, but who has been a parent in the eyes of a child, and has functioned as such by community standards (see *e.g.*, *Webster v. Lyon* discussed in Chapter 11). Why would not such *de facto* status (with the court access and due process rights increasingly conferred to it) not apply to a foster parent—particularly where the alternative is not parental return? If the distinction is a notion of "waiver" implicit or explicit in the foster arrangement "contract," how would that eliminate any right to a parent held by the child, who has not so agreed?

H. PERMANENT PLACEMENT

Drummond v. Fulton County Department of Family & Children's Services

563 F.2d 1200 (5th Cir. 1977)

RONEY, Circuit Judge:

Plaintiffs, Robert and Mildred Drummond, a white couple, acted as state-designated foster parents of a mixed race child for over two years. When the defendant state adoption agency decided to remove the child for permanent placement in another home, plaintiffs commenced this action under 42 U.S.C.A. § 1983. Alleging denial of their rights under both the equal protection and the due process clauses of the Fourteenth Amendment, they sought preliminary and permanent injunctive relief, which was denied by the district court. Although a panel of this Court reversed, *Drummond v. Fulton County Department of Family & Children's Services*, 547 F.2d 835 (5th Cir. 1977), the full Court finds no deprivation of constitutional rights and affirms the dismissal of plaintiffs' complaint.

* * *

In December 1973 in an emergency situation, a one-month-old mixed race child named Timmy was placed for temporary care in the home of Mr. and Mrs. Drummond by the Fulton County children's service agency. Lengthy proceedings were commenced to determine whether the child should be permanently removed from his natural mother's custody and placed for adoption.

Within a year, the Drummonds had become sufficiently attached to Timmy to request permission to adopt him. The Drummonds had not signed an agreement that they would not try to adopt their foster child, as is common practice with many placement agencies. Although the level of care provided by them as foster parents had consistently been rated excellent, there was an emerging consensus within the defendant child placement agency charged with Timmy's care that it would be best to look elsewhere for a permanent adoptive home. When this was explained to the Drummonds in March 1975 they appeared to acquiesce. By August of that year, however, they had renewed their request to adopt Timmy.

The child was not legally freed for adoption by the Georgia courts until September 1975. Because this signaled the end of any attempt to return Timmy to his natural mother, the agency began a more focused consideration of what ultimate placement would be best for Timmy. After a number of discussions with the Drummonds, a final decision-making meeting was held in November 1975 with 19 agency employees present. Although the Drummonds were not present at this meeting, caseworkers who had dealt with them during the past two years did attend. As a result of that meeting a final agency decision was made to remove Timmy from the Drummond home and to deny the Drummonds' adoption application. It is clear that the race of the Drummonds and of Timmy and the racial attitudes of the parties were given substantial weight in coming to this conclusion. The agency employees were also aware that as Timmy grew older he would retain the characteristics of his black father. A few months later the plaintiffs filed suit.

* * *

The manner in which race was considered in this case frames the precise issue before us. The district court found that race was not used in an automatic fashion. The Drummonds' application was not automatically rejected on racial grounds. This finding may not be disturbed here because not clearly erroneous....But can race be taken into account, perhaps decisively if it is the factor which tips the balance between two potential families, where it is not used automatically? We conclude, as did another court which grappled with the problem, that "the difficulties inherent in interracial adoption" justify the consideration of "race as a relevant factor in adoption,..."...

* * *

In concluding that there has been no denial of equal protection in these circumstances, we note the following factors.

First, consideration of race in the child placement process suggests no racial slur or stigma in connection with any race. It is a natural thing for children to be raised by parents of their same ethnic background.

Second, no case has been cited to the Court suggesting that it is impermissible to consider race in adoption placement. The only cases which have addressed this problem indicate that, while the automatic use of race is barred, the use of race as one of the factors in making the ultimate decision is legitimate....

Third, the professional literature on the subject of transracial child placement stresses the importance of considering the racial attitudes of potential parents. The constitutional strictures against racial discrimination are not mandates to ignore the accumulated experience of unbiased professionals. A couple has no right to adopt a child it is not equipped to rear, and according to the professional literature race bears directly on that inquiry. From the child's perspective, the consideration of race is simply another facet of finding him the best possible home. Rather than eliminating certain categories of homes from consideration it avoids the potentially tragic possibility of placing a child in a home with parents who will not be able to cope with the child's problems.

Fourth, in the analogous inquiry over the permissibility of considering the religion of would-be adoptive parents, numerous courts have found no constitutional infirmity....Those cases make the same distinction as this Court makes in the racial context. So long as religion is not an automatic factor, its consideration as one of a number of factors is unobjectionable.

Finally, adoption agencies quite frequently try to place a child where he can most easily become a normal family member. The duplication of his natural biological environment is a part of that program. Such factors as age, hair color, eye color and facial features of parents and child are considered in reaching a decision. This flows from the belief that a child and adoptive parents can best adjust to a normal family relationship if the child is placed with adoptive parents who could have actually parented him. To permit consideration of physical characteristics necessarily carries with it permission to consider racial characteristics. This Court does not have the professional expertise to assess the wisdom of that type of inquiry, but it is our province to conclude, as we do today, that the use of race as one of those factors is not unconstitutional.

II.

In order to make out a claim of deprivation of Fourteenth Amendment due process rights a plaintiff must demonstrate first, that he has been deprived of liberty or property in the constitutional sense, and second, that the procedure used to deprive him of that interest was constitutionally deficient. *Board of Regents v. Roth*, 408 U.S. 564 (1972).

A.

The Drummonds assert two possible constitutional liberty and property interests. The first involves a concept which plaintiffs have denominated the "psychological family"; the second, a stigma to their reputation alleged to accrue upon the rejection by the agency of their application to adopt Timmy.

Plaintiffs maintain that during the period Timmy lived with them mutual feelings of love and dependence developed which are analogous to those found in most biological families....

* * *

We conclude that there is no such constitutionally protected interest in the context of this case. An understanding of the role of the foster parent in a child placement helps make this conclusion plain. In the search for adoptive parents, thorough investigations are made so that long range considerations may be given substantial weight....Potential adoptive parents are evaluated forward in the full family context through a child's adulthood, marriage, offspring, and backward to the "adoptive" grandparents, uncles, aunts, and cousins. The attitudes of other family members are examined. In short, the goal is to duplicate the relationship that most persons have with their natural parents during their entire lives.

* * *

Here, the only time potential parents could assert a liberty interest as psychological parents would be when they had developed precisely the relationship which state law warns against the foster context....The very fact that the relationship before us is a creature of state law, as well as the fact that it has never been recognized as equivalent to either the natural family or the adoptive family by any court, demonstrates that it is not a protected liberty interest, but an interest limited by the very laws which create it....

* * *

B.

Independent counsel for Timmy claims a liberty right personal to Timmy which he asserts must be dealt with in constitutional due process terms. The interest upon which he bases this claim is one which he has chosen to call the "right to a stable environment." He argues that a child has a liberty right not to be moved from home to home, without a prior hearing, particularly in light of the significant literature which indicates a traumatic effect of such moves on young children. Counsel insists this right exists regardless of whether the child is in a natural, adoptive or foster setting and in all other temporary care situations.

* * *

Given the nature of the interests at stake, and the inquiry involved, as well as the overwhelming need for flexibility in this situation and the complexity of the decision to be made, this Court holds that whatever process was due was rendered by the state agency in this case.

AFFIRMED.

* * *

TUTTLE, Circuit Judge, with whom **GOLDBERG**, Circuit Judge, joins, dissenting:

* * *

In view of the fact that the State of Georgia has *no* "preremoval procedures" that will fit any concept of due process, a subject that will be discussed later, the case before us demands that a determination be made whether there is such protectable interest in the Drummonds.

As is sometimes the case, I believe that the concurring opinion, joined in by the Chief Justice and two of the Justices, dramatically emphasizes the importance which a majority of the court attributed to the question whether a liberty interest inheres in the relationship between the foster parents and children who have been in their care a substantial period of time....

* * *

...[T]he Court took considerable pains to analyze the assertion of the foster parents and foster children that they had a constitutionally protected liberty interest. A careful reading of the opinion indicates to me that but for the existence of the narrower ground in that case and but for the fact that the contest before the court was being waged between foster parents on the one hand and natural parents on the other, the court would readily have determined that such constitutionally protected liberty interest did exist. In the first place, the court recognized that, although "the usual understanding of 'family' implies biological relationships, and most decisions treating the relation between parent and child have stressed this element" and that "a biological relationship is not present in the case of the usual foster family" nevertheless "biological relationships are not exclusive determination of the existence of a family."...

* * *

II. TIMMY'S "LIBERTY" INTEREST

What has been said respecting the liberty interest of the Drummonds, of course, applies, possibly even more cogently, in the case of the small child whose entire life will be affected in large or small degree by his being taken away from the only parents he has known since his birth....

* * *

...[T]he defendants concede that the liberty interest exists, but that the Georgia adoptive system, taken as a whole, affords to Timmy the due process to which he is entitled and that all the process that Timmy is due at any stage of his temporary care, his foster family relationship and their terminations, the termination of parents' rights, and final adoption is that "the state structures a system *designed* to accommodate the child's best interest." In other words, appellees say that as long as the legislature decides in its wisdom that everything relating to an abandoned child's welfare and status can safely be left to the uncontrolled and unreviewable discretion of state and county employees that satisfies all due process requirements. This would include the action taken here by which the defendants seek to terminate irrevocably a relationship which the Supreme Court has, in the passages quoted above, recognized as parallel to that of a biological family, without any opportunity of the child to be heard. In any event, it appears to be a concession by the state that Timmy has a protectable interest. The question whether this interest can be taken away from him by the sort of proceedings had here is discussed below.

III. WHAT PROCESS IS DUE?

....[I]n March 1976, a "staffing" of four caseworkers or supervisors, none of whom had either seen the Drummonds or Timmy at that time, concluded ex parte that the Drummonds should be told that Timmy was to be taken from their care and "that it would be in Timmy's best interest to be adopted by a black couple." Bearing in mind that this decision was made before any of the persons involved had seen the Drummonds and before the several investigations and studies of the Drummonds as potential adoptive parents were made,[2] it is obvious, it seems to me, that Mrs. Dallinger's effort to analyze at the trial what was meant by the action taken at the staffing is an afterthought, because the only purpose for approaching the Drummonds was to explain to them that the child was to be removed and awarded to black adoptive parents. I comment on this only because the decision on whether the procedures followed provided minimal due process must necessarily depend upon when the decision was made. Miss Osgood's statement that the question was raised "that if the Drummonds were not amenable to our plan, would we move Timmy to a black foster home feeling that, you know, it would be better if we were going to have him adopted by a black couple, to have him in a black foster home if there was going to be any length of time before he was free" clearly indicates that "our plan" was that "we were going to have him adopted by a black couple." It seems apparent that this was the decision because the undisputed testimony of Mrs. Drummond following the final "consensus" was that Mrs. Dallinger said to Mr. and Mrs. Drummond: "I am sure that you are both very anxious to know what has happened and we called you in to tell you that the *decision* still stands, that we feel that Timmy will be better off adopted by a black couple or a black family." [Emphasis added]. Of course, the only "decision" that Mrs. Dallinger could have referred to is the decision made at the March staffing which I have discussed above. I suppose no one would claim that if the Drummonds and Timmy are entitled to any process at all they had received it by the time this decision was made.

---

[2] It is to be noted again here that each of the investigations resulted in fulsome praise of the Drummonds' relationship with the child.

However, the matter did not end after the March meeting between the caseworkers and the Drummonds. The latter protested and requested a reconsideration. They were put off by statements that no action would be taken until after Timmy's mother's rights had been terminated by the Juvenile Court. This was done in September, and in the meantime, several inquiries and studies were made by caseworkers or other officials of the defendant Department, most of which discussed the merits, pro and con, of the relationship between Timmy and his foster parents.[3] Finally, without giving the Drummonds an opportunity to be present and without their having been notified of the standards by which the relationship would be judged, a group meeting of 19 employees of the Department was called to obtain a "consensus" as to what should be done with Timmy in relation to his foster parents.

A written report of this meeting states in its last paragraph:

> "A vote was taken and it was a group decision that it would not be in Timmy's best interest to leave him in the Drummonds' home, and that we would begin immediately to look for an appropriate black adoptive home. Although this was a difficult decision it was felt that Timmy's long range best interest must be the focus."

The Drummonds were not present at the staffing of November 21. No physician or psychiatrist was present. There is no record of any testimony or statement made by any person present, except that we can assume that the documents heretofore referred to were available to the members of the group. The Drummonds were not given an opportunity to present any statements or evidence, much less to be represented by counsel or to present witnesses supporting their position nor were they given any notice of the basis on which the decision might rest. Of course, it is apparent from the face of the documents that no findings of fact were made as to any of the possible grounds of challenging their qualifications as adoptive parents. It is apparent from the record that they were attempting at all times merely to resist the removal of Timmy on the only ground which was explained to them, that is that it was the plan for "this type" of child to be adopted by black parents....

* * *

...[T]here is no statute and there are no regulations that cover the requirements which must be complied with by the Department before a relationship such as that enjoyed by the Drummonds and Timmy is terminated. In actual practice, moreover, there was nothing to compare with the provision described in the margin that "whenever the agency's tentative assessment of the beneficiary's condition differs from his own assessment, the beneficiary is informed that benefits may be terminated, *provided a summary of the evidence upon which the proposed determination to terminate is based, and afforded an opportunity to review the medical reports and other evidence in his case file*" nor was there anything remotely resembling the opportunity given, as described by the Supreme Court in its opinion which says "he also may respond in writing and submit additional evidence."

In the *Mathews* case, as the Supreme Court noted, the final determination by the agency is then "reviewed by an examiner in the SSA Bureau of Disability Insurance." 42 U.S.C. § 421(c);...If, as is usually the case, the SSA accepts the agency determination, it notifies the recipient in writing *informing him of the reasons for the decision, and of his right to seek de novo reconsideration by the state agency....*" 424 U.S. at 338. [Emphasis added.]

---

[3] It should be noted again that most of these reports were extravagant in their praise of the manner in which the Drummonds had developed a genuine loving family with this child...

All this is then followed if the recipient seeks reconsideration, by a federal appeal and an evidentiary hearing before an administrative law judge, as pointed out in the margin. In contrast, there is nothing in the Georgia law that permits any review, appeal or reconsideration by any tribunal or official or court of the "consensus judgment" made by this ad hoc committee.

The only kind of judicial review available is by the filing of a complaint in the United States Court where, as happened in this case, the district court had before it only an imperfect documentary record and the testimony of several of the actors in the proceeding who undertook to speak for the entire group of 19 and to explain what they had in their mind when they finally terminated Timmy's only known family relationship.

* * *

I know of no other situation under our laws in which the whole future life of a child of tender years can be gravely affected by the totally uncontrolled discretion of public officials without an opportunity for a hearing by those affected. I join in the assumption that I am sure underlies the opinion of the Court that the persons involved intended to do what they thought to be for the best of the child in the circumstances, but the law we announce today would deny relief to persons equally affected even though a strong showing could be made that the persons acting had done so capriciously, venally, or from definite racial bias, because the opinion says that the proceedings which produced the result in Timmy's case were adequate to satisfy the requirements of due process.

IV. THE RACIAL QUESTION

The complaint alleged that the action of the defendants in removing Timmy from custody of the Drummonds was motivated solely on racial grounds, that is it was done pursuant to a policy that black or part black children could not be placed for adoption with a white couple. One of the great defects in the proceeding here is the fact it is utterly impossible to determine whether or not this allegation is true. A careful reading of the documentary and oral testimony introduced at the trial gives me a strong belief that the decision made by the four or five workers in March to tell the Drummonds that they must give up Timmy so that he can be raised by a black couple was the one and only basis for all of the proceedings and the result that issued therefrom. In any event, there was no record, there was no transcript of testimony, there is no indication that any word about other reasons than Timmy's race went into any decision-making or was the basis for the final decision.

* * *

I would adhere to the mandate issued following the panel opinion of this Court.

Questions for Discussion

1. What elements of due process were missing from the procedure to decide Timmy's permanent placement? Are the Drummonds given a formal or informal hearing? An opportunity to be heard at all by the decision-makers? Is anyone independently speaking for Timmy?

2. The court opines that the State's "motive [is to move] Timmy to a better place." Is that a sufficient check on the executive branch of the state? If prosecutors are motivated to accomplish a just result, are judges, juries, or hearings rendered gratuitous?

3. If race is a legitimate factor in Timmy's permanent placement, why is he placed into foster care with the Drummonds (for two years)?

4. If Timmy is of mixed race (half black, half white), would a black couple be as racially disparate from Timmy as are the white Drummonds?

5. Can one argue that the child is living in Georgia in the 1970s and should not be subject to the torments of classmates or local discrimination because he is clearly of a different race than his parents? What is the response to the argument: "Take your liberal theories that race doesn't matter and fight your battles, but don't send a child to take the blows for you"?

6. If race is a legitimate factor in the proper placement of a child, can it be a factor in a parental rights hearing to find a white biological mother of a mixed race child unfit?

7. Timmy has been with the Drummonds from the age of one month to two years of age, when the permanent placement decision is to be made. Has Timmy bonded with these parents? Who does he call Mommy and Daddy? Who changes his diapers, feeds him, reads him books at night? Does Timmy have any procedural due process rights in the decision to permanently place him? Should constitutional doctrine permit such decisions to be made by the agency without review?

8. Supreme Court decisions have required the full panoply of procedural due process before a state taking of a welfare grant[40]and prior to the garnishment of wages by a creditor,[41] among other situations. What commends these situations for due process and judicial review over the permanent placement of Timmy?

I. PEW COMMISSION RECOMMENDATIONS

FINANCING CHILD WELFARE

1. Because every child needs a safe, permanent family, the Commission recommends:

- ***Providing federal adoption assistance to all children adopted from foster care; and***
- ***Providing federal guardianship assistance to all children who leave foster care to live with a permanent, legal guardian.***

The Commission recommends continuing federal adoption assistance as an entitlement under Title IV-E and making assisted guardianship a IV-E reimbursable expense. This will provide an additional route to permanence for children in foster care when adoption and reunification have been ruled out. Furthermore, because we believe that every child who experiences abuse and neglect–not just every poor child–deserves state and federal support in the effort to secure a permanent family, we recommend elimination of current income eligibility requirements for adoption assistance, and no income requirements for guardianship assistance.

2. Because every child needs to be protected from abuse and neglect, the Commission recommends that the federal government join states in paying for foster care for every child who needs this protection:

- ***Regardless of family income;***
- ***Including children who are members of Indian tribes; and***
- ***Including children who live in the U.S. territories.***

...Currently, the federal government shares in the cost of foster care only for children whose birth families meet outdated income eligibility requirements for cash welfare....The Commission recommends eliminating income eligibility requirements for foster care and suggests adjusting federal reimbursement rates as a means of maintaining cost neutrality. The Commission further recommends giving tribes and territories equal access to federal child welfare funds.

3. Because every child needs a permanent family, the Commission recommends allowing states to "reinvest" federal dollars that would have been expended on foster care into other child welfare services if they safely reduce foster care use. States could use these funds for any service to keep children out of foster care or to leave foster care safely. Currently, when states reduce their foster care expenditures, they"lose" the federal share of savings associated with that reduction–even though keeping children out of foster care can require substantial investments in prevention, treatment, and support once a child leaves foster care....

4. Children need skillful help to safely return home to their families, join a new family, or avoid entering foster care in the first place. For caseworkers to provide this help, states need flexible, sufficient, and reliable funding from the federal government. The Commission recommends an indexed Safe Children, Strong Families Grant that combines federal funding for Title IV-B, Title IV-E Administration, and Title IV-E Training into a flexible source of funding. The Commission recommends that additional funding be provided in the first year, and that the grant be indexed in future years.

- ***Each state's grant amount would be based on its historical spending for Title IV-B and Title IV-E Administration and Training;***
- ***In addition, the total base funding level would be enhanced by $200 million in the first year of implementation;***
- ***In subsequent years, each state's allocation would grow by 2 percent plus the inflation rate, as measured by the Consumer Price Index; and***
- ***States would be required to match the federal grant funds, just as they currently are required to match federal IV-B and IV-E dollars.***

The proposed Safe Children, Strong Families Grant would give states new flexibility to use nearly half of all current federal IV-E expenditures as they see fit to meet the unique needs of the children in their care....Recognizing that flexibility alone is not enough to enable states to build a full continuum of child welfare services, the Commission recommends providing an additional $200 million in federal funding...and an annual growth factor to ensure that funding not only keeps pace with inflation but grows over time.

5. To guarantee that public funds are used effectively to meet the needs of children who have been abused or neglected and to increase public accountability, the Commission recommends improvements to the federal Child and Family Services Reviews (CFSRs).

- ***The CFSRs should include more and better measures of child well-being, use longitudinal data to yield more accurate assessments of performance over time, and the U.S. Department of Health and Human Services (HHS) should direct that a portion of any penalties resulting from the review process be reinvested into a state's Program Improvement Plan;***

- ***The federal government should continue to help states build their accountability systems by maintaining the federal match for State Automated Child Welfare Information Systems (SACWIS); and***

- ***Congress should direct the National Academy of Sciences, through its Board on Children, Youth, and Families, to convene a foster care expert panel to recommend the best outcomes and measures to use in data collection.***

As the principal tool for assessing whether states are meeting the goals of safety, permanence, and well-being for children in foster care, the CFSRs represent a major step forward in creating real accountability in the child welfare system...the Commission...recommends that federal funding for SACWIS remain an open-ended entitlement under Title IV-E at the current 50 percent matching rate.

6. To promote innovation and constant exploration of the best ways to help children who have been abused and neglected, the Commission recommends that the federal government:

- ***Expand and improve its successful child welfare waiver program;***

- ***Continue to reserve funds for research, evaluation, and sharing of best practices; and***

- ***Provide incentives to states that make workforce improvements and increase all forms of safe permanence for children in foster care.***

Improving outcomes for children in the child welfare system will require experimentation on a broad scale, rigorous evaluation, and aggressive dissemination of proven practices. To that end, the Commission recommends building on the success of the child welfare waiver program by eliminating the cap on the number of waivers HHS may approve; permitting HHS to approve waivers that replicate demonstrations already implemented in other states....The Commission further recommends retaining the Title IV-B evaluation, research, training and technical assistance set-asides to continue to test new approaches and disseminate successful results....States that make lasting improvements in their child welfare workforce would receive a higher federal matching rate for their Safe Children, Strong Families Grant....

STRENGTHENING COURTS

1. Courts are responsible for ensuring that children's rights to safety, permanence and well-being are met in a timely and complete manner. To fulfill this responsibility, they must be able to track children's progress, identify groups of children in need of attention, and identify sources of delay in court proceedings.

- ***Every dependency court should adopt the court performance measures developed by the nation's leading legal associations and use this information to improve their oversight of children in foster care;***
- ***State judicial leadership should use these data to ensure accountability by every court for improved outcomes for children and to inform decisions about allocating resources across the court system; and***
- ***Congress should appropriate $10 million in start-up funds, and such sums as necessary in later years, to build capacity to track and analyze caseloads.***

The American Bar Association, the National Center for State Courts, and the National Council of Juvenile and Family Court Judges have developed a set of court performance outcome measures designed to help state courts improve judicial decision-making and hasten children's movement out of foster care and into safe, permanent homes. Such data are critical to improving court practice ....The Commission calls on state court systems to adopt these court performance measures and make the aggregate information publicly available...and we recommend an appropriation of at least $10 million to help state courts build their data capacity.

2. To protect children and promote their well-being, courts and public agencies should be required to demonstrate effective collaboration on behalf of children.

- ***The U.S. Department of Health and Human Services (HHS) should require that state IV-E plans, Program Improvement Plans, and Court Improvement Program plans demonstrate effective collaboration;***
- ***HHS should require states to establish broad-based state commissions on children in foster care, ideally led by the state's child welfare agency director and the Chief Justice;***
- ***Congress should appropriate $10 million to train court personnel, a portion of which should be designated for joint training of court personnel, child welfare agency staff, and***

others involved in protecting and caring for children; and

- ***Courts and agencies on the local and state levels should collaborate and jointly plan for the collection and sharing of all relevant aggregate data and information which can lead to better decisions and outcomes for children.***

Collaboration between the child welfare agency and the court is essential for lasting improvements in the child welfare system. Yet, while most federal funding for both the child welfare agency and the courts requires some type of state or court plan, there is no explicit requirement for court-agency collaboration. We recommend that states and the courts be required to demonstrate meaningful court-agency collaboration in the plans they submit to the federal government. To further collaboration, the Commission also recommends the development of multi-disciplinary, broad-based state commissions on children in foster care to ensure on-going collaboration between child welfare agencies and courts,...the Commission recommends an annual appropriation of $10 million through the Court Improvement Program to be used for court-specific training as well as cross-training initiatives....

3. To safeguard children's best interests in dependency court proceedings, children and their parents must have a direct voice in court, effective representation, and the timely input of those who care about them.

- ***Courts should be organized to enable children and parents to participate in a meaningful way in their own court proceedings;***
- ***Congress should appropriate $5 million to expand the Court Appointed Special Advocates (CASA) program;***
- ***States should adopt standards of practice, preparation, education, and compensation for attorneys in dependency practice;***
- ***To attract and retain attorneys who practice in dependency court, Congress should support efforts such as loan forgiveness and other demonstration programs; and***
- ***Law schools, bar associations, and law firms should help build the pool of qualified attorneys available to children and parents in dependency courts.***

Children, parents and caregivers all benefit when they have the opportunity to actively participate in court proceedings, as does the quality of decisions when judges can see and hear from key parties. State court leaders should consider the impact of factors such as court room and waiting area accommodations, case scheduling, use of technology in the court room, and translation of written materials. Even with the active participation of children and families, judges and attorneys will not always have the time and resources needed for the courts to make fully-informed decisions. We therefore recommend an expansion of the successful, community-based CASA program. Dissonance between state legislation, legal theory, and individual practice on the issue of legal representation of children creates confusion within the field–to the detriment of children who need strong, clear advocacy. Limited training for attorneys in dependency court contributes to the problem. The Commission recommends requiring these attorneys to complete a multi-disciplinary training program and participate in ongoing training throughout their careers. We recognize that compensation for dependency attorneys is generally low and that many law graduates leave school with substantial educational debt that can deter them from practicing in this field. We therefore recommend that Congress explore a loan forgiveness program and other demonstration programs to attract and retain competent attorneys in the dependency courts. Finally, to further develop the pool of experienced attorneys willing to represent children and parents in dependency proceedings, we call on attorneys and law firms to encourage and support the provision of more *pro bono* services to children and families in dependency court.

4. Chief Justices and state court leadership must take the lead, acting as the foremost champions for children in their court systems and making sure the recommendations here are enacted in their states.

- ***Chief Justices should embed oversight responsibility and assistance for dependency courts within their Administrative Office of the Courts;***
- ***State court leadership and state court administrators should organize courts so that dependency cases are heard in dedicated courts or departments, rather than in departments with jurisdiction over multiple issues;***
- ***State judicial leadership should actively promote: (1) resource, workload and training standards for dependency courts, judges, and attorneys; (2) standards of practice for dependency judges; and (3) codes of judicial conduct that support the practices of problemsolving courts; and***
- ***State court procedures should enable and encourage judges who have demonstrated competence in the dependency courts to build careers on the dependency bench.***

All of the recommendations for improving court performance in dependency cases require leadership from the top of the state judiciary. Establishing an office on children in the courts within the Administrative Office of the Courts would demonstrate the importance of dependency issues to the court leadership, and would help institutionalize the court's commitment to children beyond the tenure of individual Chief Justices. To ensure that dependency cases get the time, expertise, and degree of importance and attention that children deserve, we urge state court leadership to establish courts or departments dedicated to these cases. State judicial leadership should also adopt and use dependency court standards that recognize the unique nature of cases before these courts, the relatively large number of parties involved in these cases, and the often extended timeline of dependency cases. Finally, to build a cadre of experienced dependency court judges, we recommend that those judges who choose to build a career on the dependency bench be permitted to opt out of routine rotation.

Note on Pew Commission Recommendations and Five Additional Reforms

In 2005, the Pew Commission produced a seminal report with the above recommendations. The findings and conclusions of this Commission of experts has drawn widespread support, even beyond the child advocacy community. However, as the "current policy" discussion above in this chapter suggests, child advocates would supplement its recommendations with five reforms it excludes that are important to its stated goals: (a) prevention through a higher percentage of intended births; (b) family foster care supply and quality enhancement; (c) refinement of excessive confidentiality for dependency court and foster care regulation; (d) a major commitment to combat parental drug abuse —particularly of amphetamines; and (e) state assistance to foster children (and those adopted from foster care) to age 23.

Prevention through a higher percentage of intended births. The unwed birth rate remains at approximately 30%. A substantial number of children are not intended by one or both parents. These children are disproportionately subject to abuse, neglect and removal into foster care. Public programs that stimulate the ethic of a child's simple right to be intended by those persons creating him or her—and support for any measure accomplishing it—from parenting education, to sex education, to abstinence encouragement, to stimulation of the old fashioned values of marriage and commitment are all properly considered (see discussion in Chapters 2 and 3). Parenting education that extends beyond reproductive responsibility and includes basic information about child development and dangers (from shaking babies to leaving children unattended in automobile car seats during the day) also has important prevention value. Parenting education advocates argue that few high school students will actually use their trigonometry lessons, or revisit the table of elements as adults. But most will become parents and the health of their children may depend upon what they know. To the extent such education is a part of the modern curriculum, it currently is concentrated in home economics classes eschewed by the male half of the population.

Family foster care supply and quality enhancement. The family foster care supply is critical to the substitute family sought by the Pew Commission. Eighty percent of adoptions for foster children come from their family foster care providers. Historically, the demographics of stay-at-home moms produced a substantial supply of such homes. However, with real estate prices and child care costs, few adults below the upper-middle to upper classes can afford to provide a home for a child without at least receiving the cost of such care. But compensation remains low—usually in the $500 to $700 per month for a child. As a result, the supply of family foster care providers has not grown commensurate with foster child caseloads. Meanwhile, group homes are commonly paid $4,000 to $5,000 per month for each child—and more if educational services are provided. This distortion has stimulated group home placement with the lack of an intimate, permanent, committed family so essential to healthy child development. And it leaves 118,000 foster children eligible for and warranting adoption without the intimacy of a family. Where foster children have special needs, allowing substantial additional compensation to family foster care providers who obtain skills and training in their disabilities will increase supply in areas requiring special commitment.

Revision of confidentiality for dependency court and foster care regulation. Most states retain confidentiality for all juvenile proceedings. While a policy of rehabilitation justifies that secrecy in delinquency proceedings, what is its rationale in dependency court and over foster children? Some cases may warrant a protective order, as with some molestation cases. But a policy of openness subject to confidentiality when and if so warranted will have advantages for involved children. Those children are not subject to public ridicule or calumny—they are more often the heroes in the stories coming before the court. But all that has happened, and the actions of the court, and of the departments of social services—are subject to presumptive confidentiality in most states. While it may be possible to waive that secrecy, the catch-22 of not knowing to file such a petition insulates the child welfare system from public visibility and democratic accountability. Hence, a 25-year-old can assault and injure a 20-year-old spouse or friend and the proceedings and outcome are public. But if the victim is 15 or 7 or 4, it is generally adjudicated in secret. Child advocates argue that even when children die while in foster care, the circumstances of their deaths are kept effectively from public examination. And they contend that those foster care children in group homes—and who might be adoptable if more visible—are subject to less exposure for that purpose than are the abandoned dogs in the local pound.

A major commitment to combat parental drug abuse. Attorneys who represent children in dependency court generally observe a high correlation between parental drug abuse and child neglect. Some drugs, particularly so-called "speed", seem to reduce maternal and paternal instinct and at the same time speed up metabolic reactions in ways harmful to involved children. The popular culture is ambivalent about such drug use—with notions of civil liberties and personal choice dampening societal response. Those who practice in juvenile dependency court know that they are not victimless crimes when children are involved.

State assistance to foster children (and those adopted from foster care) to age 23. The average age of youth "self-sufficiency" independence in America is between 27 and 28 years of age. Until that time, most youth do not fully earn their own keep. Responsible parents assist their children as they enter adulthood, helping them with education costs, room and board, and employment. However, child advocates argue that those foster children for whom the state serves as parent are commonly abandoned to the streets at age 18. "Independent Living," tuition assistance, and other programs have increased in number and resources since the late 1990s. However, these programs do not approach the transitional help a typical parent provides. They will assist a number of emancipating youth with rent for several years. However, these youth must work full time, even with this help, to pay rent and for food and other basics given the costs of the 21st century. That burden makes higher education (even with low or subsidized tuition) problematical for most of them. The reduction of emancipation age to 18 from 21 occurred during the late 1960s and the new cut-off did not distinguish between youth obligations and protections. Child advocates argue that every child should have room and board covered to at least age 23—either at the foster home or, under careful fund dispensation, in the community. Tuition and books for higher education, from vocational training to graduate school work, should be provided as a matter of course. They contend that such an investment will yield a substantial long-run societal return.

ENDNOTES

[1] Act of April 21, 1899, [1899] Ill. Laws 131.

[2] U.S. Department of Health and Human Services, *Child Maltreatment 2003: Reports from the States to the National Child Abuse and Neglect Data System*(Washington, D.C.; 2005) (see www.acf.dhhs.gov).

[3] U.S. Department of Health and Human Services, *2006 Budget Commentary* (Washington, D.C.; 2005) (see www.hhs.gov).

[4] Pew Commission on Children in Foster Care, *Ranking of Foster Care Population by State (FY 2005)* (Washington, D.C.; 2005) (see http://pewfostercare.org/).

[5] Andrea J. Sedlak, Diane D. Broadhurst, U.S. Department of Health and Human Services, National

Center on Child Abuse and Neglect, *Third National Incidence Study of Child Abuse and Neglect* (Washington, D.C.; Sept. 1996) at v–vi (Executive Summary).

[6] Department of Health and Human Services, *Blending Perspectives and Building Common Ground, A Report to Congress on Substance Abuse and Child Protection* (Washington, D.C.; Apr. 1999) at Chapter 4.

[7] Pub. L. No. 96-272 (42 U.S.C. § 420).

[8] 42 U.S.C. §§ 671-673.

[9] *Id.*

[10] See CAL. WELF. & INST. CODE § 11401.

[11] 42 U.S.C. § 5101 *et seq.*

[12] See Pub. L. No. 104-188.

[13] The enacted version was based on a compromise between H.R. 867 and the Senate's SAFE and PASS Acts. However, it omitted a number of important provisions sought by child advocates, including more money for permanency services and training for child protection case workers. The child protection system depends critically upon the professional judgment of social workers employed by county child protection agencies (working within county departments of social services). An incompetent or strongly biased social worker can influence decisions affecting the health, safety, and future of children. Child advocates contend that the competence and expertise of this group is uneven. Civil service protection makes weeding out those who consistently manifest bad judgment difficult.

[14] H.R. 3443, Pub. L. No. 106-169; note that the pre-existing federal independent living program is renamed by this statute in honor of the late Senator John Chafee of Rhode Island.

[15] See Paul Boland, presiding Juvenile Court Judge, Los Angeles County, *Review of all New Petitions Before the L.A. County Juvenile Dependency Court* (1989).

[16] Thomas, *Drug Abuse and Child Maltreatment: A Clear and Present Danger*, 6(4) Protecting Children 4,5 (1990).

[17] In 1998, California Republican Governor Pete Wilson vetoed SB 2138 which would have implemented basic parenting education in high school, writing: "SB 2138 requires parental notification—but not consent. It...should offer to those parents and pupils who desire it, the option to satisfy the curricular requirement (here created) by alternatives...which could include church-based or home-teaching." In 1999, new Democratic California Governor Gray Davis then vetoed SB 305 to provide more modest parenting education. His veto message stated: "The primary responsibility of schools is to teach the basics....I do not believe the teaching of parenting skills is the appropriate role of schools. Rather, this is a subject that is rightfully the domain of parents, families, faith-based entities and non-profit organizations." See Children's Advocacy Institute, *Children's Legislative Report Card 1998* (San Diego, CA; October 1998) at 13; Children's Advocacy Institute, *Children's Legislative Report Card 1999* (San Diego, CA; October 1999) at 11 (http://www.sandiego.edu/childrensissues).

[18] See Administration for Children and Families, Office of Planning, Research and Evaluation, *National Survey of Child and Adolescent Well-Being* (Washington, D.C.; 2005) at Chapter 3, Table 3-2C. The percentages are obtained from the allocation of the 272,000 out-of-home placements, surveyed as the table indicates (see www.acf.hhs.gov).

[19] The percentage placed with relatives has increased dramatically over the past twenty years, from less than 20% of all placements in 1985 to almost 50% today.

[20] Barbara Needell, Daniel Webster, Richard Barth, and Michael Armijo, Child Welfare Research Center, University of California at Berkeley, School of Social Welfare, *Performance Indicators for Child Welfare Services in California: 1995, Selected Findings* (Berkeley, CA; 1997) at 37.

[21] Legislative Analyst's Office, *Child Abuse and Neglect in California* (Sacramento, CA; January 1996) at 45.

[22] Mark Nadel, *Foster Care: Challenges Faced in Implementing the Multiethnic Placement Act,* General Accounting Office, GAO/T-HEHS-98-241 (Sept. 15, 1998).

[23] See 1996 ABA Standards of Practice for Lawyers Who Represent Children in Dependency Cases; see also discussion of proposed standards by the National Association of Counsel for Children, Ventrell, *Legal Representation of Children in Dependency Court: Toward a Better Model—the ABA (NACC Revised) Standards of Practice*, NACC Children's Law Manual (Denver, CO; 1999) at 168 (www.NACCchildlaw.org).

[24] For calculation of total safety net reduction (TANF plus food stamps) to approximately 70% of the poverty line for the benchmark family of mother and two children in California by 2004-05, see Robert C. Fellmeth, *California Children's Budget 2004-05,* Children's Advocacy Institute (San Diego, CA; June 2004) at Chapter 2.

[25] Child care costs average from $4,000 to $7,000 per annum per child. Two children would consume virtually all of the net earnings of a single mother making minimum wage.

[26] These funds must not be used for services to children or families with incomes below 200% of the poverty line. Note that a small additional percentage may now be transferred for any use if related to impoverished children.

[27] See the summary of research briefly listed by Hillary Rodham Clinton, *First Lady Announces New Efforts to Support Transitioning Foster Care Youth* (Washington, D.C.; Jan. 1999). See Chapter 10 for discussion of foster care relationship to delinquency and crime.

[28] California Attorney General's Office, *Child Victim Witness Investigative Pilot Projects: Research and Evaluation Final Report* (Sacramento, CA; July 1994).

[29] See the Child Victims' and Child Witness' Protection Act of 1990, 18 U.S.C. § 3509 allowing in federal court closed circuit two way testimony by child victims of sexual abuse, or of sexual exploitation (pornography production, prostitution), or children witnessing a crime against a third party. However, the procedure requires an evidentiary finding that such a child could not communicate reasonably in the close physical presence of the defendant. Over half of the nation's states have enacted statutes allowing either two-way, or one-way video testimony by such a qualifying child. Such arrangements commonly allow for cross examination of a child by defense counsel in a less intimidating room without the jury, or defendant physically present, but with prosecutor, defense counsel and usually the court in the room with the child, with all other persons able to see the testimony via video transmission into the regular court room. See *Maryland v. Craig* and related discussion in Chapter 9 *infra.*

[30] See also *Seling v. Young*, 531 U.S. 250 (2000), allowing such statutes to be characterized as "civil" rather than criminal, thus avoiding double jeopardy, double punishment, or *ex post facto* bars were the proceeding to be considered a continuation of the criminal case.

[31] 42 U.S.C. § 14071.

[32] The use of underage performers led to the Protection of Children Against Sexual Exploitation Act of 1977 adding 18 U.S.C. §§ 2251–2252. The first section makes it a federal crime to use children in "sexually explicit" productions, with sanctions for both the producer and applicable parents or guardians allowing such labor. Section 2252 prohibits the transportation or receipt in interstate commerce for profit of such "obscene" visual or print material.

[33] 18 U.S.C. § 2255.

[34] 18 U.S.C. § 2251 *et seq.*

[35] 18 U.S.C. § 2256(8).

[36] 18 U.S.C. §§ 1460–1466.

[37] Dissenting Justice O'Connor would distinguish the two, striking the portion of the statute prohibiting depiction of those over 18 as under that age, but upholding the ban on entirely computer generated children engaged in sexual activity.

[38] Note that the statute defines prohibited "sexually explicit conduct" by apparent children, as: "actual or simulated...sexual intercourse, including genital-genital, oral-genital, anal-genital, or oral anal, whether between persons of the same or opposite sex...bestiality;...masturbation;...sadistic or masochistic abuse;...or lascivious exhibition of the genitals or pubic area of any person." 18 U.S.C. § 2256(2). Hence, the statute appears to ban specific depiction of sex acts by children; child nudity is prohibited only where "lascivious." Such nudity would require the prurient element of obscenity, but would not be subject to its "redeeming value" factor.

[39] The *Ashcroft* Court quoted from *Miller v. California*, 413 U.S. 15 (1973), discussing necessary elements for obscenity.

[40] *Goldberg v. Kelly*, 397 U.S. 254 (1970).

[41] *Sniadach v. Family Finance Corp. of Bay View*, 395 U.S. 337 (1969).

CHAPTER NINE

Child Rights as Abuse Victims/ Witnesses

A. CHILD COMPETENCY TO TESTIFY

Competency to testify traditionally requires adequate intelligence to make the testimony of value, and an understanding of the duty to tell the truth. Both tests apply to the situation at trial, not when the events testified about occurred. An exception is sometimes drawn where a child is so young when the events occurred that he or she is incapable of their accurate recall. Witness competency is traditionally determined just before trial (through a motion *in limine*) or through *voir dire* at trial (out of the presence of the jury).

At common law, children below the age of 14 have been presumed incompetent to testify as witnesses in court while those who have reached 14 are presumed competent. In either case, the presumption may be rebutted with evidence to either allow or disallow testimony. Some states draw the line for presumption shift at 10 years of age. Evidence scholars have criticized the tendency of some courts to bar testimony of child witnesses, contending that it reflects a distrust of the primary jury role—to evaluate credibility of witnesses.[1] The trend has been to more liberally allow testimony, deferring to the jury its proper weight, consistent with Rule 601 of the Federal Rules of Evidence, which presumes that every person is competent to testify.

Historically, objections about child testimony have centered around four issues: perception, memory, narration, and truthfulness. Studies during the 1970s and 1980s rebutted much of that concern, finding that children were not more prone than adults to give false testimony.[2] Language limitations and complexity may require questions to be simplified, and leading questions are commonly permitted.

The primary concern evolving in the 1990s is that children are "suggestible" as witnesses, that a parent or other authority figure can plant detailed facts or stories which children can come to believe and testify about with dangerous efficacy. Sociologically, the emotional trauma during divorce and the regrettably common use of children by one parent against the other has led to increasing accusations of child abuse or molestation. Not all of these accusations have merit, and children have been enlisted by one or both parents to buttress a case against the other. The result has been added suspicion concerning the credibility of child testimony.

Excerpts from

The Suggestibility of the Child Witness: An Historical Review and Synthesis

By
Stephen J. Ceci, Cornell University
Maggie Bruck, McGill University

More research on children's eyewitness testimony has been conducted in the past decade than in the rest of the twentieth century combined....A synthesis of this research posits three "families" of factors, cognitive, social, and biological, which must be taken into consideration if we are to understand seemingly contradictory interpretations of findings. It is concluded that there are reliable age differences in suggestibility, due to a variety of factors, but that even very young children are capable of recalling much that is forensically relevant.

* * *

The second aspect of children's testimonial credibility concerns their "suggestibility", and it is this aspect that is the focus of the present review. According to its broadest definition, suggestibility concerns the degree to which children's encoding, storage, and/or retrieval of events can be influenced by a range of internal and external factors...how easily one is influenced by both subtle suggestions and leading questions, as well as by explicit bribes, threats, and other forms of inducement. By broadening this definition of suggestibility to entail all forms of influence, not just mnemonic ones, this paper summarizes the literature that addresses the following two questions. First, are children more suggestible than adults? Second, to what degree does children's suggestibility reflect cognitive factors, social-motivated factors, and/or biological factors? The examination of these questions allows for a more precise understanding not only of the conditions under which children are suggestible, but more generally of the causal mechanisms that underlie their suggestibility.

Historical Review

* * *

During the final decade of the seventeenth century, a group of children known as the "circle girls" gave false testimony in the witchcraft trials of over 20 residents of Salem Village and Salem Farms, Massachusetts. The girls claimed to have seen the defendants flying on broom sticks, to have witnessed celestial apparitions in the form of speaking animals, and to have observed the defendants instructing insects to fly into their mouths and deposit bent nails and pins in their stomachs (which they subsequently vomited during their testimony). On the basis of their testimony, 20 defendants were convicted and put to death, and a dozen more were spared execution because they threw themselves on the mercy of the court, and admitted their participation in witchcraft. In the aftermath of the executions, some of the child witnesses publicly recanted their testimonies....

* * *

...Perhaps no other researcher has done more to redress the historical imbalance in favor of child witnesses than has Gail Goodman. After almost a century of research criticizing and belittling the accuracy and suggestibility of child witnesses, Goodman has presented a picture that is far more optimistic about children's abilities. Her work is animated in part by a desire to know whether non-abused children will make false claims of abuse in response to erroneous suggestions by adults. In order to examine this question, Goodman's strategy has been to interview nonabused children about sexual as well as non-sexual experiences.

As one example, Goodman, Rudy, Bottoms, and Aman (1990) studied eighteen pairs of same-age, same-sex 4- and 7-year-old children who were left in a trailer with a strange adult. One child played a game with the adult that involved being dressed in a clown's costume, being lifted and photographed, while the other child was encouraged to carefully observe this interchange. Approximately ten days later, both children were asked general and specific questions about the event by a different adult. During this interview, suggestive and non-suggestive questions about the event were asked. Some of these questions concerned actions that might lead to an accusation of child abuse, such as "He took your clothes off, didn't he?". Older children were more accurate on the suggestive questions. Overall, the older children also gave more accurate answers (93%) to the "abuse" questions than did the younger children (83%). However, Goodman et al. feel that these figures represent an overestimate of suggestibility in reference to courtroom issues, since a more detailed analysis of the incorrect answers to the suggestive abuse questions, revealed that there was only one false report of abuse (out of a possible 252) given by the seven-year-olds, and there were only 13 false reports given by the five-year-olds. Goodman, et al. claimed that under these circumstances child participants and bystanders are equally accurate in resisting the interviewer's erroneous suggestions about abusive actions. In fact, these children demonstrated surprise in response to the suggestive questions.

...A second study conducted by Goodman and her colleagues (Saywitz, et al., 1989) examined 5- and 7-year-old girls' memories of medical examinations. Half of each age group had a scoliosis exam and half had a genital exam. Children were tested between one and four weeks following their exam. As was true in the Goodman et al. (1990) study just described, children were asked suggestive and non-suggestive questions which are abusive or nonabusive in nature. The older children's answers to the suggestive questions, and to the abuse-related questions were more accurate than those of the younger children. However, there was essentially no difference in resistance to suggestibility for "abuse related suggestive questions" (.96 vs. .99 for the 5- and 7-year-olds, respectively). Furthermore, the seven-year-old children never made a false report of abuse, and this occurred only three times (out of a possible 215 opportunities) for the five-year-olds. These findings led the investigators to conclude that, "...our findings indicated that there are important limits on children's suggestibility" (p. 9).

* * *

Although the studies just described highlight particular aspects of an interview that may influence children's reports, the experimental settings used by the researchers are pale versions of interviews carried out in legal settings (McGough, in press). In the latter context children are questioned, on average, eleven times prior to testifying in court, often by a number of different interviewers (e.g., parents, police, therapists, child protection workers, lawyers) who usually do not have a specific set of written questions. Rather, interviewers generally employ a variety of on-line strategies before and during the interview to achieve the goal of obtaining the most detailed and accurate information about events that a child may have witnessed.

* * *

[Many] of the State's interviews in the Kelly Michaels' case [involved] highly suggestive use of props (spoons, forks, knives, dolls), and a relentless pursuit of only one hypothesis, often accompanied by bribes for the promise of disclosure (popsicles, trips to the jail, use of the tape recorder, gifts of toy police badges) and implied threats in the face of nondisclosure. For example, upon Child 43C's insistence that he had not observed any wrong-doing by Michaels, Folloneras admonished: "Don't be a baby. You're acting like a nursery school kid." (p.10 A266 in Kelly Michaels case). In a similar vein, when Child 40C requested to leave the interview to eat, McGrath asked: "You're hungry? Okay. You tell me why you want to hit the doll and I'll give you something to eat...Okay., then I'm gonna stay here and we're gonna keep on with this, its okay with me. Cause I'm here to help you, and I know you want to tell me something and I'll stay here all day 'till you tell me."

A similar pattern of threats, bribes, and strong insinuations that their friends had already told investigators of the defendant's abusive behavior can also be seen in other cases (Benedek, 1989). For example, in the celebrated McMartin Preschool sex abuse case, jurors eventually acquitted the two defendants, Peggy McMartin and Raymond Buckey, on all 65 counts against them, claiming that the videotaped interviews conducted by the social worker who headed the team revealed doubts as to what the children actually remembered versus what the interviewer had suggested to them. For example, the interviewer informed the children that other children had already told of being sexually abused by the defendants.

* * *

...Experts in psychology, social work, pediatrics, and psychiatry frequently claim in court that children are incapable of lying, or are not suggestible (e.g., *People v. Watson*, 1965; *Commonwealth v. Seese*, 1986; *Matter of Nicole V.*, 1987; also see Mason, in press; McGough, in press). It is rare to see experts presenting a careful summary of the research, because doing so would probably force them to attenuate their often strident claims for one side or another.

As a way of avoid this problem, legal jurisdictions traditionally adopted what is known as a "Frye Test" standard, or the Kelly-Frye standard, which stipulates that expert testimony is only permitted when the research that underpins the expert's testimony is "sufficiently established to have gained general acceptance in the particular field in which it belongs." (Frye v. the United States, 1923 § 1014). This ruling came about as a result of an attempt to introduce the results of an early form of polygraph testing into the record. Federal Rule 703 has diluted the Frye Test standard somewhat, allowing that the data base that expert witnesses use "must be reasonably relied upon by experts in a field in forming opinions or inferences on the subject." Hence it is permissible for experts to disagree about the meaning of research findings, as long as they are aware of them. Since we assume that this review will serve as a basis for the opinions of some who venture into court as expert witnesses on childhood suggestibility, then the following three conclusions would seem to meet a traditional Fry Test standard.

First, and foremost, preschool aged children are disproportionately more vulnerable to erroneous post-event suggestion than are older individuals, contrary to disclaimers made by some (e.g., Melton, 1990). This conclusion follows from the synopsis of past and current research, over 90% of which shows reliable age differences in children's accuracy in the aftermath of leading questions....

Differences of opinion exist as to the boundary conditions for younger children's greater suggestibility, with some researchers arguing that it is diminished or even nonexistent when the act in question concerns a child's own body, or when it is a central action (e.g., Goodman, et al., 1990; also see Amicus Brief in *Wright v. Idaho,* No. 89-260):

> Resistance to suggestion appears to be highest concerning the core aspects of events. Moreover, participation in an event, as opposed to mere observation, appears to lower children's suggestibility. (p. 80)

Others, however, have failed to provide support for these claims....

Second, contrary to some claims, children will lie when the motivational structure is tilted toward lying. In this sense they are probably no different than adults....

Extreme statements that some have proferred in the media (e.g., "Children never lie" vs. "children are incapable of getting it right because they cannot distinguish reality and fantasy") are not supported by the findings reviewed here. That children are found to lie at times ought not surprise anyone, save the rather extreme advocates who have made such baseless claims. Children are, after all, members of the human race, and as such they should be susceptible to the same influences that older members are. More research is needed into age-related shifts in motivational salience, so that we have a better understanding of whether fear of reprisals, honoring a promise, resisting bribes, for example are more or less influential for a given age group. Until such research becomes available, it is safe to conclude that sometimes children will lie, but certainly not all of the time, nor uniformly in response to all motivational forces. And when children do lie, there is some evidence that they are easier to detect than adults due to their greater leakage through nonverbal and verbal behaviors (Bussey, 1990; Goodman, 1990; Peters, 1990), though this research does not approximate the cases in which children have been rehearsed, threatened, or cajoled by powerful adults over long periods.

Third, notwithstanding the above two points, it is clear that children—even preschoolers—are capable of recalling much that is forensically relevant. That their reports are more vulnerable to post-event distortion than those of older persons, and that they can be induced to lie in response to certain motives, is not meant to imply that they are incapable of providing accurate testimony. In fact, in most of the studies that have been reported during the past decade, young children are able to accurately recollect the majority of the information that they observed, even when they did not recall as much as older children. They may be more likely to succumb to erroneous suggestions than older children and adults, but their vulnerability is a matter of degree only. Even adults are suggestible (Belli, 1989; Loftus, 1979; Loftus & Hoffman, 1989), so the question ought not be "Are children suggestible?", but rather "Is their level of suggestibility so much greater than an adult's as to: a) render them worthless as witnesses?, b) require competency hearings to determine if they ought to be allowed to provide testimony to juries?, and /or c) require judges to instruct juries about their special reliability risks?" Based on the evidence reviewed in this paper, the answer to the first two of these questions is a qualified "no."

* * *

Source: Ceci. S.J. & Bruck, M. (1993) The Suggestibility of the Child Witness: A Historical Review and Synthesis. Psychological Bulletin, 113, 403-439. See http:www.cogstud.cornell.edu.faculty/ed.ceci.html.

State v. Michaels

136 N.J. 299 (1994)

The opinion of the Court was delivered by **Handler, J.**

* * *

I

In September 1984, Margaret Kelly Michaels was hired by Wee Care Day Nursery ("Wee Care") as a teacher's aide for preschoolers. Located in St. George's Episcopal Church, in Maplewood, Wee Care served approximately fifty families, with an enrollment of about sixty children, ages three to five.

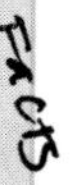

Michaels, a college senior from Pittsburgh, Pennsylvania, came to New Jersey to pursue an acting career. She responded to an advertisement and was hired by Wee Care, initially as a teacher's aide for preschoolers, then, at the beginning of October, as a teacher. Michaels had no prior experience as a teacher at any level.

Wee Care had staff consisting of eight teachers, numerous aides, and two administrators. The nursery classes for the three-year-old children were housed in the basement, and the kindergarten class was located on the third floor. During nap time, Michaels, under the supervision of the head teacher and the director, was responsible for about twelve children in one of the basement classrooms. The classroom assigned to Michaels was separated from an adjacent occupied classroom by a vinyl curtain.

During the seven-month-period that Michaels worked at Wee Care, she apparently performed satisfactorily. Wee Care never received a complaint about her from staff, children, or parents. According to the State, however, between October 8, 1984, and the date of Michaels's resignation on April 26, 1985, parents and teachers began observing behavioral changes in the children.

On April 26, 1985, the mother of M.P., a four-year-old in Michaels's nap class, noticed while awakening him for school, that he was covered with spots. She took the child to his pediatrician and had him examined. During the examination, a pediatric nurse took M.P.'s temperature rectally. In the presence of the nurse and his mother, M.P. stated, "this is what my teacher does to me at nap time at school." M.P. indicated to the nurse that his teacher, Kelly (the name by which Michaels was known to the children), was the one who took his temperature. M.P. added that Kelly undressed him and took his temperature daily. On further questioning by his mother, M.P. said that Kelly did the same thing to S.R.

The pediatrician, Dr. Delfino, then examined M.P. He informed Mrs. P. that the spots were caused by a rash. Mrs. P. did not tell Dr. Delfino about M.P.'s remarks; consequently, he did not examine M.P.'s rectum. In response to further questioning from his mother after they had returned home, M.P., while rubbing his genitals, stated that "[Kelly] uses the white jean stuff." Although M.P. was unable to tell his mother what the "white jean stuff" was, investigators later found vaseline in Wee Care's bathroom and white cream in the first-aid kit. During the same conversation, M.P. indicated that Kelly had "hurt" two of his classmates, S.R. and E.N.

M.P.'s mother contacted the New Jersey Division of Youth and Family Services ("DYFS") and Ms. Spector, Director of Wee Care, to inform them of her son's disclosures. On May 1, 1985, the Essex County Prosecutor's office received information from DYFS about the alleged sexual abuse at Wee Care. The Prosecutor's office assumed investigation of the complaint.

The Prosecutor's office interviewed several Wee Care children and their parents, concluding their initial investigation on May 8, 1985. During that period of investigation, Michaels submitted to approximately nine hours of questioning. Additionally, Michaels consented to taking a lie detector test, which she passed. Extensive additional interviews and examinations of the Wee Care children by the prosecutor's office and DYFS then followed.

Michaels was charged on June 6, 1985, in a three-count indictment involving the alleged sexual abuse of three Wee Care boys. After further investigation, a second indictment was returned July 30, 1985, containing 174 counts of various charges involving twenty Wee Care boys and girls. An additional indictment of fifty-five counts was filed November 21, 1985, involving fifteen Wee Care children. Prior to trial the prosecution dismissed seventy-two counts, proceeding to trial on the remaining 163 counts.

After several pretrial hearings, the trial commenced on June 22, 1987. The bulk of the State's evidence consisted of the testimony of the children. That testimony referred extensively to the pretrial statements that had been elicited from the children during the course of the State's investigations. The State introduced limited physical evidence to support the contention that the Wee Care children had been molested.

By the time the trial concluded nine months later, another thirty-two counts had been dismissed, leaving 131 counts. On April 15, 1988, after twelve days of deliberation, the jury returned guilty verdicts on 115 counts, including aggravated sexual assault (thirty-eight counts), sexual assault (thirty-one counts), endangering the welfare of children (forty-four counts), and terroristic threats (two counts). The trial court sentenced Michaels to an aggregate term of forty-seven years imprisonment with fourteen years of parole ineligibility.

I

The focus of this case is on the manner in which the State conducted its investigatory interviews of the children. In particular, the Court is asked to consider whether the interview techniques employed by the state could have undermined the reliability of the children's statements and subsequent testimony, to the point that a hearing should be held to determine whether either form of evidence should be admitted at re-trial.

The question of whether the interviews of the child victims of alleged sexual-abuse were unduly suggestive and coercive requires a highly nuanced inquiry into the totality of circumstances surrounding those interviews. Like confessions and identification, the inculpatory capacity of statements indicating the occurrence of sexual abuse and the anticipated testimony about those occurrences requires that special care be taken to ensure their reliability.

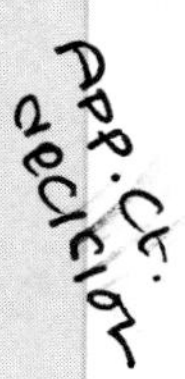

The Appellate Division carefully examined the record concerning the investigatory interviews. It concluded that the interrogations that had been conducted were highly improper....The court determined from the record that the children's accusations were founded "upon unreliable perceptions, or memory caused by improper investigative procedures," and that testimony reflecting those accusations could lead to an unfair trial....Accordingly, it held that in the event of a re-trial, a pretrial hearing would be required to assess the reliability of the statements and testimony to be presented by those children to determine their admissibility....The State appeals that determination.

Woven into our consideration of this case is the question of a child's susceptibility to influence through coercive or suggestive questioning. As the Appellate Division noted, a constantly broadening body of scholarly authority exists on the question of children's susceptibility to improper interrogation....The expanse of that literature encompasses a variety of views and conclusions....Among the varying perspectives, however, the Appellate Division found a consistent and recurrent concern over the capacity of the interviewer and the interview process to distort a child's recollection through unduly slanted interrogation techniques....The Appellate Division concluded that certain interview practices are sufficiently coercive or suggestive to alter irremediably the perceptions of the child victims....

A.

* * *

Additional factors temper our consideration of whether children are susceptible to manipulative interrogation. This Court has been especially vigilant in its insistence that children, as a class, are not to be viewed as inherently suspect witnesses. We have specifically held that age per se cannot render a witness incompetent....We declined to require or allow, absent a strong showing of abnormality, psychological testing of child-victims of sexual abuse as a predicate to a determination of the credibility of the child-victim as a witness....We have also recognized that under certain circumstances children's accounts of sexual abuse can be highly reliable....Nevertheless, our common experience tells us that children generate special concerns because of their vulnerability, immaturity, and impressionability, and our laws have recognized and attempted to accommodate those concerns, particularly in the area of child sexual abuse....

The broad question of whether children as a class are more or less susceptible to suggestion than adults is one that we need not definitively answer in order to resolve the central issue in this case. Our inquiry is much more focused. The issue we must determine is whether the interview techniques used by the State in this case were so coercive or suggestive that they had a capacity to distort substantially the children's recollections of actual events and thus compromise the reliability of the children's statements and testimony based on their recollections.

We begin our analyses by noting, as did the Appellate Division, that the "investigative interview" is a crucial, perhaps determinative, moment in a child-sex-abuse case....A decision to prosecute a case of child sexual abuse often hinges on the information elicited in the initial investigatory interviews with alleged victims, carried out by social workers or police investigators....

That an investigatory interview of a young child can be coercive or suggestive and thus shape the child's responses is generally accepted. If a child's recollection of events has been molded by an interrogation, that influence undermines the reliability of the child's responses as an accurate recollection of actual events.

* * *

The use of incessantly repeated questions also adds a manipulative element to an interview. When a child is asked a question and gives an answer, and the question is immediately asked again, the child's normal reaction is to assume that the first answer was wrong or displeasing to the adult questioner....The insidious effects of repeated questioning are even more pronounced when the questions themselves over time suggest information to the children....

The explicit vilification or criticism of the person charged with wrongdoing is another factor that can induce a child to believe abuse has occurred....Similarly, an interviewer's bias with respect to a suspected person's guilt or innocence can have a marked effect on the accuracy of a child's statements....The transmission of suggestion can also be subtly communicated to children through more obvious factors such as the interviewer's tone of voice, mild threats, praise, cajoling, bribes and rewards, as well as resort to peer pressure.

The Appellate Division recognized the considerable authority supporting the deleterious impact improper interrogation can have on a child's memory....Other courts have recognized that once tainted the distortion of the child's memory is irremediable...("Once this tainting of memory has occurred, the problem is irredeemable. That memory is, from then on, as real to the child as any other."). The debilitating impact of improper interrogation has even more pronounced effect among young children. Maryann King and John C. Yuille, Suggestibility and the Child Witness, in Children's Eyewitness Memory, 29 (Stephen J. Ceci *et al.* eds., 1987) and Stephen J. Ceci, Age Differences in Suggestibility, in Children's Eyewitness Memory 82 (Stephen J. Ceci, *et al.* ed., 1987).

The critical influence that can be exerted by interview techniques is also supported by the literature that generally addresses the reliability of children's memories. Those studies stress the importance of proper interview techniques as a predicate for eliciting accurate and consistent recollection....

* * *

B.

We next turn to an examination of the interrogations conducted in this case to determine if they were so suggestive or coercive that they created a substantial risk that the statements and testimony thereby elicited lack sufficient reliability to justify their admission at trial.

The interrogations undertaken in the course of this case utilized most, if not all, of the practices that are disfavored or condemned by experts, law enforcement authorities and government agencies.

The initial investigation giving rise to defendant's prosecution was sparked by a child volunteering that his teacher, "Kelly," had taken his temperature rectally, and that she had done so to other children. However, the overwhelming majority of the interviews and interrogations did not arise from the spontaneous recollections that are generally considered to be most reliable. See *Wright*, *supra*, 497 U.S. at 826–27,...(implying that spontaneous recall is under normal conditions an accurate indicator of trustworthiness);...Few, if any, of the children volunteered information that directly implicated defendant. Further, none of the child victims related incidents of actual sexual abuse to their interviewers using "free recall." 264 N.J.Super. at 629,...Additionally, few of the children provided any tell-tale details of the alleged abuse although they were repeatedly prompted to do so by the investigators. We note further that the investigators were not trained in interviewing young children. The earliest interviews with children were not recorded and in some instances the original notes were destroyed.[1] Many of the interviewers demonstrated ineptness in dealing with the challenges presented by pre-schoolers, and displayed their frustration with the children.

Almost all of the interrogations conducted in the course of the investigation revealed an obvious lack of impartiality on the part of the interviewer. One investigator, who conducted the majority of the interviews with the children, stated that his interview techniques had been based on the premise that the "interview process is in essence the beginning of the healing process." He considered it his "professional and ethical responsibility to alleviate whatever anxiety has arisen as a result of what happened to them." A lack of objectivity also was indicated by the interviewer's failure to pursue any alternative hypothesis that might contradict an assumption of defendant's guilt, and a failure to challenge or probe seemingly outlandish statements made by the children.

The record is replete with instances in which children were asked blatantly leading questions that furnished information the children themselves had not mentioned. All but five of the thirty-four children interviewed were asked questions that indicated or strongly suggested that perverse sexual acts had in fact occurred. Seventeen of the children, fully one-half of the thirty-four, were asked questions that involved references to urination, defecation, consumption of human wastes, and oral sexual contacts. Twenty-three of the thirty-four children were asked questions that suggested the occurrence of nudity. In addition, many of the children, some over the course of nearly two years leading up to trial, were subjected to repeated, almost incessant, interrogation. Some children were re-interviewed at the urgings of their parents.

---

[1] As a matter of sound interviewing methodology, nearly all experts agree that initial interviews should be videotaped....We have recognized generally that the existence of a video or sound recording of a statement elicited through pretrial interrogation is a factor bearing on its reliability....

In this case, fully one-half of the earliest interviews at issue here were not audio or video-taped. The record indicates that the DYFS investigator did not begin taping interviews until June 19, 1985. The Court is aware of 39 transcripts of interviews with thirty-four children, or about one-half of those interviewed by DYFS. The rest were apparently unrecorded.

The record of the investigative interviews discloses the use of mild threats, cajoling, and bribing. Positive reinforcement was given when children made inculpatory statements, whereas negative reinforcement was expressed when children denied being abused or made exculpatory statements.

Throughout the record, the element of "vilification" appears. Fifteen of the thirty-four children were told, at one time or another, that Kelly was in jail because she had done bad things to children; the children were encouraged to keep "Kelly" in jail. For example, they were told that the investigators "needed their help" and that they could be "little detectives." Children were also introduced to the police officer who had arrested defendant and were shown the handcuffs used during her arrest; mock police badges were given to children who cooperated.

* * *

IV

This Court has a responsibility to ensure that evidence admitted at trial is sufficiently reliable so that it may be of use to the finder of fact who will draw the ultimate conclusions of guilt or innocence. That concern implicates principles of constitutional due process. "[R]eliability [is] the linchpin in determining admissibility" of evidence under a standard of fairness that is required by the Due Process Clause of the Fourteenth Amendment. *Manson v. Brathwaite*, 432 U.S. 98...Competent and reliable evidence remains at the foundation of a fair trial, which seeks ultimately to determine the truth about criminal culpability. If crucial inculpatory evidence is alleged to have been derived from unreliable sources due process interests are at risk....

A.

We acknowledge that although reliability assessments with respect to the admissibility of out-of-court statements are commonplace,...assessing reliability as a predicate to the admission of in-court testimony is a somewhat extraordinary step. Nevertheless, it is not unprecedented. See *Manson*, *supra*, 432 U.S. 98,...(authorizing hearing to determine admissibility of in-court identification testimony because of pretrial suggestiveness);...When faced with extraordinary situations in which police or prosecutorial conduct has thrown the integrity of the judicial process into question, we have not hesitated to use the procedural protection of a pretrial hearing to cleanse a potential prosecution from the corrupting effects of tainted evidence....

* * *

We are confronted in this case with pretrial events relating not to the identification of an offender but, perhaps more crucially, to the occurrence of the offense itself. Those events—investigatory interviews—are fraught with the elements of untoward suggestiveness and the danger of unreliable evidentiary results. We thus concur in the determination of the Appellate Division,..., that to ensure defendant's right to a fair trial a pretrial taint hearing is essential to demonstrate the reliability of the resultant evidence.

B.

The pretrial hearing should be conducted pursuant to Evid.R. 104. The basic issue to be addressed at such a pretrial hearing is whether the pretrial events, the investigatory interviews and interrogations, were so suggestive that they give rise to a substantial likelihood of irreparably mistaken or false recollection of material facts bearing on defendant's guilt. See *Simmons v. United States*, 390 U.S. 377, 384 (1968)...

Consonant with the presumption that child victims are to be presumed no more or less reliable than any other class of witnesses, the initial burden to trigger a pretrial taint hearing is on the defendant. *Watkins v. Sowders*, 449 U.S. 341 (1981) (holding that no constitutional mandate exists for pretrial Wade hearing be held merely because counsel demands it). The defendant must make a showing of "some evidence" that the victim's statements were the product of suggestive or coercive interview techniques. *Id.*, 449 U.S. at 350,...

That threshold standard has been met with respect to the investigatory interviews and interrogations that occurred in this case. Without limiting the grounds that could serve to trigger a taint hearing, we note that the kind of practices used here—the absence of spontaneous recall, interviewer bias, repeated leading questions, multiple interviews, incessant questioning, vilification of defendant, ongoing contact with peers and references to their statements, and the use of threats, bribes and cajoling, as well as the failure to videotape or otherwise document the initial interview sessions—constitute more than sufficient evidence to support a finding that the interrogations created a substantial risk that the statements and anticipated testimony are unreliable, and therefore justify a taint hearing.

Once defendant establishes that sufficient evidence of unreliability exists, the burden shall shift to the State to prove the reliability of the proffered statements and testimony by clear and convincing evidence....Hence, the ultimate determination to be made is whether, despite the presence of some suggestive or coercive interview techniques, when considering the totality of the circumstances surrounding the interviews, the statements or testimony retain a degree of reliability sufficient to outweigh the effects of the improper interview techniques. The State may attempt to demonstrate that the investigatory procedures employed in a case did not have the effect of tainting an individual child's recollection of an event. To make that showing, the State is entitled to call experts to offer testimony with regard to the suggestive capacity of the suspect investigative procedures. The defendant, in countering the State's evidence, may also offer experts on the issue of the suggestiveness of the interrogations. However, the relevance of expert opinion focusing essentially on the propriety of the interrogation should not extend to or encompass the ultimate issue of the credibility of an individual child as a witness....

In choosing the burden of proof to be imposed on the State, we are satisfied that the clear-and-convincing-evidence standard serves to safeguard the fairness of a defendant's trial without making legitimate prosecution of child sexual abuse impossible....

* * *

C.

In conclusion, we find that the interrogations that occurred in this case were improper and there is a substantial likelihood that the evidence derived from them is unreliable. We therefore hold that in the event the State seeks to re-prosecute this defendant, a pretrial hearing must be held in which the State must prove by clear and convincing evidence that the statements and testimony elicited by the improper interview techniques nonetheless retains a sufficient degree of reliability to warrant admission at trial. Given the egregious prosecutorial abuses evidenced in this record, the challenge that the State faces is formidable. If the statements and proffered testimony of any of the children survive the pretrial hearing, the jury will have to determine the credibility and probative worth of such testimony in light of all the surrounding circumstances.

* * *

The judgment of the Appellate Division is affirmed.

* * *

APPENDIX

This Appendix presents a detailed summary of several interviews....

* * *

3. B.M.

On June 26, 1988, Investigator (I) interviewed B.M., a six year-old boy. The interview began in typical fashion with Investigator (I) asking B.M. to draw pictures of himself, his mother, his father and Kelly. After B.M. drew several pictures, Investigator (I) began asking B.M. about Kelly.

Investigator (I): I talked to all of [the kids in your class] and they were telling me how they didn't like the stuff Kelly was doing. Anyway I like talking to you older guys better because you're better to talk to, more like grownups than the little kids in the nursery school. So I'm asking you a favor—
B.M.: Why because they talked about Kelly because she did something bad to them?
Investigator (I): Uh, huh.
B.M.: What?
Investigator (I): She did bad stuff to them.
B.M.: Not me.

* * *

Investigator (I): She was hurting some kids in not some nice ways. So I'm wondering if you saw anything. You can help me to find out who some of the hurt kids are so that I can make it all better again. Because they must be pretty upset and pretty mad.
B.M.: What did she do?
Investigator (I): Well, I don't want to tell you exactly what she did because you may know something that I don't know yet, and that can really help....These are funny dolls. A little different from those you have seen before.
B.M.: I want to leave.
Investigator (I): Why.
B.M.: Because I don't like—
Investigator (I): Like what? You don't like being here: Well you'll be out of here in a couple of minutes. And you never have to come back if you don't want to. Anyway these are—what's different about these dolls, this one's a boy.
B.M.: Yeah.
Investigator (I): Because he's got a what? What do you call this?
B.M.: I don't know.

* * *

Investigator (I): I want to ask you something.
B.M.: No.
Investigator (I): Don't be a baby. You're acting like a nursery school kid. Come here. Come here a second. B.M., come here. We're not finished yet. Sit down.
B.M.: No.
Investigator (I): Come here. Seriously, we are going to need your help on this.

B.M.: No I'm not.
Investigator (I): How do you think she would hurt boys and girls, with a fork? A fork in the face? Sticking on the legs? The arms or on the neck? Does that hurt?
B.M.: [Inaudible reply.]

At that point in the questioning B.M. told Investigator (I) that he wanted to leave. Investigator (I), in an effort to put B.M. at ease, changed the tenor of the conversation and began to reassure B.M. that he was safe from Kelly.

* * *

Investigator (I): Did she try to bother you and you didn't let her?
B.M.: No.

* * *

Investigator (I): That's o.k....Believe me she is not going to be coming out of jail. She's not going to be hurting you guys anymore. That's why I'm really proud of you, and E.N. and L.J. Which one got hurt the worst?
B.M.: None of them.
Investigator (I): That's not what they told me.
B.M.: I never saw anybody get hurt.
Investigator (I): You never saw anybody get hurt? Did they ever tell you that they got hurt? See, the reason I think that you might have gotten hurt or seen them...is that you started to show me on the dolls just exactly what happened. And unless you saw it happen you wouldn't really know, would you?
B.M.: I didn't get hurt.
Investigator (I): No maybe you didn't, maybe you fought her off. Maybe you really didn't hurt then. Maybe you saw your other friends getting hurt and you didn't like it very much. You know.

* * *

B.M.: What did Kelly do?
Investigator (I): Oh I think you know. N.J. told me, and G.G. told me that she hurt them in the gym downstairs. And E.N. told me what he saw.
B.M.: What did he see?
Investigator (I): I don't want to tell you what they told me because I want to know if everybody is telling me the truth. If what you tell me goes along with what they said, then I know they were all telling the truth. You know what I mean, jellybean.
B.M.: I want to leave.—Now!

* * *

Investigator (I): Did you ever see Kelly locking any of the kids in the bathroom or closet?
B.M.: No.
Investigator (I): If you did see her hurt any kids would you tell me?
B.M.: No.

B.M. steadfastly refused to implicate Kelly in any way. The interview continued for a few more minutes, ending with Investigator (I)'s final attempts to gain "cooperation" from B.M.

* * *

Questions for Discussion

1. Why select children out for an advance hearing for admissibility? Are children more likely than adults to lie? The majority cites Stephen Ceci in support of its suspicion about child testimony. Do his conclusions support that use? Would they apply as to children who are over five years of age when testifying?

2. Do children have the adult motivations of greed, jealousy, or lust? Is the lie of a child somewhat easier to expose through cross-examination than the lie of an adult (who may be more able to fabricate consistent surrounding facts)?[3]

3. The *Michaels* court cites as a primary problem the "pursuit of a preconceived notion" implying that the questioner should believe in the "presumption of innocence". Why would the interviewer's state of mind be relevant? Do the police often have "preconceived notions" of possible guilt during investigations of adults? Do they ask leading questions? Make accusations?

4. Is the problem leading questions, or the suggestion of answers implying guilt with severe approval or disapproval based on guilt confirmation? Is the problem the court fears an adult authority figure imposing his views on a child's will and memory? Will cross-examination reveal a lack of specific facts, and inconsistencies between witnesses as to details?

5. Are children easily manipulated? The majority opinion included the most onerous interview techniques in its appendix (excerpted above). Did it indicate the children were highly responsive to suggestion?

6. The *Michaels* decision sets up an extraordinary potential pre-screening hearing to qualify a child's testimony, triggered by a showing of possible prejudice. How difficult would it be to meet the New Jersey "some evidence of pre-trial suggestion/coercion" test for pretrial hearing? Once it is met, the burden shifts to the People to show by "clear and convincing evidence" that the testimony is reliable. Where the issue is simply whether the jury will hear evidence, should the test be "clear and convincing" or "preponderance"? Or should it be "beyond a reasonable doubt"—the burden in the underlying case?

7. Criminal cases already normally involve a preliminary hearing at which children testify and are cross-examined. In the alternative, they involve sworn testimony before a grand jury, which can be challenged by motion and writ. If the *Michaels* decision forces a hearing to demonstrate truthful statements, is it effectively requiring child testimony in three formal proceedings in each case?

8. New Jersey has a liberal "tender years" hearsay exception allowing admission of statements of a sexual abuse victim under the age of 12 where the prosecution notifies the defense of its intent to introduce the statement in advance—and where there is some corroborating proof of the act. Does the extra round of qualification that the child is "trustworthy" under *Michaels* make such latitude more palatable? See *State v. R.B.*, 183 N.J. 308 (2005). Does such an intermediary "reliability" judgment satisfy the recent U.S. Supreme Court demand that hearsay not be admitted without opportunity for cross-examination? See *Crawford v. Washington*, 541 U.S. 36 (2004).

B. CHILD WITNESS/VICTIM PROTECTION

Maryland v. Craig
497 U.S. 836 (1990)

JUSTICE O'CONNOR delivered the opinion of the Court.

This case requires us to decide whether the Confrontation Clause of the Sixth Amendment categorically prohibits a child witness in a child abuse case from testifying against a defendant at trial, outside the defendant's physical presence, by one-way closed circuit television.

I

In October 1986, a Howard County grand jury charged respondent, Sandra Ann Craig, with child abuse, first and second degree sexual offenses, perverted sexual practice, assault, and battery. The named victim in each count was a 6-year-old girl who, from August 1984 to June 1986, had attended a kindergarten and prekindergarten center owned and operated by Craig.

In March 1987, before the case went to trial, the State sought to invoke a Maryland statutory procedure that permits a judge to receive, by one-way closed circuit television, the testimony of a child witness who is alleged to be a victim of child abuse....To invoke the procedure, the trial judge must first "determin[e] that testimony by the child victim in the courtroom will result in the child suffering serious emotional distress such that the child cannot reasonably communicate."....Once the procedure is invoked, the child witness, prosecutor, and defense counsel withdraw to a separate room; the judge, jury, and defendant remain in the courtroom. The child witness is then examined and cross-examined in the separate room, while a video monitor records and displays the witness' testimony to those in the courtroom. During this time the witness cannot see the defendant. The defendant remains in electronic communication with defense counsel, and objections may be made and ruled on as if the witness were testifying in the courtroom.

In support of its motion invoking the one-way closed circuit television procedure, the State presented expert testimony that the named victim, as well as a number of other children who were alleged to have been sexually abused by Craig, would suffer "serious emotional distress such that [they could not] reasonably communicate,"...if required to testify in the courtroom....The Maryland Court of Appeals characterized the evidence as follows:

> "The expert testimony in each case suggested that each child would have some or considerable difficulty in testifying in Craig's presence. For example, as to one child, the expert said that what 'would cause him the most anxiety would be to testify in front of Mrs. Craig....' The child 'wouldn't be able to communicate effectively.' As to another, an expert said she 'would probably stop talking and she would withdraw and curl up.' With respect to two others, the testimony was that one would 'become highly agitated, that he may refuse to talk or if he did talk, that he would choose his subject regardless of the questions' while the other would 'become extremely timid and unwilling to talk.'"....

Craig objected to the use of the procedure on Confrontation Clause grounds, but the trial court rejected that contention, concluding that although the statute "take[s] away the right of the defendant to be face to face with his or her accuser," the defendant retains the "essence of the right of confrontation," including the right to observe, cross-examine, and have the jury view the demeanor of the witness....The trial court further found that, "based upon the evidence presented...the testimony of

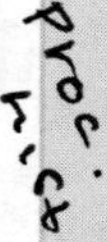

each of these children in a courtroom will result in each child suffering serious emotional distress...such that each of these children cannot reasonably communicate."....The trial court then found the named victim and three other children competent to testify and accordingly permitted them to testify against Craig via the one-way closed circuit television procedure. The jury convicted Craig on all counts, and the Maryland Court of Special Appeals affirmed the convictions,...

* * *

I

The Confrontation Clause of the Sixth Amendment, made applicable to the States through the Fourteenth Amendment, provides: "In all criminal prosecutions, the accused shall enjoy the right...to be confronted with the witnesses against him."

* * *

The central concern of the Confrontation Clause is to ensure the reliability of the evidence against a criminal defendant by subjecting it to rigorous testing in the context of an adversary proceeding before the trier of fact. The word "confront," after all, also means a clashing of forces or ideas, thus carrying with it the notion of adversariness....

...[T]he right guaranteed by the Confrontation Clause includes not only a "personal examination," 156 U.S., at 242, but also "(1) insures that the witness will give his statements under oath—thus impressing him with the seriousness of the matter and guarding against the lie by the possibility of a penalty for perjury; (2) forces the witness to submit to cross-examination, the 'greatest legal engine ever invented for the discovery of truth'; [and] (3) permits the jury that is to decide the defendant's fate to observe the demeanor of the witness in making his statement, thus aiding the jury in assessing his credibility."....

The combined effect of these elements of confrontation—physical presence, oath, cross-examination, and observation of demeanor by the trier of fact—serves the purposes of the Confrontation Clause by ensuring that evidence admitted against an accused is reliable and subject to the rigorous adversarial testing that is the norm of Anglo-American criminal proceedings....

* * *

We have accordingly stated that a literal reading of the Confrontation Clause would "abrogate virtually every hearsay exception, a result long rejected as unintended and too extreme." *Roberts*, 448 U.S., at 63. Thus, in certain narrow circumstances, "competing interests, if 'closely examined,' may warrant dispensing with confrontation at trial." *Id.*, at 64...We have recently held, for example, that hearsay statements of nontestifying coconspirators may be admitted against a defendant despite the lack of any face-to-face encounter with the accused....Given our hearsay cases, the word "confronted," as used in the Confrontation Clause, cannot simply mean face-to-face confrontation, for the Clause would then, contrary to our cases, prohibit the admission of any accusatory hearsay statement made by an absent declarant—a declarant who is undoubtedly as much a "witness against" a defendant as one who actually testifies at trial.

In sum, our precedents establish that "the Confrontation Clause reflects a *preference* for face-to-face confrontation at trial," *Roberts*, *supra*, at 63..., a preference that "must occasionally give way to considerations of public policy and the necessities of the case,"...

* * *

That the face-to-face confrontation requirement is not absolute does not, of course, mean that it may easily be dispensed with. As we suggested in *Coy*, our precedents confirm that a defendant's right to confront accusatory witnesses may be satisfied absent a physical, face-to-face confrontation at trial only where denial of such confrontation is necessary to further an important public policy and only where the reliability of the testimony is otherwise assured....

III

Maryland's statutory procedure, when invoked, prevents a child witness from seeing the defendant as he or she testifies against the defendant at trial. We find it significant, however, that Maryland's procedure preserves all of the other elements of the confrontation right: The child witness must be competent to testify and must testify under oath; the defendant retains full opportunity for contemporaneous cross-examination; and the judge, jury, and defendant are able to view (albeit by video monitor) the demeanor (and body) of the witness as he or she testifies. Although we are mindful of the many subtle effects face-to-face confrontation may have on an adversary criminal proceeding, the presence of these other elements of confrontation—oath, cross-examination, and observation of the witness' demeanor—adequately ensures that the testimony is both reliable and subject to rigorous adversarial testing in a manner functionally equivalent to that accorded live, in-person testimony. These safeguards of reliability and adversariness render the use of such a procedure a far cry from the undisputed prohibition of the Confrontation Clause: trial by *ex parte* affidavit or inquisition,...Rather, we think these elements of effective confrontation not only permit a defendant to "confound and undo the false accuser, or reveal the child coached by a malevolent adult," *Coy, supra*, at 1020, but may well aid a defendant in eliciting favorable testimony from the child witness. Indeed, to the extent the child witness' testimony may be said to be technically given out of court (though we do not so hold), these assurances of reliability and adversariness are far greater than those required for admission of hearsay testimony under the Confrontation Clause....We are therefore confident that use of the one-way closed circuit television procedure, where necessary to further an important state interest, does not impinge upon the truth-seeking or symbolic purposes of the Confrontation Clause.

The critical inquiry in this case, therefore, is whether use of the procedure is necessary to further an important state interest. The State contends that it has a substantial interest in protecting children who are allegedly victims of child abuse from the trauma of testifying against the alleged perpetrator and that its statutory procedure for receiving testimony from such witnesses is necessary to further that interest.

We have of course recognized that a State's interest in "the protection of minor victims of sex crimes from further trauma and embarrassment" is a "compelling" one....

We likewise conclude today that a State's interest in the physical and psychological well-being of child abuse victims may be sufficiently important to outweigh, at least in some cases, a defendant's right to face his or her accusers in court. That a significant majority of States have enacted statutes to protect child witnesses from the trauma of giving testimony in child abuse cases attests to the widespread belief in the importance of such a public policy....Thirty-seven States, for example, permit the use of videotaped testimony of sexually abused children;...24 States have authorized the use of one-way closed circuit television testimony in child abuse cases;...and 8 States authorize the use of a two-way system in which the child witness is permitted to see the courtroom and the defendant on a video monitor and in which the jury and judge are permitted to view the child during the testimony....

* * *

The requisite finding of necessity must of course be a case-specific one: The trial court must hear evidence and determine whether use of the one-way closed circuit television procedure is necessary to protect the welfare of the particular child witness who seeks to testify....

* * *

IV

* * *

...The trial court in this case, for example, could well have found, on the basis of the expert testimony before it, that testimony by the child witnesses in the courtroom in the defendant's presence "will result in [each] child suffering serious emotional distress such that the child cannot reasonably communicate,"....

It is so ordered.

JUSTICE SCALIA, with whom JUSTICE BRENNAN, JUSTICE MARSHALL, and JUSTICE STEVENS join, dissenting.

Seldom has this Court failed so conspicuously to sustain a categorical guarantee of the Constitution against the tide of prevailing current opinion. The Sixth Amendment provides, with unmistakable clarity, that "[i]n all criminal prosecutions, the accused shall enjoy the right...to be confronted with the witnesses against him." The purpose of enshrining this protection in the Constitution was to assure that none of the many policy interests from time to time pursued by statutory law could overcome a defendant's right to face his or her accusers in court....

Because of this subordination of explicit constitutional text to currently favored public policy, the following scene can be played out in an American courtroom for the first time in two centuries: A father whose young daughter has been given over to the exclusive custody of his estranged wife, or a mother whose young son has been taken into custody by the State's child welfare department, is sentenced to prison for sexual abuse on the basis of testimony by a child the parent has not seen or spoken to for many months; and the guilty verdict is rendered without giving the parent so much as the opportunity to sit in the presence of the child, and to ask, personally or through counsel, "it is really not true, is it, that I—your father (or mother) whom you see before you—did these terrible things?" Perhaps that is a procedure today's society desires; perhaps (though I doubt it) it is even a fair procedure; but it is assuredly not a procedure permitted by the Constitution.

Because the text of the Sixth Amendment is clear, and because the Constitution is meant to protect against, rather than conform to, current "widespread belief," I respectfully dissent.

I

* * *

..."[T]o confront" plainly means to encounter face to face, whatever else it may mean in addition. And we are not talking about the manner of arranging that face-to-face encounter, but about the manner of arranging that face-to-face encounter, but about whether it shall occur at all. The "necessities of trial and the adversary process" are irrelevant here, since they cannot alter the constitutional text.

I

Much of the Court's opinion consists of applying to this case the mode of analysis we have used in the admission of hearsay evidence. The Sixth Amendment does not literally contain a prohibition upon such evidence, since it guarantees the defendant only the right to confront "the witnesses against him." As applied in the Sixth Amendment's context of a prosecution, the noun "witness"—in 1791 as today—could mean either (a) one "who knows or sees any thing; one personally present" or (b) "one who gives testimony" or who "testifies," *i.e.*, "[i]n *judicial proceedings*, [one who] make[s] a solemn declaration under oath, for the purpose of establishing or making proof of some fact to a court." 2 N. Webster, An American Dictionary of the English Language (1828) (emphasis added). See also J. Buchanan, Linguae Britannicae Vera Pronunciatio (1757). The former meaning (one "who knows or sees") would cover hearsay evidence, but is excluded in the Sixth Amendment by the words following the noun: "witnesses *against him*." The phrase obviously refers to those who give testimony against the defendant at trial. We have nonetheless found implicit in the Confrontation Clause some limitation upon hearsay evidence, since otherwise the government could subvert the confrontation right by putting on witnesses who know nothing except what an absent declarant said. And in determining the scope of that implicit limitation, we have focused upon whether the reliability of the hearsay statements (which are not *expressly* excluded by the Confrontation Clause) "is otherwise assured."....The same test cannot be applied, however, to permit what is explicitly forbidden by the constitutional text; there is simply no room for interpretation with regard to "the irreducible literal meaning of the Clause."....

* * *

The Court's test today requires unavailability only in the sense that the child is unable to testify in the presence of the defendant.[1] That cannot possibly be the relevant sense. If unconfronted testimony is admissible hearsay when the witness is unable to confront the defendant, then presumably there are other categories of admissible hearsay consisting of unsworn testimony when the witness is unable to risk perjury, un-cross-examined testimony when the witness is unable to undergo hostile questioning, etc. *California v. Green*, 399 U.S. 149 (1970), is not precedent for such a silly system. That case held that the Confrontation Clause does not bar admission of prior testimony when the declarant is sworn as a witness but refuses to answer. But in *Green*, as in most cases of refusal, we could not know *why* the declarant refused to testify. Here, by contrast, we know that it is precisely because the child is unwilling to testify in the presence of the defendant....

III

The Court characterizes the State's interest which "out-weigh[s]" the

---

[1] I presume that when the Court says "trauma would impair the child's ability to communicate,"...it means that trauma would make it impossible for the child to communicate. That is the requirement of the Maryland law at issue here: "serious emotional distress such that the child cannot reasonably communicate." Md. Cts. & Jud. Proc. Code Ann. § 9-102(a)(1)(ii) (1989). Any implication beyond that would in any event be dictum.

[2] A different situation would be presented if the defendant sought to call the child. In that event, the State's refusal to compel the child to appear, or its insistence upon a procedure such as that set forth in the Maryland statute as a condition of its compelling him to do so, would call into question—initially, at least, and perhaps exclusively—the scope of the defendant's Sixth Amendment right "to have compulsory process for obtaining witnesses in his favor."

explicit text of the Constitution as an "interest in the physical and psychological well-being of child abuse victims,"...an "interest in protecting" such victims "from the emotional trauma of testifying,"...That is not so. A child who meets the Maryland statute's requirement of suffering such "serious emotional distress" from confrontation that he "cannot reasonably communicate" would seem entirely safe. Why would a prosecutor want to call a witness who cannot reasonably communicate? And if he did, it would be the State's own fault. Protection of the child's interest—as far as the Confrontation Clause is concerned[2]—is entirely within Maryland's control. The State's interest here is in fact no more and no less than what the State's interest always is when it seeks to get a class of evidence admitted in criminal proceedings: more convictions of guilty defendants. That is not an unworthy interest, but it should not be dressed up as a humanitarian one.

And the interest on the other side is also what it usually is when the State seeks to get a new class of evidence admitted: fewer convictions of innocent defendants—specifically, in the present context, innocent defendants accused of particularly heinous crimes. The "special" reasons that exist for suspending one of the usual guarantees of reliability in the case of children's testimony are perhaps matched by "special" reasons for being particularly insistent upon it in the case of children's testimony. Some studies show that children are substantially more vulnerable to suggestion than adults, and often unable to separate recollected fantasy (or suggestion) from reality....The injustice their erroneous testimony can produce is evidenced by the tragic Scott County investigations of 1983–1984, which disrupted the lives of many (as far as we know) innocent people in the small town of Jordan, Minnesota. At one stage those investigations were pursuing allegations by at least eight children of multiple murders, but the prosecutions actually initiated charged only sexual abuse. Specifically, 24 adults were charged with molesting 37 children. In the course of the investigations, 25 children were placed in foster homes. Of the 24 indicted defendants, one pleaded guilty, two were acquitted at trial, and the charges against the remaining 21 were voluntarily dismissed....There is no doubt that some sexual abuse took place in Jordan; but there is no reason to believe it was as widespread as charged....

* * *

The Court today has applied "interest-balancing" analysis where the text of the Constitution simply does not permit it. We are not free to conduct a cost-benefit analysis of clear and explicit constitutional guarantees, and then to adjust their meaning to comport with our findings. The Court has convincingly proved that the Maryland procedure serves a valid interest, and gives the defendant virtually everything the Confrontation Clause guarantees (everything, that is, except confrontation). I am persuaded, therefore, that the Maryland procedure is virtually constitutional. Since it is not, however, actually constitutional I would affirm the judgment of the Maryland Court of Appeals reversing the judgment of conviction.

Questions for Discussion

1. Do the "confrontation" rights litigated in *Maryland v. Craig* similarly apply to a civil proceeding (a dependency court adjudication of parental rights)?

2. How important is the physical confrontation between a victim and the defendant in determining the truth? Justice Scalia argues that a child is less likely to tell falsehoods to a father asking "is it true I did all these terrible things?" in his physical presence. If a child had been brutally raped by a powerful adult, will the violator's close presence make the child's testimony more or less accurate? Is it

permissible to assume the possibility of such guilt without violating the presumption of innocence?

3. The Maryland law requires a finding that the one-way closed circuit video is necessary for the child to testify (that she can't reasonably communicate in the physical presence of the defendant). How does a requirement of physical confrontation serve the truth by producing more honest testimony—when it eliminates the testimony?

4. The dissent considers confrontation a categorical guarantee because it is enumerated in the Constitution as intended in 1787. Does the provision specify "face to face" confrontation? Was there video in 1787? Were children testifying in such matters during this period?

5. Justice Scalia implies that children are easily manipulated to lie, citing a case where 24 were indicted and children were interrogated 50 times. Would such interrogation and other flaws in the prosecution's case be available for defense exploitation without physical confrontation?

6. The dissent acknowledges that numerous hearsay exceptions allow evidence to be introduced with no chance for cross-examination at all, but makes the distinction: If a witness appears at the trial, then physical confrontation must be permitted. Aren't statements against the interest of a co-defendant admissible without cross-examination even if present? Would the dissenters be satisfied if all child molest victim testimony at trial were to be by transcript from a preliminary proceeding (where cross-examination is allowed)? The witness is then not at trial at all.

7. Business records are admitted into evidence without cross-examination of the source, as well as statements against interest, dying statements, spontaneous declarations—because of a policy presuming some reliability excusing cross-examination. None of these exceptions are enumerated in the Constitution. Why is the defendant not deprived of his "confrontation" right in such cases, where he may be completely foreclosed from confronting the source of the evidence? Given this latitude to allow waiver of any confrontation, why would the substantial confrontation of the child, absent only the close physical proximity and presence of the defendant, be a breach of due process?

White v. Illinois
502 U.S. 346 (1992)

JUDGES: **REHNQUIST, C. J.**, delivered the opinion of the Court.

In this case, we consider whether the Confrontation Clause of the Sixth Amendment requires that, before a trial court admits testimony under the "spontaneous declaration" and "medical examination" exceptions to the hearsay rule, the prosecution must either produce the declarant at trial or the trial court must find that the declarant is unavailable. The Illinois Appellate Court concluded that such procedures are not constitutionally required. We agree with that conclusion.

Petitioner was convicted by a jury of aggravated criminal sexual assault, residential burglary, and unlawful restraint. [citation omitted] The events giving rise to the charges related to the sexual assault of S. G., then four years old. Testimony at the trial established that in the early morning hours of April 16, 1988, S. G.'s babysitter, Tony DeVore, was awakened by S. G.'s scream. DeVore went to S. G.'s bedroom and witnessed petitioner leaving the room, and petitioner then left the house....DeVore knew petitioner because petitioner was a friend of S. G.'s mother, Tammy Grigsby. DeVore asked S. G. what had happened. According to DeVore's trial testimony, S. G. stated that petitioner had put his hand over her mouth, choked her, threatened to whip her if she screamed and had "touched her in the wrong places." Asked by DeVore to point to where she had been touched, S. G. identified the vaginal area....

Tammy Grigsby, S. G.'s mother, returned home about 30 minutes later. Grigsby testified that her daughter appeared "scared" and a "little hyper." Grigsby proceeded to question her daughter about what had happened. At trial, Grigsby testified that S. G. repeated her claims that petitioner had choked and threatened her. Grigsby also testified that S. G. stated that petitioner had "put his mouth on her front part. Grigsby also noticed that S. G. had bruises and red marks on her neck that had not been there previously. Grigsby called the police.

Officer Terry Lewis arrived a few minutes later, roughly 45 minutes after S. G.'s scream had first awakened DeVore. Lewis questioned S. G. alone in the kitchen. At trial, Lewis' summary of S. G.'s statement indicated that she had offered essentially the same story as she had first reported to DeVore and to Grigsby, including a statement that petitioner had "used his tongue on her in her private parts."

After Lewis concluded his investigation, and approximately four hours after DeVore first heard S. G.'s scream, S. G. was taken to the hospital. She was examined first by Cheryl Reents, an emergency room nurse, and then by Dr. Michael Meinzen. Each testified at trial, and their testimony indicated that, in response to questioning, S. G. again provided an account of events that was essentially identical to the one she had given to DeVore, Grigsby, and Lewis.

S. G. never testified at petitioner's trial. The State attempted on two occasions to call her as a witness, but she apparently experienced emotional difficulty on being brought to the courtroom and in each instance left without testifying. The defense made no attempt to call S. G. as a witness, and the trial court neither made, nor was asked to make, a finding that S. G. was unavailable to testify. Petitioner objected on hearsay grounds to DeVore, Grigsby, Lewis, Reents, and Meinzen being permitted to testify regarding S. G.'s statements describing the assault. The trial court overruled each objection. With respect to DeVore, Grigsby, and Lewis the trial court concluded that the testimony could be permitted pursuant to an Illinois hearsay exception for spontaneous declarations.[1] Petitioner's objections to Reents' and Meinzen's testimony was similarly overruled, based on both the spontaneous declaration exception and an exception for statements made in the course of securing medical treatment.[2]...

...[W]e granted certiorari, 500 U.S. 904 (1991), limited to the constitutional question whether permitting the challenged testimony violated petitioner's Sixth Amendment Confrontation Clause right.[3]

* * *

---

[1] The spontaneous declaration exception applies to "[a] statement relating to a startling event or condition made while the declarant was under the stress of excitement caused by the event or condition."

[2] "...statements made by the victim to medical personnel for purposes of medical diagnosis or treatment including descriptions of the cause of symptom, pain or sensations, or the inception or general character of the cause or external source thereof insofar as reasonably pertinent to diagnosis or treatment shall be admitted as an exception to the hearsay rule."

...[W]e observed that there is little benefit, if any, to be accomplished by imposing an "unavailability rule."[6] Such a rule will not work to bar absolutely the introduction of the out-of-court statements; if the declarant either is unavailable, or is available and produced for trial, the statements can be introduced. Nor is an unavailability rule likely to produce much testimony that adds meaningfully to the trial's truth-determining process.....

...We note first that the evidentiary rationale for permitting hearsay testimony regarding spontaneous declarations and statements made in the course of receiving medical care is that such out-of-court declarations are made in contexts that provide substantial guarantees of their trustworthiness.[8] But those same factors that contribute to the statements' reliability cannot be recaptured even by later in-court testimony. A statement that has been offered in a moment of excitement—without the opportunity to reflect on the consequences of one's exclamation—may justifiably carry more weight with a trier of fact than a similar statement offered in the relative calm of the courtroom. Similarly, a statement made in the course of procuring medical services, where the declarant knows that a false statement may cause misdiagnosis or mistreatment, carries special guarantees of credibility that a trier of fact may not think replicated by courtroom testimony. They are thus materially different from the statements at issue in *Roberts*, where the out-of-court statements sought to be introduced were themselves made in the course of a judicial proceeding, and where there was consequently no threat of lost evidentiary value if the out-of-court statements were replaced with live testimony.

The preference for live testimony in the case of statements like those offered in *Roberts* is because of the importance of cross-examination, "the greatest legal engine ever invented for the discovery of truth." *Green,* 399 U.S. at 158. Thus courts have adopted the general rule prohibiting the receipt of hearsay evidence. But where proffered hearsay has sufficient guarantees of reliability to come within a firmly rooted exception to the hearsay rule, the Confrontation Clause is satisfied.

We therefore think it clear that the out-of-court statements admitted in this case had substantial probative value, value that could not be duplicated simply by the declarant later testifying in court. To exclude such probative statements under the strictures of the Confrontation Clause would be the height of wrongheadedness, given that the Confrontation Clause has as a basic purpose the promotion of the "'integrity of the factfinding process.'"... We therefore see no basis in *Roberts* or *Inadi* for excluding from trial, under the aegis of the Confrontation Clause, evidence embraced within such exceptions to the hearsay rule as those for spontaneous declarations and statements made for medical treatment.

As a second line of argument, petitioner presses upon us two recent decisions involving child testimony in child sexual-assault cases,...In *Craig* we upheld a conviction that resulted from a trial in which a child witness testified via closed circuit television after such a showing of necessity. Petitioner draws from

---

[3] "In all criminal prosecutions, the accused shall enjoy the right to...be confronted with the witnesses against him...." U.S. Const., Amdt. 6.

[6] By "unavailability rule," we mean a rule which would require as a predicate for introducing hearsay testimony either a showing of the declarant's unavailability or production at trial of the declarant.

[8] Indeed, it is this factor that has led us to conclude that "firmly rooted" exceptions carry sufficient indicia of reliability to satisfy the reliability requirement posed by the Confrontation Clause. [citations omitted] There can be no doubt that the two exceptions we consider in this case are "firmly rooted." The exception for spontaneous declarations is at least two centuries old,... The exception for statements made for purposes of medical diagnosis or treatment is similarly recognized in Federal Rule of Evidence 803(4), and is equally widely accepted among the States.

these two cases a general rule that hearsay testimony offered by a child should be permitted only upon a showing of necessity—i. e., in cases where necessary to protect the child's physical and psychological well-being.

Petitioner's reliance is misplaced. *Coy* and *Craig* involved only the question of what in-court procedures are constitutionally required to guarantee a defendant's confrontation right once a witness is testifying. Such a question is quite separate from that of what requirements the Confrontation Clause imposes as a predicate for the introduction of out-of-court declarations....

For the foregoing reasons, the judgment of the Illinois Appellate Court is

Affirmed.

* * *

Questions for Discussion

1. The majority concedes that the statements at issue had "great probative value," and that cross-examination is the "greatest legal engine ever invented for the discovery of truth." Does the holding reflect these observations?

2. The majority rules that *Craig* merely concerned how children would testify "once they do testify," but that out-of-court declarations have different rules. Under the *Craig* holding, the 6th Amendment right to confront compels strict face-to-face confrontation between child and defendant unless "inability to communicate" is demonstrated by the state. Does it make sense that the Court would more easily allow total exclusion of a witness than limit the manner of cross-examination?

3. Although not a child-testimony case, the U.S. Supreme Court ruled in *Crawford v. Washington*, 541 U.S. 36 (2004) that the confrontation right of an adult criminal defendant requires that he be allowed to cross-examine witnesses at trial—and effectively limited hearsay exceptions for out-of-court statements where the witness is available. Such hearsay is commonly used in juvenile court proceedings on a variety of bases, including those discussed in *White*, a so-called "tender years" exception, and others. The constitutional limitations on its use are apparently not applicable in that civil venue. However, what of its use against juvenile respondents in delinquency proceedings, where the result may be incarceration, and where the Court has required substantial adult-court due process (see *In Re Gault* and progeny discussed in Chapter 10)?

4. Is the *Crawford* holding distinguishable from *Craig* because the latter concerns not the right to cross-examine, but the physical lay-out and visibility? If so, how is it distinguishable from *White*, which concerns admission of hearsay statements against a criminal defendant and which rejects an "unavailability" rule?

C. CHILD VICTIM/WITNESS CONFIDENTIALITY

Globe Newspaper Co. v. Superior Court for the County of Norfolk
457 U.S. 596 (1982)

JUSTICE BRENNAN delivered the opinion of the Court.

Section 16A of Chapter 278 of the Massachusetts General Laws,[1] as construed by the Massachusetts Supreme Judicial Court, requires trial judges, at trials for specified sexual offenses involving a victim under the age of 18, to exclude the press and general public from the courtroom during the testimony of that victim. The question presented is whether the statute thus construed violates the First Amendment as applied to the States through the Fourteenth Amendment.

I

The case began when appellant, Globe Newspaper Co. (Globe), unsuccessfully attempted to gain access to a rape trial conducted in the Superior Court for the County of Norfolk, Commonwealth of Massachusetts. The criminal defendant in that trial had been charged with the forcible rape and forced unnatural rape of three girls who were minors at the time of trial—two 16 years of age and one 17. In April 1979, during hearings on several preliminary motions, the trial judge ordered the courtroom closed.[2] Before the trial began, Globe moved that the court revoke this closure order, hold hearings on any future such orders, and permit appellant to intervene "for the limited purpose of asserting its rights to access to the trial and hearings on related preliminary motions."....

Within hours after the court had issued its exclusion order, Globe sought injunctive relief from a justice of the Supreme Judicial Court of Massachusetts....The next day the justice conducted a hearing, at which the Commonwealth, "on behalf of the victims," waived "whatever rights it [might] have [had] to exclude the press."....[5] Nevertheless, Globe's request for relief was denied. Before Globe appealed to the full court, the rape trial proceeded and the defendant was acquitted.

* * *

---

[1] Massachusetts Gen. Laws Ann., ch. 278, § 16A..., provides in pertinent part: "At the trial of a complaint or indictment for rape, incest, carnal abuse or other crime involving sex, where a minor under eighteen years of age is the person upon, with or against whom the crime is alleged to have been committed,...the presiding justice shall exclude the general public from the court room, admitting only such persons as may have a direct interest in the case."

[2] "The court caused a sign marked 'closed' to be placed on the courtroom door, and court personnel turned away people seeking entry."....

[5] The Commonwealth's representative stated: "[Our] position before the trial judge [was], and it is before this Court, that in some circumstances a trial judge, where the defendant is asserting his right to a constitutional, public trial,...may consider that as outweighing the otherwise legitimate statutory interests, particularly where the Commonwealth [acts] on behalf of the victims, and this is literally on behalf of the victims in the sense that they were consulted fully by the prosecutor in this case. The Commonwealth waives whatever rights it may have to exclude the press."....Some time after the trial began, the prosecuting attorney informed the judge at a lobby conference that she had "[spoken] with each of the victims regarding...excluding the press."....The prosecuting attorney indicated that the victims had expressed some "privacy concerns" that were based on "their own privacy interests, as well as the fact that there are grandparents involved with a couple of these victims."....But according to the prosecuting attorney, the victims "wouldn't object to the press being included" if "it were at all possible to obtain a guarantee" that the press would not attempt to interview them or publish their names, photographs, or any personal information. *Ibid.* In fact, their names were already part of the public record. See 383 Mass. 838, 849...(1981). It is not clear from the record, however, whether or not the victims were aware of this fact at the time of their discussions with the prosecuting attorney.

I

In this Court, Globe challenges that portion of the trial court's order, approved by the Supreme Judicial Court of Massachusetts, that holds that § 16A requires, under all circumstances, the exclusion of the press and general public during the testimony of a minor victim in a sex-offense trial....

* * *

III

A

The Court's recent decision in *Richmond Newspapers* firmly established for the first time that the press and general public have a constitutional right of access to criminal trials. Although there was no opinion of the Court in that case, seven Justices recognized that this right of access is embodied in the First Amendment, and applied to the States through the Fourteenth Amendment. 448 U.S., at 558–581 (plurality opinion);...

* * *

Two features of the criminal justice system, emphasized in the various opinions in *Richmond Newspapers*, together serve to explain why a right of access to *criminal trials* in particular is properly afforded protection by the First Amendment. First, the criminal trial historically has been open to the press and general public....

Second, the right of access to criminal trials plays a particularly significant role in the functioning of the judicial process and the government as a whole. Public scrutiny of a criminal trial enhances the quality and safeguards the integrity of the factfinding process, with benefits to both the defendant and to society as a whole....Moreover, public access to the criminal trial fosters an appearance of fairness, thereby heightening public respect for the judicial process....And in the broadest terms, public access to criminal trials permits the public to participate in and serve as a check upon the judicial process—an essential component in our structure of self-government....In sum, the institutional value of the open criminal trial is recognized in both logic and experience.

B

Although the right of access to criminal trials is of constitutional stature, it is not absolute....But the circumstances under which the press and public can be barred from a criminal trial are limited; the State's justification in denying access must be a weighty one. Where, as in the present case, the State attempts to deny the right of access in order to inhibit the disclosure of sensitive information, it must be shown that the denial is necessitated by a compelling governmental interest, and is narrowly tailored to serve that interest....[17] We now consider the state interests advanced to support Massachusetts' mandatory rule barring press and public access to criminal sex-offense trials during the testimony of minor victims.

---

[17] Of course, limitations on the right of access that resemble "time, place, and manner" restrictions on protected speech,...would not be subjected to such strict scrutiny....

[19] It is important to note that in the context of § 16A, the measure of the State's interest lies not in the extent to which minor victims are injured by testifying, but rather in the incremental injury suffered by testifying *in the presence of the press and the general public.*

IV

* * *

We agree with appellee that the first interest—safeguarding the physical and psychological well-being of a minor[19]—is a compelling one. But as compelling as that interest is, it does not justify a *mandatory* closure rule, for it is clear that the circumstances of the particular case may affect the significance of the interest. A trial court can determine on a case-by-case basis whether closure is necessary to protect the welfare of a minor victim.[20] Among the factors to be weighed are the minor victim's age, psychological maturity and understanding, the nature of the crime, the desires of the victim,[21] and the interests of parents and relatives. Section 16A, in contrast, requires closure even if the victim does not seek the exclusion of the press and general public, and would not suffer injury by their presence.[22] In the case before us, for example, the names of the minor victims were already in the public record,[23] and the record indicates that the victims may have been willing to testify despite the presence of the press....If the trial court had been permitted to exercise its discretion, closure might well have been deemed unnecessary. In short, § 16A cannot be viewed as a narrowly tailored means of accommodating the State's asserted interest: That interest could be served just as well by requiring the trial court to determine on a case-by-case basis whether the State's legitimate concern for the well-being of the minor victim necessitates closure. Such an approach ensures that the constitutional right of the press and public to gain access to criminal trials will not be restricted except where necessary to protect the State's interest.[25]

Nor can § 16A be justified on the basis of the Commonwealth's second asserted interest—the encouragement of minor victims of sex crimes to come forward and provide accurate testimony. The Commonwealth has offered no empirical support for the claim that the rule of automatic closure contained in § 16A will lead to an increase in the number of minor sex victims coming forward and cooperating with state authorities.[26]...

---

[20] Indeed, the plurality opinion in *Richmond Newspapers* suggested that individualized determinations are *always* required before the right of access may be denied: "Absent an overriding interest *articulated in findings*, the trial of a criminal case must be open to the public." 448 U.S., at 581 (footnote omitted) (emphasis added).

[21] "[I]f the minor victim wanted the public to know precisely what a heinous crime the defendant had committed, the imputed legislative justifications for requiring the closing of the trial during the victim's testimony would in part, at least, be inapplicable."....

[22] It appears that while other States have statutory or constitutional provisions that would *allow* a trial judge to close a criminal sex-offense trial during the testimony of a minor victim, no other State has a *mandatory* provision excluding both the press and general public during such testimony....

[23] The Court has held that the government may not impose sanctions for the publication of the names of rape victims lawfully obtained from the public record....

[25] Of course, for a case-by-case approach to be meaningful, representatives of the press and general public "must be given an opportunity to be heard on the question of their exclusion."....This does not mean, however, that for purposes of this inquiry the court cannot protect the minor victim by denying these representatives the opportunity to confront or cross-examine the victim, or by denying them access to sensitive details concerning the victim and the victim's future testimony. Such discretion is consistent with the traditional authority of trial judges to conduct *in camera* conferences....Without such trial court discretion, a State's interest in safeguarding the welfare of the minor victim, determined in an individual case to merit some form of closure, would be defeated before it could ever be brought to bear.

[26] To the extent that it is suggested that, quite apart from encouraging minor victims to testify, § 16A improves the quality and credibility of testimony, the suggestion also is speculative. And while closure may have such an effect in particular cases, the Court has recognized that, *as a general matter, "[openness]* in court proceedings may *improve* the quality of testimony."....In the absence of any showing that closure would improve the quality of testimony of all minor sex victims, the State's interest certainly cannot justify a *mandatory* closure rule.

V

For the foregoing reasons, we hold that § 16A, as construed by the Massachusetts Supreme Judicial Court, violates the First Amendment to the Constitution.[27] Accordingly, the judgment of the Massachusetts Supreme Judicial Court is

Reversed.

* * *

CHIEF JUSTICE BURGER, with whom JUSTICE REHNQUIST joins, dissenting.

Historically our society has gone to great lengths to protect minors *charged* with crime, particularly by prohibiting the release of the names of offenders, barring the press and public from juvenile proceedings, and sealing the records of those proceedings. Yet today the Court holds unconstitutional a state statute designed to protect not the *accused*, but the minor *victims* of sex crimes. In doing so, it advances a disturbing paradox. Although states are permitted, for example, to mandate the closure of all proceedings in order to protect a 17-year-old charged with rape, they are not permitted to require the closing of part of criminal proceedings in order to protect an innocent child who has been raped or otherwise sexually abused.

The Court has tried to make its holding a narrow one by not disturbing the authority of state legislatures to enact more narrowly drawn statutes giving trial judges the discretion to exclude the public and the press from the courtroom during the minor victim's testimony....I also do not read the Court's opinion as foreclosing a state statute which mandates closure except in cases where the victim agrees to testify in open court.[1] But the Court's decision is nevertheless a gross invasion of state authority and a state's duty to protect its citizens—in this case minor victims of crime. I cannot agree with the Court's expansive interpretation of our decision in *Richmond Newspapers, Inc. v. Virginia*, 448 U.S. 555 (1980), or

---

[27] We emphasize that our holding is a narrow one: that a rule of mandatory closure respecting the testimony of minor sex victims is constitutionally infirm. In individual cases, and under appropriate circumstances, the First Amendment does not necessarily stand as a bar to the exclusion from the courtroom of the press and general public during the testimony of minor sex-offense victims. But a mandatory rule, requiring no particularized determinations in individual cases, is unconstitutional.

[1] It certainly cannot be said that the victims in this case consented to testifying in open court. During a lobby conference prior to trial, the prosecutor informed the trial judge that she had interviewed the victims, that they were concerned about publicity, and would agree to press attendance only if certain guarantees could be given:

"Each of [the three victims] indicated that they had the same concerns and basically they are privacy concerns.

"The difficulty of obtaining any kind of guarantee that the press would not print their names or where they go to school or any personal data or take pictures of them or attempt to interview them, those concerns come from their own privacy interests, as well as the fact that there are grandparents involved with a couple of these victims who do not know what happened and if they were to find out by reading the paper, everyone was concerned about what would happen then. And they stated that if it were at all possible to obtain a guarantee that this information would not be used, then they wouldn't object to the press being included. I explained that that is [a] very difficult guarantee to obtain because the Court cannot issue a conditional order, or anything like that, but I just wanted to put on the record what their concerns were and what they are afraid of." App. 48a.

It is clear that the victims would "waive" the exclusion of the press only if the trial court gave them guarantees of strict privacy, guarantees that were probably beyond the authority of the court and which themselves would raise grave constitutional problems....

its cavalier rejection of the serious interests supporting Massachusetts' mandatory closure rule. Accordingly, I dissent.

* * *

I

...The Court's wooden application of the rigid standard it asserts for this case is inappropriate. The Commonwealth has not denied the public or the media access to information as to what takes place at trial. As the Court acknowledges, Massachusetts does not deny the press and the public access to the trial transcript or to other sources of information about the victim's testimony. Even the victim's identity is part of the public record, although the name of a 16-year-old accused rapist generally would not be a matter of public record....The Commonwealth does not deny access to information, and does nothing whatever to inhibit its disclosure. This case is quite unlike others in which we have held unconstitutional state laws which prevent the dissemination of information or the public discussion of ideas....

The purpose of the Commonwealth in enacting § 16A was to give assurance to parents and minors that they would have this moderate and limited protection from the trauma, embarrassment, and humiliation of having to reveal the intimate details of a sexual assault in front of a large group of unfamiliar spectators—and perhaps a television audience—and to lower the barriers to the reporting of such crimes which might come from the victim's dread of public testimony....

Neither the purpose of the law nor its effect is primarily to deny the press or public access to information; the verbatim transcript is made available to the public and the media and may be used without limit. We therefore need only examine whether the restrictions imposed are reasonable and whether the interests of the Commonwealth override the very limited incidental effects of the law on First Amendment rights....Our obligation in this case is to balance the competing interests: the interests of the media for instant access, against the interest of the State in protecting child rape victims from the trauma of public testimony. In more than half the states, public testimony will include television coverage.

III

For me, it seems beyond doubt, considering the minimal impact of the law on First Amendment rights and the overriding weight of the Commonwealth's interest in protecting child rape victims, that the Massachusetts law is not unconstitutional. The Court acknowledges that the press and the public have prompt and full access to all of the victim's testimony. Their additional interest in actually being present during the testimony is minimal....

* * *

...Section 16A is intended not to preserve confidentiality, but to prevent the risk of severe psychological damage caused by having to relate the details of the crime in front of a crowd which inevitably will include voyeuristic strangers.[6]

---

[6] As one commentator put it: "Especially in cases involving minors, the courts stress the serious embarrassment and shame of the victim who is forced to testify to sexual acts or whose intimate life is revealed in detail before a crowd of the idly curious." Berger, Man's Trial, Woman's Tribulation: Rape Cases in the Courtroom, 77 Colum. L. Rev. 1, 88 (1977). The victim's interest in avoiding the humiliation of testifying in open court is thus quite separate from any interest in preventing the public from learning of the crime. It is ironic that the Court

In most states, that crowd may be expanded to include a live television audience, with reruns on the evening news. That ordeal could be difficult for an adult; to a child, the experience can be devastating and leave permanent scars.[7]

The Commonwealth's interests are clearly furthered by the mandatory nature of the closure statute. Certainly if the law were discretionary, most judges would exercise that discretion soundly and would avoid unnecessary harm to the child, but victims and their families are entitled to assurance of such protection....

IV

...Paradoxically, the Court today denies the victims the kind of protection routinely given to juveniles who commit crimes. Many will find it difficult to reconcile the concern so often expressed for the rights of the accused with the callous indifference exhibited today for children who, having suffered the trauma of rape or other sexual abuse, are denied the modest protection the Massachusetts Legislature provided.

* * *

---

emphasizes the failure of the Commonwealth to seal the trial transcript and bar disclosure of the victim's identity. The Court implies that a state law more severely encroaching upon the interests of the press and public would be upheld.

[7] ....Holmstrom and Burgess report that nearly half of all *adult* rape victims were disturbed by the public setting of their trials. Certainly the impact on children must be greater.

Questions for Discussion

1. The Commonwealth purportedly "waived" confidentiality on behalf of the three juvenile rape victims; does it have standing to do so?

2. Does the defendant have a constitutional right to a "public" trial, including public exposure of his accusers? Should he? Does confidentiality for testimony of victims presume the guilt of the defendant?

3. If the defendant is provided an independent judge presiding, a right to a jury, publicly paid counsel, evidence against him under oath and pursuant to the rules of evidence, the right to cross-examine the witness, and appellate review, how much quantum of due process is added by general public attendance and/or media coverage? Is it possible that widespread coverage could injure a fair trial for a defendant? Should confidentiality be allowed only if the defendant requests it?

4. If the state has a compelling state interest in protecting the privacy rights of persons possibly subjected to humiliating crimes, is the measure here narrowly enough tailored to that interest? The majority contends that it is overly broad since it applies in all cases categorically, whether the names of victims are already known, and whether they do not object to public attendance. Note that juvenile court proceedings (both delinquent and dependency courts) are confidential. Is that policy overly broad? That is, the categorical judgment of legislatures that all dependency court cases are to be confidential has been

universally upheld. Can it reconcile broad confidentiality in all cases where minors have been abused (or molested) out of concern for the child, while constitutionally barring the more limited protection in *Globe?*

5. The Court argues that there is no "empirical evidence" that a courtroom bar deters crime while a transcript of the proceedings is still available. Would it pass muster if the transcript were sealed as well? Is there a rational distinction between public attendance/media coverage and later availability of a transcript in terms of the privacy interest of victims? If those who have been victims are routinely featured ostentatiously in the media during trials, will that stimulate or discourage crime reports by victims? What empirical evidence does the Court require? If the issue is empirically grounded, is the court (as opposed to the legislature) the optimum institution to receive evidence from a wide variety of sources to decide such a policy issue?

Pennsylvania v. Ritchie
480 U.S. 39 (1987)

Justice Powell announced the judgment of the Court and delivered the opinion of the Court with respect to Parts I, II, III-B, III-C, and IV, and an opinion with respect to Part III-A, in which The Chief Justice, Justice White, and Justice O'Connor join.

The question presented in this case is whether and to what extent a State's interest in the confidentiality of its investigative files concerning child abuse must yield to a criminal defendant's Sixth and Fourteenth Amendment right to discover favorable evidence.

I

As part of its efforts to combat child abuse, the Commonwealth of Pennsylvania has established Children and Youth Services (CYS), a protective service agency charged with investigating cases of suspected mistreatment and neglect. In 1979, respondent George Ritchie was charged with rape, involuntary deviate sexual intercourse, incest, and corruption of a minor. The victim of the alleged attacks was his 13-year-old daughter, who claimed that she had been assaulted by Ritchie two or three times per week during the previous four years. The girl reported the incidents to the police, and the matter then was referred to the CYS.

During pretrial discovery, Ritchie served CYS with a subpoena, seeking access to the records concerning the daughter. Ritchie requested disclosure of the file related to the immediate charges, as well as certain records that he claimed were compiled in 1978, when CYS investigated a separate report by an unidentified source that Ritchie's children were being abused.[1] CYS refused to comply with the subpoena, claiming that the records were privileged under Pennsylvania law....

Ritchie moved to have CYS sanctioned for failing to honor the subpoena, and the trial court held a hearing on the motion in chambers. Ritchie argued that he was entitled to the information because the file might contain the names of favorable witnesses, as well as other, unspecified exculpatory evidence. He also requested

[1] Although the 1978 investigation took place during the period that the daughter claimed she was being molested, it is undisputed that the daughter did not tell CYS about the assaults at that time. No criminal charges were filed as a result of this earlier investigation.

disclosure of a medical report that he believed was compiled during the 1978 CYS investigation. Although the trial judge acknowledged that he had not examined the entire CYS file, he accepted a CYS representative's assertion that there was no medical report in the record.[3] The judge then denied the motion and refused to order CYS to disclose the files.[4]....

At trial, the main witness against Ritchie was his daughter. In an attempt to rebut her testimony, defense counsel cross-examined the girl at length, questioning her on all aspects of the alleged attacks and her reasons for not reporting the incidents sooner. Except for routine evidentiary rulings, the trial judge placed no limitation on the scope of cross-examination. At the close of trial Ritchie was convicted by a jury on all counts, and the judge sentenced him to 3 to 10 years in prison.

On appeal to the Pennsylvania Superior Court, Ritchie claimed, *inter alia*, that the failure to disclose the contents of the CYS file violated the Confrontation Clause of the Sixth Amendment, as applied to the States through the Due Process Clause of the Fourteenth Amendment.[5] The court agreed that there had been a constitutional violation, and accordingly vacated the conviction and remanded for further proceedings....

* * *

III

* * *

Ritchie argues that he could not effectively question his daughter because, without the CYS material, he did not know which types of questions would best expose the weaknesses in her testimony. Had the files been disclosed, Ritchie argues that he might have been able to show that the daughter made statements to the CYS counselor that were inconsistent with her trial statements, or perhaps to reveal that the girl acted with an improper motive. Of course, the right to cross-examine includes the opportunity to show that a witness is biased, or that the testimony is exaggerated or unbelievable....Because this type of evidence can make the difference between conviction and acquittal,...Ritchie argues that the failure to disclose information that might have made cross-examination more effective undermines the Confrontation Clause's purpose of increasing the accuracy of the truth-finding process at trial....

* * *

If we were to accept this broad interpretation..., the effect would be to transform the Confrontation Clause into a constitutionally compelled rule of pretrial discovery. Nothing in the case law supports such a view. The opinions of this Court show that the right to confrontation is a *trial* right, designed to prevent improper restrictions on the types of questions that defense counsel may ask

---

[3] The trial judge stated that he did not read "50 pages or more of an extensive record.".... The judge had no knowledge of the case before the pretrial hearing....

[4] There is no suggestion that the Commonwealth's prosecutor was given access to the file at any point in the proceedings, or that he was aware of its contents.

[5] The Sixth Amendment of the United States Constitution protects both the right of confrontation and the right of compulsory process:

"In all criminal prosecutions, the accused shall enjoy the right...to be confronted with the witnesses against him; [and] to have compulsory process for obtaining witnesses in his favor."

Both Clauses are made obligatory on the States by the Fourteenth Amendment....

during cross-examination....The ability to question adverse witnesses, however, does not include the power to require the pretrial disclosure of any and all information that might be useful in contradicting unfavorable testimony.[9] Normally the right to confront one's accusers is satisfied if defense counsel receives wide latitude at trial to question witnesses....In short, the Confrontation Clause only guarantees "an *opportunity* for effective cross-examination, not cross-examination that is effective in whatever way, and to whatever extent, the defense might wish."...

* * *

B

The Pennsylvania Supreme Court also suggested that the failure to disclose the CYS file violated the Sixth Amendment's guarantee of compulsory process. Ritchie asserts that the trial court's ruling prevented him from learning the names of the "witnesses in his favor," as well as other evidence that might be contained in the file. Although the basis for the Pennsylvania Supreme Court's ruling on this point is unclear, it apparently concluded that the right of compulsory process includes the right to have the State's assistance in uncovering arguably useful information, without regard to the existence of a state-created restriction—here, the confidentiality of the files.

1

* * *

This Court has never squarely held that the Compulsory Process Clause guarantees the right to discover the *identity* of witnesses, or to require the government to produce exculpatory evidence....Instead, the Court traditionally has evaluated claims such as those raised by Ritchie under the broader protections of the Due Process Clause....

2

It is well settled that the government has the obligation to turn over evidence in its possession that is both favorable to the accused and material to guilt or punishment....Although courts have used different terminologies to define "materiality," a majority of this Court has agreed, "[evidence] is material only if there is a reasonable probability that, had the evidence been disclosed to the defense, the result of the proceeding would have been different. A 'reasonable probability' is a probability sufficient to undermine confidence in the outcome."...

At this stage, of course, it is impossible to say whether any information in the CYS records may be relevant to Ritchie's claim of innocence, because neither the prosecution nor defense counsel has seen the information, and the trial judge acknowledged that he had not reviewed the full file. The Commonwealth, however, argues that no materiality inquiry is required, because a statute renders the contents of the file privileged. Requiring disclosure here, it is argued, would override the Commonwealth's compelling interest in confidentiality on the mere speculation that the file "might" have been useful to the defense.

---

[9] This is not to suggest, of course, that there are no protections for pretrial discovery in criminal cases....We simply hold that with respect to this issue, the Confrontation Clause only protects a defendant's trial rights, and does not compel the pretrial production of information that might be useful in preparing for trial. Also, we hardly need say that nothing in our opinion today is intended to alter a trial judge's traditional power to control the scope of cross-examination by prohibiting questions that are prejudicial, irrelevant, or otherwise improper....

Although we recognize that the public interest in protecting this type of sensitive information is strong, we do not agree that this interest necessarily prevents disclosure in all circumstances....

* * *

C

This ruling does not end our analysis, because the Pennsylvania Supreme Court did more than simply remand. It also held that defense counsel must be allowed to examine all of the confidential information, both relevant and irrelevant, and present arguments in favor of disclosure. The court apparently concluded that whenever a defendant alleges that protected evidence might be material, the appropriate method of assessing this claim is to grant full access to the disputed information, regardless of the State's interest in confidentiality. We cannot agree.

A defendant's right to discover exculpatory evidence does not include the unsupervised authority to search through the Commonwealth's files....Although the eye of an advocate may be helpful to a defendant in ferreting out information,...this Court has never held—even in the absence of a statute restricting disclosure—that a defendant alone may make the determination as to the materiality of the information. Settled practice is to the contrary. In the typical case where a defendant makes only a general request for exculpatory material under *Brady v. Maryland*, 373 U.S. 83 (1963), it is the State that decides which information must be disclosed. Unless defense counsel becomes aware that other exculpatory evidence was withheld and brings it to the court's attention,[16] the prosecutor's decision on disclosure is final. Defense counsel has no constitutional right to conduct his own search of the State's files to argue relevance....

We find that Ritchie's interest (as well as that of the Commonwealth) in ensuring a fair trial can be protected fully by requiring that the CYS files be submitted only to the trial court for *in camera* review. Although this rule denies Ritchie the benefits of an "advocate's eye," we note that the trial court's discretion is not unbounded. If a defendant is aware of specific information contained in the file (*e.g.*, the medical report), he is free to request it directly from the court, and argue in favor of its materiality. Moreover, the duty to disclose is ongoing; information that may be deemed immaterial upon original examination may become important as the proceedings progress, and the court would be obligated to release information material to the fairness of the trial.

To allow full disclosure to defense counsel in this type of case would sacrifice unnecessarily the Commonwealth's compelling interest in protecting its child abuse information. If the CYS records were made available to defendants, even through counsel, it could have a seriously adverse effect on Pennsylvania's efforts to uncover and treat abuse. Child abuse is one of the most difficult crimes to detect and prosecute, in large part because there often are no witnesses except the victim. A child's feelings of vulnerability and guilt and his or her unwillingness to come forward are particularly acute when the abuser is a parent. It therefore is essential that the child have a state-designated person to whom he may turn, and to do so with the assurance of confidentiality. Relatives and neighbors who suspect abuse also will be more willing to come forward if they know that their identities will be protected. Recognizing this, the Commonwealth—like all

---

[16] See Fed. Rule Crim. Proc. 16(d)(2); Pa. Rule Crim. Proc. 305(E) ("If at any time during the course of the proceedings it is brought to the attention of the court that a party has failed to comply with this rule [mandating disclosure of exculpatory evidence], the court may...enter such...order as it deems just under the circumstances").

other States[17]—has made a commendable effort to assure victims and witnesses that they may speak to the CYS counselors without fear of general disclosure....

IV

...An *in camera* review by the trial court will serve Ritchie's interest without destroying the Commonwealth's need to protect the confidentiality of those involved in child-abuse investigations. The judgment of the Pennsylvania Supreme Court is affirmed in part and reversed in part, and the case is remanded for further proceedings not inconsistent with this opinion.

It is so ordered.

* * *

Justice Brennan, with whom **Justice Marshall** joins, dissenting.

...I write separately to challenge the Court's narrow reading of the Confrontation Clause as applicable only to events that occur at trial. That interpretation ignores the fact that the right of cross-examination also may be significantly infringed by events occurring outside the trial itself, such as the wholesale denial of access to material that would serve as the basis for a significant line of inquiry at trial. In this case, the trial court properly viewed Ritchie's vague speculations that the agency file might contain something useful as an insufficient basis for permitting general access to the file. However, in denying access to the prior statements of the victim the court deprived Ritchie of material crucial to any effort to impeach the victim at trial. I view this deprivation as a violation of the Confrontation Clause.

* * *

The creation of a significant impediment to the conduct of cross-examination thus undercuts the protections of the Confrontation Clause, even if that impediment is not erected at the trial itself. In this case, the foreclosure of access to prior statements of the testifying victim deprived the defendant of material crucial to the conduct of cross-examination.... As we noted in *Jencks*, a witness' prior statements are essential to any effort at impeachment:

> "Every experienced trial judge and trial lawyer knows the value for impeaching purposes of statements of the witness recording the events before time dulls treacherous memory. Flat contradiction between the witness' testimony and the version of the events given in his reports is not the only test of inconsistency. The omission from the reports of facts related at the trial, or a contrast in emphasis upon the same facts, even a different order of treatment, are also relevant to the cross-examining process of testing the credibility of a witness' trial testimony." 353 U.S., at 667.

---

[17] The importance of the public interest at issue in this case is evidenced by the fact that all 50 States and the District of Columbia have statutes that protect the confidentiality of their official records concerning child abuse. See Brief for State of California *ex rel.* John K. Van de Kamp et al....

> The right of a defendant to confront an accuser is intended fundamentally to provide an opportunity to subject *accusations* to critical scrutiny....Essential to testing a witness' account of events is the ability to compare that version with other versions the witness has earlier recounted. Denial of access to a witness' prior statements thus imposes a handicap that strikes at the heart of cross-examination.
>
> * * *
>
> The Court today adopts an interpretation of the Confrontation Clause unwarranted by previous case law and inconsistent with the underlying values of that constitutional provision. I therefore dissent.
>
> * * *

Questions for Discussion

1. Is full discovery an enumerated constitutional right? Is it implied by the confrontation clause, because of the need for facts to cross-examine? Does that discovery right reach beyond information directly possessed by the state, to information possessed by third parties? Does it apply if only relevant to witnesses who are not called by the People (and hence irrelevant to cross-examination)? Or does the possibility of exculpatory evidence discovery make its production more generally compelled by the right to due process—quite apart from the confrontation clause?

2. Why might the defense find the *in camera* court examination of records insufficient? Will the court know if statements are exculpatory? Should counsel also be allowed to review the statements under a protective order of confidentiality? Would defense counsel be in a conflict situation regarding disclosure of what he knows to his client?

3. Should the court distinguish the alleged victim's psychotherapy, which occurs post-arrest and is not known to or reviewed by the prosecutors putting on the People's case? Note the strong weight given to the psychotherapy privilege privacy right of the alleged molester in *Stritzinger* (Chapter 8). If the court disallows a mandated child abuse report by his psychotherapist because of the privacy importance of the privilege, should the alleged victim's privacy be similarly respected? Or does the due process and accuracy importance of the trial trump that consideration?

ENDNOTES

[1] C. McCormick Evidence 140 (2d Ed. 1972); see also J. Wigmore, Evidence, Sections 507, 509 (3d Ed. 1940).

[2] See *e.g.*, Milton, *Children's Competency to Testify*, 5 Law & Human Behavior 73 (1981).

[3] A classic example of unsophisticated guile is provided from an early article. A child wishing to skip school for a baseball game called his teacher, pretending to be his father to report his illness: "Hello, Miss Brown, my son is very ill, and I am sorry to say he cannot come to school today." "Who is talking?" asked the teacher. "My father," replied the boy. Stephen J. Ceci, Maggie Bruck, *The Suggestibility of the Child Witness: An Historical Review and Synthesis*, citing Krout (1931) at 23.

CHAPTER TEN

Juvenile Crime and Delinquency

A. JUVENILE CRIME DEMOGRAPHIC BACKGROUND

1. National Juvenile Crime Trends

According to the Federal Bureau of Investigation, juveniles accounted for 16.4% of all arrests and 14.9% of all violent crime arrests in 2002, the most recently reported year (see Table 10-A).[1] Nationally, between 1998 and 2002, the juvenile arrest rate for Violent Crime Index offenses fell 10.2%.[2]

While the rate of juvenile arrests for murder and aggravated assaults increased somewhat in the 1990s, the consistently sharp declines in the juvenile murder arrest rate from 1993 to 2002 have returned the rate to its 1984 level, negating all of the increases that stimulated so many changes in juvenile justice policy in the 1990s. Juveniles do not account for most violent crime. For several years, arson was the only crime where juveniles comprised the majority of arrestees, but since 2001 they have comprised less than half of the individuals arrested for that offense. In terms of murder and other major violent crimes, juveniles are not markedly over-represented in relation to their percentage of the general population.

Type of Crime	Percent of all arrests involving persons under age 18 in the U.S.				
	1998	1999	2000	2001	2002
Arson	52.1%	53.6%	52.8%	49.5%	49.4%
Aggravated Assaults	14.3%	14.2%	13.9%	13.6%	13.0%
Forcible Rape	17.2%	17.0%	16.4%	16.8%	16.7%
Robbery	26.9%	25.4%	25.3%	23.6%	23.1%
Burglary	35.1%	33.5%	33.0%	31.0%	30.0%
Larceny/Theft	31.9%	31.4%	31.2%	29.6%	29.5%
Motor Vehicle Thefts	35.9%	35.3%	34.3%	32.7%	30.4%
Murder	11.9%	9.5%	9.3%	10.2%	9.6%
All Crimes	17.9%	17.2%	16.9%	16.6%	16.4%

Table 10-A. Percent of All Arrests Involving Persons Under Age 18 in the U.S.[3]

2. Child Victim Incidence

Juveniles are twice as likely as adults to be victims of serious violent crime and three times as likely to be victims of simple assault.[4] In 1997, the National Center for Health Statistics listed homicide as the fourth leading cause of death for children ages 1–4, third for children aged 5–14, and second for young people aged 15–24.[5] Of all persons murdered in 1997, 11% were under the age of 18.[6] Most juvenile victims are killed by adults, with juvenile offenders killing only 6% of murder victims under 5 years of age, 38% of those aged 12–14, and 22% of those aged 15–17. Most young child murder victims were beaten to death by family members; most older juvenile murder victims were killed with guns by an acquaintance or stranger.[7] These rates may understate the proportion of child violence victims vis-à-vis adults because of different reporting rates. While 48% of violent crimes against adults are reported, the report rate applicable where children are victims is 28%.[8]

Where youth crime does occur—particularly involving violence—its victims are most often other youth. Three-quarters of all child homicide victims aged 12–17 die from gunshot wounds. The number increased more steeply than did population to 1991. However, following the national trend, gun-related violence is declining.

3. Causal Correlations

a. Firearm Availability

Youths are able to find lethal weapons easily. One survey of inner-city high school students in four states found that 22% had possessed guns. Only 35% said it would be very difficult to obtain one.[9] There was a gun at home for 70% of respondents, 42% had friends who carried guns, and 45% had been threatened with a gun or shot at on the way to and from school.[10] A survey of youth inmates at correctional institutions in the same states found that 84% of them had possessed guns, and only 13% said it would be difficult to obtain one.[11]

A more recent survey of 4,000 arrestees in eleven cities nationally found that:

- 40% of arrested juvenile males personally possessed a firearm in the past;
- over 33% carried one within the previous month;
- 22% reported carrying a gun all or most of the time;
- 55% had been threatened with a gun;
- 50% had a gun fired at them;
- 11% had been injured by gunshot; and
- 38% believe that it is okay to shoot someone who has hurt you.[12]

A survey using answers by computer entry produced apparently more candid answers because of perceived confidentiality and anonymity. Most experts view the new results as more accurate. The 1998 study surveyed a national sample of 1,672 boys between 15 and 19 years of age. Among the answers scoring significantly higher with the more accurate procedure are the following:

- 12.4% admitted that they had carried a gun within the past 30 days;
- 27.1% carried a knife within the past 30 days;
- 34.4% had been threatened by another within the past year;

- 26.1% threatened to hurt someone else within the past year;
- 21.2% had a gun or knife pulled on them; and
- 8.9% pulled a gun or knife on someone else.[13]

About fifty percent of the respondents were under 17 years of age.

b. Schools and Safety

The special issue of weapons in schools has been highlighted by publicized school shootings, capped by tragedies at Colorado's Columbine High School in 1999 and at San Diego's Santana High School in 2001. Weapons at school can be a particularly invidious cause of juvenile violence because once there is a perception that weapon use is widespread among youth, the tendency of other youth may be to arm for self-defense.

Notwithstanding common perceptions, data indicate that school may be the safest place for children. Nationally, there were 40 shooting deaths on school property during the 1997–98 school year, down from 55 in 1992–93.[14] The trend since has continued down. In contrast, 3,000 children per year die from firearms off school property. In addition, deaths and serious injury from adult abuse and accident number in the thousands, but are relatively rare in schools, where 50 million children spend most of the waking day 180 to 200 days a year.[15] Juvenile violent crime peaks in the after school hours of the school day and in the evenings on non-school days.[16]

A recent survey on the subject involved a 1996 data sampling of 10th and 11th grade males from 53 high schools nationwide. This broad sample (beyond the juvenile justice system) surveyed a larger population (beyond the inner cities or arrestees) but focused on school safety. It found that 29% of the males possessed at least one firearm, but that only 6% had carried it outside the home within the last twelve months. The majority of gun use was related to hunting and recreational use—usually involving parental supervision—particularly in rural schools. Carrying a firearm in public was rare and carrying one to school was extremely rare.

However, as in the surveys above, 50% of respondents felt that they could obtain a firearm "relatively easily." The survey indicated that the source of firearms is most often family or friends; few had ever asked anyone else to purchase a gun for them (legally or illegally). Most respondents cited "self protection" as the motivation for carrying firearms. The survey also included the principals of the schools, with only 2% contending that guns on school grounds was a "serious problem".[17]

These surveys cumulatively infer that firearms are not often carried publicly or outside of recreational use and that they are extremely rare in school settings. However, it also supports the conclusion that guns are ubiquitously available, and that those youth who are steeped in the macho bravado gang culture and involved in delinquency are able to obtain a firearm easily, and may carry them in substantial number outside of school.[18]

c. Media and Culture

On February 7, 1996, a group of researchers released "The National Television Violence Study," commissioned by the National Cable Television Association and conducted by experts at three universities. The study monitored 2,693 shows on 23 channels and concluded that "violence predominates on television," and that the channels surveyed carried substantial violent themes in

44%–85% of their programming (HBO and Showtime at 85%, followed by basic cable channels at 59% and broadcast television at 44%). The study also noted that 73% of the perpetrators of violence were not punished in the same scene; by the end of the program, 38% of the "bad characters" received no punishment for their violent acts; 62% of the "bad characters" received some punishment. Only 15% of the "good characters" were punished or otherwise indicated regret or concern over their violent acts. Forty-seven percent of the television violence showed no harm to the victims and 58% showed no pain (where both would have occurred with the act involved).[19]

On April 16, 1998, an updated study of television violence was released by the same consortium of universities, comparing earlier findings with 6,000 hours of television on 23 channels from October 1994 to June 1997. The new study found that violence remained steady overall at 61%, that the previous level of 38% of the "bad" characters who received no punishment throughout the show has climbed to 45%. And, again, the real impact and consequences of violence were avoided. Contrary to broadcaster protests that the count failed to consider the violence "in context," the researchers counted programs which included an antiviolence theme (4% of the programs surveyed). The overall orientation toward violence was sustained consistently during daytime television, early evening, and weekends. Over 40% of the violence was initiated by the "good characters." One expert involved in the study concluded that children are taught "that violence is desirable, necessary, and painless."[20]

- While in elementary school, the average child views 100,000 violent acts (including 8,000 murders) on television.[21] Media critics contend that the problem is not any particular show, but the drumbeat of violence without consequence, and the cartoon-like characters—exaggerating good and evil with physical aggressiveness and fighting skill often determining the winner. Indeed, if the message is that the hero or "good" character usually outfights his opponent, it follows that outfighting others is an indicia of moral standing.

The *Journal of the American Medical Association* (JAMA) compiled the most comprehensive summary of literature on the influence of television violence on children, and concluded that there is "a broad consensus in the scientific literature that exposure to television violence increases children's physical aggressiveness."[22] Does it correlate with later violence? The author noted that as of 1990, the average American child was watching over 27 hours of television per week, and that children through ages 3–4 view television as depictions of factual reality; they learn better as they grow older, but does that early experience have an impact nevertheless? The JAMA presentation concludes: "Not all laboratory experiments and short-term field studies demonstrate an effect of media violence on children's behavior, but most do."[23]

The evidence from longer-range studies is more compelling: "All Canadian and U.S. studies of the effect of prolonged childhood exposure to television (two years or more) demonstrate a positive relationship between earlier exposure and later aggressiveness, although not all studies reach statistical significance."[24] Studies suggest that the most critical period is pre-adolescent childhood. One famous study involved an analysis of a small Canadian town called Notel, which acquired television for the first time in 1973 due to previous signal reception problems. Two years after introduction, tests of physical aggression among children revealed a 160% increase. Two similar control group towns nearby—still without television—showed no change.[25] Another 22-year prospective study of a semi-rural United States county correlated the television viewing of a group of 8-year-old boys and found that it "significantly predicted" serious crime incidence by age 30.[26]

The study also conducted its own survey, comparing United States, Canadian, and white South African television ownership and homicide rates (South Africa did not permit television until 1975). Following the introduction of television into the United States, the annual white homicide rate increased by 93% between 1945–74; similarly, the homicide rate in Canada increased by 92%. For both countries, there was a lag of 10–15 years before homicide rates doubled, consistent with the developmental influence theory. Examining South Africa's white population, the author analyzed an array of possibly confounding variables (age, income, urbanization, alcohol consumption, capital punishment, civil unrest, and firearm availability), and concluded that none explained the 130% increase in the white homicide rate between 1974–87 (U.S. and Canadian homicide rates did not increase markedly over the same period). The author concluded that roughly one-half of violent crime may be attributed to the influence of television and its portrayal of violence and its consequences, noting that the national cost of such an influence involves 10,000 additional homicides, 70,000 rapes, and 700,000 injurious assaults annually.[27]

A 1998 review of almost 1,000 studies presented to the American College of Forensic Psychiatry found that all but eighteen demonstrated a correlation between screen violence and human behavior; twelve of those eighteen finding no correlation were funded by the television industry.[28]

In June 1999, the House of Representatives rejected—by a vote of 282 to 146—proposed legislation which would have prohibited the sale and rental to children under the age of 17 of films, recordings, video games, books, and other media containing "explicit violent material." Media opponents to the measure contended that it was an unconstitutional effort to replace parental supervision and control with federal authority. They have similarly objected to a current and continuing investigation by the Federal Trade Commission into media marketing of violence to children.

A 1999 national survey of parents by the Kaiser Family Foundation found strong support for content-based ratings for violence and sexual themes, and for V-Chip technology to allow parental control of messages which might influence their children.[29] The same Foundation issued a report in November of 2000 tracking how much time American children spent consuming media, mostly without adult supervision. The survey found that "media," defined as television, video games, recreational reading and listening to music, consumed 38 hours a week of non-school time. Surprisingly, very little was spent on the Internet (an average of 8 minutes a day), but most of the five hours, 29 minutes per day on passive media reception is spent watching television, with an average time expended of 2 hours and 46 minutes a day. Moreover, the study found that children 8 and over spent only 5% of their television watching with a parent. The time spent subjected to cultural media influence increases for children over 8 years of age to an average of 6 hours 43 minutes a day, with non-whites spending nearly one hour more per day passively absorbing media than white children do. Tapes and radio occupied an average of 1 hour and 27 minutes a day, higher than most adults would estimate, while computer use stood at a lower rate than expected: 34 minutes (only 21 minutes non-school related).[30]

d. Poverty

The correlation between juvenile crime and a sense of personal failure or hopelessness is strong. Although child poverty has flattened since 1998, it remains near its historical high nationally, particularly for minority populations and children living in single parent families. Youth unemployment remains three times the adult level. High school drop-out rates remain substantial in many states, and are particularly high for minorities and impoverished youth.

The sense of hopelessness is underlined by the geographical concentration of the poor and by language barriers which further isolate them. Lacking the informal "friends of friends and relatives" connections of the middle class, and without mentors, these youth naturally gravitate toward those who have power within their own milieu.

e. Child Abuse and Domestic Violence

There is high statistical correlation between child abuse/family violence and later violence by juvenile victims.[31] In addition, witnessing violence within the family at a very early age appears to have an effect on later use of physical force.[32] One study found that at least 80% of children who commit homicides between the ages of 12–17 had witnessed domestic violence or had been abused themselves.[33]

Foster children or those with abused backgrounds are highly over-represented among the delinquent population. Often a child will be in both categories at the same time: in juvenile court as part of a dependency proceeding and also involved in a separate delinquency matter.[34] The correlation between child abuse and concurrent or later criminal acts by the victim is the subject of ongoing longitudinal studies by the National Institute of Justice and others. They are examining the lives of 1,575 child abuse/neglect victims from court cases dating from 1967–71. By 1994 almost half of the victims had been arrested for a nontraffic offense, 18% for a violent crime.[35] By way of comparison, the national rate of arrest for any felony is 1.4%.[36] One finding is that the arrest rate is as high in the neglect cases (defined as failure to give adequate food, clothing, shelter, and medical attention) as it is for the victims of beatings and gross physical abuse.[37]

f. Alcohol and Drugs

Alcohol and drugs are compounding factors in delinquency. Male adolescent alcohol consumption is associated with "macho" toughness. Positive association with alcohol, particularly beer, is stimulated by $2 billion in annual alcohol industry advertising and promotion. The year 2002 advertising campaigns of the major beer companies have explicitly targeted youth. Alcohol is involved in about half of the hospital-reported firearm injuries in North America.[38] Illegal drugs have similar consequences and serve as a source of income in an underground economy associated with violence.

Research indicates that most adult drug abuse begins in the early teen years. In 1993, the National Center for Education Statistics interviewed a nationally representative sample of students attending sixth through twelfth grades. Even a sample starting at the sixth grade level found 26% reporting "easy access" to beer/wine or marijuana at school, and 22% reporting that it was easy to get "other drugs" at school.[39] Students reporting easy access to alcohol and drugs were more likely than others to know of violence, and to report incidents of physical attack.[40]

In 1997, Columbia University's National Center on Addiction and Substance Abuse commissioned a poll of youths aged 12–17 and found 56%

who knew someone using cocaine, heroin, or LSD, an increase from 39% in 1996. The increase was the greatest among 12-year-olds, from 10.6% to 23.5% in one year. Citing other studies, the report noted that heroin use among eighth-graders doubled between 1991 and 1996 (to 2.4%), and that methamphetamine use had increased markedly among teens.[41]

A 1997 national survey of boys 15 to 19 years of age which likely obtained more candid results in computer-recorded responses found that 34.8% were high (or their partner was on drugs or alcohol) during their last heterosexual intercourse; 69.2% drank alcohol within the last year; 5.2% had taken street drugs with a needle; and 6.0% had used crack cocaine within the last year.[42]

The 1998 Monitoring the Future survey of high school students published percentages of high school seniors who had used alcohol, cigarettes, and various illicit drugs within their lifetime, within the past year, month, or daily. Within the last year 74% had used alcohol and 52% had "been drunk." Over 37% had used marijuana or hashish, 10% stimulants, 6% inhalants, 7.6% LSD, 5.7% cocaine (not crack), 5.5% tranquilizers, 3.6% ecstasy, 2.5% crack cocaine, 2.1% PCP, 1.7% steroids, and 1% heroin. Except for marijuana, the elicit drug rate halved with admitted use within the last month, and reduced to below 0.3% for any particular substance as used daily. However, alcohol use "within the past month" was at 52% with 33% confessing to having been drunk recently, 35% smoked cigarettes within the last month, and 22.8% marijuana or hashish. In terms of use at a daily rate, marijuana at an alarming 5.6% had passed alcohol at 3.9%. Cigarettes had by far the highest daily rate of use, at 22.4%. Although alcohol or drug use during the school day was rare, offering or selling illicit drugs at school was common, with 32% nationally reporting such an offer or transaction within the year. Significantly, the California rate of illicit drug offer or sale was at 37%, and at 46% for the state's high school males.[43] This level is of particular concern given the exclusion from the sample of the Los Angeles Unified School District where the problem is most serious, and the sample's coverage of ninth through twelfth grades (with half of the respondents 9th or 10th graders).

Another survey of children and parents released in 1998 found that the latter were generally unaware of the extent of drug use of their own children, including in particular availability to very young children. Among children 9–12 years of age, 28% had been offered illegal drugs in 1997 (up from 19% in 1993); 14% had close friends using marijuana (up from 7% in 1993); and 44% had tried marijuana (while only 21% of the parents thought it possible their children had done so). The study was the largest survey of its kind in the nation, including 1,922 preteens, 6,975 teenagers, and 815 parents.[44]

g. Paternal Abandonment; Gangs; Truancy

As Chapter 2 discusses, the absence of fathers in the home has become a growing phenomenon, and is now the case for about sixty percent of the African-American children currently being born. Single-parent incidence has apparently leveled and is retracting somewhat post-1999, but remains near historically high levels. The statistics on minority children indicate a strong possibility of their being born to an unwed mother, having little relationship with a biological father, living below the poverty line, and either dropping out of high school or being held back.

Research and correlations on the relationship between the presence or absence of fathers and sons' incarceration confirm what is intuitive. The most recent extensive longitudinal study by researchers from the University of Pennsylvania and Princeton was presented in 1998 and isolates parenting arrangement as a variable.[45] The research concluded that intact families (both mother and father present) have one-half the incidence of criminal incarceration as do other family types, *e.g.*, single parents, relatives, foster parent, orphanage. Interestingly, there was one exception. Youth in father-only (single parent) families equal the lower arrest incidence of two parent intact families. Every other combination (those lacking an involved father) consistently suffers a statistically significant 200% enhanced incarceration incidence. The marked results hold up when controlled for other factors, including: poverty, parental education, age of teen mother, race, and regional residence.[46]

Psychologists opine that one of the results of paternal absence is a lack of an involved male role model as an alternative to the action figures presented by popular culture. Youth can become hyper macho as they prematurely try to play the male leader of the family using the models available. Where such a role is frustrated by the existing family, normal adolescent peer pressures create a "gang" family as a substitute. However simplistic, the connection and correlative growth between single mother families among impoverished youth and the growth of gangs is consistent with this analysis. A 1989 survey of students aged 12 to 19 found 15% reporting "street gangs" in school. In 1993, a similar survey of a national sample of students in sixth through twelfth grades found 35% of students reporting "fighting" gangs in school; by race, 51% of surveyed Latino students, 42% of African-American students, and 31% of white students reported the existence of gangs in school.[47] The National Youth Gang Survey conducted annually for the federal Office of Juvenile Justice and Delinquency Prevention, finds gangs leveling but at a high level, with an estimated 31,000 gangs with 846,000 members in 4,800 U.S. cities. Activity by such gangs correlates closely with robbery, aggravated assault, and other violent offenses, with gang members comprising from 50% to 70% of youth arrested for such violations.[48]

Truancy and runaway rates also reflect family weakness. In 1974, federal law created the Office of Juvenile Justice and Delinquency Prevention (OJJDP) and provided grants with the intent of decriminalizing these "status offenses."[49] As recently as 1990, a national study of children living away from home concluded that 450,700 were runaways, and another 127,100 were "thrownaways"—rejected or abandoned by their parents.[50] In 1995, the U.S. Department of Health and Human Services released a 1992–93 survey of youths aged 12 to 17 living at home, and a sample of youths aged 12 to 21 living in shelters or on the streets. The survey estimated that 15% of the American youth population—or 2.8 million children—had some runaway experience in the one-year period before the survey. The study concluded that about one-half of those living apart from their families were runaways, and the other half were thrownaways. Family use of drugs correlated highly with the parental abandonment experienced by the thrownaways.[51] Conversely, research indicates that positive early experiences, either from parents or teachers, and high-quality early preschool programs, correlate with lower delinquency rates.[52]

h. Summary

One expert summarized the predictors of future delinquency as follows: "[P]ast involvement in delinquency,...drug or alcohol use, problems at school, truancy, early sexual experience,...and association with delinquent peers. Youths from impoverished homes, homes with only one parent or guardian, homes in which one or both parents exhibit some kind of problem behavior such as substance abuse, alcoholism, or mental illness, or homes in which the parents exhibit poor parenting practices are more likely to become delinquent."[53] Another source cites survey data of youths currently on probation, finding: "(1) most are more than three years below their grade level in reading and math skills, (2) 40 percent are not attending school, (3) 60 to 80 percent are abusing drugs or alcohol or both, (4) 60 percent are victims of abuse and neglect, and (5) 50 percent are from single parent homes."[54]

B. THE HISTORICAL EVOLUTION OF JUVENILE COURT

Nineteenth Century America: The Rise of the *Parens Patriae* System[1]

by Marvin Ventrell
Executive Director, National Association of Counsel for Children

* * *

Major social change is a theme of the 19th century. Early 19th century America was dominated by the "rural-communitarian-protestant triad."...That triad began to come apart in the 19th century with the industrialization and urbanization of America. Additionally, the industrialized urban areas became populated with European and Asian immigrants. An 1824 report concluded, for example, that there were approximately 9,000 children under age 14 living in poverty in New York State, and that three-fourths of the children receiving public relief were immigrant children....

1. The House of Refuge Movement

In response to the creation of the underclass of urban poor children, the House of Refuge Movement...was launched....The movement began with the Society for Prevention of Pauperism, which believed that poverty was a cause, if not the primary cause, of crime committed by children. The Society issued a report in 1819 raising concern for the number of children confined with adults in Bellevue Prison, and in 1823 the Society issued a now famous statement describing the streets as overrun with pauper children in need of saving. On January 1, 1825, New York City opened the first "House of Refuge."...

The New York House of Refuge was authorized by New York Law...which provided a charter to the Society for the Reformation of Juvenile Delinquents, the successor to the Society for Prevention of Pauperism....The authorizing legislation allowed managers of the Society to take into the house children committed as vagrants or convicted of crimes by authorities. Criminal conviction was not a condition to incarceration in the House of Refuge. Children could even be committed by administrative order or application of their parents....Neither was there any right to indictment or jury trial,...as summary conviction of disorderly persons had previously been upheld in New York in the case *In re Goodhue*....

It is a mistake to assume that the House of Refuge served as a haven for youth otherwise guilty of serious crime. Those youth were still maintained in the adult system. In the first two years of operation of the New York House of Refuge, approximately 90% of the children were housed as a result of vagrancy or minor offenses....And it is unlikely that these children would have been consequented without a House of Refuge as such minor offenses tended to go

---

[1] Excerpts from *NACC Children's Law Manual Series – 1999 Edition*, National Association of Counsel for Children (Denver, CO; 1999) at 11-20.

unpunished by the law....

Neither, however, was the Refuge movement one to protect abused children from their caretaker's authority. There is no evidence that children were placed as a result of caretaker cruelty. To the contrary, severe corporal punishment was clearly part of the House of Refuge system. In fact, conditions in many Houses were quite abusive by modern standards, including solitary confinement and beatings.

* * *

The Refuge movement spread from New York to Boston (1826) to Philadelphia (1828) to New Orleans (1827) to Baltimore (1828) to Cincinnati (1850) to Pittsburgh and St. Louis (1854). By 1860, 16 Houses of Refuge were opened in the United States....Legislation authorizing the intervention and placement of delinquent and dependent children similarly spread throughout the jurisdictions....

In addition to Houses of Refuge, Reformatories, which were entirely state-financed, began to emerge toward the middle of the century. John Watkins points out that the reformatory movement was initiated by a number of influential individuals who believed the House of Refuge system had now slowed the rate of delinquency....Reformatories were to be progressive institutions where, through civic and moral training, the youth would be reformed by his/her surrogate parent. In reality, Reformatories tended to be coercive, labor intensive incarceration....

Houses of Refuge dominated the first half, and Reformatories the last half of the century. They were characterized by an ultimate parent philosophy toward the poor, which ties the movement to the poor laws. Another link to the past was the use of apprenticeship in the Refuge movement. As Houses of Refuge became overcrowded, many children were "placed out" by being transported to rural areas of the state or placed on trains headed to the developing west where they were apprenticed to age 21. It was thought, or at least stated, that rural agrarian lifestyle would reform children from the effects of urban poverty....

2. *Ex parte Crouse* and *Parens Patriae*

The House of Refuge movement may not have had significant impact on the ultimate development of the juvenile court if the judicial system had not validated it. In a number of cases during this period, courts affirmed and authorized the practice of intervention into the lives of children through the English doctrine of *parens patriae*, which means ultimate parent or parent of the country. The courts accepted the Reformers' logic that they were entitled to take custody of a child, regardless of the child's status as victim or offender, without due process of law, because of the state's authority and obligation to save children from becoming criminal.

The 1839 Pennsylvania decision of *Ex parte Crouse*...is thought to be the first case upholding the Refuge System. The Child, Mary Ann Crouse, was committed to the Philadelphia House of Refuge by a Justice of the Peace Warrant. The warrant, executed by Mary Ann's mother essentially provided that it would be in Mary Ann's interests to be incarcerated in the House because she was "beyond her parent's control." The reported case is an appeal from a denial of the father's subsequent *habeas corpus* petition for his daughter's return. The father argued that the law allowing commitment of children without a trial was unconstitutional. The court summarily rejected the father's argument on the basis that the House was not a prison (even though Mary Ann was not free to leave), and the child was there for her own reformation, not punishment (even though Mary Ann was probably treated very harshly, a fact the court did not review). The court essentially accepted the rhetoric of the representatives of the House of Refuge. In doing so, the court acknowledged and sanctioned the state's authority to intervene into the family as ultimate parent via the doctrine of *parens patriae*. The case and the doctrine become the cornerstones of juvenile proceedings throughout the century and through the pre-*Gault* years of the juvenile court. The case was generally relied on to support "the right of the state to make coercive predictions about deviant children."...Although the distinction may have been irrelevant at the time, the case involved a dependent, not delinquent child, and in dicta, as Rendleman points out, the court argued that the state has authority to intervene into the parent-child relationship for the good of the child:

> To this end...may not the natural parents, when unequal to the task of education, or unworthy of it, be superseded by the *parens patriae*, or common guardian of the community?....That parents are ordinarily intrusted with it because it can seldom be put into better hands; but where they are incompetent or corrupt, what is there to prevent the public from withdrawing their faculties, held as they obviously are, at its sufferance? **The right of parental control is a natural, but not unalienable one....**

* * *

The lead of the *Crouse* court was followed in a series of cases involving delinquent and dependent children. In Maryland, *Roth v. House of Refuge*,...in Ohio, *Prescott v. State*,...in New Hampshire, *State ex rel. Cunnigham v. Ray*,...in Wisconsin, *Milwaukee Indus. School v. Supervisors of Milwaukee County*,...and in Illinois, *In re Ferrier*,...courts adopted the *Crouse* policy that the state's *parens patriae* duty and authority permitted seemingly unlimited intervention into family autonomy, including the child's deprivation of liberty.

F. The Juvenile Court: Institutionalizing and Developing the *Parens Patriae* System

1. Founding and Dependency Philosophy

* * *

The legislation, which led to the creation of a special tribunal which came to be called the juvenile court, was "An Act to Regulate the Treatment and Control of Dependent, Neglected and Delinquent Children."...The Juvenile Court of Cook County, Illinois opened on July 1, 1899....Although it is accurate that the Cook County Court was the first fully formalized tribunal of its kind, Massachusetts in 1874, and New York in 1892 had actually passed laws separating minors' trials from adults. While it is a mistake to assume all subsequent juvenile courts simply copied the Illinois legislation, it did serve as a model, and in less than 20 years, similar legislation had been passed in all but three states....

The Illinois legislation was largely the product of a Progressive Era movement called Child Saving. The Child Savers were individuals who viewed their cause of saving " those less fortunately placed in the social order"....as a matter of morality. The Child Savers were dominated by bourgeois women, although many were considered liberals. The movement, which was supported by the propertied and powerful, "tried to do for the criminal justice system what industrialists and corporate leaders were trying to do for the economy–that is, achieve order, stability, and control, while preserving the existing class system and distribution of wealth."...The Child Savers' rhetoric envisioned a juvenile court which would serve children and society by removing children from the criminal law process and placing them in special programs....The movement in Chicago was supported by the Illinois Conference of Charities, The Chicago Bar Association and the Chicago Women's Club.

The Illinois act provided for jurisdiction in a special court for delinquent and dependent and neglected children. A delinquent child was any child under age 16 who violated a law or ordinance, except capital offenses....

There also appears to be little, if any, support for the proposition that the juvenile court began a system of benevolent caretaking of youth by substituting a kind of therapeutic jurisprudence for harsher and limiting criminal procedure. First, serious older offenders stayed in the adult criminal system. Second, the 19th century case law reveals that juveniles brought to court under delinquency and dependency concepts received no due process. *Crouse* served to inform us they were entitled to none.

Not to suggest the juvenile court was a step backward. It was progress in the form of codification and institutionalization of the 19th century *parens patriae* system. As an institution, the juvenile court stressed centrality for dependent children. Rather than being subject to random placements without follow up, it was believed that a court could function as a centralized agency responsible for all such children from start to finish. The new court implemented the concept of probation and the founders made minimal progress toward improving placement conditions for children. Dependent children could be placed with an agency or put on probation. To at least some extent, the Child Savers' mission of creating a juvenile "statutory, non-criminal, stigma-neutral, treatment-oriented" system was achieved....

The early years of the court were characterized by continued commingling of dependency and delinquency under the courts' *parens patriae* authority. Minimal numbers of appeals validated that authority. Families remained autonomous.

2. *Gault* and the Transformation of Delinquency Out From *Parens Patriae*

The delinquency and dependency components of the juvenile court, historically connected by a "child saving" philosophy, began to separate into distinct functions in the 1960's. Driven by judicial process in delinquency, and social progress in dependency, both components were transformed.

The delinquency component of juvenile court was transformed in the late 1960s by two U.S. Supreme Court cases. In 1966, in *Kent v. United States*, the court set the stage for dismantling the *parens patriae* authority of the juvenile delinquency court by holding that the action of transferring a juvenile to criminal court required procedural due process....Then, in 1967, the Court struck down the *parens patriae* authority of the juvenile court in the context of delinquency adjudication in *In re Gault*....

* * *

C. JUVENILE JUSTICE CONSTITUTIONAL STANDARDS

1. Due Process: Notice, Counsel, Self-Incrimination, Appellate Review

In Re Gault
387 U.S. 1 (1966)

Mr. Justice Fortas delivered the opinion of the Court.

...We begin with a statement of the facts.

I.

On Monday, June 8, 1964, at about 10 a.m., Gerald Francis Gault and a friend, Ronald Lewis, were taken into custody by the Sheriff of Gila County. Gerald was then still subject to a six months' probation order which had been entered on

February 25, 1964, as a result of his having been in the company of another boy who had stolen a wallet from a lady's purse. The police action on June 8 was taken as the result of a verbal complaint by a neighbor of the boys, Mrs. Cook, about a telephone call made to her in which the caller or callers made lewd or indecent remarks. It will suffice for purposes of this opinion to say that the remarks or questions put to her were of the irritatingly offensive, adolescent, sex variety.

At the time Gerald was picked up, his mother and father were both at work. No notice that Gerald was being taken into custody was left at the home. No other steps were taken to advise them that their son had, in effect, been arrested. Gerald was taken to the Children's Detention Home. When his mother arrived home at about 6 o'clock, Gerald was not there. Gerald's older brother was sent to look for him at the trailer home of the Lewis family. He apparently learned then that Gerald was in custody. He so informed his mother. The two of them went to the Detention Home. The deputy probation officer, Flagg, who was also superintendent of the Detention Home, told Mrs. Gault "why Jerry was there" and said that a hearing would be held in Juvenile Court at 3 o'clock the following day, June 9.

Officer Flagg filed a petition with the court on the hearing day, June 9, 1964. It was not served on the Gaults. Indeed, none of them saw this petition until the habeas corpus hearing on August 17, 1964. The petition was entirely formal. It made no reference to any factual basis for the judicial action which it initiated. It recited only that "said minor is under the age of eighteen years, and is in need of the protection of this Honorable Court; [and that] said minor is a delinquent minor." It prayed for a hearing and an order regarding "the care and custody of said minor." Officer Flagg executed a formal affidavit in support of the petition.

On June 9, Gerald, his mother, his older brother, and Probation Officers Flagg and Henderson appeared before the Juvenile Judge in chambers. Gerald's father was not there. He was at work out of the city. Mrs. Cook, the complainant, was not there. No one was sworn at this hearing. No transcript or recording was made. No memorandum or record of the substance of the proceedings was prepared. Our information about the proceedings and the subsequent hearing on June 15, derives entirely from the testimony of the Juvenile Court Judge,[1] Mr. and Mrs. Gault and Officer Flagg at the habeas corpus proceeding conducted two months later. From this, it appears that at the June 9 hearing Gerald was questioned by the judge about the telephone call. There was conflict as to what he said. His mother recalled that Gerald said he only dialed Mrs. Cook's number and handed the telephone to his friend, Ronald. Officer Flagg recalled that Gerald had admitted making the lewd remarks. Judge McGhee testified that Gerald "admitted making one of these [lewd] statements." At the conclusion of the hearing, the judge said he would "think about it." Gerald was taken back to the Detention Home. He was not sent to his own home with his parents. On June 11 or 12, after having been detained since June 8, Gerald was released and driven home.[2] There is no explanation in the record as to why he was kept in the Detention Home or why he was released. At 5 p.m. on the day of Gerald's release, Mrs. Gault received a note signed by Officer Flagg. It was on plain paper, not letterhead. Its entire text was as follows:

"Mrs. Gault:

"Judge McGHEE has set Monday June 15, 1964 at 11:00 A. M. as the date and time for further Hearings on Gerald's delinquency

"/s/Flagg"

---

[1] Under Arizona law, juvenile hearings re conducted by a judge of the Superior Court, designated by his colleagues on the Superior Court to serve as Juvenile Court Judge....

[2] There is a conflict between the recollection of Mrs. Gault and that of Officer Flagg. Mrs. Gault testified that Gerald was released on Friday, June 12, Officer Flagg that it had been on Thursday, June 11. This was from memory; he had no record, and the note hereafter referred to was undated.

At the appointed time on Monday, June 15, Gerald, his father and mother, Ronald Lewis and his father, and Officers Flagg and Henderson were present before Judge McGhee. Witnesses at the habeas corpus proceeding differed in their recollections of Gerald's testimony at the June 15 hearing. Mr. and Mrs. Gault recalled that Gerald again testified that he had only dialed the number and that the other boy had made the remarks. Officer Flagg agreed that at this hearing Gerald did not admit making the lewd remarks.[3] But Judge McGhee recalled that "there was some admission again of some of the lewd statements. He—he didn't admit any of the more serious lewd statements."[4] Again, the complainant, Mrs. Cook, was not present. Mrs. Gault asked that Mrs. Cook be present "so she could see which boy that done the talking, the dirty talking over the phone." The Juvenile Judge said "she didn't have to be present at that hearing." The judge did not speak to Mrs. Cook or communicate with her at any time. Probation Officer Flagg had talked to her once—over the telephone on June 9.

At this June 15 hearing a "referral report" made by the probation officers was filed with the court, although not disclosed to Gerald or his parents. This listed the charge as "Lewd Phone Calls." At the conclusion of the hearing, the judge committed Gerald as a juvenile delinquent to the State Industrial School "for the period of his minority [that is, until 21], unless sooner discharged by due process of law." An order to that effect was entered. It recites that "after a full hearing and due deliberation the Court finds that said minor is a delinquent child, and that said minor is of the age of 15 years."

No appeal is permitted by Arizona law in juvenile cases. On August 3, 1964, a petition for a writ of habeas corpus was filed with the Supreme Court of Arizona and referred by it to the Superior Court for hearing.

At the habeas corpus hearing on August 17, Judge McGhee was vigorously cross-examined as to the basis for his actions. He testified that he had taken into account the fact that Gerald was on probation. He was asked "under what section of...the code you found the boy delinquent?"

His answer is set forth in the margin.[5] In substance, he concluded that Gerald came within ARS § 8-201-6 (a), which specifies that a "delinquent child" includes one "who has violated a law of the state or an ordinance or regulation of a political subdivision thereof." The law which Gerald was found to have violated is ARS § 13-377. This section of the Arizona Criminal Code provides that a person who "in the presence or hearing of any woman or child...uses vulgar, abusive or obscene language, is guilty of a misdemeanor...." The penalty specified in the Criminal Code, which would apply to an adult, is $5 to $50, or imprisonment for not more than two months. The judge also testified that he acted under ARS § 8-201-6 (d) which includes in the definition of a "delinquent child" one who, as the judge phrased it, is "habitually involved in immoral matters."[6]

---

[3] Officer Flagg also testified that Gerald had not, when questioned at the Detention Home, admitted having made any of the lewd statements, but that each boy had sought to put the blame on the other. There was conflicting testimony as to whether Ronald had accused Gerald of making the lewd statements during the June 15 hearing.

[4] Judge McGhee also testified that Gerald had not denied "certain statements" made to him at the hearing by Officer Henderson.

[5] "**Q.** All right. Now, Judge, would you tell me under what section of the law or tell me under what section of—of the code you found the boy delinquent?

"**A.** Well, there is a—I think it amounts to disturbing the peace. I can't give you the section, but I can tell you the law, that when one person uses lewd language in the presence of another person, that it can amount to—and I consider that when a person makes it over the phone, that it is considered in the presence, I might be wrong, that is one section. The other section upon which I consider the boy delinquent is Section 8-201, Subsection (d), habitually involved in immoral matters."

[6] ARS § 8-201-6, the section of the Arizona Juvenile Code which defines a delinquent child, reads:

"'Delinquent child' includes:

Asked about the basis for his conclusion that Gerald was "habitually involved in immoral matters," the judge testified, somewhat vaguely, that two years earlier, on July 2, 1962, a "referral" was made concerning Gerald, "where the boy had stolen a baseball glove from another boy and lied to the Police Department about it." The judge said there was "no hearing," and "no accusation" relating to this incident, "because of lack of material foundation." But it seems to have remained in his mind as a relevant factor. The judge also testified that Gerald had admitted making other nuisance phone calls in the past which, as the judge recalled the boy's testimony, were "silly calls, or funny calls, or something like that."

* * *

We do not in this opinion consider the impact of these constitutional provisions upon the totality of the relationship of the juvenile and the state. We do not even consider the entire process relating to juvenile "delinquents." For example, we are not here concerned with the procedures or constitutional rights applicable to the pre-judicial stages of the juvenile process, nor do we direct our attention to the post-adjudicative or dispositional process. See note 48, *infra*. We consider only the problems presented to us by this case. These relate to the proceedings by which a determination is made as to whether a juvenile is a "delinquent" as a result of alleged misconduct on his part, with the consequence that he may be committed to a state institution. As to these proceedings, there appears to be little current dissent from the proposition that the Due Process Clause has a role to play....The problem is to ascertain the precise impact of the due process requirement upon such proceedings.

From the inception of the juvenile court system, wide differences have been tolerated—indeed insisted upon—between the procedural rights accorded to adults and those of juveniles. In practically all jurisdictions, there are rights granted to adults which are withheld from juveniles. In addition to the specific problems involved in the present case, for example, it has been held that the juvenile is not entitled to bail, to indictment by grand jury, to a public trial or to trial by jury....It is frequent practice that rules governing the arrest and interrogation of adults by the police are not observed in the case of juveniles....

* * *

It is claimed that juveniles obtain benefits from the special procedures applicable to them which more than offset the disadvantages of denial of the substance of normal due process. As we shall discuss, the observance of due process standards, intelligently and not ruthlessly administered, will not compel the States to abandon or displace any of the substantive benefits of the juvenile process....But it is important, we think, that the claimed benefits of the juvenile process should be candidly appraised. Neither sentiment nor folklore should cause us to shut our eyes, for example, to such startling findings as that reported in an exceptionally reliable study of repeaters or recidivism conducted by the Stanford Research Institute for the President's Commission on Crime in the District of Columbia.

"(a) A child who has violated a law of the state or an ordinance or regulation of a political subdivision thereof.

"(b) A child who, by reason of being incorrigible, wayward or habitually disobedient, is uncontrolled by his parent, guardian or custodian.

"(c) A child who is habitually truant from school or home.

"(d) A child who habitually so deports himself as to injure or endanger the morals or health of himself or others."

This Commission's Report states:

> "In fiscal 1966 approximately 66 percent of the 16- and 17-year-old juveniles referred to the court by the Youth Aid Division had been before the court previously. In 1965, 56 percent of those in the Receiving Home were repeaters. The SRI study revealed that 61 percent of the sample Juvenile Court referrals in 1965 had been previously referred at least once and that 42 percent had been referred at least twice before." *Id.*, at 773.

Certainly, these figures and the high crime rates among juveniles to which we have referred (*supra*, n. 26), could not lead us to conclude that the absence of constitutional protections reduces crime, or that the juvenile system, functioning free of constitutional inhibitions as it has largely done, is effective to reduce crime or rehabilitate offenders. We do not mean by this to denigrate the juvenile court process or to suggest that there are not aspects of the juvenile system relating to offenders which are valuable. But the features of the juvenile system which its proponents have asserted are of unique benefit will not be impaired by constitutional domestication. For example, the commendable principles relating to the processing and treatment of juveniles separately from adults are in no way involved or affected by the procedural issues under discussion.[30] Further, we are told that one of the important benefits of the special juvenile court procedures is that they avoid classifying the juvenile as a "criminal." The juvenile offender is now classed as a "delinquent." There is, of course, no reason why this should not continue. It is disconcerting, however, that this term has come to involve only slightly less stigma than the term "criminal" applied to adults.[31] It is also emphasized that in practically all jurisdictions, statutes provide that an adjudication of the child as a delinquent shall not operate as a civil disability or disqualify him for civil service appointment....There is no reason why the application of due process requirements should interfere with such provisions.

Beyond this, it is frequently said that juveniles are protected by the process from disclosure of their deviational behavior. As the Supreme Court of Arizona phrased it in the present case, the summary procedures of Juvenile Courts are sometimes defended by a statement that it is the law's policy "to hide youthful errors from the full gaze of the public and bury them in the graveyard of the forgotten past." This claim of secrecy, however, is more rhetoric than reality.

---

[30] Here again, however, there is substantial question as to whether fact and pretension, with respect to the separate handling and treatment of children, coincide. See generally *infra.*

While we are concerned only with procedure before the juvenile court in this case, it should be noted that to the extent that the special procedures for juveniles are thought to be justified by the special consideration and treatment afforded them, there is reason to doubt that juveniles always receive the benefits of such a *quid pro quo.* As to the problem and importance of special care at the adjudicatory stage, cf. nn. 14 and 26, *supra.* As to treatment, see Nat'l Crime Comm'n Report, pp. 80, 87; D. C. Crime Comm'n Report, pp. 665–676, 686–687 (at p. 687 the Report refers to the District's "bankruptcy of dispositional resources"), 692–695, 700–718 (at p. 701 the Report observes that "The Department of Public Welfare currently lacks even the rudiments of essential diagnostic and clinical services");...The high rate of juvenile recidivism casts some doubt upon the adequacy of treatment afforded juveniles. See D. C. Crime Comm'n Report, p. 773; Nat'l Crime Comm'n Report, pp. 55, 78.

In fact, some courts have recently indicated that appropriate treatment is essential to the validity of juvenile custody, and therefore that a juvenile may challenge the validity of his custody on the ground that he is not in fact receiving any special treatment....

[31] "The word 'delinquent' has today developed such invidious connotations that the terminology is in the process of being altered; the new descriptive phrase is 'persons in need of supervision,' usually shortened to 'pins.'" Harvard Law Review Note, p. 799, n. 140. The N. Y. Family Court Act § 712 distinguishes between "delinquents" and "persons in need of supervision."

Disclosure of court records is discretionary with the judge in most jurisdictions. Statutory restrictions almost invariably apply only to the court records, and even as to those the evidence is that many courts routinely furnish information to the FBI and the military, and on request to government agencies and even to private employers....Of more importance are police records. In most States the police keep a complete file of juvenile "police contacts" and have complete discretion as to disclosure of juvenile records. Police departments receive requests for information from the FBI and other law-enforcement agencies, the Armed Forces, and social service agencies, and most of them generally comply....Private employers word their application forms to produce information concerning juvenile arrests and court proceedings, and in some jurisdictions information concerning juvenile police contacts is furnished private employers as well as government agencies....

In any event, there is no reason why, consistently with due process, a State cannot continue, if it deems it appropriate, to provide and to improve provision for the confidentiality of records of police contacts and court action relating to juveniles....

Further, it is urged that the juvenile benefits from informal proceedings in the court. The early conception of the Juvenile Court proceeding was one in which a fatherly judge touched the heart and conscience of the erring youth by talking over his problems, by paternal advice and admonition, and in which, in extreme situations, benevolent and wise institutions of the State provided guidance and help "to save him from a downward career."...Then, as now, goodwill and compassion were admirably prevalent. But recent studies have, with surprising unanimity, entered sharp dissent as to the validity of this gentle conception. They suggest that the appearance as well as the actuality of fairness, impartiality and orderliness—in short, the essentials of due process—may be a more impressive and more therapeutic attitude so far as the juvenile is concerned. For example, in a recent study, the sociologists Wheeler and Cottrell observe that when the procedural laxness of the "*parens patriae*" attitude is followed by stern disciplining, the contrast may have an adverse effect upon the child, who feels that he has been deceived or enticed....

Ultimately, however, we confront the reality of that portion of the Juvenile Court process with which we deal in this case. A boy is charged with misconduct. The boy is committed to an institution where he may be restrained of liberty for years. It is of no constitutional consequence—and of limited practical meaning—that the institution to which he is committed is called an Industrial School. The fact of the matter is that, however euphemistic the title, a "receiving home" or an "industrial school" for juveniles is an institution of confinement in which the child is incarcerated for a greater or lesser time. His world becomes "a building with whitewashed walls, regimented routine and institutional hours...."...Instead of mother and father and sisters and brothers and friends and classmates, his world is peopled by guards, custodians, state employees, and "delinquents" confined with him for anything from waywardness...to rape and homicide.

In view of this, it would be extraordinary if our Constitution did not require the procedural regularity and the exercise of care implied in the phrase "due process."...

If Gerald had been over 18, he would not have been subject to Juvenile Court proceedings....For the particular offense immediately involved, the maximum punishment would have been a fine of $5 to $50, or imprisonment in jail for not more than two months. Instead, he was committed to custody for a maximum of six years. If he had been over 18 and had committed an offense to which such a sentence might apply, he would have been entitled to substantial rights under the Constitution of the United States as well as under Arizona's laws and constitution. The United States Constitution would guarantee him rights and protections with respect to arrest, search and seizure, and pretrial interrogation. It would assure him of specific notice of the charges and adequate time to decide his course of action and to prepare his defense. He would be entitled to clear advice that he could be represented by counsel, and, at least if a felony were involved, the State would be required to provide counsel if his parents were unable to afford it. If the court acted on the basis of his confession, careful procedures would be required to assure its voluntariness. If the case went to trial, confrontation and opportunity for cross-examination would be guaranteed. So wide a gulf between the State's treatment of the adult and of the child requires a bridge sturdier than mere verbiage, and reasons more persuasive than cliché can provide. As Wheeler and Cottrell have put it, "The rhetoric of the juvenile court movement has developed without any necessarily close correspondence to the realities of court and institutional routines."...

* * *

We now turn to the specific issues which are presented to us in the present case.

III.
NOTICE OF CHARGES.

* * *

We cannot agree with the court's conclusion that adequate notice was given in this case. Notice, to comply with due process requirements, must be given sufficiently in advance of scheduled court proceedings so that reasonable opportunity to prepare will be afforded, and it must "set forth the alleged misconduct with particularity."...It is obvious, as we have discussed above, that no purpose of shielding the child from the public stigma of knowledge of his having been taken into custody and scheduled for hearing is served by the procedure approved by the court below. The "initial hearing" in the present case was a hearing on the merits. Notice at that time is not timely....Nor, in the circumstances of this case, can it reasonably be said that the requirement of notice was waived.[54]

IV.
RIGHT TO COUNSEL.

* * *

We conclude that the Due Process Clause of the Fourteenth Amendment requires that in respect of proceedings to determine delinquency which may result in commitment to an institution in which the juvenile's freedom is curtailed, the child and his parents must be notified of the child's right to be represented by counsel retained by them, or if they are unable to afford counsel, that counsel will be appointed to represent the child.

* * *

---

[54] Mrs. Gault's "knowledge" of the charge against Gerald, and/or the asserted failure to object, does not excuse the lack of adequate notice. Indeed, one of the purposes of notice is to clarify the issues to be considered, and as our discussion of the facts, supra, shows, even the Juvenile Court Judge was uncertain as to the precise issues determined at the two "hearings." Since the Gaults had no counsel and were not told of their right to counsel, we cannot consider their failure to object to the lack of constitutionally adequate notice as a waiver of their rights. Because of our conclusion that notice given only at the first hearing is inadequate, we need not reach the question whether the Gaults ever received adequately specific notice even at the June 9 hearing, in light of the fact they were never apprised of the charge of being habitually involved in immoral matters.

V.
CONFRONTATION, SELF-INCRIMINATION, CROSS-EXAMINATION.

* * *

...Neither Gerald nor his parents were advised that he did not have to testify or make a statement, or that an incriminating statement might result in his commitment as a "delinquent."

* * *

It is...urged, as the Supreme Court of Arizona here asserted, that the juvenile and presumably his parents should not be advised of the juvenile's right to silence because confession is good for the child as the commencement of the assumed therapy of the juvenile court process, and he should be encouraged to assume an attitude of trust and confidence toward the officials of the juvenile process. This proposition has been subjected to widespread challenge on the basis of current reappraisals of the rhetoric and realities of the handling of juvenile offenders.

In fact, evidence is accumulating that confessions by juveniles do not aid in "individualized treatment," as the court below put it, and that compelling the child to answer questions, without warning or advice as to his right to remain silent, does not serve this or any other good purpose. In light of the observations of Wheeler and Cottrell,...and others, it seems probable that where children are induced to confess by "paternal" urgings on the part of officials and the confession is then followed by disciplinary action, the child's reaction is likely to be hostile and adverse—the child may well feel that he has been led or tricked into confession and that despite his confession, he is being punished....

Further, authoritative opinion has cast formidable doubt upon the reliability and trustworthiness of "confessions" by children....

* * *

We conclude that the constitutional privilege against self-incrimination is applicable in the case of juveniles as it is with respect to adults. We appreciate that special problems may arise with respect to waiver of the privilege by or on behalf of children, and that there may well be some differences in technique—but not in principle—depending upon the age of the child and the presence and competence of parents. The participation of counsel will, of course, assist the police, Juvenile Courts and appellate tribunals in administering the privilege. If counsel was not present for some permissible reason when an admission was obtained, the greatest care must be taken to assure that the admission was voluntary, in the sense not only that it was not coerced or suggested, but also that it was not the product of ignorance of rights or of adolescent fantasy, fright or despair....

The " confession" of Gerald Gault was first obtained by Officer Flagg, out of the presence of Gerald's parents, without counsel and without advising him of his right to silence, as far as appears. The judgment of the Juvenile Court was stated by the judge to be based on Gerald's admissions in court. Neither "admission" was reduced to writing, and, to say the least, the process by which the "admissions" were obtained and received must be characterized as lacking the certainty and order which are required of proceedings of such formidable consequences....Apart from the "admissions," there was nothing upon which a judgment or finding might be based. There was no sworn testimony. Mrs. Cook, the complainant, was not present. The Arizona Supreme Court held that "sworn testimony must be required of all witnesses including police officers, probation officers and others who are part of or officially related to the juvenile court structure." We hold that this is not enough. No reason is suggested or appears for a different rule in respect of sworn testimony in juvenile courts than in adult tribunals. Absent a valid confession adequate to support the determination of the Juvenile Court, confrontation and sworn testimony by witnesses available for cross-examination were essential for a finding of "delinquency" and an order committing Gerald to a state institution for a maximum of six years.

* * *

VI.

APPELLATE REVIEW AND TRANSCRIPT OF PROCEEDINGS.

Appellants urge that the Arizona statute is unconstitutional under the Due Process Clause because, as construed by its Supreme Court, "there is no right of appeal from a juvenile court order...." The court held that there is no right to a transcript because there is no right to appeal and because the proceedings are confidential and any record must be destroyed after a prescribed period of time....Whether a transcript or other recording is made, it held, is a matter for the discretion of the juvenile court.

This Court has not held that a State is required by the Federal Constitution " to provide appellate courts or a right to appellate review at all."...In view of the fact that we must reverse the Supreme Court of Arizona's affirmance of the dismissal of the writ of habeas corpus for other reasons, we need not rule on this question in the present case or upon the failure to provide a transcript or recording of the hearings—or, indeed, the failure of the Juvenile Judge to state the grounds for his conclusion....

For the reasons stated, the judgment of the Supreme Court of Arizona is reversed and the cause remanded for further proceedings not inconsistent with this opinion.

It is so ordered.

* * *

MR. JUSTICE HARLAN, concurring in part and dissenting in part.

* * *

II.

...[O]nly three procedural requirements should, in my opinion, now be deemed required of state juvenile courts by the Due Process Clause of the Fourteenth Amendment: first, timely notice must be provided to parents and children of the nature and terms of any juvenile court proceeding in which a determination affecting their rights or interests may be made; second, unequivocal and timely notice must be given that counsel may appear in any such proceeding in behalf of the child and its parents, and that in cases in which the child may be confined in an institution, counsel may, in circumstances of indigency, be appointed for them; and third, the court must maintain a written record, or its equivalent, adequate to permit effective review on appeal or in collateral proceedings. These requirements would guarantee to juveniles the tools with which their rights could be fully vindicated, and yet permit the States to pursue without unnecessary hindrance the purposes which they believe imperative in this field....

* * *

...The Court has, even under its own premises, asked the wrong questions: the problem here is to determine what forms of procedural protection are necessary to guarantee the fundamental fairness of juvenile proceedings, and not which of the procedures now employed in criminal trials should be transplanted intact to proceedings in these specialized courts.

* * *

Mr. Justice Stewart, dissenting.

The Court today uses an obscure Arizona case as a vehicle to impose upon thousands of juvenile courts throughout the Nation restrictions that the Constitution made applicable to adversary criminal trials.[1] I believe the Court's decision is wholly unsound as a matter of constitutional law, and sadly unwise as a matter of judicial policy.

Juvenile proceedings are not criminal trials. They are not civil trials. They are simply not adversary proceedings. Whether treating with a delinquent child, a neglected child, a defective child, or a dependent child, a juvenile proceeding's whole purpose and mission is the very opposite of the mission and purpose of a prosecution in a criminal court. The object of the one is correction of a condition. The object of the other is conviction and punishment for a criminal act.

In the last 70 years many dedicated men and women have devoted their professional lives to the enlightened task of bringing us out of the dark world of Charles Dickens in meeting our responsibilities to the child in our society. The result has been the creation in this century of a system of juvenile and family courts in each of the 50 States. There can be no denying that in many areas the performance of these agencies has fallen disappointingly short of the hopes and dreams of the courageous pioneers who first conceived them....

I possess neither the specialized experience nor the expert knowledge to predict with any certainty where may lie the brightest hope for progress in dealing with the serious problems of juvenile delinquency. But I am certain that the answer does not lie in the Court's opinion in this case, which serves to convert a juvenile proceeding into a criminal prosecution.

The inflexible restrictions that the Constitution so wisely made applicable to adversary criminal trials have no inevitable place in the proceedings of those public social agencies known as juvenile or family courts. And to impose the Court's long catalog of requirements upon juvenile proceedings in every area of the country is to invite a long step backwards into the nineteenth century. In that era there were no juvenile proceedings, and a child was tried in a conventional criminal court with all the trappings of a conventional criminal trial. So it was that a 12-year-old boy named James Guild was tried in New Jersey for killing Catharine Beakes. A jury found him guilty of murder, and he was sentenced to death by hanging. The sentence was executed. It was all very constitutional.[2]

A State in all its dealings must, of course, accord every person due process of law. And due process may require that some of the same restrictions which the Constitution has placed upon criminal trials must be imposed upon juvenile proceedings. For example, I suppose that all would agree that a brutally coerced confession could not constitutionally be considered in a juvenile court hearing. But it surely does not follow that the testimonial privilege against self-incrimination is applicable in all juvenile proceedings.[3] Similarly, due process clearly

---

[1] I find it strange that a Court so intent upon fastening an absolute right to counsel upon nonadversary juvenile proceedings has not been willing even to consider whether the Constitution requires a lawyer's help in a criminal prosecution upon a misdemeanor charge....

[2] *State v. Guild*, 5 Halst. 163, 18 Am. Dec. 404 (N. J. Sup. Ct.).

"Thus, also, in very modern times, a boy of ten years old was convicted on his own confession of murdering his bed-fellow, there appearing in his whole behavior plain tokens of a mischievous discretion; and as the sparing this boy merely on account of his tender years

requires timely notice of the purpose and scope of any proceedings affecting the relationship of parent and child....But it certainly does not follow that notice of a juvenile hearing must be framed with all the technical niceties of a criminal indictment....

In any event, there is no reason to deal with issues such as these in the present case. The Supreme Court of Arizona found that the parents of Gerald Gault "knew of their right to counsel, to subpoena and cross examine witnesses, of the right to confront the witnesses against Gerald and the possible consequences of a finding of delinquency."....It further found that "Mrs. Gault knew the exact nature of the charge against Gerald from the day he was taken to the detention home."....And, as MR. JUSTICE WHITE correctly points out,...no issue of compulsory self-incrimination is presented by this case.

I would dismiss the appeal.

---

might be of dangerous consequence to the public, by propagating a notion that children might commit such atrocious crimes with impunity, it was unanimously agreed by all the judges that he was a proper subject of capital punishment."...

[3] Until June 13, 1966, it was clear that the Fourteenth Amendment's ban upon the use of a coerced confession is constitutionally quite a different thing from the Fifth Amendment's testimonial privilege against self-incrimination. See, for example, the Court's unanimous opinion in *Brown v. Mississippi*, 297 U.S. 278, at 285–286, written by Chief Justice Hughes and joined by such distinguished members of this Court as Mr. Justice Brandeis, Mr. Justice Stone, and Mr. Justice Cardozo. See also *Tehan v. Shott*, 382 U.S. 406, decided January 19, 1966, where the Court emphasized the "contrast" between "the wrongful use of a coerced confession" and "the Fifth Amendment's privilege against self-incrimination." 382 U.S., at 416. The complete confusion of these separate constitutional doctrines in Part V of the Court's opinion today stems, no doubt, from *Miranda v. Arizona*, 384 U.S. 436, a decision which I continue to believe was constitutionally erroneous.

Questions for Discussion

1. Is the ideal juvenile justice system a mimic of the adult system? Does the adult model provide ideal "*parens patriae*" proceedings? Does it encourage a child to tell the truth? To apologize? To try to make it right? Does it introduce, as its critics contend, an element of "gamesmanship" with the goal of "getting off?"

2. Is it possible to ascertain the truth without the adversary system, the right not to testify, appointed adversary counsel, *et al.?* Would a continental European "tribune" model be superior, where an independent investigation is conducted by the court? Is that closer to what a parent would do? If a state were to implement such a system, would it be constitutional under *Gault*? What is the majority's answer to the concern of the dissents about the "lock-in" nature of the majority's constitutionally-based specifics?

3. On the other hand, how many states had implemented a system at least equivalent to *Gault's* safeguards for accuracy and fairness (by any means, adversary adult system or otherwise)? Was the penalty in Gault more or less severe than that for the same offense committed by an adult? Was the proceeding as likely to yield an accurate or consistent result as typical adult proceedings?

4. The dissents in *Gault* imply that the due process requirements it imposes may fall into two categories: those which enhance accuracy in

determining guilt (notice, neutral investigation or adjudicator, right to present evidence), and those which are tied to an adversary *modus operandi* or promote ancillary social goals (right not to testify or the exclusionary rule discussed below). Is it possible to require a due process floor to assure accuracy and consistency without interposing the requirements for the latter ancillary goals?

5. The 5th Amendment guarantees against self-incrimination are intended to prevent involuntary and unreliable confessions *et al.* If a juvenile court proceeding is civil in nature, should the same right to remain silent without prejudice prevail? Would a parent advise his or her child suspected of wrongdoing that no explanation is necessary because of "a right to remain silent"?

6. Would denial of 5th Amendment right of refusal to testify be appropriate if the juvenile court decided as a threshold matter that confinement was not a remedy being considered? In such a setting, would a request to the child to explain himself or herself be permitted, with an inference of guilt allowed if the child refuses to talk?

7. How widely should *Gault* apply? To status offense proceedings (truancy, curfew, runaways)? To civil commitment cases? To school expulsion cases?

8. Should adult rules not covered by *Gault* also apply to make trials public, allow juries, exclude evidence taken in violation of the 4th Amendment? (See cases and discussion below.)

2. Unreasonable Searches and the Exclusionary Rule

New Jersey v. T.L.O.
469 U.S. 325 (1985)

JUSTICE WHITE delivered the opinion of the Court.

We granted certiorari in this case to examine the appropriateness of the exclusionary rule as a remedy for searches carried out in violation of the Fourth Amendment by public school authorities. Our consideration of the proper application of the Fourth Amendment to the public schools, however, has led us to conclude that the search that gave rise to the case now before us did not violate the Fourth Amendment. Accordingly, we here address only the question of the proper standard for assessing the legality of searches conducted by public school officials and the application of that standard to the facts of this case.

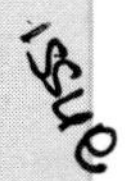

I

On March 7, 1980, a teacher at Piscataway High School in Middlesex County, N.J., discovered two girls smoking in a lavatory. One of the two girls was the respondent T.L.O., who at that time was a 14-year-old high school freshman. Because smoking in the lavatory was a violation of a school rule, the teacher took the two girls to the Principal's office, where they met with Assistant Vice Principal Theodore Choplick. In response to questioning by Mr. Choplick, T.L.O.'s companion admitted that she had violated the rule. T.L.O., however, denied that she had been smoking in the lavatory and claimed that she did not smoke at all.

Mr. Choplick asked T.L.O. to come into his private office and demanded to see her purse. Opening the purse, he found a pack of cigarettes, which he removed from the purse and held before T.L.O. as he accused her of having lied to him. As he reached into the purse for the cigarettes, Mr. Choplick also noticed a package of cigarette rolling papers. In his experience, possession of rolling papers by high school students was closely associated with the use of marihuana. Suspecting that a closer examination of the purse might yield further evidence of drug use, Mr. Choplick proceeded to search the purse thoroughly. The search revealed a small amount of marihuana, a pipe, a number of empty plastic bags, a substantial quantity of money in one-dollar bills, an index card that appeared to be a list of students who owed T.L.O. money, and two letters that implicated T.L.O. in marihuana dealing.

Mr. Choplick notified T.L.O.'s mother and the police, and turned the evidence of drug dealing over to the police. At the request of the police, T.L.O.'s mother took her daughter to police headquarters, where T.L.O. confessed that she had been selling marihuana at the high school. On the basis of the confession and the evidence seized by Mr. Choplick, the State brought delinquency charges against T.L.O. in the Juvenile and Domestic Relations Court of Middlesex County.[1] ...

* * *

Although we originally granted certiorari to decide the issue of the appropriate remedy in juvenile court proceedings for unlawful school searches, our doubts regarding the wisdom of deciding that question in isolation from the broader question of what limits, if any, the Fourth Amendment places on the activities of school authorities prompted us to order reargument on that question.[2] Having heard argument on the legality of the search of T.L.O.'s purse, we are satisfied that the search did not violate the Fourth Amendment.[3]

---

[1]T.L.O. also received a 3-day suspension from school for smoking cigarettes in a nonsmoking area and a 7-day suspension for possession of marihuana. On T.L.O.'s motion, the Superior Court of New Jersey, Chancery Division, set aside the 7-day suspension on the ground that it was based on evidence seized in violation of the Fourth Amendment. *(T.L.O.) v. Piscataway Bd. of Ed.*, No. C.2865-79 (Super.Ct.N.J., Ch.Div., Mar. 31, 1980). The Board of Education apparently did not appeal the decision of the Chancery Division.

[2] State and federal courts considering these questions have struggled to accommodate the interests protected by the Fourth Amendment and the interest of the States in providing a safe environment conducive to education in the public schools. Some courts have resolved the tension between these interests by giving full force to one or the other side of the balance. Thus, in a number of cases courts have held that school officials conducting in-school searches of students are private parties acting in loco parentis and are therefore not subject to the constraints of the Fourth Amendment....At least one court has held, on the other hand, that the Fourth Amendment applies in full to in-school searches by school officials and that a search conducted without probable cause is unreasonable...; others have held or suggested that the probable-cause standard is applicable at least where the police are involved in a search... or where the search is highly intrusive...

The majority of courts that have addressed the issue of the Fourth Amendment in the schools have, like the Supreme Court of New Jersey in this case, reached a middle position: the Fourth Amendment applies to searches conducted by school authorities, but the special needs of the school environment require assessment of the legality of such searches against a standard less exacting than that of probable cause. These courts have, by and large, upheld warrantless searches by school authorities provided that they are supported by a reasonable suspicion that the search will uncover evidence of an infraction of school disciplinary rules or a violation of the law....

Although few have considered the matter, courts have also split over whether the exclusionary rule is an appropriate remedy for Fourth Amendment violations committed by school authorities....

[3] In holding that the search of T.L.O.'s purse did not violate the Fourth Amendment, we do not implicitly determine that the exclusionary rule applies to the fruits of unlawful searches conducted by school authorities. The question whether evidence should be excluded from a criminal proceeding involves two discrete inquiries: whether the evidence was seized in violation of the Fourth Amendment, and whether the exclusionary rule is the appropriate

I

In determining whether the search at issue in this case violated the Fourth Amendment, we are faced initially with the question whether that Amendment's prohibition on unreasonable searches and seizures applies to searches conducted by public school officials. We hold that it does.

* * *

III

To hold that the Fourth Amendment applies to searches conducted by school authorities is only to begin the inquiry into the standards governing such searches. Although the underlying command of the Fourth Amendment is always that searches and seizures be reasonable, what is reasonable depends on the context within which a search takes place. The determination of the standard of reasonableness governing any specific class of searches requires "balancing the need to search against the invasion which the search entails." *Camara v. Municipal Court, supra*, 387 U.S., at 536-537. On one side of the balance are arrayed the individual's legitimate expectations of privacy and personal security; on the other, the government's need for effective methods to deal with breaches of public order.

* * *

Although this Court may take notice of the difficulty of maintaining discipline in the public schools today, the situation is not so dire that students in the schools may claim no legitimate expectations of privacy. We have recently recognized that the need to maintain order in a prison is such that prisoners retain no legitimate expectations of privacy in their cells, but it goes almost without saying that "[t]he prisoner and the schoolchild stand in wholly different circumstances, separated by the harsh facts of criminal conviction and incarceration." *Ingraham v. Wright, supra*, at 669. We are not yet ready to hold that the schools and the prisons need be equated for purposes of the Fourth Amendment.

Nor does the State's suggestion that children have no legitimate need to bring personal property into the schools seem well anchored in reality. Students at a minimum must bring to school not only the supplies needed for their studies, but also keys, money, and the necessaries of personal hygiene and grooming. In addition, students may carry on their persons or in purses or wallets such nondisruptive yet highly personal items as photographs, letters, and diaries. Finally, students may have perfectly legitimate reasons to carry with them articles of property needed in connection with extracurricular or recreational activities. In short, schoolchildren may find it necessary to carry with them a variety of legitimate, noncontraband items, and there is no reason to conclude that they have necessarily waived all rights to privacy in such items merely by bringing them onto school grounds.

Against the child's interest in privacy must be set the substantial interest of teachers and administrators in maintaining discipline in the classroom and on school grounds. Maintaining order in the classroom has never been easy, but in recent years, school disorder has often taken particularly ugly forms: drug use and violent crime in the schools have become major social problems....Even in schools that have been spared the most severe disciplinary problems, the

---

remedy for the violation. Neither question is logically antecedent to the other, for a negative answer to either question is sufficient to dispose of the case. Thus, our determination that the search at issue in this case did not violate the Fourth Amendment implies no particular resolution of the question of the applicability of the exclusionary rule.

preservation of order and a proper educational environment requires close supervision of schoolchildren, as well as the enforcement of rules against conduct that would be perfectly permissible if undertaken by an adult. "Events calling for discipline are frequent occurrences and sometimes require immediate, effective action.".... Accordingly, we have recognized that maintaining security and order in the schools requires a certain degree of flexibility in school disciplinary procedures, and we have respected the value of preserving the informality of the student-teacher relationship....

How, then, should we strike the balance between the schoolchild's legitimate expectations of privacy and the school's equally legitimate need to maintain an environment in which learning can take place? It is evident that the school setting requires some easing of the restrictions to which searches by public authorities are ordinarily subject. The warrant requirement, in particular, is unsuited to the school environment: requiring a teacher to obtain a warrant before searching a child suspected of an infraction of school rules (or of the criminal law) would unduly interfere with the maintenance of the swift and informal disciplinary procedures needed in the schools. Just as we have in other cases dispensed with the warrant requirement when "the burden of obtaining a warrant is likely to frustrate the governmental purpose behind the search," *Camara v. Municipal Court*, 387 U.S., at 532-533, we hold today that school officials need not obtain a warrant before searching a student who is under their authority.

The school setting also requires some modification of the level of suspicion of illicit activity needed to justify a search. Ordinarily, a search—even one that may permissibly be carried out without a warrant—must be based upon "probable cause" to believe that a violation of the law has occurred.... However, "probable cause" is not an irreducible requirement of a valid search. The fundamental command of the Fourth Amendment is that searches and seizures be reasonable, and although "both the concept of probable cause and the requirement of a warrant bear on the reasonableness of a search,... in certain limited circumstances neither is required.".... Thus, we have in a number of cases recognized the legality of searches and seizures based on suspicions that, although "reasonable," do not rise to the level of probable cause.... Where a careful balancing of governmental and private interests suggests that the public interest is best served by a Fourth Amendment standard of reasonableness that stops short of probable cause, we have not hesitated to adopt such a standard.

We join the majority of courts that have examined this issue in concluding that the accommodation of the privacy interests of schoolchildren with the substantial need of teachers and administrators for freedom to maintain order in the schools does not require strict adherence to the requirement that searches be based on probable cause to believe that the subject of the search has violated or is violating the law. Rather, the legality of a search of a student should depend simply on the reasonableness, under all the circumstances, of the search. Determining the reasonableness of any search involves a twofold inquiry: first, one must consider "whether the...action was justified at its inception,"...; second, one must determine whether the search as actually conducted "was reasonably related in scope to the circumstances which justified the interference in the first place,"... Under ordinary circumstances, a search of a student by a teacher or other school official[7] will be "justified at its inception" when there are reasonable

---

[7] We here consider only searches carried out by school authorities acting alone and on their own authority. This case does not present the question of the appropriate standard for assessing the legality of searches conducted by school officials in conjunction with or at the behest of law enforcement agencies, and we express no opinion on that question. Cf. *Picha v. Wielgos*, 410 F.Supp. 1214, 1219-1221 (ND Ill.1976) (holding probable-cause standard applicable to searches involving the police).

grounds for suspecting that the search will turn up evidence that the student has violated or is violating either the law or the rules of the school.[8] Such a search will be permissible in its scope when the measures adopted are reasonably related to the objectives of the search and not excessively intrusive in light of the age and sex of the student and the nature of the infraction....

This standard will, we trust, neither unduly burden the efforts of school authorities to maintain order in their schools nor authorize unrestrained intrusions upon the privacy of schoolchildren. By focusing attention on the question of reasonableness, the standard will spare teachers and school administrators the necessity of schooling themselves in the niceties of probable cause and permit them to regulate their conduct according to the dictates of reason and common sense. At the same time, the reasonableness standard should ensure that the interests of students will be invaded no more than is necessary to achieve the legitimate end of preserving order in the schools.

* * *

...[I]f Mr. Choplick in fact had a reasonable suspicion that T.L.O. had cigarettes in her purse, the search was justified despite the fact that the cigarettes, if found, would constitute "mere evidence" of a violation....

* * *

Our conclusion that Mr. Choplick's decision to open T.L.O.'s purse was reasonable brings us to the question of the further search for marihuana once the pack of cigarettes was located. The suspicion upon which the search for marihuana was founded was provided when Mr. Choplick observed a package of rolling papers in the purse as he removed the pack of cigarettes. Although T.L.O. does not dispute the reasonableness of Mr. Choplick's belief that the rolling papers indicated the presence of marihuana, she does contend that the scope of the search Mr. Choplick conducted exceeded permissible bounds when he seized and read certain letters that implicated T.L.O. in drug dealing. This argument, too, is unpersuasive. The discovery of the rolling papers concededly gave rise to a reasonable suspicion that T.L.O. was carrying marihuana as well as cigarettes in her purse. This suspicion justified further exploration of T.L.O.'s purse,...

Because the search resulting in the discovery of the evidence of marihuana dealing by T.L.O. was reasonable, the New Jersey Supreme Court's decision to exclude that evidence from T.L.O.'s juvenile delinquency proceedings on Fourth Amendment grounds was erroneous. Accordingly, the judgment of the Supreme Court of New Jersey is

Reversed.

* * *

Justice Brennan, with whom **Justice Marshall** joins, concurring in part and dissenting in part.

* * *

---

[8] We do not decide whether individualized suspicion is an essential element of the reasonableness standard we adopt for searches by school authorities. In other contexts, however, we have held that although "some quantum of individualized suspicion is usually a prerequisite to a constitutional search or seizure[,] ... the Fourth Amendment imposes no irreducible requirement of such suspicion."

...Today's decision sanctions school officials to conduct full-scale searches on a "reasonableness" standard whose only definite content is that it is not the same test as the "probable cause" standard found in the text of the Fourth Amendment. In adopting this unclear, unprecedented, and unnecessary departure from generally applicable Fourth Amendment standards, the Court carves out a broad exception to standards that this Court has developed over years of considering Fourth Amendment problems. Its decision is supported neither by precedent nor even by a fair application of the "balancing test" it proclaims in this very opinion.

I

* * *

...Such an exception, however, is not to be justified, as the Court apparently holds, by assessing net social value through application of an unguided "balancing test" in which "the individual's legitimate expectations of privacy and personal security" are weighed against "the government's need for effective methods to deal with breaches of public order.".... The Warrant Clause is something more than an exhortation to this Court to maximize social welfare as we see fit. It requires that the authorities must obtain a warrant before conducting a full-scale search. The undifferentiated governmental interest in law enforcement is insufficient to justify an exception to the warrant requirement. Rather, some *special* governmental interest beyond the need merely to apprehend lawbreakers is necessary to justify a categorical exception to the warrant requirement. For the most part, special governmental needs sufficient to override the warrant requirement flow from "exigency"—that is, from the press of time that makes obtaining a warrant either impossible or hopelessly infeasible.... Only after finding an extraordinary governmental interest of this kind do we—or ought we—engage in a balancing test to determine if a warrant should nonetheless be required.[2]

* * *

In this case, such extraordinary governmental interests do exist and are sufficient to justify an exception to the warrant requirement. Students are necessarily confined for most of the schoolday in close proximity to each other and to the school staff. I agree with the Court that we can take judicial notice of the serious problems of drugs and violence that plague our schools....

B

I emphatically disagree with the Court's decision to cast aside the constitutional probable-cause standard when assessing the constitutional validity of a schoolhouse search. The Court's decision jettisons the probable- cause standard—the only standard that finds support in the text of the Fourth Amendment—on the basis of its Rohrschach-like "balancing test."...

* * *

As compared with the relative ease with which teachers can apply the probable- cause standard, the amorphous "reasonableness under all the

---

[2] Administrative search cases involving inspection schemes have recognized that "if inspection is to be effective and serve as a credible deterrent, unannounced, even frequent, inspections are essential. In this context, the prerequisite of a warrant could easily frustrate inspection ...."...

circumstances" standard freshly coined by the Court today will likely spawn increased litigation and greater uncertainty among teachers and administrators....

* * *

I

Applying the constitutional probable-cause standard to the facts of this case, I would find that Mr. Choplick's search violated T.L.O.'s Fourth Amendment rights. After escorting T.L.O. into his private office, Mr. Choplick demanded to see her purse. He then opened the purse to find evidence of whether she had been smoking in the bathroom. When he opened the purse, he discovered the pack of cigarettes. At this point, his search for evidence of the smoking violation was complete.

* * *

Questions for Discussion

1. The Court upholds juvenile school searches on "reasonable suspicion," allowing substantial state intrusion more easily than with the "probable cause to arrest" or exigent circumstance tests applicable to adults. Did the principal have probable cause under an adult standard given the teacher's credible report and the materials viewed in plain sight?

2. If normal course adult standards applied, would the principal be required to cease his search after an initial look fails to find cigarettes? If he saw "cigarette papers" and cash "in plain sight" during his initial search of the purse, could he use this discovery as a basis to search further and read the money-owed list?

3. The Court has already created numerous exigent circumstances justifyng searches without warrants and not incident to a probable cause arrest, including: border searches, stop and frisk, murder scene, hot pursuit, traffic stops, regulatory searches, *et al.* Is there a difference in the relaxed "student search" standard here approved?

4. The Court contends that students in a school do not have as much of a "reasonable expectation of privacy" as do other citizens. To what extent is such a student expectation a reflection of the degree of intrusion traditionally exercised by school officials? Is there a self-fulfilling feature to this rationale (pattern and practice of intrusion removes an expectation of privacy which then makes the intrusion reasonable)?

5. Do the search and seizure 4th Amendment rights of a child's parents apply to social worker searches investigating child abuse? Does it matter that such searches may be executed as part of a civil rather than criminal enforcement scheme? Does it matter that the search is not for the purpose of securing evidence against a parent, but for the purpose of protecting an otherwise helpless person? What if evidence is found concerning a criminal offense (*e.g.*, child molestation or neglect) that may be used against the adults in the premises searched? What

about regulatory inspections of locations where children are placed by the court after it has assumed jurisdiction? See the latitude allowed for such child protection searches in *Wyman v. James*, 400 U.S. 309 (1971).

6. Is there an alternative to creating broad "exigent circumstance" categories? What if the court were to balance four factors: (1) justification for intrusion, (2) degree of intrusion, (3) quantum of probable cause to search, and (4) opportunity for a warrant? Should a search to find a possible explosive or firearm in the school meet the same probable cause standards as one investigating a hall pass excuse? Does the majority decision allow such a balancing? Why not use such a balancing formula in lieu of the specific search and seizure doctrines created for more than twenty different types of "exigent circumstances" applicable to adult searches?

Note on *Vernonia School District 47J v. Acton*

Following *TLO,* the Supreme Court decided *Vernonia School District 47J v. Acton*, 515 U.S. 646 (1995). The school district governing Vernonia High School in Oregon was concerned about increasing drug use on or from campus and about possible involvement of athletes as "leaders of the drug culture." A football and a wrestling coach believed that drug use was impeding the performance of some of their athletes. The District attempted drug education without improvement and turned to mandatory drug testing for all students seeking to participate in all interscholastic athletics at the start of a respective season, with 10% of participants then randomly selected for further testing each week thereafter. The policy was not framed as a law enforcement effort but to "prevent student athletes from using drugs, to protect their health and safety, and to provide drug users with assistance programs." Students were compelled to urinate under inspection (or within hearing) of an adult monitor of the same gender. A positive result (verified by a second test) would result in a choice of either a six-week assistance program with weekly testing, or suspension from the team. A further offense would lead to permanent suspension.

Justice Scalia, writing for a 6–3 majority, upheld the reasonableness of the search, citing the following three factors: decreased expectation of privacy, the relative unobtrusiveness of the search, and the severity of the need met by the search. The Court noted that it was not endorsing broadscale drug testing, distinguishing the school setting, where the institution acts as the "guardian and tutor of children entrusted to its care." The opinion noted that the searches are confined to optional athletics and the maximum sanction is a bar to participation. It also cited a district meeting with parents approving of the search, and the lack of substantial parental objection aside from the petitioner.

The dissent of Justice O'Connor, joined by Justices Stevens and Souter, argued that the search is prompted by no individualized probable cause or even suspicion, noting that "mass, suspicionless searches, however evenhanded, are generally unreasonable" in the criminal context, and that such searches have been permitted outside such a context only where not personally intrusive (such as searches of a closely regulated business), or arose out of unique contexts (such as a prison, which the dissent states is the apparent parallel). Justice O'Connor noted that the basis for "generalized suspicion" in the case arose from several specific students who were acting "in ways that plainly gave rise to reasonable suspicion." Hence, the constitutional course of action would be to test those persons, not all students in a broad class without any factual basis.

Board of Education of Independent School District No. 92 of Pottawatomie County v. Earls
536 U.S. 822 (2002)

JUSTICE THOMAS delivered the opinion of the Court.

The Student Activities Drug Testing Policy implemented by the Board of Education of Independent School District No. 92 of Pottawatomie County (School District) requires all students who participate in competitive extracurricular activities to submit to drug testing. Because this Policy reasonably serves the School District's important interest in detecting and preventing drug use among its students, we hold that it is constitutional.

• • •

The city of Tecumseh, Oklahoma, is a rural community located approximately 40 miles southeast of Oklahoma City. The School District administers all Tecumseh public schools. In the fall of 1998, the School District adopted the Student Activities Drug Testing Policy (Policy), which requires all middle and high school students to consent to drug testing in order to participate in any extracurricular activity. In practice, the Policy has been applied only to competitive extracurricular activities sanctioned by the Oklahoma Secondary Schools Activities Association, such as the Academic Team, Future Farmers of America, Future Homemakers of America, band, choir, pom pon, cheerleading, and athletics. Under the Policy, students are required to take a drug test before participating in an extracurricular activity, must submit to random drug testing while participating in that activity, and must agree to be tested at any time upon reasonable suspicion. The urinalysis tests are designed to detect only the use of illegal drugs, including amphetamines, marijuana, cocaine, opiates, and barbituates, not medical conditions or the presence of authorized prescription medications.

At the time of their suit, both respondents attended Tecumseh High School. Respondent Lindsay Earls was a member of the show choir, the marching band, the Academic Team, and the National Honor Society. Respondent Daniel James sought to participate in the Academic Team....Together with their parents, Earls and James brought a 42 U.S.C. § 1983 action against the School District, challenging the Policy both on its face and as applied to their participation in extracurricular activities....They alleged that the Policy violates the Fourth Amendment as incorporated by the Fourteenth Amendment and requested injunctive and declarative relief. They also argued that the School District failed to identify a special need for testing students who participate in extracurricular activities, and that the "Drug Testing Policy neither addresses a proven problem nor promises to bring any benefit to students or the school."

• • •

In the criminal context, reasonableness usually requires a showing of probable cause....The probable-cause standard, however, "is peculiarly related to criminal investigations" and may be unsuited to determining the reasonableness of administrative searches where the "Government seeks to *prevent* the development of hazardous conditions."...The Court has also held that a warrant and finding of probable cause are unnecessary in the public school context because such requirements "'would unduly interfere with the maintenance of the swift and informal disciplinary procedures [that are] needed.'"...

Given that the School District's Policy is not in any way related to the

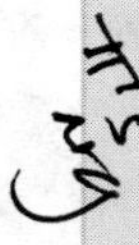

conduct of criminal investigations,...respondents do not contend that the School District requires probable cause before testing students for drug use. Respondents instead argue that drug testing must be based at least on some level of individualized suspicion....It is true that we generally determine the reasonableness of a search by balancing the nature of the intrusion on the individual's privacy against the promotion of legitimate governmental interests....But we have long held that "the Fourth Amendment imposes no irreducible requirement of [individualized] suspicion."...[I]n the context of safety and administrative regulations, a search unsupported by probable cause may be reasonable "when 'special needs, beyond the normal need for law enforcement, make the warrant and probable-cause requirement impracticable.'"...

Significantly, this Court has previously held that "special needs" inhere in the public school context....While schoolchildren do not shed their constitutional rights when they enter the schoolhouse,... "Fourth Amendment rights...are different in public schools than elsewhere; the 'reasonableness' inquiry cannot disregard the schools' custodial and tutelary responsibility for children."...In particular, a finding of individualized suspicion may not be necessary when a school conducts drug testing.

In *Vernonia*, this Court held that the suspicionless drug testing of athletes was constitutional. The Court, however, did not simply authorize all school drug testing, but rather conducted a fact-specific balancing of the intrusion on the children's Fourth Amendment rights against the promotion of legitimate governmental interests....Applying the principles of *Vernonia* to the somewhat different facts of this case, we conclude that Tecumseh's Policy is also constitutional.

• • •

· We first consider the nature of the privacy interest allegedly compromised by the drug testing....A student's privacy interest is limited in a public school environment where the State is responsible for maintaining discipline, health, and safety. Schoolchildren are routinely required to submit to physical examinations and vaccinations against disease....Securing order in the school environment sometimes requires that students be subjected to greater controls than those appropriate for adults....

• • •

Respondents argue that because children participating in nonathletic extracurricular activities are not subject to regular physicals and communal undress, they have a stronger expectation of privacy than the athletes tested in *Vernonia*....This distinction, however, was not essential to our decision in *Vernonia*, which depended primarily upon the school's custodial responsibility and authority....

In any event, students who participate in competitive extracurricular activities voluntarily subject themselves to many of the same intrusions on their privacy as do athletes....Some of these clubs and activities require occasional off-campus travel and communal undress. All of them have their own rules and requirements for participating students that do not apply to the student body as a whole....For example, each of the competitive extracurricular activities governed by the Policy must abide by the rules of the Oklahoma Secondary Schools Activities Association, and a faculty sponsor monitors the students for compliance with the various rules dictated by the clubs and activities....This regulation of extracurricular activities further diminishes the expectation of privacy among schoolchildren...."Somewhat like adults who choose to participate in a closely regulated industry, students who voluntarily participate in school athletics have reason to expect intrusions upon normal rights and privileges, including privacy."...We therefore conclude that the students affected by this Policy have a limited expectation of privacy.

Next, we consider the character of the intrusion imposed by the Policy....Urination is "an excretory function traditionally shielded by great privacy."...But the "degree of intrusion" on one's privacy caused by collecting a urine sample "depends upon the manner in which production of the urine sample is monitored."...

Under the Policy, a faculty monitor waits outside the closed restroom stall for the student to produce a sample and must "listen for the normal sounds of urination in order to guard against tampered specimens and to insure an accurate chain of custody."...The monitor then pours the sample into two bottles that are sealed and placed into a mailing pouch along with a consent form signed by the student. This procedure is virtually identical to that reviewed in *Vernonia*, except that it additionally protects privacy by allowing male students to produce their samples behind a closed stall. Given that we considered the method of collection in *Vernonia* a "negligible" intrusion,...the method here is even less problematic.

• • •

In addition, the Policy clearly requires that the test results be kept in confidential files separate from a student's other educational records and released to school personnel only on a "need to know" basis. Moreover, the test results are not turned over to any law enforcement authority. Nor do the test results here lead to the imposition of discipline or have any academic consequences....

...Rather, the only consequence of a failed drug test is to limit the student's privilege of participating in extracurricular activities. Indeed, a student may test positive for drugs twice and still be allowed to participate in extracurricular activities. After the first positive test, the school contacts the student's parent or guardian for a meeting. The student may continue to participate in the activity if within five days of the meeting the student shows proof of receiving drug counseling and submits to a second drug test in two weeks. For the second positive test, the student is suspended from participation in all extracurricular activities for 14 days, must complete four hours of substance abuse counseling, and must submit to monthly drug tests. Only after a third positive test will the student be suspended from participating in any extracurricular activity for the remainder of the school year, or 88 school days, whichever is longer....

Given the minimally intrusive nature of the sample collection and the limited uses to which the test results are put, we conclude that the invasion of students' privacy is not significant.

• • •

Finally, this Court must consider the nature and immediacy of the government's concerns and the efficacy of the Policy in meeting them....This Court has already articulated in detail the importance of the governmental concern in preventing drug use by schoolchildren....The drug abuse problem among our Nation's youth has hardly abated since *Vernonia* was decided in 1995. In fact, evidence suggests that it has only grown worse....As in *Vernonia*, "the necessity for the State to act is magnified by the fact that this evil is being visited not just upon individuals at large, but upon children for whom it has undertaken a special responsibility of care and direction."...The health and safety risks identified in *Vernonia* apply with equal force to Tecumseh's children. Indeed, the nationwide drug epidemic makes the war against drugs a pressing concern in every school.

Additionally, the School District in this case has presented specific evidence of drug use at Tecumseh schools. Teachers testified that they had seen students who appeared to be under the influence of drugs and that they had heard students speaking openly about using drugs....A drug dog found marijuana cigarettes near the school parking lot. Police officers once found drugs or drug paraphernalia in a car driven by a Future Farmers of America member. And the school board president reported that people in the community were calling the board to discuss the "drug situation."...

• • •

...the safety interest furthered by drug testing is undoubtedly substantial for all children, athletes and nonathletes alike. We know all too well that drug use carries a variety of health risks for children, including death from overdose.

We also reject respondents' argument that drug testing must presumptively be based upon an individualized reasonable suspicion of wrongdoing because such a testing regime would be less intrusive....Such a regime would place an additional burden on public school teachers who are already tasked with the difficult job of maintaining order and discipline. A program of individualized suspicion might unfairly target members of unpopular groups. The fear of lawsuits resulting from such targeted searches may chill enforcement of the program, rendering it ineffective in combating drug use....

Finally, we find that testing students who participate in extracurricular activities is a reasonably effective means of addressing the School District's legitimate concerns in preventing, deterring, and detecting drug use. While in *Vernonia* there might have been a closer fit between the testing of athletes and the trial court's finding that the drug problem was "fueled by the 'role model' effect of athletes' drug use," such a finding was not essential to the holding....

• • •

Within the limits of the Fourth Amendment, local school boards must assess the desirability of drug testing schoolchildren. In upholding the constitutionality of the Policy, we express no opinion as to its wisdom. Rather, we hold only that Tecumseh's Policy is a reasonable means of furthering the School District's important interest in preventing and deterring drug use among its schoolchildren. Accordingly, we reverse the judgment of the Court of Appeals.

Justice Ginsburg, with whom **Justice Stevens**, **Justice O'Connor**, and **Justice Souter** join, dissenting:

Seven years ago, in *Vernonia School Dist. 47J v. Acton,* 515 U.S. 646... (1995), this Court determined that a school district's policy of randomly testing the urine of its student athletes for illicit drugs did not violate the Fourth Amendment. In so ruling, the Court emphasized that drug use "increased the risk of sports-related injury" and that Vernonia's athletes were the "leaders" of an aggressive local "drug culture" that had reached "'epidemic proportions.'"...Today, the Court relies upon *Vernonia* to permit a school district with a drug problem its superintendent repeatedly described as "not...major,"...to test the urine of an academic team member solely by reason of her participation in a nonathletic, competitive extracurricular activity—participation associated with neither special dangers from, nor particular predilections for, drug use.

"The legality of a search of a student," this Court has instructed, "should depend simply on the reasonableness, under all the circumstances, of the search."...Although "'special needs' inhere in the public school context,"...those needs are not so expansive or malleable as to render reasonable any program of student drug testing a school district elects to install. The particular testing program upheld today is not reasonable, it is capricious, even perverse: Petitioners' policy targets for testing a student population least likely to be at risk from illicit drugs and their damaging effects. I therefore dissent.

• • •

A search unsupported by probable cause nevertheless may be consistent with the Fourth Amendment "when special needs, beyond the normal need for law enforcement, make the warrant and probable-cause requirement impracticable."...

"...Fourth Amendment rights, no less than First and Fourteenth Amendment rights, are different in public schools than elsewhere; the 'reasonableness' inquiry cannot disregard the schools' custodial and tutelary responsibility for children."...

The *Vernonia* Court concluded that a public school district facing a disruptive and explosive drug abuse problem sparked by members of its athletic teams had "special needs" that justified suspicionless testing of district athletes as a condition of their athletic participation.

This case presents circumstances dispositively different from those of *Vernonia*. True, as the Court stresses, Tecumseh students participating in competitive extracurricular activities other than athletics share two relevant characteristics with the athletes of *Vernonia.* First, both groups attend public schools. "Our decision in *Vernonia,*" the Court states, "depended primarily upon the school's custodial responsibility and authority."...

Those risks, however, are present for *all* schoolchildren. *Vernonia* cannot be read to endorse invasive and suspicionless drug testing of all students upon any evidence of drug use, solely because drugs jeopardize the life and health of those who use them. Many children, like many adults, engage in dangerous activities on their own time; that the children are enrolled in school scarcely allows government to monitor all such activities. If a student has a reasonable subjective expectation of privacy in the personal items she brings to school,...surely she has a similar expectation regarding the chemical composition of her urine....

The second commonality to which the Court points is the voluntary character of both interscholastic athletics and other competitive extracurricular activities. "By choosing to 'go out for the team,' [school athletes] voluntarily subject themselves to a degree of regulation even higher than that imposed on students generally."...Comparably, the Court today observes, "students who participate in competitive extracurricular activities voluntarily subject themselves to" additional rules not applicable to other students....

The comparison is enlightening. While extracurricular activities are "voluntary" in the sense that they are not required for graduation, they are part of the school's educational program; for that reason, the petitioner (hereinafter School District) is justified in expending public resources to make them available. Participation in such activities is a key component of school life, essential in reality for students applying to college, and, for all participants, a significant contributor to the breadth and quality of the educational experience....Students "volunteer" for extracurricular pursuits in the same way they might volunteer for honors classes: They subject themselves to additional requirements, but they do so in order to take full advantage of the education offered them....

Voluntary participation in athletics has a distinctly different dimension: Schools regulate student athletes discretely because competitive school sports by their nature require communal undress and, more important, expose students to physical risks that schools have a duty to mitigate. For the very reason that schools cannot offer a program of competitive athletics without intimately affecting the privacy of students, *Vernonia* reasonably analogized school athletes to "adults who choose to participate in a closely regulated industry."... Interscholastic athletics similarly require close safety and health regulation; a school's choir, band, and academic team do not.

In short, *Vernonia* applied, it did not repudiate, the principle that "the legality of a search of a student should depend simply on the reasonableness, *under all the circumstances*, of the search."...Enrollment in a public school, and election to participate in school activities beyond the bare minimum that the curriculum requires, are indeed factors relevant to reasonableness, but they do not on their own justify intrusive, suspicionless searches. *Vernonia,* accordingly, did not rest upon these factors; instead, the Court performed what today's majority aptly describes as a "fact-specific balancing,"...Balancing of that order, applied to the facts now before the Court, should yield a result other than the one the Court announces today.

• • •

Vernonia initially considered "the nature of the privacy interest upon which the search [there] at issue intruded."...The Court emphasized that student athletes' expectations of privacy are necessarily attenuated:

> "Legitimate privacy expectations are even less with regard to student athletes. School sports are not for the bashful. They require 'suiting up' before each practice or event, and showering and changing afterwards. Public school locker rooms, the usual sites for these activities, are not notable for the privacy they afford. The locker rooms in Vernonia are typical: No individual dressing rooms are provided; shower heads are lined up along a wall, unseparated by any sort of partition or curtain; not even all the toilet stalls have doors....There is an element of communal undress inherent in athletic participation."....

Competitive extracurricular activities other than athletics, however, serve students of all manner: the modest and shy along with the bold and uninhibited. Activities of the kind plaintiff-respondent Lindsay Earls pursued—choir, show choir, marching band, and academic team—afford opportunities to gain self-assurance, to "come to know faculty members in a less formal setting than the typical classroom," and to acquire "positive social supports and networks [that] play a critical role in periods of heightened stress."...

• • •

Finally, the "nature and immediacy of the governmental concern,"...faced by the Vernonia School District dwarfed that confronting Tecumseh administrators. Vernonia initiated its drug testing policy in response to an alarming situation: "[A] large segment of the student body, particularly those involved in interscholastic athletics, was in a state of rebellion . . . fueled by alcohol and drug abuse as well as the student[s'] misperceptions about the drug culture."...Tecumseh, by contrast, repeatedly reported to the Federal Government during the period leading up to the adoption of the policy that "types of drugs [other than alcohol and tobacco] including controlled dangerous substances, are present [in the schools] but have not identified themselves as major problems at this time."...

• • •

At the margins, of course, no policy of *random* drug testing is perfectly tailored to the harms it seeks to address. The School District cites the dangers faced by members of the band, who must "perform extremely precise routines with heavy equipment and instruments in close proximity to other students," and by Future Farmers of America, who "are required to individually control and restrain animals as large as 1500 pounds."...For its part, the United States acknowledges that "the linebacker faces a greater risk of serious injury if he takes the field under the influence of drugs than the drummer in the halftime band," but parries that "the risk of injury to a student who is under the influence of drugs while playing golf, cross country, or volleyball (sports covered by the policy in *Vernonia*) is scarcely any greater than the risk of injury to a student...handling a 1500-pound steer (as [Future Farmers of America] members do) or working with cutlery or other sharp instruments (as [Future Homemakers of America] members do)."...One can demur to the Government's view of the risks drug use poses to golfers,...for golfers were surely as marginal among the linebackers, sprinters, and basketball players targeted for testing in Vernonia as steer-handlers are among the choristers, musicians, and academic-team members subject to urinalysis in Tecumseh. Notwithstanding nightmarish images of out-of-control flatware, livestock run amok, and colliding tubas disturbing the peace and quiet of Tecumseh, the great majority of students the School District seeks to test in truth are engaged in activities that are not safety sensitive to an unusual degree. There is a difference between imperfect tailoring and no tailoring at all.

• • •

Nationwide, students who participate in extracurricular activities are significantly less likely to develop substance abuse problems than are their less-involved peers.... (tenth graders "who reported spending no time in school-sponsored activities were...49 percent more likely to have used drugs" than those who spent 1–4 hours per week in such activities). Even if students might be deterred from drug use in order to preserve their extracurricular eligibility, it is at least as likely that other students might forgo their extracurricular involvement in order to avoid detection of their drug use. Tecumseh's policy thus falls short doubly if deterrence is its aim: It invades the privacy of students who need deterrence least, and risks steering students at greatest risk for substance abuse away from extracurricular involvement that potentially may palliate drug problems....

To summarize, this case resembles *Vernonia* only in that the School Districts in both cases conditioned engagement in activities outside the obligatory curriculum on random subjection to urinalysis. The defining characteristics of the two programs, however, are entirely dissimilar. The Vernonia district sought to test a subpopulation of students distinguished by their reduced expectation of privacy, their special susceptibility to drug-related injury, and their heavy involvement with drug use. The Tecumseh district seeks to test a much larger population associated with none of these factors. It does so, moreover, without carefully safeguarding student confidentiality and without regard to the program's untoward effects. A program so sweeping is not sheltered by *Vernonia;* its unreasonable reach renders it impermissible under the Fourth Amendment.

• • •

> It is a sad irony that the petitioning School District seeks to justify its edict here by trumpeting "the schools' custodial and tutelary responsibility for children."...In regulating an athletic program or endeavoring to combat an exploding drug epidemic, a school's custodial obligations may permit searches that would otherwise unacceptably abridge students' rights. When custodial duties are not ascendant, however, schools' tutelary obligations to their students require them to "teach by example" by avoiding symbolic measures that diminish constitutional protections. "That [schools] are educating the young for citizenship is reason for scrupulous protection of Constitutional freedoms of the individual, if we are not to strangle the free mind at its source and teach youth to discount important principles of our government as mere platitudes."...

Questions for Discussion

1. Does the extensive categorical nature of the *Earls* search (as with the *Vernonia* search for athletes) actually help its constitutionality given the court's historical concern over excessive discretion given to state officials (particularly the police) to search or not? The majority notes that such discretion (even on the "reasonable suspicion" standard approved in *TLO*) might allow school officials to "target unpopular groups," which the mechanical search of those in extra-curricular ventures avoids? But what would prevent school officials from also selectively searching such groups on the loose "reasonable suspicion" standard of *TLO*? How does the supplemental liberal allowance of *Earls* address that alleged danger cited by the majority?

2. The Pottawatomie policy preserves confidentiality and drug results are not turned over to law enforcement. Would it make a difference if law enforcement were notified? Can that information be the basis for a "reasonable suspicion" search of the offender's locker? Can it be used for a search warrant (perhaps by sealed affidavit to preserve confidentiality)? On the one hand, the school becomes a potential "agent of the police" held to the higher standards applicable to criminal investigations. On the other hand, are not juvenile proceedings civil in nature—and designed to assist involved children? If a child is using dangerous amphetamines or opiates, should the only response be possible loss of chess club activities? If the drug problem is as serious as the majority claims, why would it not be permissible to use the information to more effectively detect the problem and treat the child?

3. Apart from the majority's stated purpose of "protecting" children from a danger, what of the implications of the concept that if a *crime* is being investigated, the state should be more constricted than if it is merely a *regulatory* matter? While precedents and both the majority opinion and dissent so assume, do not criminal offenses represent human activity of the greatest societal concern and damage? Are not most criminal acts by youth harmful to both themselves—and to other children? Why should a strong justification for a search—signaled by the criminal activity addressed—justify more restrictions on investigations, rather than less?

4. Do you agree with Justice Scalia in *Vernonia* and Justice Thomas in *Earls* that the required production of urine under the monitoring of another per-

son, including either listening for splash and feeling the warmth of the liquid, or visually inspecting genitalia while urinating—followed by the chemical testing of one's internal fluids—is a "minimal intrusion" by the state, as the majority opines? Is that judgment consistent with the extraordinary privacy accorded persons in their medical treatment and histories by custom, statute, and other precedents? One might argue that there is a compelling state interest in assuring the public that Supreme Court justices are not addicted or chemically imbalanced given the force-of-law authority of their decisions. Accordingly, would the majority justices find that a similar urine analysis of each of them before every major decision (mechanically applied) constitute only a "minimal intrusion?" Is it relevant that in 1998 the U.S. House of Representatives quietly rejected a drug testing proposal for themselves and their staffs, declaring it to be "insulting and undignified"?

5. Is death by overdose really a safety problem being addressed by comprehensive drug testing? Was there any evidence of such deaths, or of overdoses among the population here to be comprehensively tested? Justice Thomas cites teacher testimony about some students in school who were apparently on drugs and some conversations overheard about their use. Why not engage in a "reasonable suspicion" search of these students under *TLO*?

6. Is the "closely regulated industries" allowance for searches cited by the majority applicable here? Closely regulated industries are "clothed in the public interest"—a term of art implying monopoly power or "external costs" (such as the provision of medical services or hazardous activity implicating health and safety or involving extraordinary public reliance and possible irreparable harm). Would there be a basis to "closely regulate" these school clubs due to their possible external impact on the public? Is the school band, or the Future Homemakers of America club such an entity? The chess club? The after school bible-study club? If they so qualify, who does not qualify? Why would the majority's logic not apply to students who choose to eat in the cafeteria when other options may be available, or who engage in the "extra-curricular" activity of attending a football game? What is the reach of the majority's allowance of searches lacking probable cause or reasonable suspicion if the major tether is "the drug problem"?

7. May school searches such as those allowed in *Vernonia* and *Earls* be prohibited by the states under the "independent state grounds" application of their separate constitutions?

U.S. v. Frederick Doe

801 F. Supp. 1562 (E.D. Tex. 1992)

William Wayne, District Judge

On the evening of March 30, 1991, defendant was traveling northbound in an automobile on U.S. Highway 69. He was returning to his residence in Tyler, Texas, from a day long visit to his aunt in the Houston area, accompanied by two friends, Kelvin Williams and Roderick Kellum. All three vehicle occupants were African-American juveniles. Defendant was operating a maroon and black Chevrolet

Z-28 Camaro, and had just driven the car into a Chevron "Fast Fill" station located in Rusk, Texas, approximately one-half mile north of the intersection of U.S 69 and U.S. 84. Rusk Police Department Patrol Officer Otis Crow was riding that evening with reserve officer Kurt Nolan. Crow had observed defendant make a "rolling stop" at the intersection of U.S. 69 and U.S. 84. Officer Crow stopped his vehicle in front of the defendant's car, which was parked parallel to the curb in front of the convenience store. After a series of events that are in dispute, Officer Crow obtained from defendant's vehicle a large amount of cocaine, a firearm, and a box of ammunition. Defendant argues the evidence seized from his vehicle cannot be admitted without violating the Fourth Amendment.

* * *

II. Application of the Exclusionary Rule to Juvenile Proceedings

A. No Federal Case Has Determined Whether the Rule Applies

While no federal court has addressed directly the exclusionary rule's application to juvenile delinquency proceedings,...the Supreme Court has extended the search and seizure protections of the Fourth Amendment to juveniles. *New Jersey v. T.L.O.* 469 U.S. 325, 333,...

* * *

All state courts to have considered this issue have concluded that the exclusionary rule applies in juvenile delinquency adjudications, and evidence obtained by means of unlawful searches conducted by police officers is inadmissible. The Supreme Court of California in *In re Scott K.*, 24 Cal. 3d 395,...(1979), reversed a juvenile delinquency finding because the evidence against the juvenile had been seized illegally. The Justices held that juveniles are entitled to the "enforcement of search and seizure protections [to help] ensure that the factfinding process conforms with the standards of due process." *Id.* at 109. The Supreme Court of Illinois has also commanded that juveniles have a right to invoke the exclusionary rule in juvenile proceedings. *In re Marsh*, 40 Ill. 2d 53,...Lower level appellate courts have reached the same result in six other states....

B. The Exclusionary Rule Should Apply to Juvenile Delinquency Adjudication Hearings.

1. The Nature of Juvenile Delinquency Adjudications

* * *

In the quarter century since *Gault*, the Court has not retreated from its recognition that the potential penalties for being adjudicated a juvenile delinquent are on par with those resulting from a criminal conviction: "That the purpose of the commitment is rehabilitative and not punitive...[does not] change its nature.... Regardless of the purposes for which the incarceration is imposed, the fact remains that it is incarceration."....

* * *

On the other hand, the Court has not imposed the "formalities of the criminal adjudicative process" on the juvenile system...

2. The Cost Benefit Analysis of Applying the Rule

When deciding whether to apply the Fourth Amendment exclusionary rule, the court must analyze the potential costs and benefits of doing so....In decisions subsequent to *Calandra*, the Court has continually articulated that "the 'prime purpose' of the [exclusionary] rule, if not the sole one, 'is to deter future unlawful police misconduct'" *United States v. Janis*, 428 U.S. 433, 446,...(1976)...The Supreme Court has applied the exclusionary rule in forfeiture actions, which like juvenile delinquency proceedings, are nominally "civil" cases that are criminal in nature, or "quasi-criminal"....However, the Supreme Court has declined to apply the exclusionary rule in civil tax proceedings and in Immigration and Naturalization Service (INS) deportation proceedings....

* * *

The factors that counseled the Court to hold the exclusionary rule inapplicable in *Janis* and *Lopez-Mendoza* for want of deterrence value or social benefit do not apply to the juvenile context. In *Janis*, illegally seized evidence was excluded from the defendant's criminal trial. The police then turned over the evidence to the Internal Revenue Service, which filed civil tax proceeding. The Court, utilizing *Calandra*'s cost-benefit analysis, ruled that the deterrent effect was diminished under the circumstances. 428 U.S. at 447–60. Particularly significant was that the state law officials had already been "punished" by the exclusion of the evidence in a state criminal trial, and that the evidence would be excludable in any federal criminal trial that might be held....

...The officers conducting the searches in juvenile cases are the same officers who enforce the criminal laws against all persons in widely varied circumstances...The reality is that state law enforcement officers have essentially the same interest in the federal juvenile delinquency proceedings as in criminal prosecutions. The outcome of a juvenile delinquency proceeding, the incarceration of law breaker in an governmental institution, is within the arresting officer's "zone of primary interest." *Janis*, 428 U.S. at 258. In such situations, *Janis* recognizes the exclusionary [rule] should apply.

* * *

...[T]he sole deterrent for violation of the Fourth Amendment rights of juveniles is the existence of the exclusionary rule. The failure to adhere to the exclusionary rule in juvenile delinquency cases would reduce significantly the effectiveness of the rule's general deterrent powers. If the exclusionary rule is not enforced in juvenile delinquency proceedings to prevent Fourth Amendment violations, and an officer believes that the person he or she has stopped is a juvenile, the officer might feel less constrained to follow the Constitution. A holding that there is no practical remedy for the violation of the Fourth Amendment rights of suspects who will be processed by the federal juvenile delinquency system might be received by some members of the law enforcement community as tantamount to a declaration that all restraints on police behavior towards juveniles had been removed....

Furthermore, if the incidence of violations of the Fourth Amendment rights of juvenile suspects should increase, the government would be frustrated in cases where it has a strong interest in trying the juvenile as an adult. See 18 U.S.C. § 5032. In such cases, the government would be relegated to the juvenile system with its lesser punishments, if it could not convict the juvenile merely on the basis of the evidence lawfully obtained. Moreover, there likely would be cases where an officer violated the Fourth Amendment rights of a person who appeared to be a juvenile, believing there to be no sanction for such conduct, and it eventuated

> that the suspect was prosecutable only as an adult....Such a person, although perhaps factually guilty of a serious offense, might have to be set free.
>
> * * *

Questions for Discussion

1. If the juvenile courts operate in a paternalistic model to assist and rehabilitate youth who violate the law, are we compromising their purpose by excluding evidence where it is reliable and helps to ascertain the truth?

2. The court distinguishes INS proceedings where the exclusionary rule does not apply partly because of "societal costs" in allowing exclusion. Is this because those investigated by the INS are subject to routine unconstitutional intrusions and substantial numbers would be freed? Is it because the public harm from releasing an illegal immigrant based on the exclusion of evidence is greater than the release of juveniles accused of crimes? How does the Court know this to be the case? Has it received evidence to warrant the distinction made? Is it equipped to receive such evidence?

3. Does the exclusion of unconstitutionally-obtained evidence in juvenile cases extend to status offenses? To dependency court? To civil commitments? To school discipline? Should it?

3. Juveniles and the Fifth Amendment

In *Fare v. Michael C.*, 442 U.S. 707 (1979), the Court held that a juvenile's knowing and intelligent waiver of the right against self-incrimination and to counsel is weighed on a "totality of the circumstances" basis. There, a request by the minor to talk with his probation officer did not invoke the obligatory cessation of interrogation that applies when an adult requests an attorney. However, the general provisions of 5th Amendment law, including required *Miranda* warnings and a right not to speak and to consult with counsel do generally apply to youth, consistent with the importation of adult proceedings from *In Re Gault*. The general and continuing applicability of *Miranda* was upheld in *Dickerson v. United States*, 530 U.S. 428 (2000).

Some states protect juvenile 5th Amendment rights more extensively than is required under federal constitutional standards. They may do so statutorily or under their state constitutions on an "independent state" basis. State laws commonly permit waiver by a juvenile of the privilege against self-incrimination only after informed of the right to consult with (or have present) a parent, attorney, or other adult. For children under 14 years of age in some states, and under 12 years of age in some others, a parent or guardian must waive *Miranda* or must be present to explain to the child his or her rights and what such a waiver means.

The *Miranda* warnings generally apply to "custodial interrogations" by the police, or by state agents acting for the police (assisting in the enforcement of criminal statutes). However, school officials are not considered such police agents where they enforce school rules and discipline.

Some child advocates contend that juveniles, especially those under 16 years of age, do not understand the right not to speak or their rights as clients to attorneys (including the confidentiality of conversations, and the required loyalty of counsel to client). They also worry that parental presence may lead to psychological pressure to confess falsely. Others contend that the self-incrimination privilege and *Miranda* feed the "gamesmanship" atmosphere of juvenile proceedings, where the goal is to "get off" or "beat the system," rather than to admit the truth, hold yourself accountable, and try to make it right or do better.

4. Trial/Hearing Procedures

In Re Winship

397 U.S. 358 (1970)

MR. JUSTICE BRENNAN delivered the opinion of the Court.

Constitutional questions decided by this Court concerning the juvenile process have centered on the adjudicatory stage at "which a determination is made as to whether a juvenile is a 'delinquent' as a result of alleged misconduct on his part, with the consequence that he may be committed to a state institution." *In re Gault*, 387 U.S. 1, 13 (1967). *Gault* decided that, although the Fourteenth Amendment does not require that the hearing at this stage conform with all the requirements of a criminal trial or even of the usual administrative proceeding, the Due Process Clause does require application during the adjudicatory hearing of "'the essentials of due process and fair treatment.'"....This case presents the single, narrow question whether proof beyond a reasonable doubt is among the "essentials of due process and fair treatment" required during the adjudicatory stage when a juvenile is charged with an act which would constitute a crime if committed by an adult.[1]

* * *

I

The requirement that guilt of a criminal charge be established by proof beyond a reasonable doubt dates at least from our early years as a Nation. The "demand for a higher degree of persuasion in criminal cases was recurrently expressed from ancient times, [though] its crystallization into the formula 'beyond a reasonable doubt' seems to have occurred as late as 1798....

* * *

I

We turn to the question whether juveniles, like adults, are constitutionally

---

[1] Thus, we do not see how it can be said in dissent that this opinion "rests entirely on the assumption that all juvenile proceedings are 'criminal prosecutions,' hence subject to constitutional limitations." As in *Gault*, "we are not here concerned with...the pre-judicial stages of the juvenile process, nor do we direct our attention to the post-adjudicative or dispositional process."....In New York, the adjudicatory stage of a delinquency proceeding is clearly distinct from both the preliminary phase of the juvenile process and from its dispositional stage....Similarly, we intimate no view concerning the constitutionality of the New York procedures governing children "in need of supervision."....Nor do we consider whether there are other "essentials of due process and fair treatment" required during the adjudicatory hearing of a delinquency proceeding. Finally, we have no occasion to consider appellant's argument that § 744 (b) is a violation of the Equal Protection Clause, as well as a denial of due process.

entitled to proof beyond a reasonable doubt when they are charged with violation of a criminal law. The same considerations that demand extreme caution in factfinding to protect the innocent adult apply as well to the innocent child....

* * *

We conclude, as we concluded regarding the essential due process safeguards applied in Gault, that the observance of the standard of proof beyond a reasonable doubt "will not compel the States to abandon or displace any of the substantive benefits of the juvenile process."....

Finally, we reject the Court of Appeals' suggestion that there is, in any event, only a "tenuous difference" between the reasonable-doubt and preponderance standards. The suggestion is singularly unpersuasive. In this very case, the trial judge's ability to distinguish between the two standards enabled him to make a finding of guilt that he conceded he might not have made under the standard of proof beyond a reasonable doubt. Indeed, the trial judge's action evidences the accuracy of the observation of commentators that "the preponderance test is susceptible to the misinterpretation that it calls on the trier of fact merely to perform an abstract weighing of the evidence in order to determine which side has produced the greater quantum, without regard to its effect in convincing his mind of the truth of the proposition asserted."....[6]

III

In sum, the constitutional safeguard of proof beyond a reasonable doubt is as much required during the adjudicatory stage of a delinquency proceeding as are those constitutional safeguards applied in *Gault*—notice of charges, right to counsel, the rights of confrontation and examination, and the privilege against self-incrimination. We therefore hold, in agreement with Chief Judge Fuld in dissent in the Court of Appeals, "that, where a 12-year-old child is charged with an act of stealing which renders him liable to confinement for as long as six years, then, as a matter of due process...the case against him must be proved beyond a reasonable doubt."....

Reversed.

* * *

Mr. Chief Justice Burger, with whom **Mr. Justice Stewart** joins, dissenting.

The Court's opinion today rests entirely on the assumption that all juvenile proceedings are "criminal prosecutions," hence subject to constitutional limitations. This derives from earlier holdings, which, like today's holding, were steps eroding the differences between juvenile courts and traditional criminal courts. The original concept of the juvenile court system was to provide a benevolent and less formal means than criminal courts could provide for dealing with the special and often sensitive problems of youthful offenders. Since I see no constitutional requirement of due process sufficient to overcome the legislative judgment of the States in this

---

[6] Compare this Court's rejection of the preponderance standard in deportation proceedings, where we ruled that the Government must support its allegations with "clear, unequivocal and convincing evidence."....Although we ruled in *Woodby* that deportation is not tantamount to a criminal conviction, we found that since it could lead to "drastic deprivations," it is impermissible for a person to be "banished from this country upon no higher degree of proof than applies in a negligence case."....

area, I dissent from further strait-jacketing of an already overly restricted system. What the juvenile court system needs is not more but less of the trappings of legal procedure and judicial formalism; the juvenile court system requires breathing room and flexibility in order to survive, if it can survive the repeated assaults from this Court.

Much of the judicial attitude manifested by the Court's opinion today and earlier holdings in this field is really a protest against inadequate juvenile court staffs and facilities; we "burn down the stable to get rid of the mice." The lack of support and the distressing growth of juvenile crime have combined to make for a literal breakdown in many if not most juvenile courts. Constitutional problems were not seen while those courts functioned in an atmosphere where juvenile judges were not crushed with an avalanche of cases.

My hope is that today's decision will not spell the end of a generously conceived program of compassionate treatment intended to mitigate the rigors and trauma of exposing youthful offenders to a traditional criminal court; each step we take turns the clock back to the pre-juvenile-court era. I cannot regard it as a manifestation of progress to transform juvenile courts into criminal courts, which is what we are well on the way to accomplishing. We can only hope the legislative response will not reflect our own by having these courts abolished.

* * *

•Questions for Discussion

1. How would a genuinely "rehabilitative" court formulate the burden of proof? If the juvenile court remedy were actually beneficial to the child, *e.g.*, involved special schooling and elevated his prospects, would that make a preponderance test more appropriate? If a state could demonstrate that such kind paternalism were involved in an individual case, would the adult standard of *Winship* be excused? Should it be?

2. Civil proceedings which threaten one's livelihood, such as disbarment or the revocation of a license to do business, generally require "clear and convincing" evidence, which constitutes an intermediate burden of proof between New York's juvenile court preponderance test and proof beyond a reasonable doubt. Would such an intermediate step be preferable to replication of the adult standard?

3. Many jurisdictions have adopted a punitive approach to juvenile justice proceedings, including counting juvenile court "true findings" as "prior convictions" for harsh three-strike minimum penalties. Should such use require the adult standard of proof in juvenile court?

5. Jury Trial

McKeiver v. Pennsylvania
403 U.S. 528 (1971)

Mr. Justice Blackmun announced the judgments of the Court and an opinion in which The Chief Justice, Mr. Justice Stewart, and Mr. Justice White join.

These cases present the narrow but precise issue whether the Due Process Clause of the Fourteenth Amendment assures the right to trial by jury in the adjudicative phase of a state juvenile court delinquency proceeding.

* * *

I

...[W]e turn to the facts of the present cases:

No. 322. Joseph McKeiver, then age 16, in May 1968 was charged with robbery, larceny, and receiving stolen goods (felonies under Pennsylvania law, Pa. Stat. Ann., Tit. 18, §§ 4704, 4807, and 4817 (1963)) as acts of juvenile delinquency. At the time of the adjudication hearing he was represented by counsel.[2] His request for a jury trial was denied....

* * *

...McKeiver's offense was his participating with 20 or 30 youths who pursued three young teenagers and took 25 cents from them; that McKeiver never before had been arrested and had a record of gainful employment; that the testimony of two of the victims was described by the court as somewhat inconsistent and as "weak"; and that Terry's offense consisted of hitting a police officer with his fists and with a stick when the officer broke up a boys' fight Terry and others were watching.

No. 128. Barbara Burrus and approximately 45 other black children, ranging in age from 11 to 15 years,...were the subjects of juvenile court summonses issued in Hyde County, North Carolina, in January 1969.

The charges arose out of a series of demonstrations in the county in late 1968 by black adults and children protesting school assignments and a school consolidation plan. Petitions were filed by North Carolina state highway patrolmen. Except for one relating to James Lambert Howard, the petitions charged the respective juveniles with wilfully impeding traffic. The charge against Howard was that he wilfully made riotous noise and was disorderly in the O. A. Peay School in Swan Quarter; interrupted and disturbed the school during its regular sessions; and defaced school furniture. The acts so charged are misdemeanors under North Carolina law....

The several cases were consolidated into groups for hearing before District Judge Hallett S. Ward, sitting as a juvenile court. The same lawyer appeared for all the juveniles. Over counsel's objection, made in all except two of the cases, the general public was excluded. A request for a jury trial in each case was denied.

The evidence as to the juveniles other than Howard consisted solely of testimony of highway patrolmen. No juvenile took the stand or offered any witness. The testimony was to the effect that on various occasions the juveniles and adults were observed walking along Highway 64 singing, shouting, clapping, and playing basketball. As a result, there was interference with traffic. The marchers were asked to leave the paved portion of the highway and they were warned that they were committing a statutory offense. They either refused or left the roadway and immediately returned. The juveniles and participating adults were taken into custody. Juvenile petitions were then filed with respect to those under the age of 16.

---

[2] At McKeiver's hearing his counsel advised the court that he had never seen McKeiver before and "was just in the middle of interviewing" him. The court allowed him five minutes for the interview. Counsel's office, Community Legal Services, however, had been appointed to represent McKeiver five months earlier....

The evidence as to Howard was that on the morning of December 5, he was in the office of the principal of the O.A. Peay School with 15 other persons while school was in session and was moving furniture around; that the office was in disarray; that as a result the school closed before noon; and that neither he nor any of the others was a student at the school or authorized to enter the principal's office.

...The court...placed each juvenile on probation for either one or two years conditioned upon his violating none of the State's laws, upon his reporting monthly to the County Department of Welfare, upon his being home by 11 p.m. each evening, and upon his attending a school approved by the Welfare Director. None of the juveniles has been confined on these charges.

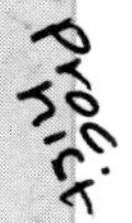

* * *

IV

The right to an impartial jury "in all criminal prosecutions" under federal law is guaranteed by the Sixth Amendment. Through the Fourteenth Amendment that requirement has now been imposed upon the States "in all criminal cases which—were they to be tried in a federal court—would come within the Sixth Amendment's guarantee." This is because the Court has said it believes "that trial by jury in criminal cases is fundamental to the American scheme of justice."....

This, of course, does not automatically provide the answer to the present jury trial issue, if for no other reason than that the juvenile court proceeding has not yet been held to be a "criminal prosecution," within the meaning and reach of the Sixth Amendment, and also has not yet been regarded as devoid of criminal aspects merely because it usually has been given the civil label....

Little, indeed, is to be gained by any attempt simplistically to call the juvenile court proceeding either "civil" or "criminal." The Court carefully has avoided this wooden approach. Before *Gault* was decided in 1967, the Fifth Amendment's guarantee against self-incrimination had been imposed upon the state criminal trial....So, too, had the Sixth Amendment's rights of confrontation and cross-examination....Yet the Court did not automatically and peremptorily apply those rights to the juvenile proceeding. A reading of *Gault* reveals the opposite. And the same separate approach to the standard-of-proof issue is evident from the carefully separated application of the standard, first to the criminal trial, and then to the juvenile proceeding, displayed in *Winship*....

Thus, accepting "the proposition that the Due Process Clause has a role to play," *Gault*, 387 U.S., at 13, our task here with respect to trial by jury, as it was in *Gault* with respect to other claimed rights, "is to ascertain the precise impact of the due process requirement."....

V

The Pennsylvania juveniles' basic argument is that they were tried in proceedings "substantially similar to a criminal trial." They say that a delinquency proceeding in their State is initiated by a petition charging a penal code violation in the conclusory language of an indictment; that a juvenile detained prior to trial is held in a building substantially similar to an adult prison; that in Philadelphia juveniles over 16 are, in fact, held in the cells of a prison; that counsel and the prosecution engage in plea bargaining; that motions to suppress are routinely heard and decided; that the usual rules of evidence are applied; that the customary common-law defenses are available; that the press is generally admitted in the Philadelphia juvenile courtrooms; that members of the public enter the room; that arrest and prior record may be reported by the press (from police sources, however, rather than from the juvenile court records); that, once adjudged delinquent, a juvenile may be confined until his majority in what amounts to a prison..., describing the state correctional institution at

Camp Hill as a "maximum security prison for adjudged delinquents and youthful criminal offenders"); and that the stigma attached upon delinquency adjudication approximates that resulting from conviction in an adult criminal proceeding.

The North Carolina juveniles particularly urge that the requirement of a jury trial would not operate to deny the supposed benefits of the juvenile court system; that the system's primary benefits are its discretionary intake procedure permitting disposition short of adjudication, and its flexible sentencing permitting emphasis on rehabilitation; that realization of these benefits does not depend upon dispensing with the jury; that adjudication of factual issues on the one hand and disposition of the case on the other are very different matters with very different purposes; that the purpose of the former is indistinguishable from that of the criminal trial; that the jury trial provides an independent protective factor; that experience has shown that jury trials in juvenile courts are manageable; that no reason exists why protection traditionally accorded in criminal proceedings should be denied young people subject to involuntary incarceration for lengthy periods; and that the juvenile courts deserve healthy public scrutiny.

VI

* * *

Despite all these disappointments, all these failures, and all these shortcomings, we conclude that trial by jury in the juvenile court's adjudicative stage is not a constitutional requirement....

* * *

...There is a possibility, at least, that the jury trial, if required as a matter of constitutional precept, will remake the juvenile proceeding into a fully adversary process and will put an effective end to what has been the idealistic prospect of an intimate, informal protective proceeding.

* * *

...The Court specifically has recognized by dictum that a jury is not a necessary part even of every criminal process that is fair and equitable....

...The imposition of the jury trial on the juvenile court system would not strengthen greatly, if at all, the factfinding function, and would, contrarily, provide an attrition of the juvenile court's assumed ability to function in a unique manner. It would not remedy the defects of the system....

* * *

...There is, of course, nothing to prevent a juvenile court judge, in a particular case where he feels the need, or when the need is demonstrated, from using an advisory jury.

* * *

...Since *Gault* and since *Duncan* the great majority of States, in addition to Pennsylvania and North Carolina, that have faced the issue have concluded that the considerations that led to the result in those two cases do not compel trial by jury in the juvenile court....

* * *

...If the jury trial were to be injected into the juvenile court system as a matter of right, it would bring with it into that system the traditional delay, the formality, and the clamor of the adversary system and, possibly, the public trial....

...Finally, the arguments advanced by the juveniles here are, of course, the identical arguments that underlie the demand for the jury trial for criminal proceedings. The arguments necessarily equate the juvenile proceeding—or at least the adjudicative phase of it—with the criminal trial. Whether they should be so equated is our issue. Concern about the inapplicability of exclusionary and other rules of evidence, about the juvenile court judge's possible awareness of the juvenile's prior record and of the contents of the social file; about repeated appearances of the same familiar witnesses in the persons of juvenile and probation officers and social workers—all to the effect that this will create the likelihood of pre-judgment—chooses to ignore, it seems to us, every aspect of fairness, of concern, of sympathy, and of paternal attention that the juvenile court system contemplates.

If the formalities of the criminal adjudicative process are to be superimposed upon the juvenile court system, there is little need for its separate existence. Perhaps that ultimate disillusionment will come one day, but for the moment we are disinclined to give impetus to it.

Affirmed.

* * *

Mr. Justice Douglas, with whom **Mr. Justice Black** and **Mr. Justice Marshall** concur, dissenting.

These cases from Pennsylvania and North Carolina present the issue of the right to a jury trial for offenders charged in juvenile court and facing a possible incarceration until they reach their majority. I believe the guarantees of the Bill of Rights, made applicable to the States by the Fourteenth Amendment, require a jury trial.

In the Pennsylvania cases one of the appellants was charged with robbery..., larceny..., and receiving stolen goods...as acts of juvenile delinquency....He was found a delinquent and placed on probation. The other appellant was charged with assault and battery on a police officer...and conspiracy...as acts of juvenile delinquency. On a finding of delinquency he was committed to a youth center. Despite the fact that the two appellants, aged 15 and 16, would face potential incarceration until their majority,...they were denied a jury trial.

In the North Carolina cases petitioners are students, from 11 to 15 years of age, who were charged under one of three criminal statutes: (1) "disorderly conduct" in a public building,...; (2) "wilful" interruption or disturbance of a public or private school,...; or (3) obstructing the flow of traffic on a highway or street,...

Conviction of each of these crimes would subject a person, whether juvenile or adult, to imprisonment in a state institution. In the case of these students the possible term was six to 10 years; it would be computed for the period until an individual reached the age of 21. Each asked for a jury trial which was denied. The trial judge stated that the hearings were juvenile hearings, not criminal trials. But the issue in each case was whether they had violated a state criminal law....

* * *

...[T]he child, the same as the adult, is in the category of those described in the Magna Carta:

> "No freeman may be...imprisoned...except by the lawful judgment of his peers, or by the law of the land."
>
> These cases should be remanded for trial by jury on the criminal charges filed against these youngsters.
>
> * * *

Questions for Discussion

1. Assuming confidentiality is important to juvenile rehabilitation goals, how much of a threat to it does a jury pose? Can juries be relied upon to maintain matters in confidence? Grand jury proceedings are universally secret, with large numbers of citizens serving on them; have those jurors commonly disclosed on-going proceedings?

2. Is the existence of a jury "audience" a possible disadvantage in its encouragement of "performing" and appeals to emotion, as opposed to a parent-like judge?

3. If adult due process includes a jury to help determine the truth (what happened), is factual accuracy for an accused youth any less important? Is it fair to require a jury in a disturbing-the-peace case against a 22-year-old with maximum jeopardy of ten days, but deny it for a child facing 6 to 15 years in custody (as with the juveniles before the *McKeiver* Court)?

4. Where a young adult is convicted of a crime, can juvenile court non-jury "convictions" be used as prior strikes in applying a three-strike adult minimum sentence—which in some states requires a 25-year minimum prison term?

5. The Constitution explicitly guarantees right of trial by jury in criminal matters. If *Gault* acknowledged modern juvenile proceedings as criminal in nature, including involuntary custody as a common outcome, is *McKeiver* consistent?

6. The Court acknowledges that juveniles are persons under the Constitution. How can the *Gault* Court constitutionally require publicly provided counsel (and other features of adult criminal court) not mentioned in the Constitution, but deprive accused juveniles of the one guarantee that is specifically enumerated?

7. Given the fact that the constitutional guarantee does not specify "twelve jurors," could states preserve juvenile court efficiency by authorizing nine-person, six-person, or even three-person juries? Do we balance such efficiency in applying jury requirements in adult proceedings?

8. The Court relied substantially on a "task force report" on juries. Was that report litigated or subject to cross examination? Is the Court the ideal forum to weigh such public policy evidence?

6. Death Penalty

Roper v. Simmons
543 U.S. 551 (2005)

JUSTICE KENNEDY delivered the opinion of the Court.

This case requires us to address, for the second time in a decade and a half, whether it is permissible under the Eighth and Fourteenth Amendments to the Constitution of the United States to execute a juvenile offender who was older than 15 but younger than 18 when he committed a capital crime. In *Stanford v. Kentucky, 492 U.S. 361 (1989)*, a divided Court rejected the proposition that the Constitution bars capital punishment for juvenile offenders in this age group. We reconsider the question.

I

At the age of 17, when he was still a junior in high school, Christopher Simmons, the respondent here, committed murder. About nine months later, after he had turned 18, he was tried and sentenced to death....

• • •

...As aggravating factors, the State submitted that the murder was committed for the purpose of receiving money; was committed for the purpose of avoiding, interfering with, or preventing lawful arrest of the defendant; and involved depravity of mind and was outrageously and wantonly vile, horrible, and inhuman. The State called Shirley Crook's husband, daughter, and two sisters, who presented moving evidence of the devastation her death had brought to their lives.

In mitigation, Simmons' attorneys first called an officer of the Missouri juvenile justice system, who testified that Simmons had no prior convictions and that no previous charges had been filed against him. Simmons' mother, father, two younger half brothers, a neighbor, and a friend took the stand to tell the jurors of the close relationships they had formed with Simmons and to plead for mercy on his behalf. Simmons' mother, in particular, testified to the responsibility Simmons demonstrated in taking care of his two younger half brothers and of his grandmother and to his capacity to show love for them.

During closing arguments, both the prosecutor and defense counsel addressed Simmons' age, which the trial judge had instructed the jurors they could consider as a mitigating factor. Defense counsel reminded the jurors that juveniles of Simmons' age cannot drink, serve on juries, or even see certain movies, because "the legislatures have wisely decided that individuals of a certain age aren't responsible enough." Defense counsel argued that Simmons' age should make "a huge difference to [the jurors] in deciding just exactly what sort of punishment to make." In rebuttal, the prosecutor gave the following response: "Age, he says. Think about age. Seventeen years old. Isn't that scary? Doesn't that scare you? Mitigating? Quite the contrary I submit. Quite the contrary."

The jury recommended the death penalty after finding the State had proved each of the three aggravating factors submitted to it. Accepting the jury's recommendation, the trial judge imposed the death penalty.

• • •

After these proceedings in Simmons' case had run their course, this Court held that the Eighth and Fourteenth Amendments prohibit the execution of a mentally retarded person. *Atkins v. Virginia, 536 U.S. 304 (2002).* Simmons filed a new petition for state postconviction relief, arguing that the reasoning of *Atkins* established that the Constitution prohibits the execution of a juvenile who was under 18 when the crime was committed.

• • •

II.

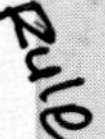

The Eighth Amendment provides: "Excessive bail shall not be required, nor excessive fines imposed, nor cruel and unusual punishments inflicted." The provision is applicable to the States through the Fourteenth Amendment....

The prohibition against "cruel and unusual punishments," like other expansive language in the Constitution, must be interpreted according to its text, by considering history, tradition, and precedent, and with due regard for its purpose and function in the constitutional design. To implement this framework we have established the propriety and affirmed the necessity of referring to "the evolving standards of decency that mark the progress of a maturing society" to determine which punishments are so disproportionate as to be cruel and unusual....

In *Thompson v. Oklahoma, 487 U.S. 815, (1988)*, a plurality of the Court determined that our standards of decency do not permit the execution of any offender under the age of 16 at the time of the crime....The plurality also observed that "[t]he conclusion that it would offend civilized standards of decency to execute a person who was less than 16 years old at the time of his or her offense is consistent with the views that have been expressed by respected professional organizations, by other nations that share our Anglo-American heritage, and by the leading members of the Western European community."...The opinion further noted that juries imposed the death penalty on offenders under 16 with exceeding rarity; the last execution of an offender for a crime committed under the age of 16 had been carried out in 1948, 40 years prior....

• • •

The next year, in *Stanford v. Kentucky, 492 U.S. 361 (1989)*, the Court, over a dissenting opinion joined by four Justices, referred to contemporary standards of decency in this country and concluded the Eighth and Fourteenth Amendments did not proscribe the execution of juvenile offenders over 15 but under 18. The Court noted that 22 of the 37 death penalty States permitted the death penalty for 16-year-old offenders, and, among these 37 States, 25 permitted it for 17-year-old offenders. These numbers, in the Court's view, indicated there was no national consensus "sufficient to label a particular punishment cruel and unusual." ...A plurality of the Court also "emphatically reject[ed]" the suggestion that the Court should bring its own judgment to bear on the acceptability of the juvenile death penalty....

• • •

III

A.

The evidence of national consensus against the death penalty for juveniles is similar, and in some respects parallel, to the evidence *Atkins* held sufficient to demonstrate a national consensus against the death penalty for the mentally retarded. When *Atkins* was decided, 30 States prohibited the death penalty for the mentally retarded. This number comprised 12 that had abandoned the death penalty altogether, and 18 that maintained it but excluded the mentally retarded from its reach....By a similar calculation in this case, 30 States prohibit the juvenile death penalty, comprising 12 that have rejected the death penalty altogether and 18 that maintain it but, by express provision or judicial interpretation, exclude juveniles from its reach.... *Atkins* emphasized that even in the 20 States without formal prohibition, the practice of executing the mentally retarded was infrequent. Since *Penry*, only five States had executed offenders known to have an IQ under 70....In the present case, too, even in the 20 States without a formal prohibition on executing juveniles, the practice is infrequent. Since *Stanford*, six States have executed prisoners for crimes committed as juveniles. In the past 10 years, only three have done so: Oklahoma, Texas, and Virginia....In December 2003 the Governor of Kentucky decided to spare the life of Kevin Stanford, and commuted his sentence to one of life imprisonment without parole, with the declaration that "'[w]e ought not be executing people who, legally, were children.'"... By this act the Governor ensured Kentucky would not add itself to the list of States that have executed juveniles within the last 10 years even by the execution of the very defendant whose death sentence the Court had upheld in *Stanford* v *Kentucky*.

There is, to be sure, at least one difference between the evidence of consensus in *Atkins* and in this case. Impressive in *Atkins* was the rate of abolition of the death penalty for the mentally retarded. Sixteen States that permitted the execution of the mentally retarded at the time of *Penry* had prohibited the practice by the time we heard *Atkins*. By contrast, the rate of change in reducing the incidence of the juvenile death penalty, or in taking specific steps to abolish it, has been slower. Five States that allowed the juvenile death penalty at the time of *Stanford* have abandoned it in the intervening 15 years—four through legislative enactments and one through judicial decision....

Though less dramatic than the change from *Penry* to *Atkins*...we still consider the change from *Stanford* to this case to be significant. As noted in *Atkins*, with respect to the States that had abandoned the death penalty for the mentally retarded since *Penry*, "[i]t is not so much the number of these States that is significant, but the consistency of the direction of change."...

• • •

As in *Atkins*, the objective indicia of consensus in this case—the rejection of the juvenile death penalty in the majority of States; the infrequency of its use even where it remains on the books; and the consistency in the trend toward abolition of the practice—provide sufficient evidence that today our society views juveniles, in the words *Atkins* used respecting the mentally retarded, as "categorically less culpable than the average criminal."...

• • •

Three general differences between juveniles under 18 and adults demonstrate that juvenile offenders cannot with reliability be classified among the worst offenders. First, as any parent knows and as the scientific and sociological studies respondent and his *amici* cite tend to confirm, "[a] lack of maturity and an underdeveloped sense of responsibility are found in youth more often than in adults and are more understandable among the young. These qualities often result in impetuous and ill-considered actions and decisions."... The second area of difference is that juveniles are more vulnerable or susceptible to negative influences and outside pressures, including peer pressure....

The third broad difference is that the character of a juvenile is not as well formed as that of an adult. The personality traits of juveniles are more transitory, less fixed....

These differences render suspect any conclusion that a juvenile falls among the worst offenders. The susceptibility of juveniles to immature and irresponsible behavior means "their irresponsible conduct is not as morally reprehensible as that of an adult." ...Their own vulnerability and comparative lack of control over their immediate surroundings mean juveniles have a greater claim than adults to be forgiven for failing to escape negative influences in their whole environment....The reality that juveniles still struggle to define their identity means it is less supportable to conclude that even a heinous crime committed by a juvenile is evidence of irretrievably depraved character. From a moral standpoint it would be misguided to equate the failings of a minor with those of an adult, for a greater possibility exists that a minor's character deficiencies will be reformed. Indeed, "[t]he relevance of youth as a mitigating factor derives from the fact that the signature qualities of youth are transient; as individuals mature, the impetuousness and recklessness that may dominate in younger years can subside."...Only a relatively small proportion of adolescents who experiment in risky or illegal activities develop entrenched patterns of problem behavior that persist into adulthood").

In *Thompson*, a plurality of the Court recognized the import of these characteristics with respect to juveniles under 16, and relied on them to hold that the Eighth Amendment prohibited the imposition of the death penalty on juveniles below that age....We conclude the same reasoning applies to all juvenile offenders under 18.

Once the diminished culpability of juveniles is recognized, it is evident that the penological justifications for the death penalty apply to them with lesser force than to adults. We have held there are two distinct social purposes served by the death penalty: "'retribution and deterrence of capital crimes by prospective offenders.'"...Retribution is not proportional if the law's most severe penalty is imposed on one whose culpability or blameworthiness is diminished, to a substantial degree, by reason of youth and immaturity.

As for deterrence, it is unclear whether the death penalty has a significant or even measurable deterrent effect on juveniles, as counsel for the petitioner acknowledged at oral argument....

• • •

...[Petitioners] assert that even assuming the truth of the observations we have made about juveniles' diminished culpability in general, jurors nonetheless should be allowed to consider mitigating arguments related to youth on a case-by-case basis, and in some cases to impose the death penalty if justified. A central feature of death penalty sentencing is a particular assessment of the circumstances of the crime and the characteristics of the offender. The system is designed to consider both aggravating and mitigating circumstances, including youth, in every case. Given this Court's own insistence on individualized consideration, petitioner maintains that it is both arbitrary and unnecessary to adopt a categorical rule barring imposition of the death penalty on any offender under 18 years of age.

We disagree. The differences between juvenile and adult offenders are too marked and well understood to risk allowing a youthful person to receive the death penalty despite insufficient culpability. An unacceptable likelihood exists that the brutality or cold-blooded nature of any particular crime would overpower mitigating arguments based on youth as a matter of course, even where the juvenile offender's objective immaturity, vulnerability, and lack of true depravity should require a sentence less severe than death. In some cases a defendant's youth may even be counted against him. In this very case, as we noted above, the prosecutor argued Simmons' youth was aggravating rather than mitigating....While this sort of overreaching could be corrected by a particular rule to ensure that the mitigating force of youth is not overlooked, that would not address our larger concerns.

It is difficult even for expert psychologists to differentiate between the juvenile offender whose crime reflects unfortunate yet transient immaturity, and the rare juvenile offender whose crime reflects irreparable corruption....

• • •

Our determination that the death penalty is disproportionate punishment for offenders under 18 finds confirmation in the stark reality that the United States is the only country in the world that continues to give official sanction to the juvenile death penalty. This reality does not become controlling, for the task of interpreting the Eighth Amendment remains our responsibility. Yet at least from the time of the Court's decision in *Trop*, the Court has referred to the laws of other countries and to international authorities as instructive for its interpretation of the Eighth Amendment's prohibition of "cruel and unusual punishments." ...

As respondent and a number of *amici* emphasize, Article 37 of the United Nations Convention on the Rights of the Child, which every country in the world has ratified save for the United States and Somalia, contains an express prohibition on capital punishment for crimes committed by juveniles under 18.... Respondent and his *amici* have submitted, and petitioner does not contest, that only seven countries other than the United States have executed juvenile offenders since 1990: Iran, Pakistan, Saudi Arabia, Yemen, Nigeria, the Democratic Republic of Congo, and China. Since then each of these countries has either abolished capital punishment for juveniles or made public disavowal of the practice.... In sum, it is fair to say that the United States now stands alone in a world that has turned its face against the juvenile death penalty.

• • •

...The Eighth and Fourteenth Amendments forbid imposition of the death penalty on offenders who were under the age of 18 when their crimes were committed. The judgment of the Missouri Supreme Court setting aside the sentence of death imposed upon Christopher Simmons is affirmed.

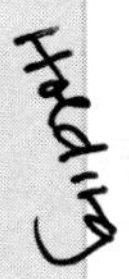

Justice Scalia, with whom **The Chief Justice** and **Justice Thomas** join, dissenting.

...What a mockery today's opinion makes of [Alexander] Hamilton's expectation, announcing the Court's conclusion that the meaning of our Constitution has changed over the past 15 years—not, mind you, that this Court's decision 15 years ago was *wrong*, but that the Constitution *has changed*. The Court reaches this implausible result by purporting to advert, not to the original meaning of the Eighth Amendment, but to "the evolving standards of decency,"...of our national society. It then finds, on the flimsiest of grounds, that a national consensus which could not be perceived in our people's laws barely 15 years ago now solidly exists. Worse still, the Court says in so many words that what our people's laws say about the issue does not, in the last analysis, matter: "[I]n the end our own judgment will be brought to bear on the question of the acceptability of the death penalty under the Eighth Amendment."...The Court thus proclaims itself sole arbiter of our Nation's moral standards—and in the course of discharging that awesome responsibility purports to take guidance from the views of foreign courts and legislatures. Because I do not believe that the meaning of our Eighth Amendment, any more than the meaning of other provisions of our Constitution, should be determined by the subjective views of five Members of this Court and like-minded foreigners, I dissent.

I

...Words have no meaning if the views of less than 50% of death penalty States can constitute a national consensus....Our previous cases have required overwhelming opposition to a challenged practice, generally over a long period of time....[W]e invalidated capital punishment imposed for participation in a robbery in which an accomplice committed murder, because 78% of all death penalty States prohibited this punishment....

• • •

Relying on...narrow margins is especially inappropriate in light of the fact that a number of legislatures and voters have expressly affirmed their support for capital punishment of 16- and 17-year-old offenders since *Stanford*. Though the Court is correct that no State has lowered its death penalty age, both the Missouri and Virginia Legislatures—which, at the time of *Stanford*, had no minimum age requirement—expressly established 16 as the minimum....The people of Arizona...and Florida...have done the same by ballot initiative. Thus, even States that have not executed an under-18 offender in recent years unquestionably favor the possibility of capital punishment in some circumstances.

The Court's reliance on the infrequency of executions, for under-18 murderers,...credits an argument that this Court considered and explicitly rejected in *Stanford*. That infrequency is explained, we accurately said, both by "the undisputed fact that a far smaller percentage of capital crimes are committed by persons under 18 than over 18,"...and by the fact that juries are required at sentencing to consider the offender's youth as a mitigating factor. Thus, "it is not only possible, but overwhelmingly probable, that the very considerations which induce [respondent] and [his] supporters to believe that death should *never* be imposed on offenders under 18 cause prosecutors and juries to believe that it should *rarely* be imposed."...

It is, furthermore, unclear that executions of the relevant age group have decreased since we decided *Stanford*. Between 1990 and 2003, 123 of 3,599 death sentences, or 3.4%, were given to individuals who committed crimes before reaching age 18....Thus, the numbers of under-18 offenders subjected to the death penalty, though low compared with adults, have either held steady or slightly increased since *Stanford*. These statistics in no way support the action the Court takes today.

• • •

Today's opinion provides a perfect example of why judges are ill equipped to make the type of legislative judgments the Court insists on making here. To support its opinion that States should be prohibited from imposing the death penalty on anyone who committed murder before age 18, the Court looks to scientific and sociological studies, picking and choosing those that support its position. It never explains why those particular studies are methodologically sound; none was ever entered into evidence or tested in an adversarial proceeding....

• • •

Even putting aside questions of methodology, the studies cited by the Court offer scant support for a categorical prohibition of the death penalty for murderers under 18. At most, these studies conclude that, *on average*, or *in most cases*, persons under 18 are unable to take moral responsibility for their actions. Not one of the cited studies opines that all individuals under 18 are unable to appreciate the nature of their crimes.

Moreover, the cited studies describe only adolescents who engage in risky or antisocial behavior, as many young people do. Murder, however, is more than just risky or antisocial behavior. It is entirely consistent to believe that young people often act impetuously and lack judgment, but, at the same time, to believe that those who commit premeditated murder are—at least sometimes—just as culpable as adults. Christopher Simmons, who was only seven months shy of his 18th birthday when he murdered Shirley Crook, described to his friends *beforehand*—"[i]n chilling, callous terms," as the Court puts it,...the murder he planned to commit. He then broke into the home of an innocent woman, bound her with duct tape and electrical wire, and threw her off a bridge alive and conscious....

• • •

That "almost every State prohibits those under 18 years of age from voting, serving on juries, or marrying without parental consent,"...is patently irrelevant—and is yet another resurrection of an argument that this Court gave a decent burial in *Stanford.* (What kind of Equal Justice under Law is it that—without so much as a "Sorry about that"—gives as the basis for sparing one person from execution arguments *explicitly rejected* in refusing to spare another?) As we explained in *Stanford*,...it is "absurd to think that one must be mature enough to drive carefully, to drink responsibly, or to vote intelligently, in order to be mature enough to understand that murdering another human being is profoundly wrong, and to conform one's conduct to that most minimal of all civilized standards." Serving on a jury or entering into marriage also involve decisions far more sophisticated than the simple decision not to take another's life.

Moreover, the age statutes the Court lists "set the appropriate ages for the operation of a system that makes its determinations in gross, and that does not conduct individualized maturity tests." *Ibid.* The criminal justice system, by contrast, provides for individualized consideration of each defendant....

• • •

The Court's contention that the goals of retribution and deterrence are not served by executing murderers under 18 is also transparently false. The argument that "[r]etribution is not proportional if the law's most severe penalty is imposed on one whose culpability or blameworthiness is diminished,"...is simply an extension of the earlier, false generalization that youth *always* defeats culpability. The Court claims that "juveniles will be less susceptible to deterrence," ...because "'[t]he likelihood that the teenage offender has made the kind of cost-benefit analysis that attaches any weight to the possibility of execution is so remote as to be virtually nonexistent'"....The Court unsurprisingly finds no support for this astounding proposition, save its own case law. The facts of this very case show the proposition to be false. Before committing the crime, Simmons encouraged his friends to join him by assuring them that they could "get away with it" because they were minors....

• • •

Though the views of our own citizens are essentially irrelevant to the Court's decision today, the views of other countries and the so-called international community take center stage.

• • •

...[I]n addition to barring the execution of under-18 offenders, the United Nations Convention on the Rights of the Child prohibits punishing them with life in prison without the possibility of release. If we are truly going to get in line with the international community, then the Court's reassurance that the death penalty is really not needed, since "the punishment of life imprisonment without the possibility of parole is itself a severe sanction,"...gives little comfort.

It is interesting that whereas the Court is not content to accept what the States of our Federal Union *say*, but insists on inquiring into what they *do* (specifically, whether they in fact *apply* the juvenile death penalty that their laws allow), the Court is quite willing to believe that every foreign nation—of whatever tyrannical political makeup and with however subservient or incompetent a court system—in fact *adheres* to a rule of no death penalty for offenders under 18. Nor does the Court inquire into how many of the countries that have the death penalty, but have forsworn (on paper at least) imposing that penalty on offenders under 18, have what no State of this country can constitutionally have: a *mandatory* death penalty for certain crimes, with no possibility of mitigation by the sentencing authority, for youth or any other reason. I suspect it is most of them....

More fundamentally, however, the basic premise of the Court's argument—that American law should conform to the laws of the rest of the world—ought to be rejected out of hand. In fact the Court itself does not believe it. In many significant respects the laws of most other countries differ from our law—including not only such explicit provisions of our Constitution as the right to jury trial and grand jury indictment, but even many interpretations of the Constitution prescribed by this Court itself. The Court-pronounced exclusionary rule, for example, is distinctively American....

• • •

And let us not forget the Court's abortion jurisprudence, which makes us one of only six countries that allow abortion on demand until the point of viability....

• • •

The Court should either profess its willingness to reconsider all these matters in light of the views of foreigners, or else it should cease putting forth foreigners' views as part of the *reasoned basis* of its decisions. To invoke alien law when it agrees with one's own thinking, and ignore it otherwise, is not reasoned decisionmaking, but sophistry....

The Court responds that "[i]t does not lessen our fidelity to the Constitution or our pride in its origins to acknowledge that the express affirmation of certain fundamental rights by other nations and peoples simply underscores the centrality of those same rights within our own heritage of freedom."...To begin with, I do not believe that approval by "other nations and peoples" should buttress our commitment to American principles any more than (what should logically follow) disapproval by "other nations and peoples" should weaken that commitment. More importantly, however, the Court's statement flatly misdescribes what is going on here. Foreign sources are cited today, *not* to underscore our "fidelity" to the Constitution, our "pride in its origins," and "our own [American] heritage." To the contrary, they are cited *to set aside* the centuries-old American practice—a practice still engaged in by a large majority of the relevant States—of letting a jury of 12 citizens decide whether, in the particular case, youth should be the basis for withholding the death penalty....

• • •

However sound philosophically, this is no way to run a legal system. We must disregard the new reality that, to the extent our Eighth Amendment decisions constitute something more than a show of hands on the current Justices' current personal views about penology, they purport to be nothing more than a snapshot of American public opinion at a particular point in time (with the timeframes now shortened to a mere 15 years). We must treat these decisions just as though they represented *real* law, *real* prescriptions democratically adopted by the American people, as conclusively (rather than sequentially) construed by this Court. Allowing lower courts to reinterpret the Eighth Amendment whenever they decide enough time has passed for a new snapshot leaves this Court's decisions without any force—especially since the "evolution" of our Eighth Amendment is no longer determined by objective criteria....

Questions for Discussion

1. The majority argues that a "bright line" of age is used to limit the rights of children to vote, drive, drink or otherwise enjoy adult privileges—all because of the generalized judgment of immaturity. The dissent counters that these policies are in gross, but that criminal trials are already individualized—and that a jury can consider precisely all appropriate factors (including immaturity) in assigning blame. But the majority cites the prosecutor's statement that the defendant's age is an *aggravating* factor militating toward the death penalty as an example of the inconsistency and danger of the individualized approach. If such a comment violates the "mitigation" that the dissent acknowledges should be considered based on youth, why could *Roper* not be reversed on that narrow basis (improper prosecutorial argument)? What is the response to the argument that the major problem is solved if state legislatures must agree to the sanction, and juries may impose it only where *admissible* factors so warrant?

2. In general, a contract can not be enforced against a child because of the bright line judgment of immaturity (see Chapter 12). Further, litigation to enforce a contract may be individualized and enforced in a particular case. Why is adequate maturity for contract execution not subject to individual determination? Would it not be possible to arrange individual exceptions to the bright line judgement that children cannot vote or drive? Aren't driving tests individualized? Are not juries selected by individual *voir dire* and examination? Is Scalia's distinction that these tasks are far more complex than "the decision not to take a life" convincing? Is the decision to execute a youth—evaluating maturity and capacity—not complex? Is it less complex than deciding whether a 16-year-old should be allowed to marry—which in many states is forbidden without parental permission?

3. Does the majority know whether the death penalty has a deterrent impact on youth? Although the statement of the defendant that nothing would happen to him because of his youth may not be dispositive, what is the evidence of deterrent impact? Is the Court the optimum forum to make such judgments, or is Scalia right that the legislature should do so—considering a broad array of evidence—and not centered on a specific fact situation?

4. How many state legislatures must act before the Court finds a practice "unusual" within the meaning of the 8th Amendment? Is it the number of legislatures who allow it? Is it the incidence of actual executions? Does it matter if the legislatures maintaining the death penalty represent relatively small populations? Does it matter if their legislative processes take time and condemned youth tend not to be a powerful political group forcing decision? If the Court must wait until virtually all state legislatures act to bar capital punishment, what is the relevance of the Court? Is it to act only when a few stragglers remain due to dilatory proceedings or inattention?

5. Is the "cruel and unusual" standard of the 8th Amendment disjunctive, so both must occur for a violation? Scalia, both in the *Roper* dissent and in his *Stanford* majority opinion, argues that "rare" does not mean "unusual." He argues that not many children are arrested for capital crimes and that the circumstances warranting a death penalty are "rare." The implication is that when the prerequisites exist for such an outcome its imposition would then not be "unusual?" But aside from the circularity of such a definition, is not capital punishment empirically "rare"—even among the population of youth convicted for capital crimes? Why is such rarity not "unusual"? If concededly "unusual", would the dissent be more effectively framed as not "cruel"?

6. The dissent cites precedent holding the execution of one who committed crimes at under 16 as violative of the 8th Amendment. Why does its reasoning about the skill of juries to make individualized decisions without arbitrary lines based on "averages" not apply to this age, or to earlier ages?

7. The dissent discounts the scientific evidence as untested by the adversary process, ambiguous, and producing generalized findings for which there are exceptions (appropriate for jury delineation). But what of the substantial evidence offered in *Roper* of brain and development change through the teen years—and cited by the majority? Do not these chemical and brain development stages apply to virtually every human as he or she grows and enters adolescence? If that evidence is weak, is not the state or its *amici* well equipped to counter such findings with contrary studies or to otherwise impeach it?

8. Is Justice Scalia correct in his opening that the majority opinion purports to "change" the "Constitution" itself? Castration was an accepted mode of punishment in 1787 (and recommended by Jefferson) and is not prohibited explicitly by the Constitution—is it permissible? Should it be left to state decision and individual cases? What of torture? Is it explicitly mentioned in the 8th Amendment?

9. Are the views of the rest of the world irrelevant to the "evolving standards" at issue? Is it relevant where the standard invoked by the court is joined in by 140 nations and 6 billion people? For those nations who historically tolerated state sponsored torture, the gassing of dissidents, the severing of hands as punishment for theft, child prostitution and slavery—would we want our standards of morality (and those of humanity in general) to be considered when they decide whether to continue such practices? Is the strong world consensus against child capital punishment credibly dismissed as simply "the subjective views of five members of the Court and like-minded foreigners," as the dissent writes?

10. The dissent argues that the world's rejection of the death penalty should not be a factor because many nations have brutal "automatic" death penalty formulae (albeit for adults), and do not otherwise follow some of our civil libertarian traditions. Justice Scalia argues that it is hypocrisy to cite international practice banning child capital punishment when we do not follow it in these other respects. Can the majority argue that world precedents are not symmetrical—but properly form a floor of civilization. Hence, is it consistent to refuse to follow practices below the libertarian policies of the United States, but still consider as relevant a universally adopted limitation on state power (the state does not execute children) to keep this nation at that international floor? Do any of the Scalia examples of foreign practices we do not follow represent libertarian principles? Are they aspirational? Universally held?

11. The United Nations Convention on the Rights of a Child has been signed by every nation of the world except the United States and Somalia (see discussion in Postscript). Both it and the Second Optional Protocol to the International Convention on Civil and Political Rights ban capital punishment based on the acts of a child (under the age of 18). What would be the effect on the four dissenters of Congressional ratification of either of these two international agreements? Ratified treaties are the equivalent of federal statutes. Would *Lopez,* striking a federal gun statute as precluded by state prerogative (see Chapter 1), disallow federal supremacy and preclude such federal policy from supersession over state laws?

12. The dissent mentions life without the possibility of parole as also an uncommon sanction for the criminal acts of children internationally. In fact, almost all of the defendants in the world so incarcerated based on crimes committed while children are in the United States. Does a term of what may be 60 or more years also conflict with the medical evidence presented in *Roper*? If there are documented stages of hormonal and brain development affecting persons through the teen years, is it not "cruel and unusual" to interpose a lifetime of incarceration, including fifty or more years after the body chemistry of adolescence has passed? Is such a policy consistent with the rehabilitation goals of juvenile justice? Is such a permanent judgment appropriate for the acts of a 15-year-old? For a 12-year-old?

D. STATUS OFFENSES

Juvenile Court jurisdiction covers children who have been abandoned (see emancipation discussion), abused or neglected, delinquent, or who commit status offenses. These status offenses include curfew violations, running away, "incorrigibility," and truancy. Statistically, strong enforcement at the status offense level correlates to reduced juvenile arrest incidence. Unsurprisingly, children who live in strong and caring families, are not out in public during late hours, and attend school—have a much lower juvenile arrest rate than their counterparts (see discussion of gangs and truancy above).

Over the last decade, curfews prohibiting juveniles from being in public and unaccompanied by an adult after certain evening hours have become common. Most are adopted by local ordinance, with over 80% of American cities of over 30,000 population so acting. Other curfews require school-age children to be "off the streets" during school hours. Courts have generally upheld such ordinances, while often finding more specific prohibitions unconstitutionally vague. For example, a Chicago prohibition on a street gang member "loitering in a public place" with one or more other such persons was so struck (see *City of Chicago v. Morales*, 527 U.S. 41 (1999)). A critical basis for rejection of such measures is the degree to which latitude is given to police authority to determine who is violating the law and who is not.

A wholesale limitation on youth movement, with defined exceptions that do not rely on police judgment, more often survives court challenge. See, *e.g.*, *Hutchins v. District of Columbia*, 188 F.3d 531 (D.C. Cir. 1999), typically affirming the District of Columbia curfew for those sixteen years of age and under without adult supervision after 11 p.m. on weekdays, and after midnight on Friday, Saturday and Sunday. As with most such ordinances, it included seven common exceptions: going on a parental errand without detour, going to or from a job without detour, an emergency, on the sidewalk abutting the residence or next door, attending an official school, religious or youth activity itself supervised by adults, or exercising 1st Amendment rights of religion, speech or assembly. Most such status offenses lead to detention at juvenile receiving facilities, followed by required community service and by fines to parents or businesses in violation.

The Supreme Court has allowed lower courts to strike such broad prohibitions on general activity for adults (see *Bykofsky v. Borough of Middletown*, 401 F. Supp. 1242 (M.D. Pa. 1975), *aff'd* without opinion 535 F.2d 1245 (3rd Cir. 1976), *cert denied* 429 U.S. 964 (1976)). But the Court has not spoken dispositively about juvenile curfews, and the circuits vary substantially (compare *Schleifer v. City of Charlottesville*, 159 F.3d 843 (4th Cir. 1998), upholding Charlottesville's ordinance, and *Nunez v. City of San Diego*, 114 F.3d 935 (9th Cir. 1997), striking San Diego's).

Most juvenile crime occurs during the three hours following school. Few studies find a strong correlation between curfews and crime reduction; most advocate after school and other programs to occupy the attention of children during the 3 p.m. to 10 p.m. period.[55] However, runaway prevention and truancy reduction do correlate with lower arrest incidence.

Truancy is dealt with somewhat differently among the states, but California's approach is typical. The state created School Attendance Review Boards (SARBs) in 1974. These SARBs include parents, school administrators, and local mental health and law enforcement representatives. Where a family fails to follow a SARB directive, the matter may be referred to the district attorney for possible status offense petition *vis-à-vis* the minor, or criminal prosecution against a parent where "willful neglect" has occurred in violation of the Penal Code.[56] As of 1994, the state had a four-step response: the first truancy triggers a written warning; the second truancy mandates attendance in a weekend program; the third requires attendance at the SARB mediation program; and the fourth triggers possible "ward of the court" designation, or a fine applied to the juvenile or to his parent, or other penalty—including loss of driving privileges.[57] Moreover, after 1995, amendments allow local jurisdictions to adopt loitering or curfew ordinances directed at youth during school hours, and authorize police to issue "notices to appear" in juvenile court. Rather than the common practice of simply returning the juvenile to school, this notice invokes court jurisdiction, and possible court orders across a panoply of remedies, including fines, driver's license suspension, required community work, or even dependency court jurisdiction and foster care placement.

Many schools deal with truancy through automatic phone calling systems where parents are notified by electronic voice that their child is absent. One does not have to replicate "Ferris Buehler's Day Off" to circumvent such a system. In contrast, the Los Angeles District Attorney initiated an aggressive program of parental notification, followed by personal service if necessary, with warnings (in groups) of the consequences of repeated truancy to the children and the parents. Such an approach has constitutional and practical difficulties where parents who are unable to control their children become the subject of criminal prosecution. However, supporters argue that the hard-line posture may give parents leverage with their children and strong motivation to monitor the school attendance of their children.

The runaway problem is significant, representing an estimated one million youth annually. Experts calculate that somewhere between 20% and 50% of these children have not fled their families as much as they were "thrownaway," either directly told to leave, or driven away through sexual abuse, beatings or extreme neglect. The problem is caused by private actors rather than the state directly. Since the Court has eschewed any affirmative duty of the state toward its children (see the leading *Deshaney* case, Chapter 12), and since the U.S. Constitution is directed toward state abuses, such abandoned children lack constitutional protection. The Congress and some states have enacted statutes directed at this population. Federally, the Runaway and Homeless Youth Act[58] provides modest grants to states to provide shelters and mental health and related services to help these youth.

E. COMMITMENT TO CIVIL INSTITUTIONS

Parham v. J.R.
442 U.S. 584 (1979)

MR. CHIEF JUSTICE BURGER delivered the opinion of the Court.

The question presented in this appeal is what process is constitutionally due a minor child whose parents or guardian seek state administered institutional mental health care for the child and specifically whether an adversary proceeding is required prior to or after the commitment.

I

(a) Appellee...J.R., a child being treated in a Georgia state mental hospital, was a plaintiff in this class action[2] based on 42 U.S.C. § 1983, in the District Court for the Middle District of Georgia. Appellants are the State's Commissioner of the Department of Human Resources, the Director of the Mental Health Division of the Department of Human Resources, and the Chief Medical Officer at the hospital where appellee was being treated. Appellee sought a declaratory judgment that Georgia's voluntary commitment procedures for children under the age of 18, Ga.

---

[2] The class certified by the District Court, without objection by appellants, consisted "of all persons younger than 18 years of age now or hereafter received by any defendant for observation and diagnosis and/or detained for care and treatment at any 'facility' within the State of Georgia pursuant to" Ga. Code § 88-503.1 (1975). Although one witness testified that on any given day there may be 200 children in the class, in December 1975 there were only 140.

Code §§ 88-503.1, 88-503.2 (1975),[3] violated the Due Process Clause of the Fourteenth Amendment and requested an injunction against their future enforcement.

* * *

(b) J.L., a plaintiff before the District Court who is now deceased, was admitted in 1970 at the age of 6 years to Central State Regional Hospital in Milledgeville, Ga. Prior to his admission, J.L. had received outpatient treatment at the hospital for over two months. J.L.'s mother then requested the hospital to admit him indefinitely.

The admitting physician interviewed J.L. and his parents. He learned that J.L.'s natural parents had divorced and his mother had remarried. He also learned that J.L. had been expelled from school because he was uncontrollable. He accepted the parents' representation that the boy had been extremely aggressive and diagnosed the child as having a "hyperkinetic reaction of childhood."

J.L.'s mother and stepfather agreed to participate in family therapy during the time their son was hospitalized. Under this program, J.L. was permitted to go home for short stays. Apparently his behavior during these visits was erratic. After several months, the parents requested discontinuance of the program.

In 1972, the child was returned to his mother and stepfather on a furlough basis, *i.e.*, he would live at home but go to school at the hospital. The parents found they were unable to control J.L. to their satisfaction, and this created family stress. Within two months, they requested his readmission to Central State. J.L.'s parents relinquished their parental rights to the county in 1974.

Although several hospital employees recommended that J.L. should be placed in a special foster home with "a warm, supported, truly involved couple," the Department of Family and Children Services was unable to place him in such a setting. On October 24, 1975, J.L. (with J.R.) filed this suit requesting an order of the court placing him in a less drastic environment suitable to his needs.

(c) Appellee J.R. was declared a neglected child by the county and removed from his natural parents when he was 3 months old. He was placed in seven different foster homes in succession prior to his admission to Central State Hospital at the age of 7.

Immediately preceding his hospitalization, J.R. received outpatient treatment at a county mental health center for several months. He then began attending school where he was so disruptive and incorrigible that he could not conform to normal behavior patterns. Because of his abnormal behavior, J.R.'s seventh set of foster parents requested his removal from their home. The Department of Family and Children Services then sought his admission at Central State....

* * *

(d) Georgia Code § 88-503.1 (1975) provides for the voluntary admission

---

[3] Section 88-503.1 provides:

"The superintendent of any facility may receive for observation and diagnosis...any individual under 18 years of age for whom such application is made by his parent or guardian....If found to show evidence of mental illness and to be suitable for treatment, such person may be given care and treatment at such facility and such person may be detained by such facility for such period and under such conditions as may be authorized by law."

Section 88-503.2 provides:

"The superintendent of the facility shall discharge any voluntary patient who has recovered from his mental illness or who has sufficiently improved that the superintendent determines that hospitalization of the patient is no longer desirable."

Section 88-503 was amended in some respects in 1978, but references herein are to the provisions in effect at the time in question.

to a state regional hospital of children such as J.L. and J.R. Under that provision, admission begins with an application for hospitalization signed by a "parent or guardian." Upon application, the superintendent of each hospital is given the power to admit temporarily any child for "observation and diagnosis." If, after observation, the superintendent finds "evidence of mental illness" and that the child is "suitable for treatment" in the hospital, then the child may be admitted "for such period and under such conditions as may be authorized by law."

Georgia's mental health statute also provides for the discharge of voluntary patients. Any child who has been hospitalized for more than five days may be discharged at the request of a parent or guardian. § 88-503.3 (a) (1975). Even without a request for discharge, however, the superintendent of each regional hospital has an affirmative duty to release any child "who has recovered from his mental illness or who has sufficiently improved that the superintendent determines that hospitalization of the patient is no longer desirable." § 88-503.2 (1975).

Georgia's Mental Health Director has not published any statewide regulations defining what specific procedures each superintendent must employ when admitting a child under 18. Instead, each regional hospital's superintendent is responsible for the procedures in his or her facility. There is substantial variation....

* * *

I

In holding unconstitutional Georgia's statutory procedure for voluntary commitment of juveniles, the District Court first determined that commitment to any of the eight regional hospitals...constitutes a severe deprivation of a child's liberty. The court defined this liberty interest in terms of both freedom from bodily restraint and freedom from the "emotional and psychic harm" caused by the institutionalization.[7] Having determined that a liberty interest is implicated by a child's admission to a mental hospital, the court considered what process is required to protect that interest. It held that the process due "includes at least the right after notice to be heard before an impartial tribunal."....

In requiring the prescribed hearing, the court rejected Georgia's argument that no adversary-type hearing was required since the State was merely assisting parents who could not afford private care by making available treatment similar to that offered in private hospitals and by private physicians. The court acknowledged that most parents who seek to have their children admitted to a state mental hospital do so in good faith. It, however, relied on one of appellees' witnesses who expressed an opinion that "some still look upon mental hospitals as a 'dumping ground.'"....[8] No specific evidence of such "dumping," however, can be found in the record.

The District Court also rejected the argument that review by the superintendents of the hospitals and their staffs was sufficient to protect the child's liberty interest. The court held that the inexactness of psychiatry, coupled

---

[7] In both respects, the District Court found strong support for its holding in this Court's decision in *In re Gault*, 387 U.S. 1 (1967). In that decision, we held that a state cannot institutionalize a juvenile delinquent without first providing certain due process protections.

[8] In light of the District Court's holding that a judicial or quasi-judicial body should review voluntary commitment decisions, it is at least interesting to note that the witness who made the statement quoted in the text was not referring to parents as the people who "dump" children into hospitals. This witness opined that some juvenile court judges and child welfare agencies misused the hospitals.

[11] In this part of the opinion, we will deal with the issues arising when the natural parents of the child seek commitment to a state hospital. In Part IV, we will deal with the situation presented when the child is a ward of the state.

with the possibility that the sources of information used to make the commitment decision may not always be reliable, made the superintendent's decision too arbitrary to satisfy due process....

III

...[W]e must consider first the child's interest in not being committed. Normally, however, since this interest is inextricably linked with the parents' interest in and obligation for the welfare and health of the child, the private interest at stake is a combination of the child's and parents' concerns.[11] Next, we must examine the State's interest in the procedures it has adopted for commitment and treatment of children. Finally, we must consider how well Georgia's procedures protect against arbitrariness in the decision to commit a child to a state mental hospital.

(a) It is not disputed that a child, in common with adults, has a substantial liberty interest in not being confined unnecessarily for medical treatment and that the state's involvement in the commitment decision constitutes state action under the Fourteenth Amendment....We also recognize that commitment sometimes produces adverse social consequences for the child because of the reaction of some to the discovery that the child has received psychiatric care....

* * *

(b) We next deal with the interests of the parents who have decided, on the basis of their observations and independent professional recommendations, that their child needs institutional care. Appellees argue that the constitutional rights of the child are of such magnitude and the likelihood of parental abuse is so great that the parents' traditional interests in and responsibility for the upbringing of their child must be subordinated at least to the extent of providing a formal adversary hearing prior to a voluntary commitment.

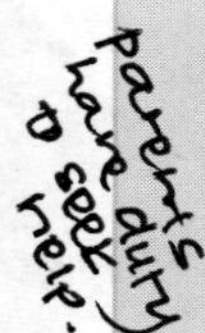

Our jurisprudence historically has reflected Western civilization concepts of the family as a unit with broad parental authority over minor children. Our cases have consistently followed that course; our constitutional system long ago rejected any notion that a child is "the mere creature of the State" and, on the contrary, asserted that parents generally "have the right, coupled with the high duty, to recognize and prepare [their children] for additional obligations." *Pierce v. Society of Sisters*, 268 U.S. 510, 535 (1925). See also *Wisconsin v. Yoder*, 406 U.S. 205, 213 (1972); *Prince v. Massachusetts*, 321 U.S. 158, 166 (1944); *Meyer v. Nebraska*, 262 U.S. 390, 400 (1923). Surely, this includes a "high duty" to recognize symptoms of illness and to seek and follow medical advice. The law's concept of the family rests on a presumption that parents possess what a child lacks in maturity, experience, and capacity for judgment required for making life's difficult decisions. More important, historically it has recognized that natural bonds of affection lead parents to act in the best interests of their children....

* * *

In defining the respective rights and prerogatives of the child and parent in the voluntary commitment setting, we conclude that our precedents permit the parents to retain a substantial, if not the dominant, role in the decision, absent a finding of neglect or abuse, and that the traditional presumption that the parents act in the best interests of their child should apply. We also conclude, however, that the child's rights and the nature of the commitment decision are such that parents cannot always have absolute and unreviewable discretion to decide whether to have a child institutionalized. They, of course, retain plenary authority to seek such care for their children, subject to a physician's independent examination and medical judgment.

(c) The State obviously has a significant interest in confining the use of its costly mental health facilities to cases of genuine need. The Georgia program seeks first to determine whether the patient seeking admission has an illness that calls for inpatient treatment. To accomplish this purpose, the State has charged the superintendents of each regional hospital with the responsibility for determining, before authorizing an admission, whether a prospective patient is mentally ill and whether the patient will likely benefit from hospital care. In addition, the State has imposed a continuing duty on hospital superintendents to release any patient who has recovered to the point where hospitalization is no longer needed.

The State in performing its voluntarily assumed mission also has a significant interest in not imposing unnecessary procedural obstacles that may discourage the mentally ill or their families from seeking needed psychiatric assistance. The *parens patriae* interest in helping parents care for the mental health of their children cannot be fulfilled if the parents are unwilling to take advantage of the opportunities because the admission process is too onerous, too embarrassing, or too contentious. It is surely not idle to speculate as to how many parents who believe they are acting in good faith would forgo state-provided hospital care if such care is contingent on participation in an adversary proceeding designed to probe their motives and other private family matters in seeking the voluntary admission.

The State also has a genuine interest in allocating priority to the diagnosis and treatment of patients as soon as they are admitted to a hospital rather than to time-consuming procedural minuets before the admission....One factor that must be considered is the utilization of the time of psychiatrists, psychologists, and other behavioral specialists in preparing for and participating in hearings rather than performing the task for which their special training has fitted them. Behavioral experts in courtrooms and hearings are of little help to patients.

* * *

(d) We now turn to consideration of what process protects adequately the child's constitutional rights....

* * *

Due process has never been thought to require that the neutral and detached trier of fact be law trained or a judicial or administrative officer....Surely, this is the case as to medical decisions, for "neither judges nor administrative hearing officers are better qualified than psychiatrists to render psychiatric judgments." *In re Roger S.*, 19 Cal. 3d 92 (1977)...Thus, a staff physician will suffice, so long as he or she is free to evaluate independently the child's mental and emotional condition and need for treatment.

It is not necessary that the deciding physician conduct a formal or quasi-formal hearing. A state is free to require such a hearing, but due process is not violated by use of informal, traditional medical investigative techniques....

* **

Here, the questions are essentially medical in character: whether the child is mentally or emotionally ill and whether he can benefit from the treatment that is provided by the state. While facts are plainly necessary for a proper resolution of those questions, they are only a first step in the process. In an opinion for a unanimous Court, we recently stated in *Addington v. Texas*, 441 U.S., at 429, that the determination of whether a person is mentally ill "turns on the meaning of the facts which must be interpreted by expert psychiatrists and psychologists."

* * *

Another problem with requiring a formalized, factfinding hearing lies in the danger it poses for significant intrusion into the parent-child relationship. Pitting the parents and child as adversaries often will be at odds with the presumption that parents act in the best interests of their child. It is one thing to require a neutral physician to make a careful review of the parents' decision in order to make sure it is proper from a medical standpoint; it is a wholly different matter to employ an adversary contest to ascertain whether the parents' motivation is consistent with the child's interests.

Moreover, it is appropriate to inquire into how such a hearing would contribute to the successful long-range treatment of the patient. Surely, there is a risk that it would exacerbate whatever tensions already exist between the child and the parents. Since the parents can and usually do play a significant role in the treatment while the child is hospitalized and even more so after release, there is a serious risk that an adversary confrontation will adversely affect the ability of the parents to assist the child while in the hospital. Moreover, it will make his subsequent return home more difficult. These unfortunate results are especially critical with an emotionally disturbed child; they seem likely to occur in the context of an adversary hearing in which the parents testify. A confrontation over such intimate family relationships would distress the normal adult parents and the impact on a disturbed child almost certainly would be significantly greater.[18]

It has been suggested that a hearing conducted by someone other than the admitting physician is necessary in order to detect instances where parents are "guilty of railroading their children into asylums" or are using "voluntary commitment procedures in order to sanction behavior of which they [disapprove]."....It is unrealistic to believe that trained psychiatrists, skilled in eliciting responses, sorting medically relevant facts, and sensing motivational nuances will often be deceived about the family situation surrounding a child's emotional disturbance.[19] Surely a lay, or even law-trained, factfinder would be no more skilled in this process than the professional.

* * *

At the regional hospital an admissions team composed of a psychiatrist and at least one other mental health professional examines and interviews the

---

[18] While not altogether clear, the District Court opinion apparently contemplated a hearing preceded by a written notice of the proposed commitment. At the hearing the child presumably would be given an opportunity to be heard and present evidence, and the right to cross-examine witnesses, including, of course, the parents. The court also required an impartial trier of fact who would render a written decision reciting the reasons for accepting or rejecting the parental application.

Since the parents in this situation are seeking the child's admission to the state institution, the procedure contemplated by the District Court presumably would call for some other person to be designated as a guardian *ad litem* to act for the child. The guardian, in turn, if not a lawyer, would be empowered to retain counsel to act as an advocate of the child's interest.

Of course, a state may elect to provide such adversary hearings in situations where it perceives that parents and a child may be at odds, but nothing in the Constitution compels such procedures.

[19] In evaluating the problem of detecting "dumping" by parents, it is important to keep in mind that each of the regional hospitals has a continuing relationship with the Department of Family and Children Services. The staffs at those hospitals refer cases to the Department when they suspect a child is being mistreated and thus are sensitive to this problem. In fact, J.L.'s situation is in point. The family conflicts and problems were well documented in the hospital records. Equally well documented, however, were the child's severe emotional disturbances and his need for treatment.

child—privately in most instances. This team then examines the medical records provided by the clinic staff and interviews the parents. Based on this information, and any additional background that can be obtained, the admissions team makes a diagnosis and determines whether the child will likely benefit from institutionalized care. If the team finds either condition not met, admission is refused.

If the team admits a child as suited for hospitalization, the child's condition and continuing need for hospital care are reviewed periodically by at least one independent, medical review group. For the most part, the reviews are as frequent as weekly, but none are less often than once every two months. Moreover, as we noted earlier, the superintendent of each hospital is charged with an affirmative statutory duty to discharge any child who is no longer mentally ill or in need of therapy.[21]

* * *

IV

(a) Our discussion in Part III was directed at the situation where a child's natural parents request his admission to a state mental hospital. Some members of appellees' class, including J.R., were wards of the State of Georgia at the time of their admission. Obviously their situation differs from those members of the class who have natural parents. While the determination of what process is due varies somewhat when the state, rather than a natural parent, makes the request for commitment, we conclude that the differences in the two situations do not justify requiring different procedures at the time of the child's initial admission to the hospital.

* * *

Indeed, if anything, the decision with regard to wards of the State may well be even more reasonable in light of the extensive written records that are compiled about each child while in the State's custody. In J.R.'s case, the admitting physician had a complete social and medical history of the child before even beginning the diagnosis. After carefully interviewing him and reviewing his extensive files, three physicians independently concluded that institutional care was in his best interests. See supra, at 590.

Since the state agency having custody and control of the child *in loco parentis* has a duty to consider the best interests of the child with respect to a decision on commitment to a mental hospital, the State may constitutionally allow that custodial agency to speak for the child, subject, of course, to the restrictions governing natural parents. On this record, we cannot declare unconstitutional Georgia's admission procedures for wards of the State.

* * *

Mr. Justice Brennan, with whom **Mr. Justice Marshall** and **Mr. Justice Stevens** join, concurring in part and dissenting in part.

I agree with the Court that the commitment of juveniles to state mental hospitals by their parents or by state officials acting *in loco parentis* involves state action that impacts upon constitutionally protected interests and therefore

---

[21] While the record does demonstrate that the procedures may vary from case to case, it also reflects that no child in Georgia was admitted for indefinite hospitalization without being interviewed personally and without the admitting physician's checking with secondary sources, such as school or work records.

must be accomplished through procedures consistent with the constitutional mandate of due process of law. I agree also that the District Court erred in interpreting the Due Process Clause to require preconfinement commitment hearings in all cases in which parents wish to hospitalize their children. I disagree, however, with the Court's decision to pretermit questions concerning the postadmission procedures due Georgia's institutionalized juveniles. While the question of the frequency of postadmission review hearings may properly be deferred, the right to at least one postadmission hearing can and should be affirmed now. I also disagree with the Court's conclusion concerning the procedures due juvenile wards of the State of Georgia. I believe that the Georgia statute is unconstitutional in that it fails to accord preconfinement hearings to juvenile wards of the State committed by the State acting *in loco parentis*.

I

RIGHTS OF CHILDREN COMMITTED TO MENTAL INSTITUTIONS

Commitment to a mental institution necessarily entails a "massive curtailment of liberty,"...and inevitably affects "fundamental rights."....Persons incarcerated in mental hospitals are not only deprived of their physical liberty, they are also deprived of friends, family, and community. Institutionalized mental patients must live in unnatural surroundings under the continuous and detailed control of strangers. They are subject to intrusive treatment which, especially if unwarranted, may violate their right to bodily integrity. Such treatment modalities may include forced administration of psychotropic medication,...aversive conditioning, ...convulsive therapy,...and even psychosurgery...Furthermore, as the Court recognizes,...persons confined in mental institutions are stigmatized as sick and abnormal during confinement and, in some cases, even after release....

Because of these considerations, our cases have made clear that commitment to a mental hospital "is a deprivation of liberty which the State cannot accomplish without due process of law." *O'Connor v. Donaldson*, 422 U.S. 563, 580 (1975)....In the absence of a voluntary, knowing, and intelligent waiver, adults facing commitment to mental institutions are entitled to full and fair adversary hearings in which the necessity for their commitment is established to the satisfaction of a neutral tribunal. At such hearings they must be accorded the right of "be present with counsel, have an opportunity to be heard, be confronted with witnesses against [them], have the right to cross-examine, and to offer evidence of [their] own."....

These principles also govern the commitment of children. "Constitutional rights do not mature and come into being magically only when one attains the state-defined age of majority. Minors, as well as adults, are protected by the Constitution and possess constitutional rights....

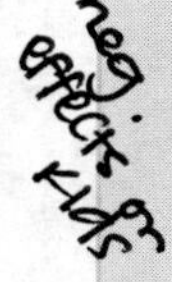

Indeed, it may well be argued that children are entitled to more protection than are adults. The consequences of an erroneous commitment decision are more tragic where children are involved. Children, on the average, are confined for longer periods than are adults....Moreover, childhood is a particularly vulnerable time of life...and children erroneously institutionalized during their formative years may bear the scars for the rest of their lives....Furthermore, the provision of satisfactory institutionalized mental care for children generally requires a substantial financial commitment...that too often has not been forthcoming.... Decisions of the lower courts have chronicled the inadequacies of existing mental health facilities for children....

In addition, the chances of an erroneous commitment decision are particularly great where children are involved. Even under the best of circumstances psychiatric diagnosis and therapy decisions are fraught with uncertainties. See O'Connor v. Donaldson, supra, at 584...These uncertainties are aggravated when, as under the Georgia practice, the psychiatrist interviews the child during a period of abnormal stress in connection with the commitment, and without adequate time or opportunity to become acquainted with the patient....These uncertainties may be further aggravated when economic and social class separate doctor and child, thereby frustrating the accurate diagnosis of pathology....

These compounded uncertainties often lead to erroneous commitments since psychiatrists tend to err on the side of medical caution and therefore hospitalize patients for whom other dispositions would be more beneficial....The National Institute of Mental Health recently found that only 36% of patients below age 20 who were confined at St. Elizabeths Hospital actually required such hospitalization....Of particular relevance to this case, a Georgia study Commission on Mental Health Services for Children and Youth concluded that more than half of the State's institutionalized children were not in need of confinement if other forms of care were made available or used. Cited in J.L. v. Parham, 412 F.Supp. 112, 122 (MD Ga. 1976).

I

Rights of Children Committed by Their Parents

A

Notwithstanding all this, Georgia denies hearings to juveniles institutionalized at the behest of their parents. Georgia rationalizes this practice on the theory that parents act in their children's best interests and therefore may waive their children's due process rights. Children incarcerated because their parents wish them confined, Georgia contends, are really voluntary patients. I cannot accept this argument.

In our society, parental rights are limited by the legitimate rights and interests of their children. "Parents may be free to become martyrs themselves. But it does not follow they are free, in identical circumstances, to make martyrs of their children before they have reached the age of full and legal discretion when they can make that choice for themselves." *Prince v. Massachusetts*, 321 U.S. 158, 170 (1944)....

* * *

Additional considerations counsel against allowing parents unfettered power to institutionalize their children without cause or without any hearing to ascertain that cause. The presumption that parents act in their children's best interests, while applicable to most child-rearing decisions, is not applicable in the commitment context. Numerous studies reveal that parental decisions to institutionalize their children often are the results of dislocation in the family unrelated to the children's mental condition....Moreover, even well-meaning parents lack the expertise necessary to evaluate the relative advantages and disadvantages of inpatient as opposed to outpatient psychiatric treatment. Parental decisions to waive hearings in which such questions could be explored, therefore, cannot be conclusively deemed either informed or intelligent. In these circumstances, I respectfully suggest, it ignores reality to assume blindly that parents act in their children's best interests when making commitment decisions and when waiving their children's due process rights.

B

This does not mean States are obliged to treat children who are committed at the behest of their parents in precisely the same manner as other persons who are involuntarily committed. The demands of due process are flexible and the parental commitment decision carries with it practical implications that States may legitimately take into account. While as a general rule due process requires that commitment hearings precede involuntary hospitalization, when parents seek to hospitalize their children special considerations militate in favor of postponement of formal commitment proceedings and against mandatory adversary preconfinement commitment hearings.

First, the prospect of an adversary hearing prior to admission might deter parents from seeking needed medical attention for their children. Second, the hearings themselves might delay treatment of children whose home life has become impossible and who require some form of immediate state care. Furthermore, because adversary hearings at this juncture would necessarily involve direct challenges to parental authority, judgment, or veracity, preadmission hearings may well result in pitting the child and his advocate against the parents. This, in turn, might traumatize both parent and child and make the child's eventual return to his family more difficult.

Because of these special considerations, I believe that States may legitimately postpone formal commitment proceedings when parents seek inpatient psychiatric treatment for their children. Such children may be admitted, for a limited period, without prior hearing, so long as the admitting psychiatrist first interviews parent and child and concludes that short-term inpatient treatment would be appropriate.

Georgia's present admission procedures are reasonably consistent with these principles....To the extent the District Court invalidated this aspect of the Georgia juvenile commitment scheme and mandated preconfinement hearings in all cases, I agree with the Court that the District Court was in error.

C

I do not believe, however, that the present Georgia juvenile commitment scheme is constitutional in its entirety. Although Georgia may postpone formal commitment hearings, when parents seek to commit their children, the State cannot dispense with such hearings altogether....

The informal postadmission procedures that Georgia now follows are simply not enough to qualify as hearings—let alone reasonably prompt hearings. The procedures lack all the traditional due process safeguards. Commitment decisions are made *ex parte*. Georgia's institutionalized juveniles are not informed of the reasons for their commitment; nor do they enjoy the right to be present at the commitment determination, the right to representation, the right to be heard, the right to be confronted with adverse witnesses, the right to cross-examine, or the right to offer evidence of their own. By any standard of due process, these procedures are deficient....I cannot understand why the Court pretermits condemnation of these *ex parte* procedures which operate to deny Georgia's institutionalized juveniles even "some form of hearing," *Mathews v. Eldridge*, *supra*, at 333, before they are condemned to suffer the rigors of long-term institutional confinement.[21]

The special considerations that militate against preadmission commitment hearings when parents seek to hospitalize their children do not militate against reasonably prompt postadmission commitment hearings. In the first place, postadmission hearings would not delay the commencement of needed treatment. Children could be cared for by the State pending the disposition decision.

Second, the interest in avoiding family discord would be less significant at this stage since the family autonomy already will have been fractured by the

---

[21]The National Institute of Mental Health has reported: "[Thousands] upon thousands of elderly patients now confined on the back wards of...state [mental] institutions were first admitted as children thirty, forty, and even fifty years ago. A recent report from one state estimates that one in every four children admitted to its mental hospitals 'can anticipate being permanently hospitalized for the next 50 years of their lives.'" Joint Commission on Mental Health of Children, *supra* n. 9, at 5-6.

institutionalization of the child. In any event, postadmission hearings are unlikely to disrupt family relationships. At later hearings, the case for and against commitment would be based upon the observations of the hospital staff and the judgments of the staff psychiatrists, rather than upon parental observations and recommendations....

* * *

Nor can the good faith and good intentions of Georgia's psychiatrists and social workers, adverted to by the Court,...excuse Georgia's *ex parte* procedures. Georgia's admitting psychiatrists, like the school disciplinarians described in *Goss v. Lopez*, 419 U.S. 565 (1975), "although proceeding in utmost good faith, frequently act on the reports and advice of others; and the controlling facts and the nature of the conduct under challenge are often disputed."....Here, as in *Goss*, the "risk of error is not at all trivial, and it should be guarded against if that may be done without prohibitive cost or interference with the...process....'[Fairness] can rarely be obtained by secret, one-sided determination of facts decisive of rights....' 'Secrecy is not congenial to truth-seeking and self-righteousness gives too slender an assurance of rightness. No better instrument has been devised for arriving at truth than to give a person in jeopardy of serious loss notice of the case against him and opportunity to meet it.'"....

III

RIGHTS OF CHILDREN COMMITTED BY THEIR STATE GUARDIANS

Georgia does not accord prior hearings to juvenile wards of the State of Georgia committed by state social workers acting *in loco parentis*. The Court dismisses a challenge to this practice on the grounds that state social workers are obliged by statute to act in the children's best interest....

* * *

To my mind, there is no justification for denying children committed by their social workers the prior hearings that the Constitution typically requires. In the first place, such children cannot be said to have waived their rights to a prior hearing simply because their social workers wished them to be confined. The rule that parents speak for their children, even if it were applicable in the commitment context, cannot be transmuted into a rule that state social workers speak for their minor clients....

* * *

IV

Children incarcerated in public mental institutions are constitutionally entitled to a fair opportunity to contest the legitimacy of their confinement. They are entitled to some champion who can speak on their behalf and who stands ready to oppose a wrongful commitment. Georgia should not be permitted to deny that opportunity and that champion simply because the children's parents or guardians wish them to be confined without a hearing. The risk of erroneous commitment is simply too great unless there is some form of adversary review. And fairness demands that children abandoned by their supposed protectors to the rigors of institutional confinement be given the help of some separate voice.

Questions for Discussion

1. Is *Parham* consistent with *Gault*? Is it appropriate to assume that parents and physicians interacting with children are acting in their best interests and do not require judicial check? Are not the police sworn to obey the law and apprehend the guilty, and are not public prosecutors sworn to seek a just resolution? Why do we not rely on their judgment in the adult criminal justice system? Why don't we rely solely on the judgment of caring relatives and physicians for the civil commitment of adults?

2. The majority opinion cites the "natural bonds of affection" which lead parents to act in the best interests of their children. Is such reliance consistent with the three million annual child abuse reports received? With the numerous adjudications of parental neglect and unfitness in juvenile dependency courts? Is it appropriate where the context is a parental attempt to remove a child from the family and place him into state institution confinement?

3. The opinion notes that there is "no evidence of bad faith" by the parents in *Parham*. If such bad faith were to exist, would it be detected under the Court's procedural rights holding?

4. The Court finds that many parents would forego mental health services if an adversary hearing were required. What is the empirical basis (evidence) for that finding? If accurate, is a check possible without a hostile adversarial approach? If an attorney is assigned to represent such a child and the parents are acting in the child's best interests, would not such an attorney be cooperative? Why should counsel be confrontational where all concerned care about and are trying to help his client?

5. The holding here finds sufficient constitutional check from the review of the hospital director. Is such an official adequately neutral? Is there a possible budgetary or other conflict that might compromise such a review? Do we allow the director of a mental hospital to serve as the primary check on adult admissions? Is it enough that an independent medical group "reviews" programs? How does such a review take place? Is the child heard? Does anybody speak for the child, separate from institution officials?

6. The decision argues that the questions at issue are "medical" and properly left to psychiatrists. Do we delegate psychiatric judgments about diminished capacity in any adult context to such experts—as the final decision makers?

7. The dissent argues for at least one post-admission hearing, and complains that juveniles are not even told the reasons for their confinement. Is the dissent an ambitious defense of the rights of children? Does it reflect a high priority that the involuntary confinement of children be considered seriously, that checks on abuse exist, and that care be taken to prevent error?

F. MAJOR FEDERAL DELINQUENCY-RELATED STATUTES AND PROGRAMS

Major federal statutes addressing juvenile justice include:

- The Juvenile Justice and Delinquency Prevention Act of 1974 (42 U.S.C. § 5601 *et seq.*) established the Office of Juvenile Justice and Delinquency Prevention (OJJDP) within the Justice Department to administer a series of state/local grants.

- The Violent Crime Control and Law Enforcement Act of 1994 (P.L. 103-322) is a major source of juvenile delinquency related funding, particularly on the prevention side. It potentially provides up to $6.9 billion for crime prevention programs which could be directed at juveniles, although little funding has been appropriated on the prevention side as of 2006.

- The 1998 Federal Juvenile Accountability Incentives Block Grant provides a national $250 million Block Grant, divided between states based on juvenile population. Three-fourths of the funds must flow through to local governments based on law enforcement spending and rate of violent crime, with the states arranging "juvenile crime enforcement coalitions" monitored by the OJJDP. Funds may be used for one or more of twelve purposes, most of which involve prosecution enhancement (additional prosecutors, specialized gang, drug, and youth violence units), "accountability based programs" for juveniles, and closer probation monitoring. Funding may also include "gun courts," "drug courts," and information sharing between criminal justice systems, schools, and social workers.[59] To be eligible, states must "actively consider" legislation to prosecute more juveniles as adults, implement graduated sanctions for juveniles, enhance record keeping, and must not enact laws which prevent judges from holding parents responsible for the actions of their children.

- The Safe Schools Initiative is funded at $225 million per year nationally, and provides grants for school security measures.

- Others. A host of minor programs exist within JJDPA jurisdiction and outside of it. During the 1990s and to 2005, the federal budget has included modestly funded grant and monitoring programs in the $5 to $50 million range for youth gang prevention, youth mentoring, creation of a National Sex Offender Registry, grants for boys and girls clubs, drug and underage drinking prevention, and a Department of Education program to train incarcerated youthful offenders for release transition to work.

Experts reviewing the federal programs note that while juvenile justice spending increased somewhat in the 1990s, most new spending remains on the punitive side. Those accounts allowing prevention programs within the states are few and there are "lots of strings attached."[60] A General Accounting Office survey of federal programs relevant to at-risk and delinquent youth found 110 different programs spending $4 billion nationally through 15 different departments and agencies, including 45 on substance abuse prevention, 20 on substance abuse treatment, and 57 on violence prevention. The GAO concluded that the programs are fragmented, uncoordinated, and lack information about results, notwithstanding recent passage of a federal Government Performance and Results Act to compel outcome measurement.[61]

In general, federal spending policy has swung from prevention funding favored by Democrats to law enforcement measures proposed by Republicans, as the political make-up of the Congress has changed. On the law enforcement side have been such measures as H.R. 3565/H.R. 3 (McCollum, R-FL), and S.10/ S. 254 (Hatch, R-UT). These have included in various versions mandatory prosecution of juveniles over the age of 14 as adults for serious federal crimes, with a federal prosecutor option to prosecute 13-year-olds as adults. Juveniles may be housed with adult prisoners, and juvenile confidentiality would be removed or altered consistent with adult proceedings. Grants would be available only to states enacting statutes similarly so providing. These bills competed from 2002 to 2006 with measures such as H.R. 278 (Schumer, D-NY), the "Balanced Juvenile Justice and Crime Prevention Act," which would provide additional authority to federal prosecutors to try children as adults, increase juvenile record disclosure where offenses are serious, and accelerate trial of gun-involved offenses, and would couple these provisions with individualized sanctions, juvenile drug courts, and after-school crime prevention programs and grants.

ENDNOTES

[1] U.S. Department of Justice, Office of Juvenile Justice and Delinquency Prevention, *Easy Access to FBI Arrest Statistics: 1994–2002: Arrest Statistics* (Washington, D.C.), available at www.ojjdp.ncjrs.org.

[2] *Id.*

[3] *Id.*

[4] Office of Juvenile Justice and Delinquency Prevention, *Juvenile Offenders and Victims: 1999 National Report* (Washington, D.C.; 1999) at 26.

[5] *Id.* at 16.

[6] *Id.* at 17.

[7] *Id.* at 18.

[8] David Finkelhor and Richard Ormrod, Office of Juvenile Justice and Delinquency Prevention, *Reporting Crimes Against Juveniles* (Washington, D.C.; Nov. 1999) at 1–7. Self-reporting is limited where the victim is inarticulate or young. Even where a report exists regarding violence against a child, it may be reported to school officials, or to local child protective services authorities and not become part of criminal justice statistics.

[9] Joseph F. Sheley, Ph.D., and James D. Wright, Ph.D., *Gun Acquisition and Possession in Selected Juvenile Samples*, Nat'l Inst. of Justice Research in Brief (1993).

[10] See Coalition for America's Children, *Children and Violence* (Washington, D.C.; 1995) at 4.

[11] *Id.*

[12] Office of Juvenile Justice and Delinquency Prevention, U.S. Department of Justice, *Juvenile Offenders and Victims: 1996 Update on Violence (Statistics Summary)* (Washington, D.C.; Feb. 1996) at 21.

[13] See Julie Marquis, *Study Finds Alarming Rate of Risky Behaviors by Boy Teens*, L.A. Times, May 8, 1998, at A-1, A-47 (reporting on a study by Charles F. Turner of the Research Triangle Institute in Washington, D.C., the findings of which were published on May 8, 1998 in Science).

[14] For a detailed statistical breakdown of crime reporting by public schools in 2000, see http://nces.ed.gov.

[15] Elizabeth Donohue, Vincent Schiraldi, and Jason Ziedenberg, Justice Policy Institute, *School House Hype: School Shootings and the Real Risks Kids Face in America* (Center on Criminal and Juvenile Justice; July 1998).

[16] Office of Juvenile Justice and Delinquency Prevention (OJJDP), *Juvenile Offenders and Victims: 1999 National Report* (Washington, D.C.; 2000) at 51 (see http://www.ncjrs.org/html/ojjdp/nationalreport99/chapter3.pdf).

[17] Joseph Sheley and James Wright, *High School Youths, Weapons, and Violence: A National Survey*, National Institute of Justice Research in Brief (Oct. 1998) at 1.

[18] *Id.* It also supports the thesis that one possible major inducement to higher rates of youth carrying guns is the impression advanced by the media that it is now more common than is the case, thus invoking the self-defense justification, and perhaps leading to a self-fulfilling result.

[19] See Paul Farhi, *Study Finds Real Harm in TV Violence*, Wash. Post (Feb. 6, 1996) at A1; see also Bill Carter, *A New Report Becomes a Weapon in Debate on Censoring TV Violence*, N. Y. Times, Feb. 6, 1996, at C11.

[20] See Richard Huff, *TV Rolls with Punches*, N.Y. Daily News, Apr. 17, 1998 (quoting Dale Kunkel, Professor of Communication at UC Santa Barbara, and discussing the National Television Violence

Study).

[21] *Children and Violence, supra* note 10, at 7, citing *Growing Up Scared*, Newsweek, Jan. 10, 1994, at 44.

[22] Brandon S. Centerwall M.D., M.P.H., *Television and Violence*, 267:22 JAMA 3059 (June 10, 1992).

[23] *Id.* at 3060.

[24] *Id.*

[25] *Id.,* citing the Joy *et al.* study; aggressiveness was measured objectively by recording rates of hitting, shoving, and biting (physical fighting).

[26] *Id.*, citing the Huesmann study of 875 children.

[27] *Id.* at 3060–62. The author cites the advice of the American Academy of Pediatrics that children be restricted to one to two hours of television per day, and recommends the now developing "V-Chip" option to enable parents to decide what their children should see.

[28] See discussion of the evidence in David Grossman, *Stop Teaching Our Kids to Kill: A Call to Action Against TV, Movie and Video Game Violence* (Crown Publishing, 1999).

[29] Kaiser Family Foundation, *How Parents Feel (and What They Know) About TV, the V-Chip, and the TV Ratings System* (Menlo Park, CA; May 1999) at 11, 13, 16. The survey found 62% favoring content based ratings as the "most useful" (at 11), that 72% would buy a television at the same cost with a V-Chip, that 77% would use it to filter shows viewed by their children. The poll, compared with one just one year earlier, shows remarkable increases in computer and internet access. As of 1999, 80% of households had cable or satellite TV, 63% had personal computers, and 50% had access to the Internet—up from 38% in 1998. *Id.* at 15.

[30] *Kids & Media–The New Millennium*, Kaiser Family Foundation (Nov. 2000), *passim.*

[31] "Comprehensive reports from the Centers for Disease Control and Prevention, The National Research Center, The American Psychological Association and the Office of Juvenile Justice and Delinquency Prevention link youth violence with these risk factors: a history of child abuse or family violence, cultural acceptance of violence, childhood behavior disorders, school failure, poor self-esteem and unemployment." *Children and Violence, supra* note 10, at 2.

[32] "The damage begins early and is often imprinted for life. A recent study...recounts the testimony of experts who have identified post-traumatic stress symptoms in infants and toddlers who were exposed to violence in their first year of life...." *Id.* at 2, quoting *Hurt, Healing, Hope: Caring for Infants and Toddlers in Violent Environments,* Zero to Three/National Center for Clinical Infant Programs (1994) at 5.

[33] The CII Forum, *Understanding Kids Who Kill*, Children's Institute International (Los Angeles, CA; Fall 1999) at 1.

[34] Child advocates generally prefer to see the dependency court proceeding take precedence to seek an outcome of close foster care supervision by a person skilled in influencing the respondent, or in adoption by attentive parents who will redirect their new child. See Sonia Nazario, *Sex, Drugs and No Place To Go*, L.A. Times, Dec. 12, 1993, at A-1; see also Chapter 8.

[35] National Institute of Justice, *The Cycle of Violence Revisited*, Research Preview (Feb. 1996) at 1.

[36] Office of Juvenile Justice and Delinquency Prevention, U.S. Department of Justice, *Juvenile Offenders and Victims: 1997 Update on Violence* (Washington, D.C.; 1997), at Arrests 1980, 1992–1997 Table; the felony arrest rate is 1,506 per 100,000, or 1.5% of the population in the same year of 1994, with the most recent 1997 figure at 1.4%

[37] *Cycle of Violence, supra* note 35, at 1.

[38] *Children and Violence*, *supra*, at 5.

[39] Office of Juvenile Justice and Delinquency Prevention, U.S. Department of Justice, *Juvenile Offenders and Victims: 1996 Update on Violence* (Statistics Summary) (Washington, D.C.; Feb. 1996) at 7.

[40] *Id.*

[41] Luntz Research Companies (for the National Center on Addiction and Substance Abuse at Columbia University), *CASA 1997 Back to School Survey* (New York, NY; Aug. 1997). See also Dina Bass, *Poll Finds Sharp Rise in Drug Use Among Youngsters*, L.A. Times, Aug. 14, 1997, at 1.

[42] See *Risky Behaviors, supra* note 13, at A-47.

[43] *Id.* at 73, presenting data from the *1997 Youth Risk Surveillance.*

[44] Partnership for a Drug-Free America, *The Boomer-Rang: Baby Boomers Seriously Underestimating Presence of Drugs in Their Children's Lives* (New York, NY; April 1998). See also Ronald J. Ostrow, *Parents Underrate Children's Exposure to Drugs*, L.A. Times, Apr. 13, 1998, at A-14.

[45] Nancy Sconyers and Monica Heuer, National Association of Child Advocates, *The Link Between Father Absence and Youth Incarceration,* Youth Development and Juvenile Justice Update (Feb. 5, 1999) at 1–2, reporting the findings of Sarah McLanahan and Cynthia Harper presented to the American Sociological Association in San Francisco in 1998, based on data from the National Longitudinal Survey on Youth.

[46] *Id.* The one exception to improvement from fathers comes from stepfather involvement. It did not improve results, a predictable outcome given the often transitory record of many stepfathers, enhanced insecurities in the relationship, and the common competitive problems involved in having someone as a parent who is focused on a child's mother as the preeminent relationship.

[47] *1996 Update on Violence, supra* note 39, at 6–7. The 1989 survey was the National Crime Victimization Survey with a national sample of students aged 12 to 19; the 1993 study was by the National Center for Education Statistics surveying a similar national sample of sixth- through twelfth-graders.

[48] See *1999 National Report, supra* note 4, at 77–79.

[49] The federal Juvenile Justice and Delinquency Prevention Act of 1974, Pub. L. No. 93-415, 42 U.S.C. § 5601 *et seq.*, requires, as a precondition of receiving certain federal grants, that truants, runaways, children "out of control" of parents, curfew violators, or the incorrigible not be held in locked facilities or housed with delinquents. The decriminalization of these offenses was intended to decrease their incidence as a gateway to criminality, treat troubled youth more humanely, with a measure of due process, and promote their rehabilitation. This Act created the Office of Juvenile Justice and Delinquency Prevention, which remains the federal government's major delinquency prevention centerpiece.

[50] David J. Steinhart, *Status Offenses*, 6:3 The Future of Children: The Juvenile Court 86, 93 (Richard E. Behrman, M.D., ed. 1996).

[51] *Id.*

[52] *Children and Violence, supra* note 10, at 3, citing J. Garbino, National Association for the Education of Young Children, *Helping Children Cope with the Effects of Community Violence* (New Orleans, LA; 1992); L. Wallach, *Helping Young Children Cope with Violence,* 48:4 Young Children 4-11; L. J. Schweinhart, H. V. Barnes, and D. R. Weikart, High/Scope Educational Research Foundation, *The High/Scope Perry Preschool Study Through Age 27* (Ypsilanti, MI; 1993).

[53] See Peter W. Greenwood, *Responding to Juvenile Crime: Lessons Learned*, 6:3 The Future of Children: The Juvenile Court 75, 77 (Richard E. Behrman, M.D., ed. 1996) at 77.

[54] Cal. Welf. & Inst. Code § 18220(h) (legislative findings for Comprehensive Youth Services Act).

[55] See *e.g,*. Howard Snyder and Melissa Sickmund, *Juvenile Offenders and Victims: 1999 National Report 65* (OJJDP 1999).

[56] Cal. Penal Code §§ 270–72.

[57] SB 1728 (Hughes) (California Chapter 1023, Statutes of 1994).

[58] 42 U.S.C. § 5700 *et seq.*

[59] See discussion in *Juvenile Justice: States May Apply for Their Share of Juvenile Crime Block Grant*, Children and Youth Funding Report (Silver Spring, MD; April 9, 1998) at 8.

[60] See *Spending of Justice Department Tackles Juvenile Crime But Ignores Prevention*, Children and Youth Funding Report (Silver Spring, MD; Nov. 25, 1997) at 11.

[61] Cornelia M. Blanchette, U.S. General Accounting Office, *At-Risk and Delinquent Youth: Multiple Programs Lack Coordinated Federal Effort* (GAO/T-HEHS-98-38) (Washington, D.C.; Nov. 5, 1997) at 1–12 (testimony before the U.S. Senate's Subcommittee on Youth Violence, Committee on the Judiciary).

CHAPTER ELEVEN

Child Rights to Custody, Family Support and Emancipation

A. CHILD CUSTODY

1. In General

Questions about child custody arise in a variety of contexts: adoption, divorce, abuse, parental death, incapacitation, or abandonment. The question of who is the parent or guardian or custodian of a child may evolve from proceedings in general civil, probate, family, or juvenile court departments—each subject to its own rules.

One of the most important differences between the respective types of courts adjudicating child custody issues is the representation of the child. Commonly, a child has no separate counsel in general civil, probate, or family court—even where his or her rights and future are at issue. Children are generally given a *guardian ad litem* in juvenile dependency court—which can assume civil jurisdiction over allegedly abused or neglected children for their protection. Federal law requires such an appointment to receive child welfare funds from the Congress. Increasingly, such appointees are attorneys. In practice, parents are assured of counsel in juvenile dependency court where their basic right to parental status is implicated. They receive an attorney at public cost if they are indigent (see below).

2. Paternal Assertion of Parental Rights

Paternal rights are most commonly litigated in family court, where child support orders may be framed obligating biological or otherwise liable fathers to support children as part of a marriage dissolution proceeding. With marriage, the involvement of the family court in arranging for child custody upon divorce creates a system for tracking parental rights and maintaining some parental role upon the separation of parents. Apart from this divorce/custody circumstance is the difficult problem of paternal status where the birth is to an unwed mother. As discussed in Chapter 2, 30% of current births are to unwed mothers, with numbers of such births increasing from 243,000 in 1960 to over 7 million by 2006. Here, assertion of paternal rights may take the form of a refusal to consent to a child's placement for adoption as sought by the child's mother, an attempt at visitation or some continuing role in the life of the child, or even full custody. This difficult context has raised emotional issues in highly publicized cases where adoptive parents were compelled to return children to the biological father even when the unwed mother had supported adoption by others. On occasion, such custody contests occur only after several years of care by prospective adoptive couples as the cases wind through the appellate courts.

The determination of paternity rights usually depends in the first instance on the "status of the father." That status is defined from a vocabulary created by applicable statutes and court decisions. The "terms of art" outline the following paternal categories:

(1) An "alleged father," refers to a person who may be a biological father, but biological paternity has not been established.

(2) A "biological" father (sometimes pejoratively referred to as a "mere biological" father in case law) refers to a person who has been confirmed as the biological father of a child, but who has not achieved "presumed" fatherhood status as defined in most state statutes.

(3) A "*Kelsey*" father refers to a biological father who promptly attempted to assume his paternal responsibility as fully as circumstances allow under the criteria of *Adoption of Kelsey S.* (1992) 1 Cal.4th 816 (see *infra*).

(4) A "*de facto*" father (or parent) may be reasonably regarded as a parent by a child and is based on actual parental performance.

(5) A "presumed" father is one who meets the criteria of state statutes allowing presumptive (but rebuttable) fatherhood status.

The Uniform Parentage Act (UPA)[1] has been adopted in eighteen states and provides for "presumed" fatherhood status where he and the child's natural mother are or have been married to each other *and* (a) the child is born during the marriage or within 300 days after the marriage is terminated by death, annulment, divorce or separation decree; *or* (b) the man receives the child into his home and openly holds the child out as his own.

In general, presumed fatherhood status is rebuttable by clear and convincing evidence; a paternity judgment establishing another man as the biological father provides such a showing. However, a practical challenge to a presumptive father from another claimant may turn on legal standing to challenge the presumed status of another, as discussed below. A common conundrum occurs when a father does not welcome a child into his home (technically required for presumed father status) only because he is deprived of the placement of the child over his objection. Where a paternal role is sought in good faith, some courts hold that "taking into the home" is not required and may be excused. Some courts give such fathers "*Kelsey*" father status just short of a presumed father, and still others would designate such a person an "equitable" father—meaning he is fulfilling the function but without all of the rights commonly ascribed to parents.

Over the past three decades, paternity rights and obligations have been much affected by:

(1) the withdrawal of marriage as a permissibly exclusive bright line test for parenthood status;

(2) the use of biology as a strong criterion for parental child *support* financial obligation (including repayment of the state for welfare paid for the children of biological fathers);

(3) the growth of single parent families, and the increasing problem of paternal abandonment of children;

(4) the assertion and exercise of a woman's prerogative to abort, and to make decisions concerning the adoption of children.

Some of these developments clash, particularly where fathers seek to claim a fatherhood role. Where large numbers of children are born not because they are intended, what are the implications for the biological father's parental rights? We do not allocate children to the wealthiest or most able or most loving available adults; historically we start with biology and marriage as the two critical factors. How does biology alone work where there is little connection between impregnation and intent or ability to be a father (or mother)? What do we do when a mother wants the child adopted by a "better" family for the child's own good and believes the biological father to be dangerous? The legal status of "father" (as with "mother") invokes a constitutionally protected "fundamental liberty interest" to parent. Is reliance on biology alone to confer that status over-inclusive? But is "marriage" as an alternative criterion under-inclusive where fathers in fact function as such without marrying the mothers of their children? What do we do when an otherwise able and willing unmarried father wanted to and would have so functioned but is deceived about his biological role and only learns of it well after the birth?

As with most legal questions, the answers are much influenced by whose shoes we occupy in answering. Are the child's shoes occupied in the decisions considering the rights and obligations of contesting parents? Is there an element viewing the child as a prize to be awarded to the adult less "in the wrong," as if an object subject to competing ownership claims? Does such an "in the wrong" analysis include recognition of children as fully participating parties?

Related questions also arise in the difficult adjudications determining these rights. Must the answer to custody questions be absolute, either "x" or "y" is the sole custodian? In divorce, there is a trend to grant "joint custody" to both parents where possible—in the interest of the child. There is a compelled sharing. Is some role possible for a biological father, who may have delayed too long to be recognized as the father without removing a happy child from a successful adoptive family, but who still may have something to contribute? We celebrate uncles and cousins and extended family involvement in the lives of children; should we allow some role for the *bona fide* assertion of another adult wanting to care for a child—particularly in a society starved for paternal concern? But what if such a claimant is a bad influence, or a danger, in the rational view of those charged with his or her custody? How do the courts draw reasonably clear and predictable lines in such matters without becoming overly enmeshed in family disputes?

One variable, not much discussed, has to do with the impact of the legal process itself: where the major harm to a child caught in a custody dispute is to bond and then to be taken from loving arms, what responsibility does the judiciary have to make a timely decision? To what extent does physical custody during adjudication determine the outcome? Where it does not determine the outcome, what is the impact of a decision to disturb the custody arrangement after a delay of two to five years and after inevitable reliance by the child on the functioning parents *pendente lite*?

Stanley v. Illinois
405 U.S. 645 (1972)

Mr. Justice White delivered the opinion of the Court.

Joan Stanley lived with Peter Stanley intermittently for 18 years, during which time they had three children...When Joan Stanley died, Peter Stanley lost not only her but also his children. Under Illinois law, the children of unwed fathers become wards of the State upon the death of the mother. Accordingly, upon Joan Stanley's death, in a dependency proceeding instituted by the State of Illinois, Stanley's children[3] were declared wards of the State and placed with court-appointed guardians. Stanley appealed, claiming that he had never been shown to be an unfit parent and that since married fathers and unwed mothers could not be deprived of their children without such a showing, he had been deprived of the equal protection of the laws guaranteed him by the Fourteenth Amendment. The Illinois Supreme Court accepted the fact that Stanley's own unfitness had not been established but rejected the equal protection claim, holding that Stanley could properly be separated from his children upon proof of the single fact that he and the dead mother had not been married. Stanley's actual fitness as a father was irrelevant....

Stanley presses his equal protection claim here. The State continues to respond that unwed fathers are presumed unfit to raise their children and that it is unnecessary to hold individualized hearings to determine whether particular fathers are in fact unfit parents before they are separated from their children. We granted certiorari, 400 U.S. 1020 (1971), to determine whether this method of procedure by presumption could be allowed to stand in light of the fact that Illinois allows married fathers—whether divorced, widowed, or separated—and mothers—even if unwed—the benefit of the presumption that they are fit to raise their children.

I

* * *

...It is first urged that Stanley could act to adopt his children. But under Illinois law, Stanley is treated not as a parent but as a stranger to his children, and the dependency proceeding has gone forward on the presumption that he is unfit to exercise parental rights. Insofar as we are informed, Illinois law affords him no priority in adoption proceedings. It would be his burden to establish not only that he would be a suitable parent but also that he would be the most suitable of all who might want custody of the children. Neither can we ignore that in the proceedings from which this action developed, the "probation officer,"...the assistant state's attorney,...and the judge charged with the case,...made it apparent that Stanley, unmarried and impecunious as he is, could not now expect to profit from adoption proceedings....

...We must therefore examine the question that Illinois would have us avoid: Is a presumption that distinguishes and burdens all unwed fathers constitutionally repugnant? We conclude that, as a matter of due process of law, Stanley was entitled to a hearing on his fitness as a parent before his children were taken from him and that, by denying him a hearing and extending it to all other parents whose custody of their children is challenged, the State denied Stanley the equal protection of the laws guaranteed by the Fourteenth Amendment.

---

[3] Only two children are involved in this litigation.

I

Illinois has two principal methods of removing nondelinquent children from the homes of their parents. In a dependency proceeding it may demonstrate that the children are wards of the State because they have no surviving parent or guardian....In a neglect proceeding it may show that children should be wards of the State because the present parent(s) or guardian does not provide suitable care....

The State's right—indeed, duty—to protect minor children through a judicial determination of their interests in a neglect proceeding is not challenged here. Rather, we are faced with a dependency statute that empowers state officials to circumvent neglect proceedings on the theory that an unwed father is not a "parent" whose existing relationship with his children must be considered.[4] "Parents," says the State, "means the father and mother of a legitimate child, or the survivor of them, or the natural mother of an illegitimate child, and includes any adoptive parent,"...but the term does not include unwed fathers.

Under Illinois law, therefore, while the children of all parents can be taken from them in neglect proceedings, that is only after notice, hearing, and proof of such unfitness as a parent as amounts to neglect, an unwed father is uniquely subject to the more simplistic dependency proceeding. By use of this proceeding, the State, on showing that the father was not married to the mother, need not prove unfitness in fact, because it is presumed at law. Thus, the unwed father's claim of parental qualification is avoided as "irrelevant."

* * *

The private interest here, that of a man in the children he has sired and raised, undeniably warrants deference and, absent a powerful countervailing interest, protection. It is plain that the interest of a parent in the companionship, care, custody, and management of his or her children "come[s] to this Court with a momentum for respect lacking when appeal is made to liberties which derive merely from shifting economic arrangements." *Kovacs v. Cooper*, 336 U.S. 77, 95 (1949) (Frankfurter, J., concurring).

The Court has frequently emphasized the importance of the family. The rights to conceive and to raise one's children have been deemed "essential," *Meyer v. Nebraska*, 262 U.S. 390, 399 (1923), "basic civil rights of man," *Skinner v. Oklahoma*, 316 U.S. 535, 541 (1942), and "rights far more precious...than property rights," *May v. Anderson*, 345 U.S. 528, 533 (1953)....

Nor has the law refused to recognize those family relationships unlegitimized by a marriage ceremony. The Court has declared unconstitutional a state statute denying natural, but illegitimate, children a wrongful-death action for the death of their mother, emphasizing that such children cannot be denied the right of other children because familial bonds in such cases were often as warm, enduring, and important as those arising within a more formally organized family unit. *Levy v. Louisiana*, 391 U.S. 68, 71–72 (1968). "To say that the test of equal protection should be the 'legal' rather than the biological relationship is to avoid the issue. For the Equal Protection Clause necessarily limits the authority of a State to draw such 'legal' lines as it chooses." *Glona v. American Guarantee Co.*, 391 U.S. 73, 75–76 (1968).

These authorities make it clear that, at the least, Stanley's interest in retaining custody of his children is cognizable and substantial.

---

[4] Even while refusing to label him a "legal parent," the State does not deny that Stanley has a special interest in the outcome of these proceedings. It is undisputed that he is the father of these children, that he lived with the two children whose custody is challenged all their lives, and that he has supported them.

For its part, the State has made its interest quite plain: Illinois has declared that the aim of the Juvenile Court Act is to protect "the moral, emotional, mental, and physical welfare of the minor and the best interests of the community" and to "strengthen the minor's family ties whenever possible, removing him from the custody of his parents only when his welfare or safety or the protection of the public cannot be adequately safeguarded without removal....".... These are legitimate interests, well within the power of the State to implement. We do not question the assertion that neglectful parents may be separated from their children.

But we are here not asked to evaluate the legitimacy of the state ends, rather, to determine whether the means used to achieve these ends are constitutionally defensible. What is the state interest in separating children from fathers without a hearing designed to determine whether the father is unfit in a particular disputed case? We observe that the State registers no gain towards its declared goals when it separates children from the custody of fit parents. Indeed, if Stanley is a fit father, the State spites its own articulated goals when it needlessly separates him from his family.

* * *

III

The State of Illinois assumes custody of the children of married parents, divorced parents, and unmarried mothers only after a hearing and proof of neglect. The children of unmarried fathers, however, are declared dependent children without a hearing on parental fitness and without proof of neglect. Stanley's claim in the state courts and here is that failure to afford him a hearing on his parental qualifications while extending it to other parents denied him equal protection of the laws. We have concluded that all Illinois parents are constitutionally entitled to a hearing on their fitness before their children are removed from their custody. It follows that denying such a hearing to Stanley and those like him while granting it to other Illinois parents is inescapably contrary to the Equal Protection Clause....

* * *

Mr. Chief Justice Burger, with whom **Mr. Justice Blackmun** concurs, dissenting.

* * *

In regard to the only issue that I consider properly before the Court, I agree with the State's argument that the Equal Protection Clause is not violated when Illinois gives full recognition only to those father-child relationships that arise in the context of family units bound together by legal obligations arising from marriage or from adoption proceedings. Quite apart from the religious or quasi-religious connotations that marriage has—and has historically enjoyed—for a large proportion of this Nation's citizens, it is in law an essentially contractual relationship, the parties to which have legally enforceable rights and duties, with respect both to each other and to any children born to them. Stanley and the mother of these children never entered such a relationship. The record is silent as to whether they ever privately exchanged such promises as would have bound them in marriage under the common law....In any event, Illinois has not recognized common-law marriages since 1905. Ill. Rev. Stat., c. 89, § 4. Stanley did not seek the burdens when he could have freely assumed them.

* * *

The Illinois Supreme Court correctly held that the State may constitutionally distinguish between unwed fathers and unwed mothers. Here, Illinois' different treatment of the two is part of that State's statutory scheme for protecting the welfare of illegitimate children. In almost all cases, the unwed mother is readily identifiable, generally from hospital records, and alternatively by physicians or others attending the child's birth. Unwed fathers, as a class, are not traditionally quite so easy to identify and locate. Many of them either deny all responsibility or exhibit no interest in the child or its welfare; and, of course, many unwed fathers are simply not aware of their parenthood.

Furthermore, I believe that a State is fully justified in concluding, on the basis of common human experience, that the biological role of the mother in carrying and nursing an infant creates stronger bonds between her and the child than the bonds resulting from the male's often casual encounter. This view is reinforced by the observable fact that most unwed mothers exhibit a concern for their offspring either permanently or at least until they are safely placed for adoption, while unwed fathers rarely burden either the mother or the child with their attentions or loyalties. Centuries of human experience buttress this view of the realities of human conditions and suggest that unwed mothers of illegitimate children are generally more dependable protectors of their children than are unwed fathers. While these, like most generalizations, are not without exceptions, they nevertheless provide a sufficient basis to sustain a statutory classification whose objective is not to penalize unwed parents but to further the welfare of illegitimate children in fulfillment of the State's obligations as *parens patriae*.[4]

Stanley depicts himself as a somewhat unusual unwed father, namely, as one who has always acknowledged and never doubted his fatherhood of these children. He alleges that he loved, cared for, and supported these children from the time of their birth until the death of their mother. He contends that he consequently must be treated the same as a married father of legitimate children. Even assuming the truth of Stanley's allegations, I am unable to construe the Equal Protection Clause as requiring Illinois to tailor its statutory definition of "parents" so meticulously as to include such unusual unwed fathers, while at the same time excluding those unwed, and generally unidentified, biological fathers who in no way share Stanley's professed desires.

Indeed, the nature of Stanley's own desires is less than absolutely clear from the record in this case. Shortly after the death of the mother, Stanley turned these two children over to the care of a Mr. and Mrs. Ness; he took no action to gain recognition of himself as a father, through adoption, or as a legal custodian, through a guardianship proceeding. Eventually it came to the attention of the State that there was no living adult who had any legally enforceable obligation for the care and support of the children; it was only then that the dependency proceeding here under review took place and that Stanley made himself known to the juvenile court in connection with these two children.[5] Even then, however, Stanley did not ask to be charged with the legal responsibility for the children. He asked only that such legal responsibility be given to no one else. He seemed, in particular, to be concerned with the loss of the welfare payments he would suffer as a result of the designation of others as guardians of the children.

---

[4] When the marriage between the parents of a legitimate child is dissolved by divorce or separation, the State, of course, normally awards custody of the child to one parent or the other. This is considered necessary for the child's welfare, since the parents are no longer legally bound together. The unmarried parents of an illegitimate child are likewise not legally bound together. Thus, even if Illinois did recognize the parenthood of both the mother and father of an illegitimate child, it would, for consistency with its practice in divorce proceedings, be called upon to award custody to one or the other of them, at least once it had by some means ascertained the identity of the father.

[5] As the majority notes, ante,..., Joan Stanley gave birth to three children during the 18 years Peter Stanley was living "intermittently" with her. At oral argument, we were told by Stanley's counsel that the oldest of these three children had previously been declared a ward of the court pursuant to a neglect proceeding that was "proven against" Stanley at a time, apparently, when the juvenile court officials were under the erroneous impression that Peter and Joan Stanley had been married....

Questions for Discussion

1. The *Stanley* Court held that the Illinois assumption that an unmarried father may have his parental rights terminated without hearing violates his due process rights. Such a father is entitled to a due process hearing. What will that hearing decide and on what basis? Is not the answer to these questions more important than the formalism of a hearing right alone? Although Illinois is required to grant Stanley a hearing, can it substantively weigh his failure to marry the mother of these children as a factor in terminating his parental rights? Can absence of marriage shift the burden from the state to Stanley to demonstrate his fitness as a parent? What if Stanley has functioned as the father, but has not married the mother of the children, *and* is not the biological father?

2. The dissent argues that the bright line distinction of marriage is constitutionally permissible as a determinant of parental rights. Arguably, children benefit from marriage incentives in a variety of ways, from inclusion in the employee health policies of fathers, to insurance and disability protections, to family court jurisdiction if the biological mother and father part. Parental status infirmity can be cured by the involved parents by marrying. However, the denial of parental rights to a father who has functioned as such can mean the permanent loss of that parent. From the child's perspective, that "taking" by the state may be momentous, and if marriage is to be the critical criterion, what opportunity do children have to determine the marital status of their parents? Is the loss of a parent entitled to the same constitutional cognizance as the right to parent? To any constitutional status? If so, is it appropriately abrogated based on circumstances over which affected children have no control?

3. Is the child's perspective discussed or considered by the majority opinion? By the dissent?

Lehr v. Robertson
463 U.S. 248 (1983)

JUSTICE STEVENS delivered the opinion of the Court.

The question presented is whether New York has sufficiently protected an unmarried father's inchoate relationship with a child whom he has never supported and rarely seen in the two years since her birth. The appellant, Jonathan Lehr, claims that the Due Process and Equal Protection Clauses of the Fourteenth Amendment, as interpreted in *Stanley v. Illinois*, 405 U.S. 645 (1972), and *Caban v. Mohammed*, 441 U.S. 380 (1979), give him an absolute right to notice and an opportunity to be heard before the child may be adopted. We disagree.

Jessica M. was born out of wedlock on November 9, 1976. Her mother, Lorraine Robertson, married Richard Robertson eight months after Jessica's birth....On December 21, 1978, when Jessica was over two years old, the Robertsons filed an adoption petition in the Family Court of Ulster County, New York. The court heard their testimony and received a favorable report from the Ulster County Department of Social Services. On March 7, 1979, the court entered an order of adoption....In this proceeding, appellant contends that the adoption order is invalid because he, Jessica's putative father, was not given advance notice of the adoption proceeding....

The State of New York maintains a "putative father registry."...A man who files with that registry demonstrates his intent to claim paternity of a child born out of wedlock and is therefore entitled to receive notice of any proceeding to adopt that child. Before entering Jessica's adoption order, the Ulster County Family Court had the putative father registry examined. Although appellant claims to be Jessica's natural father, he had not entered his name in the registry.

In addition to the persons whose names are listed on the putative father registry, New York law requires that notice of an adoption proceeding be given to several other classes of possible fathers of children born out of wedlock—those who have been adjudicated to be the father, those who have been identified as the father on the child's birth certificate, those who live openly with the child and the child's mother and who hold themselves out to be the father, those who have been identified as the father by the mother in a sworn written statement, and those who were married to the child's mother before the child was six months old.[5] Appellant admittedly was not a member of any of those classes. He had lived with appellee prior to Jessica's birth and visited her in the hospital when Jessica was born, but his name does not appear on Jessica's birth certificate. He did not live with appellee or Jessica after Jessica's birth, he has never provided them with any financial support, and he has never offered to marry appellee. Nevertheless, he contends that the following special circumstances gave him a constitutional right to notice and a hearing before Jessica was adopted.

On January 30, 1979, one month after the adoption proceeding was commenced in Ulster County, appellant filed a "visitation and paternity petition" in the Westchester County Family Court. In that petition, he asked for a determination of paternity, an order of support, and reasonable visitation privileges with Jessica. Notice of that proceeding was served on appellee on February 22, 1979. Four days later appellee's attorney informed the Ulster County Court that appellant had commenced a paternity proceeding in Westchester County; the Ulster County judge then entered an order staying appellant's paternity proceeding until he could rule on a motion to change the venue of that proceeding to Ulster County. On March 3, 1979, appellant received notice of the change of venue motion and, for the first time, learned that an adoption proceeding was pending in Ulster County.

On March 7, 1979, appellant's attorney telephoned the Ulster County judge to inform him that he planned to seek a stay of the adoption proceeding pending the determination of the paternity petition. In that telephone conversation, the judge advised the lawyer that he had already signed the adoption order earlier that day. According to appellant's attorney, the judge stated that he was aware of the pending paternity petition but did not believe he was required to give notice to appellant prior to the entry of the order of adoption.

---

[5] At the time Jessica's adoption order was entered, N. Y. Dom. Rel. Law...provided:

"2. Persons entitled to notice, pursuant to subdivision one of this section, shall include:

"(a) any person adjudicated by a court in this state to be the father of the child;

"(b) any person adjudicated by a court of another state or territory of the United States to be the father of the child, when a certified copy of the court order has been filed with the putative father registry, pursuant to section three hundred seventy-two-c of the social services law;

"(c) any person who has timely filed an unrevoked notice of intent to claim paternity of the child, pursuant to section three hundred seventy-two of the social services law;

"(d) any person who is recorded on the child's birth certificate as the child's father;

"(e) any person who is openly living with the child and the child's mother at the time the proceeding is initiated and who is holding himself out to be the child's father;

"(f) any person who has been identified as the child's father by the mother in written, sworn statement; and

"(g) any person who was married to the child's mother within six months subsequent to the birth of the child and prior to the execution of a surrender instrument or the initiation of a proceeding pursuant to section three hundred eighty-four-b of the social services law.

"3. The sole purpose of notice under this section shall be to enable the person served pursuant to subdivision two to present evidence to the court relevant to the best interests of the child."

* * *

Appellant has now invoked our appellate jurisdiction....He offers two alternative grounds for holding the New York statutory scheme unconstitutional. First, he contends that a putative father's actual or potential relationship with a child born out of wedlock is an interest in liberty which may not be destroyed without due process of law; he argues therefore that he had a constitutional right to prior notice and an opportunity to be heard before he was deprived of that interest. Second, he contends that the gender-based classification in the statute, which both denied him the right to consent to Jessica's adoption and accorded him fewer procedural rights than her mother, violated the Equal Protection Clause....

The Due Process Claim.

The Fourteenth Amendment provides that no State shall deprive any person of life, liberty, or property without due process of law. When that Clause is invoked in a novel context, it is our practice to begin the inquiry with a determination of the precise nature of the private interest that is threatened by the State....

I

The intangible fibers that connect parent and child have infinite variety. They are woven throughout the fabric of our society, providing it with strength, beauty, and flexibility. It is self-evident that they are sufficiently vital to merit constitutional protection in appropriate cases. In deciding whether this is such a case, however, we must consider the broad framework that has traditionally been used to resolve the legal problems arising from the parent-child relationship.

In the vast majority of cases, state law determines the final outcome....Rules governing the inheritance of property, adoption, and child custody are generally specified in statutory enactments that vary from State to State....Moreover, equally varied state laws governing marriage and divorce affect a multitude of parent-child relationships. The institution of marriage has played a critical role both in defining the legal entitlements of family members and in developing the decentralized structure of our democratic society....In recognition of that role, and as part of their general overarching concern for serving the best interests of children, state laws almost universally express an appropriate preference for the formal family....

* * *

The difference between the developed parent-child relationship that was implicated in *Stanley* and *Caban*, and the potential relationship involved in *Quilloin* and this case, is both clear and significant. When an unwed father demonstrates a full commitment to the responsibilities of parenthood by "[coming] forward to participate in the rearing of his child," *Caban*, 441 U.S., at 392, his interest in personal contact with his child acquires substantial protection under the Due Process Clause. At that point it may be said that he "[acts] as a father toward his children." *Id.*, at 389, n. 7. But the mere existence of a biological link does not merit equivalent constitutional protection. The actions of judges neither create nor sever genetic bonds. "[The] importance of the familial relationship, to the individuals involved and to the society, stems from the emotional attachments that derive from the intimacy of daily association, and from the role it plays in '[promoting] a way of life' through the instruction of children...as well as from the fact of blood relationship." *Smith v. Organization of Foster Families for Equality and Reform*, 431 U.S. 816, 844 (1977) (quoting *Wisconsin v. Yoder*, 406 U.S. 205, 231-233 (1972))....

The significance of the biological connection is that it offers the natural father an opportunity that no other male possesses to develop a relationship with his offspring. If he grasps that opportunity and accepts some measure of responsibility for the child's future, he may enjoy the blessings of the parent-child relationship and make uniquely valuable contributions to the child's development.[18] If he fails to do so, the Federal Constitution will not automatically compel a State to listen to his opinion of where the child's best interests lie.

In this case, we are not assessing the constitutional adequacy of New York's procedures for terminating a developed relationship. Appellant has never had any significant custodial, personal, or financial relationship with Jessica, and he did not seek to establish a legal tie until after she was two years old.[19] We are concerned only with whether New York has adequately protected his opportunity to form such a relationship.

I

The most effective protection of the putative father's opportunity to develop a relationship with his child is provided by the laws that authorize formal marriage and govern its consequences. But the availability of that protection is, of course, dependent on the will of both parents of the child. Thus, New York has adopted a special statutory scheme to protect the unmarried father's interest in assuming a responsible role in the future of his child.

* * *

Appellant argues, however, that even if the putative father's opportunity to establish a relationship with an illegitimate child is adequately protected by the New York statutory scheme in the normal case, he was nevertheless entitled to special notice because the court and the mother knew that he had filed an affiliation proceeding in another court. This argument amounts to nothing more than an indirect attack on the notice provisions of the New York statute. The legitimate state interests in facilitating the adoption of young children and having the adoption proceeding completed expeditiously that underlie the entire statutory scheme also justify a trial judge's determination to require all interested parties to adhere precisely to the procedural requirements of the statute. The Constitution does not require either a trial judge or a litigant to give special notice to nonparties who are presumptively capable of asserting and protecting their own rights.[23] Since the

---

[18] Of course, we need not take sides in the ongoing debate among family psychologists over the relative weight to be accorded biological ties and psychological ties, in order to recognize that a natural father who has played a substantial role in rearing his child has a greater claim to constitutional protection than a mere biological parent. New York's statutory scheme reflects these differences, guaranteeing notice to any putative father who is living openly with the child, and providing putative fathers who have never developed a relationship with the child the opportunity to receive notice simply by mailing a postcard to the putative father registry.

[19] This case happens to involve an adoption by the husband of the natural mother, but we do not believe the natural father has any greater right to object to such an adoption than to an adoption by two total strangers. If anything, the balance of equities tips the opposite way in a case such as this. In denying the putative father relief in *Quilloin v. Walcott*, 434 U.S. 246 (1978), we made an observation equally applicable here:

"Nor is this a case in which the proposed adoption would place the child with a new set of parents with whom the child had never before lived. Rather, the result of the adoption in this case is to give full recognition to a family unit already in existence, a result desired by all concerned, except appellant. Whatever might be required in other situations, we cannot say that the State was required in this situation to find anything more than that the adoption, and denial of legitimation, were in the 'best interests of the child.'" *Id.*, at 255.

[23] It is a generally accepted feature of our adversary system that a potential defendant who knows that the statute of limitations is about to run out has no duty to give the plaintiff advice. There is no suggestion in the record that appellee engaged in fraudulent practices that led appellant not to protect his rights.

New York statutes adequately protected appellant's inchoate interest in establishing a relationship with Jessica, we find no merit in the claim that his constitutional rights were offended because the Family Court strictly complied with the notice provisions of the statute.

- The Equal Protection Claim.

* * *

We have held that these statutes may not constitutionally be applied in that class of cases where the mother and father are in fact similarly situated with regard to their relationship with the child. In *Caban v. Mohammed*, 441 U.S. 380 (1979), the Court held that it violated the Equal Protection Clause to grant the mother a veto over the adoption of a 4-year-old girl and a 6-year-old boy, but not to grant a veto to their father, who had admitted paternity and had participated in the rearing of the children. The Court made it clear, however, that if the father had not "come forward to participate in the rearing of his child, nothing in the Equal Protection Clause [would] [preclude] the State from withholding from him the privilege of vetoing the adoption of that child." *Id.*, at 392.

Jessica's parents are not like the parents involved in *Caban*. Whereas appellee had a continuous custodial responsibility for Jessica, appellant never established any custodial, personal, or financial relationship with her. If one parent has an established custodial relationship with the child and the other parent has either abandoned...or never established a relationship, the Equal Protection Clause does not prevent a State from according the two parents different legal rights....

The judgment of the New York Court of Appeals is

Affirmed.

Justice White, with whom **Justice Marshall** and **Justice Blackmun** join, dissenting.

The question in this case is whether the State may, consistent with the Due Process Clause, deny notice and an opportunity to be heard in an adoption proceeding to a putative father when the State has actual notice of his existence, whereabouts, and interest in the child.

I

* * *

According to Lehr, he and Jessica's mother met in 1971 and began living together in 1974. The couple cohabited for approximately two years, until Jessica's birth in 1976. Throughout the pregnancy and after the birth, Lorraine acknowledged to friends and relatives that Lehr was Jessica's father; Lorraine told Lehr that she had reported to the New York State Department of Social Services that he was the father.[2] Lehr visited Lorraine and Jessica in the hospital every day during Lorraine's confinement. According to Lehr, from the time Lorraine was discharged from the hospital until August 1978, she concealed her whereabouts from him. During this time Lehr never ceased his efforts to locate Lorraine and Jessica and achieved

---

[2] Under 18 NYCRR § 369.2(b) (1982), recipients of public assistance in the Aid to Families with Dependent Children program are required as a condition of eligibility to provide the name and address of the child's father. Lorraine apparently received public assistance after Jessica's birth; it is unclear whether she received public assistance after that regulation went into effect in 1977.

sporadic success until August 1977, after which time he was unable to locate them at all. On those occasions when he did determine Lorraine's location, he visited with her and her children to the extent she was willing to permit it. When Lehr, with the aid of a detective agency, located Lorraine and Jessica in August 1978, Lorraine was already married to Mr. Robertson. Lehr asserts that at this time he offered to provide financial assistance and to set up a trust fund for Jessica, but that Lorraine refused. Lorraine threatened Lehr with arrest unless he stayed away and refused to permit him to see Jessica. Thereafter Lehr retained counsel who wrote to Lorraine in early December 1978, requesting that she permit Lehr to visit Jessica and threatening legal action on Lehr's behalf. On December 21, 1978, perhaps as a response to Lehr's threatened legal action, appellees commenced the adoption action at issue here.

* * *

The "nature of the interest" at stake here is the interest that a natural parent has in his or her child, one that has long been recognized and accorded constitutional protection....

* * *

I reject the peculiar notion that the only significance of the biological connection between father and child is that "it offers the natural father an opportunity that no other male possesses to develop a relationship with his offspring.".....A "mere biological relationship" is not as unimportant in determining the nature of liberty interests as the majority suggests.

* * *

I

In this case, of course, there was no question about either the identity or the location of the putative father. The mother knew exactly who he was and both she and the court entering the order of adoption knew precisely where he was and how to give him actual notice that his parental rights were about to be terminated by an adoption order.[5] Lehr was entitled to due process, and the right to be heard is one of the fundamentals of that right, which "'has little reality or worth unless one is informed that the matter is pending and can choose for himself whether to appear or default, acquiesce or contest.'"....

* * *

...It makes little sense to me to deny notice and hearing to a father who has not placed his name in the register but who has unmistakably identified himself by filing suit to establish his paternity and has notified the adoption court of his action and his interest. I thus need not question the statutory scheme on its

---

[5] Absent special circumstances, there is no bar to requiring the mother of an illegitimate child to divulge the name of the father when the proceedings at issue involve the permanent termination of the father's rights. Likewise, there is no reason not to require such identification when it is the spouse of the custodial parent who seeks to adopt the child. Indeed, the State now requires the mother to provide the identity of the father if she applies for financial benefits under the Aid to Families with Dependent Children Program....The State's obligation to provide notice to persons before their interests are permanently terminated cannot be a lesser concern than its obligation to assure that state funds are not expended when there exists a person upon whom the financial responsibility should fall.

face. Even assuming that Lehr would have been foreclosed if his failure to utilize the register had somehow disadvantaged the State, he effectively made himself known by other means, and it is the sheerest formalism to deny him a hearing because he informed the State in the wrong manner....

* * *

Respectfully, I dissent.

Questions for Discussion

1. Is it relevant that in *Stanley* the alternative to paternal rights is foster care, but in *Lehr* (and in *Caban v. Mohammed*[2]) there is another person competing for fatherhood status? Would it matter if Lehr is (or is likely to be) a superlative parent? If he had remarried as well to provide two parents? If the prospective adoptive father Robertson is fit, but would not prevail in a choice merely between the two based on the best interests of the child?

2. Would it make a difference if there had not been a three-year delay? Did *Lehr* "seize" his paternal opportunity? Does it matter if the child's mother misled Lehr to preclude him from invoking his paternal rights? What obligations of due diligence should be required of Lehr? Is submitting his name to the New York "registry" arranged for this purpose excused by the actual public filing of Lehr for fatherhood status? If we find for Lehr, do we remove the bright line such a registry is intended to provide and remove the certainty that children need for secure status? If we find against Lehr, do we reward the deception of a mother in foreclosing paternal rights?

3. The context of *Lehr*, unlike current divorce custody decisions, is an absolute "yes" or "no," without the middle ground of joint custody or visitation. Would Jessica benefit from the allowance of additional caring adults in her life, including her biological father? But if parental status is granted to Robertson, should the court intervene to overrule the common judgment of her mother and father as to what persons should have contact with Jessica? *E.g.*, if they believe that Lehr is a bad influence or is disruptive to their marriage? Should it matter if Lehr had, in fact, served as a psychological father to his biological child for a substantial period of time and she regarded him as her "father?"

Michael H. v. Gerald D.
491 U.S. 110 (1989)

Justice Scalia, announced the judgment of the Court and delivered an opinion, in which The Chief Justice joins, and in all but footnote 6 of which Justice O'Connor and Justice Kennedy join.

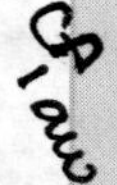

Under California law, a child born to a married woman living with her husband is presumed to be a child of the marriage. Cal. Evid. Code Ann. § 621....The presumption of legitimacy may be rebutted only by the husband or wife, and then only in limited circumstances....The instant appeal presents the claim that this presumption infringes upon the due process rights of a man who wishes to establish his paternity of a child born to the wife of another man, and the claim that it infringes upon the constitutional right of the child to maintain a relationship with her natural father.

I

The facts of this case are, we must hope, extraordinary. On May 9, 1976, in Las Vegas, Nevada, Carole D., an international model, and Gerald D., a top executive in a French oil company, were married. The couple established a home in Playa del Rey, California, in which they resided as husband and wife when one or the other was not out of the country on business. In the summer of 1978, Carole became involved in an adulterous affair with a neighbor, Michael H. In September 1980, she conceived a child, Victoria D., who was born on May 11, 1981. Gerald was listed as father on the birth certificate and has always held Victoria out to the world as his daughter. Soon after delivery of the child, however, Carole informed Michael that she believed he might be the father.

In the first three years of her life, Victoria remained always with Carole, but found herself within a variety of quasi-family units. In October 1981, Gerald moved to New York City to pursue his business interests, but Carole chose to remain in California. At the end of that month, Carole and Michael had blood tests of themselves and Victoria, which showed a 98.07% probability that Michael was Victoria's father. In January 1982, Carole visited Michael in St. Thomas, where his primary business interests were based. There Michael held Victoria out as his child. In March, however, Carole left Michael and returned to California, where she took up residence with yet another man, Scott K. Later that spring, and again in the summer, Carole and Victoria spent time with Gerald in New York City, as well as on vacation in Europe. In the fall, they returned to Scott in California.

In November 1982, rebuffed in his attempts to visit Victoria, Michael filed a filiation action in California Superior Court to establish his paternity and right to visitation. In March 1983, the court appointed an attorney and *guardian ad litem* to represent Victoria's interests. Victoria then filed a cross-complaint asserting that if she had more than one psychological or *de facto* father, she was entitled to maintain her filial relationship, with all of the attendant rights, duties, and obligations, with both. In May 1983, Carole filed a motion for summary judgment. During this period, from March through July 1983, Carole was again living with Gerald in New York. In August, however, she returned to California, became involved once again with Michael, and instructed her attorneys to remove the summary judgment motion from the calendar.

For the ensuing eight months, when Michael was not in St. Thomas he lived with Carole and Victoria in Carole's apartment in Los Angeles and held Victoria out as his daughter. In April 1984, Carole and Michael signed a stipulation that Michael was Victoria's natural father. Carole left Michael the next month, however, and instructed her attorneys not to file the stipulation. In June 1984, Carole reconciled with Gerald and joined him in New York, where they now live with Victoria and two other children since born into the marriage.

In May 1984, Michael and Victoria, through her *guardian ad litem*, sought visitation rights for Michael *pendente lite*. To assist in determining whether visitation would be in Victoria's best interests, the Superior Court appointed a psychologist to evaluate Victoria, Gerald, Michael, and Carole. The psychologist recommended that Carole retain sole custody, but that Michael be allowed continued contact with Victoria pursuant to a restricted visitation schedule. The court concurred and ordered that Michael be provided with limited visitation privileges *pendente lite*.

On October 19, 1984, Gerald, who had intervened in the action, moved for summary judgment on the ground that under Cal. Evid. Code § 621 there were no triable issues of fact as to Victoria's paternity. This law provides that "the issue of a wife cohabiting with her husband, who is not impotent or sterile, is conclusively presumed to be a child of the marriage." Cal. Evid. Code Ann. § 621(a)....The presumption may be rebutted by blood tests, but only if a motion for such tests is made, within two years from the date of the child's birth, either by the husband or, if the natural father has filed an affidavit acknowledging paternity, by the wife. §§ 621(c) and (d).

On January 28, 1985, having found that affidavits submitted by Carole and Gerald sufficed to demonstrate that the two were cohabiting at conception and birth and that Gerald was neither sterile nor impotent, the Superior Court granted Gerald's motion for summary judgment, rejecting Michael's and Victoria's challenges to the constitutionality of § 621. The court also denied their motions for continued visitation pending the appeal under Cal. Civ. Code § 4601, which provides that a court may, in its discretion, grant "reasonable visitation rights...to any...person having an interest in the welfare of the child." Cal. Civ. Code Ann. § 4601....It found that allowing such visitation would "violat[e] the intention of the Legislature by impugning the integrity of the family unit."...

On appeal, Michael asserted, *inter alia*, that the Superior Court's application of § 621 had violated his procedural and substantive due process rights. Victoria also raised a due process challenge to the statute, seeking to preserve her *de facto* relationship with Michael as well as with Gerald. She contended, in addition, that as § 621 allows the husband and, at least to a limited extent, the mother, but not the child, to rebut the presumption of legitimacy, it violates the child's right to equal protection. Finally, she asserted a right to continued visitation with Michael under § 4601....

...Before us, Michael and Victoria both raise equal protection and due process challenges. We do not reach Michael's equal protection claim, however, as it was neither raised nor passed upon below....

I

The California statute that is the subject of this litigation is, in substance, more than a century old. California Code of Civ. Proc. § 1962(5), enacted in 1872, provided that "[t]he issue of a wife cohabiting with her husband, who is not impotent, is indisputably presumed to be legitimate."....In 1980, the legislature again amended the statute to provide the husband an opportunity to introduce blood-test evidence in rebuttal of the presumption,...and in 1981 amended it to provide the mother such an opportunity....

* * *

III

We address first the claims of Michael. At the outset, it is necessary to clarify what he sought and what he was denied. California law, like nature itself, makes no provision for dual fatherhood. Michael was seeking to be declared *the* father of Victoria. The immediate benefit he evidently sought to obtain from that status was visitation rights....But if Michael were successful in being declared the father, other rights would follow—most importantly, the right to be considered as the parent who should have custody....All parental rights, including visitation, were automatically denied by denying Michael status as the father. While Cal. Civ. Code Ann. § 4601 places it within the discretionary power of a court to award visitation rights to a nonparent, the Superior Court here, affirmed by the Court of Appeal, held that California law denies visitation, against the wishes of the mother, to a putative father who has been prevented by § 621 from establishing his paternity....

* * *

Michael contends as a matter of substantive due process that, because he has established a parental relationship with Victoria, protection of Gerald's and Carole's marital union is an insufficient state interest to support termination of that relationship. This argument is, of course, predicated on the assertion that Michael has a constitutionally protected liberty interest in his relationship with Victoria.

* * *

In an attempt to limit and guide interpretation of the Clause, we have insisted not merely that the interest denominated as a "liberty" be "fundamental" (a concept that, in isolation, is hard to objectify), but also that it be an interest traditionally protected by our society. As we have put it, the Due Process Clause affords only those protections "so rooted in the traditions and conscience of our people as to be ranked as fundamental."....Our cases reflect "continual insistence upon respect for the teachings of history [and] solid recognition of the basic values that underlie our society...." *Griswold v. Connecticut*, 381 U.S. 479, 501 (1965)....

This insistence that the asserted liberty interest be rooted in history and tradition is evident, as elsewhere, in our cases according constitutional protection to certain parental rights. Michael reads the landmark case of *Stanley v. Illinois*, 405 U.S. 645 (1972), and the subsequent cases of *Quilloin v. Walcott*, 434 U.S. 246 (1978), *Caban v. Mohammed*, 441 U.S. 380 (1979), and *Lehr v. Robertson*, 463 U.S. 248 (1983), as establishing that a liberty interest is created by biological fatherhood plus an established parental relationship—factors that exist in the present case as well. We think that distorts the rationale of those cases. As we view them, they rest not upon such isolated factors but upon the historic respect—indeed, sanctity would not be too strong a term—traditionally accorded to the relationships that develop within the unitary family.[3] ...

Thus, the legal issue in the present case reduces to whether the relationship between persons in the situation of Michael and Victoria has been treated as a protected family unit under the historic practices of our society, or whether on any other basis it has been accorded special protection. We think it impossible to find that it has. In fact, quite to the contrary, our traditions have protected the marital family (Gerald, Carole, and the child they acknowledge to be theirs) against the sort of claim Michael asserts.[4]

The presumption of legitimacy was a fundamental principle of the common law....Traditionally, that presumption could be rebutted only by proof that a husband was incapable of procreation or had had no access to his wife during the relevant period....

---

[3] Justice Brennan asserts that only a "pinched conception of 'the family'" would exclude Michael, Carole, and Victoria from protection....We disagree. The family unit accorded traditional respect in our society, which we have referred to as the "unitary family," is typified, of course, by the marital family, but also includes the household of unmarried parents and their children. Perhaps the concept can be expanded even beyond this, but it will bear no resemblance to traditionally respected relationships—and will thus cease to have any constitutional significance—if it is stretched so far as to include the relationship established between a married woman, her lover, and their child, during a 3-month sojourn in St. Thomas, or during a subsequent 8-month period when, if he happened to be in Los Angeles, he stayed with her and the child.

[4] Justice Brennan insists that in determining whether a liberty interest exists we must look at Michael's relationship with Victoria in isolation, without reference to the circumstance that Victoria's mother was married to someone else when the child was conceived, and that that woman and her husband wish to raise the child as their own....We cannot imagine what compels this strange procedure of looking at the act which is assertedly the subject of a liberty interest in isolation from its effect upon other people—rather like inquiring whether there is a liberty interest in firing a gun where the case at hand happens to involve its discharge into another person's body. The logic of Justice Brennan's position leads to the conclusion that if Michael had begotten Victoria by rape, that fact would in no way affect his possession of a liberty interest in his relationship with her.

We have found nothing in the older sources, nor in the older cases, addressing specifically the power of the natural father to assert parental rights over a child born into a woman's existing marriage with another man. Since it is Michael's burden to establish that such a power (at least where the natural father has established a relationship with the child) is so deeply embedded within our traditions as to be a fundamental right, the lack of evidence alone might defeat his case. But the evidence shows that even in modern times—when, as we have noted, the rigid protection of the marital family has in other respects been relaxed—the ability of a person in Michael's position to claim paternity has not been generally acknowledged....

* * *

IV

We have never had occasion to decide whether a child has a liberty interest, symmetrical with that of her parent, in maintaining her filial relationship. We need not do so here because, even assuming that such a right exists, Victoria's claim must fail. Victoria's due process challenge is, if anything, weaker than Michael's. Her basic claim is not that California has erred in preventing her from establishing that Michael, not Gerald, should stand as her legal father. Rather, she claims a due process right to maintain filial relationships with both Michael and Gerald. This assertion merits little discussion, for, whatever the merits of the *guardian ad litem's* belief that such an arrangement can be of great psychological benefit to a child, the claim that a State must recognize multiple fatherhood has no support in the history or traditions of this country. Moreover, even if we were to construe Victoria's argument as forwarding the lesser proposition that, whatever her status vis-a-vis Gerald, she has a liberty interest in maintaining a filial relationship with her natural father, Michael, we find that, at best, her claim is the obverse of Michael's and fails for the same reasons.

Victoria claims in addition that her equal protection rights have been violated because, unlike her mother and presumed father, she had no opportunity to rebut the presumption of her legitimacy. We find this argument wholly without merit. We reject, at the outset, Victoria's suggestion that her equal protection challenge must be assessed under a standard of strict scrutiny because, in denying her the right to maintain a filial relationship with Michael, the State is discriminating against her on the basis of her illegitimacy.... Illegitimacy is a legal construct, not a natural trait. Under California law, Victoria is not illegitimate, and she is treated in the same manner as all other legitimate children: she is entitled to maintain a filial relationship with her legal parents.

We apply, therefore, the ordinary "rational relationship" test to Victoria's equal protection challenge. The primary rationale underlying § 621's limitation on those who may rebut the presumption of legitimacy is a concern that allowing persons other than the husband or wife to do so may undermine the integrity of the marital union. When the husband or wife contests the legitimacy of their child, the stability of the marriage has already been shaken. In contrast, allowing a claim of illegitimacy to be pressed by the child—or, more accurately, by a court-appointed guardian ad litem—may well disrupt an otherwise peaceful union. Since it pursues a legitimate end by rational means, California's decision to treat Victoria differently from her parents is not a denial of equal protection.

The judgment of the California Court of Appeal is

Affirmed.

Justice Brennan, with whom **Justice Marshall** and **Justice Blackmun** join, dissenting.

In a case that has yielded so many opinions as has this one, it is fruitful to begin by emphasizing the common ground shared by a majority of this Court. Five Members of the Court refuse to foreclose "the possibility that a natural father might ever have a constitutionally protected interest in his relationship with a child whose mother was married to, and cohabiting with, another man at the time of the child's conception and birth."....Five Justices agree that the flaw inhering in a conclusive presumption that terminates a constitutionally protected interest without any hearing whatsoever is a *procedural* one....Four Members of the Court agree that Michael H. has a liberty interest in his relationship with Victoria..., and one assumes for purposes of this case that he does,....

In contrast, only one other Member of the Court fully endorses Justice Scalia's view of the proper method of analyzing questions arising under the Due Process Clause....(O'Connor, J., concurring in part). Nevertheless, because the plurality opinion's exclusively historical analysis portends a significant and unfortunate departure from our prior cases and from sound constitutional decisionmaking, I devote a substantial portion of my discussion to it.

I

Once we recognized that the "liberty" protected by the Due Process Clause of the Fourteenth Amendment encompasses more than freedom from bodily restraint, today's plurality opinion emphasizes, the concept was cut loose from one natural limitation on its meaning. This innovation paved the way, so the plurality hints, for judges to substitute their own preferences for those of elected officials. Dissatisfied with this supposedly unbridled and uncertain state of affairs, the plurality casts about for another limitation on the concept of liberty.

It finds this limitation in "tradition." Apparently oblivious to the fact that this concept can be as malleable and as elusive as "liberty" itself, the plurality pretends that tradition places a discernible border around the Constitution. The pretense is seductive; it would be comforting to believe that a search for "tradition" involves nothing more idiosyncratic or complicated than poring through dusty volumes on American history. Yet, as Justice White observed in his dissent in *Moore v. East Cleveland*, 431 U.S. 494, 549 (1977): "What the deeply rooted traditions of the country are is arguable." Indeed, wherever I would begin to look for an interest "deeply rooted in the country's traditions," one thing is certain: I would not stop (as does the plurality) at Bracton, or Blackstone, or Kent, or even the American Law Reports in conducting my search. Because reasonable people can disagree about the content of particular traditions, and because they can disagree even about which traditions are relevant to the definition of "liberty," the plurality has not found the objective boundary that it seeks.

* * *

Thus, to describe the issue in this case as whether the relationship existing between Michael and Victoria "has been treated as a protected family unit under the historic practices of our society, or whether on any other basis it has been accorded special protection,"..., is to reinvent the wheel. The better approach—indeed, the one commanded by our prior cases and by common sense—is to ask whether the specific parent-child relationship under consideration is close enough to the interests that we already have protected to be deemed an aspect of "liberty" as well. On the facts before us, therefore, the question is not what "level of generality" should be used to describe the relationship between Michael and Victoria,..., but whether the relationship under consideration is sufficiently substantial to qualify as a liberty interest under our prior cases.

* * *

The evidence is undisputed that Michael, Victoria, and Carole did live together as a family; that is, they shared the same household, Victoria called Michael "Daddy," Michael contributed to Victoria's support, and he is eager to continue his relationship with her. Yet they are not, in the plurality's view, a "unitary family," whereas Gerald, Carole, and Victoria do compose such a family. The only difference between these two sets of relationships, however, is the fact of marriage. The plurality, indeed, expressly recognizes that marriage is the critical fact in denying Michael a constitutionally protected stake in his relationship with Victoria: no fewer than six times, the plurality refers to Michael as the "*adulterous* natural father" (emphasis added) or the like....However, the very premise of *Stanley* and the cases following it is that marriage is not decisive in answering the question whether the Constitution protects the parental relationship under consideration. These cases are, after all, important precisely because they involve the rights of unwed fathers. It is important to remember, moreover, that in *Quilloin*, *Caban*, and *Lehr*, the putative father's demands would have disrupted a "unitary family" as the plurality defines it; in each case, the husband of the child's mother sought to adopt the child over the objections of the natural father. Significantly, our decisions in those cases in no way relied on the need to protect the marital family. Hence the plurality's claim that *Stanley*, *Quilloin*, *Caban*, and *Lehr* were about the "unitary family," as that family is defined by today's plurality, is surprising indeed.

* * *

The plurality has wedged itself between a rock and a hard place. If it limits its holding to those situations in which a wife and husband wish to raise the child together, then it necessarily takes the State's interest into account in defining "liberty"; yet if it extends that approach to circumstances in which the marital union already has been dissolved, then it may no longer rely on the State's asserted interest in protecting the "unitary family" in denying that Michael and Victoria have been deprived of liberty.

* * *

III

Because the plurality decides that Michael and Victoria have no liberty interest in their relationship with each other, it need consider neither the effect of § 621 on their relationship nor the State's interest in bringing about that effect. It is obvious, however, that the effect of § 621 is to terminate the relationship between Michael and Victoria before affording any hearing whatsoever on the issue whether Michael is Victoria's father. This refusal to hold a hearing is properly analyzed under our procedural due process cases, which instruct us to consider the State's interest in curtailing the procedures accompanying the termination of a constitutionally protected interest. California's interest, minute in comparison with a father's interest in his relationship with his child, cannot justify its refusal to hear Michael out on his claim that he is Victoria's father.

* * *

B

The question before us, therefore, is whether California has an interest so powerful that it justifies granting Michael no hearing before terminating his parental rights.

"Many controversies have raged about the cryptic and abstract words of the Due Process Clause but there can be no doubt that at a minimum they require that deprivation of life, liberty or property by adjudication be preceded by notice and opportunity for hearing appropriate to the nature of the case."....

The purported state interests here, however, stem primarily from the State's antagonism to Michael's and Victoria's constitutionally protected interest in their relationship with each other and not from any desire to streamline procedures. Gerald D. explains that § 621 promotes marriage, maintains the relationship between the child and presumed father, and protects the integrity and privacy of the matrimonial family....It is not, however, § 621, but the best-interest principle, that protects a stable marital relationship and maintains the relationship between the child and presumed father. These interests are implicated by the determination of who gets parental rights, not by the determination of who is the father; in the hearing that Michael seeks, parental rights are not the issue. Of the objectives that Gerald stresses, therefore, only the preservation of family privacy is promoted by the refusal to hold a hearing itself. Yet § 621 furthers even this objective only partially.

Gerald D. gives generous proportions to the privacy protected by § 621, asserting that this provision protects a couple like Gerald and Carole from answering questions on such matters as "their sexual habits and practices with each other and outside their marriage, their finances, and their thoughts, beliefs, and opinions concerning their relationship with each other and with Victoria."....Yet invalidation of § 621 would not, as Gerald suggests, subject Gerald and Carole to public scrutiny of all of these private matters. Family finances and family dynamics are relevant, not to paternity, but to the best interests of the child—and the child's best interests are not, as I have stressed, in issue at the hearing that Michael seeks. The only private matter touching on the paternity presumed by § 621 is the married couple's sex life. Even there, § 621 as interpreted by California's intermediate appellate courts preempts inquiry into a couple's sexual relations, since "cohabitation" consists simply of living under the same roof together; the wife and husband need not even share the same bed....Admittedly, § 621 does not foreclose inquiry into the husband's fertility or virility—matters that are ordinarily thought of as the couple's private business. In this day and age, however, proving paternity by asking intimate and detailed questions about a couple's relationship would be decidedly anachronistic. Who on earth would choose this method of establishing fatherhood when blood tests prove it with far more certainty and far less fuss? The State's purported interest in protecting matrimonial privacy thus does not measure up to Michael's and Victoria's interest in maintaining their relationship with each other.[11]

Make no mistake: to say that the State must provide Michael with a hearing to prove his paternity is not to express any opinion of the ultimate state of affairs between Michael and Victoria and Carole and Gerald. In order to change the current situation among these people, Michael first must convince a court that he is Victoria's father, and even if he is able to do this, he will be denied visitation rights if that would be in Victoria's best interests. See Cal. Civ. Code Ann. § 4601...It is elementary that a determination that a State must afford procedures

---

[11] Thus, in concluding that § 621 "exclud[es] inquiries into the child's paternity that would be destructive of family integrity and privacy,"...the plurality exaggerates the extent to which these interests would be threatened by the elimination of § 621's presumption. On the other hand, if the State's foremost interest is in protecting the husband from discovering that he may not be the father of his wife's children, as the plurality suggests, see...at 120, n. 1, then § 621 is unhelpful indeed. Since "cohabitation" under California law includes sharing the same roof but not the same bed and since a person need only make a phone call in order to unsettle a husband's certainty in the paternity of his wife's children, § 621 will do little to prevent such discoveries.

before it terminates a given right is not a prediction about the end result of those procedures.[12]

IV

The atmosphere surrounding today's decision is one of make-believe. Beginning with the suggestion that the situation confronting us here does not repeat itself every day in every corner of the country,...moving on to the claim that it is tradition alone that supplies the details of the liberty that the Constitution protects, and passing finally to the notion that the Court always has recognized a cramped vision of "the family," today's decision lets stand California's pronouncement that Michael—whom blood tests show to a 98 percent probability to be Victoria's father—is not Victoria's father. When and if the Court awakes to reality, it will find a world very different from the one it expects.

* * *

---

[12] The plurality's failure to see this point causes it to misstate Michael's claim in the following way: "Michael contends as a matter of substantive due process that, because he has established a parental relationship with Victoria, protection of Gerald's and Carole's marital union is an insufficient state interest to support termination of that relationship."....Michael does not claim that the State may not, under any circumstance, terminate his relationship with Victoria; instead, he simply claims that the State may not do so without affording him a hearing on the issue—paternity—that it deems vital to the question whether their relationship may be discontinued. The plurality makes Michael's claim easier to knock down by turning it into such a big target.

The plurality's misunderstanding of Michael's claim also leads to its assertion that "to *provide* protection to an adulterous natural father is to *deny* protection to a marital father."...To allow Michael a chance to prove his paternity, however, in no way guarantees that Gerald's relationship with Victoria will be changed.

Questions for Discussion

1. The dissent would give Michael a due process hearing, but what would such a hearing decide and on what basis? If he demonstrates that he is the biological father, would that alone win him parental rights? What should he be required to show to win custody? Does he need parental rights status to be given court ordered visitation? (Note that Justice Stevens believes such visitation can be ordered without parental status under California law—even over the opposition of Carol and Gerald, but eight Justices disagree).

2. Should it be significant that Victoria has two half-siblings living with Carol and Gerald?

3. If, under the majority opinion, Michael is denied standing to demand paternity because Gerald was married to Carol at the time of conception and birth, what happens if Gerald and Carol divorce and *Gerald* demands a paternity test to escape child support in lieu of biological father Michael? Will he be able to transfer that obligation to Michael?

4. What if Carol divorces and then marries Michael so he has (1) substantially functioned as a father, (2) is the biological father, and (3) is married to the child's mother? Does that change the outcome under the plurality opinion?

5. Scalia's opinion rejects consideration of a child's constitutional right

to a filial (or other parental) relationship because it lacks "support in history or tradition." On what basis is a child's loss of a parent of less constitutional significance than an adult's loss of a child? Scalia argues that to permit Michael's challenge would disrupt the "peaceful union" of the marriage. Should the analysis be only of the "union," absent the children, or the "family" including them?

6. The Brennan dissent argues that biology plus a paternal relationship can trump the marriage bright line for parental status. If a wife has an affair and gives birth to a child by a third party, what are the likely outcomes of liberal paternity challenge for the survival of such marriages? For the involved children?

7. In *Michael*, both competing men have functioned to some extent as fathers. What happens where the biological father serves almost exclusively as the functioning father, and has exclusively bonded with the child. Would that make a difference to the plurality?

Note: The *Kelsey* case below presents a growing type of dispute for parental status, involving (1) a biological father unaware that he has fathered a child, or who has been misled by the mother; (2) the mother intends to place the child for adoption but regards the biological father is an unacceptable candidate, (3) the child is adopted into a family with whom the child bonds; (4) the biological father learns of the child belatedly (through no fault of his own) and seeks to rescind the adoption and assert the due process rights of a father to block adoption and to claim parental status. Such a fact pattern is more easily resolved if a measure of due diligence is required of such fathers and it is absent. Courts now regard "mere biology" alone as overly inclusive to confer upon such fathers constitutionally protected parental rights. In this context, California has attempted to fashion yet another basis for line drawing, which has been adopted in at least a substantial minority of the states.

Adoption of Kelsey S.

1 Cal. 4th 816 (1992)

OPINION BY: BAXTER

The primary question in this case is whether the father of a child born out of wedlock may properly be denied the right to withhold his consent to his child's adoption by third parties despite his diligent and legal attempts to obtain custody of his child and to rear it himself, and absent any showing of the father's unfitness as a parent. We conclude that, under these circumstances, the federal constitutional guarantees of equal protection and due process require that the father be allowed to withhold his consent to his child's adoption and therefore that his parental rights cannot be terminated absent a showing of his unfitness within the meaning of Civil Code section 221.20.

FACTS

Kari S. gave birth to Kelsey, a boy, on May 18, 1988. The child's undisputed natural father is petitioner Rickie M....He and Kari S. were not married to one another. At that time, he was married to another woman but was separated from her and apparently was in divorce proceedings. He was aware that Kari

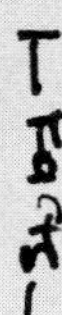

planned to place their child for adoption, and he objected to her decision because he wanted to rear the child.

Two days after the child's birth, petitioner filed an action in superior court under Civil Code section 7006 to establish his parental relationship with the child and to obtain custody of the child. (The petition erroneously stated that the child had not yet been born. His birth was earlier than expected, and petitioner had not been informed of it when he filed his action.) That same day, the court issued a restraining order that temporarily awarded care, custody, and control of the child to petitioner. The order also stayed all adoption proceedings and prohibited any contact between the child and the prospective adoptive parents.

Later that day, petitioner filed a copy of the order with law enforcement officials. He also personally attempted to serve it on the prospective adoptive parents at their home. He was unsuccessful.

On May 24, 1988, Steven and Suzanne A., the prospective adoptive parents, filed an adoption petition under Civil Code section 226....Their petition alleged that only the mother's consent to the adoption was required because there was no presumed father under section 7004, subdivision (a)....

* * *

On May 31, 1988, the prospective adoptive parents filed a petition under section 7017 to terminate petitioner's parental rights. The superior court consolidated that proceeding with the adoption proceeding. The court allowed petitioner to have supervised visitation with the child at the women's shelter where the child was living with his mother. The court also allowed the prospective adoptive parents to have unsupervised visitation at the shelter.

The parties subsequently stipulated that petitioner was the child's natural father. The superior court, however, ruled that he was not a "presumed father"...The court held four days of hearings...to determine whether it was in the child's best interest for petitioner to retain his parental rights and whether the adoption should be allowed to proceed. (The attorney appointed by the trial court to represent the child's interests advocated that petitioner should retain his parental rights.) On August 26, 1988, the court found "by a bare preponderance" of the evidence that the child's best interest required termination of petitioner's parental rights.....

Petitioner appealed. He contended the superior court erred by: (1) concluding that he was not the child's presumed father; (2) not granting him a parental placement preference; and (3) applying a preponderance-of-the-evidence standard of proof. The Court of Appeal rejected each of his contentions and affirmed the judgment.

DISCUSSION

1. The statutory framework

* * *

This statutory scheme creates three classifications of parents: mothers, biological fathers who are presumed fathers, and biological fathers who are not presumed fathers (*i.e.*, natural fathers). A natural father's consent to an adoption of his child by third parties is not required unless the father makes the required showing that retention of his parental rights is in the child's best interest. Consent, however, is required of a mother and a presumed father regardless of the child's best interest. The natural father is therefore treated differently from both mothers and presumed fathers. With this statutory framework in mind, we now examine petitioner's contentions.

* * *

...We now turn to that difficult constitutional question.[6]

* * *

The most recent relevant high court decision arose in California. (*Michael H. v. Gerald D.* (1989) 491 U.S. 110...) Michael H. claimed to be the father of a child and sought a declaration of paternity and visitation rights....Blood tests showed a 98.07 percent probability that Michael H. was the father....The mother, however, was married to and living with another man at the time of conception. On grounds not relevant to the present case, the high court upheld the denial of Michael H.'s request for a declaration of paternity and visitation rights. (A plurality of the court found to be constitutional the conclusive presumption in California Evidence Code section 621 that the mother's husband was the child's father.) Of special significance for us, however, four justices agreed that the biological father had a protected liberty interest in his relationship with his child....Justice Stevens in concurrence assumed for purposes of the decision that the natural father's relationship was entitled to constitutional protection....

Although the foregoing high court decisions do not provide a comprehensive rule for all situations involving unwed fathers, one unifying and transcendent theme emerges. The biological connection between father and child is unique and worthy of constitutional protection if the father grasps the opportunity to develop that biological connection into a full and enduring relationship.

* * *

We agree that the courts have the authority under this state's Uniform Parentage Act to grant custody to the natural father despite the mother's objection. In the present case, the superior court had the authority to grant petitioner custody of his child so that he could qualify as a presumed father under section 7004, subdivision (a). Indeed, the superior court initially did so but shortly thereafter reversed itself after enforcement of its order was thwarted.

* * *

5. The constitutionally protected interest of an unwed, natural father

* * *

Respondents do not adequately explain how an unwed mother's control over a biological father's rights furthers the state's interest in the well-being of the child. The linchpin of their position, however, is clear although largely implicit: Allowing the biological father to have the same rights as the mother would make adoptions more difficult because the consent of both parents is more difficult to obtain than the consent of the mother alone. This reasoning is flawed in several respects.

A. Respondents' view too narrowly assumes that the proper governmental objective is adoption. As we have explained, the constitutionally valid objective is the protection of the child's well-being. We cannot conclude in the abstract that adoption is itself a sufficient objective to allow the state to take whatever measures it deems appropriate. Nor can we merely assume, either as

---

[6] The nature and scope of an unwed parent's rights are questions of enormous practical significance. The United States Census Bureau recently issued "Fertility of American Women," reporting that, for the most recent statistical year (July 1989 to June 1990), 913,000 of 3.9 million births—1 in 4—were out of wedlock.

a policy or factual matter, that adoption is necessarily in a child's best interest. This assumption is especially untenable in light of the rapidly changing concept of family. As recently as only a few years ago, it might have been reasonable to assume that an adopted child would be placed into a two-parent home and thereby have a more stable environment than a child raised by a single father. The validity of that assumption is now highly suspect in light of modern adoption practice. Recent statistics show that a significant percentage of children placed for independent adoption—7.7 percent—are adopted by a single parent....The figure is even higher—21.9 percent—for children placed with agencies for adoption....

If the possible benefit of adoption were by itself sufficient to justify terminating a parent's rights, the state could terminate an unwed mother's parental rights based on nothing more than a showing that her child's best interest would be served by adoption. Of course, that is not the law; nor do the parties advocate such a system. We simply do not in our society take children away from their mothers married—or otherwise—because a "better" adoptive parent can be found. We see no valid reason why we should be less solicitous of a father's efforts to establish a parental relationship with his child. Respondents seem to suggest that a child is inherently better served by adoptive parents than by a single, biological father but that the child is also inherently better served by a single, biological mother than by adoptive parents. The logic of this view is not apparent, and there is no evidence in the record to support such a counterintuitive view.

* * *

The anomalies under this statutory scheme become readily apparent. A father who is indisputably ready, willing, and able to exercise the full measure of his parental responsibilities can have his rights terminated merely on a showing that his child's best interest would be served by adoption. If the child's mother, however, were equally of the opposite character—unready, unwilling, and unable—her rights in the child could nevertheless be terminated only under the much more protective standards of section 221.20. Such a distinction bears no substantial relationship to protecting the well-being of children. Indeed, it has little rationality.

The system also leads to irrational distinctions between fathers. Based solely on the mother's wishes, a model father can be denied presumed father status, whereas a father of dubious ability and intent can achieve such status by the fortuitous circumstance of the mother allowing him to come into her home, even if only briefly—perhaps a single day. We cannot ignore reality. Parental unfitness is considerably more difficult to show than that the child's best interest is served by adoption. Under the statutory scheme, two fathers who are by all accounts equal in their ability and commitment to fulfill their parental missions can be treated differently based solely on the mothers' decisions whether to allow the father to become a presumed father.

The system also makes little sense from a child's perspective. A child may have a wholly acceptable father who wants to nurture it, but whose parental rights can be terminated under the best-interest standard because the mother has precluded the father from attaining presumed father status. Conversely, if a presumed father is highly questionable in every respect, he is nevertheless allowed to withhold consent absent proof by clear and convincing evidence that he is unfit. (§§ 221.20 and 232.) As a practical matter, the child's best interest is largely ignored by the statutory distinction between presumed fathers and those natural fathers who are willing to assume their parental responsibilities.

* * *

E. In summary, we hold that section 7004, subdivision (a) and the related statutory scheme violates the federal constitutional guarantees of equal protection and due process for unwed fathers to the extent that the statutes allow a mother unilaterally to preclude her child's biological father from becoming a presumed father and thereby allowing the state to terminate his parental rights on nothing more than a showing of the child's best interest. If an unwed father promptly comes forward and demonstrates a full commitment to his parental responsibilities—emotional, financial, and otherwise—his federal constitutional right to due process prohibits the termination of his parental relationship absent a showing of his unfitness as a parent. Absent such a showing, the child's well-being is presumptively best served by continuation of the father's parental relationship. Similarly, when the father has come forward to grasp his parental responsibilities, his parental rights are entitled to equal protection as those of the mother....

A court should consider all factors relevant to that determination. The father's conduct both before and after the child's birth must be considered. Once he knows or reasonably should know of the pregnancy, he must promptly attempt to assume his parental responsibilities as fully as the mother will allow and his circumstances permit. In particular, the father must demonstrate "a willingness himself to assume full custody of the child—not merely to block adoption by others."....A court should also consider the father's public acknowledgement of paternity, payment of pregnancy and birth expenses commensurate with his ability to do so, and prompt legal action to seek custody of the child....

We reiterate and emphasize the narrowness of our decision. The statutory distinction between natural fathers and presumed fathers is constitutionally invalid only to the extent it is applied to an unwed father who has sufficiently and timely demonstrated a full commitment to his parental responsibilities....

* * *

Baxter, J.

We Concur: **Lucas**, C.J., **Paelll**, J., **Kennard**, J., **Arabian**, J., **George**, J.

CONCURRING AND DISSENTING OPINION BY **Mosk. J.**

I concur in the result only. My concern for the welfare of the child in cases of this sort prevents me from joining the majority's reasoning. The majority declare that Civil Code section 7004, a provision of the Uniform Parentage Act enacted in 1975, is unconstitutional as applied. The soundness of their determination is open to serious question. Its potential for mischief is not. It creates needless uncertainty in the application of statutory categories that have been consistently employed for almost 20 years. Such uncertainty will redound to the disadvantage of all parties—but especially the child.

The majority yield to the lamentable temptation to invoke the Constitution when there is a perfectly simple legal solution to the factual problem of this case. It s settled law that we should not reach constitutional questions unless absolutely required....

* * *

Though the facts are disputed, assume, *arguendo*, that in this case they can be established at trial. The biological father engaged in an adulterous relationship with the mother. A child was born. Though he had rejected the mother and returned to his wife, the biological father conceded paternity, made reasonable efforts to ascertain the whereabouts of the child and indicated a willingness to take the child into his home and to support it. In short, the biological father allegedly sought to become a presumed father within the statutory requirements of Civil Code section 7004, subdivision (a)(4), but was thwarted from achieving that status through the purported devious actions of the mother.

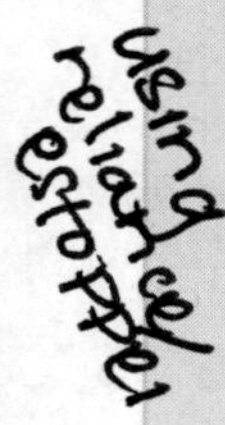

Under those circumstances, if established by a preponderance of evidence in court, I would estop the mother and the proposed adoptive parents from denying that the biological father had assumed the status of a presumed father. These are paradigm circumstances for the imposition of an estoppel....

* * *

To my mind, the choice between a declaration of unconstitutionality and a use of the doctrine of equitable estoppel is clear. The latter will yield justice for the party if he deserves justice in this individual action without providing a precedent that has the potential to produce unfortunate results in countless other proceedings, even those previously concluded.

* * *

Questions for Discussion

1. The *Kelsey* case was in litigation for four years. During this period the child was in the custody of his mother, the one party who did not want him. Now the case is to be remanded for further proceedings. Does the court take responsibility for or comment upon the impact of a four year delay before Kelsey achieves a permanent home and parents?

2. Assume that on remand the trial court finds that Rickie M. adequately attempted to assume a parental role with Kelsey and that he is not "unfit." He then blocks the proposed adoption. But he remains single and the court concludes that it is not in the best interests of the child to give him custody (only 8% of adoptive parents are single). What happens to Kelsey?

3. Scalia might argue that Rickie M. had an option to perfect his paternal rights: marry the mother of his child, and that a legislature may rationally require such a commitment prior to recognizing a father's parental rights given the ease of biology alone. What is the response of the majority to this argument?

4. Lacking marriage and presumptive father status, should "showing substantial interest" in a child by a biological father suffice to invoke constitutional parental rights? Does the vagueness of the *Kelsey* test raise problems in accomplishing expeditious adoptions?

5. Should a *Kelsey* father (a biological father who does not qualify as a "presumed father") be held to a strong "due diligence" standard to monitor and learn about any possible pregnancies he may have caused in order to claim the significant constitutional right to parenthood that can (a) veto an adoption, (b) claim custody, and (c) be extinguished only upon a showing of unfitness by clear and convincing evidence by the state at a full due process hearing, with counsel provided for him at public expense if needed?[3]

*Note on Cases Post-*Kelsey*: Baby Richard and Related Problems*

Following *Kelsey*, the Illinois Supreme Court decided the highly publicized case of Baby Richard (*In Re Petition of Doe*, 638 N.E.2d 181 (Ill. 1994). The facts as found by the Supreme Court include the following: (a) Otakar Kirchner impregnated Daniella Janikova while living with her, and intending to marry her and father their child. (b) While Otakar was visiting relatives in Czechoslovakia, Daniella received information that he may have been unfaithful to her in Europe; she then left the home two weeks before giving birth at a hospital unknown to the father, gave birth, and told Otakar the infant died at birth. (c) The mother then signed away her rights to the child, arranging for an adoption with a qualified couple (the Warburtons) who obtained custody of the child four days after his birth. (d) The father searched to verify the fate of the baby and learned 57 days after the birth that the child was alive; the father hired counsel and objected to the adoption. (e) The trial court and the appellate court considering the case find that it would be in the "best interests of the child" to remain with and be adopted by the Warburtons. (f) Otakar and Daniella then reunited and she reversed herself to support his assertion of paternal rights and to object to the adoption she had arranged. The Illinois Supreme Court granted review and issued an opinion granting a final order of habeas corpus to award the child to Otakar on approximately the child's fourth birthday.

Is Otakar a "presumed father" under the Uniform Parentage Act? Has he met the *Kelsey* standard? Is it relevant that he was misled by the mother and was prevented from bringing the child into his home or from assuming a paternal role earlier? Is it determinative? Is it relevant that four years have passed and the adoptive parents are the only parents the child has known?

Through the 1990s, a number of well-publicized cases were litigated involving biological fathers who did not marry nor live with the biological mothers, but who were interested in a parental role, and who appeared post-birth to contest adoptions arranged by the respective biological mothers. Many of them had contentions about the mother misleading them or hiding from them to prevent them from "seizing" the *Kelsey* opportunity. A substantial number sought parental rights and custody as single fathers of children who had been adopted for one to five years and more.

Justice Heiple of the Illinois Supreme Court was angry enough at the extensive press coverage of Baby Richard being torn from the arms of his adoptive parents to include an unusual emotional attack on the media's characterization of the case, accusing Chicago columnist Bob Greene of engaging in "journalistic terrorism" and bitterly criticizing the legislature, the Governor, and the Warburtons. He argued—consistent with precedent— that the "best interests" standard does not apply to deprive a fit parent of parental status. Some child advocates argued that his position begged the question in assuming that Otakar properly claimed constitutional parental status as a threshold matter. Of particular concern to child advocates was the opinion's discounting of the child's loss of his adoptive parents. Consistent with the majority rule to date, the child's right to the two parents serving this function for four years was not given constitutional dimension, in contrast to Otakar, who was afforded that status in full measure although he had not functioned as a father. The Court opined that the removal from the Warburtons will not be an "insurmountable trauma," citing the deaths of some parents and the high incidence of divorce.[4] The Illinois Court also argued that the adoptive parents bear responsibility for the delay because of their extensive litigation to keep the child.[5]

The justices here stood in the shoes of Otakar, recognized his good faith, and empathized with the denigration of his parental rights by others. Indeed, where the abdication of paternal responsibility to children has become a major societal problem, child advocates welcome a father not only willing to raise his child, but exhibiting zeal to do so. On the other hand, they also argue that Baby Richard is not a prize to be awarded to the meritorious, but a sentient human with arguably the same rights to his parents as the courts readily grant parents to their children.

The dilemma in the case stems less from the decision between the Warburtons and Otakar than from the consequence of a four-year travail while the child is parented by adults who the state will then remove from him. Accordingly, and as the *query* in *Kelsey* above asks about the similar four-year period of that litigation, should the Court take some responsibility for such a delay? Has the time period to decide these cases—arguably the source of much of the harm to involved children—ever been addressed in any pertinent court decision (other than here, where the court blames one of the parties for the decision to litigate)? How long should it take to establish the facts (a) through (f) above? The Illinois Court contends that the law applied to these facts is self-apparent and the decision reversing the trial and appellate court and awarding the child to Otakar was 7–0. Accordingly, and of import to child advocates, can the decision be made in thirty days? Ninety days? Due process takes time, but how many total hours were actually consumed with necessary fact gathering, trial, writing of briefs and oral argument over the four years while the parents of Kelsey, Richard and many other children are being determined? Does the Court have the authority to impose tight timelines on itself and its lower courts where a child is in limbo? Can it make a preliminary decision to make it more likely the child will not be moved? Would the Illinois Legislature—which responded to the publicity by attempting to legislatively reverse the Court—not serve the interests of these children by statutorily imposing tight timelines if the Court does not act through its rulemaking power to do so?

Troxel v. Granville
530 U.S. 57 (2000)

OPINION: **JUSTICE O'CONNOR** announced the judgment of the Court and delivered an opinion, in which **THE CHIEF JUSTICE**, **JUSTICE GINSBURG**, and **JUSTICE BREYER** join.

Section 26.10.160(3) of the Revised Code of Washington permits "any person" to petition a superior court for visitation rights "at any time," and authorizes that court to grant such visitation rights whenever "visitation may serve the best interest of the child." Petitioners Jenifer and Gary Troxel petitioned a Washington Superior Court for the right to visit their grandchildren, Isabelle and Natalie Troxel. Respondent Tommie Granville, the mother of Isabelle and Natalie, opposed the petition. The case ultimately reached the Washington Supreme Court, which held that § 26.10.160(3) unconstitutionally interferes with the fundamental right of parents to rear their children.

I

Tommie Granville and Brad Troxel shared a relationship that ended in June 1991. The two never married, but they had two daughters, Isabelle and Natalie. Jenifer and Gary Troxel are Brad's parents, and thus the paternal grandparents of Isabelle and Natalie. After Tommie and Brad separated in 1991,

Brad lived with his parents and regularly brought his daughters to his parents' home for weekend visitation. Brad committed suicide in May 1993. Although the Troxels at first continued to see Isabelle and Natalie on a regular basis after their son's death, Tommie Granville informed the Troxels in October 1993 that she wished to limit their visitation with her daughters to one short visit per month....

In December 1993, the Troxels commenced the present action by filing, in the Washington Superior Court for Skagit County, a petition to obtain visitation rights with Isabelle and Natalie. The Troxels filed their petition under two Washington statutes, Wash. Rev. Code §§ 26.09.240 and 26.10.160(3) (1994). Only the latter statute is at issue in this case. Section 26.10.160(3) provides: "Any person may petition the court for visitation rights at any time including, but not limited to, custody proceedings. The court may order visitation rights for any person when visitation may serve the best interest of the child whether or not there has been any change of circumstances." At trial, the Troxels requested two weekends of overnight visitation per month and two weeks of visitation each summer. Granville did not oppose visitation altogether, but instead asked the court to order one day of visitation per month with no overnight stay.... In 1995, the Superior Court issued an oral ruling and entered a visitation decree ordering visitation one weekend per month, one week during the summer, and four hours on both of the petitioning grandparents' birthdays....

Granville appealed, during which time she married Kelly Wynn. Before addressing the merits of Granville's appeal, the Washington Court of Appeals remanded the case to the Superior Court for entry of written findings of fact and conclusions of law.... On remand, the Superior Court found that visitation was in Isabelle and Natalie's best interests:

"The Petitioners [the Troxels] are part of a large, central, loving family, all located in this area, and the Petitioners can provide opportunities for the children in the areas of cousins and music.

The court took into consideration all factors regarding the best interest of the children and considered all the testimony before it. The children would be benefitted from spending quality time with the Petitioners, provided that that time is balanced with time with the childrens' *[sic]* nuclear family. The court finds that the childrens' *[sic]* best interests are served by spending time with their mother and stepfather's other six children."....

Approximately nine months after the Superior Court entered its order on remand, Granville's husband formally adopted Isabelle and Natalie....

* * *

The Washington Supreme Court ... agreed with the Court of Appeals' ultimate conclusion that the Troxels could not obtain visitation of Isabelle and Natalie pursuant to § 26.10.160(3). The court rested its decision on the Federal Constitution, holding that § 26.10.160(3) unconstitutionally infringes on the fundamental right of parents to rear their children. In the court's view, there were at least two problems with the nonparental visitation statute. First, according to the Washington Supreme Court, the Constitution permits a State to interfere with the right of parents to rear their children only to prevent harm or potential harm... Second, by allowing "'any person' to petition for forced visitation of a child at 'any time' with the only requirement being that the visitation serve the best interest of the child," the Washington visitation statute sweeps too broadly.... "It is not within the province of the state to make significant decisions concerning the custody of children merely because it could make a 'better' decision." *Ibid.*, 969 P.2d at 31. The Washington Supreme Court held that "parents have a right to limit visitation of their children with third persons," and that between parents and judges, "the parents should be the ones to choose whether to expose their children to certain people or ideas."....

We...affirm the judgment.

I

The demographic changes of the past century make it difficult to speak of an average American family. The composition of families varies greatly from household to household. While many children may have two married parents and grandparents who visit regularly, many other children are raised in single-parent households. In 1996, children living with only one parent accounted for 28 percent of all children under age 18 in the United States. U.S. Dept. of Commerce, Bureau of Census, Current Population Reports, 1997 Population Profile of the United States 27 (1998). Understandably, in these single-parent households, persons outside the nuclear family are called upon with increasing frequency to assist in the everyday tasks of child rearing. In many cases, grandparents play an important role. For example, in 1998, approximately 4 million children—or 5.6 percent of all children under age 18—lived in the household of their grandparents. U.S. Dept. of Commerce, Bureau of Census, Current Population Reports, Marital Status and Living Arrangements: March 1998 (Update), p. *i* (1998).

The nationwide enactment of nonparental visitation statutes is assuredly due, in some part, to the States' recognition of these changing realities of the American family. Because grandparents and other relatives undertake duties of a parental nature in many households, States have sought to ensure the welfare of the children therein by protecting the relationships those children form with such third parties. The States' nonparental visitation statutes are further supported by a recognition, which varies from State to State, that children should have the opportunity to benefit from relationships with statutorily specified persons—for example, their grandparents. The extension of statutory rights in this area to persons other than a child's parents, however, comes with an obvious cost. For example, the State's recognition of an independent third-party interest in a child can place a substantial burden on the traditional parent-child relationship. Contrary to JUSTICE STEVENS' accusation, our description of state nonparental visitation statutes in these terms, of course, is not meant to suggest that "children are so much chattel."...Rather, our terminology is intended to highlight the fact that these [65] statutes can present questions of constitutional import. In this case, we are presented with just such a question. Specifically, we are asked to decide whether § 26.10.160(3), as applied to Tommie Granville and her family, violates the Federal Constitution.

* * *

The liberty interest at issue in this case—the interest of parents in the care, custody, and control of their children—is perhaps the oldest of the fundamental liberty interests recognized by this Court. More than 75 years ago, in *Meyer* v. *Nebraska,* 262 U.S. 390, 399, 401....(1923), we held that the "liberty" protected by the Due Process Clause includes the right of parents to "establish a home and bring up children" and "to control the education of their own."....

* * *

Section 26.10.160(3), as applied to Granville and her family in this case, unconstitutionally infringes on that fundamental [2061] parental right. The Washington nonparental visitation statute is breathtakingly broad. According to the statute's text, "*any person* may petition the court for visitation rights *at any time,*" and the court may grant such visitation rights whenever "visitation may serve *the best interest of the child.*" § 26.10.160(3) (emphases added). That language effectively permits any third party seeking visitation to subject any decision by a parent concerning visitation of the parent's children to state-court review. Once the visitation petition has been filed in court and the matter is placed before a judge, a parent's decision that visitation would not be in the child's best interest is accorded no deference. Section 26.10.160(3) contains no requirement that a court accord the parent's decision any presumption of validity or any weight whatsoever. Instead, the Washington statute places the best-interest determination solely in the hands of the judge. Should the judge disagree with the parent's estimation of the child's best interests, the judge's view necessarily prevails. Thus, in practical effect, in the State of Washington a court can disregard and overturn *any* decision by a fit custodial parent concerning visitation whenever a third party affected by the decision files a visitation petition, based solely on the judge's determination of the child's best interests. The Washington Supreme Court had the opportunity to give § 26.10.160(3) a narrower reading, but it declined to do so....

* * *

...[T]his case involves nothing more than a simple disagreement between the Washington Superior Court and Granville concerning her children's best interests. The Superior Court's announced reason for ordering one week of visitation in the summer demonstrates our conclusion well: "I look back on some personal experiences ....We always spent as kids a week with one set of grandparents and another set of grandparents, [and] it happened to work out in our family that [it] turned out to be an enjoyable experience....

* * *

Because we rest our decision on the sweeping breadth of § 26.10.160(3) and the application of that broad, unlimited power in this case, we do not consider the primary constitutional question passed on by the Washington Supreme Court—whether the Due Process Clause requires all nonparental visitation statutes to include a showing of harm or potential harm to the child as a condition precedent to granting visitation. We do not, and need not, define today the precise scope of the parental due process right in the visitation context. In this respect, we agree with JUSTICE KENNEDY that the constitutionality of any standard for awarding visitation turns on the specific manner in which that standard is applied and that the constitutional protections in this area are best "elaborated with care." *Post*, at 9 (dissenting opinion). Because much state-court adjudication in this context occurs on a case-by-case basis, we would be hesitant to hold that specific nonparental visitation statutes violate the Due Process Clause as a *per se* matter..

* * *

Accordingly, the judgment of the Washington Supreme Court is affirmed.

* * *

JUSTICE STEVENS, dissenting.

* * *

A parent's rights with respect to her child have thus never been regarded as absolute, but rather are limited by the existence of an actual, developed relationship with a child, and are tied to the presence or absence of some embodiment of family. These limitations have arisen, not simply out of the definition of parenthood itself, but because of this Court's assumption that a parent's interests in a child must be balanced against the State's long-recognized interests as parens patriae, see, e.g., *Reno v. Flores*, 507 U.S. 292, 303-304...(1993); *Santosky v. Kramer*, 455 U.S. at 766; *Parham*, 442 U.S. at 605; *Prince v. Massachusetts*, 321 U.S. 158, 166...(1944), and, critically, the child's own complementary interest in preserving relationships that serve her welfare and protection, *Santosky*, 455 U.S. at 760.

While this Court has not yet had occasion to elucidate the nature of a child's liberty interests in preserving established familial or family-like bonds, 491 U.S. at 130 (reserving the question), it seems to me extremely likely that, to the extent parents and families have fundamental liberty interests in preserving such intimate relationships, so, too, do children have these interests, and so, too, must their interests be balanced in the equation.[8] At a minimum, our prior cases recognizing that children are, generally speaking, constitutionally protected actors require that this Court reject any suggestion that when it comes to parental rights, children are so much chattel. See ante, at 5-6 (opinion of O'CONNOR, J.) (describing States' recognition of "an independent third-party interest in a child"). The constitutional protection against arbitrary state interference with parental rights should not be extended to prevent the States from protecting children against the arbitrary exercise of parental authority that is not in fact motivated by an interest in the welfare of the child.[9]

This is not, of course, to suggest that a child's liberty interest in maintaining contact with a particular individual is to be treated invariably as on a par with that child's parents' contrary interests. Because our substantive due process case law includes a strong presumption that a parent will act in the best interest of her child, it would be necessary, were the state appellate courts actually to confront a challenge to the statute as applied, to consider whether the trial court's assessment of the "best interest of the child" incorporated that presumption. Neither would I decide whether the trial court applied Washington's statute in a constitutional way in this case, although, as I have explained,...I think the outcome of this determination is far from clear. For the purpose of a facial challenge like this, I think it safe to assume that trial judges usually give great deference to parents' wishes, and I am not persuaded otherwise here.

But presumptions notwithstanding, we should recognize that there may be circumstances in which a child has a stronger interest at stake than mere protection from serious harm caused by the termination of visitation by a "person" other than a parent. The almost infinite variety of family relationships that pervade our ever-changing society strongly counsel against the creation by this Court of a constitutional rule that treats a biological parent's liberty interest in the care and supervision of her child as an isolated right that may be exercised arbitrarily....

---

[8] This Court has on numerous occasions acknowledged that children are in many circumstances possessed of constitutionally protected rights and liberties. See *Parham v. J. R.*, 442 U.S. 584, 600...(1979) (liberty interest in avoiding involuntary confinement); *Planned Parenthood of Central Mo. v. Danforth*, 428 U.S. 52, 74...(1976) ("Constitutional rights do not mature and come into being magically only when one attains the state-defined age of majority. Minors, as well as adults, are protected by the Constitution and possess constitutional rights"); *Tinker v. Des Moines Independent Community School Dist.*, 393 U.S. 503, 506-507...(1969) (First Amendment right to political speech); *In re Gault*, 387 U.S. 1, 13...(1967) (due process rights in criminal proceedings).

[9] Cf., e.g., *Wisconsin v. Yoder*, 406 U.S. 205, 241-246...(1972) (Douglas, J., dissenting) ("While the parents, absent dissent, normally speak for the entire family, the education of the child is a matter on which the child will often have decided views. He may want to be a pianist or an astronaut or an oceanographer. To do so he will have to break from the Amish tradition. It is the future of the student, not the future of the parents, that is imperiled by today's decision. If a parent keeps his child out of school beyond the grade school, then the child will be forever barred from entry into the new and amazing world of diversity that we have today....It is the student's judgment, not his parents', that is essential if we are to give full meaning to what we have said about the Bill of Rights and of the right of students to be masters of their own destiny."). The majority's disagreement with Justice Douglas in that case turned not on any contrary view of children's interest in their own education, but on the impact of the Free Exercise Clause of the First Amendment on its analysis of school-related decisions by the Amish community.

* * *

JUSTICE SCALIA, dissenting.

In my view, a right of parents to direct the upbringing of their children is among the "unalienable Rights" with which the Declaration of Independence proclaims "all Men...are endowed by their Creator." And in my view that right is also among the "other [rights] retained by the people" which the Ninth Amendment says the Constitution's enumeration of rights "shall not be construed to deny or disparage." The Declaration of Independence, however, is not a legal prescription conferring powers upon the courts; and the Constitution's refusal to "deny or disparage" other rights is far removed from affirming any one of them, and even farther removed from authorizing judges to identify what they might be, and to enforce the judges' list against laws duly enacted by the people. Consequently, while I would think it entirely compatible with the commitment to representative democracy set forth in the founding documents to argue, in legislative chambers or in electoral campaigns, that the state has *no power* to interfere with parents' authority over the rearing of their children, I do not believe that the power which the Constitution confers upon me *as a judge* entitles me to deny legal effect to laws that (in my view) infringe upon what is (in my view) that unenumerated right.

* * *

Judicial vindication of "parental rights" under a Constitution that does not even mention them requires (as JUSTICE KENNEDY's opinion rightly points out) not only a judicially crafted definition of parents, but also—unless, as no one believes, the parental rights are to be absolute—judicially approved assessments of "harm to the child" and judicially defined gradations of other persons (grandparents, extended family, adoptive family in an adoption later found to be invalid, long-term guardians, etc.) who may have some claim against the wishes of the parents. If we embrace this unenumerated right, I think it obvious—whether we affirm or reverse the judgment here, or remand as JUSTICE STEVENS or JUSTICE KENNEDY would do—that we will be ushering in a new regime of judicially prescribed, and federally prescribed, family law. I have no reason to believe that federal judges will be better at this than state legislatures; and state legislatures have the great advantages of doing harm in a more circumscribed area, of being able to correct their mistakes in a flash, and of being removable by the people.[2]

For these reasons, I would reverse the judgment below.

* * *

JUSTICE KENNEDY, dissenting.

* * *

The first flaw the State Supreme Court found in the statute is that it allows an award of visitation to a non-parent without a finding that harm to the child would result if visitation were withheld; and the second is that the statute allows any person to seek visitation at any time. In my view the first theory is too

---

[2] I note that respondent is asserting only, *on her own behalf*, a substantive due process right to direct the upbringing of her own children, and is not asserting, *on behalf of her children*, their First Amendment rights of association or free exercise. I therefore do not have occasion to consider whether, and under what circumstances, the parent could assert the latter enumerated rights.

broad to be correct, as it appears to contemplate that the best interests of the child standard may not be applied in any visitation case. I acknowledge the distinct possibility that visitation cases may arise where, considering the absence of other protection for the parent under state laws and procedures, the best interests of the child standard would give insufficient protection to the parent's constitutional right to raise the child without undue intervention by the state; but it is quite a different matter to say, as I understand the Supreme Court of Washington to have said, that a harm to the child standard is required in every instance.

* * *

Turning to the question whether harm to the child must be the controlling standard in every visitation proceeding, there is a beginning point that commands general, perhaps unanimous, agreement in our separate opinions: As our case law has developed, the custodial parent has a constitutional right to determine, without undue interference by the state, how best to raise, nurture, and educate the child. The parental right stems from the liberty protected by the Due Process Clause of the Fourteenth Amendment....

The State Supreme Court sought to give content to the parent's right by announcing a categorical rule that third parties who seek visitation must always prove the denial of visitation would harm the child. After reviewing some of the relevant precedents, the Supreme Court of Washington concluded "'the requirement of harm is the sole protection that parents have against pervasive state interference in the parenting process.'"... For that reason, "short of preventing harm to the child," the court considered the best interests of the child to be "insufficient to serve as a compelling state interest overruling a parent's fundamental rights." ...

While it might be argued as an abstract matter that in some sense the child is always harmed if his or her best interests are not considered, the law of domestic relations, as it has evolved to this point, treats as distinct the two standards, one harm to the child and the other the best interests of the child. The judgment of the Supreme Court of Washington rests on that assumption, and I, too, shall assume that there are real and consequential differences between the two standards.

* * *

My principal concern is that the holding seems to proceed from the assumption that the parent or parents who resist visitation have always been the child's primary caregivers and that the third parties who seek visitation have no legitimate and established relationship with the child. That idea, in turn, appears influenced by the concept that the conventional nuclear family ought to establish the visitation standard for every domestic relations case. As we all know, this is simply not the structure or prevailing condition in many households. See, *e.g.*, *Moore* v. *East Cleveland,* 431 U.S. 494,...(1977). For many boys and girls a traditional family with two or even one permanent and caring parent is simply not the reality of their childhood. This may be so whether their childhood has been marked by tragedy or filled with considerable happiness and fulfillment.

Cases are sure to arise—perhaps a substantial number of cases—in which a third party, by acting in a caregiving role over a significant period of time, has developed a relationship with a child which is not necessarily subject to absolute parental veto. See *Michael H.* v. *Gerald D.,* 491 U.S. 110,...(1989) (putative natural father not entitled to rebut state law presumption that child born in a marriage is a child of the marriage); *Quilloin* v. *Walcott,* 434 U.S. 246,...(1978) (best interests standard sufficient in adoption proceeding to protect interests of natural father who had not legitimated the child); see also *Lehr* v. *Robertson,...*Some pre-existing relationships, then, serve to identify persons who have a strong attachment to the child with the concomitant motivation to act in a responsible way to ensure the child's welfare. As the State Supreme Court was correct to acknowledge, those relationships can be so enduring that "in certain circumstances where a child has enjoyed a substantial relationship with a third person, arbitrarily depriving the child of the relationship could cause severe psychological harm to the child," *In re Smith,* 137 Wn.2d at 20, 969 P.2d at 30; and harm to the adult may also ensue. In the design and elaboration of their visitation laws, States may be entitled to consider that certain relationships are such that to avoid the risk of harm, a best interests standard can be employed by their domestic relations courts in some circumstances.

Indeed, contemporary practice should give us some pause before rejecting the best interests of the child standard in all third-party visitation cases, as the Washington court has done. The standard has been recognized for many years as a basic tool of domestic relations law in visitation proceedings. Since 1965 all 50 States have enacted a third-party visitation statute of some sort. See *ante*, at 15, n. (plurality opinion). Each of these statutes, save one, permits a court order to issue in certain cases if visitation is found to be in the best interests of the child. While it is unnecessary for us to consider the constitutionality of any particular provision in the case now before us, it can be noted that the statutes also include a variety of methods for limiting parents' exposure to third-party visitation petitions and for ensuring parental decisions are given respect. Many States limit the identity of permissible petitioners by restricting visitation petitions to grandparents, or by requiring petitioners to show a substantial relationship with a child, or both....

* * *

Questions for Discussion

1. What are the proper criteria for court ordered visitation against the wishes of a parent? Does it require a biological relationship (such as a grandparent)? Does it require a previous or existing parental role or function by the person granted such visitation—as Kennedy's dissent suggests might suffice?

2. Would it matter if their son Brad had custody at the time of his death? Would it have made a difference if the Troxel grandparents were the only parents this child had ever known?

3. The opinions in *Troxel* have much in common, even between the majority opinion and the dissents. How do the Kennedy and Stevens dissents differ from the majority? From each other? Kennedy implies and Stevens states that the loss of a parental relationship from a child's perspective is a cognizable interest. Does the majority find that interest to be of constitutional dimension?

4. Note that the interests of children are often cast as a "compelling state interest" of importance—but subservient to competing adult constitutional "fundamental liberties" (such as the right to parent a child). If a child's concomitant constitutional rights are recognized and competed in a "balancing" of those rights on the same level, what would be the implications for *Troxel*? For other leading constitutional cases involving children?

Webster v. Ryan
189 Misc. 2d 86 [729 N.Y.S.2d 315] (2001)

W. DENNIS DUGGAN, J.:

In this case, the Court holds that a child has an independent, constitutionally guaranteed right to maintain contact...with a person with whom the child has developed a parent-like relationship.[1]

That right is constitutionally guaranteed because it is a fundamental liberty encompassed within the freedom of association right of the First Amendment of the United States Constitution (see the intimate personal relationship rights of *Griswold v. Connecticut* 381 US 479 (1965)), and article I, §§ 8 and 9 of the New York Constitution. This liberty is protected by the Due Process Clause of the Fourteenth Amendment and article I, § 6 of the New York Constitution. Because the state has provided no statutory basis for a child to assert such right of contact in a court of law, as it has for similar situations involving child contact with parents, grandparents and siblings, Alex Ryan, Jr., has been denied the equal protection of the laws guaranteed by the Fourteenth Amendment of the US Constitution and article I, § 11 of the New York Constitution....

• • •

...Alex, Jr., was born in 1995, with a positive toxicology for cocaine. He was removed from his mother's custody shortly after birth. Her parental rights were eventually terminated, as were the father's in 1999. Both parents' terminations were based on permanent neglect. During the time that the Department of Social Services (DSS) was providing services for the mother, the father was filing at least four custody proceedings. All of the father's petitions were dismissed by the Family Court judge without a hearing. According to the trial court, the petitions were "dismissed due to [the father's] unwillingness to partake in services recommended by [DSS]." For the years from 1995 to 1998, the father received one hour of DSS-supervised visitation each week. In reviewing the denial of the father's custody petitions, the Appellate Division held:

> "In fact, the records in these proceedings reveal no evidence that the father would not be a proper custodian for the child or that the child would be at risk in his custody. To the contrary, despite Family Court's limitation on the evidence received, the record generally supports a finding that the father is qualified to serve as a custodian for the child...."

---

[1]At the outset, the Court notes that the terms "custody" and "visitation" have outlived their usefulness. Indeed, their use tends to place any discussion and allocation of family rights into an oppositional framework. "Fighting for custody" directs the process towards determining winners and losers. The children, always in the middle, usually turn out to be losers. Churchill once said that we shape our buildings and afterwards our buildings shape us. The same can be said for our words. This Court has abandoned the use of the word "visitation" in its orders, using the phrase "parenting time" instead. If the word "custody" did not so permeate our statutes and was not so ingrained into our psyches, that would be the next phrase to go. If our Domestic Relations Law, in both substance and process, was more child focused, as I believe this decision is, there would be a better framework for determining family rights. Instead, we focus on parental rights. This misplaced focus draws parents into contention and conflict, drawing the worst from them at a time when their children need their parents' best. The Court notes, for example, that the Family Court Act of Australia uses neither the word custody nor visitation, but refers only to "parenting orders" which can include "residence orders" and "contact orders."...

Concerning the termination of parental rights finding, the Appellate Division held that DSS made no effort to satisfy its burden of showing that it had formulated a realistic plan that was tailored to fit the father's circumstances. It also held that the Family Court judge "repeatedly thwarted the father's efforts to establish the lack of any reasonable basis for the plan that was put in place....Obviously, the petition should have been dismissed at the conclusion of DSS' case, if not earlier."...The Appellate Division, in finding that the Family Court judge had demonstrated hostility toward the father and his attorney, ordered that all further proceedings be conducted before a different judge.

Upon remand, in *Ryan III,* this Court returned custody of the child to the father and entered a series of visitation orders to facilitate the transition of the child back into the father's home. During this period of time, the foster mother filed petitions seeking visitation and custody rights to Alex, Jr. This Court, in *Ryan III,* rejected the foster mother's claims. It found that there was no statutory, common law or constitutional basis to grant visitation to a nonbiological, former custodian. The Court reserved on the question of whether the child has an independent constitutional right to seek visitation with his former foster mother and allowed the parties and the Law Guardian time to brief the issue. This decision answers that question in the affirmative. From Alex, Jr.'s birth in 1995 until April 2000, when he was returned to his father, the boy had lived with the foster mother for all of his life but for a few weeks.

II. Determination of Fundamental Rights

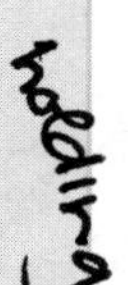

In this case, the Court has concluded that a child has a fundamental right to maintain contact, over the objection of a parent, with a person with whom the child has developed a parent-like relationship. The Court also holds that this right has constitutional protection but that this right must be balanced with the unquestionable fundamental right of the parent to raise his son without undue state interference.

The judicial determination (disparagingly described by some as "discovery") of fundamental rights has long been a subject of great debate in the legal and judicial professions.[2]...A judge, wading into the constitutional rights determination quicksand, must have an abiding concern that he not set himself up as a judicial legislature....[But] proof that the People possess other rights, not contained in or derivative of the Constitution, comes from three powerful positive sources: the Declaration of Independence, the Constitution and the Bill of Rights.

• • •

...The Constitution, as first passed, had no bill of rights at all. The Delegates to the Convention did not believe one was necessary. It was not necessary, in the Framers' view, because the Constitution, as written, gave the

---

[2] See, for example, on the restraint side: Antonin Scalia, *A Matter of Interpretation, Federal Courts and the Law* (Princeton Univ 1997); Raoul Berger, *Government by Judiciary* (Liberty Fund, Law ed 1997); and Richard A. Posner, The Problems of Jurisprudence (Harv Univ Press 1990). On the expansionist side see: Charles L. Black, Jr., *A New Birth of Freedom* (Grosset/Putnam 1997); Laurence H. Tribe, *Constitutional Choices* (Harv Univ Press 1985); and William Lusser, *The Limits of Judicial Power, The Supreme Court in American Politics* (Univ of NC Press 1988). With a foot in both camps see: John Hart Ely, *Democracy and Distrust, A Theory of Judicial Review* (Harv Univ Press 1980); Cass R. Sunstein, *The Partial Constitution* (Harv Univ Press 1993); and Alexander M. Bickel, *The Supreme Court and The Idea of Progress* (Harper and Row 1970).

Federal Government no power to abridge any fundamental rights....The final element of proof which establishes that all of our rights are not bestowed by or contained in the Constitution comes from the Bill of Rights itself—Amendment IX provides: "The enumeration in the Constitution, of certain rights, shall not be construed to deny or disparage others *retained by the people.*" (Emphasis added.)

Amendment X provides: "The powers not delegated to the United States by the Constitution, nor prohibited by it to the States, are reserved to the States respectively, *or to the people*" (emphasis added).

Amendment XIV, § 1 provides: "No State shall make or enforce any law which shall abridge the privileges or immunities of citizens of the United States."

These three Amendments all speak to rights held by the People that are not listed in the Constitution. Knowing that other rights exist, how are they to be determined and who should do the determining, the judiciary or the legislature? Most would readily agree that the legislature has the authority to determine rights or even create new rights. For example, the legislature could determine that the people have a right to universal health care. It is doubtful that the judiciary could make such a determination....The question to be asked here is, what is the judiciary's proper place in the rights determination business? It is clear that the Constitution does create some rights that would not be considered fundamental (*e.g.*, the prohibition against bills of attainder and ex post facto laws). It is also clear that the Constitution protects or guarantees many other rights, some of which are now (but were not always) universally regarded as fundamental (*e.g.*, freedom of speech and religion). Finally, it is clear that other rights determined by the courts to be possessed by the people are not specified in but are protected by the Constitution. For example, the rights to travel (*Edwards v California,* 314 US 160 [1941]), to marry (*Loving v Virginia,* 388 US 1 [1967]), and to privacy (*Griswold v Connecticut,* 381 US 479 [1965]) are rights protected by the Due Process and Equal Protection Clauses of the Fourteenth Amendment, but they are not listed anywhere in the Constitution.[3] The above discussion shows that if a right exists for a child to maintain contact with a person with whom he has developed a parent-like relationship, it will not be found explicitly or inferentially set forth in the Constitution, but it need not be. However, if such a right exists, and this Court holds that it does, that right has constitutional protection because it is a fundamental right and the Constitution protects our fundamental rights from unwarranted state intrusion or exclusion....The search for such a right must begin with the Supreme Court's Talmudic exposition of our Constitution.[4]

If one scans 200 years of Supreme Court decisions that define, determine or discover rights (however one defines the process)...and the work of legal scholars who have written on the subject, one is left quite disoriented from trying to find any consistently applied, generally agreed upon, theory of constitutional interpretation....Despite the absence of a legislative road map or clearly defined constitutional sign posts or a generally accepted method of

---

[3]...[S]ome things that most people would probably consider as a constitutional (or fundamental) right are not so at all. For example, the right of a child to an education is not constitutionally protected. (*San Antonio Ind. School Dist. v Rodriguez,*411 US 1 [1973].) One reason for this slow evolution of personal rights is that liberty rights follow property rights. Until a person's right to own and control property became protected by the Constitution, the rights to free speech, religion, and to assemble, were little more than lofty ideas. The Alien and Sedition Acts are a good example of how fragile and unprotected the rights of free speech and assembly were in 1798....

[4]The Court's use of the word Constitution in this decision includes both the New York State and Federal Constitutions. The Court finds that each Constitution's protective reach covers the right determined in this decision and should be interpreted identically.

rights determinations to provide guidance, courts, since courts began, have been determining rights....These rights have been birthed from statutes, bills of rights, constitutions, natural law and the common law.

• • •

...*Griswold* was a substantive due process case and Justice Goldberg (with Chief Justice Burger and Justice Brennan concurring) [wrote]

> "I do agree that the concept of liberty protects those personal rights that are fundamental, and is not confined to the specific terms of the Bill of Rights. My conclusion that the concept of liberty is not so restricted and that it embraces the right of marital privacy though that right is not mentioned explicitly in the Constitution is supported by both numerous decisions of this Court, referred to in the Court's opinion, and by the language and history of the Ninth Amendment....The Ninth Amendment shows a belief of the Constitution's authors that fundamental rights exist that are not deemed exhaustive."...

• • •

However these liberty rights are found, the Supreme Court's progression of rulings on issues affecting family privacy rights does show a fairly consistent trend. This trend expands the rights of families and individual family members.

1. In *Meyer v Nebraska* (262 US 390 [1923]), the Supreme Court ruled unconstitutional a Nebraska law which prohibited the teaching of any foreign language in any elementary school. 2. In *Pierce v Society of Sisters* (268 US 510 [1925]), the Supreme Court ruled unconstitutional an Oregon statute which required all children to attend public schools.

3. In *Skinner v Oklahoma* (316 US 535 [1942]), the Supreme Court declared unconstitutional the Oklahoma Criminal Sterilization Act. It declared that Skinner, who had two convictions for robbery and one for stealing chickens, had a fundamental right to procreate.

4. In *Griswold v Connecticut* (381 US 479 [1965]), the Court held unconstitutional a law which prohibited the dissemination of contraceptive materials to married couples.

5. In *Levy v Louisiana* (391 US 68 [1968]), the Court ruled unconstitutional a Louisiana law that prohibited illegitimate children from recovery for the wrongful death of their mother.

6. In *Glona v American Guar. & Liab. Ins. Co.* (391 US 73 [1968]), the Court ruled unconstitutional a Louisiana Law which denied the right of a mother to recover for the wrongful death of her child because the child was illegitimate.

7. In *Loving v Virginia* (388 US 1 [1967]), the Court held unconstitutional a Virginia law which prohibited interracial marriages.

8. In *Eisenstadt v Baird* (405 US 438 [1972]), the Court ruled unconstitutional a Massachusetts law which prohibited the distribution of contraceptives to unmarried people.

9. In *Weber v Aetna Cas. & Sur. Co.* (406 US 164 [1972]), the Court held unconstitutional a Louisiana law which denied workers' compensation benefits to an unacknowledged illegitimate child.

10. In *Carey v Population Servs. Intl.* (431 US 678 [1972]), the Court ruled unconstitutional a New York law which permitted only pharmacists to sell contraceptives to adults and a blanket prohibition on such sales to minors.

11. In *Wisconsin v Yoder* (406 US 205 [1972]), the Court held that the state could not require parents of the Amish Church to send their children to public school after the eighth grade.

12. In *Roe v Wade* (410 US 113 [1973]), the Court ruled that the state cannot prohibit a woman from terminating a pregnancy during the first two trimesters of her pregnancy because it violates her fundamental privacy right.

13. In *Gomez v Perez* (409 US 535 [1973]), the Court ruled unconstitutional a Texas law which prohibited illegitimate children from claiming child support from their father.

14. In *Cleveland Bd. of Educ. v LaFleur* (414 US 632 [1974]), the Court held unconstitutional mandatory maternity leaves.

15. In *Planned Parenthood v Danforth* (428 US 52 1976]), the Court held that the state could not require spousal consent as a predicate for a woman having an abortion or give a parent veto power over a minor's decision to have an abortion (a competing rights case).

16. In *Moore v City of E. Cleveland* (431 US 494 [1977]), the Court ruled unconstitutional a housing ordinance which prohibited a grandmother and her grandchildren from living together in a single dwelling unit.

17. In *Caban v Mohammed* (441 US 380 [1979]), the Court ruled unconstitutional New York's adoption consent statute which gave the unwed mother of a child an automatic right to veto an adoption, while the father had to show that the adoption would not be in the child's best interest.

18. In *Clark v Jeter* (486 US 456 [1988]), the Court held that a six-year statute of limitations in which to establish paternity violated the Equal Protection Clause.

Consistent with this progression of Supreme Court decisions that protect, extend and expand the liberty rights of individuals and families, and within the trajectory of the developed meaning of the Constitution, would be a holding that the state cannot deny (or in this case, refuse to enforce) the First Amendment rights of a child to associate with another person with whom the child has developed a parent-like relationship. If a child has such a right, and the Court holds that he does, and the state extends a procedure to protect or enforce similar rights of similar persons in similar situations, but excludes the child from the due process that protects that right, then the child has been denied the equal protection of the laws.

It has been firmly established that children are persons within the meaning of the Constitution and accordingly possess constitutional rights. Precisely defining these rights has not been an easy task.

"The question of the extent of state power to regulate conduct of minors not constitutionally regulable when committed by adults is a vexing one, perhaps not susceptible of a precise answer. We have been reluctant to attempt to define 'the totality of the relationship of the juvenile and the state'....Certain principles, however, have been recognized. 'Minors, as well as adults, are protected by the Constitution and possess constitutional rights'....'Watever [sic] may be their precise impact, neither the Fourteenth Amendment nor the Bill of Rights is for adults alone'....On the other hand, we have held in a variety of contexts that 'the power of the state to control the conduct of children reaches beyond the scope of its authority over adults'....Thus minors are entitled to constitutional protection for freedom of speech...equal protection against racial discrimination...due process in civil contexts...and a variety of rights of defendants in criminal proceedings." (*Carey v Population Servs.,* 431 US 678, 692 [1977].)

In this case, there is no claim that the state is intervening in a family relationship for regulatory or *parens patriae* purposes. The narrow holding in this case is that a statutory scheme that permits court intervention to order contact between a child and a parent or his sibling or grandparent is an unconstitutional denial of a child's right to equal protection of the laws when the law does not provide a procedure for the child to assert the same right with respect to a person with whom the child has a significant or substantial parent-like relationship. Since the Court holds that such a right is fundamental and constitutes a liberty interest under the Due Process Clause, the child must have an effective forum to assert that right.

III. Balancing the Fundamental Rights of a Parent and Child[30]

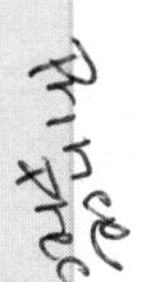

The Supreme Court has infrequently addressed the situation where constitutional interests between parents and their children compete, either with each other or with the state. In *Prince v Massachusetts* (321 US 158 [1944]), the Court held that the state's child labor laws trumped the parent's right to have her child engage in religious activity in public and the child's independent right to do so.... *Prince* stands for the proposition that the state has *parens patriae* authority over children up to a point....

• • •

In *Santosky v Kramer* (455 US 745 [1982]), the Supreme Court held that New York's statutory scheme to terminate parental rights was flawed because due process required that the fact-finding determination be made by clear and convincing evidence, as opposed to a preponderance of the evidence standard. The majority decision, essentially parent-focused, held that the risk of fact-finding error should be distributed toward the Department of Social Services and away from the parents. In so holding, the decision assumes an alliance or unity of interest between the parents and the child. The minority, in finding that due process was served by a preponderance of the evidence standard, which allocated the risk of error evenly between the parents and the agency, left the children in a neutral position.

• • •

---

[30]...See Lawrence D. Houlgate, *Three Concepts of Children's Constitutional Rights: Reflections on the Enjoyment Theory,* 2 U Pa J Const L 77 (Dec. 1999); Melinda A. Roberts, *Parent and Child in Conflict: Between Liberty and Responsibility,*10 Notre Dame JL Ethics & Pub Poly 485 (1996); Justine Witkin, *A Time For Change: Reevaluating the Constitutional Status of Minors,* 47 Fla L Rev 113 (Jan. 1995); Gilbert A. Holmes, *The Tie that Binds: The Constitutional Right of Children to Maintain Relationships With Parent-Like Individuals,* 53 Md L Rev 358 (Winter 1994); Barbara Jones, *Do Siblings Possess Constitutional Rights?,* 78 Cornell L Rev 1187 (Sept. 1993).

In *Michael H. v Gerald D.* (491 US 110 [1989]), the Court was called upon to determine the constitutionality of a California statute that provided that a child born to a married woman living with her husband, who is neither impotent nor sterile, is presumed to be a child of the marriage and that this presumption may be rebutted only by the husband or the wife....

• • •

Read one way, *Gerald D.* stands for the proposition that biology is not destiny and the court will look to the family relationships or unit that best serves the child's best interest, without regard to genetic parenthood.

• • •

The Court took 18 pages to dismiss the boyfriend/genetic-father's constitutional claims. It needed only three paragraphs to dismiss the child's....Justice Scalia does note that: "We have never had occasion to decide whether a child has a liberty interest, symmetrical with that of her parent in maintaining her filial relationship." (*Gerald D.* at 110.) However, Justice Scalia also held that the child's claim must fail because there was no basis in law, history or tradition for a child to make a claim for multiple fatherhoods.

"In contrast, allowing a claim of illegitimacy to be pressed by the child...may *well disrupt an otherwise peaceful union.* Since it pursues a legitimate end by rational means, California's decision to treat Victoria differently from her parents is not a denial of equal protection." (*Gerald D.* at 131-132 [emphasis added].)

This case, involving a married woman who had affairs of some duration with two other men and admittedly had a child out of wedlock, does not seem the best factual situation in which to raise an issue about disrupting "an otherwise peaceful union." Also, Justice Scalia, by inserting at the end the phrase, "legitimate end by rational means," puts the constitutional analysis of this case at the lowest level of scrutiny. However, the issues raised in this case and the precedents cited would support a higher level of constitutional scrutiny. Justice Stevens, concurring in the judgment, remarks...

"[Our] cases...demonstrate that enduring 'family' relationships may develop in unconventional settings. I therefore would not foreclose the possibility that a constitutionally protected relationship between a natural father and his child might exist in a case like this. Indeed, I am willing to assume for the purpose of deciding this case that Michael's relationship with Victoria is strong enough to give him a constitutional right to try to convince a trial judge that Victoria's best interest would be served by granting him visitation rights." (*Gerald D.* at 133.)

• • •

The two cases that most directly impact the holding in this case are the Supreme Court's grandparents' visitation decision, handed down last year in *Troxel v Granville* (530 US 57 [2000]) and the New York Court of Appeals "de facto" parent visitation decision in *Matter of Alison D. v Virginia M.* (77 NY2d 651 [1991])....In *Troxel...*, the Supreme Court held that the Washington statute *as applied* was unconstitutional. The first deficiency they noted in the statute was that in allowing any person at any time to apply for visitation, the law was "breathtakingly broad." Secondly, the statute contained "no requirement that a court accord the parent's decision any presumption of validity or any weight whatsoever."...At the fact-finding stage, the trial court (1) presumed that grandparent visitation was in the child's best interest, (2) placed the burden on the parents to first articulate reasonable objections to the visits, and (3) the court articulated no "special factors" which would "justify the State's interference with [the parent's] fundamental right to make decisions concerning the rearing of her two daughters."...

...Justice Stevens is the only Justice to raise the issue of the child's constitutional rights....

• • •

Justice Kennedy, also in dissent, lends support to the concept that, under appropriate circumstances, court-ordered visitation between a child and a nonparent is constitutionally permissible.

"My principal concern is that the holding seems to proceed from the assumption that the parent or parents who resist visitation have always been the child's primary caregivers and that the third parties who seek visitation have no legitimate and established relationship with the child. That idea, in turn, appears influenced by the concept that the conventional nuclear family ought to establish the visitation standard for every domestic relations case....

Cases are sure to arise...in which a third party, by acting in a caregiving role over a significant period of time, has developed a relationship with a child which is not necessarily subject to absolute parental veto."...

• • •

In balancing the unquestionable constitutionally guaranteed right of a parent to raise his or her child on one hand and the constitutional right of a child to maintain contact with a parent-substitute (and the state intrusion in giving a court forum to voice that right) on the other hand, it will be helpful to examine other areas where a state does intrude into the parent's constitutional right to raise his or her child free of state interference. By examining these circumstances, we can gauge the level of intrusion into the parent's rights that are caused by recognizing this right for the parent's child.

The bedrock principle of *Troxel* is that "the liberty interest at issue in [this] case—the interest of parents in the care, custody, and control of their children—is perhaps the oldest of the fundamental liberty interests recognized by the [Supreme Court]."...While that is undoubtedly true, the pedigree for that claim was *Meyer v Nebraska* (262 US 390), decided in 1923. Starting more than 100 years earlier than that, state courts were establishing a substantial body of law in which the state's *parens patriae* authority was used to uphold child custodial rights of nonparents against the claims of parents....

• • •

These cases illustrate a well-established policy of the judiciary to manage conflicted family relations based on the best interest of the child. There is no mention of fundamental or constitutional rights in any of these cases, or any doubt expressed by the courts that they had the authority to make these decisions. This position was not limited to state courts. Supreme Court Justice Joseph Story, riding circuit, in *United States v Green* (3 Mason 482 [1824]) held as follows:

"As to the question of the right of the father to have custody of his infant child, in a general sense it is true. But this is not on account of any absolute right of the father, but for the benefit of the infant; the law presuming it to be for its interest to be under the nurture and care of its natural protector, both for maintenance and education. When, therefore, a court is asked to lend its aid to put the infant into the custody of the father and to withdraw him from other persons, it will look into all the circumstances, and ascertain whether it will be for the real, permanent interests of the infant...."

Accompanying the judiciary's foray into the management of parent and child family relationships has been the legislature's. There are any number of laws that restrict the activities of juveniles. Most, if not all, of those laws were passed without any mention that they restrict the child's parent's right to permit the child to engage in certain activities or engage in them in a fashion that the parent feels is appropriate. Looked at from this "parent restricting" point of view, we have the following laws which illustrate that point (citations omitted):

1. A parent may not let his child purchase, or consume alcohol outside a home setting, until the child is 21....

2. A parent may not allow his child to drive a car until age 16....

3. A parent may not permit his child to be a passenger in his car unless seat belted or, if less than four, in a car seat....

4. A parent may not permit his child to ride a bike or a scooter without a helmet....

5. A parent must submit his or her child to a series of vaccinations....

6. A parent may not permit his child less than 16 to possess a BB gun, handgun, shotgun or rifle....

7. A parent may not permit his child to purchase cigarettes....

8. A parent may not permit his child less than 16 to be employed in most occupations....

9. A parent may not permit a child to marry if the child is less than 14 or, if less than 16, without the permission of a judge....

10. A parent may not permit his child less than 16 to enter a bar without adult supervision....

11. A parent may not permit his child to get a tattoo....

12. A parent may not permit a child less than 18 to hunt bear or deer or less than 16 to hunt other wildlife with a firearm....

13. A parent may not permit his child to appear in a professional wrestling or boxing match if less than 18 and, if less than 16, the child may not attend such a performance....

14. A parent may not permit his child less than 10 to operate a snowmobile off the parent's land....

15. A parent must send his child to a full-time school from age six to 16....

...Today, mandatory schooling is universally accepted. This was not always so....

• • •

...All of the regulations of children listed above were based on the police power of the state exercised in the state's capacity as *parens patriae* (parent of the country). The laws needed to have only a rational basis to sustain constitutional muster. If the state can direct a parent to send his or her child to all day school for 180 days each year, how less an intrusion into parental rights is it to permit a court to order the parent to provide visitation to a de facto parent for, say, two days each month? When balanced with the child's constitutional right, this is a fairly modest incursion into the parent's constitutional right to direct the upbringing of his or her child.

There is also a significant body of statutory law that permits a Family Court to invade the fundamental right of a parent to the control of his or her child....

These statutes clearly illustrate the accepted authority of the state to intrude into a parent's custodial rights to his or her child when the child's best interests are at stake. An even more obvious example would be the several provisions of Family Court Act article 10, which provide for the removal of children from neglectful or abusive parents. For this entire statutory framework, there is no indication from the laws' words or context that any "special weight" must be given to a parent's wishes, as that point was made in *Troxel.*

Conclusion

The historical development of family law in America, and the expansion of individual constitutional rights by the Supreme Court of the United States and the Court of Appeals of the State of New York, give foundation to a holding that a child has a constitutional right to maintain contact with a person with whom the child has developed a parent-like relationship. Accompanying that right is also a right to the equal protection of the laws. This requires that the child have the due process necessary to claim his right. This claim can be given constitutional protection, while at the same time giving due recognition, respect and protection to a parent's constitutional right to the custody, care and control of his or her child. Accordingly, with this goal in mind, the Court holds the following:...

1. That a child has certain enumerated and unenumerated constitutionally protected rights.

2. That these rights are protected coextensively by the cited provisions of the Constitution of the United States and the Constitution of the State of New York.

3. That the child's unenumerated rights include a fundamental right to maintain contact with a person with whom the child has developed a parent-like relationship.

4. That the child also has an enumerated First Amendment freedom of association right under the State and Federal Constitutions to maintain personal relations with a nonbiologically related person.

5. That the child's rights listed above are liberty interests protected by the Due Process Clauses of the Federal and State Constitutions.

6. That the child is entitled to the equal protection of the laws to be similarly situated with other children who have a statutory procedure to enforce their constitutionally or statutorily protected association rights.

7. That a child having such a right must be provided a process to enforce that

right against unwarranted restrictions by the state or a third person, in this case a parent.

8. That a parent has a fundamental right to direct the care, custody and guardianship of his or her child and is presumed to act in the child's best interest. (*Parham v J. R.,* 442 US 584 [1979].)

9. That this fundamental right of the parent must be balanced with the fundamental rights of the child. ...

Questions for Discussion

1. The court in *Webster* also holds that the court must give significant weight to the parent's determination as to what is in the child's best interest including the decision to allow a certain level of contact. It holds that the child carries the burden of proof under a preponderance test. It also holds that there must be a "parent-like relationship," taking into account its "length, nature and quality." Can a three-year-old have such a relationship justifying court-ordered visitation? A six-month old?

2. Will the (prior *de facto* parent) relationship be protected by court order until the child is 18 years of age? Will the court prevent the parent from moving the child geographically where it precludes contact from such a *de facto* parent—as in joint custody family court cases?

3. Note that an increasing number of cases recognize the rights of such "*de facto*" parents. These are parents who may not qualify as parents by virtue of biology, marriage, presumptive status (*e.g.*, under the Uniform Parentage Act), or *Kelsey* status by attempting to perform as a father. A number of these cases involve lesbian couples who agree to parent a child, so function, and then break up. The relationships are often complicated, with some of the claimants giving birth to the child, others contributing DNA material, *et al.* Some courts recognize the child's relationship with these parents as a critical factor and allow visitation for the "parent" who does not have custody, and also impose child support obligations. See *Elisa B. v. Superior Court*, 37 Cal.4th 108 (2005), with companion cases *K.M. v. E.G.* and *Kristine H. v. Lisa R.*; *see also Carvin v. Britain*, 155 Wn.2d 679 (2005). Other courts deny such status, ironically including the New York jurisdiction, as in *Alison D. v. Virginia M.*, 77 NY2d 651 (1991) (where a five-year relationship with a child did not confer any "parental" status warranting visitation). If a person functions as a parent and is reasonably so regarded by a child, *e.g.*, who provides shelter, changes diapers, feeds, medically tends, instructs, plays, nurtures, and worries—do traditional principles of equitable estoppel confer parental status? Is the parent's reliance of such a functional status relevant? Is the child's reliance?

4. As noted above, many of the cases recognizing *de facto* parental status do not involve foster parents. In *Smith v. OFFER* (discussed in Chapter 8), the Court denied any parental status whatever to foster parents, finding that they consent to a status as custodians for children pending parental return or other placement in the discretion of the local department of social services. The

Court held that they lack any proper expectation of a relationship and denied them due process standing where such children are removed from their care. In *OFFER* the removal was not to return a child to a parent, but to move a child to a different placement with strangers. The *de facto* parent in *Webster* is such a foster parent. And here the child is to be placed with a natural father who had been wrongfully denied his child, is adjudged fit, and maintained an interest and consistent visitation through most of the child's tenure away. Does the *Webster* foster parent status and return of the child to a wronged parent make its judgment problematical given the *OFFER* precedent? On the other hand, did *OFFER* analyze or fully consider the rights of the child to a relationship with a parent? If there are such rights, as *Webster* holds, how can foster care status or implied waiver of parental claim foreclose the child's right?

B. EMANCIPATION AND CHILD SUPPORT OBLIGATIONS

As a general rule, both parents are statutorily required to financially or directly support their children. State statutes that differentiate between paternal and maternal support obligations based strictly on gender raise equal protection infirmities given current case law. Most states require step-parent support of children, and the income of a step-parent living in the same household with a child is included in calculating eligibility for Temporary Aid to Needy Families (TANF) assistance, the primary cash safety-net program for children.

The obligation of support lasts until a child reaches "legal majority," which is 18 years of age in most states.[6] The obligation of support may end earlier if a child is "emancipated," has abandoned the parental home, is receiving public aid for the totally disabled, or parental rights have been terminated. Emancipation generally requires that a child function apart from parents and have verifiable independent means of support. Such support must be legal, and some courts do not permit it to consist solely of public support. Marriage and military service are relevant bases for emancipation, and are sufficient standing alone in some jurisdictions. Some states require parental consent or non-consent to be considered by the court as a factor. In most states, the court is obligated to act in "the best interests of the child" and has substantial discretion to grant or deny emancipation.

Although such emancipation may appear to be intrinsically against the best interests of a child, since it may relieve parents of support obligations, it is often necessary where a youth has been effectively abandoned or victimized by parents and needs that status to authorize benefits (from medical coverage to education subsidies) which otherwise require parental signature. Emancipation is also sought where a youth wishes to enter into a binding contract.[7] The degree of emancipation implied in such an order varies somewhat between states, but it is not necessarily a "yes or no" proposition, and may relieve parents of some obligations and grant independent authority to a child—only within a range of decisions.

Post-majority support has become more important given the lowering of the age of majority from 21 to 18 years of age over the last forty years, and the growing importance of some higher education beyond high school. Such support may be enforceable where a parent has promised it and in some states courts have required parental contribution towards such advanced schooling.[8] Some courts have held that where a support statute refers to a "child" rather than a "minor" such obligations may be conferred past the age of majority.[9]

The obligation of support is normally enforced through child support agreements or orders upon separation or divorce. Courts rarely question financial commitment decisions made within an intact family, unless they rise to the level of child neglect. However, the high incidence of divorce has led to a substantial number of such support orders applicable to the non-custodial parent post-dissolution. Most are applicable to fathers, but an increasing proportion of fathers obtain custody and the incidence of orders applying to mothers has increased. In most states, such obligations are independent of visitation rights. Contrary to common belief, the non-custodial parent does not have the right to deny such support where visitation is improperly denied. Each obligation stands independently to serve the child and each is independently enforceable in most jurisdictions.

The amount of such post-divorce child support is set by family courts based on the needs of affected children principally for shelter, food, clothing, medical care, and education, in combination with the ability to pay of the respective parents.[10] One oft-cited standard is the right of a child to a standard of living that approximates pre-divorce conditions.[11] Courts will sometimes set amounts based on earning capacity rather than on income, particularly where the court suspects an obligor is working less in order to minimize payments due.

Substantial discretion is granted to family courts in setting support amounts. It may include required in-kind contributions—among them the important inclusion of child health and other insurance available to the non-custodial parent. During the 1970s and 1980s total child support awards were criticized as inconsistent and inadequate.[12] Levels have increased somewhat to 2006, and some states have adopted "child support formulas" by statute or rule to enhance consistency. However, rates of increase appeared to flatten in real money terms after 2000. Monies received amount to a fraction of the direct costs of a child to custodial parents in the vast majority of cases.

Although many child support orders are agreed to by the involved parents, they are subject to independent court review and approval. That check is intended to preclude the bargaining away of the rights of a child. The most common example is the regrettable practice of a parent who will surrender child support for children in his or her custody in return for a surrender of visitation rights by the non-custodial parent. In such common circumstances, while the parents may be relieved of unpleasant contact between themselves, the child may be deprived of contact with one parent, and also of financial support properly due.

Child support obligations are subject to modification as circumstances change, and such circumstances increasingly involve a second family with new spouses and children imposing new obligations. Sometimes they involve new assets. Courts are divided on the impact of such subsequent choices on previous obligations, more easily adding to established amounts where additional resources arise (*e.g.*, a new spouse with substantial income) but sometimes modifying downwards, particularly where the new obligations involve children.

Many children born to unwed parents are owed child support by the non-custodial parent. This population of obligors, usually fathers, are pursued primarily by the state (see child support enforcement discussion below). A large proportion of such children receive substantial cash assistance through the TANF program (prior to 1996 termed Aid to Families with Dependent Children (AFDC)). Accordingly, the state seeks recompense from the absent parent for payments made for such children. The child support obligation extant outside of marriage is normally determined by biology (*e.g.*, paternity test results or other evidence indicating a child is the biological issue of an obligor). Increasingly, custodial parents avail themselves of these resources to collect support even where monies are not due the state. That opportunity is important because such parents lack contact with family court (no divorce decree is entered since no marriage occurred) and lack resources for private enforcement. Over half of such sums collected now pass through to involved families and children.

County of Alameda v. Kaiser
238 Cal. App. 2d 815 (1965)

OPINION, **Draper, P.J.**: Does "emancipation" of a minor by agreement with his mother relieve her of liability for his support? Does a recent decision ...bar recovery from her by the county for his treatment, in a county hospital, for physical ailments? These are the questions on this appeal.

Defendant, a widow, is the mother of Philip Kaiser, who was born August 3, 1942. He was seriously injured in an automobile accident August 13, 1962, and was treated for some time in a private hospital. On November 28, 1962, defendant made written application for county medical care for her son, representing that she had very little money or property. The next day, Philip was admitted to the county hospital, and remained hospitalized through March 28, 1963. Shortly after his admission, county officials learned that defendant had withdrawn a large amount from a bank account not listed in her financial statement. The board of supervisors then determined that defendant had financial ability to support her son (Welf. & Inst. Code, § 2576), and this action for $3,172.50 was filed in the municipal court.

At trial, defendant testified that Philip had left home in February 1962 and had resided with an aunt to the time of his injury. He had some employment while living with the aunt, but the record does not show the amount of his earnings or whether he paid the aunt for board or room. His mother had neither contributed to his support nor asked for any part of his earnings, and testified "He was living on his own, apart, permanently." The trial court concluded that the son had been "emancipated", and thus must be treated as an adult. On the theory that *Kirchner* barred recovery under these circumstances, judgment was entered for defendant. Hence, the evidence of defendant's financial ability is but sketchy. Plaintiff appealed. The appellate department expressed doubt as to the determination of "emancipation" but, assuming the son to be deemed an adult, held that *Kirchner* is inapplicable to treatment in a county hospital for physical ailments, and reversed the judgment. We accepted transfer on certification (Cal. Rules of Court, rules 62, 63).

The phrase "emancipation of a minor," as applied to agreements of parent and child, appears to have been rather loosely used. Frequently, emancipation of the minor is equated with release of the parent....In the decisions, most such statements are but dicta as to the parent's obligation, but some do hold that consensual "emancipation" of the child terminates the parent's liability....

Broad statements of this assumed rule appear infrequently in California decisions...But these cases dealt with relinquishment of the parent's rights—not with release from his liabilities. When the issue of the child's rights has been squarely presented, the California courts have held that "emancipation" by agreement does not terminate the right to support....

Logic and reason support this view. The term "emancipation" implies treatment of the individual as a chattel. Slavish adherence to definition of the word, perhaps carelessly adopted in the first place, has led some jurisdictions to infer that the obligations of the parent to his child are based wholly upon his right to the child's earnings, and that relinquishment of the right requires release from the liability. This "rule" has been contradicted or questioned by text writers (2 Armstrong, California Family Law, 1259–1260; Madden on Domestic Relations,

408–409; 5 Vernier, American Family Laws, 240). It seems apparent that the few decisions and the more frequent dicta relied upon by defendant mother confuse "emancipation" of the child with "emancipation" of the parent. The limitations upon the minor's right to make binding contracts with strangers emphasize the illogic of a rule that he may bind himself by a contractual release of his parent, the person most likely to have a strong influence upon him.

We conclude that Philip must be deemed a minor. Our question then is whether the recent ruling of our Supreme Court (Department of *Mental Hygiene v. Kirchner*, 60 Cal.2d 716) bars liability of defendant mother.

Parental liability for support of a minor child is of ancient origin. It was recognized by such writers as Coke and Blackstone (1 Schouler, Marriage, Divorce, Separation and Domestic Relations, 857), and was the subject of an old English statute (43 Eliz. I, c.2). It has long been statutory in California....One reason for imposing this obligation is to prevent the child from becoming a public charge....This long-recognized liability, often enforced, has not been held to be based upon an unreasonable classification. Thus *Kirchner's* proscription of denial of equal protection seems to have no application.

The statutes measuring liability for care and treatment of another in a county hospital..., permit recovery by the county only to the extent of the responsible party's ability to pay. To the extent that *Kirchner* turns upon possible impoverishment of the party charged for another's care, its rule is thus inapplicable here.

This case differs from *Kirchner* in another respect. Here, hospitalization was for treatment of physical injuries, a treatment essentially for the benefit of the patient. It was apparently considered beneficial by the mother who sought her child's admission to the county hospital. The element of confinement for the protection of society from the mentally ill, present in *Kirchner*, is not a factor here.

We conclude that there is no constitutional bar to the recovery here sought.

Judgment reversed. The case is remanded for trial of the issue of defendant's pecuniary ability to pay for or contribute to her son's care for which recovery is sought.

Questions for Discussion

1. Would the decision be the same if aid were being sought directly by Philip Kaiser as a minor seeking medical assistance rather than by the state for recompense? By a doctor who incurred out-of-pocket expenses in treating Philip?

2. Is it fair to consider Phil Kaiser "emancipated" based on his "agreement" when he is below the then age of majority? If a minor cannot agree to a contract which may be enforced against him, how can he agree to emancipation which deprives him of assured parental support?

3. Does the fact that Mrs. Kaiser sought hospital admission for her son contribute to her financial liability? Does maternal concern have to cease for emancipation to be effective?

Parker v. Stage
43 N.Y.2d 128 (1977)

OPINION OF THE COURT: JUDGE WACHTLER

The question on this appeal is whether the Department of Social Services can compel a father to pay for the support of his 18-year-old daughter after she has left his house, voluntarily and against his wishes, to live with her paramour and have a child. Both the Family Court and the Appellate Division held that, under the circumstances, the father should not be obligated to support his daughter even though she is receiving public assistance. The Commissioner of Social Services has appealed to this court by leave of the Appellate Division.

The facts developed at the Family Court hearing were not disputed. Respondent's daughter was born in September of 1956. Several years later the father and mother were divorced. After the divorce the girl remained in her father's custody. In early 1974 she informed her cousin that she intended to leave home to live with her paramour and have a child. Although neither she nor her boyfriend were employed, she said that she intended to support herself and her child by seeking public assistance. She did not return to school in the fall of 1974. In October, shortly after her 18th birthday, she left home while her father was at work. Nearly two weeks later he was able to locate her with the assistance of the police.

She returned home and for several months resided with her father, but only intermittently. For long periods of time she would "disappear." On each occasion her father accepted her back and continued to support her. He contacted her former guidance counselor and arranged for her to return to school. He informed her of this and continuously urged her to resume her schooling but she refused. She also refused to discuss her goals with him. At one point he helped her to obtain a job, but she quit after four weeks. For a time she was in a job training program but she quit that as well. Finally in the spring of 1975 she took up permanent residence with her paramour who was also unemployed.

In the fall of 1975 respondent's daughter gave birth to a child out of wedlock. She then applied for aid to dependent children and obtained public assistance for her child and for herself, as the mother of an eligible child (Social Services Law, § 349). In February, 1976 the Commissioner of Social Services of Orange County commenced this proceeding in the Family Court to compel the respondent to contribute toward his daughter's support.* The proceeding was brought pursuant to subdivision 3 of section 101-a of the Social Services Law which authorizes a social services official to institute a support proceeding against a parent or other responsible relative if the applicant or recipient of public assistance "fails" to do so.

At the conclusion of the hearing the Family Court Judge dismissed the petition on the ground that respondent's daughter, by leaving home to live with her paramour and have his child, had "emancipated herself from her father and his household...and...as a result of that emancipation, the respondent is relieved of any obligation to support" her.

* * *

Initially it should be noted that even in a case like *Matter of Roe v. Doe* (*supra*), when the suit is brought directly on the child's behalf pursuant to section 413 of the Family Court Act, the father's obligation to support is stated in mandatory terms. Our determination in that case, that a child who voluntarily and without good cause abandons the parent's home "forfeits her right to demand support" is not based on any express statutory exception. It rests on the State policy of fostering "the integrity of the family" by precluding the courts from interfering in the special relationship between parent and child, absent "a showing of misconduct, neglect or abuse"...It recognizes that the father's obligation to support includes

---

* It is conceded that respondent is not responsible for the support of his grandchild.

the right to exercise parental control and guidance even though the child may be old enough "to elect not to comply" (*Matter of Roe v. Doe,...*).

The question then is whether a different policy applies when the suit is brought by a public welfare official to compel a father to support a child who would otherwise become a public charge.

It was once the policy of this State to place the financial burden of supporting needy individuals upon designated relatives, rather than the public, in order to reduce the amount of welfare expenditures...Thus the common-law obligation to support wife and minor children was expanded by statute to include adult children, grandchildren and parents when they would otherwise become public charges...

In recent years however the Legislature relented. The laws were amended to relieve individuals of the obligation to support grandchildren..., adult children and parents...who were unemployed and destitute. Thereafter the burden passed to the public. In a message accompanying the 1966 bill the Governor noted that this was in part prompted by the need to comply with Federal law in order to qualify for Federal financial assistance. But he also noted that "Experience has shown that the financial responsibility of a broad class of relatives, imposed by statute, is more often a destructive, rather than cohesive, factor in family unity"...Thus the legislative history shows that the current statutory scheme recognizes the need to preserve family unity even though the consequence is to place needy relatives on the public welfare rolls.

In addition the Legislature has expressly granted the courts discretionary powers in these cases. A father, of course, is still generally obligated to support his children until they are 21 years of age...And public welfare officials may seek to enforce the obligation if the child is an applicant for or recipient of public assistance...But in such cases the obligation is not absolute....

In sum we cannot agree with the commissioner that whenever an older child chooses to leave home, for any reason, the parents must pay for the child's separate maintenance, or contribute support, if the child applies for public assistance. The courts must still consider the impact on the family relationship and the possibility of injustice in the particular case. Of course the fact that the child is eligible for public assistance may, as is evident here, permit her to avoid her father's authority and demands however reasonable they may be. But it does not follow that the parent must then finish what has been begun by underwriting the lifestyle which his daughter chose against his reasonable wishes and repeated counsel.

It should be emphasized that this is not a case of an abandoned child, but of an abandoned parent. There is nothing to indicate that the respondent abused his daughter or placed unreasonable demands upon her. There is no showing that he actively drove her from her home or encouraged her to leave in order to have the public assume his obligation of support. Indeed the contrary appears to be true. The undisputed proof in this record establishes that the father continuously supported his daughter from birth; that he urged her to remain at home and continue her schooling; that he was a forgiving parent who always accepted her back after her absences and that he made efforts to obtain employment for her. We simply hold that under these circumstances the courts below could properly refuse to compel him to pay for her support when she chose to leave home to live with her paramour.

Accordingly, the order of the Appellate Division should be affirmed.

Questions for Discussion

1. Is Angelie's mother potentially liable for Angelie's support under these facts?

2. What if Angelie recants after leaving and having a child, and asks to return to her father's care and protection? Is she irretrievably emancipated because she defied his advice and left once? Would such a judgment apply to a 12-year-old who "runs away from home?" To a 14-year-old who is starving? To a teen who is mentally/emotionally troubled?

3. Would it matter if Angelie's father were a millionaire and the outcome is substantial public expense for Angie and her child? Would it matter if Angelie's father had beaten her repeatedly? Engaged in mental or emotional cruelty? Does the broad discretion to trial courts granted in *Parker* compromise an important bright line for obligation, and invoke "who is at fault" within-the-family litigation? Before relieving a father of support obligations, should a court require at least one attempt to seek third party assistance where a child is incorrigible (*e.g.*, existing court services)?

4. Can emancipation be reversed, *i.e.*, can a child who is emancipated and economically independent then become financially dependent and again incur a parental support obligation? See *Wulff v. Wulff*, 243 Neb. 616 (1993). Note that New York law requires parental support until the child is 21 years of age. For application of support obligation up to age 21, even after consensual emancipation, see *In the Matter of Crimmins v. Crimmins,* 745 N.Y.S.2d 686 (2002).

C. CHILD SUPPORT COLLECTION

Where a traditional family court child support order is violated, it is enforced by contempt of court process—which can involve serious sanctions for a violator, including jail time. However, the American system's traditional aversion to "debtors' prisons" generally requires evidence of a willful violation of a support order to yield incarceration. Hence, such severity will require some demonstration of ability to pay (or self-manipulation so that such ability is foreclosed).

In addition to contempt of court, all states have separate statutes imposing criminal liability for "willful" non-support of children. Case law typically defines such willfulness to be a "deliberate or perverse design, malice, or an intentional or deliberate breach" of the child support duty "without just cause or excuse."[13] These laws are often invoked as a lever, with probation commonly granted pending compliance with outstanding support orders. From the perspective of most courts, a severe fine or jail time tends to undercut the purpose of the law (to provide support for affected children). The leverage of these statutes was enhanced by *Hicks v. Feiock*, 485 U.S. 624 (1988), where the Supreme Court upheld as constitutional a state law providing for civil contempt and "presuming" the ability to pay—thus shifting the burden to the parent to rebut that presumption. More recently, the Congress has made willful failure to pay child support a federal crime where (1) state lines are crossed (*e.g.*, a father who has left the state ordering payment) and (2) the debt is delinquent for more than one year or involves over $5,000.[14] Although the *Lopez* limitation on federal jurisdiction not involving "commerce" (see discussion in Chapter 1) might be invoked to void this statute, all eleven circuits have considered and upheld its jurisdiction as affecting interstate commerce (*e.g.*, see *U.S. v. Faasse*, 265 F.3d 475 (6th Cir. 2001)). However, the U.S. Supreme Court has yet to address the question.

Apart from criminal enforcement of child neglect and the contempt enforcement of family court support orders, the federal government and states have created an extensive system to collect support from absent unwed fathers where mothers and children lack family court divorce jurisdiction. As noted above, states have historically established paternity and collected such child support primarily to recoup the TANF (AFDC pre-1996) payments made to children from their absent biological parents. As noted above, such efforts increasingly include attempts to obtain child support for children in need who have not received public assistance.

A series of federal statutes, including the Revised Uniform Reciprocal Enforcement of Support Act of 1968 and the Child Support Performance and Incentive Act of 1998 (CSPIA) assist by simplifying collection between states (especially given interstate movement of obligors), and provide a system of substantial incentive payments to states based on collection performance and improvement. The Federal Office of Child Support Enforcement operates pursuant to Social Security Act Title IV-D authority[15] to help states with collection and to direct incentive payments, as well as potential penalties (reductions in federal funding). Substantial reductions have been imposed (for example, against California in 1995–2002 for its failure to implement a statewide computer system to coordinate in-state collections).

Some states provide for the identification of biological fathers at time of birth. Under the Personal Responsibility and Work Opportunity Reconciliation Act of 1996 (the federal welfare reform statute) all birth mothers are required to make a *bona fide* attempt to identify the biological father of the child, and to assist the state in finding him. Failure to so assist may yield grant reduction sanctions. (See discussion in Chapter 3.)

Most jurisdictions also provide assistance in establishing paternity where a woman seeks such an order, whether she is on welfare or not. Such paternity establishes fatherhood status for purposes of support obligations. Paternity can be established by a voluntary acknowledgment signed by both parents as part of an in-hospital or other acknowledgment program. States must have procedures that allow paternity to be established at least up to the child's eighteenth birthday. Child support paternities were established or acknowledged for about 1.6 million children in fiscal year 2004.

Although states vary in their enforcement mechanisms, many assign child support collection to offices of district attorney or state's attorney (public prosecutors). If paternity is alleged, a test can be ordered and compliance enforced. The process then involves the establishment of an order, which includes a due process hearing right for the purported biological father, and for support collection—either in court or through an administrative hearing. Almost 1.2 million orders for child support were established in fiscal year 2004.

Following the entry of an order, states are engaging in extensive new enforcement strategies, including: automatic garnishment of wages, capture of tax refunds and lottery winnings, suspension of license renewals pending order compliance (including bar admission, trade licensure, and even driver's licenses in some states). Some states assign delinquent child support orders to state income tax agencies for collection and designation as high priority "tax liens."

The federal Office of Child Support Enforcement (OCSE) reported total national support collection of $21.9 billion in year 2004 covering a caseload of 15.9 million.[16] As discussed in Chapter 2, this total amounts to $78.50 per month per child support due from an absent parent, of which about $45 per month is received by the family for the benefit of the children. The remainder recompenses federal and state jurisdictions for (TANF) welfare costs paid for affected children.

Some states (*e.g.*, New York) are implementing a "child support assurance" concept, where a parent effectively transfers her right to child support to the state in the same way a creditor may sell an account receivable to a private collection agency. The family then receives compensation not as welfare, but as monies due and owing from the absent parent, and the state then assumes the task of collection.

People v. Sorensen
68 Cal. 2d 280 (1968)

McComb, Justice.

Defendant appeals from a judgment convicting him of violating section 270 of the Penal Code (willful failure to provide for his minor child), a misdemeanor.

The settled statement of facts recites that seven years after defendant's marriage it was medically determined that he was sterile. His wife desired a child, either by artificial insemination or by adoption, and at first defendant refused to consent. About 15 years after the marriage defendant agreed to the artificial insemination of his wife. Husband and wife, then residents of San Joaquin County, consulted a physician in San Francisco. They signed an agreement, which is on the letterhead of the physician, requesting the physician to inseminate the wife with the sperm of a white male. The semen was to be selected by the physician, and under no circumstances were the parties to demand the name of the donor. The agreement contains a recitation that the physician does not represent that pregnancy will occur. The physician treated Mrs. Sorensen, and she became pregnant. Defendant knew at the time he signed the consent that when his wife took the treatments she could become pregnant and that if a child was born it was to be treated as their child.

A male child was born to defendant's wife in San Joaquin County on October 14, 1960. The information for the birth certificate was given by the mother, who named defendant as the father. Defendant testified that he had not provided the information on the birth certificate and did not recall seeing it before the trial.

For about four years the family had a normal family relationship, defendant having represented to friends that he was the child's father and treated the boy as his son. In 1964, Mrs. Sorensen separated from defendant and moved to Sonoma County with the boy. At separation, Mrs. Sorensen told defendant that she wanted no support for the boy, and she consented that a divorce be granted to defendant. Defendant obtained a decree of divorce, which recites that the court retained "jurisdiction regarding the possible support obligation of plaintiff in regard to a minor child born to defendant."

In the summer of 1966 when Mrs. Sorensen became ill and could not work, she applied for public assistance under the Aid to Needy Children program. The County of Sonoma supplied this aid until Mrs. Sorensen was able to resume work. Defendant paid no support for the child since the separation in 1964, although demand therefor was made by the district attorney. The municipal court found defendant guilty of violating section 270 of the Penal Code and granted him probation for three years on condition that he make payments of $50 per month for support through the district attorney's office.

"From the record before us, this case could be disposed of on the ground that defendant has failed to overcome the presumption that "A child of a woman who is or has been married, born during the marriage or within 300 days after the dissolution thereof, is presumed to be a legitimate child of that marriage. This presumption may be disputed only by the people of the State of California in a criminal action brought under Section 270 of the Penal Code or by the husband or wife, or the descendant of one or both of them. In a civil action, this presumption may be rebutted only by clear and convincing proof." (Evid. Code, § 661,...)

...[T]he only question for our determination is:

> Is the husband of a woman, who with his consent was artificially inseminated with semen of a third-party donor, guilty of the crime of failing to support a child who is the product of such insemination, in violation of section 270 of the Penal Code?[1]

The law is that defendant is the lawful father of the child born to his wife, which child was conceived by artificial insemination to which he consented, and his conduct carries with it an obligation of support within the meaning of section 270 of the Penal Code.

Under the facts of this case, the term "father" as used in section 270 cannot be limited to the biologic or natural father as those terms are generally understood. The determinative factor is whether the legal relationship of father and child exists. A child conceived through heterologous artificial insemination...does not have a "natural father," as that term is commonly used. The anonymous donor of the sperm cannot be considered the "natural father," as he is no more responsible for the use made of his sperm than is the donor of blood or a kidney. Moreover, he could not dispute the presumption that the child is the legitimate issue of Mr. and Mrs. Sorensen, as that presumption "may be disputed only by the people of the State of California...or by the husband or wife, or the descendant of one or both of them." (Evid. Code, § 661,...) With the use of frozen semen, the donor may even be dead at the time the semen is used. Since there is no "natural father," we can only look for a lawful father.

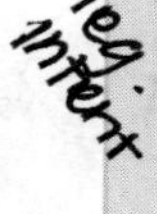

It is doubtful that with the enactment of section 270 of the Penal Code and its amendments the Legislature considered the plight of a child conceived through artificial insemination. However, the intent of the Legislature obviously was to include every child, legitimate or illegitimate, born or unborn, and enforce

---

[1] Section 270 of the Penal Code reads: "A father of either a legitimate or illegitimate minor child who...willfully omits without lawful excuse to furnish necessary clothing, food, shelter or medical attendance or other remedial care for his child is guilty of a misdemeanor and punishable by a fine not exceeding one thousand dollars ($1,000) or by imprisonment in a county jail not exceeding one year, or by both such fine and imprisonment....This statute shall not be construed so as to relieve such father from the criminal liability defined herein for such omission merely because the mother of such child is legally entitled to the custody of such child nor because the mother of such child, or any other person, or organization, voluntarily or involuntarily furnishes such necessary food, clothing, shelter or medical attendance or other remedial care for such child, or undertakes to do so.

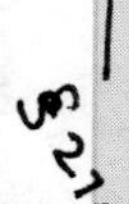

"Proof of abandonment or desertion of a child by such father, or the omission by such father to furnish necessary food, clothing, shelter or medical attendance or other remedial care for his child is prima facie evidence that such abandonment or desertion or omission to furnish necessary food, clothing, shelter or medical attendance or other remedial care is...willful and without lawful excuse.

"The court, in determining the ability of the father to support his child, shall consider all income, including social insurance benefits and gifts.

"....

"In the event that the father of either a legitimate or illegitimate minor child is dead or for any other reason whatsoever fails to furnish the necessary food, clothing, shelter or medical attendance or other remedial care for his minor child, the mother of said child shall become subject to the provisions of this section and be criminally liable for the support of said minor child during the period of failure on the part of the father to the same extent and in the same manner as the father.

"The provisions of this section are applicable whether the parents of such child are married or divorced, and regardless of any decree made in any divorce action relative to alimony or to the support of the child. A child conceived but not yet born is to be deemed an existing person insofar as this section is concerned."

the obligation of support against the person who could be determined to be the lawful parent.[3]

* * *

It is also essential to a conviction under section 270 that defendant's omission to support his child be willful. The statute provides that "Proof of...the omission by such father to furnish necessary food, clothing, shelter or medical attendance or other remedial care for his child is prima facie evidence that such...omission...is willful and without lawful excuse." This provision does not set forth a rule relating to proof but merely declares a rule of procedure that places upon defendant the duty of going forward with evidence that his omission to provide was not willful or was excusable....

Defendant failed to produce any evidence that his omission to provide for his minor child was not willful. The record shows that the district attorney requested defendant to pay $50 per month child support, but that defendant did not do so. When defendant and his wife separated she declared that she wanted no support for the child. The provisions of section 270, however, "are applicable whether the parents are married or divorced, and regardless of any decree made in any divorce action relative to alimony or to the support of the child." It is immaterial, therefore, that Mrs. Sorensen said that she wanted no support for the child, for she had no authority or power by agreement or release to deprive her child of the legal right to be supported by his father or to relieve defendant of the obligation imposed on him by law....

Rather than punishment of the neglectful parents, the principal statutory objectives are to secure support of the child and to protect the public from the burden of supporting a child who has a parent able to support him. Section 270d of the Penal Code provides that if a fine is imposed on a convicted defendant, the court shall direct its payment in whole or in part to the wife of the defendant or guardian of the child, except that if the child is receiving public assistance the fine imposed or funds collected from the defendant shall be paid to the county department either for current support of the child or as reimbursement for past support furnished from public assistance funds.

* * *

In the absence of legislation prohibiting artificial insemination, the offspring of defendant's valid marriage to the child's mother was lawfully begotten and was not the product of an illicit or adulterous relationship. Adultery is defined as "the voluntary sexual intercourse of a married person with a person other than the offender's husband or wife." (Civ. Code, § 93.) It has been suggested that the doctor and the wife commit adultery by the process of artificial insemination....Since the doctor may be a woman, or the husband himself may administer the insemination by a syringe, this is patently absurd; to consider it an act of adultery with the donor, who at the time of insemination may be a thousand miles away or may even be dead, is equally absurd. Nor are we persuaded that the concept of legitimacy demands that the child be the actual offspring of the husband of the mother and if semen of some other male is utilized the resulting child is illegitimate.

* * *

The judgment is affirmed.

---

[3] Section 270 was enacted in 1872. Prior to 1915, liability was imposed on the parents of only legitimate children. The section was then amended to include illegitimate minors as well. In the 1925 amendment a sentence was added declaring that a child conceived but not yet born was an existing person so far as this section was concerned.

Questions for Discussion

1. Can Mrs. Sorensen "agree" to forego all future support for her son from the child's father if the state does not step in to support her child? For example, would such an agreement be enforceable against a hypothetical petition by the child for such support?

2. Did it matter that Mr. Sorensen is not the biological father? Apart from specialized artificial insemination statutes, would he be a presumed father under the Uniform Parentage Act?

3. Would it be more efficient to simply garnish Mr. Sorensen's wages or attach his bank account to collect the $50 per month demanded? How much did a criminal prosecution cost the County, and what use would a jail sentence serve to provide assistance to the child? Does such a prosecution and possible incarceration "send a message" or otherwise deter the shirking of parental support obligations?

D. NOTE ON CHILD CUSTODY AND VISITATION ENFORCEMENT

Separate from child emancipation rights and child support obligations are the "parental rights" issues of child custody and visitation where parental status is acknowledged. These rights are commonly litigated in family court. Regrettably, the context for these adjudications of parental rights to children (and child rights to parents) is an often emotional divorce proceeding where children may be caught in the vortex of hostility between their parents. Unlike juvenile court, children here rarely have their own counsel. Children are often used by feuding parents to gain advantage or to vindicate perceived wrongs *vis-a-vis* each other. The children's fate in terms of custody and visitation may be determined without their input to the court—and with a factual contest unhelpful to their future relationship with their parents. One trend in these disputes is to award "joint custody" to both parents—and to thusly limit the ability of one parent to move a child far away from the other parent. But problems of movement to another state to avoid court jurisdiction, or to defy the orders of a court pertaining to custody or visitation, have remained a continuing problem.

To address some of these difficulties, many states have enacted statutes to allow enforcement of court orders establishing custody and visitation in other states. The purpose is to subject these decisions to some judicial process, and not to delegate such decisions to the parent willing or able to physically remove a child across state or national lines. Such statutes have historically been guided by the Uniform Child Custody Jurisdiction Act (UCCJA), recommended in 1968 by the National Conference of Commissioners on Uniform State Laws. All fifty states enacted statutes generally conforming to its terms—although some included significant variations.

In 1980, the Congress enacted the federal Parent Kidnapping Prevention Act (PKPA) (28 USC § 1738A) to give "full faith and credit" to the custody (and visitation) judgments of the respective courts among the several states. Section 1738(B) follows with similar terms for full faith and credit in the enforcement of child support orders between states. The crucial criterion of the statute defines the court of jurisdiction as the "home state" of the child, including a state that "had been the child's home State within six months before the date of the commencement of the proceeding and the child is absent from such State because of his removal or retention by a contestant or for other reasons, and a contestant continues to live in such State" (§ 1738A(c)(2)(A)(ii)). Allowance is made for the pick-up of jurisdiction in a non-home state where jurisdiction has not been asserted or has been rejected by other states and such jurisdiction is in the "best interest of the child"; no other state would qualify as a "home state" and there is some connection between the state and the child and at least one of the "contestants" for child custody, and the evidence as to the care and protection of the child is available in that state; the child is physically in the state and has been abandoned; or jurisdiction is necessary as an emergency to protect the child or a sibling has been "threatened with mistreatment or abuse." The most important provision of the statute is § 1738A(d), providing that the "jurisdiction of a court of a State which has made a child custody or visitation determination ... continues...[where] such State remains the residence of the child or of any contestant." Hence, the parent who remains in the jurisdiction where the court awarded custody/visitation should designedly be in a position to enforce that order in the locale of the child as moved. However, the provision applicable to where protection is necessary to prevent mistreatment or abuse of a child or sibling may be invoked if such an order has not yet been entered—perhaps encouraging movement *pendente lite*.

In 1993, the American Bar Association's Center on Children and the Law published its extensive report on the status of custody jurisdiction: *Obstacles to the Recovery and Return of Parentally Abducted Children* (1993), citing inconsistency of interpretation of the UCCJA and the technicalities of applying the PKPA and documenting a lack of consistency among the states—perhaps leading to some as destination "safe havens" for child movement in violation of adjudicated (or pending) orders. The *Obstacles Study* suggested a number of amendments, some of which were recommended in a 1997 updated statute in a new model Uniform Child Custody Jurisdiction and Enforcement Act (UCJEA) by the National Conference of Commissioners on Uniform State Laws. The UCJEA clarifies the definition of a child's "home state," provides for emergency jurisdiction in another state only until the court with original jurisdiction can act, clarifies when a court has declined jurisdiction, and importantly includes a sweeping definition of covered orders to subsume neglect, dependency, wardship, guardianship and other decisions where they involve issues of custody and visitation. It also eliminates the "best interest" criteria as an overriding basis for jurisdiction given its open-ended nature.

One purposes of the UCCJA revision was to provide a remedy for interstate visitation and custody cases. As with child support, state borders have become one of the biggest obstacles to enforcement of custody and visitation orders. As the *Obstacles Study* documents, the UCCJA does not effectively provide for a uniform method of enforcing custody and visitation orders validly entered in another state. One state might provide for a "Motion to Enforce or a Motion to Grant Full Faith and Credit" to initiate an enforcement proceeding. Another might require a Writ of Habeas Corpus or a Citation for Contempt. In some states, writs of mandamus or prohibition might be the norm. These variations increase costs and because burdens and elements of proof may vary, can create different outcomes—with some jurisdictions developing a reputation as an enforcement "safe haven," stimulating avoidance of properly litigated orders.

The provisions of Article 3 of the more recent UCCJEA provide several remedies for the enforcement of a custody determination. First, there is a simple procedure for registering a custody determination in another state to allow advance notice of its recognition. This alternative is important where a child is consistently sent to another jurisdiction—for example, visitation in another state where one parent now resides. The original court order will be honored by the state where the child is visiting. And such a provision could prove useful in international custody cases as well. The model Act provides a swift remedy along the lines of habeas corpus, preferred because time is of the essence is these adjudications—often triggered where a parent refuses to return a child after a vacation or visit. The scope of the enforcing court's inquiry is limited to the issue of whether the decree court had jurisdiction and complied with due process without further inquiry. The UCCJEA provides that the enforcing court will be able to use an extraordinary remedy. If the enforcing court is concerned that the parent, who has physical custody of the child, will flee or harm the child, a warrant allows the court to take physical possession of the child. And the new model statute provides a role for prosecutors, in the enforcement process to encourage compliance. Their involvement may be critical where the litigants are unable to afford counsel to privately enforce the law and obtain return of a child consistent with court command.

The issues are somewhat more complicated when movement of a child is across national boundaries, but some provisions of the UCCJEA pertaining to registration, *et al.*, may apply. Superimposed over the model is the Hague Convention on the Civil Aspects of International Child Abduction of 1986 and the International Child Abduction Remedies Act enacted by the Congress in 1988 to implement the Convention (42 USC § 11601 *et seq.*). Both establish administrative and judicial mechanisms to expedite the return of children (usually to their country of habitual residence) who have been abducted or wrongfully retained and to facilitate the exercise of visitation across international borders. Under the Hague Convention, children who are wrongfully removed from or retained in a contracting state (*i.e.*, a country that is party to the Convention) are subject to prompt return. The UCCJEA specifically provides for the enforcement of Hague Convention return orders and authorizes public officials to locate and secure the return of those children. As with other aspects of the rights of children, the theoretical protections of the UCCJEA—where enacted by the states—occurs in the context of continuing practicality problems: limited private resources, uncertain public authority priority, and lack of independent representation or access to the courts (or public prosecutors) by involved children.

ENDNOTES

[1] The UPA was adopted by the National Conference of Commissioners on Uniform State Laws in 1973. It was revised in 2000 to incorporate the Uniform Putative and Unknown Fathers Act and the Uniform Status of Children of Assisted Conception Act.

[2] (1979) 441 U.S. 380.

[3] For some indication that courts may apply some due diligence requirements for fathers to reach a parental rights threshold, see *In Re Baby Boy C*, 581 A.2d 1141 (D.C. App. 1990); see also *Robert O. v. Russell K.*, 604 N.E.2d 1999 (N.Y. 1992).

[4] The death of both parents would appear to be of some consequence to a child, and if the equivalent loss (from the child's perspective) were caused by the executive branch of the state, such a taking might be of some concern to the branch charged with checking the executive in the interests of potentially weak parties. Divorce usually involves retention by one parent and visitation by the other, and sometimes joint custody. However, as noted above, under the "winner take all" format of non-marital parental rights/custody law the child will likely lose all contact with the parents he has known since birth. Under current law, most jurisdictions do not acknowledge a constitutional dimension to Baby Richard's right to those he reasonably considers to be his parents—regardless of his age and passage of time, or his reliance on the state to provide parents. The issue is of particular importance given the common pattern in child abuse

cases of allowing highly marginal parents to retain parental rights while children are placed into long-term foster care, sometimes in families licensed for that purpose, sometimes with relatives. After a substantial period, such an unterminated parent may win "reunification" return of the child into his or her custody. To what extent can he or she as the "parent" with custody then bar all contact with the responsible adult who had served as the child's "parent" during the interim? See *Troxel v. Granville* and related discussion below regarding the right of "parents" to exclude visitation from other persons— including grandparents, and at least in *dicta*, those who have functioned and have been regarded as the parents by the child, perhaps for many years.

[5]As a post script, in 1997, two years after the surrender of Baby Richard to Okatar and Daniella, she petitioned the court to be declared Richard's legal mother. Her approval of the adoption had extinguished her parental legal status and she sought its reinstatement. The new case led to Child Protective Services re-entry into the setting, and facing substantial opposition to parental rights restoration, Daniella subsequently withdrew her petition. Meanwhile, Okatar moved out of the house, taking up residence with another woman and leaving Richard with Daniella—the one parent who initially rejected him and whose parental status, at least on an adoption qualification basis, was apparently problematical.

[6] The passage of the 26th Amendment to the Constitution, lowering the voting age from 21 to 18 years, led to similar age reductions for adult status during the 1970s in almost all states. However, minimum age requirements for many privileges and rights—such as drinking alcohol, smoking, driving vehicles, etc—are set at separately effective age levels by specific state statutes.

[7] Visible examples include youth sports stars or celebrities who seek to control their own affairs.

[8] See *e.g.*, *Risinger v. Risinger*, 253 S.E.2d. 652 (S.C. 1979); see also *Hinchey v. Hinchey*, 625 P.2d 297 (Alaska 1981).

[9] See *Wilkinson v. Wilkinson*, 585 P.2d 599 (Colo. 1978).

[10] See the guidelines in the Uniform Marriage and Divorce Act, Section 309, 9A ULA 167 (1967).

[11] Such support is affected by custody, with parents entitled to an offset of their support obligations if they have partial custody (since they are providing such support directly while the child is in their custody).

[12] See Bruch, *Developing Standards for Child Support, A Critique of Current Practice* 16 UCD L. Rev 49 (1982); see also Hunter, *Child Support Law and Policy: The Systemic Imposition of Costs on Women* 6 HARV. L.J. 1 (1983).

[13] *People v. Green*, 178 Colo. 77 (1972); see also *People v. Cressay*, 2 Cal. 3d 836 (1970).

[14] See the Deadbeat Parents Punishment Act of 1998, 18 U.S.C. § 228.

[15] 42 U.S.C. §§ 651-662.

[16] See http://www.acf.dhhs.gov/programs/cse.

CHAPTER TWELVE

Child Rights to Property, Contract and Tort Recovery

A. CHILD RIGHTS TO PROPERTY

1. Common Law Property Rights

Children have the right to "own" both personal and real property.[1] However, at common law they are considered incapable of managing it. Hence, parental authority generally includes the management of property owned by a child. Children can alienate and transmit title to property, but they are not permitted at common law to make irrevocable conveyances of realty without express judicial authority. Usually such a sale is approved for the maintenance or education of a minor.[2]

Parents do retain presumed title to property that they furnish to their children for support and education, such as clothing and toys. And parents have the right to earnings from their unemancipated children as concomitant to their obligation to support them. That right may take the form of child labor for a parent, or allowing children to work for others (within the limits of child labor laws) and collecting the earnings. If a parent abandons a child, the right to his or her earnings terminates.

Where parental guidance is lacking, a court may appoint a guardian for that purpose. More often, management of a child's assets is accomplished through use of trusts and gifts pursuant to the Uniform Gifts to Minors Act, which has been enacted in varying form in all fifty states. Gifts to children are presumed accepted if to their advantage. Upon receipt, the gift may be enforceable against attempted retrieval. An adult may give up to $11,000 in gifts to a child per annum without incurring federal gift taxation.

Over the last thirty years, trusts have emerged as a common vehicle for transfering property to children, and for its maintenance until they reach majority. Named trustees are appointed by the trustor, are assigned duties by the trust instrument, have a fiduciary duty to the child beneficiary and are liable for its breach.

2. Property Rights of Children of Unwed Parents

Much of the policy debate over child property rights over the past half-century has involved the rights of a particular subset of children: those born to unwed parents. What claim do such children have to property deriving from the biological parents (who owe them a duty of support)? How are such children to be treated in terms of government subsidies and payment due the children of married couples? Are such children a "suspect classification" entitled to "strict scrutiny" protection? To mid-level "heightened scrutiny"?

Levy v. Louisiana
391 U.S. 68 (1968)

Mr. Justice Douglas delivered the opinion of the Court.

Appellant sued on behalf of five illegitimate children to recover, under a Louisiana statute[1] (La. Civ. Code Ann. Art. 2315...) for two kinds of damages as a result of the wrongful death of their mother: (1) the damages to them for the loss of their mother; and (2) those based on the survival of a cause of action which the mother had at the time of her death for pain and suffering. Appellees...are the doctor who treated her and the insurance company.

We assume in the present state of the pleadings that the mother, Louise Levy, gave birth to these five illegitimate children and that they lived with her; that she treated them as a parent would treat any other child; that she worked as a domestic servant to support them, taking them to church every Sunday and enrolling them, at her own expense, in a parochial school....

* * *

We start from the premise that illegitimate children are not "nonpersons." They are humans, live, and have their being....They are clearly "persons" within the meaning of the Equal Protection Clause of the Fourteenth Amendment....

While a State has broad power when it comes to making classifications..., it may not draw a line which constitutes an invidious discrimination against a particular class....Though the test has been variously stated, the end result is whether the line drawn is a rational one....

In applying the Equal Protection Clause to social and economic legislation, we give great latitude to the legislature in making classifications....Even so, would a corporation, which is a "person," for certain purposes, within the meaning of the Equal Protection Clause...be required to forgo recovery for wrongs done its interests because its incorporators were all bastards? However that might be, we have been extremely sensitive when it comes to basic civil rights...and have not hesitated to strike down an invidious classification even though it had history and tradition on its side. (*Brown v. Board of Education*, 347 U.S. 483...) The rights asserted here involve the intimate, familial relationship between a child and his own mother. When the child's claim of damage for loss of his mother is in issue, why, in terms of "equal protection," should the tortfeasors go free merely because the child is illegitimate? Why should the illegitimate child be denied rights merely

---

[1] "Every act whatever of man that causes damage to another obliges him by whose fault it happened to repair it.

"The right to recover damages to property caused by an offense or quasi offense is a property right which, on the death of the obligee, is inherited by his legal, instituted, or irregular heirs, subject to the community rights of the surviving spouse.

"The right to recover all other damages caused by an offense or quasi offense, if the injured person dies, shall survive for a period of one year from the death of the deceased in favor of: (1) the surviving spouse and child or children of the deceased, or either such spouse or such child or children; (2) the surviving father and mother of the deceased, or either of them, if he left no spouse or child surviving; and (3) the surviving brothers and sisters of the deceased, or any of them, if he left no spouse, child, or parent surviving. The survivors in whose favor this right of action survives may also recover the damages which they sustained through the wrongful death of the deceased. A right to recover damages under the provisions of this paragraph is a property right which, on the death of the survivor in whose favor the right of action survived, is inherited by his legal, instituted, or irregular heirs, whether suit has been instituted thereon by the survivor or not.

"As used in this article, the words 'child,' 'brother,' 'sister,' 'father,' and 'mother' include a child, brother, sister, father, and mother, by adoption, respectively."

because of his birth out of wedlock? He certainly is subject to all the responsibilities of a citizen, including the payment of taxes and conscription under the Selective Service Act. How under our constitutional regime can he be denied correlative rights which other citizens enjoy?

Legitimacy or illegitimacy of birth has no relation to the nature of the wrong allegedly inflicted on the mother. These children, though illegitimate, were dependent on her; she cared for them and nurtured them; they were indeed hers in the biological and in the spiritual sense; in her death they suffered wrong in the sense that any dependent would.[5]

We conclude that it is invidious to discriminate against them when no action, conduct, or demeanor of theirs[6] is possibly relevant to the harm that was done the mother.[7]

Reversed.

Justice Harlan, whom **Mr. Justice Black** and **Mr. Justice Stewart** join, dissenting.

These decisions can only be classed as constitutional curiosities.

At common law, no person had a legally cognizable interest in the wrongful death of another person, and no person could inherit the personal right of another to recover for tortious injuries to his body....By statute, Louisiana has created both rights in favor of certain classes of persons. The question in these cases is whether the way in which Louisiana has defined the classes of persons who may recover is constitutionally permissible. The Court has reached a negative answer to this question by a process that can only be described as brute force.

One important reason why recovery for wrongful death had everywhere to await statutory delineation is that the interest one person has in the life of another is inherently intractable. Rather than hear offers of proof of love and affection and economic dependence from every person who might think or claim that the bell had tolled for him, the courts stayed their hands pending legislative action. Legislatures, responding to the same diffuseness of interests, generally defined classes of proper plaintiffs by highly arbitrary lines based on family relationships, excluding issues concerning the actual effect of the death on the plaintiff....

Louisiana has followed the traditional pattern. There the actions lie in favor of the surviving spouse and children of the deceased, if any; if none, then in favor of the surviving parents of the deceased, if any; if none, then in favor of the deceased's brothers and sisters, if any; if none, then no action lies. According to this scheme, a grown man may sue for the wrongful death of parents he did not love,[3] even if the death relieves him of a great economic burden or entitles him to

---

[5] Under Louisiana law both parents are under a duty to support their illegitimate children....

[6] We can say with Shakespeare: "Why bastard, wherefore base? When my dimensions are as well compact, My mind as generous, and my shape as true, As honest madam's issue? Why brand they us With base? with baseness? bastardy? base, base?" King Lear, Act I, Scene 2.

[7] Under Louisiana's Workmen's Compensation Act (...(1964)) an illegitimate child, who is a dependent member of the deceased parent's family, may recover compensation for his death....Employers are entitled to recover from a wrongdoer workmen's compensation payments they make to the deceased's dependent illegitimate children....

[3] He may even, like Shakespeare's Edmund, have spent his life contriving treachery against his family. Supposing that the Bard had any views on the law of legitimacy, they might more easily be discerned from Edmund's character than from the words he utters in defense of the only thing he cares for, himself.

a large inheritance. But an employee who loses a job because of the death of his employer has no cause of action, and a minor child cared for by neighbors or relatives "as if he were their own son" does not therefore have a right to sue for their death....Perhaps most dramatic, a surviving parent, for example, of a Louisiana deceased may sue if and only if there is no surviving spouse or child: it does not matter who loved or depended on whom, or what the economic situation of any survivor may be, or even whether the spouse or child elects to sue.[5] In short, the whole scheme of the Louisiana wrongful death statute, which is similar in this respect to that of most other States, makes everything the Court says about affection and nurture and dependence altogether irrelevant. The only question in any case is whether the plaintiff falls within the classes of persons to whom the State has accorded a right of action for the death of another.

* * *

The Court today, for some reason which I am at a loss to understand, rules that the State must base its arbitrary definition of the plaintiff class on biological rather than legal relationships. Exactly how this makes the Louisiana scheme even marginally more "rational" is not clear, for neither a biological relationship nor legal acknowledgment is indicative of the love or economic dependence that may exist between two persons. It is, frankly, preposterous to suggest that the State has made illegitimates into "nonpersons," or that, by analogy with what Louisiana has done here it might deny illegitimates constitutional rights or the benefits of doing business in corporate form.[8] The rights at issue here stem from the existence of a family relationship, and the State has decided only that it will not recognize the family relationship unless the formalities of marriage, or of the acknowledgment of children by the parent in question, have been complied with.

There is obvious justification for this decision....

The Equal Protection Clause states a complex and difficult principle. Certain classifications are "inherently suspect," which I take to mean that any reliance upon them in differentiating legal rights requires very strong affirmative justification. The difference between a child who has been formally acknowledged and one who has not is hardly one of these. Other classifications are impermissible because they bear no intelligible proper relation to the consequences that are made to flow from them. This does not mean that any classification this Court thinks could be better drawn is unconstitutional. But even if the power of this Court to improve on the lines that Congress and the States have drawn were very much broader than I consider it to be, I could not understand why a State which bases the right to recover for wrongful death strictly on family relationships could not demand that those relationships be formalized.

I would affirm the decisions of the state court and the Court of Appeals for the Fifth Circuit.

---

[5] ....The Court speaks in *Levy* of tortfeasors going free. However, the deceased in that case left a legitimate parent. Under the Court's opinion, the right of legitimate and perhaps dependent parents to sue will henceforth be cut off by the mere existence of an illegitimate child, though the child be a self-supporting adult, and though the child elect not to sue. Incidentally, the burden of proving the nonexistence of such a child will be on the plaintiff parent....

[8] A more obvious analogy from the law of corporations than the rather farfetched example the Court has suggested is the elementary rule that the benefits of doing business in corporate form may be denied, to the willful, the negligent, and the innocent alike, if the formalities of incorporation have not been properly complied with.

Questions for Discussion

1. Should the children of unwed parents be a suspect classification invoking strict scrutiny? Generally, the courts have held that a group held in popular disregard, politically weak, with a history of discriminatory treatment warrant such status. Don't many refer to such children as "bastards"? Are they less politically weak than racial or religious minorities? Does the fact that such children have no choice in the circumstance of their birth commend such status?

2. Assuming the more generous "rational relation" test, what is the state interest here in differentiating these children from other children? Does it stimulate marriage? What is the evidence presented of that connection? Assuming it encourages marriage, can that encouragement be constitutionally accomplished through denial of benefits to third parties?

3. Louisiana may argue that children cannot collect when their absent father dies because they are not legal heirs, that parental status can determine property rights and that marriage is a criterion for parental status. But when Louisiana seeks to collect child support for welfare it provided, does it restrict itself to married fathers? Can it take from such a source for itself because of biological tie alone, but refuse to collect for the child under the same circumstance?

4. The dissent argues that Louisiana needs a bright line, and the status of marriage provides it. But failure to marry does not necessarily preclude the constitutional rights of unmarried biological fathers seeking parental rights (see Chapter 11). That "bright line," however useful, was struck as underinclusive and abridging the parental rights of some fathers. Unlike these children, do not such fathers have the option to secure marriage prior to producing a child?

Mathews v. Lucas
427 U.S. 495 (1976)

Mr. Justice Blackmun delivered the opinion of the Court.

This case presents the issue of the constitutionality, under the Due Process Clause of the Fifth Amendment, of those provisions of the Social Security Act that condition the eligibility of certain illegitimate children for a surviving child's insurance benefits upon a showing that the deceased wage earner was the claimant child's parent and, at the time of his death, was living with the child or was contributing to his support.

I

Robert Cuffee, now deceased, lived with Belmira Lucas during the years 1948 through 1966, but they were never married. Two children were born to them during these years: Ruby M. Lucas, in 1953, and Darin E. Lucas, in 1960. In 1966 Cuffee and Lucas separated. Cuffee died in Providence, R.I., his home, in 1968. He died without ever having acknowledged in writing his paternity of either Ruby or Darin, and it was never determined in any judicial proceeding during his lifetime that he was the father of either child. After Cuffee's death, Mrs. Lucas filed an application on behalf of Ruby and Darin for surviving children's benefits under...the Social Security Act,...42 U.S.C. § 402(d)(1)..., based upon Cuffee's earnings record.

I

In operative terms, the Act provides that an unmarried son or daughter of an individual, who died fully or currently insured under the Act, may apply for and be entitled to a survivor's benefit, if the applicant is under 18 years of age at the time of application (or is a full-time student and under 22 years of age) and was dependent, within the meaning of the statute, at the time of the parent's death....A child is considered dependent for this purpose if the insured father was living with or contributing to the child's support at the time of death. Certain children, however, are relieved of the burden of such individualized proof of dependency. Unless the child has been adopted by some other individual, a child who is legitimate, or a child who would be entitled to inherit personal property from the insured parent's estate under the applicable state intestacy law, is considered to have been dependent at the time of the parent's death....Even lacking this relationship under state law, a child, unless adopted by some other individual, is entitled to a presumption of dependency if the decedent, before death, (a) had gone through a marriage ceremony with the other parent, resulting in a purported marriage between them which, but for a nonobvious legal defect, would have been valid, or (b) in writing had acknowledged the child to be his, or (c) had been decreed by a court to be the child's father, or (d) had been ordered by a court to support the child because the child was his....

An Examiner of the Social Security Administration, after hearings, determined that while Cuffee's paternity was established, the children had failed to demonstrate their dependency by proof that Cuffee either lived with them or was contributing to their support at the time of his death, or by any of the statutory presumptions of dependency, and thus that they were not entitled to survivorship benefits under the Act....

* * *

III

The Secretary does not disagree that the Lucas children and others similarly circumstanced are treated differently, as a class, from those children—legitimate and illegitimate—who are relieved by statutory presumption of any requirement of proving actual dependency at the time of death through cohabitation or contribution: for children in the advantaged classes may be statutorily entitled to benefits even if they have never been dependent upon the father through whom they claim.[7] Statutory classifications, of course, are not per se unconstitutional; the matter depends upon the character of the discrimination and its relation to legitimate legislative aims. "The essential inquiry...is...inevitably a dual one: What legitimate [governmental] interest does the classification promote? What fundamental personal rights might the classification endanger?"....

Although the District Court concluded that close judicial scrutiny of the statute's classifications was not necessary to its conclusion invalidating those classifications, it also concluded that legislation treating legitimate and illegitimate offspring differently is constitutionally suspect,[8] 390 F. Supp., at 1318–1319, and requires the judicial scrutiny traditionally devoted to cases involving discrimination

---

[7] It adds nothing to say that the illegitimate child is also saddled with the procedural burden of proving entitlement on the basis of facts the legitimate child need not prove. The legitimate child is required, like the illegitimate, to prove the facts upon which his statutory entitlement rests.

[8] Appellees do not suggest, nor could they successfully, that strict judicial scrutiny of the statutory classifications is required here because, in regulating entitlement to survivorship benefits, the statute discriminatorily interferes with interests of constitutional fundamentality....

along lines of race...or national origin....Appellees echo this approach. We disagree.[11]

It is true, of course, that the legal status of illegitimacy, however defined, is, like race or national origin, a characteristic determined by causes not within the control of the illegitimate individual, and it bears no relation to the individual's ability to participate in and contribute to society. The Court recognized in *Weber* that visiting condemnation upon the child in order to express society's disapproval of the parents' liaisons

> "is illogical and unjust. Moreover, imposing disabilities on the illegitimate child is contrary to the basic concept of our system that legal burdens should bear some relationship to individual responsibility or wrongdoing. Obviously, no child is responsible for his birth and penalizing the illegitimate child is an ineffectual—as well as an unjust—way of deterring the parent." 406 U.S., at 175. (Footnote omitted.)

But where the law is arbitrary in such a way, we have had no difficulty in finding the discrimination impermissible on less demanding standards than those advocated here....And such irrationality in some classifications does not in itself demonstrate that other, possibly rational, distinctions made in part on the basis of legitimacy are inherently untenable. Moreover, while the law has long placed the illegitimate child in an inferior position relative to the legitimate in certain circumstances, particularly in regard to obligations of support or other aspects of family law,...perhaps in part because the roots of the discrimination rest in the conduct of the parents rather than the child,[12] and perhaps in part because illegitimacy does not carry an obvious badge, as race or sex do, this discrimination against illegitimates has never approached the severity or pervasiveness of the historic legal and political discrimination against women and Negroes....

We therefore adhere to our earlier view,...that the Act's discrimination between individuals on the basis of their legitimacy does not "command extraordinary protection from the majoritarian political process," *San Antonio School Dist. v. Rodriguez*, 411 U.S. 1, 28 (1973), which our most exacting scrutiny would entail.[13]....

IV

* * *

...[W]e think it clear that conditioning entitlement upon dependency at the time of death is not impermissibly discriminatory in providing only for those children for whom the loss of the parent is an immediate source of the need....

The Court, of course, has found the privacy of familial relationships, to be entitled to procedural due process protections from disruption by the State, whether or not those relationships were legitimized by marriage under state law. *Stanley v. Illinois*, 405 U.S. 645 (1972). But the concerns relevant to that context are only tangential to the analysis here, since the statutory scheme does not interfere in any way with familial relations.

[11] That the statutory classifications challenged here discriminate among illegitimate children does not mean, of course, that they are not also properly described as discriminating between legitimate and illegitimate children....In view of our conclusion regarding the applicable standard of judicial scrutiny, we need not consider how the classes of legitimate and illegitimate children would be constitutionally defined under appellees' approach.

[12] The significance of this consideration would seem to be suggested by provisions enabling the parents to legitimatize children born illegitimate. Compare *Weber*, 406 U.S., at 170–171, with *Labine v. Vincent*, 401 U.S. 532, 539 (1971). Of course, the status of "dependency" as recognized by the statute here is wholly within the control of the parent.

[13] In *Rodriguez* the Court identified a "suspect class" entitled to the protections of strict judicial scrutiny as one "saddled with such disabilities, or subjected to such a history of purposeful unequal treatment, or relegated to such a position of political powerlessness as to command extraordinary protection from the majoritarian political process." 411 U.S., at 28.

But appellees contend that the actual design of the statute belies the Secretary's description, and that the statute was intended to provide support for insured decedents' children generally, if they had a "legitimate" claim to support, without regard to actual dependency at death; in any case, they assert, the statute's matrix of classifications bears no adequate relationship to actual dependency at death. Since such dependency does not justify the statute's discriminations, appellees argue, those classifications must fall under *Gomez v. Perez*, *supra*. These assertions are in effect one and the same.[14] The basis for appellees' argument is the obvious fact that each of the presumptions of dependency renders the class of benefit-recipients incrementally overinclusive, in the sense that some children within each class of presumptive dependents are automatically entitled to benefits under the statute although they could not in fact prove their economic dependence upon insured wage earners at the time of death. We conclude that the statutory classifications are permissible, however, because they are reasonably related to the likelihood of dependency at death.

* * *

B

Applying these principles, we think that the statutory classifications challenged here are justified as reasonable empirical judgments that are consistent with a design to qualify entitlement to benefits upon a child's dependency at the time of the parent's death. To begin with, we note that the statutory scheme is significantly different from the provisions confronted in cases in which the Court has invalidated legislative discriminations among children on the basis of legitimacy....These differences render those cases of little assistance to appellees. It could not have been fairly argued, with respect to any of the statutes struck down in those cases, that the legitimacy of the child was simply taken as an indication of dependency, or of some other valid ground of qualification. Under all but one of the statutes, not only was the legitimate child automatically entitled to benefits, but an illegitimate child was denied benefits solely and finally on the basis of illegitimacy, and regardless of any demonstration of dependency or other legitimate factor....

* * *

...[W]here state intestacy law provides that a child may take personal property from a father's estate, it may reasonably be thought that the child will more likely be dependent during the parent's life and at his death....For in its embodiment of the popular view within the jurisdiction of how a parent would have his property devolve among his children in the event of death, without specific directions, such legislation also reflects to some degree the popular conception within the jurisdiction of the felt parental obligation to such an "illegitimate" child in other circumstances, and thus something of the likelihood of actual parental support during, as well as after, life.[18]....

To be sure, none of these statutory criteria compels the extension of a presumption of dependency. But the constitutional question is not whether such

---

[14] We are not bound to agree with the Secretary's description of the legislative design if the legislative history and the structure of the provisions themselves belie it....Appellees are unable, however, to summon any meaningful legislative history to support their position regarding the congressional design....

[18] Appellees do not suggest, and we are unwilling to assume, that discrimination against children in appellees' class in state intestacy laws is constitutionally prohibited, see *Labine v. Vincent*, 401 U.S. 532 (1971), in which case appellees would be made eligible for benefits under § 216(h)(2)(A).

a presumption is required, but whether it is permitted....We conclude, in short, that, in failing to extend any presumption of dependency to appellees and others like them, the Act does not impermissibly discriminate against them as compared with legitimate children or those illegitimate children who are statutorily deemed dependent.

Reversed.

Mr. Justice Stevens, with whom **Mr. Justice Brennan** and **Mr. Justice Marshall** join, dissenting.

The reason why the United States Government should not add to the burdens that illegitimate children inevitably acquire at birth is radiantly clear: We are committed to the proposition that all persons are created equal. The Court's reason for approving discrimination against this class—"administrative convenience"—is opaque and insufficient: opaque because the difference between this justification and the argument rejected in *Jimenez v. Weinberger*, 417 U.S. 628, is so difficult to discern; insufficient because it unfairly evaluates the competing interests at stake.

I

Jimenez involved a requirement that the wage earner must have contributed to the support of his illegitimate child prior to the onset of his disability; this case involves the requirement that the deceased wage earner was contributing to the support of his illegitimate child at the time of his death. The critical objections to the classification held invalid in *Jimenez* apply with equal force in this case.

The classification in *Jimenez* was "overinclusive" because it conclusively presumed that all legitimates and some illegitimates were dependent on the disabled wage earner when many such persons were not in fact dependent. Since legitimate as well as illegitimate children are sometimes abandoned by their father before his death, precisely the same objection applies to this statutory classification. Moreover, the *Jimenez* classification was "underinclusive" because it conclusively excluded some illegitimates who were in fact dependent on the wage earner.[1] In this case the two appellee children were conclusively excluded from the class of eligibles even though they had been supported by their father for 15 years and eight years respectively. If the underinclusiveness of the *Jimenez* classification was arbitrary, this classification is even more objectionable because it attaches greater weight to support at a particular moment in time than to support of several years' duration.

* * *

I

[1] "Even if children might rationally be classified on the basis of whether they are dependent upon their disabled parent, the Act's definition of these two subclasses of illegitimates is 'overinclusive' in that it benefits some children who are legitimated, or entitled to inherit, or illegitimate solely because of a defect in the marriage of their parents, but who are not dependent on their disabled parent. Conversely, the Act is 'underinclusive' in that it conclusively excludes some illegitimates in appellants' subclass who are, in fact, dependent upon their disabled parent. Thus, for all that is shown in this record, the two subclasses of illegitimates stand on equal footing, and the potential for spurious claims is the same as to both; hence to conclusively deny one subclass benefits presumptively available to the other denies the former the equal protection of the laws guaranteed by the due process provision of the Fifth Amendment." 417 U.S., at 637.

The Court recognizes "that the legal status of illegitimacy, however defined, is, like race or national origin, a characteristic determined by causes not within the control of the illegitimate individual, and it bears no relation to the individual's ability to participate in and contribute to society."....For that reason, as the Court also recognizes, "'imposing disabilities on the illegitimate child is contrary to the basic concept of our system that legal burdens should bear some relationship to individual responsibility or wrongdoing.'"....Thus the Court starts its analysis from the premise that the statutory classification is both "'illogical and unjust.'"....It seems rather plain to me that this premise demands a conclusion that the classification is invalid unless it is justified by a weightier governmental interest than merely "administrative convenience."

* * *

In this case, the "true" classification, according to the Court, is one between children dependent on their fathers and children who are not so dependent. All of the subsidiary classifications (which have the actual effect of allowing certain children to be eligible for benefits regardless of actual dependency) are supposedly justified by the increased convenience for the agency in not being required in every case to determine dependency. But do these classifications actually bear any substantial relationship to the fact of dependency?

In this statute, one or another of the criteria giving rise to a "presumption of dependency" exists to make almost all children of deceased wage earners eligible. If a child is legitimate, he qualifies. If the child is illegitimate only because of a nonobvious defect in his parents' marriage, he qualifies. If a court has declared his father to be in fact his father, or has issued an order of support against his father, or if the father has acknowledged the child in writing, he qualifies. Apart from any of these qualifications, if the child is lucky enough to live in a State which allows him to inherit from his intestate father on a par with other children, he also qualifies. And in none of these situations need he allege, much less prove, actual dependency. Indeed, if the contrary fact is undisputed, he is nevertheless qualified.

The Court today attempts, at some length, to explain that each of these factors is rationally and substantially related to the actual fact of dependency, adopting even the somewhat tenuous rationalization of the District Court that "'[m]en do not customarily affirm in writing their responsibility for an illegitimate child unless the child is theirs and a man who has acknowledged a child is more likely to provide it support than one who does not,'"...without also noting that a man who lives with a woman for 18 years, during which two children are born, who has always orally acknowledged that the children are his, and who has lived with the children and supported them, may never perceive a need to make a formal written acknowledgment of paternity. Even more tenuous is the asserted relationship between the status of the illegitimate under state intestacy law and actual dependency. The Court asserts that "in its embodiment of the popular view within the jurisdiction of how a parent would have his property devolve among his children in the event of death, without specific directions, such legislation also reflects to some degree the popular conception within the jurisdiction of the felt parental obligation to such an 'illegitimate' child in other circumstances, and thus something of the likelihood of actual parental support during, as well as after, life."....That nebulous inference upon inference is treated as more acceptable evidence of actual dependency than proof of actual support for many years.[4]

---

[4] If the relationship between an entitling presumption and the actual fact of dependency is so nebulous that the conclusion can be supported only by resort to a supposed popular conception within a jurisdiction, the classification must either be irrational, or serve a purpose other than the one by which it is assertedly justified.

* * *

I am persuaded that the classification which is sustained today in the name of "administrative convenience" is more probably the product of a tradition of thinking of illegitimates as less deserving persons than legitimates. The sovereign should firmly reject that tradition. The fact that illegitimacy is not as apparent to the observer as sex or race does not make this governmental classification any less odious. It cannot be denied that it is a source of social opprobrium, even if wholly unmerited, or that it is a circumstance for which the individual has no responsibility whatsoever.

A fair evaluation of the competing interests at stake in this litigation requires affirmance of the judgment of the District Court.

I respectfully dissent.

Questions for Discussion

1. Isn't living with children and supporting them sufficient acknowledgment for these children to qualify? What would be Robert Cuffee's status if Ruby Lucas sought to give the children up for adoption? Would he be able to block the adoption? Would he be considered a "presumed father" under the Uniform Parentage Act (see cases and discussion in Chapter 11)?

2. Is the majority argument persuasive that illegitimate children are not a properly protected class because unlike race and gender, they do not carry the physical "badge" of their difference? Do people reliably carry such badges of their religion, which is a basis for protected group strict scrutiny status?

3. Mr. Cuffee contributed to Social Security, which funds the child survivor benefits here at issue. If the federal jurisdiction were paying welfare to these children, would this biological father be assessed child support? If he has an obligation to support the children, which the federal government is prepared to enforce, aren't his children entitled to these benefits on the same biological basis? Is it fair for government to go beyond marriage to collect for itself, but to refuse to use the same criteria when paying out?

4. The Court argues that the marriage line is administratively convenient. Is that a convincing argument? Is a less restrictive alternative available, *e.g.*, an opportunity for an illegitimate child to show actual dependency? Is categorical exclusion necessary to accomplish the stated public purpose?

5. Is "support" at the moment of death an equitable criterion where marriage is lacking under the majority decision? What about parents who provide full support for a decade or more (*e.g.*, while funding their Social Security account), are the biological parents, and then die during a brief period when they are not supporting?

6. The children of unwed parents sometimes receive "heightened" or "intermediate" scrutiny when they are differentiated by the state. Would a statute stand that allows intestate succession to nonmarital children as to their mothers' estates, but not as to their fathers'? Could the state argue that it has a compelling interest in timely and certain inheritance, and that paternal status is less certain?

Could it argue more generally that such a policy properly furthers the compelling state interest in marriage as an institution? See the striking of such a statute in *Trimble v. Gordon*, 430 U.S. 762 (1977), with explicit court rejection of a policy to influence adult behavior through the "sanctioning of children." Given *Trimble,* can a state then permit non-marital children to intestate inheritance from their fathers only "where a court has entered a filiation order" prior to death? See the affirmance of this discrimination as consistent with the state's interest in providing for the just and "orderly disposition of property at death". *Lalli v. Lalli*, 439 U.S. 259 (1978). Are these two decisions consistent with each other? With *Levy*? With *Mathews*?

7. Do DNA and other advances undermine required "filiation orders" for non-marital child inheritance from fathers? Is uncertainty really a problem now? If timeliness is an issue, would not a time limit on claims filed not satisfy such a state interest as a less restrictive alternative?

B. CHILD RIGHT OF CONTRACT

The common law acknowledges the immaturity of children to enter into the "meeting of the minds" which an enforceable contact requires.[3] Historically, contracts applied to children fell into three common law categories: (1) void (when clearly prejudicial to the child); (2) voidable (when possibly in the child's best interest); and (3) valid (when clearly in the child's best interest). The coalescence of these rules into the current "doctrine of incapacity" means that children may disaffirm contracts which are to their disadvantage, but enforce those which are of benefit. In other words, the law is not symmetrical in its application, but favors the child.

The child's disaffirmance may take place at any point during his or her minority, and perhaps for a short period after emancipation. There are some exceptions to the disaffirmance right, including contracts which are non-voidable by statute, or which provide a child with "necessaries" (*e.g.*, food, clothing, medical care). And one consequence of disaffirmance may be the remedy of rescission—including the return of items possessed by the minor. The majority rule is that such return will be limited to actual property possessed, and does not extend to restoration of full value. However, disaffirmance may be denied by some courts where minors misrepresent their age, and moreover such deceit may be a tort allowing full recovery for value received, in addition to possible damages (see tort discussion below).

C. CHILD TORT LIABILITY AND RECOVERY

1. Child Liability

Children generally are subject to the same tort rights and liabilities as adults. However, their immaturity may sometimes preclude liability for intentional torts where specific intent is required, as with slander, libel, trespass, or deceit. Such immunity is more likely where young children are implicated, with courts varying widely in their assignment of adequate capacity for liability. Some courts have formulated a "rule of 7," that children under seven years of age are presumptively unable to commit an intentional tort, those over 14 are presumed to have capacity, and liability for those 7 to 14 years of age depends on the facts. However, the majority rule is to use age simply as one factor to consider in measuring capacity. In general, courts are likely to apply the "reasonable man" standard as children exceed fourteen years of age.

2. Child Recovery from Private Parties

a. Status of Children

As a general rule, children may recover where injured by the tortious acts of others. An exception is provided by the "parental immunity" doctrine which traditionally limits such suits against parents.[4] The rationale has been the importance of family harmony. The doctrine historically was extended so far as to bar suit for incestuous rape by a father.[5] And it was extended to provide immunity for stepparents and others performing a parental role. However, the doctrine has been eroded over the last half century to the point where it no longer impedes child suit against a parent in most states.[6] The growth of liability insurance has spurred the doctrine's demise, since suit generally does not lead to collection from parents, but from insurance carriers. For example, children are almost universally allowed to sue carriers for their injuries resulting from negligent driving by their parents. Courts have also questioned the equity of denying recovery based on family harmony when many such torts are reflective of exploitive practices. Accordingly, courts rarely allow family harmony as a defense to "willful" or "wanton" (reckless) torts. Nevertheless, it may be invoked where negligence is alleged beyond the scope of insurance coverage, and its spirit is reflected in the understandable latitude afforded parents in exercising judgment about their children. "Parental discretion" stands as a formidable vestige of the parental immunity doctrine to protect good faith child rearing decisions of parents. Negligence by parents outside the penumbra of parenting, which violates the standards generally applicable, is not covered by this protection (*e.g.*, gross negligence in starting of a fire which injures a child).

Historically, children have not been allowed to recover damages for the loss of parental care and companionship occurring when a third party negligently injures or kills a parent. This omission is in contrast to the common damages for "loss of consortium" available to a spouse. However, over the last twenty years, states have started to recognize this parental loss as a possible recoverable injury.[7]

Children were not able to recover for prenatal injuries at common law. They were viewed as a "person" only as to property rights (permitting the child-as-fetus to inherit and benefit from trusts). However, over the last half-century, such rights of recovery have been increasingly recognized,[8] and now stand as the strong majority rule. Application does vary, with most jurisdictions confining it to pre-natal injuries to infants born alive. A small and declining minority confine it to injuries incurred only after the child is "viable" (sometime during the second or early third trimester of pregnancy). Thus far, no child has successfully sued a mother for injuries she caused *in utero*. However, where such injuries are the result of intentional harm (including possibly severe alcohol or drug contamination), such suits may be consistent with the trend discussed above.

b. The "Attractive Nuisance"

Perhaps the most advantageous tort doctrine applicable to children is the concept of "attractive nuisance," the liability which may attach a person who creates a hazard where children are likely to be jeopardized, particularly one reasonably expected to attract their interest. That attraction is not limited to children known to the defendant, but to any child likely to appear. The longstanding doctrine imposes an implicit duty on the citizenry to safeguard children from dangerous conditions, even on their own property where child access may be predicted.

Corson v. Kosinski

3 F.3d 1146 (7th Cir. 1993)

OPINION: **BAUER**, Chief Judge.

Lynda Lontz filed a personal injury lawsuit for herself and on behalf of her son, Kenneth Corson. Corson and Lontz are citizens of Texas and the Kosinskis are citizens of Illinois. This case is in federal court under diversity jurisdiction. 28 U.S.C. § 1332. Lontz and Corson seek $750,000 in damages from the defendants, Bruno and Carolyn Kosinski. The Kosinskis filed a motion for summary judgment, which the district court granted. Lontz and Corson appeal. We affirm.

I.

Ten-year-old Kenneth Corson, who lived with his mother in Texas, was in Chicago to spend the summer of 1989 with his father. One day, eleven-year-old Evelyn Benitz invited Kenneth and three other children over to play. Evelyn lived in an apartment in a three-story building on North Hoyne Street in Chicago which was owned by Bruno and Carolyn Kosinski. She was the only child who lived in the building.

Like many in Chicago, the building Evelyn lived in is attached to another, similar building which is also owned by the Kosinskis. The buildings share a fire wall that extends from the foundation to approximately one and a half feet beyond the roof. Both roofs are the same height, but the perimeter of the adjoining roof does not squarely abut the fire wall. Instead, eighteen feet of the wall that starts at the front of the building borders an open shaft designed to allow light to reach the ground.

Evelyn, Kenneth, and the other boys were riding bicycles and went to the basement of Evelyn's apartment building for a drink of water. The children entered the basement through a locked door for which Evelyn and the other tenants had keys. After drinking, the children left the basement via a stairwell which connects the basement to the apartments. The stairwell extends beyond the apartments and adjoins an additional stairway that leads to the roof. One of the boys ventured all the way up the stairs and found an unlocked roof door. The children went out on the roof unnoticed, played, and left. They returned later the same day and played a game that involved jumping over the fire wall that sticks out of the roof. The children jumped over the center of the wall, but Kenneth moved towards the front of the building, not knowing that the light shaft, not the roof, was on the other side of the wall. When he jumped over the wall, he fell three stories to the ground. He sustained serious, permanent injuries.

II.

* * *

Corson and Lontz sued the Kosinskis for negligence resulting in Kenneth's injury. In Illinois, a landowner is liable for an injury to a child on the owner's property if the owner knew or should have known that young children frequent the premises and a dangerous condition exists, likely to cause a child injury if the child is incapable of appreciating the risk involved, and the expense or inconvenience of remedying the dangerous condition is slight relative to the risk....

* * *

1. Premises:

Initially we must determine what constitutes the premises in this case. The plaintiff argues that the basement, back stairwell, yard, and roof should be considered part of the premises because the stairwell opens to the yard and connects the basement, the apartments, and the roof. They further argue that because children are naturally curious they will seek adventure, ostensibly by roaming to the basement and the roof. Therefore, they conclude, all the areas common to the stairwell are the premises.

The evidence shows that a separate door led to the roof. The door was normally padlocked and the tenants did not have keys. The lock was to be closed at all times, and when the lock was closed, the roof was inaccessible to the tenants (and children). This was distinct from the basement, which was also secured by a locked door for which all the tenants had keys. The basement housed circuit breakers and storage, so that tenant access to the basement was necessary. In contrast, the tenants had no reason to go to the roof. Also, the other areas of the building, such as the front porch, the yard, and the stairwell were common and accessible to all tenants, unlike the roof. We believe that the roof was effectively separated from the rest of the apartment building.

* * *

Nor will the curiosity of children serve to provide the missing evidence. We agree that children are curious. Their curiosity on this occasion turned their trip for a drink of water into an ill-fated adventure. But we do not believe that this incident is enough to find that the roof is part of the premises. Benitz lived on the second floor of the building for eleven years. The evidence showed that the children had been on the back stairwell on fewer than six occasions during that time. Moreover, when on the stairwell the children's activities were confined to talking and whispering. The plaintiffs produced no evidence that children had ever played on the back stairwell or explored the area leading to the roof.

This is not to say that the children were wholly absent from the building. They occasionally played in the yard and gathered on the front porch....

2. Frequency:

Frequency is determined by the circumstances surrounding each case... This is a factual issue that is generally left for a jury.... But we have determined that the premises encompassed by our inquiry is the roof alone, and no other part of the building. The plaintiffs provided no evidence that Evelyn or any other child had ever been on the roof.

* * *

The district court decision is AFFIRMED.

Questions for Discussion

1. What would have been the cost to mitigate the hazard? What about a sign disclosing that a blind hole lay behind the wall?

2. Would the Court's decision have been different if there had been a prior incident at the site? If there had been similar publicized incidents of such skylights causing injuries?

3. The case turns largely on whether the defendant knew or should have known if children were "frequenting the site". Isn't it reasonable to assume a child would be in that location given the unlocked door to the roof and the presence of this building in the middle of a city with many thousands of children? Wouldn't a more sensible criteria be whether it is reasonable to assume anyone, including a child, would jump over the wall in question without looking behind it?

3. Child Tort Recovery from the State

a. The Duty of Care

Deshaney v. Winnebago County
489 U.S. 189 (1989)

CHIEF JUSTICE REHNQUIST delivered the opinion of the Court.

Petitioner is a boy who was beaten and permanently injured by his father, with whom he lived. Respondents are social workers and other local officials who received complaints that petitioner was being abused by his father and had reason to believe that this was the case, but nonetheless did not act to remove petitioner from his father's custody. Petitioner sued respondents claiming that their failure to act deprived him of his liberty in violation of the Due Process Clause of the Fourteenth Amendment to the United States Constitution. We hold that it did not.

I

The facts of this case are undeniably tragic. Petitioner Joshua DeShaney was born in 1979. In 1980, a Wyoming court granted his parents a divorce and awarded custody of Joshua to his father, Randy DeShaney. The father shortly thereafter moved to Neenah, a city located in Winnebago County, Wisconsin, taking the infant Joshua with him. There he entered into a second marriage, which also ended in divorce.

The Winnebago County authorities first learned that Joshua DeShaney might be a victim of child abuse in January 1982, when his father's second wife complained to the police, at the time of their divorce, that he had previously "hit the boy causing marks and [was] a prime case for child abuse."....The Winnebago County Department of Social Services (DSS) interviewed the father, but he denied the accusations, and DSS did not pursue them further. In January 1983, Joshua was admitted to a local hospital with multiple bruises and abrasions. The examining physician suspected child abuse and notified DSS, which immediately obtained an order from a Wisconsin juvenile court placing Joshua in the temporary custody of the hospital. Three days later, the county convened an ad hoc "Child Protection Team"—consisting of a pediatrician, a psychologist, a police detective, the county's lawyer, several DSS caseworkers, and various hospital personnel—to consider Joshua's situation. At this meeting, the Team decided that there was insufficient evidence of child abuse to retain Joshua in the custody of the court. The Team did, however, decide to recommend several measures to protect Joshua, including enrolling him in a preschool program, providing his father with certain counseling services, and encouraging his father's girlfriend to move out of the home. Randy DeShaney entered into a voluntary agreement with DSS in which he promised to cooperate with them in accomplishing these goals.

Based on the recommendation of the Child Protection Team, the juvenile court dismissed the child protection case and returned Joshua to the custody of his father. A month later, emergency room personnel called the DSS caseworker handling Joshua's case to report that he had once again been treated for suspicious injuries. The caseworker concluded that there was no basis for action. For the next six months, the caseworker made monthly visits to the DeShaney home, during which she observed a number of suspicious injuries on Joshua's head; she also noticed that he had not been enrolled in school, and that the girlfriend had not moved out. The caseworker dutifully recorded these incidents in her files, along with her continuing suspicions that someone in the DeShaney household was physically abusing Joshua, but she did nothing more. In November 1983, the emergency room notified DSS that Joshua had been treated once again for injuries that they believed to be caused by child abuse. On the caseworker's next two visits to the DeShaney home, she was told that Joshua was too ill to see her. Still DSS took no action.

In March 1984, Randy DeShaney beat 4-year-old Joshua so severely that he fell into a life-threatening coma. Emergency brain surgery revealed a series of hemorrhages caused by traumatic injuries to the head inflicted over a long period of time. Joshua did not die, but he suffered brain damage so severe that he is expected to spend the rest of his life confined to an institution for the profoundly retarded. Randy DeShaney was subsequently tried and convicted of child abuse.

Joshua and his mother brought this action under 42 U.S.C. § 1983 in the United States District Court for the Eastern District of Wisconsin against respondents Winnebago County, DSS, and various individual employees of DSS. The complaint alleged that respondents had deprived Joshua of his liberty without due process of law, in violation of his rights under the Fourteenth Amendment, by failing to intervene to protect him against a risk of violence at his father's hands of which they knew or should have known....

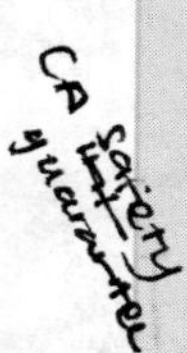

* * *

I

The Due Process Clause of the Fourteenth Amendment provides that "[n]o State shall...deprive any person of life, liberty, or property, without due process of law." Petitioners contend that the State...deprived Joshua of his liberty interest in "free[dom] from...unjustified intrusions on personal security,"...by failing to provide him with adequate protection against his father's violence. The claim is one invoking the substantive rather than the procedural component of the Due Process Clause; petitioners do not claim that the State denied Joshua protection without according him appropriate procedural safeguards, see *Morrissey v. Brewer*, 408 U.S. 471, 481 (1972), but that it was categorically obligated to protect him in these circumstances, see *Youngberg v. Romeo*, 457 U.S. 307, 309 (1982).[2]

But nothing in the language of the Due Process Clause itself requires the State to protect the life, liberty, and property of its citizens against invasion by private actors. The Clause is phrased as a limitation on the State's power to act, not as a guarantee of certain minimal levels of safety and security....

---

[2] Petitioners also argue that the Wisconsin child protection statutes gave Joshua an "entitlement" to receive protective services in accordance with the terms of the statute, an entitlement which would enjoy due process protection against state deprivation under our decision in *Board of Regents of State Colleges v. Roth*, 408 U.S. 564 (1972)....But this argument is made for the first time in petitioners' brief to this Court: it was not pleaded in the complaint, argued to the Court of Appeals as a ground for reversing the District Court, or raised in the petition for certiorari. We therefore decline to consider it here....

...If the Due Process Clause does not require the State to provide its citizens with particular protective services, it follows that the State cannot be held liable under the Clause for injuries that could have been averted had it chosen to provide them.[3] As a general matter, then, we conclude that a State's failure to protect an individual against private violence simply does not constitute a violation of the Due Process Clause.

Petitioners contend, however, that even if the Due Process Clause imposes no affirmative obligation on the State to provide the general public with adequate protective services, such a duty may arise out of certain "special relationships" created or assumed by the State with respect to particular individuals.... Petitioners argue that such a "special relationship" existed here because the State knew that Joshua faced a special danger of abuse at his father's hands, and specifically proclaimed, by word and by deed, its intention to protect him against that danger....Having actually undertaken to protect Joshua from this danger—which petitioners concede the State played no part in creating—the State acquired an affirmative "duty," enforceable through the Due Process Clause, to do so in a reasonably competent fashion. Its failure to discharge that duty, so the argument goes, was an abuse of governmental power that so "shocks the conscience," *Rochin v. California*, 342 U.S. 165, 172 (1952), as to constitute a substantive due process violation....[4]

We reject this argument. It is true that in certain limited circumstances the Constitution imposes upon the State affirmative duties of care and protection with respect to particular individuals. In *Estelle v. Gamble*, 429 U.S. 97 (1976), we recognized that the Eighth Amendment's prohibition against cruel and unusual punishment, made applicable to the States through the Fourteenth Amendment's Due Process Clause, *Robinson v. California*, 370 U.S. 660 (1962), requires the State to provide adequate medical care to incarcerated prisoners. 429 U.S., at 103–104.[5] We reasoned that because the prisoner is unable "'by reason of the deprivation of his liberty [to] care for himself,'" it is only "'just'" that the State be required to care for him....

---

[3] The State may not, of course, selectively deny its protective services to certain disfavored minorities without violating the Equal Protection Clause....But no such argument has been made here.

[4] The genesis of this notion appears to lie in a statement in our opinion in *Martinez v. California*, 444 U.S. 277 (1980). In that case, we were asked to decide, *inter alia*, whether state officials could be held liable under the Due Process Clause of the Fourteenth Amendment for the death of a private citizen at the hands of a parolee. Rather than squarely confronting the question presented here—whether the Due Process Clause imposed upon the State an affirmative duty to protect—we affirmed the dismissal of the claim on the narrower ground that the causal connection between the state officials' decision to release the parolee from prison and the murder was too attenuated to establish a "deprivation" of constitutional rights within the meaning of § 1983. *Id.*, at 284–285. But we went on to say:

"[T]he parole board was not aware that appellants' decedent, as distinguished from the public at large, faced any special danger. We need not and do not decide that a parole officer could never be deemed to 'deprive' someone of life by action taken in connection with the release of a prisoner on parole. But we do hold that at least under the particular circumstances of this parole decision, appellants' decedent's death is too remote a consequence of the parole officers' action to hold them responsible under the federal civil rights law." *Id.*, at 285 (footnote omitted).

Several of the Courts of Appeals have read this language as implying that once the State learns that a third party poses a special danger to an identified victim, and indicates its willingness to protect the victim against that danger, a "special relationship" arises between State and victim, giving rise to an affirmative duty, enforceable through the Due Process Clause, to render adequate protection....

[5] To make out an Eighth Amendment claim based on the failure to provide adequate medical care, a prisoner must show that the state defendants exhibited "deliberate indifference" to his "serious" medical needs; the mere negligent or inadvertent failure to provide adequate care is not enough. *Estelle v. Gamble*, 429 U.S., at 105–106. In *Whitley v. Albers*, 475 U.S. 312

* * *

But these cases afford petitioners no help. Taken together, they stand only for the proposition that when the State takes a person into its custody and holds him there against his will, the Constitution imposes upon it a corresponding duty to assume some responsibility for his safety and general well-being....

* * *

Affirmed.

Justice Brennan, with whom **Justice Marshall** and **Justice Blackmun** join, dissenting.

"The most that can be said of the state functionaries in this case," the Court today concludes, "is that they stood by and did nothing when suspicious circumstances dictated a more active role for them."....Because I believe that this description of respondents' conduct tells only part of the story and that, accordingly, the Constitution itself "dictated a more active role" for respondents in the circumstances presented here, I cannot agree that respondents had no constitutional duty to help Joshua DeShaney.

* * *

The Court's baseline is the absence of positive rights in the Constitution and a concomitant suspicion of any claim that seems to depend on such rights. From this perspective, the DeShaneys' claim is first and foremost about inaction (the failure, here, of respondents to take steps to protect Joshua), and only tangentially about action (the establishment of a state program specifically designed to help children like Joshua). And from this perspective, holding these Wisconsin officials liable—where the only difference between this case and one involving a general claim to protective services is Wisconsin's establishment and operation of a program to protect children—would seem to punish an effort that we should seek to promote.

I would begin from the opposite direction. I would focus first on the action that Wisconsin *has* taken with respect to Joshua and children like him, rather than on the actions that the State failed to take. Such a method is not new to this Court. Both *Estelle v. Gamble*, 429 U.S. 97 (1976), and *Youngberg v. Romeo*, 457 U.S. 307 (1982), began by emphasizing that the States had confined J. W. Gamble to prison and Nicholas Romeo to a psychiatric hospital. This initial action rendered these people helpless to help themselves or to seek help from persons unconnected to the government....

* * *

Wisconsin has established a child-welfare system specifically designed to help children like Joshua. Wisconsin law places upon the local departments of social services such as respondent (DSS or Department) a duty to investigate reported instances of child abuse. See Wis. Stat. § 48.981(3) (1987–1988). While other governmental bodies and private persons are largely responsible for the reporting of possible cases of child abuse,...Wisconsin law channels all such reports to the local departments of social services for evaluation and, if necessary, further action....Even when it is the sheriff's office or police department that receives a report of suspected child abuse, that report is referred to local social

---

(1986), we suggested that a similar state of mind is required to make out a substantive due process claim in the prison setting. *Id.*, at 326–327.

services departments for action, see § 48.981(3)(a); the only exception to this occurs when the reporter fears for the child's *immediate* safety....In this way, Wisconsin law invites—indeed, directs—citizens and other governmental entities to depend on local departments of social services such as respondent to protect children from abuse.

The specific facts before us bear out this view of Wisconsin's system of protecting children. Each time someone voiced a suspicion that Joshua was being abused, that information was relayed to the Department for investigation and possible action. When Randy DeShaney's second wife told the police that he had "'hit the boy causing marks and [was] a prime case for child abuse,'" the police referred her complaint to DSS....When, on three separate occasions, emergency room personnel noticed suspicious injuries on Joshua's body, they went to DSS with this information....When neighbors informed the police that they had seen or heard Joshua's father or his father's lover beating or otherwise abusing Joshua, the police brought these reports to the attention of DSS....And when respondent Kemmeter, through these reports and through her own observations in the course of nearly 20 visits to the DeShaney home,...compiled growing evidence that Joshua was being abused, that information stayed within the Department—chronicled by the social worker in detail that seems almost eerie in light of her failure to act upon it. (As to the extent of the social worker's involvement in, and knowledge of, Joshua's predicament, her reaction to the news of Joshua's last and most devastating injuries is illuminating: "'I just knew the phone would ring some day and Joshua would be dead.'"...

Even more telling than these examples is the Department's control over the decision whether to take steps to protect a particular child from suspected abuse. While many different people contributed information and advice to this decision, it was up to the people at DSS to make the ultimate decision (subject to the approval of the local government's corporation counsel) whether to disturb the family's current arrangements....When Joshua first appeared at a local hospital with injuries signaling physical abuse, for example, it was DSS that made the decision to take him into temporary custody for the purpose of studying his situation—and it was DSS, acting in conjunction with the corporation counsel, that returned him to his father....Unfortunately for Joshua DeShaney, the buck effectively stopped with the Department.

In these circumstances, a private citizen, or even a person working in a government agency other than DSS, would doubtless feel that her job was done as soon as she had reported her suspicions of child abuse to DSS. Through its child-welfare program, in other words, the State of Wisconsin has relieved ordinary citizens and governmental bodies other than the Department of any sense of obligation to do anything more than report their suspicions of child abuse to DSS. If DSS ignores or dismisses these suspicions, no one will step in to fill the gap. Wisconsin's child-protection program thus effectively confined Joshua DeShaney within the walls of Randy DeShaney's violent home until such time as DSS took action to remove him. Conceivably, then, children like Joshua are made worse off by the existence of this program when the persons and entities charged with carrying it out fail to do their jobs.

It simply belies reality, therefore, to contend that the State "stood by and did nothing" with respect to Joshua....Through its child-protection program, the State actively intervened in Joshua's life and, by virtue of this intervention, acquired ever more certain knowledge that Joshua was in grave danger. These circumstances, in my view, plant this case solidly within the tradition of cases like *Youngberg* and *Estelle*.

It will be meager comfort to Joshua and his mother to know that, if the State had "selectively den[ied] its protective services" to them because they were "disfavored minorities,"...their § 1983 suit might have stood on sturdier ground. Because of the posture of this case, we do not know why respondents did not take steps to protect Joshua; the Court, however, tells us that their reason is irrelevant so long as their inaction was not the product of invidious discrimination. Presumably, then, if respondents decided not to help Joshua because his name began with a "J," or because he was born in the spring, or because they did not care enough about him even to formulate an intent to discriminate against him based on an arbitrary reason, respondents would not be liable to the DeShaneys because they were not the ones who dealt the blows that destroyed Joshua's life.

* * *

As the Court today reminds us, "the Due Process Clause of the Fourteenth Amendment was intended to prevent government 'from abusing [its] power, or employing it as an instrument of oppression.'"....My disagreement with the Court arises from its failure to see that inaction can be every bit as abusive of power as action, that oppression can result when a State undertakes a vital duty and then ignores it. Today's opinion construes the Due Process Clause to permit a State to displace private sources of protection and then, at the critical moment, to shrug its shoulders and turn away from the harm that it has promised to try to prevent. Because I cannot agree that our Constitution is indifferent to such indifference, I respectfully dissent.

Justice Blackmun, dissenting.

Today, the Court purports to be the dispassionate oracle of the law, unmoved by "natural sympathy."....But, in this pretense, the Court itself retreats into a sterile formalism which prevents it from recognizing either the facts of the case before it or the legal norms that should apply to those facts....

The Court fails to recognize this duty because it attempts to draw a sharp and rigid line between action and inaction. But such formalistic reasoning has no place in the interpretation of the broad and stirring Clauses of the Fourteenth Amendment. Indeed, I submit that these Clauses were designed, at least in part, to undo the formalistic legal reasoning that infected antebellum jurisprudence,...

Like the antebellum judges who denied relief to fugitive slaves,...the Court today claims that its decision, however harsh, is compelled by existing legal doctrine. On the contrary, the question presented by this case is an open one, and our Fourteenth Amendment precedents may be read more broadly or narrowly depending upon how one chooses to read them. Faced with the choice, I would adopt a "sympathetic" reading, one which comports with dictates of fundamental justice and recognizes that compassion need not be exiled from the province of judging....

Poor Joshua! Victim of repeated attacks by an irresponsible, bullying, cowardly, and intemperate father, and abandoned by respondents who placed him in a dangerous predicament and who knew or learned what was going on, and yet did essentially nothing except, as the Court revealingly observes,..."dutifully recorded these incidents in [their] files." It is a sad commentary upon American life, and constitutional principles—so full of late of patriotic fervor and proud proclamations about "liberty and justice for all"—that this child, Joshua DeShaney, now is assigned to live out the remainder of his life profoundly retarded. Joshua and his mother, as petitioners here, deserve—but now are denied by this Court—the opportunity to have the facts of their case considered in the light of the constitutional protection that 42 U.S.C. § 1983 is meant to provide.

Questions for Discussion

1. The state's involvement with Joshua includes the creation of a mandated reporter system to detect child abuse, creation of a juvenile court system

to protect the child, funding of a local agency to detect and monitor legal compliance, receipt of information indicating his abuse, physical custody and a decision to return Joshua to his father, monthly visits, and additional information of continuing abuse. Under these circumstances, is it reasonable to conclude that the state owes "no duty" to Joshua because at the time of the beating he was not in state custody?

2. The Court rules that the state is not responsible for private action, nor can the state be liable for failure to act without a "special relationship." Is there no special relationship between Joshua and the state? Are citizens reasonably relying on the state to affirmatively protect such children? Given the statutory commands to protect children and the system purportedly set up to provide that protection, should the state be equitably estopped from claiming lack of duty?

3. The remedy here might be to pay for Joshua's care from the local agency budget. Should the possible negative impact on its resources to protect other children be considered by the Court? On the other hand, what is the financial incentive to minimize negligence in child protection if there is no accountability?

4. In *Sniadach v. Family Finance Corp. of Bay View*, 395 U.S. 337 (1969), the Court ruled that there was sufficient "state action" to require due process hearings where a private creditor garnishees wages. Another case similarly found state action in the ministerial act of court marshals enforcing court judgments (see *Fuentes v. Shevin*, 407 U.S. 67 (1972)). Still other cases found "state action" where federal funding may be involved in what is otherwise private enterprise. How can such minor state involvement trigger a "state action" determination while the child protection regulatory system and Joshua's direct involvement with it is insufficient "state action" to confer liability to the state?

Comment

Compare *DeShaney* to the subsequent New York appellate case of *Boland v. State*, 638 N.Y.S.2d 500 (1996), holding that the state had an intrinsic "special relationship" with the victims of child abuse and was not entitled to immunity for a failure to report child abuse for investigation. In *Boland*, a neighbor reported the suspected abuse of two children by a grandparent who was caring for them while their father was overseas. The report, made on the state's child protection "hotline" was assigned to the wrong county, and the investigation was delayed for two days—during which one of the children was beaten to death. The child's father filed an action and the appellate court held that there was a "special relationship" imposing a duty on the state to exercise due care through the enactment of a statutory scheme to protect children, and including its reporting-investigation mechanism. When the state's child protective intake worker deemed the allegations a qualified "abuse report," she assumed a duty to protect the children (including a reliance by the person making the report), and a failure to discharge it could be a basis for state liability where a failure to act was a proximate cause of the child's injuries.

b. Child Tort Recovery Liability Alternatives

DeShaney's denial of a state "duty of care" for children in parental custody does not preclude remedy where the state takes the child into custody and injury occurs during state-assumed care. Hence, suit may lie for injury suffered through the negligent acts of foster care providers, who function as state agents. Nor will the sovereign immunity barriers bar such suit given holdings that a child has a constitutionally (and statutory) based right to a secure placement (see immunity bar discussion in Chapter 1). However, such liability applies where removal is court ordered, and may not apply to parental voluntary placements of their children into foster care. See *Milburn v. Anne Arundel County Department of Social Services*, 871 F.2d 474 (4th Cir. 1989). Such a "voluntary surrender" category may be substantial given the common strategy of seeking "stipulated agreements" from parents to foster care placement and even for parental rights termination. Such parents may be convinced that their chances of reunification are minimal and that a quick and voluntary agreement for state assistance for their child may be in the child's best interest.

Two alternative standards of care may apply to state actors subject to civil rights cases under § 1983: (1) the traditional professional malpractice standard of "departure from accepted standards of skill and judgment for that profession in the community," or (2) a stricter standard requiring officials to manifest a "deliberate indifference" to a risk actually known to them. The latter standard poses a significant burden on a plaintiff; the injured child must show indifference notwithstanding "actual knowledge." The difficult standard has been imposed by at least two circuits. See, *e.g., White v. Chambliss*, 112 F.3d 731 (4th Cir. 1997); *K.H. ex rel. Murphy v. Morgan*, 914 F.2d 846 (7th Cir. 1990).

Can a "special relationship" creating liability arise from the failure of the executive branch to enforce a specific court order intended to protect a child? In *Town of Castlerock v. Gonzales* 125 S.Ct. 2796 (2005), a court entered a restraining order preventing the violent father from contact with the plaintiff's three daughters (ages 7, 9 and 10) or from coming within 100 yards of their home. The father violated the order, entered the home, and took all three children. The plaintiff mother reported the taking and begged the police to enforce the order. They did not do so—nor attempt to do so. All three children were murdered. The complaint alleged that the police has an official policy of not responding properly "to allegations of restraining order violations." Colorado state law makes the violation of a restraining order a crime. Colorado's law and those of other states in the domestic violence area are not comparable to "outstanding arrest warrants" issued by the court that may or may not be acted upon at a given time and place. The duty here is explicitly imposed on the police to "arrest" and to "use every reasonable means to enforce" the order—as is the case similarly in 18 other states. Nevertheless, writing for the majority, Justice Scalia held that even the direct instruction of the court to protect a child (not actually in state custody) does not create a "special relationship" creating a "duty" whose violation gives rise to damage liability under 42 USC § 1983. Rather, police have discretion and that discretion is not subject to liability based on police decisions to act or not to act. The dissent argued that a court order or judgment is a "property interest" that may be effectively "taken" from a possessor without due process by police breach of a duty to perform and constitutes a valid § 1983 claim. And it complained about the Court ignoring the judgment of Colorado state courts that the failure of the police violated a mandatory duty. The majority rather focused on the "manner" of enforcement, positing discretion as to the means and methods (apparently even where there were no means or methods).

Beyond damage actions under § 1983, standard tort suits may be brought in state court against state officials or foster care providers where children are harmed. However, the legal status of foster care providers whose negligence is often at issue is unclear. Some jurisdictions treat such providers as "state employees" or agents, affording access to public resources for compensation and treatment. Others regard foster parents as "independent contractors," in which case recovery may depend upon required or extant insurance coverage by these defendants. In addition, foster parents may receive the partial protection of "parental immunity" status given their parental role, as discussed above.[9]

4. Child Tort Recovery—Insurance Coverage

J.C. Penney Casualty Insurance Co. v. M.K.
52 Cal. 3d 1009 (1991)

OPINION: Eagleson, J.—

* * *

FACTS

In September 1984, M.K., then a five-year-old girl, told her mother, S.K., that the girl had been sexually molested by an adult male neighbor, R.H....He was a friend of the mother and had often babysat the girl. R.H. was charged with eight counts of willfully committing lewd or lascivious acts with a child under the age of fourteen years in violation of Penal Code section 288, subdivision (a).[2] R.H. pled guilty to one count in a plea bargain that dismissed the other seven counts. He was sentenced to prison for six years.

Before the molestations, J.C. Penney Casualty Insurance Company (hereafter J.C. Penney) had issued to R.H. a comprehensive homeowner's policy that provided liability insurance....

* * *

The mother and child filed an action for damages against R.H. in June 1985, alleging causes of action in negligence and intentional tort. R.H. admitted to fondling the girl's genitals with his hands, holding the girl over his head with his thumb inserted into her vagina, and orally copulating her. A medical examination confirmed vaginal penetration, which caused a ruptured hymen, and possible anal penetration.

Before trial the mother and child dismissed all causes of action for intentional tort and proceeded to trial only on theories of negligence and negligent infliction of emotional distress. At the start of the mother and child's case, R.H. stipulated that he had been negligent as to the child. Based on that stipulation, the court entered a directed verdict in the child's action that R.H. was negligent. The issue of R.H.'s negligence as to the mother was submitted to the jury, which in special verdicts found that R.H. was negligent and that his negligence was a legal cause of damage to the mother.[3] The jury awarded $400,000 to the child and $100,000 to the mother.

[2] Penal Code section 288, subdivision (a), states: "Any person who shall willfully and lewdly commit any lewd or lascivious act including any of the acts constituting other crimes provided for in Part 1 of this code upon or with the body, or any part or member thereof, of a child under the age of 14 years, with the intent of arousing, appealing to, or gratifying the lust or passions or sexual desires of that person or of the child, shall be guilty of a felony and shall be imprisoned in the state prison for a term of three, six, or eight years."

J.C. Penney's declaratory relief action was tried in May 1987. The trial court received evidence as to R.H.'s state of mind when he molested the child. More specifically, R.H. testified in deposition, admitting the following: "*Question*: You intended to do what you did, correct? *Answer*: Yes....*Question*: And you knew at the time you were doing these things that they were wrong; Isn't that correct?...*Answer*: Yes, I knew it was wrong....*Question*: And after most of these incidents, you would generally go to the bathroom to relieve yourself? *Answer*: Generally, yes. *Question*: Sexually? *Answer*: Yes. *Question*: Because you were aroused by what had happened? *Answer*: Yes." R.H. also testified, however, that he did not intend to harm the child, and a psychologist testified likewise as to R.H.'s intent.

* * *

DISCUSSION

I. Effect of the underlying judgment against the insured

* * *

We reiterate the rule that an insurer that timely and adequately reserves its right to deny coverage and that does not subsequently intentionally waive its reservation of rights is not collaterally estopped by a judgment in favor of a third party against its insured. J.C. Penney is not collaterally estopped to deny coverage in this action for declaratory relief.

II. No coverage for sexual molestation of a child

We turn now to the primary issue addressed by the parties and numerous amici curiae: Is liability coverage for R.H.'s molestations of a child excluded by the terms of the insurance policy and Insurance Code section 533? J.C. Penney contends coverage is excluded because the molestations were intentional. Defendants respond that even an intentional and wrongful act is not excluded from coverage unless the insured acted with a "preconceived design to inflict injury." They contend psychiatric testimony shows that molesters, including R.H., often intend no harm despite the depravity of their acts, and that the molestation is often a misguided attempt to display love and affection for the child.[6]

We conclude there is no coverage as a matter of law. No rational person can reasonably believe that sexual fondlings, penetration, and oral copulation of a five-year-old child are nothing more than acts of tender mercy. Except in the present case, every court to decide this issue under California law has held that a homeowner's insurance policy does not provide liability coverage for child molestation. The courts of many other states also have considered the issue and, almost without exception, have held there is no coverage.

---

[3] The award to the mother was apparently for negligent infliction of emotional distress. In *Thing v. La Chusa* (1989) 48 Cal.3d 644..., we established the requirements for recovering damages for emotional distress caused by observing a negligent injury to a third person. One of those requirements is that the plaintiff must be "present at the scene of the injury-producing event at the time it occurs and is then aware that it is causing injury to the victim."....The record in the present case reflects that the mother was never present during any of the molestations of her child....The judgment in favor of the mother is final, however, and thus not subject to collateral attack by R.H. based on the subsequent decisions in *Thing, supra*, 48 Cal.3d 644,...

[6] Amici curiae appearing on behalf of defendants are the Children's Advocacy Institute, California Trial Lawyers' Association, and the Crime Victims' Legal Clinic. Amici curiae for J.C. Penney are the Association for California Tort Reform, the Association of California Insurance Companies, the National Association of Independent Insurers, Alliance of American Insurers, and several liability insurers.

A. Insurance Code section 533

Insurance Code section 533 provides that an insurer is not liable for a "wilful act of the insured."....Section 533 is "an implied exclusionary clause which by statute is to be read into all insurance policies."....As we will explain, section 533 excludes liability insurance coverage for child molestation.[8]

* * *

Section 533 states that, "An insurer is not liable for a loss caused by the *willful* act of the insured; but he is not exonerated by the negligence of the insured, or of the insured's agents or others." (Italics added.)....The statutory language sheds little light on the precise question before us. (Nor is there any legislative history to assist us.) Read literally, section 533 is internally inconsistent. Its first sentence purports to exclude coverage for all willful acts. The second sentence, however, expressly provides that the insured's negligence does not allow an insurer to disclaim coverage.

Negligence is often, perhaps generally, the result of a "willful act," as the term is commonly understood.[11] For example, "An ordinary consequence of driving an automobile without the exercise of ordinary care or an intentional violation of a statute (speed in excess of the maximum speed limit), is injury to the person or property of the driver or a third person. Certainly no one would contend that an injury occasioned by negligent or even reckless driving was not accidental within the meaning of a policy of accident insurance...."...."It is settled that 'wilful act' in section 533 means 'something more than the mere intentional doing of an act constituting [ordinary] negligence.'"....A contrary rule would allow an insurer to deny coverage for a negligent act. That result is specifically prohibited by section 533. We long ago construed section 533's statutory predecessor (former Civ. Code, § 2629) as establishing that "[N]o form of negligence on the part of the insured, or his agents or others, leading to a loss avoids the policy, unless it amounts to a willful act on the part of the insured. The code thereby sets at rest a fruitful cause of litigation."....

In short, section 533 does not preclude coverage for acts that are negligent or reckless. We find nothing in the statute, however, to support defendants' view that a child molester can disclaim an intent to harm his victim. There is no such thing as negligent or even reckless sexual molestation. The very essence of child molestation is the gratification of sexual desire. The act is the harm. There cannot be one without the other. Thus, the intent to molest is, by itself, the same as the intent to harm.

B. Our prior decisions

The reasoning of prior decisions under section 533 also makes clear that the statute precludes coverage for child molestation. The public policy underlying section 533 is to discourage willful torts....In addition to being a crime,

---

[8] The insurance policy issued to R.H. also contains an explicit exclusion of "bodily injury or property damage which is either expected or intended from the standpoint of the insured."...J.C. Penney relies on both the explicit exclusion and section 533....Section 533 reflects a fundamental public policy of denying coverage for willful wrongs....The parties to an insurance policy therefore cannot contract for such coverage. (Civ. Code, § 1667.) We therefore need not and do not decide whether coverage would be excluded by the explicit policy exclusion in the absence of section 533.

[11] Indeed, it is hornbook tort law that an act "is a voluntary contraction of the muscles, and nothing more....When 'act' is used in this sense, it is tautological to speak of a 'voluntary act,' and self-contradictory to speak of an 'involuntary act,' since every act is voluntary." (Prosser & Keeton, The Law of Torts (5th ed. 1984) § 8, pp. 34–35.)

child molestation is indisputably a willful tort against the child. Defendants, however, contend our decision in *Clemmer v. Hartford Insurance Co., supra*, 22 Cal.3d 865 (*Clemmer*), mandates coverage unless the insurer can prove its insured acted with a "preconceived design to inflict injury."....Based on their view of *Clemmer*, defendants contend psychiatric testimony should be allowed to establish that the insured lacked such a "preconceived design."...

Clemmer, *supra*, 22 Cal.3d 865, arose from the killing of a physician (Dr. Clemmer) by his employee (Dr. Lovelace) after an employment dispute between them. The court stated the key facts as follows: "[Dr. Lovelace] greeted Dr. Clemmer, then shot him twice. These shots were followed by two more shots. Finally, Dr. Lovelace knelt close to the victim and at close range shot him in the head. The gun was placed on the ground. Dr. Lovelace remarked that he knew what he was doing and that Dr. Clemmer was destroying him professionally." (*Id.*, at p. 872.) Dr. Lovelace was convicted of second degree murder.

* * *

....We also stated, however, that even an intentional act is not excluded from coverage under section 533 unless the act is done with a "'preconceived design to inflict injury.'"....The quoted language is the linchpin of defendants' case. They argue that coverage for child sexual molestation is not excluded unless the insurer can show that the molester had a "preconceived design to inflict injury" on the child. In their view, the intent to molest is not enough.

Clemmer, *supra*, 22 Cal.3d 865, does not support defendants' contention. The brief reference in *Clemmer* to a "preconceived design to inflict injury" must be read in context. The inquiry in *Clemmer* was limited to the unresolved *mental capacity* of the insured, *i.e.*, whether he was legally sane when he committed the killing. There was no issue as to whether the insured intended to shoot his victim five times (including once in the head at close range) but not to harm the victim....

* * *

Lucas, C.J., Mosk, J., Panellli, J., Kennard, J., and Arabian J., concurred.

Broussard, J.—I dissent.

Our courts have long enforced insurance contracts for intentional and criminal acts causing injury. Rather than read Insurance Code section 533...as precluding insurance for any willful act of the insured causing injury, such as intentionally speeding or running a red light, this court has interpreted the provision as only prohibiting enforcement of contracts insuring a person from losses intentionally caused. Thus in *Clemmer v. Hartford Insurance Co.* (1978) 22 Cal.3d 865..., this court pointed out the "clear line of authority in this state to the effect that even an act which is 'intentional' or 'willful' within the meaning of traditional tort principles will not exonerate the insurer from liability under Insurance Code section 533 unless it is done with a 'preconceived design to inflict injury.'....

The majority repudiate *Clemmer*. They hold that section 533 prohibits a person from insuring against conduct that is "inherently harmful."....The opinion's construction of the provision finds no support in the language of the provision. Such a construction fails to give sufficient consideration to the interest and rights of the innocent victims of child abuse and other crimes. The construction flies in the face of our constitutional command for the "enactment of comprehensive provisions and laws ensuring a bill of rights for victims of crime...." (Cal. Const., art. I, § 28, subd. (a).) In addition, the majority's construction opens a Pandora's box such that insureds and insurers cannot know which promises of the insurer are enforceable.

• The majority hold that the insured's intent to harm must be inferred from acts of child molestation because they are inherently harmful....In view of the undisputed expert testimony in this case as well as some others that the child molester may have intended no harm, the majority appear to be practicing psychiatry without a license and doing a terrible job of it.

* * *

A vague test based on degrees of blameworthiness would be so difficult to administer justly that it should be rejected out-of-hand. Attempting to draw a line between misdemeanors or between felonies on the basis of reprehensibility or repugnance on a case-by-case basis can only bring confusion and uncertainty to insurance law.

In any event, we rejected such a test in *Peterson v. Superior Court, supra*, 31 Cal.3d 147, 158–159. In that case we held that an intoxicated driver could be liable for punitive damages when it is shown that he performed an act from which he knows, or should know, it is highly probable that harm will result. Obviously, punitive damages are permitted only in cases involving the most reprehensible and repugnant conduct. In addition to the great likelihood of harm, which in fact occurred, the conduct was criminal. While we held that punitive damages may not be indemnified, we also held that section 533 would not be applicable to bar indemnification of compensatory damages for conduct involving an extreme degree of blameworthiness.

A "wilful" act or loss is a reference to subjective intent, and, absent a clear showing of legislative intent to the contrary, it cannot reasonably be interpreted to establish tests of "inherently harmful." In short, the test established by the majority opinion finds no support in the language of the code section and must be rejected for this reason alone. To read "inherently harmful" into this straightforward statute can only be categorized as judicial legislation.[1]

Since there is no history or strong public policy indicating that the Legislature inadvertently used the language it chose, the plain language of the code section should end the case.

Moreover, even if there was some ambiguity in the language of the code section permitting it to be reasonably construed to prohibit insurance of "inherently harmful" conduct, considerations of the interests and rights of the innocent victims of child abuse and other crimes should preclude our doing so.

Liability insurance serves two functions in our society. It not only provides a fund that the wrongdoer may resort to in order to meet his just obligation, but also provides compensation for the victims of wrongful and criminal conduct. Often, the wrongdoer's insurance is the only way the innocent victims of crime, including child molestation, may recover compensation for medical expenses, their disabilities and their injuries. Particularly as to child molesters, the wrongdoers are likely to be incarcerated for lengthy periods of time (see Pen. Code, §§ 288, subd. (a), 1170.1), and there is little likelihood that a judgment recovered against the wrongdoer can be collected out of the wrongdoer's earnings. The wrongdoer will ordinarily be faced with substantial legal expenses depleting whatever assets he may have had. Liability insurers ordinarily pay to the innocent victim rather than the insured, so there is little danger that the wrongdoer insured will fatten his pocket from the insurance.

Concern for the innocent victims of crime outweighs the policy of deterrence or penalizing the wrongdoer and strongly militates against an

---

[1] The majority tell us that they decide only the wrongdoing before us, child molestation.... However, we can only expect that insurers will deny coverage in all or substantially all cases involving criminal conduct. All criminal conduct is "repugnant and reprehensible," and it will be for the courts to determine whether the particular conduct is so "repugnant and reprehensible" as to preclude insurance coverage.

interpretation expanding section 533's prohibition of insurance coverage....

If there were any doubt as to the proper balance of competing policies, it is set at rest by our Constitution. Article I, section 28, subdivision (a) commands the "enactment of comprehensive provisions and laws ensuring a bill of rights for victims of crime." When we indulge in judicial legislation, we should observe the mandates of our Constitution applicable to legislation.

* * *

I

Upon analysis, the majority theory that we must infer intent to harm from child abuse fares no better. We cannot properly infer from child molestation the intent to harm as a matter of law in the face of an overwhelming record establishing that there was no intent to harm or even in the absence of such a record. Penal Code section 288, subdivision (a) provides: "Any person who shall willfully and lewdly commit any lewd or lascivious act including any of the acts constituting other crimes provided for in Part 1 of this code upon or with the body, or any part or member thereof, of a child under the age of 14 years, with the *intent* of arousing, appealing to, or gratifying the lust or passions or sexual desires of that *person or of the child*, shall be guilty of a felony...." (Italics added.) It is clear from the italicized portion of the code section that child molestation under the section is based on the intent of the wrongdoer and that the wrongdoer may be guilty of the crime on the basis of gratifying his lust or sexual desires without regard to those of the victim. Until today, at least, neither harm to the child nor intent to harm the child was an element of the offense. Accordingly, the insured's guilty plea to one count of child molestation does not establish intent to injure.

The physical acts of child molestation are not detailed in the statute; rather, the crucial factor is the intent of the actor. The physical acts may be of a wide variety, including acts which are commonly engaged in for medical or hygienic purposes by parents, siblings, and pediatricians. However, when such acts are done with the specified intent, the conduct is criminal. The point is illustrated by the instant case where 25 of the acts of child molestation occurred while the insured was playing with the child. He touched or fondled her vaginal area while she was fully clothed. Absent criminal intent, the physical conduct would be entirely innocent. I cannot agree that the physical conduct is "inherently harmful" or that we must as a matter of law infer from such conduct, even when coupled with an intent to gratify sexual desires, that there was an intent to harm.

The expert testimony was all to the effect that there was no intent to harm. The majority opinion quotes the statements from other cases that such testimony "flies 'in the face of all reason, common sense, and experience' and is 'inherently incredible.'"....There is nothing in our record to justify this shocking attack on the science of psychiatry. Neither the majority opinion nor the cited authorities provide any empirical evidence for such an attack, and the experience involved is that of child molesters and those who work with child molesters, not judges. In the absence of experience, judges should not undertake to practice psychiatry. The opinion also states that the psychiatric testimony was "irrelevant"...but, as pointed out above, much of the physical conduct was not inherently harmful. It consisted of physical acts which, if done without criminal intent, would be lawful and innocent and not harmful at all. I do not find any reasonable basis to reject the expert testimony, and we should not do so.

III

* * *

When insurers have collected premiums and agreed to indemnify liability imposed for child molestation, we should require them to perform their promises. The interests and rights of the innocent victims of child abuse preclude our exonerating such insurers.

Questions for Discussion

1. If an adult is raped by an insured person, recovery from the policy is not categorically barred. If an adult's house is burned to the ground in an act of apparent arson, recovery is not barred. If an adult (as in the *Clemmer* case) is shot twice in the head by the insured, and then twice more for good measure, insurance recovery may be possible. On what basis is the molestation of a child uniquely selected for coverage exclusion? Would such exclusion extend to sexual intercourse with a 17-year-old?

2. The statute and public policy impose an insurance coverage bar where there is a "preconceived design to inflict injury." Notwithstanding serious error, is it possible for a person to subjectively believe that fondling a child does not inflict injury? Is a "design to inflict injury" not more likely where the insured fires four bullets into a victim's head, as in *Clemmer*—where the court holds that coverage is possible?

3. One policy behind the coverage bar for intentional torts is to avoid indemnifying and perhaps stimulating tortious behavior. Is it likely that child molestation is driven by possible insurance coverage? Of all the possible tortious or criminal acts (arson, homicide, battery, *et al.*) is any of them less likely to be influenced one way or the other by insurance coverage than a lewd act on a child?

ENDNOTES

[1] *E.g.*, see discussion in *In Re Scott K.*, 24 Cal. 3d 395 (1979).

[2] *U.S. v. Morse*, 218 U.S. 493 (1910).

[3] For example: "'[M]inors are treated differently from adults in our laws, which reflects the simple truth derived from communal experience that juveniles as a class have not the level of maturation and responsibility that we presume in adults and consider desirable for full participation in the rights and duties of modern life.' ... Adolescents 'are more vulnerable, more impulsive, and less self-disciplined than adults,' and are without the same 'capacity to control their conduct and to think in long-range terms.'"—*Stanford v. Kentucky*, 492 U.S. 361, 395 (1989) (dis. opn. of Brennan, J.)

[4] *Hewellette v. George* (1891) 68 Miss. 703.

[5] See *e.g., Roller v. Roller* (1905) 37 Wash. 242.

[6] See *e.g., Gibson v. Gibson* (1971) 3 Cal. 3d914.

[7] See *e.g.,* the precedent set in *Ferriter v. Daniel O'Connell's Sons*, 381 Mass. 507 (1980).

[8] See *e.g.,* federal recognition in *Bonbrest v. Kotz*, 65 F. Supp. 138 (D.D.C. 1946); note its incorporation into the 1977 Restatement of Torts.

[9] However, note the contradictory limited status of foster care providers in leading cases (see *Smith v. OFFER* and related cases discussed in Chapter 8). Such providers are allegedly performing an "escrow holding" function for the state and are denied constitutional parental status, *e.g.,* denied the right to hearing where assigned foster children are removed from their custody.

CHAPTER THIRTEEN

Child Civil Liberties: Speech and Religion

A. THE CONTEXT OF CONSTITUTIONAL LAW FOR CHILDREN

Children suffer from three disadvantages in securing constitution-based 1st Amendment protection: (1) "state action" asymmetry; (2) lack of access to court redress; and (3) child immaturity as a permitted distinction.

1. The "State Action" Requirement and Private Power Disadvantage

As discussed briefly in Chapter 1, the substantive constitutional guarantees of the first eight amendments originally focused on the feared federal government, seeking to limit it *vis-à-vis* the citizenry. They have been extended through the 14th Amendment also to assure individual liberties as against state governments. This requirement of "state action" to invoke protection necessarily excludes purely private parties and institutions. Some sources of such private power may operate with coercive force: from a one-company town monopoly to adult control of a child. Children suffer extraordinary disadvantage in their private bargaining power. They are subservient to the private power of adult parents, protectors, advocates, and others. Where suffering harm in their care, or from third parties or commercial exploitation or injury, children rely on the state for protection—via statutes or executive or judicial intervention. As noted above, federal and state constitutional prescriptions limit *this*, not the private power of the citizenry. Hence, the constitution functions substantially in a one-way direction for children: since they are most affected by private power abuse, constitutional limitations on the state may impede their sole remedy (state action against adults who may be their abusers). Although the state possesses extensive police powers properly subject to internal check, the state can also be a check itself to moderate private power abuse on behalf of an otherwise powerless population.

Related to "state action" asymmetry is the fact that constitutional doctrine tends to apply in the negative, to stop state intrusions rather than to compel state action. So, for example, if the basic economic or social rights of children were part of a nation's founding document (as is the case with many of the European constitutions, or would pertain if the U.S. were to ratify the Convention on the Rights of the Child) the state may be affirmatively compelled to act. For example, were children to be afforded the assured protection of minimal sustenance for survival, health care, or the right to a parental relationship, such rights could trigger an affirmative state action obligation. Our constitutional structure is not so framed.

2. Access to and Resources for Constitutional Enforcement

Even where constitutional concepts may apply to protect children, they are not effective without a mechanism to enforce them. Enforcement depends upon judicial action. As discussed in Chapter 1, the judiciary itself is passive, and depends upon public officials or private parties to bring matters before it for decision. Hence, access to its offices and the ability to obtain a judicial result substantially determine the efficacy of theoretical rights. Few public officials are assigned the task of vindicating the constitutional rights of children. And the federal courts have acted to limit constitutional enforcement where it has been attempted. The list of court-created impediments to constitutional court protection include:

(a) constitutional doctrines requiring justiciability, standing (a personal stake), and ripeness;[1]

(b) initial dismissal where moot, not a real "case or controversy," or where a dispute is in the nature of an "advisory opinion";[2]

(c) a series of decisions hostile to class certification, including requirements that common questions predominate, adequacy of representation, and "superiority" as a means of redress, *et al.* (see Chapter 1); and

(d) the refusal to grant "private attorney general" attorney's fees to counsel (provided by some states to counsel who prevail on behalf of a large group of persons where the outcome vindicates major constitutional principles in the public interest).[3]

Each of these doctrines has its own rationale, generally unrelated to child rights. When combined, they have a substantial impact on the access to the courts of those who are powerless, unorganized, inarticulate, and without resources. The interests of children are substantially affected by these limitations.

According to child advocates, constitutional private enforcement for children, including use of federal civil rights statutes, may be further limited by additional practical barriers discussed in Chapter 1, including: the failure to include children as a "protected" group for equal protection purposes; state bar policies prohibiting "solicitation of clients" in the context of a client group often unable to solicit counsel; minimal budgets for legal aid attorneys (particularly where interest rates decline given legal aid dependency on interest income from Bar trust funds); some continuing restrictions on legal aid representation in class action formats; expansion of state "sovereign immunity" and contraction of "interstate commerce" definitions to inhibit federal jurisdiction; the lack of assigned legal representation for children outside of delinquency proceedings and some dependency proceedings; and the representation of many children in dependency proceedings by counsel for the county who, due to conflicts of interest, may be unable to mount a constitutional challenge to county or state policies.

Suggestions to improve access to the judiciary for children include creation of a federal, state, or independent agency with standing to represent children, including the vindication of their constitutional rights, and financed separately from other agencies that might require such judicial check. Or, constitutional or statutory provision could allow standing and attorney fee recompense for private vindication of constitutional rights (see Chapter 1 discussion of the *Serrano* private attorney general doctrine in California).

Child advocates argue that a judiciary cognizant of the elevated status of constitutional principles will bend toward their vindication, particularly on behalf of a population least able to provide its own remedy or to reach the court's protective jurisdiction by its own devices. The courts have reached far for some other groups to accomplish this end, for example, creating the exclusionary rule to sanction police acts violative of 4th Amendment constitutional standards. Children have not often been the beneficiary of such judicial reach; child advocates contend that they have rather suffered from judicial "adult-centrism," and from antipathy toward large lawsuits, new and different parties, or unfamiliar functioning.

3. The Maturity Dilemma

The immaturity of children undeniably complicates the application of constitutional principles to them. Children are adults-in-progress. Even the most ardent child advocate acknowledges that the 1st Amendment rights of *any* two-year-old may not rise to the level of those accorded *any* adult. Indeed, many constitutional rights, *e.g.,* the right to worship the religion of our choice, may substantially be subsumed within a parental right. For example, most advocates would agree that such a parental right to require Sunday School might supercede the often child-preferred choice of morning cartoons. Even if constitutional religious rights (to worship or not to worship) applied to private action and could limit parents as such, the undeniable status of parents as having custody and control of their children within a family unit implies an authority to make decisions on their behalf.

Recognizing the immaturity of children does not, however, eliminate the application of constitutional principles for their benefit, nor does it necessarily mean that constitutional protections are only available through the vehicle of parental vindication. The constitution and courts have recognized that as children mature, their capacities and recognized rights may develop—evolving what is termed the "mature minor" doctrine. And the courts have begun to acknowledge the tragic but undeniable fact that assuring child protection through the surrogate application of parental rights does not work where parents are uncaring or absent, or where parents endanger their children. Once again, the courts may be caught in a two-party concept (state vs. adults), in a three-party setting (state vs. adults vs. children).

Further, many constitutional concepts do not involve the mature declaration of political grievances on the village green, but rather state deprivation of property, health and safety endangerment, invidious discrimination, or a host of other detriments which do not turn on maturity. For while the courts understandably discount at least by degree the speech, religion, and privacy rights of children, those rights which implicate the opportunity to develop may be arguably enhanced by the fact of immaturity.

B. FIRST AMENDMENT FREE SPEECH RIGHTS OF CHILDREN

Tinker v. Des Moines Independent Community School District
393 U.S. 503 (1969)

Mr. Justice Fortas delivered the opinion of the Court.

Petitioner John F. Tinker, 15 years old, and petitioner Christopher Eckhardt,

16 years old, attended high schools in Des Moines, Iowa. Petitioner Mary Beth Tinker, John's sister, was a 13-year-old student in junior high school.

In December 1965, a group of adults and students in Des Moines held a meeting at the Eckhardt home. The group determined to publicize their objections to the hostilities in Vietnam and their support for a truce by wearing black armbands during the holiday season and by fasting on December 16 and New Year's Eve. Petitioners and their parents had previously engaged in similar activities, and they decided to participate in the program.

The principals of the Des Moines schools became aware of the plan to wear armbands. On December 14, 1965, they met and adopted a policy that any student wearing an armband to school would be asked to remove it, and if he refused he would be suspended until he returned without the armband. Petitioners were aware of the regulation that the school authorities adopted.

On December 16, Mary Beth and Christopher wore black armbands to their schools. John Tinker wore his armband the next day. They were all sent home and suspended from school until they would come back without their armbands. They did not return to school until after the planned period for wearing armbands had expired—that is, until after New Year's Day.

* * *

I.

The District Court recognized that the wearing of an armband for the purpose of expressing certain views is the type of symbolic act that is within the Free Speech Clause of the First Amendment....As we shall discuss, the wearing of armbands in the circumstances of this case was entirely divorced from actually or potentially disruptive conduct by those participating in it. It was closely akin to "pure speech" which, we have repeatedly held, is entitled to comprehensive protection under the First Amendment....

First Amendment rights, applied in light of the special characteristics of the school environment, are available to teachers and students. It can hardly be argued that either students or teachers shed their constitutional rights to freedom of speech or expression at the schoolhouse gate. This has been the unmistakable holding of this Court for almost 50 years....

In *West Virginia v. Barnette*,..., this Court held that under the First Amendment, the student in public school may not be compelled to salute the flag. Speaking through Mr. Justice Jackson, the Court said:

> "The Fourteenth Amendment, as now applied to the States, protects the citizen against the State itself and all of its creatures—Boards of Education not excepted. These have, of course, important, delicate, and highly discretionary functions, but none that they may not perform within the limits of the Bill of Rights. That they are educating the young for citizenship is reason for scrupulous protection of Constitutional freedoms of the individual, if we are not to strangle the free mind at its source and teach youth to discount important principles of our government as mere platitudes." 319 U.S., at 637.

On the other hand, the Court has repeatedly emphasized the need for affirming the comprehensive authority of the States and of school officials, consistent with fundamental constitutional safeguards, to prescribe and control conduct in the schools....Our problem lies in the area where students in the exercise of First Amendment rights collide with the rules of the school authorities.

II.

The problem posed by the present case does not relate to regulation of the length of skirts or the type of clothing, to hair style, or deportment....It does not concern aggressive, disruptive action or even group demonstrations. Our problem involves direct, primary First Amendment rights akin to "pure speech."

The school officials banned and sought to punish petitioners for a silent, passive expression of opinion, unaccompanied by any disorder or disturbance on the part of petitioners. There is here no evidence whatever of petitioners' interference, actual or nascent, with the schools' work or of collision with the rights of other students to be secure and to be let alone. Accordingly, this case does not concern speech or action that intrudes upon the work of the schools or the rights of other students.

Only a few of the 18,000 students in the school system wore the black armbands. Only five students were suspended for wearing them. There is no indication that the work of the schools or any class was disrupted. Outside the classrooms, a few students made hostile remarks to the children wearing armbands, but there were no threats or acts of violence on school premises.

The District Court concluded that the action of the school authorities was reasonable because it was based upon their fear of a disturbance from the wearing of the armbands. But, in our system, undifferentiated fear or apprehension of disturbance is not enough to overcome the right to freedom of expression. Any departure from absolute regimentation may cause trouble. Any variation from the majority's opinion may inspire fear. Any word spoken, in class, in the lunchroom, or on the campus, that deviates from the views of another person may start an argument or cause a disturbance. But our Constitution says we must take this risk, *Terminiello v. Chicago*, 337 U.S. 1 (1949); and our history says that it is this sort of hazardous freedom—this kind of openness—that is the basis of our national strength and of the independence and vigor of Americans who grow up and live in this relatively permissive, often disputatious, society.

In order for the State in the person of school officials to justify prohibition of a particular expression of opinion, it must be able to show that its action was caused by something more than a mere desire to avoid the discomfort and unpleasantness that always accompany an unpopular viewpoint. Certainly where there is no finding and no showing that engaging in the forbidden conduct would "materially and substantially interfere with the requirements of appropriate discipline in the operation of the school," the prohibition cannot be sustained....

* * *

It is also relevant that the school authorities did not purport to prohibit the wearing of all symbols of political or controversial significance. The record shows that students in some of the schools wore buttons relating to national political campaigns, and some even wore the Iron Cross, traditionally a symbol of Nazism. The order prohibiting the wearing of armbands did not extend to these. Instead, a particular symbol—black armbands worn to exhibit opposition to this Nation's involvement in Vietnam—was singled out for prohibition. Clearly, the prohibition of expression of one particular opinion, at least without evidence that it is necessary to avoid material and substantial interference with schoolwork or discipline, is not constitutionally permissible.

* * *

...The principal use to which the schools are dedicated is to accommodate students during prescribed hours for the purpose of certain types of activities. Among those activities is personal intercommunication among the students.[6] This is not only an inevitable part of the process of attending school; it is also an important part of the educational process. A student's rights, therefore, do not embrace merely the classroom hours. When he is in the cafeteria, or on the playing field, or on the campus during the authorized hours, he may express his opinions, even on controversial subjects like the conflict in Vietnam, if he does so without "materially and substantially interfer[ing] with the requirements of appropriate discipline in the operation of the school" and without colliding with the rights of others. *Burnside v. Byars*, *supra*, at 749. But conduct by the student, in class or out of it, which for any reason—whether it stems from time, place, or type of behavior—materially disrupts classwork or involves substantial disorder or invasion of the rights of others is, of course, not immunized by the constitutional guarantee of freedom of speech....

Under our Constitution, free speech is not a right that is given only to be so circumscribed that it exists in principle but not in fact. Freedom of expression would not truly exist if the right could be exercised only in an area that a benevolent government has provided as a safe haven for crackpots. The Constitution says that Congress (and the States) may not abridge the right to free speech. This provision means what it says. We properly read it to permit reasonable regulation of speech-connected activities in carefully restricted circumstances. But we do not confine the permissible exercise of First Amendment rights to a telephone booth or the four corners of a pamphlet, or to supervised and ordained discussion in a school classroom.

If a regulation were adopted by school officials forbidding discussion of the Vietnam conflict, or the expression by any student of opposition to it anywhere on school property except as part of a prescribed classroom exercise, it would be obvious that the regulation would violate the constitutional rights of students, at least if it could not be justified by a showing that the students' activities would materially and substantially disrupt the work and discipline of the school....In the circumstances of the present case, the prohibition of the silent, passive "witness of the armbands," as one of the children called it, is no less offensive to the Constitution's guarantees.

* * *

Reversed and remanded.

* * *

Mr. Justice Black, dissenting.

The Court's holding in this case ushers in what I deem to be an entirely new era in which the power to control pupils by the elected "officials of state supported public schools..." in the United States is in ultimate effect transferred to the Supreme Court....The Court brought this particular case here on a petition for certiorari urging that the First and Fourteenth Amendments protect the right of school pupils to express their political views all the way "from kindergarten through high school." Here the constitutional right to "political expression" asserted was a right to wear black armbands during school hours and at classes in order to demonstrate to the other students that the petitioners were mourning because of

---

[6] In *Hammond v. South Carolina State College*, 272 F.Supp. 947 (D.C.S.C. 1967), District Judge Hemphill had before him a case involving a meeting on campus of 300 students to express their views on school practices. He pointed out that a school is not like a hospital or a jail enclosure....It is a public place, and its dedication to specific uses does not imply that the constitutional rights of persons entitled to be there are to be gauged as if the premises were purely private property....

the death of United States soldiers in Vietnam and to protest that war which they were against. Ordered to refrain from wearing the armbands in school by the elected school officials and the teachers vested with state authority to do so, apparently only seven out of the school system's 18,000 pupils deliberately refused to obey the order. One defying pupil was Paul Tinker, 8 years old, who was in the second grade; another, Hope Tinker, was 11 years old and in the fifth grade; a third member of the Tinker family was 13, in the eighth grade; and a fourth member of the same family was John Tinker, 15 years old, an 11th grade high school pupil. Their father, a Methodist minister without a church, is paid a salary by the American Friends Service Committee. Another student who defied the school order and insisted on wearing an armband in school was Christopher Eckhardt, an 11th grade pupil and a petitioner in this case. His mother is an official in the Women's International League for Peace and Freedom.

As I read the Court's opinion it relies upon the following grounds for holding unconstitutional the judgment of the Des Moines school officials and the two courts below. First, the Court concludes that the wearing of armbands is "symbolic speech" which is "akin to 'pure speech'" and therefore protected by the First and Fourteenth Amendments. Secondly, the Court decides that the public schools are an appropriate place to exercise "symbolic speech" as long as normal school functions are not "unreasonably" disrupted. Finally, the Court arrogates to itself, rather than to the State's elected officials charged with running the schools, the decision as to which school disciplinary regulations are "reasonable."

Assuming that the Court is correct in holding that the conduct of wearing armbands for the purpose of conveying political ideas is protected by the First Amendment,...the crucial remaining questions are whether students and teachers may use the schools at their whim as a platform for the exercise of free speech—"symbolic" or "pure"—and whether the courts will allocate to themselves the function of deciding how the pupils' school day will be spent....

While the record does not show that any of these armband students shouted, used profane language, or were violent in any manner, detailed testimony by some of them shows their armbands caused comments, warnings by other students, the poking of fun at them, and a warning by an older football player that other, nonprotesting students had better let them alone. There is also evidence that a teacher of mathematics had his lesson period practically "wrecked" chiefly by disputes with Mary Beth Tinker, who wore her armband for her "demonstration." Even a casual reading of the record shows that this armband did divert students' minds from their regular lessons, and that talk, comments, etc., made John Tinker "self-conscious" in attending school with his armband. While the absence of obscene remarks or boisterous and loud disorder perhaps justifies the Court's statement that the few armband students did not actually "disrupt" the classwork, I think the record overwhelmingly shows that the armbands did exactly what the elected school officials and principals foresaw they would, that is, took the students' minds off their classwork and diverted them to thoughts about the highly emotional subject of the Vietnam war. And I repeat that if the time has come when pupils of state-supported schools, kindergartens, grammar schools, or high schools, can defy and flout orders of school officials to keep their minds on their own schoolwork, it is the beginning of a new revolutionary era of permissiveness in this country fostered by the judiciary. The next logical step, it appears to me, would be to hold unconstitutional laws that bar pupils under 21 or 18 from voting, or from being elected members of the boards of education....

* * *

In my view, teachers in state-controlled public schools are hired to teach there. Although MR. JUSTICE MCREYNOLDS may have intimated to the contrary in *Meyer v. Nebraska*, *supra*, certainly a teacher is not paid to go into school and teach subjects the State does not hire him to teach as a part of its selected curriculum. Nor are public school students sent to the schools at public expense to broadcast political or any other views to educate and inform the public. The original idea of schools, which I do not believe is yet abandoned as worthless or out of date, was that children had not yet reached the point of experience and wisdom which enabled them to teach all of their elders. It may be that the Nation has outworn the old-fashioned slogan that "children are to be seen not heard," but one may, I hope, be permitted to harbor the thought that taxpayers send children to school on the premise that at their age they need to learn, not teach.

* * *

Mr. Justice Harlan, dissenting.

I certainly agree that state public school authorities in the discharge of their responsibilities are not wholly exempt from the requirements of the Fourteenth Amendment respecting the freedoms of expression and association. At the same time I am reluctant to believe that there is any disagreement between the majority and myself on the proposition that school officials should be accorded the widest authority in maintaining discipline and good order in their institutions. To translate that proposition into a workable constitutional rule, I would, in cases like this, cast upon those complaining the burden of showing that a particular school measure was motivated by other than legitimate school concerns—for example, a desire to prohibit the expression of an unpopular point of view, while permitting expression of the dominant opinion.

Finding nothing in this record which impugns the good faith of respondents in promulgating the armband regulation, I would affirm the judgment below.

Questions for Discussion

1. How would the majority rule if the armbands signified gang membership (*e.g.*, red for Bloods and black for Crips)? Could such clothing also be considered "symbolic speech?" (See *Bivens v. Albuquerque Public Schools*, 899 F. Supp. 556 (D. N.M. 1995).)

2. The majority notes that these armbands are akin to "pure speech," a passive, silent opinion posing no disorder. Assume that a substantial number of the siblings of students had been killed in the Vietnam War, or the sons of teachers, would that make a difference in terms of "disruption" concern? Should such disruption justifying speech denial by the state focus on the reactions of others? If a black student wears an NAACP badge in the deep south in the 1960s and provokes disruption from white students, should such reaction form the basis for state denial of that expression? What if it is a white student wearing a confederate flag symbol? (See *Phillips v. Anderson County School District Five*, 987 F. Supp. 488 (D. S.C. 1997).)

3. If a school may require students to wear uniforms to school (which has been upheld),[4] does it have a lesser included right to prescribe clothing? If it is permissible to prohibit short dresses or halter tops because of the distraction they may cause, can the same rationale extend to armbands in *Tinker?*

4. Black argues that students need to learn under the guidance of school officials, who should make decisions free from court interference. Does he recognize any quantum of free speech right applicable to students? To youth in general? Is free expression effectively taught or manifest where the message is: "Sit and listen, the state's employees shall determine when you talk and what you should be saying?" Black notes that the teaching of discipline educates students to be good citizens. Does that include training students not to disrupt other students who express heartfelt political positions?

5. Harlan's dissent would find a constitutional breach if the motivation of the state is not education enhancement, but rather to favor a dominant opinion, which he finds absent in *Tinker*. Is it likely that students who wore American flags on their clothing or other symbols expressing support for the Vietnam War would have been treated to sanctions similar to those applied to *Tinker*?

Hazelwood School District v. Kuhlmeier
484 U.S. 260 (1988)

Justice White delivered the opinion of the Court.

This case concerns the extent to which educators may exercise editorial control over the contents of a high school newspaper produced as part of the school's journalism curriculum.

I

* * *

Spectrum was written and edited by the Journalism II class at Hazelwood East. The newspaper was published every three weeks or so during the 1982–1983 school year. More than 4,500 copies of the newspaper were distributed during that year to students, school personnel, and members of the community.

The Board of Education allocated funds from its annual budget for the printing of Spectrum. These funds were supplemented by proceeds from sales of the newspaper....

* * *

The practice at Hazelwood East during the spring 1983 semester was for the journalism teacher to submit page proofs of each Spectrum issue to Principal Reynolds for his review prior to publication. On May 10, Emerson delivered the proofs of the May 13 edition to Reynolds, who objected to two of the articles scheduled to appear in that edition. One of the stories described three Hazelwood East students' experiences with pregnancy; the other discussed the impact of divorce on students at the school.

Reynolds was concerned that, although the pregnancy story used false names "to keep the identity of these girls a secret," the pregnant students still might be identifiable from the text. He also believed that the article's references to sexual activity and birth control were inappropriate for some of the younger students at the school. In addition, Reynolds was concerned that a student identified by name in the divorce story had complained that her father "wasn't spending enough time with my mom, my sister and I" prior to the divorce, "was always out of town on business or out late playing cards with the guys," and "always argued about everything" with her mother....Reynolds believed that the student's parents should have been given an opportunity to respond to these remarks or to consent to their publication. He was unaware that Emerson had deleted the student's name from the final version of the article.

Reynolds believed that there was no time to make the necessary changes in the stories before the scheduled press run and that the newspaper would not appear before the end of the school year if printing were delayed to any significant extent. He concluded that his only options under the circumstances were to publish a four-page newspaper instead of the planned six-page newspaper, eliminating the two pages on which the offending stories appeared, or to publish no newspaper at all. Accordingly, he directed Emerson to withhold from publication the two pages containing the stories on pregnancy and divorce.[1] He informed his superiors of the decision, and they concurred.

* * *

I

Students in the public schools do not "shed their constitutional rights to freedom of speech or expression at the schoolhouse gate." *Tinker*, *supra*, at 506. They cannot be punished merely for expressing their personal views on the school premises—whether "in the cafeteria, or on the playing field, or on the campus during the authorized hours,"...—unless school authorities have reason to believe that such expression will "substantially interfere with the work of the school or impinge upon the rights of other students." *Id.*...

We have nonetheless recognized that the First Amendment rights of students in the public schools "are not automatically coextensive with the rights of adults in other settings,"...and must be "applied in light of the special characteristics of the school environment." *Tinker*, *supra*, at 506;...A school need not tolerate student speech that is inconsistent with its "basic educational mission,"...even though the government could not censor similar speech outside the school. Accordingly, we held in *Fraser* that a student could be disciplined for having delivered a speech that was "sexually explicit" but not legally obscene at an official school assembly, because the school was entitled to "disassociate itself" from the speech in a manner that would demonstrate to others that such vulgarity is "wholly inconsistent with the 'fundamental values' of public school education."....We thus recognized that "[t]he determination of what manner of speech in the classroom or in school assembly is inappropriate properly rests with the school board,"...rather than with the federal courts. It is in this context that respondents' First Amendment claims must be considered.

A

We deal first with the question whether Spectrum may appropriately be characterized as a forum for public expression. The public schools do not possess all of the attributes of streets, parks, and other traditional public forums that "time out of mind, have been used for purposes of assembly, communicating thoughts between citizens, and discussing public questions."....Hence, school facilities may be deemed to be public forums only if school authorities have "by policy or by practice" opened those facilities "for indiscriminate use by the general public,"...or by some segment of the public, such as student organizations....If the facilities have instead been reserved for other intended purposes, "communicative or

[1] The two pages deleted from the newspaper also contained articles on teenage marriage, runaways, and juvenile delinquents, as well as a general article on teenage pregnancy. Reynolds testified that he had no objection to these articles and that they were deleted only because they appeared on the same pages as the two objectionable articles.

otherwise," then no public forum has been created, and school officials may impose reasonable restrictions on the speech of students, teachers, and other members of the school community...."The government does not create a public forum by inaction or by permitting limited discourse, but only by intentionally opening a nontraditional forum for public discourse."....

* * *

School officials did not deviate in practice from their policy that production of Spectrum was to be part of the educational curriculum and a "regular classroom activit[y]." The District Court found that Robert Stergos, the journalism teacher during most of the 1982–1983 school year, "both had the authority to exercise and in fact exercised a great deal of control over *Spectrum*."....

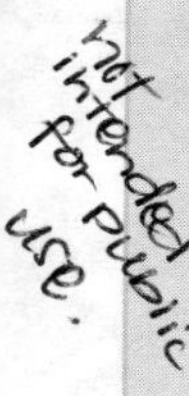

...In sum, the evidence relied upon by the Court of Appeals fails to demonstrate the "clear intent to create a public forum,"....School officials did not evince either "by policy or by practice," *Perry Education Assn.*, 460 U.S., at 47, any intent to open the pages of Spectrum to "indiscriminate use," *ibid.*, by its student reporters and editors, or by the student body generally. Instead, they "reserve[d] the forum for its intended purpos[e]," *id.*, at 46, as a supervised learning experience for journalism students. Accordingly, school officials were entitled to regulate the contents of Spectrum in any reasonable manner...It is this standard, rather than our decision in *Tinker*, that governs this case.

B

The question whether the First Amendment requires a school to tolerate particular student speech—the question that we addressed in *Tinker*—is different from the question whether the First Amendment requires a school affirmatively to promote particular student speech. The former question addresses educators' ability to silence a student's personal expression that happens to occur on the school premises. The latter question concerns educators' authority over school-sponsored publications, theatrical productions, and other expressive activities that students, parents, and members of the public might reasonably perceive to bear the imprimatur of the school. These activities may fairly be characterized as part of the school curriculum, whether or not they occur in a traditional classroom setting, so long as they are supervised by faculty members and designed to impart particular knowledge or skills to student participants and audiences.[3]

Educators are entitled to exercise greater control over this second form of student expression to assure that participants learn whatever lessons the activity is designed to teach, that readers or listeners are not exposed to material that may be inappropriate for their level of maturity, and that the views of the individual speaker are not erroneously attributed to the school. Hence, a school may in its capacity as publisher of a school newspaper or producer of a school play "disassociate itself," *Fraser*, 478 U.S., at 685, not only from speech that would "substantially interfere with [its] work...or impinge upon the rights of other students," *Tinker*, 393 U.S., at 509, but also from speech that is, for example, ungrammatical, poorly written, inadequately researched, biased or prejudiced, vulgar or profane, or unsuitable for immature audiences.[4] A school must be able to

[3] The distinction that we draw between speech that is sponsored by the school and speech that is not is fully consistent with *Papish v. University of Missouri Board of Curators*, 410 U.S. 667 (1973) (*per curiam*), which involved an off-campus "underground" newspaper that school officials merely had allowed to be sold on a state university campus.

[4] The dissent perceives no difference between the First Amendment analysis applied in *Tinker* and that applied in *Fraser*. We disagree. The decision in *Fraser* rested on the "vulgar," "lewd," and "plainly offensive" character of a speech delivered at an official school assembly

set high standards for the student speech that is disseminated under its auspices—standards that may be higher than those demanded by some newspaper publishers or theatrical producers in the "real" world—and may refuse to disseminate student speech that does not meet those standards. In addition, a school must be able to take into account the emotional maturity of the intended audience in determining whether to disseminate student speech on potentially sensitive topics, which might range from the existence of Santa Claus in an elementary school setting to the particulars of teenage sexual activity in a high school setting. A school must also retain the authority to refuse to sponsor student speech that might reasonably be perceived to advocate drug or alcohol use, irresponsible sex, or conduct otherwise inconsistent with "the shared values of a civilized social order," *Fraser*, *supra*, at 683, or to associate the school with any position other than neutrality on matters of political controversy. Otherwise, the schools would be unduly constrained from fulfilling their role as "a principal instrument in awakening the child to cultural values, in preparing him for later professional training, and in helping him to adjust normally to his environment." *Brown v. Board of Education*, 347 U.S. 483, 493 (1954).

Accordingly, we conclude that the standard articulated in *Tinker* for determining when a school may punish student expression need not also be the standard for determining when a school may refuse to lend its name and resources to the dissemination of student expression....Instead, we hold that educators do not offend the First Amendment by exercising editorial control over the style and content of student speech in school-sponsored expressive activities so long as their actions are reasonably related to legitimate pedagogical concerns.[6]

* * *

The initial paragraph of the pregnancy article declared that "[a]ll names have been changed to keep the identity of these girls a secret." The principal concluded that the students' anonymity was not adequately protected, however, given the other identifying information in the article and the small number of pregnant students at the school. Indeed, a teacher at the school credibly testified that she could positively identify at least one of the girls and possibly all three. It is likely that many students at Hazelwood East would have been at least as successful in identifying the girls. Reynolds therefore could reasonably have feared that the article violated whatever pledge of anonymity had been given to the pregnant students. In addition, he could reasonably have been concerned that the article was not sufficiently sensitive to the privacy interests of the students' boyfriends and parents, who were discussed in the article but who were given no opportunity to consent to its publication or to offer a response. The article did not contain graphic accounts of sexual activity. The girls did comment in the article, however, concerning their sexual histories and their use or nonuse of birth control. It was not unreasonable for the principal to have concluded that such frank talk was inappropriate in a

---

rather than on any propensity of the speech to "materially disrup[t] classwork or involv[e] substantial disorder or invasion of the rights of others." 393 U.S., at 513. Indeed, the *Fraser* Court cited as "especially relevant" a portion of Justice Black's dissenting opinion in *Tinker* "'disclaim[ing] any purpose...to hold that the Federal Constitution compels the teachers, parents, and elected school officials to surrender control of the American public school system to public school students.'" 478 U.S., at 686 (quoting 393 U.S., at 526). Of course, Justice Black's observations are equally relevant to the instant case.

[6] We reject respondents' suggestion that school officials be permitted to exercise prepublication control over school-sponsored publications only pursuant to specific written regulations. To require such regulations in the context of a curricular activity could unduly constrain the ability of educators to educate. We need not now decide whether such regulations are required before school officials may censor publications not sponsored by the school that students seek to distribute on school grounds....

school-sponsored publication distributed to 14-year-old freshmen and presumably taken home to be read by students' even younger brothers and sisters.

The student who was quoted by name in the version of the divorce article seen by Principal Reynolds made comments sharply critical of her father. The principal could reasonably have concluded that an individual publicly identified as an inattentive parent—indeed, as one who chose "playing cards with the guys" over home and family—was entitled to an opportunity to defend himself as a matter of journalistic fairness. These concerns were shared by both of Spectrum's faculty advisers for the 1982–1983 school year, who testified that they would not have allowed the article to be printed without deletion of the student's name.[8]

* * *

In sum, we cannot reject as unreasonable Principal Reynolds' conclusion that neither the pregnancy article nor the divorce article was suitable for publication in Spectrum. Reynolds could reasonably have concluded that the students who had written and edited these articles had not sufficiently mastered those portions of the Journalism II curriculum that pertained to the treatment of controversial issues and personal attacks, the need to protect the privacy of individuals whose most intimate concerns are to be revealed in the newspaper, and "the legal, moral, and ethical restrictions imposed upon journalists within [a] school community" that includes adolescent subjects and readers. Finally, we conclude that the principal's decision to delete two pages of Spectrum, rather than to delete only the offending articles or to require that they be modified, was reasonable under the circumstances as he understood them. Accordingly, no violation of First Amendment rights occurred.[9]

The judgment of the Court of Appeals for the Eighth Circuit is therefore

Reversed.

Justice Brennan, with whom **Justice Marshall** and **Justice Blackmun** join, dissenting.

When the young men and women of Hazelwood East High School registered for Journalism II, they expected a civics lesson. Spectrum, the newspaper they were to publish, "was not just a class exercise in which students learned to prepare papers and hone writing skills, it was a...forum established to give students an opportunity to express their views while gaining an appreciation of their rights and responsibilities under the First Amendment to the United States Constitution...." 795 F. 2d 1368, 1373 (CA8 1986). "[A]t the beginning of each school year," *id.*, at 1372, the student journalists published a Statement of Policy—tacitly approved

---

[8] The reasonableness of Principal Reynolds' concerns about the two articles was further substantiated by the trial testimony of Martin Duggan, a former editorial page editor of the St. Louis Globe Democrat and a former college journalism instructor and newspaper adviser. Duggan testified that the divorce story did not meet journalistic standards of fairness and balance because the father was not given an opportunity to respond, and that the pregnancy story was not appropriate for publication in a high school newspaper because it was unduly intrusive into the privacy of the girls, their parents, and their boyfriends. The District Court found Duggan to be "an objective and independent witness" whose testimony was entitled to significant weight. 607 F. Supp. 1450, 1461 (ED Mo. 1985).

[9] It is likely that the approach urged by the dissent would as a practical matter have far more deleterious consequences for the student press than does the approach that we adopt today. The dissent correctly acknowledges "[t]he State's prerogative to dissolve the student newspaper entirely." *Post*, at 287. It is likely that many public schools would do just that rather than open their newspapers to all student expression that does not threaten "materia[l] disrup[tion of] classwork" or violation of "rights that are protected by law," *post*, at 289, regardless of how sexually explicit, racially intemperate, or personally insulting that expression otherwise might be.

each year by school authorities—announcing their expectation that "*Spectrum*, as a student-press publication, accepts all rights implied by the First Amendment....Only speech that 'materially and substantially interferes with the requirements of appropriate discipline' can be found unacceptable and therefore prohibited." App. 26 (quoting *Tinker v. Des Moines Independent Community School Dist.*, 393 U.S. 503, 513 (1969)).[1] The school board itself affirmatively guaranteed the students of Journalism II an atmosphere conducive to fostering such an appreciation and exercising the full panoply of rights associated with a free student press. "School sponsored student publications," it vowed, "will not restrict free expression or diverse viewpoints within the rules of responsible journalism."....

This case arose when the Hazelwood East administration breached its own promise, dashing its students' expectations. The school principal, without prior consultation or explanation, excised six articles—comprising two full pages—of the May 13, 1983, issue of Spectrum. He did so not because any of the articles would "materially and substantially interfere with the requirements of appropriate discipline," but simply because he considered two of the six "inappropriate, personal, sensitive, and unsuitable" for student consumption....

In my view the principal broke more than just a promise. He violated the First Amendment's prohibitions against censorship of any student expression that neither disrupts classwork nor invades the rights of others, and against any censorship that is not narrowly tailored to serve its purpose.

I

Public education serves vital national interests in preparing the Nation's youth for life in our increasingly complex society and for the duties of citizenship in our democratic Republic....The public school conveys to our young the information and tools required not merely to survive in, but to contribute to, civilized society. It also inculcates in tomorrow's leaders the "fundamental values necessary to the maintenance of a democratic political system...."....All the while, the public educator nurtures students' social and moral development by transmitting to them an official dogma of "'community values.'"....

The public educator's task is weighty and delicate indeed. It demands particularized and supremely subjective choices among diverse curricula, moral values, and political stances to teach or inculcate in students, and among various methodologies for doing so. Accordingly, we have traditionally reserved the "daily operation of school systems" to the States and their local school boards....We have not, however, hesitated to intervene where their decisions run afoul of the Constitution. See *e.g.*, *Edwards v. Aguillard*, 482 U.S. 578 (1987) (striking state statute that forbade teaching of evolution in public school unless accompanied by instruction on theory of "creation science"); *Board of Education v. Pico*, *supra* (school board may not remove books from library shelves merely because it disapproves of ideas they express); *Epperson v. Arkansas*, *supra* (striking state-law prohibition against teaching Darwinian theory of evolution in public school); *West Virginia Board of Education v. Barnette*, 319 U.S. 624 (1943) (public school may not compel student to salute flag); *Meyer v. Nebraska*, 262 U.S. 390 (1923) (state law prohibiting the teaching of foreign languages in public or private schools is unconstitutional).

Free student expression undoubtedly sometimes interferes with the

---

[1] The Court suggests that the passage quoted in the text did not "exten[d] the *Tinker* standard to the news and feature articles contained in a school-sponsored newspaper" because the passage did not expressly mention them. *Ante*, at 269, n. 2. It is hard to imagine why the Court (or anyone else) might expect a passage that applies categorically to "a student-press publication," composed almost exclusively of "news and feature articles," to mention those categories expressly. Understandably, neither court below so limited the passage.

effectiveness of the school's pedagogical functions. Some brands of student expression do so by directly preventing the school from pursuing its pedagogical mission: The young polemic who stands on a soapbox during calculus class to deliver an eloquent political diatribe interferes with the legitimate teaching of calculus. And the student who delivers a lewd endorsement of a student-government candidate might so extremely distract an impressionable high school audience as to interfere with the orderly operation of the school. See *Bethel School Dist. No. 403 v. Fraser*, 478 U.S. 675 (1986). Other student speech, however, frustrates the school's legitimate pedagogical purposes merely by expressing a message that conflicts with the school's, without directly interfering with the school's expression of its message: A student who responds to a political science teacher's question with the retort, "socialism is good," subverts the school's inculcation of the message that capitalism is better. Even the maverick who sits in class passively sporting a symbol of protest against a government policy, cf. *Tinker v. Des Moines Independent Community School Dist.*, 393 U.S. 503 (1969), or the gossip who sits in the student commons swapping stories of sexual escapade could readily muddle a clear official message condoning the government policy or condemning teenage sex. Likewise, the student newspaper that, like Spectrum, conveys a moral position at odds with the school's official stance might subvert the administration's legitimate inculcation of its own perception of community values.

If mere incompatibility with the school's pedagogical message were a constitutionally sufficient justification for the suppression of student speech, school officials could censor each of the students or student organizations in the foregoing hypotheticals, converting our public schools into "enclaves of totalitarianism," *id.*, at 511, that "strangle the free mind at its source," *West Virginia Board of Education v. Barnette*, *supra*, at 637. The First Amendment permits no such blanket censorship authority. While the "constitutional rights of students in public school are not automatically coextensive with the rights of adults in other settings," *Fraser*, *supra*, at 682, students in the public schools do not "shed their constitutional rights to freedom of speech or expression at the schoolhouse gate," *Tinker*, *supra*, at 506. Just as the public on the street corner must, in the interest of fostering "enlightened opinion," *Cantwell v. Connecticut*, 310 U.S. 296, 310 (1940), tolerate speech that "tempt[s] [the listener] to throw [the speaker] off the street," *id.*, at 309, public educators must accommodate some student expression even if it offends them or offers views or values that contradict those the school wishes to inculcate.

In *Tinker*, this Court struck the balance. We held that official censorship of student expression—there the suspension of several students until they removed their armbands protesting the Vietnam war—is unconstitutional unless the speech "materially disrupts classwork or involves substantial disorder or invasion of the rights of others...." 393 U.S., at 513. School officials may not suppress "silent, passive expression of opinion, unaccompanied by any disorder or disturbance on the part of" the speaker. *Id.*, at 508. The "mere desire to avoid the discomfort and unpleasantness that always accompany an unpopular viewpoint," *id.*, at 509, or an unsavory subject, *Fraser*, *supra*, at 688–689 (Brennan, J., concurring in judgment), does not justify official suppression of student speech in the high school.

* * *

I

Even if we were writing on a clean slate, I would reject the Court's rationale for abandoning *Tinker* in this case. The Court offers no more than an obscure tangle of three excuses to afford educators "greater control" over school-sponsored speech than the *Tinker* test would permit: the public educator's prerogative to control curriculum; the pedagogical interest in shielding the high school audience from objectionable viewpoints and sensitive topics; and the school's need to dissociate itself from student expression....None of the excuses, once disentangled, supports the distinction that the Court draws. *Tinker* fully addresses the first concern; the second is illegitimate; and the third is readily achievable through less oppressive means.

A

* * *

The Court relies on bits of testimony to portray the principal's conduct as a pedagogical lesson to Journalism II students who "had not sufficiently mastered those portions of the...curriculum that pertained to the treatment of controversial issues and personal attacks, the need to protect the privacy of individuals..., and 'the legal, moral, and ethical restrictions imposed upon journalists....'"....In that regard, the Court attempts to justify censorship of the article on teenage pregnancy on the basis of the principal's judgment that (1) "the [pregnant] students' anonymity was not adequately protected," despite the article's use of aliases; and (2) the judgment that "the article was not sufficiently sensitive to the privacy interests of the students' boyfriends and parents...."....Similarly, the Court finds in the principal's decision to censor the divorce article a journalistic lesson that the author should have given the father of one student an "opportunity to defend himself" against her charge that (in the Court's words) he "chose 'playing cards with the guys' over home and family...."....

But the principal never consulted the students before censoring their work. "[T]hey learned of the deletions when the paper was released...." 795 F. 2d, at 1371. Further, he explained the deletions only in the broadest of generalities. In one meeting called at the behest of seven protesting Spectrum staff members (presumably a fraction of the full class), he characterized the articles as "'too sensitive' for 'our immature audience of readers,'"..., and in a later meeting he deemed them simply "inappropriate, personal, sensitive and unsuitable for the newspaper,"...The Court's supposition that the principal intended (or the protesters understood) those generalities as a lesson on the nuances of journalistic responsibility is utterly incredible. If he did, a fact that neither the District Court nor the Court of Appeals found, the lesson was lost on all but the psychic Spectrum staffer.

B

The Court's second excuse for deviating from precedent is the school's interest in shielding an impressionable high school audience from material whose substance is "unsuitable for immature audiences."....Specifically, the majority decrees that we must afford educators authority to shield high school students from exposure to "potentially sensitive topics" (like "the particulars of teen-age sexual activity") or unacceptable social viewpoints (like the advocacy of "irresponsible se[x] or conduct otherwise inconsistent with 'the shared values of a civilized social order'") through school-sponsored student activities....

Tinker teaches us that the state educator's undeniable, and undeniably vital, mandate to inculcate moral and political values is not a general warrant to act as "thought police" stifling discussion of all but state-approved topics and advocacy of all but the official position....Otherwise educators could transform students into "closed-circuit recipients of only that which the State chooses to communicate," *Tinker*, 393 U.S., at 511, and cast a perverse and impermissible "pall of orthodoxy over the classroom,"...Thus, the State cannot constitutionally prohibit its high school students from recounting in the locker room "the particulars of [their] teen-age sexual activity," nor even from advocating "irresponsible se[x]" or other presumed abominations of "the shared values of a civilized social order." Even in its capacity as educator the State may not assume an Orwellian "guardianship of the public mind,"...

The mere fact of school sponsorship does not, as the Court suggests, license such thought control in the high school, whether through school suppression of disfavored viewpoints or through official assessment of topic sensitivity.[2] The former would constitute unabashed and unconstitutional viewpoint discrimination,...as well as an impermissible infringement of the students' "'right to receive information and ideas,'"....Just as a school board may not purge its state-funded library of all books that "'offen[d] [its] social, political and moral tastes,'" 457 U.S., at 858–859 (plurality opinion) (citation omitted), school officials may not, out of like motivation, discriminatorily excise objectionable ideas from a student publication. The State's prerogative to dissolve the student newspaper entirely (or to limit its subject matter) no more entitles it to dictate which viewpoints students may express on its pages, than the State's prerogative to close down the schoolhouse entitles it to prohibit the nondisruptive expression of antiwar sentiment within its gates.

Official censorship of student speech on the ground that it addresses "potentially sensitive topics" is, for related reasons, equally impermissible. I would not begrudge an educator the authority to limit the substantive scope of a school-sponsored publication to a certain, objectively definable topic, such as literary criticism, school sports, or an overview of the school year. Unlike those determinate limitations, "potential topic sensitivity" is a vaporous nonstandard—like "'public welfare, peace, safety, health, decency, good order, morals or convenience,'"...—that invites manipulation to achieve ends that cannot permissibly be achieved through blatant viewpoint discrimination and chills student speech to which school officials might not object. In part because of those dangers, this Court has consistently condemned any scheme allowing a state official boundless discretion in licensing speech from a particular forum....

The case before us aptly illustrates how readily school officials (and courts) can camouflage viewpoint discrimination as the "mere" protection of students from sensitive topics....

C

The sole concomitant of school sponsorship that might conceivably justify the distinction that the Court draws between sponsored and nonsponsored student expression is the risk "that the views of the individual speaker [might be] erroneously attributed to the school."....Of course, the risk of erroneous attribution inheres in any student expression, including "personal expression" that, like the armbands in *Tinker*, "happens to occur on the school premises,"...Nevertheless, the majority is certainly correct that indicia of school sponsorship increase the likelihood of such attribution, and that state educators may therefore have a legitimate interest in dissociating themselves from student speech.

But "'[e]ven though the governmental purpose be legitimate and substantial, that purpose cannot be pursued by means that broadly stifle fundamental personal liberties when the end can be more narrowly achieved.'"....Dissociative means short of censorship are available to the school. It could, for example, require the student activity to publish a disclaimer, such as the "Statement of Policy" that Spectrum published each school year announcing

---

[2] The Court quotes language in *Bethel School Dist. No. 403 v. Fraser*, 478 U.S. 675 (1986), for the proposition that "'[t]he determination of what manner of speech in the classroom or in school assembly is inappropriate properly rests with the school board.'"....As the discussion immediately preceding that quotation makes clear, however, the Court was referring only to the appropriateness of the *manner* in which the message is conveyed, not of the message's *content*....

> that "[a]ll...editorials appearing in this newspaper reflect the opinions of the Spectrum staff, which are not necessarily shared by the administrators or faculty of Hazelwood East,"...; or it could simply issue its own response clarifying the official position on the matter and explaining why the student position is wrong. Yet, without so much as acknowledging the less oppressive alternatives, the Court approves of brutal censorship.
>
> * * *
>
> IV
>
> ....Instead of "teach[ing] children to respect the diversity of ideas that is fundamental to the American system,"...and "that our Constitution is a living reality, not parchment preserved under glass,"...the Court today "teach[es] youth to discount important principles of our government as mere platitudes."....The young men and women of Hazelwood East expected a civics lesson, but not the one the Court teaches them today.
>
> I dissent.

Questions for Discussion

1. Does the principal pass the *Harlan* "motivation" test? If the information published about the father was factually inaccurate and he did not have a chance to comment on it, is there a libel danger for the school? Why does the majority not discuss such a basis for non-publication?

2. Does Justice White's "special school environment" limiting student free speech rights apply only to kindergarten through twelfth grades? Does it apply to public colleges and universities as well?

3. The majority announces its agreement with the principal that "frank talk" about birth control is inappropriate for a 14-year-old. Surveys indicate that over half of U.S. high school students engage in sexual intercourse before high school graduation and approximately 20% do so before they reach 15 years of age. Is pregnancy appropriate for a 14-year-old? Does the Court believe that 14-year-olds are cut-off from sexual messages from the media or peers? Is the Court's decision partly driven by its own view of the subject matter? Isn't the point of the 1st Amendment that our own personal disagreement with a message is not itself determinative of its right to be published?

4. The Court denies "forum" status for the school newspaper. Does it analyze alternative available forums? Does it matter if there are no other realistic means for students to express themselves? Does it make sense for the majority to argue that the small number of persons controlling the primary means of communication at the school cuts against applying the 1st Amendment to that vehicle?

5. If the decision had been made by the teacher alone to cut these articles purely on grounds of poor journalism (failure to check sources, bad grammar, incomprehensible) would the dissenters join the majority? What would

the dissenters say, were the teacher to determine that the article was not sufficiently "balanced" to be in the news section, but would permit it in reduced form as a labeled "opinion" piece?

6. Does a school have a right to censor or sanction for speech by a juvenile laced with "sexual innuendo," expressing "inappropriate" thoughts for minors? See *Bethel School District No. 403 v. Fraser*, 478 U.S. 675 (1986).

7. Would a Court holding more expansively protecting unfettered student free speech decrease the number of school publications like the *Spectrum*, which could pose public relations problems for administrators?

C. CHILDREN AND FIRST AMENDMENT RELIGIOUS PRACTICE RIGHTS

Wisconsin v. Yoder

406 U.S. 205 (1972)

MR. CHIEF JUSTICE BURGER delivered the opinion of the Court.

On petition of the State of Wisconsin, we granted the writ of certiorari in this case to review a decision of the Wisconsin Supreme Court holding that respondents' convictions of violating the State's compulsory school-attendance law were invalid under the Free Exercise Clause of the First Amendment to the United States Constitution made applicable to the States by the Fourteenth Amendment. For the reasons hereafter stated we affirm the judgment of the Supreme Court of Wisconsin.

Respondents Jonas Yoder and Wallace Miller are members of the Old Order Amish religion, and respondent Adin Yutzy is a member of the Conservative Amish Mennonite Church. They and their families are residents of Green County, Wisconsin. Wisconsin's compulsory school-attendance law required them to cause their children to attend public or private school until reaching age 16 but the respondents declined to send their children, ages 14 and 15, to public school after they completed the eighth grade.[1] The children were not enrolled in any private school, or within any recognized exception to the compulsory-attendance law,...and they are conceded to be subject to the Wisconsin statute.

On complaint of the school district administrator for the public schools, respondents were charged, tried, and convicted of violating the compulsory-attendance law in Green County Court and were fined the sum of $5 each.... Respondents defended on the ground that the application of the compulsory-attendance law violated their rights under the First and Fourteenth Amendments.[4] The trial testimony showed that respondents believed, in accordance with the tenets of Old Order Amish communities generally, that their children's attendance at high school, public or private, was contrary to the Amish religion and way of life. They believed that by sending their children to high school, they would not only expose themselves to the danger of the censure of the church community, but, as found by the county court, also endanger their own salvation and that of their children. The State stipulated that respondents' religious beliefs were sincere.

In support of their position, respondents presented as expert witnesses scholars on religion and education whose testimony is uncontradicted. They

---

[1] The children, Frieda Yoder, aged 15, Barbara Miller, aged 15, and Vernon Yutzy, aged 14, were all graduates of the eighth grade of public school.

[4] The First Amendment provides: "Congress shall make no law respecting an establishment of religion, or prohibiting the free exercise thereof...."

expressed their opinions on the relationship of the Amish belief concerning school attendance to the more general tenets of their religion, and described the impact that compulsory high school attendance could have on the continued survival of Amish communities as they exist in the United States today. The history of the Amish sect was given in some detail, beginning with the Swiss Anabaptists of the 16th century who rejected institutionalized churches and sought to return to the early, simple, Christian life de-emphasizing material success, rejecting the competitive spirit, and seeking to insulate themselves from the modern world. As a result of their common heritage, Old Order Amish communities today are characterized by a fundamental belief that salvation requires life in a church community separate and apart from the world and worldly influence. This concept of life aloof from the world and its values is central to their faith.

A related feature of Old Order Amish communities is their devotion to a life in harmony with nature and the soil, as exemplified by the simple life of the early Christian era that continued in America during much of our early national life. Amish beliefs require members of the community to make their living by farming or closely related activities. Broadly speaking, the Old Order Amish religion pervades and determines the entire mode of life of its adherents. Their conduct is regulated in great detail by the *Ordnung*, or rules, of the church community. Adult baptism, which occurs in late adolescence, is the time at which Amish young people voluntarily undertake heavy obligations, not unlike the Bar Mitzvah of the Jews, to abide by the rules of the church community....

Amish objection to formal education beyond the eighth grade is firmly grounded in these central religious concepts. They object to the high school, and higher education generally, because the values they teach are in marked variance with Amish values and the Amish way of life; they view secondary school education as an impermissible exposure of their children to a "worldly" influence in conflict with their beliefs. The high school tends to emphasize intellectual and scientific accomplishments, self-distinction, competitiveness, worldly success, and social life with other students. Amish society emphasizes informal learning-through-doing; a life of "goodness," rather than a life of intellect; wisdom, rather than technical knowledge; community welfare, rather than competition; and separation from, rather than integration with, contemporary worldly society.

* * *

I

There is no doubt as to the power of a State, having a high responsibility for education of its citizens, to impose reasonable regulations for the control and duration of basic education. See, *e.g.*, *Pierce v. Society of Sisters*, 268 U.S. 510, 534 (1925). Providing public schools ranks at the very apex of the function of a State. Yet even this paramount responsibility was, in *Pierce*, made to yield to the right of parents to provide an equivalent education in a privately operated system. There the Court held that Oregon's statute compelling attendance in a public school from age eight to age 16 unreasonably interfered with the interest of parents in directing the rearing of their offspring, including their education in church-operated schools. As that case suggests, the values of parental direction of the religious upbringing and education of their children in their early and formative years have a high place in our society....Thus, a State's interest in universal education, however highly we rank it, is not totally free from a balancing process when it impinges on fundamental rights and interests, such as those specifically protected by the Free Exercise Clause of the First Amendment, and the traditional interest of parents with respect to the religious upbringing of their children so long as they, in the words of *Pierce*, "prepare [them] for additional obligations." 268 U.S., at 535.

* * *

The State advances two primary arguments in support of its system of compulsory education. It notes, as Thomas Jefferson pointed out early in our history, that some degree of education is necessary to prepare citizens to participate effectively and intelligently in our open political system if we are to preserve freedom and independence. Further, education prepares individuals to be self-reliant and self-sufficient participants in society. We accept these propositions.

However, the evidence adduced by the Amish in this case is persuasively to the effect that an additional one or two years of formal high school for Amish children in place of their long-established program of informal vocational education would do little to serve those interests. Respondents' experts testified at trial, without challenge, that the value of all education must be assessed in terms of its capacity to prepare the child for life. It is one thing to say that compulsory education for a year or two beyond the eighth grade may be necessary when its goal is the preparation of the child for life in modern society as the majority live, but it is quite another if the goal of education be viewed as the preparation of the child for life in the separated agrarian community that is the keystone of the Amish faith....

* * *

...There is no intimation that the Amish employment of their children on family farms is in any way deleterious to their health or that Amish parents exploit children at tender years. Any such inference would be contrary to the record before us. Moreover, employment of Amish children on the family farm does not present the undesirable economic aspects of eliminating jobs that might otherwise be held by adults.

* * *

Contrary to the suggestion of the dissenting opinion of MR. JUSTICE DOUGLAS, our holding today in no degree depends on the assertion of the religious interest of the child as contrasted with that of the parents. It is the parents who are subject to prosecution here for failing to cause their children to attend school, and it is their right of free exercise, not that of their children, that must determine Wisconsin's power to impose criminal penalties on the parent. The dissent argues that a child who expresses a desire to attend public high school in conflict with the wishes of his parents should not be prevented from doing so. There is no reason for the Court to consider that point since it is not an issue in the case. The children are not parties to this litigation. The State has at no point tried this case on the theory that respondents were preventing their children from attending school against their expressed desires, and indeed the record is to the contrary.[21] The State's position from the outset has been that it is empowered to apply its compulsory-attendance law to Amish parents in the same manner as to other parents—that is, without regard to the wishes of the child. That is the claim we reject today.

* * *

Indeed it seems clear that if the State is empowered, as *parens patriae*,

---

[21] The only relevant testimony in the record is to the effect that the wishes of the one child who testified corresponded with those of her parents. Testimony of Frieda Yoder, Tr. 92–94, to the effect that her personal religious beliefs guided her decision to discontinue school attendance after the eighth grade. The other children were not called by either side.

to "save" a child from himself or his Amish parents by requiring an additional two years of compulsory formal high school education, the State will in large measure influence, if not determine, the religious future of the child. Even more markedly than in *Prince*, therefore, this case involves the fundamental interest of parents, as contrasted with that of the State, to guide the religious future and education of their children. The history and culture of Western civilization reflect a strong tradition of parental concern for the nurture and upbringing of their children. This primary role of the parents in the upbringing of their children is now established beyond debate as an enduring American tradition....

* * *

Aided by a history of three centuries as an identifiable religious sect and a long history as a successful and self-sufficient segment of American society, the Amish in this case have convincingly demonstrated the sincerity of their religious beliefs, the interrelationship of belief with their mode of life, the vital role that belief and daily conduct play in the continued survival of Old Order Amish communities and their religious organization, and the hazards presented by the State's enforcement of a statute generally valid as to others. Beyond this, they have carried the even more difficult burden of demonstrating the adequacy of their alternative mode of continuing informal vocational education in terms of precisely those overall interests that the State advances in support of its program of compulsory high school education. In light of this convincing showing, one that probably few other religious groups or sects could make, and weighing the minimal difference between what the State would require and what the Amish already accept, it was incumbent on the State to show with more particularity how its admittedly strong interest in compulsory education would be adversely affected by granting an exemption to the Amish....

* * *

Affirmed.

Mr. Justice Powell and **Mr. Justice Rehnquist** took no part in the consideration or decision of this case.

* * *

Mr. Justice Douglas, dissenting in part.

I

I agree with the Court that the religious scruples of the Amish are opposed to the education of their children beyond the grade schools, yet I disagree with the Court's conclusion that the matter is within the dispensation of parents alone. The Court's analysis assumes that the only interests at stake in the case are those of the Amish parents on the one hand, and those of the State on the other. The difficulty with this approach is that, despite the Court's claim, the parents are seeking to vindicate not only their own free exercise claims, but also those of their high-school-age children.

It is argued that the right of the Amish children to religious freedom is not presented by the facts of the case, as the issue before the Court involves only the Amish parents' religious freedom to defy a state criminal statute imposing upon them an affirmative duty to cause their children to attend high school.

First, respondents' motion to dismiss in the trial court expressly asserts, not only the religious liberty of the adults, but also that of the children, as a defense to the prosecutions. It is, of course, beyond question that the parents have standing as defendants in a criminal prosecution to assert the religious interests of their children as a defense.[1] Although the lower courts and a majority of this Court assume an identity of interest between parent and child, it is clear that they have treated the religious interest of the child as a factor in the analysis.

Second, it is essential to reach the question to decide the case, not only because the question was squarely raised in the motion to dismiss, but also because no analysis of religious-liberty claims can take place in a vacuum. If the parents in this case are allowed a religious exemption, the inevitable effect is to impose the parents' notions of religious duty upon their children. Where the child is mature enough to express potentially conflicting desires, it would be an invasion of the child's rights to permit such an imposition without canvassing his views....

* * *

I

This issue has never been squarely presented before today. Our opinions are full of talk about the power of the parents over the child's education. See *Pierce v. Society of Sisters*, 268 U.S. 510; *Meyer v. Nebraska*, 262 U.S. 390. And we have in the past analyzed similar conflicts between parent and State with little regard for the views of the child. See *Prince v. Massachusetts*, *supra.* Recent cases, however, have clearly held that the children themselves have constitutionally protectible interests.

These children are "persons" within the meaning of the Bill of Rights. We have so held over and over again. In *Haley v. Ohio*, 332 U.S. 596, we extended the protection of the Fourteenth Amendment in a state trial of a 15-year-old boy. In *In re Gault*, 387 U.S. 1, 13, we held that "neither the Fourteenth Amendment nor the Bill of Rights is for adults alone." In *In re Winship*, 397 U.S. 358, we held that a 12-year-old boy, when charged with an act which would be a crime if committed by an adult, was entitled to procedural safeguards contained in the Sixth Amendment.

* * *

On this important and vital matter of education, I think the children should be entitled to be heard. While the parents, absent dissent, normally speak for the entire family, the education of the child is a matter on which the child will often have decided views. He may want to be a pianist or an astronaut or an oceanographer. To do so he will have to break from the Amish tradition.[2]

It is the future of the student, not the future of the parents, that is imperiled by today's decision. If a parent keeps his child out of school beyond the grade school, then the child will be forever barred from entry into the new and amazing world of diversity that we have today. The child may decide that that is

---

[1] Thus, in *Prince v. Massachusetts*, 321 U.S. 158, a Jehovah's Witness was convicted for having violated a state child labor law by allowing her nine-year-old niece and ward to circulate religious literature on the public streets. There, as here, the narrow question was the religious liberty of the adult. There, as here, the Court analyzed the problem from the point of view of the State's conflicting interest in the welfare of the child. But, as MR. JUSTICE BRENNAN, speaking for the Court, has so recently pointed out, "The Court [in *Prince*] implicitly held that the custodian had standing to assert alleged freedom of religion...rights of the child that were threatened in the very litigation before the Court and that the child had no effective way of asserting herself." *Eisenstadt v. Baird*, 405 U.S. 438, 446 n. 6. Here, as in *Prince*, the children have no effective alternate means to vindicate their rights. The question, therefore, is squarely before us.

[2] A significant number of Amish children do leave the Old Order. Professor Hostetler notes that "the loss of members is very limited in some Amish districts and considerable in others." J. Hostetler, Amish Society 226 (1968). In one Pennsylvania church, he observed a defection rate of 30%. *Ibid.* Rates up to 50% have been reported by others....

the preferred course, or he may rebel. It is the student's judgment, not his parents', that is essential if we are to give full meaning to what we have said about the Bill of Rights and of the right of students to be masters of their own destiny.[3] If he is harnessed to the Amish way of life by those in authority over him and if his education is truncated, his entire life may be stunted and deformed. The child, therefore, should be given an opportunity to be heard before the State gives the exemption which we honor today.

The views of the two children in question were not canvassed by the Wisconsin courts. The matter should be explicitly reserved so that new hearings can be held on remand of the case.[4]

* * *

---

[3] The court below brushed aside the students' interests with the offhand comment that "when a child reaches the age of judgment, he can choose for himself his religion."....But there is nothing in this record to indicate that the moral and intellectual judgment demanded of the student by the question in this case is beyond his capacity. Children far younger than the 14- and 15-year-olds involved here are regularly permitted to testify in custody and other proceedings. Indeed, the failure to call the affected child in a custody hearing is often reversible error....Moreover, there is substantial agreement among child psychologists and sociologists that the moral and intellectual maturity of the 14-year-old approaches that of the adult....

[4] Canvassing the views of all school-age Amish children in the State of Wisconsin would not present insurmountable difficulties. A 1968 survey indicated that there were at that time only 256 such children in the entire State....

Questions for Discussion

1. Would the Court reverse a legislatively enacted minimum educational requirement if the group seeking exception were not the Amish, but Muslims?

2. Justice Douglas notes that 30% to 50% of Amish children leave their communities. More recent data place the percentage at over two-thirds. What are the prospects for these children who will have no more than an 8th grade education? Does the state have a compelling state interest in assuring them opportunity? Does the court have adequate empirical data or appropriate breadth to reverse a legislative judgment that they warrant a minimum floor of public education beyond that level?

3. Is the state's policy to require minimum education standards for Amish children here a reflection of state *animus* toward the Amish? How would it react to a similar withdrawal from public education by other ethnic, linguistic or religious groups?

4. Could the state require the Amish to provide students with a basic high school curriculum, giving them the option of controlling the school site? Does the *Yoder* decision conflict at all with the spirit of *Brown v. Board of Education* (Chapter 4 above) which determined that in the racial context "separate but equal" was inherently discriminatory? Do the Amish children have a right to intermix with and benefit from Wisconsin children who may differ from them, and vice versa? If not constitutionally embodied, is such integration a "qualified compelling state interest"? Are the Amish regarded as having a collective right to seek to maintain

their culture, apart from religion? Do American national minorities have this right? What about Native American tribes who combine culture and religion as do the Amish?

5. The majority opines that a child who desires a high school education is "not an issue." What happens where it is an issue? According to *Planned Parenthood v. Casey*, discussed in Chapter 2, the state may provide its own information about an abortion decision to all minors who seek that procedure. Can the state provide its own information to Amish 8th graders to inform their decision about whether they wish to stop schooling at the 8th grade level?

Board of Education of the Westside Community Schools v. Mergens
496 U.S. 226 (1990)

JUSTICE O'CONNOR delivered the opinion of the Court, except as to Part III.

This case requires us to decide whether the Equal Access Act..., 20 U.S.C. §§ 4071–4074, prohibits Westside High School from denying a student religious group permission to meet on school premises during noninstructional time, and if so, whether the Act, so construed, violates the Establishment Clause of the First Amendment.

I

Respondents are current and former students at Westside High School, a public secondary school in Omaha, Nebraska. At the time this suit was filed, the school enrolled about 1,450 students and included grades 10 to 12; in the 1987–1988 school year, ninth graders were added. Westside High School is part of the Westside Community School system, an independent public school district....

Students at Westside High School are permitted to join various student groups and clubs, all of which meet after school hours on school premises. The students may choose from approximately 30 recognized groups on a voluntary basis. A list of student groups, together with a brief description of each provided by the school, appears in the Appendix to this opinion.

School Board Policy 5610 concerning "Student Clubs and Organizations" recognizes these student clubs as a "vital part of the total education program as a means of developing citizenship, wholesome attitudes, good human relations, knowledge and skills."....Board Policy 5610 also provides that each club shall have faculty sponsorship and that "clubs and organizations shall not be sponsored by any political or religious organization, or by any organization which denies membership on the basis of race, color, creed, sex or political belief."....Board Policy 6180 on "Recognition of Religious Beliefs and Customs" requires that "students adhering to a specific set of religious beliefs or holding to little or no belief shall be alike respected."....In addition, Board Policy 5450 recognizes its students' "Freedom of Expression," consistent with the authority of the Board....

There is no written school board policy concerning the formation of students clubs. Rather, students wishing to form a club present their request to a school official who determines whether the proposed club's goals and objectives are consistent with school board policies and with the school district's "Mission and Goals"—a broadly worded "blueprint" that expresses the district's commitment to teaching academic, physical, civic, and personal skills and values....

In January 1985, respondent Bridget Mergens met with Westside's principal, Dr. Findley, and requested permission to form a Christian club at the school. The proposed club would have the same privileges and meet on the same terms and conditions as other Westside student groups, except that the proposed club would not have a faculty sponsor. According to the students' testimony at trial, the club's purpose would have been, among other things, to permit the students to read and discuss the Bible, to have fellowship, and to pray together. Membership would have been voluntary and open to all students regardless of religious affiliation.

Findley denied the request, as did associate superintendent Tangdell. In February 1985, Findley and Tangdell informed Mergens that they had discussed the matter with superintendent Hanson and that he had agreed that her request should be denied. The school officials explained that school policy required all student clubs to have a faculty sponsor, which the proposed religious club would not or could not have,...and that a religious club at the school would violate the Establishment Clause. In March 1985, Mergens appealed the denial of her request to the Board of Education, but the Board voted to uphold the denial.

* * *

I

A

In *Widmar v. Vincent*, 454 U.S. 263 (1981), we invalidated, on free speech grounds, a state university regulation that prohibited student use of school facilities "'for purposes of religious worship or religious teaching.'"....In doing so, we held that an "equal access" policy would not violate the Establishment Clause under our decision in *Lemon v. Kurtzman*, 403 U.S. 602, 612–613 (1971). In particular, we held that such a policy would have a secular purpose, would not have the primary effect of advancing religion, and would not result in excessive entanglement between government and religion....We noted, however, that "university students are, of course, young adults. They are less impressionable than younger students and should be able to appreciate that the University's policy is one of neutrality toward religion."....

In 1984, Congress extended the reasoning of *Widmar* to public secondary schools. Under the Equal Access Act, a public secondary school with a "limited open forum" is prohibited from discriminating against students who wish to conduct a meeting within that forum on the basis of the "religious, political, philosophical, or other content of the speech at such meetings."...A "limited open forum" exists whenever a public secondary school "grants an offering to or opportunity for one or more noncurriculum related student groups to meet on school premises during noninstructional time." § 4071(b). "Meeting" is defined to include "those activities of student groups which are permitted under a school's limited open forum and are not directly related to the school curriculum." § 4072(3). "Noninstructional time" is defined to mean "time set aside by the school before actual classroom instruction begins or after actual classroom instruction ends." § 4072(4). Thus, even if a public secondary school allows only one "noncurriculum related student group" to meet, the Act's obligations are triggered and the school may not deny other clubs, on the basis of the content of their speech, equal access to meet on school premises during noninstructional time.

The Act further specifies that "schools shall be deemed to offer a fair opportunity to students who wish to conduct a meeting within its limited open forum" if the school uniformly provides that the meetings are voluntary and student-initiated; are not sponsored by the school, the government, or its agents or employees; do not materially and substantially interfere with the orderly conduct of education activities within the school; and are not directed, controlled, conducted, or regularly attended by "nonschool persons.".... "Sponsorship" is defined to mean "the acting of promoting, leading, or participating in a meeting. The assignment of a teacher, administrator, or other school employee to a meeting for custodial purposes does not constitute sponsorship of the meeting." § 4072(2). If the meetings are religious, employees or agents of the school or government may attend only in a "nonparticipatory capacity." § 4071(c)(3). Moreover, a State may not influence the form of any religious activity, require any person to participate in such activity, or compel any school agent or employee to attend a meeting if the content of the speech at the meeting is contrary to that person's beliefs....

* * *

III

Petitioners contend that even if Westside has created a limited open forum within the meaning of the Act, its denial of official recognition to the proposed Christian club must nevertheless stand because the Act violates the Establishment Clause of the First Amendment, as applied to the States through the Fourteenth Amendment. Specifically, petitioners maintain that because the school's recognized student activities are an integral part of its educational mission, official recognition of respondents' proposed club would effectively incorporate religious activities into the school's official program, endorse participation in the religious club, and provide the club with an official platform to proselytize other students.

We disagree....

* * *

...First, although we have invalidated the use of public funds to pay for teaching state-required subjects at parochial schools, in part because of the risk of creating " a crucial symbolic link between government and religion, thereby enlisting—at least in the eyes of impressionable youngsters—the powers of government to the support of the religious denomination operating the school,"...there is a crucial difference between *government* speech endorsing religion, which the Establishment Clause forbids, and *private* speech endorsing religion, which the Free Speech and Free Exercise Clauses protect. We think that secondary school students are mature enough and are likely to understand that a school does not endorse or support student speech that it merely permits on a nondiscriminatory basis....

* * *

Second, we note the Act expressly limits participation by school officials at meetings of student religious groups, §§ 4071(c)(2) and (3), and that any such meetings must be held during "noninstructional time," § 4071(b). The Act therefore avoids the problems of "the students' emulation of teachers as role models" and "mandatory attendance requirements,"... To be sure, the possibility of *student* peer pressure remains, but there is little if any risk of official state endorsement or coercion where no formal classroom activities are involved and no school officials actively participate. Moreover, petitioners' fear of a mistaken inference of endorsement is largely self-imposed, because the school itself has control over any impressions it gives its students....

Third, the broad spectrum of officially recognized student clubs at Westside, and the fact that Westside students are free to initiate and organize additional student clubs,...counteract any possible message of official endorsement of or preference for religion or a particular religious belief....Although a school may not itself lead or direct a religious club, a school that permits a student-initiated and student-led religious club to meet after school, just as it permits any other student group to do, does not convey a message of state approval or endorsement of the particular religion....

Petitioners' final argument is that by complying with the Act's requirement, the school risks excessive entanglement between government and religion. The proposed club, petitioners urge, would be required to have a faculty sponsor who would be charged with actively directing the activities of the group, guiding its leaders, and ensuring balance in the presentation of controversial ideas....

Under the Act, however, faculty monitors may not participate in any religious meetings, and nonschool persons may not direct, control, or regularly attend activities of student groups....Moreover, the Act prohibits school "sponsorship" of any religious meetings,...which means that school officials may not promote, lead, or participate in any such meeting,...Although the Act permits "the assignment of a teacher, administrator, or other school employee to the meeting for custodial purposes,"....

Accordingly, we hold that the Equal Access Act does not on its face contravene the Establishment Clause. Because we hold that petitioners have violated the Act, we do not decide respondents' claims under the Free Speech and Free Exercise Clauses. For the foregoing reasons, the judgment of the Court of Appeals is affirmed.

* * *

Justice Stevens, dissenting.

....Can Congress really have intended to issue an order to every public high school in the nation stating, in substance, that if you sponsor a chess club, a scuba diving club, or a French club—without having formal classes in those subjects—you must also open your doors to every religious, political, or social organization, no matter how controversial or distasteful its views may be? I think not. A fair review of the legislative history of the Equal Access Act (Act),...20 U.S.C. §§ 4071–4074, discloses that Congress intended to recognize a much narrower forum than the Court has legislated into existence today.

I

The Act's basic design is easily summarized: when a public high school has a "limited open forum," it must not deny any student group access to that forum on the basis of the religious, political, philosophical or other content of the speech of the group. Although the consequences of having a limited open forum are thus quite clear, the definition of such a forum is less so. Nevertheless, there is considerable agreement about how this difficulty must be resolved....

* * *

The forum at Westside is considerably different from that which existed at the University of Missouri. In *Widmar*, we held that the University had created "a generally open forum,"...Over 100 officially recognized student groups routinely participated in that forum....They included groups whose activities not only were unrelated to any specific courses, but also were of a kind that a state university could not properly sponsor or endorse. Thus, for example, they included such political organizations as the Young Socialist Alliance, the Women's Union, and the Young Democrats....The University permitted use of its facilities for speakers advocating transcendental meditation and humanism. Since the University had allowed such organizations and speakers the use of campus facilities, we concluded that the University could not discriminate against a religious group on the basis of the content of its speech. The forum established by the state university accommodated participating groups that were "noncurriculum related" not only because they did not mirror the school's classroom instruction, but also because they advocated controversial positions that a state university's obligation of neutrality prevented it from endorsing.

* * *

Accordingly, as I would construe the Act, a high school could properly sponsor a French club, a chess club, or a scuba diving club simply because their activities are fully consistent with the school's curricular mission. It would not matter whether formal courses in any of those subjects—or in directly related subjects—were being offered as long as faculty encouragement of student participation in such groups would be consistent with both the school's obligation of neutrality and its legitimate pedagogical concerns. Nothing in *Widmar* implies that the existence of a French club, for example, would create constitutional obligation to allow student members of the Ku Klux Klan or the Communist Party to have access to school facilities....More importantly, nothing in that case suggests that the constitutional issue should turn on whether French is being taught in a formal course while the club is functioning.

Conversely, if a high school decides to allow political groups to use its facilities, it plainly cannot discriminate among controversial groups because it agrees with the positions of some and disagrees with the ideas advocated by others. Again, the fact that the history of the Republican party might be taught in a political science course could not justify a decision to allow the young Republicans to form a club while denying Communists, white supremacists, or Christian Scientists the same privilege. In my judgment, the political activities of the young Republicans are "noncurriculum related" for reasons that have nothing to do with the content of the political science course. The statutory definition of what is "noncurriculum related" should depend on the constitutional concern that motivated our decision in *Widmar*.

* * *

...The Court focuses upon whether the Act might run afoul of the Establishment Clause because of the danger that some students will mistakenly believe that the student-initiated religious clubs are sponsored by the school....I believe that the plurality's construction of the statute obliges it to answer a further question: whether the Act violates the Establishment Clause by authorizing religious organizations to meet on high school grounds even when the high school's teachers and administrators deem it unwise to admit controversial or partisan organizations of any kind.

Under the Court's interpretation of the Act, Congress has imposed a difficult choice on public high schools receiving federal financial assistance. If such a school continues to allow students to participate in such familiar and innocuous activities as a school chess or scuba diving club, it must also allow religious groups to make use of school facilities. Indeed, it is hard to see how a cheerleading squad or a pep club, among the most common student groups in American high schools, could avoid being "noncurriculum related" under the majority's test. The Act, as construed by the majority, comes perilously close to an outright command to allow organized prayer, and perhaps the kind of religious ceremonies involved in *Widmar*, on school premises.

* * *

Questions for Discussion

1. *Yoder* acknowledged the strength of "peer pressure" on children. The prospect of Amish defection based on the required immersion of their children into a public school system with a majority of school children possibly ridiculing the dress and customs of their children was a factor for the Court. What if *Yoder* had been decided differently and its students were integrated into public schools, typically making up 5% of the student body? What would be the consequence of widely attended non-Amish, or perhaps anti-Amish religious meetings right after school and in the same location, attended by teachers and announced by school media? Would it constitute a state (school) arranged or facilitated intrusion into parental religious direction of their children? If a parental fundamental liberty interest is invoked, is there a less restrictive alternative to the *Mergens* practice?

2. Would it matter if the club were to engage in social or charitable activities as opposed to the actual exercise of religious worship?

3. The dissent fears excessive state advancement of religion. The state already grants religion property tax subsidies and income tax subsidies (deductions) for any person who contributes to a church or religion, and our libraries spend substantial public funds on the literature and teachings of various religions. What is the distinction to prohibit public school buildings (which are otherwise unused) to be the site of such activities?

4. Justices Scalia and Kennedy concurred in *Mergens*, but would go further and allow the state to "endorse a religion" so long as it did not persecute or affirmatively discriminate against others. Would such a view be likely if such sponsorship were of the teachings and policies of a non-Christian religion? Do religions discriminate against members of other religious groups, agnostics and atheists when they claim that their beliefs are valid and those of other religions are "false," and that those worshiping falsely are foreclosed from heaven and perhaps are affirmatively evil? Does the historical record of religious "tolerance" commend the assumption that state sponsorship would be benign for the unsponsored? Is such persecution more likely to be prevented if the line is drawn to preclude state sponsorship of a religion, or to allow such sponsorship and to prohibit subsequent acts of discrimination or coercion?

5. If the school had an "atheists" or "agnostics" club, could it be denied access to school facilities under *Mergens*?

Zobrest v. Catalina Foothills School District
509 U.S. 1 (1993)

JUDGES: **REHNQUIST, C. J.**, delivered the opinion of the Court, in which **WHITE**, **SCALIA**, **KENNEDY**, and **THOMAS**, JJ., joined.

Petitioner James Zobrest, who has been deaf since birth, asked respondent school district to provide a sign-language interpreter to accompany him to classes at a Roman Catholic high school in Tucson, Arizona, pursuant to the Individuals with Disabilities Education Act (IDEA), *20 U.S.C. § 1400* et seq., and its Arizona counterpart [cite omitted]. The United States Court of Appeals for the Ninth

Circuit decided, however, that provision of such a publicly employed interpreter would violate the Establishment Clause of the First Amendment. We hold that the Establishment Clause does not bar the school district from providing the requested interpreter.

James Zobrest attended grades one through five in a school for the deaf, and grades six through eight in a public school operated by respondent. While he attended public school, respondent furnished him with a sign-language interpreter. For religious reasons, James' parents (also petitioners here) enrolled him for the ninth grade in Salpointe Catholic High School, a sectarian institution.[1] When petitioners requested that respondent supply James with an interpreter at Salpointe, respondent referred the matter to the County Attorney, who concluded that providing an interpreter on the school's premises would violate the United States Constitution....

* * *

We have never said that "religious institutions are disabled by the First Amendment from participating in publicly sponsored social welfare programs." *Bowen v. Kendrick*,...For if the Establishment Clause did bar religious groups from receiving general government benefits, then "a church could not be protected by the police and fire departments, or have its public sidewalk kept in repair."...Given that a contrary rule would lead to such absurd results, we have consistently held that government programs that neutrally provide benefits to a broad class of citizens defined without reference to religion are not readily subject to an Establishment Clause challenge just because sectarian institutions may also receive an attenuated financial benefit....

* * *

Respondent contends, however, that this case differs from *Mueller* and *Witters*, in that petitioners seek to have a public employee physically present in a sectarian school to assist in James' religious education. In light of this distinction, respondent argues that this case more closely resembles *Meek v. Pittenger*,...According to respondent, if the government could not place a tape recorder in a sectarian school in *Meek*, then it surely cannot place an interpreter in *Salpointe*. The statute in *Meek* also authorized state-paid personnel to furnish "auxiliary services" — which included remedial and accelerated instruction and guidance counseling — on the premises of religious schools. We determined that this part of the statute offended the First Amendment as well. *Id., at 372. Ball* similarly involved two public programs that provided services on private school premises; there, public employees taught classes to students in private school classrooms.[9] ...

Respondent's reliance on *Meek* and *Ball* is misplaced for two reasons. First, the programs in Meek and Ball — through direct grants of government aid — relieved sectarian schools of costs they otherwise would have borne in educating their students. See *Witters, supra,* at 487 ("The State may not grant aid to a religious school, whether cash or in kind, where the effect of the aid is 'that of a direct subsidy to the religious school' from the State") (quoting *Ball*, *supra*, at 394). For example, the religious schools in *Meek* received teaching material and equipment from the State, relieving them of an otherwise necessary cost of

---

[1] The parties have stipulated: "The two functions of secular education and advancement of religious values or beliefs are inextricably intertwined throughout the operations of Salpointe."

[9] Forty of the forty-one private schools in *Ball* were pervasively sectarian. 473 U.S. 384 at 384-385.

performing their educational function. *421 U.S. at 365-366* . "Substantial aid to the educational function of such schools," we explained, "necessarily results in aid to the sectarian school enterprise as a whole," and therefore brings about "the direct and substantial advancement of religious activity." *Id., at 366.* So, too, was the case in *Ball:* The programs challenged there, which provided teachers in addition to instructional equipment and material, "in effect subsidized the religious functions of the parochial schools by taking over a substantial portion of their responsibility for teaching secular subjects." *473 U.S. at 397* . "This kind of direct aid," we determined, "is indistinguishable from the provision of a direct cash subsidy to the religious school." *Id., at 395.* The extension of aid to petitioners, however, does not amount to "an impermissible 'direct subsidy'" of Salpointe. *Witters, 474 U.S. at 487* . For Salpointe is not relieved of an expense that it otherwise would have assumed in educating its students. And, as we noted above, any attenuated financial benefit that parochial schools do ultimately receive from the IDEA is attributable to "the private choices of individual parents." *Mueller, 463 U.S. at 400* . Handicapped children, not sectarian schools, are the primary beneficiaries of the IDEA; to the extent sectarian schools benefit at all from the IDEA, they are only incidental beneficiaries....

Second, the task of a sign-language interpreter seems to us quite different from that of a teacher or guidance counselor. Notwithstanding the Court of Appeals' intimations to the contrary, [citation omitted] the Establishment Clause lays down no absolute bar to the placing of a public employee in a sectarian school.[10] Such a flat rule, smacking of antiquated notions of "taint," would indeed exalt form over substance.[11] Nothing in this record suggests that a sign-language interpreter would do more than accurately interpret whatever material is presented to the class as a whole. In fact, ethical guidelines require interpreters to "transmit everything that is said in exactly the same way it was intended." James' parents have chosen of their own free will to place him in a pervasively sectarian environment. The sign-language interpreter they have requested will neither add to nor subtract from that environment, and hence the provision of such assistance is not barred by the Establishment Clause.

The IDEA creates a neutral government program dispensing aid not to schools but to individual handicapped children. If a handicapped child chooses to enroll in a sectarian school, we hold that the Establishment Clause does not prevent the school district from furnishing him with a sign-language interpreter there in order to facilitate his education. The judgment of the Court of Appeals is therefore

Reversed.

DISSENT: **JUSTICE BLACKMUN**, with whom **JUSTICE SOUTER** joins, and with whom **JUSTICE STEVENS** and **JUSTICE O'CONNOR** join as to Part I, dissenting.

Today, the Court unnecessarily addresses an important constitutional issue, disregarding longstanding principles of constitutional adjudication. In so

---

[10] For instance, in *Wolman v. Walter* [citation omitted] we made clear that "the provision of health services to all schoolchildren — public and nonpublic — does not have the primary effect of aiding religion," even when those services are provided within sectarian schools. We accordingly rejected a First Amendment challenge to the State's providing diagnostic speech and hearing services on sectarian school premises...

[11] Indeed, respondent readily admits, as it must, that there would be no problem under the Establishment Clause if the IDEA funds instead went directly to James' parents, who, in turn, hired the interpreter themselves. Brief for Respondent 11 ("If such were the case, then the sign language interpreter would be the student's employee, not the School District's, and governmental involvement in the enterprise would end with the disbursement of funds").

doing, the Court holds that placement in a parochial school classroom of a public employee whose duty consists of relaying religious messages does not violate the Establishment Clause of the First Amendment. I disagree both with the Court's decision to reach this question and with its disposition on the merits. I therefore dissent.

* * *

I

* * *

Let us be clear about exactly what is going on here. The parties have stipulated to the following facts. Petitioner requested the State to supply him with a sign-language interpreter at Salpointe High School, a private Roman Catholic school operated by the Carmelite Order of the Catholic Church. Salpointe is a "pervasively religious" institution where "the two functions of secular education and advancement of religious values or beliefs are inextricably intertwined." Salpointe's overriding "objective" is to "instill a sense of Christian values." Its "distinguishing purpose" is "the inculcation in its students of the faith and morals of the Roman Catholic Church." Religion is a required subject at Salpointe, and Catholic students are "strongly encouraged" to attend daily Mass each morning. Salpointe's teachers must sign a Faculty Employment Agreement which requires them to promote the relationship among the religious, the academic, and the extracurricular....They are encouraged to do so by "assisting students in experiencing how the presence of God is manifest in nature, human history, in the struggles for economic and political justice, and other secular areas of the curriculum."...The Agreement also sets forth detailed rules of conduct teachers must follow in order to advance the school's Christian mission....

At Salpointe, where the secular and the sectarian are "inextricably intertwined," governmental assistance to the educational function of the school necessarily entails governmental participation in the school's inculcation of religion. A state-employed sign-language interpreter would be required to communicate the material covered in religion class, the nominally secular subjects that are taught from a religious perspective, and the daily Masses at which Salpointe encourages attendance for Catholic students. In an environment so pervaded by discussions of the divine, the interpreter's every gesture would be infused with religious significance. Indeed, petitioners willingly concede this point: "That the interpreter conveys religious messages is a given in the case."...By this concession, petitioners would seem to surrender their constitutional claim.

* * *

"Although Establishment Clause jurisprudence is characterized by few absolutes," at a minimum "the Clause does absolutely prohibit government-financed or government-sponsored indoctrination into the beliefs of a particular religious faith."...In keeping with this restriction, our cases consistently have rejected the provision by government of any resource capable of advancing a school's religious mission. Although the Court generally has permitted the provision of "secular and nonideological services unrelated to the primary, religion-oriented educational function of the sectarian school," *Meek,* 421 U.S. at 364, it has always proscribed the provision of benefits that afford even "the opportunity for the transmission of sectarian views," *Wolman,* 433 U.S. at 244.

Thus, the Court has upheld the use of public school buses to transport children to and from school, *Everson v. Board of Education,*...while striking down the employment of publicly funded buses for field trips controlled by parochial school teachers, *Wolman,* 433 U.S. at 254. Similarly, the Court has permitted the provision of secular textbooks whose content is immutable and can be ascertained in advance, *Board of Education v. Allen,*...while prohibiting the provision of any instructional materials or equipment that could be used to convey a religious message, such as slide projectors, tape recorders, record players, and the like, *Wolman,* 433 U.S. at 249. State-paid speech and hearing therapists have been allowed to administer diagnostic testing on the premises of parochial schools, *Wolman,* 433 U.S. at 241-242, whereas state-paid remedial teachers and counselors have not been authorized to offer their services because of the risk that they may inculcate religious beliefs, *Meek,* 421 U.S. at 371.

These distinctions perhaps are somewhat fine, but "'lines must be drawn.'" *Grand Rapids,* 473 U.S. at 398 (citation omitted). And our cases make clear that government crosses the boundary when it furnishes the medium for communication of a religious message. If petitioners receive the relief they seek, it is beyond question that a state-employed sign-language interpreter would serve as the conduit for petitioner's religious education, thereby assisting Salpointe in its mission of religious indoctrination. But the Establishment Clause is violated when a sectarian school enlists "the machinery of the State to enforce a religious orthodoxy."...

* * *

III

The Establishment Clause "rests upon the premise that both religion and government can best work to achieve their lofty aims if each is left free from the other within its respective sphere."...To this end, our cases have strived to "chart a course that preserves the autonomy and freedom of religious bodies while avoiding any semblance of established religion."...I would not stray, as the Court does today, from the course set by nearly five decades of Establishment Clause jurisprudence. Accordingly, I dissent.

* * *

Questions for Discussion

1. Does *Zobrest* signal the Court's acceptance of "voucher" financing of sectarian schools (each school age child is assigned a sum of money which may be redeemed by parents in any school of choice: public, private, or sectarian)? Its discussion distinguishes *Zobrest* from prior cases prohibiting aid because the latter do not provide expenses they would otherwise have incurred, but merely allow additional sums not otherwise to be expended for religious or instructional purposes in furtherance of a non-sectarian policy of disability assistance. But it also distinguishes *Zobrest* from such prior cases by noting that the subsidy does not go "to the schools, but essentially runs with the child or the parents, with the decision on where to spend it left to individuals." Footnote 11 indicates that this rationale alone provides an adequate distinction from prior law and makes such indirect funding of sectarian schools constitutional. What then is the constitutional bar to wholesale voucher funding?

2. The majority seems to be saying that the act of giving educational tax money back to parents and allowing them to decide where it is expended may not be a "public subsidy" violating the establishment clause. How would the majority

answer the following: (1) if the gravamen of the wall between church and state is constitutional, it will apply even if a majority vote through their legislature, or directly, to publicly fund religion. How does the additional "vote" of individual allocation supersede constitutional bar? (2) Although individual parents may make decisions apart from state compulsion under the majority's discussion, are not the taxes collected and redistributed coercively by the state using its generic police power—deriving from the people at large? (3) Large numbers of Americans, who disagree with certain religious precepts, will be taxed and those sums redistributed to others to finance religious teaching. Does the fact that parents in the religious sects one finds abhorrent have made a decision to place their children in sectarian schools resolve one's objection?

Zelman v. Simmons-Harris
536 U.S. 639 (2002)

MR. JUSTICE REHNQUIST delivered the opinion of the Court:

The State of Ohio has established a pilot program designed to provide educational choices to families with children who reside in the Cleveland City School District. The question presented is whether this program offends the Establishment Clause of the United States Constitution. We hold that it does not.

There are more than 75,000 children enrolled in the Cleveland City School District. The majority of these children are from low-income and minority families. Few of these families enjoy the means to send their children to any school other than an inner-city public school. For more than a generation, however, Cleveland's public schools have been among the worst performing public schools in the Nation. In 1995, a Federal District Court declared a "crisis of magnitude" and placed the entire Cleveland school district under state control....The district had failed to meet any of the 18 state standards for minimal acceptable performance. Only 1 in 10 ninth graders could pass a basic proficiency examination, and students at all levels performed at a dismal rate compared with students in other Ohio public schools. More than two-thirds of high school students either dropped or failed out before graduation. Of those students who managed to reach their senior year, one of every four still failed to graduate. Of those students who did graduate, few could read, write, or compute at levels comparable to their counterparts in other cities.

It is against this backdrop that Ohio enacted...its Pilot Project Scholarship Program, financial assistance to families in any Ohio school district that is or has been "under federal court order requiring supervision and operational management of the district by the state superintendent." ... The program provides two basic kinds of assistance to parents of children in a covered district. First, the program provides tuition aid for students in kindergarten through third grade, expanding each year through eighth grade, to attend a participating public or private school of their parent's choosing..... Second, the program provides tutorial aid for students who choose to remain enrolled in public school. § 3313.975(A).

The tuition aid portion of the program is designed to provide educational choices to parents who reside in a covered district. Any private school, whether religious or nonreligious, may participate in the program and accept program students so long as the school is located within the boundaries of a covered district and meets statewide educational standards....Participating private schools must agree not to discriminate on the basis of race, religion, or ethnic background, or to "advocate or foster unlawful behavior or teach hatred of any person or group on the basis of race, ethnicity, national origin, or religion." Any public school located in a school district adjacent to the covered district may also participate in the program. Adjacent public schools are eligible to receive a $ 2,250 tuition grant for each program student accepted in addition to the full amount of per-pupil state funding attributable to each additional student....

Tuition aid is distributed to parents according to financial need. Families with incomes below 200% of the poverty line are given priority and are eligible to receive 90% of private school tuition up to $ 2,250....For these lowest-income families, participating private schools may not charge a parental co-payment greater than $ 250....For all other families, the program pays 75% of tuition costs, up to $ 1,875, with no co-payment cap....Where tuition aid is spent depends solely upon where parents who receive tuition aid choose to enroll their child. If parents choose a private school, checks are made payable to the parents who then endorse the checks over to the chosen school....

• • •

In *Mueller* (463 U.S. 397), we rejected an Establishment Clause challenge to a Minnesota program authorizing tax deductions for various educational expenses, including private school tuition costs, even though the great majority of the program's beneficiaries (96%) were parents of children in religious schools. We began by focusing on the class of beneficiaries, finding that because the class included "*all* parents," including parents with "children [who] attend nonsectarian private schools or sectarian private schools,"...viewing the program as a whole, we emphasized the principle of private choice, noting that public funds were made available to religious schools "only as a result of numerous, private choices of individual parents of school-age children." This, we said, ensured that "'no imprimatur of state approval' can be deemed to have been conferred on any particular religion, or on religion generally."...

• • •

Finally, in *Zobrest*, we applied *Mueller* and *Witters* to reject an Establishment Clause challenge to a federal program that permitted sign-language interpreters to assist deaf children enrolled in religious schools. Reviewing our earlier decisions, we stated that "we observed that the program "distributes benefits neutrally to any child qualifying as 'disabled.'" Its "primary beneficiaries," we said, were "disabled children, not sectarian schools."...

We further observed that "by according parents freedom to select a school of their choice, the statute ensures that a government-paid interpreter will be present in a sectarian school only as a result of the private decision of individual parents....

• • •

Mr. Justice Souter, with whom **Justice Stevens**, **Justice Ginsburg**, and **Justice Breyer** join, dissenting:

The Court's majority holds that the Establishment Clause is no bar to Ohio's payment of tuition at private religious elementary and middle schools under a scheme that systematically provides tax money to support the schools' religious missions. The occasion for the legislation thus upheld is the condition of public education in the city of Cleveland. The record indicates that the schools are failing to serve their objective, and the vouchers in issue here are said to be needed to provide adequate alternatives to them. If there were an excuse for giving short shrift to the Establishment Clause, it would probably apply here. But there is no excuse. Constitutional limitations are placed on government to preserve constitutional values in hard cases, like these. "Constitutional lines have to be drawn, and on one side of every one of them is an otherwise sympathetic case that provokes impatience with the Constitution and with the line. But constitutional lines are the price of constitutional government."...

The applicability of the Establishment Clause[1] to public funding of benefits to religious schools was settled in *Everson* v. *Board of Ed. of Ewing,* 330 U.S. 1 (1947) which inaugurated the modern era of establishment doctrine. The Court stated the principle in words from which there was no dissent:

"No tax in any amount, large or small, can be levied to support any religious activities or institutions, whatever they may be called, or whatever form they may adopt to teach or practice religion." *Id.*, at 16. The Court has never in so many words repudiated this statement, let alone, in so many words, overruled *Everson.*

Today, however, the majority holds that the Establishment Clause is not offended by Ohio's Pilot Project Scholarship Program, under which students may be eligible to receive as much as $ 2,250 in the form of tuition vouchers transferable to religious schools. In the city of Cleveland the overwhelming proportion of large appropriations for voucher money must be spent on religious schools if it is to be spent at all, and will be spent in amounts that cover almost all of tuition. The money will thus pay for eligible students' instruction not only in secular subjects but in religion as well, in schools that can fairly be characterized as founded to teach religious doctrine and to imbue teaching in all subjects with a religious dimension.[2] Public tax money will pay at a systemic level for teaching the covenant with Israel and Mosaic law in Jewish schools, the primacy of the Apostle Peter and the Papacy in Catholic schools, the truth of reformed Christianity in Protestant schools, and the revelation to the Prophet in Muslim schools, to speak only of major religious groupings in the Republic. How can a Court consistently leave *Everson* on the books and approve the Ohio vouchers? The answer is that it cannot. It is only by ignoring *Everson* that the majority can claim to rest on traditional law in its invocation of neutral aid provisions and private choice to sanction the Ohio law. It is, moreover, only by ignoring the meaning of neutrality and private choice themselves that the majority can even pretend to rest today's decision on those criteria.

• • •

...it seems fair to say that it was not until today that substantiality of aid has clearly been rejected as irrelevant by a majority of this Court, just as it has not been until today that a majority, not a plurality, has held purely formal criteria to suffice for scrutinizing aid that ends up in the coffers of religious schools. Today's cases are notable for their stark illustration of the inadequacy of the majority's chosen formal analysis.

II.

Although it has taken half a century since *Everson* to reach the majority's twin standards of neutrality and free choice, the facts show that, in

---

[1] "Congress shall make no law respecting an establishment of religion," U.S. Const., Amdt. 1.

[2] See, *e.g.*, App. 319a (Saint Jerome School Parent and Student Handbook 1999-2000, p. 1) ("FAITH must dominate the entire educational process so that the child can make decisions according to Catholic values and choose to lead a Christian life"); *id.*,at 347a (Westside Baptist Christian School Parent-Student Handbook, p. 7) ("Christ is the basis of all learning. All subjects will be taught from the Biblical perspective that all truth is God's truth").

the majority's hands, even these criteria cannot convincingly legitimize the Ohio scheme.

A

Consider first the criterion of neutrality. As recently as two Terms ago, a majority of the Court recognized that neutrality conceived of as evenhandedness toward aid recipients had never been treated as alone sufficient to satisfy the Establishment Clause....But at least in its limited significance, formal neutrality seemed to serve some purpose. Today, however, the majority employs the neutrality criterion in a way that renders it impossible to understand.

Neutrality in this sense refers, of course, to evenhandedness in setting eligibility as between potential religious and secular recipients of public money....Thus, for example, the aid scheme in *Witters* provided an eligible recipient with a scholarship to be used at any institution within a practically unlimited universe of schools....; it did not tend to provide more or less aid depending on which one the scholarship recipient chose, and there was no indication that the maximum scholarship amount would be insufficient at secular schools. Neither did any condition of Zobrest's interpreter's subsidy favor religious education. See 509 U.S. at 10.

In order to apply the neutrality test, then, it makes sense to focus on a category of aid that may be directed to religious as well as secular schools, and ask whether the scheme favors a religious direction. Here, one would ask whether the voucher provisions, allowing for as much as $ 2,250 toward private school tuition (or a grant to a public school in an adjacent district), were written in a way that skewed the scheme toward benefiting religious schools.

This, however, is not what the majority asks. The majority looks not to the provisions for tuition vouchers,... but to every provision for educational opportunity: "The program permits the participation of *all* schools within the district, [as well as public schools in adjacent districts], religious or nonreligious." The majority then finds confirmation that "participation of *all* schools" satisfies neutrality by noting that the better part of total state educational expenditure goes to public schools, thus showing there is no favor of religion.

The illogic is patent. If regular, public schools (which can get no voucher payments) "participate" in a voucher scheme with schools that can, and public expenditure is still predominantly on public schools, then the majority's reasoning would find neutrality in a scheme of vouchers available for private tuition in districts with no secular private schools at all. "Neutrality" as the majority employs the term is, literally, verbal and nothing more. This, indeed, is the only way the majority can gloss over the very nonneutral feature of the total scheme covering "*all* schools": public tutors may receive from the State no more than $ 324 per child to support extra tutoring (that is, the State's 90% of a total amount of $ 360),...whereas the tuition voucher schools (which turn out to be mostly religious) can receive up to $ 2,250....

• • •

B

The majority addresses the issue of choice the same way it addresses neutrality, by asking whether recipients or potential recipients of voucher aid have a choice of public schools among secular alternatives to religious schools. Again, however, the majority asks the wrong question and misapplies the criterion. The majority has confused choice in spending scholarships with choice from the entire menu of possible educational placements, most of them open to anyone willing to attend a public school. I say "confused" because the majority's new use of the choice criterion, which it frames negatively as "whether Ohio is coercing parents into sending their children to religious schools,"...ignores the reason for having a private choice enquiry in the first place. Cases since *Mueller* have found private choice relevant under a rule that aid to religious schools can be permissible so long as it first passes through the hands of students or parents....The majority's view that all educational choices are comparable for purposes of choice thus ignores the whole point of the choice test: it is a criterion for deciding whether indirect aid to a religious school is legitimate because it passes through private hands that can spend or use the aid in a secular school. The question is whether the private hand is genuinely free to send the money in either a secular direction or a religious one. The majority now has transformed this question about private choice in channeling aid into a question about selecting from examples of state spending (on education) including direct spending on magnet and community public schools that goes through no private hands and could never reach a religious school under any circumstance. When the choice test is transformed from where to spend the money to where to go to school, it is cut loose from its very purpose.

• • •

There is, in any case, no way to interpret the 96.6% of current voucher money going to religious schools as reflecting a free and genuine choice by the families that apply for vouchers. The 96.6% reflects, instead, the fact that too few nonreligious school desks are available and few but religious schools can afford to accept more than a handful of voucher students. And contrary to the majority's assertion, public schools in adjacent districts hardly have a financial incentive to participate in the Ohio voucher program, and none has....For the overwhelming number of children in the voucher scheme, the only alternative to the public schools is religious. And it is entirely irrelevant that the State did not deliberately design the network of private schools for the sake of channeling money into religious institutions. The criterion is one of genuinely free choice on the part of the private individuals who choose, and a Hobson's choice is not a choice, whatever the reason for being Hobsonian.

• • •

The scale of the aid to religious schools approved today is unprecedented, both in the number of dollars and in the proportion of systemic school expenditure supported. Each measure has received attention in previous cases. On one hand, the sheer quantity of aid, when delivered to a class of religious primary and secondary schools, was suspect on the theory that the greater the aid, the greater its proportion to a religious school's existing expenditures, and the greater the likelihood that public money was supporting religious as well as secular instruction. As we said in *Meek*, "it would simply ignore reality to attempt to separate secular educational functions from the predominantly religious role" as the object of aid that comes in "substantial amounts."...

• • •

The gross amounts of public money contributed are symptomatic of the scope of what the taxpayers' money buys for a broad class of religious-school students. In paying for practically the full amount of tuition for thousands of qualifying students,...compare *Nyquist*, 413 U.S. at 781-783 (state aid amounting to 50% of tuition was unconstitutional), the scholarships purchase everything that tuition purchases, be it instruction in math or indoctrination in faith....[T]he majority makes no pretense that substantial amounts of tax money are not systematically underwriting religious practice and indoctrination.

B

It is virtually superfluous to point out that every objective underlying the prohibition of religious establishment is betrayed by this scheme, but something has to be said about the enormity of the violation. I anticipated these objectives earlier,... in discussing *Everson*, which cataloged them, the first being respect for freedom of conscience. Jefferson described it as the idea that no one "shall be compelled to...support any religious worship, place, or ministry whatsoever,"...even a "teacher of his own religious persuasion," and Madison thought it violated by any "'authority which can force a citizen to contribute three pence . . . of his property for the support of any . . . establishment.'"...

• • •

...Nor is the State's religious antidiscrimination restriction limited to student admission policies: by its terms, a participating religious school may well be forbidden to choose a member of its own clergy to serve as teacher or principal over a layperson of a different religion claiming equal qualification for the job....Indeed, a separate condition that "the school...not...teach hatred of any person or group on the basis of...religion,"...could be understood (or subsequently broadened) to prohibit religions from teaching traditionally legitimate articles of faith as to the error, sinfulness, or ignorance of others, if they want government money for their schools.

• • •

When government aid goes up, so does reliance on it; the only thing likely to go down is independence. If Justice Douglas in *Allen* was concerned with state agencies, influenced by powerful religious groups, choosing the textbooks that parochial schools would use, 392 U.S. at 265 (dissenting opinion), how much more is there reason to wonder when dependence will become great enough to give the State of Ohio an effective veto over basic decisions on the content of curriculums? A day will come when religious schools will learn what political leverage can do, just as Ohio's politicians are now getting a lesson in the leverage exercised by religion.

• • •

...Religious teaching at taxpayer expense simply cannot be cordoned from taxpayer politics, and every major religion currently espouses social positions that provoke intense opposition. Not all taxpaying Protestant citizens, for example, will be content to underwrite the teaching of the Roman Catholic Church condemning the death penalty....Nor will all of America's Muslims acquiesce in paying for the endorsement of the religious Zionism taught in many religious Jewish schools, which combines "a nationalistic sentiment" in support of Israel with a "deeply religious" element....Nor will every secular taxpayer be content to support Muslim views on differential treatment of the sexes,...or, for that matter, to fund the espousal of a wife's obligation of obedience to her husband, presumably taught in any schools adopting the articles of faith of the Southern Baptist Convention....Views like these, and innumerable others, have been safe in the sectarian pulpits and classrooms of this Nation not only because the Free Exercise Clause protects them directly, but because the ban on supporting religious establishment has protected free exercise, by keeping it relatively private. With the arrival of vouchers in religious schools, that privacy will go, and along with it will go confidence that religious disagreement will stay moderate.

Questions for discussion

1. What if the average expenditure in public school is $7,500 per student, and the vouchers (substantially going to parochial schools) amount to $8,000? What additional issues does such a format raise? What if the average expenditure in public school is $7,500 and the voucher amounts to $6,000, but those students who remain in the public schools include a higher percentage of disabled or language deficient student who require $2,000 more per student than the previous population (prior to voucher departures) to educate? What if the vouchers amount to less than public school costs, but fail to count the parochial school public subsidy from tax deductible contributions they receive?

2. Is the state "establishing religion" constitutionally if it provides open competition and allows parents (or students) to choose public, private or parochial as they desire and as is consistent with their religious belief? If parochial schools outperform public schools academically, why should the fact of religious teaching preclude subsidy?

3. What action should the state take, if any, where a voucher financed parochial school admits persons of other religions, but requires them to learn and take examinations in the school's faith? What if it requires them to participate in the prayers and religious practice that is part of the parochial school's tradition? If state schools are permitted to take a "pledge of allegiance" including the group chant "under God", why cannot a parochial school impose similar faith-based practices? Can a Muslim school qualify for vouchers under *Zelman*? Can it include an opening group pledge of allegiance to "one nation under Allah?" Do we approve of the *Zelman* model in parts of the Middle East—where the education of young children is controlled by dogmatic Mullah's who purport to know how and why we were created and which people live in sin? Is our concern affected by the subsidy of those schools by the "civil" government that exercises taxation powers? Is it lessened by parental agreement to their child's attendance at such schools where financed by or through the state?

4. Ohio law purportedly prohibits schools from teaching "hatred of any person or group on the basis of race, ethnicity, national origin, or religion." Is it a violation of such a standard to teach that those of other religions live in sin? Is the definition of "hate" limited to personal *animus*, or does it include the teaching—through voucher (state tax sourced) finances that other groups will not and cannot be "saved" and are bound to suffer everlasting perdition? How is the state to police its tolerance standards? Is Souter concerned about the public law pressure on parochial schools to limit their religious message—or the prospect that they will not limit it and the state will benignly tolerate that intolerance?

ENDNOTES

[1] See, *e.g.*, *Baker v. Carr*, 369 U.S. 186 (1962).

[2] See, *e.g.*, *Flast v. Cohen*, 392 U.S. 83 (1968).

[3] See *Alyeska Pipeline v. Wilderness Society*, 421 U.S. 240 (1975), and discussion in Chapter 1.

[4] See *Canady v. Bossier Parish School Bd.*, 240 F.3d 437 (5th Cir. 2001), upholding uniform requirements where parents may "opt out." Note that most states have enacted statutes authorizing school districts to limit dress or prescribe uniforms.

POSTSCRIPT

Child Rights and International Law

The empirical reality and legal status of children discussed in Chapters 1–13 above have international counterparts. Although beyond the scope of this text, the contraction of the world through the momentous communications and transportation advances of the last fifty years reduces the psychological distance between the children of the disparate nations of the world.

The empirical status of children internationally varies radically by nation-state, with child measures of family wealth, health, and education high in North America and Western Europe and extremely low in much of the developing world. Notwithstanding some improvement over the last two decades, overpopulation, poverty, illness, and lack of education afflict most of the children of the world. Millions are directly subject to extreme poverty to the point of hunger and malnutrition, abusive child labor, problematical health, and relatively short life spans.[1] One in twelve children in the world dies before reaching the age of five.[2] Any examination of the status of children in the United States properly notes on the one hand, the prevalence of the disadvantaged, even desperate, straits of their peers in the developing world, and on the other hand, the relatively higher standing of children in other industrialized countries, whose wealth is closer to that of the U.S.

Within that international community, the United States exercises a leadership role on many levels. Our nation's scientific advances in electronics, biology and medicine, agriculture, and other technologies have produced profound worldwide change. The cultural and entertainment products of the nation proliferate the media throughout the world.

Child advocates argue that the political and moral leadership of the United States should address the plight of children internationally, including not only the promotion of private reproductive responsibility, but also the modeling and funding of successful social service precedents, the protection of the earth, and the enhancement of opportunity for the benefit of future generations worldwide. Such leadership would include the promotion of effective and adequate child investment in U.S. bilateral aid policies, and our support of international organizations and ratification of relevant international treaties. The United Nations' Convention on the Rights of the Child and other international efforts to protect or advance children require each participating nation to commit beyond its own immediate self-interest for a larger and long-term gain.

A. THE INTERNATIONAL CONVENTION ON THE RIGHTS OF THE CHILD

In 1966, the United Nations adopted the International Covenant on Civil and Political Rights. Entered into force in 1976, the Covenant included the legally binding provision that all children "shall have, without any discrimination as to race, colour, sex, language, religion, national or social origin, property or birth, the right to such measures of protection as are required by his status as a minor, on the part of his family, society and the State." The United States signed and ratified the 1966 Covenant. Also adopted in 1966, and effective in 1976, was the U.N.'s International Covenant on Economic, Social, and Cultural Rights, providing that "[s]pecial measures of protection and assistance should be taken on behalf of all children and young persons without any discrimination for reasons of parentage or other conditions." The U.S. signed but did not ratify this Economic, Social, and Cultural Rights Covenant.

The first and major general agreement focusing on children is the United Nations' Convention on the Rights of the Child. Drafting began on the Convention in 1979, declared the "Year of the Child" internationally. It was adopted by the General Assembly in 1989. The Convention has been signed and ratified by all but two U.N. member states: the United States and Somalia.

The Convention sets forth the rights of children in over 54 articles in three categories: (1) participation in society and in decisions affecting their future, (2) protection against discrimination, neglect, and exploitation, and (3) assistance for basic needs.[3]

Important provisions include the following:

Article 3

1. In all actions concerning children, whether undertaken by public or private social welfare institutions,...the best interests of the child shall be a primary consideration.

2. States Parties undertake to ensure the child such protection and care as is necessary for his or her well-being, taking into account the rights and duties of his or her parents, legal guardians, or other individuals legally responsible....

3. States Parties shall ensure that the institutions, services and facilities responsible for the care or protection of children shall conform with the standards established by competent authorities, particularly in the areas of safety, health, in the number and suitability of their staff, as well as competent supervision.

Article 6

1. States Parties recognize that every child has the inherent right to life.

2. States Parties shall ensure to the maximum extent possible the survival and development of the child.

Article 7

1. The child shall be registered immediately after birth and shall have the right from birth to a name, the right to acquire a nationality and, as far as possible, the right to know and be cared for by his or her parents.

Article 9

1. States Parties shall ensure that a child shall not be separated from his or her parents against their will, except when competent authorities subject to judicial review determine, in accordance with applicable law and procedures, that such

separation is necessary for the best interests of the child. Such determination may be necessary in a particular case such as one involving abuse or neglect of the child by the parents, or one where the parents are living separately and a decision must be made as to the child's place of residence.

2. In any proceedings pursuant to paragraph 1 of the present article, all interested parties shall be given an opportunity to participate in the proceedings and make their views known.

3. States Parties shall respect the right of the child who is separated from one or both parents to maintain personal relations and direct contact with both parents on a regular basis, except if it is contrary to the child's best interests.

Article 12

1. States Parties shall assure to the child who is capable of forming his or her own views the right to express those views freely in all matters affecting the child, the views of the child being given due weight in accordance with the age and maturity of the child.
2. For this purpose, the child shall in particular be provided the opportunity to be heard in any judicial and administrative proceedings affecting the child, either directly, or through a representative or an appropriate body, in a manner consistent with the procedural rules of national law.

Article 13

1. The child shall have the right to freedom of expression; this right shall include freedom to seek, receive and impart information and ideas of all kinds, regardless of frontiers, either orally, in writing or in print, in the form of art, or through any other media of the child's choice.

2. The exercise of this right may be subject to certain restrictions, but these shall only be such as are provided by law and are necessary:

(a) For respect of the rights or reputations of others; or

(b) For the protection of national security or of public order (ordre public), or of public health or morals.

Article 14

1. States Parties shall respect the right of the child to freedom of thought, conscience and religion.

2. States Parties shall respect the rights and duties of the parents and, when applicable, legal guardians, to provide direction to the child in the exercise of his or her right in a manner consistent with the evolving capacities of the child.

3. Freedom to manifest one's religion or beliefs may be subject only to such limitations as are prescribed by law and are necessary to protect public safety, order, health or morals, or the fundamental rights and freedoms of others.

Article 15

1. States Parties recognize the rights of the child to freedom of association and to freedom of peaceful assembly.

Article 18

1. States Parties shall use their best efforts to ensure recognition of the principle that both parents have common responsibilities for the upbringing and development of the child. Parents or, as the case may be, legal guardians, have the primary responsibility for the upbringing and development of the child. The best interests of the child will be their basic concern.

Article 19

1. States Parties shall take all appropriate legislative, administrative, social and educational measures to protect the child from all forms of physical or mental violence, injury or abuse, neglect or negligent treatment, maltreatment or exploitation, including sexual abuse, while in the care of parent(s), legal guardian(s) or any other person who has the care of the child.

Article 23

1. States Parties recognize that a mentally or physically disabled child should enjoy a full and decent life, in conditions which ensure dignity, promote self-reliance and facilitate the child's active participation in the community.

2. States Parties recognize the right of the disabled child to special care and shall encourage and ensure the extension, subject to available resources, to the eligible child and those responsible for his or her care, of assistance for which application is made and which is appropriate to the child's condition and to the circumstances of the parents or others caring for the child.

Article 24

1. States Parties recognize the right of the child to the enjoyment of the highest attainable standard of health and to facilities for the treatment of illness and rehabilitation of health. States Parties shall strive to ensure that no child is deprived of his or her right of access to such health care services forth in the present Convention and in other international human rights or humanitarian instruments to which the said States are Parties.

Article 25

States Parties recognize the right of a child who has been placed by the competent authorities for the purposes of care, protection or treatment of his or her physical or mental health, to a periodic review of the treatment provided to the child and all other circumstances relevant to his or her placement.

Article 26

1. States Parties shall recognize for every child the right to benefit from social security, including social insurance.

Article 27

1. States Parties recognize the right of every child to a standard of living adequate for the child's physical, mental, spiritual, moral and social development.

2. The parent(s) or others responsible for the child have the primary responsibility to secure, within their abilities and financial capacities, the conditions of living necessary for the child's development.

3. States Parties, in accordance with national conditions and within their means, shall take appropriate measures to assist parents and others responsible for the child to implement this right and shall in case of need provide material assistance and support programmes, particularly with regard to nutrition, clothing and housing.

Article 28

1. States Parties recognize the right of the child to education, and with a view to achieving this right progressively and on the basis of equal opportunity, they shall, in particular:

(a) Make primary education compulsory and available free to all;

(b) Encourage the development of different forms of secondary education,...

(c) Make higher education accessible to all on the basis of capacity by every appropriate means;

Article 32

1. States Parties recognize the right of the child to be protected from economic exploitation and from performing any work that is likely to be hazardous or to interfere with the child's education, or to be harmful to the child's health or physical, mental, spiritual, moral or social development.

2. States Parties shall take legislative, administrative, social and educational measures to ensure the implementation of the present article. To this end, and having regard to the relevant provisions of other international instruments, States Parties shall in particular:

(a) Provide for a minimum age or minimum ages for admission to employment;

Article 34

States Parties undertake to protect the child from all forms of sexual exploitation and sexual abuse. For these purposes, States Parties shall in particular take all appropriate national, bilateral and multilateral measures to prevent:

(a) The inducement or coercion of a child to engage in any unlawful sexual activity;

(b) The exploitative use of children in prostitution or other unlawful sexual practices;

(c)The exploitative use of children in pornographic performances and materials.

Article 37

States Parties shall ensure that:

(a) No child shall be subjected to torture or other cruel, inhuman or degrading treatment or punishment. Neither capital punishment nor life imprisonment without possibility of release shall be imposed for offences committed by persons below eighteen years of age;

(b) No child shall be deprived of his or her liberty unlawfully or arbitrarily. The arrest, detention or imprisonment of a child shall be in conformity with the law and shall be used only as a measure of last resort and for the shortest appropriate period of time;

> (c) Every child deprived of liberty shall be treated with humanity and respect for the inherent dignity of the human person, and in a manner which takes into account the needs of persons of his or her age. In particular, every child deprived of liberty shall be separated from adults unless it is considered in the child's best interest not to do so and shall have the right to maintain contact with his or her family through correspondence and visits, save in exceptional circumstances;
>
> (d) Every child deprived of his or her liberty shall have the right to prompt access to legal and other appropriate assistance, as well as the right to challenge the legality of the deprivation of his or her liberty before a court or other competent, independent and impartial authority, and to a prompt decision on any such action.

The U.S. government's opposition to the Convention centers on five of its aspects: (1) Article 37's prohibition on child capital punishment, which the United States uniquely imposed until 2005, as discussed in Chapter 10); (2) the child labor limitations of Article 32, which some contend may be broader than current U.S. standards; (3) the promise of economic/health/special needs/ education support from the state; (4) the possible application of minimum standards against the prerogatives of parents; and (5) the supersession of state sovereignty (including possible funding obligations) given the incorporation of its provisions into federal law entitled to constitutional supremacy were it to be ratified.

Although not ratified, some commentators contend that, given their virtual universal acceptance, the provisions of the Convention have achieved the status of "international common law," and as such are binding on the United States under international law theory, irrespective of its nonratification by any single nation.

B. OTHER CHILD-RELATED INTERNATIONAL AGREEMENTS AND AGENCY ACTIVITY

More specific international agreements affect children, including those pertaining to the environment, child labor, land mines, and other subjects. International agencies advance the goals of the U.N. Convention on the Rights of the Child in similar ways, with the United Nations International Children's Emergency Fund (UNICEF), the World Health Organization (WHO), the International Labor Organization (ILO), and the United Nations Educational, Scientific, and Cultural Organization (UNESCO) working to protect child refugees, address health crises, advance family planning, and limit child labor.

Another set of international agreements and intra-national enforcement by nation-states affects the environment in many ways, of obvious concern to children who will inhabit what is left behind by current adult generations. The issues appropriate for such attention include the exhaustion of non-renewable resources, erosion of top soil , long-term pesticide contamination, alteration of weather patterns, ozone depletion, loss of rain forest and wetlands worldwide, ocean pollution, destruction of the great barrier reef, extinction of plant and animal species, and other environmental abuses. They raise a seminal ethical question for humans: to what extent will we take for ourselves and in so doing deprive children who will survive us?

C. INTERNATIONAL ECONOMIC AGREEMENTS

Separate from the various international and bilateral efforts to protect children are a series of international agreements designed to promote international trade, but with a potentially profound effect on the environmental and child labor purposes of the agreements listed above. For example, child advocates contend that one impediment to the creation of a child labor floor (or other external-cost-ameliorating standard) is the trend toward trade barrier reductions, which would inhibit a nation from barring products made from the abusive child labor practices of others and which would violate its own national standards.

The international system of trade has been much affected by the General Agreement on Tariffs and Trade (GATT), the North American Free Trade Agreement (NAFTA), and the rise of the World Trade Organization (WTO) as a potential arbiter of what had been a nationally determined and enforceable floor for child safety, and environmental protection. The primary job of the WTO is to judge the laws of trading nations for compliance with its standards. It conducts its business in Geneva, Switzerland without the public notice and public participation structure common to public bodies, and assured by law for such decisions within the United States. No outside appeal is available. Such disputes are determined by three panelists nominated to hear each such dispute. Once the WTO has declared a law that bars an import to be WTO-illegal, the nation must allow the import or face trade sanctions.

To date, the WTO has yet to create a clear body of law on the right of a nation to refuse goods based on child labor or other child-related practices of the exporting nation. That failure is not the result of its recognition that such import exclusions are in compliance with their standards, but largely reflect the rarity of importation restrictions by the receiving nation based on such abuses in the nation of origin. Should such refusals occur to move child protection and standards up as child advocates would aspire, will the WTO focus on trade "efficiency" threaten such a raising of the bar? What are the remedies for those representing the interests of children where WTO decisions sanction nations for such child protection in their import policies?

Questions for Discussion

A detailed discussion of the international aspect of child rights is beyond the scope of this text. However, questions of primary concern to child advocates include the following:

1. Should the United States ratify the U.N. Convention on the Rights of the Child?

2. Existing land mines maim or kill 15,000–20,000 persons annually, most of them civilians and 30% of them children. The 1997 Convention on the Prohibition of the Use, Stockpiling, Production and Transfer of Anti-Personnel Mines agreement has been signed by 142 nations. Should the United States sign and ratify it?

3. Given the special harm to children from war crime offenses (child hunger/starvation, orphan and refugee status, illness, and death), should the United States support a permanent U.N. War Crimes Tribunal? Should it recognize the International Court of Justice?[4]

4. Should the United States join most other nations in limiting greenhouse gases, given global warming evidence? Should it work more cooperatively and actively for environmental preservation of the ocean, rain forest, and soil, and for animal and plant species survival?

5. Should the United States alter its opposition to international family planning given continued population growth in Third World countries and its implications?[5] Should it at least fund non-abortion birth control consistent with the religious beliefs of the population served?

6. What should be the contribution of the federal government to other nations with children in trouble in the form of bilateral aid? Currently, twenty-one nations with a lower standard of living contribute a substantially higher percentage of their GNP for health and child-related assistance to developing nations.[6] While representing only a small fraction of the world's population, the United States currently accounts for more than half of the world's total military spending.[7] Should the same ratio apply to U.S. economic assistance and education investment in the world's children?

7. Should the United States permit the sale ("dumping") of dangerous products internationally to the detriment of children? For example, tobacco exports continue at high rates and addiction incidence among children outside the United States is now substantially higher than for U.S. youth. Should American tobacco firms be prohibited from manipulating nicotine to enhance addiction and from targeting children in their advertising and promotion overseas, as we have now required for the protection of our own children?

8. The United States has acceded to the jurisdiction of the WTO, an international body representing corporate and trade interests, as discussed above. This submission allows the WTO's undemocratic commercial tribunals to override (or sanction) the democratically determined standards enacted by the United States to protect children where these are in conflict with trade standards. Is such a position consistent with national insistence on sovereign prerogative where the international agency or agreement seeks to protect and advance children—as current policies relevant to questions (1) - (5) above indicate?

ENDNOTES

[1] See U.N. Secretary General, *We the Children (Updated Report)* (Sept. 2001) *passim*, at http://www.unicef.org.

[2] U.N. Department of Public Relations, *U.N. Finds One in Twelve Children Dies Before Age Five* (2002), at http://www.unicef.org.

[3] For the full text of the Convention and related international agreements, see http://www.hrweb.org/legal/undocs.html.

[4] The International Court of Justice is the major tribunal of international law. It operates at the Hague as part of the United Nations Charter. Fifteen independent judges are elected by the Security Council and the General Assembly of the United Nations. After the 1984 filing by Nicaragua against it, the United States withdrew from its agreement to voluntarily comply with the decisions of the Court. During the 1980s, the United States withheld dues from the Court and has encouraged "voluntary" negotiations between parties with disputes that might come within Court jurisdiction. The U.S. has independently refused to support the U.N. establishment of a War Crimes Tribunal.

[5] The United States has haltingly supported the United Nations Population Fund, which serves 120 million women in developing countries who wish to space their births or stop having children and require contraceptive help. Demand is expected to rise 40% to 2017. In April 2002, the Bush Administration withheld $34 million appropriated by the Congress for the Fund, representing 13% of its budget and

compelling substantial cutbacks. The Fund's official estimated the cuts would result in "2 million unwanted pregnancies, 800,000 induced abortions, 4,700 maternal deaths, and 77,000 infant and child deaths." The cuts were reportedly based on false charges by a pro-life organization that U.N. and U.S. funds were used by China for its coercive one-child family policy. Barbara Crossett, *U.N. Agency on Population Blames U.S. for Cutbacks*, N. Y. TIMES, Apr. 7, 2002, at 13.

[6] Five nations of Northern Europe invest in the world's children seven to ten times the U.S. GNP percentage contribution. The U.S. average for year 2000 represents a commitment of one-tenth of one percent of its GNP, one-half the average of giving nations, and one-seventh the U.N. target expectation. *We the Children*, *supra* note 1, at 15.

[7] The United States will spend $490 billion for military purposes in fiscal 2006. The 47 other major nations of the world combined spend substantially less (see http://www.cdi.org).

APPENDIX

Child Advocacy Website Glossary

A. Selected Child Advocacy Web Sites

ABA Center on Children and the Law
www.abanet.org/child

ABA Family Law Section
www.abanet.org/family

American Professional Society on the Abuse of Children
www.apsac.org

Child Welfare League of America, Inc.
www.cwla.org

Children Now
www.childrennow.org

Children's Advocacy Institute
www.caichildlaw.org

Children's Defense Fund
www.childrensdefense.org

Connect for Kids
www.connectforkids.org

First Star
www.firststar.org

International Society for the Prevention of Child Abuse and Neglect
www.ispcan.org

Kempe Children's Center
www.kempecenter.org

National Association of Counsel for Children
www.naccchildlaw.org

National Center for Children in Poverty
www.cpmcnet.columbia.edu/dept/nccp/

National Center for Missing and Exploited Children
www.missingkids.org

National Center for Youth Law
www.youthlaw.org

National Network for Youth
www.nn4youth.org

Voices for America's Children
www.childadvocacy.org

B. Key Government Resources

Library of Congress, Legislative Information on the Internet
http://thomas.loc.gov

U.S. Department of Health and Human Services' Children's Bureau
www.acf.dhhs.gov/programs/cb

U.S. Department of Health and Human Services' Family and Youth Services Bureau
www.acf.dhhs.gov/programs/fysb

U.S. Department of Justice's Office of Juvenile Justice and Delinquency Prevention
http://ojjdp.ncjrs.org

U.S. Government Printing Office
www.access.gpo.gov/su_docs

U.S. Supreme Court
www.supremecourtus.gov

Index